# Family Law

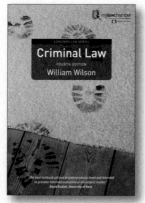
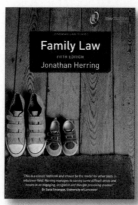

# Family Law

## Fifth Edition

## Jonathan Herring

Exeter College
Oxford University

**Longman**
**is an imprint of**

Harlow, England • London • New York • Boston • San Francisco • Toronto
Sydney • Tokyo • Singapore • Hong Kong • Seoul • Taipei • New Delhi
Cape Town • Madrid • Mexico City • Amsterdam • Munich • Paris • Milan

**Pearson Education Limited**
Edinburgh Gate
Harlow
Essex CM20 2JE
England

and Associated Companies throughout the world

*Visit us on the World Wide Web at:*
www.pearsoned.co.uk

First published 2001
Second edition published 2004
Third edition published 2007
Fourth edition published 2009
**Fifth edition published 2011**

ISBN: 978-1-4082-5552-0

100641545X

**British Library Cataloguing-in-Publication Data**
A catalogue record for this book is available from the British Library

**Library of Congress Cataloging-in-Publication Data**
Herring, Jonathan.
  Family law / Jonathan Herring. – 5th ed.
     p. cm
  Includes bibliographical references and index.
  ISBN 978-1-4082-5552-0 (pbk.)
  1. Domestic relations–England.   I. Title.
  KD750.H47 2011
  346.4201'5–dc22

                            2011004369

10  9  8  7  6  5  4  3  2  1
14  13  12  11

Typeset in 9/12pt Giovanni by 35
Printed and bound in Great Britain by Henry Ling Ltd., at the Dorset Press, Dorchester, Dorset

To Kirsten, Laurel, Jo and Darcy
In memory of Professor John Usher

# Brief contents

# Contents

Contents

**mylaw**chamber
*unrivalled support for legal education*

## Your complete learning package

Visit **www.mylawchamber.co.uk/herring** to access a wealth of resources to support your studies and teaching.

### Self study resources

Use **Case Navigator**\* for help and practise with **case reading and analysis** in **Family Law**.

### In addition access:
● Interactive multiple choice questions to test your understanding of each topic
● Weblinks to help you read more widely around the subject and really impress your lecturers
● Discussion questions to help you get to grips with some of the more difficult concepts
● Legal updates to help you stay up to date with the law and impress examiners

### Teaching support materials
● **Case Navigator** is easy to integrate into any course where case reading and analysis skills are required

**Also:** The regularly maintained mylawchamber site provides the following features:
● Search tool to help locate specific items of content.
● Online help and support to assist with website usage and troubleshooting.

\*Please note that access to Case Navigator is free with the purchase of this book, but you must register with us for access. Full registration instructions are available on the website. The LexisNexis element of Case Navigator is only available to those who currently subscribe to LexisNexis Butterworths online.

# Preface

This textbook tries to present family law in its context. I hope readers will gain not only an understanding of what the law actually is, but also an awareness of the complex tensions in social, philosophical and political forces which surround 'family life'. This means the book contains much law, but also a little sociology, political theory and philosophy. Of course a little of anything might be said to be a bad thing and the book can only give a flavour of the wide-ranging issues surrounding family life and its regulation. Still, it is hoped the reader can see that family law is not simply a set of rules cast down from upon high, but rules that have to operate in the messy world of personal relations where many people do not know what the law says, and even if they do, do not care very much about it.

I am extremely grateful for the support of the team at Pearson Education and particularly Cheryl Cheasley. Barbara Massam, who has in various ways been involved in all five editions of this book, has done an excellent job. I am also grateful for the support and help of colleagues and friends while writing this book, and in particular Shazia Choudhry, John Eekelaar, Michelle Madden Dempsey, Lucinda Ferguson, Sandra Fredman, Rob George, Stephen Gilmore, Rebecca Probert, Helen Reece, George P. Smith, Rachel Taylor and Julie Wallbank. In all sorts of ways they have helped with the book. Of course my wife Kirsten, and children Laurel, Joanna and Darcy, have been a constant source of fun, laughs and encouragement. In the preface to the third edition I wrote: 'Each new edition of this book appears linked to the birth of a new child for us. That must stop!' It has indeed stopped, so no new family members to greet the next editions.

The book seeks to present the law as at 1 August 2010.

*Jonathan Herring*
*Exeter College, Oxford University*
*November 2010*

The publishers would like to thank Gil Chapman, Senior Lecturer at the University of Glamorgan.

# Guided tour

'a bid by a joint purchaser to establish a greater beneficial interest than a joint interest will involve the steepest of climbs, usually resulting in a failure to attain the summit'.[125]

> **CASE: *Kernott v Jones* [2010] EWCA Civ 578**
>
> The couple bought a property in joint names. They later separated and for twelve years the woman lived in the property and paid for its maintenance and mortgage, while the man made no contribution at all. It was found that this conduct was insufficient to rebut the presumption of an intention to share the property equally. The fact that one party had made a greater financial contribution to the property or that one party had not lived in the property for some time was not sufficient to rebut the presumption of shared ownership. Rimmer LJ interpreted *Stack v Dowden* to mean that the courts could not invent an intention to rebut the presumption in a joint names case, the search had to be made for a real intention. As he noted, it would be difficult to find one in the absence of an actual conversation.[126] In this case there was no evidence of an actual intention which could rebut the presumption that because the property was in joint names it should be jointly owned.

**Essential cases** boxes allow you to easily identify the most important cases for your study of family law.

[117] *Fowler v Barron* [2008] 2 FCR 1.
[118] *Holman v Howes* [2007] EWCA Civ 877.

1. Under s 2 of the Domestic Proceedings and Magistrates' Court Act 1978, periodical payments orders and lump sum orders for less than £1,000[49] can be made. Section 1 sets out the criteria:

> **LEGISLATIVE PROVISION**
>
> **Domestic Proceedings and Magistrates' Court Act 1978, section 1**
>
> Either party to a marriage may apply to a magistrates' court for an order under section 2 of this Act on the ground that the other party to the marriage—
>
> (a) has failed to provide reasonable maintenance for the applicant; or
>
> (b) has failed to provide, or to make a proper contribution towards, reasonable maintenance for any child of the family; or
>
> (c) has behaved in such a way that the applicant cannot reasonably be expected to live with the respondent; or
>
> (d) has deserted the applicant.

**Legislative provision** boxes identify the key aspects of pertinent statutes that feature in family law.

[46] Discussed in Chapter 6.
[47] Section 198.
[48] Cretney, Masson and Bailey-Harris (2002: 78).
[49] There is no such limitation if there is a consent order.

> **TOPICAL ISSUE**
>
> **Childhood in crisis?**
>
> In recent years the media paid much attention to the 'crisis' of childhood. In 2006 a letter was sent to the *Daily Telegraph* signed by leading academics and public figures. They expressed grave concern at the rates of depression and behavioural problems experienced by children. They saw 'modern life' as being part of the problem, explaining: 'Since children's brains are still developing, they cannot adjust – as full-grown adults can – to the effects of ever more rapid technological and cultural change. They still need what developing human beings have always needed, including real food (as opposed to processed "junk"), real play (as opposed to sedentary, screen-based entertainment), first-hand experience of the world they live in and regular interaction with the real-life significant adults in their lives.'[33] The Archbishop of Canterbury joined the expression of concern, complaining that children had become 'infant adults'.[34] A 2008 report blamed excessive individualism by adults as creating a mass of problems for children.[35] In one survey 89 per cent of adults felt that children had been damaged by materialsim.[36] But children are regarded not just as disadvantaged but dangerous. In one poll 43 per cent agreed with the statement that 'something has to be done to protect us from children'.[37] Whether children 'have never had it so bad' is hard to assess. In material ways there is much evidence that children are better off than their predecessors, but that seems to be bringing with it a range of other problems. The Children's Commissioner states that 'one in ten children and young people aged 5–16 have a mental disorder that is associated with "considerable distress and substantial interference with personal functions"'.[38]

**Topical issue** examples demonstrate the application of family law to everyday life, through analysis of contemporary and controversial stories, events or scenarios.

## DEBATE

### Should all fathers automatically get parental responsibility?

1. *The balance of power between mothers and fathers.* The case for awarding parental responsibility to only a selection of unmarried fathers runs as follows. Why does the father need parental responsibility? He can carry out all the duties and joys of parenthood (feeding, clothing, playing with the child) without parental responsibility. He only needs parental responsibility when he is dealing with third parties such as doctors and schools. At such times the mother can provide the necessary consent. He would only need parental responsibility if he were wishing to exercise it in a way contrary to the mother's wishes.[335] An unmarried father who has been fully involved in the raising of the child might be thought validly to have an important say in the raising of children. But an unmarried father who had limited or no contact with the child should surely not be able to override the mother's wishes. Ruth Deech has argued that parental responsibilities:

> include feeding, washing and clothing the child, putting her to bed, housing her, educating and stimulating her, taking responsibility for arranging babysitting and day-care, keeping the child in touch with the wider family circle, checking her medical condition, arranging schooling and transport to school, holidays and recreation, encouraging social and possibly religious or moral development. Fatherhood that does not encompass a fair share of these tasks is an empty and egotistical concept and has the consequence that the man does not know the child sufficiently well to be able sensibly to take decisions about education, religion,

**Debate** sections put forward arguments both for and against contentious issues, and stimulate both further thinking and reflection.

## KEY STATISTICS

- Between 1961 and 1991 there was a fivefold rise in the divorce rate. But currently we are seeing a rapidly declining number of divorces.
- In 2007 there was a drop to 121,799 divorces; this was a notable drop from the figure of 153,282 in 2004.[1] It is lower than the number of divorces in 1976. It has been estimated that 45% of marriages end in divorce.[2]
- The divorce rate (the number of divorces per 1,000 marriages per year) has risen from 4.7 in 1970 to 13.7 in 1999, and since then has steadied, with the rate at 14.0 in 2005. In 2007 the divorce rate in England and Wales fell to 11.2 divorcing people per 1,000 married population.[3]
- In 2007 the median duration of a marriage was 11.5 years. This is an increase from 1993–6 when it hovered between 9.8 and 9.9 years.[4]
- There were 106,763 children aged under 16 who were in families where the parents divorced in 2008. Twenty-one per cent of these children were under five and 63% were under eleven.[5]
- 67% of divorces are granted to wives.[6]

**Key statistics** provide you with interesting and relevant facts applied to family law.

## Further reading

Archard, D. (2004b) *Children: Rights and Childhood*, London: Routledge.

Archard, D. and Skivenes, M. (2009) 'Balancing a Child's Best Interests and a Child's Views', *International Journal of Children's Rights* 17 (2009) 1–21.

Bainham, A. (2009d) 'Is anything now left of parental rights?' in R. Probert, S. Gilmore and J. Herring, *Responsible Parents and Parental Responsibility*, Oxford: Hart.

Bridgeman, J. (2007) *Parental Responsibility, Young Children and Healthcare Law*, Cambridge: CUP.

**Further reading** sections, located at the end of each chapter, guide you to additional sources for deeper levels of study/ research.

Visit **www.mylawchamber.co.uk/herring** to access a wealth of resources to support your studies:

- Case Navigator to help improve your case reading and analysis skills
- Interactive multiple choice questions to test your understanding of each topic
- Weblinks to help you read more widely around the subject and really impress your lecturers
- Discussion questions to help you get to grips with some of the more difficult concepts
- Legal updates to help you stay up to date with the law and impress examiners.

# Table of cases

Visit **www.mylawchamber.co.uk/herring** to access unique online support to improve your case reading and analysis skills.

**Case Navigator provides:**
- **Direct deep links** to the core cases in family law.
- **Short introductions** provide guidance on what you should look out for while reading the case.
- **Questions** help you to test your understanding of the case, and provide feedback on what you should have grasped.
- **Summaries** contextualise the case and point you to further reading so that you are fully prepared for seminars and discussions.

*Please note that access to Case Navigator is free with the purchase of this book, but you must register with us for access. Full registration instructions are available on the website. The LexisNexis element of Case Navigator is only available to those who currently subscribe to LexisNexis Butterworths online.

Case Navigator cases are highlighted in bold.

# Table of statutes

# Table of statutory instruments

# Table of European legislation

# 1     What is family law?

Families can be the scenes of some of the greatest joys, as well as some of the greatest sadnesses, that life can bring. Surveys suggest that for a substantial majority of people families are more important to them than jobs or status.[1] The interaction of law and the family therefore gives rise to questions of enormous importance to the individuals who appear before the courts and to society at large.[2] In *Huang v Secretary of State for the Home Department*[3] the House of Lords emphasised the importance of families to individuals:

> Human beings are social animals. They depend on others. Their family, or extended family, is the group on which many people most heavily depend, socially, emotionally and often financially. There comes a point at which, for some, prolonged and unavoidable separation from this group seriously inhibits their ability to live full and fulfilling lives.

In 2008 the Labour Government agreed:

> Families are the bedrock of our society. They nurture children, help to build strength, resilience and moral values in young people, and provide the love and encouragement that helps them lead fulfilling lives.[4]

This first chapter will consider some key questions about families: What are families? What is family law? Is family life in crisis? It will also highlight some of the most controversial issues which face family lawyers today and which will appear throughout the book. First, it is necessary to attempt a definition of a family.

## 1 Seeking a definition of the family

The notion of a 'family' is notoriously difficult to define.[5] Many people have a stereotypical image of what the 'ideal family' is like – a mother, a father and two children. Yet this family composition is not the family form that most people will have experienced. Only 24 per cent of households in 2009 consisted of a couple with dependent children.[6] So the image of two

---

[1] Future Foundation (1999). Yet Babb et al. (2006) report that one in five full-time employees usually works at least 48 hours a week.
[2] For a remarkable history of family law during the twentieth century see Cretney (2003a).
[3] [2007] UKHL 11, [2007] 2 AC 167, para 18.
[4] Cabinet Office (2008: 1).
[5] See Hantrais (2004) for a discussion of definitional problems facing statisticians seeking to work in the area of families.
[6] National Statistics (2010).

parents and two children as the ideal family is just that, an ideal; a powerful ideal, but not the most common family form.[7]

It is possible to distinguish families (a group of people related by blood, marriage or adoption); a nuclear family (parents and their dependent children); extended families (the nuclear family plus the wider kin, e.g. grandparents); kinships (the larger family groups related by blood or marriage); and households (a group of people sharing accommodation).[8] One of the difficulties in defining 'family' is the power of the definition and especially the stigma that follows from denying that a certain group of people is a family.[9] In part this explains the strong objections from the gay and lesbian community to the now repealed s 28 of the Local Government Act 1988, which referred to gay and lesbian relationships as a 'pretended family relationship'.[10]

'Family' is presently a term that is of limited legal significance. As we shall see, much effort has been made in attempting a legal definition of 'marriage', 'parent' and 'parenthood', but relatively few cases have defined 'a family'. However, following the Human Rights Act 1998 and the importance of the right to respect for family life, the concept of family will grow in legal significance.[11]

How might the law define a family?[12]

## A The person in the street's definition

In an attempt to define a 'family', the law could rely on common usage: how would the person in the street define a family? The difficulty with this is that although there may be some cases where everyone would agree that a particular group of people is a family, there are many other cases where, when asked, people would answer 'I don't know', or there would be conflicting answers, reflecting different values, religious beliefs or cultural perspectives. So, asking a person in the street does not help to clarify the definition of family in ambiguous cases. When children have been asked to define families they have revealed a broad understanding of the term and even included pets.[13] Studies of children also suggest that they define families in terms of those people they feel very close to, rather than the standard structure of blood relations.[14]

## B A formalistic definition

The law could rely upon a formalistic approach.[15] Such definitions would focus on whether the group of individuals in question has certain observable traits that can be objectively proved. These definitions often focus on criteria such as marriage or the existence of children. The benefit of formalistic definitions is their clarity and ease of proof. The approach therefore has a strong appeal to lawyers. The definitions avoid involving the court in time-consuming or unnecessarily controversial questions.

---

[7] Krause and Meyers (2002) provide an excellent discussion.
[8] Day Sclater (2000). See also Archard (2003: ch. 2) for further discussion, although he takes the view that a family must involve children.
[9] Douglas (2005: 3).
[10] The section was repealed by the Local Government Act 2003, Sch 8(1), para 1.
[11] Munby J (2004c) provides a useful summary of the significance of the Act for family lawyers.
[12] See Diduck (2005) for an excellent discussion of the changing legal understanding of families.
[13] Morrow (1998); Smart, Neale and Wade (2001: 52).
[14] Smart, Neale and Wade (2001: 52).
[15] See Glennon (2008) and Leckey (2008) for an informative analysis.

The main disadvantage is that the approach can be rather technical. If the group of people failed to meet the formal requirements of the definition even though they functioned as a family, should they be denied the status of family? For example, some people argue that it would be bizarre if the law treated an unmarried couple who had lived together for 20 years and raised children together any differently from a married couple who had been married 20 years. Should the fact that the married couple undertook a short ceremony 20 years previously make a difference? Those who take such a view may prefer a definition that considers the function the relationship performs, rather than its technical nature.

## C  A function-based definition

A function-based definition[16] examines the functions of families in our society.[17] If a group of people perform certain functions then the law can term them a family. The law would be less concerned with the formal nature of relationship between the group of people (e.g. whether they were married or not) and more concerned with their relationship in day-to-day practicalities and their contribution to society. In other words, the approach focuses on what they do, rather than what they are. This has led David Morgan to argue that although we may not be able to define what a family is, we can identify what 'family practices' are.[18] If such an approach were to be adopted, the law might describe the functions of a family as: providing security and care for its members; producing children; socialising and raising of children; and providing economically for its members.[19] However, whether a family needs to fulfil all or only some of these functions is controversial. Some have argued that a family's existence should be focused around children.[20] Others suggest that a sexual relationship, or a potential sexual relationship is essential if families are to be distinguished from friendship.[21] Still others have argued that caring and sharing is what is central to a family.[22]

Opponents of a function-based approach claim that it presupposes that the traditional family is the ideal, and only permits other family forms to be included within the definition if they are sufficiently close to the functions of that ideal.[23] Hence it is argued that it is only because of the dominant position marriage has held in our society that a sexual element is seen as important to the definition of marriage.[24] There is also the problem of proof. Determining what the group of people does is normally far harder than determining whether or not they have undergone a formal ceremony of some kind.

## D  An idealised definition

Another approach suggests that a workable definition of what a family is does not exist, but that a definition of an idealised family can be provided. In our society many would see this as a married couple with children.[25] The difficulty is that this idealised picture has become tarnished through evidence of domestic violence; abuse of children within the home; and the

---

[16] The term 'functionalist definition' would be neater, but within sociological writing the term 'functionalism' has become associated with one particular view of the function of a family: a highly traditional one.
[17] Glennon (2000).
[18] Morgan (2003).
[19] See Veitch (1976); Rusk (1998).
[20] Bainham (1995b).
[21] See Lord Clyde in *Fitzpatrick v Sterling Housing Association* [2000] 1 FCR 21 at p. 35.
[22] See Bottomley and Wong (2009).
[23] *Harvard Law Review* (1991).
[24] Fineman (2004).
[25] Morgan (2007).

oppression of women within marriage. But some still promote a highly traditional family form as the ideal, with the father as the head of the household, to be respected and honoured by his wife and children.[26] In one major survey of opinion only one in ten people agreed that it was the man's job to earn money and the woman's job was to stay at home and look after the family.[27]

To others this picture would be far from ideal. We could try to 'update' the traditional image and create an ideal of a mutually supportive family where the children are cared for in a non-patriarchal, caring environment. But such an image of an ideal family is very much a western European one. Where are the grandparents, the uncles and aunts, nephews and nieces? And is it really impossible to be a family without children? So, in a culturally diverse nation such as ours it would be impossible to agree on an idealised family form that would be acceptable to everyone.[28]

## E A self-definition approach

This approach would state 'you are a family if you say you are'. Eekelaar and Nhlapo[29] have suggested that societies are gradually accepting an increasing variety of family forms and are reaching the position that a family is any group of people who regard themselves as a family. The benefit of such an approach is that it does not stigmatise people as 'not family' unless they do not wish to be regarded as a family. In 2008 the then Labour Government accepted there was no ideal family:

> There is no single family form that guarantees happiness or success. All types of family can, in the right circumstances, look after their family members, help them get on in life and, for their children, have high hopes and the wherewithal to put them on the path to success.[30]

By contrast, the Conservative Party has been dismissive of such an approach, believing that the Government should be bold in declaring that marriage is the best option for families:

> Politicians and policy makers have typically shied away from distinguishing between family structures. They have become scared they might upset someone if they talk about two-parent families. Too many hide behind the mantra that it is just about personal choice and that Government has no opinion . . . The difference in stability between marriage and cohabitation is of fundamental importance, yet Government policy has failed to recognise that [there is] a 'marriage effect'.[31]

It will be interesting to see the extent to which the prevailing (2010) Coalition Government adopts a pro-marriage stance.

## F Do we give up?

So there are severe difficulties in defining families. There is little agreement within society over exactly what constitutes family or what the purposes of a family are. Does this lead us to throw up our hands and say there is no such thing as a family, as so many sociologists do?

---

[26] Priolo (2007).
[27] National Centre for Social Research (2010).
[28] See Bainham (1995b).
[29] Eekelaar and Nhlapo (1998: ix).
[30] Cabinet Office (2008: 5). See also DCSF (2010).
[31] Centre for Social Justice (2009: 8–9).

The argument for not doing so is that most people regard their family (whatever they mean by that) as of enormous importance, and indeed families are seen as having great social significance. Promoting the family is one of the few political ideals with which most people agree.

What this demonstrates is that there are dangers in seeking to promote family life or talk about family law unless we are clear what it is we mean by families. We need to be precise about what aspect of the family a law is seeking to promote, or which group of people is intended to be covered by a particular law. Indeed, it may be that some parts of family law will apply to some families and not to others. It is not that some groups are family and some are not, but that some family groups may need the benefits of a particular law and others not.[32] What is clear is that the definition of a family may change over time. Gittens writes:

> Just as it would be ludicrous to argue that a society or an era is characterised by one type of individual, so it is ludicrous to argue that there can only be one type of family. Families are not only complex, but are also infinitely variable and in a constant state of flux as the individuals who compose them age, die, marry, reproduce and move.[33]

## G Discussion of how the law defines families

The legal definition of families has changed over time. In 1950 in *Gammans v Ekins*,[34] talking of an unmarried couple, it was stated: 'to say of two people masquerading as these two were as husband and wife, that they were members of the same family, seems to be an abuse of the English Language'. This approach would no longer represent the law.

The leading case on the meaning of family in the law is *Fitzpatrick v Sterling Housing Association Ltd*,[35] a decision of the House of Lords. Although their Lordships were careful to explain that they were just considering the meaning of family in the Rent Act 1977, the decision will be highly influential in defining family in other contexts.

---

**CASE: *Fitzpatrick v Sterling Housing Association Ltd* [2000] 1 FCR 21**

The case concerned a Mr Thompson and a Mr Fitzpatrick, who had lived together in a flat for 18 years until Mr Thompson died. Under the Rent Act 1977 Mr Fitzpatrick could succeed to the tenancy of the flat, which had been in Mr Thompson's name alone, if he was a member of Mr Thompson's family. So, the core issue was whether a gay or lesbian couple could be a family. By a three to two majority the House of Lords held that Mr Thompson and Mr Fitzpatrick were a family. The majority accepted that the meaning of family is not restricted to people linked by marriage or blood. Lord Slynn suggested that the hallmarks of family life were 'that there should be a degree of mutual inter-dependence, of the sharing of lives, of caring and love, or commitment and support'.[36] He later added that the relationship must not be 'a transient superficial relationship'.[37] ➡

---

[32] Ghandhi and MacNamee (1991).
[33] Gittens (1993: 5).
[34] [1950] 2 KB 328 at p. 331.
[35] [2000] 1 FCR 21.
[36] [2000] 1 FCR 21 at p. 32.
[37] [2000] 1 FCR 21 at p. 35.

Applying these criteria to the couple in question, they were certainly family members. Mr Fitzpatrick had cared for Mr Thompson during the last six years of his illness. Lord Clyde, unlike the others in the majority, thought that it would be difficult for a couple to show that they were a family unless there was an active sexual relationship or the potential for one.[38] He felt that the sexual element was important if a distinction was to be drawn between families and acquaintances. The dissenting judges argued that the paradigm of the family was a legal relationship (e.g. marriage or adoption) or by blood (e.g. parent–child). As the couple did not fall into these definitions, nor did they mirror them, they could not be regarded as a family, although the minority added that they believed Parliament should consider reforming the law so that a survivor of a gay or lesbian relationship could take on a tenancy.

In *Mendoza v Ghaidan*[39] it was held that a same-sex couple were living 'as [the tenant's] husband or wife' for the purposes of para 2(2) of Sch 1 to the Rent Act 1977, which lists those entitled to succeed to a statutory tenancy. Relying on the Human Rights Act 1998 the House of Lords interpreted the paragraph to read 'as if he or she were his wife or husband' and held that this would cover long-term same-sex partners. In *Joram Developments Ltd v Sharratt*[40] a 24-year-old man and a 75-year-old woman shared a flat, enjoying each other's company and living communally, although there were no sexual relations. The House of Lords was willing to say they shared a household, but not that they were members of a family.

So, to summarise the law's approach to defining a family, the law does not restrict the definition of family life to those who are married or those who are related by blood. It is willing to accept that other less formal relations can be family if they can demonstrate a sharing of lives and degree of intimacy and stability. However, it would be wrong to say that the law takes a pure function-based approach because if a couple are married they will be regarded as a family, even though their relationship is not a loving, committed, or stable one.

The law, therefore, in defining families, uses a combination of a formalist and function-based approach. Despite these developments recognising a variety of family forms it can be argued that there is a hierarchy of families in family law: the top position being taken by married couples, with unmarried heterosexual couples and same-sex couples below them.[41] Certainly the closer a relationship is to the 'ideal' of marriage the more likely it is to be recognised as a family.

## H New families?

Some commentators believe that at the beginning of the twenty-first century we are witnessing some fundamental changes in the nature of families.[42] Others argue that family life has been in constant flux across the centuries.[43] Certainly some current statistics make dramatic reading. The more detailed figures are given at relevant parts throughout the book, but some of the main changes in family life in recent years include the following:

---

[38] [2000] 1 FCR 21 at p. 47.
[39] [2004] UKHL 30.
[40] [1979] 1 WLR 928.
[41] Bailey-Harris (2001c).
[42] Silva and Smart (1999).
[43] Fox Harding (1996).

## KEY STATISTICS

- People are now marrying at an older age; the rate of marriage is dropping; and there are projections that fewer and fewer people will marry.[44] In 2007 of those aged over 30 only 55% were married.

- Increasingly people are cohabiting outside of marriage. In 2008, 45% of children were born to a mother who was unmarried.[45] In 2007, of those aged 16–29 10% were married, while 16% were cohabiting.[46] In 2007 around 10% of the adult population were cohabiting.[47]

- Same-sex relationships are increasingly acceptable. It has been estimated that there are between 2.3 and 3.2 million gay, lesbian or bisexual people in the UK.[48]

- In the 1970s and 1980s there were sharp increases in the rate of divorce. In recent years the divorce rate appears to have levelled off, and even slightly declined. However, it has been projected that 41% of marriages entered into in the 1990s will end in divorce.[49]

- An increasing proportion of children lives in lone-parent households. In 2007, 20% of households with dependent children were headed by a single parent.[50] In 2009 only 63% of children lived with a married couple.[51]

- The average size of households is in decline (in 2009 it was 2.4 people)[52] and there is a significant increase in the number of people living alone. In 2009, 29% of households contained a single person.[53] It has been estimated that this will rise to 35% by 2021.[54]

- The proportion of the population over the age of 65 is ever increasing.[55]

- There has been a sharp decline in birth rates. In a survey of women aged 21–23 only 40% said they expected to have a baby in the next five years.[56] Women are leaving having children until later. In 2007 20% of births were to women over the age of 35.[57] Two thirds of mothers are in paid employment.[58]

- More and more children are living with their parents even after their eighteenth birthday: in 2006, 58% of men and 39% of women aged 20–24 in England still lived at home with their parents.[59]

- There were more than seven million people (12% of the population) living alone in the UK in 2009.[60]

---

[44] See Chapter 2.
[45] National Statistics (2010a).
[46] National Statistics (2010a).
[47] National Statistics (2010a).
[48] Equal Opportunities Commission (2006a).
[49] Haskey (1996a).
[50] National Statistics (2010a).
[51] National Statistics (2010a).
[52] National Statistics (2010a).
[53] National Statistics (2010a).
[54] Lewis (2005).
[55] See Chapter 12.
[56] Muir (2003).
[57] National Statistics (2010a).
[58] Family and Parenting Institute (2009).
[59] National Statistics (2008b).
[60] National Statistics (2010a).

As these statistics indicate, the nature of family life is certainly undergoing a change. Geoff Dench and Jim Ogg have suggested that we are experiencing a dramatic shift from the traditional model of 'mother–father–child' family to one based on 'mother–grandmother–child', with fathers (and fathers' sides of the family) becoming irrelevant for many children. They argue:

> We can see a clear tendency at the moment for matrilineal ties (through the mother) to become the more active, while patrilineal, through the father, may often be very tenuous or even non-existent . . . [There is now] a growing frailty in ties between parents . . . an increasing marginalisation of men, and of ties traced through men, and a stronger focusing of families around women.[61]

Certainly there has been a dramatic increase in the extent to which child care is undertaken by grandparents, so that now four in five pre-school children are to some extent cared for by grandparents. By contrast, there has been a decreasing significance in the roles played by aunts, uncles and wider relatives.[62]

However, contrary to the views of Dench and Ogg, others have argued we are witnessing a significant change in family life because fathers are seeking to play an increasing role in the lives of their children.[63]

## TOPICAL ISSUE

### New men, old fathers?

Fathers 4 Justice and other such groups[64] have gained notoriety with campaigns that have included throwing purple flour at the Prime Minister, parading across Buckingham Palace and wearing costumes of male superhero figures:[65] all of this in the name of promoting the role of fathers, particularly after divorce, and campaigning against what they regard as discrimination against fathers. Whether we are witnessing a change in the role men play in family life is hotly debated.[66] Traditionally the family could be seen as a central way in which sex roles were created and reinforced.[67] Women were to be bearers and carers of children and other dependants. Men were to be providers. The woman's role and place was in the home. The man's domain was in the 'real world' of commerce and business.[68]

This is now changing; although quite how is unclear.[69] There certainly appears to be an increased acceptance that the traditional model of the family is not how things should be. In a recent survey only 17 per cent of men thought the traditional model still desirable.[70] Surprisingly, perhaps, of teenagers questioned, 21 per cent of boys believed women should adopt a traditional role.[71] Many couples seek to ensure that there is an equal sharing of household tasks and child care. However, most fail, and in heterosexual couples women still end up performing the clear majority of household labour and child care.[72]

---

[61] Dench and Ogg (2002: x–xiii).
[62] Willmott and Nelson (2003).
[63] Collier (2010); Fatherhood Institute (2008).
[64] Fathers 4 Justice is now said to be disbanded: Collier (2009b).
[65] Collier (2005, 2007); Jordan (2009).
[66] Fineman (2004).
[67] Collier and Sheldon (2008).
[68] Collier (2010).
[69] Featherstone (2009 and 2010).
[70] National Centre for Social Research (2008).
[71] Park, Phillips and Johnson (2004).
[72] Björnberg and Kollind (2005). For some practical suggestions on how to increase men's involvement in child rearing, see O'Brien (2005).

Most people accept that there has been a change in public perception about what is expected of a 'good father' although it is unclear how much this has affected the practice of fathering.[73] Looking at the new paternity leave of two weeks given to fathers following the birth of a child, a recent study found that only 50 per cent of fathers took the full two weeks available.[74] Less than 20 per cent took up the right to claim more than that.[75] That said, other studies showed that over 70 per cent of fathers wished they had been able to take more leave than they did in fact take.[76] Whether this is rhetoric not matching reality or a demonstration of the financial pressures many couples are under is a matter for debate. Even if fathers are spending more time with children they are not doing so in a way which impacts on their career progression. While for mothers childbirth often signals a move into no paid work or part-time work, for fathers it rarely does.[77] Even in cases where both partners work more than 48 hours a week, only 20 per cent of women said their partner had the main responsibility for the washing and the cooking.[78]

A significant study in the role of the modern father found that, although the majority of fathers were spending more time with their children, their care was often mediated through the mother. In other words, the mother enabled the care, for example, by supervising it, or suggesting what the father might do with the child.[79] Further, there is good evidence of many fathers 'cherry picking' the fun parts of child care (e.g. playing with the child), leaving the more mundane roles to mothers.[80] Perhaps this is indicated by a survey of children who were asked 'who understands you best?': 53 per cent said 'mum'; 19 per cent said a best friend and only 13 per cent said 'dad'.[81] Furthermore, in a different survey 65 per cent of fathers felt that mothers were 'naturally' better at looking after children than fathers.[82] In any event, an optimist may hope that we are seeing the start of an acceptance that the raising of children should be undertaken equally by men and women. The image of fathers in the law has certainly changed, with Sheldon and Collier noting that

> the image of unmarried fathers as unworthy, irresponsible and disengaged has been increasingly supplemented, if not entirely supplanted, by a very different depiction of unmarried fathers: as a discriminated group who are often deeply committed to their children yet find themselves denied access to them, being left unfairly dependent on the whims of sometimes hostile mothers.[83]

The extent to which this is a truthful representation will be considered further in Chapter 9.

Evidence concerning the importance or otherwise of a father figure is in dispute.[84] Studies showing the success of lesbian couples in raising children together may suggest that, although there may be a benefit from having two or more people sharing the load of parenting and providing the child with a variety of input, whether they happen to be male or female does not matter.[85] Others, however, believe there is something unique that a male parent has to offer.[86]

---

[73] Featherstone (2009).
[74] Smeaton (2006).
[75] According to Thompson et al. (2005: viii) only one in five fathers altered their work patterns following the birth of a child.
[76] Yaxley, Vinter and Young (2005). But see BBC Newsonline (2009d) for evidence of a reluctance by fathers to take paternity leave.
[77] Featherstone (2009).
[78] Family and Parenting Institute (2009).
[79] Lewis and Welsh (2006); Welsh et al. (2004).
[80] Featherstone (2009: 34).
[81] ICM (2004).
[82] Thompson et al. (2005).
[83] Collier and Sheldon (2008: ch. 6).
[84] Maccullum and Golombok (2004).
[85] Dunne (2000).
[86] Hauari and Hollingworth, K. (2010).

Not only has the image of what makes a 'good father' changed, so too has the notion of what makes a 'good mother'.[87] There has been an increased responsibility placed on parents if their children behave badly[88] and it has been mothers in particular who have been penalised for the misbehaviour of their children.[89] Certainly the acceptability, and even necessity, of 'working mothers'[90] has increased.[91] Of teenagers questioned, 78 per cent thought that working mothers could have just as strong a relationship with their children as those at home.[92] During the last few years we have seen significant steps being taken by the Government to facilitate 'working motherhood': improvements in the provision of child care[93] (although it is still inadequate in many areas); an increase in provision for maternity leave;[94] much effort to encourage lone parents to take up employment;[95] and the development by companies of 'family friendly policies' for their staff.[96] Despite this, there are enormous pressures on mothers seeking to combine their paid and caring work.[97] Especially so, now that we live in the era of the Domestic Goddess.

Sylvia Hewlett[98] argues there is a battle for motherhood. Mothers are finding the tension between a desire to maintain a career and to have children complex. She notes that 59 per cent of Britain's top female executives do not have children. Among professional women in the United States 42 per cent do not have children. One recent study argued that in the UK a third of graduate women will not have children.[99] The pressure on women seeking to combine work and raising a child is increased given the growing perception that by undertaking paid work a woman will harm family life. In 1998 51 per cent of women believed that family life would not suffer if a woman worked, but this had fallen to 46 per cent in 2002.[100] A different study found that 61 per cent of those questioned believed that parents did not get to spend enough time with their children. Some 48 per cent admitted that they chose to pursue their career even if that affected their family life.[101]

Some sociologists believe we are witnessing an increase in individualisation, with personal development being a key aspect of people's lives.[102] Elisabeth Beck-Gernsheim explains the individualisation thesis in this way:

> On the one hand, the traditional social relationships, bonds and belief systems that used to determine people's lives in the narrowest detail have been losing more and more of their meaning . . . New space and new options have thereby opened up for individuals. Now men and women can and should, may and must, decide for themselves how to shape their lives – within certain limits, at least.

---

[87] For a discussion of the idealisation of mothers see Herring (2008a).
[88] Kaganas (2010).
[89] Featherstone (2010a).
[90] The idea that mothers who are not in paid employment are not working is, of course, false.
[91] See the discussion in Churchill (2008).
[92] Park, Phillips and Johnson (2004).
[93] HM Treasury (2004b). In one study of parents with young children, nine out of ten parents had used some form of child care or early years provision in the previous year: Bryson, Kazimirski and Soutwood (2006).
[94] See Work and Families Act 2006. However, there is still ample evidence of discrimination against workers who become pregnant: Adams, McAndrew and Winterbrotham (2005).
[95] Especially through the Sure Start Programme. Government consultation has indicated a widespread concern that lone parents are in fact feeling pressured to take up employment: DWP (2006a).
[96] Lewis (2009); James (2009).
[97] Gatrell (2005).
[98] Hewlett (2003).
[99] Leapman (2007).
[100] BBC Newsonline (2008l).
[101] BBC Newsonline (2007i).
[102] Beck (2002); Daly and Scheiwe (2010) but see Smart (2007a) and Eekelaar (2009) for a questioning of this.

On the other hand, individualization means that people are linked into [social] institutions . . . these institutions produce various regulations . . . that are typically addressed to individuals rather than the family as a whole. And the crucial feature of these new regulations is that they enjoin the individual to lead a life of his or her own beyond any ties to the family or other groups – or sometimes even to shake off such ties and to act without referring to them.[103]

This vision of an individualised society is rejected by some as failing to pay sufficient account to the sense of obligation that family ties do generate.[104] Others argue it is simply impossible for an individual to pursue their vision for their life without forming relationships with others.[105]

There is, however, little doubt that many people experience tensions between their family responsibilities and their personal aspirations. Many parents value their role as care-giver, but, to the outside world, status and power are achieved through career development, rather than child-care responsibilities.[106] Indeed, as already mentioned, it may even be that the pursuit of personal fulfilment is putting people off becoming parents. In a recent survey,[107] 64 per cent of men and 51 per cent of women agreed that it was more important for women to enjoy themselves than to have children (the fact that the question sees these as alternatives is revealing!). A majority of those questioned believed doing well at work and earning money can 'count for more' than bringing up children. Two thirds of men and women said that career pressures made it harder to bring up children and explained decreases in the birth rate.[108] It is difficult to know what to make of surveys of this kind, but they do reflect a widespread belief that children are expensive, take up too much time and represent an end of fun and youth.[109]

So, with the changing understanding of what it means to be a mother or father, and indeed whether being a mother or father is a good thing, the meaning of family is under challenge. Moreover, gay and lesbian relationships are offering a challenge to traditional heterosexual models of relationship.[110] The future for families is hard to predict. Shelley Roseneil and Sasha Budgeon[111] have suggested that rather than talking of families we should refer to 'cultures of intimacy and care'. They even suggest that for many people the role played by close friends is more important than that played by those with whom people have sex, who flit in and out of life more quickly than best friends. Indeed it has been suggested that we are seeing a rapid increase in friends sharing homes together and this will be an increasingly common social phenomenon.[112]

## 2 Should family life be encouraged?

Most people regard families as beneficial. Indeed the Universal Declaration of Human Rights proclaims that the family is 'the natural and fundamental group unit of society'. However,

---

[103] Beck (2002: ix).
[104] Smart (2007a).
[105] Herring (2009b).
[106] Ghysels (2004).
[107] BBC Newsonline (2006a).
[108] A different poll found that 72% of parents said that pressures at work adversely affected their ability to be a good parent: ICM (2004).
[109] That is utter nonsense of course. Although see Twenge, Campbell, and Foster (2003) for a link between the existence of children and marital dissatisfaction.
[110] Weeks (2004); Lind (2004).
[111] Roseneil and Budgeon (2004).
[112] Scott Hunt, S. (2009); Heath (2004).

there are those who oppose families.[113] The benefits and disadvantages of family life will now be briefly summarised.

---

**DEBATE**

## Is family life good?

### Arguments in favour of family life

1. Emotional security. Family members can provide crucial emotional support and care for each other. Parents can furnish the love and security that children need as they are growing up. As Schaffer has argued:

   > Families are ideally suited for the bringing up of children: they are small, intimate groups, making it easy for children to acquire consistent rules of behaviour; they are linked to various outside settings (other families, work, leisure, and so forth) to which children can gradually be introduced; and they are usually composed of individuals deeply committed to the child whose security and care can therefore be guaranteed. The family is thus the basic unit within which the child is introduced to social living.[114]

2. Families can be regarded as essential to the development of people's identity and to the pursuit of their goals in life. Similarly, families enable children to develop their own characters and personalities.[115]

3. The advantages of family life are not limited to the benefits received by the members themselves. Families benefit the state. Ronald Reagan[116] captured a popular perception that: 'Strong families are the foundation of society. Through them we pass our traditions, rituals and values. From them we receive the love, encouragement and education needed to meet human challenges. Family life provides opportunity and time for the spiritual growth that fosters generosity of spirit and responsible citizenship.'

4. The family can also be supported as an institution which protects people from powerful organisations within the state.[117] It is harder for the state to misuse its powers against groups of people living together, than to oppress individuals living alone.

### Arguments against families

1. A major concern over families is the level of abuse that takes place against the weakest members. It has been claimed that around a quarter of all young females are abused within the home.[118] Levels of domestic violence are strikingly high.[119] Certainly, behind the screen of 'respectable family life' appalling abuse of children and women has occurred. Whether the amount of interpersonal violence would decrease if there were no families may be open to doubt.

---

[113] Barrett and MacIntosh (1991).
[114] Schaffer (1990: 204).
[115] Parsons and Bales (1955).
[116] Quoted by White House Working Group on the Family (1985).
[117] Mount (1982: 1).
[118] Cawson, Wattam, Brooker and Kelly (2000) cite 21% of girls having suffered sexual abuse; 82% of abuse of girls is by parents or relatives.
[119] See Chapter 6.

2. There is a major concern that families are a means of oppression of women. Delphy and Leonard argue:

> We see men and women as economic classes with one category/class subordinating the other and exploiting its work. Within the family system specifically, we see men exploiting women's practical, emotional, sexual and reproductive labour. For us 'men' and 'women' are not two naturally given groups, which at some point in history fell into a hierarchical relationship. Rather the reason the two groups are distinguished socially is because one dominates the other in order to use its labour.[120]

The argument is not necessarily that every family involves oppression, but that the structure of family life too readily enables oppression to occur.

3. Barrett and MacIntosh[121] argue that families encourage the values of selfishness, exclusiveness and the pursuit of private interest, which undermine those of altruism, community and the pursuit of the public good.[122] They insist: 'The world around the family is not a pre-existing harsh climate against which the family offers protection and warmth. It is as if the family has drawn comfort and security into itself and left the outside world bereft. As a bastion against a bleak society it has made that society bleak.'[123] If, rather than spending time on DIY and gardening, family members spent time on community projects, would society be a better place?

## Questions

1. *What, if anything, is good about family life? Are those goods found in all families?*
2. *Imagine we had a completely different society. What forms and structures of intimate relationships could be possible? Would they be better or worse than we currently have?*

## Further reading

Read **Herring** (2010c) and **Fineman** (2004) for a discussion of whether family law should be arranged around caring relationships, rather than sexual ones.

## A Proposing new visions for families

If the law and society were to attempt to promote a radically different form of family life, what might that be?

1. Martha Fineman has suggested that we should view the carer–dependant[124] relationship as the core element of a family.[125] She is therefore seeking to move away from seeing the sexual relationship between a man and a woman as the core element of family life and instead is focusing on dependent relationships.[126] It is these caring relationships which are of real value to society, certainly more so than a couple having just a sexual relationship. Adopting such an approach I have argued in favour of a 'sexless family law':

---

[120] Delphy and Leonard (1992: 258).
[121] Barrett and MacIntosh (1991).
[122] See also Brecher (1994).
[123] Barrett and MacIntosh (1991: 80).
[124] Although see Herring (2007a) for an argument that the distinction between carer and cared for is not straightforward.
[125] Fineman (2004). In Fineman (1995) she had suggested the mother–child dyad as the key relationship. See the excellent discussion of Fineman's work in Reece (2008).
[126] See also Deech (2010a).

We must ask what kinds of relationship require the ministrations of family law: its protective; adjustive; and supportive functions. The answer is not marriage, civil partnership and cohabitation. In other words a sexual relationships is not what marks a relationship as one requiring the functions of the law. Rather it is relationships marked by care and interdependency. These are the relationships which are of greater importance to society and need promotion. These are the relationships which are likely to cause the greatest disadvantage, especially in economic terms, and therefore need the protective and adjustive work of family law.[127]

Anne Bottomley and Simone Wong have suggested that the law should centre around 'shared households'.[128] Property law for intimate relations should depend on the sharing of a home and care, rather than any sexual or formal relationship between the parties.[129] The kinds of approaches mentioned here would all include relationships such as a daughter caring for her elderly father within the purview of family law.

2. Barrett and MacIntosh argue that society should move away from small units towards collectivism. They would like to see a range of favoured patterns of family life, involving larger groups of people living together in a variety of relationship forms.[130] As noted above, increasing numbers of people live alone and this might suggest a model where people throughout their lives engage in a variety of relationships, but without cohabiting with anyone. Sociologists have recognised 'living apart together relationships', where a couple have a monogamous sexual relationship, but live in separate places.[131] Levin suggests three conditions to be regarded as a couple who are 'living apart together': that the couple agree they are a couple; others see them as such; and they live in separate houses.[132] E-mail, texting and other IT makes such relationships easier to maintain. A device that allows couples who are separated by distance to have long-distance sex by drawing in light on each other's bodies may be of assistance too![133] It has been estimated that there are 2 million men and 2 million women in England and Wales who are 'living apart together'.[134]

3. Weeks et al., looking at the meaning of 'family' within the gay and lesbian community, talk of 'families of choice'. Families are seen as 'an affinity circle which may or may not involve children which has cultural and symbolic meaning for the subjects that participate or feel a sense of belonging in and through it'.[135] Family in this definition are those people to whom a person feels particularly close, rather than those with whom there is a blood tie.

4. Beck-Gernsheim[136] argues that for many people there is a pressure between people pursuing their own goals for their lives and the obligations they feel they owe to their families. She argues this will not lead to the end of the family: 'The answer to the question "What next after the family" is thus quite simple: the family! Only different, more, better: the negotiated family, the alternating family, the multiple family, new arrangements after divorce, remarriage, divorce again, new assortments from your, my, our children, our past and present families.'[137]

---

[127] Herring (2010c: 16).
[128] Bottomley and Wong (2007).
[129] Bottomley and Wong (2009).
[130] Barrett and MacIntosh (1991: 134).
[131] Haskey and Lewis (2006); Carling (2002).
[132] Levin (2004: 227).
[133] BBC Newsonline (2009c).
[134] Haskey (2005).
[135] Weeks, Donovan and Heaphy (2001: 86).
[136] Beck-Gernsheim (2002).
[137] Beck-Gernsheim (2002: 8).

## 3 Approaches to family law

### A What is family law?

There is no accepted definition of family law. Family law is usually seen as the law governing the relationships between children and parents, and between adults in close emotional relationships.[138] Many areas of law can have an impact on family life: from taxation to immigration law;[139] from insurance to social security.[140] Therefore, any book that attempts to state all the laws which might affect family life would be enormous, and inevitably textbooks have to be selective in what material is presented. Conventions have built up over the kinds of topics usually covered, but these are in many ways arbitrary decisions. For example, the laws on social security benefits and taxation can have a powerful effect on family life, but they are usually avoided in family law courses. This book has a chapter on family issues surrounding older people, but this topic is not included in many family law courses. Rebecca Probert recently edited a book on the law on intact families (i.e. families which have not experienced relationship breakdown), highlighting how family lawyers tend to focus on issues which arise when families break up, and ignore the many families who stay together.[141]

### B How to examine family law

There has been much debate over how to assess family law.[142] What makes good family law? How do we know if the law is working well? This chapter will now consider some of the approaches that are taken to answer these questions, although no one approach is necessarily the correct one and perhaps it is best to be willing to look at the law from a number of these perspectives.

### (i) A functionalist approach

This approach regards family law as having a series of goals to be fulfilled. We can then assess family law by judging how well it succeeds in reaching those goals.[143] For example, if we decide that the aim of a particular law has the purpose of increasing the number of couples who marry, then we can look at the rate of marriages to see if the law has succeeded in its aim. So what might be the objectives of family law?

Eekelaar[144] has suggested that, broadly speaking, family law seeks to pursue three goals:

1. Protective – to guard members of a family from physical, emotional or economic harm.

2. Adjustive – to help families which have broken down to adjust to new lives apart.

3. Supportive – to encourage and support family life.

It might be thought that functionalism is such a straightforward approach that it would be uncontroversial. However, there are difficulties with the functionalist approach:

---

[138] See Murphy (2005) and B. Stark (2005) on the growing significance of international family law.
[139] Hale (2009a).
[140] See Wikeley (2007a).
[141] Probert (2007c).
[142] O'Donovan (1993).
[143] Millbank (2008b).
[144] Eekelaar (1984: 24–6); Eekelaar (1987b).

1. One difficulty is that a law rarely has a single clearly identified goal. More often it is attempting a compromise between competing claims. A recent Act on divorce claims that it is seeking both to uphold marriage and to make it possible to divorce with as little bitterness or expense as possible.[145] These are contradictory aims. The Act may or may not strike an appropriate balance between them, but we cannot judge the success of the Act by deciding whether or not it reaches a particular goal, because it has several.

2. Another problem with the functionalist approach is that the law is only one of the influences on the way that people act in their family life. So an Act designed to reduce the divorce rate may have little effect if other social influences cause an increase in the divorce rate. The fact that the divorce rate has not fallen may not be the fault of the Act. The rise might be the result of a complex interaction between the law and all sorts of other influences on family life.[146]

3. With the functionalist approach there is a danger of not questioning whether the aims of the law are the correct ones to pursue. So, just asking whether an Act designed to reduce the divorce rate has actually helped reduce divorce sidesteps asking whether we want to reduce the divorce rate. It is even a little more complex than this because sometimes the law appears to create the very problem it is seeking to fix. For example, it is only because we have legal marriage that we have 'a problem' with divorce.

4. A further difficulty with functionalism is that it overlooks what the law does not try to do. The fact that the law does not regulate a particular area can be as significant as a decision of the law to regulate.

These are powerful criticisms of the functionalist perspective, but do not render it invalid. The approach is so tied to common sense that it cannot be denied as a useful method. However, as the criticisms demonstrate it does have serious limitations.

## (ii) Feminist perspectives

Feminist contributions to family law have been invaluable.[147] At the heart of feminist approaches is the consideration of how the law impacts on both men and women; in particular, how the law is and has been used to enable men to exercise power over women. Alison Diduck and Katherine O'Donovan explain:

> The importance of feminist perspectives on family law . . . is to bring to light the ways in which the legal regulation of private, family relations are also about the regulation of social and political relations; they are about the nature and value of dependence and independence, about the balance of social and economic power and about the part that law plays in this regulation. A feminist perspective emphasizes the personal as political, and, born as it was of feminist activism, feminist theory is also about the possibility of the transformation or reconstruction of both.[148]

It is important to appreciate the richness of the feminist perspectives:

1. At a basic level, feminist writers point to ways in which the law directly discriminates against women. For example, at one point in history a husband could divorce his wife on

---

[145] Family Law Act 1996, s 1.
[146] Hill (1995) discusses the wide variety of influences on family life.
[147] For excellent recent discussions of family law from feminist perspectives see Diduck and O'Donovan (2007); Diduck (2003); Fineman (2004: ch. 6) and Munro (2007).
[148] Diduck and O'Donovan (2007: 3).

the ground of adultery, but a wife could only divorce her husband on the adultery ground if there was also some aggravating feature, for example that the adultery was incestuous. Nowadays there are relatively few provisions that discriminate in such an overt way.[149]

2. Feminist writers also highlight aspects of family law which are indirectly discriminatory: that is, laws which on face value do not appear to discriminate against women, but in effect work against women's interests. An example is the rule that financial contributions to a household are far more likely to give rise to a share of ownership in the house than non-financial ones through housework.[150] This indirectly discriminates against women because it is far more likely that women provide only non-financial contributions to a household than men.

3. Feminists have also sought to challenge the norms that form the foundation of the law. Terms which the law might regard as having a given meaning, such as 'family', 'marriage', 'work' and 'mother', have been shown in fact to be 'constructs', images which the law has wished to present as uncontroversial, but which are in fact value-laden. Feminists argue that the law has a construct of what is a 'good mother' and penalises those who are not regarded as 'proper mothers', such as lone parents. Smart[151] suggests that society believes a good mother 'can prevent delinquency by staying at home to look after the children, she can reduce unemployment by staying at home and freeing jobs for men, she can recreate a stable family unit by becoming totally economically dependent on her husband so that she cannot leave him. *She* is the answer.' Mothers who depart from this ideal, for example lone mothers, are penalised by the law and blamed for all kinds of social harms.[152] Rather less work has been done on the way the law constructs men and what makes a good father.[153]

4. Some feminist perspectives have also challenged what are sometimes called 'male' forms of reasoning. These feminists have categorised reasoning which focuses on individual rights as 'male' and as undermining the values that women prize, such as relationship and interdependency.[154] Gilligan has written of a distinction between the ethic of care (which rests on responsibilities, relationships and flexible solutions rather than on fixed long-term solutions) and the ethic of justice (which focuses on abstract principles from an impartial stance and stresses the consistency and predictability of results).[155] This has led to much dispute over whether rights or ethic of care are a more appropriate way to develop feminist thought.[156] Elizabeth Kiss has summarised many of these concerns:

> Feminists who embrace an ethic of care contrast their approach with an ethic of rights which they seek to supplement or even supplant. Cultural feminists and feminist communitarians criticize rights for being overly abstract and impersonal and for reflecting and endorsing a selfish and atomistic vision of human nature and an excessively conflictual view of social life. Feminist legal scholars argue that rights analysis obscures male dominance, while feminist poststructuralists charge that rights language is bound up with socio-linguistic hierarchies of gender and with the outdated patriarchal fiction of a unitary self. Finally, many

---

[149] See **Runkee v UK** [2007] 2 FCR 178 where a challenge to the payment to widows but not widowers failed. Now the benefits for widows and widowers are the same.
[150] See Chapter 4.
[151] Smart (1984: 136).
[152] See e.g. Herring (2008a).
[153] But see Collier (1995; 2000; 2003; 2008).
[154] Gilligan (1982).
[155] For further elaboration on ethic of care see Held (2006) and Herring (2007a).
[156] Wallbank, Choudhry and Herring (2009).

theorists argue that feminist political strategies should not be centred around rights, claiming that such an approach reinforces a patriarchal status quo and, in effect, abandons women to their rights.[157]

5. Feminists have also been concerned with how the law operates in practice and not just with what the law says.[158] For example, although the law might try to pretend that both parents have equal parental rights and responsibilities,[159] in real life it is mothers who carry out the vast majority of the tasks of parenthood. So, it is argued, the legal picture of shared parental roles does not match the reality.[160]

There are, of course, divisions among feminist commentators and there are dangers in referring to 'the feminist response' to a question. Most notably for family law there is a disagreement between those who espouse feminism of difference and those who endorse feminism of equality. Feminism of equality (sometimes called liberal feminism) argues that women and men should be treated identically. Okin,[161] for example, would like to see a world where gender matters as little as eye colour.[162] Feminism of difference argues that the law should accept that men and women are different, but should ensure that no disadvantages follow from the differences. The issue of child care is revealing.[163] Feminists of equality might argue that we should seek to encourage men and women to have an equal role in child rearing so that they also have an equal role in the workforce. Feminists of difference would contend that we need to ensure that child rearing is valued within society and recompensed financially.[164] Society needs to esteem the nurturing work traditionally carried out by women, rather than forcing women to have to adopt traditionally male roles if they are to receive financial reward. The root problem with these approaches is that they can both work against some women.[165] Feminism of equality might work to the disadvantage of the woman who does not want to enter the world of employment but wants to work at home child caring and homemaking. Indeed, arguably, middle-class women have only felt able to go out to work because they have been able to employ other women to provide housework and child-care services. The difficulty with feminism of difference is that, by stressing differences, it can be seen as exacerbating and reinforcing the traditional roles that men and women play and so can limit the options for women. Much work is therefore being done to produce a third model which values the caring and nurturing work traditionally carried out by women, but at the same time protects the position of women in the workforce.[166] Dunn[167] argues there is a need for:

> recognising and celebrating the value of women's traditional areas of work and influence rather than accepting a masculine and capitalist hierarchy of value which can lead to women passing on their responsibilities to less powerful women. In conjunction with this would be the view that this valuable work is something that male peers can and should do, the aim being to facilitate and insist upon change in men's lives – enabling them to become more like women to the same degree that women have become more like men.

---

[157] Kiss (1997: 2).
[158] Wallbank (2009).
[159] This is only true if both have parental responsibility. See Chapter 8.
[160] Wallbank (2009); Day Sclater and Yates (1999).
[161] Okin (1992: 171).
[162] For an argument for gender neutrality in family law from a perspective which is not explicitly feminist see Bainham (2000c).
[163] See Boyd (2008) for an excellent discussion of the uses of equality made by fathers' groups and feminists.
[164] Laufer-Ukeles (2008).
[165] Gregson and Lowe (1994).
[166] For an excellent discussion of equality and discrimination generally see Fredman (2002).
[167] Dunn (1999: 94).

But until men are more willing to undertake this change and value the caring work women do, women are left to carry on their caring work unvalued. As should be clear, the law can only supply part of the impetus for equality for women. Political, cultural and psychological changes are necessary if there is ever to be an end to disadvantages for women.[168]

### (iii) The public/private divide

Traditionally it has been thought appropriate to divide life into public and private arenas.[169] Family law has been seen as the protector of private life. Notably, the European Convention on Human Rights upholds 'a right to respect for private and family life'. The significance of this distinction between public and private life is twofold. First, the traditional liberal position is that there are some areas of our lives that are so intimate that it is inappropriate for the state to intervene.[170] It is argued that it is quite proper for the law to regulate aspects of public life, such as contracts, commercial dealings, and governments, but that other areas of life are so private that they are not the state's business. Goldstein et al. argue that protection of family privacy is essential to promote the welfare of the child:

> When family integrity is broken or weakened by state intrusion, her [the child's] needs are thwarted, and her belief that her parents are omniscient and all-powerful is shaken prematurely. The effect on the child's developmental progress is likely to be detrimental. The child's needs for security within the confines of the family must be met by law through its recognition of family privacy as the barrier to state intervention upon parental autonomy.[171]

Not only, it is contended, should the state not intervene in private areas, it cannot. Imagine a law that makes adultery illegal. This might be opposed on the basis that it infringes people's privacy. It might also be argued that it would be unfeasible. The police cannot keep an eye on the nation's bedrooms and hotels[172] to monitor whether adultery is taking place!

Secondly, it is maintained that where it does intervene in the public arena, the law seeks to promote different kinds of values than it does on the rare occasions when it deals with private law issues. In the public law sector people are presumed to be self-sufficient and able to look after themselves, whereas in the private arena the law stresses mutual co-operation and dependency.[173]

The distinction between private areas of life (into which the law should not intervene) and public areas of life (where the law may intervene) is deeply embedded in many people's thinking and much liberal political philosophy. The differentiation is particularly important in family life, although it is far from straightforward. The following are some of the difficulties with the distinction:

1. Is there really a difference between intervention and non-intervention? Imagine a family where the husband regularly assaults his wife. The law might take the view that this is a private matter and that it should not intervene. But, with this approach, what is the law doing? It could be argued that by choosing not to intrude, the law has permitted the existing power structure to be reinforced. In other words, the husband's power can be exercised by him only because of the state's decision not to step in. So a decision not to intervene

---

[168] Lewis and Campbell (2007); Day Sclater and Yates (1999).
[169] See the discussion in Gavison (1994); Oliver (1999).
[170] See Herring (2009b) for a discussion of the role played by autonomy.
[171] Goldstein, Solnit, Goldstein and Freud (1996: 90).
[172] To make a rather conservative selection of venues.
[173] A distinction is sometimes drawn between *Gemeinshaft*: the values of love, duty, and common purpose (private values) and *Geschellshaft*: the values of individualism, competition and formality (public values).

should not be seen in a neutral light, but as a decision to accept the status quo.[174] This makes the distinction between intervention and non-intervention more complex than at first appears.[175]

2. Can we distinguish the public and the private? Take the example of child abuse. Although this takes place within the home, the consequences of it can affect all of society. The state will have the cost of providing alternative care for the child and of dealing with the social harms that flow from child abuse. This indicates that although the conduct takes place in private it has public consequences. Nicola Lacey argues that all areas of life – both public and private – involve interlocking arrangements, institutions and relationships between different kinds of people and bodies.[176] To classify a particular area of life as public or private is to oversimplify the complex interplay between governments, corporations and citizens.[177] As one commentator has put it: 'government does indeed have an interest in who does the dishes, given that patterns of inequality and inequity in the home may shape both adults' and children's capacities for and opportunities for self-government'.[178]

3. Why exactly might we want to protect the private? The argument for respecting private life is that it enables people to make decisions about how to live their lives free from state intervention. The traditional liberal approach is that each person should be able to develop his or her own beliefs and personality, free from state intervention unless there is a very good reason for the state to intrude.[179] However, this argument does not necessarily support a neutral stance from the state. Take a wife being regularly assaulted by her husband: it is arguable that to enable her to develop her own beliefs and personality the law must intervene.[180] In other words, the promotion of her autonomy (the freedom to choose how she wishes to live her life) which underpins the notion of privacy doctrine does not necessarily require the law to be non-interventionist. In fact to promote an individual's privacy might require intervention in her private life. I have controversially suggested that there are some forms of family life (e.g. those characterised by abuse) that do not deserve respect and so are not protected by article 8.[181] But it may be argued that undesirable forms of family life still deserve prima facie protection, even though there will be very good reasons which justify intervention.

4. Is respecting privacy in fact about promoting societal interests? Eekelaar argues that, rather than dividing the world into public and private, it is more effective to recognise that the state has an interest in all areas of life, and the question is how the state best promotes its interests.[182] In relation to families, non-intervention often best promotes the state's interests. Andrew Bainham[183] suggests that: 'Child-rearing may be seen with equal justification as either a private matter, subject to state involvement only when public norms are transgressed, or as a public matter in the sense that the task of giving effect to the community's standards and expectations for child-rearing is delegated to parents.' So this approach

---

[174] This may be because the law is happy with the status quo or because the law is concerned that legal intervention would cause even more harm. See further Eekelaar (2000a).
[175] See also Freeman (1985).
[176] Lacey (1993).
[177] Schneider (2000a: ch. 6).
[178] Maclean (2007: 77).
[179] Herring (2009b).
[180] Gavison (1994).
[181] Herring (2008c).
[182] Eekelaar (1989).
[183] Bainham (1990).

would require us to ask whether society's goals are best furthered by intervention or non-intervention in this particular area, rather than asking whether this is a private or public area of life.

5. A further argument is that the image of the home and family as a private place is an ideal that may be true for some middle-class couples, but for those reliant on social housing and benefits the home can be seen as replete with social intrusion. In fact the state may police families in a less obvious way than direct legal intervention: health visitors,[184] teachers, neighbourhood watch schemes and social workers could all be thought a form of policing of families outside formal legal regulation.[185] The argument here is that to regard legal intervention in family life as the only form of state intervention is unduly narrow.

6. Some commentators challenge not the existence of the public/private distinction, but the way in which it has been used to women's disadvantage. Such people suggest that, for example, the way that the law has classified domestic violence as a private matter, and the 'problem of lone parents' as a public one, works against women's interests. Indeed a critic would argue that those areas of life which are traditionally the preserve of women are labelled as private and so not worthy of legal intervention, whereas the men's world is labelled public and so deserving of regulation. Further, that by describing the care of children and vulnerable adults as private, the state has avoided much of the cost of care which has fallen particularly on women.[186]

## (iv) Family law and chaos

Any image that family law controls family life in Britain is clearly false. It has been said that 'the law of the family is the law of the absurd'.[187] The point here is that people do not live their family lives only after considering the legal niceties involved. People do not (normally) consult their lawyers before making love, moving in together, or even getting married. The notion that people treat each other in intimate relationships by following the requirement of the law is clearly unrealistic. Indeed family law has been criticised for failing to pay sufficient attention to the emotions that govern how people act in their intimate lives.[188] The vast majority of people simply do not know what the law relating to families is, and, even if they did, it would be very unlikely that the law would influence the way they would act in their family lives.[189] This is not to say that family law is utterly powerless. First, in the cases that actually reach the court, a court order usually has a strong influence on the lives of the parties thereafter. Secondly, the law and legal judgments[190] act as one part of the maelstrom of general attitudes within society towards the family, and the general attitudes of society can affect the way people think they ought to behave and hence the way they do behave.

Family law has to deal with people who act in the heat of love, hate, fury or passion, and so it is not surprising that it cannot itself be entirely rational. Like human beings, the law seeks to pursue contradictory objectives with inconsistent means. There is nothing necessarily wrong with this. To seek coherence and consistency in family law may therefore be a false

---

[184] Health visitors regularly visit a mother in her house following the birth of a child.
[185] Donzelot (1980); Parton (1991); Rodger (1996).
[186] Fineman (2004: 228).
[187] Schneider (1991).
[188] Huntington (2008). See Collier (2009a) for an interesting discussion of the role of emotion in the fathers' rights groups.
[189] Rose (1987).
[190] Especially when reported in the media.

goal. The law is dealing with the chaotic relationships of inconsistent and unreliable people, and so it is not surprising that the law reveals these characteristics too.[191] There is a futher issue and that is that social attitudes and practices are changing fast. Carol Smart has written that family law is 'hurrying along in the wake of changes brought about by people themselves'.[192]

### (v) Autopoietic theory

Autopoietic theory has been developed from the ideas of Teubner. Its main proponent in the family law arena is Michael King.[193] He argues that society is made up of systems of discourse, and that law is but one system of communication within society.[194] One significance of the theory is that it recognises that there are difficulties in one system of communication working with another. In other words, the law has a certain way of looking at the world and interacting with it. The law classifies people and disputes in particular ways ('a mother'; 'a father'; 'a contact dispute'; 'a child abuse case'), applies the legal rules to it, and produces the appropriate legal response. This process may transform the problem, as the parties understood it, into a quite different form of dispute and then produce an answer inappropriate to the parties' actual needs. Further, when other systems of communication attempt to interact with the legal system, unless they are able to put their arguments into the form of legal communication, the legal system cannot deal with them. For example, when social workers or psychologists are called upon by the courts to advise on what is in the best interests of the child, their evidence will be transformed into a legal communication. This may not be easy for lawyers. The law tends to concentrate on sharp conclusions: guilty or not guilty; abuse or no abuse. Social workers, by contrast, concentrate on on-going relationships and working in flexible methods over time, rather than setting down in a written order what should happen to children for the future.

## 4 Current issues in family law

Some of the general issues that affect family law will now be considered.

### A How the state interacts with families

Fox Harding has suggested seven ways in which the state could interact with families.[195] Although only sketched here at a superficial level, they demonstrate the variety of attitudes the state could have towards families.

1. *An authoritarian model.* Under this approach the state would set out to enforce preferred family behaviour and prohibit other conduct. The law could rely on both criminal sanctions and informal means of social exclusion and stigmatisation. This approach would severely limit personal freedom.

---

[191] Dewar (1998).
[192] Smart (2009: 7).
[193] King (2000); James (1992). For a more critical discussion see Eekelaar (1995).
[194] E.g. King (2000).
[195] Fox Harding (1996).

2. *The enforcement of responsibilities in specific areas.* This model would choose the most important family obligations which the state would then seek to enforce. It is similar to the
   authoritarian model, but recognises that some family obligations are unenforceable.

3. *The manipulation of incentives.* Here the aim is to encourage certain forms of family behaviour through use of rewards (for example, tax advantages), rather than discourage undesirable behaviour through punishment.[196]

4. *Working within constraining assumptions.* Here the state does not overtly advocate particular
   family forms, but bases social resources on presumptions of certain styles of family life.
   For example, especially in the past, benefit and tax laws were based on the presumption
   that the wife was financially dependent on her husband.

5. *Substituting for and supporting families.* In this model the state's role is limited to supporting
   or substituting for families if they fail. In other words, the state does not seek to influence
   the running of the family until the family breaks down, but if it does then the state will
   intervene.

6. *Responding to needs and demands.* Here the law intervenes only when requested to do so by
   family members. Apart from responding to such requests, the state does not intrude in
   family life.

7. *Laissez-faire model.* Under this approach the state would seek to exercise minimal control of family life, which would be regarded as a private matter, unsuitable for legal
   intervention.

## B Privatisation of family law

There is much debate over whether there is a lessening of the legal regulation of family life.
Some believe that we are witnessing the privatisation of family life, with the law regulating it
less and less.[197] For example, the Government has attempted to encourage couples who are
divorcing to use mediation to resolve financial disputes and disagreements about what
should happen to the children after divorce, rather than using lawyers and court procedures.
On the other hand, there are other areas of family law where the law appears more interventionist. There has been an increased use of the criminal law against parents whose children
misbehave.[198] So, the picture is not a straightforward one of intervention or deregulation.
Dewar has argued that, rather than experiencing deregulation, the law is focusing its resources
on cases where there is a need for legal intervention.[199] An example to illustrate his argument
concerns parental arrangements for children on divorce. Previously, in divorce cases involving children there would be a hearing where a judge would meet the parties and consider the
arrangements for the children. However, now there is no such hearing and, unless either
party applies for a court order, the judge will not consider the arrangements for the children
in depth. This could be seen as privatisation of family law, but it could also be seen as focusing judicial time on those cases which need it – those where the parents cannot agree what
should happen to the child. Such an attitude can be seen in *Re G (Children) (Residence
Order: No Order Principle)*[200] where it was held that if the parties have reached a carefully

---

[196] See further Roberts (2001).
[197] Herring (2009b). Fink and Carbone (2003) foresee a form of family law based on contracts agreed by the
parties. See further Barton (2007).
[198] See Keating (2008).
[199] Dewar (1992: 6–7).
[200] [2006] 1 FLR 771.

negotiated agreement over the children the court should normally make an order in the terms agreed and not seek to produce an alternative solution.

The law does seem more ready to intervene in family life once the family has broken up. For example, while the family is together there is no direct attempt to ensure that a child is receiving a reasonable level of financial support from his or her parents. However, once the couple separate, the Child Support legislation comes into operation to ensure that a wage-earning parent financially supports the child at a suitable level. The law appears to assume that where a family lives together any difficulties can be resolved by the parties themselves within the ongoing relationship; the law is only needed when the parents separate.[201]

Some research has been conducted into why people seek court orders in relation to children.[202] One might suspect that the reason found was that court orders were sought where the parties were in disagreement. However, the researchers found that this was only one reason why an order might be sought. The other two were:

1. *Authority.* The parents wanted to be able to rely on the authority that a court order gave them, in particular where they felt they lacked control in a specific situation and wanted the confidence that a court order would provide.

2. *Vindication.* Here what was sought was the approval of the court for the parties' agreement and a formal record of it. Also researchers felt that sometimes an application to the court was used to send a message to the child. For example, a father might make an application for a residence order which was doomed to failure so that he could say to the child that it was the court's choice rather than the father's that the child should live with the mother.

Of course, often parties avoid seeking court orders. This may be because of the expense,[203] or the fact that the wrong they wish to be righted is not one recognised by the law. The law cannot usually prevent one spouse spreading gossip about the other, for example.

It is perhaps ironic that at the same time as many call for family law to become increasingly privatised, there has been increasing pressure on the Government to open up the family courts.[204] Traditionally, family cases, especially those involving children, have been held in private, and publication not permitted without express permission of the judge. This has enabled some to say that the family law courts are secretive and are able to pass judgments free of public scrutiny and accountability. Behind closed doors judges and social workers conspired to remove children from their parents and make judgments which were anti-fathers, it was alleged. Cynics might argue that the press were frustrated in not being able to report sordid tales of child abuse and family breakdown which would sell newspapers. The fact that the media were not allowed access to the courts and were restricted in their reporting was seen as meaning the courts were neither transparent nor accountable. Indeed, claims were made that the bar on press attendance and reporting infringed the rights to freedom of the press in article 10 of the European Convention on Human Rights (ECHR). Increasing pressure led to a change in the law.[205] The Family Proceedings (Amendment) (No 2) Rules[206] permit accredited members of the press to attend most proceedings in family courts. This includes ancillary relief proceedings as well as disputes over children.[207] The press can be

---

[201] Eekelaar and Maclean (1997: 2).
[202] Pearce, Davis and Barron (1999).
[203] And/or being refused legal aid funds to bring the application.
[204] E.g. Munby J (2005). For the latest proposals see Ministry of Justice (2007).
[205] Crawford and Pierce (2010)and George and Roberts (2009) provide useful discussion of the issues.
[206] SI 2009/857.
[207] Practice Direction: Attendance of Media Representatives at Hearings in Family Proceedings [2009] 2 FLR 157.

excluded to protect the privacy of the parties, especially children,[208] or where their presence will impact on the evidence given to the court.[209] Those seeking to exclude the press must offer justification for this.

No reporting is allowed concerning cases involving children without the leave of the court. The Children, Schools and Families Act 2010, once in force, will expand what issues journalists can report and will give them access to documents produced for court proceedings. It confirms that the publication of court proceedings is an offence unless it is permitted under the Act, or authorised by the judge.[210] Section 12 permits publication if the information was obtained by an accredited news representative,[211] the information does not identify the parties to the proceedings[212] and is not 'sensitive personal information relating to the proceedings.[213] The Act allows in the future judges to give permission to allow sensitive information to be published where:

(a) it is in the public interest to give the permission;

(b) it is appropriate to give the permission so as to avoid injustice to a person involved in, referred to in or otherwise connected with the proceedings;

(c) it is necessary to give the permission in the interests of the welfare of a child or vulnerable adult involved in, referred to in or otherwise connected with the proceedings;

(d) an application for permission has been made by a party to the proceedings, or on behalf of a child who is the subject of the proceedings, and granting the permission is appropriate in all the circumstances.[214]

When this is in force much weight is likely to depend on whether the interest in the case is simply prurient or whether there are genuine issues of public concern.[215]

In *Re Child X (Residence and Contact: Rights of Media Attendance: FPR Rule 10.2 8 (4)*[216] a celebrity father was seeking contact and residence for his children. The media wished to attend. Sir Mark Potter held that the press should be excluded. In this case evidence of the child's views had been given on the basis of confidentiality. To make the child's views public would breach that confidence. The ECHR article 10 rights of press were therefore outweighed by the article 8 rights of the child. This decision provides a welcome emphasis on the interests of the child. Indeed the reasons provided for excluding the press would apply in many cases.

Critics have complained that although the interests of the press have been taken into account the privacy rights of children have not.[217] Julia Brophy's survey of young people found that 96 per cent of them said that they would be much less willing to talk to experts or give evidence if they knew reporters would have access to what they said.[218] There are also severe dangers that cases will be sensationalised and misreported by the press.[219]

---

[208] *Re Child X (Residence and Contact: Rights of Media Attendance*: FPR Rule 10.2 8 (4) [2009] EWHC 1728.

[209] *Spencer v Spencer*[2009] EWHC 1529 (Fam).

[210] Section 12.

[211] That representative must agree to the publication.

[212] Journalists will be permitted to report and name expert witnesses, but no sensitive details of the parties can be included.

[213] That explicitly includes restricted adoption information.

[214] Section 13.

[215] *Independent News and Media Ltd and others v A (by his litigation friend, the Official Solicitor)* [2010] 2 FCR 187.

[216] [2009] EWHC 1728.

[217] Crawford and Pierce (2010).

[218] Brophy (2010).

[219] See Crawford and Pierce (2010) for some examples.

For those with concern about the increasing potential for press reporting of family cases, some reassurance can be found in the words of the President of the Family Division:

> In my judgment it is grotesquely contrary to the interests of children to allow journalists access to sensitive court documents. Quite apart from the desire to encourage frankness in what may well be very personal and sensitive areas of a case, are lawyers now to draft documents with one eye to them being published in the press? What a charter for the tendentious litigant and the downright publicity seeker! It is simply unacceptable that such documents should be available and, presumably, capable of being selectively reproduced. And if they are to be redacted, who is to do the redacting? And who will pay? Practitioners will be on fixed fees, irrespective of whether you think the process acceptable. Surely the judge cannot be expected to do it.[220]

Assuming this is the approach the rest of the judges take there will be little or no reporting of sensitive material. However, that is perhaps still not entirely reassuring. The presence of the media in the court and the potential for access to documentation will have a significant impact on children and couples going through times of considerable personal stress.

## C Autonomy

Linked to the public–private debate is the role attached to autonomy. Autonomy has become a major theme in family law in recent years.[221] In basic terms autonomy is the principle that people should be able make their own decisions about how to live their lives, as long as in doing so they do not harm others. Joseph Raz defines it in this way:

> The ruling idea behind the ideal of personal autonomy is that people should make their own lives. The autonomous person is a (part) author of his own life. The ideal of personal autonomy is the vision of people controlling, to some degree, their own destiny, fashioning it through successive decisions throughout their lives.[222]

In terms of family law this means that we should respect individual's decisions about how they wish to live their family lives, and the state should not interfere. People should be free to leave relationships without undue hardship. Similarly, in the case of disputes between the parties, we should respect their decisions about how to resolve them. The state should not be telling people how to run their families, or imposing solutions on their disputes. Autonomy appears to be playing a more prominent role in family law with increasing weight being placed on enabling couples to resolve disputes themselves and with the law taking a less interventionist stance.[223] This emphasis on autonomy could be explained in part by it falling in with Government attempts to reduce legal aid and general legal expenditure. It might also reflect the fact that the issues raised in family cases are often contentious: relying on autonomy avoids the Government having to take sides. However, not everyone supports the emphasis on autonomy. I have argued that the image of individuals making choices to pursue their goals in life is anathema to family life:

> Individualism ignores the complex web of relations and connections which make up most people's lives. The reality for everyone, but in our society particularly women, is that it is the values of inter-dependence and connection, rather than self-sufficiently and independence, which reflect their reality. People do not understand their family lives as involving clashes of

---

[220] Wall (2010).
[221] Herring (2010b); Ryder (2009).
[222] Raz (1986: 369).
[223] Herring (2010b).

individual rights or interests, but rather as a working through of relationships. The muddled give and take of everyday family life where sacrifices are made, and benefits gained, without them being totted up on some giant familial star chart, chimes more with everyday family life than the image of independent interests and rights.[224]

Some writers have supported the use of relational autonomy, where the focus is on the making of choices within the context of relationships.[225]

## D The decline in 'moral judgements'

It is arguable that the law is increasingly reluctant to make what some see as moral judgements.[226] At one time the courts were happy to state what had caused the breakdown of a marriage; who was a good mother or a good father; or what was the best way to raise a child.[227] However, increasingly the courts have been unwilling to do this, and have accepted that there is not necessarily one right answer in difficult cases.[228] In particular, the courts are more and more reluctant to accept that a party's bad conduct should affect the outcome of a case. At one time the question of whether a party had engaged in bad conduct was highly relevant in divorce cases, custody disputes and financial cases. Nowadays behaviour is rarely relevant.[229]

Another notable example of the law's reluctance to impose moral standards is the fact that the House of Lords or Court of Appeal will only overturn a lower court's decision if it is shown that the judgment was clearly outside the range of decisions that the court could reasonably make.[230] The higher courts will not overturn a ruling simply because it is not the decision that they would have made. There is some evidence that judges are becoming increasingly less willing to hear cases and make decisions, and rather seek to persuade or encourage the parties to reach their own agreement.[231]

It may be that the law's increasing reluctance to make moral judgements represents increasing uncertainty over moral absolutes in society at large.[232] Bainham[233] questions the assumption that there is a shared body of common values about family life and the role of family in society. He even questions whether it can be said that society accepts that adultery is morally wrong. He argues: 'It seems likely that if we were to concentrate on the practice rather than the theory of matrimonial obligations, at least as strong a case could be made for identifying a community norm of marital infidelity.' If we cannot even agree that adultery is wrong, there are few areas indeed where the law could set down moral judgements. However, Regan has argued that the law cannot avoid making moral judgements.[234] Even declining to express a moral judgement is in a way expressing a moral view. Also, as Bainham argues, the courts are willing to use bad behaviour as evidence of how an individual may behave in the future. So, although a father who has been violent may not be denied contact with his child

---

[224] Herring (2010b: 266).
[225] Rhoades (2010 a and b); Herring (2010b).
[226] For a discussion of the interaction between legal and social norms see Eekelaar (2000a).
[227] King (1999). For a wide-ranging discussion on the role of fault in family law see Bainham (2001a).
[228] *Piglowska v Piglowski* [1999] 2 FLR 763.
[229] Bainham (2001a).
[230] *Re C (A Minor) (Adoption: Parental Agreement: Contact)* [1993] 2 FLR 260 at p. 273.
[231] E.g. Bailey-Harris, Barron and Pearce (1999).
[232] Munby J (2005: 502); Bainham (2000c). This is often put down to a decline in religious belief. However, note that in a recent large-scale study 19% of those questioned said they went to a religious service at least once a month (Babb et al. (2006: 200)).
[233] Bainham (1995b: 239).
[234] Regan (2000).

on the basis that he has behaved immorally, he might be denied contact on the basis that his past bad conduct indicates that he might pose a risk to the child in the future.[235] It is also notable that family lawyers have generally been rather reluctant to discuss the notions of responsibilities in family law. In part this may be due to a concern about the moral assessment that may be implied. Nevertheless it is clear that the notion of responsibility is a key one in family law.[236] Baroness Deech[237] makes the interesting point that we are happy to attach responsibilities and make moral judgements about some areas of life – the environment, diet or smoking – but not in relation to intimate family life.

Criticism of the law's reluctance to uphold moral principles has come from a leading feminist writer, Carol Smart.[238] She argues that there is an overemphasis on 'psy professions' who focus on children's welfare and fathers' rights, while a mother's interests are lost. She is not, of course, calling for the courts to uphold 'traditional morality', but rather wishes to emphasise 'the morality of caring'. This is tied in with an argument that the law should focus on what family members 'do' rather than what their rights are. She argues that the 'doing' of parenthood – providing the day-to-day care of the child – should be given far more weight than in the present law, which instead emphasises rights, such as 'the father's right to contact the child'.[239] Janet Finch has recently argued that as well as family being about 'doing' it is also about displaying. She explains:

> By 'displaying' I mean to emphasize the fundamentally social nature of family practices, where the meaning of one's actions has to be both conveyed to and understood by relevant others if those actions are to be effective as constituting 'family' practices.[240]

## E Sending messages through the law

The number of cases where the courts actually decide what happens to a family is small. Of far more importance is the general message that the law sends to individuals and to the solicitors who advise them. The ability of the law to send messages has been recognised by the Law Commission, which concluded, in a discussion on the law of divorce, that: 'for some of our respondents, as for our predecessors, it was important that divorce law should send the right messages, to the married and the marrying, about the seriousness and the permanence of the commitment involved. We agree.'[241] The law can also send messages through the language it uses.[242] For example, judges have said that it is no longer appropriate in legal terms to speak of illegitimacy, because whether a child's parents are married or not does not affect the child's status.[243]

The problem with using the law as a means of sending messages is that, as regards the general public, the message that the law wishes to send is transmitted by the news media. The reliability of the media as conveyors of legal messages is certainly open to doubt. The Government can, of course, send messages of its own about family life outside the context of the law. For example, the Government has created the National Family and Parenting Institute

---

[235] Bainham (2001a). See Chapter 9 for a discussion of the law on contact.
[236] Bridgeman, Keating and Lind (2008).
[237] Deech (2010d).
[238] Smart (1991).
[239] Smart (2007a: 45).
[240] Finch (2007: 66).
[241] Law Commission Report 192 (1990: para 3.4).
[242] Bainham (1998b). This question becomes particularly important in discussing the enforcement of court orders: see Bainham (2003a).
[243] Though it is not as straightforward as this; see Chapter 7.

to advise people on parenting and family matters.[244] However, Eekelaar has expressed some concern that using the law to send 'messages' concerning how individuals live their intimate lives may infringe the principle that 'aspects of an individual's life are matters for determination by that individual alone'.[245]

## F Legal aid and costs

The role that costs and legal aid plays in family law is crucial.[246] The aim of legal aid, as defined by the Lord Chancellor at the time, 'is to provide a reasonable level of help in legal matters to people in genuine need, who could not afford that help without some subsidy or guarantee from the public'.[247] If legal aid is not available for certain kinds of proceedings then access to that part of the law is effectively denied to a section of the population.[248] Indeed a leading judge has commented that family courts appear to be witnessing an increase in cases where people are representing themselves, which makes cases last longer, and may impede justice.[249]

One notable example is the right to defend a divorce petition. Although this right exists in theory, it would be very unlikely that someone would be granted legal aid to defend a divorce petition. So the right to defend a divorce petition in effect is a right only for the wealthy. Further, there is some evidence that at least in some parts of the country it has become difficult to find a solicitor or barrister to deal with legal aid work.[250] Therefore, in some places the only sources of advice are through volunteers who are not legally qualified (e.g. at a Citizens' Advice Bureau). Even the judiciary have accepted that the family justice system is 'stretched to breaking point'.[251]

Most concerning is the dramatic increase in fees for local authorities seeking to bring care proceedings (in May 2008 the fees were increased from £150 to £4,825), which many believe has deterred local authorities bringing proceedings to protect children. As a result in 2010 the Government announced plans to abolish the court fees for care proceedings. In *R (Hillingdon London Borough Council) v Lord Chancellor*[252] an unsuccessful legal challenge was brought against the increase. The increase in fees has, remarkably, produced strong statements opposing them by both groups representing Circuit Judges and District Judges.[253] Wall LJ has argued that the Government's lack of legal aid funding is exploiting the family law system. In a remarkably unrestrained speech he stated:

> Our dedication, our goodwill, our passionate belief that our function is to address the best interests of vulnerable children and families is not being recognized by a government which, however much it pays lip service to the welfare of children, is frankly indifferent to disadvantaged children and young people who are the subject of proceedings, and simply refuses properly to fund the family justice system, relying instead on the fact that we have always got by in the face of government indifference, and will continue to do so.[254]

---

[244] Home Office (1998).
[245] Eekelaar (2001c: 190).
[246] The detailed law on legal aid is now found in the Access to Justice Act 1999, as amended.
[247] Lord Chancellor's Department (1996).
[248] See *Moses-Taiga v Taiga* [2008] 1 FCR 696 where a husband was ordered to make payments to his wife during the litigation of her ancillary relief claim so that she could afford to instruct a firm of experienced solicitors.
[249] Wall LJ (2008a).
[250] Davis, Finch and Barnham (2003).
[251] *Re C (Domestic Violence: Fact-Finding Hearing)* [2010] 1 FLR 1728, para 18.
[252] [2009] 1 FLR 39.
[253] Circuit Judges Family Sub-Committee (2008).
[254] Wall LJ (2008b: 584). See also Coleridge J (2008).

Mr Justice Coleridge in a speech noted the dramatic fall in the number of child-care lawyers and the shortage of social workers in local authorities children's departments.[255]

A further significant effect of the costs issue is that now all questions of reform of family law must consider the potential impact on the legal-aid bill and the general cost to government. Arguably, the Child Support legislation and the proposed divorce reform in the Family Law Act 1996 were both driven at least in part by a desire to cut the cost to the Government of legal aid. In 2010 the Government announced huge cuts to the family legal aid budget.

## G Families in crisis

There are some who believe that families are in crisis. Typical of such a view is the following statement of the Conservative Party's Centre for Social Justice:[256]

> A strong, successful and cohesive Britain needs strong families. Family stability in Britain has been in continuous decline for four decades. Since the 1970s there has been a decline in marriage. Over the same period there has been a marked increase in the number of lone parents, with a quarter of all children now growing up in single parent households. A further one in four children are born to cohabiting couples. Around one in ten families with dependent children are stepfamilies. Sadly, 15 per cent of all babies are born and grow up without a resident biological father, and seven per cent are born without a registered father on their birth certificate. Britain has the highest divorce rate and highest teenage pregnancy rate in Europe, with the teenage pregnancy rate actually rising between 2006 and 2007. . . . Tragically, at least one in three children will experience family breakdown, in the form of parental separation, by age 16.

Not only are they dismayed at such facts, they are dismayed at changing social attitudes towards sex, family life and the importance of marriage. There is no doubt that there has been a notable shift in public attitudes in these areas. In the British Social Attitudes Survey 2008[257] 70 per cent of people thought there was nothing wrong with sex outside of marriage; the figure in 1984 was just 48 per cent. Only 28 per cent of those questioned thought that married parents were better than unmarried ones. But other attitudes and practice have proved harder to shift: 77 per cent of people in couples say that the woman usually does the laundry, a percentage little changed since 1994.

Despite the wringing of hands over the 'decline in family life', a recent survey found 93 per cent of those questioned were happy with their family life.[258] Seventy-five per cent of people questioned said they were happiest when with their family, only 17 per cent said they were happier with friends. For family lawyers immersed in the problems that arise on family breakdown it is easy to forget that families are a source of great joy for many people. Further, it is arguable that the increased rates of marriage breakdown show that more is expected of intimate relationships, and people are not willing to put up with low quality relationships.[259] That might not be a bad thing. There is also little evidence that family ties not based on marriage become weakened. Marriage may be in crisis, that does not mean families are. There is often political talk of promoting family values,[260] by which is usually meant: stable marriages; gendered division of roles; the confinement of sexuality to the married heterosexual

[255] Coleridge J (2008).
[256] Centre for Social Justice (2010). See the discussion of moral panics in Krinsky (2008).
[257] National Centre for Social Research (2008).
[258] BBC Newsonline (2007e).
[259] Smart (2007a: 15).
[260] For a discussion of the difficulty in finding agreed 'family values' in today's society see Carbone (2000).

unit; and the support of these patterns through government policy.[261] These have been championed in particular by some on the 'new right'. Alison Diduck has suggested that when people mourn the loss of the traditional family they are in fact grieving for the loss of the values of loyalty, stability, co-operation, love and respect, rather than the traditional image of the married couple with children.[262] Others speak of the 'new family', where the traditional notions of family have been cast aside to make room for multifarious forms of family life. So, whether family life is in crisis or simply undergoing change is a matter for debate.[263]

Anthony Giddens[264] suggests that there has been a fundamental shift in the nature of intimate relationships. He suggests that today the typical relationship is one

> entered into for its own sake, for what can be derived by each person from a sustained association with another; and which is continued only in so far as it is thought by both parties to deliver enough satisfaction for each individual to stay within it.

This is a highly individualised concept of relationships.[265] It has been criticised by some feminist commentators for failing to recognise the role that dependency and caring plays in the lives of women particularly. Lewis has argued that although individualism is a significant influence in many people's lives, it should not be thought that this means that people do not value commitment. Rather this commitment is negotiated and the result of 'give and take' within a relationship. This means that the value of the relationship is found by the couple themselves, rather than in the form it takes. In other words people no longer feel there are social expectations on how relationships should develop (e.g. that they should lead to marriage).[266] Rather, people develop their own relationships in their own way.

## H Solicitors, barristers and family law

As we have already noted, the vast majority of disputes between family members do not reach the courts. Many are resolved by negotiation using solicitors. Hence the position of the family law solicitor is a crucial one in the working out of family law in everyday life. Ingleby has suggested the term 'litigotiation'[267] as appropriate to explain what many family lawyers do. The word suggests a combination of litigation and negotiation, meaning that the parties negotiate through the mechanisms put in place to prepare for litigation. The 'guess' or prediction of what a court will order shapes the bargaining of the solicitors. If, for example, the solicitors are negotiating a financial settlement after divorce, they will normally be able to estimate the range within which a court is likely to make an order. The negotiations will then concern where in that range the parties can reach agreement. Further, there is increasing interest in the attitudes and practices of family lawyers.[268] Piper has suggested that 'solicitors appear to have internalised an agreed set of "rules" which must be followed by those aspiring to be good family lawyers'.[269] Even if the case reaches barristers they too make extensive efforts to reach settlement.[270]

---

[261] Jagger and Wright (1999: 1–2).
[262] Diduck (2003: 23).
[263] Howard and Wilmot (2000).
[264] Giddens (1992: 58).
[265] For arguments against such increased individualism see Eekelaar and Maclean (2004).
[266] Lewis (2001b); Eekelaar and Maclean (2004).
[267] Ingleby (1992). See also Wright (2007).
[268] Eekelaar, Maclean and Beinart (2000).
[269] Piper (1999: 101). See also Diduck (2000).
[270] Eekelaar and Maclean (2009).

## I Non-legal responses to family problems

No family lawyer would claim that the law provides the solutions to all problems that families might face.[271] The importance of the role played by social workers, psychiatrists, psychologists and mediators in resolving difficulties families face should not be under-estimated. Thorpe LJ,[272] in an important case concerning disputes over contact with children, stated:

> The disputes are often driven by personality disorders, unresolved adult conflicts or egocentricity. These originating or contributing factors would generally be better treated therapeutically, where at least there would be some prospect of beneficial change, rather than given vent in the family justice system.

It is notable that solicitors are being expected not only to provide legal advice, but also point clients in the direction of other sources of help.[273] In part this is in response to recognition that litigation can be distressing for the child.[274]

As we shall see in Chapter 9, Thorpe LJ's suggestions have been adopted by the Government, with legislation now encouraging non-legal means of resolving contact disputes. In Chapter 3 the benefits and disadvantages of using mediation rather than lawyers will be discussed and it will be noted that recent suggestions of reform of the divorce law have been dominated by attempts to encourage parties to rely on mediation, rather than using lawyers.

## J Rights and consequentialism

The tension in family law between the wish to promote the welfare of the child and the concern to protect the rights of family members has been emphasised by many writers and it gives rise to some fascinating theoretical issues. In an insightful article[275] Stephen Parker has analysed how the approach of family law has swung between 'utility' and 'rights'. A utilitarian approach, he argues, 'evaluates acts and institutions in terms of their consequences for reaching' a goal; in this context the goal is the promotion of the welfare of the child, whereas a rights-based approach seeks 'not to evaluate an act or institution solely in terms of its consequences' (for example, promoting the welfare of the child) but in terms of 'the right of an actor to do it'. Parker suggests that in Anglo-Australian law there had been a gradual shift from rights to utility, but there is now gradual reversion to rights. In fact the picture is confused, as Parker acknowledges, because there is not a clear attachment to either rights or utility across family law at present. He suggests that this represents 'normative anarchy'[276] and Dewar has stated that this is part of the 'normal chaos of family law'.[277] Dewar argues that rights and utility are 'simply different and incompatible ways of approaching the tasks of conceptualising children and their needs and of decision making in such cases'.[278] As we shall see repeatedly in this book, the Human Rights Act 1998 has highlighted this tension between rights and welfare.

---

[271] Wall LJ (2009).
[272] *Re L (A Child) (Contact: Domestic Violence)* [2000] 2 FCR 404 at p. 439. See further Smart (2007a).
[273] Melville and Laing (2010).
[274] *Re N (Section 91(14))* [2010] 1 FLR 1110.
[275] Parker (1992). See also Eekelaar (1994d); Parker (1998).
[276] Parker (1992: 312).
[277] Dewar (1998).
[278] Dewar (1998: 472).

## K Rules or discretion

There is a debate over the extent to which family law cases should be resolved by relying on rules and the extent to which they should be decided on a discretionary basis.[279] Put simply, should a judge decide each case on its merits and be given a wide discretion in reaching a solution appropriate to a particular case or should we have rules to ensure consistency,[280] save costs, and protect the rights of individual family members?[281] In fact the distinction is not that sharp because there is a continuum between wide discretion and inflexible rules.[282] The more family law is seen as a set of fixed rights and responsibilities, the more likely it is for a rule-based system to be used; but if family law is seen as being about achieving justice for the particular individuals involved, it is more likely that a discretionary-based system will be employed. With a discretionary-based system, if the case is going to be decided on its own special facts then the court will require all the relevant evidence to be heard, and this creates more costs in both the preparation of and hearing of a case. So the expense involved is another important factor in deciding the balance between the two regimes.[283]

## L Multiculturalism and religious diversity

To what extent should family law take into account the variety of cultural practices in British society?[284] The question can be framed as how to balance the desire to protect the values of the dominant culture with a need to recognise and respect the values of minority cultures. For example, in relation to marriage, should the law permit polygamous marriages out of respect for minority cultures which may encourage polygamy, or should it rather reflect the disapproval of the majority culture towards polygamy? Corporal punishment of children is another issue over which different cultures may have different practices. Alternatively, the issue can be seen as this: does the law believe that people have rights which should be protected, regardless of their cultural background, or does the law encourage cultural groups to adopt different practices, regardless of whether the majority approves of them?[285]

There are various strategies that could be adopted including the following:[286]

1. *Absolutism*. This view is that the values of the majority are the only correct values. Absolutism would lead to a strategy of complete non-recognition of the values of minority cultures. Minority cultures would have to adopt the values of the majority. This is not an approach that would be acceptable to most western democracies.

2. *Pluralism*. This approach recognises that there are some issues where minority values should be protected, but others where the majority's values must be preserved.[287] Poulter argues that minority cultural values should be restricted in instances where human rights

---

[279] Schneider (1991).
[280] As Dewar (2000b) points out, clear rules would ensure that there is consistency between decisions reached not only in the courtroom but also between settlements negotiated by the parties and their lawyers.
[281] Dewar (1997).
[282] Schneider (1991).
[283] For further discussion see Dewar and Parker (2000).
[284] For some useful discussions see Barton (2009); Banda (2005 and 2003); Brophy (2000); Khaliq and Young (2001) and Malik (2007).
[285] Mouffe (1995).
[286] For a thorough discussion see Freeman (1997a; 2002b).
[287] For further discussion see Raz (1994).

as set out in international agreements must be protected.[288] For example, if the practices of a minority culture infringe children's rights, the law is permitted to outlaw those practices. Parkinson suggests that 'the importance of preserving the inherited cultural values of the majority must be balanced against the effects of such laws on the minority's capacity for cultural expression'. Parkinson insists, in reference to Australia, that there are some aspects of the majority's culture which are fundamental and should be fixed.[289] He refers to the minimum age of marriage, to laws prohibiting incest, and to the need for consent for marriage as being some of the fundamental values. On these issues, minority family practices which contravened these principles could be outlawed. However, on less fundamental values, the minority practices should be respected, even if the majority found them distasteful.

3. *Relativism.* This view states that there are no moral absolutes; that different values may be acceptable for particular cultures at particular times[290] Therefore, if a form of conduct is accepted in a minority culture the majority has no ground upon which to forbid it. If this approach were adopted there might be difficulties over issues where the minority practice is based on a mistaken factual premise. For example, if female circumcision was acceptable in a minority culture because it was thought to provide medical benefits, would the majority be entitled to forbid it because they 'know' that it has no medical benefits? In a more positive light, relativism claims that society benefits from there being a wide variety of different cultural practices and beliefs – it creates a richer and more diverse society.[291] However, most relativists accept that there might be some forms of cultural practice that so infringe the rights of others to live their lives as they wish that they should be prohibited.[292] Opponents of relativism argue that once society accepts that people have certain rights, these rights should not be lost simply because a citizen is from a minority culture. If, for example, children's rights require that the law forbids corporal punishment, children should not lose those rights because they belong to a culture which accepts corporal punishment.

Freeman has argued that a degree of scepticism is justifiable when considering cultural practices:

> Many cultural practices when critically examined turn upon the interpretation of a male elite (an oligarchy, clergy or judiciary): if there is now consensus, this was engineered, an ideology construction to cloak the interests of only one section of society.[293]

He stated that the way ahead is to develop, through dialogues across communities, versions of 'common sense' values.[294]

One of the few occasions on which the English courts[295] have addressed these issues was *R v Derriviere*,[296] where a father gave his son, aged under 13, heavy corporal punishment because he had stayed out late at night. The father argued that the level of punishment was normal by the standards of his culture. However, the Court of Appeal held: 'Once in this

---

[288] Poulter (1987).
[289] Parkinson (1996: 148).
[290] See the discussion in Tilley (2000).
[291] Raz (1994).
[292] Raz (1994).
[293] Freeman (2000d: 13).
[294] Freeman (2002b).
[295] Poulter (1998) provides a thorough discussion of the response of English law to cultural diversity.
[296] (1969) 53 Cr App R 637. 6).

country, this country's laws must apply; and there can be no doubt that, according to the law of this country, the chastisement given to this boy was excessive and the assault complained of was proved.' However, in sentencing the father, the fact that he was unaware of the acceptable standards of corporal punishment was taken into account.[297] Another example was *A v T (Ancillary Relief: Cultural Factors)*[298] which involved a divorce between an Iranian couple, who had recently moved to England. On their divorce the husband was refusing to grant his wife a talaq divorce which meant that even though the couple might be divorced in the eyes of the law, they remained married in the eyes of their religion. Baron J ordered that if the husband did not provide the wife with the talaq divorce he was to pay her an extra £25,000. He did this having heard evidence that this was the approach that Sharia courts would have taken, arguing that where the spouses have only a 'secondary attachment' to English jurisdiction and culture, then due weight could be given to factors relevant to their 'primary culture'. It will be interesting to see whether courts in other cases will accept an argument that a different family law might apply to different cultures.

The issue has come to the public attention with speeches by the Archbishop of Canterbury and Lord Chief Justice attracting much attention because they were (inaccurately) reported as saying that English family law should adopt principles from Sharia law.[299] The question being addressed was, in fact, the extent to which secular courts should recognise or be willing to give effect to decisions of Sharia courts, if a couple have chosen to have their disputes settled by those religious courts. Some feel the courts should respect the decision of a couple to have their disputes resolved by an extra-legal alternative. However, Penny Booth voices the concerns of others with such proposals: 'The danger is in the development of a parallel system of (any) law where the choice as to which system or principle is used is determined not by the individual or the issue but by the group bullies. In family law this danger could arise where the determination of system and approach is not made by the woman but the man: not through the female but through the male-dominated system.'[300]

In recent times it seems that there is particularly a tension between religion and family law.[301] For those with conservative religious values many of the developments in family law are antagonistic to fundamental beliefs, particularly in the area of same-sex relationships.[302] Of course, there are plenty of religious people who take a liberal approach to same-sex relationships. The law must find a way of balancing respect for human rights and respect for religious freedom. This raises broad issues, ranging from whether owners of bed and breakfast establishments can refuse same-sex couple as guests on religious grounds, to whether or when women should be permitted to wear the burkha. These issues are hotly contested. There is a further issue too and that is the extent to which an individual's religious choice should be respected if it is developed in a culture which does not respect individual choice. For example, if a woman chooses to be utterly subservient to her husband after being raised in a culture that teaches that women must be subservient to men, is that a choice to be respected or should it be regarded as a coerced choice.[303]

---

[297] For a useful discussion of how cultural values and human rights interrelate see Freeman (2002a: ch1).
[298] [2004] 1 FLR 977. See also S. Edwards (2004).
[299] Booth (2008).
[300] Booth (2008: 395). For further discussion see Ahmed (2010).
[301] Cahn and Carbone (2010).
[302] See e.g. *Islington LBC v Ladele* [2009] EWCA Civ 1357 where a registrar refused on religious grounds to conduct a civil partnership and was sacked.
[303] Chambers (2007); Mookherjee (2008).

## 5 The Human Rights Act 1998 and family law

The Human Rights Act 1998 protects individuals' rights under the European Convention on Human Rights.[304] That Convention sets out the minimum standards of treatment under the law that people are entitled to expect.[305] The Human Rights Act 1998 has had a significant impact on the way that family cases will be argued. Parents, children and families now regularly bring cases referring to their rights under the Act. There are two important aspects of the Human Rights Act. First, the rights in the Act (which are essentially the rights protected in the European Convention on Human Rights) are directly enforceable against public authorities (e.g. local authorities) and all public authorities must act in a way that is compatible with these rights unless required not to do so by other legislation.[306] The court is a public authority and hence it is generally thought that no court order should infringe an individual's rights as defined in the Human Rights Act, unless compelled to do so by other legislation. Secondly, under s 3 of the Human Rights Act all legislation is to be interpreted, if at all possible, in line with the Convention rights. If it is not possible to interpret the legislation in accordance with these rights, then the legislation should be enforced as it stands and a declaration of incompatibility issued: this requires Parliament to confirm or amend the offending legislation.[307] In interpreting the extent of the rights protected in the Human Rights Act, the decisions of the European Court of Human Rights and European Commission will be taken into account by the courts.[308] The possible relevance of rights under the Act will be considered at the relevant points throughout this book. However, the impact has been less in family law than in other areas. Sonia Harris-Short[309] suggests two reasons why family law judges have taken a 'minimalist' approach to the use of the Act. First, there is a long-standing suspicion of rights among family lawyers, especially because the notion of parental rights[310] might be used to usurp the fundamental principle that the welfare of the child should be the law's paramount concern. Secondly, many family law cases involve complex issues of moral, social and political significance and the courts wish to avoid being brought into such disputes. Hence we will see in Chapter 11 that courts are very reluctant to use the Human Rights Act to order local authorities to provide children in care with particular services.

## 6 The UN Convention on the Rights of the Child

Although the UN Convention on the Rights of the Child (UNCRC) is not technically binding in the English courts, it is frequently referred to by the courts and plays a role in influencing the development of the law. The Convention will be referred to at various points in this book where appropriate. The rights include, for example, a right to life,[311] a right to know and be cared for by his or her parents,[312] and a right to freedom of expression.[313]

---

[304] See Choudhry and Herring (2010) for a detailed examination of human rights and family law.
[305] This point is emphasised in Bainham (2000c).
[306] Human Rights Act 1998, s 6.
[307] Secondary legislation which does not comply with the Human Rights Act can be disapplied: *Re P* [2008] UKHL 38, discussed Herring (2009a).
[308] Human Rights Act 1998, s 2.
[309] Harris-Short (2005).
[310] Perhaps most especially fathers: Fortin (1999a: 251).
[311] Article 6.
[312] Article 7.
[313] Article 13.

## 7 Conclusion

This chapter has considered the nature of families and family law. One point that has emerged is that the terms 'family' and 'law' do not have a fixed meaning. The understanding of a family has changed over time. For example, although at one point a family would have been defined as a married couple with children, the House of Lords recently accepted that a gay couple can be a family.[314] The Civil Partnership Act has now given the chance for same-sex couples to have an officially recognised status. John Eekelaar has even suggested that rather than talking about family law it would be more appropriate to talk about the 'personal law'.[315] Despite the lack of clarity over what a family is, it is clear that it is a powerful ideal: no major political party would openly advocate 'family unfriendly policies'. The chapter has also noted the diversity of ways that family law can be approached. There is no one correct way of viewing the law, and each approach has its benefits and limitations. However, the discussion demonstrates that the interaction between families, law and socio-political forces is complex. The tensions between the traditional ideal of what a family should be like and the realities of family life today are revealed in the topical issues discussed throughout the chapter. As these controversies indicate, family law today is quite different from family law 30 years ago; and where family law will be in 30 years' time is hard to predict.

## Further reading

Bainham, A. (1995b) 'Family Law in a pluralistic society', *Journal of Law and Society* 23: 234.

Bottomley, A. and Wong, S. (2009) *Changing Contours of Domestic Life, Family and Law*, Oxford: Hart.

Bridgeman, J., Keating, H. and Lind, C. (2008) *Responsibility, Law and the Family*, London: Ashgate.

Collier, R. (2008) 'Engaging fathers? Responsibility, law and the "problem of fatherhood"', in J. Bridgeman, H. Keating, and C. Lind (eds) *Responsibility, Law and the Family*, London: Ashgate.

Collier, R. (2009a) 'Fathers' rights, gender and welfare: some questions for family law', *Journal of Social Welfare and Family Law* 31: 237

Collier, R. and Sheldon, S. (2008) *Fragmenting Fatherhood*, Oxford: Hart.

Diduck, A. (2003) *Law's Families*, London: LexisNexis Butterworths.

Diduck, A. (2005) 'Shifting Familiarity', in J. Holder and C. O'Cinneide (eds) *Current Legal Problems*, Oxford: OUP.

Diduck, A. and O'Donovan, K. (eds) (2007) *Feminist Perspectives on Family Law*, London: Routledge.

---

[314] *Fitzpatrick v Sterling Housing Association Ltd* [2000] 1 FCR 21.
[315] Eekelaar (2006b: 31). Although his use of this phrase is potentially misleading because by 'personal' he means 'personal relationships with others'. It is not, therefore, as individualistic a concept as at first appears. See further the discussion in Diduck (2008).

**Eekelaar, J.** (2006b) *Family Life and Personal Life*, Oxford: OUP.

**Featherstone, B.** (2009) *Contemporary Fathering*, Bristol: Policy Press.

**Fineman, M.** (2004) *The Autonomy Myth*, New York: The New Press.

**Glennon, L.** (2008) 'Obligations between adult partners: Moving from form to function?', *International Journal of Law Policy and the Family* 22: 22.

**Herring, J.** (2010c) 'Sexless Family Law', *Lex Familiae* 11: 3.

**King, M. and Piper, C.** (1995) *How the Law Thinks About Children*, Aldershot: Arena.

**Laufer-Ukeles, P.** (2008) 'Selective recognition of gender difference in the law: revaluing the caretaker role', *Harvard Journal of Law and Gender* 31: 1.

**Lewis, J.** (2009) *Work–Family Balance, Gender and Policy*, Cheltenham: Edward Elgar.

**Morgan, P.** (2007) *The War between the State and the Family*, London: IEA.

**Smart, C.** (2007a) *Personal Life*, Bristol: Polity.

**Wallbank, J. Choudhry, S. and Herring, J.** (eds) (2009) *Rights, Gender and Family Law*, London: Routledge.

Visit **www.mylawchamber.co.uk/herring** to access study support resources including interactive multiple choice questions, weblinks, discussion questions and legal updates.

mylawchamber

*unrivalled support for legal education*

# 2 Marriage, civil partnership and cohabitation

## 1 Introduction

In most societies around the world it is widely accepted that it is best for children to be brought up in 'stable intimate partnerships' and that such partnerships can provide adults with much personal fulfilment. The regularisation of these stable relationships has in England and Wales been channelled through marriage, but marriage worldwide is a hugely varied phenomenon.[1] For example, there is no agreement over whether marriage is polygamous or monogamous (i.e. how many parties there should be to a marriage); whether or not the upbringing and/or nurturing of children is central to the concept of marriage; whether marriage partners should be chosen by the parties themselves or by their wider family; or at what age marriage is appropriate. In Britain, in our culturally diverse society, it would be difficult to say anything about the nature of marriage that would be true for all married couples. Traditionally, it has been the Christian conception of marriage which has been dominant, although it is far from clear exactly what that conception is.[2] Increasingly, there is a divide between the church's and the law's understanding of marriage. Legal marriages can take place in circumstances which would not be approved by many churches.[3] It is interesting that some religious groups have even seen the need for legal marriages to be bolstered by special religious pledges, involving commitments beyond the legal obligations of marriage.[4] In England and Wales we have recently seen the creation of civil partnerships, an alternative to marriage which is open only to couples of the same sex. As we shall see later, the fact that it was felt necessary to create a status different from marriage, although very similar to marriage in legal effect, shows how powerful the traditional understandings of marriage still are.

Marriage used to be the main focus of family law. Textbooks would concentrate on discussion of the formalities of marriage, the consequences of marriage, and its dissolution. However, today, many commentators on family law feel that parenthood is the core concept in family law and that marriage is of limited legal significance. Diduck and Kaganas have suggested that 'marriage is both central and peripheral to family law but arguably remains at the heart of family ideology'.[5] Their argument is that, while the legal consequences of marriage are limited, the symbolic nature of marriage still plays an important part as providing an

---

[1] For a wonderful history of marriage see Probert (2009a).
[2] Thatcher (1999).
[3] National Statistics (2008d) records that 68% of all marriages were civil ceremonies (i.e. not in a church or other religious building).
[4] E.g. the Promise Keepers movement in the United States, discussed critically in Fineman (2004: 130–1).
[5] Diduck and Kaganas (2006: 30).

image of what the ideal family should be. That said, marriage still creates some important legal consequences – it would not be possible for a lawyer to advise a client over a family matter unless the lawyer knew whether the couple were married. There are two particular challenges that threaten to limit the legal significance of marriage even further. First, there are calls for the traditional definition of marriage to be widened, for example that two adults be permitted to marry, and that divorce should be more readily available. As marriage has become easier to enter and to exit, any claim that it is a special relationship deserving of particular respect becomes harder to maintain. Secondly, there are arguments that those who are unmarried but live together in many ways like a traditionally married couple should be treated in the same way as a married couple.[6] These pressures make it harder to claim a unique status for marriage.

## 2 Statistics on marriage

The significance of marriage as a cultural concept appears to be changing. This leads many commentators to believe that marriage is in decline. Some statistics certainly suggest that it is.

### KEY STATISTICS

There was a 40% drop in the number of marriages between 1972 and 1998.[7] In 2008 there were 232,990 marriages in England and Wales.[8] Although there had been a rise in the number of marriages at the turn of the century, this has not continued and the current figure is well below the 480,300 marriages in 1972. In 2008, the number of men marrying per 1,000 unmarried men aged 16 or over was 21.6; for women the rate was 10.6.[9] These rates were a drop from the rates in the year 2000, which were 29.5 and 25.7. These are the lowest rates since calculations were first done in 1862.

Significantly, in 2008, 37% of marriages were second or further marriages for at least one of the parties.[10] This suggests that there are numbers of people marrying, divorcing and remarrying who are keeping the numbers of marriages at their present rate.

The number of people who choose not to marry at all has greatly increased. Soon we will be in the position of marriage not being the norm for adults in the UK. Barlow et al. suggest that we are at a time 'where unmarried cohabitation is quite normal and where marriage is more of a lifestyle choice rather than an expected part of life'.[11]

Whether or not marriage is in terminal decline remains to be seen. It is clear that the nature of marriage is changing. Three points in particular are worth noting. First, the average age of first marriage in England and Wales has changed – the average age of marriage has risen from 23 for men and 21.4 for women in 1975 to 32.1 for men and 29.9 for women in 2008.[12]

---

[6] Thornton Azinn and Xie (2007).
[7] Barton (2002b: 437).
[8] National Statistics (2010b).
[9] National Statistics (2010b).
[10] National Statistics (2010b).
[11] Barlow et al. (2005: 49).
[12] National Statistics (2010b).

Secondly, it is now commonplace for a couple to cohabit before marriage.[13] Thirdly, the likelihood that marriage will end in divorce has greatly increased.[14]

## 3  What is marriage?

### A  The meaning of marriage

It is impossible to provide a single definition of marriage. Indeed, one approach is to say that one cannot define marriage because marriage is whatever the parties to a marriage take it to mean. Thus, a Christian couple seeking to base their marriage on biblical principles may well see their marriage in very different terms from a couple who understand their marriage to be open and short-term, entered into for tax purposes. Further, the wife's experience and understanding of marriage may be very different from the husband's. At one time a common marriage vow of a wife was that she be 'bonny and buxom in bed and board'![15] As this indicates expectations of the obligations of marriage have changed over time.

Martha Fineman has written:

> Marriage, to those involved in one, can mean a legal tie, a symbol of commitment, a privileged sexual affiliation, a relationship of hierarchy and subordination, a means of self-fulfilment, a social construct, a cultural phenomenon, a religious mandate, an economic relationship, the preferred unit for reproduction, a way to ensure against poverty and dependence on the state, a way out of the birth family, the realization of a romantic ideal, a natural or divine connection, a commitment to traditional notions of morality, a desired status that communicates one's sexual desirability to the world, or a purely contractual relationship in which each term is based on bargaining.[16]

And this, she suggests, is not an exhaustive list. The lack of a clear definition of marriage may be a sign of the times. It reflects the religious, cultural and ethnic diversity within our society.[17] As Glendon writes:

> the lack of firm and fixed ideas about what marriage is and should be is but an aspect of the alienation of modern man. And in this respect the law seems truly to reflect the fact that in modern society more and more is expected of human relationships while at the same time social changes have rendered those relationships increasingly fragile.[18]

But it would be too easy to see marriage as simply being whatever the parties want it to be, because this denies a wider understanding of marriage within society, in particular the role it plays as an ideal that people aspire towards. Not everyone agrees that marriage is still something aspired too. Rosemary Auchmuty suggests it is generally regarded as old-fashioned and based on sexist assumptions. People feel they need to justify why they are getting married these days, rather than having to explain why they are not.[19] Marriage can be examined from a number of perspectives:

[13] Kiernan and Mueller (1999).
[14] See Chapter 3.
[15] Instone-Brewer (2002: 231).
[16] Fineman (2004: 99).
[17] Eekelaar (2007).
[18] Glendon (1989).
[19] Auchmuty (2009).

### (i) Functional

From a functionalist approach it would be necessary to decide what the purpose of marriage is. Some insist that children are at the heart of marriage. Hoggett et al. suggest: 'If nothing else, then, marriage is about the licence to beget children.'[20] Engels,[21] on the other hand, saw the role of marriage and family as an integral part of the regulation of private property and the creation of legitimate heirs. Others would emphasise the role of creating an environment of love and comfort for the husband, wife and any children.

### (ii) Psychological

Others analyse marriage by considering the psychological need to marry and the psychological interactions between the two marriage partners. For example, one perspective is to see marriage as a conversation between the spouses, formulating their own relationship and their common view of the world.[22] Anthony Giddens has argued that modern intimate relations are entered into 'for what can be derived by each person from a sustained association with another; and . . . is continued only in so far as it is thought by both parties to deliver enough satisfaction for each individual to stay within it'.[23] In other words, people are now more individualistic and are only willing to stay in relationships so long as they feel they personally are benefiting from them.[24]

### (iii) Political

It is also possible to consider the role marriage plays in wider society. Some see the subjugation of women as the essence of marriage. Marriage has been described as 'a public form of labour relationship between men and women, whereby a women pledges for life (with limited rights to quit) her labour, sexuality and reproductive capacity, and receives protection, upkeep and certain rights to children'.[25] Baroness Hale has, however, rejected the argument that there should nowadays be a feminist objection to marriage: 'These are not the olden days when the husband and wife were one person in law and that person was the husband. A desire to reject legal patriarchy is no longer a rational reason to reject marriage.'[26] Mount has suggested that marriage is far from a conservative institution, but rather it is subversive, protecting individuals from the power of the state and the church.[27]

### (iv) Religious

There is a wide variety of religious understandings of marriage.[28] Some religions teach of a spiritual union between spouses on marriage, with the spouses' love reflecting God's love.[29] Some religions regard marriage as indissoluble, although others do not take a hard line on divorce. In England and Wales the law's understanding of marriage has historically been  strongly influenced by Christian theology.[30] In *Sheffield CC v E and S*, Munby J stated that

---

[20] Hoggett et al. (2003).
[21] Engels (1978).
[22] Berger and Kellner (1980).
[23] Giddens (1992: 58).
[24] Beck and Beck-Gernsheim (1995); Lewis (2001a; 2001b).
[25] Lenard (1980).
[26] *Re P* [2008] UKHL 38, para 109.
[27] Mount (1982).
[28] Thatcher (1999).
[29] Pontifical Council for the Family (2000).
[30] For a collection of writing on modern theological understandings of marriage see Scott and Warren (2001).

'although we live in a multi-cultural society of many faiths, it must not be forgotten that as a secular judge my concern . . . is with marriage as a civil contract, not a religious vow'.[31] This is hardly controversial, but the fact that Munby J felt it was necessary to say what he did indicates the hold of religion over the notion of marriage.

## B The legal definition of marriage

The most widely accepted definition of marriage in the law is that in *Hyde v Hyde and Woodhouse*:[32] 'the voluntary union for life of one man and one woman to the exclusion of all others'. This is perhaps better understood as an ideal promoted by the law rather than a definition as such. As we shall see, it is quite possible to have a legally valid marriage which is entered into involuntarily,[33] is characterised by sexual unfaithfulness, and is ended by divorce. Contrast the *Hyde* definition with the more recent definition of marriage provided by Thorpe LJ: 'a contract for which the parties elect but which is regulated by the state, both in its formation and in its termination by divorce because it affects status upon which depend a variety of entitlements, benefits and obligations'.[34] Notably this has no requirement that the parties are opposite sex; that the marriage is for life; or monogamous. Indeed it seems only the 'voluntariness' element of the *Hyde* definition remains in his formulation. It should not, however, be thought that Thorpe LJ's definition represents the current law. Lord Millet demonstrated that some members of the judiciary have a more traditional understanding of the concept when he stated:

> Marriage is the lawful union of a man and a woman. It is a legal relationship between persons of the opposite sex. A man's spouse must be a woman; a woman's spouse must be a man. This is of the very essence of the relationship, which need not be loving, sexual, stable, faithful, long-lasting, or contented.[35]

The law has had much to say about who can marry whom and how the relationship can be ended, but says very little explicitly about the content of the relationship itself. In fact, it would be possible for a couple to be legally married but never to have lived together or had any kind of relationship.[36] In *R (On the Application of the Crown Prosecution Service) v Registrar General of Births, Deaths and Marriages*[37] the Crown Prosecution Service sought an order preventing a marriage between a man charged with murder and the woman intended to be the main prosecution witness at his trial. It was argued that the marriage was being entered into so that she would not be a compellable witness against him. However, the Court of Appeal refused to grant the order. It would not examine the reason why the couple wanted to marry and consider if it was a valid one.[38] This is not surprising because the law cannot force a married couple to live in any particular relationship. The law on marriage merely provides parameters within which the couple are free to develop the content of their marriage as they wish.

---

[31] [2004] EWHC 2808 (Fam), para 116.
[32] (1866) LR 1 PD 130 at p. 133, per Lord Penzance. This definition is discussed in Poulter (1979) and Probert (2007e).
[33] If a marriage is not entered into voluntarily then the marriage will be voidable, which will mean that it is a legally valid marriage, but can still be set aside if the pressurised party wishes to have the marriage annulled.
[34] *Bellinger v Bellinger* [2001] 2 FLR 1048, at para 128.
[35] *Ghaidan v Godin-Mendoza* [2004] UKHL 30.
[36] *Vervaeke v Smith* [1983] 1 AC 145.
[37] [2003] 1 FCR 110; [2003] QB 1222.
[38] See also *M v H* [1996] NZFLR 241 where the New Zealand court upheld the marriage of two students entered into solely so that their parents' wealth would not be taken into account in calculating the level of their grant. Note also that in *Frasik v Poland* (22933/02) the ECtHR confirmed that prisoners had a right to marry.

## C Why do people marry?

Several recent studies have sought to discover why people marry.[39] Of course, the decision is rarely made entirely on rational grounds.[40] Hibbs et al.[41] carried out an interesting study into why people married. Forty-two per cent of those engaged people questioned gave 'love' or 'love and . . .' as the reason for marriage. A further 13 per cent stated the reason for marriage as being a sign of commitment and 9 per cent as marriage being a sign of progression of their relationship. Three per cent said they did not know why they were getting married! Three factors which might have been expected to appear were rarely mentioned: only 4 per cent mentioned children being a reason to marry; less than 1 per cent mentioned religion;[42] and none gave legal reasons for getting married.[43] A study by Eekelaar and Maclean[44] emphasised that different ethnic groups gave different reasons for marriage. They found that among some communities religious reasons and a desire to please parents constituted an important reason for marrying. They suggested that reasons for marrying could be divided into three categories: pragmatic (e.g. for legal reasons); conventional (e.g. pressure from parents, religious belief); or internal (e.g. to affirm their commitment to each other). They found that the vast majority of their respondents referred to conventional or internal reasons in explaining their decision to marry.

Alissa Goodman and Ellen Greaves[45] in a recent survey of the evidence concluded that a couple are more likely to marry rather than cohabit if:

- the mother is of Indian, Pakistani or Bangladeshi ethnicity;
- the mother is religious;
- the mother's parents did not separate;
- there are no children of previous partners in the household;
- the mother and father have high levels of education;
- the parents own their own home;
- the couple lived together for longer prior to the child's birth;
- the pregnancy was planned;
- the mother was 20 or older when her first child was born;
- there is more than one child in the household;
- the parents have a higher relationship quality when the baby is 9 months old.

Another study, looking at why people did not marry, found that the most common reason given was that people could not afford it (21.8 per cent of those questioned).[46] The cost of marriage is also sometimes given as a reason for delaying marriage. One report[47] suggested that the

---

[39] Much less research has been carried out on why people cohabit, but see Smart (2000a) and Barlow et al. (2005).

[40] Barlow (2009a).

[41] Hibbs, Barton and Beswick (2001). See also Barlow et al. (2003).

[42] Kiernan (2001) found a strong link between marriage rates and religious belief.

[43] Although 3% stated that legal considerations had influenced their decision to get married. In fact 41% of those questioned thought (quite incorrectly) that marriage would not change their legal rights and responsibilities towards each other. See also Barlow et al. (2005: 56).

[44] Eekelaar and Maclean (2004).

[45] Goodman and Greaves (2010b: 5).

[46] Lewis (2001b: 135).

[47] Biz/ed (2005). See also Carter (2003).

average cost of marriage was between £16,000 and £25,000. This will represent many years' savings for most couples. A marriage need cost only £94 (the registry office fee), but the reception, honeymoon, etc. that go along with the modern wedding create significant additional expense. One couple attracted publicity recently, spending 'only' £480 on a 'bargain wedding'.[48]

## 4 Marriage as a status or contract

Marriage could be regarded as either a status or a contract. In law, a status is regarded as a relationship which has a set of legal consequences flowing automatically from that relationship, regardless of the intentions of the parties. A status has been defined as 'the condition of belonging to a class in society to which the law ascribes peculiar rights and duties, capacities and incapacities'.[49] So, the status view of marriage would suggest that, if a couple marry, then they are subject to the laws governing marriage, regardless of their intentions or choices.[50] The alternative approach would be to regard contract as governing marriage. The legal consequences of marriage would then flow from the intentions of the parties as set out in an agreement rather than any given rules set down by the law. In English law marriage is best understood as a contract.

Baroness Hale has stated:

> Marriage is, of course, a contract, in the sense that each party must agree to enter into it and once entered both are bound by its legal consequences. But it is also a status. This means two things. First, the parties are not entirely free to determine all its legal consequences for themselves. They contract into the package which the law of the land lays down. Secondly, their marriage also has legal consequences for other people and for the state.[51]

However, Dewar and Parker have suggested marriage should be regarded as 'a contractually acquired status'.[52] There are some legal consequences which flow automatically from marriage, and other consequences which depend on the agreement of the parties. The law sets out: who can marry; when the relationship can be ended; and what are the consequences for the parties of being married. However, following the Children Act 1989 and Family Law Act 1996, increasing emphasis is placed on encouraging the parties to resolve their disputes at the end of their relationship themselves without referring them to court.

Some have argued that it would be preferable to move towards a more contractarian view of marriage.[53] The law could require each couple wishing to marry to decide for themselves exactly what the legal consequences of their marriage would be in a pre-marriage contract. If necessary, the law could produce some sample contracts that people might choose to use.[54] The supporters of such a proposal tend to fall within three camps. First, some feminists argue that a contractarian view of marriage would enable women to avoid the traditional marital roles that are disadvantageous to them. Secondly, from a libertarian perspective some argue that the law should not impose upon people any regulation of their intimate lives. Spouses should choose their own form of regulation[55] rather than there being one kind of marriage

[48] BBC Newsonline 16 August 2008.
[49] *The Ampthill Peerage Case* [1977] AC 547.
[50] For support for marriage as a status see Regan (1993a).
[51] *Redmacher v Granatino* [2010] UKSC 42, para 132.
[52] Dewar and Parker (2000: 125).
[53] Rasmusen and Evans State (1998).
[54] Pre-marriage contract forms are available on the Internet, according to Kavanagh (2000).
[55] McLellan (1996).

sanctioned by the state.[56] After all, there are many different kinds and understandings of marriage and a contractual-based approach can recognise those differences.[57] Thirdly, there are traditionalists who believe that the present law on marriage is too liberal and that a couple should be allowed to contract to enter a 'traditional' marriage, for example severely restricting access to divorce.[58]

Opponents of contractual marriage argue that pre-marriage contracts are unpopular among the general public because they are 'not very romantic'.[59] They implicitly accept that marriage may not be for life. Perhaps more significantly, it is argued that entering a fair contract is only possible if the parties are fully aware of each other's financial position, are independently advised and have equality of bargaining power.[60] In only a few cases will this be so. Even if the parties do have full information and equality of bargaining power, the parties cannot foresee the future, and so the contract may rapidly become outdated and need to be continually renegotiated.[61] Other opponents argue that the contract approach overlooks the interests the state might have in the marriage: the state might wish to support marriage because it has benefits for society as a whole; or the state may have an interest in ensuring that people are not taken advantage of within intimate relationships.[62] If this is so, the state will not want to leave the law of marriage entirely up to the parties themselves. Mary Lyndon Shanley has suggested that the contractual view of marriage 'fails to take into account the ideal of marriage as a relationship that transcends the individual lives of the parties'.[63] Margaret Brinig[64] argues that marriage represents public support and reinforcement for relationships that enable trust to be built up because they rest on a long-term commitment. A compromise solution would be for the state to offer people who wish to marry a range of alternative forms of marriage from which they can choose. For example, some states in the United States offer, as an alternative to the standard marriage, 'covenant' marriage, which permits divorce in limited circumstances only.[65]

## 5 The presumption of marriage

If a man and a woman live together, believe themselves to be married, and present themselves as married, the law presumes that they are legally married.[66] Where the presumption does apply anyone who seeks to claim that the couple are not married must introduce evidence to rebut this presumption. The policy behind this is that a couple who believe themselves to be married should not suffer the disadvantages that would follow from being found not to be married without there being clear evidence.[67] In many cases the presumption can be rebutted by showing that they do not appear on the register of marriage.

---

[56] Evans State (1992).

[57] Shultz (1982).

[58] See Chapter 3 for a discussion of these arguments.

[59] Bridge (2001: 27).

[60] McLellan (1996).

[61] Alexander (1998).

[62] Herring (2009b).

[63] Lyndon Shanley (2004: 6). Regan (2004: 69) argues that marriage is a way of upholding and reinforcing commitments.

[64] Brinig (2010).

[65] Waddington (2000: 251–2). Fineman (2004: 133) reports that where these are available only 1.5% of marriages have been covenant marriages.

[66] The presumption was preserved by s 7(3)(b)(i) of the Civil Evidence Act 1995. A detailed discussion of the presumption is found in Borkowski (2002).

[67] Borkowski (2002).

The presumption is most often used where the marriage took place a long time ago or abroad[68] and so official records are not be available. In *Martin v Myers*,[69] where the couple had never travelled abroad, the court held that as there was no record of their marriage in the register of marriage this was strong evidence to rebut the presumption. In *A-M v A-M (Divorce: Jurisdiction: Validity of Marriage)*[70] a couple, originally from the Middle East, who had travelled extensively and had cohabited for around twelve years were regarded as married: the court was willing to presume that the couple had married overseas. In such a case it will be extremely difficult to show that a couple had not married somewhere overseas.[71] In *A v H (Registrar General for England and Wales and another intervening)*[72] a cohabitation of a year and a half was insufficient,

The presumption can be rebutted if it can be shown that the parties did not undergo a legal marriage. However, the longer the parties have cohabited, the stronger the presumption is that they are legally married.[73] In order to rebut the presumption of marriage, clear and positive evidence must be introduced.[74] In *Pazpena de Vire v Pazpena de Vire*[75] a distinction was drawn between cases where the couple have cohabited following a ceremony but there are doubts whether the ceremony is valid, and cases where there is no evidence of a ceremony but there has been a lengthy cohabitation, with the couple believing themselves to be, and being regarded by others as being, married. Where there has been some kind of ceremony then it must be shown beyond reasonable doubt that the ceremony was an invalid marriage, otherwise the presumption will apply. Where there is no evidence of a ceremony there must be firm evidence that there was no marriage. It is important to appreciate that the law is not saying that couples who live together are married because they cohabit, but that there is a presumption that they have undergone a ceremony of marriage unless proved otherwise. If the validity of a marriage is ambiguous, there is power under s 55 of the Family Law Act 1986 for a court to make a declaration clarifying the status of the marriage.

## 6 Non-marriages, void marriages and voidable marriages

Although it is relatively rare for a party to seek to have a marriage annulled in law, nullity is particularly important because, in effect, it defines who may or may not marry and reveals what the law sees as the essential ingredients of marriage. What might appear to be a ceremony of marriage can either be:

1. a valid marriage;

2. a voidable marriage;

3. a void marriage; or

4. a non-marriage, a ceremony of no legal significance.[76]

It is necessary to draw some important distinctions at this point:

---

[68] *A-M v A-M (Divorce: Jurisdiction: Validity of Marriage)* [2001] 2 FLR 6.
[69] [2004] EWHC 1947 (Ch).
[70] [2001] 2 FLR 6.
[71] Welstead and Edwards (2006: 19).
[72] [2009] 3 FCR 95
[73] *Chief Adjudication Officer v Bath* [2000] 1 FLR 8.
[74] *Chief Adjudication Officer v Bath* [2000] 1 FLR 8.
[75] [2001] 1 FLR 460.
[76] See the useful discussion on the distinction between these in Probert (2002b).

## A The difference between divorce and nullity

The law relating to marriage draws an important distinction between those marriages which are annulled and those which are ended by divorce. Where the marriage is annulled the law recognises that there has been some flaw in the establishment of the marriage, rendering it ineffective. Where there is a divorce the creation of the marriage is considered proper but subsequent events demonstrate that the marriage should be brought to an end.

## B The difference between a void marriage and non-marriage

A void marriage is one where, although there may have been some semblance of a marriage, there is in fact a fundamental flaw in the marriage which means that it is not recognised in the law as valid. This needs to be distinguished from a non-marriage, where the ceremony that the parties undertook was nothing like a marriage and so is of no legal consequence. It is a nothing in the eyes of the law. The distinction is of great practical significance because if it is a void marriage then the court has the power to make financial orders, redistributing property between the couple. If the ceremony is a non-marriage the court has no power to redistribute property and the couple will be treated as an unmarried couple. In **Hudson v Leigh (Status of Non-Marriage)**[77] Bodey J listed the following factors as indicating whether a marriage was a void marriage or a non-marriage.

> (a) whether the ceremony or event set out or purported to be a lawful marriage;
> (b) whether it bore all or enough of the hallmarks of marriage;
> (c) whether the three key participants (most especially the officiating official) believed, intended and understood the ceremony as giving rise to the status of lawful marriage; and
> (d) the reasonable perceptions, understandings and beliefs of those in attendance.[78]

In that case it was clear the event was a non-marriage. Neither the parties nor the celebrant intended the ceremony to be a marriage and the normal wording of a marriage service was altered so it did not appear to be a marriage. By contrast in **Gereis v Yagoub**[79] the couple went through a purported marriage at a Coptic Orthodox Church without going through the legal formalities. Although the priest had encouraged the parties to have a civil ceremony of marriage, they had not done so. Judge Aglionby stressed the following facts in deciding this was a void marriage: the ceremony had the 'hallmarks of an ordinary Christian marriage'; the parties regarded themselves as married (they had sexual intercourse only after the service); the couple held themselves out as a married couple by, for example, claiming married couples' tax allowance. He therefore decided that the marriage was void in that the parties had knowingly and wilfully intermarried in disregard of the formalities under the Marriage Act 1949. In **B v B**[80] a couple got married in a hot air balloon in California. The marriage had not complied with the formality requirements of English or Californian law. It was emphasised in this case that the couple had tried to marry. The husband argued it was all intended as a sham, but the court thought a couple would not go to all the effort they had to undertake a sham. The marriage was therefore void, rather than being a non-marriage.

---

[77] [2009] 3 FCR 401.
[78] Para 75.
[79] [1997] 1 FLR 854, [1997] 3 FCR 755.
[80] [2007] EWHC 2472 (Fam).

It could be argued that the case law is discriminating against ethnic minorities because their ceremonies do not 'bear the hallmarks of a marriage' as understood in a Christian context.[81] Indeed an Islamic ceremony in a private flat[82] and a Hindu ceremony in a restaurant[83] have been held to be non-marriages, being too far distant from what one would expect from a marriage ceremony.

In *Muñdoz Díaz v Spain*[84] the ECtHR rejected an argument that the non-recognition of a Roma marriage by Spanish law was an interference in their right to marry under article 12 or was discriminatory and breaching article 14. The court noted that civil marriage in Spain was open equally to everyone. However, they did find a breach of the woman's rights under the first protocol, combined with article 14, because the state had led her to believe her marriage was recognised, in which case denying her claims to her husband's pension on the basis that there was no marriage breached her rights. So there is no right of a minority culture to have its marriages recognised in the law, but the state must be careful to ensure people know what does or does not count as a marriage.

## C The difference between a void and a voidable marriage

A void marriage is one that in the eyes of the law has never existed. A voidable marriage exists until it has been annulled by the courts and, if it is never annulled by a court order, it will be treated as valid. This distinction has a number of significant consequences:

1. Technically, a void marriage is void even if it has never been declared to be so by a court, whereas a voidable marriage is valid from the date of the marriage until the court makes an order. That said, a party who believes his or her marriage to be void would normally seek a court order to confirm this to be so. This avoids any doubts over the validity of the marriage and also permits the parties to apply for court orders relating to their financial affairs.[85]

2. A child born to parties of a void marriage would be technically 'illegitimate', unless at the time of the conception either parent reasonably believed that they were validly married to the other parent.[86] The concept of illegitimacy is now not part of the law, but still there are a very few consequences that depend on whether a child's parents are married or unmarried.[87]

3. The distinction between a void and a voidable marriage may also be important in determining one person's rights to the other's pension.[88]

4. Any person may seek a declaration that the marriage is void,[89] but only the parties to the marriage can apply to annul a voidable marriage. This reflects a fundamental distinction in the grounds on which marriage can be declared void or voidable. The grounds on which a marriage may be declared void are those circumstances in which there is an element of public policy against the marriage – hence any interested person can seek a declaration of

---

[81] See the discussion in Probert (2002b).
[82] *A-M v A-M (Divorce: Jurisdiction: Validity of Marriage)* [2001] 2 FLR 6.
[83] *Gandhi v Patel* [2002] 1 FLR 603.
[84] [2010] 1 FLR 1421.
[85] *Whiston v Whiston* [1995] 2 FLR 268, [1995] 2 FCR 496; discussed in Cretney (1996a).
[86] Legitimacy Act 1976, s 1(1).
[87] See Chapter 7.
[88] See *Ward v Secretary of State for Social Services* [1990] 1 FLR 119, [1990] FCR 361.
[89] Matrimonial Causes Act 1973 (hereafter MCA 1973), s 16. This section applies to decrees after 31 July 1971.

nullity. The grounds on which a marriage may be voidable do not indicate that there is a public policy objection to the marriage, but rather that there is a problem in the marriage which is so significant that, if one of the parties wishes, the marriage can be annulled.

Having discussed these distinctions it is now necessary to consider the grounds on which a marriage may be void or voidable.

## D  The grounds on which a marriage is void

As already noted, the grounds[90] on which a marriage is void are those which reflect a public policy objection to the marriage. The grounds[91] are set out in the Matrimonial Causes Act 1973, s 11:

---

### LEGISLATIVE PROVISION

**Matrimonial Causes Act 1973, section 11**

(a)  that it is not a valid marriage under the provisions of the Marriage Acts 1949 to 1986 (that is to say where—

  (i)  the parties are within the prohibited degrees of relationship;
  (ii)  either party is under the age of sixteen; or
  (iii)  the parties have intermarried in disregard of certain requirements as to the formation of marriage);

(b)  that at the time of the marriage either party was already lawfully married;

(c)  that the parties are not respectively male and female;

(d)  in the case of a polygamous marriage entered into outside England and Wales, that either party was at the time of the marriage domiciled in England and Wales.

---

These grounds will now be considered separately.

### (i)  Prohibited degrees

The marriage between two people who are related to each other in certain ways is prohibited. It is interesting that nearly all societies across the world have bars on marriages between people who are related. In Britain the restrictions are based on two groups of relations: those based on blood relationships (consanguinity) and those based on marriage (affinity). The details of the law are set out in the Marriage (Prohibited Degrees of Relationship) Act 1986, s 6(2).[92]

1.  The prohibited consanguinity restrictions mean that marriage between the following is not permitted: parent–child; grandparent–grandchild; brother–sister; uncle–niece; aunt–nephew. These include relations of the half-blood as well as those relationships based on the whole blood. It will be noted that cousins may marry under English law.[93]

---

[90]  *Re Roberts (dec'd)* [1978] 1 WLR 653 at p. 656, per Walton J.
[91]  Walton J suggested that the set of grounds set out in MCA 1973 is exhaustive and so there is no jurisdiction for the courts to create new grounds: *Re Roberts (dec'd)* [1978] 1 WLR 653 at p. 658.
[92]  As amended by the Marriage Act 1949 (Remedial) Order 2007 No 438.
[93]  For a discussion of whether cousin marriage should be permitted see Deech (2010c) and Taylor (2008) who both express concerns about the potential genetic harms to children of such marriages.

2. The affinity restrictions are traditionally based on the 'unity of husband and wife'. This is the notion that, on marriage, a husband and wife become one. These prohibited degrees based on marriage are controversial because some believe that the doctrine of unity upon which they are based is outdated. Only one remains: *Marrying a stepchild*. A step-parent can marry the child of a former spouse if: (i) both parties are aged 21 or over; and (ii) the younger party has not been a child of the family in relation to the other while under the age of 18. The effect of the law is that if a step-parent acts in a parental role towards a stepchild, the two can never marry. The bar on parents-in-law and children-in-law that used to exist was abolished by the Marriage Act 1949 (Remedial) Order 2007 No 438. This follows the decision in *B v UK*[94] where a man wanted to marry his daughter-in-law. The law (at the time) prohibited this and they challenged it in the European Court of Human Rights. The Court held that the UK law improperly interfered with the couple's right to marry under article 12 of the ECHR. The UK Government argued that the policy was justified in order to discourage sexual rivalry between parents and children and to protect a child from confusion over who their parents and grandparents were. However, the Court felt that the fact that parents- and children-in-law could cohabit meant that these risks existed anyway and the marriage bar did not prevent them arising. The Government responded by removing the bar.

3. Even though adoption normally ends the relationship between the adopted child and his or her birth family, the restrictions on marriage between an adopted child and members of his or her birth family apply as above. An adoptive child and adoptive parent are also within the prohibited degrees of relationship.[95] However, an adopted child can marry other relations that arise from the adoption. So a man could marry the daughter of his adopted parents.[96]

The restrictions based on these relationships are justified by three arguments.[97] The first is the fear of genetic dangers involved in permitting procreation between close blood relations. This would not justify bars based on affinity[98] and with the availability of genetic screening may be harder to support. A second argument in favour of these bars is that permitting marriage between close relations may undermine the security of the family. The argument is that children should be brought up without the possibility of approved sexual relations later in life with members of their family. A third argument can be based on the widespread instinctive moral reaction against such relationships.

It should be recalled that although these restrictions prevent, say, a father marrying his daughter, there would be nothing to prevent them cohabiting, although any sexual relations would constitute the crime of incest.

## (ii) Age

There are two requirements that relate to the age of the parties:

1. A marriage will be void if either party to the marriage is under 16.[99] All western societies have some kind of age restrictions on who may marry and a minimum age for legal sexual

---

[94] [2005] 3 FCR 353, discussed in Cretney (2006b) and Gaffney-Rhys (2005).

[95] This is a permanent bar and applies even if the child is adopted for a second time.

[96] Assuming the daughter is not his half-sister.

[97] For an argument that the list of prohibited relationships should be added to, see Cretney, Masson and Bailey-Harris (2002: 42).

[98] Interestingly, Australia has removed all restrictions on marriage based on affinity: see Finlay (1976).

[99] Marriage Act 1949, s 2. On the issue of under-age marriage see Bunting (2005) and Gangoli, McCarry, and Razak (2009).

relations, although exactly what that age is varies from state to state and generation to generation.[100] The choice of the age 16 in England and Wales reflects the policy of the criminal law that it is unlawful for a man to have sexual intercourse with a girl under 16. It also reflects the concern of society about any children that may be born of such a union: the parents may be too young to care for the children and the burden could then fall on the state. There is also the argument that, below that age, the parties may not fully understand the consequences of marriage.

2. The second requirement is that if either party is between the age of 16 and 18 then it is necessary to have the written consent of each parent with parental responsibility.[101] It is possible for the teenager to apply to the court to have the parental consent requirement revoked. However, if the marriage goes ahead without that consent (or on the basis of a forged consent), it would still be valid. The significance of this requirement, then, is that it permits a registrar to refuse to carry out a wedding without this consent. Rebecca Probert has questioned whether requiring parental consent to marry is appropriate in this day and age.[102]

### (iii) Formalities

There are complex rules governing the legal formalities required for a marriage. The exact requirements depend on whether the marriage was performed within the rites of the Church of England or outside. The detailed provisions will not be discussed here.[103]

The purposes of having formalities can be said to be as follows:

1. The formality requirements help to draw a clear line between a marriage, an engagement, and an agreement to cohabit.

2. The formality requirements ensure that the parties do not enter into marriage in an ill-considered or frivolous way. To fulfil the requirements takes some time and effort. Further, they ensure that the moment of marriage is a solemn event. This reinforces the seriousness of marriage to the parties and those present.

3. The existence of the formalities helps to ensure that there is a formal record of marriages.[104]

4. The formalities also ensure that anyone who wishes to object to the marriage can do so.

There are, however, dangers that formalities can be too strict. There are two particular concerns. The first is that couples may be discouraged from marrying if the formalities are too onerous. This concern led to the passing of the Marriage Act 1995, which has greatly increased the number of places where a marriage can take place. Secondly, if the law were interpreted too strictly, a minor breach of the rules could invalidate what might appear to be a valid marriage. The law has dealt with this concern under ss 25 and 49 of the Marriage Act 1995,

---

[100] Indeed, until 1929 in England a girl could marry from the age of 12.

[101] Unless there is a residence order, in which case only the parents with parental responsibility and residence order need consent: Marriage Act 1949, s 3, as amended. A guardian or local authority can also provide consent in certain circumstances.

[102] Probert (2009).

[103] See Cretney, Masson and Bailey-Harris (2002: ch. 2).

[104] Although see the remarkable case of *Islam v Islam* [2003] FL 815 where, although the evidence showed that the woman had been married, she was not able to show that she had married the man she claimed to be her husband. The judge asked the papers to be sent to the Crown Prosecution Service so that it could consider possible criminal proceedings against the wife.

which state that a marriage is void for breaching the formalities only if the parties marry knowingly and wilfully in breach of the requirement.[105]

One further issue is whether the parties should be required to undergo biological tests, in order to see if either party is suffering from an infectious illness. There have been calls for genetic testing to be carried out on the parties before marriage.[106] At present no biological tests are required in England and Wales. The reason may be that a requirement of tests would discourage marriage.

There have also been some calls that couples be required to attend marriage counselling sessions before marriage. The closest the Government has come is the proposal that a 'clear and simple guide' detailing the rights and responsibilities of marriage should be made available to all couples planning to marry.[107] This seems very sensible given the lack of under-standing over the legal consequences of marriage.[108] In the USA a computer questionnaire has become a popular way for a couple to check compatibility before marriage. Apparently, having taken the test and considered the results, 10 per cent of couples decided not to marry.[109]

## (iv) Bigamy

If at the time of the ceremony either party is already married to someone else, the 'marriage' will be void. The marriage will remain void even if the first spouse dies during the second 'marriage'.[110] So, if a person is married and wishes to marry someone else, he or she must obtain a decree of divorce or wait until the death of his or her spouse. If the first marriage is void it is technically not necessary to obtain a court order to that effect before marrying again, but that is normally sought to avoid any uncertainty. In cases of bigamy, as well as the pur-ported marriage being void, the parties may have committed the crime of bigamy.[111] Chris Barton[112] has argued that there is little justification for making bigamy a crime and instead more could be done at the time of marriage to check whether parties are free to marry.

Many cultures do permit polygamous marriages, although in British society monogamous marriages are the accepted norm, which is rarely challenged.[113] There are concrete objections to polygamous marriages. Some argue that polygamy may create divisions within the family, with one husband or wife vying for dominance over the others, and particularly that divisions may arise between the children of different parents.[114] Supporters of polygamous marriage argue that polygamy leads to less divorce and provides a wider family support network in which to raise children. Polygamy could also be regarded as a form of sex discrimination unless both men and women were permitted to take more than one spouse. There have also been suggestions that permitting polygamous marriages involves an insult to the religious sensitivities of the majority.[115]

---

[105] See *Chief Adjudication Officer* v *Bath* [2000] 1 FCR 419, [2000] 1 FLR 8 for an example of a case where the parties were unaware of the non-compliance with the formalities.

[106] Discussed in Deech (1998).

[107] Home Office (1998: 4.15).

[108] Hibbs, Barton and Beswick (2001).

[109] Hibbs, Barton and Beswick (2001). See Simons (1999) for a detailed discussion of marriage preparation.

[110] *Dredge* v *Dredge* [1947] 1 All ER 29.

[111] In *Khan* v *UK* (1986) 48 DR 253 the European Court of Human Rights rejected an argument that the bar on polygamous marriage infringed the parties' rights under article 12 of the European Convention.

[112] Barton (2004).

[113] For a detailed discussion see Bradney (1993); Parkinson (1996). Shah (2003) discusses the extent of unofficial polygamy in the UK and highlights the problems in regulating against it.

[114] See Bala and Jaremko Bromwich (2002: 166–9) for a discussion of the arguments against polygamy. See Kaganas and Murray (1991) and Emens (2004) for a more supportive approach.

[115] Devlin (1965).

## (v) The parties must be respectively male and female

A marriage is void if the parties are not respectively male and female in a biological sense. This gives rise to two separate issues. The first is deciding what is a man and what is a woman: in particular, how the law should deal with transsexual and intersex people. The second is whether the law should permit two people of the same sex to marry if they wish. As these situations raise different problems they will be considered separately. The first shall be discussed here, but the issue of same-sex marriage will be considered when civil partnerships are discussed.

### (a) Transsexual people

The question of deciding how to define sex has arisen in particular because of the law's treatment of transsexual people.[116] These are people who are born with some or all of the biological characteristics of one sex, but psychologically feel they belong to the other sex.[117] There is a treatment available on the National Health Service[118] and in private hospitals, known as 'gender realignment surgery' (popularly known as a 'sex change operation'[119]). This, combined with hormonal drug treatment, has the effect that the outward appearance of the patient matches their 'psychological sex'. Such a person can then operate in society to a large extent as the sex they feel they ought to be. It should be stressed that this complaint is well recognised medically and some clinicians believe that the condition may have a physical, rather than a psychological, cause.

The law relating to transsexual people is now dominated by the Gender Recognition Act 2004. Before that legislation the leading case on transsexual people and marriage was *Corbett v Corbett*,[120] a decision of Ormrod J. He argued that for the purpose of the law an individual's sex is fixed at birth: 'The law should adopt in the first place the first three of the doctor's criteria, i.e., the chromosomal, gonadal and genital tests, and if all three are congruent, determine the sex for the purpose of marriage accordingly, and ignore any operative intervention.'[121] So, in the case before him, April Ashley, born as a man but having undergone a 'sex change operation' and living as a woman, was a man and could not enter into a marriage with a man.[122] The law based on that case was found incompatible with the ECHR in *Goodwin v UK*[123] and *I v UK*.[124] Following *Goodwin*, the case of *Bellinger v Bellinger*[125] issued a declaration that the definition of sex in s 11(c) of the Matrimonial Causes Act 1973 which prohibited a transsexual person marrying in her declared sex was incompatible with articles 8 and 12 of the European Convention on Human Rights.

---

[116] Taitz (1988); Khaliq (1996); Sharpe (2002); Whittle (2002).

[117] There is no definitive data on the number of transsexual people, but estimates vary between 2,000 and 5,000: Home Office (2000a).

[118] Although there is no right to such treatment: *R v North West Lancashire HA, ex p A* [2000] 2 FCR 525.

[119] This term is disliked by many transsexual people who argue that the operation is not changing their sex, but rather is bringing their body in line with their true sex. By contrast see Eekelaar (2006b: 55) who sees the Gender Recognition Act as creating a clash between legal truth and physical truth.

[120] [1971] P 83.

[121] At p. 106.

[122] Sharpe (2002) and Whittle (2002: ch. 7) provide a detailed analysis and criticism of his decision. See also Chau and Herring (2002: 347–51).

[123] [2002] 2 FCR 577.

[124] [2002] 2 FCR 613.

[125] [2003] UKHL 21, [2003] 2 FCR 1. See Gilmore (2003b) for a powerful critique of the decision.

The Government responded by producing the Gender Recognition Act 2004. Under the Act a person can apply for a Gender Recognition Certificate. Section 9(1) explains:

## LEGISLATIVE PROVISION

### Gender Recognition Act 2004, section 9(1)

Where a full gender recognition certificate is issued to a person, the person's gender becomes for all purposes the acquired gender (so that, if the acquired gender is the male gender, the person's sex becomes that of a man and, if it is the female gender, the person's sex becomes that of a woman).

There are two alternative grounds on which a person may apply to the Gender Recognition Panel for a certificate.[126] First that they have 'changed their gender'[127] under the law of another country. Secondly, they are living in the gender which is not that on their birth certificate. To issue a certificate on the second ground the panel must be persuaded that the applicant:

## LEGISLATIVE PROVISION

### Gender Recognition Act 2004, section 2(1)

(a) has or has had gender dysphoria,

(b) has lived in the acquired gender throughout the period of two years ending with the date on which the application is made,

(c) intends to continue to live in the acquired gender until death.[128]

The applicant is required to produce reports from experts in the field to establish these facts.[129] It should be noted that it is not necessary for a person to have undergone any surgery. Once a certificate is issued the individual's gender is changed for all purposes. In *R (AB)* v *Secretary of State for Justice*[130] AB had been issued with a certificate meaning she was a woman and it was therefore held to be unlawful to place her in a man's prison.

Where the individual is married the Panel cannot issue a full gender recognition certificate, the reason being that otherwise the result would be a same-sex marriage.[131] Instead an interim gender recognition certificate is issued to the applicant.[132] This will become a full certificate if their spouse dies or the marriage comes to a legal end. The issuing of an interim gender

---

126 www.grp.gov.uk is the website of the Gender Recognition Panel and contains some useful material on its work.

127 This phrase is given in quotation marks because many transsexual people do not regard themselves as having changed sex, but as having their body altered to align to their true sex.

128 Gender Recognition Act 2004 (GRA 2004), s 2(1).

129 GRA 2004, s 3.

130 [2009] EWHC 2220 (Admin).

131 These provisions reveal the desperate lengths to which Parliament feels it needs to go in order to ensure there cannot be a same-sex marriage.

132 GRA 2004, s 4.

recognition certificate can be a ground for annulment or a fact to be relied upon to establish the ground of divorce.[133] In *Parry v UK*[134] a husband, with the support of his wife, had undergone gender reassignment surgery. The couple were devout Christians and wished to remain married, but the husband wanted a full recognition certificate. As we have seen she could not do both: she either could get the certificate[135] or remain married. The ECtHR rejected their complaint that the current English law infringed their ECHR rights. The fact that they could get a gender recognition certificate and then enter a civil partnership meant their rights were not infringed.

As already stated, the full certificate changes the legal categorisation of the person's sex, but it does 'not affect the status of the person as the father or mother of a child'.[136] As Stephen Gilmore has pointed out, this means that a person could be the mother of one child and the father of another.[137] It should also be noted that those transsexual people who do not apply for a certificate have their sex determined by the *Corbett* test set out above.[138] Between 4 April 2005 and 31 January 2010 1,443 full certificates have been granted; and 46 interim certificates. Only 46 applications were refused and 7 withdrawn.[139]

Generally the Act has been welcomed. At last individuals suffering from gender identity dysphoria can be recognised in law as having the sex with which they identify. Yet there are some who raise concerns about the legislation. Alison Diduck[140] has expressed concern that the legislation appears to regard gender dysphoria as an abnormal dysfunction that needs special medical and legal treatment. It is almost as if it is some highly contagious condition which needs careful control and monitoring. Certainly the wait for two years is a long time. While a wait before undergoing surgery may be sensible given it is so hard to reverse, is there a need for a wait before obtaining a certificate? John Eekelaar objects to the fact that on the issue of a gender recognition certificate a new birth certificate is issued. He argues doing so feeds the climate of discrimination and harassment that the legislation is designed to combat. If society approves of gender reassignment surgery it should 'shout about it from the rooftops'.[141] However, transsexual people claim that the surgery is bringing their body in line with their true sex. So reissuing the birth certificate is correcting an erroneous document. Andrew Sharpe notes that the Act makes a failure to disclose gender a ground of annulment of a marriage. This, he suggests, reveals the suspicion the law retains about transsexual people.[142]

Others have complained that the legislation does nothing for a transsexual or an intersex person who wishes to be regarded as neither male nor female. Indeed the legislation can be said to reflect the law's obsession with categorising people into being either male or female.[143] Some commentators have argued that far from there being two boxes for male and female, there is rather a scale of maleness and femaleness.[144]

---

[133] GRA 2004, Sch 2.
[134] Application No. 42971/05.
[135] They were unkeen on the option of getting a gender recognition certificate and entering a civil partnership.
[136] GRA 2004, s 12.
[137] Gilmore (2003b). Where a woman gives birth to a child, is later given a gender recognition certificate and thereafter, with his new female partner, receives fertility treatment at a licensed clinic and a child is born as a result.
[138] Probert (2005).
[139] Gender Recognition Users Panel (2010).
[140] Diduck (2003: ch. 1).
[141] Eekelaar (2006b: 76).
[142] Sharpe (2007).
[143] Chau and Herring (2004: 201); Sandland (2005).
[144] O'Donovan (1993); Chau and Herring (2004).

## (b) Intersex people

Transsexual people must be clearly differentiated from intersex people who are born with sexual or reproductive organs of both sexes. As the biological sex of an intersex person is ambiguous at birth, the doctors, in consultation with the family, will select a sex for the child.[145] Tragically it can later become clear that the doctors made the wrong choice and the child's body develops in a way clearly in line with the opposite sex. In such cases it is possible to amend the birth certificate to reflect the fact that an error was made in determining the sex at birth and the child will be regarded as having the later sex.

The leading case in this area is now *W v W (Nullity)*,[146] where Charles J held that if a person was born with ambiguous genitalia the individual's sex was to be determined by considering: (i) chromosomal factors; (ii) gonadal factors; (iii) genital factors; (iv) psychological factors; (v) hormonal factors; and (vi) secondary sexual characteristics (such as distribution of hair, breast development, etc.). Notably, Charles J accepted that a decision as to someone's sex could be made at the time of the marriage, taking these factors into account. As we have seen, some commentators take the view that the position of intersex people reveals that there is no hard and fast division between male and female, but rather there is a scale between maleness and femaleness and people are placed at various points on that scale.[147] To them we should simply treat everyone as a person and not classify people as male or female. That would mean, in this context, that any two people should be allowed to marry. Objectors to this view might reply that it overlooks the reality that the vast majority of people clearly do strongly regard themselves as either male or female. It is highly artificial to refer to a scale when virtually everyone is at either end of it.

### (vi) Public policy

There is one reported case where a marriage was rendered void on the basis of public policy. In *City of Westminster v C*[148] the Court of Appeal held a marriage between a man with severe intellectual impairment and a woman in Bangladesh performed over the telephone void. He lacked capacity to have any understanding of the nature of marriage and would be unable to consent to sexual relations. The marriage was described as exploitative of the woman and of the man. Although normally lack of capacity would render a marriage voidable rather than void, public policy justified this marriage being declared void.

### (vii) Marriages entered into abroad

Complex issues of private international law arise over the recognition of marriages conducted abroad, and these are not discussed in this book.[149]

## E The grounds on which a marriage is voidable

The grounds on which a marriage is voidable are set out in the Matrimonial Causes Act 1973, s 12:

---

[145] For a detailed discussion of the medical and legal issues surrounding intersexual people see Chau and Herring (2002 and 2004).

[146] [2000] 3 FCR 748; discussed in Herring and Chau (2001). See also *B v B* [1954] 2 All ER 598.

[147] The argument is developed in Chau and Herring (2002). See also the interesting discussion of the meaning of sex in Grenfell (2003).

[148] [2008] 2 FCR 146, see Probert (2008a) for a discussion of this case.

[149] See, e.g., Murphy (2005).

> ## LEGISLATIVE PROVISION
>
> **Matrimonial Causes Act 1973, section 12**
>
> (a) that the marriage has not been consummated owing to the incapacity of either party to consummate it;
>
> (b) that the marriage has not been consummated owing to the wilful refusal of the respondent to consummate it;
>
> (c) that either party to the marriage did not validly consent to it, whether in consequence of duress, mistake, unsoundness of mind or otherwise;
>
> (d) that at the time of the marriage either party, though capable of giving a valid consent, was suffering (whether continuously or intermittently) from mental disorder within the meaning of the Mental Health Act 1983 of such a kind or to such an extent as to be unfitted for marriage;
>
> (e) that at the time of the marriage the respondent was suffering from venereal disease in a communicable form;
>
> (f) that at the time of the marriage the respondent was pregnant by some person other than the petitioner.

These grounds will now be considered separately.

### (i) Inability or wilful refusal to consummate

The importance of consummation was originally based on the theological ground that the act of sexual intercourse united the two spouses in a spiritual union and was therefore necessary to complete the sacrament of marriage. The requirement of consummation can also be explained in non-religious terms in that it is the act of sexual intercourse that most clearly distinguishes marriage from a close relationship between two platonic friends. However, given the increase in sexual relations outside of marriage it is harder to argue that sexual intercourse has a unique place in marriage. It has even been suggested that it is a sexist requirement in that it is easier for a man to show he has the capacity to engage in sexual intercourse than it is for a woman.[150] The importance of consummation could also be said to amount to an encouragement for married couples to produce children.[151]

In order for a marriage to be consummated there need only be one act of consummation; but the act must take place after the solemnisation of the marriage.[152] So in *P v P*,[153] where a husband only had sexual relations eight times in 18 years, the marriage was not voidable and divorce was the only way to end the marriage. There are two grounds of voidability connected to consummation. The first ground is a wilful refusal by a spouse to consummate the marriage, and the second is the incapacity of either party to consummate the marriage. The applicant for the nullity application can rely on his or her own inability to consummate but not on his or her own wilful refusal. This is because a party should not be able to rely on his or her own decision not to consummate in order to annul a marriage. It is useful to have the two alternative grounds as it may be difficult in a particular case to discover whether the non-consummation was due to inability or wilful refusal.

---

[150] Welstead and Edwards (2006: 35).
[151] *Baxter v Baxter* [1948] AC 274.
[152] *Dredge v Dredge* [1947] 1 All ER 29.
[153] [1964] 3 All ER 919.

What is meant by consummation? 'Consummation' is defined as an act of sexual intercourse. Consummation can only be carried out by the penetration of the vagina by the penis. No other form of sexual activity will amount to consummation. Intercourse needs to be 'ordinary and complete, and not partial and imperfect'.[154] There needs to be full penetration, but there is no need for an ejaculation or orgasm.[155] In *Baxter v Baxter*[156] the House of Lords held that consummation took place even though the man was wearing a condom.[157] There have even been cases where a pregnancy resulted from a sexual act but the court decided there was no consummation because there was no penetration.[158] This reveals that the consummation requirement is not explained by the state's interest in the potential production of children.

'Inability to consummate' means that the inability cannot be cured by surgery[159] and is permanent. Inability can be either physiological or psychological. Inability also includes 'invincible repugnance', where one party is unable to have sexual intercourse due to 'paralysis of the will',[160] but this must be more than lack of attraction or a dislike of the other partner.[161]

There has been much debate over whether the incapacity to consummate marriage has to exist at the time of the marriage. In other words, what would happen if the husband was rendered impotent as a result of a fight he had with the bride's father during the reception? Under Canon Law impotence could be relied upon only if the impotence existed at the time of marriage. This reflected the crucial distinction between nullity and marriage: nullity applies when defects exist at the time of marriage, while divorce is used when defects occur after the time of the marriage itself. However, the Matrimonial Causes Act makes no reference to the inability existing 'at the time of the marriage', whereas it makes explicit reference to 'at the time of the marriage' in relation to other grounds of voidability. It is therefore submitted that there is a strong case that the inability can occur at any time before or during the marriage as long as the union has not yet been consummated.

'Wilful refusal to consummate' requires a 'settled and definite decision not to consummate without wilful excuse'.[162] If there has been no opportunity to consummate the marriage[163] then it will be hard to show that there has been a wilful refusal unless one party has shown 'unswerving determination' not to consummate the marriage.[164] 'Wilful refusal' may also occur where the parties have agreed only to have intercourse under certain circumstances (e.g after a religious ceremony). In such a case then a refusal by one party to abide by the condition may constitute 'wilful refusal'.[165] For example, in *Kaur v Singh*[166] a couple agreed they would be legally married and then undergo a religious ceremony, and only after that would the marriage be consummated. The couple were legally married but the man then refused to undergo the religious ceremony, although he was willing to consummate the marriage. The wife was unwilling to consummate the marriage until the religious ceremony was performed.

---

[154] *D-E v A-G* (1845) 1 Rob Eccl 279 at p. 298.

[155] *R v R* [1952] 1 All ER 1194.

[156] [1948] AC 274.

[157] There is some doubt about coitus interruptus (where the man withdraws before ejaculation): *Cackett v Cackett* [1950] P 253; *White v White* [1948] P 330; *Grimes v Grimes* [1948] 2 All ER 147. The issue was left open in *Baxter v Baxter* [1948] AC 274.

[158] *Clarke v Clarke* [1943] 2 All ER 540. The marriage here had lasted 15 years.

[159] If the inability to consummate can only be cured by potentially dangerous surgery then the inability will be treated as permanent: *S v S* [1956] P 1.

[160] *G v G* [1924] AC 349.

[161] *Singh v Singh* [1971] P 226.

[162] *Horton v Horton* [1972] 2 All ER 871.

[163] Perhaps because the parties are living in different places (e.g. the husband is in prison).

[164] *Ford v Ford* [1987] Fam Law 232.

[165] *A v J* [1989] 1 FLR 110.

[166] [1972] 1 All ER 292.

She applied for and was granted a nullity decree on the basis of wilful refusal to consummate.[167] There is some doubt over the position of the law where the parties agree before the marriage that they will not consummate the marriage at all. It seems to be that such an agreement would be regarded as contrary to public policy[168] unless the parties have a good reason for the agreement.[169] The marriage will not be annulled on the ground of wilful refusal if the lack of consummation is due to a just excuse,[170] although the case law reveals very little on the exact meaning of this.[171]

### (ii) Lack of consent

The Matrimonial Causes Act recognises four circumstances which may cause a person to be unable to give consent so as to render a marriage voidable. These are 'duress, mistake, unsoundness of mind or otherwise'.[172] The law seeks to resolve a tension here. On the one hand there is the view that it should not be too easy to have a marriage annulled. On the other hand, at least in the West, consent is regarded as a highly important factor in marriage. At one time the law required that the lack of consent was apparent at the time of the ceremony.[173] Although the appearance of consent may be important as a matter of evidence, it is now clear that it is not a formal requirement.

It should be noted that lack of consent renders a marriage voidable rather than void. This means that if a party does not consent to the marriage but later changes his or her mind and is happy with the marriage, the marriage will be valid and there is no need to remarry. The separate ways in which a lack of consent may be demonstrated will now be discussed.

### (a) Duress

If it could be shown that someone was compelled to enter a marriage as a result of fear or threats, the marriage may be voidable due to duress. The following issues have been discussed in the case law:

1. *What must the threat or fear be of?* At one time it was thought that it was only possible for duress to render a marriage voidable if there was a threat to 'life, limb or liberty'.[174] The Court of Appeal in *Hirani v Hirani*[175] suggested that the test for duress should focus on the effect of the threat rather than the nature of the threat. In other words, the threats can be of any kind, but it must be shown that 'the threats, pressure or whatever it is, is such as to destroy the reality of the consent and overbear the will of the individual'.[176] In the case of *Hirani v Hirani*[177] the court accepted that social pressure could overbear the consent. The woman was threatened with ostracism by her community and her family if she did not go through with the marriage, and the fear of complete social isolation was such that there was no true consent. In *P v R (Forced Marriage: Annulment: Procedure)*[178] Colderidge J

---

[167] See also *A v J* [1989] 1 FLR 110.
[168] *Brodie v Brodie* [1917] P 271.
[169] *Morgan v Morgan* [1959] P 92.
[170] Borkowski (1994).
[171] *Horton v Horton* [1972] 2 All ER 871.
[172] Article 16(2) of the Universal Declaration of Human Rights 1948 states that: 'Marriage shall be entered into only with the free and full consent of the intending spouses.'
[173] *Cooper v Crane* [1891] P 369.
[174] *Szechter v Szechter* [1971] P 286; *Singh v Singh* [1971] P 226.
[175] (1982) 4 FLR 232; noted Bradney (1983).
[176] *Hirani v Hirani* (1982) 4 FLR 232 at p. 234.
[177] (1982) 4 FLR 232.
[178] [2003] 1 FLR 661. See also *NS v MI* [2006] EWHC 1646 (Fam) where the *Hirani* approach was adopted.

followed *Hirani* and held that severe emotional pressure could be such as to mean that there was no genuine consent to marry. *Hirani* should be contrasted with *Singh v Singh*,[179] where the couple had not met before the marriage and the wife agreed to marry only out of respect for her parents. As the wife entered the marriage, not out of fear, but out of a sense of duty, it could not be said that she did not consent to the marriage. The effect of the *Hirani* decision is that those who have undergone an arranged marriage in the face of a serious threat have the choice of either accepting their culture and the validity of the marriage or accepting the dominant culture's view that marriage should be made voidable.[180] This could be regarded as an appropriate compromise between respecting the cultural practice of arranged marriages and respecting people's right to choose whom to marry.[181]

2. The Law Commission has suggested that really what is at issue is the legitimacy of the threat rather than the lack of consent. After all, many people feel a pressure from family or society to get married.[182] This approach is reflected in other areas of law where duress is an issue, for example contract law, where reference to the 'overborne will' has largely been abandoned.[183] When someone is acting under duress it is not that they do not make a choice but rather that the choice is made in circumstances in which it should not lead to legal effect. This then requires the court to make a judgment on whether the horrors of the alternative meant that the choice should not be given effect, rather than considering whether there was true consent.[184] It may be that when the issue next comes before the Court of Appeal it will focus on the legitimacy of the threat as well as the impact of the threat on the victim.

3. *Must the fear be reasonably held?* What if a threat was made, but a reasonable person would not have taken it seriously? In *Szechter* it was suggested that duress could not be relied upon unless the fear was reasonably held.[185] Against this is *Scott v Selbright*,[186] in which it was suggested that as long as the beliefs of threats were honestly held, duress could be relied upon. The *Scott v Selbright* view seems preferable because it would be undesirable to punish a person for their careless mistake by denying them an annulment.

4. *Was the threat reasonably made?* In *Buckland v Buckland*[187] a man was alleged to have made a young woman pregnant while he was in Cyprus. The police threatened him with arrest and prosecution unless he married the woman. He denied the allegation but, fearing the police's threats, agreed to marry the woman. Simon J agreed that the marriage was voidable due to lack of consent on the grounds of duress. However, he stressed that this was because he believed the young man's version of events, namely that he had barely met the woman and was not responsible for the pregnancy. The threat was therefore 'unjust'. However, had he been responsible for the pregnancy, Simon J's judgment seems to imply that the marriage would not have been annulled. Some commentators have argued that this is a wrong approach and that if there is a genuine lack of consent the marriage should

---

[179] [1971] P 226.
[180] See also *Re KR (Abduction: Forcible Removal by Parents)* [1999] 2 FLR 542, where the court was willing to use wardship to protect a 17-year-old from being taken abroad for an arranged marriage.
[181] Parkinson (1996). In *NS v MI* [2006] EWHC 1646 (Fam) Munby J emphasised that the court must beware of stereotyping.
[182] Diduck and Kaganas (2006: 42).
[183] *Lynch v DPP* [1980] AC 614; *Universal Tankships Inc v I.T.W.F.* [1983] AC 366. See Atiyah (1982).
[184] Bradney (1994).
[185] [1971] P 286. See also *Buckland v Buckland* [1968] P 296 at p. 301 (per Scarman J); *H v H* [1954] P 258 at p. 269 (per Karminski J).
[186] (1886) 12 PD 21 at p. 24.
[187] [1968] P 296.

be voidable regardless of whether the party was at fault in causing the duress. Even if *Buckland* is followed in future cases, surely it can never be reasonable to impose a threat requiring someone to enter into a marriage?

5. *By whom must the threat be made?* The threat can emanate from a third party; it need not emanate from the spouse.[188]

### (b) Mistake

A mistake can also negate consent. So far the law has only allowed two kinds of mistake to negate consent. The first is a mistake as to the other party's identity. It must be a mistake as to identity rather than a mistake as to attribute.[189] So, for example, a marriage would not be voidable if one party wrongly thought the other was rich,[190] or a marvellous cook.[191] But a marriage would be voidable if a party to the marriage thought the person they were marrying was someone else (e.g. if there was a case of impersonation).[192] The second kind of mistake that will make a marriage voidable is when there is a mistake as to the nature of the ceremony. So, if one party believes the ceremony is one of engagement, say, then this can invalidate the marriage.[193] However, a mistake as to the legal effects of marriage is insufficient.[194]

It is arguable that in the light of *Hirani* this area of the law is open to reconsideration; that the law should focus not on the kind of mistake, but the effect of the mistake on a person's consent. So, for example, if it was crucial to a wife that her husband belonged to a particular religion then a mistake as to his religion could invalidate her consent. Only future cases will tell whether such a liberal approach can be taken, or whether the traditional approach of accepting only mistakes as to the person or the nature of the ceremony will negate consent.

### (c) Unsoundness of mind

If a person lacks the capacity to marry, no one else can consent on their behalf. Unsoundness will only lead to a marriage being voidable if it exists at the time of the marriage. So a marriage will not be void if someone becomes mentally ill after the marriage. There is a presumption that people are of sound mind, and so the burden of proof lies on the person seeking to have the marriage annulled. To determine whether there is sufficient unsoundness of mind to render the marriage voidable, Singleton LJ in *In the Estate of Park*[195] stated that it is necessary to ask whether the person was:

> capable of understanding the nature of the contract into which he was entering, or was his mental condition such that he was incapable of understanding it? To ascertain the nature of the contract of marriage a man must be mentally capable of appreciating that it involves the responsibilities normally attaching to marriage. Without that degree of mentality, it cannot be said that he understands the nature of the contract.

In *Sheffield City Council v E and S*[196] it was emphasised that every adult is presumed to have the capacity to consent. The test for capacity did not focus on whether the individual understood

---

[188] *H v H* [1954] P 258; *NS v MI* [2006] EWHC 1646 (Fam).
[189] *Moss v Moss* [1897] P 263.
[190] *Wakefield v Mackay* (1807) 1 Hag Con 394 at p. 398; *Ewing v Wheatly* (1814) 2 Hagg Cas 175.
[191] See *C v C* [1942] NZLR 356 for a New Zealand case where a woman who married a man she believed (incorrectly) to be a famous boxer failed in her attempt to have the marriage annulled.
[192] E.g. *Militante v Ogunwomoju* [1993] 2 FCR 355.
[193] An example of this can be found in *Valier v Valier* (1925) 133 LT 830.
[194] *Messina v Smith* [1971] P 322.
[195] [1954] P 112.
[196] [2004] EWHC 2808 (Fam), discussed in Gaffney-Rhys (2006).

that they were getting married, but rather whether they understood the nature of the duties and responsibilities attached to marriage: that spouses were to live together and to love each other to the exclusion of all others. Normally it involved sharing a common domestic life, sharing each other's society, comfort and assistance. Marriage was not meant to be a difficult concept to understand. Munby J emphasised that if a person's competence was challenged in court the judge must focus on whether the person had capacity to marry, not on whether it was wise for them to marry. Controversially he held that it was not necessary to show that the person understood the character of the person they were marrying. In this case there were concerns that the man was a violent and abusive man, and that the woman, who suffered various learning difficulties, did not appreciate that. It might be thought the character of one's partner is central to marriage. A violent abusive marriage is a very different thing from a loving one.

In *X City Council v MB*[197] it was held that to have capacity to marry, a person would have to have capacity to consent to sexual intercourse. That meant they would need to understand the character and nature of sexual intercourse and the reasonably foreseeable consequences of it. They would also need the capacity to be able to choose whether or not to engage in it. The case demonstrates the way the law regards sexual intercourse as an essential element of marriage. Given the fact that much sexual intercourse takes place outside marriage, it may be questioned whether sexual relations should be seen as central to the notion of marriage.[198]

### (d) Otherwise

The statute refers to a lack of consent through factors other than duress or mistake. These include the following:

1. *Drunkenness.* There is no clear authority on whether the marriage is voidable where one party was drunk and so did not consent to the marriage. There are two views here. One is that drunkenness should be seen as analogous to being of unsound mind and so would make a marriage voidable. Another view is that a party should not be able to rely on a lack of consent that arises due to their own fault, and so voluntary intoxication should not render a marriage voidable. In *Sullivan v Sullivan*[199] it was suggested that the groom was so drunk that he was unable to understand the nature of the ceremony and so the marriage was voidable.

2. *Fraud and misrepresentation.* Neither fraud nor innocent misrepresentation will on its own affect the validity of the marriage.[200] However, if the fraud or misrepresentation leads to a mistake as to the identity of the other party or the nature of the ceremony then, as discussed above, the marriage will be voidable.

### (iii) Mental disorder

A marriage is also voidable if either party is suffering from a mental disorder[201] at the time of the marriage to such an extent that they are unfit for marriage: that is, 'incapable of carrying out the ordinary duties and obligations of marriage'.[202] It is necessary to distinguish this from

---

[197] [2007] 3 FCR 371.
[198] Some religions teach that sexual intercourse should only take place in marriage. This has been the traditional Christian view and may explain why sexual relations are regarded as central to marriage.
[199] (1812) 2 Hag Con 238 at p. 246.
[200] *Swift v Kelly* (1835) 3 Knapp 257 at p. 293; *Moss v Moss* [1897] P 263.
[201] As defined by the Mental Health Act 1983.
[202] *Bennett v Bennett* [1969] 1 All ER 539.

the lack of consent through unsoundness of mind. The mental disorder ground covers those who are able to understand the nature of a marriage but are unable to perform the duties of marriage due to a mental illness.

It should be stressed that both of the grounds relating to mental illness only make the marriage voidable and not void, so there is nothing to stop those with mental illnesses, even extreme ones, from marrying, the one exception being where the court finds a public policy objection to the marriage.[203]

### (iv) Venereal disease and pregnancy

A marriage is voidable if the respondent is suffering from venereal disease[204] at the time of the ceremony or if the respondent was pregnant by someone other than the petitioner. It should be noted that a wife cannot seek nullity on the ground that the husband has fathered a child through another woman prior to the marriage. It may be thought that venereal disease and pregnancy should no longer be regarded as sufficient grounds to annul a marriage, although, as we shall see, a petitioner will not be able to use these grounds if they were aware of the disease or the pregnancy at the time of the marriage. The continued use of the term 'venereal disease' is a little unfortunate because it is one that is no longer used in medical circles. 'Sexually transmitted disease' is the preferred phrase.[205]

### (v) Sham marriages

What is the position of a couple who go through a marriage purely for the purpose of pretending to be married, even though they never intend to live together as husband or wife? This is most likely to arise in a case involving immigration.[206] The House of Lords in **Vervaeke v Smith**[207] suggested that such marriages are valid, even though in that case the parties only saw each other on a few occasions after the marriage and the aim of the marriage was to enable the wife to obtain British citizenship and so avoid deportation.[208] Although such a marriage was valid, it may not be sufficient for the purposes of immigration rules. So a person entering a sham marriage in order to enter the UK might find themselves unable come to Britain, but married to someone they do not know. It seems the use of marriage purely for immigration purposes is not uncommon.[209]

## F  Bars to relief in voidable marriages

There are no bars to a marriage being void, although there are some circumstances which prevent the petitioner from seeking to annul a voidable marriage. These bars are found in s 13(1) of the Matrimonial Causes Act 1973. If the bar is established the court may not annul the marriage. The burden is on the respondent to raise the bar as a defence. If the respondent

---

[203] *City of Westminster* v *C* [2008] 2 FCR 146, see Probert (2008) for a discussion of this case.

[204] The term is not defined in the Act.

[205] It is not clear whether the courts would be willing to stretch the meaning of venereal disease to include HIV.

[206] See Asylum and Immigration (Treatment of Claimants etc.) Act 2004, s 19 which was used to introduce a regime requiring those subject to immigration control to obtain a certificate from the Secretary of State before marrying (unless they were marrying within the rites of the Church of England). This scheme was designed to prevent sham marriages entered into for immigration purposes, but see e.g. *R (On the application of Baiai)* v *Secretary of State* [2008] 3 FCR 1 which declared such schemes as discriminatory and incompatible with the right to marry in the ECHR.

[207] [1983] 1 AC 145.

[208] Divorce may well be possible, of course: e.g. *Silver* v *Silver* [1955] 1 WLR 728.

[209] BBC Newsonline (2009a).

does not mention the bar, the court cannot raise it on his or her behalf. If no statutory bar is established the court cannot bar the annulment on the basis of public policy.[210] This indicates that the bars exist not for public policy reasons but for the protection of the petitioner. We will now consider the different bars.

## (i) Approbation

Section 13(1) of the Matrimonial Causes Act 1973 states:

---

### LEGISLATIVE PROVISION

**Matrimonial Causes Act 1973, section 13(1)**

The court shall not . . . grant a decree of nullity on the ground that a marriage is voidable if the respondent satisfies the court—

(a) that the petitioner, with knowledge that it was open to him to have the marriage avoided, so conducted himself in relation to the respondent as to lead the respondent reasonably to believe that he would not seek to do so; and

(b) that it would be unjust to the respondent to grant the decree.

---

It is essential that both paragraphs (a) and (b) be proved to the court's satisfaction. The basis of this bar is that it is seen as contrary to public policy and unjust to allow a person to seek to annul the marriage after leading the other party to believe he or she would not challenge the marriage. For example, in *D v D (Nullity)*[211] the husband relied on his wife's refusal to consummate the marriage in a nullity petition. However, he had previously agreed to the adoption of a child. It was held that his action indicated to the wife that he intended to treat the marriage as valid. Similarly, a man marrying a woman who he knows suffers from a mental disorder or is pregnant would be barred from seeking to annul the marriage on these grounds.[212] It may be that if the marriage has lasted some time the court might imply from the delay in bringing the petition that the petitioner had consented to the marriage.

In order to establish the bar it must be shown that to annul the marriage would be unjust. For example, in *D v D* it might have been unjust to leave the wife caring for the children on her own. However, in that case the wife consented to the nullity decree and so it was thought not to be unjust to her to grant the decree. In considering justice under (b) the court is likely to consider factors such as the length of the marriage, financial implications of the nullity, and social implications of granting a decree.

## (ii) Time

A decree of nullity will normally not succeed unless brought within three years of the date of the marriage,[213] the exception being a petition based on impotence. The policy behind this is clear: parties need a degree of security in their marriage – if three years have passed, then to claim that the marriage is fundamentally flawed seems unrealistic. In *B v I (Forced Marriage)*[214]

---

[210] *D v D (Nullity)* [1979] Fam 70.
[211] [1979] Fam 70.
[212] See, e.g., *Morgan v Morgan* [1959] P 92.
[213] MCA 1973, s 13(2). There is an exception if the petitioner suffered from some kind of mental disorder.
[214] [2010] 1 FLR 1721.

a 16-year-old girl was forced into a marriage in Bangladesh and was only able to alert someone over three years later. The court was unable to declare the marriage a nullity, but could declare it to be a marriage which was incapable of recognition within the UK. It was significant in that case that the woman would have faced significant stigma within her community if she had relied on divorce. Otherwise the obvious solution to her situation would have been to seek a divorce.

### (iii) Estoppel

Can a party ever be prevented from obtaining a nullity decree on the basis of estoppel? There are two kinds of estoppel that might be relevant. The first is estoppel by conduct where one party so conducts himself or herself that it would be unjust for him or her to deny the facts that he or she has led the other to believe are true. *Miles v Chilton*[215] provides an example of the kind of situation under discussion. A husband sought annulment on the ground that his wife was already married at the time of the marriage. The wife argued that the husband had deceived her into believing that her 'first' husband had divorced her. The court held that this was no answer to the husband's petition, because otherwise the court would be prevented from discovering the true state of affairs.[216] So estoppel by conduct was not found relevant in this case.

The other kind of estoppel is *estoppel per rem judicatam*, meaning that a party cannot seek to overturn a court's decision. A decree of nullity is what is known as a judgment *in rem*: proceedings cannot be started which seek to undermine such a judgment. However, if the nullity petition is dismissed this affects only the parties themselves. So, if a man is granted a nullity petition on the ground that the wife is married to another man, no one can seek to undermine the basis of the annulment by suggesting in a court that the first marriage was invalid. However, if the petition had been dismissed on the ground that the first marriage was invalid this does not bar anyone except the parties themselves from seeking to show that the first marriage was in fact valid.

## G Effects of a decree of nullity

Section 16 of the Matrimonial Causes Act 1973 states:

### LEGISLATIVE PROVISION

**Matrimonial Causes Act 1973, section 16**

A decree of nullity granted after 31st July 1971 in respect of a voidable marriage shall operate to annul the marriage only as respects any time after the decree has been made absolute, and the marriage shall, notwithstanding the decree, be treated as if it had existed up to that time.

A child of a void marriage is treated as legitimate due to s 1(1) of the Legitimacy Act 1976, as long as at the time of the marriage either (or both) parties reasonably believed that the marriage was valid.[217] *Re Spence*[218] has clarified the law and said that if the marriage was annulled after the birth then the child was legitimate.

[215] (1849) 1 Rob Eccl 684.
[216] There are contrary dicta in *Bullock v Bullock* [1960] 2 All ER 307 at p. 309.
[217] Under the Family Law Act 1986, s 56 a declaration of legitimacy can be made if there is any doubt.
[218] [1990] 2 FLR 278, [1990] FCR 983.

Due to ss 23 and 24 of the Matrimonial Causes Act 1973 on granting a decree of nullity, the court has the power to make ancillary relief orders to the same extent as if a divorce order was being made. However, following **Whiston v Whiston**,[219] as interpreted in **Rampal v Rampal (No. 2)**,[220] if the marriage is void on the ground of bigamy then the court might decide that the applicant's conduct was such that the court should not award her any ancillary relief. In **J v S-T**[221] the applicant was born a woman, underwent a partial sex-change operation, lived as a man, and then married a woman. After 17 years of marriage the wife[222] petitioned for a declaration that the marriage was void on the ground that the parties were not respectively male and female. The husband applied for ancillary relief. The court held that there was a discretion in the court to award ancillary relief. However, in exercising its discretion the court decided not to make any award bearing in mind his deception as to his sex.[223] By contrast in **Ben Hashem v Al Shayif**[224] as both the husband and wife had been fully aware of the bigamous nature of their marriage, the bigamy had no impact on the amount awarded.

## H Reform of nullity

There were 331 petitions for annulments in 2008, of which 200 were granted.[225] The tiny numbers involved raise the question of whether we need all the complex law on nullity that we have. The concept of a void marriage is necessary if there are to be limits on who may marry and to whom. However, there has been some debate over whether the concept of voidable marriage should be abolished. The Law Commission[226] supported the retention of voidable marriage by arguing that to some couples it is particularly important that annulment rather than divorce ends their marriage. This tends to be for religious reasons. Cretney has argued that the law on voidable marriage could be abolished, leaving questions of annulment to the church or other religious bodies.[227] There is much to be said for this approach, given that the vast majority of annulment petitions are brought for religious reasons.

## I Forced marriages

The Government's Forced Marriage Unit dealt with 420 cases of forced marriage in 2009. Of these, 30 per cent concerned under-18s, and 86 per cent were women.[228] Most cases involved members of south Asian communities.[229] Article 12 of the European Convention on Human Rights protects the right to marry. This includes the right not to be forced into a marriage against your will. The problem of 'forced marriages' is one which the courts have had to deal with increasingly often.[230] We have already seen that if a party is forced into a marriage as a result of threats or pressures then the marriage can be annulled on the basis of no consent.

---

[219] [1995] 2 FLR 268, [1995] 2 FCR 496; discussed Cretney (1996a).

[220] [2001] 2 FCR 552.

[221] [1997] 1 FLR 402, [1997] 1 FCR 349.

[222] It took the wife 17 years to find out that her husband had not been born a man. The facts of the case reveal the dangers of looking in a man's sock drawer.

[223] As a result of ss 1(1)(a) and 25(4) of the Inheritance (Provision for Family and Dependants) Act 1975 a person who in good faith has entered into a void marriage may apply to the court for reasonable provision out of the estate.

[224] [2009] 1 FLR 115.

[225] Ministry of Justice (2009).

[226] Law Commission Report 33 (1970).

[227] Cretney (1972). See also Probert (2005).

[228] Walsh (2009a).

[229] Department for Children, Schools and Families (2009).

[230] See Dauvergne and Millbank (2010) for a discussion of the international dimension.

Here we will consider how the court will deal with a case where there are concerns that a forced marriage is about to take place. Hogg J has described forced marriage as 'abusive'.[231]

It should be emphasised that there are no legal objections to an arranged marriage, where the parents determine who their adult child should marry. Parents may encourage or persuade their child to marry the person they propose. There are many communities where this is common practice and the courts will not invalidate a marriage or seek to prevent the parents urging their child to marry, unless the pressure used becomes illegitimate. In *A Local Authority* v *N*[232] Munby J warned that courts must be sensitive to cultural, social and religious circumstances and the courts should not assume that an arranged marriage is a forced one. The Government is aware that it is necessary to draw a clear distinction between a forced marriage and an arranged marriage:

> There is a clear distinction between a forced marriage and an arranged marriage. In arranged marriages, the families of both spouses take a leading role in arranging the marriage but the choice whether or not to accept the arrangement remains with the prospective spouses. In forced marriage, one or both spouses do not (or, in the case of some adults with disabilities, cannot) consent to the marriage and duress is involved. Duress can include physical, psychological, sexual, financial and emotional pressure.[233]

An arranged marriage is entered into freely by both people, although their families take a leading role in the choice of partner.[234] However, the point at which the encouragement of the family members crosses the line to become duress – changing an arranged marriage to a forced marriage – is not easy to pinpoint.

It is easy to be over-simplistic in an understanding of forced marriages. In fact, they involve a complex interplay of gender and age discrimination. They should not be seen simply as the product of a minority cultural practice, as economic difficulties and immigration policies also play an important role.[235] Nor should it be assumed that only young women are affected – men can be,[236] as can older women.[237] It should be remembered, too, that it is not just the entry into forced marriages that needs tackling, but women need to be enabled to leave such marriages.[238] The issue needs also to be seen in the broader context of so-called 'honour' based violence.[239]

The courts have shown an increased willingness to make orders to protect someone from a forced marriage. There are three jurisdictions the courts can use: Forced Marriage (Civil Protection) Act 2007; the Mental Capacity Act 2005; and the inherent jurisdiction. Where the only issue of concern is the forced marriage, then the 2007 Act should be used. Where, however, there are a range of issues over which the court needs to make orders, the Mental Capacity Act 2005 should be used if the person lacks mental capacity; or the inherent jurisdiction order if the person does not.

## (i) Forced Marriage (Civil Protection) Act 2007

The 2007 Act was passed to provide specific protection to people at risk of being forced into a marriage. The Act does not deal with the validity of forced marriages, those are dealt with by the law on voidability. The Act enables the court to make 'forced marriage protection orders'.

---

[231] *Re B; RB v FB and MA (Forced Marriage: Wardship: Jurisdiction)* [2008] 2 FLR 1624.
[232] [2005] EWHC 2956.
[233] HM Government (2009: 10).
[234] Forced Marriage Unit (2006: 1).
[235] Gill and Anitha (2009); Chantler, Gangoli and Hester (2009).
[236] Samad (2010).
[237] Gangoli and Chantler (2009).
[238] Chantler, Gangoli and Hester (2009).
[239] *Re B-M (Care Orders)* [2009] 2 FLR 20.

A forced marriage is defined as one where one person forces another to enter into a marriage without their 'full and free consent.'[240] Force here includes physical and psychological threats; and includes threats, whoever they are directed towards.[241] The Act gives the court a broad discretion to make whatever order is necessary to protect the individual at risk: it can order 'such prohibitions, restrictions or requirements . . . and . . . other terms . . . as the court considers appropriate for the purposes of the order'.[242] This could include surrendering a passport, or prohibiting a party from contacting another. In deciding whether to make an order the court must have regard to 'all the circumstances including the need to secure the health, safety and well-being of the person to be protected'. Notably the Act states that in ascertaining that person's well-being, the court is to have regard to his or her wishes and feelings (so far as reasonably ascertainable) and giving them 'such weight as the court considers appropriate given his or her age and understanding'.[243] To date there has been little litigation using the Act.

## (ii) Mental Capacity Act 2005

The Mental Capacity Act 2005 enables courts to make orders to promote the best interests of mentally incompetent people.[244] The Act can only be used in relation to issues over which a person lacks capacity.

## (iii) The inherent jurisdiction

Recently, the courts have also shown a willingness to use the inherent jurisdiction to protect individuals who are at risk of being forced into a marriage. It has even been used in respect of British nationals living overseas.[245] The jurisdiction can be exercised over vulnerable adults. These are people who might have capacity to make the decision on whether or not to marry, but are for some other reason vulnerable. This may be because they have some disability or because someone is exercising undue influence over them. In *Re SK (An Adult) (Forced Marriage: Appropriate Relief)*[246] the court was told about a young British citizen who it was believed was facing threats from her family urging her to marry. Even though she was currently in Bangladesh, Singer J was willing to make orders under the inherent jurisdiction to prevent her parents from 'causing or permitting' her being married or betrothed. Subsequently the young woman appeared before the court and told it that she did not need the protection of the court and the orders were discontinued.[247] In *M v B*[248] the inherent jurisdiction was used to protect S who was aged 23 and suffering from learning difficulties. There were concerns that S was to be married without her consent. Having found that she lacked the capacity to consent, orders were made prohibiting her parents from entering her into a formal or informal contract for marriage.[249] The inherent jurisdiction can still be used for those who have capacity but who are in some other way vulnerable.[250]

---

[240] Family Law Act 1996 (FLA), s 63A(4).
[241] FLA, s 63A(4).
[242] FLA, s 63B.
[243] FLA, s 63A.
[244] See the discussion in *Re SK* [2008] EWHC 636 (Fam).
[245] *Re B; RB v FB and MA (Forced Marriage: Wardship: Jurisdiction)* [2008] 2 FLR 1624.
[246] [2005] 2 FCR 459.
[247] In *X CC v MB, NB and MAB* [2006] EWHC 168 (Fam) it was emphasised that courts should not make excessive orders in protecting people from forced marriages. Munby J held that there needed to be a real risk of harm before the jurisdiction was used.
[248] [2005] EWHC 1681 (Fam).
[249] See also *Re SA* [2006] Fam Law 268 where a woman was mentally competent but was deaf, dumb and blind in one eye – orders were made protecting her from a forced marriage. The concern was that she would not be able effectively to communicate her opposition to any marriage.
[250] *Re SA (Vulnerable Adult with Capacity: Marriage)* [2007] 2 FCR 563.

## 7 Civil partnerships

A same-sex couple cannot marry.[251] They can, however, enter a civil partnership. This status was created by the Civil Partnership Act 2004 (CPA 2004).[252] In 2008 there were 7,169 civil partnerships entered into in the UK. This was a significant decrease from the figure of 16,106 in 2006. That is not so surprising, because 2006 was the first full year during which civil partnerships were available and no doubt many couples had been waiting for some time. However, it was an 18 per cent drop on the figures for 2007. Indeed, notably, the average age of entering a civil partnership in 2007 was 42.8 for men and 41.2 for women, while it had been respectively 47.0 and 43.6 in 2006.[253] By the end of 2008 a total of 33,956 civil partnerships had been formed since the introduction of the legislation;[254] 53 per cent of couples entering civil partnerships were male and 47 per cent were female.

 As we shall see, in many ways civil partnerships are 'marriage in all but name'.[255] The President of the Family Division in *Wilkinson v Kitzinger*[256] has explained:

> Parliament has taken steps by enacting the CPA to accord to same-sex relationships effectively all the rights, responsibilities, benefits and advantages of civil marriage save the name, and thereby to remove the legal, social and economic disadvantages suffered by homo-sexuals who wish to join stable long-term relationships.

The reader may well wonder why the Government did not take the simple step of allowing same-sex marriage. The reason was essentially political.[257] There was remarkably little opposition to the CPA 2004 because it did not create same-sex marriage. To create this status, which is legally equivalent to marriage, we needed an Act with 264 sections and 30 schedules.

### A  Who can enter a civil partnership?

Civil partnerships can only be entered into by same-sex couples.[258] Opposite-sex couples can either marry or cohabit. A civil partnership is created when the parties sign a civil partnership document 'at the invitation of, and in the presence of, a civil partnership registrar' and 'in the presence of each other and two witnesses'.[259]

There are other restrictions on who can enter a civil partnership: the parties must not be married or already a civil partner; they must both be over the age of 16[260] and they must not be within the prohibited degrees of relationship.[261] These restrictions match the equivalent to the ones found in marriage.

---

[251] Wintemute and Andenaes (2001) provide a very useful collection of essays on the legal regulation of same-sex relationships.

[252] Mallender and Rayson (2006) provides book-length descriptions of the Act. For critical discussion of the Act see Barker (2006).

[253] National Statistics (2010a).

[254] National Statistics (2010c).

[255] This was the description used by Baroness Hale (2004a) writing extra-judicially. See further Bamforth (2007).

[256] [2006] EWHC 2022 (Fam) at para 121. See Harding (2007) and Eekelaar (2007) for a discussion of this case.

[257] Stychin (2006). Crompton (2004) suggests the Act created the best of both worlds for the Government in appeasing both the 'gay' and 'anti-gay' lobbies.

[258] Civil Partnership Act 2004 (CPA 2004), s 1(1).

[259] CPA 2004, s 2(1).

[260] Where a person is under 18 parental consent is required: s 4.

[261] CPA 2004, s 3.

## B How do you form a civil partnership?

In many ways the creation of a civil partnership is much like a civil wedding. There are two important differences, however. First, in a civil wedding it is the exchange of vows, rather than the signing of the register, which creates the marriage.[262] Secondly, no religious services can be used while a civil partnership registrar is officiating at the signing of the register.[263] Of course, there is nothing to stop the couple from having a religious service after they have become civil partners. However the Equality Act 2010[264] allows for the creation of regulations that will permit religious groups to have a civil partnership as part of a religious service. This recognises the fact that some religious groups are supportive of same-sex relationships.

## C Annulling a civil partnership

A civil partnership can be void or voidable. It will be void if:[265]

1. the parties were not of the same sex;
2. either of them was already a civil partner or married;
3. either of them was under the age of 16;
4. the parties were within the prohibited degrees of relationship; or
5. they both knew that certain key formality requirements had not been complied with.[266]

A civil partnership will be voidable on the following grounds:[267]

---

**LEGISLATIVE PROVISION**

**Civil Partnership Act 2004, section 50**

(a) either of them did not validly consent to its formation (whether as a result of duress, mistake, unsoundness of mind or otherwise);

(b) at the time of its formation either of them, though capable of giving a valid consent, was suffering (whether continuously or intermittently) from a mental disorder of such a kind or to such an extent as to be unfitted for civil partnership;

(c) at the time of its formation, the respondent was pregnant by some person other than the applicant;

(d) an interim gender recognition certificate under the Gender Recognition Act 2004 has, after the time of its formation, been issued to either civil partner;

(e) the respondent is a person whose gender at the time of its formation had become the acquired gender under the 2004 Act.

---

These match the void and voidable grounds for marriage, with two notable exceptions: the non-consummation grounds are not included, nor is the venereal disease ground. We will

---

[262] Cretney (2006a: 23).
[263] CPA 2004, s 2(5).
[264] Equality Act 2010, s 202.
[265] CPA 2004, s 49.
[266] CPA 2004, s 49.
[267] CPA 2004, s 50.

look at the reasons for this later. The Act also contains bars to relying on annulment and these match those discussed above for marriage.[268]

## D The end of the civil partnership

Civil partnerships will end on the death of the party or on an order for dissolution (the equivalent of divorce). The law on dissolution of a civil partnership is very similar to the law on divorce and will be discussed in Chapter 3. For now, it is worth noting that adultery is a fact which establishes the ground for divorce, but not dissolution.

## E The effect of a civil partnership

Baroness Hale in *Secretary of State for Work and Pension* v *M*[269] explained that civil partnerships have 'virtually identical legal consequences to marriage'. We shall be looking at the consequences of marriage and civil partnerships later in this chapter. Jill Manthorpe and Elizabeth Price have argued that although civil partnership has enabled same-sex couples to have the relationship between themselves formally recognised, their relationship with their partner's children or wider family is not recognised in law or socially to the same extent as occurs in marriage.[270] In particular a civil partner of a woman may not be in as strong a position as a husband in relation to their children. This is explored further in Chapter 9.

## F The differences between civil partnership and marriage

As has been repeated several times, there are very few differences between spouses and civil partners. As Stephen Cretney explains, the care taken by Parliament to ensure that marriage and civil partnerships were treated in the same way is revealed by the fact that the CPA 2004 amends legislation as diverse as the Explosive Substances Act 1883 and the Law of Property Act 1925.[271] The most important differences between marriage and civil partnership are the following:

1. The formalities at the start of the relationship: in a civil partnership it is the signing of the register, rather than the exchange of vows, which creates the legal relationship. Further, unlike a marriage, a civil partnership ceremony cannot contain a religious service.[272] However, section 202 of the Equality Act 2010 allows for regulations to be passed which will permit religious groups to have civil partnership ceremonies in the context of a religious service.

2. The non-consummation grounds and venereal disease ground are not present as a ground of voidability in civil partnerships, while they are in marriage.

3. Adultery is not a fact establishing the ground for dissolution of a civil partnership, although it is for divorce.

4. If a woman receives assisted reproductive services her husband will be regarded as the father of the child. Her civil partner would not be regarded as a parent of the child.[273]

---

[268] CPA 2004, s 51.
[269] [2006] 1 FCR 497 at para 99.
[270] Manthorpe and Price (2005).
[271] Cretney (2006a: 29).
[272] Interestingly, a survey of same-sex couples found that a significant minority wanted a religious element in the civil partnership celebration: Readhead (2006).
[273] The Court of Appeal recognised this in *Re G (Children)(Residence: Same-Sex Partner)* [2006] 1 FCR 681.

What are we to make of these differences? One response is to suggest that they are so minor as to be of negligible practical significance. The exact moment when the status is created is of no practical relevance; nullity is very rarely used and is mainly of significance for those with strong conservative religious beliefs; and in a case of adultery a civil partner can rely on a behaviour ground for dissolution.[274] Another response is to be more cynical. The lack of reference to adultery and non-consummation demonstrates the law's failure to recognise that gay sex is real sex. Baroness Scotland, a Government minister at the time of the passing of the CPA, explained: 'There is no provision for consummation in the Civil Partnership Bill. We do not look at the nature of the sexual relationship, it is totally different in nature.' The coyness apparent in the Government's explanation that it was not possible to produce a same-sex equivalent to consummation and adultery, may indicate a reluctance to accept same-sex relationships at full value. Is the law suggesting that same-sex sexual behaviour is something that should not be talked about?

## G Is the Civil Partnership Act to be welcomed?

### TOPICAL ISSUE

#### Are civil partnerships good news?

Supporters of the Civil Partnership Act see it as an important step towards recognising the equality of same-sex relationships. It means that same-sex couples can now have, effectively, the same rights and responsibilities as married couples; same-sex couples are as worthy of recognition and as socially valuable as opposite-sex ones.[275] The Act ensures that same-sex couples need not suffer legal disadvantage, in the sense that they can, if they wish, have the legal rights open to a married opposite-sex couple.[276] As Baroness Hale eloquently explained in **Ghaidan v Godin-Mendoza**:[277]

> Homosexual couples can have exactly the same sort of interdependent couple relationship as heterosexuals can. Sexual 'orientation' defines the sort of person with whom one wishes to have sexual relations. It requires another person to express itself. Some people, whether heterosexual or homosexual, may be satisfied with casual or transient relationships. But most human beings eventually want more than that. They want love. And with love they often want not only the warmth but also the sense of belonging to one another which is the essence of being a couple. And many couples also come to want the stability and permanence which go with sharing a home and a life together, with or without the children who for many people go to make a family. In this, people of homosexual orientation are no different from people of heterosexual orientation.

The Government explained its thinking behind the Act in this way:

> Today there are thousands of same-sex couples living in stable and committed partnerships. These relationships span many years with couples looking after each other, caring for their loved ones and actively participating in society; in fact, living in exactly the same way as any other family. They[278] are our families, our friends, our colleagues and our neighbours. Yet the law rarely recognises their relationship . . . in so many areas, as far as the law is concerned, same-sex relationships simply do not exist. That is not acceptable.[279]

---

[274] Spon-Smith (2005: 271).
[275] Readhead (2006); Weeks (2004).
[276] Hale (2004); Murphy (2004).
[277] [2004] 2 FCR 481 at para 142.
[278] The 'them' and 'us' terminology might be thought revealing.
[279] Women and Equality Unit (2003).

Public opinion is divided on the acceptability of same-sex behaviour. There is still a notable minority of people for whom it is unacceptable. In a 2002 survey, 23 per cent of people questioned thought that same-sex conduct should be illegal.[280] In a survey in 2010 only 36 per cent of people thought that same-sex behaviour was 'always or mostly wrong'. In 1983 the figure had been 62 per cent.[281] Even among religious people only a half believed that same-sex sexual activity was always or almost always wrong.[282] Notably the surveys suggest that opposition to same-sex relationships is largely found in older sections of the population and that the rate of opposition in decreasing year on year.

The Act has also received criticism from those who think that same-sex couples should be treated in the same way as opposite-sex couples. They should be allowed to marry. The Act is an inappropriate sop to those whose prejudice prevents them recognising the equal value of same-sex and opposite-sex relationships. Michael Freeman[283] has pointed out that the law is not very strict over who is granted the special benefits of being married: paedophiles and murderers can marry. So why should same-sex couples not be allowed to marry? As one protest banner put it, 'Charles can marry twice! Gays can't marry once!'[284]

Are those who object to the Act on the basis that it does not provide marriage making a mountain out of a molehill? After all, what is in a name? Civil partnership offers same-sex couples all the same rights as marriage; who cares what it is called? To supporters of gay marriage it is a matter of equality. The difference in name indicates that same-sex couples are regarded as somehow 'different' from opposite-sex couples.[285] And there is much symbolic significance attached to the name marriage, which is still seen as the ideal form of family life.[286] On the other hand, it might be thought that the lack of any effective opposition to the CPA 2004 depended on the terminology used in the Act. Is it better to have civil partnerships which have widespread acceptability or gay and lesbian marriage which would be controversial and antagonistic to some?

A rather different point is taken by Stephen Cretney who is concerned that the lack of a requirement that the civil partnership be consummated means that it could be open to misuse by those seeking to take advantage of its provisions for financial reasons. He asks:

> could it, in the twenty-first century, really have been intended to create such a huge marketing opportunity for all those financial advisers with their glossy pamphlets inciting elderly gentlemen who want to spend their days pottering quietly off to Lords or the Oval secure in the knowledge that their financial futures are mutually secured or indeed elderly ladies who like sharing visits to art exhibitions or needlework competitions?[287]

However, it should be pointed out that marriage, too, can be (and is) entered into purely for financial or immigration purposes, despite the fact that there is the consummation requirement. His point really is that the sexual element of the civil partnership, although pointedly not referred to in the Act, is in fact very important as it helps to distinguish a civil partnership (and a marriage) from a friendship.

---

[280] ICM (2002b). Christian Institute (2002) calls civil partnership 'counterfeit marriage'.
[281] National Centre for Social Research (2010).
[282] National Centre for Social Research (2010).
[283] Freeman (1999).
[284] Spotted by Cretney (2006a: 20). The reference is to Prince Charles.
[285] For support for this perception from analysis of conversations see Land and Kitzinger (2007).
[286] See Chapter 1.
[287] Cretney (2006a: 50).

In the first in-depth study of same-sex couples who had entered civil partnerships a number of interesting points emerged.[288] Among civil partners it was common to refer to themselves as 'married' and few had faced negative reactions to their status. Many couples noted that they had been accepted as sons-in-law or daughters-in-law and as full members of their partner's family. Interestingly, while 80 per cent of the members of the gay and lesbian community welcomed the Act, only 50 per cent wanted marriage to be extended to include same-sex couples. Another study found ambivalence towards civil partnership in the gay and lesbian community, with some describing it as 'pretend marriage' or 'second class'. Others were, however, wary of marriage, seeing it as a 'church thing' and not a label they would feel comfortable with.[289]

## H The future: gay marriage?

It is possible to identify a journey which several countries have already taken in response to same-sex couples.[290] First, the law removes criminal offences outlawing same-sex activity. Secondly, the law grants same-sex couples an increasing set of rights. Thirdly, a status equivalent to marriage, but different from it, is granted to same-sex couples. Finally, same-sex couples are allowed to marry. If this path is followed in the UK then civil partnership may well be no more than a stepping stone on the way to recognising same-sex marriage.[291] Only then will same-sex and opposite-sex relationships be regarded as of equal value.[292] Of course another option will be for civil partnerships to become open to both same-sex and opposite-sex couples and for marriage to cease to have legal relevance.[293]

Pubic opinion remains divided on the question of whether same-sex couples should be allowed to marry. In a survey in 2002, 50 per cent of those questioned thought 'yes' and 50 per cent thought 'no'.[294] But it appears that the percentage in favour of permitting same-sex marriage increases every time a survey is done. In a 2004 survey, only 11 per cent of those questioned said they would be very disappointed if their child was gay or lesbian.[295] Another recent public opinion poll found that 61 per cent of the public supported gay marriage[296] and 51 supported children being taught in schools that gay relationships are of equal value to marriage. This suggests that gay relationships are receiving increasing public support. It may be that the existence of civil partnerships will increase the acceptability of the concept of same-sex marriage. Indeed it is notable that the media often incorrectly refer to civil partnerships as 'gay marriage'.[297]

Indeed, arguably it is the cultural significance of the Act that is of greater importance than the legal consequences.[298] However, critics will argue that by keeping same-sex couples out of marriage, a homophobic message is reinforced by the Act. In *Home Affairs v Fourie*[299] a South African case, Justice Albie Sachs, argued:

[288] Smart, Masson and Shipman (2006).
[289] Clarke, Burgoyne and Burns (2007).
[290] Glennon (2005).
[291] Bamforth (2001) argues for same-sex marriage as a matter of justice.
[292] Wintemute (2005).
[293] Beresford and Falkus (2009).
[294] ICM (2002).
[295] ICM (2004b).
[296] Bennett (2009).
[297] 'Sir Elton John heads England's gay wedding rush' declared the *Daily Telegraph* (2005).
[298] Hull (2005).
[299] [2005] ZACC 19, para 71.

The exclusion of same sex couples from the benefits and responsibilities of marriage, accordingly, is not a small and tangential inconvenience resulting from a few surviving relics of societal prejudice destined to evaporate like the morning dew. It represents a harsh if oblique statement by the law that same sex couples are outsiders, and that their need for affirmation and protection of their intimate relations as human beings is somehow less than that of heterosexual couples. It reinforces the wounding notion that they are to be treated as biological oddities, as failed or lapsed human beings who do not fit into normal society, and, as such, do not qualify for the full moral concern and respect that our Constitution seeks to secure for everyone. It signifies that their capacity for love, commitment and accepting responsibility is by definition less worthy of regard than that of heterosexual couples.

There are, of course, voices against same-sex marriage. Many of these are based on religious beliefs,[300] arguing that marriage is a religious concept and that allowing same-sex marriage would infringe their religious concepts of marriage. One conservative Christian group has complained of 'cultural genocide' as a result of legislation prohibiting hate speech and equal treatment of same-sex couples.[301] Miss California claimed to have been robbed of the chance to become Miss USA 2009 because of her anti-gay marriage stance.[302] However, there is no need for the legal concept of marriage to match religious ones; indeed it does not, at present, for many religions. Even if it was thought that the law should match religious views of marriage, then which religious view should be followed? There are plenty of religious groups who support same-sex marriage. More importantly, the offence caused to those who have religious objections to same-sex marriage must be weighed against the harm caused to those same-sex couples who wish to marry. In weighing these it may be thought that harm to the same-sex couple would be greater and more personal than that to those with religious objections.[303]

Lynn Wardle, seeking to present a non-religious argument against same-sex marriage, argues:

> The union of two persons of different genders creates a union of unique potential strengths and inimitable potential value to society. It is the *integration* of the universe of gender differences – profound and subtle, biological and cultural, psychological and genetic – associated with sexual identity that constitutes the core and essence of marriage. Just as men and women are different, so a union of two men or of two women is not the same as the union of a man and a woman.[304]

Notice that this view is based on a strong belief in the differences between the genders. Indeed a strong case can be made for saying that the opposition to same-sex marriage inevitably reflects a desire to maintain a difference between sexual roles.[305] Even if you agreed with Wardle that there is a benefit in integrating the universes of two different people, does that only occur when they are of different sex? Others argue that same-sex relationships are less desirable than opposite-sex ones in other ways: they are less stable, less likely to raise children, or less effective in raising children.[306] The argument that appears to carry the most merit

---

[300] But see White (2010) for a discussion of economic arguments against same-sex marriage.

[301] Christian Concern for the Nation (2009).

[302] BBC Newsonline (2009i).

[303] In *Islington LBC* v *Ladele* [2009] EWCA Civ 1357 a registrar who was sacked after refusing to conduct a civil partnership because of her religious beliefs was found to have been justifiably dismissed.

[304] Wardle (2006: 53). See also Stewart (2004), Regan (1993a), Finnis (1994), Jones-Purdy (1998), George (1999: ch. 8), Pontifical Council for the Family (2000), Duckworth (2002b) outlining some of the non-religious arguments against permitting same-sex marriage. Bamforth (2001) and Woelke (2002) respond to some of these arguments.

[305] Case (2010).

[306] Duckworth (2002a: 91); Gallagher (2001). See Eskridge and Spedale (2006) and Kurdek (2004) for evidence rejecting such claims.

is that a same-sex couple will not be able to produce a child together, without medical intervention. But we allow opposite-sex couples who are infertile, or who have no intention of having children, to marry.[307]

Not all members of the gay and lesbian community are supporters of 'gay marriage'. The main concern is that by adopting marriage gay relationships may start to mimic heterosexual ones. Lesbians and gay men should be seeking to develop their own kinds and forms of relationship, rather than adopting heterosexual models.[308] However, even those who adopt this view are likely to accept that the law should give same-sex couples the option of marriage, even if they think that same-sex couples should not take up that right.[309] There is also a concern among some that although civil partnership will offer recognition and protection for 'orthodox' same-sex couples, those gay men and lesbians who do not match the marriage model (e.g. they have more than one regular partner) will be further ostracised.[310] More cynically, Adam has argued that the Civil Partnership Act is just a way for the state to get gay men and lesbians to take on financial responsibility for children or other adults who would otherwise be the responsibility of the state.[311]

A rather different concern has been voiced by Rosemary Auchmuty.[312] That is, that calls for same-sex marriage might be seen as suggesting that marriage is something good that should be encouraged and is an ideal to aspire to. However, she sees marriage as being an institution which has and still does oppress women. She is not opposed to gay marriage, but believes it should not be seen as the most important issue for those promoting the interests of the gay community. She explains:

> whether you see marriage as an oppressive bastion of male power, as the second-wave feminists did, or simply as outmoded and irrelevant, as many contemporaries do, the goal should surely be to get rid of it, or at least to let it die out of its own accord – not to try to share in its privileges, leaving the ineligible out in the cold.

A rather different set of objections to the Civil Partnership Act is that it is only open to same-sex couples. Why should an unmarried heterosexual couple wishing to register their relationship not be able to take advantage of this legislation? It has even been suggested (somewhat ironically) that the legislation discriminates on grounds of sexual orientation in making civil partnerships open only to same-sex couples.[313] The Government's answer to such complaints was that opposite-sex couples had marriage available to them and therefore had no need for civil partnership. This, however, overlooks the argument that an opposite-sex couple may dislike marriage with its historical and religious baggage and wish to formalise their relationship in another way. It also overlooks the case of couples who wish to have a legal formality for their relationship, but cannot marry, such as two sisters who in old age have shared a home together, or an elderly parent cared for by her son. Indeed, in the House of Lords' debates on the CPA 2004 a 'wrecking amendment' was introduced to the Act which was designed to permit such couples to register their relationships. It failed; and rightly so. Although there is a good case for better legal recognition of those caring for others, the CPA 2004 was not the place in which to do it. What the argument showed is that it is the sexual

---

[307] Cretney (2006a: 14–15).
[308] Weeks (2004: 35); Boyd and Young (2003); Ettlebrick (1992).
[309] Glennon (2006); Auchmuty (2004); Toner (2004).
[310] See the discussion in Lind (2004); Barker (2004).
[311] Adam (2004).
[312] Auchmuty (2008: 485).
[313] Wong (2005) considers this argument.

element of the relationship, with what that represents, which leads us to regard a relationship as being different from a relationship between friends.[314]

The issue arose in **Burden v UK**[315] where two unmarried sisters had lived together for many years. They were concerned that if either of them died the other would be liable to pay inheritance tax. They complained to the European Court of Human Rights that they were denied the exemption from inheritance tax that was available to married couples and civil partners. The Grand Chamber of the ECtHR rejected their complaint stating that a relationship between siblings is 'qualitatively of a different nature to that between married couples and [civil partners] . . . The very essence of the connection between siblings is consanguinity, whereas one of the defining characteristics of a marriage or Civil Partnership Act union is that it is forbidden to close family members.' They went on to explain that what is special about a civil partnership is the existence of the public undertaking and the rights and obligations that go with that. That makes civil partnership (and marriage) different from cohabitation. This seems the correct response to this case. What the sisters really wanted was to be exempt from inheritance tax, rather than become civil partners.[316] The strength of their case indicates a need to reform inheritance tax, rather than extend the law on civil partnerships.

The legal challenge to the absence of same-sex marriage came hard on the heels of the implementation of the Civil Partnership Act 2004.

---

### CASE: *Wilkinson v Kitzinger* [2006] EWHC 2022 (Fam)

In **Wilkinson v Kitzinger**[317] a Canadian lesbian couple, who had married in Canada (which permits same-sex marriage), sought a declaration as to their marital status under English law. If English law did not recognise their marriage they wanted a declaration of incompatibility in respect of the Matrimonial Causes Act under the Human Rights Act 1998. They failed. The case was heard by Sir Mark Potter, the President of the Family Division. The fact that they lost is perhaps not surprising, although the strength of language in the rejection of their argument is. He started with the easy question: under English law a same-sex couple could not marry and so their marriage could not be recognised. The wording of the Matrimonial Causes Act was quite clear about that.

The harder question was whether this was compatible with the European Convention on Human Rights (ECHR). Sir Mark Potter pointed out that the European Court of Human Rights had consistently said it would be inappropriate to use the Convention in areas of considerable social, political and religious controversy in respect of which there was no consensus across Europe. Gay marriage was such an area.[318] A key point in the judgment was that Parliament had very recently debated the issue of regulation of same-sex relationships and had passed the Civil Partnership Act. This, the President thought, could not be considered to be an unacceptable compromise for the issue.

> He rejected the view that civil partnership was second-class marriage, but said it was a parallel and equalizing institution designed to redress a perceived inequality of treatment of long-term monogamous same-sex relationships, while at the same time demonstrating support for the long established institution of marriage.

---

[314] Cretney (2006a).
[315] [2008] ECHR 357, [2008] 2 FCR 244.
[316] Auchmuty (2009).
[317] [2006] EWHC 2022 (Fam).
[318] The Netherlands, Belgium and Spain permit same-sex marriage.

Quite why the reference is to only 'perceived' inequality is a mystery. More controversially, he went on to indicate that he thought the compromise adopted by Parliament was appropriate. Parliament, he explained, had declined to alter the deep-rooted and almost universal recognition of marriage as a relationship between a man and a woman. He approved of Lord Nicholls's statement in *Bellinger v Bellinger*:[319] 'Marriage is an institution or a relationship deeply embedded in the religious and social culture of this country. It is deeply embedded as a relationship between two persons of the opposite sex.'

The President rejected the argument that there were rights to same-sex marriage to be found in either article 8 or 12 of the ECHR.[320] Article 12 provided for the right to marry, but marriage here he interpreted in its traditional sense. As to the right to family life in article 8, the House of Lords in *M v Secretary of State for Work and Pensions*[321] had made it clear that a same-sex couple currently did not fall within the definition of 'family life'. In any event, the CPA 2004 provided a same-sex couple with all the legal benefits of marriage. There was no aspect of their private life which was interfered with by not being able to marry. It could not, therefore, be said that there was an interference with Convention rights which was discriminatory on the basis of sexual orientation and therefore contrary to article 14.[322] Even if there was any discrimination it could be justified with the aim of protecting the traditional understanding of marriage.[323]

Perhaps the most surprising passage is the following, which is worth quoting at length:

**118** It is apparent that the majority of people, or at least of governments, not only in England but Europe-wide, regard marriage as an age-old institution, valued and valuable, respectable and respected, as a means not only of encouraging monogamy but also the procreation of children and their development and nurture in a family unit (or 'nuclear family') in which both maternal and paternal influences are available in respect of their nurture and upbringing.

**119** The belief that this form of relationship is the one which best encourages stability in a well-regulated society is not a disreputable or outmoded notion based upon ideas of exclusivity, marginalisation, disapproval or discrimination against homosexuals or any other persons who by reason of their sexual orientation or for other reasons prefer to form a same-sex union.

**120** If marriage is, by longstanding definition and acceptance, a formal relationship between a man and a woman, primarily (though not exclusively) with the aim of producing and rearing children as I have described it, and if that is the institution contemplated and safeguarded by Article 12, then to accord a same-sex relationship the title and status of marriage would be to fly in the face of the Convention as well as to fail to recognise physical reality.

He went on to explain that the CPA 2004 was a recognition that same-sex relationships were not inferior to opposite-sex ones, but rather, as a matter of nature and common understanding, different.[324]

---

[319] [2003] 2 AC 467 at para 46.

[320] See Murphy (2004) for an argument that a proper interpretation of the ECHR is that same-sex couples should have a right to marry. See the response by Bamforth (2005), challenging his approach to the issue and arguing that focusing on justice and autonomy, rather than the wording of the ECHR articles, is a more effective approach.

[321] [2006] 2 WLR 637.

[322] See W. Wright (2006) for a discussion of such an argument.

[323] He referred to the unreported decision of the European Court of Human Rights in *Estevez v Spain*, 10 May 2001, which quoted the promotion of family life based on marriage as a legitimate state aim.

[324] [2006] UKHL 11 at para 113. It is not quite clear how he thought they were different.

As indicated already, the fact that the application was unsuccessful is not surprising; what is, is the manner of its rejection. The President could have left the issue as a matter for Parliament given the social and political issues raised. The fact that he went on to make a detailed argument against recognising same-sex marriage is interesting, because it was unnecessary. Opponents of his view would reject the idea that support for traditional married family life justifies discrimination against same-sex couples. As Baroness Hale, dissenting in M v *Secretary of State for Work and Pensions*,[325] stated:

> No one has yet explained how failing to recognise the relationships of people whose sexual orientation means that they are unable or strongly unwilling to marry is necessary for the purpose of protection or encouraging the marriage of people who are quite capable of marrying if they wish to do so.

The President's judgment repeats the argument at several points that opposite-sex and same-sex relationships are 'equal but different', but he fails to make it clear what he thinks is different about a same-sex and an opposite-sex couple. Presumably it is the nature of the sexual relations, but what exactly is it about the difference that is thought worthy of a comment or a legal distinction? Even if one can locate a difference between same-sex and opposite-sex couples, is it one that should matter? Nicholas Bamforth[326] argues:

> Love, mutual commitment and long-term emotional, physical and moral support are among the most important ingredients of a decent human life. To those who support – normatively speaking – the rights to autonomy (or dignity) or equality, it is morally unimportant whether such things are provided by a partner of the opposite sex or one of same sex.

Although it was suggested earlier that in time civil partnerships will be regarded as a stepping stone on the way to recognising same-sex marriage, that is not the only possible consequence of official recognition of same-sex relationships. Will it (further) challenge the traditional gender roles within marriage and heterosexual relationships? Will it open up the possibility of a child having two fathers or two mothers?[327] Will it further challenge the legal distinction between male and female?[328]

## 8 Unmarried cohabiting couples

There is enormous difficulty in discussing unmarried couples because there are so many forms of cohabitation. The term 'cohabiting couple' can range from a group of students living together in a flat-share, to a boyfriend and girlfriend living together while contemplating marriage, to a couple who have deliberately decided to avoid marriage but wish to live together in a permanent stable relationship. Lord Hoffmann in *Re P*[329] stated: 'Statistics show that married couples, who have accepted a legal commitment to each other, tend to have more stable relationships than unmarried couples, whose relationships may vary from quasi-marital to ephemeral.' Baroness Hale in the same case stated:

> Some unmarried relationships are much more stable than some marriages, and vice versa. The law cannot force any couple, married or unmarried, to stay together. But being married does at least indicate an initial intention to stay together for life. More important, it makes a great legal

---

[325] [2006] 1 FCR 497.
[326] Bamforth (2005: 272).
[327] Kelly (2004).
[328] Chau and Herring (2004).
[329] [2008] UKHL 38.

difference to their relationship. Marriage brings with it legal rights and obligations between the couple which unmarried couples do not have.[330]

One set of researchers[331] suggested that there are essentially four categories of cohabitants:

- the Ideologues: those in long-term relationships, but with an ideological objection to marriage;
- the Romantics: those who expect to get married eventually and see cohabitation as a step towards marriage, which they saw as a serious commitment;
- the Pragmatists: who decided whether or not to get married on legal or financial grounds;
- the Uneven Couples: where one partner wanted to marry and the other did not.

The law has not yet provided a coherent approach to cohabitation, but in several statutes married and unmarried couples have been treated in the same way. Apart from these special provisions, the law treats unmarried couples as two separate individuals, without regard to their relationship. If there is no specific statutory provision then the law treats an unmarried couple in the same way as it would two strangers.[332]

Same-sex couples who have not entered into a civil partnership can claim many of the rights that are available to opposite-sex unmarried couples.[333] In 1999 the House of Lords in *Fitzpatrick v Sterling Housing Association Ltd*[334] accepted that a gay person was a member of his partner's family. Lord Nicholls in *Secretary of State v M*[335] has stated that 'under the law of this country as it has now developed a same sex couple are as much capable of constituting a "family" as a heterosexual couple'. Little could Sister Sledge have foreseen that the theme from their song 'We are family' would be repeated by a Law Lord, albeit in a slightly more erudite way. In *Ghaidan v Godin-Mendoza*[336] the House of Lords accepted that the phrase 'a person who was living with the original tenant as his or her wife or husband' could include a same-sex couple.[337]

Perhaps a key legal difference is that a same-sex relationship does not fall within the scope of respect for family life under article 8 of the European Convention on Human Rights, although it would fall within the definition of private life.[338] However, it is unlawful under the European Convention to discriminate upon the grounds of sexual orientation.[339]

Tyrer J in *Kimber v Kimber*[340] suggested the following factors be considered in deciding whether there is cohabitation:

1. whether the parties were living together under the same roof;
2. whether they shared in the tasks and duties of daily life (e.g. cooking, cleaning);
3. whether the relationship had stability and permanence;

---

[330] *Re P* [2008] UKHL 38, para 108.
[331] Barlow, Burgoyne and Smithson (2007).
[332] See Smart and Stevens (2000) for a discussion of the wide range of cohabiting relationships.
[333] CPA 2004, Sch 24 amends statutes to ensure that same-sex and opposite-sex cohabitees are treated in the same way. Bailey-Harris (2001c: 605; 2000) provides a powerful argument that same-sex and opposite-sex cohabitants should be treated in the same way.
[334] [2000] 1 FCR 21. The case is discussed in Glennon (2000) and Diduck (2001a).
[335] [2006] 1 FCR 497 at para 506.
[336] [2004] UKHL 30.
[337] In *Nutting v Southern Housing Group* [2004] EWHC 2982 (Ch) it was emphasised that to be living as a spouse one had to have a life-long commitment.
[338] *ADT v UK* [2000] 2 FLR 697.
[339] *EB v France* [2008] 1 FCR 236; *Da Silva Mouta v Portugal* [2001] 1 FCR 653, discussed in Herring (2002b).
[340] [2000] 1 FLR 232. See also *Re J (Income Support Cohabitation)* [1995] 1 FLR 660 and *Kotke v Saffarini* [2005] EWCA Civ 221 for other discussion of what cohabitation means.

4. how the parties arranged their finances;

5. whether the parties had an ongoing sexual relationship;

6. whether the parties had any children and how the parties acted towards each other's children; and

7. the opinion of the reasonable person with normal perceptions looking at the couple's life together.

There are some statutory attempts at defining cohabitation. Section 144 (4)(b) of the Adoption and Children Act 2002 states that 'two people (whether of different sexes or the same sex) living as partners in an enduring family relationship' can adopt. A more common form of definition of cohabitation is found in the Family Law Act 1996: 'two persons who, although not married to each other, are living together as husband and wife or (if of the same sex) in an equivalent relationship'.[341]

What is clear is that more and more couples are choosing to cohabit.[342] In 2008, 45 per cent of children were born to a mother who was unmarried.[343] In 2007, of those aged 16–29 10 per cent were married, while 16 per cent were cohabiting.[344] In 2007 around 10 per cent of the adult population were cohabiting.[345] Cohabiting couples tend to be younger than married couples, with half being headed by a person under the age of 35. Only 10 per cent of married households are headed by someone under 35. Of women in the age group 18 to 59, 25 per cent were cohabiting outside marriage.[346]

The evidence suggests that some cohabitants are living together, but planning to marry; while others see cohabitation as an alternative to marriage. In one study only 9.7 per cent of cohabiting couples said that they were not considering getting married,[347] although 22.7 per cent stated that they did not regard marriage as important. Certainly cohabitation before marriage has become the norm.[348] Where cohabitation does not end in marriage it tends to break up. The average length of cohabitation is about two years, after which the couple tend either to marry or split up.[349] But, as already emphasised, we must be careful not to make generalisations: many long-term cohabiting relationships do exist.

## 9 Comparisons between the legal position of spouses or civil partners and unmarried couples

It is surprisingly difficult to compile a complete list of the differences between the legal positions of spouses or civil partners and unmarried couples, primarily because the law does not provide a clear statement of the rights and responsibilities of marriage. Some of the main differences in the legal treatment of married and unmarried couples will now be discussed.[350]

---

[341] FLA, s 62(1)(a) (as amended by the Domestic Violence, Crimes and Victims Act 2004).
[342] This is a Europe-wide phenomenon: see Kiernan (2001). For a thorough discussion of the statistics on cohabitation, see Haskey (2001).
[343] National Statistics (2010a).
[344] National Statistics (2010a).
[345] National Statistics (2010a).
[346] Babb et al. (2006: 27).
[347] Lewis (2001b: 135).
[348] Haskey (2001: 57).
[349] Ermisch and Francesconi (1998).
[350] See also Barlow et al. (2005: 7–11).

## A Formalities at the beginning and end of a relationship

The law closely regulates the beginning and end of a marriage or civil partnership. It sets out certain formalities that must be complied with in order for a legal marriage or civil partnership to start, and it only ends when the court grants a decree absolute of divorce, or a dissolution. An unmarried cohabiting relationship can, by contrast, begin or end without any notification to any public body. While every marriage and civil partnership is centrally registered, there is no such record of cohabitation. One consequence of these formalities is that, although the law can restrict who can enter marriage or civil partnership, there is obviously no restriction as to who may cohabit – there is nothing to stop any number of men or women, unmarried or married, from cohabiting.

It is easy to overestimate the practical importance to the parties of the legal formalities at the beginning and end of a relationship. The legal requirements of marriage or civil partnership are not particularly difficult to comply with, and the legal formalities take up little time when compared with the non-legal trappings that often accompany marriage or civil partnership, which take up much more of the money and attention of the parties. Similarly, in relation to separation, although divorce or dissolution does include legal formalities, when compared with the paperwork and practical arrangements of the ending of a long-term relationship the legal formalities of divorce or dissolution can be of minor importance. The paperwork concerned over, for example, separating joint bank accounts, resolving the occupation of the home, dealing with the mortgage or tenancy, changing arrangements over electricity, gas bills, etc. can make the formalities connected to the divorce or dissolution itself seem small.

## B Financial support

During the marriage or civil partnership itself each party can seek a court order requiring one to pay maintenance to the other,[351] but one unmarried cohabitant cannot seek maintenance from another. In fact, it is very rare for one spouse to seek maintenance from the other except in the context of divorce. Where it is sought, the amounts awarded tend to be low and difficult to collect.[352]

Of far more significance is the fact that on divorce or dissolution the court has the power to redistribute property owned by either party. However, on the ending of an unmarried relationship the court only has the power to declare who owns what and has no power to require one party to transfer property to the other or to pay maintenance. Although this is a crucial distinction between spouses or civil partners and unmarried couples, three important factors need to be stressed. The first is that for many couples the Child Support Act 1991 and Children Act 1989 cover the maintenance for children. These Acts apply equally to married and unmarried couples. Secondly, once the child support has been resolved, there is often not enough spare money to consider spousal or partner support. In fact, in fewer than half of all divorces do the courts make any order dealing with the parties' financial resources.[353] The third distinction is that, as we shall see later, in resolving disputes between unmarried cohabitants over property the courts have utilised various equitable doctrines (for example, constructive trusts) which have in effect given the courts wide discretion in deciding the appropriate share of the equitable interest. Indeed in some cases involving unmarried couples

---

[351] See Chapter 5.
[352] The common law duty on a husband to maintain a wife was abolished in s 198 of the Equality Act 2010.
[353] Barton and Bissett-Johnson (2000).

the results using the equitable doctrines are those which would be expected if the couple were married and the court were hearing the case under the Matrimonial Causes Act 1973.

Cohabiting couples, unlike spouses or civil partners, can enter binding cohabitation contracts which will determine what will happen to their property on separation.[354] However, care must be taken in the wording of such contracts. In *Sutton v Mischon de Reya*[355] the claimant asked a firm of solicitors to draft a cohabitation contract. Sutton and a Swedish businessman, Mr Stahl, wished to conduct a 'master–slave' relationship. They asked that the contract back this up by confirming that Sutton was to have absolute power over Stahl, to obey him in everything he said on pain of punishment and to hand over to Sutton all his property. Charles J held that such a contract amounted to, in effect, a contract for sexual services. He saw a key distinction between a contract for sexual relations outside marriage which was not enforceable and a contract between people who are cohabiting in a relationship which involves sexual relations. Charles J, in a surprising turn of phrase, stated that 'even a moron in a hurry'[356] could tell that the contract in this case fell into the former category and so was not enforceable.

## C Children

There used to be a crucial distinction drawn between 'legitimate' and 'illegitimate' children. This affected the status of children and the nature of parental rights over children. The label of illegitimacy has now been abolished by the Family Law Reform Act 1987 and only minor differences exist in the legal position of 'legitimate' and 'illegitimate' children.[357] However, there are still important differences between the legal position of married and unmarried fathers. As we shall see, one of the key concepts of the law relating to parenthood is parental responsibility. Every mother of a child automatically acquires parental responsibility for her child, but the father of the child will automatically acquire parental responsibility only if he is married to the mother. An unmarried father may acquire parental responsibility by being registered as the father on the child's birth certificate, lodging at the court a parental responsibility agreement, or the father may apply to the court for a parental responsibility order. This is a significant difference between married and unmarried fathers, but is of less importance than it might at first appear, for two reasons. First, the courts have been very willing to award parental responsibility to a father who applies for it. The second is that in day-to-day issues parental responsibility is of limited importance. Many unmarried fathers carry out their parental role unaware that they do not have parental responsibility. Whether or not a father has parental responsibility is only really of significance when major decisions have to be made in respect of the child, such as whether a child should have a medical operation.

## D Inheritance and succession

Where a person dies without having made a will, the person is intestate. In such a case the deceased's spouse or civil partner will be entitled to some or all of the estate, depending on the application of various rules which will be discussed in Chapter 12. However, an unmarried partner of the deceased is not automatically entitled to an intestate estate. All an unmarried partner can do is to apply under the Inheritance (Provision for Family and Dependants) Act

---

[354] They cannot contract out of child support obligations, however: *Morgan v Hill* [2006] 3 FCR 620.
[355] [2004] 3 FCR 142; [2004] 1 FLR 837.
[356] At para 23.
[357] See Chapter 7.

1975 for an order that in effect alters the intestacy rules and awards them a portion of the estate. So, a bereaved unmarried partner must apply to the court in order to be put in the same position as the bereaved spouse if his or her partner is intestate.

## E Criminal law

There used to be important distinctions between married and unmarried couples in criminal law, but many of these have been removed.

1. *Rape.* It used to be a common law rule that a husband could not be guilty of raping his wife.[358] This was justified in two ways. First, there was an emphasis on the concept of the unity of husbands and wives – as a husband and wife are one in the eyes of the law, sexual intercourse between them could be no crime.[359] Secondly, it was argued that on marriage the wife impliedly consents to intercourse at any time during that marriage and that such consent was irrevocable. Eventually the House of Lords in *R v R (Rape: Marital Exemption)*[360] abolished the marital exception for rape and this was confirmed by Parliament in the Criminal Justice and Public Order Act 1994. Lord Keith explained that marriage 'is in modern times regarded as a partnership of equals and no longer one in which the wife must be the subservient chattel of the husband'.[361] So now the substantive law on rape is the same whether the defendant be the victim's husband or not.[362]

2. *Actual bodily harm and grievous bodily harm.* There is some confusion in the criminal law over the circumstances in which one person may injure another with their consent. In *R v Brown*[363] the House of Lords confirmed the conviction of some sadomasochists who were convicted of assaulting each other even though their 'victims' had consented to the infliction of the pain. In *R v Wilson*[364] a husband was convicted of assault occasioning actual bodily harm for branding his initials on his wife's buttocks in spite of her consent. The Court of Appeal overturned the conviction. There is some dispute over how to reconcile these two cases. One argument is that the courts distinguished between injuries caused within marriage and injuries caused by gay couples.[365]

3. *Coercion.* The defence of coercion[366] is available to a wife who has committed a crime (apart from murder or treason) as a result of threats from her husband. If a wife commits an offence in the presence of her husband there is a rebuttable presumption that she should not be convicted because she was acting as a result of her husband's coercion. The defence is very similar to duress, the main difference being that coercion does not require a threat of death or serious injuries. The defence is not available to an unmarried couple[367] or even to those with void marriages.[368] It has been widely criticised as based on an outdated presumption that wives are under the thumb of their husbands.

---

[358] Although he could be guilty of other criminal offences against his wife.
[359] This was never a very convincing explanation, because a husband could be convicted of assaulting his wife.
[360] [1991] 4 All ER 481, [1992] 1 FLR 217. See now Sexual Offences Act 2003, s 1.
[361] [1991] 4 All ER 481 at p. 484.
[362] Although it appears that marital rapists still receive lower sentences than non-marital rapists (Warner (2000)).
[363] [1993] 1 AC 212.
[364] [1996] 3 WLR 125.
[365] Although in *Emmett*, unreported, 15.10.99 a man's conviction following injuries caused to his partner during an (alleged) sadomasochistic incident with his fiancée was upheld. For an alternative explanation and discussion see Herring (2009c: ch. 6).
[366] Criminal Justice Act 1925, s 47.
[367] *R v Court* (1912) 7 CAR 127.
[368] *R v Ditta, Hussain and Kara* [1988] Crim LR 42.

4. *Theft*. Under s 30 of the Theft Act 1968 a person can only be prosecuted for theft against his or her spouse if the Director of Public Prosecutions has given consent.

5. *Conspiracy*. A person cannot be guilty of conspiring with his or her spouse or civil partner, unless it is alleged that they conspired with other people.[369]

## F Contract

It was only after the Law Reform (Married Women and Tortfeasors) Act 1935 that wives were able themselves to enter contracts that were legally effective. Husbands and wives can enter into contracts with each other, but will have to show that there is intent to create legal relations. For example, in *Balfour v Balfour*[370] the Court of Appeal held that a promise by a husband to pay his wife £30 per week while he was abroad was unenforceable. This was because there is a presumption that spouses do not intend to be legally bound by such agreements. The rule does not apply to spouses who have separated. A married couple cannot enter into an enforceable contract which excludes the jurisdiction of the divorce court. So, a court can make orders in relation to children or financial matters regardless of any contracts the spouses have signed. The position for unmarried couples is similar. Although they may enter a contract they must persuade a court that their agreement was intended to be legally binding. A crucial difference is that a married couple or civil partners cannot enter into a contract which governs what would happen to their property in the event of their divorce or dissolution because that would be to interfere with the court's jurisdiction under the Matrimonial Causes Act 1973. An unmarried couple can sign a contract which will determine what happens to their property when the relationship ends.

## G Tort

The rule that a spouse could not sue his or her spouse in tort was revoked by the Law Reform (Husband and Wife) Act 1962 and the rule that a husband had to be joined in any tortious action brought by or against a wife was abolished by statute in 1935.[371] In relation to tort, married and unmarried couples are therefore now treated in the same way. The most remarkable case of partners suing in tort is *P v B (Paternity; Damages for Deceit)*[372] where a man sued in deceit after his partner had falsely told him he was the father of her child, as a result of which he claimed he paid her £90,000 to support the child. His action was held not to be barred on the grounds of public policy.[373]

## H Evidence

There are two issues here: can a spouse give evidence against the other spouse (is he or she competent), and can a spouse be forced to give evidence against the other spouse (is he or she compellable)?[374] At one time spouses were not compellable[375] witnesses in civil or

---

[369] Criminal Law Act 1977, s 2(2)(a).
[370] [1919] 2 KB 571.
[371] Married Women's Property Act 1882 and Law Reform (Married Women and Tortfeasors) Act 1935.
[372] [2001] 1 FLR 1041.
[373] A spouse will not be permitted to sue a former spouse in tort if this is regarded as an attempt to unsettle the financial orders reached on divorce: *Ganesmoorthy v Ganesmoorthy* [2003] 3 FCR 167.
[374] Creighton (1990).
[375] By saying a witness is compellable it is meant that a witness can be forced to give evidence.

criminal proceedings against their spouses, the idea being that a spouse should not be forced into the appalling dilemma of either committing perjury or giving evidence which would harm his or her spouse in the proceedings. The spouse was considered an incompetent witness in criminal proceedings because the evidence would be so tainted that a jury would not be able to treat it fairly. These positions have been changed by statute.

The present law is now that in civil proceedings a spouse or civil partner is both a compellable and a competent witness. In criminal proceedings generally the spouse or civil partner is competent, but not compellable.[376] In other words, if a spouse or civil partner is willing to give evidence against his or her spouse or partner he or she may do so, but will not be forced to. The exceptions are that if the husband and wife or civil partners are jointly charged for an offence, then neither is competent to give evidence for the prosecution (unless the charges against them are dropped or they plead guilty). Under s 80 of the Police and Criminal Evidence Act 1984 there is a shortlist of offences for which the spouse or civil partner is compellable. These are offences which involve an assault or injury or threat of injury to the spouse or any person under the age of 16, or a sexual offence against a person under 16.[377] There are no special rules relating to the evidence of cohabitants.[378]

## I Matrimonial property

The Family Law Act 1996 provides married couples and civil partners with home rights which provide a right to occupy the matrimonial home.[379] There are also special provisions relating to family property during bankruptcy, and pension rights, which we will discuss later. These provisions do not apply to cohabitants, who are given no particular protection on bankruptcy.

## J Marital confidences

Communication between spouses used to be subject to special protection so that a spouse who disclosed confidential information about the other could be found in breach of confidence. However, the law on confidential information has now developed so that it covers cohabitants.[380] It has even been found that there could be confidential relations between a husband and the person he was having an adulterous relationship with.[381]

## K Taxation and benefits

There are special exemptions from tax that apply to married couples and civil partners but not unmarried couples. The most important are in respect of inheritance tax and capital gains tax allowance.[382] The Labour Government removed the married couples' tax allowance, which was an allowance against income tax available to married couples but not to unmarried

---

[376] In *R (On the Application of the Crown Prosecution Service) v Registrar General of Births, Deaths and Marriages* [2003] 1 FCR 110 a defendant to a charge of murder married the chief prosecution witness to take advantage of this rule. The Crown Prosecution Service in that case unsuccessfully applied to prevent that marriage.

[377] This includes attempting, conspiring, aiding, abetting, counselling, procuring or inciting their commission.

[378] This was confirmed by the Court of Appeal in *R v Pearce* [2001] EWCA Crim 2834, [2002] 3 FCR 75. It rejected an argument that, following the Human Rights Act 1998, cohabitants should not be compellable witnesses.

[379] See Chapter 4.

[380] *Stephens v Avery* [1988] 1 Ch 449; *A v B (a company)* [2002] 1 FCR 369.

[381] *CC v AB* [2008] 2 FCR 505. See also *John Terry (previously 'LNS') v Persons Unknown* [2010] EWHC 119 (QB).

[382] Tax Law Review Committee (2003) provides a useful summary of the differences between married and unmarried couples' taxation.

couples. The removal of this tax advantage has been strongly criticised. For example, Mary Corbett of the Catholic Family Group wrote: 'Only naive people would think that the marriage allowance would have kept anyone together, but the allowance was a symbol worth keeping because it pointed to marriage as a worthwhile commitment.'[383] It is significant that the Labour Government replaced the married couples' tax allowance with a tax credit for those who care for children. In relation to state benefits, unmarried couples and married couples are generally treated in the same way. It has been alleged that now some married couples are disadvantaged as compared to lone parents in the tax and benefits systems.[384] The Prime Minister has announced that he intends the Government to provide tax advantages for married couples and those in civil partnerships.

## L Citizenship

Anyone who is not a citizen of the UK and colonies does not become a citizen by marrying someone who is. She or he may obtain nationality by naturalisation or by one of the other methods. The spouse's requirements for naturalisation are less strict than for others. If a person is settled in the UK then the spouse will be given entry clearance as long as he or she can show the marriage is not a sham and that the couple are able to accommodate and maintain themselves. There is a similar power for engaged couples, but not unmarried cohabitants.[385] Following the Civil Partnership Act spouses and civil partners are treated in the same way for immigration purposes.

## M Statutory succession to tenancies

Statute has provided rights to a tenant's family to succeed to the tenancy on the death of a tenant. The phrase 'family' has been interpreted to include opposite-sex or same-sex cohabitants.[386] The phrase 'as husband and wife' includes opposite-sex or same-sex couples.[387]

## N Domestic violence

Married couples, civil partners and cohabitants are associated persons and so can apply for non-molestation injunctions. Cohabitants can also apply for occupation orders, although if the applicant does not have property rights in the property she will be treated less favourably than she would have been had she been married or a civil partner.[388]

## O Fatal Accident Act 1976

The Fatal Accident Act 1976 permits a spouse or civil partner of a deceased killed in an accident to claim damages under certain circumstances. Under this Act a cohabitant is able to have a claim in the same way as a spouse or civil partner if he or she had been living with the deceased for at least two years immediately before the date of death.[389]

The next two issues are differences of a theoretical rather than practical nature.

---

[383] Corbett (1999).
[384] BBC Newsonline (2007a).
[385] Cretney, Masson and Bailey-Harris (2002: 92–3) for the detail of the law.
[386] *Fitzpatrick v Sterling Housing Association Ltd* [2000] 1 FCR 21.
[387] *Ghaidan v Godin-Mendoza* [2004] 2 FCR 481.
[388] See Chapter 6.
[389] It does not cover those who were 'going out' together but not cohabiting: *Kotke v Saffarini* [2005] 1 FCR 642.

## P The doctrine of unity

The principal effect of marriage at common law is that the husband and wife become one. The doctrine of unity finds its basis in Christian theology.[390] Blackstone[391] wrote:

> By marriage, the husband and wife are one person in law; that is, the very being or legal existence of the woman is suspended during the marriage, or at least is incorporated and consolidated into that of the husband; . . . Upon this principle of a union of person in husband and wife, depend almost all the legal rights, duties, and disabilities, that either of them acquire by the marriage.

The effects of this doctrine were never fully explained in the law and today the doctrine is regarded with cynicism. Lord Denning MR in *Midland Bank Trust Co Ltd v Green (No. 3)*[392] explained that the position used to be that '. . . the law regarded the husband and wife as one and the husband as that one'. However, he made it clear that the doctrine of unity is now of very limited application.[393]

## Q Consortium

The concept of consortium is not clear but has been defined by Munby J in *Sheffield CC v E and S*[394] as 'the sharing of a common home and a common domestic life, and the right to enjoy each other's society, comfort and assistance'. At one time there was an obligation on the wife to provide her husband with 'society and services', although a husband did not owe the wife a corresponding duty. However, Munby J emphasised that nowadays spouses are 'joint co-equal heads of the family' and any rights of consortium are equal and reciprocal. However, the concept of consortium is rarely enforced in law. In *R v Reid*[395] it was confirmed that a husband could be guilty of kidnapping his wife and that the right of consortium did not provide a defence to such a charge.

## 10 Engagements

Before marriage it is common for couples to enter into an engagement, when the parties agree to marry one another.[396] In the past, under common law, such agreements were seen as enforceable contracts, and so if either party, without lawful justification, broke the engagement then it would be open for the other to sue for breach of promise and to obtain damages. Such an action was abolished by the Law Reform (Miscellaneous Provisions) Act 1970, s 1,[397] which stated that no agreement to marry is enforceable as a contract. The abolition was justified on the basis that it was contrary to public policy for people to feel forced into marriages through fear of being sued.

---

[390] The Bible, Genesis 2: 24; Genesis 3: 16.

[391] Blackstone (1770: 442).

[392] [1982] Ch 529 at p. 538.

[393] In *Ünal Tekeli v Turkey* [2005] 1 FCR 663 it was said to be contrary to the ECHR to require a married couple to both take the husband's surname; that was sex discrimination and could not be justified in the name of promoting marital unity. The Court left open the question of whether it would be permissible to require the couple to share a surname.

[394] [2004] EWHC 2808 (Fam) at paras 130–1. The case is discussed in Gaffney-Rhys (2006).

[395] [1973] QB 299.

[396] It is possible for a party to be engaged even though he or she is married to someone else: *Shaw v Fitzgerald* [1992] 1 FLR 357, [1992] FCR 162.

[397] Law Commission Report 26 (1969), although Bagshaw (2001) discusses the possibility of an action being brought in the tort of deceit if a person promised to marry another, without ever intending to do so.

In general, engaged couples are treated in the same way as unmarried couples, though engagement and agreement to enter a civil partnership still has legal significance in a number of ways:

1. *Property of engaged couples.* When resolving property disputes between an engaged couple s 37 of the Matrimonial Proceedings and Property Act 1970 applies.[398] The effect of this provision is described in detail in Chapter 4, but, in brief, it states that if someone improves a house he or she thereby acquires an interest in it. Apart from this provision, the property of an engaged couple is treated in the same way as that of an unmarried couple.[399]

2. *Gifts between engaged couples.* The Law Reform (Miscellaneous Provisions) Act 1970, s 3(1) states that: 'A party to an agreement to marry who makes a gift of property to the other party to the agreement on the condition (express or implied) that it shall be returned if the agreement is terminated shall not be prevented from recovering the property by reason only of his having terminated the agreement.' So each case will turn on its own facts and depend on whether the gift was subject to an implied condition that the gift should be returned if the marriage did not take place. For example, furniture bought for the intended matrimonial home may be thought to be conditional upon marriage and therefore should be returned if the engagement is broken. A Christmas gift would probably be regarded as unconditional.

3. The gift of an engagement ring is presumed to be an absolute gift and therefore can be kept by the recipient, but this presumption can be rebutted if it can be shown there was a condition that the ring be returned in the event of the marriage not taking place.[400] For example, if the ring had belonged to the man's grandmother and was intended to be passed down within her family, it may be presumed that the ring should be returned if the engagement is broken.

4. *Domestic violence.* Engaged couples are 'associated' people for the provisions of Part IV of the Family Law Act 1996 and so can automatically apply for a non-molestation order against one another. However, the Act requires the engagement be proved in one of a number of distinct ways (see Chapter 6).

## 11 Should the law treat cohabitation and marriage or civil partnership in the same way?

It should be noted that many European countries have legislated to treat married and unmarried couples in the same way.[401] There are various ways of considering this question.

### A Does the state benefit from cohabitation to the same extent as from marriage or civil partnership?

The state has traditionally favoured marriage and sought to encourage people to marry, most explicitly by providing tax advantages to married couples which are not available to unmarried

---

[398] *Mossop v Mossop* [1988] 2 FLR 173 CA, because of s 2(1) of the Law Reform (Miscellaneous Provisions) Act 1970.
[399] See Chapter 5.
[400] Law Reform (Miscellaneous Provisions) Act 1970, s 3(2). See *Cox v Jones* [2004] 3 FCR 693 for a case where the man was not able to show that the ring was not intended as a gift.
[401] Thorpe LJ (2002: 893).

people. However, marriage is not encouraged only through such explicit means. As Katherine O'Donovan explains: 'Marriage endures as symbol . . . it may be presented as private but it is reinforced everywhere in public and in political discourse.'[402] A study of attitudes among the general public towards marriage revealed that two thirds of those interviewed saw marriage as an ideal family form, although notably only 28 per cent of respondents thought marriage made couples better parents.[403] In another poll only 44 per cent of those questioned thought marriage was essential to ensuring a lasting relationship.[404] Most recently a poll found that 70 per cent of those aged between 20 and 35 wanted to marry, including 79 per cent of those currently cohabiting.[405] But why is it that the Government, through public statements and policies, seeks to encourage marriage and civil partnership?

There are five particular advantages to the state which are often cited:

1. Sir George Baker, a former President of the Family Division, has argued that marriage provides the 'building blocks' of society and is 'essential to the well-being of our society, as we understand it'.[406] Lord Hoffmann has declared: 'The state is entitled to take the view that marriage is a very important institution and that in general it is better for children to be brought up by parents who are married to each other than by those who are not.'[407] This view, although a popular notion amongst politicians, lacks precision. What does it mean that marriage is a building block or the foundation of society? It could be argued that a married couple may feel they have a greater stake in society than two single people, and so may be more willing to contribute to it.[408] This is certainly open to debate as, for example, single people may well be more likely to use public transport and perhaps even be more vulnerable to crime. It could be suggested that marriage or civil partnership provides psychological benefit to the couple themselves, which might in turn make them better citizens.[409] It has been suggested that marriage makes a couple wealthier, happier and healthier.[410] These arguments are all hard to prove either way. We have not tried a society without marriage, and so do not know whether society would be different without marriage.

2. It may be that the state wishes to support marriage and civil partnership in order to promote the production of and caring for children. The Labour Government's view was that: 'many lone parents and unmarried couples raise their children every bit as successfully as married parents. But marriage is still the surest foundation for raising children and remains the choice of the majority of people in Britain. We want to strengthen the institution of marriage to help more marriages to succeed.'[411] The Conservative Party's Centre for Social Justice has also voiced its support for the institution of marriage.[412] It claimed that those children not in two-parent families are:[413]

   – 75 per cent more likely to fail at school
   – 70 per cent more likely to be a drug addict

---

[402] O'Donovan (1993: 57).

[403] Barlow et al. (2001).

[404] ICM Poll (2002b).

[405] de Waal (2008).

[406] *Campbell v Campbell* [1977] 1 All ER 1 at p. 6.

[407] *Re P (Adoption: Unmarried Couple)* [2008] UKHL 38, para 13.

[408] Berger and Kellner (1980).

[409] There is some evidence of a higher incidence of premature death among unmarried rather than married men: McAllister (1995).

[410] Waite and Gallagher (2001).

[411] Home Office (1998).

[412] Centre for Social Justice (2009).

[413] Centre for Social Justice (2010).

- 50 per cent more likely to have an alcohol problem
- 40 per cent more likely to have serious debt problems
- 35 per cent more likely to experience unemployment/wefare dependency.

They claimed that married relationships were more stable than unmarried relationships[414] and so it was in society's interests to promote marriage. This claim is controversial and we shall return to it shortly.

3. A third alleged benefit to the state is that by managing the start of a relationship the state is able to regulate the relationship if it breaks down. The state may wish to ensure that at the end of a relationship the arrangements for children will promote the child's welfare, and that the spouse's or civil partner's property is divided between them in a way that is just. If a marriage or civil partnership breaks down, the couple must turn to the courts for a divorce or dissolution so that the marriage or civil partnership can be officially terminated; however, if an unmarried couple separate, the court may well not be involved at the end of the relationship. The strength of this view is weakened in the light of the present law. First, the law, in both financial and child-related matters, essentially allows the parties themselves to resolve these matters and intervenes only if there is a dispute. Secondly, this view does not explain why the law does not try to provide the same intervention for unmarried couples.

4. A fourth benefit is economic. If a person falls ill, or becomes unemployed, and so no longer has an income, then the financial responsibility is likely to fall on the state if that person is single, whereas spouses or civil partners would depend on each other. A further economic benefit is the straightforward fact that a couple sharing accommodation require less housing than two single people.

5. Marriage and civil partnership can be used as an effective evidential tool. If the law were to abolish the legal significance of marriage then it would be necessary to create some kind of alternative in order legally to regulate family life. Perhaps cohabitation would provide that alternative. The difficulty is that a couple might be sharing a house, but not necessarily sharing their lives. The definition of cohabitation and the investigation that would be necessary to decide whether or not a couple were sharing their lives would be far more complex and expensive than deciding whether a person is married. The couples who marry or enter civil partnerships therefore save the state's and courts' time and effort in formally establishing the nature of their relationship.

Many of these benefits of marriage or civil partnership to the state are also provided by cohabiting relationships. Further, it is unclear whether all or even most married couples or civil partners provide these benefits.[415] However, the core question is whether unmarried cohabiting couples are as stable as married or civilly partnered ones.[416] This is especially important when considering their role in raising children. It is very difficult to obtain statistics on cohabiting relationships because there are no formalities marking their beginning and end. The evidence available suggests that unmarried cohabiting relationships are shorter lived.[417]

---

[414] The Labour Government claimed this too: HM Government (2010a).

[415] Huston and Melz (2004) argue that although there are benefits in some couples marrying, that is not true for all couples.

[416] For the case that cohabitation does not benefit the state to the same extent as marriage, see Morgan (2000). She argues that there are higher rates of domestic violence, child abuse and alcohol abuse. For a study arguing for similar findings in the United States (including an argument that married couples record higher levels of sexual satisfaction than unmarried ones) see Waite (2000).

[417] McRae (1997); Haskey (2001); Kiernan (2001).

One study found that around 27 per cent of couples that were cohabiting when their child was born have separated by the time the child is aged 5, compared with 9 per cent of couples that were married when their child was born.[418]

However, it is also clear that unmarried cohabitants tend to be economically less well off, and it may be their economic position rather than their marital status that truly affects the stability of their relationship.[419] In other words, even if the cohabiting couple had married, their relationship would not have lasted any longer.

After an extensive review of the literature Alissa Goodman and Ellen Greaves conclude:[420]

> Our findings suggest that while it is true that cohabiting parents are more likely to split up than married ones, there is very little evidence to suggest that this is due to a causal effect of marriage. Instead, it seems simply that different sorts of people choose to get married and have children, rather than to have children as a cohabiting couple, and that those relationships with the best prospects of lasting are the ones that are most likely to lead to marriage.

Similarly Miles, Pleasence and Balmer found that, once age and socio-economic factors were taken into account, 'there was little difference in breakdown rates between married and cohabiting respondents'.[421]

Goodman and Greaves make similar findings in relation to child welfare,[422] concluding that encouraging parents to marry is unlikely to lead to significant improvements in young children's outcomes. They found that there are differences in development between children born to married and cohabiting couples but this reflects differences in the sort of parents who decide to get married rather than to cohabit. For example, compared to parents who are cohabiting when their child is born, married parents are more educated, have a higher household income and a higher occupational status, and experience a higher relationship quality early in the child's life. It is these and other similar factors that seem to lead to better outcomes for their children. Having taken account of these (largely pre-existing) characteristics, the parents' marital status appears to have little or no additional impact on the child's development.

We might ask if there are any rational reasons why married relationships or civil partnerships might be stronger than unmarried ones. Four reasons will be suggested. The first is that marriage or civil partnership may indicate a deeper commitment to the relationship.[423] This may be true for many couples but is clearly not true for all. The current divorce rate demonstrates that marriage is not a guarantee of lifelong commitment. Indeed in Eekelaar and Maclean's research[424] no difference in the level of commitment to the relationship was found between married and unmarried couples. There is, however, one sense in which it might be argued that a spouse or civil partner has a greater commitment to the relationship and that is in terms of the legal responsibilities undertaken. The potential financial liability of a spouse or civil partner is certainly greater than that undertaken by a cohabitee.[425] In financial and legal terms, at least, a child is likely to be better off if his or her parents are married than if they are unmarried.[426] Anita Bernstein sees one of the strongest arguments in favour of

---

[418] Benson (2009). See also Kiernan and Mensah (2010).
[419] See Ermisch (2006) for a discussion of how being raised in a single parent household can affect a child.
[420] Goodman and Greaves (2010b).
[421] Miles, Pleasence and Balmer (2009: 54).
[422] Goodman and Greaves (2010a).
[423] Morgan (2000); Gallagher and Waite (2001).
[424] Eekelaar and Maclean (2004).
[425] Cleary (2004).
[426] Lewis (2006) rejects the arguments that attitudes of married and unmarried couples towards their relationship are identical, especially in cases of recoupling.

marriage being that 'as a form of enforced commitment, state-sponsored marriage facilitates investment – that is, the sacrifice of short-term gain for the prospect of returns in the long term'.[427] This may well be true but, as Maclean and Eekelaar[428] point out, 'marriage is neither a necessary nor sufficient condition for the acceptance of personal obligation'. They argue:

> It becomes increasingly difficult to identify being married in itself as necessarily, or even characteristically, constituting a significant source of personal obligations in the eyes of the participants in such relationships.[429]

They suggest it is the obligations negotiated by the parties which are the source of the obligation for all couples, be they married or cohabiting.

The second reason why one might believe that marriages or civil partnerships are more enduring than cohabitation is that the social pressure against ending a marriage or civil partnership may be greater than the pressure against ending an unmarried relationship. Again this may be true, depending on the attitude and culture of the parties, their families and communities.

Thirdly, the legal barriers to divorce or dissolution may slow down the marital breakdown process, which might increase the chance of reconciliation. The strength of these arguments is very much open to debate. Even if it could be shown that marriage itself makes couples more stable, it could still be argued that the state should do more to encourage and support unmarried relationships rather than privileging married relationships. Fourthly, it can be suggested that the characteristics or values of cohabiting couples differ from married ones and these make them more likely to separate.[430]

An argument that is sometimes made in this debate is that treating unmarried couples in the same way as married couples will discourage marriage or civil partnership, thereby harming society.[431] The Conservative Party's Centre for Social Justice[432] commissioned research which suggested that 58 per cent of those questioned thought giving cohabitants the same rights as married couples would undermine marriage. This argument is weak. Kiernan, Barlow and Merlo[433] have analysed marriage rates in Australia and Europe and have found 'little evidence of a relationship between the introduction of legislation giving rights to cohabiting couples with subsequent changes in the propensity to marry'.

As has already been mentioned, it is very unlikely that people decide not to marry because of the legal consequences. Simply put, few people know the law in this area.[434] Even those who do are more likely to base their decision to marry on religious and social views, or to be influenced by their families, friends and culture.

## B Choice

An alternative approach is to focus on 'choice'.[435] Deech[436] has argued that if a couple choose not to marry it is wrong for the law to treat them as if they were married as this would negate their choice and show a lack of respect for their decision. She argues:

---

[427] Bernstein (2003: 203).
[428] Maclean and Eekelaar (2005b).
[429] Eekelaar (2004: 536).
[430] See, e.g., Lye and Waldron (1997).
[431] Morgan (2000).
[432] Centre for Social Justice (2009).
[433] Kiernan, Barlow and Merlo (2007: 72).
[434] Smart and Stevens (2000).
[435] Deech (1980); Dnes (2002). See Glennon (2010) for a very helpful discussion of choice in this context.
[436] Deech (2010d). See also Garrison (2004) who takes a similar line.

My preference is for the rights of the individual, or human rights, in this instance autonomy, privacy, a sphere of thought and action that should be free from public and legal interference, namely the right to live together without having a legal structure imposed on one without consent or contract to that effect. It is better not to have legal interference in cohabitation and leave it to be dealt with by the ordinary law of the land, of agreements, wills, property and so on.[437]

There are perhaps three difficulties with this view, despite its persuasive power.[438] The first is that it is doubtful to what extent many couples *choose* not to marry, at least to what extent they choose not to take on the legal consequences of marriage.[439] In reality few couples decide positively not to get married because of the legal differences in treatment and, indeed, few marry because of the legal benefits.[440] Indeed in one survey 69 per cent of those questioned thought living together outside marriage created legal rights.[441] A major Government campaign to combat this has had limited effects. In a recent study only 38 per cent of people knew that cohabiting did not give you the same rights as being married.[442] A second problem is that some couples disagree over whether or not to marry. It may be, for example, that the woman wants to get married but the man does not. It seems a little harsh to say she has chosen not to marry. Deech, rather bluntly, replies that such a person should either leave her partner or accept the unmarried status. A third argument is that some of the legal consequences of marriage do not reflect the couple's decision but rather the justice of the situation or the protection of a state interest (for example, protecting the interests of children).[443] One might take the view that it should not be possible to choose not to have justice or not to protect a state interest. Alternatively, it could be said that although cohabiting couples might not want all of the consequences of marriage, this does not mean they do not want the law to intervene at all at the end of their relationship.[444] In spite of these responses, where both members of a couple have decided firmly to reject the legal consequences of marriage, to deny respect to that choice seems unduly interventionist.

It may be that Deech's argument is more persuasive when seen as a call for marriage to be treated in the same way as cohabitation. In other words, regardless of whether the couple are married or not, the law's response should focus on their commitment to each other, rather than having the consequences of the status of marriage 'imposed upon them'.

## C Reflecting current attitudes

Another approach is to argue that the law should reflect current attitudes. Studies suggest that many people do not regard cohabitation outside marriage as immoral and indeed there is often talk in the media of 'a common law wife', suggesting that if a couple have lived together for a certain time they are treated as married.[445] In a recent study, 51 per cent of people believed that 'common law marriage' existed.[446] A survey of media references found that media use of the terms 'common law husband' or 'common law wife' vastly outnumbered

---

[437] Deech (2010d).

[438] The argument is rejected in Law Commission Consultation Paper 179 (2006: 19).

[439] Oliver (1982).

[440] Hibbs, Barton and Beswick (2001).

[441] Hibbs, Barton and Beswick (2001: 202).

[442] National Centre for Social Research (2008).

[443] Herring (2005a).

[444] Haskey (2001: 53).

[445] See the discussion of the common law marriage myth in Barlow, Burgoyne, Clery and Smithson (2008) and Probert (2008b).

[446] National Centre for Social Research (2008).

articles emphasising that the concept does not exist.[447] This meaning of 'common law marriage' is not legally recognised. Unmarried couples are often under the misapprehension that once they have cohabited for a while they will be treated as if they are married.[448] It may be argued that the law should reflect this popular (mis)understanding. Of those interviewed in a recent survey, 61.4 per cent suggested that cohabitants who had lived together for ten years should have the same maintenance rights as married couples, and 92.1 per cent thought they should have the same inheritance rights.[449] However, another study[450] found a significant difference in the attitudes towards financial matters of those married couples divorcing and cohabiting couples who were separating. Divorcing couples talked about ensuring there were fair financial arrangements for the children and then dividing what was left, while separating cohabitants talked about each partner taking back what they had brought into the relationship. Interestingly, the role of children appeared to play a much smaller part in the discussions of cohabitants.

Although it appears now to be generally accepted that it is 'all right' for a couple to live together without intending marriage, this does not mean that marriage has lost its meaning.[451] In one study of people in their twenties 75 per cent disagreed with the statement that there was no point getting married anymore.[452] Further, a majority of people still see marriage as the ideal basis for child raising;[453] although it should be noted that cultural and religious factors can greatly influence attitudes towards marriage. Despite these positive attitudes to marriage the majority of the public appears to support giving couples who have cohabited for a considerable period of time the same rights as spouses or civil partners.[454] Another survey found a strongly and widely held view that children of unmarried parents should not be treated any differently from those of married ones.[455]

## D Discrimination

It might be argued that to treat married and unmarried people's family rights and responsibilities differently amounts to discrimination of their rights under article 8 of the European Convention on Human Rights in a way prohibited by article 14. The European Court has not yet specifically stated that discrimination on the grounds of marital status is covered by article 14, but it has been implied in several cases. In *Re P*[456] the House of Lords held that for the purposes of the Human Rights Act 1998 treating cohabitants differently from married couples did amount to discrimination, although that could be justified in some cases. In *Gomez v Spain*[457] a woman who separated from her cohabitant of 18 years complained that her inability to make the financial claims that a wife could make against her husband on divorce infringed her convention rights. The Commission held that any difference in treatment was justifiable by the need to protect the traditional family. She had chosen not to take up the

---

[447] Probert (2007b).
[448] Pickford (1999). In their survey Barlow and James (2004: 161) found that 56% of respondents believed that people who had cohabited for a period of time were 'common law spouses'. Among cohabitants the figure was 59%.
[449] Barlow et al. (2001; 2003).
[450] Maclean et al. (2002).
[451] In Barlow et al. (2005: 124) 84% of those aged 18 to 24 agreed with that statement.
[452] Wicks and Asato (2002). In MORI (1999) 77% disagreed with the statement that marriage is dead.
[453] Barlow et al. (2005: 21).
[454] Barlow et al. (2005: 51).
[455] Barlow, Burgoyne, Clery and Smithson (2008).
[456] [2008] UKHL 38, discussed Herring (2009a).
[457] Application 37784/97 (19 January 1998).

advantages of marriage and therefore the discrimination was proportionate. The implication of this might be that some differences in treatment between married and unmarried couples will be unlawful discrimination under the ECHR and others will not. It may be, for example, that parental rights should not differ as between married and unmarried parents, but the rights they have between themselves can.[458]

## E  Should marriage be discouraged?

There are, of course, arguments that the state should not encourage marriage.[459] Some feel that marriage is an institution which has helped perpetuate disadvantage against women.[460] Katherine O'Donovan has sought 'to break free from marriage as a timeless unwritten institution whose terms are unequal and unjust'.[461] The argument is that marriage ensures the maintenance of patriarchal power, through the power given to husbands as 'head of the household'.[462] Martha Fineman[463] has argued 'Marriage allows us to ignore dependency in our policy and politics' and that means care-givers (normally women) bear the burden of caring with no social reward. Other criticisms have been similar to those launched against the family, namely that marriage can be self-centred, with the couple focusing on preparing their home rather than working in the community around them. From an opposite perspective, marriage can be seen as anti-individualist. O'Donovan summarises Weitzman's view of marriage:

> this unwritten contract, to be found in legislation and case-law, is tyrannical. It is an unconstitutional invasion of marital privacy, it is sexist in that it imposes different rights and obligations on the husband and wife, and it flies in the face of pluralism by denying heterogeneity and diversity and imposing a single model of marriage on everyone.[464]

Other commentators detect a modern understanding of marriage among younger people which is based on a partnership of equals, sharing the burdens of homemaking, child-caring and wealth creation,[465] although the extent to which such marriages occur in reality, rather than as an aspiration, is a matter of debate.

## F  Protection

Baroness Hale, writing extra-judicially, has argued that the law needs to protect cohabitants from inequality. She writes:

> Intimate domestic relationships frequently bring with them inequalities, especially if there are children. They compromise the parties' respective economic positions, often irreparably. This inequality is sometimes compounded by domestic ill-treatment. These detriments cannot be predicted in advance, so there should be remedies that cater for the needs of the situation when it arises. They arise from the very nature of intimate relationships, so it is the relationship rather than the status that should matter.[466]

---

[458] Although see *B v UK* [2000] 1 FCR 289 where the ECHR upheld differences in relation to parental responsibility between married and unmarried fathers.

[459] See Chapter 1.

[460] For an economic analysis supporting this conclusion see Slaughter (2002).

[461] O'Donovan (1993).

[462] Smart (1984).

[463] Fineman (2006: 63).

[464] O'Donovan (1984: 114).

[465] Schwartz (2000) describes such marriages as 'peer' marriages.

[466] Hale (2004a).

Notably this argument does not necessarily require that cohabitation be treated identically to marriage, but it does call for protection from inequality that flows from cohabitation – particularly the unfairness that women face as a result of undertaking the child-caring role in the relationship.

## 12 The Law Commission's proposed reforms

The Law Commission's Consultation Report 2007, *Cohabitation: The Financial Consequences of Relationship Breakdown*, proposes reform to the law. This is discussed in Chapter 4. Their proposal will give cohabitants some financial remedies on separation, but these will be less extensive than available to married couples.[467] The Government announced in 2008 that it will delay responding to the Law Commission proposals until it has seen the impact of similar proposals which have been enacted in Scotland. The Government has particular concerns over the costs to the state of enacting such a scheme.

## 13 What if the state were to abolish legal marriage?

One point of view is that marriage should cease to have any legal significance, although holders of this view would be happy for marriage to continue to have religious and social significance.[468] This would mean that any legal regulation of relationships would not depend on whether couples are married or not, but rather on different criteria: for example, whether a couple have children, or the length of time a cohabitation has existed.[469] So, for example, if the Government wishes to give benefits to stable couples who care for children, these could be directed towards couples with children who have stayed together for five years, rather than giving the benefit to all married couples, which would be over-inclusive.[470] Glendon foresaw the withering away of marriage. She argued that the law was moving to 'break the family down into its component parts and treat family members as separate and independent'.[471]

---

**DEBATE**

### After marriage?

If the law does not rely on marriage, how might the law distinguish two strangers from two people in a close relationship, assuming it wishes to?[472] The following are some possibilities:

1. The law could rely on cohabitation. This proposal could be that if a couple have cohabited for two years and/or have a child then they are given the rights married couples and civil partners currently have.[473] In effect this would create a system where you must 'opt out'

---

[467] Hale (2009b).
[468] See Bernstein (2006) for a useful set of essays discussing this. For support for this from a religious perspective see Barrow and Bartley (2006).
[469] Clive (1994). But see Bridge (2001: 9) who questions whether such an approach is compatible with article 12 of the European Convention on Human Rights.
[470] Such a proposal is developed in Law Commission of Canada (2002).
[471] Glendon (1989: 296).
[472] For a discussion of whether family law could be reduced to a network of personal rights and obligations, without obligations emanating from 'the family', see Eekelaar (2000a).
[473] See Baker (2009b) for a discussion of Australian law which has taken an approach similar to this.

of marriage if you are cohabiting. Most proponents of such a scheme would accept that people could marry in the 'normal' way too. The difficulty is in defining cohabitation. Does it require staying overnight: how many nights a week are necessary?[474] Proof of cohabitation (or non-cohabitation) may also prove difficult. Fineman would seek to regulate relationships of dependency and care, rather than cohabitation.[475] There would be problems in defining this too.

2. An alternative approach is to focus on the kind of relationship. Has the relationship reached a depth where it deserves a particular benefit? Simon Gardner, in the context of property rights, has suggested considering whether the relationship displays 'communality'. The difficulty with this approach is that it is very difficult for a third party (e.g. a judge) to understand the nature of a particular relationship. Some people, for example, would attach great significance to a sexual relationship; others would pay little attention to this.

3. Another approach is to focus on the agreement between the parties.[476] This could require or encourage the parties to prepare and sign a legal agreement.[477] This is only satisfactory where the parties are aware of the benefits of doing so. It is notoriously difficult to persuade people to make wills. It is doubtful we will be more successful in persuading people to make cohabitation contracts. We will return to this issue in Chapter 5.

4. It would be possible for the state to create an alternative to marriage, for example registered partnerships.[478] However, it is unlikely that people who do not wish to marry would choose to register their partnerships. Partnerships would, however, be useful for those who are legally barred from marriage.

5. To some commentators the significance attached to parenthood reflects the decreasing importance of marriage. Dewar[479] suggests 'that family law is increasingly emphasising the maintenance of economic and legal ties between parents and children after separation, as if to create the illusion of permanence in the face of instability. Since, by definition, neither marriage nor cohabitation are available for the purpose, these continuing links are founded on parenthood.'

## Questions

1. If two friends came to see you asking your advice as a lawyer as to whether they should enter a civil partnership or whether they should cohabit, what would you recommend and why?

2. Would it really make any difference to the law if it was decided that marriage was of no legal significance?

## Further reading

Read **Deech** (2010d) for a passionate argument against treating unmarried couples in the same way as married ones. Read **Auchmuty** (2008) for an argument that marriage is outdated and is on its way out.

---

[474] Cf. *Santos v Santos* [1972] Fam 247.
[475] Fineman (2004: 99).
[476] For a useful discussion see Lewis (2001b).
[477] Todd (2006).
[478] Anderson (1997); Bradley (2001). See Francoz-Terminal (2009) for a discussion of the French approach.
[479] Dewar (2000a: 63).

## 14 Conclusion

This chapter has considered the nature of marriage, civil partnership and cohabitation. Increasing numbers of people are deciding to live together outside marriage and, in response, the legal distinctions between married and unmarried couples are lessening. Most significantly, the tax advantages awarded to married couples and civil partners have been replaced by a tax credit to those caring for children (whether married or not). This reflects a suggestion that it is parenthood rather than marriage or civil partnership that is at the heart of family law. This is not to say there are no legal differences between married and unmarried couples, but those differences that remain are controversial and many argue that the distinctions should be removed. As the legal consequences of marriage lessen, it is harder to justify the restrictions on who can marry whom. Further, if marriage or civil partnership is not to be the touchstone for deciding who are a legally recognised couple, what should replace it? There are great difficulties in finding an alternative: cohabitation or the intentions of the parties, for example, are not susceptible to ready proof, particularly when compared to examining the marriage register to see if a couple are married. The truth is that the term 'cohabitants' can cover a vast range of different kinds of relationship. The bureaucratic difficulties caused by defining cohabitation[480] might ultimately lead to the law deciding that intimate relationships between adults give rise to no legal obligations whatsoever and that obligations should flow instead from parenthood.[481]

## Further reading

**Auchmuty, R.** (2008) 'What's so special about marriage? The impact of *Wilkinson* v *Kitzinger*' *Child and Family Law Quarterly* 20: 475.

**Bamforth, N.** (2007) '"The benefits of marriage in all but name?" Same-sex couples and the Civil Partnership Act 2004', *Child and Family Law Quarterly* 19: 133.

**Barker, K.** (2006) 'Sex and the Civil Partnership Act: the future of (non) conjugality?', *Feminist Legal Studies* 14: 214.

**Barlow, A., Duncan, S., James, G. and Park, A.** (2005) *Cohabitation, Marriage and the Law*, Oxford: Hart.

**Bernstein, A.** (ed.) (2006) *Marriage Proposals: Questioning A Legal Status*, New York: New York University Press.

**Chau, P.-L. and Herring, J.** (2004) 'Men, Women and People: The Definition of Sex', in B. Brooks-Gordon, L. Goldsthorpe, M. Johnson and A. Bainham (eds) *Sexuality Repositioned*, Oxford: Hart.

**Cretney, S.** (2006a) *Same-sex relationships*, Oxford: OUP.

**Deech, R.** (2010d) 'Cohabitation', *Family Law* 40: 39.

---

[480] See Garrison (2007) who regards this as one of the great benefits of marriage. *Kotke* v *Saffarini* [2005] EWCA Civ 221 shows the difficulties the courts can face in defining cohabitation.

[481] See Bernstein (2006) for a useful collection of essays on the legal regulation of family life without reference to marriage.

**Eekelaar, J.** (2007) 'Why people marry: The many faces of an institution', *Family Law Quarterly* 41: 413.

**Eekelaar, J. and Maclean, M.** (2004) 'Marriage and the moral bases of personal relationships', *Journal of Law and Society* 4: 510.

**Gill, A. and Anitha, S.** (2009) 'The illusion of protection? An analysis of forced marriage legislation and policy in the UK', *Journal of Social Welfare and Family Law* 31: 257.

**Glennon, L.** (2006) 'Strategizing for the future through the Civil Partnership Act', *Journal of Law and Society* 33: 244.

**Harding, R.** (2007) 'Sir Mark Potter and the protection of the traditional family: why same sex marriage is (still) a feminist issue', *Feminist Legal Studies* 15: 223.

**Law Commission Consultation Paper 179** (2006) *Cohabitation: The Financial Consequences of Relationship Breakdown*, London: TSO.

**Lewis, J.** (2001b) *The End of Marriage?* Cheltenham: Edward Elgar.

**Lyndon Shanley, M.** (2004) *Just Marriage*, Oxford: OUP.

**Probert, R.** (2002b) 'When are we married? Void, non-existent and presumed marriages', *Legal Studies* 22: 398.

**Regan, M.** (1999) *Alone Together: Law and the Meaning of Marriage*, New York: OUP.

**Sharpe, A.** (2007) 'Endless sex: the Gender Recognition Act 2004 and the persistence of a legal category', *Feminist Legal Studies* 15: 57.

**Stychin, C.** (2007) 'Family friendly? Rights, responsibilities and relationship recognition', in A. Diduck and K. O'Donovan (eds) *Feminist Perspectives on Family Law*, London: Routledge.

## 3 Divorce and mediation

## 1 Statistics on divorce

### KEY STATISTICS

- Between 1961 and 1991 there was a fivefold rise in the divorce rate. But currently we are seeing a rapidly declining number of divorces.

- In 2007 there was a drop to 121,799 divorces; this was a notable drop from the figure of 153,282 in 2004.[1] It is lower than the number of divorces in 1976. It has been estimated that 45% of marriages end in divorce.[2]

- The divorce rate (the number of divorces per 1,000 marriages per year) has risen from 4.7 in 1970 to 13.7 in 1999, and since then has steadied, with the rate at 14.0 in 2005. In 2007 the divorce rate in England and Wales fell to 11.2 divorcing people per 1,000 married population.[3]

- In 2007 the median duration of a marriage was 11.5 years. This is an increase from 1993–6 when it hovered between 9.8 and 9.9 years.[4]

- There were 106,763 children aged under 16 who were in families where the parents divorced in 2008. Twenty-one per cent of these children were under five and 63% were under eleven.[5]

- 67% of divorces are granted to wives.[6]

- There were 180 civil partnership dissolutions granted in the UK in 2008.[7]

These statistics are alarming to many. The high divorce rates suggest significant levels of personal unhappiness for the adults and children involved. True, the divorce rate is falling dramatically, but that is principally because fewer people are marrying. That said, the seeming picture of gloom painted by these figures could be misleading. Between 1978 and

[1] National Statistics (2010d).
[2] Haskey (2008).
[3] National Statistics (2010d).
[4] National Statistics (2010d).
[5] National Statistics (2010d).
[6] National Statistics (2010d).
[7] National Statistics (2010c).

1988 the total number of divorces rose by 6 per cent but the number of *first* marriages ending in divorce fell by 6 per cent.[8] Indeed, 20 per cent of those divorcing in 2008 had been divorced previously.[9] What this reveals is that the divorce rate figures are somewhat skewed by the number of people marrying, divorcing, remarrying and divorcing again. Further, it is clear that the divorce rate for marriages which have lasted at least eight years is the same today as it was in 1970. In other words, well-established marriages are as stable now as they were 30 years ago. As Eekelaar and Maclean explain, 'the increase in the divorce rate for people marrying in the 1970s is almost entirely an increase during the first four to eight years of marriage';[10] although the fact that the median duration of marriages at the time of divorce has increased from 10.1 years in 1981 to 11.5 years in 2004 may suggest that even well-established marriages are more at risk.[11]

The projected rate of divorce stands at 45 per cent.[12] This means that of every 100 people who marry, 45 will divorce. Almost half of divorces will occur before the tenth wedding anniversary. However, it is crucial to appreciate that this is the average rate. A couple who are both marrying for the first time in their mid-twenties and who have not cohabited before marriage, will have a much lower projected rate of divorce. Even with the 45 per cent figure, this still means that the clear majority of marriages last for life. In the current climate it is easier to forget that if you marry it is more likely that you will be with your partner for life than you will divorce.

## 2 Causes of divorce

Here we will consider the factors that are statistically linked to divorce. It must be stressed that these are only statistical links, so it does not mean that because one of these factors is present the couple will divorce; it is simply more likely that they might.

1. *Age.* There is a close link between divorce and being married at a young age. An 18-year-old bride has twice the risk of marital breakdown as that of a 21-year-old. This is particularly so where the marriage follows a pregnancy.[13]

2. *Previously married.*[14] A second marriage is much more prone to divorce than a first marriage.[15] However, this does depend on the cause of the end of the first marriage. A woman who remarries after divorcing her first husband is six times more likely to be divorced a second time than a woman who remarries after the death of her first husband. Some argue that the existence of stepchildren puts particular strains on second marriages.[16]

3. *Education.* There is a link between low-level educational achievement and the divorce rate, although most of the evidence to support this is based on studies in the USA. It may be that poor education is reflected in poor communication skills, which could be directly linked to divorce.

---

[8] Eekelaar (1991a: 55).
[9] National Statistics (2010d).
[10] Eekelaar and Maclean (1997: 22).
[11] Eekelaar (2006b: 24).
[12] Wilson and Smallwood (2008: 29).
[13] E.g. Bracher, Morgan and Trussell (1993).
[14] E.g. Haskey (1983).
[15] Gibson (1994: 163).
[16] Kiernan and Wicks (1990).

4. *Children*. There is some evidence that having children can produce a strain on the marriage.[17] The huge life changes children can bring, not to mention the exhaustion, inevitably produce tensions.

5. *Poverty*. There is a strong link between divorce and poverty, unemployment and receipt of benefits.[18] A man who becomes unemployed is nearly two and a half times more likely to separate within the year following the loss of the job than an employed man.[19] There is also some evidence that where the husband earns less than the wife this can increase the likelihood of divorce significantly;[20] although recent decreases in house prices have been said to lead to a reduction in the number of relationship breakdowns.[21]

6. *Cohabitation prior to marriage*. If a couple cohabit prior to marriage there is clear evidence that they are more likely to divorce than a couple who do not cohabit prior to marriage.[22] For example, between 1980 and 1984 a couple who cohabited prior to marriage were 50 per cent more likely to divorce within the first 5 years than a couple who had not cohabited.[23] Even 15 years from the start of the relationship the fact that a couple cohabited before marriage affects the likelihood of their divorce by a 20 per cent increase.[24] To many these are surprising statistics. Two explanations are offered. First, if a couple cohabit and then choose to marry, it must be asked why they have decided to marry. It may be that the cohabiting couple decide to marry in order to feel more secure within their relationship, whereas the feeling of a lack of security may, in fact, indicate a weakness in the relationship. This explanation could be supported by reference to the fact that the longer the cohabitation before marriage the greater the risk of divorce. The second explanation of why cohabitation affects the divorce rate is that those who choose not to cohabit prior to marriage may do so because of religious beliefs and those same religious beliefs may disincline a couple to divorce.[25]

7. *Experiencing divorce in childhood*. Those whose parents divorce during their childhood are more likely to experience divorce in their own marriages.[26]

8. *Higher expectations*. It may be that higher expectations of marriage cause divorce. Of those born in 1970 one in four women and one in five men say they are unhappy with their partner. In 1958 the figure was one in thirty.[27]

## 3 Social explanations for increasing divorce

Although the factors above are statistically linked to divorce, they do not necessarily provide an explanation for why the divorce rate has risen. The following have been proposed as some of the reasons why the divorce rate has increased:

---

[17] Twenge, Campbell and Foster (2003).
[18] Kiernan and Mueller (1999).
[19] Haskey (1984).
[20] Cronin and Curry (2000).
[21] Rainer and Smith (2008).
[22] E.g. Haskey (1992); Kamp Dush, Cohan and Amato (2003). Although see Kiernan (1999) for a contrary finding looking at statistics across Europe.
[23] Kiernan and Mueller (1999).
[24] Kiernan and Mueller (1999).
[25] Kiernan and Wicks (1990) suggest that seven out of ten couples cohabit prior to marriage.
[26] E.g. McLanahan and Bumpass (1988).
[27] Iacovou (2004).

1. One explanation for the increased divorce rate is that society's attitude towards marriage has changed. Some have argued that a higher degree of satisfaction is now expected from marriage.[28] Anthony Giddens has maintained that in modern times people stay in intimate relationships only for as long as the relationships meet their own goals of personal autonomy and fulfilment.[29] Shelley Day Sclater summarises his view: 'we no longer look for Mr or Mrs Right, but rather we search for the perfect relationship; when one fails to satisfy, the individual in late modernity increasingly feels free to move on to try another'.[30] This increased individualism and the increased expectations of marriage may therefore help explain the increase in divorce rates. Notably, the majority of divorce petitions are presented by women. It may be that women are increasingly less willing to accept a traditional subservient role in marriage; although it should be noted that a recent study of those who had divorced did not record that life after divorce was any happier, just different.[31]

2. Another explanation is that increased life expectancy affects the divorce rate.[32] The potential length of marriages increased by 15 years during the course of the twentieth century.[33] In other words, the average length of a marriage is now similar to that in the Victorian era; marriages now end in divorce at a time when they used to be ended by death.

3. Hochschild[34] has suggested that increased work pressures mean that there is less time to spend on family activities and this causes marital breakdown. Further, combining the career aspirations of both the husband and the wife with child care can cause great tensions within a marriage.

4. One factor that affects the divorce rate is that now divorce is economically a possibility for women. Improvements in benefits for lone parents and increased employment opportunities for women mean that a wife can leave her husband without falling into utter poverty. In the first half of the twentieth century the wife was dependent on her husband to support her; few women would have been economically able to leave their husbands. In 2008, 67 per cent of those petitioning for divorce were women.[35]

## 4 What should be the aims of divorce law?

There has been much debate over what the role of the law is on divorce or dissolution. Some possibilities will now be considered. The first six are set out as the guiding principles for the divorce law in s 1 of the Family Law Act 1996. Notably, when the Lord Chancellor announced that the proposals in the Act would not be implemented, he confirmed the Government's support for the principles declared in s 1.[36]

1. Divorce law should seek to support the institution of marriage.[37] Divorce is not only a tragedy for the couple; it also involves expense to the state. It has been suggested that the

---

[28] Gibson (1994: 214).
[29] Giddens (1992).
[30] Day Sclater (2000: 68).
[31] Newcastle Centre for Family Studies (2004).
[32] Gibson (1994: 127).
[33] Eekelaar and Maclean (1997: 17).
[34] Hochschild (1996).
[35] National Statistics (2010a).
[36] Lord Chancellor's Department (2001).
[37] Family Law Act 1996 (hereafter FLA 1996), s 1(1)(a).

cost of family breakdown on the state is £37 billion.[38] Divorce may also be said to shake social stability by challenging the image of the family as comforting, secure and enduring.[39] However, these arguments assume that there is a link between divorce law and the rate of divorce. Ruth Deech argues:

> every successive attempt during this century to bring statute law into line with 'reality' has resulted in an increase in the divorce rate. The increased divorce rate results in greater familiarity with divorce as a solution to marital problems, more willingness to use it and to make legislative provision for its aftermath. The resultant pressure on the divorce system leads to a relaxation of practice and procedure . . . , then to a call for a change in the law in order to bring it into line with 'reality', and then to yet another increase in divorce.[40]

In this way, she argues, the changes in divorce law have led to an increase in the divorce rate. Indeed the statistics appear to support Deech's argument, although some commentators see the legislation as a response to the divorce statistics, rather than a cause of them.[41] What is far from clear is *how* changes in the divorce law could cause marital breakdown.[42] Clearly the rate of divorce and law on divorce are linked. We could have no legal divorce at all, and so a divorce rate of nil. That would not mean, of course, that all the couples who would have divorced would still be living together. No doubt, they would simply separate. We would therefore have a large number of 'empty shell' marriages. So, the real question is whether the divorce law affects the marital *breakdown* rate. If the divorce procedure is perceived to be difficult, spouses may be reluctant to seek the advice of a solicitor until they think that they would be entitled to a divorce. Delaying the visit to the solicitor and the institution of legal proceedings may possibly help reduce breakdown rates. So it is possible that the *perception* of the divorce law might affect the breakdown rate. However, it should be stressed that there is a whole range of factors that might affect marital breakdown.

If the law did wish to discourage divorce, it might do so more effectively by making marriage – rather than divorce – harder.[43] Increasing the age at which one could marry might well reduce the divorce rate, as might requiring the parties to have a year of reflection and consideration before being permitted to marry. However, both of these proposals might lead to a reduction of the marriage rate,[44] as well as the divorce rate. Certainly the Government has accepted that much more than manipulation of the divorce law is required if marriages are to be supported by the state.[45]

2. Divorce law should seek to save marriages if possible.[46] The argument here is that if a couple seeks a divorce the legal procedure should do all it can to persuade them to be reconciled and to turn back from divorce.[47] However, opponents of this aim argue that people do not normally turn to lawyers when their marriage first hits the rocks, but only

---

[38] Centre for Social Justice (2009).
[39] Day Sclater (1999: 4).
[40] Deech (1994: 121). Deech (1990), Eekelaar and Maclean (1990), Brinig (2000) and Ellman (2000a) discuss whether the law on divorce can affect the rates of breakdown.
[41] Davis and Murch (1988: 22–3). Mansfield, Reynolds and Arai (1999) claim that changes in the law have only a slight impact on divorce rates.
[42] Richards (1996b).
[43] Scott (1990).
[44] Which may or may not be objectionable.
[45] Home Office (1998).
[46] FLA 1996, s 1(1)(b).
[47] For a discussion of how the FLA 1996 sought to encourage reconciliation, see McCarthy, Walker and Hooper (2000).

when it is irreparable,[48] and often at the time when one or both of the parties wishes to remarry. It is also argued that some marriages should not be saved: for example, where there has been serious domestic violence, or where the unhappy marriage is harming the children.[49]

3. If there is to be a divorce, the law should not exacerbate the bitterness between the parties.[50] Sir Paul McCartney described his divorce from Heather Mills as 'going through hell'[51] and many who have experienced divorce will empathise with that. The aim of reducing bitterness, one might think, is uncontroversial; however, opponents point out that increased bitterness is an inevitable aspect of divorce. To expect a legal system to enable the parties to separate happily and then have a good post-divorce relationship is pure idealism. This is why the stated purpose is that the law should *not exacerbate* the bitterness, rather than *remove* it.

4. The divorce law should seek to promote a continuing relationship between the spouses as far as possible, particularly where there are children.[52] This is clearly desirable. As Beck and Beck-Gernsheim explain:

> Only someone equating marriage with sex, loving and living together can make the mistake that divorce means the end of marriage. If one concentrates on problems of material support, on the children and on a long common biography, divorce is quite obviously not even the legal end of marriage but transforms itself into a new phase of post-marital 'separation marriage'.[53]

Whether the divorce process is the correct mechanism for helping the parties to communicate after divorce, or is used at the best time, may be open to debate, but if the law can do anything to improve the parties' relationship after divorce, clearly it should.

5. The divorce process should not involve unnecessary expenditure for the state or the parties.[54] This is relatively uncontroversial. The difficulty is over the meaning of the word 'unnecessary'. In the bitterness of the moment, the parties might wish their lawyers to dispute every fact claimed by the other party or to hide as many assets as possible from the other party. Lawyers are certainly expensive, but that is in part, and only in part, because the parties misuse their lawyers' time to negotiate about matters which are, from one perspective, not worth the money involved. That said, it is much easier for an outsider to state what is and is not worth litigating, than it is for the divorcing couples themselves.

6. The divorce law should ensure that any risk to one of the parties, and to any children, of violence from the other party during the breakdown of the relationship, so far as is reasonably practicable, be removed or diminished. This is certainly a laudable aim of the divorce law. It may, however, conflict with the above aims. For example, the 'harder' divorce is, in the name of reinforcing the institution of marriage, the more likely it is that the abused party may have to put up with higher levels of abuse.

7. Some argue that the law should permit divorce in order to enable remarriage because otherwise there will be increased unmarried cohabitation after the breakdown of the

---

[48] Hasson (2004); Walker (2000a).
[49] Richards and Dyson (1982). Walker and McCarthy (2004) interviewed couples two years after they had considered, but decided against, divorce: they found some 'appalling' marriages.
[50] FLA 1996, s 1(1)(c)(i).
[51] BBC Newsonline (2007c).
[52] FLA 1996, s 1(1)(c)(ii).
[53] Beck and Beck-Gernsheim (1995: 147).
[54] FLA 1996, s 1(1)(c)(iii).

spouses' relationship. One of the major aims of the Divorce Reform Act 1969 was to reduce the number of children born to unmarried parents by enabling people to remarry after divorce. In fact the number of such children increased.

8. The law should seek to deal with the emotional turmoil of the parties.[55] Whether the emotional side of divorce should be dealt with through the legal process itself or by co-ordinating counselling and legal services is open to debate. There is particular concern with the lack of support children receive when their parents separate. One recent study found that one-quarter of children said that no one had talked to them about their parents' separation. Only 5 per cent felt they had been given a full explanation and the opportunity to ask questions.[56]

## 5 The present law on divorce: Matrimonial Causes Act 1973

### A The background to the Matrimonial Causes Act 1973

Prior to 1857 the ecclesiastical (church) courts determined the law on divorce.[57] This meant that although nullity decrees could be made, divorce was not available through the courts. The only form of divorce was by an Act of Parliament, a hugely expensive procedure that was open only to a few people. The Matrimonial Causes Act 1857 was the first Act to create an alternative to divorce by Act of Parliament. It created a divorce procedure through the courts. However, there was a difference between the grounds available to a husband and those open to a wife. For example, a husband could rely on his wife's adultery, but a wife could rely on a husband's adultery only if there were aggravating circumstances (e.g. the adultery was incestuous or there was some 'unnatural offence'). The Matrimonial Causes Act 1923 put the husband and wife in the same position – simple adultery was a ground of divorce for both. The grounds were extended further in the Matrimonial Causes Act 1937 to include cruelty, desertion, or incurable insanity. The last ground was of particular significance because for the first time it recognised that a party could be divorced even though they had not behaved in a blameworthy way.

The Second World War led to an increase in the number of divorces. During the 1960s there was an increasing acceptance of divorce, even by religious bodies. There were growing calls for divorce to be available simply on the ground that the marriage had irretrievably broken down. The arguments in favour of making divorce easier particularly focused on couples whose marriages had failed and who were forced to form relationships out of marriage with new partners because they were unable to prove the grounds of divorce. There were particular concerns over the number of children being born to unmarried parents. It was argued that liberalising the divorce law would lead to a reduction in the number of children born outside marriage.[58] Rather surprisingly, in 1966 a group created by the Archbishop of Canterbury produced one of the leading documents (*Putting Asunder*) in favour of liberalising the law. The fact that the Church of England had come to accept the need for a liberalisation of the divorce law indicated that society's attitude towards divorce had truly changed. The

---

[55] Brown and Day Sclater (1999).
[56] Dunn and Deater-Deckard (2001).
[57] For a discussion of the history of divorce law see Smart (2000a); Cretney (2003a).
[58] In fact the number of children born to unmarried parents did not fall following the relaxing of the divorce laws.

report was referred to the Law Commission, who produced their own report: *Reform of the Grounds of Divorce: The Field of Choice*.[59] The Archbishop's group had suggested that the judge should consider each and every case to decide whether the marriage had irretrievably broken down. But the Law Commission thought the ideal was not practical, and instead proposed creating a new ground of divorce based on a period of separation.

The Government decided not to adopt all of the Law Commission's proposals, and the Divorce Reform Act 1969 sought to create a compromise between the different views. The decision was to abolish the old grounds for divorce and replace them with a single ground for divorce – that the marriage had irretrievably broken down. However, the only way of proving irretrievable breakdown was by establishing one of five facts. The divorce law was consolidated in the Matrimonial Causes Act 1973. Before turning to the present law, it is important to appreciate that the Family Law Act 1996 has since been passed, which sets out a complete reform of the law. However, the Lord Chancellor has announced that the Act will not be implemented.[60] This means that the present law is in a strange hiatus: the Matrimonial Causes Act 1973 is the present law but Parliament has indicated that it believes the Act needs to be reformed.[61] This chapter will therefore consider the current law in the Matrimonial Causes Act 1973; the rejected proposals of the Family Law Act 1996; and how the law might be reformed in the future.[62]

## B The current law: the Matrimonial Causes Act 1973

To understand how the Matrimonial Causes Act 1973 works in practice it is crucial to appreciate the court procedures that are in place to deal with petitions for divorce.

### (i) The special procedure

Prior to 1973 each divorce required a hearing where the petitioner in open court would have to present evidence to support the grounds set out in the petition, by introducing witnesses if necessary. This was expensive, embarrassing and stressful for the parties and it involved the judiciary in lengthy hearings. A special procedure was introduced that, by 1977, covered all grounds for divorce where the petition was undefended.[63] Under the special procedure the petitioner simply needs to lodge at the court the petition outlining the grounds for the divorce; a statement concerning the arrangements for the children; and an affidavit confirming the truth of these documents.[64] If the petition is undefended the case is entered onto the special procedure list and the district judge just has to read through the documents and, if satisfied that the petitioner has proved his or her case, pronounces a decree nisi. This is done in an open court, although usually the parties are not present and the judge simply announces that a decree nisi is granted in cases numbered one to twenty (for example).[65] So although there is some scrutiny to ensure that the formal paperwork is present, there is no attempt to ensure that what is stated on the petition is true. Indeed the petition may be entirely false; there is no need to prove the veracity of what is stated, unless the respondent defends the divorce.

---

[59] Law Commission Report 6 (1966).
[60] Dyer (2000).
[61] Lord Chancellor's Department (2001).
[62] According to Thorpe LJ (2000), there is a widespread feeling amongst family lawyers that there is a need for some reform.
[63] The procedural change was reinforced by the withdrawal of legal aid for divorce.
[64] It is also necessary to provide other documents in some cases.
[65] See *Practice Direction: Requests to Inspect Files Following Pronouncements of Decrees Nisi* [2009] 2 FLR 1079 for protection of the parties' privacy.

The law works on the assumption that if the respondent does not attempt to defend the petition then it can be assumed to be true. This assumption is in fact unreliable. If a respondent receives a petition based on falsehoods, he or she must decide whether or not to defend the petition. The expense involved in defending the petition (there is no community legal services funding available) and the reluctance of lawyers to become involved in defended divorces[66] means that very few petitions are defended. Even where divorces are defended, the vast majority of defences are unsuccessful.[67] The procedure can be said to increase bitterness between the parties, by denying the respondents opportunity to defend themselves from the allegations in the petition.[68] There would therefore be more than an element of truth in saying that the present law of divorce in England and Wales is *in effect* divorce on demand.[69]

---

### CASE: *B v B (Divorce: Dismissal: Sham Marriages)* [2003] Fam Law 372

In *B v B (Divorce: Dismissal: Sham Marriages)*[70] a judge refused to grant five undefended petitions of divorce, having received evidence from the Queen's Proctor that the marriages had been entered into purely for immigration purposes and that the divorces were being sought shortly after indefinite leave to remain in the country had been granted. To grant the divorces in such a case, it was held, would be an abuse of the divorce system, although it must be said that there is something a little strange in punishing such abusers of the system by requiring them to remain married.

---

The divorce decree is completed in two stages. First the decree nisi is pronounced and later the decree absolute is declared. The divorce does not take effect until the decree absolute. Any time after six weeks from the decree nisi the petitioner can apply for a decree absolute; if the petitioner fails to apply then the respondent can apply for the decree to be made absolute any time after three months from the decree nisi.[71] The purpose of the gap in time between the decree nisi and decree absolute is to give time for any appeal against the decree nisi to be lodged.

About three-quarters of petitions are based on either adultery or unreasonable behaviour as these grounds do not involve delay. In 1994 the median length of time the divorce procedure took when the petition was based on one of the fault facts was 6.8 months for petitioning wives and 6.3 months for petitioning husbands.[72]

### (ii) The ground for divorce

Divorce under the Matrimonial Causes Act 1973 is granted on the basis of a petition where one party (the petitioner) presents an application for divorce which the other party (the respondent) may choose either to defend or not. It is not possible to petition for divorce until the couple have been married for one year. The sole ground for divorce is set out in s 1(1) of

---

[66] They are widely regarded by lawyers as a waste of time. If one party is determined to obtain a divorce, is there any practical benefit in preventing them?

[67] In only 4 in 1,000 divorces did the judge reject the petition in 1988: Law Commission Report 170 (1988).

[68] Cretney (2003a: 383).

[69] This has even been acknowledged by Munby J, albeit extra-judicially: Munby J (2005: 503).

[70] [2003] Fam Law 372.

[71] Although if the respondent applies the court has a discretion to refuse to make the decree absolute if there are financial matters unresolved (Matrimonial Causes Act 1973 (hereafter MCA 1973), s 9(2)). See, e.g., *Manchanda v Manchanda* [1995] 2 FLR 590.

[72] Haskey (1996a).

the Matrimonial Causes Act 1973: that the marriage has irretrievably broken down. But the only way of proving irretrievable breakdown is by proving one of the five facts in s 1(2). If none of the five facts is proved then a divorce cannot be granted, even if the court is convinced that the marriage has irretrievably broken down.[73] Even if one of the facts is made out, if the court is convinced that the marriage has not irretrievably broken down, a divorce should not be granted. The five facts are as follows.

## (a) *The respondent's adultery*

---

**LEGISLATIVE PROVISION**

**Matrimonial Causes Act 1973, section 1(2)(a)**

Section 1(2)(a) of the Matrimonial Causes Act 1973:

'that the respondent has committed adultery and the petitioner finds it intolerable to live with the respondent'.

---

The petitioner can rely on the fact that the respondent has committed adultery and that the petitioner finds it intolerable to live with the respondent. Three points should be stressed. First, a petitioner cannot rely on his or her own adultery. Secondly, it is not enough just to show that the respondent had committed adultery – it is also necessary to demonstrate that the petitioner finds it intolerable to live with the respondent. Thirdly, in *Cleary v Cleary*[74] it was established that it is not necessary to show that the reason why the petitioner cannot live with the respondent is due to the adultery. So if the husband commits adultery which the wife forgives, but then later the relationship breaks down for some other reason, the adultery fact can be made out. This suggests that the law believes that adultery is a symptom of a broken marriage, but does not of itself indicate that a marriage has broken down. However, s 2(1) of the Matrimonial Causes Act 1973 states that if the parties live together for more than six months after an act of adultery then the petition cannot be based on that act of adultery.

Adultery is defined as involving a voluntary act of sexual intercourse between the husband or wife and a third party of the opposite sex.[75] Homosexual intercourse or other forms of sexual activity not involving sexual intercourse will not constitute adultery, but may well constitute unreasonable behaviour under s 1(2)(b). If the respondent defends the petition and denies the adultery then the petitioner must prove it. The court will be willing to find that adultery took place if it could be demonstrated that the parties had the inclination and opportunity to commit adultery. For example, if the husband was seen dining with a woman and then retiring to a room to spend the night with her the court may be willing to assume that adultery took place.

In relation to the intolerability, the question is whether *this* petitioner finds it intolerable to live with this respondent. It does not matter whether most people would or would not find it intolerable to live with the respondent; it is only the reaction of the petitioner which is relevant.[76]

---

[73] *Buffery v Buffery* [1988] 2 FLR 365, [1988] FCR 465.
[74] [1974] 1 All ER 498.
[75] *Dennis v Dennis* [1995] 2 All ER 51. Solicitors are urged by the Law Society to encourage their clients not to name in any petition the person with whom the adultery took place (2006: 28).
[76] *Goodrich v Goodrich* [1971] 2 All ER 1340.

## (b) The respondent's behaviour

> **LEGISLATIVE PROVISION**
>
> **Matrimonial Causes Act 1973, section 1(2)(b)**
>
> Section 1(2)(b) of the Matrimonial Causes Act 1973: 'that the respondent has behaved in such a way that the petitioner cannot reasonably be expected to live with the respondent'.

The petitioner can rely on the ground that the respondent has behaved in such a way that the petitioner cannot reasonably be expected to live with him or her. A crucial point is that it is not enough just to prove that the respondent has engaged in unreasonable behaviour. It must be behaviour that a right-thinking person would think was such that this petitioner cannot reasonably be expected to live with the respondent.[77] So the court should take into account the personality of the parties in deciding whether the conduct was sufficient to prove the ground.[78] However, if the petitioner is reacting unreasonably to the respondent's behaviour the petitioner may fail.

Domestic violence would obviously fall within the definition of unreasonable behaviour, but a wide range of conduct can be included under this heading. It is also possible to rely on a series of incidents which, although minor in themselves, cumulatively establish that the petitioner cannot live with the respondent. There are probably few marriages where a party would not be able to recall a few incidents of unreasonable behaviour by his or her spouse. Ruth Deech suggests it is 'very easy' to rely on the behaviour ground.[79] The Law Commission has acknowledged that 'virtually any spouse can assemble a list of events which, taken out of context, can be presented as unreasonable behaviour sufficient to found a divorce petition'.[80] The cases reveal a wide range of conduct constituting unreasonable behaviour, ranging from a DIY enthusiast husband who removed the door of the toilet and took eight months to replace it,[81] to a husband who required his wife to tickle his feet for hours every evening leaving his wife with uncontrollable movements in her hands.[82] One journalist claims that facebook 'sex chats' are responsible for one in five divorces. That seems hard to believe, but the internet may well have facilitated infidelity.[83]

It should be stressed that although the behaviour must be unreasonable, there is no need for the respondent to be blameworthy.[84] For example, if a spouse suffers from an illness which causes him or her to behave in an unreasonable way, the fact that the behaviour was 'not their fault' would be irrelevant.[85] However, this rule causes difficulties. In *Pheasant* v *Pheasant*[86] the husband presented a petition on the behaviour factor, based on a claim that the wife did not provide spontaneous displays of emotion. It was held that this could not

---

[77] *Birch* v *Birch* [1992] 1 FLR 564, [1992] 2 FCR 564.
[78] *Birch* v *Birch* [1992] 1 FLR 564, [1992] 2 FCR 564.
[79] Deech (2009b).
[80] Law Commission Report 170 (1988: 3.8).
[81] *O'Neill* v *O'Neill* [1975] 3 All ER 289.
[82] *Lines* v *Lines* (1963) *The Times*, 16 July. See also *Le Brocq* v *Le Brocq* [1964] 3 All ER 464 where the wife claimed that her husband's submissive character and refusal to argue infuriated her.
[83] See Herring (2009b: ch. 1).
[84] *Gollins* v *Gollins* [1964] AC 644.
[85] *Katz* v *Katz* [1972] 3 All ER 219.
[86] [1972] 1 All ER 587.

constitute unreasonable behaviour, as the wife had not breached any marital obligation. The case is perhaps better understood as revealing a reluctance of the courts to accept that omissions by a spouse can constitute unreasonable behaviour,[87] rather than setting up a requirement that behaviour has to constitute a breach of an obligation in order to constitute unreasonable behaviour. However, it would be wrong to suggest that a decree cannot be based on the omissions of a spouse; it is just that the court will require more convincing that omissions can constitute unreasonable behaviour.[88] *Pheasant* v *Pheasant* can be contrasted with *Livingstone-Stallard* v *Livingstone-Stallard*,[89] where the divorce was granted on the basis of the constant criticisms and rudeness of the husband. In *Hadjimilitis (Tsavliris)* v *Tsavliris (Divorce: Irretrievable Breakdown)*[90] the unreasonable behaviour was claimed to be the husband's constant criticism; lack of warmth; controlling and demanding behaviour; public humiliation; lack of respect, insight, sensitivity and understanding, causing the wife depression and nervous strain.

If the spouses live together for six months after the last incident of unreasonable behaviour referred to in the petition then the court must take this into account when considering whether it was reasonable to expect the petitioner to live with the respondent.[91] However, if the period is less than six months the fact that the parties lived together after the incident cannot be taken into account. The reason for this is that parties should not be deterred from attempting reconciliation for fear that it would make it harder to establish a fact.

## (c) The respondent's desertion

> ### LEGISLATIVE PROVISION
>
> **Matrimonial Causes Act 1973, section 1(2)(c)**
>
> Section 1(2)(c) of the Matrimonial Causes Act 1973: 'that the respondent has deserted the petitioner for a continuous period of at least two years immediately preceding the presentation of the petition'.

If the petitioner can show that the respondent has deserted the petitioner for a continuous period of two years preceding the petition, this could form the basis of the divorce application. Desertion has been defined as an unjustifiable withdrawal from cohabitation, without the consent of the remaining spouse and with the intent of being separated permanently. If the desertion is justifiable then it cannot be relied upon. It was justifiable for a wife to leave when the husband took in a 'second wife'.[92] It is also possible to rely on two years' separation with consent to the divorce,[93] so desertion is rarely used.[94]

---

[87] The courts have been reluctant to accept that refusal to engage in sexual relations was necessarily unreasonable behaviour: *Mason* v *Mason* (1981) 11 Fam Law 143.

[88] *Thurlow* v *Thurlow* [1975] 2 All ER 979.

[89] [1974] 2 All ER 766.

[90] [2002] Fam Law 883.

[91] It is still quite possible for a petition to be granted, despite the period of living together, where, for example, there was no alternative accommodation available for the petitioner: *Bradley* v *Bradley* [1973] 3 All ER 750.

[92] *Quoraishi* v *Quoraishi* [1985] FLR 780.

[93] MCA 1973, s 1(2)(d).

[94] Haskey (1996a).

## (d) Two years' separation with the respondent's consent to the divorce

> **LEGISLATIVE PROVISION**
>
> **Matrimonial Causes Act 1973, section 1(2)(d)**
>
> Section 1(2)(d) of the Matrimonial Causes Act 1973: 'that the parties to the marriage have lived apart for a continuous period of at least two years immediately preceding the presentation of the petition . . . and the respondent consents to a decree being granted'.

If the petitioner can establish that there has been two years' separation immediately before the presentation of the petition and that the respondent consents to the petition a divorce can be granted. This ground is significant because the law has accepted that divorce can be obtained by consent without proof of wrongdoing. The intention was that this would be the most commonly used fact, but actually has never been more popular than behaviour.[95]

A couple are living apart unless they are living with each other in the same household.[96] It is possible for them to be living apart in the same accommodation, if they are living separate lives. For example, in *Hollens* v *Hollens*[97] the husband and wife both lived in a house but did not speak, eat or sleep together. They were held to be living apart. However, in *Mouncer* v *Mouncer*,[98] where the spouses ate together and spoke to each other, it was decided that they were not living apart. The strict interpretation has been criticised on the basis that the more civilised the parties are towards each other during the 'separation', the more likely it is that the courts will find the fact not made out.[99] The situation can be particularly harsh on a couple who cannot afford alternative accommodation and where one of the first three grounds cannot be made out. The courts' approach can be explained on the basis that the more liberal the interpretation given to living apart, the closer the law is to accepting divorce on demand.

Not only must the parties be physically apart, there must also be a wish by one spouse to live apart, explained the Court of Appeal in *Santos* v *Santos*.[100] This need not be a mutual wish, nor need it be communicated. So, if the husband is imprisoned and the spouses live separately for over two years, this ground can be made out if one of the parties formed the intention to live separately. The requirement in *Santos* v *Santos*[101] of a mental element is controversial because there is no reference to it in the statute.

Section 2(5) permits the spouses to resume living together for one or more periods totalling six months. Such a period will not count towards the two years' living apart, but it will not stop the period running.

[95] National Statistics (2010d).
[96] MCA 1973, s 2(6).
[97] (1971) 115 SJ 327.
[98] [1972] 1 All ER 289.
[99] Hayes and Williams (1999: 529).
[100] [1972] Fam 247.
[101] [1972] Fam 247.

## (e) Five years' separation

> ### LEGISLATIVE PROVISION
>
> **Matrimonial Causes Act 1973, section 1(2)(e)**
>
> Section 1(2)(e) of the Matrimonial Causes Act 1973: 'that the parties to the marriage have lived apart for a continuous period of at least five years immediately preceding the presentation of the petition . . .'

The petitioner can rely on the fact that the parties have been separated for five years prior to the date of the petition. This was the most controversial ground because it permitted divorce to be ordered against a spouse without his or her consent and without any proof of wrongdoing. Opponents called the section a 'Casanova's charter', although with a five-year wait between marriages, a Casanova would require patience!

## (iii) Defences to petitions

1. If the petitioner relies on the ground of five years' separation,[102] s 5 of the Matrimonial Causes Act 1973 provides a defence to a respondent who does not wish the divorce to go through.[103] The defence is available if the divorce would result in grave financial or other hardship to the respondent and it would be wrong in all the circumstances to dissolve the marriage. A good example of how s 5 could be used is *K v K (Financial Provision)*,[104] where the court lacked the power to require the husband to make certain orders to equalise the position of the parties in respect of pension provision. The court felt that in the absence of such provision the wife would suffer grave financial hardship. The court adjourned the husband's petition for divorce until the husband voluntarily made the necessary financial arrangements. In *Archer v Archer*,[105] where the wife had considerable assets, the court refused to find that she would suffer grave financial hardship if the divorce were granted. In general the courts have been very reluctant to use s 5 even if divorce causes financial losses[106] or social ostracism.[107] It should be stressed that it is not enough just to show the hardship; it is also necessary to show that it would be wrong in all the circumstances to grant the decree.

2. If the petition is based on the two or five years' separation grounds then decree absolute should not be made unless the court is satisfied that the petitioner should not be required to make financial provision for the respondent, or that the financial provision made by the petitioner for the respondent is reasonable and fair, or the best that can be made in the circumstances.[108]

---

[102] MCA 1973, s 1(2)(e).
[103] FLA 1996, s 10 proposed a similar provision to the divorce procedure under MCA 1973, s 5. Notably, s 10 would have also permitted a court to make an order preventing divorce if there was evidence that the children involved would suffer substantial harm.
[104] [1996] 3 FCR 158, [1997] 1 FLR 35.
[105] [1999] 1 FLR 327.
[106] *Julian v Julian* (1972) 116 SJ 763.
[107] *Banik v Banik* [1973] 3 All ER 45; *Rukat v Rukat* [1975] Fam 63.
[108] MCA 1973, s 10(2), (3). See *Wickler v Wickler* [1998] 2 FLR 326 for an example of when the section was used and *Re G (Decree Absolute: Prejudice)* [2003] 1 FLR 870 where it was not.

3. Under s 9(2) if three months have passed from the making of the decree nisi and the petitioner has not applied to have it made absolute then the respondent can apply to have the decree nisi made absolute. However, the court has the power to refuse to make the decree absolute on the respondent's application if that is appropriate in all the circumstances. In *O v O (Jurisdiction: Jewish Divorce)*[109] the respondent husband refused to supply his wife with a *get*, which she required if her divorce was to be recognised within the Jewish religion. The wife petitioner therefore refused to apply to have the decree made absolute. The respondent husband applied under s 9(2) but the court refused to make the decree absolute until he supplied the *get*.[110]

4. Viljeon J in *O v O (Jurisdiction: Jewish Divorce)*[111] also suggested a court had the power to delay making absolute a decree nisi under the inherent jurisdiction if there were special reasons for doing so.[112] The failure of the husband in that case to supply the *get* was a sufficiently special circumstance.

5. Under the Divorce (Religious Marriages) Act 2002 the court can refuse to make a decree absolute until the arrangements for a religious divorce have been made. The Act will be discussed further, below.

6. Where the couple have children of the family under the age of 16, the court, when considering whether to make a decree nisi, must consider the parties' proposals concerning the future of the child. On divorce the court must decide whether it should make any orders under the Children Act 1989. The same is true if the court directs that it should consider the arrangements for a child over 16. The court rarely so directs, but may do so if there are special circumstances: for example, if the child is disabled. The court may ask for further evidence and even delay the making of the decree absolute in exceptional cases until it is in a position to make any appropriate orders in respect of the children. In practice, whatever the age of the child, unless either spouse has applied for an order, the court is unlikely to make one of its own volition. As Douglas et al. explain: 'The assumption which lies behind this approach is that parents may be trusted in most cases, to plan what is best for their children's futures, and that, where they are in agreement on this, it is unnecessary and potentially damaging for the state, in the guise of the court, to intervene.'[113]

## 6 Problems with the present law

Moves to reform the Matrimonial Causes Act 1973 started with the Booth Committee Report in 1985. The report argued that defended divorces led to increased bitterness and disappointment. Parties, it was argued, should resolve issues themselves and disputes taken to court should be kept to a minimum. Subsequently, Law Commission Report 192[114] suggested significant reforms of the law. The report began by criticising the present law. These criticisms will now be considered.

---

[109] [2000] 2 FLR 147.
[110] For another example, where there was a fear that the respondent would leave the jurisdiction without enabling the court to make effective ancillary relief orders, see *W v W (Decree Absolute)* [1998] 2 FCR 304.
[111] [2000] 2 FLR 147.
[112] See also *Miller Smith v Miller Smith (No 2)* [2009] EWHC 3623 (Fam).
[113] Douglas, Murch, Scanlan and Perry (2000: 178).
[114] Law Commission Report 192 (1990).

## A 'It is confusing and misleading'

The confusion is said to flow from the fact that although irretrievable breakdown is stated to be the ground for all divorces, it is in fact insufficient simply to show that the marriage is irretrievably broken down: one of the five facts must also be proved. A linked complaint is that the law requires the parties to cite a fact as the cause of the marital breakdown, a fact that might not actually be the real cause of the marital breakdown. Mears,[115] however, claims that the law is not misleading because lawyers can always explain the true position of the law to their clients. This is not, it must be said, a very satisfactory excuse for having a confusing law. That said, as Mears points out, this is not an area of the law which the public complains about on the grounds of it being impenetrable.

The law can also be criticised on the basis that its practice differs so much from the law as it appears in the statute books. Cretney puts it this way:

> English divorce law is in a state of confusion. The theory of the law remains that divorce is a matter in which the State has a vital interest, and that it is only to be allowed if the marriage can be demonstrated to have irretrievably broken down. But the practical reality is very different: divorce is readily and quickly available if both parties agree, and even if one of them is reluctant he or she will, faced with a divorce petition, almost always accept the inevitable: there is no point in denying that the marriage has broken down if one party firmly asserts that it has.[116]

## B 'It is discriminatory and unjust'

The Law Commission suggests that the ground of two years' separation is not readily available to those who are unable to afford alternative accommodation for those two years.[117] Those who cannot afford to live separately must use one of the fault-based grounds or wait for five years.[118] Mears[119] argues that this is also an unfair criticism because the only discrimination is against those who are unable to prove the ground of divorce. The validity of his objection depends on whether there is a good reason for requiring separation. If there is not, the Law Commission's argument is valid.

It is also said by some to be unjust that the fault-based grounds do not necessarily reflect who is really responsible for the marital breakdown. For example, the fact that one party has committed adultery might imply that he or she is solely responsible for the breakdown of the relationship – while in fact the other party's bad behaviour may be said to have caused the adultery.

## C 'It distorts the parties' bargaining positions'

The argument here concerns the situation where one spouse is desperate for the divorce to go through as quickly as possible but the other spouse is happy for there to be a delay in the divorce. As the party who is desperate for a divorce is dependent on the other party's consent (if it is a two-year petition) or willingness not to defend the petition, either way, this gives the non-consenting spouse a weapon that can be used to advantage in the bargaining process.

---

[115] Mears (1991).
[116] Cretney (2003a: 391).
[117] If the couple are in local authority housing they may not be entitled to separate housing until they have officially divorced.
[118] It is possible for two parties to live separately under one roof.
[119] Mears (1991).

For example, if the spouses had separated and found new partners, and the husband for religious reasons wished to marry his new partner, but the wife was happy to cohabit with hers, then the wife could use the husband's desire for a divorce as soon as possible to extract a more generous settlement from him, by threatening not to consent to the divorce and thereby requiring him to wait until five years after their separation. Those who would seek to counter this argument would reply that the non-consenting spouse only has a tool if the consenting spouse cannot prove one of the grounds that Parliament has set down and, if so, the non-consenting spouse is within his or her rights to withhold consent.

### D 'It provokes unnecessary hostility and bitterness'

The system encourages the parties to use the fault-based grounds because they are so much quicker to use.[120] This can produce distress, bitterness and embarrassment in the making of that allegation, particularly because such allegations are made in public documents. The legal process, it is said, requires the parties to look to the past and at the bad aspects of their marriage. This might destroy any last hope of reconciliation. If a wife visits her solicitor and informs him or her that she wants to divorce her husband then the first thing the solicitor will do[121] will be to ask the wife to recount all the very worst things that her husband has done during the marriage. These will be typed up into a draft petition and sent to the husband. It would be hard to imagine a procedure better designed to increase the parties' ill feelings towards each other. Supporters of the present law would argue that ill feeling and bitterness are an inevitable part of divorce. This will be discussed further below.

### E 'It does nothing to save the marriage'

The parties are required to concentrate on making allegations rather than saving the marriage. The only provision specifically designed to assist reconciliation in the Matrimonial Causes Act 1973 is s 6. This states that if a petitioner consults a solicitor in connection with a divorce, the solicitor is required to certify whether or not the possibility of a reconciliation has been discussed and, if appropriate, whether the names and addresses of organisations or people that can help have been provided.[122] The aim is to ensure that a solicitor reflects carefully on whether the parties ought to consider reconciliation. The provisions are, of course, of little use to those who do not instruct a solicitor.[123] It is notable that in one recent survey only 53 per cent of those divorcing were sure that divorce was what they wanted.[124]

### F 'It can make things worse for the children'

Children whose parents divorce may suffer more if the parents are in conflict. The law does not attempt to reduce conflict; indeed, it may exacerbate conflict by focusing on one party's blameworthy conduct. However, in a recent study 30 per cent of those questioned thought it should be harder for couples with children to divorce; only 38 per cent disagreed with that view.[125]

---

[120] A divorce based on the fault-based grounds can often take between four and six months to complete.
[121] After discussing fees.
[122] MCA 1973, s 6(1).
[123] Booth J (1985: paras 4.42–4.23).
[124] Newcastle Centre for Family Studies (2004).
[125] National Centre for Social Research (2008).

# 7 Reforming the divorce law: the failure of the Family Law Act 1996

Although the criticisms have persuaded many commentators and practitioners that the divorce law is in urgent need of reform, it must be pointed out that (unlike many other areas of family law) members of the public do not appear to get particularly agitated about it.[126] There have not been demonstrations in the streets calling for reform of divorce law, even though there have in several other areas of the law. Nevertheless, the criticism contained in the Law Commission report persuaded the Government, and Parliament decided to reform the law through the Family Law Act 1996. However, before putting the Act into effect, it was decided to try out the proposals in various pilot studies around the country. The results of the pilot studies were regarded by the Government as very disappointing. It therefore decided not to implement the Family Law Act 1996 and Part II of the Act (which deals with the divorce procedure) will be repealed.[127] This chapter will still discuss the Act in outline because there is a widespread acceptance that the divorce law should be reformed in some way.[128] The reasons for the rejection of the law as set out in the Family Law Act 1996 will play a key role in discussions over how the divorce law should be reformed in the future.

## A General principles of the Family Law Act 1996

Section 1 of the Family Law Act, which sets out the general principles which would govern the law under the divorce part of the Act, provides:

### LEGISLATIVE PROVISION

**Family Law Act 1996, section 1**

The court and any person, in exercising functions under or in consequence of Parts II and III, shall have regard to the following general principles—

(a) that the institution of marriage is to be supported;

(b) that the parties to a marriage which may have broken down are to be encouraged to take all practicable steps, whether by marriage counselling or otherwise, to save the marriage;

(c) that a marriage which has irretrievably broken down and is being brought to an end should be brought to an end—

    (i) with minimum distress to the parties and to the children affected;

    (ii) with questions dealt with in a manner designed to promote as good a continuing relationship between the parties and any children affected as is possible in the circumstances; and

    (iii) without costs being unreasonably incurred in connection with the procedures to be followed in bringing the marriage to an end; and

(d) that any risk to one of the parties to a marriage, and to any children, of violence from the other party should, so far as reasonably practicable, be removed or diminished.

---

[126] Although see Shepherd (2009) for a renewed call for divorce reform.

[127] Lord Chancellor's Department (2001).

[128] The Lord Chancellor indicated he would continue to consider ways of reforming the divorce procedure despite the failure of the Family Law Act 1996 (Lord Chancellor's Department 2001).

These general principles were to guide not only judges but others carrying out activities relating to the divorce, including lawyers acting for clients, mediators, and Legal Services Commission officers.

## B A timetable for divorce procedures under the Family Law Act 1996

At the heart of the thinking behind the Act is that divorce should be a process over time rather than a one-off event. Before looking at some of the detailed provisions of the Act, a general outline of the proposed procedures will be provided by means of a timetable.[129] The procedures set out in the Act were in fact complicated, and this timetable is a simplification. It is based on the parties moving through the procedure as quickly as possible.

| | |
|---|---|
| *0 months* | The spouse wishing to initiate the procedure must attend an 'information meeting'. The other spouse, if he or she wishes, can also attend the meeting. Following the information meeting, the parties should spend the next three months considering whether they really want to get divorced. |
| *3 months* | One or both parties may file a statement of marital breakdown.[130] The statement of marital breakdown cannot be made until the parties have been married at least one year.[131] |
| *3 months, 14 days* | The period of reflection and consideration starts.[132] During this time the parties should continue to consider whether they want to get divorced. Marriage counselling facilities will be available. The parties should also look to the future and consider their relationship after divorce. In particular, arrangements should be made for residence and contact relating to any children, and any financial arrangements should be considered. The parties may consult a lawyer or mediator, if they have not done so already. |
| *12 months, 14 days* | If there are no children and neither party has applied for an extension of time, the parties can apply for the divorce order.[133] The court will grant the divorce order if applied for, providing the parties have been able to satisfy s 9 (requiring in essence that the arrangements over the parties' finances and children have been resolved). A party can apply for an order under s 10 to prevent the granting of the divorce order if there would be substantial financial or other hardship to the applicant spouse or the child if the divorce order were granted. |
| *18 months, 14 days* | Those unable to apply at the 12-month stage (e.g. those with children or where a party has applied for an extension) may apply for a divorce order. The court will grant a divorce order subject to ss 9 and 10. |

---

[129] Bird and Cretney (1996) provide a useful analysis of the Act.
[130] FLA 1996, s 6.
[131] FLA 1996, s 6(2), (3).
[132] The 14 days are the period allowed for service of the statement of marriage breakdown on the other party.
[133] In cases where there are children of the parties or one spouse has applied for an extension of time, the period of reflection and consideration will be extended by a further six months. This extension will not apply if an occupation order or non-molestation order is in force, or if the court is satisfied that delaying the making of the divorce order would be significantly detrimental to the welfare of any child: FLA 1996, s 7.

Some of the more controversial aspects of the proposals and the difficulties with them revealed by the pilot studies will now be considered in further detail.

## C The information meeting

The information meeting was to start the whole divorce procedure. Apart from a few exceptions,[134] anyone intending to initiate divorce proceedings was to attend an information meeting. It was not necessary for both spouses to attend a meeting but they could. The aims of the information meeting were as follows:[135]

1. To communicate a range of information on the divorce process and its consequences. This would cover information about the procedure of the divorce; the availability of mediation; the existence of free marriage guidance facilities and other counselling facilities; the possibility of seeking legal advice; and advice on matters associated with marriage breakdown such as housing and domestic violence.

2. To 'mark the seriousness of the step taken'. The parties were to be informed of the possible consequences of divorce and in particular the ways in which a child may suffer during a divorce. They were to be encouraged to think again about whether they really wished to obtain a divorce. The parties at the meeting were to be offered marriage guidance counselling and were to be encouraged to take it.[136]

3. To encourage the parties to use mediation, rather than relying on lawyers.

The pilot studies used a range of styles of information meetings including one-to-one meetings; group sessions; using CD-ROMs and computer technology; or a mixture of the three. The meetings were conducted by 'information providers', who were not necessarily lawyers, and who were employed on the basis of their communication skills.[137] The highest levels of satisfaction in the pilot studies were found with individual meetings; next came the group sessions; and the least popular were the CD-ROMs.[138]

The Government's decision to abandon the implementation of the 1996 Act was largely caused by the lack of satisfaction with the information meetings.[139] The major concern was that the meetings did not succeed in encouraging the parties to attend mediation. Other statistics reveal successes: 90 per cent of attendees found the meetings useful and 13 per cent of those attending went to see a marriage counsellor, half of those with their spouse.[140] Most people found the meetings positive.[141] These have led at least one leading researcher to suggest the Government should not have regarded the meetings as a failure, but rather that it had unrealistic expectations about what they could achieve.[142]

The key complaint made about the information meetings was that they were too 'structured, impersonal and routine'.[143] Many participants felt that they were being subjected

---

[134] Famous and disabled people were to be exempt from attending the meetings.
[135] FLA 1996, s 8(9) provides a complete list.
[136] FLA 1996, s 8(6)(b).
[137] Out-of-work actors were a popular category.
[138] Walker (2001a), although in part the lack of satisfaction with the CD-ROMs may result from lack of familiarity with computers.
[139] Walker (1998; 1999; 2001a).
[140] Walker (2001a). Walker and McCarthy (2004) report that those who met with counsellors found their meetings useful, even though few marriages were saved.
[141] Walker (2001b).
[142] Walker (2001b). See also Hale LJ (2000) who suggests that there were unrealistic expectations for the information meetings.
[143] Walker (2000b: 6).

to a prepared package, rather than being treated as individuals. In particular there were complaints that:

1. The 'information providers' were able only to provide information and were not able to give individual advice. This meant that, although the parties were given general principles, they could not be given advice on how these principles applied to their particular case. This was particularly frustrating for some participants.

2. Some of the information given at the meeting was not relevant. For example, some participants found it irritating to listen to information about domestic violence injunctions when such information was not useful for them. Those who did not have children found the information relating to children unnecessary.

3. Part of this dissatisfaction was caused by the fact that those attending the information meeting had different purposes in mind. Some were attending the meeting in order to gain advice on a particular question; some simply had problems with their marriage and were not sure how to proceed; and some wished to pursue divorce proceedings.[144] It is not surprising that the same information was not appropriate for all these groups.

4. There were concerns that members of religious or ethnic minorities would be deterred from attending information meetings because the meetings were public and alien to their culture.[145]

What lessons for future law reform are to be learned from the failure of the information meetings in the pilot studies? First, no two divorces are the same. The information that one couple may require to guide them through their divorce may be quite irrelevant for another divorcing couple.[146] As Professor Walker, in her in-depth study of the pilot information meetings, explains:

> People want an individual meeting to be sensitive to their personal situation and the stage they have reached in the process of marriage breakdown, and flexible enough to focus on providing information which is relevant to their needs at that time. Relevance and timing are key factors in the provision of information.[147]

Secondly, those involved in the divorcing process strongly dislike being 'lectured to' and prefer discussions with information providers to being passive recipients of information. Indeed, attempts by the state to force divorcing couples to 'behave well' during divorce are likely to be of very limited effect. However, research in Scotland reported very positive outcomes to programmes aimed to assist separating parents understand and support their children.[148]

One aspect of the information meetings that proved useful was that they enabled participants to have access to a wide range of information and services. The Government has now encouraged solicitors to take up the role of providers of information about services that may be useful to divorcing couples. Solicitors are to be encouraged to be part of Family Advice and Information Networks which will provide information and resources to those considering divorce.[149]

---

[144] Walker (2000b).

[145] Bridge (2000).

[146] Arnold (2000). Interestingly, only 66% of women who said that in theory information about violence was relevant to them found the information provided useful: Bridge (2000: 546), although it should be noted that there are concerns that victims of domestic violence may be reluctant to describe themselves as such: Richards and Stark (2000).

[147] Walker (2001a).

[148] Mayes, Gillies, MacDonald and Wilson (2000).

[149] Walker (2004a).

## D  Encouragement of reconciliation

One of the main aims of the Family Law Act 1996 was to persuade couples to become reconciled.[150] At the information meeting, couples were to be encouraged to consider saving their marriage, and counsellors were available to assist those who wished to pursue this option. Further, the Act required a three-month gap between the information meeting and the making of the statement of marital breakdown.[151] The aim of this gap was to provide a 'cooling off' period, a time for the parties to consider reconciliation and the offer of marriage guidance facilities. These facilities were to be available free of charge throughout the period of 'reflection and consideration'. Indeed, it was hoped that through the process of mediation the couple might decide to seek reconciliation. Mediators, it was thought, might be more willing than lawyers to encourage parties to consider reconciliation.[152]

Initial research from the pilot studies indicated that this aim was not being achieved. In fact, there was some evidence that the information meetings inclined those who were uncertain about their marriage towards divorce. Further, the information meetings were usually attended by only one of the parties (the one seeking the divorce), in which case talking about reconciliation was of little effect.[153] Interestingly, just under a half of respondents at the pilot studies attended a meeting with a marriage counsellor. However, many of those did not want to save their marriages, but wanted emotional support.[154] As the Lord Chancellor has indicated,[155] the story of the Family Law Act's attempts to save marriages is that efforts to rescue marriages need to focus on the period of time *before* the parties reach the stage of considering divorce. Indeed, the Government announced that £5 million was to be given to Marriage and Relationship Support, a body which offers marriage guidance for couples whose relationship is going through a difficult time before they reach the stage of divorce.[156]

A more recent study of those who went through the information meetings reveals a more complex picture. In Walker's study[157] 19 per cent of those who attended information meetings made some attempt to save their marriage and were cohabiting two years later. However, this, as she points out, is not necessarily a success. Many of the couples two years after the information meeting were suffering severe marital difficulties and were desperately unhappy. Although cohabiting, the sense in which their marriages were 'saved' may be questioned: 'there are couples who endure what can only be described as ghastly marriages which appear to offer little in the way of happiness, and much in the way of misery'.[158]

## E  The length of the process

As noted earlier, under the present law (under the Matrimonial Causes Act 1973) a divorce could take 4 months where reliance is placed on a fault-based ground. Under the Family Law Act 1996 the length of the proposed divorce procedure was a minimum of 12 months and

---

[150] Mackay (2000).
[151] FLA 1996, s 8(2). There were exceptional circumstances where this requirement could be waived.
[152] This appears to be an unfounded hope: Dingwall and Greatbatch (2001). Walker (2001a).
[153] Walker (2001a).
[154] McCarthy (2001); Walker (2004b) found that only 45% of those who attended marriage counselling under the FLA 1996 did so with the purpose of trying to save their marriage.
[155] Lord Chancellor's Department (2001).
[156] Lord Chancellor's Department (2003c). Such money has been used to support, for example, the 'Keep Love Alive' campaign.
[157] Walker (2004b).
[158] Walker (2004b: ch. 2).

14 days. Where the divorcing spouses have children under 16[159] or one of the parties requests extra time for consideration,[160] the minimum could[161] increase to 18 months and 14 days. Cretney had doubts about whether people will spend the period of reflection and consideration reflecting and considering: 'May not some of those concerned prefer to spend their time in the far more pleasurable activity of conceiving – necessarily illegitimate – babies?'[162] It was comments like these that led the Lord Chancellor to mention the length of time for the divorce procedures in the Family Law Act 1996 as one of the reasons for proposing the repeal of Part II of the Act.

## F Counselling and mediation

When the Family Law Act 1996 was passed, the Government intended mediation to be at the heart of the new divorce law.[163] For example, at the information meeting the parties were to be informed of the availability of mediation and they were to be encouraged to use it during the period of reflection and consideration.[164] There were to be special provisions to encourage those reliant on public funding to use mediation.[165] The pilot studies found that mediation was not popular. Only 7 per cent of those attending the information meetings wanted to use mediation and 39 per cent said that they were *more* likely to see a solicitor than they had been before the meeting.[166] This was said by the Lord Chancellor to be a disappointment.[167] It may be that in the light of the experience of the Family Law Act the Government will be less keen to promote mediation than it was. As Wilson J (writing extra-judicially) put it:

> Mediation is a seductive figure whom government has been quick to embrace. But, like a mistress whose lover expected not to have properly to support her, she currently senses that her affair with government has cooled and is left worried about its long-term intentions.[168]

## G Divorce order to be granted only once the financial orders and arrangements for children are made

Under the procedure as set out in the Family Law Act 1996[169] the divorce order could normally only be granted when parties had made arrangements for the future.[170] This included arrangements concerning financial matters and their children. This marks a crucial difference between the law under the Family Law Act 1996 and that under the Matrimonial Causes Act 1973.

---

[159] FLA 1996, s 7(11).

[160] FLA 1996, s 7(10), (13).

[161] The extensions to the period of reflection would not have applied automatically, for example, if the delay in making the divorce order would be significantly detrimental to the welfare of any child.

[162] Cretney (1996b).

[163] In Home Office (1998) mediation is presented as being generally preferable to litigation for disputes between family members.

[164] Although this is only open to those eligible for free legal aid and mediation (FLA 1996, s 23(3)). Others must fund mediation themselves.

[165] Legal Aid Act 1988, ss 15F–15H; discussed in King (1988).

[166] Walker (2004a).

[167] Whether these findings should be regarded as a failure is discussed in Collier (1999) and Walker (2000b).

[168] Wilson J (2003: 35).

[169] FLA 1996, s 5.

[170] FLA 1996, s 9. There were various exceptional circumstances in which this requirement need not be complied with, which are set out in FLA 1996, Sch 1.

Under the Family Law Act, in most cases, the divorce would only be granted if the parties had reached an agreement over the financial matters. However, under the Matrimonial Causes Act it is perfectly possible (and quite common) to obtain a divorce and only then turn to consider the financial orders that should be made. It is likely that in this regard, in any future reform, the Family Law Act's proposals will be adopted.

## H Protecting children's interests during divorce

The Family Law Act 1996 had a number of other special provisions seeking to promote the interests of children:

1. There was no general duty on the courts to consider the interests of the children during the divorce procedure. Under s 11 the court had a duty to pay particular regard to the wishes and feelings of children. However, it seems the section only operated where the court was considering whether or not to permit a divorce if the arrangements concerning the children were not yet resolved, and was not of wider application.

2. Under s 10 an order preventing divorce could be made if a divorce would cause a child substantial financial or other hardship and it would thus be wrong to dissolve the marriage. However, there was no wider power to prevent divorce in order to promote the interests of any child.

3. The information meetings were to stress to the attendees the importance of promoting any child's welfare and might offer advice on how to help children through the divorce. Information about counsellors trained to work with children was to be offered (s 8(9)(b)). There is much evidence that during a divorce children can feel helpless and do not understand what is happening.[171] The research on pilot study information meetings indicated that the information on children was useful, although parents 'found it difficult to bridge the gap between knowing what to do to help their children and actually doing it'.[172]

4. The Lord Chancellor was empowered to make rules requiring lawyers to inform their clients that children's wishes, feelings and welfare should be considered.

5. There were duties on state-funded mediators: they were required 'to have arrangements designed to ensure that the parties are encouraged to consider the wishes and feelings of each child'; and to consider whether the children should attend the mediation sessions (s 27(8)).[173]

## I 'Quickie divorce'

There was concern that some of the media, having picked up on the fact that under the proposals proof of fault would no longer be required, had presented the proposed law as a 'quick and easy' divorce. In fact, as noted above, the procedure under the 1996 Act was to take much

---

[171] Lyon (1997b: 70).
[172] Walker (2001b: 4).
[173] There are codes of practice for mediators which cover when children should be involved: UK College of Mediators (1998).

longer in most cases than the present law under the Matrimonial Causes Act 1973. The worry was that such misinformed perceptions might undermine marriage. Further, those who seek a divorce might be disappointed to find that a divorce could actually take over one and a half years. Supporters of the present law argue that the Matrimonial Causes Act 1973 presents a clever fiction: it appears very difficult to divorce, but in fact it can be quick and easy to do so.[174] Indeed, Cretney has argued that the Government should have been more open about this effect of its proposals: 'It is in concealing the reality – that divorce is to be available at the unilateral wish of either party, behind a comforting façade of consideration, reflection, reconciliation and counselling – that the government's proposals are most vulnerable to the charge of perpetuating the tradition of hypocrisy and humbug.'[175] In a more positive light, John Eekelaar has called the proposal that either party be permitted to bring the marriage to an end 'a radical empowerment of married people'.[176]

## J Idealisation of divorce

The Family Law Act 1996 can be criticised for presenting an idealised vision of divorce. It assumes that a fair number of couples will be reconciled; that people will wish to sit in a room together and mediate their dispute; and that time will be spent reflecting on and considering their relationship and the future. The pilot studies show that such aspirations for divorcing couples may be unrealistic. The law may hope that divorcing couples will behave in a 'sensible' way, but such wishes may ignore the psychological effects of divorce.[177] The law has only limited ability to influence social behaviour.[178] As Hasson puts it, 'marital breakdown is a fact of life to be dealt with, rather than something to be corrected or discouraged'.[179]

Reece has interpreted the Family Law Act as an attempt to encourage people to divorce responsibly.[180] It was recognising that people's relationships are based on choice; you cannot force someone to be happily married. However, when people make the momentous choice of divorce the law should ensure that that decision is taken with proper care and due consideration of the consequences. The information meetings and times for reflection and consideration were an attempt to do this. Other commentators have interpreted these periods of reflection as a punishment (a 'time out') imposed by the state on divorcing couples.[181] John Eekelaar has written of the way the Act sought 'to enhance people's freedom to pursue goals of their own choosing, but to exercise state power surreptitiously by influencing them to choose goals which the state believes to be in their interests, or those of the community'.[182] If that was its goal, it failed.

Cynically, perhaps, Davis has suggested that giving the couple time for reflection was more about assuaging society's anxieties about divorce than being for the benefit of the couple.[183] He argues that we must never forget that there is little the law can offer to heal the pain of divorce and there is much the law can do to make it worse.[184]

---

[174] Deech (1990).
[175] Cretney (1996b: 52).
[176] Eekelaar (2006b: 21).
[177] Brown and Day Sclater (1999).
[178] James (2002).
[179] Hasson (2003: 362).
[180] Reece (2003); Dewar (1998); Eekelaar (1999).
[181] Reece (2000).
[182] Eekelaar (2006b: 21).
[183] Davis (2001).
[184] See the discussion in Douglas, Murch, Scanlan and Perry (2000); Davis (2001).

## 8 Some general issues on divorce

Following the failure of the Family Law Act 1996 it is 'back to the drawing board' so far as reform of the divorce law is concerned. This section will now consider some key issues which will need to be taken into account when deciding how the law should be reformed.

### A Individualisation of divorce

In the United States in particular there have been moves towards offering people a range of marriages from which they can choose the model which suits them best.[185] For example, a couple could choose a marriage that could end in divorce whenever either party chooses, in other words divorce on demand. However, if they wished, the parties could select a divorce clause stating that the marriage could only come to an end if adultery was proved, or maybe even that the marriage could never be ended.[186] These are sometimes known as 'covenant marriages'. The main argument in favour of this approach is that it provides freedom of choice, that parties should be able to choose to limit their freedom to divorce in order to give deeper commitment to the marriage. The argument can be made that in some marriages sacrifices need to be made early on in the marriage, for the long-term benefits of a committed relationship. For a party to leave after the other party has made sacrifices and before the benefits arrive is unjust. For example, a wife may decide to give up work, and concentrate on caring for the children and making the home. From her perspective, entering into a marriage where her husband is bound to stay with her for at least ten years may in fact be a more attractive option than a marriage where he could leave at any time. Opponents of this approach argue that it would be very difficult to enforce. In the above example, preventing the husband from divorcing for ten years will not keep him from simply leaving his wife. Alternatively, the proposed clause could be redefined so that if either party ceases to cohabit with the other there would be a financial penalty. This could create problems of its own; in particular, there are concerns that it could lead to domestic violence. Further, the financial penalty might work against the interests of a poorer spouse who would be unable to make the payments necessary if she or he wished to separate.

Reece[187] sees a post-liberal approach to divorce in the Family Law Act 1996: that divorce should be an exercise of choice, but that this choice should be a carefully thought out and considered one. She explains: 'For the post-liberal, it is no longer sufficient to establish whether the subject wants to divorce: instead, we need to discover whether divorce would help him or her to realise himself or herself, or whether remaining married would more authentically reflect him or her.'[188]

### B No-fault versus fault-based divorce

There has been much debate over whether there should be a fault- or no-fault-based divorce system. In fact this rather simplifies the options available to the law. The forms of divorce law most discussed have been the following:

---

[185] Scott (1990); Lacey (1992); Rasmusen and Evans State (1998); Shaw Spaht (2002). The take-up rate for the 'covenant marriage' (with fault-based divorce) has been low (Ellman (2000b)).
[186] See discussion in Brinig (2000).
[187] Reece (2003).
[188] Reece (2003: 18).

1. *A pure fault-based system.* This system allows divorce only if one party proves that the other party has wronged them in a particular way. The most common faults cited are that one party has committed adultery, or otherwise behaved in an unacceptable way.

2. *Requiring proof of irretrievable breakdown.* Here divorce would be granted if there is proof that the marriage has broken down and cannot be saved.

3. *Divorce over a period of time.* Divorce would be available after the spouses had waited a period of time following an indication that they wished to separate.

4. *Divorce by agreement.* If both parties agreed to a divorce, that would be available without proof of any fault on either side.

5. *Divorce on demand.* In this form divorce is granted at the request of one of the parties. There is no need to prove fault or irretrievable breakdown.

In modern times models 1 and 2 have few supporters,[189] mostly on the basis that it is impossible for a court to ascertain whether there is irretrievable breakdown or who was at fault in causing the end of the marriage.[190] Around the world, legal systems have been moving towards a no-fault divorce procedure. Thorpe LJ[191] argues that no-fault divorce is 'the highest legislative priority for the family justice system'. Despite the wide support in academic circles for no-fault divorce, the arguments are not all one way and it is useful to consider the advantages and disadvantages of both fault and no-fault systems.

---

**DEBATE**

## Should divorce or dissolution be fault based?

### Arguments in favour of fault-based divorce

#### (a) Psychology

Richards argues that although the law may seek to discourage parties from asking who is to blame for the ending of the marriage, this is unrealistic:

> The coming of legal 'no fault' divorce has perhaps allowed us to believe that couples separate with a similar detached view of divorce. They don't. Blame, accusation, and strong feelings of injustice are the norm at divorce and they get in the way of couples making reasonable arrangements about children and money. Neither legal fiction of the lack of fault or imposed orders do anything to relieve the situation, rather the reverse.[192]

A no-fault system can therefore be criticised on the basis that it does not deal with the issues which really concern the parties.[193] Indeed, in one study of divorcing couples' attitudes to divorce the law's failure to address who was at fault in causing the breakdown of the marriage was cited as a major flaw.[194] To some divorcing spouses justice is served only if the court

---

[189] Though see Hood (2009).
[190] Bainham (2001a) discusses the role fault plays in family law generally.
[191] Thorpe LJ (2000).
[192] Richards (1994: 249).
[193] Davis and Murch (1988); Day Sclater (1999). See also the discussion in Smart and Neale (1999: 138) suggesting the law fails to appreciate the different kinds of power exercisable on divorce.
[194] Davis and Murch (1988); Deech (1990). See also Smart et al. (2005) which emphasises how important fault is to those actually divorcing.

declares that the other party was the cause of the marriage breakdown.[195] Psychologists argue that blame is a psychologically crucial part of the divorce process,[196] and that making allegations of fault can even be cathartic.[197] As one experienced mediator put it, for most of his clients: 'their marriage has not died, it has been killed'.[198] It has been suggested that ignoring fault in the divorce petition means that proceedings over divorce or money become more acrimonious.[199]

While these arguments reveal the importance to divorcing parties of finding fault, some argue that it is not the place of the courtroom to explore these issues, especially at the taxpayer's expense.[200] Perhaps one benefit of mediation is that it can do something to deal with the parties' allegations of fault in a private setting, although most mediators try to persuade clients to focus on the future rather than the past.

### (b) Justice

Linked to the argument above is a further point that it is not only the parties' psychological needs that are relevant here, but that it is the law's responsibility to uphold society's values and to discourage conduct which damages society.[201] Where one spouse is to blame for ending the marriage and thereby harming the children, the law should declare the wrongdoing and, if appropriate, punish it.[202] However, others reply that the law cannot prevent marital misconduct or even be responsible for deciding who has caused the end of a relationship.[203] For example, Bainham[204] has argued that the party who commits adultery may not be the one who is at fault, because they may have been driven to do so as a result of the coldness of their spouse. This is controversial but demonstrates that it is far from easy to determine who is at fault.

### (c) Marriage

It can be argued that having no-fault divorce undermines marriage: no-fault divorce permits a spouse to end a marriage whenever she or he wishes and this undermines the ideal of marriage being a life-long obligation. As Baroness Young has argued:

> The message of no fault is clear. It is that breaking marriage vows, breaking a civil contract, does not matter. It undermines individual responsibility. It is an attack upon decent behaviour and fidelity. It violates common sense and creates injustice for anyone who believes in guilt and innocence.[205]

Others reply that if a couple are staying together only because of what the law says, their marriage is worth little; what makes marriages strong or weak is the love and commitment of the spouses, and not the legal regulation. As already noted, there is much debate over whether the law on divorce can in fact affect the rate of marital breakdown.[206]

➡

---

[195] Davis, Cretney and Collins (1994).
[196] Day Sclater and Piper (1999).
[197] Hood (2009).
[198] Richards (2001).
[199] Deech (2009b).
[200] Rasmusen (2002) surveys the range of legal remedies there may be to penalise adultery, apart from denying divorce.
[201] Law Commission Report 192 (1990: 181) found that 84% of people in a survey agreed with the present law that adultery should be a ground for divorce (suggesting that the general public favours fault-based grounds).
[202] Swisher (1997).
[203] O'Donovan (1993).
[204] Bainham (1995b).
[205] Baroness Young, Hansard (HL) Vol. 569, col. 1638.
[206] Ellman (2000b).

Some economists have entered the debate to argue in favour of using divorce to maintain the stability of marriage. Rowthorn[207] argues that a no-fault divorce system undermines the notion of commitment that is key to the nature of marriage.[208] It provides men, in particular, the opportunity to leave the marriage when it is opportune for them, leaving women severely disadvantaged. Cohen puts the argument this way:

> At the time of formation, the marriage contract promises gains to both parties. Yet the period of time over which these gains are realized is not symmetrical. As a rule, men obtaining early in the relationship, and women late. This follows from women's relative loss in value. Young women are valued as mates by both old and young men. When they choose to marry a particular man they give up all their other alternatives. . . . The creation of this long-term imbalance provides the opportunity for strategic behaviour whereby one of the parties, generally the man, will perform his obligations under the marriage contract only so long as he is receiving a net positive marginal benefit and will breach the contract unless otherwise constrained once the marginal benefit falls below his opportunity cost.[209]

Scott is sympathetic to the aims of those who seek a fault-based system of divorce. She argues that the law should impose restrictions on exiting marriage as these will 'discourage each spouse from pursuing transitory preferences that are inconsistent with the couple's self-defined long-term interest' and therefore 'each spouse, knowing the other's commitment is enforceable, receives assurance that his or her investment in the relationship will be protected'.[210] However, Scott argues that fault is not the most effective way of doing this and instead suggests three other ways of providing a disincentive to divorce: mandatory waiting periods before divorce;[211] mandatory marital counselling before a divorce petition can be presented; and that on divorce most marital property be held on trust to provide for the children. Reece considers a similar argument from a different perspective. She suggests that it could be argued that no-fault divorce denies the parties the opportunity of engaging in a long-term committed project, fully immersing themselves in the marriage, confident that the other party cannot (without good reason) withdraw from the marriage.[212]

## Arguments in favour of no-fault systems

### (a) 'Empty shell'

It has been maintained that if one spouse wishes to divorce there is little value in forcing the couple to stay married. There is no point in keeping 'empty shell' marriages alive. Making divorce available only on proof of fault does not lead to happier marriages, but to parties separating, although legally married, or to cantankerous divorce. After all 'no statute, no matter how carefully and cleverly drafted, can make two people love each other'.[213] A recent poll suggested that only 17 per cent of the public thought a couple should stay together 'for the sake of the children'.[214] Evidence from psychologists suggests children living in unhappy homes do worse on a number of levels than children in separated homes.[215]

---

[207] Rowthorn (1999).
[208] Lewis (1999: 125).
[209] Cohen (2002: 25).
[210] Scott (2003: 162).
[211] Ellman (2000b) argues that such waiting periods do more harm than good.
[212] Reece (2003: 121).
[213] Lord Chancellor's Department (1995: para 3).
[214] Resolution (2010).
[215] See Chapter 9 for further discussion.

### (b) The 'right to divorce'

Some argue that it is now a human right to divorce.[216] Forcing someone to remain married against their wishes is an infringement of their right to marry or right to family life. However, the European Court of Human Rights has made it clear that the European Convention does not include a right to divorce.[217]

### (c) Bitterness

A common complaint is that a fault-based system promotes bitterness. By focusing the spouses' minds on the past and the unhappiness of the marriage and making these public, it is argued that fault-based systems exacerbate the anger and frustration they feel towards each other.

### (d) The impossibility of allocating blame

We have already referred to this argument – that the law cannot really determine who was truly to blame for the break-up. There are practical difficulties in discovering the facts of the case, particularly as the husband and wife are often the only two witnesses. But even if all the facts were known, the court may still not be in a position to allocate blame. Bainham suggests that many people would take the view that for 'a very large number of people, the obligation of *lifelong* fidelity to one partner was at best an impossible dream'.[218]

### Questions

1. If there is a psychological imperative for spouses to blame each other on divorce, what is the best way to channel those feelings?

2. What would be wrong with having a system where simply filling in a form led to a divorce? Is that, in fact, much different from what we have at the moment?

3. Is there a good reason for treating marriages differently from other contracts, where we do seek to establish fault?

4. Do you agree that divorce is a disaster for society and the individuals? What can be done about it?

### Further reading

Read **Eekelaar** (1999) for a discussion of the attempts to control people during the divorce process. Read **Reece** (2003) for a consideration of the 1996 Family Law Act reforms.

Although this chapter has summarised the arguments for and against fault-based divorce, it should be noted that the weight of opinion among practising and academic family lawyers is in favour of a no-fault-based system. A recent opinion poll suggested that 68 per cent of the public were, too.[219] Future reforms of the divorce law in England and Wales are very likely to abandon fault-based grounds of divorce. Indeed, Cretney has argued that the courts on divorce should seek to do little more than they do on marriage, namely record-keeping. The court cannot even properly decide whether or not a marriage has irretrievably broken down.[220]

---

[216] Bradley (1998).
[217] *Johnston v Ireland* (1986) 9 EHRR 203.
[218] Bainham (2002c: 177).
[219] Resolution (2010).
[220] Cretney (2002).

## C Length of time for the divorce process

The length of time a divorce should take is inherently problematic. On the one hand, there is concern that if the process moves too quickly then people who are having difficulties with their marriage and consult a solicitor for advice might find themselves divorced before they have had time to think about whether divorce is appropriate. Indeed, under the present law some people have complained that once they consulted a solicitor the matter was taken out of their hands and they lost control of what was happening. On the other hand, the longer the divorce takes, the greater the risk of increased domestic violence and bitterness, especially if the couple are not able to fund two homes until the financial settlement is made. Others suggest that the increased length of the divorce process will discourage people from marrying in the first place.[221] Ruth Deech has advocated a three-month period of delay before a divorce decree be granted.[222] Certainly the length of a divorce under the proposals in the Family Law Act do not sit easily with the 'no delay' principle in s 1(2) of the Children Act 1989.[223] The most obvious effect of the length of time that the divorce procedure takes is that it delays remarriage. It might be argued that, given the vulnerability of second marriages to divorce, this might be seen as sensible.[224]

## D Reconciliation and divorce

We have already discussed the difficulties of using the law on divorce to encourage reconciliation. Attempting to save a marriage once one of the parties has taken the drastic step appears to be far too late. As indicated by the Lord Chancellor, in future, attempts to save marriages in trouble will primarily focus on the period of time before the parties seek to divorce.[225] Indeed, perhaps the possibility of requiring couples who are planning to marry to receive advice and counselling may be investigated.[226]

## E The Human Rights Act 1998 and divorce

According to *Johnston v Ireland*,[227] although the European Convention recognises a right to marry, this does not necessarily include a right to divorce. In *F v Switzerland*[228] it was confirmed that it was contrary to the Convention to forbid a man who had divorced three times from marrying for a fourth time until three years had elapsed. It was held that although stability of marriage was a legitimate aim, the length of the time restriction was unreasonable and disproportionate. These cases suggest that the Convention will allow the state to restrict access to divorce, but not unduly restrict access to marriage or remarriage.[229] Further, they suggest that neither the law of divorce as set out in the Matrimonial Causes Act 1973 nor the rejected proposals under the Family Law Act 1996 could be challenged under the Human Rights Act 1998.

---

[221] Bainham (1998b).
[222] Deech (2009b).
[223] See Chapter 9.
[224] Eekelaar and Maclean (1997: 145) are concerned that the length of the period of reflection might increase cohabitation.
[225] Lord Chancellor's Department (2001). Concrete proposals are found in Lord Chancellor's Department (2002b).
[226] Barton (2003).
[227] (1986) 9 EHRR 203.
[228] (1987) 10 EHRR 411.
[229] *Dennis v Dennis* [2000] 2 FLR 231.

## F Financial arrangements to be made before divorce

As noted above, one of the significant effects of the Family Law Act 1996 was to be that a divorce order could not be granted until the arrangements for the future were resolved. By contrast, the present law under the Matrimonial Causes Act 1973 allows divorce to be granted without the arrangements concerning financial matters and children being completely resolved. In fact, it might be years after the divorce when the financial orders are finally made. The Government justified the Family Law Act approach by arguing that 'people who marry should discharge their obligations undertaken when they contracted their earlier marriage and also their responsibilities which they undertook when they became parents, before they become free to remarry'.[230] But there was more to it than that, because it was hoped that, as the parties made their arrangement for the future, they might in fact decide to abandon their divorce plans. For example, the hope was that a father, upon realising he would see his children only once a fortnight after the divorce, might decide to be reconciled with his wife.

Another argument in favour of the Family Law Act approach is that it ensures that the negotiations over the financial matters do not go on indefinitely. In contrast, the argument in favour of the Matrimonial Causes Act's approach is that a spouse may not be able emotionally to face deciding what should happen after the divorce until the divorce order is actually made, particularly if that spouse is opposed to the making of the decree.

## G Religion and divorce

Problems arise when the requirements for divorce in a religion do not match the legal requirements. For example, as we have seen, under Jewish religious law unless the former husband provides what is known as a *get*, the wife is not permitted to remarry.[231] She can remarry under secular law, but not under religious law.[232] At first sight this appears to be solely a religious matter and it would be inappropriate for the law to intervene. But Hamilton has suggested four reasons why the state might want to intervene in these types of situations:[233]

1. To promote remarriage. Marriage and family are seen as the framework of society, and the state should have the power to intervene to permit remarriage and to require a religion to recognise the marriage.
2. The right to marry under the European Convention[234] could be said to justify intervention by the law to recognise remarriage.
3. General perceptions of fairness and equality require that the courts and legislature intervene where a religious divorce is unjustly withheld.
4. An unscrupulous husband may use his control of the religious divorce to get a more favourable settlement.

However, there are serious problems for legal intervention in this area. The main one is that under Jewish law the *get* must be provided voluntarily, and so a court order to provide a *get* might be counterproductive.[235] So far the courts have been very unwilling to intervene where a *get* has not been provided.[236]

---

[230] Lord Chancellor's Department (1995: para 4.26).
[231] She will then be an *agunah* (a 'chained wife').
[232] There can be similar problems under Islamic law.
[233] Hamilton (1995: ch. 3).
[234] Article 12.
[235] Schuz (1996).
[236] *Brett v Brett* [1969] 1 All ER 1007.

The Divorce (Religious Marriages) Act 2002 enables the courts to refuse to make a decree of divorce absolute unless a declaration has been made by both parties that they have taken such steps as are required to dissolve the marriage in religious terms.[237] This does not resolve all the problems because it does not help in situations where the wife seeks a divorce but the husband refuses to grant it, or in cases where the couple have already divorced. There one option may be to require a husband to pay a further lump sum if he fails to comply with the religious aspects of the divorce.[238]

## H  Children and divorce

There has been much concern expressed that discussion of reform of divorce does not take sufficient account of the feelings and wishes of children. Day Sclater has summarised the research on children and divorce in this way: 'they want their views to be taken account of; they do not want to choose between parents, neither do they want to feel responsible for post-divorce arrangements for their care, but they do want to be involved in the changes that affect their lives, and to have a chance to contribute to the decision-making process'.[239] As we have seen, in relation to the present system and the Family Law Act 1996 proposals there are only limited procedures that permit children's voices to be heard. A recent survey found that only 34 per cent of parents in the sample had discussed the arrangements concerning children after divorce with their children.[240] This alone lends weight to a requirement that the court should consider the interests of children.[241] To what extent the law can or should seek to involve children in the divorce and court proceedings will be discussed further in Chapter 9.

## 9  Pursuing an action for inducing divorce

There has been some debate over whether a spouse can sue a person who has broken up the marriage. For example, could a wife sue the woman who committed adultery with her husband if the adultery was the cause of the marital breakdown? This has been done in the United States, but it is very unlikely that such an action would be recognised in the UK. The action would have to be based in tort and probably on inducing a breach of contract. However, it is very likely that the court would see such an action as contrary to public policy.[242]

## 10  Separation orders

The effect of a separation order is that, although the parties remain married, there is no legal obligation to cohabit. The significance of the order lies in the fact that it enables the court to make orders relating to financial provision for spouses.[243] A separation order is likely to

---

[237] See Morris (2005) for a useful summary of the religious requirement for divorce in a number of jurisdictions. The Law Society (2006) encourages solicitors to be aware of any religious issues when advising clients.

[238] *A v T (Ancillary Relief: Cultural Factors)* [2004] 1 FLR 977.

[239] Day Sclater (2000: 80).

[240] Murch, Douglas, Scanlan et al. (1999).

[241] Lowe and Murch (2003).

[242] See Pascoe (1998). See also Bagshaw (2001) and the possible use of the tort of deceit in family cases.

[243] Under FLA 1996, s 21, if one spouse dies intestate then the property shall devolve as if the other spouse had died prior to the intestacy.

be made where the parties have religious objections to divorce but have decided to live separately, or where there are financial benefits to the parties if they remain married (e.g. a widow's pension that will only be payable to a woman who has remained married to her husband). Few judicial separation orders are made: only 214 were made in 2008.[244]

## 11 Death and marriage

A marriage comes to an end on the death of one of the parties. Usually there will be no doubt that a person has died.[245] However, there can be situations where, although it is suspected that someone has died, it cannot be proved: for example, if a husband fails to return home from work and his car is found abandoned near a cliff but his body is never found. This kind of situation puts the wife in a difficult position. Is she free to remarry or is she prevented from remarrying until she can prove that her husband has died?

There are two circumstances in which a person is entitled to assume that his or her spouse has died. The first is based on the seven-year ground. To rely on the seven-year ground it is necessary to show that there is no affirmative evidence that the person was alive for the seven years or more since their disappearance, and:

1. that there are persons who would be likely to have heard from the spouse during that period;
2. that those persons have not heard from him or her; and
3. all appropriate enquiries have been made.[246]

This will give rise to a presumption of death, which could be rebutted if other evidence arises that shows that the spouse might still be alive. In *Thompson v Thompson*[247] it was stressed that 'pure speculation' that the spouse may be alive is insufficient to defeat the presumption of death.

The second ground for presuming death under s 19 of the Matrimonial Causes Act 1973 is:

Any married person who alleges that reasonable grounds exist for supposing that the other party to the marriage is dead may present a petition to the court to have it presumed that the other party is dead and to have the marriage dissolved, and the court may, if satisfied that such reasonable grounds exist, grant a decree of presumption of death and dissolution of marriage.[248]

There is no need to show that seven years have passed since the spouse was last seen, but there must be convincing circumstantial evidence of death. It may be that the discovery of the car by the cliff in the example mentioned above would be insufficient on its own. In *Chard v Chard*,[249] where there was no reason why anyone would have heard from the missing wife, the court refused to presume her death even some 16 years after the wife was last seen. She had broken contact with her family and her husband, but it could not be presumed from the fact that she had not contacted anyone that she was dead.

[244] Ministry of Justice (2009).
[245] Normally death and marriage are clearly evidenced by the registers of death and marriage.
[246] MCA 1973, s 19.
[247] [1956] P 414.
[248] MCA 1973, s 19.
[249] [1956] P 259.

## 12 Dissolving a civil partnership

When a civil partnership comes to an end the parties can seek to dissolve it. The law on dissolution of civil partnerships is almost exactly the same as divorce for married couples. Just like divorce, the ground for dissolution is that the civil partnership has broken down irretrievably.[250] This can only be proved by establishing one of four facts. These match four of the five facts for divorce: 'unreasonable behaviour'; desertion; two-year separation with consent; five-year separation.[251] These grounds are explained above. Notably absent from the list is the fact of adultery. The explanation for this was that the legal definition of adultery is in terms of heterosexual intercourse and it would not transmit to the same-sex context. This is not very convincing; it would not seem to be beyond the wit of man to produce a definition of adultery in the same-sex context. Perhaps it indicates a squeamishness about same-sex relations which reveals a lack of acceptance of the validity of same-sex behaviour. Nevertheless, if adultery has taken place the injured partner could no doubt rely on the behaviour fact to obtain a dissolution. There is, therefore, no practical consequence that flows from this distinction between divorce and dissolution.

### TOPICAL ISSUE

#### 'Gay divorce'

Will 'gay divorces' (properly dissolutions of civil partnerships) be any different from 'heterosexual divorces'? This is a topic which has interested many commentators.[252] Will dissolutions be less bitter than divorces? Will the facts relied upon be any different?

The media reported the first English 'gay divorce' in May 2006. The reports were that a couple who had entered a civil partnership in February 2006 had ended their relationship just three months later.[253] One party is reported as saying, 'Liz told me she didn't love me any more, that she hadn't done for years. I was absolutely flabbergasted. I asked her why she'd gone through with the wedding and she said it was to make me happy.' She complains that her partner was seeing a guest at their 'wedding'. If this is anything to go by, perhaps not surprisingly, gay divorces are likely to be just as rancorous as heterosexual ones.

## 13 Mediation

### A Introduction

In recent years there have been attempts to persuade divorcing couples[254] to make greater use of mediation rather than resorting to lawyers.[255] Indeed, before their solicitors can be granted

---

[250] Civil Partnership Act 2004 (CPA 2004), s 44(1).
[251] The CPA 2004 has provisions which match those in the MCA 1973 to deal with periods of attempted reconciliation which will not (if less than six months) interrupt the time periods mentioned in the facts.
[252] E.g. Butler-Sloss (2006).
[253] Petre (2006).
[254] Indeed, in many areas of the law there have been moves to encourage the use of alternative dispute resolution techniques.
[255] Davis (1988); Walker, McCarthy and Timms (1994).

Legal Services Commission funding all publicly funded clients must meet with a mediator and their case be assessed to see if it is suitable for mediation.[256] A recent survey found that in fact in a third of cases solicitors had not discussed the option of mediation involved in cases of family breakdown.[257] In 2006–07 the Legal Services Commission spent £13 million on 13,889 mediations.[258] In 1997–98 only 406 mediations had been funded.[259] The Conservative Party has stated alternative dispute resolution (or mediation) 'should be regarded as the primary method of dispute resolution, keeping family disputes out of court unless really necessary . . . In children disputes there should be a mandatory attempt at pre-court resolution via ADR.'[260] It will be interesting to see how this makes its way into the Coalition Government's policies. Given the desire to cut back on legal aid it may well be that mediation is set to play an even more prominent role in family law. The Government has announced a review of family justice, part of which will consider the role mediation should play in family law.[261]

Baroness Hale in *Holmes-Moorhouse v Richmond-Upon-Thames London Borough Council*[262] set out the law's approach to mediation:

> The reality is that every effort is made, both before and during any family proceedings, to encourage the parents to agree between themselves what will be best for their children. There are many good reasons for this. The parents know their own children better than anyone. They also know their own circumstances, what will suit them best, what resources are available and what they can afford. Agreed solutions tend to work much better and last much longer than solutions imposed by a court after contested proceedings. The contest is likely to entrench opposing viewpoints and inflame parental conflict. Conflict is well known to be bad for children. Not only that, the arrangements made when the couple separate are bound to have to change over time, as the children grow up and their own and their parents' circumstances change. Parents who have been able or helped, through mediation or in other ways, to agree a solution at the outset are more likely to be able to negotiate those changes for themselves, rather than to have to return to court for further orders.

These alleged benefits are controversial, as we shall see. However, first, mediation must be defined.

## B What is mediation?

It is important to distinguish between reconciliation and mediation. The aim of reconciliation is to encourage the parties to abandon the divorce petition and to rescue their marriage. Mediation, however, accepts the fact of breakdown and attempts to assist the parties in deciding what should happen in the future.[263] It may happen that in the course of working together to arrange their life post-divorce, the parties become reconciled, but that is not the purpose of mediation. The Government White Paper on divorce reform defines mediation as 'a process in which an impartial third person, the mediator, assists couples considering separation or divorce to meet together to deal with the arrangements which need to be made

---

[256] FLA 1996, s 29. See the discussion and criticism of this provision in Davis, Bevan and Pearce (2001). Davis et al. (2000) found that the provision had not led to an increase in the number of mediations.
[257] House of Commons Public Accounts Committee (2007).
[258] Legal Services Commission (2007).
[259] Barton (2005: 992).
[260] Centre for Social Justice (2010).
[261] Ministry of Justice (2010b).
[262] [2009] 1 FLR 904, para 31.
[263] See Leach (2005) for a discussion of what mediation is.

for the future'.[264] The core goal in mediation is 'to help separating and divorcing couples to reach their own agreed joint decisions about future arrangements; to improve communications between them; and to help couples work together on the practical consequences of divorce with particular emphasis on their joint responsibilities to co-operate as parents in bringing up their children'.[265] A variety of different styles of mediation have been developed.[266] There are two main points of distinction. The first lies in how closely the mediation process is tied in with the court. The second involves the role played by the mediator. Regarding the first point of distinction, there are two basic forms of mediation in use: out-of-court mediation and in-court mediation.

### (i) Out-of-court mediation

Out-of-court mediation is mediation that takes place outside of the court system. The benefit of this scheme is that it can be used before the legal process has begun: the parties have not yet met lawyers and do not yet have entrenched positions. Indeed, there is no need for the court to be notified that the mediation is taking place. At the end of the mediation it is common for the court to be presented with the agreement and be asked to formalise it by means of a consent order.[267]

### (ii) In-court mediation

The aim of in-court mediation is to incorporate mediation within a court-based process.[268] The Private Law Programme seeks to facilitate in-court mediation. A typical system might be as follows: the district judge would meet the solicitors and the parties. If it is an appropriate case the district judge may direct the parties to attend a mediation meeting with a court welfare officer who will help the parties reach an agreement. A mediation meeting may involve any children over the age of 9, and the parties' solicitors may attend as well.[269] The district judge will be available to make consent orders. If the parties cannot reach an agreement, a different court welfare officer may be required to produce a report. So, although the mediation itself does not involve the judge, the mediation procedure is in a sense supervised by the judge and can be taken into account if the judge has to resolve the dispute.

The main disadvantage of the in-court mediation scheme is the fact that the parties may feel under pressure from the district judge to reach an agreement. Some have felt that in-court mediation blurs the distinction between adjudication and mediation.[270] In other words, although the mediated agreement is meant to be determined by the parties, in reality the judge or welfare officer makes the final decision and persuades the parties to agree to it. Therefore, to talk of the decision as the parties' agreement is something of a fiction. Certainly with in-court mediation, the exact line between mediation and a court-imposed solution becomes ambiguous. Another concern is that in cases of embedded conflict, it may simply delay a resolution of the difficulties for the parties, which may not be beneficial for the children.[271]

---

[264] Lord Chancellor's Department (1995: para 5.4).
[265] Lord Chancellor's Department (1995: para 6.17). See also S. Roberts (1995).
[266] Lord Chancellor's Advisory Committee on Legal Education and Conduct (1999) for recommendations to improve the training and accreditation of mediators.
[267] See Chapter 11.
[268] For an example see Brasse (2004).
[269] See L. Parkinson (2006) for a discussion of involving children in mediation.
[270] Davis, Cretney and Collins (1994: ch. 8); Davis (2000).
[271] Trinder (2008).

Under the Family Proceedings Rules 1999 a couple using court procedures to resolve financial issues between them must attend a Financial Dispute Resolution appointment,[272] where the judge will encourage the parties and the lawyers to reach a settlement. The parties and their lawyers will be expected to attend and make offers to settle. The Rules are designed to encourage lawyers to negotiate a settlement in as many cases as possible.

## C The role of the mediator

The other variable in forms of mediation is the function that the mediator plays. Roberts has suggested three roles a mediator could adopt:[273]

1. *Minimal intervention*. This model requires the mediator to ensure there is effective communication between the parties, but it is not the job of the mediator to influence the content of the agreement. So even if the mediator believes that the parties are reaching an agreement that is wholly unfair to one side, the mediator should not try to correct the balance. At the heart of this model is the notion that the agreement should be the parties' own decision. If the agreement seems fair to them then it is not for anyone else to declare it unfair.

2. *Directive intervention*. Under this model the mediator might provide additional information and seek to influence the content of the agreement if the proposed agreement is clearly unfair to one side or the other. He or she may try to persuade one or both parties to change their views, and may attempt to persuade the parties to agree to the arrangements the mediator believes are most suitable. One trainer of mediators encourages them to 'take their gloves off' and fight for the interests of children, ensuring that the parents reach agreements in the child's best interests.[274] However, most mediators accept that ultimately the decision is for the parties to reach themselves.

3. *Therapeutic intervention*. Here the mediator focuses on the relationship between the parties. This model promotes the belief that the dispute is merely a symptom of a broken relationship. The time spent in mediation may not therefore focus on the actual issues in dispute, but on trying to improve the parties' relationship generally.

In the English and Welsh family law context the model of minimalist intervention is often used.[275] But this model does not render the mediator powerless.[276] Most mediators hold a screening meeting before starting mediation and if, for example, it becomes clear that there has been serious violence in the past, they will refuse to go ahead with the mediation. Further, if during the course of the mediation the mediator is concerned that one party is being taken advantage of, it is always open to the mediator to stop the mediation and suggest that the parties seek legal advice.[277] It may be that there is a changing attitude to this issue[278] and that increasingly mediators in England are being interventionist. All mediators would encourage parties to have good relationships with each other and to put the interests of their

---

[272] Family Proceedings Rules 1999 (SI 1999/3491), r 2.61.
[273] Roberts (1988).
[274] Schaffer (2007).
[275] UK College of Family Mediators 2000, para 42. But see S. Roberts (2000) who suggests there is variation in practice over the style of mediation used.
[276] Waldman (1997).
[277] The contents of mediation are to be kept privileged and cannot usually be referred to in later proceedings: *DB v PO* [2004] EWHC 2064 (Fam).
[278] Wilson (2009).

children first.[279] But that is seeking to influence the parties agreements, albeit in an uncontroversial way. It may simply be impossible for a mediator not to rely on norms of some kind.[280] Some mediators claim that it is permissible to seek to persuade the parties to adopt current societal or cultural norms, such as that the interests of children should come first.[281] What is not permissible is for the mediator to seek to impose their own norms on the couple.[282] However, this view is based on being able to draw a reasonably clear line between which norms are social and which are personal. One suggestion is that as long as the mediator is open about what norms he or she is bringing to the discussion, and the couple accept this, the mediator is acting appropriately.[283]

Now the arguments over the benefits and disadvantages of mediation must be considered.[284]

## D The benefits of mediation

The following are some of the possible benefits of mediation:

1. Central to the arguments in favour of mediation is the idea that there is no 'right answer' to a particular dispute. If the parties reach a solution which is right for them, no one else should be able to regard their agreement as the wrong one. It could be said to be none of the state's business to seek to interfere in the arrangement the parties have reached. In part, mediation is fuelled by a belief that the court cannot claim that there is a particular solution that is 'just' or 'in the best interests of the child' because there are no agreed community values the law could use as a basis for such a solution. Indeed the House of Lords itself has accepted that in many cases a variety of solutions could be appropriate and there is not necessarily a right or wrong one.[285]

    There are three key issues here. The first is whether it is correct that there is no right answer for a court to declare. If there is not, then the solution reached by the parties is likely to be as good as the solution reached by anyone else. If, however, you do not accept this and believe that it is possible to state that some solutions are better than others, then the second key issue is whether there is a good reason to believe that the court is more likely to find a better solution than the parties in mediation. Thirdly, even if you accept that some solutions are better than others and that the court is more likely than the parties to find a better solution, there is still the issue of whether the state, through the courts, should be able to impose the right answer (or *a* right answer) on the parties. The law might want to set down a right answer on the divorcing couple because there are interests of either third parties or of the state which justify forcing a solution on the parties.[286] So, for example, many argue that mediation is not acceptable because it does not adequately protect the interests of the child. There is nothing to prevent the parents reaching an agreement in mediation which does not promote the interests of the child. However, such an argument would need to demonstrate that allowing judges to resolve disputes over children has a better chance of promoting children's interests than letting parents reach the decision.

---

[279] Stepan (2010).
[280] MacFarlane (2002).
[281] Belhorn (2005).
[282] See the discussion in Stepan (2010).
[283] Irvine (2009).
[284] As Mantle (2001: 151) argues, much more research is required before it is possible properly to assess the advantages of mediation.
[285] *Piglowska* v *Piglowski* [1999] 2 FLR 763 HL.
[286] Or even that there are rights that the divorcing couple have themselves which they should not be permitted to negotiate away in the process of mediation.

2. Supporters of mediation claim that the solutions agreed by the parties are more effective than court orders in the long term,[287] although one study found that only one half of all mediated agreements were intact six months after they were reached.[288] There are three aspects to the argument that mediation produces more effective results. The first is that because the parties have reached the agreement themselves they will more easily be able to renegotiate it together if difficulties with the agreement subsequently arise. Secondly, the solution reached through mediation will be one which the parties can tailor to their particular lifestyles rather than being a formula applied by lawyers or judges to deal with 'these kinds of cases'. Thirdly, it is argued that, as mediation can be hard work and emotionally exhausting, the parties will therefore feel more committed to the agreement than if it had been given to them by a judge.

3. Mediation enables the parties to communicate more effectively. The White Paper on mediation criticises the use of lawyers as detrimental to communication:

> Marriage breakdown and divorce are . . . intimate processes, and negotiating at arm's length through lawyers can result in misunderstandings and reduction in communication between spouses. Lawyers have to translate what their clients say and pass it on to the other side. The other party's lawyers then translate again and pass this on to his or her client. There can thus be a good deal of misunderstanding and a good deal of anger about what is said and how it is said.[289]

Opponents of mediation argue that lawyers can filter out particularly offensive communications and so in fact reduce bitterness, while mediation, by contrast, can increase bitterness. It is said that placing people whose relationship is breaking down in a room together is bound to generate animosity and discord. Despite these arguments, it must be agreed that if mediation enables the parties to talk to each other effectively it has given them an invaluable gift. The question is: how many couples are helped and how many might find that the process of mediation exacerbates bitterness? To this we have no clear answer.

Another aspect of this argument is that supporters of mediation claim that family disputes are unsuitable for court hearings. It is argued that court hearings work reasonably well in finding out past facts: 'who did what to whom and when'; but are less effective in building up ongoing relationships. In other words, the court procedure works best if the parties are never going to have to see one another again. Mediation, it is claimed, is a more suitable basis for a long-term relationship.

4. A linked argument to the one made above is that mediation is a better forum for resolving the emotional issues involved in divorce. The mediation process can not only help to resolve the dispute but perhaps also help the parties to come to terms with their feelings about the other person and begin the post-breakdown healing process. One mediator claims that mediation enables parties to express their anger and notions of blame more effectively than the legal process.[290] This might be why, on successful mediation, parties report high levels of satisfaction with the result.[291] While this is true where the procedure is successful,

---

[287] HM Government (2004: para 2). For a discussion of the evidence against this proposition see Eekelaar, Maclean and Beinart (2000: 16) and Wright (2007).

[288] Mantle (2001: 141). He regards this rate as impressive, given the level of conflict between many parties in court cases. For other studies finding no evidence that mediated agreements were longer lasting than court orders see Davies et al. (2000: 101) and Walker (2004a: 142).

[289] Lord Chancellor's Department (1995: para 5.19).

[290] Richards (2001).

[291] Teitelbaum and Dupaix (1994).

where it is unsuccessful the failure might simply increase the emotional anguish. Indeed one psychologist has warned of the dangers of encouraging parties to put their anger to one side 'for the sake of the children', as mediators often encourage parties to do.[292]

5. Mediation gives time for all issues which are important to the parties to be discussed. It has been a complaint of the legal process that it 'transforms' the parties' disputes. Their arguments are put into legal terminology and some issues that might be of concern to them are ignored.[293] For example, if a husband and wife were using lawyers and wanted help in resolving a dispute over who should keep their goldfish, lawyers would refuse to spend much time on this, regarding it as a trivial issue. Certainly a judge would not be impressed if asked to rule on who should keep the goldfish. By contrast, in mediation any matter which is important to the parties can be discussed and they can put their arguments in the language they wish to use rather than transforming the issue through legal terminology. Perhaps the real concern here is public funding. Should public funds be used to resolve what appear to be trivial issues, whether in mediation or the courts? It could also be argued that the use of formal lawyer's language helps avoid antagonism between the parties, which might occur if more open language was used.

6. Mediation saves costs, or at least the Government certainly hoped that mediation would save costs. By using just one mediator rather than two lawyers, and with the hourly rate for mediators being generally less than that for lawyers, savings could be made. The Law Commission suggested that the average mediation was £550 per case, while £1,565 was the average legal aid bill per case using lawyers.[294] In fact, whether or not mediation saves money depends on the success rate of mediation. The present research indicates that if all couples were required to attend state-subsidised mediation it would be likely to lead to increased, not reduced, costs.[295] This is because of the extra costs involved where mediation fails. The Newcastle study (based on people volunteering for mediation) suggested that only about 39 per cent of mediations were wholly successful, 41 per cent were partially successful and 20 per cent failed.[296] For the 20 per cent of totally failed mediations[297] there are inevitably greater costs than if the parties had gone to lawyers to begin with, without using mediation.[298] If mediation is partly successful the parties still need to consult lawyers to resolve the remaining issues. But asking a lawyer to resolve 50 per cent of a dispute does not mean incurring only 50 per cent of what the cost would have been had he or she been asked to resolve the whole of the dispute. This is because it is the gathering together of all the facts and information that takes up most of a lawyer's time and this will need to be done whether the lawyer is resolving all or only a part of a dispute. So resolving 50 per cent of a dispute may cost 75 per cent of what the fee would have been for resolving all of a dispute, in which case it is not clear that mediation actually saves costs.[299] Even if the mediation is completely successful, there are some who believe the costs will be greater.[300]

---

[292] Day Sclater (1999: 180).
[293] Sarat and Felstiner (1995).
[294] Law Commission Report 192 (1990).
[295] Walker (2004a: 134).
[296] Newcastle Conciliation Project (1989). In Davis's (2000) research there was 45% agreement on all issues and 24% on some. In Walker (2004) only 25% reached agreement on all issues.
[297] The success rate would be likely to be significantly lower if mediation were forced on all divorcing couples, as the survey covered those who had volunteered to participate in mediation.
[298] Ogus, Jones-Lee, Cloes and McCarthy (1990).
[299] Davis, Clisby, Cumming et al. (2003: 5) found that 57% of their sample stated that their partner was not keen to resolve the legal disputes and compromise.
[300] Burrows (2000).

An important study looking at the comparative costs of mediation and solicitor-based negotiation found that mediation could cost between 65 per cent and 115 per cent of the solicitor-based negotiation.[301] The study suggested that if the success rate for mediation fell below 60 per cent (which the evidence suggests it would be very likely to do), there would be no savings. The success rate of mediation for couples who sought mediation after attending an information meeting under the study for the Legal Services Commission was only 34 per cent for financial cases and 45 per cent for children cases.[302] A more recent study found that 59 per cent of cases were wholly or partially successful for mediation.[303] A study[304] found that the modal costs for non-for-profit mediators was £700; and £1,200 for solicitor-mediators. However, it is impossible to know how much these would have cost had lawyers dealt with these cases. Another survey[305] found that on average a referral to court funded by legal aid cost £930 more than a mediated case. Such statistics are of limited use because it cannot be assumed that the cases that went to court could have been successfully mediated. More importantly it should not just be a question of whether mediation is cheaper, but whether its benefits (or disadvantages) are worth the expenditure (or savings).[306]

## E  The disadvantages of mediation

1. Some opponents of mediation argue that it is in fact impossible for a mediator to be purely impartial.[307] A mediator can influence the content of the agreement, through explicit as well as indirect means, such as body language or the way a mediator responds to one party's proposal.[308] For example, a husband might make a proposal and whether the mediator immediately asks the wife what she thinks about the proposal or asks the husband to expand on the proposal might have a profound effect on the course of the negotiation. Piper,[309] in her study of mediation, notes that a mediator's summaries of what has been said to date plays a crucial role in the mediation and yet often excludes what the mediator believes to be 'non-relevant matters'.[310] Dingwall and Greatbatch found that mediators had 'the parameters of the permissible',[311] in other words a band of orders they thought acceptable. There would be no intervention as long as the negotiations were within that band, but if the mediation appeared to be going beyond that band the mediator would seek to influence the discussion.[312]

   If the mediator does directly or indirectly affect the content of the agreement then there are concerns that mediation will become, in effect, adjudication in secret. The mediator will act like a judge but without having to give any reasons or be publicly accountable for the outcome. For example, one recent study suggested that mediators often spoke of a

---

[301] Bevan and Davis (1999).

[302] Davis, Finch and Barnham (2003: 9). See similar figures for the success rate for mediation in the pilot studies: Walker (2001b: 3).

[303] House of Commons Public Accounts Committee (2007).

[304] Davis, Finch and Barnham (2003).

[305] Walker (2004a).

[306] Reid (2009).

[307] Piper (1993); Dingwall and Greatbatch (1994). As Wilson (2004: 685) points out, a mediator needs to 'connect' with clients and it is difficult to do this without becoming involved.

[308] Dingwall (1988). See Richards (2005: 390) where a mediator discusses the techniques used by mediators if the negotiations are going to lead to what is thought by the mediator to be an inappropriate result.

[309] Piper (1996).

[310] See also Kruk (1998).

[311] Dingwall and Greatbatch (2001).

[312] One example given was that the mediator did not mind whether the father saw the children one weekend in three or four, but would not be happy if the father was to have no contact.

father's right of contact with his children, even though the courts have expressly denied such a right.[313]

2. One powerful criticism of mediation is that mediation can work against the interests of the weaker party.[314] Weakness in the bargaining position may stem from three sources: first, a lack of information, coupled with the inability to verify presented information. Every family lawyer would say that it is common for rich spouses to portray themselves as impoverished. As mediation has a less effective method of checking levels of wealth compared with disclosure mechanisms used by lawyers, it is likely to work against the interests of the less-well-off spouse.[315] A party's lack of personal expert knowledge may also impede their bargaining position. For example, if one party is a trained accountant and the other has an aversion to figures then when the parties discuss what should happen to the pension or the endowment mortgage there might be an inequality of power. The second weakness in the bargaining process may result from a lack of negotiation skills. One party may regularly take part in negotiations in the course of his or her work and may be trained to push for an agreement, while the other may not. The third weakness can be psychological. Women,[316] it is argued by some, are, in general, by nature conflict-averse.[317] They may more readily agree rather than argue, partly as a result of being socially conditioned to avoid conflict.[318] There is also an argument that women generally may put greater value on things that are not material in value and/or they may have lower self-esteem.[319] It may well be that the wife's primary concern is that she keeps the children, and is willing to agree to anything in order to achieve that goal.[320] One survey of the research concluded that generally women were not putting their own interests first in mediation and therefore were losing out to men, who were.[321] There is some evidence that women are more likely to suffer depression than men at the end of a relationship, and this may affect their bargaining ability.[322] However, these points are controversial and there is in fact much debate over whether women do better or worse using mediation.

There are particular concerns about using mediation where the relationship has been characterised by violence.[323] In such cases mediators themselves accept that mediation is unsuitable because co-operation and proper negotiations can only take place where there is no abuse or fear.[324] The concern is whether the mediators can always ascertain those cases where there has been domestic violence.[325] Particularly difficult are cases where the

---

[313] Davis, Pearce, Bird et al. (2000). See further the discussion on contact in Chapter 9.

[314] One study of mediation at a county court found that one quarter mediated without being legally represented.

[315] In their sample, Davis, Clisby, Cumming et al. (2003: 5) found high levels of mistrust among those who were mediating.

[316] Doughty (2009). One does not have to accept the gendered way the argument is presented in order to appreciate its weight. For example, if one party is conflict-averse, regardless of whether they are a man or a woman, they may be at a disadvantage.

[317] Dingwall and Greatbatch (1994) express concerns that mediation may work against people from certain cultural and ethnic backgrounds.

[318] Grillo (1991) argues that women are more concerned than men with keeping the relationship amicable. See Walker (2004a: 138) for research supporting this argument.

[319] Bryan (1992).

[320] Davis and Roberts (1989) argued that there was no evidence that women did worse in mediation, but Bryan (1992), for example, strongly disagrees.

[321] Tilley (2007).

[322] Bryan (1992).

[323] Kaganas and Piper (1994). Contrast Roberts (1996).

[324] Where mediators detect a clear imbalance of power which they cannot counter they should terminate the mediation: Law Society Code of Practice 2004, paras 6.2–6.4.

[325] Diduck and Kaganas (2006: ch. 11).

parties do not regard themselves as victims of domestic violence.[326] In a recent study of mediation it was found that mediators used a variety of techniques to put domestic violence issues to one side.[327]

3. Mediation can be skewed by the norms of society. Neale and Smart have argued that even if one accepts that the mediators and the law are not influencing the agreement, it is wrong to believe that the values of the parties are the only ones that shape the agreement. The norms of society (which may not be legal norms) will predominate.[328] Researchers have found that 'folk myths' concerning what should happen on divorce can play an important part in the mediation.[329] Specifically, Neale and Smart are concerned that if the parties focus on protecting the children's welfare, then the burden of caring for the children will fall mostly on mothers, based on the common assumption that the woman should look after the children.[330] Further, Neale and Smart are concerned that the money and property will be seen as belonging to the wage earner, most often the husband. So the wife will be in the weaker position of arguing for some of 'his' money, rather than discussing how to distribute 'their' money.[331] This may be partly circumvented by allowing the parties to receive legal advice before or during mediation, although the more legal advice is used the greater the costs.

4. There is concern that if mediation becomes widely used, the quality of the court-based procedure and the law itself will suffer, because it will be less often used.[332]

5. As already mentioned, there are concerns over whether mediation affects children's interests. As Richards explains:

> while mediation may do much to help parents reach agreements and set up workable arrangements for children, it cannot protect children's interests. It must rely on the informa-tion about children that the parties bring to the sessions. Necessarily this information will be presented in the light of parental perceptions, hopes, fears, anxieties, and guilt. In most cases this will serve children's interests well enough, but it cannot be termed protection as it is not based on an independent view.[333]

As well as the question of whether mediation will protect the interests of children, there is also the question of whether children should be involved in the proceedings. Many think that children should not be involved in mediation, especially given the tension that is often felt early on in a mediation. There may be a case for having a session with the children once the parties have reached a basic agreement.

6. There are doubts whether mediators have the expertise to consider the complex tax and financial issues which may have to be dealt with on divorce.[334] For example, even experi-enced solicitors struggle with the valuation and sharing of pensions on divorce and most seek expert advice. To expect mediators and the couple to deal with such issues is to expect too much.

---

[326] Davis, Clisby, Cumming et al. (2003: 5) found that 41% of women and 21% of men in their sample stated that fear of violence made it difficult to resolve issues in their case.

[327] Trinder, Firth and Jenks (2010).

[328] Neale and Smart (1997).

[329] Piper (1996).

[330] Walker, McCarthy and Timms (1994) found that women felt greater guilt at the occurrence of the divorce and might therefore be in a weaker bargaining position.

[331] Smart and Neale (1997). The difficulty in distinguishing offers from threats is discussed in Altman (1996).

[332] Ingleby (1997: 400).

[333] Richards (1995b: 225).

[334] Dingwall and Greatbatch (2001).

7. An argument can be made that mediation does not acknowledge the psychological realities of many divorces.[335] Although it would be nice if every divorcing couple amicably reached an agreement over their children and finances, and that would reassure us that all was well with 'the family', the anger, fear and bitterness means such a pleasant picture is for the few. It is anger, bitterness and fear that dominate, rather than a desire to sit down and talk the matter out. In a recent study, 25 per cent of those involved in mediation were dissatisfied with the mediation they received.[336] This was of those who had chosen to receive mediation.

## F The false dichotomy of mediation and litigation

In considering the benefits and disadvantages of mediation it is important to stress that the choice is not between mediation and litigation in the courtroom, but rather between mediation and negotiation between lawyers.[337] The image of lawyers aggressively fighting cases out in the courtroom is exceptional.[338] In fact, few cases actually reach the courts for settlement. In a major study by Ingleby not one case in his sample resulted in a contested final hearing.[339] Davis et al. noted:

> . . . some solicitors gave us the impression that they regarded trials of the ancillary relief issue in much the same light as they viewed the white rhino – a possibly mythical creature which was outside their immediate experience.[340]

A recent study of clients' experiences of solicitors and mediators found no evidence of lawyers as 'aggressive troublemakers'.[341]

Supporters of a lawyer-based approach argue that negotiations between lawyers ensure that the bargaining process is on an equal footing and that values which the law wishes to promote can infiltrate the negotiations. The lawyer also plays an important role in being partisan: being on the side of the client.[342] It is, of course, possible to go through the divorce procedure without using lawyers and mediators. To many clients, having someone to take their side and fight their corner is of great psychological benefit during the trauma of divorce. Interestingly, of clients who had used both lawyers and mediators in one study, 60 per cent stated that their lawyers had been helpful, but only 35 per cent their mediators.[343] In a recent study[344] 67 per cent of those who had divorced said they were satisfied or fairly satisfied with their solicitors; 22 per cent were dissatisfied or very dissatisfied. The complaints particularly centred on the failure of solicitors to take account of the stressful and emotional aspects of the divorce. Satisfaction with solicitors was notably higher than with mediators.[345] A particularly popular form of negotiation through lawyers relies on 'collaborative law'. Lawyers who

---

[335] Day Sclater (1999).
[336] House of Commons Public Accounts Committee (2007).
[337] Eekelaar, Maclean and Beinart (2000).
[338] Davis (2000).
[339] Ingleby (1992).
[340] Davis, Cretney and Collins (1994: 40).
[341] Davis, Finch and Fitzgerald (2001).
[342] Davis, Finch and Fitzgerald (2001).
[343] Davis, Clisby, Cumming et al. (2003: 11).
[344] Newcastle Centre for Family Studies (2004).
[345] For a more negative view of the relationship between solicitors and clients see C. Wright (2006) who finds that clients and solicitors face difficulties in communicating.

sign up to this agree to work together to find a solution that works for both parties. It has received judicial endorsement.[346]

The Legal Services Commission requires all people seeking public funding for a family dispute to attend a meeting with a mediator, who will assess their suitability for mediation.[347] They are only entitled to legal aid if their case is unsuitable for mediation. Research suggests that few of those attending such meetings are enthusiastic or interested in mediation and that in the majority of cases the mediator assesses the case unsuitable for mediation.[348] However, worryingly, a recent study found that 57 per cent of parents who indicated a fear of violence were still deemed suitable for mediation by mediators at the initial meeting.[349] This scheme can be regarded as putting pressure on legal aid clients to use mediation rather than lawyers (a pressure that privately funded clients do not have). Some 13,552 mediations were funded in 2008–09.[350] Given the number of family law cases this is relatively small. Of those funded (presumably just those cases where mediation was particularly suitable) only 68 per cent reached a full or partial agreement.

## 14 Conclusion

The present law on divorce is in a strange state. Although the Matrimonial Causes Act 1973 represents the present law, Parliament has indicated that it regards it as unsatisfactory and proposed reforms through the Family Law Act 1996. However, because of the difficulties revealed in the pilot studies, the Act's divorce reforms have been abandoned. The chapter has focused on the complexity of the role of the state during divorce. On the one hand, there are concerns that if divorce is 'too easy' this may be thought to destabilise marriage. On the other hand, any attempt to make divorce available only to those who can prove that their marriage has broken down may involve the parties in costly and bitter disputes over whether the marriage can be saved. The Family Law Act 1996 can be seen as an attempt by the law to persuade the parties to behave in particular ways on divorce: namely to act without anger or bitterness and to reach amicable settlements. The pilot studies reveal that human nature is not so readily manipulated. The difficulty for the law here is how to channel the strong feelings often produced during divorce through a legal system traditionally designed to be governed by rational thought rather than wild emotion. As Eekelaar suggests:

> We may, however, become uncomfortable when the government intervenes at these points in the institutional processes of marriage and divorce and attempts to impose its own vision of how people should be behaving at these times. At best it risks being made to appear foolish and ineffectual. Worse it can appear heavy-handed, domineering and insensitive . . .[351]

Perhaps the last word should rest with children. A survey of under 10s said that if they could invent a new rule it would be to ban divorce. Parents arguing was the second worst thing in the world; after being fat![352]

---

[346] *S v P (Settlement by Collaborative Law Process)* [2008] 2 FLR 2040.
[347] Legal Services Commission (2004). Davis, Clisby, Cumming et al. (2003) discuss the operation of this provision in practice.
[348] Davis, Pearce, Bird et al. (2000); Davis, Clisby, Cumming et al. (2003).
[349] Davis, Pearce, Bird et al. (2000: 58).
[350] Legal Services Commission (2010).
[351] Eekelaar (1999: 387).
[352] Quoted in Deech (2009b).

## Further reading

**Davis, G.** (2000) *Monitoring Publicly Funded Family Mediation*, London: Legal Services Commission.

**Day Sclater, S. and Piper, C.** (1999) *Undercurrents of Divorce*, Aldershot: Ashgate.

**Deech, R.** (2009b) 'Divorce – A disaster?', *Family Law* 39: 1048.

**Eekelaar, J.** (1991a) *Regulating Divorce*, Oxford: Clarendon Press.

**Eekelaar, J.** (1999) 'Family law: Keeping us "on message"', *Child and Family Law Quarterly* 11: 387.

**Hasson, E.** (2003) 'Divorce law and the Family Law Act 1996', *International Journal of Law, Policy and the Family* 17: 338.

**Irvine, C.** (2009) 'Mediation and Social Norms', *Family Law* 39: 351.

**MacFarlane, J.** (2002) 'Mediating Ethically: the Limits of Codes of Conduct and the Potential of a Reflective Practice Model', *Osgoode Hall Law Journal* 40: 49.

**Reece, H.** (2003) *Divorcing Responsibly*, Oxford: Hart.

**Family property**

The courts' power to redistribute the property of spouses on divorce and make orders for maintenance will be discussed in Chapter 5. In this chapter the parties' financial position during their relationship, whether they are spouses, civil partners or unmarried, will be considered. There are two themes which run through the chapter. The first is to what extent the family should be regarded as individuals each with their own property interests, and to what extent the law should recognise that property is owned by the family as a group of people. Lorna Fox has warned that there are dangers in seeing property as owned by the family as a unit, because that would weaken the interests of each individual member of the family.[1] On the other hand, emphasising the formal property rights of individuals can mean that technicalities of property law dominate, which may not reflect the real intentions of the parties or produce fairness. The second issue is how to deal with disputes between family members and third parties. The difficulty is this: in cases involving disputes between family members the law may want to protect the interests of each member by giving them each an interest in the property, even if the property is formally in the name of only one person. However, so doing causes difficulties when a third party is involved because property which might appear to belong to one person may be subject to the rights of other family members.

## 1 The reality of family finances

As shall be seen, the law does not normally intervene in the way in which the family distributes its money among its members. It is therefore important to understand how families deal with their money and property in the absence of formal legal regulation.

One notable feature of the latter half of the twentieth century was the increasing number of women in paid employment. Now, around 70 per cent of working age women are in employment.[2] Indeed, it has been argued that the lifestyle of many families can only be maintained by having two wage earners.[3] This has led Morgan to maintain that some couples cannot afford a 'traditional marriage' (i.e. where the husband is employed, but the wife does not seek paid employment) and married couples relying on one income cannot afford to have children.[4]

Although at one time stigma attached to a mother who was in employment while raising children, a survey into women's attitudes to combining paid work and raising children

[1] Fox (2005).
[2] Harkness (2005).
[3] Irvine (1999).
[4] Morgan (1999b: 82).

suggested that the stigma is now less.[5] Eight out of ten women accepted that most mothers have to do paid work to support their families these days. However, more than eight out of ten women said that they thought mothers felt guilty about 'leaving' their children, especially if below school age. Notably, the Government launched a scheme known as the 'New Deal',[6] specifically designed to encourage lone parents (the large majority of whom are women) to seek employment.[7]

Despite the widespread existence of families with dual earners, there is still a common presumption that men are the main breadwinners, and this presumption has a powerful effect. For example, even if both people are working, research indicates that if the child falls ill it is far more often the mother rather than the father who takes time off work to care for the child.[8] Pahl argues that:

> inequality in the wider society meshes with inequality within the household. A woman may contribute a higher proportion of her earnings to housekeeping than her husband, but her income is still likely to be regarded as marginal; a man may contribute a lower proportion of his earnings, but he still feels justified in spending more than his wife on leisure because both define him as the breadwinner.[9]

Many more women than men fall into the category of homemakers. Homemakers are largely unpaid and have no access to unemployment or sickness benefits.[10] Further, in social terms the work is undervalued and lacks prestige.

Pahl has identified four systems of money management adopted in families:

1. *Wife management of the whole wage system*. The wife is responsible for managing the finances of the household and is responsible for all expenditure, except for the personal spending of the husband.

2. *Allowance system*. Typically this involves the husband giving the wife a set amount every week or month. She is responsible for paying for specific items of household expenditure and the rest of the money remains under the control of the husband.

3. *Pooling system or shared management*. Here the couple have a joint account or common kitty into which both pay in and from which both draw out.

4. *Independent management system*. Here each spouse has his or her own separate fund and there is no mixing of funds. They reach an agreement over who pays which bills.

Pahl argues that the system adopted can have important consequences on the way money is spent. She explains:

> Where wives control finances a higher proportion of household income is likely to be spent on food and day-to-day living expenses than is the case where husbands control finances; additional income brought into the household by the wife is more likely to be spent on the food than additional money earned by the husband . . . husbands are more likely to spend more on leisure than wives.[11]

In her more recent work Pahl argues that there is increasing individualisation of the control of money within couples, with each to some extent retaining control over his or her own

---

[5] Bryson, Budd, Lewis and Elam (2000).
[6] Outlined in Douglas (2000a).
[7] See further the discussion in Chapter 1 on what constitutes a 'good mother'.
[8] Harkness (2005).
[9] Pahl (1989: 170).
[10] Employment Rights Act 1996, s 161.
[11] Pahl (1989: 151–2).

income and being responsible for 'his or her' expenses. She warns that this has the danger of impoverishing women, especially where women earn less than men, or where women are seen as being responsible for child-care expenses.[12] This view has been backed up by a study of cohabiting couples which found that women often did less well than men out of the way the couple arranged their finances.[13]

Children are also engaged in unpaid work, particularly in babysitting or working in the family business.[14] Children are protected by the Children and Young Persons Act 1933 and the Children (Protection at Work) Regulations 1998,[15] which provide that no child under the age of 14 can be employed in any work other than on an occasional basis or as an employee of the parents in light agricultural or horticultural work. The light work must not jeopardise the child's safety, health, development, attendance at school, or participation in work experience.[16]

## 2  The ownership of family property: general theory

Who owns the family's property?[17] Of course, most of the time there is no need for members of a family to know who in law owns a particular piece of family property. In most families 'who owns the television?' is not a question that is usually asked. (Ownership of the remote control is, of course, another question!) There are, however, a number of reasons why it can be important to know who owns a certain piece of property:

1. If the couple are unmarried then it is crucial to know who owns what because there is no power in the court to redistribute property if the relationship breaks down. Therefore, when the couple separate, each person is entitled to take whatever property is theirs.

2. If someone becomes bankrupt then all of their property falls into the hands of the trustee in bankruptcy. The property of the bankrupt's spouse or partner does not. It is therefore necessary to know whether certain property belongs to the bankrupt person or their partner.

3. If a third party wishes to purchase property it may be important to know who is the owner. Particularly when a house is to be sold, it is necessary to know who the owner of the house is so that he or she can sign the appropriate paperwork. There have been cases where husbands have sold the family home behind their wives' backs. In such cases it is important to know whether the wife had an interest in the property and, if so, whether the purchaser is bound by her interest.

4. On the death of a family member it is important to know who owns what. So, if a wife left all her books to her brother in her will, it would be important to know which books were hers and which books belonged to her husband.

5. Ownership of family property has important symbolic power. At one time the husband owned all of his wife's property. This reflected the fact that he was regarded as in control of all of the family's affairs. It is arguable that if the law were to state that family property is jointly owned, this would reflect a principle of equality between spouses in marriage.

---

[12] Pahl (2004 and 2005).
[13] Vogler (2009).
[14] Discussed in Diduck and Kaganas (2006: ch. 5).
[15] SI 1998/276.
[16] Children and Young Persons Act 1933, s 18.
[17] Under s 17 of the Married Women's Property Act 1882 an application can be made to a court for a declaration of ownership if the couple are married.

Law in this area should seek to pursue three particular aims. First, the law should produce as high a degree of certainty as possible. Secondly, the law should reflect the wishes and expectations of most couples. Thirdly, the law should be practical and easy to apply. Some of the approaches the law could take are as follows:

1. *Sole ownership*. The law could decide that one spouse owns all the family's property. Historically, a woman could not own property in her own right[18] and so the husband owned all the family's property. This approach might have the benefit of certainty, but it would not reflect the expectations of many couples nowadays and would be unacceptable in a society committed to equality between men and women.

2. *Community of property*.[19] The law could state that on marriage (or cohabitation) all property becomes jointly owned.[20] This may be thought to reflect the expectations of most couples, but does it? On marriage would the husband expect a half interest in his wife's collection of shoes? The law could deal with such concerns by producing exceptions to the rule, but these might create uncertainty.[21] Many European regimes have some form of community of property regime and, if harmonisation of the law in this area were to take place across Europe, England and Wales may be required to adopt it.[22]

3. *Community of gains*. The law could be that each party owns the property he or she owned before the marriage (or cohabitation), but all property acquired during the relationship will be jointly owned. Many countries that have adopted this approach have created exceptions for special gifts or inheritance received during the relationship.

4. *Community of common property*. The law could take the approach that all items intended for joint use would be jointly owned.[23] So the car, television, cooker, etc. would be jointly owned but the wife's golf clubs would not. This approach could be criticised on the basis that in some cases there might be doubt whether a particular item was for common use, and this could cause uncertainty over ownership.

5. *Purchaser-based ownership*. Another option is simply to use the normal rules of property and not create any particular regime for couples. In effect this would mean that the person who buys a piece of property owns it. The objection to this is that it may be a matter of chance whose money happened to be used to buy a piece of property.

6. *Intention-based ownership*. The law could decide that ownership would be determined by the intentions of the parties. There would have to be rules that would apply if it were not possible to discover the parties' intentions. This approach would have the disadvantage of making it particularly difficult for third parties to ascertain the ownership of a piece of property.

As we shall see, the law of England and Wales does not plump for one or other of these approaches but instead is based on a rather arbitrary set of rules, which have developed over the years. Cretney[24] has argued that, following the decision in *White v White*,[25] 'in substance (albeit not in form) English law now has a matrimonial regime of deferred community of

---

18. The Married Women's Property Act 1882 has removed the incapacity of the wife to own property.
19. Barlow, Callus and Cooke (2004). Some countries have 'deferred community of property', which only comes into play on separation.
20. See, e.g., Family Law (Scotland) Act 1985.
21. Law Commission Report 175 (1988: para 3.2).
22. Barlow, Callus and Cooke (2004).
23. Basically the approach proposed by Law Commission Report 175 (1988).
24. Cretney (2003d: 412).
25. [2001] AC 596.

property'. That case (and the law on financial orders on divorce generally) is discussed in detail in Chapter 5. For now, suffice it to say that it advocates equal division of a couple's assets on divorce in some cases. Cretney's argument has not received widespread support, not least because the equal division of assets following **White** applies only in a minority of cases. The Law Commission did produce a report in an attempt to formulate a more coherent approach, although it found it difficult to find a single principle that could apply across the board, and its proposals were not implemented by Parliament.[26]

Before setting out the law it is necessary to distinguish between real property and personal property. Basically, real property is land and buildings, personal property is all other kinds of property (e.g. books, cars, CDs).

## 3 The ownership of personal property

So, how do the courts decide who owns what? The law can be summarised with the following statements:

1. Income belongs to the person who earns it.[27] So if a wife is employed, her salary belongs to her.

2. Personal property prima facie belongs to the person whose money was used to buy the property.[28] This is a presumption which can be rebutted.[29] For example, if a husband bought his wife perfume it may well be that the court would find the presumption rebutted and that the perfume belonged to the wife, not the husband.

3. Ownership of property can be transferred from one person to another if there is effective delivery of the property[30] with evidence that it is intended as a gift. So, if a wife hands a piece of property to her husband saying that it is a present for him, this would be an effective transfer of ownership from her to him.

4. The act of marriage, engagement or cohabitation itself does not change ownership of property.

There are a number of scenarios where the law is a little more complicated, and these will now be discussed in detail.

### A Jointly used bank accounts

Where the parties pool their incomes into a common account, it seems that normally they both have a joint interest in the whole fund.[31] The crucial question is: what is the purpose for which the fund is held? The leading case is **Jones v Maynard**.[32] The husband authorised his wife to draw from his bank account. Although the husband's contribution to the account was greater than the wife's, they treated the account as a joint account. When the marriage was dissolved the ownership of the account became an issue. Vaisey J argued:

---

[26] Law Commission Report 175 (1988).
[27] *Heseltine v Heseltine* [1971] 1 All ER 952.
[28] *The Up-Yaws* [2007] EWHC 210 (Admlty).
[29] *Re Whittaker* (1882) 21 Ch D 657.
[30] *Re Cole* [1904] Ch 175.
[31] This is so regardless of in whose name the account stands.
[32] [1951] Ch 572.

In my view a husband's earnings or salary, when the spouses have a common purse and pool their resources, are earnings made on behalf of both; and the idea that years afterwards the contents of the pool can be dissected by taking an elaborate account as to how much was paid in by the husband or the wife is quite inconsistent with the original fundamental idea of a joint purpose or common pool. In my view the money which goes into the pool becomes joint property.

So the court should focus on the intentions of the parties. Was the account intended to be a 'common purse'? If the account was in both names then it is very likely it will be regarded as joint. This is true whether the couple are spouses, civil partners or cohabitants. Even if it was in only one person's name the court will examine whether in fact the fund was used jointly.

Where property is bought using a joint bank account the key issue will be the intentions of the parties.[33] If the purchased item was for joint use it is likely to be jointly owned. However, if the property was bought for the use of one of the parties then it seems likely that it will be regarded as belonging to that party. So, if a woman bought a rare stamp for her stamp collection using money from a joint bank account then the stamp is likely to be seen as hers, but if she bought a sofa it will probably be seen as for joint use and therefore jointly owned.[34] In *Re Bishop*[35] investments were purchased from the common fund. Some were purchased in joint names, others in the name of the husband and one in the wife's name. It was held that the fact that the investments were put in specified names indicated they were owned by the named parties.

## B Housekeeping and maintenance allowance

According to s 1 of the Married Women's Property Act 1964:

### LEGISLATIVE PROVISION

**Married Women's Property Act 1964, section 1**

If any question arises as to the right of a husband or wife to money derived from any allowance made by either of them for the expenses of the matrimonial home or for similar purposes, or to any property acquired out of such money, the money or property shall, in the absence of any agreement between them to the contrary, be treated as belonging to them in equal shares.

The provision was amended in the Equality Act 2010[36] so that it applies to husbands and wives in the same way.[37] The Act only applies to spouses or civil partners. It does not apply to cohabitants, nor engaged couples. However, for engaged couples and cohabitants the courts may still decide that the parties intended to share such property. Little use seems to be made of the Act, perhaps because it is based on a rather outdated scenario of family finances.

## C Gifts from one partner to the other

Where it is clear that one party intended to make a gift and transferred possession of the property to the other party, then ownership passed from one to the other. So if a wife

[33] See *Re Northall* [2010] EWHC 1448.
[34] A specific agreement could rebut these presumptions.
[35] [1965] Ch 450.
[36] Section 200.
[37] Section 70A of the Civil Partnership Act 2004 has a similar provision for civil partners.

purchased a book using money from her own bank account the law will presume it belongs to her. However, if she wrapped it up and presented it to her husband on his birthday ownership passed to him.[38]

## D Gifts to partners from third parties

Where a third party makes a gift to a couple, ownership of the gift depends on the donor's intention. This intention can be inferred from the surrounding circumstances. For example, it is reasonable to assume that a wedding gift was intended for joint ownership unless there is evidence to the contrary.[39] By contrast, a birthday present given to the husband will be presumed to belong to him alone.

## E Improvements to personal property

If a spouse, civil partner or fiancé(e) (but not a cohabitant) does work that improves a piece of property, then he or she can rely on s 37 of the Matrimonial Proceedings and Property Act 1970 to establish an interest in the property. We will discuss this provision later when real property is considered.[40]

## F Express declarations of trust

An owner of a piece of personal property can declare him or herself trustee of it. The declaration can be oral and does not require the use of formal language. For example, in *Rowe v Prance*[41] a man bought a boat and wrote to his lover referring to what he would like to do with her on 'our boat'. This was held by the court to be sufficient evidence of an express declaration of trust and he therefore shared equitable ownership with his lover.[42]

## G Criticisms of the present law

The present law has been widely criticised.[43] The Law Commission has characterised the existing rules as arbitrary, uncertain and unfair.[44] There is too much emphasis placed on who purchased a piece of property, while this is often a matter of chance. Some of the presumptions seem out of date and based on sexist presumptions no longer appropriate for our law. Further, there is also much uncertainty over when an express trust can be found. The case of *Rowe v Prance*, which we have just discussed, demonstrates that even casual comments can have legal significance attached to them, perhaps out of all proportion to their intended effect. By contrast, there may be couples whose general lifestyle demonstrates that they wish to share everything, but if there are no statements which reflect this, they may have difficulty in proving co-ownership.[45] An unmarried couple who go to court for an order deciding who owns their collection of CDs could find themselves in for a protracted court case.

---

[38] The presumption of advancement (that a husband intended to give his wife a gift when transferring property to her) was abolished by Equality Act 2010, s 199.
[39] *Midland Bank v Cooke* [1995] 4 All ER 562, [1995] 2 FLR 915.
[40] See pages 167–8.
[41] [1999] 2 FLR 787.
[42] See also *Haywood v Haywood*, unreported, 13.7.2000.
[43] See, e.g., Tee (2001).
[44] Law Commission Report 175 (1988: para 1.4).
[45] Although the court has shown a willingness to find a common intention in *Haywood v Haywood*, unreported, 13.7.2000.

## 4 Maintenance during marriage

The law on the payment of maintenance on divorce will be discussed in Chapter 5. This section will consider maintenance payments during marriage and cohabitation.

### A Unmarried cohabitants

There is no obligation on one unmarried partner to support the other. However, there is an obligation on a parent to provide for children whether the parents are married or not. This will be discussed in Chapter 5. Income could result, however, from an order under s 40 of the Family Law Act 1996, requiring a party to make payments of maintenance for the dwelling house, or rent or mortgage, in connection with an occupation order.[46]

### B Married couples

There are two potential sources of maintenance liability for spouses while the couple are married: from statutes and from separation agreements reached between themselves. We will discuss the liability to maintain spouses on divorce in Chapter 5. The common law duty on a husband to maintain a wife was abolished by the Equality Act 2010.[47]

#### (i) Statutory obligations to maintain

Research suggests that although there are statutory means of enforcing an obligation to pay maintenance during the marriage, in practice very small sums are involved and they are rarely collected.[48] No doubt many spouses who have separated rely on benefits or earnings while pursuing divorce proceedings. The liability to support a child under the Child Support Act 1991 dominates the financial relationship between parties prior to divorce.

There are four statutory provisions that are relevant for spousal maintenance during marriage:

1. Under s 2 of the Domestic Proceedings and Magistrates' Court Act 1978, periodical payments orders and lump sum orders for less than £1,000[49] can be made. Section 1 sets out the criteria:

---

**LEGISLATIVE PROVISION**

**Domestic Proceedings and Magistrates' Court Act 1978, section 1**

Either party to a marriage may apply to a magistrates' court for an order under section 2 of this Act on the ground that the other party to the marriage—

(a) has failed to provide reasonable maintenance for the applicant; or

(b) has failed to provide, or to make a proper contribution towards, reasonable maintenance for any child of the family; or

(c) has behaved in such a way that the applicant cannot reasonably be expected to live with the respondent; or

(d) has deserted the applicant.

---

[46] Discussed in Chapter 6.
[47] Section 198.
[48] Cretney, Masson and Bailey-Harris (2002: 78).
[49] There is no such limitation if there is a consent order.

In calculating the level of spousal maintenance, the first consideration is the welfare of any minors and there is a list of factors to consider, virtually identical to those in s 25 of the Matrimonial Causes Act 1973.[50] Sums that are awarded are usually small. In *E v C (Child Maintenance)*[51] it was held to be inappropriate to order a man on income support to pay £5 per week. In fact if someone is on income support it would only be appropriate to order a nominal sum. Applications under this statute are made to the magistrates' court. This is a cheaper procedure than the other three provisions and is therefore the most popular.

2. Under s 27 of the Matrimonial Causes Act 1973 periodic payment and lump sum orders can be made without limit. It is necessary to show that the respondent has failed to provide reasonably for the spouse or for a child of the family. The provision is only available for married couples.

3. Prior to divorce and nullity or judicial separation it is possible to apply for maintenance pending suit.[52] Interim lump sum orders can now be made.[53]

4. Section 40 of the Family Law Act 1996 can require the payment of rent, mortgage, and outgoings in respect of a property when an occupation order is made.[54]

### (ii) Separation agreements

Especially before divorce became more readily available, private agreements were a popular option for couples who could not divorce (or did not want to divorce) but intended to separate. Nowadays separation agreements are often used by couples to deal with the parties' financial affairs while waiting for the final financial orders to be made. An agreement is only binding if the normal requirements of contract law are in place. In particular, there must be an intention to create legal relations.[55] There is a presumption that agreements between married couples are not intended to be legally binding.[56] The law's approach to such agreements is that they can be legally enforced, but are open to alteration by the courts. In other words, the court's jurisdiction to redistribute property on divorce cannot be ousted by private agreements.[57] The issue is considered further in Chapter 5.

## 5 Ownership of real property: the family home

The home is the most valuable asset that many people own. This is true not just in monetary terms but in emotional terms: to many people the home is of great psychological importance.[58] A dispute over ownership of the home can therefore be particularly heated. We will first consider how the law determines who owns a house.[59] This is particularly important for unmarried couples because at the end of their relationship the court has no jurisdiction to require one party to transfer their share of the home to the other and can only declare who at the moment owns the house.

[50] Discussed in Chapter 5.
[51] [1995] 1 FLR 472, [1996] 1 FCR 612.
[52] Matrimonial Causes Act 1973, s 22; see *G v G (Maintenance Pending Suit: Costs)* [2003] Family Law 393.
[53] Matrimonial Causes Act 1973, s 22A(4).
[54] See Chapter 6.
[55] *Soulsbury v Soulsbury* [2007] 3 FCR 811.
[56] *Balfour v Balfour* [1919] 2 KB 571.
[57] *Jessell v Jessell* [1979] 1 WLR 1148 at p. 1152.
[58] Indeed article 8 of the ECHR protects the right to respect for one's home. See further Barlow (2007) and Fox (2007).
[59] Although references will be made to a house, the law is essentially the same over flats.

English and Welsh law has not developed a special regime for dealing with family homes.[60] So the law governing the family home is the same as that concerning any two people who happen to share a house, whether they be business partners or lovers.[61] As a result of the way in which the law has evolved, it is necessary to distinguish ownership of property at law and at equity.

## A  Legal ownership

Determining ownership of land[62] is not difficult. If the land is registered,[63] the legal owner can be determined by discovering who is registered as the owner of the land. If the land is not registered, it is necessary to discover into whose name the lease or property was conveyed. Section 52(1) of the Law of Property Act 1925 makes clear that legal title can only be conveyed by deed.[64] So words alone cannot transfer legal ownership.

Just because someone owns the property at common law, it does not mean they are the absolute owner, because the legal owner may hold the property on trust for someone else. It is therefore necessary to consider who owns the property in equity.

## B  Equitable ownership

In the eyes of equity it matters not in whose name the property is registered, nor into whose name the property was conveyed. In equity the legal owner of the property may be found to hold the property on trust for someone else who will then have an equitable interest in the property. A trust may be express or implied.

### (i) Express trusts

The leading statutory provision is s 53(1)(b) of the Law of Property Act 1925, which states that a declaration of trust in respect of land must be manifested and proved in writing. So an oral statement from the owner that they wish to hold the land on trust for someone else would not be sufficient for an express trust.[65] It may be that there is a trust deed that sets out the shares of the parties in equity. The deed may be part of the conveyance (for example, the conveyance may specifically state that the property is transferred 'to A to hold on trust for A and B in shares of 60 per cent and 40 per cent respectively') or there may be a separate document signed by the owner setting out the terms of the trust. In these cases, unless there is any fraud or mistake, this document will identify the shares and there will be no need for the court to consider the ownership question further.[66] This was made clear in *Goodman* v *Gallant*.[67] It is therefore highly advisable for a couple purchasing a house to make it quite clear the shares they are to own in equity.[68] It should be noted that simply putting the house into joint names leads to a presumption that they intend each other to have an equal share of the equitable interest, but that presumption can be rebutted.[69]

---

[60] For an excellent discussion see Mee (1999).
[61] *Pettitt* v *Pettitt* [1970] AC 777; *Gissing* v *Gissing* [1971] 1 AC 886.
[62] Land here includes ownership of the house on the land.
[63] Eventually the Land Registration Act 2002 will end unregistered title.
[64] Law of Property (Miscellaneous Provisions) Act 1989, s 2.
[65] Although such a statement may well form the basis of an implied trust.
[66] *Clarke* v *Harlowe* [2006] Fam Law 846.
[67] [1986] 1 FLR 513.
[68] *Springette* v *Defoe* [1992] 2 FLR 388 at p. 390, per Dillon LJ.
[69] *Stack* v *Dowden* [2007] UKHL 17.

However, all too often there is no written declaration of interests. Typically this arises where one person buys a house and later on his or her partner moves in. The parties do not think about seeing a lawyer to produce a written document. In such cases s 53(2) of the Law of Property Act 1925 is crucial, because it states that s 53(1) does not affect the creation of implied, resulting and constructive trusts. So in the absence of a formal document it is necessary to turn to the law of implied trusts.[70]

## (ii) Implied trusts

There are three areas that need to be considered: resulting trusts, constructive trusts and proprietary estoppel. As we shall see, the role now played by resulting trusts in relation to the family home is small.[71]

### (a) Resulting trusts

The presumption of a resulting trust is that if A and B both contribute to the purchase price[72] of a house and the property is put into B's name then, although B will be owner at common law, she will hold it on trust (a resulting trust) for herself and A. Similarly, if A transfers property into B's name, without B providing any consideration,[73] then B will hold the property on trust solely for A. Both of these resulting trusts are presumptions, based on the belief that people do not give money or property expecting nothing in return. The presumption can be rebutted if it can be shown that the contribution to the purchase price was given as a gift or a loan.[74] For example, if an aunt helps provide the purchase price for her nephew's first house it may readily be shown that she intended this money to be a gift and did not intend him to hold it on trust for her.

At one time the presumption of the resulting trust did not apply if there is a close relationship between A and B.[75] In such a case it was presumed that A intended to make a gift to B. This was known as the presumption of advancement. It was abolished in section 199 of the Equality Act 2010.

### (b) Constructive trusts

The law on constructive trusts is now governed by the decision of the House of Lords in *Lloyds Bank v Rosset*,[76] although it has been developed by some more recent decisions.[77] To appreciate the decision it is important to consider some of the earlier case law. Some of the cases prior to *Rosset* had suggested that the court could find a constructive trust if it thought that the fairness of the case demanded it; other cases had suggested that a constructive trust could be found if this accorded with the parties' intentions, but that these intentions could be inferred (invented, critics would say) by the courts. Lord Bridge feared that such approaches led to too much uncertainty and so he sought to tighten up the circumstances in which the courts could find a constructive trust. He stated that a constructive trust could be found only if: (1) there is a common intention to share ownership; and (2) the party seeking to establish the constructive trust has relied on the common intention to his or her detriment. These two requirements need to be considered in further detail.

---

[70] *Gissing v Gissing* [1971] 1 AC 886.
[71] *Fowler v Barron* [2008] EWCA Civ 377.
[72] See *Huntingford v Hobbs* [1993] 1 FLR 736 for a discussion of the position where a mortgage is used.
[73] E.g. a payment.
[74] *Sekhon v Alissa* [1989] 2 FLR 94.
[75] *Lavelle v Lavelle* [2004] 2 FCR 418 at p. 421.
[76] [1991] 1 AC 107. For a useful discussion of the law on constructive trusts see Sawyer (2004).
[77] In particular *Stack v Dowden* [2007] UKHL 17 and *Abbott v Abbott* [2007] UKPC 53.

### 1. *Common intent*

There are two well-established ways of establishing common intent:

(i) 'Any agreement, arrangement or understanding reached between them that the property is to be shared beneficially.'[78]

(ii) A common intent can be inferred from a direct contribution to the purchase price or mortgage instalment.

It seems that the courts may be willing to find evidence of a common intention, even if neither of these is established. However, in the absence of these two well-established ways, proving a common intention will be an uphill task.

The above means of establishing a common intention will now be considered separately. We will then consider when the courts might be willing to find a common intention in their absence.

First let us consider the agreement to share ownership. This requires evidence of an actual conversation between the parties in which it was agreed that the parties would share owner-ship. It is not enough that there is a mutual, but uncommunicated, belief.[79] There must be proof that a conversation took place.[80] It should be stressed that the agreement must be to share ownership, not just to share occupation.[81] It seems an agreement that a party might have a share of the ownership in certain circumstances in the future would be sufficient if those circumstances indeed materialised.[82]

Lord Bridge accepted that it is not easy to prove an oral agreement, but that evidence of agreements can be introduced 'however imperfectly remembered and however imprecise their terms must have been'.[83] The difficulties with this have been recognised in *Hammond* v *Mitchell* by Waite J who noted that:

> the tenderest exchanges of a common law courtship may assume an unforeseen significance many years later when they are brought under equity's microscope and subjected to an analysis under which many thousands of pounds of value may be liable to turn on this fine question as to whether the relevant words were spoken in earnest or in dalliance and with or without representational intent.[84]

Cases following *Rosset* have been very willing to find evidence of common intention. The following comments have been evidence of an agreement: 'Don't worry about the future because when we are married [the house] will be half yours anyway and I'll always look after you and [our child]';[85] and 'You need a secure home.'[86] These examples are controversial because the promises appear to relate to rights in the future, rather than being agreements to share in the present, which is what Lord Bridge required. It may be that the judgments after *Rosset* are trying to loosen the strictness of the approach taken by Lord Bridge, although, in a

---

[78] *Lloyds Bank* v *Rosset* [1991] 1 AC 107.

[79] *Fowler* v *Barron* [2008] EWCA Civ 377, discussed in Hayward (2009).

[80] Although the Court of Appeal has suggested it might be willing to infer from the surrounding circumstances that there was a conversation agreeing to share the property: *Springette* v *Defoe* [1992] 2 FLR 388 at p. 395; *Hyett* v *Stanley* [2003] 3 FCR 253.

[81] *Lloyds Bank* v *Rosset* [1990] 1 All ER 1111 at p. 1115; *G* v *G (Matrimonial Property: Rights of Extended Family)* [2005] EWHC 1560 (Admin).

[82] *Ledger-Beadell* v *Peach and Ledger-Beadell* [2006] EWHC 2940 (Ch).

[83] In *Lightfoot* v *Lightfoot-Brown* [2005] EWCA Civ 201, Arden LJ (at para 23) said that even if the terms of the agreement were 'imprecise' the court could still find a common intent.

[84] *Hammond* v *Mitchell* [1992] 2 All ER 109 at p. 121. See also *Buggs* v *Buggs* [2003] EWHC 1538 (Fam).

[85] *Hammond* v *Mitchell* [1992] 2 All ER 109, [1992] 1 FLR 229.

[86] *Savil* v *Goodall* [1993] 1 FLR 755, [1994] 1 FCR 325.

more recent decision, the comment concerning improvements to a property 'this will benefit us both' and an assurance to his partner that if he were to die 'you will be well provided for' were insufficient to found a claim for a constructive trust.[87]

Lord Bridge stated there were two 'outstanding examples' of the kind of agreements revealing common intention that he had in mind. Both cases involved property which was in the man's name and he gave an excuse to his partner for not putting the property into their joint names.[88] In *Eves v Eves*[89] the man (untruthfully) stated that his partner was too young to be put on the title deed. In *Grant v Edwards*[90] the man involved (again untruthfully) said he would not put the property into their joint names because it would prejudice a dispute between her and her husband (whom she was divorcing). Some commentators have pointed out that these cases, far from showing a common intention that the property was to be shared, in fact indicate that the men did not intend that their partners should have a share. Others have supported these cases on the basis that in each instance the men, having led the women to believe it was their intent that the property should be in their joint names, cannot deny there was a common intention to share ownership.

If it is not possible to find evidence of an express agreement to share, then it will be necessary to infer an agreement to share. The only circumstance in which Lord Bridge was willing to accept that such an inference could be made was where there was a direct contribution to the purchase price or at least one of the mortgage instalments. It should be stressed that Lord Bridge required a *direct* contribution. Arden LJ in *Lightfoot v Lightfoot-Brown*[91] said that the payment had to be 'referable to the acquisition of the house'. This appears to mean that if the woman paid all of the household expenses while the man paid the mortgage instalments then she would not be able to rely on an implied common intention, even though the man could only meet the mortgage instalments because she had paid the household bills.[92]

But what if the claimant is not able to show that there was an agreement to share ownership nor able to show a financial contribution to the purchase price? Lord Bridge in *Rosset* appeared to suggest that in such a case a constructive trust cannot be found. However, we now have several dicta from law lords questioning whether Rosset should be interpreted so strictly. In *Stack v Dowden*[93] Baroness Hale suggested that Rosset had set the hurdle for a constructive trust 'rather too high'.[94] Lord Walker questioned whether 'the law had moved on' and questioned whether it had been consistent with earlier decisions.[95] In *Abbott v Abbott*[96] the Privy Council stated that 'the law has undoubtedly moved on' since *Rosset*. They suggested that the whole course of conduct of the parties could be examined in order to consider whether the parties intended to share the property. However, these dicta leave it unclear quite what the current law is and when the courts will be willing to find a common intention in the absence of the *Rosset* grounds. In *Thomson v Humphrey*[97] Warren J held that it would not be helpful to set out precisely what kinds of conduct could or could not lead to a finding of common intention. Each case should be deal with on its own merits. Certainly something more than simply

[87] *James v Thomas* [2007] 3 FCR 696; discussed in Piska (2009).
[88] See, for a more recent example, *Van Laethem v Brooker* [2006] 1 FCR 697.
[89] [1975] 3 All ER 768.
[90] [1987] 1 FLR 87.
[91] [2005] EWCA Civ 201, para 23.
[92] *Ivin v Blake* (1993) 67 P&CR 263. Although there is notable academic support for the kind of approach adopted in *Le Foe v Le Foe* [2007] 1 FCR 107. See, for example, Douglas (2004: 103).
[93] [2007] UKHL 17.
[94] Para 63.
[95] Para 63.
[96] [2007] UKPC 53.
[97] [2009] EWHC 3576 (Ch).

living in the house will be required. A financial contribution will be sufficient, but there may be other forms of conduct from which the courts will find intention. As yet it is far from clear what that will be. One possibility is that the courts will ask whether the best explanation for the behaviour of the parties is that they were assuming they equally owned the property.

### 2. Detrimental reliance

According to *Rossett* a common intent to share is not in and of itself sufficient for a constructive trust. There must also be acts showing that a party has relied on that common intention to his or her detriment.[98] However, considerable uncertainty surrounds this requirement. First, it is far from clear what constitutes detrimental reliance. Second, there are some doubts over whether the requirement exists at all.

The approach with the most authority is that detrimental reliance requires conduct upon which the claimant 'could not reasonably have been expected to embark unless she was to have an interest in the house'.[99] In *Eves v Eves*[100] the act of reliance was the woman's manual work on the property, including breaking up concrete, demolishing and rebuilding a shed, and renovating the house. This conduct was held to be detrimental reliance because it was not the kind of conduct one would expect from a 'normal' female cohabitant. It could therefore be inferred that she must have acted in this way because she believed she had an interest in the property. By contrast, in *Thomas v Fuller-Brown*[101] a man who moved in with a woman and carried out various pieces of DIY around the house did not thereby acquire an interest in it. This was partly because the acts of DIY were the kind of things a man living in the house could be expected to have done, and so was not the type of conduct he would only have performed had he believed he had an interest in the property. In *Rosset* the wife's conduct in supervising the builders because her husband was abroad was insufficient to amount to detrimental reliance as 'it would seem the most natural thing in the world for any wife, in the absence of her husband abroad, to spend all the time she could'[102] working on the house, and therefore did not reveal that she believed that she had an interest in the house. In *Crossley v Crossley*,[103] assuming joint liability for the mortgage payments on the property was detrimental reliance. Several of these examples demonstrate the danger that gender stereotyping can determine whether a party is able to establish detrimental reliance or not.

There is some authority for alternative approaches. Sir Nicholas Browne-Wilkinson V-C (as he then was) suggested that detrimental reliance requires any conduct of the kind that relates to a couple's 'joint lives' together.[104] This is a very liberal interpretation of the requirement; it simply stipulates that there were detrimental acts that related to the couple's joint lives. This might include caring for the couple's children or a substantial amount of housework. If a couple were living together it would almost be inevitable that there would be acts that were referable to their joint lives together. Whichever approach is taken, a direct contribution to the purchase price or mortgage instalments can constitute detrimental reliance. This means that such payments will be evidence from which both a common intention can be inferred

---

[98] *Chan Pui Chun v Leung Kam Ho* [2003] 1 FCR 520 CA. See also *Churchill v Roach* [2004] 3 FCR 744 where, although detrimental acts were found before the agreement to share ownership, none were found after and so there could be no constructive trust.

[99] Nourse LJ in *Grant v Edwards* [1986] Ch 638, [1987] 1 FLR 87. See also *Chan Pui Chun v Leung Kam Ho* [2003] 1 FCR 520.

[100] [1975] 3 All ER 768.

[101] [1988] 1 FLR 237.

[102] [1990] 1 All ER 1111 at p. 1117.

[103] [2005] EWCA Civ 1581.

[104] *Grant v Edwards* [1986] Ch 638 at p. 657.

and detrimental reliance shown and therefore in and of them establish a constructive trust. Notably *Stack v Dowden*[105] and *Abbott v Abbott*[106] do not mention the requirement of reliance, causing one leading commentator to refer to 'the demise' of the reliance requirement.[107] In *de Bruyne v de Bruyne*[108] it was held that a constructive trust could be imposed even in the absence of detrimental reliance, as long as there were other circumstances which meant that it would be unconscionable for the owner to hold the property absolutely. Perhaps the best view is that proof of detrimental reliance will assist a party seeking to establish a constructive trust, but its absence is not necessarily fatal to a claim.

### 3. Calculating what share a party is entitled to under a constructive trust

The shares the parties are entitled to under a constructive trust are determined by the parties' intentions.[109] However, if we do not know what the parties intended because, for example, the couple never discussed sharing, then the court must attempt to infer their intention by referring to all the evidence in the case. This was the approach as stated by the House of Lords in *Stack v Dowden*.[110] They rejected an approach of asking: 'What would be a fair share for each party having regard to the whole course of dealing between them in relation to the property?'[111] The focus must be on the intentions of the parties, rather than fairness.

The court, in seeking to ascertain the common intention of the parties, should consider the whole of their course of conduct.[112] Baroness Hale held that financial contributions would be an important factor to take into account; so, too, would the following:

> any advice or discussions at the time of the transfer which cast light upon their intentions then; . . . the purposes for which the home was acquired; the nature of the parties' relationship; whether they had children for whom they both had responsibility to provide a home; how the purchase was financed, both initially and subsequently; how the parties arranged their finances, whether separately or together or a bit of both; how they discharged the outgoings on the property and their other household expenses.[113]

She explained that although how much each contributed financially was relevant, it would be quite possible to conclude that 'they intended that each should contribute as much to the household as they reasonably could and that they would share the eventual benefit or burden equally'.[114] In such a case an applicant may be entitled to a 50 per cent share even though she had contributed to less than 50 per cent of the purchase price. In the particular case before their lordships the parties kept their financial affairs 'rigidly separate' and took careful notice of who paid for what. In that case it was found that the financial contributions should be particularly significant in ascertaining their contributions.[115] Where the property purchased is an investment property held in joint names, with no declaration of beneficial interest, the court will focus only the financial contributions of the parties.[116]

---

[105] [2007] UKHL 17.
[106] [2007] UKPC 53.
[107] Gardner (2008).
[108] [2010] 2 FCR 251.
[109] *Crossley v Crossley* [2006] 1 FCR 655. There it was emphasised that if it is clear what the parties' intentions were there is no need to consider what a 'fair share' of the equitable interest would be.
[110] [2007] UKHL 17; followed in *Qayyum v Hameed* [2009] 2 FLR 962.
[111] As proposed *Oxley v Hiscock* [2004] 2 FCR 295 at para 69.
[112] *Fowler v Barron* [2008] EWCA Civ 377.
[113] Para 69.
[114] Para 69. See Burgoyne et al. (2006) for a sociological discussion of how unmarried couples understand their finances.
[115] See also *Fowler v Barron* [2008] 2 FCR 1.
[116] *Laskar v Laskar* [2008] EWCA Civ 347.

As Baroness Hale's quote demonstrates, in ascertaining the parties' intentions, financial matters are just one factor to take into account, albeit a very important one. The court will be willing to look at all of the circumstances of the case to ascertain their intentions as to shares. However, a secret intention of one of the parties will not be relevant.[117] The court should not take into account factors that do not shed light on the intentions of the parties, even though fairness might suggest they should be taken into account.[118] Baroness Hale did acknowledge that the intentions of the parties may change over time.[119] The fact that early on in their relationship it was decided that just the man would own the property does not preclude a conclusion that by the end of the relationship they were intending to share the property equally.

Where the parties have put the property in joint names[120] but not indicated their beneficial interests there is a presumption that they intended to share it equally.[121] That presumption applies even if one or both of the parties did not appreciate the significance of putting the property in joint names.[122] However, the presumption can be rebutted if there is clear evidence as to the parties' intentions.[123] What is unclear after *Stack v Dowden* is how strong the evidence has to be to rebut the presumption.[124] The most that can be said is that their lordships stated the presumption is hard to rebut. Rimmer LJ has subsequently explained 'a bid by a joint purchaser to establish a greater beneficial interest than a joint interest will involve the steepest of climbs, usually resulting in a failure to attain the summit'.[125]

---

**CASE: *Kernott v Jones* [2010] EWCA Civ 578**

The couple bought a property in joint names. They later separated and for twelve years the woman lived in the property and paid for its maintenance and mortgage, while the man made no contribution at all. It was found that this conduct was insufficient to rebut the presumption of an intention to share the property equally. The fact that one party had made a greater financial contribution to the property or that one party had not lived in the property for some time was not sufficient to rebut the presumption of shared ownership. Rimmer LJ interpreted *Stack v Dowden* to mean that the courts could not invent an intention to rebut the presumption in a joint names case, the search had to be made for a real intention. As he noted, it would be difficult to find one in the absence of an actual conversation.[126] In this case there was no evidence of an actual intention which could rebut the presumption that because the property was in joint names it should be jointly owned.

---

[117] *Fowler v Barron* [2008] 2 FCR 1.
[118] *Holman v Howes* [2007] EWCA Civ 877.
[119] Para 62.
[120] While this presumption can play an important role only 30% of cohabitants live in accommodation that is in joint names: Probert (2007a).
[121] *Stack v Dowden* [2007] UKHL 17. For an excellent discussion of this case see George (2008). Due to a change in the forms used in conveyancing it should be rare in the future for property to be held in joint names but for there to be no indication as to how the property is to be held.
[122] *Fowler v Barron* [2008] 2 FCR 1.
[123] *Stack v Dowden* [2007] UKHL 17.
[124] Probert (2007a) suggests that there was little exceptional about the facts in the case itself, where the presumption was rebutted.
[125] *Kernott v Jones* [2010] EWCA Civ 578, para 72.
[126] See also *Walsh v Singh* [2010] 1 FLR 1658.

> Jacob LJ dissented. He complained:
>
> Even though this case is a 'cautionary tale', decisions of this Court will not change the way people behave. In the real world unmarried couples seldom enter into express agreements into what should happen to property should the relationship fail and often do not settle matters clearly when they do. Life is untidier than that. In reality human emotional relationships simply do not operate as if they were commercial contracts and it is idle to wish that they did.[127]
>
> He supported the approach of the trial judge in looking at all the circumstances and imputing an intention that the woman have 90 per cent of the property.

Simon Gardner proposes the following as a possible summary of the current law. He distinguishes the single name scenario (where legal title to a house is held by D alone; there is no express trust in favour of C); and the joint names scenario (where the title is in the names of D and C, without an express trust).

(i)   In the single name scenario, C prima facie has no interest, while in the joint names scenario C prima facie has a 50 per cent interest ('equality follows the law').

(ii)  But C can claim more if C and D had a common intention (or shared intention, or understanding, or agreement) that this should be the case. In the joint names scenario, this common intention should be found only if the circumstances show C and D, despite their joint transfer, to have chosen not to share equally, or to have discarded their initial agreement to do so.

(iii) The question of quantum – i.e. the size of the interest that C can claim – is also governed by the parties' common intention.

(iv)  The 'common intention' may be express, or implied, or imputed. To find an implied or imputed common intention, the court will draw upon the parties' 'whole course of conduct in relation to [the property]'; a 'holistic approach', 'undertaking a survey of the whole of the course of dealing between the parties and taking account of all conduct which throws light on what shares were intended'.[128]

Notably this view presents a significant liberalisation from *Rosset* with courts being able to find a common intention from a consideration of all evidence. A more restrictive interpretation of the current law would suggest that Gardner's proposal is placing too much weight on some rather unclear obiter dicta from *Abbott* and *Stack*. Notably, some of the most recent cases[129] suggest that courts are taking a restrictive interpretation of when a constructive trust will be found.

### (c) Proprietary estoppel

For A to establish a proprietary estoppel claim over B's property it is necessary to show:[130]

1. A reasonably believes she has or is going to be given an interest over B's property;

2. A must act reasonably in reliance on this belief; and

3. It must be conscionable (fair) in all the circumstances to give A a remedy.

The law has recently been examined by the House of Lords.

---

[127] Para 90.
[128] Gardner (2008). The quotations are from *Abbott* v *Abbott* [2007] UKPC 53.
[129] *Negus* v *Bahouse* [2007] EWHC 2628 (Ch); *Tackaberry* v *Hollis* [2007] EWHC 2633 (Ch); *James* v *Thomas* [2007] EWCA Civ 1212; *Morris* v *Morris* [2008] EWCA Civ 257.
[130] *Re Basham (Deceased)* [1987] 1 All ER 405; *Gillet* v *Holt* [2000] FCR 705.

## CASE: *Thorner* v *Major* [2009] UKHL 18

Thorner had worked on his cousin's farm for 29 years without pay. The cousin was said by the court to be a man of few words. However, some statements were made which led Thorner to believe he would leave him the farm in his will. For example, he gave some life insurance policy documents to Thorner, saying they were for his 'death duties'. The cousin did make a will leaving the farm to Thorner, but then revoked the will, having fallen out with another legatee. He made no other will. Under the rules of intestacy the farm passed to the cousin's siblings. Thorner argued that the farm was his. At first instance it was found that the vague comments were sufficient for a proprietary estoppel. However, the Court of Appeal allowed an appeal, principally on the basis that the statements were not promises and had not been relied upon by Thorner.

The House of Lords held that to establish a propriety estoppel the assurance had to be 'clear enough'. Whether the assurance was clear enough depended on the context of the words or actions. Insisting that statements had to be 'clear and unambiguous' would be too strict a test and would be unrealistic. Normally it would be sufficient if the claimant could show that he or she reasonably understood the words or conduct to be an assurance on which he could rely. In this case given that the cousin was 'taciturn and undemonstrative' the judge was entitled to accept the words and conduct as amounting to an estoppel. What the cousin actually intended was not really relevant, because the focus was on Thorner's reasonable interpretation of what was said. Nor was it relevant to consider whether a reasonable person would have relied on what the cousin said, the question was whether it was reasonable for Thorner to rely on it. Only in exceptional cases might a person seek to defend a propriety estoppel on the basis that they did not intend to convey the promise as it was reasonably understood by the claimant. Their lordships also confirmed that a proprietary estoppel claim had to relate to an identified property. In this case it was clear what property was being talked about.

As a result of this decision the key question in estoppel is whether it was reasonable for the claimant to believe an assurance or promise was made and reasonable to rely on it. Their lordships approved *Gillet* v *Holt* which had stressed that the crucial principle underlying proprietary estoppel is conscionability.[131] Conscionability in essence means fairness.[132] However, they made it clear that proprietary estoppel was not solely an issue of unconscionability. Even substantial detriment will not found a claim for a proprietary estoppel without some representation.[133] The assurance need not be to a specific property right, but must refer to a piece of property.[134] So, the statement to a girlfriend that she 'would not want for anything' could not form the basis of an estoppel claim.[135] Nor was an assurance that a woman would have a roof over her head.[136]

Having established a proprietary estoppel claim, the next question is: What interest in the property should thereby be acquired by the plaintiff?[137] The simple answer is that the remedy

---

[131] *Gillet* v *Holt* [2000] FCR 705.
[132] For a detailed discussion see Dixon (2010), who offers a much narrower definition of unconscionability in the context of proprietary estoppel.
[133] *Walsh* v *Singh* [2010] 1 FLR 1658.
[134] See for further discussion McFarlane and Robertson (2009), Mee (2009) and Dixon (2010).
[135] *Lissimore* v *Downing* [2003] 2 FLR 308.
[136] *Negus* v *Bahouse* [2008] 1 FCR 768.
[137] Gardner (2006).

given is that which would 'satisfy the equity'; in other words, that remedy which would be just. The courts have been willing to grant a wide range of remedies including a fee simple[138] or a sum of money.[139] In particular the courts will consider the nature of the interest that was promised or assured by the owner and the amount of detriment suffered by the claimant.[140] Although ultimately the question is a matter for the court's discretion, any remedy should be proportionate to the financial value of the detriment.[141]

### (d) The interrelation of constructive trusts and proprietary estoppel

It will have been noticed that the requirements of a constructive trust and proprietary estoppel are very similar. Indeed some commentators take the view that proprietary estoppel and constructive trusts should be amalgamated.[142] Certainly the courts have not taken great efforts to distinguish the two. Lord Bridge, for example, said that where a person has acted to his or her detriment on reliance of an agreement to share property, this will 'give rise to a constructive trust or proprietary estoppel'. The Court of Appeal has accepted that the requirements for the two are very similar.[143] However, the current view of the courts is that, although at some point the doctrines might be merged, they are not yet assimilated.[144] Carnwath LJ will have expressed the views of many experienced practitioners on the history of the case law in this area when saying:

> To the detached observer, the result may seem like a witch's brew, into which various esoteric ingredients have been stirred over the years, and in which different ideas bubble to the surface at different times. They include implied trust, constructive trust, resulting trust, presumption of advancement, proprietary estoppel, unjust enrichment, and so on. These ideas are likely to mean nothing to laymen, and often little more to the lawyers who use them.[145]

## C Improvements to the home

Section 37 of the Matrimonial Proceedings and Property Act 1970 states that if a spouse, civil partner or fiancé(e) (but not an unmarried cohabitant) makes a substantial contribution to the improvement of property[146] in which the other spouse, civil partner or fiancé(e) has an interest, the improvement will create an interest in the property. However, the section states that this rule is subject to any agreement that the parties reach. A number of requirements need to be satisfied if the section is to apply:

1. The improvement must be of monetary value. Section 37 applies whether the contribution is in real money or money's worth. The improvement may be made by the claimant him- or herself or by someone employed by the claimant.[147] So if an incompetent husband carries out DIY work on the house, which in fact decreases the value of the house, he will be unable to invoke this section, as no improvement of monetary value has been made.

---

[138] *Pascoe v Turner* [1979] 1 WLR 431; *Q v Q* [2009] 1 FLR 935. A fee simple is absolute ownership.

[139] *Dodsworth v Dodsworth* (1973) 228 EG 1115.

[140] *Jennings v Rice* [2003] 1 FCR 501.

[141] *Jennings v Rice* [2003] 1 FCR 501. The question of whether a proprietary estoppel creates an interest in land and, if so, when is discussed in Bright and McFarlane (2005).

[142] See the debate between Hayton (1993) and Ferguson (1993). See also the discussion in Nield (2003).

[143] *Yaxley v Gotts* [2000] Ch 162, [1999] 2 FLR 941.

[144] *Stokes v Anderson* [1991] 1 FLR 391. See also *Churchill v Roach* [2004] 3 FCR 744 at p. 759 where Judge Norris QC suggested that while constructive trusts focus on the intention of the parties at the time of purchase, proprietary estoppel focuses on the time when a party seeks to go back on an assurance or promise.

[145] *Stack v Dowden* [2005] 2 FCR 739, at para 75.

[146] The section applies to real and personal property.

[147] *Griffiths v Griffiths* [1979] 1 WLR 1350.

2. The contribution must be identifiable with the improvement in question. So if it could be shown that a wife pays the household expenses thereby enabling the husband to pay for the improvements to a piece of property, s 37 could be relied upon by the wife.[148]

3. The contribution must be of a substantial nature. *Re Nicholson (Deceased)*[149] provides a good example of this: installing central heating worth £189 in a house worth £6,000 was substantial, but spending £23 on a gas fire was not.

4. The contribution must constitute an improvement to the property and not merely maintenance of it.[150]

The share acquired will be that which reflects any agreement of the parties, and if there is not one, then what the court regards as just. Normally the party will receive a share in the property reflecting the increase in the value of the property that the improvements caused.

There is some debate over the policy behind this section. It could be regarded as putting into legal effect the presumed intentions of the parties: that is, what the parties themselves would have expected to happen as a result of their actions to improve the property had they thought about it. Alternatively, s 37 could be seen as a way of achieving a just result in recognition of a party's contribution to improving the house, regardless of the parties' intentions. The fact that the parties can reach an agreement which negates the effect of the section would suggest that the statute is primarily seeking to reflect the parties' intentions.[151] The section is rarely relied upon because works carried out on the house will often form the basis of a proprietary estoppel or constructive trust claim.

## D Criticism of the present law

The law on ownership of the family home has been heavily criticised.[152] The Law Commission has stated that: 'Current property law rules are generally agreed to be highly complicated and uncertain. In addition to the technical difficulties they present, the nature of the evidence required to prove the elements of a claim makes it difficult in practice to predict the likely outcome of cases. Most significantly, the rules lead to outcomes which many people would consider to be unfair.'[153] Martin Dixon has said that little could be worse than the law after *Stack v Dowden*.[154] The law can especially lead to great injustice for unmarried cohabitants. Injustice was revealed in the following dicta of Johnson J in *T v S (Financial Provision for Children)*:[155]

> the sadness here is that, after a long and seemingly happy relationship, this mother of five children, never having been married to their father, has no rights against him of her own. She has no right to be supported by him in the short, still less in the long term; no right in herself to even have a roof over her head.

There is much academic support for the need to change the law.[156] The following are some of the main criticisms:

1. The requirement in *Rosset* for an oral agreement between the parties or a direct financial contribution has been heavily criticised. It is unrealistic to expect all couples to discuss the

---

[148] *Harnett v Harnett* [1973] 2 All ER 593 at p. 603.
[149] [1974] 1 WLR 476.
[150] *Re Nicholson (Deceased)* [1974] 1 WLR 476.
[151] It is therefore analogous to the working of resulting trusts.
[152] See Douglas, Pearce and Woodward (2007) and Gardner (2008).
[153] Law Commission Consultation Paper (Overview) (2006: 15).
[154] Dixon (2007: 256).
[155] [1994] 2 FLR 883.
[156] See Gardner (1993); Bailey-Harris (1995; 1996); Law Commission Report 278 (2002).

legal ownership of their property.[157] The cases demonstrate that the courts have had to pick up on casual comments made during the relationship.[158] A further difficulty with the approach in *Rosset* is that the parties' recollections of their 'tenderest exchanges' may well be contradictory and the only way to decide which of the two is telling the truth would be to look at the nature of their relationship (which was the kind of approach Lord Bridge was trying to move away from). Supporters of the current law's foucs on intentions might argue that it enables the court to look at the situation from the parties' perspectives, rather than seeking to impose a law on them.[159]

2. The emphasis on requiring a spoken promise in both constructive trusts and proprietary estoppel works against the less articulate or assertive partner, who may not seek an unequivocal promise from the owner.[160] Ruth Deech says that she warned her male students to conduct their love affairs in silence to ensure they would not unintentionally create a constructive trust![161]

3. It has been argued that the law reveals gender bias. In the absence of a conversation, common intention can only be established through a direct contribution to the purchase price or mortgage instalments. It is far more likely that men will be able to contribute in these ways than women, given the greater rates of employment among men.[162] Further, the law devalues non-financial contributions to the household by treating them as insufficient to establish a constructive trust. Olsen suggests that the law reveals an underlying distrust of unmarried women. She argues: 'Unmarried women involved in sexual relations are either good women who should be married or bad women who should not be able to make demands upon a man beyond whatever he chooses to give her.'[163] Notably, in relation to the redistribution of property of married couples on divorce, the House of Lords has held that there should be no discrimination between the money-earner and the homemaker or child-carer.[164]

4. The emphasis placed on whether the property is in joint names has also been challenged. It has been argued that whether the property is in joint names is often a matter of chance and often does not reflect a careful consideration by the parties as to ownership of the property.[165] Indeed it has been claimed by psychological economists that financial payments are a very unreliable guide to intentions.[166]

5. We have already noted that the results of these cases can be particularly unpredictable. This produces uncertainty and causes particular difficulties for negotiations between the parties before the case reaches the court.

## E Reform of the law

The Law Commission for many years has been considering the law relating to the ownership of property of unmarried couples and has finally produced a report.[167] The Law Commission

[157] Hayes and Williams (1999: 688).
[158] Rippon (1998).
[159] See the discussion in Harding (2009).
[160] Gardner (1993); Mee (1999).
[161] Deech (2010d).
[162] Wong (2005) suggests this leaves the law open to challenge under the Human Rights Act 1998.
[163] Olsen (1998).
[164] *White v White* [2001] AC 596; see Chapter 5.
[165] Douglas, Pearce and Woodward (2009a).
[166] Burgoyne and Sonnenberg (2009).
[167] Law Commission Report 307 (2007). The proposals and surrounding issues are discussed in Bridge (2007a, b and c) and Wong (2006). Law Commission Report 278 (2002), discussed in Probert (2002a). See Fox (2003) for a discussion of how other jurisdictions have dealt with this issue.

proposes allowing cohabiting couples to make some financial claims against each other, but these will be normally be at a lower level than would be available if they were married. It is proposed that a claim can be made if the couple meet the 'eligibility criteria': these should be either that the couple have a child or that they have lived together for a certain period of time.[168] By cohabitation the Law Commission means that a couple are living as a couple in a joint household.[169] A couple would be free to opt out of the scheme if they wished.[170] However, the court could set aside an opt-out if following it would cause manifest unfairness. An applicant would need to prove that:

1. the respondent has a retained benefit; or

2. the applicant has an economic disadvantage;

as a result of qualifying contributions the applicant has made.[171]

A qualifying contribution is 'any contribution arising from the cohabiting relationship which is made to the parties' shared lives or to the welfare of the members of their families'.[172] Contributions can include financial, non-financial and future contributions, but they must have an enduring consequence for the couple at the time of the separation. An economic disadvantage could, therefore, include loss of earning potential as a result of caring for children during the relationship and afterwards. A retained benefit could be capital acquired during the relationship or enhanced earning capacity created during the relationship. The court would make an order ensuring a fair sharing of the gains and losses resulting from the relationship. This might require a party who had made a benefit from the relationship to share that, or require a party who had suffered a disadvantage to be compensated. However, the court would take into account, as first consideration, the welfare of any child of both parties. The court could make lump sum orders, property transfers and pension sharing orders. However, it could not make ongoing periodic payment orders.[173]

The Law Commission rejects an argument that once a couple satisfy the 'eligibility criteria' they should be treated in the same way as a married couple for financial relief purposes. It argues that the notion of 'equal partnership' which applies to marriage cannot necessarily be said to apply to cohabitants.

> Where parties are married, the formal commitment that they have entered into may be taken as good evidence that they have assumed mutual responsibilities to support each other in case of need . . . Cohabitants currently have no legal obligation of mutual support either during or after their relationship. Even in long relationships, there may be no clear basis for concluding that the parties have assumed that sort of responsibility towards each other.[174]

Whether treating couples in the same way as a married couple would undermine marriage is a matter for debate. One study of what has happened in Australia where those living together for two years or more are treated in the same way as a married couple, suggests that reform had no effect on marriage rates.[175]

The Government has announced that it will delay responding to the Law Commission proposals until it has seen the impact of similar proposals which have been enacted in

---

[168] The Law Commission suggested that a figure between two and five years might be appropriate.
[169] Couples who were closely related or one or both of whom were under age 16 would be excluded.
[170] Any opt out would need to be in writing and signed by both parties.
[171] Law Commission Report 307 (2007: para 4.33).
[172] Law Commission Report 307 (2007: para 4.33).
[173] See Douglas, Pearce and Woodward (2008) for a survey of cohabitants' options of how the Law Commission proposals would work.
[174] Law Commission Consultation Paper 179 (2006: 3.36).
[175] Kiernan, Barlow and Merlo (2006).

Scotland. The Government has particular concerns over the costs to the state of enacting such a scheme.

Here is a summary of some of other ways which could be used to reform the law in this area:[176]

1. The law could give the courts the power to redistribute the property of cohabitants in the same way as they can redistribute the property of married couples.[177] This proposal was discussed in Chapter 2. It should be noted that such a proposal would leave those people sharing homes who are not in a marriage-like relationship (e.g. three friends sharing a house or an older person and their carer) with the current legal regulation.

2. The law could focus on the intentions of the parties. This approach might encourage unmarried cohabitants to draw up cohabitation contracts, but, if they did not, the courts would seek to ascertain the parties' intentions from what was said and done during the relationship. The benefit of this approach is that it would promote the parties' autonomy – the law would be seeking to enforce their intentions, rather than telling them what to do. The disadvantages are shown by the law on constructive trusts. Snippets of vaguely recalled conversations may have far more emphasis placed upon them than was intended. Further, in many of these cases the intention of the owner of the property may be quite different from the intention of the cohabitee, and so seeking any kind of *common* intention could be a futile task.

3. The law could focus on the reasonable expectations of the party who is seeking an interest in the property. The difficulty with this approach is revealed by the following scenario. An owner tells the claimant that she can live with him but she will never acquire an interest in his house. If the claimant were then to move in and spend an enormous amount of effort in maintaining and improving the property, she could not reasonably expect the owner to intend that she thereby acquires an interest in the house, even though justice may call out for her to be awarded an interest. The approach also suffers from the difficulty that establishing that the claimant's belief that she had an interest in the property was reasonable is likely to require proof of conversations of the kind which bedevil the present law.

   These concerns have produced an interesting variant of the reasonable expectation approach and this is to focus on what share the claimant might reasonably believe he or she *ought* to have.[178] In the scenario discussed in the previous paragraph, although the owner made it clear that the claimant was not to acquire an interest in the property and so she cannot reasonably believe that she was to acquire an interest, she might nevertheless reasonably expect that she ought to. The problem of this variant centres on the concept of reasonableness. Our society does not have a fixed set of views on when people should be entitled to a share in houses, so it is hard to say what is reasonable or not. In effect this model is similar to option 1 above – it is simply a question of judicial discretion. So it may be more desirable to give the judiciary such discretion explicitly.

4. The courts could focus on the actions performed on the property by the party who has no legal interest in the property. The law should then seek to value the work they have performed. This approach could be based on a form of unjust enrichment. This means that if the owner has received a benefit of the other party's work, the owner would be unjustly enriched by retaining the benefits of the work unless the other party acquires an interest

---

[176] Miles (2003) and Probert (2003) provide excellent discussions on this.
[177] Discussed in Bailey-Harris (1996); Wong (2009).
[178] Eekelaar (1994b).

in the property.[179] The benefit of this approach is that by focusing on what was done (rather than said, foreseen or intended), a more concrete concept is used. It is certainly easier to prove. The difficulty with this approach is twofold. The first is valuation of the benefit. This is a particular problem where the benefit is in the form of work which is not usually valued in economic terms, such as housework, and which at the time the parties themselves may not have regarded as of economic value.[180] Joanna Miles suggests that it should be recognised that the 'entitlement to a share in the property derives not from any presumed economic value of the contributions, but from an acknowledgement of their unique, socially valuable contribution to the joint enterprise entailed in the parties' relationship'.[181] Secondly, there is difficulty with the unjustness element. Could the owner argue that in return for housework he permitted the claimant to stay in the house, or provided for her financially in other ways and it is therefore not unjust to deny her an interest in the property?

5. The court could focus on the nature of the parties' relationship. Gardner[182] has argued that the court should consider whether the relationship of the parties has reached the stage of 'communality'. He criticises the present approach for being individualistic: dealing with disputes using the values of commercial law. It would be better to use values which governed the parties' relationship to resolve their dispute. Gardner suggests that the values promoted by a loving relationship are sharing and communality: 'that the parties have committed themselves to sharing the incidents of the relationship between them – good and bad; wealth and costs; work and enjoyment'.[183] The example he gives, however, demonstrates the great difficulties with his approach. He considers a situation where one person invites another to a meal, but the other is unable at the last minute to turn up. He suggests that if they were not yet a couple there would be no expectation to pay for their share of the food, but if they had reached communality, the one unable to attend would expect to pay for his or her share of the meal. Whether most couples would regard there to be an obligation to pay in such cases is very much open to question. Therein lies the problem: it is extremely difficult for someone from the outside to judge the nature of a relationship. Take sexual relations. For some couples the onset of sexual relations may indicate that the relationship has become a deeply committed one; for other couples sexual relations may not indicate this at all. These concerns are greater if one considers that judges may not be best placed to assess the nature of younger people's relationships. The communality approach might also require deeply personal details of a relationship to be aired before the court. A further difficulty is that one party may regard the relationship to have reached communality and the other party not. These arguments suggest that although this approach might be the most attractive in theory, there are grave practical problems with it.

6. Another option is to rely on the law of unjust enrichment.[184] The benefit of this approach is that it shifts the focus from why the applicant should be entitled to have a share, to asking whether the defendant should be entitled to keep all the ownership of the property. There may be political benefits too as the argument is no longer attempting to put a cohabitant in the position of a married person, but is seeking to prevent a cohabitant from engaging in fraud-like behaviour.

---

[179] See, e.g., Dickson J in *Pettkus v Becker* (1980) 117 DLR (3d) 257 at p. 274.
[180] Gupta et al. (2010).
[181] Miles (2003: 641).
[182] Gardner (1993). See also Gardner (2004).
[183] Gardner (1993).
[184] Douglas, Pearce and Woodward (2009b).

# 6 Rights to occupy the home

A person has the right to occupy the house if they have an interest in the property under an express trust, resulting trust, constructive trust or a proprietary estoppel. Even if the claimant is unable to establish such an interest, he or she may be able to establish a constructive trust, or a spouse may have a right to occupy the property under a contractual licence or a home right.

## A Contractual licences

A contractual licence is a contract under which the owner permits the licensee to occupy the property.[185] The claimant needs to show all the requirements of an ordinary contract. There can be particular difficulties for family members in demonstrating that the owner intended to create legal relations.[186] The holder of the contractual licence might be able to obtain damages if the owner excludes him or her, but the contractual licence will not bind third parties.[187]

## B Home rights

### (i) When are home rights conferred?

Section 30(1) of the Family Law Act 1996[188] explains when a home right is bestowed. Home rights are conferred in respect of a dwelling-house,[189] which has been or was intended to be the home of the spouses where:

---

**LEGISLATIVE PROVISION**

**Family Law Act 1996, section 30(1)**

(a) one spouse or civil partner ('A') is entitled to occupy a dwelling-house by virtue of—

    (i) a beneficial estate or interest or contract; or
    (ii) any enactment giving A the right to remain in occupation; and

(b) the other spouse or civil partner ('B') is not so entitled.

---

The right is also awarded to spouses or civil partners who have an equitable interest in the home.[190] The home right ceases on divorce, dissolution or death of either spouse or civil partner,[191] unless a court orders otherwise.[192]

---

[185] *Tanner v Tanner* [1975] 3 All ER 776.
[186] *Horrocks v Forray* [1976] 1 All ER 737.
[187] *Tanner v Tanner* [1975] 3 All ER 776.
[188] As amended by Civil Partnership Act 2004, Sch 9.
[189] Defined widely in Family Law Act 1996 (hereafter FLA 1996), s 63 to include, e.g., a caravan.
[190] FLA 1996, s 30(9).
[191] FLA 1996, s 30(8).
[192] FLA 1996, s 33(5).

## (ii) What do home rights consist of?

A home right consists of:

### LEGISLATIVE PROVISION

**Family Law Act 1996, section 30(2)**

(a) if in occupation, a right not to be evicted or excluded from the dwelling-house or any part of it by the other spouse except with the leave of the court given by an order under section 33;

(b) if not in occupation, a right with leave of the court so given to enter into and occupy the dwelling-house.[193]

The real significance of the right is that, otherwise, the spouse or civil partner without it could be evicted by the other.

Section 30(3) of the 1996 Act states that payments made by the person with the home right in respect of rent or mortgage should be treated by the recipient as if made by the owner or tenant of the property. So, if a husband stops paying rent on a house taken in his name, the wife can pay the rent and the landlord would have to accept the payment as if made by the husband, and so cannot evict her for non-payment of rent.

## (iii) Protection of home rights against third parties

The home rights should be protected by a notice on the land register if the land is registered under the Land Registration Act 2002, or as a class F Land Charge if the land is unregistered.[194] The significance of this is that if the owner sells the house to a third party and the home right is registered then the third party must permit the home rights holder to occupy the property.

## 7 The sale of a family home: enforcing trusts

If a cohabiting couple split up there are two questions for the court. The first is: who owns or has the right to occupy the property? That is the question we have just discussed. The second is whether the property should or may be sold. This is the question which will now be addressed.

If two unmarried cohabitants[195] co-own a property (for example, under a constructive trust), there may then be a dispute over whether or not the property should be sold. The Trusts of Land and Appointment of Trustees Act 1996 governs the present law. Land that is co-owned is now held under a trust of land. The trustees have a power to sell and also a power to postpone sale. Section 14(1) permits any trustee or beneficiary under a trust to apply to the court for an order. The court then has the power to make any order relating to the exercise

[193] FLA 1996, s 30(2).
[194] The home right is not an overriding interest, even if the holder is in occupation: FLA 1996, s 31(10)(b).
[195] Disputes between married couples over whether a house should be sold should normally be resolved under the Matrimonial Causes Act 1973, although see *Miller Smith v Miller Smith* [2010] 1 FLR 1402 where the wife was obstructing the divorce and the court was willing to make an order under the Trusts of Land and appointment of Trustees Act 1996.

of the trustees' functions as it sees fit.[196] Most significantly, the court can order the trustees to sell the property and pay the beneficiaries their cash share of the property.[197] The court could also refuse to order sale but require the party remaining in occupation of the home to pay the other 'rent'.[198]

There is a set of guidelines to be considered by the court when deciding whether to exercise its powers.[199] The guidelines are set out in s 15 of the Trusts of Land and Appointment of Trustees Act 1996. These do not rob the courts of a wide discretion, but rather give them some factors to take into account.[200]

---

## LEGISLATIVE PROVISION

### Trusts of Land and Appointment of Trustees Act 1996, section 15

(a)  the intentions of the person or persons (if any) who created the trust,

(b)  the purpose for which the property subject to the trust is held,

(c)  the welfare of any minor who occupies or might reasonably be expected to occupy any land subject to the trust as his home, and

(d)  the interests of any secured creditor of any beneficiary.[201]

---

Different guidelines apply to a trustee in bankruptcy; these will be discussed shortly.

The general attitude of the courts has been that a house is bought by the couple as a home, but if they split up then the purpose of the trust has failed (factor (b) above) and a sale can be ordered.[202] If there are children living in the house, the interests of the children will often be an important consideration, particularly if ordering the sale of the property will disrupt their education.[203] The aim of the Act is to give the courts wide discretion, and so each case will be decided on its own special facts.[204] Notably, this is one of those areas of the law where the interests of children are not made paramount.[205]

There have been some attempts to use s 14 where the parties are divorcing or have divorced. The courts have adopted a strict approach: couples who are divorcing or have divorced must apply for orders under the Matrimonial Causes Act 1973 and may not use the Trusts of Land and Appointment of Trustees Act 1996.[206]

## 8 Protection of beneficial interests against purchasers

We have seen how a cohabitant or spouse who is not a legal owner can establish an interest in a property via a constructive trust or a proprietary estoppel. However, this interest would

---

[196]  According to *Lawrence v Bertram* [2004] FL 323 one party can be ordered to buy out the other party.
[197]  Trusts of Land and Appointment of Trustees Act 1996, s 15.
[198]  Trusts of Land and Appointment of Trustees Act 1996, s 13.
[199]  These were intended to consolidate the previous case law.
[200]  *TSB v Marshall and Rodgers* [1998] 2 FLR 769; *The Mortgage Corp v Shaire* [2000] 1 FLR 973.
[201]  Under s 15(3) the wishes of the majority of the beneficiaries should be taken into account.
[202]  *Jones v Challenger* [1961] 1 QB 176 CA. But see *Holman v Howes* [2005] 3 FCR 474 where the woman was promised on purchase that she could stay in the house as long as she needed, and so no sale was ordered.
[203]  *Bernard v Joseph* [1982] Ch 391; *Edwards v Lloyds TSB Bank* [2005] 1 FCR 139.
[204]  *The Mortgage Corp v Shaire* [2000] 1 FLR 973.
[205]  Warren (2002) discusses the impact of bankruptcy on children.
[206]  *Laird v Laird* [1999] 1 FLR 791; *Tee v Tee and Hamilton* [1999] 2 FLR 613.

be of limited value if the owner could sell the property and thereby extinguish the other party's interest. Imagine this situation: A owns a house in law; his girlfriend, B, moves in and in due course acquires an interest in the house under a constructive trust; A then sells the house to C: what is B's position?

The answer depends on whether the land is registered or not. If the land is registered then B's interest can be protected if her interest is registered on the land register with a caution, or if she can claim to have an overriding interest under Schedules 1, 2 and 3 to the Land Registration Act 2002. If the land is not registered then the question is whether the purchaser had notice of the interest, that is, whether the purchaser was aware or ought to have been aware of B's interest.[207] Both of these provisions have the same basis: C ought to have been able to discover the interests of B by following ordinary conveyancing practice, and by failing to do so deserves to be bound by B's interests.

## 9 Protection of family property on bankruptcy

The law in relation to bankruptcy and the family requires a delicate balance between the rights of the creditors and the rights of the bankrupt's family.[208] There are strong economic arguments in favour of encouraging people to embark on entrepreneurial activities, even if there is a risk of failure. Part of this incentive is to ensure that it is not too difficult for business people to acquire capital for the start-up and support of their businesses. In practice, banks and other lending institutions are only willing to provide credit where there is a degree of security and this involves enabling business people to use their family home as collateral or security for loans. Few people have any other assets which would provide adequate security. The effect of using a family home as collateral or security for a loan is that if the debtor fails to make the required payments the bank can then seize the house, sell it and pay off the loan with the proceeds. However, the consequences of this on bankrupts and their families are severe. The Court of Appeal has referred to the 'melancholy consequences of debt and improvidence with which every civilised society has been familiar'.[209] The problem for the law is that if it protects the interests of the bankrupt's family members too strongly, then the family home will cease to be regarded as valuable security and this will discourage loans to entrepreneurs, which will have undesirable economic consequences. The difficulty was neatly summarised by Lord Browne-Wilkinson in *Barclays Bank v O'Brien*: 'It is essential that a law designed to protect the vulnerable does not render the matrimonial home unacceptable as security to financial institutions.'[210] Creditors may have no way of knowing whether the debtor has (or will have) a family, and any protection for family members would create greater uncertainty in the loan market. On the other hand, is it fair that a person should lose his or her home due to the business failure of someone else? This is connected to the questions of to what extent the law should regard family members as each having their own property and to what extent the law should recognise a kind of community property. It has been pointed out that if a wife can gain from the family business when it does well, she should suffer when it does not.

---

[207] *Kingsnorth Trust v Tizard* [1986] 1 WLR 783.
[208] The leading works on this area are Fox (2007), Miller (2004), and Probert (2007d).
[209] *Re Citro* [1991] Ch 142 at p. 157.
[210] [1994] 1 AC 180 at p. 188.

The law on bankruptcy as it affects family members will now be briefly discussed. On bankruptcy all of the bankrupt's property[211] is vested in the trustee in bankruptcy.[212] The trustee in bankruptcy is appointed by the court to act on behalf of the creditors and is 'in charge' of the bankrupt's assets, with the power to sell or transfer them.[213] The trustee in bankruptcy is under a duty to sell the assets and to distribute the proceeds among the creditors.[214] It is a fundamental principle of the law of bankruptcy that the trustee steps into the shoes of the bankrupt and so cannot assume rights that a bankrupt does not have. There are two main issues: the first is how the law protects creditors from family members. It would be all too easy for bankrupts to transfer their assets to their family members in an effort to put the assets out of the reach of the creditors, and the law shields creditors from such attempts. The second issue is how the law guards family members from creditors.

## A Protecting creditors from family members

### (i) Setting aside transactions

There is the danger that if one spouse is engaged in a business which is in severe financial difficulties he or she will attempt to avoid the unpleasant consequences of bankruptcy by transferring assets to his or her spouse in an attempt to keep them out of the hands of creditors. This danger has been addressed by two provisions in particular:

1. Section 423 of the Insolvency Act 1986 deals with transactions which defraud creditors.[215] If a person enters into a transaction at an undervalue in order to defeat the claims of his or her creditors, the transaction can be set aside. So, for example, if a wife whose business is failing transfers some shares into her husband's name without receiving sufficient payment from him, this transaction can be set aside and the shares returned to the wife (in effect therefore to her trustee in bankruptcy).[216] For the provision to operate, the following criteria apply:

   (a) There must be a transaction: a transaction includes any kind of transfer, gift or arrangement.[217]

   (b) The transaction was at an undervalue: it will be regarded as at an undervalue if there was no consideration,[218] or the consideration given was significantly less than the value of the asset.

   (c) The purpose of the transaction must be to place the asset outside the reach of the creditors or any person who might at some point in time become a creditor. This can be inferred from the circumstances if necessary.

   (d) The transaction cannot be set aside if the property was acquired in good faith and for value,[219] and without awareness of the facts on which an order under s 423 could be made.

---

[211] Defined in the Insolvency Act 1986 (hereafter IA 1986), s 283, notably excluding clothes, bedroom furniture, and provisions for satisfying the basic domestic needs of the bankrupt and his family (s 283(2)(b)).

[212] IA 1986, s 306.

[213] The bankruptcy will sever a joint tenancy: *Re Gorman (A Bankrupt)* [1990] 2 FLR 289.

[214] Insolvency Rules 1986, SI 1986/1925, and IA 1986 set out the law in detail.

[215] See *Ram v Ram* [2004] 3 FCR 425 for a rejection by the Court of Appeal of an argument that the provision infringes rights protected by the Human Rights Act 1998.

[216] Parties to an ancillary relief order do give each other consideration. It is not, therefore, possible to set aside an ancillary relief order on the basis that there was no consideration: *Hill v Haines* [2007] EWCA Civ 1284 (see Capper (2008)).

[217] IA 1986, s 436.

[218] That is, nothing of value in the eyes of the law was given in return for the transfer.

[219] In other words, that a reasonable price was paid.

Proceedings to set aside the transaction can be brought by anyone prejudiced by the transaction; by a party to the transaction; or by the trustee in bankruptcy.[220] Courts will order that assets are returned so that the parties are in the position they would have been in had the transaction not been made.[221]

2. Section 339 deals with transactions at an undervalue entered into by a bankrupt. It is therefore different from s 423, which addresses situations where a debtor is seeking to avoid the consequences of bankruptcy, but need not actually be bankrupt. Under s 339 the trustee of the bankrupt's estate may apply to the court for an order if the bankrupt entered into a transaction at an undervalue. The application can be made in respect of any transaction entered into up to five years prior to the bankruptcy. But if the transaction was more than two years prior to the bankruptcy then it is necessary to show that the bankrupt was insolvent at the time of the transaction. The insolvency will be presumed if the transaction was entered into with 'an associate' (which includes a spouse, former spouse, reputed spouse[222] or relative).[223] There is no need to prove an intent to defraud, and so the section is simpler to prove than s 423.

These provisions sit a little uneasily with the general law on personal property of family members which regards cohabitants or spouses as two separate individuals. In this context, the law in effect treats the property of the family as a single unit and not owned as individuals.

### (ii) Bankruptcy and the family home

The trustee in bankruptcy, acting on behalf of the creditors, can seek an order for sale of the family home under s 14 of the Trusts of Land and Appointment of Trustees Act 1996.[224] The court may make such order as is just and reasonable having regard to: the interests of the creditors, the conduct of the spouse or former spouse so far as contributing to the bankruptcy, the needs and resources of that person, the needs of any children, and all the circumstances of the case other than the needs of the bankrupt.[225] If the application is lodged more than one year after the making of the bankruptcy order, the interests of the creditors should outweigh any other consideration unless the facts of the case are exceptional. The court has accepted that a case may be exceptional where the bankrupt's spouse is seriously ill;[226] or if the couple are caring for a seriously disabled adult child;[227] but, if there are not extreme circumstances of this kind, the law explicitly prefers the interests of the creditors.[228] Indeed, even if the circumstances are exceptional it is still open to the court to order sale.[229] However, the Court of Appeal has suggested that although the courts have greater flexibility they should not forget that it is always a 'powerful consideration' whether the creditor is receiving proper recompense for not receiving their money.[230] In *Barca v Mears*[231] it was stated that the Human

---

[220] IA 1986, s 423(5).

[221] IA 1986, s 423(3).

[222] The meaning of the phrase is unclear, but presumably it is intended to include a stable cohabiting relationship.

[223] IA 1986, ss 339, 341, 435.

[224] An occupation order under FLA 1996, s 33 may be available, but s 14 seems more appropriate.

[225] IA 1986, s 335A; *Avis v Turner* [2007] EWCA Civ 748.

[226] *Re Raval* [1998] 2 FLR 718; *Judd v Brown* [1998] 2 FLR 360. In another case, *Re Bremner (A Bankrupt)* [1999] 1 FLR 912, the spouse's needs in looking after the seriously ill bankrupt were regarded as exceptional.

[227] *Re Haghighat (A Bankrupt)* [2009] 1 FLR 1271.

[228] The existence of a consent order will not be regarded as an exceptional factor: *Turner v Avis and Avis* [2009] 1 FLR 74.

[229] *Dean v Stout* [2005] EWHC 3315 (Ch).

[230] *Bank of Ireland v Bell* [2001] 3 FCR 134, [2001] 2 FLR 809.

[231] [2005] Fam Law 444; see also *Jackson v Bell* [2001] Fam Law 879 and *Hosking v Michaelides* [2004] All ER (D) 147 (May).

Rights Act 1998 requires the court, when considering whether the circumstances were exceptional, to take into account the article 8 rights of the family members.

## B Protecting the families from the creditors

Clarke[232] argues that there is certainly a public interest in discouraging bankruptcy, but on the other hand it would not be in the public interest if the bankrupt's family could be left with literally nothing. Section 283(2) of the Insolvency Act 1986 states that 'such clothing, bedding, furniture, household equipment and provisions as are necessary for meeting the basic domestic needs of the bankrupt and his family' are excluded from the bankrupt's estate. Section 310(2) states that the income of the bankrupt should not fall 'below what appears to the court to be necessary for meeting the reasonable needs of the bankrupt and his family'. In deciding the appropriate sum it is important to achieve 'proportionality' between the creditors and the bankrupt;[233] this does not necessarily mean that the bankrupt and his or her family are limited to the minimum sum requisite for the family to survive and so could even include private school fees.[234] This provision should ensure that the bankrupt and his or her family do not become dependent on benefits, and shows that society's interest of saving public costs is even more important than the interests of any creditors.

Section 336 of the Insolvency Act 1986 offers some protection to the occupation rights of the bankrupt's spouse. Once the bankrupt's property is placed in the hands of the trustee, no homes rights[235] can be acquired. However, existing rights will bind a trustee, even if they are unregistered.[236] This is because the trustee steps into the shoes of the bankrupt and takes the property with the same limitations that bound the bankrupt. Children are offered some protection under s 337. If the bankrupt was entitled to occupy a dwelling-house by virtue of any estate or interest, and any person under the age of 18 was living with the bankrupt when the petition was presented, the trustee cannot evict the child. The protection is in addition to any protection available under s 336.

## 10 Spouses, partners and mortgages

There are particular problems where one spouse, civil partner or cohabitant signs a mortgage, with the family home as security, and then defaults on the mortgage. Imagine a husband who takes out a loan or mortgage, using the family home as collateral, and fails to make the necessary payments.[237] The bank will then try to enforce the security by seeking an order for sale of the property. If the wife is seeking to prevent the sale, she will have an uphill task.[238] The following stages indicate the approach the law would take.

1. The first question is whether the wife has an interest in the property. She might seek to demonstrate that she has an interest under an express or implied trust, or has rights of occupation under a home right. If she has no interest[239] then she will not be in a position to halt the order for sale.

[232] Clarke (1993).
[233] *Kilvert v Kilvert* [1998] 2 FLR 806.
[234] *Re Rayatt* [1998] 2 FLR 264.
[235] Under FLA 1996, Part IV.
[236] The trustee can apply to have the rights terminated under IA 1986, s 336(1)–(2).
[237] The law will be the same if it is the wife who takes out the loan and substantially the same if the couple are unmarried, but in the section that follows it will be assumed that the husband takes out the loan.
[238] Davey (1997).
[239] A wife will inevitably have a home right if the home was intended to be both spouses' home together.

2. The next question is whether the mortgage covers the wife's share of the property or whether it only covers the husband's share. Clearly if the wife was a party to the mortgage (i.e. if she signed the mortgage) and the mortgage states that it covers the wife's share, it would.[240] However, even if she did not sign the mortgage she may have ceded priority of her interest over to the bank. This means that her share in the property would only be paid over to her after the bank was paid the sum owed to it. So if the house is worth £100,000 and there is a mortgage of £70,000 and the wife's share in the house is 50 per cent (i.e. £50,000), then when the house is sold the bank's mortgage would be paid first and the wife could claim her share from what was left (i.e. about £30,000 in this example). In fact this scenario is not realistic, as attempts to enforce an order for sale by the bank are likely to be preceded by a period of non-payment of mortgage instalments and second mortgages. Usually, therefore, the mortgage would take up the total value of the house, leaving nothing for the wife.

The wife would be deemed to have ceded priority of her interest to the bank in the following cases:

(i) She signed a document ceding priority.

(ii) She knew that her husband had taken out the mortgage and had voiced no objection.[241]

(iii) The mortgage was essential to the purchase of the property.[242]

(iv) The mortgage was a second mortgage, replacing a mortgage to which the wife had ceded priority.[243]

The case law developments in (ii), (iii) and (iv) are controversial. In effect they make it very unlikely that a wife or cohabitant would be able to claim priority over a mortgage in respect of a mortgage on the family home.

3. There are three ways in which a wife may attempt to prevent the mortgagee from enforcing a sale:

(i) The wife could argue that the mortgage was void or voidable. She could show that she and/or her husband had signed the mortgage as a result of misrepresentation or undue influence, or that the mortgage was unconscionable. Alternatively, she could rely on the Unfair Terms in Consumer Contracts Regulations 1999.[244] The normal rules of contract law would apply. A special set of rules has been developed in this area in relation to undue influence and we will discuss these in detail shortly.

(ii) If the wife's share in the home is independent of the mortgage she and the trustee in bankruptcy will be co-owners. The trustee can make an application under s 14 of the Trusts of Land and Appointment of Trustees Act 1996. This has already been discussed.

(iii) The wife could seek an order suspending enforcement of the mortgage under s 36 of the Administration of Justice Act 1970.[245]

---

[240] Unless the contract specifically states otherwise, the creditor cannot increase the liability of a guarantor in a way which prejudices the position of the guarantor without the consent of the guarantor (*Lloyds TSB Bank v Shoney* [2001] EWCA Civ 1161, [2002] 1 FCR 673).

[241] *Paddington Building Society v Mendelsohn* (1985) 50 P&CR 244.

[242] *Abbey National Building Society v Cann* [1990] 2 FLR 112.

[243] *Equity and Law Home Loans v Prestidge* [1992] 1 WLR 137.

[244] SI 1999/2083.

[245] For a discussion of the recent case law, see Dixon (1998); Pawlowski and Brown (2002).

Dewar[246] has pointed out that this area of the law involves give and take. On the one hand, the law has been making it increasingly easy for the spouse or cohabitant to establish an interest in the family home. However, this interest is almost inevitably worthless if the bank or building society seeks to enforce a mortgage on the home. The law here is seeking to protect the cohabitant or spouse as against his or her partner, but not so as to prejudice the rights of the lending institutions.

## A  Undue influence

There have been a large number of recent cases resulting from the decision of the House of Lords in *Barclays Bank* v *O'Brien*.[247] The kind of situation under discussion has arisen where one spouse or cohabitant (it has most often been the wife or female cohabitant) agreed to act as a surety or guarantant for her spouse's or cohabitant's loan. When the bank came to enforce the surety or guarantee, the wife or cohabitant sought to escape liability from acting as surety because of her husband's undue influence. At first sight such a claim seems unlikely to succeed. Normally, a contract between two parties (here the bank and the wife) will not be set aside on account of the wrongdoing of a third party (the husband). However, in *Barclays Bank* v *O'Brien*[248] the House of Lords found a novel way around this difficulty by arguing that the bank could be bound by the misrepresentation or undue influence of the husband if it had notice of it. So if the spouse or partner could show: (1) that there was undue influence or a misrepresentation made by her husband or cohabitant; and (2) that the bank had notice of the undue influence or misrepresentation, then the contract of surety or guarantee signed by the wife or cohabitant would be unenforceable.

The requirements will be considered separately.

### (i)  Proof of undue influence or misrepresentation

The concept of misrepresentation is clearly governed by contract law and does not usually give rise to particular difficulties in this area.[249] In *Hewett* v *First Plus Financial Group*[250] a husband who failed to disclose to his wife that he was having an affair when persuading her to guarantee his loans was found to have made a misrepresentation. Given the relationship of trust between them he was under a duty of candour.

The doctrine of undue influence requires more explanation. Undue influence arises in cases where there is a relationship where one party has a measure of influence over another and takes unfair advantage of the relationship. Unfair advantage may be taken by blatant acts of persuasion, exploitation[251] or by less overt acts of pressure.[252] The burden of proving the undue influence is on the wronged person. Sometimes it is possible to prove 'actual undue influence' where the one party exploited the other and 'twisted' their mind.[253] More commonly the applicant has to ask the court to presume undue influence.[254] The kind of evidence

---

[246] Dewar (2000b).
[247] [1994] 1 FLR 1, [1994] 1 FCR 357.
[248] [1994] 1 FLR 1, [1994] 1 FCR 357.
[249] See Beatson (2002).
[250] [2010] EWCA Civ 312.
[251] *Drew* v *Daniel* [2005] 2 FCR 365.
[252] *Royal Bank of Scotland* v *Etridge (No. 2)* [2001] 3 FCR 481, para 11.
[253] *Drew* v *Daniel* [2005] 2 FCR 365.
[254] *Drew* v *Daniel* [2005] 2 FCR 365 suggested that cases of presumed undue influence often focus on what the donee failed to do, rather than what they did.

which will lead to a presumption of undue influence was explained by Lord Nicholls in *Royal Bank of Scotland* v *Etridge (No. 2)*:[255]

> Proof that the complainant placed trust and confidence in the other party in relation to the management of the complainant's financial affairs, coupled with a transaction which calls for explanation, will normally be sufficient, failing satisfactory evidence to the contrary, to discharge the burden of proof.[256]

This can be broken down into the following elements:

1. the relationship between the parties was of a kind in which undue influence could be exercised;[257] and

2. the transaction calls for an explanation;[258] and

3. there is no evidence to rebut the presumption that there was undue influence.

Regarding element 1, there are some relationships which automatically give rise to a presumption that undue influence could be exercised. An example would be a doctor and patient relationship.[259] Others depend on the facts of the particular circumstances. So in one case, involving a man and his gardener, it was held that the presumption of undue influence could apply because the gardener had come to dominate the man. In later cases the courts have also been very willing to find that a variety of relationships have been of the kind that undue influence could be exercised.[260] This is especially where one party is vulnerable and has come to trust the other.[261] But what about husbands and wives? Lord Browne-Wilkinson in *Barclays Bank* v *O'Brien* held that there is no automatic presumption that the relationship between a husband and wife is one where undue influence could be exercised. However, on the facts of a particular case a claimant may be able to persuade a court that he or she relied on his or her spouse in all financial matters, therefore was open to having his or her trust abused.[262]

In relation to element 2, it used to be the law that it was necessary to show that the claimant suffered manifest disadvantage as a result of the transaction. However, in *Royal Bank of Scotland* v *Etridge (No. 2)*[263] Lord Nicholls took the view that the correct test is to ask whether the transaction was readily explicable by the relationship of the parties. The significance of this is twofold. First, there may be a transaction which is to the disadvantage of the weaker party, but which is readily explicable by the relationship between the parties and so does not give rise to a presumption of undue influence (for example, where a child gives her father a Christmas present).[264] Secondly, there may be a transaction which does call for explanation, even if not to the manifest disadvantage of the parties (for example, where a client sells his solicitor his house for the market value). Applying that to the kind of cases under discussion,

---

[255] [2001] 3 FCR 481.

[256] Para 14.

[257] Normally this will be a well-established relationship, but it can be one which arises from the circumstances of the transaction itself: *Macklin* v *Dowsett* [2004] EWCA Civ 904.

[258] See *Turkey* v *Awadh* [2005] 2 FCR 7 for a case where the transaction was explicable by 'the ordinary motives of the people concerned' and there could therefore be no undue influence.

[259] Others include guardian and ward, trustee and beneficiary, solicitor and client (*Royal Bank of Scotland* v *Etridge (No. 2)* [2001] 3 FCR 481 at para 18).

[260] E.g. *Crédit Lyonnais Bank* v *Burch* [1997] 2 FCR 1.

[261] E.g. *Abbey National* v *Stringer* [2006] EWCA Civ 338.

[262] Most cases have involved husbands taking advantage of their wives, but *Simpson* v *Simpson* [1992] 1 FLR 601 and *Barclays Bank* v *Rivett* [1999] 1 FLR 730 are examples of cases where a wife was found to have exercised undue influence over her husband. See *Wallbank* v *Wallbank* [2007] EWHC 3001 (Ch) for a case where the wife failed to show her husband was dominant.

[263] [2001] 3 FCR 481 at paras 21–31.

[264] E.g. *Karsten* v *Markham* [2010] 1 FCR 523.

is a transaction where a wife guarantees payment of her husband's business debts one which calls for explanation? Lord Nicholls in *Royal Bank of Scotland* thought not, 'in the ordinary case'.[265] He explained that 'the fortunes of husband and wife are bound up together. If the husband's business is the source of the family income, the wife has a lively interest in doing what she can to support the business.'[266] In other cases a court will be more willing to find that the transaction requires an explanation. In *Humphreys v Humphreys*,[267] a woman who 'disclaim[ed] any pretensions to being . . . brainy' signed an unusual trust deed in favour of her son. Rimer J described the trust deed as 'one-sided' and calling out for an explanation. The court will also consider the size of the gift: the larger it is the more likely there will need to be an explanation for it.[268]

In relation to the third element, the most common way of rebutting a presumption of undue influence is by showing that the claimant received independent financial advice. However, even though a claimant received independent financial advice it may still be found that the transaction was the result of undue influence.[269] Further, there may be other ways, apart from independent advice, which would rebut the presumption of undue influence. Once the first two factors are established, the burden is on the recipient of the property to show that the transfer was made freely and in a properly informed way.[270]

### (ii) Notice to the bank of undue influence or misrepresentation

The bank will be put on inquiry where a wife offers to stand surety for her husband's debts; similarly, in relation to unmarried couples, where the bank is aware of the relationship. This can be where the couple are heterosexual or homosexual, or may or may not be cohabiting.[271] A joint advance to a couple will not put the bank on inquiry. Once the bank is on inquiry it is under an obligation to take reasonable steps to satisfy itself that the wife understood the practical implications of the transaction. In *Etridge* Lord Nicholls accepted that this would not mean that the wife was not suffering from undue influence, but it would mean that the wife was aware of the basic elements of the transaction. The most common way for a bank to carry out its obligation would be to ensure that the wife receives independent legal advice. It would not be enough for the bank simply to be aware that the wife had a solicitor acting for her.[272]

### (iii) Discussion of the *O'Brien/Etridge* case law

---

**DEBATE**

## Has the O'Brien/Etridge case law helped vulnerable partners?

Lord Bingham has described transactions whereby a partner guarantees a loan as being of 'great social and economic importance'.[273] The law is seeking to protect the position of a spouse (or partner) who is offering their interest in a matrimonial home to secure the borrowing of a spouse. It is necessary to ensure that he or she fully understands the transaction into

---

[265] Para 30.
[266] Para 28.
[267] [2005] 1 FCR 712.
[268] *Watson v Huber* (2005) unreported, 9 March 2005.
[269] *Jennings v Cairns* [2003] EWCA Civ 1935.
[270] *Smith v Cooper (by her litigation friend, the Official Solicitor)* [2010] 2 FCR 551.
[271] *Royal Bank of Scotland v Etridge (No. 2)* [2001] 3 FCR 481 at para 47. See Auchmuty (2003) for an argument that same-sex couples should not be regarded as liable to be unequal.
[272] *First National Bank v Achampong* [2004] 1 FCR 18.
[273] *Royal Bank of Scotland v Etridge (No. 2)* [2001] 3 FCR 481 at para 21.

which the party entered. On the other hand it is necessary also to protect the position of lenders, so that they can advance money confident that the transaction will not be undone if appropriate procedures are undertaken.[274]

The ultimate effect of *O'Brien* cases is that banks now ensure that any spouse or partner guaranteeing a loan will be required by the bank to see a solicitor first.[275] Arguably, all this does is lead to increased expenses for the spouse, with little practical benefit to him or her. However, others see it as an attempt by the law to do the best it can to protect the independent financial interests of wives, without unduly prejudicing the interests of banks and other lending institutions. The law recognises that the financial interests of husbands and wives may not be identical. The normal privacy that surrounds marital finances does not apply here. Under *O'Brien* the courts will be willing to look at the way in which money matters were dealt with within the marriage.

Some complain that the law 'depicts wives as passive, ill-informed and obedient to the will of their partners'.[276] Then again, there is evidence that the majority of wives do defer to their husbands over important financial decisions and so the law is perhaps simply being realistic.[277] Gardner neatly sums up the alternative approaches here:

> Some may see [the law] as appropriately standing for the recognition and correction of what they see as the disadvantaged position of wives and other emotional dependants in the kind of matter under discussion. Others, however, whilst agreeing that wives and other emotional dependants occupy a disadvantaged position, may believe that the appropriate answer is to encourage such people to take better care of themselves, and/or to alter social structures in such a way that the disadvantage is less likely to arise; and that the law should remain neutral as between classes of citizens, seeing this as important either as the correct position for the law in principle, or as marking the equal status which it is hoped wives and other emotional dependants will attain. Others still may find the very idea that specially generous treatment is merited an insulting one.[278]

## Questions

1. *Is there anything the law can do to stop partners pressuring each other into guaranteeing loans?*
2. *Would the law be clearer and fairer if we treated all property belonging to spouses or civil partners as jointly owned?*

## Further reading

Read **Miles and Probert** (2009) for an excellent set of essays on how couples regard their assets during their relationship.

## 11 Conclusion

This chapter has revealed that the law has failed to find a consistent approach to family property. On the one hand, generally the law treats spouses or cohabitants as two individuals and the normal property rules apply. On the other hand, some of the rules on bankruptcy or

---

[274] *Royal Bank of Scotland* v *Etridge (No. 2)* [2001] 3 FCR 481 at para 2.
[275] Oldham (1995).
[276] Thornton (1997: 491).
[277] Fehlberg (1997).
[278] Gardner (1999: 6).

mortgages accept that, even if property may be technically owned by one family member, in practice it is enjoyed by them all and so there are special rules designed to ensure that one family member does not avoid the consequences of insolvency by claiming that his or her property is actually owned by other family members. The law in this area is interesting in its treatment of the ownership of the family home. As there is no discretion in the court to redistribute the property of unmarried couples on the breakdown of their relationship, the law on who owns the family home is particularly important for them. This has led the court to develop (manipulate, some would say) land law to enable a cohabitant to establish an interest in a home even if the normal formality requirements that attach to the transfer of interests in land have not been complied with.

## Further reading

**Dixon, M.** (2010) 'Confining and defining proprietary estoppel: the role of unconscionability', *Legal Studies* 30: 408.

**Fehlberg, B.** (1997) *Sexually Transmitted Debt*, Oxford: OUP.

**Fox, L.** (2006) *Conceptualising Home: Theories, Law and Policies*, Oxford: Hart.

**Gardner, S.** (1993) 'Rethinking family property', *Law Quarterly Review* 109: 263.

**Gardner, S.** (2008) 'Family property today', *Law Quarterly Review* 122: 422.

**Harding, M.** (2009) 'Defending *Stack v Dowden*', *Conveyancer and Property Lawyer* 73: 309.

**Law Commission Report 278** (2002) *Sharing Homes*, London: The Stationery Office.

**Miles, J. and Probert, R.** (eds) (2009a) *Sharing Lives, Dividing Assets*, Oxford: Hart.

**Miller, G.** (2004) *The Family, Creditors and Insolvency*, Oxford: OUP.

**Pahl, J.** (2005) 'Individualisation in couple's finances', *Social Policy and Society* 4: 4.

**Probert, R.** (2007d) 'The security of the home and the home as security', in R. Probert (ed.), *Family Life and the Law*, Aldershot: Ashgate.

**Wong, S.** (2009) 'Caring and sharing: Interdepency as a basis for property redistribution' in A. Bottomley and S. Wong (eds) *Changing Contours of Domestic Life, Family and Law*, Oxford: Hart.

Visit **www.mylawchamber.co.uk/herring** to access study support resources including interactive multiple choice questions, weblinks, discussion questions and legal updates.

Use **Case Navigator** to read in full some of the key cases referenced in this chapter with commentary and questions:

*White v White* [2001] 1 All ER 1

# 5  Property on separation

In 2009 a man who was divorcing his wife sought the return of his kidney that he donated to her when she needed a transplant.[1] He failed, of course, but it's a powerful metaphor for the difficulties that can arise in seeking to divide a couple's property on divorce or dissolution. There is a widespread perception that divorce causes financial ruin for a wealthy spouse. The truth, as we shall see, is that divorce or dissolution causes enormous financial hardship for both parties, but especially women.

It is notable that while a couple are married or civil partners the law does little to interfere in the property interests of the parties. By contrast, on separation the law is willing to intervene to ensure that the spouse's or civil partner's financial interests are adequately protected. The law distinguishes financial support for children from financial support for partners. In relation to child support, the law is now governed by the Child Maintenance and Other Payments Act 2008 and, to a lesser extent, the Children Act 1989. The 2008 Act replaces the previous child support scheme in the Child Support Act 1991. The child support legislation applies equally to parents who are married, civil partners and those who are unmarried. However, in relation to financial support for partners an important distinction is drawn between spouses or civil partners and unmarried couples. For married couples and civil partners the courts have the power to redistribute the family's property between the parties as they consider just, taking into account all the circumstances of the case.[2] For unmarried couples the courts can simply declare who owns what, and have no power to require one party to transfer property to another, except as a means of providing child support. We have discussed the law on property ownership in Chapter 4.

## 1  Child support: theoretical issues

There is grave concern over the economic circumstances in which many children are brought up in the UK.[3] Twenty two percent of all households in the UK are in poverty and 53 per cent of these involve a child.[4] 3.9 million do according to the figures for 2008–09.[5] For several years the Government has promised to eradicate child poverty, but current figures indicate it

---

[1] BBC Newsonline (2009d).

[2] It seems to be generally agreed that the courts will use the same principles for civil partnerships that are used in marriages: Allen and Williams (2009).

[3] Wikeley (2006c) is the leading work on the law and policy relating to child support.

[4] Child Poverty Action Group (2010).

[5] Department for Work and Pensions (2010). Poverty here defined as below 60% of contemporary median net disposable household income after housing costs.

has fallen behind its target.[6] The Child Poverty Act 2010 places a statutory duty on the Secretary of State to eradicate child poverty by 2020.[7] There are particular concerns about children of lone parents. Almost half of all lone parent households are in poverty.[8]

Child poverty is not restricted to children of lone parents. Seven per cent of children do not have properly fitting shoes; 3 per cent go without three meals a day; 10 per cent go without celebration on special occasions; 6 per cent without a waterproof coat.[9] The statistics on child poverty are particularly concerning because poverty is linked with low birth weight,[10] poor levels of psychological health,[11] higher levels of exclusions from schools and teenage pregnancies,[12] drug misuse and high unemployment.[13]

As already mentioned the Child Poverty Act 2010 is designed to impose on the Government an obligation to end poverty by 2020. The new Coalition Government's policies are still being developed but the policies are likely to be directed towards encouraging parents to work (e.g. by increasing the provision of child care), not by giving increased benefits to non-working parents.[14] Fortin is critical of such an approach. She claims that

> despite the Government's assertions that 'Work is good for you' work clearly does not increase the income of all families and may not benefit all children . . . The confident claims that work produces good outcomes for children are also surprising given the lack of agreement over the potential impact on young children of long term nursery care, rather than full-time maternal care at home.'[15]

As this discussion demonstrates, the question of financial support is crucial if children's interests are to be adequately protected. The issue raises some important questions of theory, which will now be discussed.

## A Does the obligation to support children fall on the state or on the parents?

A key issue concerning child support is: on whom does the burden of support for children primarily fall?[16] Ultimately, is the state responsible for the financial support of children (although the state can recoup the money from parents) or are the parents responsible (although the state can step in to support children if the parents fail)? In other words, is it the state's primary role to enforce parental responsibility to pay child support, or to provide guaranteed support itself for the child? Krause suggests that the obligation is shared between society and the parents: 'children have a right to a decent start in life. This right is the obligation of the father and equally of the mother, and in recognition of a primary and direct responsibility, equally the obligation of society.'[17]

Looking at this issue from another angle, it is possible to regard the question as one of children's rights. If it is accepted that children should have rights then it seems inevitable that

---

[6] Department for Work and Pensions (2010).
[7] Although see Palmer (2010) for a sceptical consideration of the statute.
[8] Department for Work and Pensions (2010).
[9] Gordon, Adelman, Ashworth et al. (2000: 34).
[10] Palmer, Rahman and Kenway (2002: 32 and 38).
[11] Meltzer and Gatward (2000).
[12] Palmer, Rahman and Kenway (2002: 31–2).
[13] Child Poverty Action Group (2010).
[14] Daly and Scheiwe (2010).
[15] Fortin (2009b: 340–1).
[16] See the excellent discussion in Ferguson (2008).
[17] Krause (1994: 232).

children have a right to the financial support necessary so that they can, at least, be fed and clothed.[18] Article 27(4) of the United Nations Convention on the Rights of the Child declares: 'State parties shall take all appropriate measures to secure the recovery of maintenance for the child from the parents or other persons having financial responsibility for the child, both within the State Party and from abroad . . .' Given that the state is a more reliable supporter than the parent, it is in the child's interests that the state should have the primary obligation to ensure children receive sufficient support, but how the state's obligation is performed may vary from family to family.

The Government's White Paper, *Children's Rights and Parents' Responsibilities*, regards the burden of child support as clearly on the parents, and sees the Government's role as 'helping' parents to meet their responsibility.[19] The Child Poverty Act 2010, however, recognises that the state has obligations too. The question is made even more complex in that the state's approach to child support may seek to pursue a variety of aims. As well as ensuring that the child is adequately provided for, a scheme may also endeavour to discourage births out of marriage; to punish unmarried fathers; or to decrease the legal aid costs associated with relationship breakdown.[20]

There are three main aspects of the State's response to poverty among children. First, there is a complex system of benefits and tax credits for low-income and unemployed parents. The state does recognise some obligation to *all* children by providing child benefit payments to all parents regardless of wealth.[21] Although in 2010 it was announced that child benefit would in the future not be paid to higher rate tax payers. Secondly, there are the incentives on all parents to seek employment, especially on those currently claiming benefits.[22] Thirdly, there is the Child Maintenance and Enforcement Commission, which seeks to collect money from non-residential parents (those parents who no longer live with the child). A recent Government document on child support states:

> Parents, whether they live together or not, have a clear moral as well as legal responsibility to maintain their children. Relationships end. Responsibilities do not.
>
> Government and society as a whole have a clear interest in making sure these responsibilities are honoured.[23]

Sheldon, by contrast, is not convinced that the present law adequately protects the interests of children. She argues: 'Leaving children dependent on the economic means of their parents has contributed significantly to the widespread poverty of women and children and, in countries where the wealth to rectify this situation exists, this should be cause for national shame.'[24] She therefore argues that the state should be regarded as primarily responsible for the financial support of children.

Scott has argued that parents can be said to be liable to pay child support because they have wronged the child by allowing their relationship to become unhappy.[25] The enforcement of child support punishes this wrong and deters such behaviour. It also requires people to consider carefully about having children if they are unsure that their relationship is going to last. To some this argument will appear to be an expression of moral disapproval for sexual behaviour outside committed relationships, which is inappropriate in a pluralistic society.[26]

---

[18] Wikeley (2006c).
[19] Department of Social Security (2000: 1).
[20] Krause (1994).
[21] See Ferguson (2008) for further discussion of the state's responsibility to children.
[22] A useful summary is Douglas (2000a).
[23] Department for Work and Pensions (2006c: 1).
[24] Sheldon (2003: 193).
[25] Scott (1990). See also Altman (2003).
[26] Bainham (2001a).

## B Are the parents' obligations independent or joint?

Accepting that parents are obliged to support their children, the question is then whether parents are separately responsible for the support of the child or whether they share this burden, in that each parent should only be expected to pay their own half of the child support. If, for example, a mother who is receiving income support is raising the child, should a non-residential employed father be required to pay all the expenses of the child or only 'his half' of them? It is arguable that the residential parent provides her 'share' of the child support through the time and effort she puts in day to day for the child, and that therefore the full financial burden should fall on the non-residential parent.[27]

## C Biological or social parents?

If children should be supported jointly by their parents, the next question is: What is meant by parents in this context? Specifically, where a parent has both stepchildren and biological children, how should his or her resources be shared between them?[28] Imagine A and B have a child, Y. A moves out and later lives with C, who has a child, X, by a previous relationship. Should A support Y or X? Or should he try to support both? Prior to the Child Support Act 1991, the practice in many cases was that if a man left his first family and later moved in with a second family, he would provide for the second family and the state would support the first family through benefits. The Child Support Act 1991 and Child Support, Pensions and Social Security Act 2000 have changed this fundamentally and now liability is attached to biological parenthood and the 2008 Act continues that approach. So, in our example, A is liable in law to support Y and not X.[29] Interestingly, a study suggests that this is in line with the views of children whose parents have separated.[30]

There are a number of issues here:

1. *Should financial responsibility be linked with parental responsibility?* Is it fair that under English and Welsh law an unmarried father is automatically required to support the child financially, but is not automatically granted parental responsibility? It can be argued that as it is inevitably in the child's interests to receive financial support from his or her father, but not inevitably in the child's interest for his or her father to have parental responsibility, the position can be justified. For example, if the father does not know the child at all, it may be in the child's interests to require him to pay but not to permit him to make decisions on the child's behalf. However, from a father's perspective the position appears most unjust.[31] Indeed there is some evidence that both mothers and fathers in their minds link the payment of child support and contact.[32]

2. *Should financial responsibility be coupled with social parenting?* It could be argued that the law should match fiscal legal liability with the feelings of social or moral obligation that parents have. This, it has been maintained, would make the law more effective and acceptable. Eekelaar and Maclean found in their survey that fathers thought financial obligations

---

[27] Eekelaar (1991a: 111).
[28] Bennett (1997).
[29] See Chapter 7 for a general discussion on the differences between biological and social parenthood.
[30] Peacey and Rainford (2004) found that 81% of respondents agreed that non-resident parents had an obligation to support their child.
[31] By contrast, in *P v B (Paternity; Damages for Deceit)* [2001] 1 FLR 1041 a father sued in deceit his cohabitant whom he claimed had falsely told him her child was his, leading to him paying £90,000 by way of child support.
[32] Herring (2003a).

should be tied to the social role played by fathers, but mothers thought the obligations should follow the blood tie.[33] The study demonstrated that there was a strong link between payment of financial support and contact with the child. Where the father had contact with the child he was more likely to support the child than where he did not. Eekelaar and Maclean argued:

> A support obligation which accompanies or arises from social parenthood is embedded in that social parenthood; thus the payment of support can be seen as part of the relationship maintained by continued contact. But an obligation based on natural parenthood rests on the policy of instilling a sense of responsibility for individual action and equity between fathers who do and fathers who do not exercise social parenthood.[34]

The workings of the child support legislation in practice has revealed that where there is an ongoing level of contact between the non-resident parent and the child there is more likely to be payment of child support and that such payments are perceived to be fair.[35]

3. *Should it matter whether the pregnancy was planned or not?* Hale J in **J v C (Child: Financial Provision)**[36] confirmed that liability under the Children Act 1989 and the Child Support Act 1991 did not depend on whether the pregnancy was planned or not. Although it may be understandable that, from a parent's perspective, whether the pregnancy was planned or not should be relevant in determining liability, from the child's viewpoint he or she should not be prejudiced because of his or her parents' attitudes at the time of the conception.[37] That said, some commentators have argued that the man should be liable only if he has intentionally impregnated the mother and thereby can be said to have consented to taking on the financial liability.[38] As Kapp has argued:

> To saddle a man with at least eighteen years of expensive, exhausting child support liability on the basis of a haphazard vicissitude of life seems to shock the conscience and be arbitrary, capricious, and unreasonable, where childbirth results from the mother's free choice . . . a man no longer has any control over the course of a pregnancy he has biologically brought about [and] it is unjust to impose responsibility where there is no ability to exercise control.[39]

Others argue that, at least, a father should not be liable if he has been misled by the mother into believing that she is using contraception or is infertile.[40] There is, perhaps, here a clash between what may be fair to the father and what is in the interests of the child. Nick Wikeley[41] has written:

> There is an unspoken value judgment that child support is not a right of the child but an imposition on the father which must be construed as restrictively as possible . . . such a perspective is based upon the Lockean philosophical tradition which emphasizes property rights and individual autonomy and views child support as a taking which demands a justification. The result is that the rights of the parent and the children inevitably come a poor second to those of the non-resident parent.

---

[33] Eekelaar and Maclean (1997). These might not reflect the views of the public at large: Herring (1998b: 214).
[34] Eekelaar and Maclean (1997: 150).
[35] Davis and Wikeley (2002).
[36] [1999] 1 FLR 152, [1998] 3 FCR 79.
[37] Spon-Smith (2002: 29) notes a case in which a man who was deceived into thinking that he was the father of a child was refunded by the CSA £30,000 that he had paid by way of child support when it turned out he was not the father.
[38] Brake (2005).
[39] Kapp (1982: 376–7).
[40] See further the discussion in Sheldon (2001a).
[41] Wikeley (2005: 98).

4. *Should the level of child support depend on whether the parents were married?* Although the child support legislation applies to both married and unmarried couples, the argument is that a child should not lose out because his or her parents were unmarried or were not civil partners. However, it would be wrong to assume that the financial position of the child is the same whether the parents are married or not.[42] The ability of the courts to redistribute property between spouses or civil partners can significantly benefit the child.

## D  What level should the support be?

There are many options for setting the correct level of child support. Some of the options are:

1. *Subsistence costs.* This would be the amount of money that would be necessary to support the child at a minimally decent level. It could be assumed to be the amount of the welfare payment from the state that would be paid in respect of the child.

2. *Acceptable costs.* This would be the estimated level of support required to keep a child at a reasonably acceptable standard of living. It might be suitable to look at the level of payments made by local authorities to foster parents as a guide for the appropriate figure.

3. *Expected lifestyle costs.* This would be the amount needed to keep the child at the lifestyle level which would have been expected had the parents not separated. Another way of putting this test is that the child should be kept at the lifestyle standard enjoyed by children in two-parent households of the separating parents' income level.[43]

4. *Actual expenditure.* The law could focus on the amount actually spent by the residential parent, in so far as it was reasonable, and require the non-residential parent to share these costs. The difficulty with this approach would be the ambiguity which surrounds the term 'reasonableness'. The average cost of raising a child until the age of 21 has recently been calculated at £180,137.[44]

5. *Income percentage.* The level of child support could be a fixed percentage of the non-residential parent's income.

6. *Cost-effective level.* The amount of support should be fixed at a level which can be regularly paid. This approach is highly pragmatic. It focuses not on the child but on the expense to the state of enforcing and collecting the payments. It argues that, whatever the ideal, if the level is fixed at too high a rate and seen as unfair, then the money will not be paid. It is therefore better to set a lower rate which is more likely to be paid and thereby avoid the costs of enforcement.

7. *Equality of households.* This approach would seek to achieve an equal standard of living between the father's and mother's households.[45] This would not necessarily mean fixing equal income, because the cost of caring for the child would involve the residential parent in greater expense. This method requires integration of the maintenance of the parent with support for the child.

8. *Utilitarian.* This approach would fix child support at a level at which the removal of any asset from the non-residential parent's house would lead to a greater reduction in that

---

[42] Munby J (2005: 497).
[43] Parker (1991).
[44] BBC Newsonline (2006g).
[45] Parker (1991).

household's welfare than the gain which would be received by the residential parent's household. The approach focuses not on sums of money, but on the welfare and happiness of the parties. It would, however, be extremely difficult to measure these.

## E Paternity fraud

There have been cases where a man has paid child support after being falsely told that he was the father of a child. In *A v B (Damages: Paternity)*[46] a man obtained damages against a former partner for deceit in relation to a paternity issue. He was awarded damages to compensate him for sums paid for the benefit of the child, but he could not recover the sums spent on his partner.

## F 'The lone-parent crisis'

In the present political climate it is difficult to separate the question of child support from the concerns over the 'crisis of lone parents'.[47] There has been a substantial increase in the number of lone-parent households. In 2008 in England and Wales a lone parent headed 12 per cent of households; in 1972 the figure was 4 per cent.[48] The reaction to the increase in lone parenthood has been varied.[49] Some see lone parents as an alarming sign of social disintegration, while others view lone parenthood as a crucial aspect of the liberation of women from the traditional family.[50] As discussed in Chapter 1 while there is general agreement that children in lone parents families do less well than children raised in two parent households, there is much debate as to why this is so. Some argue that the root cause of the disadvantage faced by children of lone parents is the poverty associated with lone parenthood, while others cite the lack of a father figure or stable family background as the primary cause.[51] In political terms, these arguments lead to debates over whether state benefits to lone parents encourage lone parenthood and so should be restricted or whether such benefits help alleviate the disadvantages attached to lone parenthood and should be increased.

Although it is common to refer to 'the problem of lone mothers', it might be more appropriate to refer to 'the problem of non-residential fathers'. One survey found that only 77 per cent of non-residential fathers had paid maintenance at least once and 57 per cent were doing so currently. Twenty-one per cent had not seen their children in the last year, although 47 per cent saw their children at least every week.[52] Lady Thatcher, who as Prime Minister had steered the Child Support Act 1991 through Parliament, notably recalled in her memoirs that she was 'appalled by the way in which men fathered a child and then absconded, leaving the single mother – and the tax payer – to foot the bill for their irresponsibility and condemning the child to a lower standard of living'.[53] Similar attitudes were expressed when it was recently disclosed that a 21-year-old man had just fathered his seventh child.[54]

---

[46] [2007] 3 FCR 861, discussed in Wikeley and Young (2008). See also *P v B (Paternity: Damages for Deceit)* [2001] 1 FLR 1041.

[47] For criticism of lone-parent families see, e.g., Galston (1991); for a more positive response see Young (1999).

[48] National Statistics (2010a).

[49] Fox Harding (1996).

[50] Morgan (2007).

[51] Edwards and Halpern (1992).

[52] Bradshaw, Stimson, Skinner and Williams (1999).

[53] Thatcher (1995: 630).

[54] BBC Newsonline (2006h).

## G  Child support and parental support

If a parent is obliged to support a child, should he or she necessarily be required to provide for the residential parent?[55] There is no point in supplying a child with food and clothing if there is no one to feed or clothe the child. So a strong case can be made that if a child is to be cared for by a residential parent, then the non-residential parent should be liable to support the residential parent at some level. Another key question is how to balance the claims of children and spouses on divorce. A straightforward approach could be that first the courts should resolve the issues related to the child's support, and then turn to spousal support. In truth, for most couples nowadays, child support takes up such a large part of income that very limited resources are available for spousal support.

## H  Should child support be a private issue?

Should the level of child support be fixed by the Government or is it a private matter to be left to negotiation between the parties? In considering this issue it is useful to distinguish cases where the child and resident parent are receiving state benefits and cases where they are not. Where they are, the state has a clear interest in ensuring that the non-resident parent recompenses the state for the amount paid out in benefits, if he or she can afford to do so. But if neither party is in receipt of benefits, does the state have an interest, justifying intervention, in how the parties decide to arrange child support? For example, if a couple decide that the best way to arrange their post-separation finances is that the wife and children will receive the former matrimonial home, but to compensate the husband for his loss in the share of the house he will have to pay less by way of financial support than he would have done, is it proper for the state to intervene to require the husband to pay a certain minimum amount? Or should this be regarded as a private matter which should be left to the decision of the couple themselves? It could be argued that the issue of child poverty is an important one for the state, and parents should not be permitted to enter an agreement which leaves the child only barely provided for.[56] However, the Child Maintenance and Other Payments Act 2008 is based on the principle that individuals should negotiate for themselves child payments, and the primary role of the state is to assist in these negotiations and give effect to them.

## 2  Financial support of children

### A  Financial support of children living with both parents

A crucial point about the present law is that generally it does not intervene in the financial affairs of a family who are living together. As long as the child is provided for at a basic level and the child is not suffering significant harm, the state will not interfere. Indeed many fathers have complained that they are required to pay more for their child after the separation than they did when living with the child. It is on parental separation that the law intervenes and can require a parent not just to provide for the basic needs of the child, but also to apply a fair level of support. This non-intervention in family life except upon the separation of parents is one aspect of the weight the law places on the protection of the private life of the

---

[55] See the discussion on Children Act 1989, Sch 1 below.
[56] Wikeley (2006c).

family.[57] In fact, a child who wishes to complain that he or she is not being given enough pocket money could seek an order under s 8 of the Children Act 1989, but it is hard to imagine a court being willing to hear such a case.

## B The Child Support Act 1991

The original child support scheme is found in the Child Support Act 1991. The scheme has been reformed by the Child Maintenance and Other Payments Act 2008. Nevertheless, we will very briefly describe the 1991 Act because it still applies to some cases and an understanding of it helps explain the 2008 Act. The 2008 Act will not fully come into force until 2011.

The CSA 1991 was born out of a deep dissatisfaction with the system of child support that existed at the time. The system prior to the 1991 Act was administered by the courts. The burden lay on the residential parent to apply to the court for an order against the other parent. Many parents did not think it was worth applying or found the system too difficult to use. Even when they did use the courts the sums awarded were low and very hard to enforce.

The 1991 Act was only concerned with non-resident parents. It had no impact for children whose parents were living together. It imposed liability on 'parents'.[58] This covers only those who are in law the mother or father of the child. Under the CSA 1991 parents had a duty to maintain their children until the child was 16, or until their nineteenth birthday if they were receiving full-time education.[59]

The Child Support Agency had responsibility for administering the Act.[60] This means that the duty for assessing and enforcing the payments lies with the Agency and not with the residential parent or the courts. Indeed, if the residential parent is receiving benefits, he or she must notify the Agency of the identity of the other parent.[61] The Agency will then enforce the orders for payments made against the non-residential parent, whether the residential parent wishes the Agency to become involved or not.[62]

The Act provided a formula which determined the liability of parents. The original formula in the Child Support Act 1991 was extraordinarily complicated and was replaced with a new one in the Child Support, Pensions and Social Security Act 2000. Only four pieces of information will be required for assessment: the non-residential parent's income;[63] the number of children they have; the number of nights the children stay overnight with the non-resident parent; and whether they live in a household with other children. If the non-residential parent earned over £200 per week net and has one qualifying child, he or she must pay 15 per cent of his or her income;[64] if he or she has two qualifying children he or she must pay 20 per cent; if he or she has three or more he or she must pay 25 per cent.[65] The maximum assessable weekly income is £2,000 per week. So the most a non-resident parent would have to pay under the new scheme is £26,000 per year for three or more children. Some account is taken of any other children living with the non-residential parent. So, if a

---

[57] See Chapter 1.

[58] CSA 1991, s 1.

[59] CSA 1991, s 55.

[60] A role now performed by the Child Maintenance and Enforcement Commission; CSA 1991, Sch 1.

[61] CSA 1991, s 6.

[62] CSA 1991, s 9.

[63] If the children are spending an equal amount of time with both parents the resident parent is the person who is receiving the payment. If the child is at boarding school the resident parent is the parent with whom the child would be living if not at school (!).

[64] This is income after tax, national insurance and pension contributions.

[65] Child Support, Pensions and Social Security Act 2000 (hereafter CSPSSA 2000), s 1, Sch 1.

father (F) leaves his partner (M) and their child (A) and moves in with another woman (W) who has a child (B) by another man, the existence of B will affect the amount payable by F for A.[66] His notional income is reduced in relation to the number of children living with him by 15 per cent, 20 per cent or 25 per cent, as above. So if F earned £1,000 per week, because of B his notional income would be reduced by 15 per cent, making it £850. He would then have to pay 15 per cent of that for A (i.e. £127.50).

The formula is a little rough and ready and takes only a few factors into account. No account is taken of exceptional costs, except under an application to the tribunal. The Government hopes that, although the formula is a little crude, the percentages are low enough that only rarely will the tribunal have to depart from the calculation.[67] The figure of 15 per cent was justified on the basis that an unseparated two-parent family spent 30 per cent of their income on their children and so the non-resident parent should pay his or her half on separation.[68] The flaw in this explanation (as the White Paper admitted) is that normally the father contributes far more than half of the costs of the child's upbringing and so he will be paying far less under the 2000 Act than he would have done when the couple were together. It might be thought impossible to come up with a formula that can be applied to all applicants given the huge variety in people's family lives and incomes.[69]

One important rule is that if the non-residential parent has his or her child to stay with him or her for more than 52 nights per year there will be a reduction in the levels paid. If the child stays with the payer 52 to 103 nights per year[70] the level payable will be reduced by one-seventh; 104 to 155 nights by two-sevenths; 156 to 174 by three-sevenths;[71] and 175 or more by one-half. Payers whose income is less than £100 per week need make no payment at all if there is staying contact for one or more nights per week. This policy may well lead to an increase in the level of overnight contact.[72] Whether this will always be in the interests of the child is open to debate.[73]

As we shall see shortly, the Child Support Act 1991, as amended, suffered enormous problems in practice. The Child Support Agency struggled to collect effectively the payments and was strongly opposed by fathers. This led to a series of legal challenges to the Agency by both resident and non-resident parents. They failed.[74] Most notably the House of Lords in *R (On the Application of Kehoe)* v *Secretary of State for Work and Pensions*[75] held that the lack of effective legal remedy for resident parents who were not receiving payments from non-resident parents was not consistent with the Human Rights Act 1998. Predictably the Court of Appeal in *Rowley* v *Secretary of State for the Department of Work and Pensions*[76] found that the Secretary of State did not owe a duty of care in tort law to qualifying children or their parents

---

[66] CSPSSA 2000, s 1, Sch 1.

[67] Department of Social Security (2000: 1.12).

[68] Department of Social Security (2000: 9).

[69] Pirrie (2005).

[70] That is one or two nights a week.

[71] At first sight, reduction by three-sevenths seems appropriate but, according to the pressure group Families Need Fathers, a six-sevenths reduction is appropriate, as the non-residential parent has one day a week less care than the residential parent, although this overlooks the fact that the non-residential parent has to provide support for the primary carer.

[72] A one-seventh reduction in child support for the cost of a burger and a DVD is a bargain.

[73] See Chapter 9 for a discussion about the benefits of contact.

[74] E.g. *R (Mantle)* v *Secretary of State for Work and Pensions* [2010] 1 FLR 541; *Treharne* v *Secretary of State for Work and Pensions* [2009] 1 FLR 853.

[75] [2005] UKHL 48, [2005] 4 All ER 905. See Wikeley (2006a) for an excellent commentary on the judgment. An appeal by Ms Kehoe to the ECtHR failed: *Kehoe* v *UK* [2008] 1 FCR 461.

[76] [2007] 3 FCR 431.

in exercising their function under the CSA. The Government has announced that in cases of maladministration compensation will be available, but this is on a voluntary basis.[77]

## (i) The Child Support Agency in crisis

By 2006 it was undeniable that the Child Support Agency was in crisis. There had been a number of reports revealing its difficulties, most notably by the Ombudsman[78] and the House of Commons Work and Pensions Committee,[79] the latter stating that the Agency was a failing organisation needing rapid and radical change.[80] A glance at some of the statistics indicates the depth of the problem.[81]

---

### KEY STATISTICS

- By April 2005 the accumulated debt owed by non-resident parents since 1993 stood at over £3.3 billion. Much of that was believed to be uncollectable. In 2008 it was estimated that £3.8 billion was owed and that £1.8 billion will not be collected.[82] In the same time period £5 billion was collected.[83]

- Over a quarter of a million applications under the scheme had not yet been cleared. There were 70,000 applications under the old scheme which were yet to be cleared.

- 30% of non-resident parents who had been assessed did not pay.

- It cost around 60 pence in administration costs to get each £1 of maintenance to a child.

- Only one-half of lone parents had a maintenance order or agreement in their favour. Where they did, only 64% received anything.[84] Of all parents with care on benefits only 25% were actually receiving any money from the Agency.[85] As the legislation was especially designed to help this group, this is particularly disappointing.

---

These figures represent but the tip of the iceberg of a range of problems. There was widespread miscalculation of the sums due; those seeking to contact the Agency found it almost impossible to get through on the telephone;[86] morale among staff at the Agency was generally seen as appallingly low; and there was little use of the Agency's enforcement powers.[87] The Government announced that the Child Support Agency would be abandoned and replaced.

Many looking at the mess in 2006 blamed the policy framework and the scheme. Others criticised those running the CSA; the computer software designers; and the Government itself. But it should not be forgotten that the real cause of the problem was non-resident fathers failing to pay the sums they were assessed to pay. The problems facing the Agency would have

---

[77] *R (Humphries) v Secretary of State for Work and Pensions* [2008] 2 FLR 2116.
[78] Ombudsman (2004).
[79] House of Commons Work and Pensions Committee (2005).
[80] In *Giltane v CSA* [2006] EWHC 423 (Fam) the Agency accepted that figures given to the court were incorrect.
[81] Child Support Agency (2006).
[82] BBC Newsonline (2008i).
[83] Department for Work and Pensions (2006c: 5).
[84] Willitts et al. (2005).
[85] Wikeley (2006b).
[86] House of Commons Work and Pensions Committee (2005).
[87] Wikeley (2006b).

been far fewer if non-resident parents had been willing to pay the sums they were legally required to.

Certainly there were some problems with the formula, even in its simplified version in the 2000 Act. There are particular difficulties in calculating correctly the appropriate payments for those whose income is constantly changing: for example, those who are self-employed.[88] But that would be so whatever statutory formula were used. Further, there was no doubt that the Child Support Agency lacked support from the general public. It has been argued that the CSA 1991 put the Treasury, rather than the child, first.[89] There is much to uphold such an allegation. If payments are made to the Agency they did not actually benefit the residential parent and the child because any payment received will lead to a 'pound for pound' reduction in the benefits they receive. Bradshaw et al.[90] found that 57 per cent of non-residential fathers were paying child support. The main reasons given by the fathers who were not paying child support was that the father was unemployed or could not afford the payments. If the aim was to save the Government money the Agency failed spectacularly as it cost more to run than it collected for the state.[91]

It should not, of course, be thought that the Child Support Agency was good for nothing. It did collect maintenance and for over 100,000 children and this was enough to raise them out of poverty. Over half a million children received payments from money paid via the Agency.[92] In June 2008, 684,400 children were benefiting from over £1 billion in maintenance payments per year.[93] Not everyone agrees that the CSA was a complete failure. As Maclean and Fehlberg argue:

> It has provided a service for all children, not only those whose parents divorce. Amounts of support are significantly higher than under the previous court based system, and enforcement is slightly better and was never at any stage worse. . . . above all, the CSA gave prominence and clarity to the concept of support for the child in its own right. And although most non-resident parents criticize their own assessment for support, the concept of the financial responsibility of parents for children whether or not they share or ever shared a household is now well established.[94]

## C The Child Maintenance and Other Payments Act 2008

Acknowledging the problems facing the child support system, the Government has set out some of the principles that have guided the reforms in the 2008 Act:

> . . . The system should be simpler, less bureaucratic and more cost-effective.
>
> Whether or not a person decides to use the state system to arrange child maintenance should be their choice. The system should prioritise the needs of children. It must help engender a new climate where parents can more easily come to their own financial arrangements concerning the maintenance of their children. And it should mark a clean break with the past, with a new organisation being created to give the delivery of child support a fresh start.[95]

---

[88] See *Smith v Secretary of State for Work and Pensions* [2006] UKHL 35 and Wikeley and Young (2005) for a detailed discussion of this issue.

[89] Child Poverty Action Group (1994).

[90] Bradshaw, Stimson, Skinner and Williams (1999).

[91] Jones and Perrin (2009).

[92] Child Maintenance and Enforcement Commission (2010).

[93] Child Maintenance and Enforcement Commission (2010a). There are still massive arrears of child support which have not been paid: Burrows (2010).

[94] Maclean and Fehlberg (2009: 9).

[95] Department for Work and Pensions (2006c: 1).

The Government, in its paper entitled *A Fresh Start*, outlined what it regarded as the key objectives for the 2008 Act:

- help tackle child poverty by ensuring that more parents take responsibility for paying for their children and that more children, especially the poorest, benefit from this;

- promote parental responsibility by encouraging and empowering parents in their role and, where necessary, requiring them to meet their obligations;

- provide an efficient and professional service that gets money to children in the most cost-effective way for the taxpayer; and

- be simple and transparent, and provide an accessible, reliable and responsive service that is understood and accepted by users and their advisers and capable of being administered by staff.

The Child Maintenance and Other Payments Act 2008 establishes the framework. It will not come fully into force until 2011. The Child Support Agency will be replaced by the Child Maintenance and Enforcement Commission (CMEC). From 14 July 2008 any parent with care who makes a claim for income support will no longer be treated as making a claim for child support and there will be no penalties for those who fail to apply for child support. So, all those with care will now be able to agree a private maintenance agreement with their ex-partner; or, if they wish, can apply to the CMEC for an assessment; or indeed they may wish to make no arrangements at all.

The role of the new CMEC is notably different from the old CSA. Its role is to promote child maintenance and to provide information and guidance to separated parents.[96] Indeed CMEC is able to charge for providing its services.[97] The hope of the Government is that the services will enable parents to make their own voluntary arrangements. Whether that is a realistic goal or not remains to be seen. If a government found it impossible to produce a formula which was regarded as fair or to enforce effectively child support payments, is there any reason to suspect parents will be any more effective at doing so? Indeed it is worth remembering that the whole reason the CSA was created was due to the problems lone parents faced in seeking to collect child maintenance. The House of Commons Work and Pensions Committee[98] has expressed the concern that the new law will see a return to the position before the CSA when little child support was collected.

Section 2 of the 2008 Act states that the main objective of the CMEC is 'to maximize the number of those children who live apart from one or both of their parents for whom effective arrangements are in place'. However, given the inability of the Commission to force couples to reach agreement or impose payment arrangements on them, it is hard to see how the Commission can be blamed if children do not receive adequate child support payments. The Commission is also given the aim of supporting and encouraging parents to make and keep 'appropriate voluntary maintenance arrangements for their children'.[99] The second objective is to ensure that there is compliance with child support orders.[100]

It seems that the primary aim of the Commission will be to encourage people to reach private arrangements over child support.[101] It has a duty to take appropriate steps to 'raise

---

[96] Child Maintenance and Other Payments Act 2008 (CMOPA), ss 4 and 5.
[97] CMOPA, s 6.
[98] House of Commons Work and Pensions Committee (2010).
[99] CMOPA, s 2(2).
[100] CMOPA, s 2(2). See further Wikeley (2008b).
[101] Child Maintenance and Enforcement Commission (2008b).

awareness among parents' of taking responsibility for maintenance and making appropriate arrangements.[102] A CMEC guide states:

> Doing things yourself can be quicker and easier than through the CSA (as long as you and the other parent are able to work together). There is no bureaucracy to deal with or set rules to follow. You can be more flexible about how, what and when payments should be made. If you can keep solicitors and the CSA out of it, it's a lot easier to keep things friendly. It can be a good way to rebuild trust for the future. . . . A private agreement is totally private. No one else needs to get involved in your affairs.[103]

However, it is suggested, there is much to be concerned about in leaving the issue of child support to parental agreement. Baroness Hollis noted that non-resident fathers were likely to welcome the reforms:

> They think that they will get a better deal; they think that they will pay less money; they think that there will be less pressure on them to pay; and they think that they will be able to hug knowledge and information that she – the parent with care – will not have and which will allow them, to a degree, to control what they pay.[104]

As Nick Wikelely puts it 'There is a clear risk, in the absence of adequate advice and support services, that any existing power imbalances between parents will simply be reinforced, to the detriment of children's interests.'[105]

If a couple cannot make their own arrangement the parent can still apply for an assessment using the child support formula, as set out in the CSA 1991. However, the CMEC will only make an assessment where either party requests an assessment to be made. The formula has been slightly amended by the 2008 Act to mean that the assessment will be of the non-resident parent's gross income.[106] This reflects the fact that the CMEC will be able to use data from HM Revenue and Customs, rather than relying on a non-resident's disclosure of information. A non-resident will be required to pay 12 per cent for one child, 16 per cent for two children and 19 per cent for three or more children.[107]

No longer will benefits be reduced if a parent is receiving child support. So all money paid in maintenance will reach children.[108] This indicates a shift from child support being the primary source of financial support for children to the state accepting responsibility for meeting the basic need of children and child support payments being a top-up. There is now a complete separation between benefits payments and child support.[109]

Where an assessment is made, there are new enforcement mechanisms availiable to the CMEC. These include imprisonment, driving disqualification, removal of travel authorisation (e.g. passport) and even a curfew order. However, to repeat, assessment and enforcement will only take place where either parent requests it. The legislation indicates that the preference is for couples to reach their own agreement. Where they do, the CMEC will not have power to enforce them, although the couple present the agreement to a court to be made into a consent order. The Henshaw Report, which played an important role in the background to the new legislation, explained this approach:

---

[102] CMOPA, s 4.
[103] Child Maintenance and Enforcement Commission (2008c).
[104] Quoted in Wikeley (2008a: 1027).
[105] Wikeley (2008a: 1027).
[106] CMOPA, Sch 4.
[107] Lower percentages of 9, 12 and 15 will apply to gross income of over £800 per week.
[108] Child Maintenance and Enforcement Commission (2008a).
[109] Jones and Perrin (2009).

Many parents would prefer to make their own child maintenance arrangements and could often do so amicably. The existing child maintenance system, however, does not provide a framework to facilitate this. Where parents with care make a claim for benefits, the system overturns any arrangements that may already be in place. This undermines the very parental responsibility it is seeking to enforce and can be to the detriment of the children concerned. Reclaiming most of the money for the State, rather than passing it through to the children, means that neither parent has a strong enough incentive to co-operate. This undermines the extent to which child maintenance can contribute to the eradication of child poverty.[110]

A recent survey found that 24 per cent of those on benefits said that if left to their own devices they would agree that the non-resident parent would not have to pay child support.[111] If that reflects what happens when the Act is in operation it will mean that children will lose out significantly under the new legislation. Not surprisingly, surveys suggest that the new regime is welcomed by twice as many non-resident parents as resident parents.[112]

There is no doubt that the 2008 Act is designed to ease the problems which the Child Support Agency had faced of complexity and widespread non-compliance. As the level and enforcement of child maintenance is going to be in the hands of parents rather than the Government, one of its aims may be to deflect criticisms about child support away from the politicians.[113] However, as Nick Wikeley puts it:

> The central tenet of the Child Support Act 1991 was the principle of parental (and especially paternal) financial responsibility, which was allowed to trump any concerns about operational effectiveness. The danger is that the pendulum has now swung too far the other way, and that the [2008 Act] has been dominated by operational concerns at the expense of the consideration of principle.[114]

## D The Children Act 1989 and child support

The Children Act 1989 can require parents to support children, regardless of whether the parents are married or unmarried. This is an important part of ensuring that the law governing the financial support of children does not depend on whether the parents were married or not. However, in practice the Children Act 1989 has been very little used, in part because so few separating cohabitants seek advice from solicitors.[115]

### (i) Who can apply under the Children Act 1989?

The following people can apply for a financial order under s 15 of the Children Act 1989 in respect of a child:

1. A parent. This includes adoptive parents as well as natural parents. It also includes 'any party to a marriage (whether or not subsisting) in relation to whom the child . . . is a child of the family'.[116] A step-parent would be covered by the definition.

2. A guardian.

3. Any person who has a residence order in force in respect of a child.

---

[110] Henshaw (2006: para 21).
[111] Wikeley, Ireland et al. (2008).
[112] Wikeley, Ireland et al. (2008).
[113] Maclean and Fehlberg (2009); Masson (2009).
[114] Wikeley (2007b: 457). See also Wikeley (2009).
[115] Maclean, Eekelaar, Lewis et al. (2002). In 2004 only 389 orders were made: Law Commission Consultation Paper 179 (2006: 17).
[116] See Chapter 7 for further discussion of this term.

4. An adult student, or trainee, or other person who can show special circumstances can apply for an order against his or her parents.[117] This order cannot be made if both parents are living together in the same household. So, for example, if the child's parents are still happily married or cohabiting the law will not intervene to force them to provide for the student's upkeep.[118]

The court in its own discretion can make an order under the section, even if there has been no application. For example, if the child has been made a ward of court, the court might make an award under the Act.

## (ii) Who is liable to pay?

1. *Parents.* This includes biological parents and adoptive parents. A parent is liable to pay even if he or she does not have parental responsibility or never sees the child. A person who has played the role of a parent, but is not a parent in the eyes of the law cannot be made liable.[119]

2. *Those who have treated the child as a child of the family.* This can only apply to spouses or civil partners. An unmarried cohabitant of the mother, who is not the father of the child, will not be liable.[120]

## (iii) Orders which can be made

Under the Children Act 1989 periodical payments and lump sum orders can be made.[121] A party can also be required to make a transfer of property. This is most likely to be used in relation to the family home and may, for example, direct that a child and the residential parent stay in a property until the child ceases education. There is also the power to transfer a secure tenancy to the other parent for the child's benefit.[122]

## (iv) Factors that the court will consider

The courts will take into account the following factors in deciding whether to make an order:

---

### LEGISLATIVE PROVISION

**Children Act 1989, Schedule 1, para 4(1)**

(a) the income, earning capacity, property and other financial resources which [the applicant, parents and the person in whose favour the order would be made] has or is likely to have in the foreseeable future;

(b) the financial needs, obligations and responsibilities which [each of those persons] has or is likely to have in the foreseeable future;

➡

---

[117] E.g. *C v F (Disabled Child: Maintenance Orders)* [1999] 1 FCR 39, [1998] 2 FLR 1.
[118] The only orders these applicants can claim are periodical payments or lump sum orders.
[119] *T v B* [2010] EWHC 1444 (Fam).
[120] *J v J (A Minor: Property Transfer)* [1993] 1 FCR 471, [1993] 2 FLR 56; *T v B* [2010] EWHC 1444 (Fam).
[121] This can include a lump sum to meet expenses incurred before the court hearing, including expenses connected to the birth of a child (Children Act 1989, Sch 1, para 5(1)).
[122] *K v K (Minors: Property Transfer)* [1992] 2 FCR 253, [1992] 2 FLR 220; although the courts have indicated that they will be cautious in exercising this power: *J v J (A Minor: Property Transfer)* [1993] 1 FCR 471, [1993] 2 FLR 56.

(c) the financial needs of the child;

(d) the income, earning capacity (if any), property and other financial resources of the child;

(e) any physical or mental disability of the child;

(f) the manner in which the child was being, or was expected to be, educated or trained.

Where the liability of a person who is not the child's legal parent is taken into account the court should also consider:

## LEGISLATIVE PROVISION

### Children Act 1989, Schedule 1, para 4(2)

(a) whether that person had assumed responsibility for the maintenance of the child and, if so, the extent to which and basis on which he assumed that responsibility and the length of the period during which he met that responsibility;

(b) whether he did so knowing that the child was not his child;

(c) the liability of any other person to maintain the child.

The welfare of the child is not the paramount consideration because, as is made clear by s 105(1), property orders are not deemed concerned with the upbringing of the child and so fall outside the scope of s 1(1) of the Children Act 1989.[123] However, the child's welfare will be an important consideration.[124] The following points will influence the court in deciding the appropriate level of the award:

1. The level of the award should not depend on whether the child's parents were married or not.[125]

2. The child should be brought up in a manner which is in some way commensurate with the non-residential parent's lifestyle.[126] In *J v C (Child: Financial Provision)*[127] the child's non-residential father became a millionaire and it was held that the child should be brought up in a way appropriate for a millionaire's daughter, including living in a four-bedroomed house and being driven around in a Ford Mondeo(!) In other cases it has been emphasised that where the child is having contact with the father the child will feel uncomfortable if his or her home circumstances are vastly different from those enjoyed by his or her father. In *Re P (A Child) (Financial Provision)*[128] the mother's claim for a top-of-the-range Range Rover from the very wealthy father was found to be excessive. However, she could expect a £20,000 car and £450,000 for a house in a 'suitable' part of London. In *F v G (Child: Financial Provision)*[129] the father was worth over £4.5 million and earned over half a million pounds a year. It was held that the level of award should enable the

---

[123] *J v C (Child: Financial Provision)* [1999] 1 FLR 152; *Re P (A Child) (Financial Provision)* [2003] 2 FCR 481.
[124] *Re P (A Child: Financial Provision)* [2003] EWCA Civ 837.
[125] In *A v A (A Minor: Financial Provision)* [1994] 1 FLR 657 at p. 659.
[126] *H v P (Illegitimate Child: Capital Provision)* [1993] Fam Law 515.
[127] [1999] 1 FLR 152.
[128] [2003] 2 FCR 481.
[129] [2005] 1 FLR 261.

mother to raise the child in a manner 'not too brutally remote' from the father's lifestyle. In *T v T (Financial Provision: Private Education)*[130] a lump sum order was made under Sch 1 to cover the children's private school fees, that being commensurate with the parents' wealth.

3. The court should be wary of making an award which will benefit the resident parent but not the child.[131] Of course some provision for the child will inevitably also benefit the resident parent and other children living with them (e.g. a house) and there can be no objection to this.[132] Payment for nanny care could be expected, even if the mother was not working.[133] In *Re P (A Child: Financial Provision)*[134] it was held that the mother was entitled to an allowance in her capacity as the child's carer, even though she could not make any claim in her own right. In *H v C*[135] private health insurance for the mother was included as part of her carer's allowance. In *F v G (Child: Financial Provision)*[136] £60,000 was awarded for the mother to use either to employ a nanny or to herself as full-time carer. Sums for child care can even be ordered if the child is a teenager.[137] These sums can be used by the mother to 'pay herself' and the mother is not required to account for how the money is spent. However, payments must be seen as support for the child, rather than maintenance for the mother in her own right.[138] In *Re S (Child: Financial Provision)*[139] where the Court of Appeal said that the phrase 'for the benefit of the child' in para 1(2) of Sch 1 would be interpreted widely. It could therefore include awarding the mother money so that she could travel to see the child, who had been abducted to Sudan.[140]

4. A parent is liable to support a child only during the child's minority.[141] So, if a large sum is provided for accommodation for the child, the sum will normally be held on trust to revert to the paying parent on the child reaching the age of 18 or finishing his or her education.[142] This means that, when the child reaches 18, if a house was provided it may be sold and the sum returned to the paying parent.[143] Similarly funds to support the child will cease on majority, unless there are exceptional circumstances such as disability of the child.[144]

5. If the court is considering the liability of a step-parent, it will take into account their liability to support any biological child of theirs.

6. Where the applicant is a disabled adult, they can claim against their parents. Although the expenses are restricted to expenses that directly relate to the disability while under the jurisdiction of the Child Support Act, under the Children Act other expenses can be considered.[145]

---

[130] [2005] EWHC 2119 (Fam).
[131] *Re P (A Child) (Financial Provision)* [2003] 2 FCR 481. See the useful commentary in Gilmore (2004d).
[132] *J v C (Child: Financial Provision)* [1998] 3 FCR 79.
[133] *Re P (A Child) (Financial Provision)* [2003] 2 FCR 481.
[134] [2003] 2 FCR 481.
[135] [2009] 2 FLR 1540.
[136] [2005] 1 FLR 261.
[137] *N v D* [2008] 1 FLR 1629.
[138] *MT v OT* [2007] EWHC 838 (Fam).
[139] [2004] EWCA Civ 1685.
[140] Followed in *CF v KM* [2010] EWHC 1754 (Fam).
[141] *Re N (A child) (Payments for benefit of child)* [2009] 1 FCR 606.
[142] *H v P (Illegitimate Child: Capital Provision)* [1993] Fam Law 515; *T v S* (Financial Provision for Children) [1994] 1 FCR 743, [1994] 2 FLR 883.
[143] Although the order may provide for the residential parent to have an option to purchase the house.
[144] *Re N (A Child) (Payments for Benefit of Child)* [2009] 1 FCR 606.
[145] *C v F (Disabled Child: Maintenance Orders)* [1999] 1 FCR 39, [1998] 2 FLR 1.

7. It is not possible for the parents to enter a contract which prevents them applying for an order under Sch 1.[146]

## 3 Matrimonial Causes Act 1973 and children

### A Powers of the court on divorce or dissolution

On divorce or dissolution the court has wide powers to redistribute the parties' property. This includes the power to make orders especially designed to benefit children. For example, an order could demand regular payment of money to the child or, more commonly, a payment to the resident parent for the benefit of the child.

### B 'Child of the family'

Many of the court's powers to redistribute in divorce proceedings apply in respect of 'a child of the family'. The meaning of this phrase will be discussed in Chapter 7. The definition most notably includes a stepchild. Such a child can be treated under the child support legislation as the biological parents' responsibility, but under the Matrimonial Causes Act 1973 (hereafter MCA 1973) as the step-parents' responsibility.

The MCA 1973 does list special considerations that apply where a step-parent is being asked to pay. The following factors must be taken into account:

---

**LEGISLATIVE PROVISION**

**Matrimonial Cause Act 1973, section 25(4)**

(a) to whether that party assumed any responsibility for the child's maintenance, and, if so, the extent to which, and the basis upon which, that party assumed such responsibility and the length of time for which that party discharged such responsibility;

(b) to whether in assuming and discharging such responsibility that party did so knowing that the child was not his or her own;

(c) to the liability of any other person to maintain the child.[147]

---

### C Applications by children

A child who is over the age of 18 can apply for a financial or property order if his or her parents are divorcing, or apply for a variation of an order made earlier.[148] Although normally orders will cease once the child reaches the age of 18, the court can order that periodical payments extend beyond the eighteenth birthday if the child is or will be receiving instruction at an educational establishment or undergoing training and there are special circumstances which justify the order.[149]

---

[146] *Morgan v Hill* [2006] 3 FCR 620.
[147] Matrimonial Causes Act 1973 (hereafter MCA 1973), s 25(4).
[148] See *Downing v Downing* [1976] Fam 288.
[149] MCA 1973, s 29.

## D Factors to be taken into account

The factors to be considered in deciding the appropriate level of an award under the MCA 1973 will be discussed in detail shortly. It should be noted that the welfare of any child is to be regarded as the first consideration[150] and the courts regard ensuring the children are adequately housed as especially important.[151] The courts have indicated that the amount that would be awarded under the CSA 1991 will be a starting point.[152] However, in wealthy cases, substantial sums of maintenance can be ordered and can include private school fees, university tuition fees, funding for gap years and private medical insurance.[153]

## 4 Theoretical issues concerning financial support on divorce or dissolution

As we noted in Chapter 2, the powers of the court to redistribute property and make orders on dissolution of a civil partnership match those available for marriage under the Matrimonial Causes Act. For ease of expression we will discuss how the courts will deal with property and income on the breakdown of a marriage. Everything that is said could apply equally to the dissolution of a civil partnership.[154]

The redistribution of property on divorce is a controversial issue. There is a wide range of competing policies that the law seeks to hold together. There is a desire to ensure that on divorce a fair redistribution of the property takes place so that one party is not unduly disadvantaged by the divorce. On the other hand there is the desire to enable the parties to achieve truly independent lives after the divorce. To do both is often impossible. The truth is that for many couples suitable financial orders cannot be made. Neither party will be able to live at a standard of living they regard as acceptable. Both will feel they have been hard done by. As Symes explains:

> Quite clearly, marriage as it has traditionally been practised, is not intended to be ended by divorce. Indeed, traditional housewife marriage has a most potent feature of indissolubility built right into it – dependency . . . The accumulation of responsibilities and obligations, the consequences of an unequal partnership based on dependency – all mean that an absolute severance of the bond without massive adjustment would be manifestly unjust, more likely impossible.[155]

There is simply not enough money for most married couples to support two individuals in separate households after divorce, certainly not at the level to which they had become accustomed.[156]

## A The economic realities of divorce

There is convincing evidence that following divorce women who are caring for children suffer a detrimental downturn in their finances, while their ex-husbands do not.[157] The conclusions of a recent study of the impact of divorce on women was blunt:

---

[150] MCA 1973, s 25.
[151] *M v B (Ancillary Proceedings: Lump Sum)* [1998] 1 FLR 53, [1998] 1 FCR 213.
[152] *GW v RW* [2003] Fam Law 386.
[153] *H v H (Financial Relief)* [2010] 1 FLR 1864.
[154] See Wilson (2007) and Allen and Williams (2009) for a discussion of whether there are any arguments that civil partnerships will be treated any differently from marriages in this area.
[155] Symes (1985: 57).
[156] Barton and Bissett-Johnson (2000) noted that in the majority of cases no financial orders are made by the court. In some cases this will reflect the fact that there are simply no assets to redistribute.
[157] Sigle-Rushton, W. (2009); Davis et al. (1991); Perry et al. (2000).

The stark conclusion is that men's household income increases by about 23 per cent on divorce once we control for household size, whereas women's household income falls by about 31 per cent. There is partial recovery for women, but this recovery is driven by repartnering: the average effect of repartnering is to restore income to pre-divorce levels after nine years. [For] those who do not repartner . . . the long term economic consequences of divorce are serious.[158]

The extent of disadvantage for women on divorce is closely related to their employment history during marriage.[159] There is convincing evidence that following divorce those who have undertaken primary care of the child (normally the wife) suffer significantly.[160] Child-care responsibilities mean that women are far more likely to have given up employment than men; where they are employed, mothers are more often in part-time low status, poorly paid jobs.[161] Even where they have returned to full-time employment, the time taken out to care for children will have set back their earning potential.[162] In part, ex-wives' financial hardships also reflect the wage differences which exist generally between men and women: average earnings of women are 22 per cent lower than men.[163] Women face discrimination in finding employment, both on the basis of their sex and on the basis that they are caring for children and therefore in a weaker position to advance their careers.[164] It is not just child care that can restrict a woman's ability to advance her career. Women still carry the primary duty of housework.[165] In one survey 48 per cent of men did no or a little housework.[166] The impact of this becomes especially apparent on retirement where women suffer particular poverty as compared with men.[167]

## B  Why should there be any redistribution?

To assist in the discussion of this question, it will be assumed that the husband is in the stronger position economically, and that the wife is seeking a court order. Similar arguments can, of course, be made if it is the wife who is the higher earner.[168]

1. *Spousal support and the care of children.* Supporting the child should inevitably require providing benefits to the residential parent. So if it is decided that the child should live in a luxury-level house, this will benefit both the child and the parent with whom they are living. Further, included in the support required for the child must be an element to provide personal care for the child. So one ground for spousal support is that the spouse be maintained at the level required to ensure adequate care of the child. Eekelaar and Maclean have supported the 'equalisation of the standard of living of the two households, and thus of the children within them'.[169] They argue that this equalisation is not due to any kind of implied undertaking between the parents (as some of the models below emphasise), but

---

[158] Fisher and Low (2009: 254).
[159] Funder (1988).
[160] Dex, Ward and Joshi (2006) and Bourreau-Dubois, Jeandidier and Berger (2003).
[161] Scott and Dex (2009); Fawcett Society (2010).
[162] Scott and Dex (2009).
[163] National Statistics (2009a).
[164] Maclean (1991).
[165] Trew and Drobnic (2010); Crompton and Lyonette (2008); Sayer (2010); Brannen, Meszaros, Moss and Poland (1994).
[166] Mintel (2004). Geist (2010) notes that in surveys men tend to exaggerate the amount of housework they do.
[167] See Chapter 12.
[168] See Fehlberg (2004) for a useful discussion of some of the theories discussed here.
[169] Eekelaar and Maclean (1997: 197).

due to the moral claim of the child; that is, the child's household should not be disadvantaged to the benefit of the non-residential parent's household.

2. *Contract.* It could be argued that it is a part of the marriage contract that, on breach of the contract, one party will pay the other 'damages'; that on marriage the spouses promise to support each other for the rest of their lives. If a husband decides to divorce his wife he must pay her damages so that she is in the economic position she would have been in had he not broken the contract. This would mean that the husband would have to pay the wife financial support so that she could enjoy the level of wealth she experienced during the marriage.[170] Nowadays this theory does not really explain the English law: first, because it might be questioned whether marriage does include a promise to remain with the other spouse forever, given the ready availability of divorce; secondly, because the law has abandoned trying to work out which party breached the contract, that is, who it is that has caused the marriage breakdown. However, as will be seen, in cases involving very rich couples, aspects of this approach are still used in the reasoning of the courts.[171]

3. *Partnership.* The view here is that marriage should be regarded as analogous to a partnership.[172] The husband and wife co-operate together as a couple as part of a joint economic enterprise.[173] It may be that one spouse is employed and the other works at home, but they work together for common benefits. Therefore, on divorce each spouse should be entitled to their share, normally argued to be half each.[174] Lord Nicholls in *Miller v Miller*[175] accepted the validity of what he called the 'equal sharing' principle. He put the argument this way:

> [in marriage] the parties commit themselves to sharing their lives. They live and work together. When their partnership ends each is entitled to an equal share of the assets of the partnership, unless there is a good reason to the contrary. Fairness requires no less.

But the partnership model does not necessarily lead to an equal division. John Eekelaar suggests:

> at the end of the relationship, the investment which each party has put into the marriage is assessed on one side of the balance sheet and set against the value of the assets which each is taking out of it and also the earning power which each has at that time. If there is a disparity between the parties with regard to what was put in and what is being taken out, an adjustment will be made to equalize the position between them. Marriages is a joint enterprise in a capitalist society demanding, at least prima facie, equal rewards for effort.[176]

It could also be argued that on marriage the parties will bring to the relationship a variety of different assets, skills, personalities, interests, etc. Throughout the marriage each party will enjoy and share their personalities, interests and skills. If the relationship involves the mutual sharing of all aspects of their lives, this should include their material assets.

At first consideration this argument might justify redistributing assets that have accumulated during the marriage, but would not apply to assets owned by the parties before entering the marriage or assets acquired after the marriage breakdown. However, the

---

[170] This would justify the minimal loss theory behind the Matrimonial Proceedings and Property Act 1970.
[171] Deech (2010a).
[172] See the approach of the Canadian Supreme Court in *Moge v Moge* (1993) 99 DLR (4th) 456, discussed in Diduck and Orton (1994). See also Bailey-Harris (2001b).
[173] Fehlberg (2005).
[174] See Burch (1983).
[175] [2006] 2 FCR 213 at para 16.
[176] Eekelaar (2007: 431).

approach can be developed to extend to future assets. It is possible to argue that the partnership assets are not limited to tangible assets, but extend to the earning capacity of the parties.[177] So, if the wife had supported the husband at home while he developed his career, she could argue that he has only been able to reach the position where he is able to earn as much money as he does because of the help she provided. This argument would entitle the wife to a share in his future earnings, reflecting the increase in his earning potential acquired during the marriage. The approach could also be said to justify a sharing of assets acquired before the marriage. But there are difficulties with the partnership approach:

(i)  Some argue that the partnership approach is inappropriate in the absence of an express agreement to share the family assets. It could be replied that the partnership concept is part of the marriage package, and is an obligation which the parties accept by marrying. Another response is that the partnership approach is not necessarily designed to reflect the intentions of the parties, but rather what is conscionable or fair; that, as the spouses worked together on a common enterprise, they should share the fruits, even if they had not explicitly agreed to do so. Seen in this way the partnership approach is closer to unjust enrichment, than contract law. Regan has argued that marriage is a distinctive relationship based on mutuality, interdependence and care. Therefore responsibilities can arise from it even though there has not been an express agreement to undertake them.[178]

(ii)  Where the argument extends to future earnings, the partnership approach requires the court to calculate what share of the husband's earning capacity is a result of the marriage. This is difficult to ascertain.[179] Also, if the husband could show that, had he not married, he would have done just as well in his career, he could argue that no proportion of his earning capacity could be said to result from the partnership.[180] Finally, if one friend helps another to advance in her career we do not normally think this creates a financial obligation, even if the friend has been instrumental in obtaining the break.[181] Why should it be different in marriage?

(iii) It can be argued that the approach takes insufficient account of the needs of the parties. Particularly where one spouse is raising the child, a one-half share may not adequately meet his or her needs.[182] In other words, dividing the assets equally might leave the spouse with the child effectively in a worse-off financial position (because of the extra expenses of child care) and not receiving a 'fair' share of the economic benefits of the joint enterprise.

Despite these objections, the partnership approach certainly provides a sound basis for financial support. It is important to appreciate that the approach is not arguing that one spouse should transfer money to the other, but rather that the family assets should be regarded as jointly owned. So a home-working mother is not asking for some of her husband's money on divorce; she is seeking her share of their assets.[183]

---

[177] This argument is developed in Frantz and Dagan (2002 and 2004). It was rejected in *Q v Q* [2005] EWHC 402 (Fam) by Bennett J.

[178] Regan (1999: 188).

[179] See further Ellman (2005); and the American Law Institute proposals discussed by Ellman (2005) and Eekelaar (2006b: 51–2).

[180] Singer (1997).

[181] Eekelaar (2006b: 48).

[182] Forder (1987).

[183] Weitzman (1985: 360).

4. *Equality.* Some argue that on the breakdown of the marriage the parties should be treated equally as a basic aspect of justice.[184] As Eekelaar has pointed out, this could mean two things: first, equality of outcome; and, secondly, equality of opportunity.[185] Equality of outcome requires that at the point of divorce each spouse has the same total value of assets. Equality of opportunity is that 'each former spouse should be in an equal position to take advantage of the opportunities to enhance her or his economic position in the labour market'.[186] Neither in its most simple form is satisfactory. The difficulty with equality of outcome is that as the needs of the parties (particularly in relation to children) are different, giving the parties equal assets will not truly produce an equal standard of living. The problem with the equality of opportunity approach is that the prevailing social structures (such as discrimination against women in the employment market) are such that perfect equality of economic opportunity would be impossible to achieve.

A more sophisticated version of equality of income for both households post-divorce would have to take carefully into account the costs of raising children. This might involve ensuring that each household has the same amount of spare cash after the payment of essential expenses.[187] That would normally involve giving more money to the household that has children living in it.

Ingleby[188] has questioned the use of equality. He argues that our society is characterised by inequality, in part due to the abilities of families to pass on wealth to their members. Why is equality in the abstract important or significant? He sees equality as too easy a way of avoiding the difficult question of assessing the contributions of the parties to the marriage.

5. *Compensation.*[189] Here the argument is that on divorce the non-earning spouse should be compensated for the disadvantages she has suffered as a result of the marriage.[190] This was accepted as a principle in *Miller v Miller*,[191] where Lord Nicholls explained:

> [Compensation] is aimed at redressing any significant prospective economic disparity between the parties arising from the way they conducted their marriage. For instance, the parties may have arranged their affairs in a way which has greatly advantaged the husband in terms of his earning capacity but left the wife severely handicapped so far as her own earning capacity is concerned. Then the wife suffers a double loss: a diminution in her earning capacity and the loss of a share in her husband's enhanced income.

Baroness Hale referred to the need to compensate for 'relationship-generated dis-advantage'. The compensation argument can take two forms (assuming the wife to be the non-earning spouse):

(i) The non-earning spouse should be compensated for loss of the earnings which she would have gained had she not been at home caring for the children or the home.

(ii) The non-earning spouse should in retrospect be paid an appropriate wage for her work by the husband. A court could assess how much the house-cleaning and child-caring would have cost the husband had he employed people to do it. Some who adopt this

---

[184] Parkinson (2005).
[185] Eekelaar (1988).
[186] Eekelaar (1988: 192).
[187] Weitzman (1985).
[188] Ingleby (2005: 147).
[189] For a useful discussion of compensation claims see Murray (2008).
[190] In *VB v JP* [2008] 2 FCR 682 the wife refused to take up a promotion because the husband did not want to move. This was regarded as an economic disadvantage due to the marriage.
[191] [2006] 2 FCR 213 at para 13. See the discussion in Ellman (2007).

approach accept that, as the non-earning spouse herself benefits from the housework, the cost should be shared and so the husband should only pay for half of this work.

There are difficulties with the compensation approach. Those criticising the first option argue that the non-earning spouse chose to bear and raise children, maybe for personal motives. She may have chosen the joys of child-raising over the world of work, just as some people take a lower-paid job due to the pleasure it provides.[192] Therefore, any loss is as a result of her choice and is not a ground for compensation. This argument, however, overlooks the fact that the choice of bearing and raising children is one that is essential to society's well-being. It is therefore a choice which society must seek to encourage and support. Others argue that the costs that women who care for children suffer are due to the inequalities of society, rather than being married. It is the state's failure to provide adequate child-care facilities and employment protection for mothers that is the root cause of the disadvantages suffered. The losses women suffer should be compensated for by the state rather than by husbands.[193] However, in the absence of state support, it is surely unfair for mothers alone to have to carry the burden of financial sacrifice for the raising of children.

Eekelaar sees a different objection to the compensation approach, arguing that even if the wife had not married her husband she would have married someone else, and so it is not realistic to claim that the lack of development in her career is this man's fault.[194] Funder has argued that if, say, the wife gives up her career to care for the children then the resulting loss of income is a loss for both parties because they would have shared her income. The wife cannot therefore claim compensation for it, because the couple would have already equally shared the loss of the income.[195] Carbone and Brinig[196] refute these kinds of arguments by suggesting that, as the husband himself has benefited from his wife's sacrifices (by having the pleasure of fatherhood and a pleasant home life), it can be seen as reasonable to require him to compensate the wife for her loss of earnings. A difficulty then arises in calculating what the wife would have earned had she not given up her career in order to undertake family responsibilities.[197] A final argument against compensation is that it can act as a deterrent against a wife who undertakes paid work during the marriage. She may find herself on divorce no better off, or even worse off, than a wife who gives up her career early in the marriage.[198]

6. *The state's interests.* The arguments so far have assumed that the issue is about achieving fairness between the parties themselves.[199] It is arguable that financial orders on divorce can be justified by interests of the state, regardless of what would be fair or just between the parties.[200] So what state interests are there here? The following are suggested:[201]

(i) Saving public money. Orders should be made to avoid costs to the state of the children or either spouse becoming dependent on welfare payments now or in the future.

---

[192] Maclean and Eekelaar (2005b) find that there is widespread awareness of the financial losses that will often flow from motherhood.
[193] Fergusson (2008).
[194] Eekelaar (1988).
[195] Funder (1994).
[196] Carbone and Brinig (1991).
[197] Mee (2004: 437).
[198] Davis (2008).
[199] Many commentators make the assumption that redistribution of property on divorce is a private matter: see, e.g., Cretney (2003b).
[200] Herring (2005b).
[201] Herring (2005b). But see also Bailey-Harris (1998b).

(ii) Child-care issues. The state might take the view that each member of society should be as economically productive as possible, and so it would want to discourage a spouse giving up employment to take up child care, in which case the state might want to limit financial awards on divorce. If there were no financial orders on divorce then this would discourage a spouse from thinking of giving up employment to care for children; instead they would be likely to rely on day care. However, the state might believe that children's interests are promoted if one spouse gives up work to care for the children, in which case some form of protection from financial disadvantage would be necessary. Hale J in the Court of Appeal in *SRJ v DWJ (Financial Provision)*[202] has stated:

> It is not only in [the child's] interests but in the community's interests that parents, whether mothers or fathers, and spouses, whether husbands or wives, should have a real choice between concentrating on breadwinning and concentrating on home-making and child-rearing, and do not feel forced, for fear of what might happen should their marriage break down much later in life, to abandon looking after the home and the family to other people for the sake of maintaining a career.

(iii) The symbolic valuing of child care. The state should place a far higher value on the unpaid work of raising children than is done at present.[203] Financial orders on divorce are one way of demonstrating that the state treasures child care as an important social activity.[204]

(iv) The interests of children. The level of support for the spouse with primary care of the child will have a significant impact on the welfare of the child. It will affect whether the primary carer will need to undertake work to earn money; their state of emotional and their material well-being; and their sense of self-respect. All of these will have an impact on the well-being of the child.

(v) Stability of marriage. Some economists have argued that the level of maintenance can act as a deterrent against divorce.[205] Whether this is correct and whether we wish to pressure people into remaining in a marriage which they wish to leave is a matter for debate.

(vi) Post-divorce life. The level of financial support after divorce will affect the behaviour of the spouses after divorce. Do we want ex-wives to find employment and seek to become financially self-sufficient or is it proper to recognise that the duties owed to a spouse continue after divorce because the disadvantages flowing from the marriage do?[206] Whatever one's view on such questions the kind of orders made on divorce will affect the spouse's behaviour.

(vii) Sex discrimination. The state is entitled to seek to promote equality between men and women. As already mentioned, divorce plays a significant role in leading to equality among women. The state can legitimately seek to combat discrimination through state orders.

Not everyone, by any means, will agree that all of these state interests are weighty. But they do demonstrate that the issue of financial orders on divorce is not just of significance to

---

[202] [1999] 2 FLR 176 at p. 182.

[203] Burggraf (1997). See the National Family and Parenting Institute (2001b) for the data on work and family life. See Mumford (2007) on how tax credits could be used to recognise and value child care.

[204] It might be thought that orders on divorce are not an effective way of getting this message across. Unmarried parents are not rewarded and the level of the award does not reflect the amount or quality of the work done.

[205] Dnes (1998). See also the discussion in Cohen (2002: 24–5).

[206] See Regan (1993a).

the parties themselves, but can have effects on the wider society. Lucinda Ferguson argues that the state has over-extended the appropriate interpersonal obligations owed between spouses and by parents to children in order to deal with poverty which should be resolved by state support:

> The notion of interpersonal obligation has been distorted in both contexts in an attempt to respond to social inequality. More concerning than this distortion, however, is the fact that neither of these support obligations manages to successfully respond to social inequality anyway. Separated and divorced women and children raised in single-parent families represent a disproportionate percentage of those Canadians[207] living below the low income cutoff. Focus on expanding and strengthening these interpersonal obligations has distracted us from the urgent need to address the root causes of the inequality that these obligations have been adapted to address.[208]

Many of the difficulties that this chapter deals with are caused by the unequal sharing of child care. Although there is evidence of fathers seeking to play an increased role in child care[209] the vast majority is still undertaken by women.[210] Some commentators take the view that the Government should attempt to encourage a more equal division of child-caring roles. However, the trend is for those working to be working for longer and longer hours, making it harder for couples to share child care and work.[211] The alternative is to encourage both parties to work and for even greater use to be made of day care. However, this raises the debate over whether day care or care at home is preferable for children. This is a heated debate. Although the evidence suggests that there are some advantages and disadvantages to both, there is controversy as to whether overall one is preferable.[212]

Having spent all this time considering the academic justifications for financial orders on divorce, it is regrettable to note that they have not impressed the judiciary. Thorpe LJ has stated:

> [I]n this jurisdiction we should not flirt with, still less embrace, any of the categorisations of the defining purposes of periodical payments advanced by academic authors. The judges must remain focused on the statutory language, albeit recognising the need for evolutionary construction to reflect social and economic change . . . [T]o adopt one model or another or a combination of more than one is to don a straitjacket and to deflect concentration from the statutory language.[213]

## C The case for the abolition of maintenance

There is a case for the abolition of maintenance. The argument is that the existence of maintenance perpetuates the fact that women are dependent upon men.[214] A vicious circle exists in that, because the law tells wives that they will be entitled to financial support if their relationships ends, they are willing to take lower-paid jobs and they thereby do become

---

[207] The point could equally well be made about this in England.

[208] Ferguson (2008: 75).

[209] Maushart (2001: 129–34) and see Chapter 1.

[210] E.g. Eekelaar and Maclean (1997: 137).

[211] Moen (2003). Hakim (2003) argues that although most couples want a better home life–work balance most believe that one spouse should be primarily responsible for raising the children.

[212] Ermisch and Francesconi (2001; 2003) argue that children whose parents both work suffer in a variety of ways. The Daycare Trust (2003) paints a much more positive view of day care.

[213] Thorpe LJ in *Parlour* v *Parlour* [2004] EWCA Civ 872 at para 106. See Miles (2005) for an insightful discussion of his statement.

[214] In practice it is far more common for a wife to be awarded maintenance than a husband.

dependent upon their husbands.[215] If maintenance were abolished and financial independence encouraged, women would have to find jobs that paid adequately.[216] Although there may be a short period during which women would suffer from the lack of maintenance, over time the market would have to provide adequately paid jobs for women, or provide economic rewards for homemaking and child-rearing activities. O'Donovan,[217] although sympathetic to this argument, has suggested that the abolition of maintenance can only fairly be accomplished when there:

1. is equality of division of labour during marriage, including financial equality;

2. is equal participation in wage-earning;

3. are wages geared to people as individuals and not as heads of families;

4. is treatment of people as individuals (rather than family units) by the state in taxation and benefit provision.

A second objection to maintenance has already been mentioned: that the economic disadvantages that women suffer are due to inequalities within society, such as the lack of provision of child-care services and family-friendly working practices, etc. Therefore, the state, and not husbands, should recompense wives on the breakdown of their marriage for the losses that society has caused.

## D Certainty or discretion?

### DEBATE

#### Certainty or discretion?

A major issue in the area of spousal financial support is whether the financial support for spouses should be based on some formula to ensure certainty of result and consistency or whether the case should be resolved in reliance upon discretion. As we shall see, spousal financial support is at present based on a very broad discretion, considering a list of factors. This can be contrasted with the Child Support Act, where the level of the award was based upon a mathematical calculation, with only a limited discretion to depart from the calculation. Some of the arguments for and against discretion will now be considered:

1. *Enforcement.* One of the arguments against discretion is that enforcement is easier if the system is seen to be fair and consistent. One common reason for non-payment of maintenance is that the amount payable is seen to be unfair. Having a clearly applied formula, which the parties could be made aware of before marriage, might improve enforcement levels.[218]

2. *Certainty.* Another argument against discretion is that the parties in negotiations are assisted by having clear guidance on what amount the law regards as fair in a particular case.[219] The problem with the present law is that it can be very difficult for solicitors to predict how

➡

---

[215] Deech (2009a).

[216] Although the levels of maintenance are low, and it is unlikely that women would choose not to work in the hope of getting maintenance should they divorce. Perhaps more convincing is the argument that maintenance is symbolic of the culture of dependency.

[217] O'Donovan (1982).

[218] Jackson, Wasoff, Maclean and Dobash (1993).

[219] Jackson, Wasoff, Maclean and Dobash (1993).

much a court will award a client.[220] Not only does a discretion-based system make negotiations harder, it also increases the powers of solicitors.[221] As Jackson et al. argue:

> along with discretion goes uncertainty; the elevation of professional judgement (because only lawyers, who deal with these matters all the time, have the necessary knowledge and skill to weigh up the competing factors); an almost limitless need for information about family finances (because discretion, if it is to [be] justified at all, has to be based on a minute examination of differing circumstances) and the demand for large amounts of professional time (because discretion, if it is not to be exercised arbitrarily, takes time).[222]

Dewar, however, argues that there is no evidence that less discretion means it will be easier for the parties to reach an agreement, because the parties can disagree how even a rigid formula should apply.[223] Lord Nicholls in **Miller; McFarlane** accepted there was a difficulty for the courts here. On the one hand ensuring fairness between the parties meant that the court needed flexibility, but that created unpredictability and that conflicted with another aspect of fairness: that like cases should be treated alike.[224] Practitioners claim that if you 'know your District Judge' (i.e. the arguments that that judge is usually persuaded by) this can be an advantage for your client.[225] This is in part due to the discretionary nature to the system.[226]

3. *Flexibility*. A benefit of the discretion-based system is that it can apply unique solutions that may better fit the circumstances of individual parties. As discussed when considering the CSA 1991, one of the most common complaints about the formula around which the Act is based is that it is too rigid and creates injustices in many cases.

The benefits or disadvantages of discretion change from case to case.[227] Davis et al. suggest that:

> One possible conclusion to draw from our research is that a discretionary system is not geared to mass proceedings such as we have in divorce these days. The proposal that outcomes may be determined by the application of a formula, and usually by an administrative authority, can certainly be supported in relation to the relatively straightforward cases which comprised the bulk of our sample.[228]

Perhaps the core question is: to what extent are we willing to put up with injustices in a few cases to enable speedy and efficient responses for the majority?

Lord Nicholls in **White v White**[229] accepted that there were both advantages and disadvantages to a discretion-based system. He argued that even though English and Welsh law had a discretionary system, there still should be principles which guide the discretion:

> It goes without saying that these principles should be identified and spelled out as clearly as possible. This is important, so as to promote consistency in court decisions and in order to assist parties and their advisers and mediators in resolving disputes by agreement as quickly and inexpensively as possible.

---

[220] Davis, Cretney and Collins (1994).
[221] Davis, Cretney and Collins (1994).
[222] Jackson, Wasoff, Maclean and Dobash (1993: 256).
[223] Dewar (1997).
[224] [2006] 1 FCR 213 at para 6.
[225] Watson-Lee (2004: 349).
[226] Although similar claims are made about district judges in areas of the law where there is much less discretion.
[227] Acknowledged by Lord Nicholls in *White v White* [2000] 3 FCR 555, [2000] 2 FLR 981.
[228] Davis, Cretney and Collins (1994: 270).
[229] [2000] 2 FLR 981, [2000] 3 FCR 555.

---

**Questions**

1. *Do you think there would be disputes even if the law were crystal clear?*

2. *Should a judge use his or her own moral values when exercising discretion? Or the values of society at large? Or the values of the couple?*

**Further reading**

Read **Cooke** (2007) for a helpful discussion of the nature of uncertainty in this area of the law.

---

## E The Human Rights Act 1998 and maintenance

Article 1 of the first Protocol of the European Convention on Human Rights protects the right to peaceful enjoyment of property:

> Every natural or legal person is entitled to the peaceful enjoyment of his possessions. No one shall be deprived of his possessions except in the public interest and subject to the conditions provided for by the law and by the general principles of international law. The preceding provisions shall not, however, in any way impair the right of a State to enforce such laws as it deems necessary to control the use of property in accordance with the general interest or to secure the payment of taxes or other contributions or penalties.

At first sight, a person ordered to make any payment on divorce could invoke this article. In *Charman* v *Charman (No. 2)*[230] Colderidge J firmly rejected a suggestion that an order under the MCA could breach Article 1.[231]

Article 5 of the seventh Protocol on the equality between spouses states:

> Spouses shall enjoy equality of rights and responsibilities of a private law character between them, and in their relations with their children, as to marriage, during marriage and in the event of its dissolution. This article shall not prevent States from taking such measures as are necessary in the interests of the children.

There is an explanatory memorandum which states that article 5 'should not be understood as preventing the national authorities from taking due account of all relevant factors when reaching decisions with regard to the divisions of property in the event of the dissolution of marriage'. This article was not included within the Human Rights Act 1998 due to potential conflict with English and Welsh law,[232] although the Government has promised to implement the Protocol in due course. Even if it does, these provisions are unlikely greatly to affect English and Welsh law, given the uncertainty over the term equality, discussed above.

## F The importance of discovery

Crucial to the success of the parties' negotiations and any court hearing is having full disclosure of each party's assets, income and liabilities. There is a duty on both clients and lawyers to make a full frank and clear disclosure of the parties' present assets. In *Bokor-Ingram*

---

[230] [2006] EWHC 1879 (Fam), para 126.
[231] For further discussion see Choudhry and Herring (2010: ch 10).
[232] Home Office (1997: 4.15, 4.16).

v *Bokor-Ingram*[233] a husband did not disclose that he was negotiating for a new job with significantly increased salary. That was held not to have been made a clear disclosure. A form must be filed with the court, which sets out income and assets. However, it is 'all too common'[234] for people to try to hide their assets. Indeed for lawyers in practice, far more time is often spent ascertaining the other party's true wealth than in deciding what would be a fair division of the property. The problem can be a simple failure to disclose, but in more sophisticated forms can involve hiding income and property behind companies or trusts controlled by the parties. Although the courts have powers for ordering discovery of relevant documents, too often it is impossible to be sure that all the relevant material has been provided. The court has two further tools at its disposal if it cannot ascertain a party's true financial position. First, the court can order that the non-disclosing party be punished by being ordered to pay all or some of the legal costs incurred in the attempt to ascertain his or her wealth.[235] Further, the court can, if it is convinced that it does not have the full picture, presume that a party has a certain level of wealth.[236] This will certainly be done where the court decides that a person's lifestyle is not commensurate with their claimed income.[237] If a non-disclosure only comes to light after an order has been made the court can give leave to appeal out of time, even if that is years later.[238]

The difficulty in ascertaining the wealth of the parties is likely to work in favour of the richer party. It is far harder to hide the income of a part-time worker than to hide the true income of a managing director of a company whose salary may be but a small portion of his or her true income. An argument could be made that a failure to provide an effective means of ascertaining the assets available on divorce interferes with the article 6 ECHR rights to a fair trial.[239]

At the other end of the spectrum, the courts have complained of solicitors seeking too much information from the other side in the hope of uncovering assets which may be available to their clients. Intensive financial questioning[240] can lead to enormous solicitors' costs; £1.5 million in one notorious case.[241] The Family Proceedings Rules 1999[242] are designed to prevent unnecessary investigation, but the practitioner is in a difficult position. There is a danger that if he or she does not follow up a lead in disclosure, they may be sued in negligence, but if the practitioner does they may be penalised in costs for unnecessary work.

An issue of considerable importance in practice arose in *Tchenguiz v Imerman*.[243] The wife had obtained information about her husband's assets from a computer, which she was not authorised to access. This amounted to a breach of his rights of confidentiality, the court held, and so she was not permitted to use the information in the court hearing. Although it was accepted there was a real problem with spouses not disclosing their assets, that did not justify a party breaking the law in order to discover the truth. The difficulty is that if it is discovered that a spouse has misled the court the intrusion into privacy seems justified. A party should

---

[233] [2009] 2 FLR 922.

[234] Thorpe LJ in *Purba v Purba* [2000] 1 FLR 444.

[235] *W v W (Ancillary Relief: Non-Disclosure)* [2003] 3 FCR 385.

[236] *Pasha v Pasha* [2001] EWCA Civ 466, [2001] 2 FCR 185.

[237] *Thomas v Thomas* [1996] 2 FLR 544, [1996] FCR 668; *Al Khatib v Masry* [2002] 2 FCR 539; *Minwalla v Minwalla* [2005] 1 FLR 771.

[238] *Burns v Burns* [2004] 3 FCR 263.

[239] *Švenčionienė v Lithuania* [2009] 1 FLR 509 demonstrates that article 6 claims can be made in ancillary relief cases. See further Choudhry and Herring (2010: ch. 10).

[240] *Evans v Evans* [1990] 1 FLR 319, [1990] FCR 498.

[241] *F v F (Ancillary Relief: Substantial Assets)* [1995] 2 FLR 45.

[242] SI 1999/3491.

[243] [2010] EWCA Civ 908.

not be able to rely on claims of privacy in relation to material they should have disclosed to the court. However, if they have made proper disclosure and the breach of confidentiality was a mere 'fishing expedition' then the rights to confidentiality seem to be infringed. One issue argument the court, perhaps surprisingly, did not find convincing was that in marriage a spouse loses the right of confidentiality in relation to the other. Perhaps the better argument in this context is that on divorce the couple's assets become available for redistribution and cease to be regarded as his or her assets. The conclusion in this case that information obtained without consent of the other spouse sometimes cannot be used in evidence is likely to make disclosure of the truth of the parties positions even harder and lead to an increase in the number of orders made on the basis of false facts. Rich spouses will be delighted.

## 5 Orders that the court can make

The court has a range of orders that it can make. It is useful to divide these up into those orders that relate to income, and those that relate to capital and property.

### A Income orders

The main income order is the periodical payments order (PPO) under s 23 of the MCA 1973.[244] These payments can be weekly, monthly or annual. For example, a husband could be ordered to pay his ex-wife £400 per month. The order can be secured or unsecured. If it is a secured PPO and the payments are not made, then the property providing the security can be sold to enable payment. The security could be, for example, shares or the matrimonial home. This is an attractive option for the recipient, as she will not have to worry about non-payment, and also secured periodical payments can continue after the death of the payer. However, if there are sufficient assets to provide security for periodical payments, then it might be better simply to transfer those assets over to the wife as a lump sum instead of requiring regular payments. It is, therefore, not surprising that Thorpe LJ has suggested that secured PPOs 'have [been] virtually relegated to the legal history books'.[245]

A payments order will cease on any of the following events:

1. The death of either party.[246] However, if the order is a secured periodical order, the order need not cease on the death of the payer.[247]
2. The remarriage of the recipient.[248] The explanation is that on remarriage the new spouse would be financially responsible for the recipient. While that might have some validity if the payments are in the nature of support, that argument does not apply where the maintenance payments represent a share in the assets the couple have built up together during the marriage.

[244] MCA 1973, s 22 allows for 'maintenance pending suit' which allows for payments prior to the litigation being completed. Its primary use today is to enable a party to pay their solicitors: *Moses-Taiga v Taiga* [2008] 1 FCR 696.

[245] *AMS v Child Support Officer* [1998] 1 FLR 955 at p. 964. Although 4,721 periodic payment orders were made in 2005 (Department of Constitutional Affairs, 2006a: 74).

[246] MCA 1973, s 28(1)(a).

[247] MCA 1973, s 28(1)(b).

[248] MCA 1973, s 28(1)(a). Remarriage will not prevent a court making a lump sum order, if the application for such an order was made before the remarriage: *Re G (Financial Provision: Liberty to Restore Application for Lump Sum)* [2004] 2 FCR 184.

3. The court order may specify a date on which the payments will end. For example, the order may state that there are to be periodical payments for the next three years only.[249]

Maintenance orders can be made against either parent for the benefit of a child. If the child is over 18 years of age then PPOs can be made only if the child is in full-time education or under specific circumstances, such as disability.

## B Property orders

There are three main types of property orders:

1. *Lump sum orders.* A lump sum order (LSO) requires a lump sum of money to be handed over by one spouse to the other. The LSO may be made to a parent for the benefit of a child. It is possible to order that the LSO be paid in instalments. The LSO is often used when considering housing issues: assuming one party is to stay in the matrimonial home, the other will need some money to use as a deposit to rent or buy a home.

2. *Transfer of property orders.* The most common transfer of property order is an order that one party transfers a share in the matrimonial home to the other. A transfer of property order could also be used to transfer ownership of other property, such as a car or piece of furniture. The court can make an order to transfer property to the other spouse or to an adult for the benefit of a child under a trust.

3. *Power to order sale.* Under s 24A of the MCA 1973 the court can order the sale of property which either spouse owns outright or which the spouses own jointly.[250] The order is effectively ancillary to an LSO. The owner is normally required to sell the item and then the proceeds are divided between the spouses by means of an LSO.[251]

## C Clean break orders

### (i) What is a clean break order?

When considering what financial order to make, the court must consider whether to make a clean break order. If a clean break order is not made then the parties can potentially have further financial obligations placed upon them after divorce for the rest of their lives. For example, if on divorce the husband is required to pay the wife £100 per month, and two years after the divorce the husband wins the national lottery, the wife could apply to the court for a significant increase in the amount she should receive. Similarly, if she won the national lottery, the husband could apply to have the payments ended. By contrast, if a clean break order is made, it ends any continuing obligation between the spouses. So the court may make a lump sum or property adjustment order, and neither party would be able to make any further applications to the court.[252] The financial responsibilities to each other in relation to

---

[249] The recipient could apply to vary the order so as to extend that period unless the order contains a direction under s 28(1A) or the date on which the payments are due to cease has passed, in which case it is not possible to apply for variation.

[250] *Ram v Ram (No. 2)* [2004] 3 FCR 673 confirmed that property which is co-owned by a spouse and trustee in bankruptcy cannot be the subject of a s 24 order.

[251] MCA 1973, s 24A(6): if a third party has an interest in the property this does not mean that there cannot be an order for sale, but that third party's interests must be taken into account.

[252] Although it would be possible to appeal against the making of the order, discussed below.

the divorce are at an end.[253] However, it should be stressed that the clean break cannot end the possibility that a spouse may be liable under the CSA 1991. It is only spousal support that can be cleanly broken; child support cannot.

A delayed clean break order is also possible.[254] This is where the periodical payments order is set for a certain period, say two years, and after that period the payments will end, with no option for the spouse receiving the payments to apply to extend that period.

## (ii) The statutory provisions

In every divorce case there is an obligation on the court to consider whether to make a clean break order. Under s 25A(1) of the MCA 1973 there is a duty on the court in all cases to consider 'whether it would be appropriate so to exercise [its] powers that the financial obligations of each party towards the other will be terminated as soon after the grant of the decree as the court considers just and reasonable'.[255]

If the court is making a periodic payments order, it should consider whether to limit the length of time over which payments will be made, and whether a delayed clean break order would be appropriate.[256] A clean break should not be regarded as something to be achieved at all costs. Certainly it would be wrong to make an order which produced an unfair or unjust division in the name of achieving a clean break order.[257]

## (iii) The benefits and disadvantages of a clean break order

The benefits of a clean break order include:

1. The parties are each free to pursue their own careers or start new careers without fear that their actions will lead to applications to vary maintenance payments. If the husband is paying maintenance, he may be reluctant to increase his income for fear that such an increase would simply result in his ex-wife seeking a larger maintenance payment. The wife might be deterred from seeking a new job for fear that if she had more income her husband would seek to have the maintenance payments reduced.

2. There may be emotional reasons for having a clean break: the parties may not feel that they are completely released from the marriage until all financial issues are resolved;[258] although if there are children the parties will be encouraged to keep in contact,[259] and so the strength of this benefit may be questioned.[260]

3. If the recipient intends to remarry, she may prefer a lump sum clean break arrangement as this will free her to remarry without the risk of losing her maintenance.

4. It avoids the future problems in the payment and collection of periodic payments. As Baroness Hale put it in *Miller; McFarlane*:[261] 'Periodical payments are a continuing source of stress for both parties. They are also insecure. With the best will in the world the paying

---

[253] A clean break order should also contain a term making it impossible to apply under the Inheritance (Provision for Family and Dependants) Act 1975 should the paying spouse die: *Cameron v Treasury Solicitor* [1996] 2 FLR 716 CA.

[254] MCA 1973, s 28(1A).

[255] MCA 1973, s 25(1)(a), (2).

[256] MCA 1973, s 25A(2).

[257] *S v S* [2008] EWHC 519 (Fam); *F v F (Clean Break: Balance of Fairness)* [2003] 1 FLR 847.

[258] Lord Scarman in *Minton v Minton* [1979] AC 593 at p. 608.

[259] And financial liability may continue under the CSA 1991.

[260] See Hale J in *SRJ v DWJ (Financial Provision)* [1999] 2 FLR 176.

[261] [2006] 2 FCR 213 at para 133.

party may fall on hard times and be unable to keep them up. Nor is the best will in the world always evident between formerly married people.'

The main disadvantage of the clean break is that the court ties its hands and, whatever tragedy befalls the parties, the courts cannot reopen the court order. For example, if the court assumes that the wife will be able to support herself with the income from a new job and therefore makes a clean break order, nothing can be done if, a few months later, she is made redundant.

### (iv) When a clean break order is appropriate

Although the court must consider in each case whether or not to make a clean break order,[262] there is no presumption in favour of making the order.[263] Baroness Hale referred to the benefits of a clean break as producing 'independent finances and self-sufficiency'.[264] Clean break orders have been considered appropriate in the following circumstances:

1. *When continuing support offers no benefit to the wife.* In *Ashley v Blackman*[265] the wife was unemployed. The husband was of limited means. The court accepted that the wife would see a very limited benefit if the husband were ordered to pay maintenance because any small amounts of money transferred to her would lead to a corresponding reduction in her state benefits.[266] The court therefore made a clean break order.

2. *Short, childless marriages.* If the marriage was short and childless, and the parties are easily able to return to the position they were in before they married, a clean break order may be appropriate.[267] Even if the marriage is short, if there is a child the court may well decide that the future for mother and child is too uncertain to make a clean break order.[268]

3. *The very wealthy.* With wealthy people it is often particularly appropriate to require one spouse to pay the other a substantial lump sum as part of a clean break order.[269] A 'Duxbury' calculation is widely used, which involves calculating a lump sum which, if suitably invested, will produce enough income to meet the reasonable requirements of the recipient spouse for the rest of their life.[270] The House of Lords in *White v White*[271] has, however, referred to the *Duxbury* paradox, which is that the longer the marriage, the older the claimant will be and the shorter the life expectancy, and so the lower the award.

4. *Both spouses have well-established careers.* In *Burgess v Burgess*[272] the wife was a doctor in general practice and the husband was a partner in a firm of solicitors. Both were well established in their careers and their children were students at university. It was held that dividing all the family assets equally and making a clean break order was the most appropriate course, given that they were both clearly able to support themselves from their careers.

---

[262] MCA 1973, s 25A(1).
[263] *Fisher v Fisher* [1989] 1 FLR 423, [1989] FCR 308.
[264] *Miller; McFarlane* [2006] UKHL 24.
[265] [1988] FCR 699, [1988] 2 FLR 278.
[266] *Seaton v Seaton* [1986] 2 FLR 398.
[267] E.g. *Hobhouse v Hobhouse* [1999] 1 FLR 961.
[268] *B v B (Mesher Order)* [2003] Fam Law 462.
[269] For a rare case where despite the parties' wealth a clean break order was not appropriate, see *F v F (Clean Break: Balance of Fairness)* [2003] 1 FLR 847.
[270] Actuarial calculations are made, estimating the life expectancy of the recipient spouse, the rate of inflation, etc.
[271] [2000] 2 FLR 981, [2000] 3 FCR 555.
[272] [1996] 2 FLR 34, [1997] 1 FLR 89.

5. *Where there is antagonism between the spouses.* A clean break between spouses is appropriate where the relationship has broken down. In such a case continuing financial responsibility may only increase the bitterness affecting the relationship. However, even if the relationship is an unhappy one it might still be impossible to make a clean break order which achieves fairness.[273]

## (v) When a clean break order is inappropriate

1. *Where there are still young children.* In **Suter v Suter and Jones**[274] there were children, but very limited capital assets. It was held that it was not appropriate to make a clean break order and that the husband should be required to pay a nominal sum of £1 a year. The court stressed that simply because there were dependent children did not mean that there was no possibility of making a clean break order. However, in this case it was necessary to provide a 'backstop' in case there were future unforeseen events which might lead the court to want to make ancillary relief orders.

2. *Where there is too much uncertainty over the recipient's financial future.* In **Whiting v Whiting**[275] the wife had, at the time of the divorce, started a job. The husband, who had been well paid, had recently been made redundant, but had become self-employed earning at that time £4,500. The trial judge decided that the husband should be ordered to pay a nominal sum and declined to make a clean break order. This was because, although it appeared that the wife was in a position where she would be able to become financially independent, it was not possible to predict her future.[276] The majority of the Court of Appeal decided that the judge's decision could not be said to be entirely wrong, even though they would have made a clean break order. Balcombe LJ, in the minority, thought the trial judge's ruling was fundamentally wrong and should be overturned. Less controversial was *M v M (Financial Provision)*,[277] where a woman, aged 47, had a limited earning capacity. Here the court declined to make a clean break order as she had not worked for the last 20 years and there was no certainty that she would be able to become self-sufficient in the future. In *D v D*[278] the uncertainty of the value of the husband's private company was said to justify not making a clean break.[279]

3. *Where there is a lengthy marriage.* In **SRJ v DWJ (Financial Provision)**[280] the couple had been married for 27 years, during which the wife had spent most of her time caring for the children and the house. The Court of Appeal felt that this strongly militated against a clean break order.

4. *To achieve fairness.* Where one spouse has undertaken child-care responsibilities during the marriage, while the other has pursued his or her career and this causes economic disparity after the marriage which cannot be rectified by provision of a lump sum then ongoing periodic payments may be required to achieve fairness.[281] In such a case to make a clean break order would not be fair.[282]

---

[273] **Parra v Parra** [2002] 3 FCR 513, although the judgment was overturned on the facts by the Court of Appeal ([2003] 1 FCR 97).
[274] [1987] 2 FLR 232, [1987] FCR 52.
[275] [1988] 2 FLR 189, [1988] FCR 569.
[276] See also *H v H (Financial Provision)* [2009] 2 FLR 795.
[277] [1987] 2 FLR 1.
[278] [2007] 1 FCR 603.
[279] See also *P v P* [2010] 1 FLR 1126.
[280] [1999] 2 FLR 176.
[281] **Miller; McFarlane** [2006] 2 FCR 213 at para 39.
[282] Ouazzani (2009).

## (vi) Deferred clean break orders

If the court decides that a clean break order is not appropriate, then the next question is whether a delayed clean break order can be made. A delayed clean break order is useful where a party could adjust, without undue hardship, to the termination of financial provision orders in the foreseeable future.

In *Flavell v Flavell*[283] Ward LJ was concerned that the lower courts were too ready to make these delayed clean break orders. He stated:

> There is in my judgment, often a tendency for these orders to be made more in hope than in serious expectation. Especially in judging in the case of ladies in their middle years, the judicial looking into a crystal ball very rarely finds enough of substance to justify a finding that adjustment can be made without undue hardship. All too often these orders are made without evidence to support them.

As Ward LJ put it in *C v C (Financial Provision: Short Marriage)*,[284] 'Hope, without pious exhortations to end dependency, is not enough.' The court therefore must have clear evidence that the recipient will certainly be financially independent come the end of the period of maintenance payments if a delayed clean break order is to be appropriate. Such comments may be welcomed by those who believe that the courts have too readily decided that a wife who has been out of the job market for a long time can easily find employment, particularly women from minority cultural groups.[285]

## D Interim orders

Given the length of time that litigation and negotiations can take, it is understandable that a divorcing spouse might need financial support before the making of a final court order. Hence the MCA 1973 permits the court to order interim support under s 22. There are no formal guidelines, but the courts will take into account all the circumstances of the case. In fact, it seems that interim awards are 'almost unknown', according to Thorpe J in *F v F (Ancillary Relief: Substantial Assets)*.[286] This is because the courts do not want to tie their hands before they have heard all the facts in a full hearing. They have been used to assist a party pay for their lawyers fees, although only in cases of very wealthy couples.[287]

## 6 Statutory factors to be taken into account when making orders

The factors to be taken into account by a court in deciding which orders to make are listed in s 25 of the MCA 1973. Key to understanding the way judges decide what financial orders to make under the MCA 1973 is to appreciate that they are given wide discretion. The House of Lords has accepted that different judges may quite properly reach different conclusions as to what the most appropriate order is in a particular case.[288] The Act deliberately has no one overall objective[289] and it is permissible for the court to take into account factors not listed in

---

[283] [1997] 1 FLR 353, [1997] 1 FCR 332.
[284] [1997] 2 FLR 26, [1997] 3 FCR 360.
[285] S. Edwards (2004: 811).
[286] [1995] 2 FLR 45.
[287] *F v F (Ancillary Relief: Substantial Assets)* [1995] 2 FLR 45.
[288] *Piglowska v Piglowski* [1999] 2 FLR 763.
[289] *White v White* [2001] AC 596 HL at pp. 316–17.

s 25, if it believes them to be relevant.[290] However, Lord Nicholls in the House of Lords in *White v White*[291] has suggested that fairness is the overriding purpose of the Act. Fairness here means the judge's objective assessment of fairness, not the parties' subjective assessment of what they think might be fair.[292] That said, the concept of fairness is not particularly useful. Lord Nicholls accepted that this guidance was not of enormous assistance: as he put it, 'fairness, like beauty, lies in the eye of the beholder'.[293] In *Miller; McFarlane* he said: 'Fairness is an illusive concept. It is an instinctive response to a given set of facts. Ultimately it is grounded in social and moral values. These values, or attitudes, can be stated. But they cannot be justified, or refuted, by any objective process of logical reasoning.'[294] Baroness Hale was perhaps more helpful in suggesting that 'The ultimate objective is to give each party an equal start on the road to independent living.'[295]

We shall now consider the various factors which s 25 of the MCA 1973 requires the court to take into account.[296]

## A The welfare of children

The court must take into account all the factors listed in s 25. However, it is required 'to have regard to all the circumstances of the case, first consideration being given to the welfare while a minor of any child of the family who has not attained the age of eighteen'.[297] It was made clear in *Suter v Suter and Jones*[298] that although the child's welfare is the first consideration, that does not mean that it is the overriding consideration; that is to say, it is the most important factor, but not the only factor. The Court of Appeal explained that, as well as protecting the child's interests, it is necessary to reach 'a financial result, which is just as between husband and wife'.

The criteria to be taken into account when considering awards to spouses with children are set out in s 25(3):

---

**LEGISLATIVE PROVISION**

**Matrimonial Causes Act, section 25(3)**

(a)  the financial needs of the child;

(b)  the income, earning capacity (if any), property and other financial resources of the child;

(c)  any physical or mental disability of the child;

(d)  the manner in which he was being and in which the parties to the marriage expected him to be educated or trained;

(e)  the considerations mentioned in relation to the parties to the marriage in paragraphs (a), (b), (c) and (e) of [s 25(2) of the MCA 1973].

---

[290]  *Co v Co* [2004] EWHC 287 (Fam).
[291]  [2000] 2 FLR 981, [2000] 3 FCR 555.
[292]  *Lambert v Lambert* [2002] 3 FCR 673 at para 39.
[293]  *White v White* [2000] 3 FCR 555 at para 1.
[294]  [2006] 2 FCR 213 at para 4.
[295]  Para 144.
[296]  It is important to note that less than half of cases lead to ancillary relief orders (Barton and Bisset-Johnson (2000)). Many couples have so few assets that a court order is unnecessary.
[297]  MCA 1973, s 25(1). 'Child' here includes any child of the family of the couple (see Chapter 7 for further discussion of this term).
[298]  [1987] 2 FLR 232, [1987] FCR 52.

The child's interests are obviously significant when considering the appropriate level of child support but are also very relevant when deciding the financial support for spouses. The child's interests can be pertinent in a number of ways:

1. It has been held that it would be contrary to the child's interests if either of his or her parents had to live in straitened circumstances, as this would cause the child distress[299] and affect the parents' ability to care for him or her. Baroness Hale in *Miller; McFarlane* explained that part of promoting the child's welfare was to ensure that the primary carer is 'properly provided for, because it is well known that the security and stability of children depends in large part upon the security and stability of their primary carers'.[300]

2. The child's interests can also be important in deciding what should happen to the matrimonial home. It may well be thought that it is in the child's best interests if he or she and the parent who is caring for him or her remain in the matrimonial home. In *B v B (Financial Provision: Welfare of Child and Conduct)*[301] the need to ensure that the child (who had had a disturbed background) had a secure and satisfactory home meant that there was no money to enable the husband to purchase a house. This was justified by Connell J on the basis that the child's welfare was to be the first consideration.

3. The child's interests are also relevant in deciding whether or not the court should expect the residential parent to go out to work to support him- or herself, or order the other spouse to pay maintenance support.[302] The courts generally accept that a parent caring for young children should not be expected to seek employment.[303]

The court will take into account the future interests of children, even beyond their minority, as well as the interests of children already over the age of minority, even though the interests of such children are not the first consideration.[304]

## B Financial resources

### LEGISLATIVE PROVISION

**Matrimonial Causes Act 1973, section 25(2)(a)**

The income, earning capacity, property and other financial resources which each of the parties to the marriage has or is likely to have in the foreseeable future, including in the case of earning capacity any increase in that capacity which it would in the opinion of the court be reasonable to expect a party to the marriage to take steps to acquire.

Clearly, the financial resources of the parties are a key element, although the truth is that in most cases the courts are dealing with the debts, rather than the assets, of the parties.[305] All of the assets of a party will be considered, even those they owned before the marriage. A number of controversial issues have been discussed by the courts in regard to financial resources:

---

[299] *E v E (Financial Provision)* [1990] 2 FLR 233 at p. 249.
[300] [2006] 2 FCR 213 at para 128.
[301] [2002] 1 FLR 555.
[302] *Waterman v Waterman* [1989] 1 FLR 380, [1989] FCR 267.
[303] *Leadbeater v Leadbeater* [1985] 1 FLR 789.
[304] *Richardson v Richardson* (No. 2) [1997] 2 FLR 617.
[305] Eekelaar and Maclean (1986); Fisher (2002).

1. The court cannot take into account the resources of a third party.[306] So, if the wife now has a rich boyfriend, his income cannot be taken into account. However, the court may assume that a spouse's new partner might be in a position to contribute to her household expenses thereby reducing her needs.[307] Another circumstance in which this issue is relevant is if a spouse's wealth is hidden within a company that he or she controls. The court may assume that the company could make payments to the spouse to meet any order that the court may impose,[308] as long as there are no third party's interests which may be endangered.[309] In *TL v ML*[310] it was held that it might be appropriate to make an award on the assumption that a third party (such as a parent) would meet the award, but only if that would be fair to do so, for example where the third party has indicated they are willing to provide the funds to meet any court order.[311]

2. 'Other resources' include income from discretionary trusts; personal injury damages;[312] and even inheritance received after the divorce.[313] Property inherited during the marriage can be divided on divorce, although the fact that it was inherited by one spouse should be taken into account in determining whether it would be fair to distribute it.[314] In *B v B (Ancillary Relief)*[315] it was held to be unfair to divide assets equally on divorce after a 12-year marriage where all of the available capital had been brought into the marriage by the wife from an inheritance. Only very rarely will the court assume that one spouse will receive money under someone's will at some point in the future.[316] However, in *C v C (Ancillary Relief: Trust Fund)*[317] a husband was due to acquire a quarter share in a substantial trust fund on the death of a 74-year-old widow. The court held that given that the woman was likely to live another 15 years and that the husband would definitely be entitled to the share on her death under the terms of the trust, it was an asset that could be taken into account, although 'at the outer limits' of what would count. Had the widow been much younger it is unlikely the court would have considered it.

3. The court will consider not only the spouse's present income, but also the extra earnings that could be gained by working overtime[318] or taking out loans.[319] If a person is unemployed then he or she may be expected to find work. One difficult issue involves the earning capacity of spouses, normally wives, who have dedicated their lives to child care. The courts will not generally expect a middle-aged spouse who has been out of the job

---

[306] *Re L (Minors) (Financial Provisions)* [1979] 1 FLR 39; *Duxbury v Duxbury* [1987] 1 FLR 7.

[307] *Atkinson v Atkinson (No. 2)* [1996] 1 FLR 51, [1995] 3 FCR 788 CA.

[308] Especially where the company has provided the paying spouse with money when needed in the past.

[309] *Thomas v Thomas* [1996] 2 FLR 544, [1996] FCR 688. A similar point was made in this case about a discretionary trust, but see *Re C (Divorce: Ancillary Relief)* [2007] EWHC 1911 (Fam) and *A v A and St George Trustees Ltd* [2007] EWHC 99 (Fam).

[310] [2006] 1 FCR 465.

[311] Although in *Re C (Divorce: Ancillary Relief)* [2007] EWHC 1911 (Fam) Baron J was more willing to assume that a wife who was a beneficiary under a discretionary trust could expect to receive money from the trust. See also *A v A and St George Trustees Ltd* [2007] EWHC 99 (Fam).

[312] *C v C (Financial Provision: Personal Damages)* [1995] 2 FLR 171, [1996] 1 FCR 283. But the court will not assume an outcome in proceedings which are yet to be concluded: *George v George* [2003] 3 FCR 380.

[313] *Schuller v Schuller* [1990] 2 FLR 193, [1990] FCR 626.

[314] *White v White* [2000] 2 FLR 981, [2000] 3 FCR 555.

[315] [2008] 1 FCR 613.

[316] Although in rare cases it might even be appropriate to adjourn the court until a relative's death has occurred: *MT v MT (Financial Provision: Lump Sum)* [1992] 1 FLR 362, [1991] FCR 649.

[317] [2010] 1 FLR 337.

[318] *J-PC v J-AF* [1955] P 215.

[319] *Newton v Newton* [1990] 1 FLR 33, [1989] FCR 521.

market to find employment.[320] Hence in *A v A (Financial Provision)*[321] it was held not to be reasonable to expect a woman of 45 to seek full-time employment or set up her own business, even though she had an engineering degree. Had she been much younger, or had there been no children, the court might have reacted differently.[322]

## C The needs, obligations and responsibilities of the parties

> ### LEGISLATIVE PROVISION
>
> **Matrimonial Causes Act 1973, section 25(2)(b)**
>
> The financial needs, obligations and responsibilities which each of the parties to the marriage has or is likely to have in the foreseeable future.

Having looked at the plus side (the resources of the parties), the court will then turn to the minus side (the needs, obligations and responsibilities of the parties). Needs here are not restricted to those that arise directly from the marriage.[323] The concept of 'needs' is inevitably subjective. Do you *need* a sofa? If so, should it be from Argos, Habitat, or Harrods? The courts have interpreted 'needs' loosely. The needs of a rich couple are not the same as the needs of a poor couple. This has, in fact, caused the courts some embarrassment, in that saying a spouse *needs* three houses[324] sounds peculiar, and so the courts have suggested that, at least in the context of the rich, 'reasonable requirements' of the spouses should be referred to, rather than their 'needs'. Reasonable requirements are not limited to essentials, and so, for example, in *Gojkovic v Gojkovic*[325] £1.3 million was given to enable a wife to start up her own business. In *Miller* Baroness Hale said that in relation to wealthy couples needs had to be interpreted 'generously'.[326] Although slightly earlier in her judgment she referred to needs 'generated by the relationship'.[327] It would be surprising if the need of a spouse not generated by the marriage (e.g. a disability) did not count as a need for the purposes of the legislation. Maybe Baroness Hale was simply emphasising that special weight would attach to needs which were caused by the marriage.[328] Lord Nicholls spoke of marriage as a relation of interdependence and stated that 'Mutual dependence begets mutual obligations of support.'[329] That might suggest there is no requirement that needs flow from the relationship.[330]

In many cases the first need the court will consider is housing. As Thorpe LJ put it in *Cordle v Cordle*: 'nothing is more awful than homelessness'.[331] The court will therefore always seek to ensure that the children and their carer are housed. Where possible the next concern will be to provide money for the non-resident parent to be rehoused.

---

[320] *Barrett v Barrett* [1988] 2 FLR 516, [1988] FCR 707.
[321] [1998] 2 FLR 180, [1998] 3 FCR 421.
[322] See *N v N (Consent Order: Variation)* [1993] 2 FLR 868, [1994] 2 FCR 275.
[323] *Miller; McFarlane* [2006] 2 FCR 213 at para 11.
[324] *F v F (Ancillary Relief: Substantial Assets)* [1995] 2 FLR 45.
[325] [1990] FLR 140, [1990] FCR 119.
[326] *Miller; McFarlane* [2006] 2 FCR 213, para 142.
[327] Emphasised in *R v R* [2009] EWHC 1267 (Fam).
[328] See Hale (2009b).
[329] *Miller; McFarlane* [2006] 2 FCR 213 at para 11.
[330] See Bridge (2006: 642) for a useful discussion.
[331] [2002] 1 FCR 97 at para 33.

The court will not normally take into account obligations which are voluntarily assumed. If a spouse has increased expenditure because he or she insists on living in an unduly large house,[332] or lives a long way from work and so has high travel expenses,[333] then the court may regard these as voluntarily assumed obligations and therefore will not include them when considering the appropriate award. But the court may be willing to take into account the costs of a new family and the needs of a new spouse.[334]

It should be stressed that the courts are concerned with what a spouse needs, not with what he or she might actually spend the money on. The court's responsibility is to ensure that there is enough money, as far as possible, to meet the spouse's needs, and it is the spouse's responsibility to spend it appropriately.[335] A spouse cannot refuse to pay maintenance on the basis that the recipient would spend it in an inappropriate manner.[336]

The courts will also consider the obligations the parties have. In particular any debts or other legal obligations they owe. Occasionally the courts will consider a moral obligation (e.g. to support an elderly parent), but they will rarely play a significant role.[337]

## D 'The standard of living enjoyed by the family before the breakdown of the marriage'[338]

This factor tends to be relevant to rich couples in particular.[339] For wealthy couples a spouse's reasonable requirements are calculated by considering the expenditure during the marriage.[340] So, if the wife during the marriage normally spent £50,000 per annum on clothes then, when calculating her reasonable requirements, it will be assumed that that figure represents her reasonable requirements for clothing.[341] In *S v S*[342] the couple had both been heavily involved in horses during the marriage. It was held that after the divorce the wife should be given enough money so that she could continue her love of horses. As the court emphasised, that was only appropriate because the husband was a wealthy man. An exception to this approach was highlighted in *A v A (Financial Provision)*,[343] where the spouse lived a frugal life despite being extremely wealthy.[344] In such a case the court suggested that the wife's reasonable requirements could be calculated by asking what standard of life she might have expected to enjoy being married to a man of that wealth. In *Miller v Miller*[345] the trial judge had placed weight on the wife's expectation (following comments made by the husband) that she would enjoy a rich lifestyle even in the event of a divorce. In the House of Lords it was said that hopes and expectations were not to be taken into account, although the standard of living during the marriage could be.

---

[332] *Slater v Slater* (1982) 3 FLR 364 CA.
[333] *Campbell v Campbell* [1998] 1 FLR 828, [1998] 3 FCR 63.
[334] *Barnes v Barnes* [1972] 3 All ER 872.
[335] *Duxbury v Duxbury* [1987] 1 FLR 7.
[336] *Duxbury v Duxbury* [1987] 1 FLR 7.
[337] *Judge v Judge* [2009] 1 FLR 1287.
[338] MCA 1973, s 25(2)(c).
[339] *Leadbeater v Leadbeater* [1985] 1 FLR 789.
[340] *Dart v Dart* [1996] 2 FLR 286, [1997] 1 FCR 21.
[341] The media reported one case where there was an award of £50,000 to ensure that the couple's horses were maintained at the level to which they were accustomed: BBC Newsonline (2008d).
[342] [2008] 2 FLR 113.
[343] [1998] 2 FLR 180, [1998] 3 FCR 421.
[344] Singer J suggested that their frugality was revealed by the fact their sofa was purchased at Ikea rather than Harrods.
[345] [2006] 2 FCR 213.

## E 'The age of each party to the marriage and the duration of the marriage'[346]

The shorter the marriage, the less likely the court will make a substantial award.[347] In *Attar v Attar*,[348] where the couple had lived together as a married couple only for six months, it was suggested that the sum awarded should reflect the amount necessary to return the parties to the position they were in before they were married.[349] However, just because a marriage is short does not mean that an order will not be made. This was clearly revealed in *C v C (Financial Provision: Short Marriage)*,[350] where the marriage had lasted only nine months. However, a child had been born during the marriage. As the wife could not be expected to enter employment[351] and the child's health was uncertain, there was no likelihood that the wife would be able to become independent. Therefore, a substantial lump sum order and periodical payments order were made. In *Miller v Miller*[352] a wife was awarded £5 million after a marriage of under three years. The House of Lords explained that such a large sum could be justified because during the course of the short marriage the husband had made a significant amount of money. The wife was entitled to her share of the money generated during the marriage, even in the case of a short marriage. Lisa Glennon has argued that the courts should focus on the length of caregiving undertaken during the marriage, rather than the length of the marriage.[353]

In considering the length of the marriage the court will also take into account the total length of the relationship. In *Krystman v Krystman*[354] a couple were married for 26 years but they had actually lived together for only two weeks and so no order was made. Where the couple have cohabited before the marriage the court will take into account the total length of the relationship. Ewbank J in *W v W (Judicial Separation: Ancillary Relief)*[355] and Mostyn QC in *GW v RW*[356] drew no distinction between the period of cohabitation and the period of marriage.[357] In *Co v Co*[358] Coleridge J preferred to see pre-marital cohabitation not as a factor which was relevant when considering 'the length of the marriage', but as part of the general circumstances of the case. In *Miller; McFarlane* Baroness Hale stated that when considering whether property was 'marital property' acquired during the marriage a court should 'probably' include property acquired during pre-marital cohabitation or engagement.[359] Courts have also had to consider cases where the same couple have divorced, later cohabited and then broken up again. The cohabitation can be taken into account in reopening the original divorce.[360] The courts are yet to consider a case involving a civil partnership where a couple

---

[346] MCA 1973, s 25(2)(d).
[347] See the discussion in Eekelaar (2003c).
[348] [1985] FLR 649.
[349] See also *Hobhouse v Hobhouse* [1999] 1 FLR 961.
[350] [1997] 2 FLR 26, [1997] 3 FCR 360 CA.
[351] The wife had worked as a prostitute (her husband had met her in her 'professional capacity') but the husband could not expect her to return to her former 'occupation'.
[352] [2006] 2 FCR 213 at para 55. See further Cooke (2007).
[353] Glennon (2008).
[354] [1973] 3 All ER 247.
[355] [1995] 2 FLR 259.
[356] [2003] EWHC 611, [2003] 2 FCR 289.
[357] See Gilmore (2004a) for criticism of this, arguing that it will penalise those who do not cohabit prior to marriage and undermines personal choice as to when the obligations of marriage begin.
[358] [2004] EWHC 287 (Fam). See Douglas (2004) for academic support for this approach.
[359] [2006] UKHL 24 at para 149.
[360] *Hill v Hill* [1998] 1 FLR 198, [1997] FCR 477.

cohabited prior to the partnership. It is very likely the courts will look at the whole length of the relationship as they do with marriage.[361]

## F  'Any physical or mental disability of either of the parties to the marriage'[362]

In reality this factor is subsumed under the needs heading. The most notable case is *C v C (Financial Provision: Personal Damages)*[363] where a husband who was badly disabled was held entitled to £5 million, even though the wife was to be left on social security benefits. The husband's disabilities meant he required constant care and complex equipment, and this meant that he had to have all the assets.

## G  Contributions to the welfare of the family

---

**LEGISLATIVE PROVISION**

**Matrimonial Causes Act 1973, section 25(2)(f)**

The contributions which each of the parties has made or is likely in the foreseeable future to make to the welfare of the family, including any contribution by looking after the home or caring for the family.

---

Under this heading the courts have discussed two issues. The first is the position of the spouse (normally wife) who has not been earning, but who has worked as a homemaker and child carer. The courts have recognised this to be an important contribution to the welfare of the family. In *White v White*[364] Lord Nicholls explained:

> whatever the division of labour chosen by the husband and wife, or forced upon them by circumstances, fairness requires that this should not prejudice or advantage either party when considering [MCA 1973, s 25(2)(f)] . . . If in their different spheres, each contributed equally to the family, then in principle it matters not which of them earned the money and built up the assets. There should be no bias in favour of the money earner and against the home-maker and the child-carer.[365]

The importance of not discriminating between the contributions of the money-earner and the homemaker or child carer was repeated by the House of Lords in *Miller; McFarlane*.[366] Coleridge J in *RP v RP* put it this way:

> At the end [of the marriage] both are entitled to a full share of the fruits of their combined and equal contribution; she to ensure that she has a secure future both with and later without the children, and the husband so that he can re-establish himself. She has earned it . . . and so has he. This is not largesse by the husband, it is her entitlement deriving from her valuable contribution.[367]

---

[361] Allen and Williams (2009).
[362] MCA 1973, s 25(2)(e).
[363] [1995] 2 FLR 171, [1996] 1 FCR 283.
[364] [2000] 2 FLR 981, [2000] 3 FCR 555; see Diduck (2001b) for a useful discussion.
[365] This was repeated in *Miller; McFarlane* [2006] 2 FCR 213, para 1 and said to be true for all marriages.
[366] [2006] UKHL 24.
[367] [2008] 2 FCR 613, para 63.

## H Conduct

---

**LEGISLATIVE PROVISION**

**Matrimonial Causes Act 1973, section 25(2)(g)**

The conduct of each of the parties if that conduct is such that it would in the opinion of the court be inequitable to disregard it.

---

At one time conduct was considered very important. A wife who was regarded as guilty of marital misconduct could expect a low award.[368] However, in line with the trend generally in family law, it is now rare for conduct to be taken into account.[369] As the statute states, the conduct must be 'such that it would . . . be inequitable to disregard'. The cases suggest that the conduct must be of an extreme kind in order to be relevant. Sir George Baker P suggested that conduct should be 'of the kind that would cause the ordinary mortal to throw up his hands and say, "surely that woman is not going to be given any money" or "is not going to get a full award"'.[370] Burton J[371] suggested that to be taken into account the conduct had to be such that to ignore it would produce a 'gasp'. Conduct which only led to a 'gulp' would be insufficient. For example, in *K v K (Financial Provision: Conduct)*[372] the wife helped her depressed husband's suicide attempt as she wished to acquire his estate and to set up a new life with her lover. Her conduct was such that it should be taken into account and her award was reduced from the £14,000 she would have received but for her misconduct to £5,000.[373] Notably conduct, even in these extreme cases, does not lead to the award being reduced to nil. In *H v H (Financial Relief: Attempted Murder as Conduct)*[374] the husband attacked the wife with knives in front of the children. He was sentenced to 12 years' imprisonment for attempted murder. It will not surprise the reader to learn that this was regarded as conduct which it was inequitable to disregard. In *K v L*[375] the husband sexually abused the wife's grandchildren. The Court of Appeal agreed that this entitled the judge to award the husband nothing, even though the wife owned property valued at over £4 million. It was explained that his conduct was so appalling and its 'legacy of misery' so profound that a nil award was appropriate. Where the conduct in question is financial misconduct (e.g. one of the spouses has wasted money on gambling or wild living) the court will be particularly willing to take it into account. Normally this is done by 're-attributing' the wasted money to the spouse who spent it.[376]

Where a court decides that conduct is sufficiently serious to be taken into account, the judge must explain how it affects the level of the award. In *Clark v Clark*[377] the Court of

---

[368] *Wachtel v Wachtel* [1973] Fam 72 marked the change in the courts' attitude.

[369] Eekelaar (1991a); although Inglis (2003) argues that judges should be far more willing to allow domestic violence to affect the level of the award.

[370] *W v W* [1976] Fam 107 at 110.

[371] In *S v S (Non-Matrimonial Property: Conduct)* [2006] EWHC 2793 (Fam).

[372] [1990] 2 FLR 225, [1990] FCR 372.

[373] *HM Customs and Excise and another v A* [2002] 3 FCR 481 held that the fact that the husband was a convicted drug dealer was conduct which it was inequitable to ignore.

[374] [2006] Fam Law 264.

[375] [2010] EWCA Civ 125.

[376] *Vaughan v Vaughan* [2007] 3 FCR 532.

[377] [1999] 2 FLR 498.

Appeal held that the wife's misconduct was so bad 'it would be hard to conceive graver misconduct'.[378] The Court of Appeal criticised the lower court judge, who accepted that the conduct was bad but had decided that it should not affect the level of the award. The Court of Appeal felt that serious misconduct should be taken into account in deciding the appropriate order, although it was open to a court to decide that no deduction would be made. In *H v H (Financial Relief: Attempted Murder as Conduct)*[379] Coleridge J held that in assessing the significance of conduct the court should not be punitive, but rather it should lead the court to place greater emphasis on the needs of the 'victim' and less on the blameworthy party. Conversely, as the House of Lords made clear in *Miller; McFarlane*,[380] if conduct is not sufficiently serious to fall within subsection (g) it should not be taken into account.[381] In that case the conduct of the husband was not conduct which was 'obvious and gross' so as to require being taken into account. There the fact that the husband had ended the marriage by committing adultery was not sufficiently serious to be relevant. Surprisingly in *FZ v SZ*[382] it was held that a false allegation of domestic violence by the wife was sufficient to amount to conduct. That is surprising because in other cases actual domestic violence has not been regarded as relevant unless it is especially serious.

The court will consider not only the bad conduct, but also the good conduct of the spouses. In *A v A (Financial Provision: Conduct)*[383] the husband gave up his job and made no effort to work, while the wife undertook a degree course and started a new career. The court thought that the contrast between what they regarded as the good conduct of the wife and the bad conduct of the husband should be taken into account in calculating the correct award.

Whether conduct should or should not be relevant has given rise to some debate.[384] There are some who argue that if the court is to achieve justice, it must ensure that grossly wrong conduct is taken into account. Others argue that, with the increasing acceptance of no-fault divorce, it is harder to justify the relevance of fault here, except in the most extreme cases. Shazia Choudhry and I have criticised the failure of the courts to attach weight to domestic violence in financial cases.[385] That said, as Lord Nicholls in *Miller; McFarlane* acknowledged, there is a widespread feeling among the public that conduct is relevant. He suggested that the average person would think: 'If a wife walks out on her wealthy husband after a short marriage it is not "fair" this should be ignored. Similarly if a rich husband leaves his wife for a younger woman.' However, Lord Nicholls said that it would be impossible for a judge to 'unravel mutual recriminations about happenings within the marriage'.[386]

---

[378] [1999] 2 FLR 498 at p. 509. The wife (described by the judge as a woman of considerable charm and physical attraction) was in her early 40s and the husband nearly 80. She oppressed the husband, refused to consummate the marriage and virtually imprisoned the husband in a caravan in the garden of his house.

[379] [2006] Fam Law 264.

[380] [2006] 2 FCR 213 at para 61.

[381] See Eekelaar (2005a) for a powerful critique of the Court of Appeal's approach on this. See Hodson (2006) who argues that domestic violence should play a far more important role in this area than it does at present.

[382] [2010] EWHC 1630 (Fam).

[383] [1995] 1 FLR 345.

[384] Carbone and Brinig (1991). See also Carbone and Brinig (1988).

[385] Choudhry and Herring (2010: ch. 10).

[386] [2006] 2 FCR 213 at para 60.

## I Loss of benefits

---

**LEGISLATIVE PROVISION**

**Matrimonial Causes Act 1973, section 25(2)(h)**

The value to each of the parties to the marriage of any benefit (for example, a pension) which, by reason of the dissolution or annulment of the marriage, that party will lose the chance of acquiring.

---

The most obvious issue here is the pension rights that a spouse may lose the right of acquiring, although rights under an inheritance might be relevant. The law on pensions will be discussed shortly.

## 7 Interpretation of the statute by the courts

We have just been considering the factors listed in section 25 of the MCA. However, the courts, particularly in the past few years, have been producing further guidelines and principles to govern the courts' discretion. In most cases the decision of the court will be dominated by the needs of the parties. The judge will be trying to do his or her best to meet as many of the parties' needs, and especially those of the children, with the limited resources. It is only in cases involving wealthier couples that the principles we will now consider come into play. In *Miller v Miller; McFarlane v McFarlane*,[387] it was held that there were three key principles: needs, equality and compensation. We have discussed needs already, but will now say more about the other two ideas.

### A The principle of equality

The principle of equality was introduced by the decision of the House of Lords in *White v White*.

---

**CASE: *White v White* [2000] 3 FCR 555**

The Whites had assets of roughly £4.5 million when their marriage ended after 33 years together. The trial judge awarded the wife £800,000 which he assessed as meeting the wife's reasonable needs for the rest of her life. The judgment was appealed to the Court of Appeal and then to the House of Lords. In a major reconsideration of the exercise of discretion, the House of Lords suggested that equality of division of the family assets should be seen as a 'yardstick'. Lord Nicholls explains:

> As a general guide equality should only be departed from if, and to the extent that, there is good reason for doing so. The need to consider and articulate reasons for departing from equality would help the parties and the court to focus on the need to ensure the absence of discrimination. This is not to introduce a presumption of equal division under another guise.[388]

---

[387] [2006] 1 FCR 213.
[388] *White v White* [2000] 3 FCR 555 at para 24. Singer HHJ (2001) provides a useful discussion of discrimination in this context.

Equal division is an appropriate starting point because each party has contributed to the marriage, be it financially or through child care or housework. There was to be no discrimination between contributions through child care and housework and monetary contributions. Lord Nicholls, however, makes it clear, then, that the equality principle is not to be regarded as a presumption, but rather a yardstick. On the facts of the case the wife ended up with less than half because of the significant contribution of the husband's family to the family business.

In *Lambert* Thorpe LJ described the yardstick of equality as a 'cross check'.[389] However, in *Charman v Charman*[390] the Court of Appeal stated that the principle should be used as a starting point and that is how it is generally understood. Hughes LJ in *B v B (Ancillary Relief)*[391] saw the importance of the principle as being twofold: 'First, it underlines the necessity not to treat financial contributions differently from those in non-monetary form. Second, it underlines the essential fairness of equal division in a large number of cases of shared matrimonial life.' Lord Nicholls made it clear that very often there will be a reason for departing from equality. In *Miller; McFarlane*[392] Lord Nicholls emphasised that the yardstick was intended as 'an aid, not a rule'. Indeed, given that in many cases there are insufficient assets to meet the needs of the couple and children, it will, in fact, be rare for there not be a good reason for departing from the starting point of equal division.

The decision in *White* has left many questions unanswered:

### (i) When should the principle of equality be departed from?

The following are some of the circumstances in which it may be appropriate to depart from equality:

(a) *The needs of the parties.* In most cases the needs of the children and resident parent will require a departure from equality.[393] Couples may lack sufficient assets to meet the most basic needs of the children and primary carer. In such a case an equal distribution will be unacceptable; indeed the children and carer may well need all of the assets and, in addition, ongoing maintenance payments. Only where the couple are very rich will there be sufficient assets to meet the basic needs of the parties and equal division can be considered as a possibility. In *Lambert* Lord Justice Thorpe suggested that in many cases the courts should seek to divide equally those assets which were surplus once the needs of the parties had been met.[394] In *S v S*[395] the husband was living with a woman and her children. It was held he therefore had greater needs than the wife who was living alone. This justified giving him slightly more than half the assets. However, subsequently *H-J v H-J (Financial Provision: Departing from Equality)*[396] and *Norris v Norris*[397] have suggested that it is wrong in principle for a wife to get less than she would otherwise have been awarded because her husband has left her for another woman and has had children with her.

---

[389] [2002] 3 FCR 673 at para 38.
[390] [2006] EWHC 1879 (Fam); [2007] EWCA Civ 503.
[391] [2008] 1 FCR 613.
[392] [2006] UKHL 24 at para 16.
[393] *J v J* [2009] EWHC 2654 (Fam). In *Miller; McFarlane* [2006] 1 FCR 213 at para 13, Lord Nicholls said that most cases begin and end with a consideration of needs.
[394] *Lambert v Lambert* [2002] 3 FCR 673 at para 39.
[395] [2001] 3 FCR 316.
[396] [2002] 1 FLR 415.
[397] [2003] 2 FCR 245.

(b) *Extraordinary contribution.* In **Lambert v Lambert**[398] Thorpe LJ made it clear that only in exceptional cases will the contribution to the marriage of one of the parties be regarded as a good reason for departing from equality.[399] In **Sorrell v Sorrell**[400] Bennett J found one of the 'exceptional' cases where it could be said that the husband had made an outstanding contribution. The husband was 'regarded within his field and the wider business community as one of the most exceptional and most talented businessmen'; his 'spark of genius' had created the family fortune; he should be given 60 per cent of the family assets. In the reported cases this has been applied to husbands who have made extraordinary sums of money in their careers.[401] In **Charman v Charman**,[402] where the husband was an extraordinarily successful business man, creating £131 million, it was accepted that his contribution was such that it would be inequitable not to have regard to it. The mere fact that a substantial sum of money has been generated will be insufficient. It will be necessary to show that there was a 'genius element' making the contribution special. This is interesting because it suggests that a windfall, not reflecting genius (e.g. a win on the National Lottery), will not constitute a special contribution. The Court of Appeal refused to set a figure at which it would be said that the contribution was special, but did state that where the contribution did justify a departure the maximum departure would be to a 66/33 division and the minimum 55/45. In the case before the court, the husband's contribution in generating the enormous wealth of the couple was 'special' and so a departure from equality was appropriate. The district judge's granting of 36.5 per cent of the assets to the wife was upheld.

Thorpe LJ in **Lambert** made the point that if the money-earner's contribution can be assessed to ascertain whether it was outstanding, then in fairness the child-carer's or homemaker's contribution should be assessed to see if it was outstanding.[403] The obstacle is, of course, that it is extremely difficult to calculate how good someone is at being a child carer.[404] The courts do not want to get into the position where they are deciding whether the wife was a domestic goddess or not.[405]

However, in **Miller; McFarlane**, Baroness Hale emphasised that s 25(2)(f) (the subsection which refers to contribution) requires the court to consider not the contribution to the accumulated wealth, but rather the contribution to the family. She said that 'only if there is such a disparity in their respective contributions to the welfare of the family that it would be inequitable to disregard should this be taken into account in determining their shares'.[406] This seems to raise the spectre of considering the quality of a child-carer's contribution.[407] But later cases, such as **Charman**, seem to have been rather reluctant to made adverse findings on a wife's contributions.

(c) *Parental contribution or inheritance.* In **White** itself and **Dharamshi v Dharamshi**[408] the fact that the family business had been started by money from the father's parents was

---

[398] [2002] 3 FCR 673.
[399] This was approved by Lord Nicholls in *Miller; McFarlane* [2006] 2 FCR 213 at para 68. See *Norris v Norris* [2003] 2 FCR 245 where the wife's contribution to the marriage was 'as full as it could have been', but not exceptional.
[400] [2006] 1 FCR 62.
[401] *Cowan v Cowan* [2001] 2 FCR 332.
[402] For a helpful discussion see Miles (2008).
[403] Hodson, Green and De Souza (2003). It will be no easier if it is the wife who is claiming to be exceptional: *Norris v Norris* [2003] 2 FCR 245, [2003] Fam Law 301.
[404] *Miller; McFarlane* [2006] 2 FCR 213 at para 27.
[405] Baroness Hale, in *Miller; McFarlane* [2006] 2 FCR 213 at para 146.
[406] [2006] 2 FCR 213 at para 146.
[407] Meehan (2006).
[408] [2001] 1 FCR 492.

a reason for giving him slightly more than half the family assets. In **B v B** *(Ancillary Relief)*[409] the fact that the wife had inherited the money that made up nearly all the couple's wealth justified a departure from equality.[410]

(d) *Property brought into the marriage or acquired after it.* If one party was already rich when they married, their pre-marital wealth may provide a reason for departing from equality.[411] Similarly if they acquired the wealth after the end of the relationship that too could provide a reason to depart from equality. We shall discuss this issue further below.

(e) *Obvious and gross misconduct.* As discussed above (see pages 230–1) in extreme cases the conduct of a party may be relevant and that might justify a departure from equality.

(f) *Difficulties in liquidation.* If it is not possible to liquidate assets (e.g. they are tied up in a business in a way which makes their extraction impossible) this will be a reason to depart from equality.[412]

(g) *To achieve a clean break.* A court may be persuaded that in order to achieve a clean break a departure from equality may be required. For example, if the wife is not to have periodic payments she may need a lump sum to replace them and may, therefore, get over 50 per cent of the assets.[413]

(h) *To ensure there was adequate compensation for losses caused during a relationship to a spouse.* We shall return to this later, but the courts will try to ensure there is compensation for a spouse who suffers a loss as a result of the marriage. Most obviously this would arise if one spouse gave up a career to care for children, during the marriage. In such a case the court will consider whether an equal division of the property will ensure there is adequate compensation. If not then periodic payments or a share greater than 50 per cent may need to be given to her.[414]

(i) *The way the parties organised their marriage.* In **J v J**[415] Charles J suggested the court would take account of the way the couple arranged their finances and treated their property. He did not expand on this but it may be that if a couple have throughout their marriage kept their financial arrangements separate, this may mean it would be unfair to divide their property equally.

## (ii) What property is to be divided equally?

Is the property to be divided equally under the *White* yardstick only the property which was acquired by the couple during the marriage, or is all of the property that the couple possess available for redistribution? The position the courts appear to have reached at present is that all of a couple's property is available for redistribution, especially where the needs of the parties require it.[416] That is, all of the assets the couple have at the time of the hearing.[417] But in a 'big money' case where there are sufficient funds to meet the parties' needs then the court may take into account that some property is non-marital. In other words that it is acquired before the marriage started, or after it ended. This issue, and others, was considered in the

[409] [2008] 1 FCR 613.
[410] See also *Re V (Financial Relief: Family Farm)* [2005] Fam Law 101.
[411] *Miller; McFarlane* [2006] 2 FCR 213.
[412] *N v N (Financial Provision: Sale of Company)* [2001] 2 FLR 69; *A v A* [2004] EWHC 2818 (Fam).
[413] *Vaughan v Vaughan* [2007] 3 FCR 532.
[414] *McFarlane* [2006] UKHL 24.
[415] [2009] EWHC 2654 (Fam).
[416] *Charman v Charman* [2007] EWCA Civ 503; *J v J* [2009] EWHC 2654 (Fam), discussed Herring (2010d).
[417] *H v H (Financial Provision)* [2009] 2 FLR 795; *J v J* [2009] EWHC 2654 (Fam); *R v R* [2009] EWHC 1267 (Fam).

very important decisions of *Miller* and *McFarlane* (two cases heard together by the House of Lords):

---

### CASE: *Miller; McFarlane* [2006] UKHL 24

The House of Lords heard two cases together. In *Miller* the marriage had lasted a little under three years. The husband, at the time of divorce, owned assets in excess of £17 million. The trial judge, approved by the Court of Appeal, granted the wife £5 million. The Court of Appeal, in justifying such a sum, emphasised the fact that the husband had caused the breakdown of the marriage (by 'running off' with another woman) and that he had caused the wife reasonably to expect a generous provision in the event of a divorce. The House of Lords rejected both these arguments as irrelevant. However, it held that even though it was a short marriage she was entitled to an equal share in the assets acquired during the marriage. The husband's wealth had increased significantly during their short marriage and the £5 million could be said to be a fair share of that money.

---

In *Miller v Miller*[418] Lord Nicholls held that in a short marriage it may be fair only to divide marital property, that is, the property acquired during the marriage. It does not include non-marital assets, assets acquired outside the marriage, such as property brought into the marriage or inherited property. Charles J in *J v J*, subsequently explained that 'that property acquired and built up during the marriage through the respective efforts and roles of the couple should be shared equally. Such property is a product of the relationship'.[419] The same could not be said of marital assets. In *Miller* this meant the wife was awarded £5 million after a marriage of under three years: the couple had generated about £15 million during the short marriage.

Baroness Hale and Lord Nicholls agreed that in a case of a lengthy marriage whether the assets were family assets or marital assets would become increasingly irrelevant and it would be likely that the court would simply divide everything the couple had in half. But their lordships made it clear they were not setting down a hard and fast rule that in long marriages you divide all the property equally and in short marriages you divide only the marital property. In each case the judge must seek to determine what would be fair in the circumstances at hand. For example, in *N v N*[420] despite a marriage of over 32 years it was held to be fair to award the wife 32 per cent of the assets.

So, it seems after *Miller*, that especially in short marriages, an important distinction is drawn between marital and non-marital property. However, the exact distinction between marital and non-marital assets is hard to draw. Lord Nicholls in *Miller* understood marital property[421] to be all assets acquired by either party during the marriage, save those acquired by gift or inheritance. He also included the matrimonial home as 'matrimonial property' even if one party had brought it into the marriage. Baroness Hale, by contrast, used a narrower understanding of 'marital assets', preferring the phrase 'family assets'. These were restricted to assets generated by the family: it could include the family home, family savings, income generated by a business organised by both parties. It would not include assets which were

---

[418] [2006] 2 FCR 213, at para 19.
[419] *J v J* [2009] EWHC 2654 (Fam), para 304.
[420] [2010] EWHC 717 (Fam).
[421] He used the phrase 'matrimonial property', but later cases have preferred the terminology 'marital property'.

produced by the efforts of one party alone. She explained that in relation to non-family assets 'it simply cannot be demonstrated that the domestic contribution, important though it has been to the welfare of the family as a whole, has contributed to their acquisition'.[422] The difference between the views would be revealed in a case involving a business project in which the wife was not involved in any way (perhaps she did not even know about it). This could be a marital asset for Lord Nicholls because it was an asset acquired during the course of the marriage. But it would not be a family asset under Baroness Hale's test if the wife could not be said to have contributed to its acquisition. In the House of Lords, Lord Hoffmann agreed with Baroness Hale, and Lord Hope (diplomatically, but unhelpfully) agreed with both. Lord Mance did not express a clear view, but he did advocate flexibility. John Eekelaar has suggested that this would indicate a view closer to Baroness Hale's.[423]

The *Charman v Charman*[424] Court of Appeal preferred Baroness Hale's approach, which Sir Mark Potter summarised in this way:

> a distinction fell to be made between 'family assets' and the fruits of a business in which both parties had substantially worked, on the one hand, and the fruits of a business in which only one party had substantially worked, i.e. unilateral assets, on the other. The suggestion was that it was property only of the former character which was subject to the sharing principle.[425]

Lord Nicholls's approach, which would apply the sharing principle to any asset generated during the marriage, but not income generated prior to marriage, was rejected. The Court of Appeal stated: 'We suggest with respect that, while the approach of Lord Nicholls was perhaps the more logical, the approach . . . of Baroness Hale . . . was perhaps the more pragmatic.'[426] Whether Baroness Hale's approach is more pragmatic may be open to question. It will inevitably lead to a flood of arguments over precisely the extent to which a spouse was working or helping in the business, precisely the kinds of arguments which *White* was seeking to avoid. It could introduce a discrimination between the homemaker who also helps in business matters and the homemaker who does not. For example, is it right that a wife who has a severely disabled child to care for and so does nothing to help in her husband's business should be disadvantaged as compared with a spouse who has time to spare to do so? In *S v S (Non-Matrimonial Property: Conduct)*[427] following Baroness Hale's approach it was held that commercial properties owned by a husband before the marriage and which he did not deal with during the marriage were non-marital property. The wife could not claim a share of an increase in their value during the marriage. By contrast, a share portfolio he brought into the marriage, but which he dealt with during it, could be marital property. The wife could claim a share in the increase in their value during the marriage. Although in reaching this distinction Baron J claimed to be following Baroness Hale, her focus appears primarily to be on whether the husband worked on the properties during the marriage, rather than the wife's contribution to the increases in wealth. It may be that the courts in applying Baroness Hale's approach will assume that if a spouse did nothing in relation to property during the marriage then it will remain non-marital; but that if the spouse does increase its value, it will be marital, unless it can be clearly shown that the other spouse made no contribution to the increase in its value.

---

[422] [2006] 2 FCR 213 at para 151.
[423] At para 160. Eekelaar (2006a: 755).
[424] [2007] EWCA Civ 503.
[425] Para 82.
[426] Para 85.
[427] [2006] EWHC 2793 (Fam).

A possible further complexity was introduced in *J v J*[428] Charles J suggested that in deciding whether an asset was a marital asset the court should consider whether the couple enjoyed the asset together during the marriage. This implies that even if an asset was inherited or brought into the marriage, if it was used jointly by the couple then it may thereby become marital property. That would tie in with the approach taken by the courts to the matrimonial home which will be treated as marital property, even if it was brought into the marriage by one spouse. This approach was followed in *K v L*[429] where during the marriage the husband received a substantial inheritance. This he kept in his name and was put to one side. The parties lived a relatively simple lifestyle. It was held that in the light of the way the couple had treated the inheritance during the marriage it would be unfair to divide it on divorce. Subsequently in *N v N*[430] and *Charman (No. 4)*[431] it was emphasised that the courts should not undertake lengthy and time-consuming investigations as to which assets are or are not marital assets; fairness, if the overarching principle, means that a detailed analysis of the origins of assets is not normally necessary.[432]

The significance of the meaning of marital assets in the case of short marriage was central to one of the most notorious divorce cases in recent years:

---

**CASE: *McCartney v Mills-McCartney* [2008] 1 FCR 707**

The husband, Paul McCartney, a famous musician and composer, had been married to Heather Mills for four years. At the time of divorce the wife claimed that the husband was worth £400 million. Bennett J held that it was important to note that the vast bulk of the husband's fortune was made before the marriage and indeed before the couple met. The amount of money generated during the marriage was very small. There was no evidence that Heather Mills had suffered a financial loss as a result of the marriage. In the light of these facts the primary focus of the courts would be to ensure that the wife and child's reasonable needs (interpreted in a generous way) were met. Focusing on those, he was ordered to pay her £16.5 million, meaning she would leave the marriage worth £24.3 million. Maintenance for the child was set at £35,000 per annum and the nanny's salary at £30,000.

---

## B Compensation

If one spouse is a wage earner and the other is not, then equal division of assets on divorce will mean equality at that point in time, but a few years down the line there is likely to be a sharp inequality.[433] Baroness Hale in *Miller v Miller*[434] explained that the court is concerned with fairness not just at the time of divorce but also with the 'foreseeable (and on occasions more distant) future'. The unfairness of future inequality is particularly acute when one

---

[428] [2009] EWHC 2654 (Fam).
[429] [2010] EWHC 1234 (Fam).
[430] [2010] EWHC 717 (Fam).
[431] [2007] EWCA Civ 503.
[432] *H v H* [2008] 2 FLR 2092.
[433] But see the warning of Thorpe LJ in *Parra v Parra* [2003] 1 FCR 97 at para 27 of relying on speculation as to what the parties' financial position might be in the future.
[434] [2006] 2 FCR 213 at para 129.

spouse has given up a career to pursue child care, leaving the other to generate substantial earning potential.[435] The leading case is *McFarlane*.

---

**CASE: *McFarlane* [2006] UKHL 24**

At the time of the marriage, both had been in successful careers. However, the wife gave up her career to care for the children and family. The marriage ended after 16 years. The couple had assets of around £3 million which they agreed to share; they could not agree on the periodic payments. The House of Lords ordered payments of £250,000 per year (the husband earned about £1 million per annum): these would ensure that the wife was compensated fairly for the losses created during the marriage, particularly to her earning potential. Unlike the Court of Appeal, the House of Lords refused to make a s 28(1A) order that the length of time for the payments could not be extended.

---

This point in *McFarlane*[436] was that equal division would not have produced fairness. The couple had assets worth around £3 million, the husband was earning about £1 million a year. If the £3 million were divided equally (£1.5 million each), within a few years the husband would be many times wealthier than the wife. The wife had lost significant earning potential as a result of the marriage. The periodic payments were necessary to compensate her for this.

Mrs McFarlane returned to the courts several years later (*McFarlane v McFarlane*).[437] She applied for an increase in maintenance payments for herself and the children. Charles J agreed, although he ordered that the payments would stop in 2015, that being the date when the husband was due to retire. Interestingly the order was made in terms of a percentage of the husband's earnings, rather than a specific sum. That meant that the parties would not need to return to court if the husband's income fluctuated.

In *VB v JP*[438] Sir Mark Potter suggested that compensation was just one of the strands of fairness and it would not necessarily be appropriate to try to calculate a precise figure as to the loss of earnings caused by the marriage. In a big money case he suggested that normally an equal division of the assets would compensate the wife for her lost career prospects, although it was always a question of what would be fair. In *RP v RP*[439] Coleridge J held that it would be undesirable to break up ancillary relief claims into headings: needs; sharing and compensation. Nevertheless those three principles were clearly articulated as factors to take into account by the House of Lords in *Miller; McFarlane*.[440]

## C Balancing needs, compensation and fairness

In *Charman*, guidance was provided on how to balance the competing principles of sharing, compensation and needs, outlined by the House of Lords in *Miller; McFarlane*.[441] The Court of Appeal explained that if an assessment of the wife's needs was greater than the sum that she would be granted on the basis of sharing or compensation then she should be awarded

---

[435] See also *Murphy v Murphy* [2009] EWCA Civ 1258.
[436] [2006] 2 FCR 213.
[437] [2009] 2 FLR 1322.
[438] [2008] 2 FCR 682.
[439] [2008] 2 FCR 613.
[440] See Duckworth and Hodson (2001); Eekelaar (2001a).
[441] *Charman v Charman* [2007] EWCA Civ 503, para 73; *Miller; McFarlane* [2006] 2 FCR 213, paras 11–13.

that sum. If, however, the sum she would be awarded on the basis of sharing was greater than her needs, she should be awarded the sharing sum. In short, she should receive the sharing amount or the needs amount, whichever was greater. As regards what to do if the sum to be awarded under the principle of compensation was greater than the award based on needs or sharing, the court decided that that question was best left to another case. Despite making these points, it was emphasised that, at the end of the day, the key issue is fairness. None of the Court of Appeal's comments was intended to be setting down a rule.[442]

## D A claim on spouse's future earnings?

It is well established that in order to meet the needs of a spouse or a child, a spouse may be required to pay some of their future earnings by way of financial support. However a different kind of claim can be made against future earnings. The Court of Appeal in *Charman* referred to an argument that the husband's earning capacity was an asset which the wife had helped generate and that therefore she should be entitled to a share of his future earnings. The Court of Appeal described the issue as complex and felt it was unnecessary to address it. In *H v H*[443] the argument was accepted by Charles J, but in restrictive terms. First, a wife would need to show that 'but for' her contribution the husband would not have been earning at the level he was. In many cases this will be hard to do. Second, even where the wife can demonstrate this she will not be entitled to substantial sums because the balance of his income will be earned by his work and endeavours after the marriage, rather than relating back to the help the wife offered during the marriage. In that case the wife was awarded one-third, one-sixth and one-twelfth of his income for the three years after the marriage. This decision is a welcome acknowledgement that a money-earner benefits financially from the support of the homemaker/child-carer not only during the marriage but also after it. It remains to be seen whether future cases will be more or less willing to accept such arguments.[444]

In *Rossi v Rossi*[445] it was suggested there was a one-year watershed, meaning that a wife could not claim that she had contributed to the husband's income if he received it a year after the separation. However that was dismissed in *H v H (Financial Provision)*[446] as over-simplistic.[447] In that case a husband was receiving bonuses and other payments after the end of the marriage, which related to work he had done during the marriage. There was no difficulty in finding that the wife could make a claim to those.[448] However, Singer J accepted that a husband's earning potential could be regarded as a fruit of the partnership. But he also accepted that there could be cases where the subsequent earnings were in truth the result of the husband's hard work and endeavours and did not relate back to the marriage.[449] Then it would not be fair to make an award to a wife in respect of those earnings.[450] He also agreed that the efforts of the wife after the relationship had ended as carer of the children did not count as a contribution to his income. It remains to be seen how willing the courts will be to acknowledge a claim on future income.[451] It seems generally, in big money cases, the courts will

---

[442] *C v C* [2007] EWHC 2033 (Fam).
[443] [2008] 2 FCR 714.
[444] [2009] 2 FLR 1322.
[445] *Rossi v Rossi* [2006] EWHC 1482 (Fam).
[446] [2009] 2 FLR 795.
[447] Para 75. See also *H v H* [2007] EWHC 459 (Fam).
[448] *B v B* [2010] EWHC 193 (Fam).
[449] *H v H* [2007] EWHC 459 (Fam).
[450] *B v B* [2010] EWHC 193 (Fam).
[451] *P v P (Post-Separation Accruals and Earning Capacity)* [2008] 2 FLR 1135 advocates a flexible approach.

decide that an equal division will provide an adequate acknowledgement of the spouse's contributions during the marriage. Only where his earning potential will mean that very soon after the divorce a husband will be significantly richer than his wife is the court likely to consider giving her a share in his future income on the basis that she helped generate his earning power.

## E A discussion of the case law

Before discussing the approach taken by the courts it is worth recapping the central principles.

1. In all cases the overarching objective of the courts is to reach a fair result.
2. The courts will consider all of the factors listed in section 25 of the Matrimonial Causes Act 1973.
3. The court will be guided by the three principles of: meeting needs; sharing; and compensation. In most cases the principle of needs will determine the result.
4. Where there are more assets than needs the courts will use equal division of all the couple's assets as a starting point. However, there may be a good reason why it is necessary to depart from equality in order to achieve a fair result.

There has been much debate over the rulings in *White v White* and *Miller; McFarlane*.[452] Perhaps it is still too early to assess properly the impact of the decision because its ramifications are still being worked out by the Court of Appeal. But the essential argument that in all but exceptional cases the contributions of the money-earner and the child-carer/homemaker should be regarded as equal is controversial. Stephen Cretney asks:

> is it far-fetched to suggest that there is something rather simplistic about the notion that home-making contributions are to be equated in terms of economic value with commercially motivated money-making activity? And even if right-thinking people now want to make such an equation, is this not essentially a matter of social judgment for decision by Parliament rather than the courts?[453]

Cretney's point about whether the approach in *White* was a matter for Parliament rather than the courts is a matter for debate. If the House of Lords felt that the lower courts' interpretation of the word 'contribution' in s 25 was effecting gender discrimination and was misconceived was it not right to set out what the word should mean?[454] That is a normal aspect of the House of Lords' role in statutory interpretation.

Francis has also challenged the assumption of equal contribution: 'If . . . a lazy spouse with round-the-clock support staff, who spends his or her life lunching and playing tennis is to receive half, how is the hard-working spouse who has assisted the other in running the (family) business, looked after the children and run the home to be rewarded?'[455] However, it is interesting that the principle of equality appears to accord with the general public's views on what is appropriate on the breakdown of a relationship. One study found that equal division was felt by many people to be a fair way of dividing matrimonial assets on divorce, although (*inter alia*) where one party had given up earning prospects to look after a child or there was fault in the ending of relationships many felt there should be a departure from equality.[456] Perhaps the response to Francis is that non-monetary contributions to marriage are so varied

---

[452] See Duckworth and Hodson (2001); Eekelaar (2001a).
[453] Cretney (2001: 3).
[454] See the discussion in Hale (2009b).
[455] Francis (2006: 105). See also Brasse (2006) who criticises *Miller; McFarlane* as reflecting a 'compensation culture'.
[456] Lewis, Arthur, Fitzgerald and Maclean (2000).

and valued by spouses in different ways that we cannot in each case calibrate the contribution. What the courts are saying is that we assume in marriages that both parties are giving something and that they are different, but of equal value.

An aspect of *White* which has been less discussed by the courts and commentators is Lord Nicholls's argument that focusing on the needs of the party would mean that an older wife after a long marriage would receive less than a younger wife with a shorter marriage. Focusing on contributions rather than needs avoided this. Eekelaar has suggested that the shift in the approach of the courts indicated a shift from a welfare-based approach (meeting the needs of the parties) to an entitlement-based approach (what the spouse has 'earned' through the marriage).[457] In other words, it is no longer a case of the money-earner having to give the child-carer/homemaker some of 'his' money; rather it is the court dividing the couple's joint assets. Opponents of this suggestion might argue that English and Welsh law clearly does not recognise community of property (i.e. that on marriage the couple's property becomes jointly owned).[458]

There has been much criticism of the current state of the law. Coleridge J in *RP v RP*[459] stated that:

> After three decades of silence (1970–2000) when the House of Lords declined to give any guidance, there have now been two momentous decisions in six years. They run to hundreds of paragraphs. In addition they have been subjected to further interpretation in cases in the Court of Appeal and/or below. A new statute could not have had more far reaching social or forensic consequences. At present, on the ground, considerable confusion abounds.

He called for a plea for 'reflective tranquillity', concluding: 'Section 25 says it all, thereafter perhaps for the moment, the least said the better.'[460]

Despite Coleridge's wise words the discussion has continued.[461] The judgment in *Charman* ended with a call for the issues raised to be considered by the Law Commission.[462] The difficulties in finding a common European approach to the issue was discussed, as was the possibility of giving greater effect to pre-marital assets.[463] The Court of Appeal offered no ready solutions and, given the political minefield in reforming the law in this area, it is unlikely Parliament will be amending the law on ancillary relief in the near future.

The complaints about the current law are often exaggerated. The complexity of the issues raised by big money ancillary relief questions should not be underestimated. Any attempt to produce a clear formula to deal with these cases is unlikely to be sufficiently nuanced to provide the certainty so many crave. At least it would do so only at the cost of unfairness in individual cases. In fact Emma Hitchings[464] in her study of 'everyday' cases found little uncertainty in the law. She writes:

> I would suggest that the findings in this study do not support the argument that the law of ancillary relief is uncertain and chaotic. At the everyday level at least, there does not appear to be a pressing need for additional principle to increase certainty of outcome. In the everyday case where needs dominate, the findings demonstrate that the advice given to clients is pretty consistent, subject to local court culture and the practicalities of the individual case.

---

[457] Eekelaar (2001a).

[458] *Miller; McFarlane* [2006] 2 FCR 213 at para 123. Eekelaar (2003c). Cretney's (2003c) suggestion that the recent case law had created a community of property regime was rejected in *Sorrell v Sorrell* [2006] 1 FCR 62 at para 96.

[459] [2008] 2 FCR 613, at para 77.

[460] This, notably, is at para 78 of his judgment.

[461] Harris (2008).

[462] [2007] EWCA Civ 503, at para 121.

[463] See also Cooke (2009).

[464] Hitchings (2009b: 204).

Even in relation to big money cases, the general principles can be stated reasonably clearly, as they were at the start of this section. It is not surprising that it is taking time to work out precisely how these principles operate in practice, and understandably the judiciary insist that the only thing that can be said for certain is that the courts should seek to ensure there is fairness in every case.[465] Indeed there is evidence that the cause of disputes over financial orders is not so much uncertainty over the law as a distrust between the parties and disputes over disclosure.[466]

The principles articulated by the House of Lords are to be welcomed, especially the value placed on child care and the need to combat gender discrimination.[467] It *Charman* it was complained that London was regarded as 'the divorce capital of the world', given its perceived generous awards to wives. Quite why that is a bad thing is unclear. If our law is more progressive in its recognition of the value of child care than other legal systems we should celebrate, not complain.

## 8 Particular issues relating to redistribution of property on divorce

### A The poor

The case law has established that a spouse cannot expect the state to meet his or her liability towards the other spouse. It is very unusual for a party on benefits to be ordered to make payments.[468] More commonly, a nominal order is made that could be varied if the person ever got a job. The courts have also made it clear that a payer in employment should not be made to pay so much that he or she is left with only the same income he or she would have if receiving benefits, because that would rob him or her of the incentive to be employed. In *Ashley* v *Blackman*[469] the wife was a 48-year-old schizophrenic woman on state benefits and the husband was a 55-year-old on an income of £7,000 per annum. The judge thought it important to allow the husband to see the 'light at the end of the tunnel' and be spared paying the few pounds that separated him from penury as there was no corresponding benefit to the wife. In *Delaney* v *Delaney*[470] the husband was left with insufficient income to pay his mortgage and support his new cohabitant. The Court of Appeal balanced the availability of state benefits and the husband's need to support his new cohabitant. A nominal payments order in favour of the children was all the court was willing to make. The court thought it important to be aware that there was 'life after divorce'. However, it must be appreciated that, after the Child Support Act 1991 and the Child Support, Pensions and Social Security Act 2000, any attempt by the courts to make a clean break order is impossible in regard to children.

It is easy to overlook the fact that the kind of cases which have troubled the House of Lords and Court of Appeal in recent years have been 'big money cases'. Although the principles articulated in those cases are relevant for the few who have great wealth and can afford to finance litigation, the principles are of limited relevance to the 'everyday case'. In a study of practitioners by Emma Hitchings[471] it was found that for most high-street practitioners these

---

[465] Although some commentators are not even willing to agree with that: Herring (2005a).
[466] See Eekelaar and Maclean (2009) and Maclean and Eekelaar (2009).
[467] Diduck (2010).
[468] *Billington v Billington* [1974] Fam 24 at p. 29.
[469] [1988] FCR 699, [1988] 2 FLR 278.
[470] [1990] 2 FLR 457, [1991] FCR 161.
[471] Hitchings (2008).

cases are of little relevance. The everyday case is met with trying to meet the basic needs of the parties.[472]

## B Pensions

For most couples the home and pension are the two most valuable family assets.[473] The difficulty arises where one spouse, normally the husband, has substantial pension provision, but the other, normally the wife, has wholly inadequate provision. As Lord Nicholls in **Brooks v Brooks** [474] explained, the 'major responsibility for family care and home-making still remains with women' and 'the consequent limitations on their earning power prevents them from building up pension entitlements comparable with those of men'. Twice as many women as men (two-thirds of the female population) have an income below poverty level on their retirement.[475] If the couple remain married then the wife will be able to share in her husband's pension and, if her husband dies while he is receiving a pension, his widow will be entitled to payments. However, if they divorce, the wife's financial position will be much weaker than had she remained married.[476] Joshi and Davis state:

> where domestic responsibilities have not been divided it is not equal treatment to expect women to carry the double burden of society's unpaid work and earn themselves as individuals the pension rights that their husbands and ex-husbands managed to earn freed from the need to run the unpaid side of life.[477]

A different view is expressed by Deech, who suggests that it is arguable that wives who do not ensure that they have adequate pension provision in their own name are negligent.[478]

There is now a duty on the court to consider the pension position of the parties on divorce under the MCA 1973, s 25B.[479] Under s 25B(1) of the Act the courts are under a duty to consider the parties' pension entitlements:

---

### LEGISLATIVE PROVISION

**Matrimonial Causes Act 1973, section 25B(1)**

(a)  . . . any benefits under a pension scheme which a party to the marriage has or is likely to have, and

(b)  . . . any benefits under a pension scheme which, by reason of the dissolution or annulment of the marriage, a party will lose the chance of acquiring.

---

Singer J, in *T v T (Financial Relief: Pensions)*,[480] has made it clear that this provision does not require the courts to compensate a party for loss of a share in a pension, but it does mean that the courts have to consider any loss of pension rights. The court, in deciding what (if any) order to make, has the following options. In explaining these options it will be

---

[472] Hitchings (2010).
[473] See Ellison (1998); Salter (2000); Hanlon (2001) for relevant discussions of the pension issue.
[474] [1995] 2 FLR 13 at p. 15.
[475] Masson (1996: 109).
[476] Price (2009).
[477] Joshi and Davies (1992).
[478] Deech (1996).
[479] Pensions Act 1995, s 166.
[480] [1998] 1 FLR 1072, [1998] 2 FCR 364.

assumed that it is the husband who has substantial pension provision and the wife whose pension position is inadequate.

1. *'Set off'*. The husband could be ordered to pay the wife money in order to ensure she has adequate provision.[481] So a husband might be ordered to pay his wife a lump sum which the wife should invest so that it will provide for her retirement. The difficulty is that there are few couples who have sufficient funds to provide an adequate sum for a pension.

2. *'Earmarking' part of pension*. This is a delayed LSO or PPO. The court has power to order the trustees or managers to make payments (including lump sums) for the benefit of a pensioner's spouse when sums become payable to the pensioner under the terms of the pension.[482] From 1 December 2000 earmarking orders must be expressed in percentage terms.

3. *Delay*. The court may prefer to delay deciding what should happen to the pension until the husband retires.[483] On divorce the court will therefore make a PPO and not dismiss the application for an LSO. The issue will therefore be delayed until the husband retires and at that point the wife should apply for an LSO and/or a variation of the PPO.

4. *Commutation of pension*.[484] The court can order the pension to be commuted:[485] that is, that the pension fund be turned into a lump sum, which can then be divided by means of an LSO. Normally, to commute a pension is financially disadvantageous and is therefore rarely ordered.[486]

5. *Undertakings*. If the court lacks the jurisdiction to order a particular kind of provision, it may still be able to accept an undertaking. For example, a court cannot order a husband to take out a policy of insurance on his own life for his wife's benefit, but the court may be willing to accept an undertaking from a husband that he will do so.[487]

6. *Pension sharing*. Since December 2000 the court has been able to split the husband's pension into two portions on the spouses' divorce. The husband will thus have his share and the wife will have her share and each will be responsible for paying into their pensions as appropriate. The two pensions will then operate independently.[488] This order is available only as a result of the Welfare Reform and Pensions Act 1999.[489] The wife will be entitled to keep her share of the pension with the provider of her husband's pension scheme or transfer her share to a different company. The Government has stressed that there is no presumption that there should be a 50:50 split or indeed any form of order at all.[490] It may be that **White v White** implies that an equal split of the pension should be ordered in a case of a long marriage unless there is a good reason not to.[491] However, in shorter marriages account should be taken of what proportion of the pension is referable to the marriage and what proportion relates to payments made before the marriage.[492] In **Martin-Dye v Martin-Dye**[493] the Court of Appeal suggested that, as it had been decided that the other assets would be allocated

---

[481] *MD v D* [2009] 1 FCR 731; *Richardson v Richardson* [1978] 9 Fam Law 86.
[482] MCA 1973, s 25B(4).
[483] *Burrow v Burrow* [1999] 1 FLR 508.
[484] MCA 1973, s 25B(7).
[485] Since 1 December 2000 the court can require a portion of the pension to be commuted (MCA 1973, s 25B(7)).
[486] *Field v Field* [2003] 1 FLR 376.
[487] *W v W (Periodical Payments: Pensions)* [1996] 2 FLR 480.
[488] *R (on the application of Smith) v Secretary of State for Defence* [2004] EWHC 1797 (Admin), confirmed in *R (Thomas) v Ministry of Defence* [2008] 2 FLR 1385.
[489] In the unusual facts of *Brooks v Brooks* [1995] 2 FLR 13, [1995] 3 FCR 214 the House of Lords was willing to split a one-person pension scheme under the MCA 1973, treating it as a prenuptial contract.
[490] Baroness Hollis, Official Report (HL) 6 July 1999, col. 776.
[491] *SRJ v DWJ (Financial Provision)* [1999] 2 FLR 176.
[492] Salter (2003).
[493] [2006] 2 FCR 325.

57 per cent to the wife and 43 per cent to the husband, the pensions should be divided in the same proportions. The Court of Appeal in that case warned of the danger of treating a pension valued at a certain sum as equivalent to cash of that value. That would be wrong.[494]

The pension sharing option is certainly the most desirable option for many wives.[495] As mentioned already, a set-off is available only for the richest of couples. The difficulty with earmarking and delay (options 2 and 3 above) is that, if the wife remarries, this will end her PPO. A further difficulty with earmarking is that the husband may be deterred from paying into the pension scheme after the order is made and may prefer to set up a separate pension scheme.[496] There is also a concern that the parties may not want to have their relationship reawakened maybe 20 years after the divorce when the husband retires. It is not surprising to learn that the number of earmarking orders has been small.[497] With option 3 there is the difficulty that, by the time the husband retires, he may have several ex-wives who seek to claim a portion of the pension. We will now look in further detail at pension sharing, which will be the most appropriate option for most couples with a substantial pension. In 2008 there were 10,417 pension sharing orders.[498]

### (i) What pensions can be split?

Pension sharing is available 'in relation to a person's shareable rights under any pension arrangement other than an excepted public service pension scheme'.[499] The basic state pension cannot be split, although the State Earnings Related Pension Scheme (SERPS) can be.

### (ii) What is a pension sharing order?

A pension sharing order is defined in s 21A(1) of the MCA 1973 as:

---

**LEGISLATIVE PROVISION**

**Matrimonial Causes Act 1973, section 21A(1)**

. . . an order which—

(a) provides that one party's—

    (i) shareable rights under a specified pension arrangement, or
    (ii) shareable state scheme rights,

    be subject to pension sharing for the benefit of the other party, and

(b) specifies the percentage value to be transferred.[500]

---

[494] See Salter (2008) and Rosettenstein (2005) for a discussion of the problems in valuing pensions and other financial products.
[495] Ginn and Price (2002).
[496] There are also difficulties where the husband dies before the pension is payable.
[497] Bird (2000).
[498] Ministry of Justice (2009).
[499] MCA 1973, s 27(1) explains that a person's shareable rights under a pension arrangement are 'any rights of his under the arrangement' other than rights of a description specified by regulations made by the Secretary of State for Social Security (MCA 1973, s 27(3)). See also Pension Sharing (Valuation) Regulations 2000, SI 2000/1052, reg 2.
[500] A pension sharing order can be made only in respect of petitions filed after 1 December 2000 (Welfare Reform and Pensions Act 1999, s 85(2)(a)). If the petition is filed before that date there is conflicting case law on whether a decree nisi can be rescinded in order to permit the petitioner to re-petition and be able to take advantage of the new provisions (*S v S (Rescission of Decree Nisi: Pension Sharing Provision)* [2002] FL 171; *H v H (Pension Sharing: Rescission of Decree Nisi)* [2002] 2 FLR 116; but see *Rye v Rye* [2002] FL 736).

The essence of the order is therefore that a portion of one party's shareable rights is transferred to the other party. The order transfers rights to the other party and it must specify the percentage value to be transferred.[501]

### (iii) The effects of pension sharing

The effects of pension sharing are defined in s 29 of the Welfare Reform and Pensions Act 1999:

---

**LEGISLATIVE PROVISION**

**Welfare Reform and Pensions Act 1999, section 29**

(a) the transferor's shareable rights under the relevant arrangement become subject to a debit of the appropriate amount, and

(b) the transferee becomes entitled to a credit of that amount as against the person responsible for that arrangement.

---

The transferor therefore loses the percentage required to be transferred, so that his pension fund is reduced in value, and the transferee acquires the right to require the pension scheme trustee or manager to credit her with that amount so that she gains a pension fund of that value. The transferee in effect has a pension of her own.[502]

### (iv) Factors to be taken into account

Under s 25(2) of the MCA 1973 the court is to have regard to all the circumstances of the case and include 'any benefits under a pension arrangement which a party to the marriage has or is likely to have' and 'any benefits under a pension arrangement which . . . a party to the marriage will lose the chance of acquiring'.

The court cannot make a pension sharing order if there is in force an earmarking order in respect of that pension.[503] Similarly, an earmarking order cannot be made if a pension sharing order is in force.

## C Family businesses

If a husband and wife co-own a business, effectively as business partners, the law treats financial settlements differently from other divorce cases.[504] The court starts by deciding what share in the business each spouse has. In many cases this will be 50:50, but the proportion is determined by commercial law principles. The court must then decide who should continue running the business (assuming that the couple cannot continue running the business together after the divorce). If the business is profitable then only as a last resort should the court stop the business operating.[505] However, following *White v White*, the need in some cases to

---

[501] The order must rely on percentages rather than a cash sum. See further *H v H* [2009] EWHC 3739 (Fam).
[502] *Slattery v Cabinet Office* (Civil Service Pensions) [2009] 1 FLR 1365.
[503] MCA 1973, s 24B(5).
[504] For a useful discussion of such cases see P. Marshall (2003).
[505] *B v B (Financial Provision)* [1989] 1 FLR 119, [1989] FCR 146.

achieve equality may require the sale of businesses more often than before.[506] The court begins with a presumption that the spouse leaving the business should receive compensation for his or her share. Only if the factors in s 25 of the MCA 1973 compel it, will this be departed from. The other spouse can be required to transfer his/her shares and assets of a co-owned partnership or company as payment of an order.[507] The most difficult problem is to find a way for one spouse to buy the other spouse's share of the business.[508] One option is to give the spouse who lost his or her share in the business a charge[509] over the business property and over the profits made by the business.[510]

## D Housing

In many cases the matrimonial home is the most valuable asset that the parties have. There is real difficulty in balancing the interests of the husband, the wife and the children in deciding who should occupy the family home. *M v B (Ancillary Proceedings: Lump Sum)*[511] provides some indication of how these interests are to be ranked:

> In all these cases it is one of the paramount considerations, in applying the s 25 criteria, to endeavour to stretch what is available to cover the need of each for a home, particularly where there are young children involved. Obviously the primary carer needs whatever is available to make the main home for the children, but it is of importance, albeit it is of lesser importance, that the other parent should have a home of his own where the children can enjoy their contact time with him. Of course there are cases where there is not enough to provide a home for either. Of course there are cases where there is only enough to provide for one. But in any case where there is, by stretch and a degree of risk-taking, the possibility of a division to enable both to rehouse themselves, that is an exceptionally important consideration and one which will inevitably have a decisive impact on the outcome.[512]

These dicta were approved by the House of Lords in *Piglowska v Piglowski*.[513] So the first aim is to house the children and then, if possible, to enable both spouses to be housed. There are three good reasons for permitting the children to remain in the matrimonial home if at all possible. First, the children will benefit from the security of staying in the house they have been brought up in, given the other huge changes that are going on around them. Secondly, there are educational reasons for keeping the children in their present home, as they can continue to attend their present school. Thirdly, it may be important for the children's psychological welfare that they keep up their friendships with other children who live nearby.

Clearly, whether the parties have alternative accommodation is an important consideration. So in *Hanlon v Hanlon*,[514] where the husband had a flat that came with his job, the court readily required him to transfer to his wife his interest in the matrimonial home. By contrast, if a spouse has special needs then this is an important factor. In *Smith v Smith*[515]

---

[506] Although see *N v N (Financial Provision: Sale of Company)* [2001] 2 FLR 69 where the difficulty in liquidating assets provided a reason for departing from equality.
[507] *Harwood v Harwood* [1991] 2 FLR 274, [1992] 1 FCR 1.
[508] See, e.g., *Thomas v Thomas* [1996] 2 FLR 544, [1996] FCR 668.
[509] A little like a mortgage.
[510] *Belcher v Belcher* [1995] 1 FLR 916.
[511] [1998] 1 FLR 53 at p. 60.
[512] Approved in *Piglowska v Piglowski* [1999] 2 FLR 763.
[513] [1999] 2 FLR 763.
[514] [1978] 2 All ER 889.
[515] [1975] 2 All ER 19n.

the wife was awarded the house as she suffered from a kidney complaint. Despite these observations, the House of Lords has stressed that the court in each case has a discretion and that it would be wrong to see these cases as setting down any rigid rule.[516]

The harsh truth is that if the house were to be sold and the equity divided[517] then it may be that neither spouse would have sufficient cash to purchase another house of the same size. On the other hand, not selling the house and permitting the children and the residential parent to remain in the house may seem harsh on the non-residential spouse. So the courts have sought ways of enabling one spouse to stay in the house with the children while seeking to protect the other spouse's financial interest in the property.[518] If the couple own a house, then on divorce the court can consider the following options:

1. The court might order one spouse to pay money in exchange for the other's share in the property. So if the husband is ordered to give up his share in the matrimonial home so that the wife and children can stay there, the wife may be required to pay money to the husband by way of compensation. This is likely to be an option only for reasonably well-off couples. The money given in exchange for the share in the property should be sufficient so as to enable the husband to purchase his own property, with the aid of a mortgage if necessary.

2. The court could order that the house be sold under s 24A of the MCA 1973 and the proceeds be divided between the parties in such proportion as the court orders. This might be particularly appropriate if there are no children and the sale would provide enough money to enable both parties to buy their own homes. Such orders require careful wording over payment of mortgage until sale, occupation with the sale, and control of the sale. There is obviously a fear that the party who is allowed to occupy the house until the sale might try to delay the sale.

3. The court can postpone the sale of the property until a specified event has occurred. There are two main kinds of orders that can been used:

   (i) A *Mesher* order.[519] The parties will hold the property as equitable tenants in common and the sale will be deferred until the children reach the age of 17; or complete their full-time education; or the wife dies or remarries; or until further order. If one of these events occurs, the house will be sold and the equity divided as decided by the court. The option 'or until further order' enables the court to preserve a discretion in cases where an unforeseen event occurs. Until the sale the wife (or residential parent) will be permitted to occupy the property with the children. Until recently it had been thought that the *Mesher* had fallen out of favour.[520] There are a number of disadvantages with it:

       (a) The wife and husband will have to communicate and discuss the sale many years after the divorce. It thereby keeps a certain tie between the couple years after the marriage has formally ended.

       (b) When the children have finished their education they may still be reliant on the mother for accommodation, and the sale of the house could cause them harm.

---

[516] *Piglowska v Piglowski* [1999] 2 FLR 763.
[517] Under MCA 1973, s 24A.
[518] *Fisher-Aziz v Aziz* [2010] EWCA Civ 673.
[519] *Mesher v Mesher* [1980] 1 All ER 126.
[520] Eekelaar (1991a) found that only 18% of registrars regarded *Mesher* orders in a favourable light.

(c) The time when the mother is forced to leave her home is at a time in her life when she is most vulnerable. She may be middle-aged, with limited earning capacity and in no position to find appropriate alternative housing.

However, in *Elliott v Elliott*[521] the Court of Appeal supported the making of a *Mesher* order on the basis of *White v White*. It was held that to avoid gender discrimination and to promote equality the husband was prima facie entitled to half the value of the family home. Although the needs of the children justified delaying the husband's access to his share, once the children no longer needed the home the husband should be entitled to his share. A *Mesher* order enabled that to occur. *White* might therefore lead to an increase in the number of *Mesher* orders.[522]

An interesting twist on the *Mesher* order was provided by *Sawden v Sawden*[523] where the Court of Appeal made an order with the triggering event not being that the children had finished their full-time education but rather that the children had left the home and were living independently of the mother. This recognises the reality that children nowadays often remain living with their parents, not just during education but for some time afterwards.

(ii) A *Martin* order.[524] The *Martin* order is similar to a *Mesher* order in that the property is jointly owned, but the wife (or residential parent) can stay in the home for as long as she wishes. A common form of the order is that she can stay in the house until she dies or remarries. In *Clutton v Clutton*[525] the Court of Appeal approved a *Martin* order where the sale was to take place on the death, remarriage or cohabitation of the wife. There is concern over this kind of 'cohabitation clause', as it might lead to spying by the husband and involve an invasion of the wife's privacy.[526] The Court of Appeal in *Clutton* suggested that this concern was outweighed by the bitterness the husband would otherwise feel if the wife were to cohabit in 'his' house with another man.[527]

4. The court can give a spouse occupation rights. If, say, a husband was the beneficial owner of the property, it would be possible to give the wife a right to occupy without giving her ownership of the property. There is no provision for such an order under the MCA 1973, but it can be achieved through an order under s 30 of the Family Law Act 1996 that a wife's home rights continue after divorce.

5. The court could order a transfer of the house from one spouse to the other, subject to a charge in the transferor's favour. For example, a husband could be ordered to transfer to his wife his share in the house, subject to a charge in his favour. So he would not own the house, but when the house is sold he would be entitled to a share in the proceeds.[528] The benefit of this order is that, as the wife would be the owner, she would decide when the house should be sold, but the husband does not completely lose his financial interest in the property.

---

[521] [2001] 1 FCR 477.

[522] Fisher (2002: 111). Although see *B v B (Mesher Order)* [2003] Fam Law 462 for an expression of judicial concern about *Mesher* orders.

[523] [2004] 1 FCR 776.

[524] *Martin BH v Martin BH* [1978] Fam 12.

[525] [1991] 1 FLR 242, [1991] FCR 265.

[526] For an example of such spying see *B v B (Mesher Order)* [2003] Fam Law 462.

[527] Hayes (1994).

[528] It is not normally appropriate to phrase the order in terms of a sum of money but rather a percentage, as a specific sum would be ravaged by inflation: *S v S* [1976] Fam 18n at p. 21.

6. The court could order that the house be held on trust for the child. In *Tavoulareas* v *Tavoulareas*[529] the husband was ordered to purchase a house to provide accommodation for his wife and child during the child's dependency. The house was to be held on trust for the husband with the fund reverting to the child rather than to the husband. Once the child reached majority he could, in theory, remove his mother from the home.

## E  Pre-marriage or prenuptial contracts

The traditional position in English and Welsh law is that pre-marriage contracts carry little weight in a court's consideration of an application under the MCA 1973.[530] However, as we shall see shortly, that view is under challenge. The reasoning behind the traditional approach is that Parliament has given the courts the job of determining how property should be distributed on divorce, and the parties cannot rob the court of its jurisdiction.[531] It used to be said that pre-marriage contracts were contrary to public policy in that they require people to enter marriage while contemplating its breakdown. However, the courts do not seem to find this a convincing argument given the high rates of divorce.[532]

The current approach of the courts is governed by the following decision:

---

**CASE: *Radmacher v Granatino* [2010] UKSC 42**

A German wife and French husband had signed a pre-nuptial agreement in Germany which stated that neither would have a financial claim on the other in the event of a divorce. Baron J, the judge at first instance, placed negligible weight on the agreement and granted the husband (the less wealthy of the two spouses) over £5 million. The Court of Appeal held that Baron J had erred. The law on pre-marriage contracts was moving on and there was a clear trend to give greater weight than previously to pre-marriage contracts. The agreement should have carried due weight. In some cases the agreements should have 'decisive weight' and even be of 'magnetic importance'. The husband appealed to the Supreme Court.

The Supreme Court divided 8:1. The majority summarised their views by saying: 'The court should give effect to a nuptial agreement that is freely entered into by each party with a full appreciation of its implications unless in the circumstances prevailing it would not be fair to hold the parties to their agreement.'[533]

The agreement could only carry weight if the spouses 'enter into it of their own free will, without undue influence or pressure, and informed of its implications'.[534] If there was a material non-disclosure by one of the parties to the agreement that could render it of no or little effect. Normally each party would need legal advice, but not if each understood the implications of the agreement. Similarly any 'unworthy conduct, such as exploitation of a dominant position to secure an unfair advantage' could mean that little

---

[529] [1998] 2 FLR 418, [1999] 1 FCR 133.
[530] See Miller (2003) and Barton (2008a) for a general discussion of the issue and the law. Barton (2005: 994) suggests that rather than saying civil partners enter 'prenups' they must enter 'pre-reggies'!
[531] Hence contracts between a spouse and a parent-in-law providing for what should happen in the event of a divorce are similarly not enforceable: ***Uddin v Ahmed*** [2001] 3 FCR 300.
[532] Connell J in *M v M (Prenuptial Agreement)* [2002] Fam Law 177.
[533] Para 75.
[534] Para 68.

or no weight would attach to the agreement. The parties' emotional state would be considered when deciding whether the agreement had been entered into freely. Their Lordships felt that in this case the husband was an experienced businessman and, although not legally advised, he did understand the nature of the agreement.

The agreement would carry weight only if it was fair. An agreement which failed to take into account the needs of the children would lack fairness. Similarly an agreement which failed to meet the needs of either spouse, or failed to compensate them for losses caused by the marriage, would not be covered. As the majority explained:

> The parties are unlikely to have intended that their ante-nuptial agreement should result, in the event of the marriage breaking up, in one partner being left in a predicament of real need, while the other enjoys a sufficiency or more, and such a result is likely to render it unfair to hold the parties to their agreement. Equally if the devotion of one partner to looking after the family and the home has left the other free to accumulate wealth, it is likely to be unfair to hold the parties to an agreement that entitles the latter to retain all that he or she has earned.[535]

A contract may also lack fairness if there had been an unforeseen event after the making of the contract during the marriage. As their Lordships pointed out, this is particularly likely to have occurred in the case of longer marriages. However, an agreement which tried to ensure that the other party did not claim on existing property (i.e. property acquired before the marriage) would be likely to be seen as fair.

If the court concluded that the contract had been properly entered into and was not unfair then the court would give effect to it when making an order for ancillary relief. *Obiter* the majority held that a pre-marriage agreement could be regarded as a contract and could be enforced as such, although that would be subject to any application to the court under the MCA.

At the heart of the approach of the majority in **Radmacher** is an appeal to autonomy. As the majority stated:

> The reason why the court should give weight to a nuptial agreement is that there should be respect for individual autonomy. The court should accord respect to the decision of a married couple as to the manner in which their financial affairs should be regulated. It would be paternalistic and patronising to override their agreement simply on the basis that the court knows best. This is particularly true where the parties' agreement addresses existing circumstances and not merely the contingencies of an uncertain future.[536]

The decision of their Lordships is controversial. The benefits of prenuptial agreements (prenups as they are often called) appear exaggerated. It is far from obvious that having prenups will make the law more certain. Assuming there is to be some limit on prenups, for example that they must not be unfair, we need to have a yardstick against which to measure fairness. So to advise a client the solicitor will need to know what order a court would be likely to make in order to check whether the order in the prenup is close enough to be fair.[537] It will be extremely difficult for lawyers to draft a prenup.[538] As Rix LJ stated in

---

[535] Para 81.
[536] Para 78.
[537] George, Harris and Herring (2009).
[538] Scherpe (2010).

*Radmacher*: 'Over the potential many decades of a marriage it is impossible to cater for the myriad different circumstances which may await its parties.'[539] To cover all eventualities in a fair way will require an extensive document. And where there are extensive documents there are hefty bills!

Any attempt to set down in advance the responsibilities of parties could work against the interests of a party who had to undertake unexpected care work. That is likely to be women. As I have written:

> Relationships are unpredictable and messy. The sacrifices called for can be unpredictable and obligations without limit. Ask any partner caring for their demented loved one. To seek to tie these down at the start of the relationship in some form of 'once and for all' summation of their claims against each other, ignores the realities of intimate relationships.[540]

Nor is it certain either that prenups will reduce litigation. There is ample room to challenge a prenup. A person unhappy with the prenup could claim there was inadequate disclosure at the time of the agreement; they were not given adequate advice at the time of entering the agreement; there was undue influence or misrepresentation; the contract has been frustrated by later unforeseen events; that the contract is manifestly unfair. Further there might be all kinds of disputes over the correct interpretation of the wording of the prenup. Even if all of that were clear many of the problems which beset the current law would still be there: non-disclosure of assets; attempts to dispose of assets; excessive expenditure. Indeed whole new areas of dispute could arise if ownership of assets had to be determined for the purposes of the contract.[541] At least under the current law the court does not normally have to determine issues of ownership on a divorce or dissolution. Jurisdictions which have enforced prenups have faced substantial levels of litigation challenging them.[542] So a hefty lawyer's bill to get the prenup arranged in the first place and a hefty lawyer's bill to undo it when you divorce. No wonder prenups are so popular among the lawyers![543] And perhaps no wonder so few people choose to enter them.[544]

Perhaps the most significant argument against prenups is that financial orders on divorce should not reflect simply the interests of the two parties, as supporters of prenups seem to assume; they should also protect the interests of the state.[545] For example, much of the case law from *White* onwards has aimed to ensure women are not discriminated against. That work will be undone if parties are able to contract in a discriminatory way. It was left to Baroness Hale to bravely point out the gendered dimensions of the case (and, even more bravely, of the make-up of the Supreme Court):

> Would any self-respecting young woman sign up to an agreement which assumed that she would be the only one who might otherwise have a claim, thus placing no limit on the claims that might be made against her, and then limited her claim to a pre-determined sum for each year of marriage regardless of the circumstances, as if her wifely services were being bought by the year? Yet that is what these precedents do. In short, there is a gender dimension to the issue which some may think ill-suited to decision by a court consisting of eight men and one woman.[546]

---

[539] Para 73.
[540] Herring (2010b: 270).
[541] *F v F (Pre-Nuptial Agreement)* [2010] 1 FLR 1743.
[542] Fehlberg and Smyth (2002).
[543] George, Harris and Herring (2009).
[544] Hitchings (2009).
[545] Herring (2005a).
[546] Para 137.

While the majority stated that a contract would not carry weight if it was unfair in not meeting the needs of the parties or compensating for losses caused by the marriage, they specifically did not include the sharing principle as an aspect of fairness. Yet, in a marriage, the parties share their characters, hobbies and bodies. Is it not fair they share their finances too?

Despite these points the arguments relied upon by the House of Lords based on autonomy do chime with other moves in family law, which attach greater weight to autonomy.[547] The move to no fault divorce and increased use of mediation encourage parties to decide for themselves the nature of their legal relationship.[548] Of course many people will not be interested in pursuing pre-marriage contracts. Even the Beckhams have, apparently, decided against having a prenup on the basis that it is 'unromantic'.[549]

The position on pre-marriage contracts should be contrasted with unmarried couples where cohabitation contracts are enforceable.[550] The difference is that cohabitation contracts cannot be seen as robbing the courts of any jurisdiction to redistribute property. Such contracts are rarely made, although they are increasing in popularity.[551]

## 9 Consent orders

Increasingly, parties are being encouraged to resolve their financial disputes on divorce without going to court, either through negotiation between their lawyers, or more rarely through mediation. Further impetus is given by the Family Proceedings Rules 1999,[552] which have as their aim the enabling of parties to reach agreement. If the parties do reach an agreement then it is normally incorporated into the form of a draft court order which is presented to court for formal approval. The court retains the power to examine the contents of the agreement and consider the factors in s 25 of the MCA 1973. Ward LJ in *Harris v Manahan*[553] described the role of the court in these cases: 'the court is no rubber stamp nor is it some kind of forensic ferret'. In other words, the court will not blindly accept the parties' proposed orders, nor will it spend enormous effort considering the proposal with a high level of scrutiny.[554] The court will assume that if the parties were advised independently then the terms are reasonable and will make an order on the terms agreed by the parties.[555] Once the consent order has been made, it has the same legal effect as if it had been made by the court after a contested hearing.

### A The status of agreement before a court order has been made

What if the parties have reached an agreement, but before the agreement is turned into a consent order by the court one of the parties seeks to resile from it?

The position is that the court must then hold a contested hearing, but, following *Macleod v Macleod*,[556] then providing the agreement is in writing it will bind the parties, subject to

---

[547] Centre for Social Justice (2010).
[548] Franck (2009).
[549] Barton (2008a).
[550] *Sutton v Mischon de Reya* [2003] EWHC 3166 (Ch), discussed in Probert (2004b).
[551] Barlow, Burgoyne, Clery and Smithson (2008).
[552] SI 1999/3491.
[553] [1997] 1 FLR 205, [1997] 2 FCR 607.
[554] Davis, Pearce, Bird et al. (2000) in empirical research found that there was rarely sufficient information before a judge properly to evaluate the proposed order.
[555] *Xydhias v Xydhias* [1999] 1 FLR 683, [1999] 1 FCR 289.
[556] [2008] UKPC 64.

three important caveats.[557] First, the agreement could be challenged because of the circumstances of the agreement. For example, if the parties were not adequately advised or if there was a misrepresentation or undue pressure. Second, it may be varied under section 35 MCA if there has been change of circumstance which would make the arrangement 'manifestly unjust'[558] or where the agreement fails to make adequate provision for the child. Third, the court would not enforce the agreement if it was an improper attempt to 'cast a public obligation on the public purse'. That would occur if the parties arranged the agreement on the basis that one spouse would claim benefits, even though the other spouse could easily afford to pay them maintenance.

It should be remembered that there is nothing to stop spouses entering into a contract as long as the contract does not prohibit either party from seeking ancillary relief orders. In *Soulsbury v Soulsbury*[559] the husband promised to pay his wife a lump sum in his will if she did not enforce her claim for maintenance. As the agreement did not prevent the wife from seeking enforcement of the court order, it was a valid agreement.

## 10 Enforcement of financial orders

### A Avoiding enforcement problems

At least half of the financial orders made are not paid without the use of enforcement.[560] Problems over enforcement are so common that it is better to find a way of avoiding having to use enforcement in the first place. For example, obtaining a lump sum order instead of a periodical payments order can help, as it would only need to be enforced once. Indeed, if there are difficulties in enforcing a periodical payments order, the court may order a lump sum order in its place.[561] The problem is that few couples have sufficient spare capital to enable such a lump sum to be ordered. For some couples a more realistic option is for the court to make a secured periodical payments order. Such an order means that an asset (such as a house) is used as collateral so that if the periodical payments are not made the asset can be sold to supply the necessary money to meet the order.

### B Enforcement of periodical payments

Bankruptcy cannot be used as a means of enforcing periodical payments orders, but if the orders are not secured then the following forms of enforcement may be used:

1. A judgment summons under the Debtors Act 1869. This means that if a payment is not made then the debtor can be liable to imprisonment.[562]

2. An attachment of earnings order.[563] This requires payment to be made by the employer directly out of the earnings of the payer.

---

[557] The court developed the law from *Edgar v Edgar* [1980] 2 FLR 19.
[558] Para 41.
[559] [2007] 3 FCR 811.
[560] Edwards, Gould and Halpern (1990). See also Eekelaar and Maclean (1986).
[561] *Fournier v Fournier* [1998] 2 FLR 990, [1999] 2 FCR 20.
[562] Family Proceedings Rules 1991, SI 1991/1247, r 2. The Court of Appeal in *Murbarak v Murbarak* [2001] 1 FCR 193 warned that great care had to be taken to ensure that the requirements of article 6 of the European Convention were complied with when relying on a judgment summons. See now Family Proceedings (Amendment) Rules 2003 (SI 2003/184), which should ensure the procedures are Human Rights Act compliant.
[563] Attachment of Earnings Act 1971; Maintenance Enforcement Act 1991, s 1(5).

3. An order can be made requiring the payer to set up a standing order from a bank account to the recipient.[564]

The debtor who is in arrears may apply to have a periodical payments order varied, or even to have the arrears remitted. There is a general rule that arrears should not be allowed to build up for over 12 months.[565] This approach can be justified on the basis that, if no attempt is made to enforce the arrears, the recipient can be deemed to have acquiesced in the non-payment. In practice this means that arrears need to be enforced reasonably swiftly.

### C Enforcement of lump sum orders and property adjustment orders

Lump sums are not payable on the bankruptcy of the payer spouse,[566] although in exceptional circumstances a bankruptcy order could be made to enable payment of a lump sum.[567] They can be enforced in the same way as any other debt. The most common means will be through the attachment of an earnings order, or by a judgment summons.

### D Defeating claims: Matrimonial Causes Act 1973, section 37

The MCA 1973, s 37 seeks to prevent people disposing of assets in an attempt to minimise the award that can be made to their husbands or wives. The court has wide powers to prevent or set aside dispositions of property which have been made for the purpose of defeating a financial relief claim. The difficulty is often in proving that the intent of the person was to defeat a spouse's claim, although there is no need to show it was his or her sole – or even dominant – intention.[568] When deciding whether the maker of the payments had such an intention the court will look at whether he knew that the claimant might be applying for ancillary relief; the amounts of the payments compared with his overall wealth; and the reasons he had for making the payments.[569] Section 37 can only be used where the party who has made the disposition is the other spouse. It cannot be used to, for example, seek to set aside a bank's charge.[570]

## 11 Bankruptcy and ancillary relief

There are some complex provisions dealing with the interaction of bankruptcy and ancillary relief orders.[571] Here the bankrupt's estate is subject to competing claims: from the bankrupt's creditors and from the bankrupt's spouse. How should the law reconcile these? The key elements of the law are as follows:

1. *Using bankruptcy to avoid financial orders on divorce.* If a spouse has petitioned for bankruptcy merely as a device to avoid ancillary relief orders then the bankruptcy order can be set aside, but only if he used fraud or misrepresentation in his bankruptcy petition.[572] A

---

[564] Maintenance Enforcement Act 1991, s 1(5).
[565] *R v Cardiff Magistrates' Court, ex p Czech* [1999] 1 FLR 95.
[566] Insolvency Rules 1986, SI 1986/1925, r 13.3(2)(a).
[567] *Wheatley v Wheatley* [1999] 2 FLR 205. For a thorough discussion see Miller (2002).
[568] *Kemmis v Kemmis* [1988] 1 WLR 1307.
[569] *Trowbridge v Trowbridge* [2004] 2 FCR 79.
[570] *Ansari v Ansari* [2009] 1 FLR 1121.
[571] Powell and Iowe (2009).
[572] Insolvency Act 1986, s 282. See *Paulin v Paulin* [2009] 2 FLR 354 for an example.

spouse cannot claim to have a bankruptcy petition set aside on the basis that the husband had entered into it in order to frustrate the wife's ancillary relief claim.[573]

2. *Financial relief orders on bankruptcy.* A financial obligation arising from a divorce order is not provable in bankruptcy.[574] This means that if a husband is ordered to pay his wife a lump sum on divorce under the MCA 1973 and before he pays it he becomes bankrupt, his wife will not be able to claim against the trustee in bankruptcy along with other creditors.[575] However, in the unlikely event that all the creditors are paid off and there are still funds available, she may be able to enforce the order.

Normally, the fact that a person goes bankrupt will not upset any earlier transfers of property to the former spouse. However, this rule is subject to provisions of the Insolvency Act 1986 designed to secure for the benefit of creditors certain property transferred by the bankrupt within a specified period before the bankruptcy, which were discussed in Chapter 4.[576] In *Haines v Hill*[577] it was held that an order of the court following contested ancillary relief proceedings could not amount to a transaction at an undervalue and be set aside under s 339 of the Insolvency Act 1986, although if it were shown that the order was vitiated by fraud, mistake or misrepresentation it could be.[578]

3. *Transfers after the bankruptcy.* Once a spouse has become bankrupt then any transfers of his or her property will be void,[579] unless leave of the court is given.[580] *Re Flint (A Bankrupt)*[581] stated that where a husband transferred the house to his wife after he was bankrupt, but under the terms of a consent order made before the bankruptcy, the transfer was void. The same will be true if the order had been one made by a court following a contested hearing. This does not mean that the court cannot make an order against a bankrupt, although it would usually only be appropriate to do so if there is likely to be a surplus at the end of the bankruptcy (*Hellyer v Hellyer*[582]).

These cases demonstrate a clear preference for the bankrupt's creditors above the interests of the bankrupt's divorcing wife. As was noted earlier in this chapter, there is much debate over whether the financial orders on divorce are providing the wife (or whoever is the less well-off spouse) with *her* share of the assets or whether the husband (or better-off spouse) is required to pay her some of *his* assets. The law in bankruptcy seems based on the latter view.

## 12 Variation of, appeals against, and setting aside court orders

It may be that some time after the order has been made, one of the parties believes that the order is no longer appropriate. It may be that, since the making of the order, the needs of one

---

[573] *Whig v Whig* [2007] EWHC 1856 (Fam).

[574] Insolvency Rules 1986, r 12(3); *Woodley v Woodley (No. 2)* [1992] 2 FLR 417, [1993] 1 FCR 701.

[575] Although if the lump sum order referred to money in a specific account, the order may have had the effect of transferring the equitable interest in it: *Re Mordant* [1996] 1 FLR 334.

[576] See Insolvency Act 1986 (hereafter IA 1986), ss 339, 400.

[577] [2007] 3 FCR 785.

[578] See *Re Jones (A Bankrupt)* [2008] 2 FLR 1969 for a discussion of when a consent order will be regarded as dishonest.

[579] Though if a bankrupt has been ordered to transfer property to a spouse it is possible that the effect of the order is that the beneficial interest ceases to belong to the bankrupt: *Harper v O'Reilly and Harper* [1997] 2 FLR 816; *Re Mordant* [1996] 1 FLR 334.

[580] IA 1986, s 284.

[581] [1993] 1 FLR 763.

[582] [1996] 2 FLR 579.

of the parties has increased (for example, he or she suffers a serious injury following a car crash) or that one of the parties has greater resources (for example, he or she has won the national lottery). One of the most dramatic examples of events after the making of an order which justified amending the order is *Barder v Barder (Caluori Intervening)*,[583] where following a divorce the wife killed the family's two children and committed suicide. In her will she left the property to her mother.

It is important to distinguish three ways of challenging an order.

1. The applicant could apply to vary or discharge orders. The amount payable under a periodical payments order may be increased or decreased, or the order discharged and brought to an end.[584] An application to vary an order is based on an argument that, although the order was correct at the time when it was made, subsequent events mean that the order should be varied to reflect the new positions of the parties. It is not possible to apply to vary a lump sum order.[585]

2. The applicant could appeal against an order. Here the claim is that there was a fundamental flaw in the judge's reasoning, and the order should not have been made.

3. The applicant could apply to have the order set aside. This is normally done on the grounds of fraud or non-disclosure of property,[586] although not every non-disclosure will justify setting an order aside.[587] The approach is similar to an appeal but the crucial difference is that the application to set aside accepts that the correct decision was made by the judge on the facts as presented, but maintains that the other party misled the court into making the wrong order.

## A Variation

The power of the courts to vary the order is highly controversial (unlike the power to vary or set aside the order which exists for all court orders). If the couple have divorced and an appropriate order is made by the court, why should the fact that, say, the husband wins the national lottery justify the wife in being entitled to more money? Looking back at the justifications discussed earlier in this chapter, apart from the contract approach the others would not seem to justify a claim to the lottery winnings. However, a case can be made to justify variation. This is that on divorce all too often there are not sufficient assets to make the order that the court may believe just, bearing in mind all the circumstances. For example, even though the marriage may be a long one and the wife may have contributed significantly to it through care of the children and the home, the husband may have disposed of his assets and so there are not enough to give her the level of income she deserves. In such a case, if the husband subsequently does receive a lottery winning and the court can now make the order which would be just and appropriate, should it not do so? Against this is the argument that court orders should represent finality, so that the parties can plan for the future. Further, there is a fear that the power to vary court orders may discourage the parties from seeking to improve their financial position. Payers may fear that if they increase their income the payee will apply to increase the level of payments; similarly, payees may be concerned that any improvement in their standard of living will lead to an application to reduce the level of payments.

---

[583] [1987] 2 FLR 480.
[584] MCA 1973, s 31.
[585] Unless it is a lump sum order in instalments.
[586] *Bokor-Ingram v Bokor-Ingram* [2009] 2 FLR 922.
[587] *I v I (Ancillary Relief: Disclosure)* [2008] EWHC 1167 (Fam).

## (i) Which orders can be varied?

An application can be made to vary a periodical payments order.[588] The court could increase, decrease or terminate the payments, or could vary for how long the payments are to be made. It can also terminate a periodical payments order and replace it with a lump sum order. Any application for variation must be made before the order expires.[589] In other words, if the order states that periodical payments are to be made to the wife until 1 January 2013, the wife can only apply to extend the period of payments if she applies to do so before 1 January 2013. If a court wants to make an order for periodical payments which cannot be extended then an order under s 28(1A) of the MCA 1973 must be made.[590] On hearing an application for variation the court could decide to terminate payments altogether.[591] The court can also vary a PPO by making an LSO in its place.[592] So if a husband had been paying a wife £1,000 per year maintenance and he acquired some capital, the court might decide to order him to make a lump sum payment of, say, £25,000 and then end his PPO. When making orders of this kind the court should use the lump sum as payment in place of the ongoing periodical payments order. It should not reopen arguments about how the couple's assets should be distributed.[593]

As property adjustment orders (PAOs) and lump sum orders are designed to produce finality the general principle is that they cannot usually be varied.[594]

## (ii) Factors to be taken into account

In considering variation of a PPO the court will have regard to all the circumstances of the case, the first consideration being the welfare of the child. This includes any change in matters to which the court had regard when first making the order. Under s 31(7) of the MCA 1973, in considering variation the court is also to consider:

---

**LEGISLATIVE PROVISION**

**Matrimonial Causes Act 1973, section 31(7)**

(a) . . . whether in all the circumstances and after having regard to any such change it would be appropriate to vary the order so that payments under the order are required to be made or secured only for such further period as will in the opinion of the court be sufficient to enable the party in whose favour the order was made to adjust without undue hardship to the termination of those payments;

(b) in a case where the party against whom the order was made has died, the circumstances of the case shall also include the changed circumstances resulting from his or her death.

---

[588] A lump sum order cannot be varied, unless it is a lump sum order payable in instalments.
[589] *Jones v Jones* [2000] 2 FCR 201.
[590] *Richardson v Richardson (No. 2)* [1997] 2 FLR 617, [1997] 2 FCR 453; discussed in Cooke (1994).
[591] *Penrose v Penrose* [1994] 2 FLR 621.
[592] MCA 1973, s 31(7B), as inserted by the Family Law Act 1996 (hereafter FLA 1996). See *Harris v Harris* [2001] 1 FCR 68 where the Court of Appeal refused to set down guidelines on how the power under this section should be used, although in *Cornick v Cornick (No. 3)* [2001] 2 FLR 1240 it was suggested that the principles in *White v White* could be applied.
[593] *Pearce v Pearce* [2003] 3 FCR 178.
[594] Although the time of payment can sometimes be changed: *Omelian v Omelian* [1996] 2 FLR 306, [1996] 3 FCR 329 CA.

Section 31(7)(a) therefore specifically requires the court to consider the possibility of ending the payments altogether to enable the parties to become financially independent. Most cases for variation will involve a fundamental change in circumstances since the order was made,[595] although this is not essential according to the Court of Appeal in *Flavell v Flavell*.[596] In *North v North*[597] the husband had been paying the wife nominal periodical payment orders. Some 20 years after the divorce she had gone to Australia, lived a lavish lifestyle and used up her money. On her return to the UK she sought an increase in the level of payments. The Court of Appeal held that the husband was an 'insurer against all hazards'. Here the wife had created her needs from her own extravagance or irresponsibility. The periodical payments should not be increased. In *Hvorostovsky v Hvorostovsky*[598] the husband's income has increased substantially after the divorce (he was an international singer) and this justified an increase in the level of maintenance paid to the wife. The Court of Appeal emphasised that in such a case an ex-wife could not claim more than her reasonable needs.

On a hearing to vary a periodical payments order the court should not reopen the division of capital. In *Lauder v Lauder*[599] the husband became very wealthy in the years following the divorce. However, that did not justify the court varying the PPO to give the wife a share of his wealth. The court would only consider whether in the light of her current needs and the economic disadvantages caused to her by the marriage, there was a justification for increasing the order. As the current order met her needs there was not.

There is a strict rule that if the spouse who is in receipt of periodical payments remarries then the payments will automatically come to an end.[600] But what if she or he cohabits rather than remarries? In *Atkinson v Atkinson (No. 2)*[601] the Court of Appeal rejected an argument that, as the wife was now cohabiting, the periodical payments should come to an end. However, the Court of Appeal accepted that the ex-wife's needs were less on the basis that her cohabitant could be expected to contribute to her household expenses and so the level of maintenance should be reduced. On the husband's behalf it was argued that an ex-wife who remarries should not be disadvantaged compared to an ex-wife who cohabits and that therefore cohabitation and marriage should automatically end the payments. The court rejected this argument, stating that if the court did end the wife's payments on cohabitation this would pressurise her into marrying her new cohabitant to ensure she had financial security. The court stated that it would be wrong for the law to place such pressure on her. This approach was recently approved by the Court of Appeal in *Fleming v Fleming*,[602] where an argument that changing social attitudes meant that marriage and cohabitation should be treated in the same way in this context was rejected.[603] However, in *K v K (Periodic Payment: Cohabitation)*[604] Coleridge J thought that a cohabiting couple should strive towards financial

---

[595] A party will be prevented from seeking to vary an order if they have led the other party to act to his or her detriment on an assumption that they will not apply for variation.

[596] [1997] 1 FLR 353, [1997] 1 FCR 332.

[597] [2007] 2 FCR 601.

[598] [2009] 2 FLR 1574.

[599] [2008] 3 FCR 468.

[600] Although this will not necessarily defeat a claim for a lump sum or for child maintenance: *Re G (Financial Provision: Liberty to Restore Application for Lump Sum)* [2004] Fam Law 332.

[601] *Atkinson v Atkinson* [1995] 2 FLR 356, [1995] 2 FCR 353; *Atkinson v Atkinson (No. 2)* [1996] 1 FLR 51, [1995] 3 FCR 788.

[602] [2003] EWCA Civ 1841.

[603] Although the court decided that given the wife's cohabitation and current financial position there was no reason to extend the period of her periodic payments.

[604] [2005] EWHC 2886 (Fam).

independence from a husband.[605] He thought the law had to acknowledge that a 'social revolution' had taken place in connection with cohabitation. Nothing in the earlier case law stopped a judge from deciding that in the light of the cohabitation periodical payments should cease. However, in *Grey v Grey*[606] the Court of Appeal approved the approach in *Fleming*. So a judge should now consider what financial contribution the new cohabitant was, or could, make to the spouse's household and take that into account in assessing the level of periodic payments.[607]

To deal with the problem with the spouse receiving payments living with someone else, it is possible to draft the PPO or PAO to cease if there is cohabitation. For example, a typical order relating to the home is 'the wife to have occupation of the former matrimonial home, sale of the property to be postponed until such time as she remarry or cohabit with another man'; a typical PPO is that 'the order for periodical payments shall terminate in the event of the wife's cohabitation with another man'.[608] There are difficulties with such orders. The first is the complexity of cohabitation. If the wife has a partner who visits her regularly, when does this amount to cohabitation?[609] Further, such clauses can even lead to spying by the paying spouse to try to discover whether there is cohabitation.

In *Vaughan v Vaughan*[610] an ex-wife sought to increase her period payments or to have them capitalised. The primary issue was that her husband had remarried. He argued that if he paid his ex-wife a capital sum that would leave his present wife in a vulnerable position if ever they were to split up. The Court of Appeal disagreed. Although it was proper for the court to take account of the husband's obligation to support his current wife, they should not consider the hypothetical possibility of him divorcing his current wife. Notably the court thought it important that the ex-wife receive a level of maintenance that was adequate compensation for her loss of earning potential caused by the marriage.[611]

## B  Setting aside a consent order

Once a consent order has been made by the court, the court will be very reluctant to permit any challenges to the order. The following are examples of the circumstances upon which an application can be made to set aside a consent order:

1. *Non-disclosure.* The court, in deciding whether to set aside a consent order on the basis of non-disclosure, will consider whether the non-disclosure was fundamental enough to merit setting the order aside. In *Livesey v Jenkins*[612] the House of Lords thought the failure by the wife to reveal that she was engaged to remarry was of sufficient importance that the order should be set aside. The test, their Lordships suggested, was that had the court been aware of the information that had not been disclosed it would have made a substantially different order. This test strikes the balance between on the one hand ensuring fairness between the parties and discouraging non-disclosure, and on the other hand preventing a

---

[605] The husband had argued in that case that it was inconsistent that cohabitation prior to marriage could be taken into account when assessing the length of a marriage (*Co v Co* [2004] 1 FLR 1095), but was not relevant when considering termination of spousal maintenance.
[606] [2010] 1 FCR 394.
[607] *Grey v Grey* [2010] 1 FCR 394.
[608] Hayes (1994).
[609] See *Kimber v Kimber* [2000] 1 FLR 383.
[610] [2010] 2 FCR 509.
[611] See also *McFarlane (No. 2)*.
[612] [1985] FLR 813.

large number of appeals on the basis of the tiniest non-disclosures. A mistake as to value will not be sufficient to justify setting aside a court order.[613]

2. *Bad legal advice.* In **B v B (Consent Order: Variation)**[614] it was accepted that 'manifestly bad advice' could be a ground for setting aside a consent order. In **Harris v Manahan**[615] the Court of Appeal seemed to restrict this to cases where there was an exceptional case of the 'cruellest injustice'. It might be more profitable in such cases for a person to bring negligence proceedings against his or her solicitors.

## C Appeal

It is possible to appeal against a court order. However, there are time restrictions on when an application can be made. A crucial issue is when it is possible to appeal against an order out of time. This is particularly relevant in relation to clean break orders when variation cannot be relied upon. There is a balance to be drawn between on the one hand ensuring there is finality of litigation, so that the parties are not constantly challenging the orders made in the court, while, on the other hand, it could be seen to be contrary to justice to uphold a judgment known to be based on a falsehood. The leading case is **Barder v Barder (Caluori Intervening)**,[616] which suggested that an application to appeal out of time will occur only if the following conditions are shown:

1. The basis of the order, or a fundamental assumption underlining the order, has been falsified by a change of circumstances since the making of an order. Perhaps the most common example of this is where a valuation relied upon by the court of, for example, a business or a house, has proved inaccurate,[617] although it should be stressed that an application for leave can only rely on an unsound valuation as the basis of appeal if they have sought leave as quickly as possible and are not at fault for the misvaluation.[618] Even then the courts take the view that valuations are an 'inexact science' and so only if they are very badly wrong will they form the basis of a successful appeal.[619] Where the value of the property has fallen as a result of fluctuation in the property market that will not be a *Barder* event.[620] Similarly a mistake as to the value of an item by the parties will not be a *Barder* event.[621] Another example may be where one spouse unexpectedly dies shortly after an order has been made.[622] In **Williams v Lindley**[623] an order was made which included a lump sum to meet the wife's housing needs. A few weeks after the order was made the wife became engaged and subsequently married a very wealthy man. The Court of Appeal by a majority found that this destroyed the foundation of the order which was to meet her housing needs. Also, where the couple reconcile and cohabit after the divorce only to separate many years later it is open to appeal out of time against the original order; the

---

[613] *Judge v Judge* [2008] EWCA Civ 1458, [2009] 2 FCR 158.
[614] [1995] 1 FLR 9, [1995] 2 FCR 62.
[615] [1997] 1 FLR 205, [1997] 2 FCR 607.
[616] [1988] AC 20.
[617] E.g. *Kean v Kean* [2002] 2 FLR 28.
[618] *Kean v Kean* [2002] 2 FLR 28.
[619] *B v B* [2007] EWHC 2472 (Fam).
[620] *Horne v Horne* [2009] 2 FLR 1031.
[621] *Walkden v Walkden* [2009] 3 FCR 25.
[622] *Barder v Barder (Caluori Intervening)* [1988] AC 20; *Reid v Reid* [2004] Fam Law 95.
[623] [2005] 1 FCR 813.

reconciliation and cohabitation is an event of sufficient importance to justify giving leave out of time.[624] In *Maskell v Maskell*[625] it was held that the husband's redundancy could not be regarded as a supervening event. It was not an unpredicted event, but part of life's normal difficulties.

2. Such change is within a relatively short time of the order, usually two years at most.[626] However, the court may be sympathetic if the applicant has applied as quickly as could reasonably be expected once he or she knew of the change of circumstances, especially in cases of fraud.[627]

3. The applicant must show that had the true situation been known or event foreseen the court would have made a materially different order.[628]

4. The application for leave must have been made reasonably promptly once the change of circumstances was known about.

5. The granting of leave should not prejudice unfairly third parties who have acquired interests for value in the property affected.

6. Only in an 'exceptionally small number of cases' will these factors justify the overruling of a decision in a family law case.[629]

In *Myerson v Myerson (No. 2)*[630] there was a huge drop in the value of the husband's assets soon after the making of an order. The value of his assets were now 14 per cent of what they had been valued to be at the time of the order. However this was held not to be a *Barder* event. It represented the normal process of price fluctuation. When he had agreed to the order the husband had realised that his assets were volatile and could increase or decrease in value. In *Dixon v Marchant*[631] a husband claimed that his wife's remarriage just seven months after the making of a clean break order amounted to a *Barder* event. The majority of the Court of Appeal disagreed. The husband realised that a clean break order carried the risk the wife might remarry soon after it was made and so he would end up paying more than he would have done had he been paying periodical payments (which would stop on remarriage). Importantly the court found that there was no evidence that the wife had deceived her husband during the negotiations leading up to the clean break order. The case can be contrasted with *Williams v Lindley*[632] where the wife's remarriage shortly after the making of a consent order did justify variation. In that case it seems that the wife's need for housing had dominated the negotiations prior to the order. As her housing needs were met on the unforeseen marriage so soon after the making of the order, this was held to be a *Barder* event.

---

[624] *Hewitson v Hewitson* [1995] 1 FLR 241; see *Hill v Hill* [1998] 1 FLR 198 for an alternative way of dealing with these cases.

[625] [2001] 3 FCR 296.

[626] *Worlock v Worlock* [1994] 2 FLR 689 (four years after application and two years after change then 'far too late').

[627] Although see *Burns v Burns* [2004] 3 FCR 263 where the applicant was so slow in bringing the matter to court that leave was not granted. However, note *Den Heyer v Newby* [2005] EWCA Civ 1311 where it was said that, if such a delay in bringing the matter to court was caused by the respondent's failure to make proper disclosure, the respondent could not complain.

[628] *S v S (No. 2) (Ancillary Relief: Application to Set Aside Order)* [2010] 1 FLR 993.

[629] *Shaw v Shaw* [2002] 3 FCR 298 at para 44.

[630] [2009] 2 FLR 147.

[631] [2008] 1 FCR 209.

[632] [2005] 1 FCR 269.

## 13 Transfer of tenancies

Under Sch 7 to the Family Law Act 1996 the court has the power to transfer certain tenancies from one spouse or cohabitant to another.

### A Who can apply?

Spouses or civil partners can apply where 'one spouse or civil partner is entitled, either in his own right or jointly with the other spouse or civil partner, to occupy a dwelling-house by virtue of a relevant tenancy'.[633] Cohabitants or former cohabitants can apply where 'one cohabitant is entitled, either in his own right or jointly with the other cohabitant, to occupy a dwelling-house by virtue of a relevant tenancy'.[634] Cohabitants are defined in the Family Law Act 1996 in such a way as to include same-sex couples.

### B Which tenancies can be transferred?

The statute applies only to certain kinds of tenancy[635] and the tenancy must be of a dwelling-house which was the home of the spouses or cohabitants. A tenancy must still be in existence when the application for a transfer is made. An important restriction on the availability of the Schedule was revealed in *Gay v Sheeran*,[636] where Mr Sheeran was a joint tenant with Ms Gunn of a property. Ms Gunn moved out; Ms Gay subsequently moved in; and finally Mr Sheeran moved out. Ms Gay sought an order transferring the tenancy to her. However, she failed because neither she nor Mr Sheeran were 'entitled in [their] own right or jointly with the other cohabitant' to occupy the property. So a cohabitant cannot seek a transfer of a tenancy which is jointly held by his or her partner and a third party.

### C Orders that can be made

In essence the tenancy can be transferred from one spouse or cohabitant to the other; or be transferred from the joint names of both cohabitants or spouses into the name of one of them.[637] If the tenancy is transferred then the new tenant takes on the tenancy subject to all the burdens as well as the benefits of the tenancy. There is no power to alter the terms of the agreement. But there is the power to require the transferee to pay compensation to the transferor for the loss of any interest in the tenancy.[638]

### D Factors to be taken into account

The court must consider:

1. the circumstances in which the tenancy was granted;
2. the housing needs and resources of the parties and any relevant child;

---

[633] FLA 1996, Sch 7, para 2.
[634] FLA 1996, Sch 7, para 3.
[635] A protected tenancy or statutory tenancy within the meaning of the Rent Act 1977; a statutory tenancy within the meaning of the Rent (Agriculture) Act 1976; a secure tenancy within the meaning of s 79 of the Housing Act 1985; and an assured or assured agricultural occupancy within the meaning of Part I of the Housing Act 1988.
[636] [1999] 2 FLR 519.
[637] The detailed terms are set out in FLA 1996, Sch 7, Part II.
[638] A list of the effects to be taken into account is found in Sch 7 to the FLA 1996.

3. the financial resources and obligations of the parties and any child;

4. the likely effect of transferring or not transferring the tenancy on the health, safety or well-being of the parties and any relevant child; and

5. the suitability of the parties as tenants.[639]

In a case involving cohabitants the courts should also consider:

1. the nature of the parties' relationship, including the fact that they have not given each other the commitment involved in marriage;

2. the length of time the parties have cohabited;

3. the length of time since they ceased to cohabit;

4. whether they have any children together or whether they had parental responsibility for any children.[640]

In *Lake v Lake*[641] the Court of Appeal held that conduct could be taken into account in deciding whether to order a transfer of a tenancy, even though it is not listed in Sch 7 as a factor to consider. *B v M*[642] gives a good example of where an order to transfer a tenancy may be appropriate. A woman moved in to her partner's rented property. She started up a successful florist business in the property. On the breakdown of the relationship she successfully applied for a transfer of the tenancy; the court focused on the fact that her business was flourishing and that the man could find alternative accommodation, as he was in receipt of housing benefit.

## 14 Reform of the law on financial support for spouses

In recent years there has been some discussion about whether the law needs to be reformed to give it a clearer structure.[643] Although there have been many voices calling for change there is little agreement over what system would be better.[644] There are a number of options that have been mooted including the following:

1. In the government paper, *Supporting Families*, some overarching criteria were proposed as giving the courts clearer guidance:

   First, to promote the welfare of any child of the family under the age of eighteen, by meeting housing needs of any children and the primary carer, and of the secondary carer; both to facilitate contact and to recognise the continuing importance of the secondary carer's role. Second, the court would take into account the existence and content of any written agreement about financial arrangements . . . third, . . . the court would then divide any surplus so as to achieve a fair result, recognising that fairness will generally require the value of the assets to be divided equally between the spouses. Fourth, the court would try to terminate financial relationships between the parties at the earliest date practicable.[645]

---

[639] FLA 1996, Sch 7, para 5.
[640] FLA 1996, Sch 7, para 5.
[641] [2006] EWCA Civ 1250.
[642] [1999] FLP, 16 March.
[643] Barlow (2009b); Bailey-Harris (2005); Miles (2005); Thorpe LJ (1998a); Bird (2002).
[644] Maclean and Eekelaar (2009).
[645] Home Office (1998: para 4.49).

The Law Society has produced a report with ten guidelines to govern the exercise of discretion.[646] They draw a notable distinction between cases where the assets of the parties exceed the family's needs and where they do not. Where they do not exceed needs, then the assets should be used to meet the housing needs of the children, followed by the parties; and any remaining assets should be 'distributed in accordance with the remaining needs of the parties in proportion to their separate abilities to meet those needs'. If there are assets which exceed needs these should be distributed according to any pre-marriage agreement, or, if none, in such a way as would be fair, that often being equally. Apart from the weight given to pre-marriage agreements these appear to reflect the current law.

2. *Pre-marriage contracts.* There has been much dispute whether more weight should be given to contracts.[647] We discussed arguments about these above. Eekelaar predicts that the basis of the law in the future will take into account the agreements of the parties. He suggests that the law is moving towards the following position:

> the law should first look to securing the circumstances of children when any relationship breaks down, then to making sure (if possible) that the role of the children's carer is properly recognized, and that includes characterizing that role as one which generates entitlements to capital or, in some cases, to ongoing support. Beyond that, parties will be given wide freedom to determine their own interests.[648]

3. *Equal distribution.* Some have proposed that there should be a presumption of equality in distribution of assets.[649] The Conservative Party's Centre for Social Justice[650] argues:

> Our proposal on financial provision is that all assets of the couple on divorce should be categorised into marital assets and non-marital assets and divided differently. Marital assets should be divided equally subject to overriding calls on those assets, and non-marital assets should stay with the relevant spouse again subject to overriding calls on those assets and unless there is any good reason to make any distributive orders. Non-marital assets would be pre-marital assets, inheritances or gifts and certain postseparation assets with provision that some non-marital assets would become marital assets in particular circumstances and over time. The court would have power to make different orders if there was significant injustice but otherwise the present very wide discretion would be fettered.

That is close to the current law as it applies to big money cases, but it appears that they want it to apply to all cases. Their proposals should be understood bearing in mind they also would like to see pre-marriage contracts enforced unless they would cause significant injustice. The major concern with their equal divison proposal is that in many cases there is an unequal division in order to meet the basic needs of the children and their carer. A strong equality approach would be likely to work against the interests of children and their carers.[651] As Baroness Hale has acknowledged: 'Too strict an adherence to equal sharing and the clean break can lead to a rapid decrease in the primary carer's standard of living and a rapid increase in the breadwinner's.'[652]

---

[646] Law Society (2003).
[647] See Fehlberg and Smyth (2002) for a discussion of the Australian experience, and Atwood (1993) on the American.
[648] Eekelaar (2000b: 421).
[649] Thorpe LJ (1998c).
[650] Centre for Social Justice (2009), discussed in Hodson (2009).
[651] Wilson J (1999).
[652] *McFarlane*, para 142.

4. In *Wachtel v Wachtel*[653] Denning LJ suggested that the wife should be entitled to one-third of the family's assets. He explained that the husband would have to find 'some woman to look after his house', while it would be unlikely a woman would need to. This view has few supporters nowadays. It is clearly based on traditional gender roles and, even from its own sexist perspectives, overlooks the need of the wife to employ a handyman to help with house repairs!

5. John Eekelaar[654] has suggested an approach which attaches greater significance to the length of time the parties have lived together than the current law.[655] He explains that 'duration of marriage is an excellent proxy for measuring a number of factors which are important in achieving a "fair" outcome. They include: the degree of commitment to a relationship; the value of contributions made to it, which is not susceptible of straightforward economic measurement; and the extent of disadvantage undergone on separation.'[656] By contrast Thorpe LJ has stated: 'What a party has given to a marriage and what a party has lost on its failure cannot be measured by simply counting the days of its duration.'[657] John Eekelaar accepts that in a lengthy marriage equality is appropriate, but where one party brings to the marriage substantial assets the poorer party should be regarded as gradually earning an increasing share in the other's assets. He suggests 2.5 per cent per annum, leading to an equal share after 20 years. Similarly, in relation to maintenance he suggests that the person who has taken on the majority of child care receive an award of 30 per cent of the income at the time of separation after a 20-year marriage, scaled down if the marriage is shorter. Payments should last for 60 per cent of the duration of the marriage.[658]

Eekelaar's argument is strongest when considering an extreme case: if, for example, a woman marries a multi-millionaire but the marriage lasts only a few weeks she should not be entitled to half the fortune. But if the marriage has lasted 30 years she has a strong claim for an equal share of the fortune. Against his argument is the view that it does not accord with how most couples understand their marriage and finances. The notion of the child-carer/homemaker day by day earning a little more in his or her spouse's assets is not one with which many couples would feel an affinity. Rebecca Bailey-Harris[659] also argues that it is discriminatory that domestic contributions earn equal value only over time, whereas financial ones do not. Eekelaar responds to this comment by suggesting that unlike financial contributions homemaking is linked to duration. His point is that one day's housework cannot be worth more or less than one day's housework; however, the money-earner's value depends on the amount brought home. So homemaking can be valued only by time, but money-earning need not be.[660] 'Homemaking for one day, however brilliantly done, is in itself of relatively little value,' he says. This, at least if it includes child care (as it appears to), is debatable. Would that be true of the day of birth? Or the day the child finally was helped by the parent to understand multiplication? Or the day the teenager was given comfort for their first broken heart?

[653] [1973] Fam 72.
[654] Eekelaar (2001a; 2003c).
[655] See also Ellman (2005).
[656] Eekelaar (2006a: 756).
[657] *Miller* [2005] EWCA Civ 984, para 34.
[658] Eekelaar (2006a: 758).
[659] Bailey-Harris (2003a).
[660] The argument is less convincing if one includes as a contribution to the marriage not only money-earning, child care and household tasks, but also emotional support, love, etc.

6. Others argue that if there is to be financial fairness between spouses on divorce, some fundamental change in society is required. Diduck and Orton look forward to a better future:

> Along with true equality in employment and pay and affordable good quality child care, an adequate valuation of domestic work would mean it would not be necessary that each partner play exactly the same role in wage earning . . . Roles in marriage could be adopted based on the partners' actual interests and skills. Maintenance on divorce would still sometimes be necessary, then, but it would no longer overwhelmingly be women who require it and it would no longer result in economic disadvantage for the recipient. Maintenance would be seen as a right, expected and earned, rather than as a gift, act of benevolence or based on a notion of women's dependency on men.[661]

As it is, many of the problems with finding a fair law of ancillary relief are due to the fact that we live in a flawed society with gendered inequalities in term of wages, child care, housework and discrimination, a society which does not recognise caring for others in financial terms. Given such a background, the law on ancillary relief is bound to fail. Much of the approach of the current law is based on trying to enable a woman to enter the job market or to compensate her for 'missing out' on employment. The assumption is that care work is not valuable and that the ideal wives should be striving for is to match the 'male' ideal of employment. An alternative would be to recognise the value of care work not just for the couple themselves, but for society in general.[662]

## 15 Conclusion

Ruth Deech opens her recent discussion of financial orders on separation by asking her readers to consider three sisters:

> One is very pretty and marries a national footballer; they have no children and it is a short marriage before she leaves him for an international celebrity. The second sister marries a clergyman and has several children; the marriage ends after 30 years as he is moving into retirement. The third sister never marries; she stays at home and nurses first their mother, who has a disability, and then their father, who has Alzheimer's, and dies without making a will. Which of the three sisters will get the windfall: an amount sufficient to keep her in luxury for the rest of her days, when her relationship with a man comes to an end? And which one most needs and deserves financial support, even of the bare minimum? The message is that getting married to a well-off man is an alternative career to one in the workforce.[663]

Her implied message is that the current law on financial orders on separation has gone badly wrong. The undeserving footballer's wife ends up with millions, the carer of the demented mother ends up with nothing. She is right that this seems unfair. But, of course it does not follow that the problem is the award to the footballer's wife. It may be the real issue is the lack of provision for carers, rather than excessive awards to wives. And the way resources are distributed in the world is generally unfair.

This chapter has focused on the financial position of partners on the breakdown of their relationship. For many couples it is the financial support for children which is the key issue,

---

[661] Diduck and Orton (1994: 686–7).
[662] Glennon (2010).
[663] Deech (2009a).

with limited resources available for spousal support. For both married and unmarried couples, child support is calculated by means of a rigid formula, set out in the Child Support Act 1991. This is by contrast with the wide discretion the courts have to determine spousal support under the Matrimonial Causes Act 1973. The two systems reveal the contrasting benefits and disadvantages of rule-based and discretion-based systems. The chapter also reveals the different bases upon which financial support obligations are based. In *White* v *White* the House of Lords has stressed the importance of fairness between spouses, which will often require an equal division of assets between a husband and wife, although in many ordinary cases it is enough of a struggle meeting the basic needs of the parties and the children, let alone considering broader theoretical concepts. The Child Support Act 1991, despite its focus on the parental obligation to support children, primarily seeks to reduce government expenditure on welfare payments. Running through this chapter is the requirement for the law to be realistic. Imposing obligation which cannot be enforced, or requiring people to support those to whom they feel no particular moral obligation, is unlikely to result in an effective law. That said, finding a law on financial support for family members which is regarded as fair, reflects the social obligations which people feel, and is practicably enforceable, might be an impossible task.

## Further reading

**Altman, S.** (2003) 'A theory of child support', *International Journal of Law, Policy and the Family* 17: 173.

**Bailey-Harris, R.** (1998a) 'Dividing the Assets on Breakdown of Relationships Outside Marriage: Challenges for Reformers', in R. Bailey-Harris (ed.) *Dividing the Assets on Family Breakdown*, Bristol: Jordans.

**Cooke, E.** (2007) 'Miller/McFarlane: law in search of a definition', *Child and Family Law Quarterly* 19: 98.

**Eekelaar, J.** (2000b) 'Post-Divorce Financial Obligations', in S. Katz, J. Eekelaar and M. Maclean (eds) *Cross Currents*, Oxford: OUP.

**Eekelaar, J.** (2006a) 'Property and Financial Settlement on Divorce – Sharing and Compensating', *Family Law* 36: 754.

**Ellman, I.** (2005) 'Do Americans Play Football?', *International Journal of Law, Policy and the Family* 19: 257.

**George, R. H., Harris, P. and Herring, J.** (2009) 'Pre-Nuptial Agreements: For Better or for Worse?', *Family Law* 39: 934.

**Glennon, L.** (2010) 'The limitations of equality discourses on the contours of intimate obligations' in J. Wallbank, S. Choudhry and J. Herring (eds) *Rights, Gender and Family Law*, Abingdon: Routledge.

**Herring, J.** (2005a) 'Why Financial Orders on Divorce should be Unfair', *International Journal of Law, Policy and the Family* 19: 218.

**Miles, J.** (2005) 'Principle or pragmatism in ancillary relief: the virtues of flirting with academic theories and other jurisdictions', *International Journal of Law, Policy and the Family* 19: 242.

Miles, J. (2008) '*Charman* v *Charman* (No. 4) [2007] EWCA Civ 503 – making sense of need, compensation and equal sharing after Miller; McFarlane', *Child and Family Law Quarterly* 20: 378.

O'Donovan, K. (2005) 'Flirting with academic categorisations', *Child and Family Law Quarterly* 17: 415.

Perry, P., Douglas, G., Murch, M. et al. (2000) *How Parents Cope Financially on Marriage Breakdown*, London: Joseph Rowntree.

Wikeley, N. (2006c) *Child Support: Law and Policy*, Oxford: Hart.

Wikeley, N. (2007b) 'Child support reform – throwing the baby out with the bathwater', *Child and Family Law Quarterly* 19: 435

Wikeley, N. (2009) 'Financial support for children after parental separation: Parental responsibility and responsible parenting', in R. Probert, S. Gilmore and J. Herring, *Responsible Parents and Parental Responsibility*, Oxford: Hart.

# 6 Domestic violence

## 1 Introductory issues

### A Terminology of topic and definitions

There is no agreement over the correct terminology to be used to describe violence that takes place between adults in a close relationship. At one time it was common to talk about domestic violence or 'battered wives', but now the violence between those in close emotional relationships is seen as a wider problem, being restricted not just to wives nor even to domestic situations.[1] Despite its drawbacks, the term 'domestic violence' will be employed here because it has become so widely accepted.

The definition of domestic violence used by the Government has varied over time. The one used currently by the Government is:

> Any incident of threatening behaviour, violence or abuse (psychological, physical, sexual, financial or emotional) between adults who are or have been intimate partners or family members, regardless of gender or sexuality.[2]

There are two things in particular to note about this definition. First, it is not restricted to physical attacks, but is widely drafted to include financial and emotional abuse. Secondly, it is not restricted to people living together, but includes violence between family members. This wide definition is not universally supported. Helen Reece has expressed grave concern that employing a definition of domestic violence that includes emotional abuse is a 'remarkable downplaying of the physical'.[3] Ward LJ has acknowledged the breadth of the term saying: 'Domestic violence, of course, is a term that covers a multitude of sins. Some of it is hideous, some of it is less serious.'[4]

Michelle Madden Dempsey has suggested that we need to draw a distinction between domestic violence in the 'strong sense' and domestic violence in the 'weak sense'. Domestic violence in a 'strong sense' requires the intersection of three elements: illegitimate violence, domesticity and structural inequality in the relationship,[5] while domestic violence in its 'weak sense' only requires domesticity and structural inequality. Adopting this approach it is possible to recognise that violence is especially serious, while still retaining the label of

---

[1] See Kaganas (2007a) for a refutation of claims that women are often violent to men.
[2] Home Office (2005a: para 10).
[3] Reece (2009a).
[4] *Re P (Children)* [2009] 1 FLR 1056, para 12.
[5] See Madden Dempsey (2006: 332) for a very useful article on the definition of domestic violence. See also Kelly and Johnson (2008).

domestic violence for not physical but abusive behaviour. In a later work she has replaced 'structural inequality' in the relationship with 'domesticity'.[6] Although by domesticity she appears to mean 'a relationship characterized by intimacy, familial ties, or a shared household'.[7]

Madden Dempsey's emphasis on the role played by structural inequality highlights the way that domestic violence can involve and build on coercive control exercised by one party over the other in a myriad of ways.[8] It recognises that physical violence is part of a relational inequality that enables, reinforces and is reinforced by the violence. However, as she explains there is more to the notion of structural inequality than this. It reflects and is reinforced by sexist structures within society. She explains:

> the patriarchal character of individual relationships cannot subsist without those relationships being situated within a broader patriarchal social structure. Patriarchy is, by its nature, a social structure – and thus any particular instance of patriarchy takes its substance and meaning from that social context. If patriarchy were entirely eliminated from society, then patriarchy would not exist in domestic arrangements and thus domestic violence in its strong sense would not exist . . . Moreover, if patriarchy were lessened in society generally then *ceteris paribus* patriarchy would be lessened in domestic relationship as well, thereby directly contributing to the project of ending domestic violence in its strong sense.[9]

Helen Reece has argued that isolation and inequality are the touchstones of the rationale of domestic violence.[10] These are experienced by those female cohabitants suffering domestic violence as part of an ongoing unequal relationship, from which there is no easy exit, but not non-cohabiting relatives.[11] Reece argues that the wide definition used by the Government loses sight of the fact that domestic violence involves the abuse of unequal cohabiting relations.

Michael Johnson has suggested we can separate three forms of domestic violence:[12]

1. 'Intimate terrorism' (IT)—When one intimate partner uses a variety of tactics to exert power and control over another;

2. 'Situational couple violence' (SCV)—When an argument between partners gets 'ugly' and escalates out of control; and

3. 'Violent resistance' (VR)—When a victim, usually a female, uses violence to retaliate against being abused.

Not everyone would agree that the third category should be regarded as domestic violence at all. Nevertheless, this categorisation is helpful in bringing out the different contexts in which domestic violence can occur.

The forms of abuse are distressingly varied.[13] The abuse is not limited to physical abuse, but includes emotional abuse and intimidation.[14] Of course, physical abuse can also in turn lead to depression and other mental disorders.[15] Indeed, some have argued that domestic

---

[6] Madden Dempsey (2009: ch 6).
[7] Madden Dempsey (2009: 111).
[8] Stark (2007).
[9] Madden Dempsey (2007).
[10] Reece (2006a).
[11] Reece's (2006a) survey of the statistics indicates that violence between relatives outside the context of cohabitation is very rare.
[12] Johnson et al. (2010: 2).
[13] Home Office (2000d: 1.15). The variety of forms of abuse is revealed in Jones et al. (1995).
[14] A powerful and perceptive discussion can be found in Edwards (1996: ch. 5). See also Barnish (2004) and Smith (1989).
[15] Johnson et al. (2010: 2).

violence should be seen as but part of the spectrum of violence faced by women.[16] The lines between domestic violence and stalking, violence by children against parents and elder abuse, 'honour violence' and 'date rape' are not easy to draw.[17] There are dangers in conceiving of domestic in too narrow a way and not seeing it as one part of a wider range of forces.[18]

To some extent the phrase 'domestic violence' is a 'culturally specific term'. What this means is that the understanding of domestic violence is determined by the norms of a particular culture, a particularly dramatic example being cases of so-called 'honour killings'.[19] So, in some cultures, if a husband refused to permit his wife to leave the home unaccompanied, this would not be regarded as abuse, whereas in other cultures it would. There are real difficulties here. Should the definition of abuse be determined by the victim or by society? Are there rights that should not be infringed even if it is acceptable to do so in a particular culture? This refers back to the discussion of cultural pluralism that was undertaken in Chapter 1. One difficulty is that victims do not necessarily regard themselves as victims of domestic violence.[20] A woman might think that she deserved to be hit, for example, or that pushing and punching is normal in intimate relationships. Smart and Neale have found that the versions of events given by men and women of an incident of domestic violence are often quite different.[21] This means that, even if a woman believes an incident constitutes domestic violence, her partner may not see it in that way.

The vast majority of domestic violence takes place against women,[22] although many men are subject to violence from their partners.[23] It has been argued that most violence by women against men is quite different from violence by men against women because women's violence is often in self-defence rather than being an aspect of an ongoing oppressive relationship.[24] Also where men are the victims the injuries involved tend to be less serious.

Domestic violence can also include abuse against elderly people. This raises particular issues and will be considered separately in Chapter 12. The issue of children who are violent to their parents will be discussed further towards the end of this chapter.

## B The incidence of domestic violence

The occurrence of domestic violence is often underestimated in the public consciousness. Giddens has written: 'The home is, in fact, the most dangerous place in modern society. In statistical terms, a person of any age or of either sex is far more likely to be subject to physical attack in the home than on the street at night.'[25] It is not easy to gather comprehensive statistical information on domestic violence, given that so little of it is reported.[26] However, the following shocking array of statistics demonstrates the prevalence of domestic violence:

---

[16] Kelly and Lovett (2005).
[17] Stewart et al. (2006).
[18] See for example the analysis of domestic violence against those with disabilities: Hague, Thiara and Mullender (2010).
[19] See also Patel (2009) writing on 'dowry abuse'.
[20] Mahoney (1991); Smart and Neale (1999).
[21] Smart and Neale (1999).
[22] For a discussion of the ethnic issues in domestic violence see Mama (2000). For a discussion of violence in lesbian relations see Eaton (1994). See also Kaganas (2007a).
[23] Mirless-Black (1999). Where men are abused the degree of violence tends to be less: Buzawa and Buzawa (2003: 13). See Families Need Fathers (2003) for an argument that it is too often assumed that domestic violence is only perpetrated by men against women.
[24] Dobash and Dobash (2004: 343); Day Sclater (2000: 105–6).
[25] Giddens (1989).
[26] Home Affairs Select Committee (2008).

## KEY STATISTICS

- 'Domestic violence is the largest cause of morbidity worldwide in women aged 19–44, greater than war, cancer or motor vehicle accidents.'[27]

- The British Crime Survey found that one in four women and one in six men had been or will be physically assaulted by a current or former partner at some point in their lives.[28]

- 28% of people aged 16 to 59 had experienced any domestic (partner or family) abuse since the age of 16.[29] In 2009/10 7% of women in that age group had suffered domestic abuse, as had 4% of men.[30]

- An incident of killing, stabbing or beating takes place on average every six minutes in a home in Britain.[31]

- Around two women a week are killed by a current or former partner.[32] 47% of all female murder victims are killed by a current or former partner.[33]

- One in five of all violent crimes reported are related to domestic abuse[34]

- Mooney found that 61% of women questioned said that they could imagine their male partners using violence against them in a hypothetical scenario.[35]

- A recent survey of teenagers found 25% of girls and 18% of boys reported some form of physical partner violence.[36] Another survey of teenage girls found that 31% thought it acceptable for a boy to be 'aggressive' to his girlfriend if he thought she had been unfaithful to him.[37]

- There are significant financial costs which fall on the state as a result of domestic violence. Domestic violence is estimated to have cost the UK £25.3 billion in 2005–06.[38]

- Of women who had been the subject of domestic violence who left home, 76% suffered continued violence.[39]

- 30% of cases of domestic violence start during the victim's pregnancy.[40]

- On average women are attacked 35 times before seeking assistance.[41] One study looking at only the very worst cases of domestic violence found that only 23% were reported to the police.[42]

- Around 50% of women in contact with mental health services have experienced child sexual abuse; a significant number have also suffered abuse as adults. The majority of women in prison have a background of child abuse or domestic violence.[43]

---

[27] The first two statistics are found in Home Affairs Select Committee (2008: 1).
[28] Thompson (2010).
[29] Povey (2008).
[30] Flatley et al. (2010).
[31] Stanko (2000).
[32] Home Affairs Select Committee (2008).
[33] Thompson (2010).
[34] Home Office (2009a).
[35] Mooney (2000).
[36] Barter, McCarry, Berridge, and Evans (2009).
[37] BBC Newsonline (2005b).
[38] Home Affairs Select Committee (2008).
[39] Humphreys and Thiara (2002).
[40] Home Office (2003a: 20). See also Burch and Gallup (2004).
[41] Falconer (2004).
[42] Walby and Allen (2004).
[43] Home Office (2009a).

> • Far more domestic violence is performed by men than women. The CPS reports 94% of cases involved a male perpetrator.[44] Where it does involve women it is usually verbal or in a situation where both parties are using violence.[45]

An issue of particular recent concern is the impact of domestic violence on children.[46] A UNICEF report suggests that up to 1 million children in the UK are living with domestic violence.[47] There is widespread acceptance that children raised in a household where there is domestic violence suffer in many ways, as compared to households where there is not.[48] This includes psychological disturbance and often a feeling that they are to blame for the violence.[49] The impact of the domestic violence on the mother may itself harm the child.[50] Indeed, one study of children who had suffered abuse showed that 39 per cent of them had come from families in which there was domestic violence.[51] Marianne Hester found that children were present in 55 per cent of cases of domestic violence.[52] Ten per cent of children who witnessed domestic violence witnessed their mother being sexually assaulted.[53]

## C Causes of domestic violence

The explanations of the causes of domestic violence fall into three categories:[54]

1. *Psychopathological explanations.* These tend to see the problem of domestic violence as flowing from the psychological make-up of the abuser. It is said that domestic violence is caused by the abuser having an underdeveloped personality, including an inability to control his anger or deal with conflict. There is also a strong link between alcohol and abuse, although the alcohol may just exacerbate other factors.[55] Some even argue that male violence is natural, pointing to the fact that male animals are more violent than female animals. The psychopathological approach is criticised by others on the ground that pathology cannot be the only explanation for domestic violence, as abusers are able to control their tempers outside the home, when dealing with people at work, for example. The Government has sought opinions on whether there should be a register of domestic violence abusers.[56]

2. *Theories about the position of women in society.* These theories focus on patriarchy and the domination of women by men, throughout society.[57] One argument is that the attitude of

[44] Thompson (2010).
[45] Hester (2009):
[46] Hester, Pearson and Harwin (2007).
[47] UNICEF (2006).
[48] Kitzmann et al. (2003); Mullender et al. (2002); Humphreys (2001).
[49] Barnardo's (2004).
[50] Radford and Hester (2006).
[51] Farmer and Pollock (1998).
[52] Hester (2009). According to a study by the charity Barnardo's (2004) in 9 out of 10 cases of domestic violence children are in the room of, or in the room next door to, the violence.
[53] Mullender (2005).
[54] A useful discussion on the causes of domestic violence is found in Miles (2001: 80–7).
[55] Home Office (2003a: 18) reports that 32% of victims of domestic violence reported that their abusers were drunk at the time. See Home Office (2004) on the links between alcohol and domestic violence.
[56] Home Office (2003a: 36).
[57] See, for example, Freeman (1984); Hanmer (2000).

the law and state authorities perpetuates abuse. Society, through the multifarious ways that men are permitted to exercise power over women, makes domestic abuse appear acceptable to the abuser. This can be supported by evidence which shows that violence often occurs when women do not fulfil their traditional roles and men use violent means to reassert their authority.[58] Further, the lack of an effective response by the law means that women are unable to find suitable ways to escape from abuse.[59] Although this is a convincing explanation of domestic violence, there is a danger that it can lessen the responsibility of the individual abuser for his actions. Elizabeth Schneider states:

> [H]eterosexual intimate violence is part of a larger system of coercive control and subordination; this system is based on structural gender inequality and has political roots . . . In the context of intimate violence, the impulse behind feminist legal arguments [is] to redefine the relationship between the personal and the political, to definitively link violence and gender.[60]

3. *The family relationship.* Some argue that the failure of family relationships leads to domestic violence. Poor communication skills or volatile partnerships are to blame as the causes of violence.[61] This is a controversial approach, because it suggests that it is the fault of both the abuser and the victim that the violence has occurred. Dobash and Dobash point out that this fails to explain why it is the man rather than the woman who is usually violent.[62]

The truth, no doubt, is that domestic violence occurs as a result of the complex interaction between these and many other factors.

## D The development of the law on domestic violence

A famous statement of the lawyer Hale describes the attitude of the law to domestic violence in the past: he suggested that a husband could beat his wife with a stick no wider than his finger.[63] This was seen as an aspect of the husband's right to control his household. The law did not really recognise domestic violence until the feminist movement brought it to the attention of a male-dominated media and legislature in the 1970s. It was either regarded as so rare as not appropriate for legal intervention, or as simply part of the 'rough and tumble of marital life'. It was the refuge/shelter movement and the growth of feminist writings, in particular *Scream Quietly or the Neighbours will Hear* by Pizzey, which made domestic violence a public issue.[64] There was subsequently a report of a Select Committee of the House of Commons which found there was a strong case for improving the assistance available to women who were the victims of domestic violence.[65] At that time legal remedies were limited to the general criminal law and tort law. The increased interest in protecting human rights led to arguments that safeguarding victims of domestic violence was an aspect of protecting their human rights. Indeed, domestic violence was the subject of an optional protocol attached to the United Nations Convention on the Elimination of All Forms of Discrimination against Women.

---

[58] Yllo and Bograd (1988).
[59] Hester and Westmarland (2005).
[60] Schneider (2000a: 5–6).
[61] Borkowski, Murch and Walker (1983).
[62] Dobash and Dobash (1992).
[63] Cited in Doggett (1992).
[64] Pizzey (1978).
[65] Select Committee (1975; 1977).

In the UK a series of statutes was passed by Parliament, presenting a rather haphazard scheme of protection: Matrimonial Homes Act 1967; Domestic Violence and Matrimonial Proceedings Act 1976; and Domestic Proceedings and Magistrates' Courts Act 1978. We will not go into the details of these pieces of legislation, but they displayed a confusing array of law. The three Acts used different criteria; were available to different kinds of relationships; used different courts; and provided different kinds of remedies. In addition to the statutes, the courts sometimes relied upon their power to make orders under tort and the courts' inherent jurisdiction.[66] The Family Law Act 1996 was introduced in an attempt to bring coherence to the civil remedies for domestic violence.

To understand fully the law on domestic violence it is necessary to appreciate aspects of criminal law, tort law and housing law, as well as legislation specifically designed to deal with domestic violence.[67] Traditionally, a distinction has been drawn between civil proceedings and criminal proceedings. In civil proceedings it is the victim herself who is bringing the proceedings to pursue applications against the abuser, as compared with the criminal law, where the proceedings are brought on behalf of the state. The rest of the chapter will proceed as follows. First, it will consider the injunctions and orders that can be obtained to protect a victim of domestic violence from abuse under the Family Law Act 1996. Secondly, the remedies available under the Protection from Harassment Act 1997 will be examined. Thirdly, the chapter will outline the provision of alternative accommodation by local authorities to victims of domestic violence. Fourthly, it will consider the criminal law's response to this problem. The chapter will end with a consideration of why the law finds domestic violence such an intractable problem.

## 2 Injunctions and orders under the Family Law Act 1996

This section will discuss orders available under the Family Law Act 1996. There are essentially two kinds of order available. The victim of domestic violence (the applicant) can seek a court order that the abuser (the respondent), first, does not molest her and, secondly, that he leave and stay away from the family home. These are known as non-molestation orders and occupation orders respectively. Both are primarily designed to deter the respondent from abusing the applicant in the future. If he does so in breach of a non-molestation or occupation order, he could face imprisonment.

### A The non-molestation order

The non-molestation order is an order that one party does not molest the other.[68] Molestation here is not defined in the Act but includes conduct that harasses or threatens the applicant. Such an order is less intrusive than an order forcing someone to leave his or her home and so is more readily and widely available. Indeed, many acts that would constitute molestation are crimes (especially after the Protection from Harassment Act 1997). So viewed, the non-molestation order can be regarded as odd – an order that someone not commit a crime against another. Cynics argue that the use of non-molestation orders is merely a means

---

[66] Reserved by s 37 of the Senior Courts Act 1981 and s 38 of the County Courts Act 1984.

[67] Humphreys, Hester, Hague et al. (2002) discuss the importance of a multifaceted response to domestic violence.

[68] Family Law Act 1996 (hereafter FLA 1996), s 42.

of delaying treating an act as a crime.[69] It is common for police to suggest that a victim seek non-molestation injunctions, rather than themselves having to institute criminal proceedings.[70]

### (i) Who can apply for a non-molestation order?

There was much debate over who should be able to apply for non-molestation injunctions under the Act. On the one hand, there was a desire that people who needed protection receive it; on the other hand, if too many people could seek non-molestation injunctions this could lead to excessive litigation. For example, it was thought inappropriate that disputes between neighbours and employees should be resolved by using non-molestation injunctions. Hence the Law Commission Report preceding the Family Law Act 1996 suggested that remedies should be limited to those who have an especial emotional tie.[71] 'Associated persons' are defined in s 62(3). Before listing those who come under this heading, it is important to note that Wall J in *G v F (Non-Molestation Order: Jurisdiction)*[72] suggested that if it is unclear whether the relationship between two people falls within one of these definitions, it should be treated as if it does. Indeed, he thought that unless it was clear that the couple were not associated, it should be presumed that they were. A person is associated with another person if:

1. They are or have been either civil partners or married to each other.

2. They are cohabitants or former cohabitants. Under s 62(1)(a) 'cohabitants' are defined as 'two persons who are neither married to each other nor civil partners of each other but are living together as husband and wife or as if they were civil partners'. In *G v F (Non-Molestation Order: Jurisdiction)*[73] the respondent stayed with the applicant a few nights a week in her home and she visited him for two nights a week at his home. Wall J held that this should be regarded as cohabitation. Particular weight was placed on the fact that they had had a sexual relationship, had lived in the same household, and had had a joint account.[74]

3. They have or have had an intimate personal relationship with each other which is or was of a significant duration. This category was added in by the Domestic Violence, Crime and Victims Act 2004. Before then couples who were going out together but not actually cohabitants or were not engaged could not apply for non-molestation orders as they were not associated people. Now they are. We will look forward to the courts' attempts to define an 'intimate personal relationship' and 'significant duration'. District Judge Robert Hill has suggested that it is unclear whether a relationship of 'several months' will be of 'significant duration'.[75] Other people will regard a relationship of 'several months' as a lengthy one and believe that a relationship lasting over a week is of 'significant duration'. Given the approach in *G v F (Non-Molestation Order: Jurisdiction)*[76] it may well be that borderline cases will be included in the definition.

---

[69] Connelly and Cavanagh (2008) see their value as being a route to criminal law intervention.
[70] Although in Humphreys and Thiara (2002) 75% of women who had non-molestation orders said the order had helped.
[71] Law Commission Report 207 (1992), paras 3.17 and 3.19.
[72] [2000] 2 FCR 638.
[73] [2000] 2 FCR 638.
[74] See *Clibbery v Allan* [2002] 1 FLR 565 where the couple were not found to be cohabiting.
[75] Hill (2005: 283). He suggests a relationship over several years definitely would be.
[76] [2000] 2 FCR 638.

4. They live or have lived in the same household, otherwise than merely by reason of one of them being the other's employee, tenant, lodger or boarder. This category includes many people living together and would cover, for example: students living together in a student house; or two elderly people sharing accommodation companionably. A sexual relationship is not required. It should be noted that just because one of a couple is the other's employee, tenant, lodger or boarder does not mean the couple are necessarily excluded: the question is whether they live together merely because of that relationship. So if a landlord and tenant are lovers they may be associated. Under this heading a child may claim to be associated with a parent and therefore be entitled to apply for a non-molestation order against a parent.[77]

5. They are relatives. This is given a very wide definition in s 63(1):

    (a) the father, mother, stepfather, stepmother, son, daughter, stepson, stepdaughter, grandmother, grandfather, grandson, or granddaughter of that person or of that person's spouse or former spouse, or

    (b) the brother, sister, uncle, aunt, niece, nephew or cousin (whether of the full blood or of the half blood or by affinity) of that person or of that person's spouse or former spouse; and includes, in relation to a person who is cohabiting or has cohabited with another person as husband and wife, any person who would fall within paragraph (a) or (b) if the parties were married to each other.

    This is a wide definition and is rather arbitrary. It includes, for example, a former cohabitant's half-niece, although it does not include cousins.

6. They have agreed to marry one another or enter a civil partnership (whether or not that agreement has been terminated). It should be stressed that this is not as broad a category as it may at first appear. This is because there are only three ways one can prove that there is an agreement to marry.[78] First, that there is evidence in writing of the agreement to marry. Secondly, that there was the gift of an engagement ring by one party to the agreement to the other in contemplation of the marriage. Thirdly, that there was a 'ceremony entered into by the parties in the presence of one or more other persons assembled for the purpose of witnessing the ceremony'.[79] There has been some debate over whether an engagement party would be sufficient for the third method of proof. It seems unlikely that a court would accept a party as 'a ceremony', although a religious service on engagement would certainly be sufficient. It is rather odd that if a couple can prove that they are engaged, but not in one of the ways above, they would not necessarily be associated. It should be noted that a formerly engaged couple can only apply for a non-molestation order if the agreement to marry was terminated less than three years previously.[80] There are no restrictions in the statute on the means of proving the termination of the agreement.

7. In relation to any child, a parent of a child or someone who has parental responsibility for the child. In relation to any child who has been adopted, the natural parent of the child; a parent of the natural parent; or a person with whom a child has been placed for adoption.

---

[77] *Re Alwyn (Non-Molestation Proceedings By A Child)* [2010] 1 FLR 1363.
[78] FLA 1996, s 44. See Civil Partnership Act 2004, s 73 for the definition of a 'civil partnership agreement'.
[79] FLA 1996, s 44.
[80] FLA 1996, s 44(4).

8. They are parties to the same family proceedings (other than proceedings under Part IV of the 1996 Act). Family proceedings are defined in s 63. The list includes, for example, parties to a contact application. The list also includes the Adoption Act 1976 and so if there was tension between the potential adopters and the genetic parents an application for a non-molestation injunction can be made.

If the applicant is associated with the respondent she can apply for a non-molestation injunction against him, even if the dispute between them is not a family dispute. In **Chechi v Bashier**[81] the Court of Appeal rejected the argument that the Family Law Act 1996 could not apply to two brothers who had a business dispute. Although their dispute was not a family one, they were associated by virtue of being brothers and so the court had jurisdiction to make a non-molestation order.[82]

The court can make a non-molestation order on its own motion.[83] This might be appropriate where the court decides that a party or a child needs the protection of the order but is for some reason (maybe fear) unwilling to apply for the order.[84] Similar concerns have led to s 60 being inserted into the 1996 Act, which permits approved third parties to bring proceedings on behalf of victims of domestic violence. Local authorities are now approved as 'third parties' for the purposes of this section.[85]

A child can apply for an order with the leave of the court if he or she is under the age of 16 but the 'court may grant leave for the purposes of subsection (1) only if it is satisfied that the child has sufficient understanding to make the proposed application for the occupation order or non-molestation order'.[86] In making its decision the court is likely to consider the kinds of factors that are relevant when a child applies for an order under the Children Act 1989.[87]

### (ii) On what grounds can the order be granted?

Under s 42(5) of the Family Law Act 1996:

---

**LEGISLATIVE PROVISION**

**Family Law Act 1996, section 42(5)**

In deciding whether to exercise its powers under this section and, if so, in what manner, the court shall have regard to all the circumstances including the need to secure the health, safety and well-being—

(a) of the applicant or, in a case falling within subsection (2)(b), the person for whose benefit the order would be made; and

(b) of any relevant child.

---

This is clearly a very widely drawn test, permitting the court to take into account any circumstances it believes relevant. The aim of the test is to focus on the need for protection in the

---

[81] [1999] 2 FLR 489.
[82] But declined to do so.
[83] But only to protect parties to the proceedings before it.
[84] FLA 1996, s 42(2).
[85] Family Law Act 1996 (Forced Marriage) (Relevant Third Party) Order 2009.
[86] FLA 1996, s 43.
[87] See Chapter 8.

future rather than requiring proof of the fact or threat of violence in the past.[88] 'Health' is defined to include 'physical or mental health' and so it is not necessary to show that there is even a threat of physical violence. One factor the court will consider is whether the order may be misused. If the court fears that the order will simply be used as a weapon in the party's disagreements, rather than to provide protection, the court may decline to make the order.[89]

### (iii) What can the order contain?

A non-molestation order will prohibit one person from molesting another. Molestation is not defined in the statute. That is a deliberate omission and was recommended by the Law Commission, which argued that there should not be a definition for fear that it might provide loopholes that a respondent could exploit.[90] It was noted that the lack of a definition had not led to grave difficulties with the law to date. The Law Commission stated that molestation could encompass 'any form of serious pestering or harassment and applies to any conduct which could properly be regarded as such a degree of harassment as to call for the intervention of the court'.[91] It could range from rifling through a handbag[92] to shouting obscenities.[93] In *C v C (Non-Molestation Order: Jurisdiction)*[94] the Court of Appeal stated that a husband could not obtain a non-molestation order to prevent his former wife making revelations in newspapers about their relationship. It was explained that molestation does not involve simply a breach of privacy but 'some quite deliberate conduct which is aimed at a high degree of harassment of the other party'. Here it was felt that the husband was seeking protection of his reputation rather than protection from molestation. This case might be contrasted with *Johnson v Walton*,[95] where a man sent semi-naked photographs of his former girlfriend to the press. It was held that this could constitute molestation. A distinction between these cases may be made on the basis that the press involvement was directly aimed at humiliating the woman in *Johnson v Walton*, whereas in *C v C (Non-Molestation Order: Jurisdiction)*[96] the wife's conduct was intended to explain her version of events rather than disgracing her husband.[97]

Under s 42(6) the order can refer to specific acts of molestation. This might be appropriate where the applicant wishes to prevent a particular kind of conduct which the respondent (or the police) might not appreciate would constitute molestation. Persistent telephone calls might be an example. There are some lower court unreported decisions which indicate that s 42(6) can include prohibiting a person from entering a specified area around a person's house.[98] This may well be open to challenge before the Court of Appeal, as it could be seen as obtaining an occupation order through the back door.[99] It seems certain that a non-molestation order could not be used to remove someone from a house.

---

[88] Law Commission Report 192 (1990: 3.6).
[89] *Chechi v Bashier* [1999] 2 FLR 489.
[90] Law Commission Report 207 (1992: 3.1).
[91] Law Commission Report 207 (1992: 3.1).
[92] *Spencer v Camacho* [1984] 4 FLR 662.
[93] *George v George* [1986] 2 FLR 347.
[94] [1998] 1 FLR 554, [1998] 1 FCR 11.
[95] [1990] 1 FLR 350, [1990] FCR 568.
[96] [1998] 1 FLR 554, [1998] 1 FCR 11.
[97] The court in *C v C (Non-Molestation Order: Jurisdiction)* [1998] 1 FLR 554, [1998] 1 FCR 11 also took into account the importance of freedom of the press.
[98] These unreported decisions are discussed in Da Costa (1998).
[99] See FLA 1996, s 33(3)(g).

There is no limit to the duration of a non-molestation order. It can be stated to last until a further order is made.[100]

### (iv) Can the order be made against someone who is unable to control his or her actions?

Prior to the Family Law Act 1996, case law suggested that only deliberate acts could constitute molestation.[101] This is probably no longer correct. In *Banks v Banks*[102] it was seen as inappropriate to make a non-molestation injunction against a woman who was suffering from a manic depressive disorder and therefore unable to control her behaviour. The reasoning was that it would be wrong if she were to be guilty of contempt of court through conduct that was beyond her control. This was only a decision of a county court and so is not a strong precedent. The concern is that a similar argument could be used to prevent an injunction being made against an alcoholic abuser. It is arguable that in this area the law should focus on protection of the victim rather than fairness to the perpetrator of the violence. In the light of these arguments and the decision of the Court of Appeal in *G v G (Occupation Order: Conduct)*[103] that an occupation order could be made after unintentional conduct,[104] it is submitted that a non-molestation injunction should be able to be made even following unintentional conduct. However, it should be borne in mind that a person can only be guilty of contempt if he or she has sufficient mental capacity to understand that a court order has been made forbidding certain conduct, under threat of punishment.[105]

### (v) Enforcement of the orders

Section 42A of the Family Law Act (inserted by the Domestic Violence, Crime and Victims Act 2004) states that it is an offence for a person to do something he is prohibited from doing by a non-molestation order without reasonable excuse.[106] A person can only be guilty of the offence if when they engaged in the conduct they were aware[107] of the existence of the order.[108] The prosecution has the burden of proof of showing that the defendant did not have a reasonable excuse.[109] Prior to the insertion of section 42A a breach of a non-molestation order would be dealt with by the victim applying to court for an order of contempt of court. The significance of this change in the law is that if there is a breach it no longer lies in the hands of the victim to decide whether or not to bring contempt proceedings; it is the decision of the police. Before the Act, following a breach, if the victim decided not to instigate contempt proceedings nothing further would happen. Now, even if the victim objects, the police may decide to bring proceedings for the offence under s 42A.[110] This has led to complaints by some that this provision disempowers the victim in taking away the choice of whether or not to bring proceedings if an order is breached.[111] Supporters claim that police prosecution

---

[100] *Re B-J (A Child) (Non-Molestation Order: Power of Arrest)* [2000] 2 FCR 599.
[101] *Johnson v Walton* [1990] 1 FLR 350, [1990] FCR 568, but contrast *Wooton v Wooton* [1984] FLR 871.
[102] [1999] 1 FLR 726.
[103] [2000] 2 FLR 36.
[104] *G v G (Occupation Order: Conduct)* [2000] 2 FLR 36.
[105] *P v P (Contempt of Court: Mental Capacity)* [1999] 2 FLR 897.
[106] See Platt (2008) for a useful discussion of the practical significance of this section.
[107] Normally this will be because he has formally been served with the order, but it need not.
[108] FLA 1996, s 42A(2). As well as committing the s 42A offence the person will be guilty of a contempt of court. They cannot be convicted in respect of both (s 42A(4)). See Bessant (2005) for a discussion of s 42A.
[109] *R v Richards* [2010] EWCA Crim 835.
[110] The court can no longer attach a power of arrest to a non-molestation order (para 38 of Sch 10 to the Domestic Violence, Crime and Victims Act 2004).
[111] Hitchings (2005).

protects victims from being pressurised into not commencing enforcement proceedings, and demonstrates how seriously society regards such breaches. However, there is evidence that the police are using cautions or informal warnings, rather than prosecuting for this offence.[112] If this happens victims may be worse off than they would have been in the past. Another concern is the delay in police procedures, and particularly those of the Crown Prosecution Service, before a decision over prosecution is taken. This can mean it might be weeks before the offender is brought to court, while under the previous system a respondent who was arrested under a power of arrest for a breach of a non-molestation could be brought before the court to be sentenced the next day.[113] Later in this chapter we will consider the decline in the use of civil remedies. One explanation is that s. 42A had put claimants off seeking a non-molestation order.[114]

If the order is breached by acts of violence then the respondent is likely to be prosecuted under s 42A.[115] In deciding what sentence is appropriate, the court should focus on the act that constitutes the breach, rather than the facts that led to the making of the injunction in the first place. In *Cambridgeshire CC v D*[116] a non-molestation injunction was obtained after serious violence. In breach of the injunction, D wrote love letters. The Court of Appeal overturned a sentence of 12 months for contempt, saying that that was an excessive punishment for writing love letters, despite the serious violence in the past.[117]

Where the act which breaches the order is a criminal offence then the defendant can face proceedings for both the s 42A offence (or contempt of court) and a criminal prosecution for the offence committed. In such a situation a court should not sentence in contempt proceedings for conduct which has already been punished in the criminal courts.[118] However in sentencing for contempt the fact that the conduct was a contempt of court was a factor to take into account. The focus must be on the severity of the contempt, rather than the severity of the conduct. In recent years the courts have indicated that they are taking violent acts that breach court orders more seriously than they might have done in the past.[119]

## B Occupation orders

An occupation order can remove an abuser from the home and can give a right to the victim to enter or remain in the home. Although the occupation order is most commonly used in cases of domestic violence it can be applied for if there is no violence, but simply a dispute over who should occupy the property. Where the order is that someone be removed from their home, this is a severe infringement of the rights of the person who is removed from their home. However, the order may be the only way possible to provide effective protection for the victim(s). In the very worst cases it might be crucial that the abuser does not know where the victim is, in which case alternative accommodation will be essential. Given the greater infringement of the rights of the respondent, access to occupation orders is far more restricted than to non-molestation orders. There are five different sections, which apply to different

---

[112] Home Office Affairs Select Committee (2008); Platt (2008).

[113] Hester, Westmarland, Pearce and Williamson (2008).

[114] Platt (2008).

[115] *G v C (Residence Order: Committal)* [1998] 1 FLR 43. It is perfectly proper to imprison a person for contempt who is also due to face criminal proceedings for the same incident (*DPP v Tweddell* [2002] 1 FCR 348).

[116] [1999] 2 FLR 42.

[117] For a general discussion on sentencing in these cases, see *Hale v Tanner* [2000] 3 FCR 62.

[118] *Slade v Slade* [2010] 1 FLR 160, distinguishing *Lomas v Parle* [2004] 1 All ER 1173, discussed in Burton (2004).

[119] *H v O (Contempt of Court: Sentencing)* [2004] EWCA Civ 1691; *Lomas v Parle* [2004] 1 All ER 1173.

groups of applicants, and each section has slightly different requirements, some being harder to satisfy than others.

It is only possible for an applicant to obtain an occupation order against a respondent to whom she is associated. If the applicant is married to the respondent or is entitled to occupy the property, she should use s 33.[120] However, if the applicant is not entitled to occupy the property, the key question is whether the applicant is the ex-spouse of the respondent or is the cohabitant or former cohabitant of the respondent. If she is the ex-spouse, s 35 is appropriate; if she is the cohabitant or ex-cohabitant then an application should be made under s 36. In the very unlikely event that neither the applicant nor the respondent are entitled to occupy the dwelling-house then s 37 or s 38 should be used. It seems unlikely that a child could seek an occupation order against a parent as they would not fall within any of these categories.[121] This chapter will now consider these different sections in further detail.

## (i) Section 33: married and entitled applicants

### (a) Who can apply?

'Entitled' applicants can use s 33. An entitled person is a person who:

---

**LEGISLATIVE PROVISION**

**Family Law Act 1996, section 33**

(a)  is entitled to occupy a dwelling-house by virtue of a beneficial estate or interest or contract or by virtue of any enactment giving him the right to remain in occupation, or

(b)  has home rights in relation to a dwelling-house.

---

Nearly all spouses or civil partners are therefore 'entitled' because they will have home rights.[122] Also, anyone who has a right to occupy a dwelling-house is entitled. This includes those who own the house (for example, those who are registered owners) and those who, although not registered owners, have a beneficial interest in the property by virtue of a resulting trust, a constructive trust, a proprietary estoppel or an interest under a trust for land.[123] The question of whether a person has a right to reside in the property under a proprietary estoppel or trust can be highly complex. Cases deciding such issues have been known to go on for weeks.[124] It might seem odd that an applicant seeking urgent protection from violence could need to introduce evidence of promises made often years earlier in order to determine which section of the Act should be used.[125] To amount to an interest sufficient to be able to use s 33 it must not be insubstantial. For example, a contractual licence to occupy the home for four days would be insufficient.[126]

---

[120] Except in the very unusual situation where neither spouse is entitled to occupy their home (e.g. if they are squatters).

[121] *Re Alwyn (Non-Molestation Proceedings By A Child)* [2010] 1 FLR 1363.

[122] The exception being where neither is entitled to occupy the house, in which case either s 37 or s 38 applies.

[123] But not a contractual licence: *Ashburn Anstalt v Arnold* [1989] Ch 1.

[124] *Hammond v Mitchell* [1992] 1 FLR 229, [1991] FCR 938.

[125] In *S v F (Occupation Order)* [2000] 1 FLR 255 Judge Cryan found that there was not enough time at the hearing to hear all the evidence necessary to decide whether the applicant had an interest and so treated the application as if made under s 35.

[126] *Moore v Moore* [2004] 3 FCR 461.

### (b) In respect of what property can the order be sought?

There are two requirements here. The first is that the property is a dwelling-house. So if a couple ran a business together it would not be possible to get an order in respect of the business premises. The second is that the home must be or was intended to be the home of the applicant and a person to whom she is associated. So if a flat was bought with the sole intention of it being the wife's pied-à-terre while she worked in London, an occupation order could not be obtained concerning the flat as it was never meant to be the home of the couple together. Similarly, if the applicant left the marital home and moved in with her mother she could not get an occupation order requiring the respondent to stay away from her mother's home.[127] Whether a holiday cottage would be defined as a home is open for debate.

### (c) Against whom can the order be made?

The order can be sought by the applicant against any person with whom she is associated and with whom she shared or intended to share a home.

### (d) What factors will the court take into account?

#### The 'significant harm test'

The starting point for the court's deliberations is the significant harm test set out in s 33(7):

---

**LEGISLATIVE PROVISION**

**Family Law Act 1993, section 33(7)**

If it appears to the court that the applicant or any relevant child is likely to suffer significant harm attributable to conduct of the respondent if an order under this section containing one or more of the provisions mentioned in subsection (3) is not made, the court shall make the order unless it appears to it that—

(a) the respondent or any relevant child is likely to suffer significant harm if the order is made; and

(b) the harm likely to be suffered by the respondent or child in that event is as great as, or greater than, the harm attributable to conduct of the respondent which is likely to be suffered by the applicant or child if the order is not made.

---

The court must first ask itself what will happen if the court makes no order: is it likely that the applicant or relevant child will suffer significant harm attributable to the conduct of the respondent? If the answer is 'no' then the significant harm test is not satisfied. If the answer is 'yes' then the court must consider what will happen if the court does make an order: will the respondent or any relevant child suffer significant harm? If the answer to that question is 'no' then the court *must* make an occupation order. If the answer is 'yes', then the question is whose risk of harm is greater. If the harm the applicant or child will suffer is greater than that which the respondent and any relevant child will suffer then an order *must* be made. Otherwise the significant harm test is not satisfied.

*B v B*[128] shows how the subsection operates.

---

[127] Although a non-molestation order may offer some protection here.
[128] [1999] 1 FLR 715, [1999] 2 FCR 251.

> **CASE: B v B** [1999] 1 FLR 715, [1999] 2 FCR 251
>
> The case concerned a married couple who had two children living with them: the hus-
> band's son from his previous relationship and a baby of their own. The husband was
> extremely violent and so the wife and baby moved out to temporary accommodation,
> leaving the husband and his son in the flat. The court considered the significant harm
> test. They were satisfied that if they made no order the mother and baby who were living
> in unsatisfactory temporary accommodation would continue to suffer significant harm
> and that this was attributable to the husband's violence. However, the court also
> accepted that if the husband and his son were ordered from the flat they would suffer
> significant harm too. In particular, the local authority would not be under any obligation
> to house them and so the son's education and general welfare would suffer.[129] The court
> decided that the harm, especially to the son, if the order was made would be greater than
> the harm that the mother and baby would suffer if the order was not made, and so the
> significant harm test was not satisfied.

A few points on the wording of the test will now be considered:

1. *Who is a 'relevant child'?* A relevant child here is broadly defined to include 'any child
   whose interests the court considers relevant'.[130] The child does not need to be the biological
   child of either the applicant or the respondent. In most cases the child will be living with
   the applicant and respondent, but conceivably the interests of a child not living with them
   will also be relevant, for example if the making or not making of an occupation order
   prevents the child having contact with the parties.

2. *What is harm?* Harm is defined as including 'ill-treatment and the impairment of health'
   (which includes emotional health).[131] For a child, harm also involves impairment of
   development. Ill-treatment 'includes forms of ill-treatment which are not physical and, in
   relation to a child, includes sexual abuse'.[132] It is rather surprising that the statute makes it
   clear that sexual abuse is harm to a child but does not state this in respect to an adult.
   There is probably no significance in this because sexual abuse of an adult would inevitably
   constitute ill-treatment or impairment of health. Also, although the definition of harm in
   the Children Act 1989[133] does not specifically apply to the Family Law Act 1996, presumably the court would willingly accept that a child who witnessed domestic violence was
   being harmed.

3. *What is significant harm?* There is no definition of significant harm in the Family Law Act
   1996, although in a similar context Booth J suggested it was harm that was 'considerable,
   noteworthy or important'.[134] In *Chalmers v Johns*[135] the Court of Appeal rejected an argument
   that a one-and-a-half mile walk to school for the mother and child was 'significant harm'.
   The court stressed that in order to be 'significant harm' some kind of exceptional harm
   needed to be shown.

---

[129] A similar fear was expressed in *Re Y (Children) (Occupation Order)* [2000] 2 FCR 470.
[130] FLA 1996, s 62(2).
[131] FLA 1996, s 63(1).
[132] FLA 1996, s 63(1).
[133] Section 31.
[134] *Humberside CC v B* [1993] 1 FLR 257 at p. 263.
[135] [1999] 1 FLR 392.

4. *What does 'attributable' mean?* One point of particular importance on the wording of the test is that when considering whether the applicant or relevant child will suffer significant harm it must be shown that the significant harm will be attributable to the conduct of the respondent. In *B v B*, the facts of which are explained above, the mother was able to show that it was her husband's extreme violence which had forced her from the house and so the significant harm was attributable to her husband's conduct. If there had been no violence and she had moved out simply because she did not like her husband any more, she would have had grave difficulty in showing that the significant harm was attributable to the husband's conduct. However, notably, when considering the risk of significant harm to the respondent there is no need to show that it is attributable to the conduct of the applicant. So in *B v B* it was irrelevant that the significant harm that the son and husband would suffer if the order was made would not be due to the wife's conduct. *G v G (Occupation Order: Conduct)*[136] makes it clear that conduct is attributable to the respondent even if it is unintentional conduct: the court's focus is on the effect of the respondent's conduct, not his or her intention.

5. *What does 'likely' mean?* It is not clear what 'likely' means here. The word 'likely' in s 31 of the Children Act 1989 has been defined by the House of Lords to signify 'a real possibility'. It is suggested that a similar interpretation is given to the term here. It seems that the degree of likelihood of significant harm is not relevant in the significant harm test. In other words, if it is almost certain that the applicant will suffer significant harm, but there is a real possibility that the respondent will suffer a higher level of harm, the significant harm test will not be satisfied.

6. *What if the risks of significant harm are equal?* It should be noted that if the harm likely to be suffered by the applicant is equal to the harm that may be suffered by the respondent then an order does not have to be made.

The significant harm test sets out the circumstances in which the court *must* make an order. It is important to appreciate that simply because the significant harm test is not satisfied does not mean that an order cannot be made.[137]

### General factors

If the significant harm test is satisfied then the court must make an order. If, however, it is not, the court must then consider the general factors. These are set out in s 33(6):

---

### LEGISLATIVE PROVISION

**Family Law Act 1996, section 33(6)**

(a) the housing needs and housing resources of each of the parties and of any relevant child;

(b) the financial resources of each of the parties;

(c) the likely effect of any order, or of any decision by the court not to exercise its powers . . . , on the health, safety or well-being of the parties and of any relevant child; and

(d) the conduct of the parties in relation to each other and otherwise.

---

[136] [2000] 2 FLR 36.
[137] *Chalmers v Johns* [1999] 1 FLR 392.

The courts have in fact been reluctant to grant occupation orders.[138] Thorpe LJ in *Chalmers v Johns*[139] held that when considering the general factors a judge should bear in mind that an occupation order 'overrides proprietary rights and . . . is only justified in exceptional circumstances'.[140] Occupation orders should be seen as 'draconian'.[141] In *G v G (Occupation Order: Conduct)* it was stressed that to succeed, an applicant must show that more tensions exist than normally surround a family during a divorce.[142] In *Re Y (Children) (Occupation Order)*[143] Sedley LJ suggested occupation orders should be seen 'as a last resort in an intolerable situation'.[144] These decisions of the Court of Appeal emphasise that occupation orders should be made only in exceptional cases. Critics would argue that these statements are excessively restrictive. Had Parliament intended that occupation orders should only be available in exceptional cases, it would have said so.

The Court of Appeal in *B v B*[145] considered the position had the father not had the son with him. The court suggested that in that case, even if the significant harm test might not have been satisfied,[146] the court would still be minded to make an order, when looking at the general factors and in particular bearing in mind his violence towards the wife. This suggests that where the court is dealing with a violent spouse the conduct factor ((d)) may become very important.

However, it would be wrong to state that an occupation order is only available when there is serious violence. In *S v F (Occupation Order)*[147] the children were residing with the mother, who had decided to leave London to live in the country. One son wished to remain in London, especially because he was soon going to be taking examinations at school. The court was willing to make an occupation order granting the father the right to live in the matrimonial home in London so that he could provide a house for his son for the completion of the schooling, while the mother moved to the country.

### (e) What orders can be made?

These will be divided into three categories:

1. *Declaratory orders under s 33(4) and (5)*. These orders simply enable the court to declare that a party has a right to remain in the property. This may forestall any attempt by the respondent to bring court proceedings to evict the applicant.

2. *Orders under s 33(3)*:

---

[138] Although evidence looking at cases shortly after the Act was implemented suggests that more occupation orders are being granted than were under the previous legislation (Edwards (2000)).

[139] [1999] 1 FLR 392 CA.

[140] [1999] 1 FLR 392 at p. 397; see also *Re Y (Children) (Occupation Order)* [2000] 2 FCR 470 at p. 477.

[141] See also *G v G (Occupation Order: Conduct)* [2000] 2 FLR 36.

[142] [2000] 2 FLR 36.

[143] [2000] 2 FCR 470.

[144] [2000] 2 FCR 470 at p. 480.

[145] [1999] 1 FLR 715, [1999] 2 FCR 251.

[146] Because the husband being rendered homeless would be a greater harm than the mother and baby living in poor accommodation.

[147] [2000] 1 FLR 255.

---

**LEGISLATIVE PROVISION**

**Family Law Act 1996, section 33(3)**

An order under this section may—

(a) enforce the applicant's entitlement to remain in occupation as against the other person ('the respondent');

(b) require the respondent to permit the applicant to enter and remain in the dwelling-house or part of the dwelling-house;

(c) regulate the occupation of the dwelling-house by either or both parties;

(d) if the respondent is entitled as mentioned in subsection (1)(a)(i), prohibit, suspend or restrict the exercise by him of his right to occupy the dwelling-house;

(e) if the respondent has matrimonial home rights in relation to the dwelling-house and the applicant is the other spouse, restrict or terminate those rights;

(f) require the respondent to leave the dwelling-house or part of the dwelling-house; or

(g) exclude the respondent from a defined area in which the dwelling-house is included.

---

These orders can be divided into three categories: first, there are those which enforce the applicant's existing rights ((a), (b)); secondly, orders used to regulate the rights of both parties ((c)); thirdly, those that prevent the respondent from enforcing his rights ((d), (e), (f), (g)). The strongest order that the court could make would require the respondent to leave the dwelling-house;[148] remove his rights to re-enter;[149] and exclude him from the area surrounding the house.[150] Subsection (c) gives the court great flexibility and permits the court to make all kinds of arrangements for the occupation of the home. It might decide that the applicant can live there during the weekdays and the respondent at the weekends, or that the respondent live on the top floor and the applicant on the ground floor.

3. *Section 40 orders.* There would be little point in removing the respondent from the house if the applicant was unable to pay for the rent for the house or meet the mortgage payments and so could be removed by the landlord or mortgagee. Therefore, under s 40 four kinds of supplemental orders can be made. First, either party can be ordered to pay the rent, mortgage payments, or general household expenses;[151] secondly, either party can be ordered to maintain or repair the house;[152] thirdly, the party who is to remain in the property can be required to make payments to the party who is to be removed (in effect this

---

[148] FLA 1996, s 33(3)(f).

[149] FLA 1996, s 33(3)(d).

[150] FLA 1996, s 33(3)(g). There is some debate over what exactly an 'area' is in this context. Would it be possible to exclude someone from the village in which the home is situated?

[151] FLA 1996, s 40(1)(a)(ii).

[152] FLA 1996, s 40(1)(a)(i).

will be equivalent to a payment of rent);[153] and, fourthly, orders can be made to deal with disputes over use and care of furniture.[154] When considering an application under s 40 the court should consider all the circumstances, including the parties' financial needs, obligations and resources.[155] Unfortunately, because statute does not provide for any method of enforcing orders requiring payment under s 40, the Court of Appeal in *Nwogbe* v *Nwogbe*[156] has recommended that financial orders are not made under s 40 until Parliament has rectified this error.[157]

### (f) Duration

An order under s 33 can be of fixed or unlimited length, until the court next hears the matter.[158] The length of the order does not seem to be limited by the extent of the property right or the duration of the marriage.

### (ii) Section 35: one ex-spouse or ex-civil partner with no existing right to occupy

### (a) Who can apply?

This section applies only to situations where the applicant has no right to occupy the property but the respondent (the applicant's ex-spouse or civil partner) does. If the couple are still married or civil partners and the applicant is entitled to occupy the property then s 33 should be used.

### (b) In respect of what property?

An order under s 35 is available only in respect of a dwelling-house which was the actual or intended home of the applicant and the respondent.

### (c) What orders are available?

The list of orders is similar to those in s 33(3). However, there is an important difference in that if the court is going to make any order under s 35 then the applicant must be given the right to enter or remain in the property, and the respondent must be prohibited from evicting the applicant. These orders are known as the mandatory orders. The thinking behind these provisions is that it would be quite wrong to evict the respondent but not give the applicant the right to enter or remain in the property. Otherwise, it would be possible to end up with a situation where neither party would have the right to live in the property. In addition to the mandatory orders, the court can make a discretionary order. Those are any of the other orders available under s 33(3): for example, an order excluding the respondent from a defined area around the dwelling-house.

### (d) What factors are to be taken into account?

When considering a mandatory order the general factors as listed in s 33(6)[159] apply, although there are some extra factors which are to be taken into account for the ex-spouse, and these are (s 35(6)):

---

[153] FLA 1996, s 40(1)(b).
[154] FLA 1996, s 40(1)(c), (d), (e).
[155] FLA 1996, s 40(2).
[156] [2000] 2 FLR 744, [2000] 3 FCR 345.
[157] Parliament's response is still awaited.
[158] FLA 1996, s 33(10).
[159] See page 292.

---

**LEGISLATIVE PROVISION**

**Family Law Act 1996, section 35(6)**

(e)  the length of time that has elapsed since the parties ceased to live together;

(f)  the length of time that has elapsed since the marriage was dissolved or annulled; and

(g)  the existence of any pending proceedings between the parties—

   (i)  for an order under section 23A or 24 of the Matrimonial Causes Act 1973 (property adjustment orders in connection with divorce proceedings, etc.);

   (ii)  for a property adjustment order under Part 2 of Schedule 5 to the Civil Partnership Act 2004; or

   (iii)  for an order under paragraph 1(2)(d) or (e) of Schedule 1 to the Children Act 1989 (orders for financial relief against parents); or

   (iv)  relating to the legal or beneficial ownership of the dwelling-house.

---

These three factors are to turn the court's mind to the nature of the parties' marriage or civil partnership. The shorter the marriage or civil partnership and the longer the time since the separation, the harder it will be for the applicant to succeed.

If the court decides not to make a mandatory order the court should then consider making a discretionary order. When considering whether to make a discretionary order the court must first consider the significant harm test which operates in exactly the same way as described above in relation to s 33. If the test does not require the court to make an order, the court will then consider the general factors listed in ss 33(6) and 35(6)(e). This is rather odd because it means that a more wide-ranging investigation is made when the court considers making the discretionary order than when it makes a mandatory order, even though the mandatory orders involve a greater invasion of the respondent's property rights. The explanation may be that having found that the applicant deserves to have a right to occupy the property (in deciding whether to make a mandatory order) the case then involves two people who both should be entitled to occupy the dwelling-house and so the case is similar to a case involving an entitled applicant under s 33 and the criteria for further orders should then be the same.[160]

### (e) Duration

The duration of an order under s 35 is more limited than a s 33 order. The order cannot exceed six months, although at the end of the six months the applicant can reapply for further extensions not exceeding six months each.[161]

### (iii) Section 36: one cohabitant or former cohabitant with no existing right to occupy

### (a) Who can apply?

This section applies to an applicant who is not entitled to occupy the property and who is the cohabitant[162] or former cohabitant of the respondent. Cohabitants are defined as 'two

---

[160]  Although that would not explain why (e) is taken into account when considering the discretionary stage.

[161]  FLA 1996, s 35(10).

[162]  As defined in FLA 1996, s 62(3).

persons who are neither married to each other nor civil partners of each other but are living together as husband and wife or as if they were civil partners'.[163]

### (b) In respect of what property?

The orders are available only in respect of a property that was or was intended to be the home of the applicant and the respondent.

### (c) What orders can be made?

The orders available are exactly the same as under s 35.

### (d) What factors are to be taken into account?

When considering whether to make a mandatory order the court must consider the general factors listed in s 33(6) and, in addition, the following extra criteria:

---

**LEGISLATIVE PROVISION**

**Family Law Act 1996, section 36(6)**

(e) the nature of the parties' relationship and in particular the level of commitment involved in it;

(f) the length of time during which they have lived together as husband and wife;

(g) whether there are or have been any children who are children of both parties or for whom both parties have or have had parental responsibility;

(h) the length of time that has elapsed since the parties ceased to live together; and

(i) the existence of any pending proceedings between the parties

    (i) for an order under paragraph 1(2)(d) or (e) of Schedule 1 to the Children Act 1989 (orders for financial relief against parents); or

    (ii) relating to the legal or beneficial ownership of the dwelling-house.

---

When considering whether to make a discretionary order the court begins by asking the 'significant harm' questions. These are:

---

**LEGISLATIVE PROVISION**

**Family Law Act 1996, section 33(7)**

(a) whether the applicant or any relevant child is likely to suffer significant harm attributable to conduct of the respondent if [a discretionary order is not made]; and

(b) whether the harm likely to be suffered by the respondent or child if [the discretionary order is made] is as great as or greater than the harm attributable to conduct of the respondent which is likely to be suffered by the applicant or child if the provision is not included.

---

[163] FLA 1996, s 62(1)(a).

This is very similar to the significant harm test, but it does not compel the court to make an order if the applicant's significant harm is greater than the respondent's harm would be. The significant harm that the parties are at risk of suffering are simply factors to be considered, along with the general factors in s 33(6). Given the argument earlier that once a mandatory order is made an applicant should be viewed in the same light as an entitled applicant under s 33(6), it is hard to justify using the significant harm questions rather than the significant harm test.[164]

### (e) Duration

An order under s 36 cannot exceed six months in duration and can be extended on one occasion for a period of six months. This is similar to s 35, with the important limitation that under s 36 only one extension can be applied for, but there is no limit on the number of extensions under s 35.

## (iv) Section 37: neither spouse nor civil partner entitled to occupy

### (a) Who can apply?

This section applies to spouses or former spouses or civil partners or former civil partners where neither party is entitled to occupy the property. It would, in fact, be very unusual for neither party to be entitled to occupy the matrimonial home. If the spouses were squatters then this may be so.[165] There will be very few applications under this section.

### (b) In respect of what property?

The orders are available only in respect of a property that was or was intended to be the home of the applicant and the respondent.

### (c) What can the order contain?

Under s 37(3):

---

**LEGISLATIVE PROVISION**

**Family Law Act 1996, section 37(3)**

An order under this section may—

(a) require the respondent to permit the applicant to enter and remain in the dwelling-house or part of the dwelling-house;

(b) regulate the occupation of the dwelling-house by either or both of the spouses;

(c) require the respondent to leave the dwelling-house or part of the dwelling-house; or

(d) exclude the respondent from a defined area in which the dwelling-house is included.

---

These orders are much more limited than those under ss 33, 35 and 36 because neither party is entitled to occupy the home and so they have no rights that can be restricted or removed.

---

[164] The significant harm questions are one of the provisions inserted late in the legislative process to distinguish the treatment of married and unmarried couples.

[165] Or if they were bare licensees (e.g. if a friend had invited the couple to stay).

### (d) What factors are to be taken into account?

Section 33(6) (the general factors) and (7) (the significant harm test) apply.

### (e) Duration

An order under s 37 can be made for a period not exceeding six months, but may be extended on any number of occasions for a further period not exceeding a total of six months.

## (v) Section 38: neither cohabitant nor former cohabitant entitled to occupy

### (a) Who may apply?

This section applies to a cohabitant or former cohabitant where neither the applicant nor the respondent is entitled to occupy the property. Again it will be very rare for applications to fall within this section.

### (b) In respect of what property?

The orders are available only in respect of a property that was or was intended to be the home of the applicant and the respondent.

### (c) What orders can be made?

The same orders that were listed as available under s 37(3) (quoted above) are available under s 38.

### (d) What factors are to be taken into account?

Section 36(6) (the general factors) and (7) (the significant harm questions) apply.

### (e) Duration

As under s 36, the order can be for a maximum of six months, and be extended on one occasion for a maximum period of six months.

## (vi) Those who cannot apply for an occupation order

As should be clear from the above, a person who is not entitled to occupy the property and is not the spouse, former spouse, cohabitant or former cohabitant of the respondent cannot apply for an occupation order. In particular, relatives and non-cohabiting couples cannot apply for an occupation order in respect of a dwelling-house unless they are entitled to occupy it.

## (vii) Some core issues in occupation orders

### (a) Conduct

The original Law Commission proposals did not refer to the conduct of the parties.[166] Orders, it was suggested, should be granted solely by considering the parties' needs, resources, and obligations – in effect a 'no-fault' scheme to resolve disputes over the occupation of the home. It is understandable that Parliament was reluctant to follow these proposals. It would have meant that if there was a case where the violent party was less well off and not in a position to find alternative accommodation then the victim of domestic violence could be

---

[166] Nor in the significant harm test (s 33(7)) did the applicant's significant harm have to be attributable to the respondent's conduct.

the one ordered out of the house for her own protection. This would be unacceptable to the majority of people. That said, the parts of the Family Law Act 1996 relating to domestic violence do not sit easily with the parts intended to deal with divorce, which stress the importance of 'no-fault' divorce and discourage the parties from making allegations of misconduct against one another.

### (b) Property interests

When considering occupation orders, property rights are of significant importance. Cohabitants and former spouses with property interests are treated differently from those without property interests. The importance of property interests is also revealed by the fact that cohabitants with property interests are treated in the same way as married couples with property interests. A critic would argue that considering the property interests of the parties is inappropriate when deciding how to protect an applicant from violence: are not people more important than property rights?[167] Can it be justifiable that if two victims of domestic violence in similar circumstances need the protection of an occupation order, one may be granted the order and one not, as the result of their property entitlement under the rules of land law? Those who seek to justify the relevance of property interests do so on two bases. First, it has been argued that an order removing a party's property rights is a greater infringement of a party's rights than removing a party from a house in which they have no property interest, and therefore requires stronger justification. Secondly, it has been maintained that entitled and non-entitled applicants should be treated differently because different kinds of issues are involved. The Law Commission suggested that cases involving non-entitled applicants are 'essentially a short-term measure of protection intended to give them time to find alternative accommodation or, at most, to await the outcome of an application for a property law remedy'.[168] By contrast, cases of entitled applicants may involve imposing long-term solutions. These arguments, although powerful in theory, lose some of their force when it is recalled that the law on whether or not a person has an interest in property under a constructive trust or proprietary estoppel is so controversial and appears to draw arbitrary distinctions.[169] Another argument is that a property right carries with it obligations, including the obligation not to enable the property to be used for criminal purposes.[170] Could it be said that a person who commits violence in his or her home thereby forfeits his or her property right?

### (c) Children's interests

It is notable that the interests of children are not paramount, as they are in other issues involving children. The Law Commission was concerned that placing children's interests as paramount 'might lead to more specious applications by fathers for custody, and encourage more mothers to use "I've got the kids so kick him out" arguments'.[171] The concern is understandable, but a similar argument could be used in many circumstances where the welfare test applies. Although the child's welfare is not paramount under the Family Law Act 1996, the Act does have provisions which protect children.[172] There are three in particular:

---

[167] Law Commission Report 207 (1992).
[168] Law Commission Report 207 (1992: para 4.7).
[169] See Chapter 4.
[170] *Tuck v Robson* [1970] 1 All ER 1171.
[171] Law Commission Report 207 (1992).
[172] For a discussion of the impact of domestic violence on children see McGee (2000).

1. Children can now, under s 43, apply for an occupation or non-molestation order. If under the age of 16, the child needs the leave of the court and can apply only if 'the child has sufficient understanding to make the proposed application'.[173] If a child has applied to the court for a non-molestation order, the court is likely to make one if possible.[174] Only rarely will the child be able to establish a property interest and so be able to apply for an occupation order.[175]

2. When considering the significant harm test it is important to note that if there is a relevant child who is likely to suffer significant harm attributable to the conduct of the respondent, the court must make an order unless greater or equal harm will be caused to the respondent if the order is made. However, it is notable that there is no attempt to attach greater importance to the harm suffered by the child than the harm suffered by the respondent or applicant.

3. The needs of the child are factors that should be taken into account when considering the general factors.

The failure to prioritise the needs of the child in the Family Law Act 1996, Part IV does not fit comfortably with the weight placed on children's interests under the Children Act 1989, Adoption and Children Act 2002 and Human Rights Act 1998.[176] Notably, children who are suffering significant harm can be removed from their parents and taken into care under s 31 of the Children Act 1989. However, the fact that the child is suffering significant harm does not necessarily require the making of an occupation order under the significant harm test, if it can be shown that the respondent will suffer a greater level of harm.[177] This may be a particular concern because there is increasing evidence that children who witness domestic violence suffer in a variety of ways.[178] Some commentators, however, have expressed concern that putting children at the forefront of domestic violence issues will lead to lack of focus on the woman who is the direct victim of domestic violence.[179] There is also a broader concern that professional intervention to assist in cases of domestic violence fail to adequately take account of the interests of children.[180]

### (d) The distinction between married and unmarried couples

The Family Law Act 1996 does distinguish between unmarried and married couples or civil partners, but only where the applicant has no interest in the property. If the applicant does have an interest in the property there is no difference in the law that applies. Where the applicant does not have an interest in the home the law draws three distinctions:

1. The significant harm test is not used for non-entitled applicants; the significant harm questions are used and only once, using the general factors, it has been decided that a mandatory order must be made.[181]

2. There is a difference in the general factors that are taken into account. In particular, the court is required to consider the nature of the parties' relationship.

---

[173] FLA 1996, s 43(1).
[174] Bainham (1998a: 428).
[175] *Re Alwyn (Non-Molestation Proceedings by A Child)* [2010] 1 FLR 1363.
[176] Choudhry and Herring (2006a). See also Westendorp and Wolleswinkel (2005).
[177] Although the court may still make an occupation order when considering the general factors.
[178] Parkinson and Humphreys (1998).
[179] Davies and Krane (2006).
[180] Stanley, Miller, Richardson, Foster, and Thomson (2010b).
[181] FLA 1996, s 36.

3. The maximum duration of orders for non-entitled cohabitants is shorter than for non-entitled spouses or ex-spouses or civil partners.

As suggested earlier, it is hard to see how any of these differences could be thought to uphold marriage, and some commentators have suggested that in this context no distinction should be drawn between married and unmarried couples.

### (e) *Human Rights Act 1998*
The Human Rights Act 1998 may be relevant to domestic violence in the following ways:[182]

1. Article 3 requires the state to protect citizens from torture or inhuman or degrading treatment from other people.[183] Article 2 requires the state to protect citizens from a risk of death at the hands of others.[184] A state will infringe an individual's right under articles 2 or 3 if it is aware that she or he is suffering the necessary degree of abuse at the hands of another and fails to take reasonable[185] or adequate[186] or effective[187] steps to protect that individual.[188] The phrase 'inhuman treatment' in article 3 includes actual bodily harm or intense physical or mental suffering.[189] 'Degrading treatment' includes conduct which humiliates or debases an individual; or shows a lack of respect for, or diminishes, human dignity. It also includes conduct which arouses feelings of fear, anguish or inferiority capable of breaking an individual's moral and physical resistance.[190] In considering whether treatment is 'degrading' the court will have regard to whether its object was to humiliate and debase the victim, and the effect on the victim. The fact the abuse take place over a long period of time can bring it within article 3.[191] It is clear, then, that the more serious forms of domestic violence that involve physical abuse are likely to fall within article 3. If the police, prosecuting authority or courts fail to take positive steps to provide an effective remedy for someone suffering torture or inhuman or degrading treatment, they will be in breach of article 3.[192] The court must ensure, in considering an application for an occupation order, that an applicant who is suffering torture or inhuman or degrading treatment is provided protection.

2. Article 8 protects an individual's right to respect for their private and family life. The right to private life includes the right to personal integrity, both physical and psychological.[193] Domestic violence which imposes physical or psychological harm could therefore infringe this. If the violence interfered in the way that a mother was able to care for her children this could amount to an interference in her right to respect for her family life. As with article 3, the state has a positive obligation to ensure that one individual does not interfere with another individual's article 8 right. The obligation can arise where it would be reasonable

---

[182] Choudhry and Herring (2010: ch. 9); Burton (2010).
[183] *A v UK (Human Rights: Punishment of Child)* [1998] 2 FLR 959, [1998] 3 FCR 597; *E v UK* [2002] 3 FCR 700.
[184] *Opuz v Turkey* (App. No.33401/02); *Van Colle v CC of Hertfordshire* [2008] UKHL 50.
[185] *Z v UK* [2001] 2 FCR 246.
[186] *A v UK* [1998] 3 FCR 597, para 24.
[187] *Z v UK* [2001] 2 FCR 246, para 73.
[188] *E v UK* [2002] 3 FCR 700; *Van Colle v CC of Hertfordshire* [2008] UKHL 50.
[189] *Ireland v United Kingdom* (1978) 2 EHRR 25.
[190] See, amongst recent authorities, *Price v United Kingdom*, no. 33394/96, (1988) 55 D&R 1988, paras 24–30 and *Valašinas v Lithuania* [2001] ECHR 479.
[191] *Opuz v Turkey* (App. No.33401/02).
[192] *MC v Bulgaria* (2005) 40 EHRR 20; *ES v Slovakia* (Application No.8227/04).
[193] *Anufrijeva v Southwark LBC* [2003] 3 FCR 673; *Pretty v UK* (2002) 12 BHRC 149, para 61.

for the state to intervene to protect someone's rights and there is an 'element' of culpability in the state's failure to intervene.[194]

An occupation order requiring someone to leave their home would appear clearly to breach the right under article 8 of the Convention to respect for private and family life.[195] However, the making of orders could readily be justifiable under para 2 of article 8 on the grounds of public safety; prevention of disorder or crime; protection of health or morals; or protection of rights and freedoms of others. In particular, an occupation order could be justified in order to protect the rights of the applicant or the child. It might even be argued that an abuser loses his rights in his home by using his home as a place in which to be violent to others.[196] A more interesting question is whether the high hurdles placed in the way of obtaining occupation orders adequately protect the right to respect for the private and family life of the applicant and child.

3. Article 6 is relevant in requiring a public hearing. As will be discussed later, it is arguable that an *ex parte* occupation order infringes a party's rights under article 6. Of potentially more significance is a suggestion that an occupation order could be regarded as punishment following a criminal charge and so the requirements of article 6 must be complied with,[197] the argument being that removal from one's home is equivalent to a criminal punishment.[198] In deciding whether a law involves punishment, the European Court of Human Rights has suggested that there are three factors to be taken into account: the legal classification of the provision; the nature of the offence; and the nature and degree of severity of the penalty.[199] If article 6 does apply, then all the paragraphs of article 6 apply:

(a) a presumption of innocence;

(b) a right to be informed of the accusation;

(c) a right to have adequate time and facilities for the defence;

(d) the right to defend oneself, to have representation and legal aid;

(e) the right to call and cross-examine witnesses.

It is not clear that (a) would be protected in law on occupation orders. The other requirements may be infringed in relation to *ex parte* applications (which will be discussed later). However, there are good reasons for arguing that occupation orders do not constitute criminal proceedings and punishment. First, the application is not brought by the state but by an individual. Secondly, the purpose of the remedy is not to punish the respondent, but to protect the applicant.

4. Article 1 of the first Protocol of the European Convention states that: 'Every person shall be entitled to the peaceful enjoyment of his possessions. No one shall be deprived of his possessions except in the public interest and subject to the conditions provided for by the law and by the general principles of international law.' Although an occupation order might deprive a person of his or her right to enjoyment of his or her possession, in most cases where such an order will be made it could be justified as being in the public interest.[200]

---

[194] *Anufrijeva v Southwark LBC* [2003] 3 FCR 673.

[195] See *McCann v The United Kingdom* [2008] 2 FLR 899; HMIC/CPSI (2004: para 7.20) states that the most common human rights argument made in the courts is by respondents arguing that an occupation order will infringe their rights.

[196] Choudhry and Herring (2006b).

[197] See Swindells, Neaves, Kushner and Skilbeck (1999: ch. 13).

[198] *Öztürk v Germany* (1984) 6 EHRR 409.

[199] *Ravnsborg v Sweden* (1994) 18 EHRR 38.

[200] *Sporrong and Lönnroth v Sweden* (1986) 5 EHRR 35.

5. Article 14 prohibits discrimination. A failure by a state to properly respond to domestic violence has been held to be sex discrimination.[201] Domestic violence far more commonly affects women than men and therefore an inadequate legal response disproportionately impacts women. It might also be argued that the law on occupation orders discriminates against unmarried couples. If an applicant is able to show that because she was not in a married relationship or a civil partnership she was not able to get an order under the Family Law Act, she could argue that this amounts to discrimination contrary to article 14.

### (f) Wider consequences of domestic violence orders

As well as resolving a dispute between two parties as to who can live in a property, the occupation order can in fact have far wider impact. For example, there can be consequences in relation to the children. If, say, the husband is removed from the house, and the wife and children remain there, it may well be that the father will lose contact with the children. Certainly by the time the court comes to consider the residence of the children, the children will have settled with the mother and the 'status quo principle' (see Chapter 9) will mean that the father will be very unlikely to obtain a residence order. Further, in ancillary relief applications, if the husband has found alternative accommodation and the children and wife are living in the house, the court may well make an order transferring the house into the wife's name.[202] Indeed studies have suggested that in a significant number of cases domestic violence is connected in complex ways with a whole range of family disputes.[203]

## C Ex parte non-molestation and occupation orders under the Family Law Act 1996

An *ex parte* application is an application made by one party without the other party being present or being given notice of the proceedings. Such an application will most often be used when there is a need for the immediate protection of the victim and any delay in serving papers on the respondent and giving him time to reply may endanger the applicant. In offering the applicant some immediate protection, the statute makes it clear that an *ex parte* hearing should be followed by an *inter partes* hearing, at which both parties will be able to put forward their arguments.[204] It should be stressed that the *ex parte* court order is effective only once it has been served on the respondent. So there is no danger that a respondent will breach an order of which he or she is unaware. There is a careful balancing exercise required here. On the one hand, there is the difficulty of ensuring that the evidence is sufficient to make an order, particularly an order removing someone from his or her home, when only one side of the case is heard. On the other hand, it is necessary to make available fast and effective remedies to those in dire need of them. Section 45 of the Family Law Act 1996 states that a court can make an *ex parte* occupation or non-molestation order 'in any case where it considers that it is just and convenient to do so'. In deciding whether this is so, the court shall have regard to all the circumstances, including:

---

[201] *Opuz v Turkey* (App. No.33401/02).
[202] See Chapter 5.
[203] Pleasence, Balmer, Buck et al. (2003).
[204] FLA 1996, s 45(3).

LEGISLATIVE PROVISION

**Family Law Act 1996, section 45(2)**

(a) any risk of significant harm to the applicant or a relevant child, attributable to conduct of the respondent, if the order is not made immediately;

(b) whether it is likely that the applicant will be deterred or prevented from pursuing the application if an order is not made immediately; and

(c) whether there is reason to believe that the respondent is aware of the proceedings but is deliberately evading service and that the applicant or a relevant child will be seriously prejudiced by the delay involved [in effecting service or substituted service].

It is arguable that making an *ex parte* order could deny people the right to a fair and public hearing under article 6 of the European Convention on Human Rights. However, in a different context, the Court of Appeal in *Re J (Abduction: Wrongful Removal)*[205] rejected such an argument on the basis that the right to the full *inter partes* hearing and the right to apply to have an *ex parte* order set aside protects the right to a fair hearing.

## D Undertakings

An undertaking is a promise by the respondent in clear terms, which is made formally in court. The court can accept an undertaking in any case where it has the power to make a non-molestation or occupation order. Where the court accepts the undertaking, an order is normally not made.[206] Section 46(4) states that an undertaking can be enforced as if it were an order of the court.[207] However, some have claimed that the police are far less willing to intervene if a victim claims that an undertaking has been breached than where she claims that a court order has been breached.[208]

The one restriction on the power of the court to accept an undertaking is s 46(3), which provides that 'the court shall not accept an undertaking . . . in any case where apart from this section a power of arrest would be attached to the order'.[209] The significance of this is that, under s 47(1), if the respondent has used or threatened violence against the applicant or a relevant child, a power of arrest *must* be attached to an occupation order or a non-molestation order unless the court is satisfied that the applicant or relevant child will be adequately protected without such a power of arrest.[210] It is therefore arguable that where the court is required to attach a power of arrest under s 47(1) it cannot accept an undertaking. However, it may be that the court will readily hold that if an undertaking is offered, the applicant and child will be adequately protected without the power of arrest and so the undertaking can be accepted. Certainly research suggests that it has become the norm to accept undertakings in non-molestation cases when offered.[211] Section 47(3A) states:

---

[205] [2000] 1 FLR 78.
[206] FLA 1996, s 46(1).
[207] FLA 1996, s 46(4), although a power of arrest cannot be attached to an undertaking (s 46(2)).
[208] Barron (2002).
[209] It is unclear whether the court can issue a warrant for arrest on the basis of a breach of an undertaking: Gerlis (1996).
[210] A more restrictive test applies where the application is *ex parte* (FLA 1996, s 47(3)).
[211] Bird (1996: 4.12).

> **LEGISLATIVE PROVISION**
>
> **Family Law Act 1996, section 47(3A)**
>
> The court shall not accept an undertaking under subsection (1) instead of making a non-molestation order in any case where it appears to the court that—
>
> (a) the respondent has used or threatened violence against the applicant or a relevant child; and
>
> (b) for the protection of the applicant or child it is necessary to make a non-molestation order so that any breach may be punishable under section 42A.

## E  Powers of arrest

Section 47(1) creates a strong presumption in favour of attaching a power of arrest in nearly all cases of occupation injunctions because it is rare for one of those injunctions to be applied for unless there is at least a threat of violence.[212] The significance of having a power of arrest attached to an order is that, if a person breaches the order, the police automatically have the power to arrest him or her. If a power of arrest is not attached, then the victim will have to apply to the court for a warrant for arrest,[213] unless the actions constitute a criminal offence.

## F  Punishment for breach of an order

It must not be assumed that just because an order has been made, the victim is now protected from domestic violence.[214] If a person has breached a non-molestation or occupation order then he or she is liable to be punished for contempt of court. This may involve imprisonment or a fine. Where the act breaching an occupation or non-molestation order is a violent one then there should be an immediate custodial sentence.[215] In some cases a defendant imprisoned for contempt can apply to 'purge' his contempt and seek early release.[216]

## G  The reduction in the use of civil remedies

In the past few years there has been a noticeable reduction in the use of civil remedies in domestic violence cases. In 2004, 32,891 occupation and non-molestation orders were made, while in 2008 this had fallen to 24,466.[217] That is a drop of nearly a third.[218]

There are a number of possible explanations for this. One is that section 42A Family Law Act 1996, introduced in 2004, with the creation of an offence of breaching a non-molestation order, has deterred applicants.[219] However, the percentage drop in the number of occupation orders has been higher than in relation to non-molestation orders and so that cannot be a major cause.

---

[212] In *Chechi v Bashier* [1999] 2 FLR 489.

[213] The application needs to be supported by a statement on oath and there must be reasonable grounds to believe that a respondent has failed to comply with the order (s 47(9)).

[214] Humphreys and Thiara (2003).

[215] *Wilson v Webster* [1998] 1 FLR 1097, [1998] 2 FCR 275.

[216] *CJ v Flintshire Borough Council* [2010] EWCA Civ 393.

[217] Ministry of Justice (2009).

[218] See also Walsh (2009c).

[219] Platt (2008).

A more plausible explanation may be that the police are now taking domestic violence more seriously and are prosecuting domestic violence cases with greater vigour. That might mean that fewer people are seeing the need to rely on domestic violence remedies.

Another explanation is that there has been a decrease in the number of public funding (legal aid) certificates for domestic violence proceedings.[220] It is difficult to know whether that is because fewer clients are seeking such orders or whether it is becoming harder to get public funding to seek them. What certainly seems to be true is that there are a decreasing number of solicitors' firms doing publically funded work. It may be that the difficulty in accessing legal advice is causing a decrease in the numbers.[221]

However, a closer look at the figure suggests another explanation. There has not been a huge drop in the number of applications. Indeed there was only a drop of a few hundred in the number of applications for non-molestation orders between 2004 and 2008. It may be that judges are being less willing to grant domestic violence orders. This might indicate a scepticism about allegations of domestic violence, particularly in cases where there is a dispute over contact and the allegation may be regarded as being made to assist in the contact case, rather than being a genuine case. If so, this is very worrying. The statistics on domestic violence indicate that many more people suffer domestic violence than seek legal remedies and that where they do seek legal assistance this is after a lengthy period of abuse.

## 3 Injunctions under the Protection from Harassment Act 1997 and tort

Prior to the Protection from Harassment Act 1997, the law of tort had been strained in the attempt to find a tort of harassment.[222] For example, one case found that persistent telephone calls constituted the tort of nuisance.[223] Stretching the traditional categories of the law of tort is no longer necessary, as the 1997 Act in effect creates a new tort of harassment. It is possible to obtain an injunction if there is an actual or anticipated breach of s 1.[224] Under s 1:

---

**LEGISLATIVE PROVISION**

**Protection from Harassment Act 1997, section 1**

(1) A person must not pursue a course of conduct—

    (a) which amounts to harassment of another, and

    (b) which he knows or ought to know amounts to harassment of the other.

(2) For the purposes of this section, the person whose course of conduct is in question ought to know that it amounts to harassment of another if a reasonable person in possession of the same information would think the course of conduct amounted to harassment of the other.

---

[220] Burton (2009a).
[221] Burton (2009a).
[222] See Burton (2008b) for a discussion of the use of ASBOs to deal with domestic violence.
[223] *Khorasandjian v Bush* [1993] 2 FCR 257, [1993] 2 FLR 66; overruled in *Hunter v Canary Wharf Ltd* [1997] 2 FLR 342.
[224] Protection from Harassment Act 1997, s 3.

> (3) Subsection (1) does not apply to a course of conduct if the person who pursued it shows—
>
> (a) that it was pursued for the purpose of preventing or detecting crime,
>
> (b) that it was pursued under any enactment or rule of law or to comply with any condition or requirement imposed by any person under any enactment, or
>
> (c) that in the particular circumstances the pursuit of the course of conduct was reasonable.

This section requires proof of three elements:

1. First, it must be proved that the defendant harassed the victim. The Act does not define harassment and so the word is to be given its normal meaning. However, the Act makes it clear that 'references to harassing a person include alarming the person or causing the person distress'.[225] This reveals that there is no need to demonstrate that physical harm is caused, nor that the victim suffers a psychological injury.[226] Only a person can be harassed for the purposes of the Act; a local authority cannot.[227]

2. The offence can be committed only where there is a course of conduct, which must involve conduct on at least two occasions.[228] So a single incident, however terrifying, cannot amount to an offence under the Act. Two incidents separated by four months were found not to be a 'course' of conduct in *Lau v DPP*.[229] However, it all depends on the nature of the conduct. If there was a threat to do an act and a year later the threat was carried out, this linked form of conduct could constitute a course of conduct.[230] What is required is some kind of nexus or theme which connects the behaviour into a course of conduct.[231] In *R v Hills*[232] there were two incidents of violence separated by six months. However, between the two incidents the couple had cohabited and had sexual relations. This, the Court of Appeal felt, meant that there could not be a course of conduct. Indeed they doubted that the Protection from Harassment Act 1997 was suitable in cases where the defendant and victim were living together, as such cases were a long way from the stalking cases at which the Act was primarily aimed. That said, the 1997 Act has been used for a wide variety of cases beyond the traditional stalking cases, ranging from animal rights protesters, to neighbours falling out with each other, and it is hard to see why cohabitants should be seen as outside the Act's scope.

3. It is enough if it is shown that the defendant *ought* to have been aware that his or her conduct was harassing. It is therefore no defence for defendants to claim that they were unaware that their behaviour was harassing. In *R v Colohan*[233] the schizophrenic

---

[225] Section 7(2). There is no need for the prosecution to prove that the victim suffered a psychologically recognised illness, as is required under the Offences Against the Person Act 1861, ss 47, 20 and 18.

[226] Although Lord Steyn, in *R v Ireland and Burstow* [1998] AC 147, thought that most cases under the Act would involve violence.

[227] *Tameside MBC v M (Injunctive Relief: County Courts: Jurisdiction)* [2001] FL 873, although in that case the judge in the county court was willing to use the court's statutory jurisdiction under s 38 of the County Courts Act 1984 to protect the council and its staff.

[228] Protection from Harassment Act 1997, s 7(3): conduct includes speech.

[229] [2000] 1 FLR 799.

[230] *Lau v DPP* [2000] 1 FLR 799.

[231] *R v Patel* [2004] EWCA Crim 3284. But repeated 'spontaneous' acts can be a course of conduct: *Hipgrave v Jones* [2005] FL 453.

[232] [2001] 1 FCR 569.

[233] [2001] 3 FCR 409.

defendant argued that the jury should consider whether a reasonable schizophrenic person would be aware that his or her conduct was harassing. The argument was rejected: the jury or magistrates should simply consider what an ordinary reasonable person would have known.

There are various defences available listed in s 3(3). The one most likely to be relied upon is the defence that the course of conduct was reasonable. A defendant's mental illness will not render his or her conduct reasonable.[234] Once s 1 is established then an injunction can be made. In addition, s 3(2) states that damages can be awarded for anxiety and any financial loss.[235]

It should be stressed that this Act does not require there to be any kind of relationship between the parties. It is therefore potentially very wide. Interestingly, the first reported case under the section involved animal rights protesters picketing an animal laboratory.[236] This was not the kind of case the Government had in mind in passing the legislation, but demonstrates the potential width of the statute.

## 4 The Children Act 1989 and domestic violence

It is not possible to obtain a prohibited steps order or specific issue order under s 8 of the Children Act 1989, which has the same effect as an occupation or non-molestation order.[237] There are two reasons for this. The first is that the basis of making an order under the Children Act 1989 is the welfare principle, whereas Parliament has set out different criteria in the Family Law Act 1996 for occupation and non-molestation orders. To allow someone to be able to get an occupation order under the Children Act 1989 would be to bypass the criteria in the Family Law Act 1996. The second is that an order under s 8 of the Children Act 1989 can be made only in respect of an issue which relates to an exercise of parental responsibility. An order that one partner does not molest the other would not relate to an exercise of parental responsibility and so could not be made under s 8 of the Children Act 1989.

## 5 Domestic violence and housing law

A crucial part of legal protection for abused adults is the provision of alternative affordable accommodation by the state.[238] One scandalous aspect of the law's present approach is the lack of support for battered women's refuges to which women can turn in emergencies.[239] These are largely run by voluntary agencies on very tight budgets.[240] However, shelters are intended only as a short-term solution. For long-term solutions the local authorities need to provide housing. The abused spouse, who is not able to afford rented accommodation and is seeking alternative accommodation, must rely on the legislation relating to homelessness.[241]

---

[234] *R v Colohan* [2001] 3 FCR 409.
[235] In *Singh v Bhakar* [2006] FL 1026, £35,000 was awarded to a wife harassed by her mother-in-law.
[236] *Huntingdon Life Services Ltd v Curtis* (1997) *The Times*, 11 December.
[237] *Re H (A Minor) (Prohibited Steps Order)* [1995] 1 FLR 638, [1995] 2 FCR 547.
[238] Recognised by the Government in Home Office (2000b: 12.1).
[239] Home Office Affairs Select Committee (2008). Some refuges do not allow women with older boys to use their facilities.
[240] Humphreys, Hester, Hague et al. (2002).
[241] Rubens (2008).

Indeed it has been suggested that 15 per cent of those who are homeless have been victims of domestic violence.[242] For the year 2002–03, 22 per cent of homeless families had become homeless following relationship breakdown. In 70 per cent of these cases violence had caused the breakdown.[243]

Under the Housing Act 1996 there is a duty on all local authorities:

1. To ensure that any person who requires support in their area has access to advice and information about homelessness.

2. To enquire whether a person is eligible for assistance if the local authority has reason to believe that a person is threatened with homelessness.

3. To house a person who is in priority need, and not intentionally homeless.[244]

It is this third duty which is of the most practical significance and so it will be considered in more detail.

## A  The definition of 'homeless'

A person is homeless if they have no accommodation available for their use in the UK or elsewhere. The accommodation must be available[245] for the person together with any other person who lives with them as a member of their family, or any other person who might reasonably be expected to live with them. However, to be available it must be reasonable to expect the person to occupy the property. It would not be reasonable for the person to occupy a property they have had to leave due to domestic violence.[246] The relevant section of the Housing Act 1996 (s 177(1)) states:

---

**LEGISLATIVE PROVISION**

**Housing Act 1996, section 177(1)**

It is not reasonable for a person to continue to occupy accommodation if it is probable that this will lead to domestic violence against him, or against—

(a)  a person who normally resides with him as a member of his family; or

(b)  any other person who might reasonably be expected to reside with him.

---

Hence, once it is shown that the person is likely to be the victim of domestic violence from a person with whom they live, they will automatically be found to be homeless.[247] 'Domestic violence' here means 'violence from a person with whom he is associated, or threats of violence from such a person which are likely to be carried out'.[248] The Homelessness Act 2002 provides

---

[242] Morley and Pascall (1996: 328).
[243] Shelter (2003).
[244] Housing Act 1996, s 175(4).
[245] This includes property which the person has an interest in or a licence to occupy or a right not to be evicted from.
[246] Or if the property is, for example, occupied by a squatter who could be removed only by legal action or force (s 175(2)(a)).
[247] *Bond v Leicester City Council* [2002] 1 FCR 566.
[248] Housing Act 1996, s 177(1).

that violence from a non-associated person may also be included if it is racially motivated, for example. Accommodation need not be settled or permanent.[249] Thus it can include temporarily staying with friends or relatives. This is problematic because it is common for victims of domestic violence to seek refuge with friends or relatives.[250] More importantly, the question has been raised whether a shelter may be regarded as accommodation. In *Moran v Manchester City Council*[251] it was held that a shelter could be regarded as accommodation.

## B Priority need

Those who are in priority need include, *inter alia*:

---

**LEGISLATIVE PROVISION**

**Housing Act 1996, section 189(1)**

(a) a pregnant woman or a person with whom she resides or might reasonably be expected to reside;

(b) a person with whom dependent children reside or might reasonably be expected to reside;

(c) a person who is vulnerable as a result of old age, mental illness, or handicap, or physical disability or other special reason,[252] or with whom such a person resides or might reasonably be expected to reside.[253]

---

Category (b) includes those with whom a child stays only several days a week.[254] To fall within category (b) the courts[255] have held that it is not necessary for a parent to have a residence order in respect of a child, although some local authorities might still require this.[256] Under category (c) a victim of domestic violence will be regarded as a vulnerable person.[257] In 2002 statutory instruments[258] added to the categories of those in priority need, including (in England[259]) those who are vulnerable as a result of ceasing to occupy accommodation by reasons of violence or realistic threats of violence from another person. The requirement of vulnerability is meant to distinguish between cases where a person flees domestic violence but is surrounded by a network of friends and family and cases where the person in flight is left desperate and destitute.[260]

---

[249] *R v Brent LBC, ex p Awua* [1995] 2 FLR 819, [1995] 3 FCR 278.

[250] Department of Health (2002a: para 6.37) accepts that overcrowding may mean that staying with a relative or friend is no longer feasible.

[251] [2008] EWCA Civ 378, rejecting the view in *R v Ealing LBC, ex p Sidhu* [1982] 3 FLR 438.

[252] This has been said to include a young person escaping a violent home life: *R v Kensington and Chelsea LBC, ex p Kihara* (1996) 29 HLR 147.

[253] See also Homeless Persons (Priority Need for Accommodation) (England) Order 2002 (SI 2002/2051) and Homeless Persons (Priority Need) (Wales) Order 2001 (SI 2001/607) which add to this list for England and Wales respectively.

[254] *R v Lambeth LBC, ex p Vagiviello* (1990) 22 HLR 392.

[255] *R v Ealing LBC, ex p Sidhu* [1982] 3 FLR 438.

[256] Barron (2002); Yell (1992: 20).

[257] *R v Kensington and Chelsea LBC, ex p Kihara* (1996) 29 HLR 147.

[258] Homeless Persons (Priority Need for Accommodation) (England) Order 2002 (SI 2002/2051) and Homeless Persons (Priority Need) (Wales) Order 2001 (SI 2001/607).

[259] The provisions for Wales are slightly wider, most notably not requiring proof of vulnerability.

[260] Department of Communities and Local Government (2006); Department of Health (2002a: para 8.26).

## C Unintentionally homeless[261]

A person is intentionally homeless if they do or fail to do something that leads to them not occupying property that it would have been reasonable for them to carry on occupying.[262] A person is unintentionally homeless unless it is shown that they caused their own homelessness.

The difficulty is that local authorities have found the burden of caring for homeless people a heavy one, so it is not surprising that they have attempted to treat their obligations as strictly as possible. This has worked to the disadvantage of many victims of domestic violence: some authorities have taken the view that a woman who is the victim of violence should seek an occupation order (or ouster order as it was); a failure to do this, simply leaving her home instead, may make her intentionally homeless.[263] Such an attitude was strongly criticised by the Court of Appeal in *R v Westminster CC, ex p Bishop*.[264] However, the approach reveals the reluctance of local authorities to house victims of domestic violence unless they feel compelled to do so by the state. In *Moran v Manchester City Council*[265] it was held that the local authority were permitted to take the view that as the woman had a place in a refuge she was not homeless. The Home Office has recently stressed to local authorities the importance of ensuring that victims of domestic violence are provided with accommodation.[266]

## 6 Domestic violence and the criminal law

The fact that a violent incident occurred in a home does not affect its position in the criminal law.[267] An assault in a home is as much an assault as if it took place in a pub; at least, that is the theory. However, the history of the criminal law in this area shows that the police and courts have often regarded domestic violence as a less serious offence than other crimes. In recent years Parliament, the courts and police have shown an increasing awareness of the problems of molestation, domestic violence and stalking, but there is still much dissatisfaction with the operation of the criminal law.

## A The substantive law

As already stated, the fact that an offence takes place in a home makes no difference to the substantive law. It is nowadays uncontroversial to say that a domestic assault is as serious as any other. However, some commentators have gone further and argued that in fact domestic assaults should be regarded as aggravated assaults. There could be special offences connected with domestic violence in the same way as there are offences dealing with racist assaults.[268] This section will concentrate on how the criminal law has responded to the increasing awareness of domestic violence problems.

---

[261] For a discussion on unintentional homelessness see Rubens (2008). If the person is intentionally homeless then the duty is only to give accommodation for such period as is reasonable for him or her to find alternative accommodation, and to provide advice and assistance to help find accommodation.

[262] Housing Act 1996, s 191 (as amended by Homelessness Act 2002). If a person is intentionally homeless then only temporary accommodation and advice and assistance need be offered (s 190).

[263] Thornton (1989).

[264] [1994] 1 FLR 720.

[265] [2008] EWCA Civ 378.

[266] Home Office (2000c: 2c.iii.1). See also Department of Health (2002a: ch. 7).

[267] Edwards (1996: ch. 5); Cowan and Hodgson (2007).

[268] Conway (2004).

## (i) Rape

There used to be a common law rule that a husband could not be guilty of raping his wife. The reasoning behind this rule was that, on marriage, a wife gave her irrevocable consent to sexual relations throughout marriage. In *R v R (Rape: Marital Exemption)*[269] the House of Lords stated that the traditional view that a husband could not be guilty of raping his wife was now unacceptable and the common law rule was abolished. Now, a husband can be guilty of raping his wife. The fact that the law did not change until 1992 reveals the reluctance of Parliament and the courts to deal with domestic violence.[270]

## (ii) Assaults

Concerning the law on assaults, there have been difficulties with the areas of stalking and harassment. The House of Lords has been willing to extend the understanding of assault occasioning actual bodily harm[271] and causing grievous bodily harm[272] to cover harassing conduct. In *R v Ireland and Burstow*[273] the House of Lords accepted that the phrase 'bodily harm' included psychological injuries as well as physical injuries. This enabled the House of Lords to uphold the conviction of a man who had been persistently telephoning women with silent phone calls, for an offence contrary to s 47 of the Offences Against the Person Act 1861. Their Lordships also confirmed the conviction of a man for causing grievous bodily harm contrary to s 18 of the Offences Against the Person Act 1861 after he fought a campaign of harassment against a woman and caused her a severe psychological illness.[274]

## (iii) Sentencing of domestic crimes

The Court of Appeal has made it clear that marital disharmony will never in itself constitute a justification for violence.[275] Also, the fact that the parties are married is not a reason for giving a lower sentence.[276] However, a survey of cases by Edwards has suggested that some judges regard domestic violence as less serious than other assaults.[277] Another survey has found widespread use of binding over to keep the peace in these cases.[278]

## (iv) Protection from Harassment Act 1997

The Protection from Harassment Act 1997 was produced after a number of high-profile cases involving stalking were thought to reveal inadequacies in the law.[279] Stalkers may be complete strangers to the victim or be former partners. In fact this statute covers a far wider range of behaviour than stalking. It is an offence to breach s 1 of the Protection from Harassment Act 1997, which was quoted above. The maximum sentence for the offence under s 1 is

---

[269] [1992] 1 AC 599. The decision was put into statutory form in Criminal Justice and Public Order Act 1994, s 142 and see now Sexual Offences Act 2003.
[270] Herring (2011).
[271] Offences Against the Person Act 1861, s 47.
[272] Offences Against the Person Act 1861, ss 18 and 20.
[273] [1998] AC 147, discussed by S. Gardner (1998); Herring (1998c).
[274] *R v Bretton* [2010] EWCA Crim 207, extended sentences may be available in cases of domestic violence.
[275] *R v Rossiter* [1994] 2 All ER 752 at p. 753.
[276] *R v W* (1993) 14 Cr App R (S) 256; *R v Cutts* [1987] Fam Law 311.
[277] Edwards (1996).
[278] Cretney and Davis (1996) found that domestic violence resulted in a bind-over in 16% of cases, whereas for assaults in non-domestic assaults only 4% of cases resulted in a bind-over.
[279] Wells (1997).

six months[280] and it is possible for the court to make a restraining order.[281] A more serious offence is set out in s 4 of the Act, which concerns a course of conduct which causes a victim to fear on two occasions that violence will be used against him or her. The requirements for this offence are similar to s 1, with two main differences: the focus is on causing fear of violence rather than on harassment; and the reasonableness defence is available only if the conduct is deemed reasonable for the protection of the defendant or the defendant's or another's property. The maximum sentence is five years.[282]

## (v) Compensation

Financial compensation is probably very low down the list of priorities for a victim of domestic violence but payment can have practical importance as well as being a public recognition of the wrong done to the victim.[283] It is unrealistic that a victim will sue a perpetrator in tort, and so any compensation is likely to come from the Criminal Injuries Compensation Scheme.[284] An award under the scheme is available where there is a conviction and domestic violence is covered by the scheme, although awards are not high.

## (vi) Crimes committed by victims of domestic violence

There have been cases where a victim of domestic violence has killed her abuser and been charged with murder. The courts have been willing to develop the law on the defence of loss of control and diminished responsibility to deal with such cases.[285] However, there are still grave concerns over whether the current defences work effectively in these cases.[286]

Section 5 of the Domestic Violence, Crime and Victims Act 2004 creates an offence of failing to protect a child who was at risk of death. While this has been welcomed by some as an important aspect of protecting children from violence, others have expressed concern that the offence has to date been used against mothers who were themselves the victims of domestic violence from the person who killed the child.[287] It is suggested that the state would do better offering effective protection to victims of domestic violence, rather than prosecuting them for failing to protect their children, when the state itself has so manifestly failed to protect them.[288]

## B  The criminal law in practice

There has been a history of the criminal law not, in practice, taking domestic violence seriously. A report by Her Majesty's Inspectorate of Constabulary and Crown Prosecution Service Inspectorate admitted:

> Until relatively recently for example, dominant police culture depicted violence in the home as 'just another domestic' – a nuisance call to familiar addresses that rarely resulted in a satisfactory

---

[280] Or a level 5 fine (s 5).
[281] This order prohibits the defendant from conduct which would constitute harassment or cause a fear of violence. The order can be of fixed or indefinite duration (s 5(3)(b)).
[282] Section 4(4).
[283] Cobley (1998).
[284] Now set out in the Criminal Injuries Compensation Act 1995.
[285] See Herring (2010i) for a detailed discussion of the law.
[286] McColgan (1993) and Kaganas (2002).
[287] Herring (2007a).
[288] Herring (2008b).

policing outcome. To the service's credit, tremendous efforts have been made in the last five years or so to overturn this stereotype and ensure that domestic violence is treated as a serious incident, requiring a high standard of professional investigation. The CPS too has raised the profile of domestic violence, issuing revised policy and guidance and setting up a network of Area domestic violence coordinators. But all too often, policies and rhetoric are not matched on the ground by effective responses and solid investigative practice.[289]

As these comments indicate, although at present much work is being done to change attitudes, for too long the approach of the police was that 'domestics' were not proper crimes which warranted a thorough investigation.[290] Further, the prosecution authorities were reluctant to take such cases to court unless there was a very high chance of success. Indeed the report noted that there was a 50 per cent attrition rate at each stage of process (the police being called; the making by the police of a potential crime report; the making of a full crime report; the making of an arrest; the charging of the defendant; the conviction). As a result only a tiny percentage of domestic assaults were ending up in court. There is a determination within the police to change the attitudes of officers towards domestic violence and within the CPS to pursue, where appropriate, prosecutions for domestic violence.[291] The Government has declared it as an aim of its domestic violence policy to increase arrest and prosecution rates.[292] Early signs are of an improvement: the rate of 'successful' prosecutions for domestic violence has increased from 46 per cent in 2003 to 67 per cent in 2007–08.[293] In one small study only 27 of the 54 respondents who had contacted the police after an incident of domestic violence said they would contact the police if there was another incident.[294]

There are basically three stages at which an incident of domestic violence may fail to lead to a successful prosecution: the arrest; the decision to prosecute; and the trial.[295]

## (i) Arrest policies

Criminologists have written much on the importance of police culture[296] and have argued that in police culture domestic violence is often not taken seriously enough. Using the database of one domestic violence unit, Stanko[297] found that only 12 per cent of recorded cases of domestic violence resulted in arrest. At present in England and Wales when police are informed of a domestic violence incident, in 21 per cent of cases there is an arrest.[298] In 42 per cent of cases the abuser was 'spoken to' by the police; in 29 per cent of cases he was neither arrested nor spoken to.

There are three main problems which limit the likelihood of arrest. First, for various reasons, the victim may fail to contact the police after an assault. For example, the victim may feel that what happened was not a crime, or she may feel that she would not be taken seriously. Secondly, the police may not make an arrest because they themselves do not regard domestic violence as a 'proper crime', or because they find it impossible to discover what actually happened. The police arrive at scenes which are often emotionally charged and not easy to

---

[289] HMIC/CPSI (2004: 6). See also Burman, Smailes and Chantler (2004).
[290] See also Hester and Westmarland (2005).
[291] HMIC/CPSI (2004).
[292] Home Office (2006a).
[293] Burton (2009a).
[294] Musgrove and Groves (2007). Among minoritised cultures only 4 of the 17 women who had reported incidents to the police said they would again.
[295] Lazarus-Black (2007); Hoyle (1998).
[296] Edwards (1996: 196–8).
[297] Stanko et al. (1998).
[298] Walby and Allen (2004).

deal with.[299] Certainly a domestic violence incident is not as clear-cut an issue as dealing with a fight outside a pub. Thirdly, the victim, even though she may have contacted the police, may not actually want an arrest, but just want the man to be removed.[300] This decision might be encouraged explicitly or implicitly by the police's reaction to the situation.

The Home Office issued guidance[301] on arrest and domestic violence, suggesting that there should be an arrest in all cases of domestic violence unless there are exceptional circumstances.

### (ii) 'Down-criming' and decisions not to prosecute

Some people have alleged that although there has been an increase in the number of arrests for domestic violence following changes made in police practice, the number of convictions has not changed, because of the attitude of the Crown Prosecution Service (CPS).[302] It is the job of the CPS to decide either to prosecute the offence; to 'down-crime' (that is, to charge a lesser offence than the one the victim alleges); or not to pursue the case to a court hearing.[303] Following arrest, 30 per cent of cases are withdrawn; 7 per cent are not charged; and 52 per cent are discontinued. Only 11 per cent of cases are brought to trial.[304] The decision not to prosecute, or to 'down-crime', may be caused by difficulties of proof, especially as often the only witnesses to the incident are the victim and the defendant. It may be that the victim is unwilling to pursue the prosecution because of her fear of reprisals or because she believes that it will be of no tangible benefit to her. Indeed the imprisonment of the abuser might cause the victim financial and emotional harm. One study found that in 46 per cent of cases victims withdrew their support for a prosecution, having initially reported the incident to the police.[305] In cases where a victim withdraws her testimony, the CPS have been instructed to investigate to ensure that her decision truly reflects her wishes.[306] The Home Office has suggested that it may be appropriate to bring proceedings even if the victim does not wish to give evidence, and that the CPS should consider adopting such a policy.[307] However, in practice it is rare for there to be a prosecution if the victim is unwilling to co-operate. The CPS guidance now requires consideration of bringing a prosecution even if the victim does not want one.[308]

### (iii) The trial

Even if the case reaches trial, a conviction is, of course, not guaranteed. There are particular problems if the victim does not want to give evidence.[309] Under s 23 of the Criminal Justice Act 1988 a written statement of the victim of an assault may[310] be admissible as evidence.[311] So in suitable cases there may be no need for the victim to give evidence in court. Nevertheless,

---

[299] Edwards and Halpern (1991).

[300] Hoyle (1998: 214) found that only one-third of the women in her study wanted the police officers to arrest the suspect, and many of those did not want the matter taken further.

[301] Home Office (2000c: ch. 2).

[302] See Crown Prosecution Service (2009) for their current policy.

[303] 'Down-criming' occurs in all offences but it appears to be particularly common in offences of domestic violence: Cretney and Davis (1996).

[304] Cretney and Davis (1996)

[305] Crown Prosecution Service Inspectorate (1998).

[306] Home Office (2000c: 2b:ii.4).

[307] Home Office (2000c: 2b.ii.6).

[308] Crown Prosecution Service (2009).

[309] Home Office (2000b: ch. 2) sets out guidance for courts in order to make the experience of giving evidence as untraumatic as possible.

[310] The court has a discretion to decide whether to admit the statement, and in particular to rule whether the evidence can be subject to the scrutiny of cross-examination.

[311] Although only if the witness was able to give that evidence 'live'.

live evidence is likely to be more persuasive to a jury. It would be possible to compel the victim to give oral evidence, by threatening them with contempt of court if they fail to testify in person.[312] In one case a victim refused to give evidence and this led to the case being dropped against her attacker, but as a result the judge decided to sentence the victim to prison for contempt of court.[313]

The low rate of successful prosecutions thus results from victims not wishing to pursue criminal prosecutions, and the state agencies being reluctant to press for such prosecutions.[314]

## C Reforming the criminal procedure

A more radical approach could be taken by the criminal law in dealing with domestic violence. Some of the options are as follows.

### (i) Pro-arrest guidelines or pro-prosecution

Some jurisdictions have adopted 'pro-arrest' policies or even 'mandatory arrest' policies.

---

**TOPICAL ISSUE**

## Pro-arrest policies

With pro-arrest policies the police are required or strongly encouraged to arrest an abuser if the victim of domestic violence makes a complaint.[315] Even if the victim subsequently withdraws her consent the prosecution should still continue. In the UK the closest statement to a mandatory arrest policy is the most recent guidance of the Home Office, suggesting that, unless there are good reasons not to, an arrest should be carried out in cases of domestic violence.[316] Further, there could be a strong presumption in favour of prosecuting domestic violence cases, even where the victim opposes this.

One argument in favour of a mandatory arrest and prosecution policy is that a potential abuser, aware of the high likelihood of being arrested, may be deterred from violence. Others suggest that it is unlikely that batterers would be aware of the policy, and, even if they were, it would not operate as a deterrent in the 'heat of the moment'. A further justification of a pro-arrest or mandatory arrest policy is that the batterer will automatically be publicly labelled as an abuser. The publicity that would surround such a policy might make a powerful statement to society in general that domestic violence is unacceptable.[317] The policy would also lead to less pressure being put on victims, who would not have to decide whether or not to seek arrest or prosecution, and because of this might also be more willing to assist police officers.[318] This, supporters claim, will disempower batterers, by removing their ability to thwart criminal procedures by terrifying the victim into withdrawing her complaint.[319] Critics could reply that such policies in fact disempower the victim by assuming that society knows

---

[312] Police and Criminal Evidence Act 1984, s 80.
[313] *R v Renshaw* [1989] Crim LR 811.
[314] Cretney and Davis (1996).
[315] Ellison (2002a).
[316] Home Office (2000c: ch. 2).
[317] Madden Dempsey (2007 and 2009) describes how effective prosecution of domestic violence can exhibit the characteristics of a feminist state.
[318] Ellison (2002a).
[319] Hunter, Nixon and Parr (1996); Schneider (2000b: 488).

what is best for her, rather than letting her decide whether to pursue her complaint.[320] Such policies, some claim, work against the interests of women and racial minorities.[321]

One well-known example of a mandatory arrest policy in practice was the Minneapolis Experiment in the United States. Although this policy led to a reduction in the rate of reported domestic violence, it was unclear whether this was because victims were not reporting violence because of the policy or whether the policy did indeed reduce the level of violence.[322] Further replica studies in Omaha, Nebraska and Charlotte, North Carolina failed to replicate the Minneapolis results.[323] There is therefore no conclusive evidence that such a policy would lead to a reduction in the level of violence. The argument that such a policy would send out a clear message of society's disapproval of domestic violence still stands.

Carolyn Hoyle and Andrew Saunders have argued:

> The pro-arrest approach assumes a position opposite to that of the victim choice model approach: that victims have little agency and that the police and policy makers know what is best for them. It seems presumptuous that policy makers or the feminist advocates who have influenced them can easily determine what is best for, or in the interests of, a diverse group of battered women. It is as much a conceit as the theory of deterrence in this area, which assumed that violent men are a homogeneous group.[324]

This, however, assumes that it is straightforward to ascertain what a victim wants. Even in cases where the victim is saying that she does not want a prosecution, this may not represent her true wishes. She may be acting out of fear of reprisal or she may have contradictory wishes: I do not want the violence to continue, but I do not want a prosecution. In such a case, ascertaining her wishes is not straightforward.

A pro-arrest policy could also be supported on human rights grounds.[325] As explained earlier in this chapter the state has an obligation to take reasonable steps to protect citizens from inhuman and degrading treatment.[326] A failure to arrest or prosecute a perpetrator of domestic violence could infringe the victim's rights under articles 2, 3 or 8 of the ECHR.[327] This could lead to a claim for damages under sections 7 and 8 of the Human Rights Act 1998.

## (ii) 'Rehabilitative psychological sentences'

An alternative approach would be for the criminal law to focus on the rehabilitation of domestic violence offenders rather than on punishment. In other jurisdictions those arrested for domestic violence offences can be sent on 'batterers' programmes'.[328] Linda Mills has argued for a model 'therapeutically fostering reconciliation' loosely modelled after the Truth and Reconciliation Commission in South Africa.[329] Other models focus on the apparent

---

[320] Dayton (2003); Miccio (2005).
[321] Gruber (2007).
[322] Buzawa and Buzawa (2003).
[323] A further difficulty with the approach is that it might lead to both parties being arrested, if both have been violent. It might be possible to require arrest of the primary aggressor, but this would not be an easy policy to implement on the ground.
[324] Hoyle and Sanders (2000: 19).
[325] Choudhry and Herring (2010: ch. 9); Choudhry (2010).
[326] *Opuz v Turkey* (App. No.33401/02). For a recent case where it was alleged the police failed to protect a victim of domestic violence see BBC Newsonline (2009f).
[327] Burton (2010).
[328] According to evidence to House of Commons Home Affairs Select Committee (2008), such programmes have huge waiting lists and few resources.
[329] Mills (2003) and Stark (2005) are strongly critical of approaches of this kind.

psychological inadequacies of the aggressor: they can teach the aggressor acceptable ways of expressing anger; challenge the abuser's general attitude towards women; or treat both the abuser and the victim together by finding ways to improve their communication.[330] Supporters of such programmes suggest that in this way the law can actually prevent future violence, but opponents argue that the method fails to take violence seriously enough and treats it as an illness rather than as criminal behaviour. Further, there is little evidence yet that they are effective.[331] Hoyle's study[332] found that a large majority of victims did not want prosecutions of the alleged abuser, some because they did not want to break up their relationships.[333] For such cases the psychological course may find favour with victims. The Home Office has recognised the benefits of some programmes of this kind, but has not suggested that they should replace the sanctions of the criminal law.[334] There is, however, much debate over the effectiveness of such programmes.[335]

### (iii) Not using the criminal law at all

It could be argued that the criminal law is inappropriate in cases of domestic violence. Given that there are such difficulties in proof and in finding punishments that meet the victims' needs, rather than developing criminal law and policing, the law should focus on attempting to find alternative housing for abused women. Some say that imprisoning the abuser can only worsen the position of the victim.[336] However, this approach fails to recognise the interest that society has in preventing domestic violence and in expressing its condemnation of such acts through the criminal law. Offering alternative accommodation can be used in conjunction with the criminal law, but should not be a replacement for it.

## 7 Children abusing their parents

One problem that is only recently receiving the attention it deserves is that of teenagers abusing their parents. In one small sample 11 per cent of families were found to be affected by this issue.[337] Understandably, parents are reluctant to voice their concerns about such a problem. Few parents would want to see their children prosecuted or removed from them. Indeed in many cases parents will feel that they are to blame, due their failure to parent their children effectively.

The issue does not neatly fall into the categories of family law. Is it best regarded as an issue of domestic violence or child protection? Does the fact that child is being violent indicate that they need to be taken into care or receive punishment? It may be that there are elements of both issues in some of these cases.

---

[330] Adams (2000), Dobash and Dobash (2000) and Bowen, Brown and Gilchrist (2002) describe such programmes.
[331] Mullender and Burton (2000).
[332] Hoyle (1998: 214).
[333] Some victims are concerned that informing public authorities about violence will lead to investigation by social workers into the welfare of their children: McGee (2000).
[334] Home Office (1999).
[335] Bullock, Sarre, Tarling and Wilkinson (2010); Morley and Mullender (1992: 284–5).
[336] Hoyle (1998).
[337] Hunter, Nixon and Parr (2010).

# 8  Why the law finds domestic violence difficult

Around the world, legal systems struggle to find the correct response to domestic violence. There are a number of reasons for the difficulties.

## A  The traditional image of the family

Domestic violence challenges the traditional images within family law of the family as a place of safety, a haven in a harsh world.[338] The presumption of non-intervention in family life is based on this peaceful view of families, although, as we saw when considering the statistical information on domestic violence, abuse is common in the home. The strength of the image of the family may explain why some victims refuse to regard themselves as the victims of crime, even regarding violence as an aspect of 'normal life'.[339]

## B  Privacy

In Chapter 1 the importance of the concept of privacy in family law was stressed.[340] O'Donovan[341] suggests: 'Home is thought to be a private place, a refuge from society, where relationships can flourish uninterrupted by public interference.' So not only is the home regarded as a refuge; some consider it essential that the law should 'stay out of the home'. Catharine Mackinnon characterised the ideology of privacy as 'a right of men "to be let alone" to oppress women one at a time'.[342] However, despite the strength that has traditionally been attached to the privacy argument, there are good reasons in favour of state intervention in cases of domestic violence.

1. Battering can be seen as causing public harm: it can cause increased costs to the NHS; extensive loss to the economy of police time, victims having to take time off work, etc. It has been estimated that domestic violence alone costs the economy £5.8 billion per year, once the costs to the National Health Service, police and lost work have been taken into account.[343] Notably, half of women seeking help for mental health problems have been the victim of domestic violence.[344]

2. It could be said that domestic violence is caused by and reinforced by patriarchy. As the state upholds and maintains patriarchy, it has responsibility for it and so is under a duty to mitigate its effects.

3. Intervention in domestic violence could be required in order to uphold the equal rights of men and women. If there is to be equality between the sexes in the home, there must be effective remedies for domestic violence.

It has been argued that if society focuses on the victim's privacy rather than the privacy of the 'home', intervention is justified. Schneider[345] maintains that the state needs to promote

[338]  Lasch (1977).
[339]  Kaganas and Piper (1994).
[340]  Schneider (1994).
[341]  O'Donovan (1993: 107).
[342]  Mackinnon (1987: 32).
[343]  Walby (2004).
[344]  Home Office (2003a: 10); Walby (2004).
[345]  Schneider (1994: 37).

'a more affirmative concept of privacy, one that encompasses liberty, equality, freedom of bodily integrity, autonomy and self-determination, which is important to women who have been battered'. Intervention in domestic violence can therefore be justified in order to promote the privacy of the victim.

## C Difficulties of proof

One of the difficulties of domestic violence is that often the only witnesses to the violence are the two parties themselves. In many cases it is one person's word against another's. This requires the courts to make orders that may infringe important rights of either party on the basis of meagre evidence. If the court makes the wrong decision, an innocent person may be removed from his or her home, or a victim may be denied protection from further violence. An obvious objection to mandatory prosecution is that without the evidence of the victim it is going to be extremely difficult to obtain a conviction. The incident is often only witnessed by the victim: so, in a practical sense, is it possible to prosecute where the victim opposes the prosecution? Those who wish to see more extensive prosecution in this area might suggest two solutions. One would be to compel victims of domestic violence to testify under pain of imprisonment for contempt of court. This has few supporters. As the primary justification offered for intervention is the protection of the rights of the victim and any children, to imprison the victim would undermine that aim. The second alternative has more support. This involves a prosecution without the involvement of the victim. At present it is very rare for this to happen.[346] Louise Ellison[347] has argued that 'victimless prosecution' is the way forward.[348] She argues that, although it is often assumed that without victim involvement a prosecution is not possible, more imaginative policing and prosecution techniques would make it feasible. She discusses, for example, the use of cameras as soon as the police arrive on the scene, to capture objective evidence of injuries.[349] She recommends that police procedure in domestic violence cases should be premised on the assumption that there will be a 'victimless prosecution'.[350] There may also need to be changes to the law of evidence – and in particular the hearsay rule and the admissibility of previous convictions – to assist in victimless prosecution. The advantages of victimless prosecution are clear: it involves less invasion of the victim's autonomy if the victim is opposed to it; the victim can avoid the pressures associated with giving evidence in these kinds of cases; and it can prevent threats or other pressures being used to dissuade victims from participating in litigation. Of course none of this should be seen as seeking not to prosecute with the victim's consent; much more should be done to enable and encourage the victim to support the litigation. The use of specialist domestic violence police, advisors,[351] prosecutors and courts might assist in these procedures.[352] The pilot studies to date indicate that in specialist domestic violence courts victimless prosecutions have been successfully brought.[353]

[346] Edwards (2000).
[347] Ellison (2002a and b).
[348] See also Edwards (2000) arguing for a greater willingness to use victim's written statements in cases where victims are unwilling to give evidence in court.
[349] HMIC/CPSI (2004: 10) and Staffordshire Police (2005) contain useful discussions of some of the practical steps that can be taken.
[350] Ellison (2002b) and Crown Prosecution Service (2005).
[351] Howarth, Stimpson, Baran and Robinson (2009).
[352] Lewis (2004). Crown Prosecution Service and Department of Constitutional Affairs (2004) reports particularly favourably on developing a multi-agency framework to provide improved support to victims.
[353] Burton (2006).

## D Occupation or protection

There are two kinds of cases in which someone may apply for an order relating to the occupation of a home: the first type involves domestic violence, where the applicant is seeking protection; the second kind involves no violence and the dispute concerns who should occupy the home until a final resolution is reached regarding the financial affairs of the couple (this being more in the nature of a property dispute). Although these are quite different kinds of cases, the Family Law Act 1996 deals with them both under ss 33, 35 and 36.

## E Victim autonomy

> ### DEBATE
>
> ### What weight should be attached to the wishes of the victim?
>
> There can be real difficulties in finding a correct solution to a situation once domestic violence is proved. In some cases the ideal solution from the victim's point of view is that her partner returns to the home but ceases to be violent.[354] The victim may be emotionally and financially dependent on the abuser and to imprison him might cause her further harm.[355] It can be argued that a victim who wishes to remain in a violent relationship is not expressing her genuine wishes, and that, rather than respect what the victim says she wants, we should seek to put the victim where the victim, free from violence, can make genuine choices.[356] Another argument is that the common attitudes of victims to domestic violence – 'I want the relationship to continue, but the violence to stop' – represent incompatible wishes. The law is not able to respect both of these desires of the victim. The law could take the view that the desire for the violence to stop is the more important aspect of the wishes of the victim.
>
> There may also be a conflict here between the interests of the state and the victim. The state may wish to express its abhorrence of domestic violence by a severe punishment, whereas the victim may not seek such stern treatment. This tension is revealed in civil law in that s 60 of the Family Law Act 1996 permits third parties to bring proceedings on a victim's behalf, but the courts may make orders on their own motion under s 42 of the Family Law Act 1996. Both sections suggest that it may be proper to provide a victim with protection which she does not want. In criminal law, encouraging arrest and pressurising a victim into providing evidence demonstrates the tension between protecting the victim's right to choose what should happen and voicing society's opposition to domestic violence. A leading body representing family lawyers has urged that protection rather than punishment should be at the heart of law on domestic violence.[357] At the extreme it might even be alleged that a victim's autonomy is threatened, on the one hand, by her abusive partner and, on the other, by state agencies acting to 'protect her' contrary to her wishes.[358] However, whether an abused woman is in a position to exercise autonomy following what might be years of abuse is also open to question.[359] Further, it could be argued that the interests of potential future victims ➡

[354] Hoyle (1998).
[355] In certain cultures there may be severe social disadvantages following public intervention in domestic violence.
[356] The argument is discussed in Miles (2001: 101).
[357] Solicitors Family Law Association (2003).
[358] Mills (2003).
[359] Hoyle and Sanders (2000).

of domestic violence justify a tough approach against current incidents of violence.[360] The reasons for this reluctance on the part of the victim may include: a fear of retaliation if they are seen to co-operate in legal proceedings; a desire that the relationship with the abuser continue; concerns about the welfare of children; difficulties in obtaining legal aid for civil proceedings;[361] a failure on the part of the police and others in supporting victims;[362] and a sense that none of the 'remedies' on offer by the law is helpful.

## Questions

1. *Is it demeaning to treat victims of domestic violence as 'vulnerable adults' who do not deserve the full protection of autonomy?*

2. *Do you think that domestic violence crimes are not really 'crimes against the state' and therefore can be treated differently from assaults in public places?*

## Further reading

Read **Hoyle and Sanders** (2000) and **Choudhry and Herring** (2006a) for contrasting views on the correct response to whether mandatory arrest and prosecution would be a good idea.

Peter De Cruz, after overviewing the law of domestic violence, writes:

> Overall, this overview has revealed that endemic and entrenched problems remain, namely: the difficulty in persuading victims (predominantly female) to make complaints, testify in court or to leave violent and abusive relationships. Another disturbing finding is the passivity of certain female victims, especially those from ethnic minorities or who are immigrants in certain countries and therefore more vulnerable to such abuse and open to exploitation.[363]

This quote might be read as blaming the victims for the problems the law faces: they are failing to leave their abusers or make complaints. To take that approach would be to fail to appreciate the impact on the victim of violence and the many obstacles that face those who seek to leave abusers or pursue them in the courts.

## F  Integrated approaches

One of the difficulties that the law has faced in this area has been integration of the work of the civil courts and criminal courts. An incident of domestic violence can lead to both a criminal prosecution and a civil application by the victim. If the courts which hear the different applications are not co-ordinated there is a danger of conflicting remedies being provided. One solution is the creation of specialist domestic violence courts which hear all kinds of cases of domestic violence.[364] The other benefit of this is that the courts become expert in the law and issues surrounding domestic violence.[365] A further example of integrating civil and

---

[360] Ellison (2002b).
[361] Rights of Women (2004: 5).
[362] See, e.g., Plotnikoff and Woolfson (1998: 12). In this study only 3 of 71 Domestic Violence Officers (4%) interviewed said unreservedly that domestic violence work was valued within their force.
[363] De Cruz (2010: 315).
[364] Crown Prosecution Service and Department of Constitutional Affairs (2004). See Burton (2006) for an excellent discussion of the work of these courts.
[365] Burton (2004).

criminal remedies is s 5A of the Protection from Harassment Act 1997: a court which acquits a defendant on a charge under the Act may nevertheless make a restraining order protecting the alleged victim. This might be appropriate in a case where, although it has not been proved that the defendant committed an offence, there is enough evidence to demonstrate that the 'victim' requires protection. Certainly it must not be forgotten that the making of a court order is only the start of the process of responding to domestic violence. There are often long-term issues arising from it which require extensive involvement from a range of agencies.[366]

A different issue of integration is the need to achieve co-operation between the different groups who work with victims of domestic violence: battered women's refuges, the police, local authority housing departments and benefits agencies might all need to work together to provide effective protection for victims of domestic violence. The Government has been seeking to improve communication between the different groups.[367] Ninety per cent of police forces have now appointed domestic violence officers who will co-ordinate the responses to domestic violence cases.[368]

## G The law not appropriate

Some feminists argue that the law's treatment of domestic violence is doomed to fail, given the patriarchal domination of the language, procedures and personnel of the legal process.[369] They maintain that domestic violence can only be combated if the domination of women by men throughout society is brought to an end. Until then the law can only tinker at the edges of the problem.

## H Solicitors

The professionals involved can create problems in the law's response to domestic violence. We have already discussed the attitudes of the police, but there may be problems with the mindset of those whose role is to assist the victim. Lawyers are traditionally seen as slow acting and the hectic life of many practising solicitors makes problematic the rapid applications that are necessary in domestic violence cases. Ingleby, in his work on family solicitors, argues: 'The solicitor's role in these violent situations might be seen in terms of preserving non-violent arm's-length lines of communication within which to negotiate the other aspects of the dispute in the hope that the passage of time will defuse the situation.'[370] It may also be that some solicitors lack awareness of the problems surrounding domestic violence. One study suggested that solicitors do not, as a matter of routine, ask family clients about domestic violence.[371] A different problem is the lack of lawyers who specialise in this underpaid, but vitally important, area of work.[372]

---

[366] Abrahams (2010).
[367] Home Office (2006a).
[368] HMIC/CPSI (2004: 3.26).
[369] Smart (1984).
[370] Ingleby (1992: 36).
[371] Kaganas and Piper (1999: 194).
[372] Burton (2009b).

## 9 Conclusion

This chapter has considered the law on domestic violence. This is an area where the notion of privacy has been particularly influential: that behaviour between partners in their home is their own business and the state should not interfere. In recent years the extent of domestic violence has become more widely acknowledged, both in terms of the severity of the violence and the number of people involved. However, acknowledgement of the problem is but a small step towards providing a solution. The Family Law Act 1996 and the judicial interpretation of that statute reveal that ousting abusive partners runs counter to the protection of property rights and (now) the right to respect for family and private life under the Human Rights Act 1998. So, even if ousting will provide the most effective protection to a victim of domestic violence, the courts will require convincing evidence before being willing to do so. A further difficult issue is to what extent the law should respect the right of autonomy of the victim of domestic violence and therefore rely on her to pursue the remedy she wishes; and to what extent the state should seek to protect the victim (regardless of whether she wants the intervention). This is an area where, perhaps, the solution lies not so much in the hands of the law, but in a wholesale change in attitudes towards violence in the home.[373]

## Further reading

**Burton, M.** (2008a) *Legal Responses to Domestic Violence*, London: Routledge.

**Choudhry, S.** (2010) 'Mandatory prosecution and arrest as a form of compliance with due diligence duties in domestic violence – the gender implications', in J. Wallbank, S. Choudhry and J. Herring (eds) *Rights, Gender and Family Law*, Abingdon: Routledge.

**Choudhry, S. and Herring, J.** (2006a) 'Righting Domestic Violence', *International Journal of Law, Policy and the Family* 20: 95.

**Freeman, M.** (1984) 'Legal Ideologies: Patriarchal Precedents and Domestic Violence', in M. Freeman (ed.) *The State, The Law and the Family*, London: Sweet & Maxwell.

**Harne, L. and Radford, J.** (2008) *Tackling Domestic Violence: Theories, Policies and Practice*, Maidenhead: Open University Press.

**Herring, J.** (2007b) 'Familial Homicide, Failure to Protect and Domestic Violence: Who's the victim?', *Criminal Law Review* 923.

**Hoyle, C.** (1998) *Negotiating Domestic Violence: Police, Criminal Justice and Victims*, Oxford: Clarendon Press.

**Hoyle, C. and Sanders, A.** (2000) 'Police responses to domestic violence: from victim choice to victim empowerment', *British Journal of Criminology* 40: 14.

**Madden Dempsey, M.** (2006) 'What counts as domestic violence? A conceptual analysis', *William and Mary Journal of Women and the Law* 12: 301.

---

[373] Home Office (2000d and 2000e) discuss how the Government intends to change attitudes towards domestic violence.

**Madden Dempsey, M.** (2009) *Prosecuting Domestic Violence*, Oxford: OUP.

**Reece, H.** (2006a) 'The End of Domestic Violence', *Modern Law Review* 69: 770.

**Reece, H.** (2009a) 'Feminist Anti-Violence Discourse as Regulation', in E. Jackson et al. (eds) *Regulating Autonomy: Sex, Reproduction and Families*, Oxford: Hart.

**Rubens, T.** (2008) 'Domestic violence and priority need', *Journal of Housing Law* 11: 28.

**Schneider, E.** (2000a) *Battered Women and Feminist Law Making*, New Haven: Yale University Press.

**Stark, E.** (2007) *Coercive Control: How Men Entrap Women in Personal Life*, Oxford: OUP.

Visit **www.mylawchamber.co.uk/herring** to access study support resources including interactive multiple choice questions, weblinks, discussion questions and legal updates.

**my**law**chamber**

*unrivalled support for legal education*

Use **Case Navigator** to read in full some of the key cases referenced in this chapter with commentary and questions:

*Re Y (Children) (Occupation Order)* [2000] 2 FCR 470

POWERED BY LexisNexis

# 7    Who is a parent?

It may seem rather odd to ask, 'Who is a parent?'[1] But the concept of parenthood is far from straightforward. It is often assumed that the parents of a child are those who genetically produce the child. The woman whose egg and the man whose sperm together ultimately produce the child are its parents. In the past, although there may have been practical problems in proving who was the biological father, that definition of parenthood was generally agreed. In recent times this definition has become problematic.[2] Four developments in particular have caused a re-examination of the concept of parenthood. The first is the advent of new reproductive technologies.[3] Now the woman who carries the child need not be genetically related to the child; a man may donate sperm to a hospital without ever intending to play a parental role; a whole range of options have been opened up for same-sex couples wishing to produce a child. Technologies continue to evolve and in 2008 it was announced that a man had been enabled to become pregnant.[4] It has become plausible to talk of a right to procreate.[5] Secondly, with increased rates of divorce and breakdown of relationships it is now common for a child to be cared for by someone who is not necessarily a genetic parent but, for example, a step-parent. Indeed a child may have a series of adults who carry out the social role of being a parent.[6] For such children there has been a separation between who is the person caring for them day to day and who is their genetic parent. Thirdly, there has been an increased interest in child psychology among lawyers, and an acceptance that children may have a 'psychological parent' who is not genetically the parent. Fourthly, what it means to be a mother or father in our society is undergoing complex and interesting changes. Men are sometimes seen as dispensable in the reproductive process, yet many men greatly value the paternal tie.[7] Sally Sheldon and Richard Collier have written of the 'fragmentation' of fatherhood, with it appearing to involve a number of disparate roles.[8]

Shortly, the law on parenthood will be considered, but it will be useful to consider briefly the understanding of parenthood from three other disciplines.

---

[1] The United Nations Convention on the Rights of the Child does not include a definition of a parent. For a general discussion on defining parenthood see Bainham (1999) and Steinbock (2005).
[2] Jones (2007).
[3] Sheldon (2005).
[4] BBC Newsonline (2008c).
[5] Eijkholt (2010).
[6] Haskey (1997) states that only three-quarters of children in their mid-teens live with both their biological parents.
[7] See Collier (2009a) and Daniels (2006) for the tensions between reproduction and notions of masculinity.
[8] Collier and Sheldon (2008).

## 1 Psychological, sociological and biological notions of parenthood

### A Child psychologists

One influential group of child psychologists has argued that, from a child's perspective, 'psychological parenthood' is of greater significance than biological parenthood.[9] Goldstein et al. write:

Whether any adult becomes the psychological parent of a child is based on day-to-day interaction, companionship and shared experiences. The role can be fulfilled either by a biological parent or by an adoptive parent or by any other caring adult – but never by an absent, inactive adult, whatever his biological or legal relationship to the child may be.[10]

They explain that children's and adults' perceptions of parenthood may differ:

Unlike adults, children have no psychological conception of blood tie relationship until quite late in their development. For the biological parents, the experience of conceiving, carrying and giving birth prepares them to feel close to and responsible for their child. These considerations carry no weight with children who are emotionally unaware of the events leading to their existence. What matters to them is the pattern of day-to-day interchanges with adults who take care of them and who, on the strength of such interactions, become the parent figures to whom they are attached.[11]

Although this notion of a psychological parent is important, research on adopted children suggests that some children may also regard genetic parentage of great importance,[12] as it provides an important part of the child's sense of identity.

### B Sociologists

Some sociologists have argued that parenthood is a socially constructed term, meaning that the rules on who is a parent reflect common norms within society, rather than reflecting an inevitable truth. Indeed anthropologists looking at different societies in different parts of the world and at different times have found a wide variety of understandings of parenthood. For example, Goody has noted the following different aspects of parenthood: bearing and begetting children; endowment with civil and kinship status; nurturance; and training and sponsorship into adulthood.[13] Different people in different cultures may carry out these roles.

### C Biological perceptions

Johnson has usefully distinguished four kinds of parenthood in a biological sense.[14] First, there is genetic parentage. At present, there is a need for sperm from the man and an egg from the woman to produce a conceptus which will ultimately develop into a person.[15] Secondly,

---

[9] For discussion of the psychological importance to a child of 'attaching' to a parent-figure see Bowlby (1973); Aldgate and Jones (2006); Howe, Brandon, Hinings and Schofield (1999).
[10] Goldstein, Solnit, Goldstein and Freud (1996: 19).
[11] Goldstein, Solnit, Goldstein and Freud (1996: 9).
[12] Thoburn (1988).
[13] Goody (1982).
[14] Johnson (1999). See also Rothstein et al. (2006).
[15] It may be that technology will develop so that in the future more than two people could be genetically related to a child.

there is coital parentage, which involves the meeting or joining of the sperm and egg.[16] Thirdly, there is a gestational or uterine component of parentage, involving the rearing and support of the foetus, which in humans is undertaken by the mother in pregnancy. Finally, there is the post-natal component: the raising of the child after birth.

It is obvious from this very brief outline that the definition of a parent is unclear and the term 'parent' can cover a wide range of ideas. Baroness Hale in *Re G (Children) (Residence: Same-Sex Partner)*[17] has looked at different aspects of parenthood and has usefully suggested that it is necessary to distinguish three key elements: legal, genetic and social parenthood.[18] Legal parenthood is concerned with who is deemed in the eyes of the law to be the parent. Genetic parenthood relates to whose sperm or eggs led to the creation of the child. Thirdly, the social parent is the person who carries out the day-to-day nurturing role of a parent. These roles are often acted out by the same person, but can be carried out by different people. For example, a step-parent may be the social parent of a child without being the biological or legal parent.

## 2 The different meanings of being a parent in law

It is not surprising that the law has a variety of understandings on being a parent. Bainham has usefully explained that the law distinguishes between parentage, parenthood and parental responsibility:[19]

1. *Parentage*: those who are genetically related to the child; in other words, the man who provided the sperm and the woman who provided the egg, which were combined to produce the foetus which became the child.[20]

2. *Parenthood*: those who are regarded in the law as parents. In many cases they will be those who have parentage, but it need not be so. For example, the law may decide that a man who donates sperm to a clinic will not be legally regarded as the father of the child.

3. *Parental responsibility*: those who are to have the legal responsibilities and rights that are attached to being a parent.

The benefit to the law in having these different understandings of 'parent' is that it increases flexibility. The law can decide that some people will have parenthood but not parental responsibility, or indeed that some people will be regarded as having parental responsibility but not parenthood. For some children it is possible that different people will have parentage, parenthood and parental responsibility under the present law. For example, imagine a woman who gives birth following assisted reproductive services provided to her and her unmarried partner but using the sperm of a sperm donor. After the birth she leaves her partner and marries another man, who is awarded a residence order in respect of the child. In such a case the sperm donor would have parentage; the partner parenthood; and the husband parental responsibility.

---

[16] For the majority of human parents this will be through sexual intercourse.
[17] [2006] 1 FCR 436 at paras 32–5. See the excellent discussion in Diduck (2007).
[18] A similar distinction had been earlier drawn by Eekelaar (1991c).
[19] Bainham (1999). See also Callus (2008), Masson (2006c) and Hubin (2003) who also discusses ways of breaking down aspects of being a parent.
[20] See Archard (1995) for a discussion of the significance that should attach to a genetic link between an adult and a child.

The law could be much simpler. We could have just two categories for adults: they either are or are not parents of a child. But having only two categories would lead to a less subtle law. By accepting different forms of parents the law is able to capture the variety of ways in which an adult can act in a parental role. Bainham argues that having different ways of being a parent assists in the debate over whether social or biological parenthood should be regarded by the law as the crucial element of parenthood: 'Increasingly the question will not be whether to prefer the genetic or social parent but how to accommodate both on the assumption that they both have distinctive contributions to make to the life of the child.'[21]

However, Bainham's enthusiasm for accepting a wide range of different kinds of parent is controversial. It is important to note that the 'problem' in defining parenthood is largely one of defining fathers. There is relatively little difficulty in defining motherhood. In the vast majority of cases there is no separation between parentage, parenthood and parental responsibility for mothers, as they relate to the same person. Increasing the number of people who can be regarded as parents is in reality increasing the number of people who can be regarded as fathers.[22] From the mother's viewpoint, the greater the recognition given to different kinds of fathers, the weaker the mother's position may become.[23] For example, a requirement that mothers should consult with a child's father(s) over important issues is a more onerous requirement if several men are regarded as father, rather than just one. Indeed, some commentators argue that the only kind of parenthood the law should be interested in is the 'doing' of parenting: the person who undertakes the day-to-day care of the child. A person whose only link to the child is one of blood has no link which deserves any recognition. But that goes against the very strong feelings about blood ties which many people have.

This chapter will now consider the legal definitions of who is the mother and who is the father of a child.[24]

## 3 Who is the child's mother?

The mother of a child is the woman who gives birth to the child.[25] This is so even where there is assisted reproduction and the woman who carries and gives birth to the child is not genetically related to the child. Section 33(1) of the Human Fertilisation and Embryology Act 2008 (hereafter HFEA 2008) states:

### LEGISLATIVE PROVISION

**Human Fertilisation and Embryology Act 2008, section 33(1)**

The woman who is carrying or has carried a child as a result of the placing in her of an embryo or of sperm and eggs, and no other woman, is to be treated as the mother of the child.

---

[21] Bainham (1999: 27).
[22] Masson (2006c: 135).
[23] See further Herring (2001: 137).
[24] For a discussion of the medical law issues surrounding reproduction see Herring (2010e: ch. 7).
[25] *Ampthill Peerage Case* [1977] AC 547 at p. 577.

This indicates that, in relation to motherhood, it is the gestational rather than the genetic link which is crucial. In fact the genetic link is irrelevant in establishing legal motherhood.[26] This could be explained in any one of three ways. The most convincing argument is that the pain and effort of childbirth and the closeness of the bond which develops through pregnancy[27] and birth justifies the status of motherhood.[28] The gestational mother has given more of herself to the child than the genetic mother. In other words the law emphasises the social aspect of parenting over the genetic link. Secondly, the law could be justified on the basis of certainty. It is far easier to discover who gave birth to the child than to ascertain who (if anyone) donated the egg.[29] Thirdly, the law might be seen as a way of encouraging egg donation.[30] Egg donors may be deterred from donating if they were to be regarded as the parents of the child.[31] Baroness Hale in *Re G (Children) (Residence: Same-Sex Partner)*[32] explained the law in this way:

> While this may be partly for reasons of certainty and convenience, it also recognises a deeper truth: that the process of carrying a child and giving him birth (which may well be followed by breast-feeding for some months) brings with it, in the vast majority of cases, a very special relationship between mother and child, a relationship which is different from any other.

A woman can also become a child's mother through the making of an adoption order or a parental order.[33] It should be noted that, unlike the position in France, a woman who gives birth does not have the chance to disclaim motherhood.[34] However, if the child is adopted the birth mother will cease to be the legal mother.

The definition of mother may be challenged by lesbian couples seeking assisted reproductive treatment together or making private arrangements for one of them to become pregnant.[35] They may argue that they wish to raise the child as a couple together and so both should be recognised as parents. The current law is clear: only the woman who gives birth is the mother. Her partner can be recognised as a 'second parent', but rather oddly, she will not, as a matter of law, be defined as the mother. There is no legal significance. If the mother and her partner have entered a civil partnership then under section 42(1) HFEA 2008 the partner will be treated as a parent, unless it can be shown she did not consent to the placing of the sperm or eggs into the mother. If the mother (W) and other women (P) are not in a civil partnership then the partner can become a parent if she meets the 'agreed female parenthood provisions':

---

[26] Contrast *Johnson v Calvert* [1993] 851 P 2d 774. Discussed in Douglas (1994b). See also *Moschetta v Moschetta* (1994) 25 Cal App 4th 1218.

[27] There is some psychological evidence for such a bond which is discussed in Hill (1991), although see Jenks (1996: 42) who sees it as an artificial concept to reinforce the view that women are natural carers.

[28] Douglas (1991).

[29] This argument was stressed by the Warnock Report (1984: 6.6–6.8).

[30] Kandel (1994).

[31] Surveys of egg donors suggest that the vast majority do not regard themselves to be mothers of the children produced using their eggs: Ahuja et al. (1998).

[32] [2006] 1 FCR 436, para 34.

[33] These will be discussed shortly.

[34] See the discussion in Marshall (2008) and Lefaucheur (2004).

[35] Sifris (2009); Dempsey (2004); Dunne (2000). See also Almack (2006).

LEGISLATIVE PROVISION

**Human Fertilisation and Embryology Act 2008, section 44(1)**

(1) The agreed female parenthood conditions referred to in section 43(b) are met in relation to another woman ('P') in relation to treatment provided to W under a licence if, but only if,—

(a) P has given the person responsible a notice stating that P consents to P being treated as a parent of any child resulting from treatment provided to W under the licence,

(b) W has given the person responsible a notice stating that W agrees to P being so treated,

(c) neither W nor P has, since giving notice under paragraph (a) or (b), given the person responsible notice of the withdrawal of P's or W's consent to P being so treated,

(d) W has not, since the giving of the notice under paragraph (b), given the person responsible—

(i) a further notice under that paragraph stating that W consents to a woman other than P being treated as a parent of any resulting child, or

(ii) a notice under section 37(1)(b) stating that W consents to a man being treated as the father of any resulting child, and

(e) W and P are not within prohibited degrees of relationship in relation to each other.

(2) A notice under subsection (1)(a), (b) or (c) must be in writing and must be signed by the person giving it.

(3) A notice under subsection (1)(a), (b) or (c) by a person ('S') who is unable to sign because of illness, injury or physical disability is to be taken to comply with the requirement of subsection (2) as to signature if it is signed at the direction of S, in the presence of S and in the presence of at least one witness who attests the signature.

It is worth noticing that it is not actually necessary for the mother and partner to be in a sexual relationship. Although the clinic is unlikely to agree to treat a couple if it is felt they do not have a close relationship.

The fact that the female partner is not described as a mother is odd. Especially given that the male partner of the mother (as we shall see shortly) in equivalent circumstances is treated as a father.[36] One possible explanation is that the law is wedded to the idea that a child can have only one mother and one father. Indeed the HFEA 2008 seems to go to considerable lengths to ensure that a child does not have two of one kind of parent. It may be thought to be to stretch the conventional understanding of a family too far to hold that a child has two mothers. Alternatively it might be thought simply to amount to a fiction to say a child has two mothers. The child will know that cannot be true. However in cases of assisted reproduction, it is no more of a fiction to say a woman's female partner is the mother, than to say a male partner is a father.

---

[36] Leanne Smith (2007). See also Wallbank (2004a).

## 4 Who is the child's father?

The law on fatherhood is much more complex. A man[37] who wishes to prove that he is the father of a child must show:

1. that he is genetically the father of the child;[38] or

2. that one of the legal presumptions of paternity applies and has not been rebutted; or

3. that he is a father by virtue of one of the statutory provisions governing assisted reproduction; or

4. that an adoption order or parental order has been made in his favour.

The core notion of paternity has traditionally been seen as a biological or genetic concept. A man is the father of a child genetically related to him.[39] Until recently it was difficult to prove whether a father was genetically related to a child and so the law had to rely on certain presumptions. Now DNA testing can prove conclusively whether a man is the father of a child. However, the legal presumptions are still of importance because they explain who the father of a child is if no tests have been carried out.[40]

### A Legal presumptions of paternity

These are the circumstances in which fatherhood is presumed:

1. If a married woman gives birth it is presumed that her husband is the father of the child.[41] This presumption is sometimes known as *pater est quem nuptiae demonstrant* (or *pater est* for short). It does not apply to unmarried cohabitants.[42] If the birth takes place during the marriage but conception took place before the marriage the *pater est* presumption still applies. The presumption also applies if it is clear[43] that the conception took place during a marriage, even if death or divorce has ended that marriage by the time the birth occurs.[44] There will therefore be conflicting presumptions if the child could have been conceived during a first marriage but is born during the course of the wife's second marriage. It is not clear who the law would regard as the father in such a situation. It is suggested that the second husband should be regarded as the father, it being more likely that he is the genetic father. He is also the man who would act in the parental role during the child's upbringing. Against this view is the argument that it would be wrong to presume that the wife committed adultery.

   The *pater est* presumption is controversial, although no doubt statistically it is more likely than not that a husband is the father of his wife's child. It is also possible to see the presumption as being based on the policy of seeking to avoid a child not having a

---

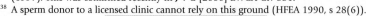

[37] Only a man can be a father: *X, Y, Z v UK* [1997] 2 FLR 892, [1997] 3 FCR 341 ECtHR, discussed in Lind (1997). This was confirmed recently in *J v C* [2006] EWCA Civ 551.

[38] A sperm donor to a licensed clinic cannot rely on this ground (HFEA 1990, s 28(6)).

[39] This was confirmed in *Leeds Teaching Hospital NHS Trust v A* [2003] EWHC 259, [2003] 1 FCR 599.

[40] See Freeman and Richards (2006) for a fascinating study of the legal and social ramifications of DNA testing.

[41] *Banbury Peerage Case* (1811) 1 Sim & St 153 HL.

[42] Although it does to parties in a void marriage: Legitimacy Act 1976, s 1.

[43] The court will refer to the normal gestation period, although the House of Lords in *Preston-Jones v Preston-Jones* [1951] AC 391 HL could not agree on the definition of a gestational period.

[44] A cynic might regard this presumption as unrealistic in some cases. If a child is conceived and shortly afterwards there is a divorce, that may well suggest a third party is the father.

father. Thorpe LJ in *Re H and A (Children)*[45] has doubted the relevance of the presumption. He explained, 'as science has hastened on and as more and more children are born out of marriage it seems to me that the paternity of any child is to be established by science and not by legal presumption of inference'.[46] Without the presumption, however, children will have no legal father until tests are carried out. There is some doubt over the extent to which children of married couples are the children of the husband. It has been claimed that around 15 per cent of children born to married couples are in fact not the children of their husband.[47] A more reliable estimate puts the figure at 4 per cent.[48]

2. The law presumes that if a man's name appears on the birth certificate of a child, he is the child's father.[49] If the couple are married then there is a statutory obligation on both parties to register the birth within 42 days. If the mother is unmarried the obligation rests on the mother alone. The unmarried father does not have a right to have his name registered and a blank can be left in that space if the mother wishes.[50] If the unmarried father wishes to be registered as the father then it is necessary for either the mother to consent or for the father to prove his genetic fatherhood through a court order.[51] As we shall discuss below, the law on birth registration is soon to be amended to encourage both parents to jointly register the birth.[52]

3. It is not clear whether the making of a parental responsibility agreement will be regarded as prima facie evidence of paternity, although the Lord Chancellor's Consultation Paper[53] believes it does. *R v Secretary of State for Social Security, ex p West*[54] suggests that a parental responsibility order by consent can be regarded as evidence of paternity by the Child Support Agency.

4. The court may also infer paternity simply from the facts of the case. For example, if it were shown that the mother and the man spent the night together at the time the conception is said to have taken place, this would be evidence of the man's paternity.

## B Reforming the law on birth registration

The Welfare Reform Act 2010 has put in place the framework for amending the law on birth registration. The provisions of the Act state that regulations will provide the detail of the new approach. Consultation is currently taking place on the content of those regulations.[55] The purpose of the reforms is to encourage the registration of the birth by both the mother and father. The Green Paper preceding the 2010 Act stated:

> Our proposal is that legislation around birth registration for unmarried parents should reflect that parenting is a joint undertaking and it should therefore make both parents equally

---

[45] [2002] 2 FCR 469.

[46] At p. 479.

[47] Sterling (2009). This figure was based on the percentage of CSA paternity tests which were false. But that is hardly a representative sample of the population.

[48] King and Jobling (2009).

[49] Births and Deaths Registration Act 1953, s 34(2); *Brierley v Brierley* [1918] P 257.

[50] See *A v H (Registrar General for England and Wales and another intervening)* [2009] 3 FCR 95 for a case where an unmarried father told a registrar untruthfully he was married and was thereby wrongly registered as the father.

[51] Births and Deaths Registration Act 1953, s 10(1)(a).

[52] Department for Work and Pensions (2008).

[53] Lord Chancellor's Department (1998).

[54] [1999] 1 FLR 1233.

[55] Department for Work and Pensions (2008a).

responsible for registering the birth of their child . . . The key benefit of an approach that places equal responsibility on both parents to register is that it is in keeping with the Government's desire to promote responsible fatherhood.[56]

It is likely that the new regulations will impose a duty on the mother when registering the birth of the child to state who the father is. Currently there is no such obligation. The Government acknowledges that there are some cases where this will not be possible: impossibility (the father's identity is unknown); impracticability (e.g. the current whereabouts of the father are unknown) or unreasonableness (where the mother or child will be in danger if there is a registration).[57] Currently some 84 per cent of children born to unmarried couples are jointly registered and the proposals will therefore only aim to deal with a small minority. What is far from clear about the government proposals is the sanction that will be imposed on a mother who refuses to disclose the identity of the father. Or, more to the point, what a registrar can do if a mother says that she met the father only once in a pub and does not remember much about him. Whether she is telling the truth or not cannot be ascertained. It is hard to imagine how the proposed reforms will be workable.

The issue of birth registration has proved a highly controversial one. As Andrew Bainham points out there are four interests at stake in the process: the state, the mother, the father and the child.[58]

1. *The State.* Bainham argues that the state has an interest because the state has an interest in ensuring the 'orderly assumption of responsibility by parents from the moment of the child's birth'.[59] This is true, but it is debatable whether registration has much to do with ensuring parents look after their children. One area where the state might is in relation to enforcement of child support. As seen in Chapter 5, child support rests in biological parentage, but it is not always clear who is a child's father and in such a case child support may not be collectable. If all fathers were registered then this difficulty could be overcome. Less important interests of the state may include the collection of demographic data and the creation of identity confirming documentation.

2. *The child.* Bainham claims that a child has a right to be registered at birth.[60] This right is included in the United Nations Convention on the Rights of the Child.[61] It can be seen as a way of protecting the right of the child to know their genetic origins, which is protected in article 8 of the ECHR. We will be discussing this alleged right later in this chapter. Jane Fortin[62] notes that the child also has interests to ensure that the mother is not caused emotional harm or put in physical danger as a result of the registration process.

3. *The mother.* Bainham[63] sees the interest of the mother as being part of her right to respect for private life under article 8. By being registered as the mother she can establish herself as having the legal rights and responsibilities of parenthood. He notes that she has an interest in the naming of the father under the current law, in that the registered father will thereby acquire parental responsibility. Another interest (not emphasised by Bainham) is

---

[56] Department for Work and Pensions (2008a).
[57] As Barton (2008b) points out these can also arise in the case of married fathers. He questions whether there need to be exemptions in such cases from joint registration in marriage.
[58] Bainham (2008c).
[59] Bainham (2008c: 450).
[60] Bainham (2008c).
[61] Article 7.
[62] Fortin (2009a).
[63] Bainham (2008c).

that the mother may wish to keep the identity of the father hidden, either to protect her private life or to protect herself or the child from violence.

4. *The father.* As Bainham argues, the father has a particular interest in registration because although birth is a readily observable event establishing maternity, the birth registration document is the most obvious way a father can establish paternity. It enables the possibility of establishing a relationship with the child at some point. If his name is not on the birth certificate and the mother does not want the father to see the child, there is little likelihood of the child and father having a relationship at any point.

Bainham's conclusion in weighing up these interests is that the fundamental rights of the child should be central. As he emphasises, these rights are not based in welfare, but autonomy. The significance being, he argues, that simply showing that the registration will cause harm to the child will not necessarily be sufficient to defeat a claim based on autonomy. In putting the argument this way he does not support the approach of the Government which puts the case for joint birth registration on the basis that it is beneficial for the child to know who the father is.[64] Bainham sees the current law as giving primary weight to the interests of the mother rather than being based on seeking to promote the welfare of the child. He argues with this in mind there should be a clear legal duty on mothers to identify the father wherever possible. Except in a case of rape he does not think that mothers have a good reason not to name the father. As Jane Fortin[65] notes it is hard to see why only rape counts as an exception. If the father has been abusive to the mother in the past, he may well pose a serious risk to the mother and child in the future. However, as she points out, article 8 is not an absolute right and needs to be balanced against the interests of others. Bainham's assumption that the right to know one's genetic origins necessarily trumps the interests of the mother is not made out in the ECHR case law.

It is interesting that Bainham does not go so far as to suggest there should be a DNA test of all children and their alleged parents, 'something which would be a move too far for almost everyone'.[66] It is not clear why he thinks this is 'too far'. If we think registration of genetic parentage is a fundamental right the minor inconvenience for adults of the test or the expense involved does not seem a good enough reason not to do this. Perhaps the fact that DNA tests of all do not seem plausible and few suggest it, indicate that in fact even supporters of the importance of gentic parentage, like Bainham, accept it is not that fundamental a right.

Julie Wallbank has also written opposing the Government's proposals and Bainham's support of them.[67] She argues that we need to remember the social class of the group of people targeted in these proposals: unmarried mothers who are not registering births jointly. She refers to sociological research into these women which suggests that they are socially and economically vulnerable. They are often fearful of the father and it cannot be assumed that the father wishes to be involved in the child's life, or if he does that it will be beneficial. To impose obligations to name fathers on this group of women is unjustifiable. Wallbank doubts joint registration will provide any practical benefit to the children in question and may create risks for them.

Another issue to consider is that the reforms may work against the interests of lesbian couples who have used a friend as a sperm donor, on the understanding that he is to play no role in the child's life.[68] Having to register the man as the father may not reflect the intentions of any of the parties, nor the reality of the child's life.

[64] Department for Children, Schools and Families (2009).
[65] Fortin (2009a).
[66] Bainham (2008c: 459).
[67] Wallbank (2009).
[68] Sheldon (2009).

The resolution of these debates turns on two questions. First, how important is the right to know one's genetic origins. This is an issue we shall look at later in this chapter. Second, how much weight do we attach to a woman's choice not to register the father? Do we respect her assessment of what is best for the child, bearing in mind the socio-economic circumstances of the couples in question, or is it necessary to override her concerns in order to protect the child and the father's rights?

## C Rebutting legal presumptions of paternity

Section 26 of the Family Law Reform Act 1969 states that the legal presumptions of paternity can be rebutted on the balance of probabilities. In *S v S, W v Official Solicitor (or W)*[69] Lord Reid thought that the presumptions should be regarded as weak, and could be rebutted with only a little evidence.[70] There are two main ways whereby a man presumed to be the father could rebut the presumption. The first and most reliable is to seek a court order for genetic tests (normally through comparing DNA samples). There is power to order such tests under s 20 of the Family Law Reform Act 1969, although, as will be noted later, the court in some cases will refuse to order tests to be performed. If a man is shown to be the father of the child through genetic tests then he is legally the father of the child, and if another man was presumed to be the father he is no longer so regarded. In *F v CSA*[71] it was unclear whether the father of the child was the mother's husband or her lover. The lover was assessed by the Child Support Agency. He refused to undergo blood tests: this refusal led to a presumption that he was the father.[72] This presumption was held to be stronger than the presumption of legitimacy. The second way that a man could seek to rebut a presumption that he was the father would be to introduce evidence to undermine the logical basis of the presumption. So a husband could rebut the presumption that he was the father of his wife's child by introducing evidence that he was abroad at the time of the alleged conception, or that he was impotent.

## D Fathers and assisted reproduction

There are various forms of assisted reproduction:[73]

1. *Assisted insemination.* This refers to the placing of sperm into the mother (other than by sexual intercourse) leading to fertilisation. It is common to distinguish insemination using the husband's sperm (AIH) and insemination using a donor's sperm (AID).

2. *In vitro fertilisation (IVF).* This technique involves mixing in a dish an egg and sperm. The fertilised egg is then placed in the woman's uterus. The sperm and/or egg may come from the couple themselves or donors.

3. *Gamete intrafallopian transfers (GIFT).* Here a donated egg is placed with the sperm (either of the husband or a sperm donor) in the womb.

---

[69] [1972] AC 24.
[70] In *Re Moynihan* [2000] 1 FLR 113 a higher standard of proof was suggested, but the Court of Appeal in *Re H and A (Children)* [2002] 2 FCR 469 preferred *S v S*.
[71] [1999] 2 FLR 244.
[72] See also *Secretary of State for Work and Pensions v Jones* [2003] EWHC 2163 (Fam).
[73] A thorough analysis of the law on assisted reproduction can be found in Deech and Smajdor (2007) and Herring (20010d: ch. 7). See Horsey (2007) and Probert (2004b) on the law prior to the HFEA 2008.

4. *Intra-cytoplasmic sperm injection (ICSI)*. This involves the injection of a sperm into an egg with a very fine needle. The resulting embryo is placed in the woman.

The law governing assisted reproduction is found in the Human Fertilisation and Embryology Acts 1990 and 2008. The starting point in ascertaining parenthood in cases of assisted reproduction is that the same rules that govern fatherhood in other cases apply. The genetic father, or a man presumed to be the father by virtue of one of the presumptions above, will be the father in a case of assisted reproduction unless he can find a statutory provision that states otherwise. In other words, the 'default' position, in the absence of any provision to the contrary, is that the genetic father is the legal father. Any man who is a father as a result of provisions in the Act is a father in the full sense of the law and cannot, for example, seek to escape liability under the Child Support legislation on the basis that he is not the biological father.[74]

The Human Fertilisation and Embryology Acts provides for the following exceptions to the basic rule that the genetic father is the child's father:

1. Section 41 HFEA 2008 makes clear that a man who donates sperm to a licensed clinic is not the father of any child born using that sperm as long as his sperm is used in accordance with his consent under Sch 3 of the 1990 Act. The protection does not cover the donor who consents to sperm for use with his wife, but it is used for another woman.[75] He will be regarded as the father of any child born. The donor must trust the clinic not to use his sperm outside the terms of his consent. The sperm donor's identity can be revealed to a child who seeks to discover the donor's identity if the sperm was donated after April 2005.[76]

2. A man who has died before his sperm is used in procedures leading to pregnancy is not the father of any child born using that sperm.[77] A dead man's sperm can only be used where he has consented to its use.[78] A man can be a father and registered on the birth certificate if the child is conceived after his death using sperm where he had given permission, or if donor sperm is used before his death.[79]

The HFEA 2008 also provides that a man not genetically related to a child is the legal father in the following circumstances:

1. Under s 35 the husband of a woman who gives birth as a result of a licensed clinic's assisted reproductive treatment is presumed to be the child's father unless he shows that he did not consent *and* that he is not the child's genetic father.[80] It should be noted that a clinic is very unlikely to provide services to a married woman without her husband's consent[81] and so it should be rare that the question of consent will be raised. In *Leeds Teaching Hospital NHS Trust v A*[82] a wife's egg was mixed by mistake with the sperm of Mr B, rather

---

[74] *Re CH (Contact Parentage)* [1996] 1 FLR 569, [1996] FCR 768; *Leeds Teaching Hospital NHS Trust v A* [2003] EWHC 259 (Fam), [2003] 1 FCR 599.

[75] *Leeds Teaching Hospital NHS Trust v A* [2003] EWHC 259 (Fam), [2003] 1 FCR 599.

[76] Human Fertilisation and Embryology Authority (Disclosure of Donor Information) Regulations 2004.

[77] HFEA 2008, s 42(1).

[78] In *Centre for Reproductive Medicine v U* [2002] FL 267, Butler-Sloss P rejected an argument that the husband's withdrawal of his consent before his death was the result of undue influence.

[79] HFEA 2008, ss 39, 40.

[80] HFEA 1990, s 28(2).

[81] The Human Fertilisation and Embryology Authority Code of Practice, para 5.7 makes this clear.

[82] [2003] 1 FCR 599, discussed Ford and Morgan (2003).

than that of her husband (Mr A). It was held that Mr A had not consented to the treatment of his wife *with that sperm* and therefore he was not the father under s 28 of the 1990 (which is in similar terms to s 35 of the 2008 Act). As Mr B's sperm had been used without his consent, s 28(6) (the equivalent to s 41, discussed above) did not apply and so he was the father. Sally Sheldon[83] makes the interesting point that had it been the eggs that had been mixed the position would have been different. Mrs A would be the mother because she gave birth. Why should it matter whether it was the sperm or the eggs that were muddled up?

2. Under s 37 a man will be treated as the father of a child born to a woman[84] as long as the 'agreed fatherhood conditions' are satisfied. These are as follows:

---

## LEGISLATIVE PROVISION

**Human Fertilisation and Embryology Act 2008, section 37(1)**

(1) The agreed fatherhood conditions referred to in section 36(b) are met in relation to a man ('M') in relation to treatment provided to W under a licence if, but only if,—

(a) M has given the person responsible a notice stating that he consents to being treated as the father of any child resulting from treatment provided to W under the licence,

(b) W has given the person responsible a notice stating that she consents to M being so treated,

(c) neither M nor W has, since giving notice under paragraph (a) or (b), given the person responsible notice of the withdrawal of M's or W's consent to M being so treated,

(d) W has not, since the giving of the notice under paragraph (b), given the person responsible—

   (i) a further notice under that paragraph stating that she consents to another man being treated as the father of any resulting child, or

   (ii) a notice under section 44(1)(b) stating that she consents to a woman being treated as a parent of any resulting child, and

(e) W and M are not within prohibited degrees of relationship in relation to each other.

---

Notice that for this provision to apply there is no need to show that the man and woman are in a sexual relationship or even living together. However, a clinic is only likely to provide treatment to a couple in a close relationship. To rely on s 37 the treatment must take place in a licensed clinic,[85] registered by the British Human Fertilisation and Embryology Authority.[86] Cases of so-called DIY treatment will be discussed next.

---

[83] Sheldon (2005).

[84] The provision does not apply to married women receiving treatment with their husbands (s 28(2) is the relevant provision for them): *Leeds Teaching Hospital NHS Trust v A* [2003] EWHC 259 (Fam), [2003] 1 FCR 599.

[85] *U v W (Attorney-General Intervening)* [1997] 2 FLR 282, [1998] 1 FCR 526.

[86] Department of Health (2010) indicates the Human Fertilisation and Embryology Authority may be abolished and merged into the Care Quality Commission.

## E DIY assisted reproduction

> **TOPICAL ISSUE**
>
> ## Why not DIY?
>
> In a case of do-it-yourself insemination, where, for example, a woman obtains sperm via the Internet[87] or from a friend and uses a syringe to impregnate herself, the normal rules apply. The donor of the sperm will be treated as the father, and the woman who gives birth as the mother. The Human Fertilisation and Embryology Acts do not alter these basic rules as the procedures do not take place within a licensed clinic. There is one exception to this: s 35 of the Human Fertilisation and Embryology Act 2008 suggests that if the mother is married then her husband (and not the sperm donor) is the father, unless it can be shown that the husband did not consent to the use of the sperm.[88] In all other cases, the sperm donor in a DIY case will be the father and can thereby become liable to pay child support for the child.[89]

## F An analysis of the allocation of parenthood in HFE Acts

There are several notable features of the law on allocation of parenthood following the HFEA 2008. One is that in cases of assisted reproduction the father's status is secured through the mother.[90] He acquires parental status through being her husband or as a result of her consenting to him being recognised as the father in order to satisfy the agreed parenthood conditions. That might reflect a lingering suspicion that a non-genetic father is not a real father and that there is a need for the mother to vet and approve him as a suitable man.

As a result of the provisions in the Human Fertilisation and Embryology Acts 1990 and 2008, some children can be deemed fatherless. This might arise where a single woman (or a married woman acting without her husband's consent) becomes pregnant as a result of AID provided by a licensed clinic. The donor could not be the father due to s 41, and the legislation does not provide for anyone else to be the father. A similar situation arises if a man's sperm is used after his death. Some have criticised the fact that the law allows a child to be fatherless; but, without breaching the principle that sperm donors should not be fathers, it is hard to see how the law can avoid this. However, it fits uneasily with the approach taken elsewhere in the law that assumes it is important for a child to have a link with a father.[91]

One interesting observation on these legally fatherless children is that the law here, for the first time, is moving away from the view that a child must have one father and one mother.[92] Hale LJ has stated that it is clearly in the child's interests to have a father, if possible.[93]

---

[87] Try http://www.mannotincluded.com if you are interested! There have been reports of the first child born in the UK as a result of Internet sperm (BBC (2003)). According to BBC Newsonline (2009g) there is an 'underground world' of sperm donation through the Internet.

[88] An unmarried couple cannot rely on s 28(3) because that applies only where the couple receive treatment in a licensed clinic.

[89] BBC Newsonline (2007h).

[90] Lind and Hewitt (2008).

[91] Smith (2010).

[92] Lind and Hewitt (2009).

[93] *Re R (A Child)* [2003] 1 FCR 481, para 27.

However, she went on to accept that that was not always possible. One prominent theme within the present law is that a child, as far as possible, should have one father and one mother, and can never have more than one mother or one father. Richards has complained of the 'very persistent prejudice that children should never have more than two parents and when a new one arrives, an old one has to go'.[94] The assumption that there can be only one mother and one father is, presumably, tied to genetic parentage. However, technological advances mean that it would now be possible for a child to be born genetically related to two women. It was recently announced that scientists were able to create an embryo which was genetically related to three people.[95] Techniques involving artificial sperm are progressing quickly.[96] If biology no longer necessitates the two-parent rule, maybe it is time to abandon it.[97] Also it restricts the law and means that the law cannot recognise that there may be a number of men or women playing a parental role in the child's life.[98]

These points may reflect a broader point that the law seems fixated on the traditional family form of a mother and father for each child.[99] This explains why the law is reluctant to accept a parent having two mothers, which produces such a strange set of provisions dealing with same-sex parents. As Alison Diduck[100] puts it:

> Like fatherhood under the Human Fertilisation and Embryology Act 1990, lesbian parenthood is acquired on a basis that mimics rather than overcomes traditional norms and biology.
>
> It applies a type of presumption of paternity to partnered lesbian women and instantiates rather than challenges hetero normativity and 'nature'. It both biologises and heterosexes 'parent' by ascribing that status on the basis of a person forming an exclusive sexual link with the biological parent . . . [W]e are left with a situation in which legal parenthood remains limited in number and subtly gendered.

From a different perspective there have been complaints that the HFEA 2008 departs too much from the principle that parentage should match genetics. However, not everyone is happy about the extension to the notion of parenthood provided for in the 2008 Act reforms. Thérèse Callus[101] objects that the reforms confuse parental role and parental status. She thinks the parental role is very important, but carrying out a parental role is different from having a parental status. Andrew Bainham argues:

> The fact that someone is doing some of the things which parents do does not make that person the parent. The true claim which same-sex partners and other social parents have is that they should be given the legal powers which are necessary to enable them to look after a child properly and it is the status of possessing parental responsibility which is best designed to achieve this.[102]

Such arguments lead some to the conclusion that parentage should follow genetics and that we should use parental responsibility to recognise the role played by the partners of women receiving assisted reproduction using donated sperm.[103]

---

[94] Richards (1995a: 21). See also Kandel (1994).
[95] BBC Newsonline (2008f).
[96] BBC Newsonline (2009b).
[97] Wallbank (2004a).
[98] Lind and Hewitt (2009).
[99] Lind and Hewitt (2009); McCandless and Sheldon (2010).
[100] Diduck (2007: 465).
[101] Callus (2008).
[102] Bainham (2008a: 348).
[103] See the discussion in Bainham (2008a).

## G Parental orders: surrogacy

A married couple can become parents through a parental order. This is designed for use following a surrogacy arrangement.[104] Surrogacy involves an agreement whereby the 'gestational mother'[105] agrees to bear a child for someone else ('the commissioning parent or parents'). The Surrogacy Arrangements Act 1985 defines a surrogacy arrangement as one made before the woman began to carry the child 'with a view to any child carried in pursuance of it being handed over to, and parental responsibility being met (so far as practicable) by another person or persons'.[106] The aim is that the gestational mother will hand over the baby after birth to the commissioning parent and that the gestational mother will not exercise parental responsibility. Surrogacy can cover a wide range of different forms. The genetic link between the commissioning parents can vary: the gestational mother could be impregnated with both the sperm and the egg of donors; or the child could be born through the gestational mother being artificially inseminated with either the father's or a sperm donor's sperm.

Whatever the form of the surrogacy, the legal attribution of parenthood is straightforward. It is clear that the gestational mother is the mother and the genetic father is the legal father unless he is a sperm donor providing sperm to a licensed clinic. However, it is possible for the commissioning couple to apply to a court for a parenting order, the effect of which is that they will be treated as the parents of the child. On the making of the order the child will be treated as the child of the applicants.[107] The order will vest parental responsibility exclusively in the applicants, and the parental status and parental responsibility of anyone else (and specifically the gestational mother) will be thereby extinguished.[108] The order will be registered in the Parental Order Register.[109] To obtain an order it is necessary to show:

1. Either the sperm, or eggs, or both, came from the commissioning husband or wife.

2. The applicants are married, civil partners or in 'an enduring family relationship and are not within prohibited degrees of relationship in relation to each other'.[110]

3. The applicants must both be over 18.

4. At least one of the applicants must be domiciled in the UK.[111]

5. The child must, at the time of the order, live with the applicants.[112]

6. The order must be made within six months of the child's birth.[113]

---

[104] Douglas (1991: ch. 7); Hibbs (1997); and Cook, Day Sclater and Kaganas (2003) provide useful discussions of surrogacy.

[105] Often known as the surrogate mother, although there has been some debate over whether it is the commissioning mother or the gestational mother who is the surrogate: see Morgan (1994).

[106] Section 1(2) (as amended by Children Act 1989, Sch 13, para 56).

[107] Although the child will still be within the prohibited degrees of the birth family for marriage purposes and the law of incest.

[108] HFEA 2008, s 54.

[109] When someone is 18 he or she can be supplied with a copy of his or her birth certificate (which will reveal the identity of the birth family), and counselling facilities will be available: Adoption Act 1976, s 51, applied by Parental Orders (Human Fertilisation and Embryology) Regulations 1994.

[110] Section 54, Human Fertilisation and Embryology Act 2008 amended the 1990 Act to extend the list of those who can apply beyond married couples.

[111] This includes the Channel Islands or Isle of Man.

[112] Human Fertilisation and Embryology Act 2008, s 54(4).

[113] Human Fertilisation and Embryology Act 2008, s 54(3).

7. The father must give full and unconditional consent[114] to the making of the order.[115]

8. The gestational mother must give her full and unconditional consent to the making of the order, at least six weeks after the birth.

9. The husband of the woman who gave birth to the child must give his full and unconditional consent.[116]

10. Money or other benefits have not been given to the surrogate mother, unless they are reasonable expenses or the court has retrospectively authorised the payments.

11. The pregnancy was not the result of sexual intercourse between the surrogate mother and male applicant.

12. The court must decide to make the order with the child's welfare being the paramount consideration and the checklist of factors in section 1 of the Adoption and Children Act 2002 being applied.[117]

It should be stressed that this is a highly restrictive list of requirements. Most notably, the applicants must be married and at least one of them have a genetic link to the child. However, there is no requirement that the couple be approved by the local authority as suitable parents, as would be the case if they wished to adopt the child. If the commissioning couple are unable to apply for a parenting order, or if the application fails, then it is still open to ask for a residence order authorising that the child live with the commissioning couple.

There has been some litigation over the obligation to expenses. In *Re S (Parental Order)*[118] Hedley J was willing to reptrospectively authorise payments of $23,000 in excess of expenses because they 'do not offend any broad issue of principle in relation to the buying of children and are not greatly disproportionate to expenses reasonably incurred; nor are they tainted by any issues of bad faith'. In *Re X (Foreign Surrogacy)*[119] it was held that although the sum paid exceeded the expenses it was not 'disproportionate'. In that case it was also emphasised that the surrogate had not been taken advantage of, nor had there been deception of the authorities. These decisions suggest that relatively small payments to surrogates may be retrospectively approved, providing there is no deception or abuse.

We will discuss surrogacy in detail later in this chapter.

## H Adoption

Adoption will be discussed in detail in Chapter 11. There are two points to be stressed here. The first is that before adoption takes place, prospective adoptive parents must undergo close scrutiny through the adoption panel of the local authority. The court will further consider whether the adoption is in the child's best interests. The court can make the order only if the parents consent or, *inter alia*, the court decides that it would be in the child's welfare for the parents' consent to be dispensed with. Secondly, once the adoption order is made, the adoptive couple acquire the full status of parenthood. They do not merely obtain parental responsibility but are considered by the law to be the child's parents.

---

[114] The consents mentioned are unnecessary if the person cannot be found or is incapable of giving agreement.
[115] This requirement is of consent to the order, not just consent to the application: Human Fertilisation and Embryology Act 2008, s 54.
[116] *Re X and another (foreign surrogacy)* – [2009] 2 FCR 312.
[117] Human Fertilisation and Embryology (Parental Orders) Regulations 2010, SI 985/2010, sch 1.
[118] [2010] 1 FLR 1156.
[119] [2009] 2 FCR 312.

# 5 Losing parenthood

Legal parenthood will only come to an end if an adoption order is made or a parental order under s 54 of the Human Fertilisation and Embryology Act 2008 is awarded. In either of these cases the original parents (the parents at birth) cease to be the legal parents and the applicants take over as parents.

# 6 Social parents

Under this heading we will discuss the various ways the law treats those who are caring for the child in a parental way, even though they may not actually be the parents. There are several categories: guardianship; foster parents; special guardians; treating a child as a child of the family; step-parents; and others caring for children.

## A Guardianship

The law is naturally concerned about children whose parents die. In part this is dealt with by enabling parents with parental responsibility to appoint someone to be a guardian of their children in the event of their death. The courts can also appoint a guardian. There is no restriction over who can be appointed as a guardian[120] and more than one guardian can be appointed.[121] The parents may appoint anyone they choose, although step-parents are common choices. A local authority cannot be appointed as a guardian.[122]

### (i) The appointment of guardians by parents

Parents with parental responsibility can appoint guardians,[123] as can people who are guardians themselves. But a father without parental responsibility cannot appoint a guardian; nor can a non-parent with parental responsibility. The appointment of a guardian must be written, dated, and signed.[124] Usually the appointment is made as a term in a will, although this is not necessary.

At what point does the guardianship come into effect? This depends upon whether or not one of the parents has a residence order at the time when a parent dies:

1. Where a residence order has been made in favour of one of the parents the guardianship will take effect on the death of the parent with the residence order, even if the other parent is still alive and has parental responsibility. In such a case the child will have both a parent and a guardian.

2. Where there is no residence order in place, the guardianship only comes into effect once the last remaining parent with parental responsibility dies.[125] So, if a couple are married and the mother appoints a guardian and then dies, the appointed guardian will not

---

[120] It seems even a child can be a guardian of a child, but this would be highly unusual.
[121] Children Act 1989 (hereafter CA 1989), s 6.
[122] Nor can the director of social services be appointed in order to circumvent this restriction (*Re SH (Care Order: Orphan)* [1995] 1 FLR 746 at p. 749).
[123] Although a guardian can only be appointed by a person over the age of 18.
[124] CA 1989, s 5(5).
[125] CA 1989, s 5(7), (8). The surviving parent can apply for the appointment to be ended if he or she wishes.

actually become a guardian until the father also dies. By contrast, if a father is unmarried and without parental responsibility then the mother can appoint a guardian who will take office immediately on her death.

The explanation for the distinction between cases where there are or are not residence orders seems to lie in the fact that if there has been a residence order the court may have decided not to give residence to the other parent because they were unsuitable. In such a case, enabling the parent with the residence order to appoint a guardian may in effect protect the child. However, the law has been criticised. There are two particular concerns. The first is that the law produces uncertainty: both the parent and the guardian may have parental responsibility,[126] but the law does not say with whom the child should live. This need not cause us too much concern because the parties could resolve any dispute by applying to the court for a residence order if they are not able to reach agreement between themselves. The second concern is one of principle: Bainham argues that the position is contrary to the principle of continuing parental responsibility.[127] In theory, both parents with parental responsibility are on an equal footing and if one dies the other should take over. Certainly the law does not sit easily with the 'natural parent presumption' (that the child is better off with the natural parent unless the natural parent is manifestly unsuitable).[128] The law could be supported on the basis that the parent with the residence order has been given the right to decide with whom the child will live and that this power should continue after death. More convincing is the argument that, by giving both the guardian and the parent the authority to care for the child, the law maximises the chances that someone will be able to take over care of the child on the death of the parent with the residence order.

The person appointed to be guardian does not need to have been approved by the court or the local authority. It is notable that there is a very limited control on the making of an appointment; the absence of control over such appointments is in marked contrast to adoption or fostering.[129] However, there is power in the court to revoke a guardianship and this power could be used if the guardian was unsuitable. It is still arguable that a power to revoke guardianship once it has become apparent the guardian is unsuitable is not as effective protection for a child as requiring a would-be guardian to undergo some kind of vetting process.

### (ii) The appointment of guardians by courts

The court may consider appointing a guardian where the parents have both died without either of them appointing anyone as guardian of their children.[130] The court can also appoint a guardian even though the parents have appointed other guardians. This might occur if the person appointed by the parents as guardian is unable or unwilling to carry out the role. The court only has the power to appoint a guardian if there is no parent with parental responsibility who is alive, or if the parent with the residence order has died.[131] Usually this will follow an application to the court by the proposed guardian, although the court can act on its own motion. In deciding who to appoint, the child's welfare is to be the paramount consideration.[132] Clearly the court is likely to want to appoint someone who knows the child well.[133]

---

[126] If the parent was an unmarried father he may not have parental responsibility.
[127] Bainham (1998a: 181–5).
[128] Discussed further in Chapter 9.
[129] Douglas and Lowe (1992).
[130] Or having appointed an unsuitable or unwilling guardian.
[131] CA 1989, s 5(2).
[132] Though there is no requirement to consult the checklist in s 1(3) of CA 1989.
[133] *Re C (Minors) (Adoption by Relatives)* [1989] 1 FLR 222, [1989] FCR 744.

### (iii) The legal effects of guardianship

The effects of guardianship are as follows:

1. The guardian acquires parental responsibility.

2. The guardian can object to adoption.

3. The guardian can appoint a guardian to replace them on their death.

4. A guardian is not liable to provide financially for a child under the Children Act 1989 or child support legislation, nor under social security legislation.[134]

5. There are no succession rights on the intestate death of the guardian.[135]

6. No citizenship rights pass through a guardian.

It should be noted that guardians are given more 'rights' than a non-parent with parental responsibility (e.g. the rights on adoption), although they are not given all of the rights and responsibilities of a parent with parental responsibility. Although guardians are not liable for assessment under the child support legislation, guardians are under a legal duty to maintain the children and provide education, adequate food, clothing, medical aid and lodging. The explanation is that there was a fear that guardians would be deterred from accepting guardianship if they could become financially responsible for the child under the child support legislation.

### (iv) Revoking an appointment

Section 6 of the Children Act 1989 deals with revocation of a guardianship appointment. The guardianship can be revoked in the following ways:

1. The parent who made the appointment makes a subsequent appointment. This will revoke the first appointment unless it is clear the parent was seeking to appoint a second guardian.[136]

2. The parent who made the appointment can revoke it by a signed and dated document.[137]

3. If the appointment is made in a will it is revoked if the will or codicil is revoked.[138]

4. If the appointment is made by a document, the destruction of the document will end the appointment.[139]

5. If a spouse is appointed as guardian[140] this will be revoked by a subsequent divorce.[141]

### (v) Disclaimer

A guardian can disclaim the appointment within a reasonable length of time.[142] The disclaimer must be in writing. Once someone disclaims guardianship he or she ceases to have

---

[134] Social Security Administration Act 1992, s 78. It should be noted that guardians might be liable to support the child on their divorce under the Matrimonial Causes Act 1973 if the child were regarded as a 'child of the family'.

[135] Nor can the guardian claim in the event of the child's death.

[136] CA 1989, s 6(1).

[137] CA 1989, s 6(2).

[138] CA 1989, s 6(4).

[139] CA 1989, s 6(3).

[140] For example, if a step-parent is appointed as guardian.

[141] CA 1989, s 6(3A).

[142] CA 1989, s 6(5).

the rights and responsibilities of guardianship. There is no need for a person to consent to becoming a guardian, so the burden rests on the guardian to make the non-acceptance of the appointment clear as soon as possible.

### (vi) Termination

A court order can terminate guardianship. Anyone with parental responsibility, or the child him- or herself, can apply for a revocation, as can the court on its own motion.[143] The welfare principle governs the issue. The court may also decide to appoint a replacement guardian. The kind of circumstances in which the court may terminate a guardianship are where the guardian is failing properly to care for the child or where there is a dispute between, say, an unmarried father and the guardian which cannot be resolved, and the court decides the child's long-term future is with the father.

Termination of guardianship will occur on the death of the child, the death of the guardian, or on the child reaching majority. It may well be that the guardian's powers will terminate on the minor's marriage, but there is no clear provision to this effect.

## B Foster parents

### (i) The nature of foster parenthood

Foster parents[144] are people who look after children on a long-term basis, but are not related to them. The term therefore covers a wide variety of arrangements: from a friend asked by a mother to care for her child while the mother has a lengthy time in hospital, to a family approved by a local authority to look after children who have been taken into local authority care. The law draws an important distinction between those placements which are private (arranged by parents) and those which are public (arranged by the local authority).

### (ii) Private foster parents

The Children Act 1989 defines a 'privately fostered child'[145] as a child under 16 years of age cared for by someone who:

1. is not a parent;
2. does not have parental responsibility for the child;
3. is not a relative; and
4. has accommodated the child for at least 28 days.

The requirement that a foster parent must accommodate a child for at least 28 days means that babysitters, day-care centres, playgroups and nurseries are not classified as foster parents.

There is, in practice, limited regulation of private foster parents.[146] There is no need for a court or local authority to approve a private fostering arrangement, although the local authority should be notified by the foster parents of the fact they are fostering or intend to foster.[147] The local authority, in theory, can inspect the house where the child is living to

---

[143] CA 1989, s 6(7).

[144] Although the statute refers to 'foster parents', local authorities prefer to refer to 'foster carers'.

[145] CA 1989, s 66. See Laming (2003) for a call that the Government reconsider the law on private foster arrangements.

[146] It is now possible for a person who is thought by a local authority to be unsuitable to be a foster parent to be disqualified.

[147] Children (Private Arrangements for Fostering) Regulations 1991, SI 1991/2050, r 4.

check that it is suitable for fostering and may even supervise the fostering. In practice, many private fostering arrangements go unreported to any organ of the state.[148] Even where the local authority is notified of the arrangement, it is unlikely to intervene unless there is evidence that the child is being harmed.

Foster parents do not automatically acquire parental responsibility.[149] They are normally in the same position as anyone else who happens to be caring for a child at a particular time. They can rely on s 3(5) of the Children Act 1989:

---

**LEGISLATIVE PROVISION**

**Children Act 1989, section 3(5)**

A person who—

(a)  does not have parental responsibility for a particular child; but

(b)  has care of the child

may (subject to the provisions of this Act) do what is reasonable in all the circumstances of the case for the purpose of safe-guarding or promoting the child's welfare.

---

### (iii) Local authority foster parents

Local authority foster parents have a very special position in the Children Act 1989. The details of their position will be discussed in Chapter 11, but the law seeks to hold together two policies. On the one hand, there is the realisation that foster parents and children can form a close relationship which should be recognised and protected.[150] On the other hand, local authority foster parents are not normally intended to be permanent carers and it is necessary to ensure that local authorities can remove the child (perhaps with a view to placing the child with prospective adopters) when necessary. The balance is struck by restricting the foster parent's ability to apply for a residence order until the foster parents have cared for the child for three years.

## C Special guardians

The Adoption and Children Act 2002 created the status of special guardianship. This is intended to cover those who are full-time carers of children but are not going to take on the full status of parenthood. This is discussed further in Chapter 11.

## D Those who treat a child as a child of the family

Even if an adult is not a child's genetic parent, legal consequences will follow if he or she treats a child as 'a child of the family'.

---

[148]  Barton and Douglas (1995: 107) suggest that compiling the register is not high on the list of priorities of a local authority and that the power of inspection is rarely used; see Laming (2003).

[149]  In *Re M (A Child)* [2002] 1 FCR 88 the child was found to have family life with the foster carers for the purposes of article 8 of the European Convention on Human Rights.

[150]  Foster carers and their children can have family life together for the purposes of article 8: *R (On the Application of L)* v *Manchester CC* [2002] Fam Law 13.

## (i) What does 'a child of the family' mean?

The phrase 'child of the family' means any child of a married couple and any child treated by a married couple as a child of their family.[151] The definition therefore covers both genetic children of the marriage and a child to whom the spouses are not genetically related, but whom they have brought up as their child.[152] It covers stepchildren who are treated by step-parents as their own child. The phrase does not cover children brought up by unmarried couples.[153] To decide whether a child is a child of the family the Court of Appeal has proposed the test: 'the independent outside observer has to look at the situation and say: "does the evidence show that the child was treated as a member of the family?"'.[154] Therefore, the test focuses on the conduct of the adult rather than their beliefs.[155] The child must be treated as a child of *a family*. There must be a family – a husband and wife living together.[156] The child cannot be treated as a child of a family due to actions before he or she was born.[157] In *A v A (Family: Unborn Child)*[158] the man married a pregnant woman, believing the child to be his, but after the marriage, yet before the birth, the wife left the man. It was decided that he had not treated the child as a child of the family because the only way in which the husband had treated the child as if it were his own was before the birth. The decision has been criticised by some as being unduly narrow. It certainly could be that a wife could decide to go ahead with a pregnancy because of her husband's support. If he leaves her just before the birth there is an argument that he should be responsible for financial support.

One case which indicates how difficult the definition can be to apply is *Re A (Child of the Family)*.[159] Here two grandparents were looking after their grandchild after the mother fell ill. The grandparents in due course divorced and the issue arose whether the child was treated as a child of their family. The grandfather argued that he had treated the child as a grandchild and not as a child of his marriage. The court disagreed, relying on the following facts: the child called him 'dad'; the grandparents made important decisions relating to the child without referring to the mother; and the grandparents paid for the child's food and expenses without seeking recompense from the mother.[160]

## (ii) The consequences of treating a child as a child of the family

1. On divorce a spouse is liable to provide financial support for any child he or she treated as a child of the family under s 52 of the Matrimonial Causes Act 1973.[161]

2. A person who has treated a child as a child of the family may be liable to provide financial support under Sch 1 to the Children Act 1989.[162]

3. A person who has treated a child as a child of the family may be liable to provide financial support under the Domestic Proceedings and Magistrates' Courts Act 1978, s 38.

---

[151] CA 1989, s 105(1).
[152] Foster children placed by a local authority or voluntary agency are excluded from the definition.
[153] *J v J (A Minor: Property Transfer)* [1993] 2 FLR 56, [1993] 1 FCR 471.
[154] *D v D (Child of the Family)* (1981) 2 FLR 93 at p. 97, per Ormrod LJ.
[155] *Carron v Carron* [1984] FLR 805.
[156] Cohabiting for a fortnight was sufficient in *W v W* [1984] FLR 796.
[157] *A v A (Family: Unborn Child)* [1974] Fam 6.
[158] [1974] Fam 6.
[159] [1998] 1 FLR 347.
[160] Financial support on its own is not sufficient to establish that a man is treating the child as a child of the family: *M v M (Child of the Family)* [1984] FLR 796.
[161] See Chapter 5.
[162] See Chapter 5.

4. A person who has treated a child as a child of the family can apply as of right for a residence or contact order without needing to apply to the court for leave.[163]

5. A child may be able to claim against the estate of a deceased adult who has treated them as a child of the family under the Inheritance (Provision for Family and Dependants) Act 1975.[164]

By using the concept of a child of the family the law gives some recognition to social parenthood, although it is restricted to those who are married. The emphasis is on the imposition of responsibilities rather than granting rights. The person treating the child as if the child is his or hers acquires responsibilities towards the child as listed above, although he or she does not thereby acquire parental responsibility. The biological parents will still be liable to support the child under the Child Support, Pensions and Social Security Act 2000, the Children Act 1989 or the Matrimonial Causes Act 1973; and the social parent may also be liable to support the child under the concept of a child of the family. From the child's viewpoint this greatly increases the chances that someone will support them financially.

## E Step-parents

### (i) The legal position of step-parents

A step-parent is a person who marries the mother or father of a child.[165] Inaccurately, but commonly, the term is also used for an unmarried cohabitant who moves in with a child's parent.[166] It has been estimated that one in eight children will at some point in their childhood live in a household with a step-parent.[167] Step-parents, and particularly stepmothers, have often been stigmatised in fairy tales as terrifying figures for children. Research backs up the common perception that relationships between children and step-parents can be difficult, particularly where there are stepbrothers and stepsisters.[168] Of course, the quality of relationship between stepchildren and step-parents varies enormously, as indeed does the relationship between genetic parents and their children.[169] A recent study by Marjorie Smith found that many stepfamilies did not describe themselves using the label 'step-' but simply as families.[170] Another recent study on step-parenthood found that most children felt a continuing commitment to blood ties *and* a commitment to their stepfamilies.[171] In other words, the child felt able to accept the new step-parent but also wished to retain the relationship with the genetic parent. The researchers found 'commitment to the idea of family as a set of flexible interconnecting and supportive relationships'.[172] However, the research suggested that, in times of family stress, the stepfamily emphasised the genetic relationships, rather than the step-relationships.[173]

The law's treatment of step-parents is ambiguous. Even though a step-parent in practice often acts towards the child as a parent and indeed may be treated by the child as if they were

---

[163] CA 1989, s 10(5)(a).
[164] Inheritance (Provision for Family and Dependants) Act 1975, s 1(1)(d). See Chapter 12.
[165] The social and legal position of step-parents is discussed in M. Smith (2003). Ribbens McCarthy et al. (2003) found that many stepfamilies reject the 'step-' terminology and regard themselves simply as families.
[166] Barton (2009).
[167] Haskey (1994).
[168] Bar-Hava and Pryor (1998).
[169] Ferri and Smith (1998); Ribbens McCarthy et al. (2003).
[170] M. Smith (2003).
[171] Bornat, Dimmock, Jones and Peace (1999).
[172] Bornat, Dimmock, Jones and Peace (1999).
[173] See also Edwards, Gillies and McCarthy (1999).

their biological parent, the step-parent does not automatically acquire parental responsibility on marrying the parent.[174] However, if the step-parent reaches an agreement with the child's parents with parental responsibility, he or she can thereby gain parental responsibility.[175] It should be noted that a step-parent will need the consent of the non-resident parent (if he or she has parental responsibility) for this to happen. The alternative for a step-parent is to apply to the court for a parental responsibility order. This will be used, no doubt, mainly where the non-resident parent is refusing to consent to the sharing of the parental responsibility. The step-parent who acquires parental responsibility in either of these two ways will not lose it if their marriage to the parent comes to an end. However, they can have that parental responsibility brought to an end by a court order.[176] These provisions apply only to a person who marries a parent; they do not apply to a cohabitant of a parent. Another option for a step-parent is to adopt the child.[177] The step-parent is not under a legal obligation to support stepchildren, although if he or she treats a child as a child of the family he or she may be liable on divorce or separation to support the child, under the Matrimonial Causes Act 1973. On divorce a court may award a step-parent a contact order, but there is no presumption in favour of such an order.[178]

## F Others caring for the child

A family friend or relative may care for a child on a day-to-day basis without having an official role. Such a person does not acquire parental responsibility simply because he or she is caring for a child. However, the law does provide some ways in which day-to-day carers are regulated by the law:

1. It is possible to delegate parental responsibility. Under s 2(9) of the Children Act 1989 a person with parental responsibility may 'arrange for some or all of it to be met by one or more persons acting on his behalf'.[179] Hence a parent may delegate responsibility to a babysitter or childminder.[180] There is no need to obtain court approval of the delegation. However, delegation does not absolve someone with parental responsibility from any legal liability. For example, a parent may be guilty of a criminal offence involving neglect of children, even though they have delegated parental responsibility to someone else, as s 2(11) makes clear.

2. Under s 3(5) of the Children Act 1989 if an adult is caring for a child he or she 'may . . . do what is reasonable in all the circumstances of the case for the purpose of safeguarding or promoting the child's welfare'. The exact scope of this power and to what extent such a carer must consult with the parent is unclear.[181] It is generally accepted that a person

---

[174] Bartlett (1984: 914) argues that the step-parent should gain parental rights on marriage to the parent, but lose them on divorce. See Bainham (2006a: 61) for an argument for not treating a step-parent the same as a natural parent.

[175] CA 1989, s 4A. This section was added by the Adoption and Children Act 2002. For a discussion of the vulnerable position of the step-parent before these reforms see Masson (1984: ch. 14); Lowe (1997c).

[176] The application to do so can be brought by a person with parental responsibility or the child.

[177] See, further, Chapter 11.

[178] A contact order is available but there is no presumption of contact between a child and a step-parent, as was made clear in *Re H (A Minor) (Contact)* [1994] 2 FLR 776, [1994] FCR 419.

[179] CA 1989, s 2(9).

[180] Department for Children, Schools and Families (2008a: para 2.18).

[181] In *B v B (A Minor) (Residence Order)* [1992] 2 FLR 327, [1993] 1 FCR 211 a grandmother without parental responsibility caring for a child had difficulty in dealing with doctors and the educational authority in cases relating to children.

relying on s 3(5) cannot overrule a decision of a person with parental responsibility, but there is no provision explicitly to this effect.

3. A social parent with leave could apply to the court for a s 8 order.[182] If the child is living with that adult then he or she could acquire parental responsibility by virtue of a residence order.

4. A carer could seek to use wardship. The best-known circumstances are *Re D (A Minor) (Wardship: Sterilisation)*,[183] in which there were plans to sterilise an 11-year-old girl. Her parents did not object, but an educational psychologist who had been seeing the girl was concerned and used wardship to bring the issue to the court. However, wardship is available only in extreme cases. Following the Children Act 1989, in most cases an application for such a s 8 order will be most appropriate.

5. People caring for children have responsibilities. They commit criminal offences if they assault, ill-treat, neglect, abandon or expose a child in a way likely to cause unnecessary suffering or injury. Also a child can be taken into care on the basis of the lack of care provided by a carer.[184]

## 7 Relatives

Here we will consider the position of those who are a child's relatives.[185] First, we will look at the rights of family members under the Children Act 1989. It will also be necessary to examine the right to respect for family life protected under the Human Rights Act 1998. The Children Act defines relatives as including 'a grandparent, brother, sister, uncle, or aunt (whether of the full blood or half blood or by affinity) or step-parent'.[186] In the Children Act there is no clear legal status which flows from being a relation. There are some who argue for a more formalised position for relatives, giving them a clear set of rights.[187] The arguments are made especially in respect of grandparents.[188] Sociological studies demonstrate that most children hold their grandparents in special affection[189] and indeed grandparents often play a major role in child-care arrangements.[190] Over one-half of women in paid work with a child under five left the child with the child's grandparents.[191] Where a child is disabled, the role played by grandparents can be particularly significant.[192] There are dangers in talking about grandparents as a general group. One study suggested that grandmothers tended to play a more significant role in children's lives than grandfathers, and maternal grandparents than paternal grandparents.[193] In a recent study it was found that, on parental divorce, paternal

[182] CA 1989, s 10.
[183] [1976] Fam 185.
[184] *Lancashire CC v B* [2000] 1 FLR 583, [2000] 1 FCR 509.
[185] For a useful discussion of the psychological role that relatives can play, see Pryor (2003).
[186] CA 1989, s 105. The Family Law Act 1996 gives a much longer list of relatives, which is discussed in Chapter 6.
[187] Family Matters Institute (2009) See Masson and Lindley (2006) for an argument that relatives caring for children lack adequate support from the state.
[188] See Herring (2008c: ch. 7) for a detailed discussion on the law and social practice of grandparenting.
[189] Step-grandparents can play a significant role too.
[190] Hill and Tisdall (1997: 89–90); Douglas and Murch (2002a). For a discussion of the support siblings can offer each other, see Beckett and Hershman (2001).
[191] Social and Community Planning Research (2000).
[192] *Re J (Leave to Issue Application for Residence Order)* [2003] 1 FLR 114.
[193] Douglas and Ferguson (2003); Hunt (2006b)

grandparents often lost contact with their grandchildren and that grandparents suffered depression as a result.[194] This has led some to call for the law to grant grandparents a special legal status with attendant rights.

Opponents of such suggestions reply that giving wider family members rights will impinge on the rights of parents to raise their children as they think fit;[195] further, that to give grandparents and others rights would be to give them rights without having responsibilities for the child.[196] Douglas and Ferguson,[197] arguing against giving grandparents special legal rights, maintain that this would work against the norms that generally govern relations between grandparents, their children and grandchildren. They argue that these relationships are governed by 'the norm of non-interference': that is, that grandparents seek to support but not interfere in the role carried out by parents. Further, they argue that the sacrifices that grandparents make for their grandchildren are not seen as part of a reciprocal relationship (i.e. grandparents do not expect anything back from their labours of love for their grandchildren).[198]

This is a complex issue, partly because the nature of the relationships varies so much. For example, some children never see their aunts and to others an aunt may be a 'second mother'. It is therefore perhaps not surprising that the law is reluctant to set out specified rights and obligations flowing from a particular blood relationship. One danger in this area is that, by giving relatives parental responsibility, the child might become confused. An aunt is an aunt, not a parent. That said, parental responsibility is a legal term of art and a phrase unlikely to be used in everyday family life.

Under the Children Act 1989 there are various consequences of being a relative:

1. A relative can apply for a residence order or contact order without leave of the court where the child has lived with the relation for one year (or with the consent of the parents). Even if the child has lived with the relatives less than one year, the relative can still apply for a s 8 order, but leave of the court will be required.[199] A relative is unlikely to be successful in applying for a residence order against the wishes of the parents unless it is shown that the parents are clearly unsuitable.[200] In *Re D (Care: Natural Parent Presumption)*,[201] for example, the court had to decide whether a child should live with his father or grandmother. The Court of Appeal preferred the father, even though he had a history of drug abuse and had a number of children with different women, with some of whom he had no links. However, in *Re H (Residence: Grandparent)*[202] grandparents who had cared for a child for six years were granted a residence order, which was confirmed, despite the mother's objection. This was because there was such a strong relationship between the child and the grandparents. More commonly, a relative may apply for a contact order. In *Re A (Section 8 Order: Grandparent Application)*[203] the grandmother wanted contact with her young grandchildren after a bitter divorce. The Court of Appeal stated that, although

[194] Merrick (2000).
[195] See Crook (2001).
[196] Kaganas (2007b); Kaganas and Piper (2001: 268).
[197] Douglas and Ferguson (2003).
[198] Ferguson (2004).
[199] CA 1989, s 10(5B). For an argument that in relation to grandparents leave should not be required, see Drew and Smith (1999).
[200] *Re D (Care: Natural Parent Presumption)* [1999] 1 FLR 134.
[201] [1999] 1 FLR 134.
[202] [2000] Fam Law 715.
[203] [1995] 2 FLR 153, [1996] 1 FCR 467.

there was a presumption in favour of contact between a parent and a child, there was no such presumption of contact between a grandparent and a child, nor between any other relative and a child. It is clear that in each case the court will need to be persuaded that the relationship between the grandparent and the child is a close one and that contact will benefit the child. In many cases the court will be readily persuaded that the relationship is close.[204] The courts have acknowledged that to force a parent to permit contact between a child and a grandparent may be counter-productive if, for example, the parents regard the grandmother as interfering.[205] Siblings, of course, have a strong right to contact, but more distant relatives have been less successful than grandparents in contact cases.[206] In *W v W (Abduction: Joinder as Party)*[207] a 17-year-old was joined as a party to a child abduction case, after arguing that her mother was unable to protect her younger sister from the abusive father.

2. A grandparent and other relatives will have a strong case for contact with a child who is in care. If a local authority is 'looking after a child' then it is under a duty to promote contact between the child and the wider family.[208] The cases certainly suggest that contact between a grandparent and a child in care will normally be granted. So in *Re M (Care: Contact: Grandmother's Application for Leave)*[209] the Court of Appeal granted an order in favour of reasonable contact between a child and the grandparent. The court noted that grandparents have a special place in any child's affections. The court felt that when a child was in care a local authority had the burden of proof in proving why contact should not go ahead. In *Re W (A Child) (Contact: Leave to Apply)*[210] Wilson J accepted that the question of whether there was a presumption of contact between grandparents and children would need to be reconsidered.

3. Where the parents of a child have died without appointing a guardian, the courts are likely to consider appointing a relative as guardian.

4. The local authority is under an obligation to consider placing a child with relatives before taking a child into care.[211] Further, a local authority which is considering putting a child up for adoption should consider the possibility of placing a child with a relative before considering adoption by a stranger.[212] In *Re K (Adoption and Wardship)*,[213] where a Bosnian child was adopted in the UK, the fact that the grandfather and extended family were not consulted was seen as a serious flaw in the procedure, although in *Re R (A Child) (Adoption: Disclosure)*[214] Holman J held that the relatives should not be informed of the proposed adoption of a newborn baby, after the mother asked that the birth be kept confidential. Section 14A(5) of the Children Act 1989 allows a relative to apply for a special guardianship order.

---

[204] *Re M (Care: Contact: Grandmother's Application for Leave)* [1995] 2 FLR 86, [1995] 3 FCR 550.
[205] *Re F and R (Section 8 Order: Grandparent's Application)* [1995] 1 FLR 524. See also *Re S (Contact: Grandparents)* [1996] 1 FLR 158, [1996] 3 FCR 30.
[206] *G v Kirkless MBC* [1993] 1 FLR 805, [1993] 1 FCR 357 and *Re A (A Minor) (Residence Order: Leave to Apply)* [1993] 1 FLR 425, [1993] 1 FCR 870.
[207] [2010] 1 FLR 1342.
[208] See Chapter 11.
[209] [1995] 2 FLR 86, [1995] 3 FCR 550.
[210] [2000] 1 FCR 185.
[211] Adoption and Children Act 2002, s 1(4)(f) requires the court to consider the child's relationship with her relatives before making an adoption order.
[212] *Re R (A Child) (Adoption: Disclosure)* [2001] 1 FCR 238.
[213] [1997] 2 FLR 221; [1997] 2 FLR 230.
[214] [2001] 1 FCR 238.

5. Domestic violence injunctions. Under the Family Law Act 1996 non-molestation injunctions are available between 'associated persons', which includes relatives.[215]

6. Relatives may treat a child as a child of their family and this will trigger a series of rights and responsibilities.[216]

7. In certain circumstances a relative may be in a position to invoke wardship.[217]

## 8 The Human Rights Act 1998 and the right to respect for family life

Under article 8 of the ECHR:

---

**LEGISLATIVE PROVISION**

**European Convention on Human Rights, article 8**

1. Everyone has the right to respect for his private and family life, his home and his correspondence.
2. There shall be no interference by a public authority with the exercise of this right except such as is in accordance with the law and is necessary in a democratic society in the interests of national security, public safety or the economic well-being of the country, for the prevention of disorder or crime, for the protection of health or morals, or for the protection of the rights and freedoms of others.[218]

---

This is a clear recognition that family members other than parents can be protected through the law. The relevance of this article will be discussed throughout the book, but here a few general points will be made.[219]

### A What is family life?

In defining family life it is clear that the paradigm of family life for the European Court of Human Rights has been a husband and wife and children.[220] In *B v UK*[221] the European Court expressed this when explaining that there could be a variety of kinds of unmarried father, ranging from an ignorant or indifferent father to the relationship with the child being 'indistinguishable from the conventional family-based unit'. Clearly, here the court regarded the 'conventional family-based unit' as a married couple with children.[222] However,

---

[215] See Chapter 6.
[216] See pages 343–5.
[217] See *Re H (A Minor) (Custody: Interim Care and Control)* [1991] 2 FLR 109, [1991] FCR 985.
[218] Article 8 of the European Convention.
[219] See Choudhry and Herring (2010) for a detailed discussion.
[220] Liddy (1998).
[221] [2000] 1 FLR 1, [2000] 1 FCR 289.
[222] In *Ahmut v The Netherlands* (1997) 24 EHRR 62 it was stated that once two people have family life, only in exceptional circumstances will that be lost.

the European Court has not restricted family life to married couples and relationships through blood.[223] In *Kearns v France*[224] it was held that it covered a mother and child in a case where the mother had given her child up for adoption shortly after birth. Article 8 has been found to cover unmarried couples;[225] siblings;[226] uncle/nephew;[227] grandparents/grandchild;[228] and foster parents/foster child.[229] However, it appears that the further the relationship departs from the paradigm (i.e. the more remote the blood relationship), the more evidence is needed to show that there was a close social relationship between the parties. For example, in *Boyle v UK*[230] it was accepted that the uncle and nephew had 'family life' because the uncle proved he was a father figure to the boy. Had he actually been the boy's father, the court would readily have accepted that their relationship constituted family life and there would have been no need to show that their relationship was especially close. The English courts have been more willing to assume family life exists with wider relatives. In *Re R (A Child) (Adoption: Disclosure)*[231] Holman J was willing to hold that a newborn baby had family life with her wider family, including uncles and aunts. If the relationship does not fall within family life, it may still be protected by article 8 as an aspect of the parties' private life. In *Znamenskaya v Russia*[232] it was held that 'close relationships short of "family life" would generally fall within the scope of "private life"'.

If the case involves a married couple the court will willingly find family life even if the spouses are not living together.[233] An unmarried couple can demonstrate family life, but it depends on the nature of the relationship: the court will consider whether the parties live together; the length of the relationship; and whether they have demonstrated commitment to each other, for example by having children.

Perhaps the most controversy surrounds fathers and children. Although mothers inevitably have family life with their children,[234] this is not true of fathers. As the European Court in *Lebbink v Netherlands*[235] stated: 'The court does not agree with the applicant that a mere biological kinship, without any further legal or factual elements indicating the existence of a close personal relationship, should be regarded as sufficient to attract the protection of art 8.' It explained that in considering a claim of a father the court would consider 'the nature of the relationship between the natural parents and the demonstrable interest in and commitment by the father to the child both before and after its birth'.[236] It appears that fathers can acquire family life with their children in two ways:

---

[223] *X, Y, Z v UK* [1997] 2 FLR 892, [1997] 3 FCR 341.

[224] [2008] 2 FCR 1.

[225] *X, Y, Z v UK* [1997] 2 FLR 892, [1997] 3 FCR 341. A suggestion that, on divorce, a couple ceases to have family life was made by the court in *L v Finland* [2000] 2 FLR 118 at p. 148; but this seems inconsistent with the general approach in the previous cases: e.g. *Keegan v Ireland* (1994) 18 EHRR 342.

[226] *Moustaquim v Belgium* (1991) 13 EHRR 802 and *Senthuran v Secretary of State for the Home Department* [2004] 3FCR 273.

[227] *Boyle v UK* (1994) 19 EHRR 179.

[228] *L v Finland* [2000] 2 FLR 118; *Adam v Germany* [2009] 1 FLR 560.

[229] *X v Switzerland* (1978) 13 DR 248.

[230] (1994) 19 EHRR 179. See also *Jucius and Juciuvienė v Lithuania* [2009] 1 FLR 403

[231] [2001] 1 FCR 238.

[232] [2005] 2 FCR 406 at para 27.

[233] *Abdulaziz et al. v UK* (1985) 7 EHRR 471.

[234] *Re B (Adoption by One Natural Parent to Exclusion of Other)* [2001] 1 FLR 589, per Hale LJ.

[235] [2004] 3 FCR 59 at para 37.

[236] At para 36.

1. By actually caring for the child in a practical way and thereby demonstrating his interest in and commitment to the child.[237] This does not require the father to live with the child,[238] but must involve some kind of contact.[239]

2. If the conception of the child takes place in the context of a committed relationship. Therefore, if the father was married, engaged or in a permanent cohabiting relationship at the time of the conception he will have family life with the resulting child.[240]

This means that if the conception is part of a casual relationship and the man does not under-take a significant role in the care of a child, he will not be regarded as having family life with a child. In *G v The Netherlands*[241] a man donated sperm to a lesbian couple. After the child's birth he sought to have regular contact with the child. The European Court held that he did not have family life with the child.[242] Similarly, in **Leeds Teaching Hospital NHS Trust v A**[243] it was held that a man who provided sperm to enable a woman to become pregnant through assisted reproduction could not thereby claim to have family life with the child. In *Haas v The Netherlands*[244] the European Court of Human Rights held there was no family life between a deceased man and a man who claimed to be his son. Although the deceased had financially supported the child, he had never lived with the applicant nor his mother, nor had he ever recognised him as his son. In *Görgülü v Germany*,[245] where a mother gave up a child for adoption shortly after birth, the court was willing to find that the father had 'family life' with the child. However, due to his limited involvement in the child's life it might be easier to justify an interference in his family life rights than it would have been if he had spent many years caring for the child. To some these cases constitute gender discrimination and there is no justification for assuming that a mother, but not a father, deserves family life with the child.[246] To others the courts are recognising that through pregnancy and birth all mothers have demonstrated a relationship which deserves protection under the European Convention on Human Rights, while fathers' relationships with their children can be so minimal that they do not automatically justify protection.

## B What is respect?

The European Court has made it clear that the requirement of respect for family life places both positive and negative obligations on the state. Article 8 may not only require the state not to interfere in family life but it may on occasions require the state to act positively to promote family life. For example, in *Hokkanen v Finland* the European Court held that the failure of the state to provide an effective mechanism for enforcing a contact order between

---

[237] *Lebbink v Netherlands* [2004] 3 FCR 59.

[238] *Lebbink v Netherlands* [2004] 3 FCR 59.

[239] *Söderbäck v Sweden* [1999] 1 FLR 250.

[240] *Keegan v Ireland* [1994] 3 FCR 165 although subsequently the European Commission on Human Rights in *M v The Netherlands* (1993) 74 D&R 120 stated that there had to be some close personal ties to establish family life.

[241] (1990) 16 EHRR 38.

[242] See also *Mikulic v Croatia* [2002] 1 FCR 720 where a father who had only ever had a casual relationship with the mother and had played no significant role in the care of the child was held not to have family life.

[243] [2003] 1 FCR 599.

[244] [2004] 1 FCR 147.

[245] [2004] 1 FCR 410.

[246] Bainham (2005: 216) argues the approach is inconsistent with art. 7 of the UNCRC which recognises the right of the child to know both parents from birth.

a father and his child was an infringement of the right to respect for family life.[247] In *Stubbings v UK*[248] it was explained:

> although the object of article 8 is essentially that of protecting the individual against arbitrary interference by the public authorities, it does not merely compel the state to abstain from such interference: there may, in addition to this primary negative undertaking, be positive obligations inherent in an effective respect for private or family life. These obligations may involve the adoption of measures designed to secure respect for private life even in the sphere of the relations of individuals between themselves.

Thus the Court has reasoned that some positive acts may be a necessary part of respect for family or private life and so a failure to provide these can be an interference with respect for family life. This is certainly so where the state has intervened in family life (e.g. by taking a child into care) in which case a duty arises requiring steps to be taken to reunite the child and family.[249] It also means the state must take steps to enable family ties to be established. For example, *Raumussen v Denmark*[250] suggests that respect for family life may involve providing an effective and accessible remedy so that a man can establish that he is the father of a child. Another important example will be discussed in Chapter 11: if the state takes a child into care then it is under an obligation to enable contact between the child and his or her family to take place, unless to do so would harm the child.

The word respect does not necessarily involve approval. One might respect a person's religious beliefs, without agreeing with them. All that would be needed for respect would be an acknowledgement that the thing to be respected has some value. This suggests that the ECHR requires the state to value all forms of family life which have value, even if the Government believes they are below the ideal forms of family life.[251] More controversially it might be suggested that some forms of family life are so devoid of value that they do not deserve respect. That might be so where the relationship is characterised by abuse.[252]

## C  When can infringement be justified?

Paragraph 2 of article 8 sets out the circumstances in which an infringement of the right to respect for family life is justified. To justify the interference in the right it must be shown that:

1. The interference was in accordance with the law.

2. The interference was in pursuance of one of the listed aims (e.g. national security).

3. The interference must be necessary. It is not enough to show that the interference was reasonable or desirable; it must be shown that there was a pressing need for the interference.[253] Further, it must be shown that the extent of the intervention was proportionate; in other words, there was not a less interventionist measure which would have adequately protected national security (or whichever of the listed aims was being pursued).

It is submitted that the nature of the quality of relationship between the parties is relevant, not only in deciding whether there is family life, but also in deciding whether the interference is justified under para 2. The further the applicant is from the paradigm of a married parent/child

---

[247] [1996] 1 FLR 289, [1995] 2 FCR 320 ECtHR; Feldman (1997).
[248] (1997) 1 BHRC 316.
[249] See Chapter 11.
[250] (1985) 7 EHRR 371. See also *Paulik v Slovakia* [2006] 3 FCR 323.
[251] Herring (2008c).
[252] Herring (2008c).
[253] *Dudgeon v UK* (1982) 4 EHRR 149.

relationship, the more likely it is that state action will not be regarded as interference in the relationship; or if it is interference that it will be seen as justifiable. Thus to prevent a grandparent from visiting a child in care requires less justification than preventing a parent from having contact.[254]

## 9 Who has parental responsibility?

In many ways this is a more important question than 'who is a parent?', but, as we shall see, 'who is a parent?' and 'who has parental responsibility?' are actually linked questions. It is necessary to distinguish the way mothers, fathers, non-parents and local authorities may obtain parental responsibility. First, the law will be set out in broad outline and then more detailed points will be discussed.

### A Outline of the law

#### (i) Mothers

All mothers[255] automatically have parental responsibility.

#### (ii) Fathers

A father[256] will have parental responsibility in any of the following circumstances:

1. he is married to the mother;[257] or
2. he is registered as the father of the child on the birth certificate;[258] or
3. he enters into a parental responsibility agreement with the mother; or
4. he obtains a parental responsibility order from the court;[259] or
5. he has been granted a residence order;[260] or
6. he has been appointed to be a guardian;[261] or
7. he has adopted the child.

#### (iii) Non-parents

Someone who is not a parent can obtain parental responsibility in the following ways:

1. He or she will acquire parental responsibility if appointed as a guardian.[262]
2. A person who is not a parent or a guardian will acquire parental responsibility when he or she obtains a residence order.
3. A person who is granted an emergency protection order thereby acquires parental responsibility.

---

[254] *Price v UK* (1988) 55 D&R 1988; *L v Finland* [2000] 2 FLR 118.
[255] That is, the woman regarded as the mother in the eyes of the law.
[256] That is, a man who is regarded as a father under the legal definition.
[257] The phrase 'married to the mother' has a wide definition. This includes a child born as a result of assisted reproduction (CA 1989, s 2).
[258] CA 1989, s 4, as amended by the Adoption and Children Act 2002.
[259] CA 1989, s 4.
[260] CA 1989, s 12(2).
[261] CA 1989, s 5(6).
[262] CA 1989, s 5(6).

It should be noted that, in these circumstances, although the non-parent will have parental responsibility, he or she will not obtain the rights that flow from being a parent.

### (iv) Local authorities

Local authorities can acquire parental responsibility as follows:

1. When a local authority obtains a care order it acquires parental responsibility.[263]

2. When a local authority obtains an emergency protection order it acquires parental responsibility.

## B  Consideration of the law in more detail

It is necessary to discuss some specific aspects of some of the points above.

### (i) Mothers

The rule that all mothers automatically have parental responsibility for their children can be explained on the basis that the mother throughout the pregnancy has sustained the child and has undergone great sacrifices for her child. As she has demonstrated her commitment to the child through pregnancy and has accepted that she will be involved in the care for the child after the birth, it is in the child's interests that she obtains parental responsibility.

### (ii) Fathers

There is much debate over whether all fathers should automatically obtain parental responsibility. The present law restricts which fathers might obtain parental responsibility. For a father there are two sources of parental responsibility: first, the mother (if she has married him or has permitted him to be registered as the father on the birth certificate or has entered a parental responsibility agreement with him); secondly, the court (if the unmarried father is granted one of the orders mentioned above). The law appears to take the view that a father needs to be vetted and approved before he can acquire parental responsibility. But it should also be noted that a father (unlike the mother) has a choice: if a man wishes to father a child without having parental responsibility he may do so. There is no way that a mother can force the unmarried father of her child to have parental responsibility against his wishes.[264] The mother does not have the option of giving birth to a child but not taking parental responsibility. This may well indicate cultural assumptions that it is 'natural' for mothers to care for children, but this is not necessarily expected of fathers.

We shall consider in further detail the different ways in which an unmarried father can acquire parental responsibility.

#### (a) The registered father

The Adoption and Children Act 2002 amended s 4 of the Children Act 1989 to provide that fathers who are registered as the father of the child on the birth certificate will automatically acquire parental responsibility.[265] This significant change in the law will greatly increase the

---

[263] CA 1989, s 44(4)(c).

[264] She cannot register him on the birth certificate without his consent.

[265] Of course a father who misleads a registrar into putting his name on the certificate cannot thereby acquire parental responsibility: *A v H (Registrar General for England and Wales and another intervening)* [2009] 3 FCR 95.

number of unmarried fathers who have parental responsibility. Eighty per cent of births to unmarried couples are registered by both mother and father. However, it is important to appreciate that an unmarried father can only appear on the birth certificate if the mother agrees to this.[266] So in a way this is simply a particular kind of parental responsibility agreement.[267] On the birth of the child the mother is specifically given the chance to share responsibility with the father. There have been concerns that this change in the law will in fact deter fathers from being registered because they falsely believe that if they are given parental responsibility they will become financially liable for the child.[268] Eekelaar voices a different concern, that mothers may be deterred[269] from registering the father's name for fear that doing so would give him rights he could use to interfere with her upbringing of the child.[270] If either of these concerns materialised this would work against the policy of enabling children readily to discover the identity of their birth parents, discussed later in this chapter. Another concern is that a mother may not appreciate the significance of registering the child's father.[271]

### (b) Parental responsibility agreements

A father and a mother can enter a parental responsibility agreement under s 4(1)(b) of the Children Act 1989. The agreement must be in the prescribed form and recorded.[272] It must be signed by both parties and taken to a court where the certificate will be witnessed and signed. Critics of the procedure argue that the technicalities that surround it deter fathers from using it. Indeed, the number of parental responsibility agreements has not been high.[273] The reason, no doubt, is that if the parents are happy together they do not see the need for a formal agreement, but if they are in dispute then there will be no agreement. On the other hand, there are those who suggest that the procedure is too easy. There is no effective check to ensure that the applicant is the father of the child; that the mother's consent is freely given;[274] or that the man is suitable to have parental responsibility.

In *Re X (Parental Responsibility Agreement)*[275] the Court of Appeal regarded the right of a mother and father to enter into a parental responsibility agreement 'free from state intervention'[276] as an important aspect of the right of respect for family life under article 8. The right to enter into the parental responsibility agreement exists even though the child has been taken into care.[277]

---

[266] *A v H (Registrar General for England and Wales and another intervening)* [2009] 3 FCR 95.

[267] For an argument that the new provision robs mothers of their powers to control a father's access to parental responsibility see Wallbank (2002a). This is significant in the light of the possible reforms to birth registration in the Welfare Reform Act 2010.

[268] In fact fathers are liable under the Child Support Act 1991 whether or not they have parental responsibility.

[269] In fact he suggests they would be 'well advised' not to (Eekelaar (2001d: 430)).

[270] Although he points out that having the father registered may make it easier to claim child support against him.

[271] Diduck and Kaganas (2006: 229). See Department for Work and Pensions (2006d: 40) for proposals to give information to parents at the time of birth registration about the legal rights and responsibilities of parenthood.

[272] An oral agreement could amount to a delegation of parental responsibility under CA 1989, s 2(9).

[273] About 3,000 parental responsibility agreements are registered each year. This is, of course, a tiny percentage of the children born to unmarried parents.

[274] There was some evidence that the mother's signature has been forged (Children Act Advisory Committee (1993: 13)), although since the Parental Responsibility Agreement Regulations 1994, SI 1994/3157 the agreement must now be signed in the local court and witnessed by a court official before being lodged at the court. A copy is then sent to the mother and father.

[275] [2000] 1 FLR 517.

[276] This is perhaps a little misleading, as the agreement does have to be lodged at the court and so the state is involved.

[277] In *Re X (Parental Responsibility Agreement)* [2000] 1 FLR 517.

## (c) Section 4 applications

If the father is not registered on the birth certificate and is unable to obtain the mother's consent, he can apply under s 4 of the Children Act 1989 for a parental responsibility order. Only genetic fathers can apply under s 4, and if there is any doubt whether the applicant is the father, DNA evidence will be required. Orders are available only in respect of a child under 18.[278]

In deciding whether to grant parental responsibility, s 1(1) of the Children Act 1989 applies,[279] and therefore the welfare of the child is to be the paramount consideration.[280] Although the Court of Appeal in *Re H (Parental Responsibility)*[281] has stated that it is wrong to suggest that there is a presumption in favour of awarding parental responsibility, we shall see that the cases demonstrate that only in unusual circumstances will parental responsibility not be granted. The statistics show that in 90 per cent of cases the application succeeds.[282]

Most of the cases considering applications under s 4 use as a starting point *Re H (Minors) (Local Authority: Parental Responsibility) (No. 3)*,[283] where it was stated that these factors should be taken into account:

(1) the degree of commitment which the father has shown towards the child;

(2) the degree of attachment which exists between the father and the child; and

(3) the reasons of the father applying for the order.

A little more focus to the test was set out by Mustill LJ in *Re C (Minors)*:

> . . . was the association between the parties sufficiently enduring; and has the father by his conduct during and since the application shown sufficient commitment to the child to justify giving the father a legal status equivalent to that which he would have enjoyed if the parties had married?[284]

The fact that the applicant has applied for an order shows commitment in itself,[285] but the Court of Appeal has stressed that even if there is attachment and commitment the court still might not award parental responsibility if other factors indicate that it would be contrary to the child's interests.[286] Each case depends very much on its own facts, but the following points have arisen in previous cases and will be considered:[287]

1. *Contact with the child.* Where there is regular contact and financial support the court will readily find there is sufficient commitment between the father and the child for a parental responsibility order to be appropriate.[288] However, just because there has never been contact between the father and the child, it does not necessarily mean that parental responsibility will not be granted, especially if the father can demonstrate that the lack of contact was due to the mother's actions. That said, as yet there is no case where a father has never seen the child but was awarded parental responsibility. Indeed in *Re J (Parental*

---

[278] There is no need to demonstrate that the circumstances are exceptional: cf. CA 1989, s 9(6).

[279] As does CA 1989, s 1(5): *Re P (Parental Responsibility)* [1998] 2 FLR 96, [1998] 3 FCR 98, although Gilmore (2003a) suggests that whether the welfare principle applies to applications for a parental responsibility order is yet to be definitively decided.

[280] Ward J in *D v Hereford and Worcester CC* [1991] 1 FLR 215, [1991] FCR 56; *Re F (A Minor) (Parental Responsibility Order)* [1994] 1 FLR 504 CA; *Re H (Parental Responsibility)* [1998] 1 FLR 855.

[281] [1998] 1 FLR 855.

[282] Six per cent of the applications are refused and in 4 per cent of cases no order is made.

[283] [1991] 1 FLR 214, [1991] FCR 361.

[284] *Re C (Minors) (Parental Rights)* [1992] 2 All ER 86 at p. 93.

[285] *Re S (A Minor) (Parental Responsibility)* [1995] 2 FLR 648 at p. 659.

[286] *Re P (Parental Responsibility)* [1998] 2 FLR 96, [1998] 3 FCR 98.

[287] Gilmore (2003a) provides a very useful discussion of the case law.

[288] *Re S (A Minor) (Parental Responsibility)* [1995] 2 FLR 648.

*Responsibility)*[289] parental responsibility was refused on the basis that the child never knew her father, he was 'almost a stranger'.

2. *Status.* In *Re S (A Minor) (Parental Responsibility)*[290] the Court of Appeal emphasised that parental responsibility gave an unmarried father the status 'for which nature had already ordained that he must bear responsibility'. This judgment suggests that the parental responsibility order merely confirms what the father's status is according 'to nature'. The parental responsibility order was referred to as a 'stamp of approval'. In this case, even though the father had been convicted of possessing paedophilic literature, he was still awarded parental responsibility. It is not clear what to make of these statements of the Court of Appeal. They certainly suggest that there need to be good reasons if an unmarried father is not to be granted parental responsibility. In *Re D (Contact and Parental Responsibility: Lesbian Mothers and Known Father)*[291] Black J gave parental responsibility to a man who had been selected by a lesbian couple to impregnate one of them so that the couple could raise a child together. Justifying his decision he said that 'perhaps most importantly of all' is the reality that the man *was* the child's father. This suggests that biological parenthood itself is a good reason for granting parental responsibility. By contrast, in *R v E and F (Female Parents: Known Father)*[292] a father who donated sperm to a lesbian couple was not granted parental responsibility on the basis that there was no doubt he was the father and did not need parental responsibility to reinforce that.

3. *Child's reaction to failed application.* In *C and V (Minors) (Parental Responsibility and Contact)*[293] Ward LJ stated that it was good for a child's sense of self-esteem that the child thought positively about an absent parent and so 'wherever possible the law should confer on a concerned father that stamp of approval because he has shown himself willing and anxious to pick up the responsibility of fatherhood and not to deny or avoid it'. Similarly, in *Re S (A Minor) (Parental Responsibility)*[294] it was stated that:

> . . . the law confers upon a committed father that stamp of approval, lest the child grow up with some belief that he is in some way disqualified from fulfilling his role and that the reason for the disqualification is something inherent which will be inherited by the child, making her struggle to find her own identity all the more fraught.[295]

4. *The child's view.* If the child is sufficiently mature, the child's views on whether the application should succeed can be taken into account.[296] In *Re G (A Child) (Domestic Violence: Direct Contact)*[297] the fact that a child (aged nearly 4) did not want to have any contact with the father and was fearful when he was mentioned led Butler-Sloss P to hold that it was inappropriate to grant him parental responsibility.

5. *Misuse.* A father should not be denied a parental responsibility order simply because there are fears that the father may misuse the order.[298] If necessary, the court can make

---

[289] [1999] 1 FLR 784.
[290] [1995] 2 FLR 648.
[291] [2006] 1 FCR 556.
[292] [2010] EWHC 417 (Fam).
[293] [1998] 1 FLR 392, [1998] 1 FCR 57; see Eekelaar (1996).
[294] [1995] 2 FLR 648.
[295] At p. 657. A cynic might doubt whether the child will appreciate the significance of parental responsibility if he or she does not see his or her father. The order is more likely to affect the father's image of himself than his child's.
[296] *Re J (Parental Responsibility)* [1999] 1 FLR 784.
[297] [2001] 2 FCR 134.
[298] *Re S (A Minor) (Parental Responsibility)* [1995] 2 FLR 648 at p. 657.

orders restricting the father's use of parental responsibility[299] or requiring him to obtain the leave of the court before bringing any proceedings.[300] It is even possible to remove parental responsibility from a father.[301] In *Re S (A Minor) (Parental Responsibility)*[302] the mother's argument that the father might misuse the order on the basis that he had been unreliable about providing financial support for the child and had been convicted of possessing paedophilic literature failed. It was stated that it was wrong to focus on the potential misuse of the order and, instead, a father wishing to undertake the responsibilities associated with parenthood should be entitled to do so. That said, if there is very clear evidence that the father is determined to disrupt the mother's care of the child and is applying for parental responsibility to enable him to do so then the court will decline to grant the order.[303] Alternatively the court might grant him parental responsibility and at the same time make an order that he must not exercise his parental responsibility in a particular way. In *Re D (Contact and Parental Responsibility: Lesbian Mothers and Known Father)*[304] the father was given parental responsibility but then prohibited from interfering in medical or schooling issues.

6. *Parental responsibility and other orders.* A parental responsibility order can be made even though a contact or residence order is inappropriate.[305] In other words, it is not necessary to show that the father will ever practically be able to exercise parental responsibility in order for him to be awarded it. So, parental responsibility can be ordered even though the child is about to be adopted.[306] A good example of this point is *Re C and V (Minors) (Parental Responsibility and Contact)*,[307] where a father had a close relationship with a child. Unfortunately, the child had severe medical problems and needed constant medical attention. The mother had learned the skills necessary to care for the child, but the father had not. It was therefore felt inappropriate to grant contact to the father, but still he was granted parental responsibility as a mark of his commitment to the child. By contrast in *R v E and F (Female Parents: Known Father)*[308] a father was to have contact with the child, but was not granted parental responsibility. It was held that section 3(5) Children Act 1989 enabled him to make decisions about the child during the contact session and so he did not need parental responsibility.

7. *Reprehensible conduct of the father.* Simply because the father has harmed the child in the past does not necessarily mean that a father will be denied parental responsibility. However, in *Re T (Minor) (Parental Responsibility)*[309] the application was denied because the father had shown no understanding of the child's welfare and had treated the mother with violence and hatred.[310] In *Re P (Parental Responsibility: Change of Name)*[311] the Court of Appeal refused to interfere with a refusal to grant parental responsibility on the basis that the father's repeated criminal offences and resulting imprisonment demonstrated

---

[299] For example, through a prohibited steps order or a specific issue order.
[300] CA 1989, s 91(14).
[301] CA 1989, s 4(3).
[302] [1995] 2 FLR 648.
[303] *Re P (Parental Responsibility)* [1998] 2 FLR 96, [1998] 3 FCR 98; *Re M (Handicapped Child: Parental Responsibility)* [2001] 3 FCR 454.
[304] [2006] 1 FCR 556.
[305] *Re P (A Minor) (Parental Responsibility Order)* [1994] 1 FLR 578.
[306] *Re H (Minors) (Local Authority: Parental Responsibility) (No. 3)* [1991] 1 FLR 214, [1991] FCR 361.
[307] [1998] 1 FLR 392, [1998] 1 FCR 57.
[308] [2010] EWHC 417 (Fam).
[309] [1993] 2 FLR 450, [1993] 1 FCR 973.
[310] See also *Re G (A Child) (Domestic Violence: Direct Contact)* [2001] 2 FCR 134.
[311] [1997] 2 FLR 722, [1997] 3 FCR 739.

(the court felt) his lack of commitment to the child. In *Re H (Parental Responsibility)*[312] the father had injured the son deliberately and there was even some suggestion that sadism was involved, and therefore the court did not grant parental responsibility as there was a future risk. So it appears that if the misconduct reveals a lack of commitment to the child or that the man is a danger to the child then the misconduct may be a strong reason to deny parental responsibility.

8. *Mother's possible reaction to the granting of the order.* The fact that the mother might bitterly oppose the order and there is hostility is not a reason for refusing the order,[313] although if the child's mother will be so upset that this may affect her parenting ability and cause the child to suffer, then parental responsibility may be denied.[314]

9. *Mother's death.* In some cases the argument had been accepted that parental responsibility should be granted to a father so that he can take over care of the child if anything happens that might prevent the mother from caring for the child: for example, if she dies.[315]

10. *The father's ability to exercise parental responsibility.* In *M v M (Parental Responsibility)*[316] the father suffered from learning disability and head injuries and Wilson J argued that therefore he was incapable of exercising the rights and responsibilities of parental responsibility.

11. *The father's standing under the Hague Convention.* If there are concerns that the child may be abducted and the father needs to use the Hague Convention, the father needs parental responsibility to do so. In *Re J-S (A Child) (Contact: Parental Responsibility)*[317] the mother was Australian and the father English, and this was, the Court of Appeal held, an argument in favour of granting the father parental responsibility.

As the above discussion demonstrates, the cases do not always reveal a consistent approach, but it appears that if a father has shown sufficient commitment to the child then a parental responsibility order will be made unless there are serious concerns that he may harm the child. This has led one leading family lawyer to complain of the 'degradation of parental responsibility'.[318] Indeed it is striking that we needed a decision of the Court of Appeal (in *Re H (Parental Responsibility)*[319]) to tell us that a father who had sadistically injured his child should not have parental responsibility. One of the few cases where a father was not successful in an application for parental responsibility was *Re B (Role of Biological Father)*[320] where a lesbian couple asked the brother of one of them to provide sperm for assisted conception. The three agreed at the time of conception that the child would be raised by the two women alone. However, after the birth the man wanted to take on the role of father and sought parental responsibility and contact. Hedley J emphasised that the key issue was the child's welfare and here the two women were to be the child's nuclear family. Despite the fact the man met the *Re H* criteria, he should not be given parental responsibility. Contact four times per year would be allowed so that the child could explore his link with the man.

---

[312] [1998] 1 FLR 855.
[313] *D v S* [1995] 3 FLR 783; *Re P (A Minor) (Parental Responsibility Order)* [1994] 1 FLR 578.
[314] *Re K* [1998] Fam Law 567.
[315] *Re E (Parental Responsibility: Blood Test)* [1995] 1 FLR 392, [1994] 2 FCR 709; *Re H (A Minor) (Parental Responsibility)* [1993] 1 FLR 484, [1993] 1 FCR 85.
[316] [1999] 2 FLR 737.
[317] [2002] 3 FCR 433.
[318] Reece (2009b).
[319] [1998] 1 FLR 855.
[320] [2008] FL 411.

In 2008, 7,072 parental responsibility orders were granted and in only 108 cases did the court refuse to grant a parental responsibility order.[321] The readiness of the courts to award parental responsibility is controversial. In discussing these cases it is crucial to remember that they all involve families where the mother is opposing the grant of parental responsibility. If she was in accord, the couple would lodge a parental responsibility agreement. What from one perspective appears to be the court encouraging the father to play his role in the child's life might appear to the mother to be a licence to the man who may have abused her child to interfere in every aspect of the child's life. The real difficulty here is that perhaps the notion of parental responsibility is not sufficiently fine-tuned. There is a strong argument for possibly creating two levels of parental responsibility: one giving all the rights of parenthood and the other giving a lesser level of rights (for example, the right to be consulted on a list of crucial decisions). Returning to *Re S (A Minor) (Parental Responsibility)*, discussed above, to give a father who had a conviction for possession of paedophilic literature the right to clothe, feed and bathe a child might seem inappropriate, even if there is an argument that he can have a say in fundamental issues, such as where the child should be educated. The difficulty is that the present law on parental rights requires us to give him all or none of the legal rights of a parent.

### (iii) Non-parents

It is sensible that if a non-parent is given a residence order, parental responsibility will also be granted because this will reflect the fact that he or she will be carrying out the parental roles. At present only parents or those with residence orders can be granted parental responsibility. There is an argument that the court should have a wider power to make parental responsibility orders. The court has certainly called for this. A good example of the problems of the present law is *Re WB (Residence Order)*,[322] where a man had brought up and cared for a child with the mother. He separated from the mother but it was found (to his surprise) that he was not a father. The court could only grant him parental responsibility by giving him a residence order, but the court felt unable to do so as it was in the child's welfare to stay with her mother. However, the courts have shown greater willingness to make a shared residence order in order to grant parental responsibility if to do so would not be completely artificial.[323] Nevertheless in *Re A (A Child) (Joint Residence: Parental Responsibility)*[324] a child was raised by a man (A) and a woman. A believed himself to be a father and played a full role in raising the child. However, it was found after the child's second birthday that in fact A was not the father. The Court of Appeal approved the making of a shared residence order in order to recognise the role that he played as the child's social and psychological parent and to ensure he had parental responsibility. The making of the joint residence order was the only way of granting him parental responsibility. The order was made even though in reality the child was to live with the mother, and A was to have regular contact with the father.

### (iv) Local authorities

This will be discussed in Chapter 10.

---

[321] Ministry of Justice (2009).
[322] [1995] 2 FLR 1023.
[323] *Re H (Shared Residence: Parental Responsibility)* [1995] 2 FLR 883, [1996] 3 FCR 321.
[324] [2008] 3 FCR 107. See Wallbank (2007) for criticisms of this use of parental responsibility.

## 10 Who should get parental responsibility?

### A Unmarried fathers[325]

As we have explained, unmarried fathers in English law do not obtain parental responsibility automatically. An unmarried father may acquire parental responsibility in three ways. The first is by agreement with the mother and being registered as the father on the birth certificate or registering a parental responsibility agreement with the court. The second is by marrying the child's mother.[326] The third is by persuading the court to make a parental responsibility order. Whether this law is satisfactory is hotly disputed and there is much debate over whether unmarried fathers should get parental responsibility automatically.[327]

The difficulty is that the term 'unmarried father' covers a wide range of relationships. The European Court of Human Rights in *B v UK*[328] has explained the dilemma: 'The relationship between unmarried fathers and their children varies from ignorance and indifference to a close stable relationship indistinguishable from the conventional family-based unit.' In 2007, 44 per cent of births in England and Wales were outside marriage, but in the same year only 9,674 parental responsibility orders were made.[329] About 3,000 parental responsibility agreements are registered each year.[330] This indicates that only a tiny proportion of unmarried fathers have parental responsibility, even though 82 per cent of births to unmarried parents were joint registrations, suggesting that at least that percentage of fathers intended to play an important role in the child's life.[331] Research by Pickford[332] found that although four-fifths of fathers were aware that they were financially liable to support their children, only one-quarter of all fathers were aware that there was a difference in the legal rights of married and unmarried fathers. Elmalik and Wheeler[333] found that more than 80 per cent of couples incorrectly believed a father cohabiting with his child had parental responsibility, even if unmarried. Indeed, they found doctors' ignorance of law led them to operate on children on the basis of consent from an unmarried father and thereby, technically, acting without lawful authorisation. So, ignorance of the law is not just found among the parents, but those professionals dealing with them.

Very broadly, five approaches could be taken to unmarried fathers and parental responsibility:

1. All unmarried fathers could be given parental responsibility automatically.

2. All unmarried fathers could be given parental responsibility, but this could be removed on application to the court.[334]

3. A group of unmarried fathers could be given parental responsibility. There could be removal or addition to this group on application to the court.

---

[325] There has been a real problem in finding a term to describe the father of a child who is not married to the mother. The phrase unmarried father has become widely accepted, although he may well be married – to someone other than the mother.

[326] Only the father of a child obtains parental responsibility of the child by marrying the mother. A step-parent does not thereby acquire parental responsibility.

[327] Sheldon (2001b); Bainham (1989); Lowe (1997c); Lord Chancellor's Department (1998).

[328] [2000] 1 FLR 1 at p. 5.

[329] Ministry of Justice (2008).

[330] Lord Chancellor's Department (1998).

[331] National Statistics (2005a: table 3.2).

[332] Pickford (1999).

[333] Elmalik and Wheeler (2007).

[334] Parental responsibility for mothers cannot be revoked, except when following the making of an adoption order or a parental order.

4. No unmarried fathers could be automatically given parental responsibility, but a procedure could exist whereby they could acquire parental responsibility (or to remove parental responsibility). This is the position in England and Wales at present.

5. No unmarried father is given parental responsibility.

The essential question is, where should the burden lie? Should it be on the mother or the state to establish that the father is unsuitable, or on the father to show that he is suitable? At the heart of this issue is what parental responsibility means. The stronger the 'rights' that parental responsibility provides, the more reluctant the law will be in granting it to a wide group of people. However, the more limited the rights the more willing a legal system may be to grant all fathers parental responsibility. The meaning of parental responsibility is discussed in Chapter 8. There is also a dispute over the role of the law here. On the one hand, there are those who emphasise the 'message' that the law gives. They often argue that fathers should be encouraged and expected to fulfil their role as parents and this should be emphasised by giving as many unmarried fathers as possible parental responsibility. Others emphasise the practical effect of giving unmarried fathers parental responsibility and are concerned by the fact that parental responsibility could be misused.

Some of the key issues that have been raised in the debate are as follows:

---

## DEBATE

### Should all fathers automatically get parental responsibility?

1. *The balance of power between mothers and fathers.* The case for awarding parental responsibility to only a selection of unmarried fathers runs as follows. Why does the father need parental responsibility? He can carry out all the duties and joys of parenthood (feeding, clothing, playing with the child) without parental responsibility. He only needs parental responsibility when he is dealing with third parties such as doctors and schools. At such times the mother can provide the necessary consent. He would only need parental responsibility if he were wishing to exercise it in a way contrary to the mother's wishes.[335] An unmarried father who has been fully involved in the raising of the child might be thought validly to have an important say in the raising of children. But an unmarried father who had limited or no contact with the child should surely not be able to override the mother's wishes. Ruth Deech has argued that parental responsibilities:

   > include feeding, washing and clothing the child, putting her to bed, housing her, educating and stimulating her, taking responsibility for arranging babysitting and day-care, keeping the child in touch with the wider family circle, checking her medical condition, arranging schooling and transport to school, holidays and recreation, encouraging social and possibly religious or moral development. Fatherhood that does not encompass a fair share of these tasks is an empty and egotistical concept and has the consequence that the man does not know the child sufficiently well to be able sensibly to take decisions about education, religion, discipline, medical treatment, change of abode, adoption, marriage and property.[336]

   Julie Wallbank[337] has argued that because women assume the primary responsibility for the child their views should be given priority in decisions about whether the father should ➡

---

[335] Eekelaar (1996); Kaganas (1996).
[336] Deech (1993: 30).
[337] Wallbank (2002a).

acquire parental responsibility. She suggests that those who support giving all fathers parental responsibility rely on the 'ethic of justice' (which emphasises the importance of formal equality and general rules), rather than 'the ethic of care' (which emphasises the importance of responsibilities and relationships).[338] She supports privileging the position of mothers who undertake the bulk of the day-to-day work with the child.[339] Opponents of such views will claim that it is wrong to presume that unmarried fathers do not take part in the 'work' of parenting or do not have relationships with their children that are of equal worth to those mothers have.

2. *Fears of misuse.* There is a concern that the non-residential father may misuse parental responsibility. He may see it as a justification for 'snooping' on the mother and continuing to exercise power over her, although it may be said that if a man is of the kind who will pester the mother with legal actions and 'snooping' to check she is being a good mother, he will do so whether or not he has parental responsibility.

3. *Parental responsibility should reflect the social reality.* The argument here is that if a father is carrying out a parental role he should receive parental responsibility. This would mean that the legal position of the father and his social position would match. The parental responsibility could then be seen as the law's stamp of approval for the task he is carrying out.[340]

4. *Rights of the child.*[341] The issue could be examined from the perspective of the rights of the child. It could be argued that a child has a right to have the responsibilities of parenthood imposed on both his or her mother and father. Deech strongly opposes such an argument: 'The basic rights of the child are not furthered by delivering more choice to the unmarried father. Legal rights which he may acquire are choices for him; that is, he may or may not choose to exercise them. Such choice is a limitation on the rights of the child.'[342]

5. *The rights of the father.* Some claim that the English law, in failing to provide an unmarried father with parental responsibility, breaches the Human Rights Act 1998.[343] There are ways that such a claim may be made:

   (a) *Discrimination on the grounds of sex.* Article 14 states: 'The enjoyment of the rights and freedoms set forth in this convention shall be decreed without discrimination on any ground such as sex, race, colour, language, religion, political or other opinion, natural or social origin in association with a natural minority, property, birth or other status.' It might be argued that, by giving mothers but not fathers automatic parental responsibility, this is discrimination on the ground of sex. However, this was rejected in *McMichael v UK*[344] and *B v UK*.[345] This, it is argued, is correct because of the greatly differing roles that men and women play during pregnancy.

   (b) *Discrimination on the grounds of marital status.* Again, referring to article 14, it could be said that the list of prohibited grounds of discrimination is not closed (the article

---

[338] See further Sevenhuijsen (1997); Smart and Neale (1999).
[339] Sheldon (2001b: 105) argues there is not yet sufficient evidence to demonstrate that unmarried fathers undertake sufficient child care to be in a position to make important decisions for children. There is sufficient evidence in relation to mothers to make this assumption.
[340] Eekelaar (1996).
[341] See also Fortin (1998: 323).
[342] Deech (1993: 30).
[343] Booth (2004: 355).
[344] (1995) 20 EHRR 205.
[345] [2000] 1 FLR 1, [2000] 1 FCR 289.

says 'such as', indicating that there could be other grounds apart from the ones mentioned in the article). It could therefore be argued that marital status could be added as another prohibited ground and that denying automatic parental responsibility to unmarried fathers is therefore prohibited. *B v UK*[346] accepted that it is permissible under the European Convention on Human Rights for a state to treat married and unmarried couples in different ways, if a sound reason for doing so exists. It was suggested that, given the wide varieties of unmarried fathers, it was legitimate for the state to restrict which could receive parental responsibility.[347]

(c) *Breach of right to respect for family life*. Article 8 of the European Convention on Human Rights states that: 'Everyone has the right to respect for his private and family life, his home and his correspondence.' This article certainly protects unmarried fathers[348] but this does not require automatic legal status. The approach taken by the European Court seems to be that, as long as there is a route available by which a father can establish that he should be given parental responsibility, there is no breach of the Convention.

In response to such arguments John Eekelaar has rejected an argument that a father has, by virtue of being a father, a right over the child. He explains: 'It is hard for a man to have the prospect of the exercise of fatherhood plucked away by the collapse of his relationship with the mother . . . It is hard for a mother to have her hopes of a father bringing up her child dashed. But the frailties of the adults can be harder for the child.'[349]

6. *Wrong to impose responsibilities but no rights*. An unmarried father is liable to pay child support under the Child Support Act 1991 but is not automatically awarded parental responsibility. Is it fair that he should suffer the burdens but not gain the benefits that flow from parental responsibility? Deech has argued the opposite. If the father is not willing to show the commitment to the mother and the child by marriage, he should not receive parental responsibility, but should bear financial responsibility.[350] Indeed it could be argued that although it always promotes a child's welfare to have both parents under a duty to support him or her financially, it is not true that it is necessarily in a child's interests to have both parents having the power to make decisions over his or her upbringing. This is true especially if a parent with that power does not know the child.

7. *The rapist father*. The argument that carried much weight in the parliamentary discussion of the issue was that a man who fathered a child through rape should not obtain parental responsibility. To require a victim of rape to persuade a court that the rapist father should have his parental responsibility removed was clearly inappropriate and it was therefore better not to give the unmarried father automatic parental responsibility.[351] This argument is perhaps not as strong as might at first sight appear. It would be possible to have a specific statutory provision excluding convicted rapists[352] (although this would

---

[346] [2000] 1 FLR 1, [2000] 1 FCR 289.

[347] Hofferth and Anderson (2003) argue that the sociological data (at least from the USA) indicates that a marriage to the mother is a better indication of parental commitment than a genetic tie.

[348] E.g. *Johnston v Ireland* (1986) 9 EHRR 203.

[349] Eekelaar (2006b: 116).

[350] Deech (1993).

[351] The argument overlooks the fact that a husband who rapes his wife gets parental responsibility under the law.

[352] Bainham (1989: 231).

deal only with those rapists who were convicted). In any event there is a danger in relying on a rare situation to establish a general rule.

8. *Uncertainty*. This is one of the strongest arguments in favour of the present law. One benefit of the present law is that it is relatively easy to know whether a man has parental responsibility for a child. He will need to produce his certificate of marriage with the mother, the child's birth certificate, a parental responsibility order or copy of a parental responsibility agreement. If the law were to state that all unmarried fathers automatically obtained parental responsibility then, unless biological tests were done, it would be impossible to know whether a man claiming to have parental responsibility was or was not the father of the child. As the most common situation where it really matters whether a man has parental responsibility or not is when a child needs medical treatment, it is important that doctors can readily discover whether a father has parental responsibility. Bainham's response to such a point is to suggest that from birth a father should be recognised as having 'inchoate' rights which are 'perfected and converted into recognisable' legal rights when paternity is established in the legal process.[353] If this suggests that a father's rights will be enforceable only when his paternity is recognised in the law then few unmarried fathers will be able to rely on these rights because few of them will have their paternity established at law, except those named on the birth certificate, who have parental responsibility under the current law.

9. *Efficiency and public resources*. The present law seems to suggest that it is not at all difficult for an unmarried father to obtain parental responsibility (although it does involve expense and time) and, if so, it may be asked whether there is any point in having these administrative hoops, with the public costs they involve.[354] On the other hand, it may be that increasing the number of people with parental responsibility will merely increase the scope for bringing disputes to court.

10. *Marriage promotion*. It might be argued that the distinction between married and unmarried fathers is important as part of the promotion of marriage. The belief of the majority of people that marriage does not affect parental rights undermines this argument to a large extent.[355]

## Questions

1. *Which is worse: that a deserving father is not given parental responsibility or that an undeserving father is given parental responsibility?*

2. *Are there good reasons for treating mothers and fathers differently in the allocation of parental responsibility?*

3. *Is the concept of parental responsibility trying to do too many things?*

## Further reading

Read **Gilmore** (2003) for a discussion of the arguments around the allocation of parental responsibility. Consider the arguments in **Masson** (2006c) over whether parental responsibility should be about a blood tie or caring.

---

[353] Bainham (2006b: 163).
[354] In terms of judicial resources and legal aid.
[355] Pickford (1999).

The arguments over who should get parental responsibility are well balanced.[356] The difficulty is that the cases where parental responsibility matters the least (where the mother and father are jointly raising the child together) are the cases where there are strongest arguments for awarding both parents parental responsibility, and the cases where parental responsibility matters the most (the parents have separated and are in dispute over the raising of the child) are the cases where there is the strongest case for putting special weight on the wishes of the parent who carries out the bulk of the day-to-day caring for the child. The truth is that the law is requiring too much of responsibility. A single concept cannot do the job of an acknowledgement of a parent's commitment; be a stamp of approval for their parenting role; provide a parent with all the rights and responsibilities of parenthood; and decide who can make important decisions in relation to children. At a risk of further complicating the law, it is suggested that the law should develop two categories of parental responsibility: that which acknowledges that the father has shown commitment to the child and that which reflects the reality that he is sharing in the day-to-day upbringing of the child.

## 11  Losing parental responsibility

A person with parental responsibility cannot give up parental responsibility just because he or she does not want it any more. Even if the child has to be taken into care because of the parent's abuse, parental responsibility does not come to an end.[357] In *Re M (A Minor) (Care Order: Threshold Conditions)*[358] the father had killed the mother in front of the children and was sentenced to a lengthy term of imprisonment. He still retained parental responsibility. However, parental responsibility can be extinguished in a few ways:

1. Anyone with parental responsibility will lose it when an adoption order is made. Once an adoption order is made, only the adoptive parents will have parental responsibility.

2. A child's birth mother and her husband will lose parental responsibility when a parental order under s 30 of the Human Fertilisation and Embryology Act 1990 is made.[359]

3. Once a child reaches 18, all parental responsibility for the child comes to an end.[360]

4. If a father has parental responsibility through a parental responsibility order, this can be brought to an end if the court so orders under s 4(3) of the Children Act 1989. An application to do so can be brought by someone with parental responsibility (including the father applying himself) or the child.[361] The welfare principle governs the issue. However, the court may not end a parental responsibility order if there is a residence order still in force in favour of the father. In *Re P (Terminating Parental Responsibility)*,[362] although the parents had made a parental responsibility agreement under s 4, it became clear that the father had caused the baby severe injuries, causing permanent disability. It was held that by his conduct he had forfeited his entitlement to parental responsibility and it was removed. It will require extreme conduct of this kind if the court is to remove parental responsibility under s 4(3).

---

[356] Although most of the academic writing supports a change in the law to permit all fathers to acquire parental responsibility automatically (see Gilmore (2003a)).

[357] See Chapter 11.

[358] [1994] 2 FLR 577, [1994] 2 FCR 871.

[359] See pages 337–8.

[360] CA 1989, s 91(7), (8).

[361] With leave of the court: see Chapter 9.

[362] [1995] 1 FLR 1048, [1995] 3 FCR 753.

5. If a person has parental responsibility by virtue of being granted a residence order then when the residence order comes to an end so does the connected parental responsibility. However, a father who has been awarded a residence order (and therefore parental responsibility) will retain parental responsibility even if the residence order is ended.

6. Parental responsibility will, of course, end on the death of the child, although there may be separate rights in respect of burial of the child's body.[363]

## 12 Wider issues over parenthood

Having looked through the law regulating parents, we can now look at some of the key issues of debate in this area.

### A What is the basis for granting parenthood?

There has been much discussion on what is at the heart of the concept of parenthood. Four main views will be considered: first, that genetic parenthood is the core idea in the law; secondly, that the law focuses on intent to be a parent; thirdly, that parenthood is earned by commitment to and care of the child; fourthly, that social parenthood (the day-to-day caring of the child) is the most important part of parenthood. Before considering the arguments in favour of these approaches, it should be noted that they are not necessarily incompatible. All four could be persuasive. As Bainham has argued,[364] by using a variety of understandings of 'parent' the law can recognise different aspects of parenthood. For example, it is then possible for the law to acknowledge that both genetic parent *and* social parent have a role to play in a child's life.

### (i) Genetic parentage

It could be claimed that the core notion of parenthood is genetic parenthood. It is clear that there is not an exact correlation between genetic parentage and legal parenthood. The circumstances where a man who is not biologically the father of the child can still be recognised as the father were discussed above. The circumstances where the legal father will not be the genetic father are as follows:

1. A husband may be presumed to be the father of his wife's child, but in fact not be the genetic father. If the genetic father does not seek to challenge the presumption, the husband will be treated as the father.

2. In cases of AID treatment where either the husband is the father under s 28(2), or the partner is the father under s 28(3) of the Human Fertilisation and Embryology Act 1990, the child's father will not be the genetic father.

3. An adopted father will be a father in the eyes of the law, even if he is not the genetic father.

4. Where a father has the benefit of a parental order, he will be the legal father but may not be the genetic father.

However, these circumstances are all rare. The vast majority of genetic parents are parents in law, although not all genetic fathers are awarded parental responsibility, as we have seen.

---

[363] *R v Gwynedd, ex p B* [1992] 3 All ER 317.
[364] Bainham (1999).

That said, if genetic parentage is at the heart of legal parenthood, it is surprising that the law does not take stronger steps to determine genetic parenthood. It would be possible for our legal system to require genetic testing of every child born to ensure that paternity is known, but it does not.[365] Instead, we are happy to rely on the presumptions of law. One journalist[366] has suggested that 30 per cent of husbands are unaware that they are not the father of their wife's children. If this figure is anything like accurate, then it must bring into question whether genetic parentage is in reality of significance for parenthood, because these husbands will be presumed to be the father in the law's eyes without being genetically the father. Further, there are claims which emphasise that genetic parentage can be unfair in cases of 'sperm bandits' (where men claimed that women obtained their sperm either by lying about whether they were using contraception or when the men were asleep or unconscious).[367]

But why should genetic links be regarded as important at all? There are two main arguments that have been relied upon in favour of biology:[368]

1. *Genetic identity*. It is argued that our genetic parents play a crucial role in our self-identity. The strongest evidence for this is in relation to adopted children, who often seek to find information about their genetic parents. To recognise genetic parenthood acknowledges the importance to the child of the genetic link. It also recognises the importance many parents place on the genetic link to their children.

2. *Genetic contribution*. Some argue that the genetic link is important because the child has been born out of the genetic contribution of the parents. As the child's being results from the contribution of the two genetic parents that contribution must be recognised.

Baroness Hale in *Re G (Children) (Residence: Same-Sex Partner)*[369] explained the significance of genetic parentage in this way:

> For the parent, perhaps particularly for a father, the knowledge that this is 'his' child can bring a very special sense of love for and commitment to that child which will be of great benefit to the child (see, for example, the psychiatric evidence in *Re C (MA) (An Infant)* [1966] 1 WLR 646). For the child, he reaps the benefit not only of that love and commitment, but also of knowing his own origins and lineage, which is an important component in finding an individual sense of self as one grows up. The knowledge of that genetic link may also be an important (although certainly not an essential) component in the love and commitment felt by the wider family, perhaps especially grandparents, from which the child has so much to gain.

## (ii) Intent

Some have argued that the law should now place less emphasis on genetic parentage and that, instead, intent to be a parent is of far more importance.[370] A parent is a parent only if he or she intends to be a parent. Or as Katharine Baker[371] prefers, a man is the father if he has struck a bargain to take on that role with the gestational mother. There is no doubt that there are some situations where intent to be a parent can be seen as crucial:

1. In assisted reproduction a man jointly receiving treatment with a woman can be treated as the father, even though he has no genetic link. Here his intention to be a parent is respected.

---

[365] Eekelaar (2006b: 75) argues that to do so would be too great an intrusion into a private area of life.
[366] Illman (1996).
[367] Sheldon (2001a).
[368] J. Hill (1991).
[369] [2006] UKHL 43 at para 33. See Leanne Smith (2007) for further discussion.
[370] Vonk (2007).
[371] Baker (2004).

2. A sperm donor can waive his parental status. Here the law respects an intention not to be a parent.

3. Guardianship seems based on intention, but in a negative way in that, unless the guardian expressly disclaims the guardianship, they will be a guardian.[372]

4. Adoption is intent based. An adoption order is made only after a person volunteers to be an adoptive parent.

However, there are problems in emphasising intent when considering the most common origin of parenthood, where normal sexual intercourse is involved. It could be argued that to have sexual intercourse reveals an intent to be a parent. At first this seems an implausible argument, given the rate of unintended pregnancies. However, it is possible to argue that, given the availability of contraception and abortion, where the couple decide to go ahead with a pregnancy they manifest their intent to be parents. But there are difficulties with this. First, a father will have a limited role in law in the decision whether or not the mother has an abortion.[373] Secondly, the decision not to abort may be due to religious or moral beliefs and not necessarily indicate an intention to become a parent. It could be argued that each time a couple engage in sexual intercourse they willingly accept the risk of becoming parents, and this is sufficient intent to be a parent. However, where contraception is used but fails, such a presumption would appear to fly in the face of the facts.[374] Further, it seems a very odd test for parenthood. If Y notices that a neighbour is pregnant and would like to act as a father of the child, Y cannot claim Y has an intent to be the child's parent, which should be recognised by law. There is also a concern that such an approach would lead to uncertainty. For example, how does one prove one's intent? What exactly is an intent to be a parent? There are also fears that, under the guise of using intent to be a parent, different policies could be used.[375] Could it be said, for example, that a drug addict could have no intent to be a parent because he or she would not be capable of being an effective parent?[376] There are also concerns that focusing on intent might lead to the burdens of parenthood falling on more women than men because it is more likely that a man than a woman will successfully be able to argue that he did not intend to be a parent.[377]

There might, however, be an argument that the intent to be a parent is useful where there are competing claims based on biology. For example, in **Johnson v Calvert**,[378] a Californian case, the mother gave birth following a surrogacy arrangement, the commissioning mother having provided the egg. Here both could be said to be the biological parent (the commissioning mother by providing the egg, the gestational mother through the care provided during the pregnancy). The court said that intent could be used to resolve the dispute. The court argued that 'but for' the intent of the commissioning parents, the child would not have been born and so they should therefore be regarded as the parents. It was held by Panelli J that it was the commissioning mother 'who intended to procreate the child – that is, she who intended to bring about the birth of a child that she intended to raise as her own – is the natural mother under Californian law'. The argument is not straightforward, as it could equally be suggested that if the gestational mother had not been involved, the child would

---

[372] It does reflect the intention of the parent of who should carry on the parenting role.
[373] A father cannot stop a mother having an abortion: *C v S* [1987] 2 FLR 505 CA. For a critique of such arguments see Sheldon (2003).
[374] Stumpf (1986: 187).
[375] Dolgin (1998).
[376] Douglas (1991: ch. 9).
[377] See the interesting discussion in Sheldon (2001a).
[378] [1993] 851 P 2d 774.

not have been born. A similar claim could be made for the medical team involved in the assisted reproduction.[379]

It is certainly true that intent-based parenthood would help avoid gender stereotypes or overemphasis of traditional family structures.[380] Recognising intent rather than the stereo-typical male and female roles would acknowledge a variety of parenting forms. It would permit more than two people to be parents of a child, and parents would not need to be of the opposite sex. This could be seen as a great benefit of the approach or a great disadvantage, depending on one's view on the traditional family form.[381]

### (iii) Earned parenthood

It can be argued that parenthood must be earned: the mother, through pregnancy, has demon-strated her commitment to the child and has formed a bond with the child. If the father has married the mother and can therefore be presumed to have offered the mother support through the pregnancy, this also indicates a commitment to the child. But the unmarried father has not earned the parenthood, as he has not shown the commitment to the mother and child by marrying the mother. Although this could be a test for parental responsibility, it is not an explanation of who is a parent. A genetic father can be regarded as a father even though he has done nothing to 'earn the parentage'.

### (iv) Social parenthood

At the start of this chapter it was noted that psychologists have stressed the importance of psychological parents. This has led some to argue that the law should recognise the day-to-day work of parenting, rather than the more abstract notions of intended parenthood or genetic parenthood.[382] As noted earlier, psychological evidence suggests that, for children, it is the person who provides their constant care and with whom they have an emotional relationship who is most important. The emphasis on social parenthood would also appeal to those who would argue that the law should emphasise and value caring interdependent relationships between parties.

### (v) Child welfare

James Dwyer[383] claims that the welfare of the child should be key to the allocation of parent.[384] We should not, therefore, 'thrust a parent–child relationship on a child where the adult is presumptively unfit to parent'.[385] This leads him controversially to suggest that where a biological parent is too young;[386] has committed serious crimes; has an IQ less than 70;[387] or is drug dependent, she or he should not be treated as a parent, unless they can show they are competent. He complains that the current law pays inadequate attention to the character or capacity of those it creates as parents.[388] Critics may reply that this is entering dangerous

---

[379] See Probert (2004a) who suggests a definition of parent based on who was the legal cause of the child com-ing into existence.
[380] Shultz (1990), discussed in Douglas (1994b).
[381] See Chapter 1.
[382] Schaffer (1990).
[383] Dwyer (2006).
[384] See Masson (2006c) who also suggests that the welfare of children should determine the allocation of par-enthood, but with very different results from Dwyer.
[385] Dwyer (2006: 35).
[386] He suggests under the age of 18.
[387] Dwyer (2006: 260).
[388] Dwyer (2006: 255).

territory. Once we start trying to predict who may be a good or bad parent we are slipping into 'social engineering'. It is simply impossible to predict who will be a good parent or not.

## B Is there a right to know one's genetic parentage?

### (i) What could such a right entail?

The question: 'Does a child have a right to know genetic parentage?' is often asked, but is ambiguous. It is necessary to be quite clear about what such a right would entail. The following could be included:

1. A right to know some non-identifying information about genetic parents.

2. A right to be told the names of genetic parents.

3. A right to meet one's genetic parents.

These rights might arise from as early an age as possible, or only once the child has reached the age of majority. It should be borne in mind that it is arguable that a child has a right *not* to know his or her genetic parentage. Even if we recognise the child's rights, it is necessary to appreciate that as well as these rights there are rights of parents that might also be relevant. There may be a right for a genetic parent to be acknowledged as the parent of a child. There may also be said to be a right of privacy: the right *not* to be acknowledged as the parent. There may also be rights of the social parent – that unwanted revelation of genetic parentage may amount to interference with their family life. Some countries in Europe offer a mother the opportunity to denounce her status of motherhood: the state will arrange alternative carers for the child and there will be no link between the mother and child.[389] Such laws are said to encourage women not to abandon their babies or to abort unwanted children. There are no equivalent laws in England and Wales.[390] There may also be rights of the social parent – that unwanted revelation of genetic parentage may amount to interference with their family life.

### (ii) Does the law recognise the right to know one's genetic parentage?

It is clear that the law does not recognise this right as a general one. We do not test every child at birth to determine genetic parentage. That said, with the Child Support Act 1991 and the expense that can fall on a non-residential father, it is likely that more fathers will seek to deny parentage and require tests which will establish the genetic truth. There are certain specific circumstances where the right to know one's genetic parentage arises.

#### (a) Children born as a result of sexual intercourse

A child can discover from his or her birth certificate who are registered as his or her parents. Once a child is 18 he or she can obtain a copy of the birth certificate, although the name of the father might have been left blank on the certificate. Even if it was filled in, there is no guarantee that the named man is the true father. A child might also discover his or her genetic parenthood if his or her mother is assessed by the Child Support Agency. However, the child has no right to be told who his or her father is by the Child Support Agency[391] and after the 2008 Child Maintenance and Other Payments Act there is no obligation on a parent to name a father.

---

[389] See the discussion in O'Donovan (2000).
[390] Although a mother can shortly after birth place her child with the local authority and ask for an adoption to be arranged.
[391] *Re C (A Minor) (Child Support Agency: Disclosure)* [1995] 1 FLR 201.

An adult may seek to rebut one of the presumptions of parentage. However, it is not possible to make a free-standing application for a declaration of parenthood.[392] In other words, a man cannot seek a declaration that he is or is not the father simply out of curiosity. Instead, there must be some other application to which parenthood is relevant; for example, if a man is seeking to have contact with the child or if there is a dispute over whether a man should be financially responsible for a child. Even then the court may decide that the application can be decided without recourse to tests. For example, in *O v L (Blood Tests)*[393] the mother argued that her husband was not the father of the child three years after their separation when the husband sought contact. During the marriage the husband had assumed that he was the father of the child and the court held that, given the close relationship between the husband and the child, contact would be ordered regardless of what the blood tests showed. There was therefore no need to pursue the tests.[394]

*When should tests be ordered?*

In deciding whether to order tests, the child's welfare is not the paramount consideration. This is because the child's upbringing is not in question and so s 1 of the Children Act 1989 does not apply. Instead, the test is as set out in *S v S, W v Official Solicitor (or W)*,[395] a decision of the House of Lords: 'the court ought to permit a blood test of a young child to be taken unless satisfied that that would be against the child's interests'.[396] The case law on whether tests should be ordered reveals that the courts are pulled by two countervailing arguments. On the one hand, the courts have placed importance on the child's right to know their genetic origins; on the other hand, the courts have placed weight on the concern that if it is found that the child's father is not the mother's husband or present partner, the child's family unit will be disrupted and this will harm the child. The cases show that it can be hard to predict which argument will carry the day.

The leading case emphasising the importance of the child knowing the truth is the Court of Appeal decision in *Re H (A Minor) (Blood Tests: Parental Rights)*.[397] The mother and her husband cared for three children. It was alleged that the youngest of the children was the result of an affair the mother had had. All three children and the husband had a good relationship. Ward LJ argued that 'every child has a right to know the truth unless his welfare clearly justifies the cover-up'.[398] He claimed that such a right was apparent in article 7 of the UN Convention on the Rights of the Child: 'The child should be registered immediately after birth and shall have the right from birth to a name, the right to acquire a nationality and, as far as possible, the right to know and to be cared for by his or her parents.'[399] Ward LJ did add that it was important here that the child's relationship with the husband was not likely to be harmed by finding out the truth about his biological paternity and that the child was likely to find out in any event, as the older brothers were aware of the doubt over the child's paternity. It was better to have the issue resolved now than for the child to find out later.[400]

---

[392] *Re E (Parental Responsibility: Blood Test)* [1995] 1 FLR 392.
[393] [1995] 2 FLR 930, [1996] 2 FCR 649.
[394] See also *K v M (Paternity: Contact)* [1996] 1 FLR 312, [1996] 3 FCR 517.
[395] [1972] AC 24.
[396] As summarised in *Re F (A Minor) (Blood Test: Parental Rights)* [1993] Fam 314 at p. 318; see also Fortin (1996).
[397] [1996] 2 FLR 65, [1996] 3 FCR 201.
[398] *Re H (A Minor) (Blood Tests: Parental Rights)* [1996] 2 FLR 65 at p. 80.
[399] The importance of ascertaining the truth was emphasised by the Court of Appeal in *Re H and A (Children)* [2002] 2 FCR 469, [2002] 1 FLR 1145.
[400] This case has been followed in several other cases: e.g. *Re G (Parentage: Blood Sample)* [1997] 1 FLR 360, [1997] 2 FCR 325.

The arguments in favour of ordering tests have been strengthened after the Human Rights Act 1998.[401] In *Mikulic v Croatia*[402] the European Court of Human Rights held that a child had a right to know her biological parenthood as part of her right to respect for private life under article 8. The state was required to put in place procedures which would protect that right. Notably the court did not claim that a father has the right to establish his paternity under article 8.[403] Indeed, in *Yousef v The Netherlands*[404] the European Court held that even though a father had family life with his child it was not in the child's interests to declare formally that he was the father. However, *Yousef* could be criticised on the basis that it failed to consider the child's right to have his paternity declared. In *Shofman v Russia*[405] it was confirmed that a fair balance had to be struck between the protection of legal certainty of family relations and the right of a party to challenge presumptions of paternity.[406] In that case not allowing a man to challenge a presumption that he was the father if the child was over one year old did not strike the correct balance and interfered with his rights under article 8. The strength the court might put on the right to know one's genetic background was revealed in *Re J (A Minor) (Wardship)*,[407] where the court accepted that an injunction could be granted to prevent a mother (who was seeking to avoid the carrying out of tests) leaving the country.[408] In *Secretary of State for Work and Pensions v Jones*[409] weight was placed on the child's right to know who his father was under article 8 in supporting the presumption of paternity in a case where a man without a good excuse failed to undergo a DNA test to establish whether or not he was the father of a child.

The leading case in favour of not ordering tests is *Re F (A Minor) (Blood Test: Parental Rights)*.[410]

---

### CASE: *Re F (A Minor) (Blood Test: Parental Rights)* [1993] Fam 314

A wife became pregnant at a time when she was having sexual relations with both her husband and another man. After the affair she was reconciled with her husband and they raised the child together. There had been no contact between the alleged father and the child. The lover applied for parental responsibility. It was claimed that the blood tests would not benefit the child. Indeed there was evidence that the mother's marriage would be harmed and the security of the child's upbringing would be diminished if the blood tests showed the lover to be the father. The Court of Appeal stressed that the welfare of the child depended upon the stability of the family unit, which included the mother's husband. The advantages to the child of the blood tests were, the court thought, minimal, when compared with the benefits of a secure family upbringing.[411]

---

[401] See Beesson (2007) for a discussion of the ECHR caselaw.

[402] [2002] 1 FCR 720.

[403] *Re T (A Child) (DNA Tests: Paternity)* [2001] 3 FCR 577. But see *Rozanski v Poland* [2006] 2 FCR 178 where a father who had helped raise a child did have a right to be recognised legally as father.

[404] [2002] 3 FCR 577.

[405] [2005] 3 FCR 581.

[406] See also *Mizzi v Malta* [2006] 1 FCR 256 at para 114.

[407] [1988] 1 FLR 65.

[408] *Re E (A Minor) (Blood Tests: Parental Responsibilities)* [1993] 3 All ER 596.

[409] [2003] Fam Law 881.

[410] [1993] Fam 314, discussed in Fortin (1996).

[411] A similar attitude was taken in *Re CB (Unmarried Mother) (Blood Test)* [1994] 2 FLR 762, [1994] 2 FCR 925.

In *Re K (Specific Issue Order)*[412] Hyam J stated that the child's right to know the identity of his father could be outweighed by the child's welfare. There the mother had an obsessive hatred of the biological father, and if the child was told about the father's identity the child would suffer due to the mother's emotional turmoil. He therefore refused to require the mother to inform the child who her father was.

The most recent cases have favoured ordering tests: *Re H (A Minor) (Blood Tests: Parental Rights)*;[413] *Re T (A Child) (DNA Tests: Paternity)*;[414] and *Re H and A (Children)*.[415] This suggests that only in cases where there is overwhelming evidence that children will suffer grave harm if tests are ordered are the courts likely to decline to order tests. However, it is clear that the court still will on occasion refuse to order tests:

---

**CASE: *J v C* [2006] EWHC 2837 (Fam)**

A man sought tests to establish paternity and contact in respect of his child in 2004. The hearing was adjourned and there were further delays in the litigation. By the time of the hearing in October 2006 the father had disappeared and it became clear that the child, now aged 10, believed that the mother's current partner was his father. As the man was no longer pursuing the litigation, the court considered whether the court on its own motion should order that the child be told the truth. A psychiatric report before the court advised against this, stating that the mother was vulnerable and to tell the child the truth would have been detrimental to her health. A CAFCASS report also agreed that telling the truth would harm the mother and child. Sumner J started by confirming that a court was entitled to make orders on its own motion, if necessary to protect the welfare of the child. He emphasised that the mother agreed that the child should be told the truth when he reached 16, but not at the moment. Sumner J held that in this case the harm to the child and his family of knowing the truth outweighed the benefits.

---

**CASE: *Re D (Paternity)* [2006] EWHC 3545 (Fam), [2007] 2 FLR 26**

A man claimed to be the father of a child (D) aged 11. D had been raised by a woman he believed to be his paternal grandmother. D's only stability in his troubled life had been living with this woman. A man (not the person assumed by the boy to be his father) sought blood tests to establish that he was the father and then contact to be ordered. He and D's mother had a relationship at the time D was conceived. D, described by the judge as a troubled and angry person, strongly objected to the applications. Hedley J accepted that there was a serious possibility that the man was the father. He also confirmed that, as established in the earlier case law (e.g. *Re H and A (Children)*[416]), the general approach was that in a case of disputed paternity the truth should be known and tests performed. He referred to: 'the general proposition that truth, at the end of the day, ➡

---

[412] [1999] 2 FLR 280.
[413] [1996] 3 FCR 201.
[414] [2001] 3 FCR 577, [2001] 2 FLR 1190.
[415] [2002] 2 FCR 469, [2002] 1 FLR 1145.
[416] [2002] 2 FCR 469.

is easier to handle than fiction', and explained that the courts' approach 'is designed to avoid information coming to a young person's attention in a haphazard, unorganised and indeed sometimes malicious context and a court should not depart from that approach unless the best interests of the child compel it so to do'.[417]

However, he held that this principle could be departed from where the best interests of the child compelled the court to decide otherwise. In this case the strong objections of the child played an important role in the decision-making. Even though the child may not have been *Gillick* competent,[418] Hedley J found that he understood the issues and had a strong view. As this stage of his life it was best not to press the issue. Interestingly, the court ordered that the man supply samples and these be stored so that if the child later wanted tests to be done they could be performed quickly.

These two cases demonstrate that there can be circumstances in which the child's welfare will outweigh any 'right to know'.[419] Two particular points of interest are, first, that the courts have seen these cases as a matter of welfare and made no reference to the now extensive jurisprudence of the European Court of Human Rights on rights to know (e.g. *Mikulic v Croatia*).[420] Second, the weight placed on the child's views in *Re D* is notable, especially given that he was found not to be *Gillick* competent. Analysed in terms of rights, it raises the issue of the extent to which a child has the right *not* to know their genetic origins. That is a question yet to receive sufficient judicial or academic attention. Third, the cases were, in part, driven by a reluctance to force a mother to disclose information she so clearly did not want to disclose. In *Re F (Children) (Paternity: Jurisdiction)*[421] the court showed a more robust approach with a mother being ordered through a specific issue order to inform the children of their father's identity.

### Tests and consent

Section 21 of the Family Law Reform Act 1969 states that the court can direct biological tests but not force adults to take blood tests.[422] A child can be tested if the person with 'care and control' of the child consents, or if they do not then the court can order that the tests be carried out if that would not be contrary to the best interests of the child.[423] In In *Re L (A Child)*[424] it was held that tests could be ordered against a presumed sibling of a child to determine the child's identity if it could be shown that doing so would not harm the sibling.

### Adverse inferences and refusals to be tested

Section 23(1) of the Family Law Reform Act 1969 states that if a person fails to take a biological test then the court will draw inferences.[425] If a man is seeking to show that he is the father of a child but refuses to undergo blood tests it will be presumed that he is not the

---

[417] *Re D (Paternity)* [2006] EWHC 3545 (Fam), [2007] 2 FLR 26 at para 22.
[418] See Chapter 8.
[419] See also *Re L (Identity of Birth Father)* [2009] 1 FLR 1152.
[420] [2002] 1 FCR 720.
[421] [2008] 1 FCR 382.
[422] Section 21(1).
[423] Section 21(3)(b), inserted by Child Support, Pensions and Social Security Act 2000. Blood Tests (Evidence of Paternity) (Amendment) Regulations 2001, SI 2001/773.
[424] [2010] FL 132.
[425] *Re A (A Minor) (Paternity: Refusal of Blood Tests)* [1994] 2 FLR 463.

father.[426] Similarly, if a man is seeking to show he is not the father but refuses to undergo blood tests, it will be presumed that he is the father.[427] If a mother refuses to allow a child to be tested when a man claims he is the father it will be presumed that the man is the father. If a mother refuses to consent to the child being tested when her husband claims he is not the father then it will be presumed that the husband is not the father. In effect, the law is saying that if a person refuses to undergo blood tests, which will establish the truth, then it must be that he or she knows the test will show his or her claim to be false. The position is summarised by Ward LJ in *Re G (Parentage: Blood Sample)*:[428] 'the forensic process is advanced by presenting the truth to the court. He who obstructs the truth will have the inference drawn against him.' The inferences are also a way of encouraging the parties to undergo tests.

An adverse inference will not be drawn if there is a reason for refusing a biological test which is fair, just and reasonable,[429] rational, logical and consistent.[430] For example, if it was contrary to someone's religious beliefs to give a sample for testing then this might be accepted as a valid reason.

### (b) Children born as a result of assisted reproduction

Following the Human Fertilisation and Embryology Authority (Disclosure of Donor Information) Regulations 2004[431] all children born as a result of donated gametes can discover the donor's name; the donor's date of birth and town of birth; the appearance of the donor; and (if provided) a short statement made by the donor. This applies to all children born from donations provided after 1 April 2005. Before that date a child could discover only certain information necessary for medical purposes and whether they were related to a person they wished to marry.[432] The change in the law was promoted as an important part of ensuring that a child has a right to know their genetic origins.[433] The Human Fertilisation and Embryology Act 2008 requires the Human Fertilisation and Embryology Authority to keep a register of gamete donors. Once an individual has reached the age of 16 he or she can request information about those whose gametes were used to produce them, subject to regulations which will be produced later. This can include information about genetic siblings. A gamete donor can also find out limited information about the number and sex of children born using their gametes. Interestingly the debate tends to surround sperm donors, there seem to be little consideration of egg donors.[434]

However, all those sources of information presume that a child knows that he or she has been born as the result of assisted reproductive technology. There is no requirement that a child's birth certificate indicate that a child was born as a result of donated sperm or eggs and there is no legal obligation on parents to tell their children of the circumstances of their conception.[435] There is evidence that over 70 per cent of parents who use reproductive

---

[426] *Re G (Parentage: Blood Sample)* [1997] 1 FLR 360, [1997] 2 FCR 325.

[427] *Re A (A Minor) (Paternity: Refusal of Blood Tests)* [1994] 2 FLR 463.

[428] [1997] 1 FLR 360, [1997] 2 FCR 325.

[429] *Re A (A Minor) (Paternity: Refusal of Blood Tests)* [1994] 2 FLR 463.

[430] *Re G (Parentage: Blood Sample)* [1997] 1 FLR 360, [1997] 2 FCR 325.

[431] SI 2004/1511.

[432] HFEA 1990, s 31(4)(b). Marrying your half-sibling may seem fanciful, but in cities where there is a severe shortage of sperm donors (such as Glasgow apparently) this is not so far-fetched.

[433] In *Rose v Secretary of State for Health* [2002] 2 FLR 962 it was accepted that children had a right to know the identity of their sperm donor fathers as part of their right to respect for their private and family life. However, the court left open the question of whether respect for the sperm donors' rights justified an interference in the child's rights.

[434] Jones (2010).

[435] See M. Roberts (2000) and Blyth, Frith, Jones and Speirs (2009) for further discussion.

techniques do not tell children of their genetic origins,[436] although the Human Fertilisation and Embryology Authority encourages parents to tell their children.[437] Without a legal require-ment that children born of donated sperm be told of their origins, the law's protection of their right to know their genetic origins is rather half-hearted.[438] Bainham[439] and others strongly assert that since children have a right to know the truth about their biological parentage, the law should oblige parents to tell their children that they are donor-conceived.

The change in the law has had predictable results. There has been a dramatic drop in the number of men donating sperm and there is evidence of infertile couples seeking treatment abroad in order to avoid the sperm donor father's identity ever being discovered.[440] A BBC report claims that 70 per cent of clinics are unable to access donor sperm, or find it extremely difficult to. It may also be that the reforms have made it even less likely that a couple will inform their child that he or she has been born as a result of assisted reproduction.[441] Turkmendag, Dingwall and Murphy express their objections strongly:

> The removal of anonymity has had identifiable detrimental effects: donors are reluctant to donate, UK clinics cannot meet the demand for gametes, there are long waiting lists for patients who wish to get treatment, and increasing use of international travel to avoid the law. None of these consequences were unforeseen or unpredictable: worries about donor shortage were voiced by major stakeholders (e.g. clinics, BFS, Royal College of Obstetricians and Gynaecologists, and British Medical Association) before the new law was introduced.[442]

### (c) Adopted children

This is discussed in Chapter 11.

### (d) Establishing parentage

The court has two jurisdictions under which it may seek to determine or declare parenthood. Under s 56 of the Family Law Act 1986 a child can seek a declaration that a named person is his or her parent.[443] Section 27 of the Child Support Act 1991 also allows the Secretary of State or person with care to apply for a declaration of parentage in connection with the operation of the Child Support Act.

If the law took seriously a child's right to know his or her genetic origins the legal position would be quite different. At present the birth register is not an accurate source of genetic information.[444] The state could require tests to be carried out at birth to ensure there was an accurate statement of a child's genetic background. At the very least there could be a require-ment for children born using donated gametes to have that registered as such.[445] The effect of the present law is that the child's right to know who his or her father was is only given effect

---

[436] Maclean and Maclean (1996). See also the studies by Cook (2002) and Golombok, MacCallum, Goodman and Rutter (2002) also finding widespread secrecy surrounding assisted reproduction.

[437] See Grace and Daniels (2007) for an interesting discussion of what causes parents to either disclose or not disclose their child's genetic origins.

[438] In J v C [2006] EWCA Civ 551 at para 13. Wall LJ had grave doubts whether a specific issue order could be made to require a parent to tell their child of the circumstances of their birth.

[439] Bainham 2008c.

[440] Turkmendag et al. (2008: 293).

[441] Blyth and Frith (2009).

[442] Turkmendag et al. (2008: 293).

[443] The courts will be wary about attempts to get a declaration of parenthood without using one of these statutory routes: see Re B (A Child) (Parentage: Knowledge of Proceedings) [2004] 1 FCR 473.

[444] Freeman (1992b).

[445] Glazebrook (1984: 209).

when the father seeks to establish his paternity. It would be more accurate to say that the present law protects a father's rights to establish his paternity than that a child has a right to know his or her genetic parents. Notably children whose mothers are in receipt of benefits have the right protected, because their mother may be required by the Child Maintenance and Enforcement Commission to declare who their father is.[446] Any father receiving an assessment from the agency who has any doubts over whether or not he is the father of the child is likely to insist that tests are carried out.

### (e) *The Human Rights Act 1998 and the right to know one's parentage*

As already indicated, the Human Rights Act can be relied upon to support a claim that a child has a right to know his or her genetic origins.[447] Although the European Courts have not been sympathetic to a claim that a father has a right to establish his paternity if he is unable to establish that he has family life with the child,[448] they have been more accepting of the argument that a child has a right to know who his or her parents are. In *Mikulic v Croatia*[449] the European Court of Human Rights found that a child's right to respect for private life included the right to establish who is his or her father. However, this right is not an absolute right. In *Odievre v France*[450] it was held to be permissible for France not to inform adopted children of their biological origins in the name of protecting the privacy of mothers who had given up their children for adoption.[451]

### (iii) Should there be a right to know one's parentage?

> **DEBATE**
>
> ## Should there be a right to know one's parentage?
>
> The main arguments in favour of recognising a right to know one's parentage include the following:[452]
>
> 1. Eekelaar argues that there is a right to be informed of one's parentage.[453] He asks whether anyone would choose to live their life on the basis that they had been deliberately deceived about their genetic origin.[454] On that basis he suggests we should recognise the right to know one's parentage.
> 2. There are claims that knowing parentage produces psychological benefits.[455] There is evidence that some adopted children feel that unless they find out about their genetic origins they suffer psychologically. Barbara Almond seeks to explain the importance of knowing one's genetic origins:

---

[446] See further Chapter 5.
[447] See also Blyth and Farrand (2004) on the approach of the UNCRC on donor anonymity.
[448] *MB v UK* [1994] 77 A DR 108.
[449] [2002] 1 FCR 720.
[450] [2003] 1 FCR 621, discussed in Steiner (2003) and Callus (2004).
[451] The argument was that if confidentiality was not respected, women who did not want to care for the children they were carrying would be more likely to abort or abandon them.
[452] Richards (2003) provides a useful summary of the arguments in favour of the right to know in the context of children born as a result of assisted reproduction.
[453] Eekelaar (1994a). See also Wallbank (2004b).
[454] Eekelaar (1994a).
[455] Wilson (1997).

Without this, [the children] are born as exiles from the kinship network and are orphans in a sense previously unknown to human beings. They may in fact have unknown half-siblings, cousins, aunts, grandparents, but they will never meet them. Of course, there is every chance that they will be provided by an alternative family network that will provide love and security, but the subtle similarities of genetic relationships may come to haunt them in the future, particularly when they have children of their own and start to look for such things as shared resemblances, attitudes, interests, tendencies, qualities of character and physical features in their own offspring.[456]

3. There is no evidence that children of assisted reproduction are harmed on discovering their origins.[457] Freeman notes that Sweden, Germany, Austria and Switzerland do permit disclosure, without there being disadvantageous consequences.[458]

4. O'Donovan[459] notes that there are medical reasons why one needs to know one's parentage. For example, if a child is aware that he or she is genetically predisposed to a particular illness, it might be possible to receive preventive treatment.

The main arguments against the right to know one's parentage are:

1. Some argue that social parents have an interest in not having their family life disrupted by information being given to the child they are caring for about his or her genetic origins.[460] Values of caring and relationship are valid can be undermined by emphasis on genetic truth.[461] Carol Smart argues 'secrets may be felt to be necessary for the preservation of relationships, and the "truth" may be taken to be less important than stabilising fictions'.[462]

2. The genetic parents may have a right to privacy, which would be infringed by informing the child of their existence. There is evidence parents who have used assisted reproductive services would suffer grave emotional harm if they were forced to disclose to their child that they were born as a result of assisted reproductive services.

3. The child may have the right not to know his or her genetic parentage. This argument would be that the law should wait until the child is old enough to be able to decide for him- or herself. The fact that some adopted children choose not to discover their genetic parentage suggests that they would rather not know the information.

4. In the context of assisted reproduction there are concerns that giving children the right to discover their parentage may discourage donation.[463] Many donors are not particularly interested in contact.[464] This will depend on the motivation behind the donation of the sperm or egg. Empirical evidence suggests that the typical sperm donor is a student donating for beer money;[465] although, now that anonymity of sperm donors has changed, the kind of men who will donate sperm may well change.[466] Egg donors seem to be motivated more strongly by altruism; indeed egg donation (unlike sperm donation) is not paid.[467] This is partly

---

[456] Almond (2006: 116).
[457] Golombok, Cook, Bish and Murray (1995).
[458] Freeman (1996).
[459] O'Donovan (1988).
[460] Discussed in Maclean and Maclean (1996).
[461] Smart (2009).
[462] Smart (2009: 558).
[463] Price and Cook (1995).
[464] Lui and Weaver (1994).
[465] Golombok and Cook (1993). At £15 a go (Horsey (2006)), it won't buy many rounds! An HFEA (2006) review suggested £250 plus expenses for a 'course' of sperm donation. It is not quite clear what a 'course' would be.
[466] Turkmendag et al. (2008).
[467] Plomer and Martin-Clement (1996).

because egg donation involves a higher degree of risk and injury[468] than sperm donation. More controversially, the technology exists to extract eggs from foetuses. The benefit of this might be thought to be that there would be no possible genetic mother who could seek to play a role in the resulting child's life.

5. Genetic origins are not very important. We each share 99.9 per cent of our genes with each other. Indeed, you share 50 per cent of your genes with a banana according to Professor John Harris![469] So, perhaps the importance given to our unique genetic inheritance is over-emphasised.[470] Many millions of people over the centuries have been brought up deceived as to their genetic origins, they don't seem to have suffered too much. It is only because we have the technology to do tests that this right has arisen.

6. Claims that a child has a right to know can easily be misused by adults to pursue their own agendas. Jane Fortin argues:[471]

> The DNA testing applications brought by putative fathers are not brought to provide the child with information alone, they are the initial stages of attempts to establish a social relationship between father and child based on assumptions about biological connectedness. The putative fathers' assumption that once the biological ties between father and child have been clearly identified, they should be fulfilled by a social relationship, produces an elision of the right to know the parent's identity, with the right to know and have a relationship with that parent. Whether or not claims can be justified by reference to the child's own rights, such an elision concentrates the court's attention on the putative father's position and his own interests – countered by those of the mother. Such an approach thereby produces considerable tensions, not least those arising from the false assumption that the biological link between child and parent can magically transform a previously non-existent relationship into a fruitful one for both parties.

## Questions

1. *Is a child who does not know their genetic origins harmed?*
2. *Are the issues of a right to know genetic origins and the definition of parenthood linked?*
3. *Why do some people seem to value the blood tie so much and others not?*

## Further reading

Compare **Bainham** (2008c) and **Fortin** (2009a) on the importance of the blood tie and the right to know one's genetic origins.

## C Is there a right to be a parent?

### (i) What might the 'right to procreate' mean?

It is hard to claim a positive right to procreate, not least because natural procreation requires two people. Few people would seriously suggest that the state should be obliged to provide partners for anyone who wishes to produce a child! Article 12 of the European Convention

---

[468] Smith and Cook (1991).
[469] Harris (2003).
[470] Richards (2006: 61) questions whether one's genetic origins are central to one's sense of identity given that twins can have identical DNA, but clearly separate identities.
[471] Fortin (2009a).

states that 'men and women of marriageable age have the right to marry and according to national laws governing the exercise of this right found a family'. Although this might suggest a positive right to procreate on a literal reading, this notion has been rejected in *Paton v UK*.[472] In *R v Secretary of State for the Home Office, ex p Mellor*[473] the Court of Appeal held that a married prisoner had no right under article 12 to have access to artificial insemination services to enable his wife to have a child. Such services were a privilege or benefit and no one could claim them as of right.[474] However, the Court of Appeal went on to suggest that there might be exceptional circumstances in which it would be a disproportionate interference in a prisoner's article 8 rights to deny access to assisted reproduction.[475] However, the Grand Chamber of the European Court of Human Rights in *Dickson v UK*[476] held by a narrow majority that a prisoner had a right under article 8 to receive assisted reproductive services. That right could be interfered with bearing in mind the interests of the child to be born and the wider state interests, but the state must ensure each prisoner's request to be able to use assisted reproduction was considered carefully on its own merits.

First, it can be said there is a right not to have one's natural ability to procreate removed by the state.[477] The notion of compulsory sterilisation, or having to be approved as a suitable parent before engaging in sexual intercourse, would not be acceptable in most democracies.[478] Further, in some of the cases involving sterilisation of adults with a mental disability, references have been made to the 'right of a woman to reproduce'.[479] The issue was considered by the courts in *Briody v St Helens and Knowsley HA*,[480] where, due to the alleged negligence of a health authority, the claimant was unable to bear children. She sought damages to enable her to enter a surrogacy contract in California, so that a surrogate could be impregnated with the claimant's egg, fertilised with her partner's sperm. She failed but, interestingly, Ebsworth J did not reject the claim on the basis that she had no right to a child but on the basis that she was seeking money to acquire a child by means of a commercial contract that would not comply with UK law. He foresaw that there may be cases where an award could be made to enable a woman rendered infertile to acquire a child.[481]

The second sense in which one might claim a right to procreate is to argue that one should not be denied fertility treatment without good reason.[482] For example, lesbian women, gay men or single people should not be prevented from using such techniques, without good reason.[483] It can be claimed that infertility should be treated as an illness and a would-be parent should be entitled to treatment for this as with any other medical condition. Mary Warnock[484] argues that a person is only entitled to claim as a right a basic need. Although couples might desperately want a child it is not a need that is basic to human well-being. Further she is concerned that children should not be regarded as an entitlement, but should remain a gift

---

[472] (1981) 3 EHRR 408 ECtHR.

[473] [2000] 3 FCR 148.

[474] For an interesting discussion of this case see Williams (2002).

[475] [2003] 3 FCR 148, at para 45.

[476] Application 44362/04, discussed in Jackson (2007).

[477] Although not expressed in such terms, *R v Human Fertilisation and Embryology Authority, ex p Blood* [1999] Fam 151, [1997] 2 FCR 501 could be regarded as accepting a right to procreate.

[478] Archard stresses that a right to bear children must be conditional on the ability to provide for one's offspring: Archard (1993).

[479] *Re B (A Minor) (Wardship: Sterilisation)* [1988] AC 199; *Re F (Mental Patient: Sterilisation)* [1990] 2 AC 1; *Re D (A Minor) (Wardship: Sterilisation)* [1976] Fam 185.

[480] [2000] 2 FCR 13. The Court of Appeal upheld the judgment in [2002] QB 856.

[481] [2000] 2 FCR 13 at p. 37.

[482] For further discussion see Robertson (1994); Harris (1999); Sutherland (2003).

[483] Douglas (1991: 21).

[484] Warnock (2002: 53). See further Warnock (2006).

to be received with gratitude.[485] The law governing the provision of treatment by fertility clinics will be discussed further shortly, but it should be noted that if there is such a right, it is limited. Under the NHS any right to claim treatment must be regarded in the context of the whole NHS system and there may be monetary or medical reasons why a particular form of treatment is not available.[486] It should be noted that those who are able to afford it may well be able to obtain infertility treatment that is not available on the NHS. This means that maybe the question, 'Can you buy a baby in the UK?' cannot be answered with a definite 'No'.[487] In *R (On the Application of Assisted Reproduction and Gynaecology Centre and H)* v *HFEA*[488] Sedley LJ took the view that neither articles 8 nor 12 gave a woman a right to a particular type of assisted reproductive treatment. However, if they did the HFEA might well be able to show reasons justifying why it should not be provided. That said, if a clinic refused to provide treatment on the grounds of race or sex (or perhaps sexual orientation) it is arguable that the rights under the European Convention would be engaged.[489]

Some writers have claimed there is a right to reproductive autonomy – the right to choose whether or not to reproduce.[490] It is argued that the choice to have a child is intimately bound up with our sense of identity and can therefore be analogous to other rights that are protected, such as the right to religion. The argument most often made to support such a claim is that, as there are no tests or restrictions on fertile couples who wish to produce a child, there should be no restrictions on those who need the assistance of fertility treatment.[491] Indeed, to impose such restriction could amount to discrimination on the grounds of disability. Opponents of such a right reject these arguments. O'Neill points out that the right to reproduce involves the creation of a third party, and this distinguishes it from other rights, such as to religion or free speech.[492] She argues that reproduction 'can never be justified simply by the fact that it expresses the individual autonomy of one or two (or more) would-be reproducers'.[493]

The issue of a 'right to be a parent' came to the fore in *Evans* v *Amicus Healthcare Ltd and others*.[494]

---

### CASE: *Evans* v *Amicus Healthcare Ltd and others* [2004] 3 All ER 1025

In October 2001 Natalie Evans and Howard Johnston, who were engaged, underwent IVF treatment. It was discovered that Natalie Evans had tumours on her ovaries. Her ovaries had to be removed as soon as possible and she was required quickly to make a decision on whether she wanted any ova removed and frozen. There were three main options: either that she freeze her ova; or her eggs be fertilised with donated sperm and frozen; or that her ova be fertilised with Mr Johnston's sperm and then frozen. She chose the last option, a decision she would subsequently deeply regret. There were two main ➡

---

[485] Warnock (2002: 53 and 112).
[486] *R (On the Application of Assisted Reproduction and Gynaecology Centre and H)* v *HFEA* [2002] Fam Law 347.
[487] Brazier (1999).
[488] [2002] Fam Law 347.
[489] For a comparison of how different countries approach issues surrounding assisted reproduction see Blyth and Landau (2004).
[490] Alghrani and Harris (2006). Spencer and Pedain (2006) for a useful collection of essays on this.
[491] Robertson (1994); Harris (1998).
[492] O'Neill (2002: 61).
[493] O'Neill (2002: 62). See also Cahn and Collins (2009) for a discussion of an American woman who had octuplets.
[494] [2004] 3 All ER 1025.

reasons for it. The first was that frozen ova do not freeze well and many do not survive. The second was that Mr Johnston assured her that he wanted to be the father of her children; that they were not going to split up; and that she should not be negative. Six eggs were harvested, fertilised and frozen. Later that month her ovaries were removed. In May 2002 the couple separated and Mr Johnston wrote to the clinic asking them to destroy the embryos. Ms Evans sought an order preventing the destruction of the embryos.

The Court of Appeal found the case straightforward in legal terms and decided against Ms Evans and authorised the destruction of the embryos. The decision was reached primarily on the basis of the interpretation of the Human Fertilisation and Embryology Act 1990 (HFEA 1990). That Act makes it clear that a licensed clinic is only permitted to store an embryo which has been brought about in vitro if there is effective consent by each person whose gametes were used to bring about the creation of the embryo (HFEA 1990, Sch 3, paras 6(3), 8(2)). Although Mr Johnson had consented to the original storage of the sperm and its use in fertilising the egg, he had now withdrawn his consent and so the clinic was no longer permitted to store it. It was not just the wording of the statutory provisions which convinced the Court of Appeal that this was the correct interpretation of the Act; they emphasised that there were two principles underlying the Act:

(i)   The welfare of any child born by treatment was to be of fundamental importance.

(ii)  The requirement of informed consent, capable of being withdrawn at any point prior to the transfer of the embryos to the woman receiving treatment.

Both of these principles supported the conclusion that the embryos should be destroyed. As to the first, it was not in the child's interests to be born to a father who did not want the child to be born. As to the second, it clearly required the destruction of the embryo.

The Court of Appeal also considered whether the Human Rights Act 1998 required the Court to reinterpret the HFEA 1990 in a way which was consistent with the parties' rights under the European Convention on Human Rights. The court quickly concluded that the embryo had no rights under the Convention.[495] As to the rights to respect for private and family life, it was noted that Ms Evans's right to reproduce had to be balanced against Mr Johnston's right not to reproduce. This was problematic because it involved 'a balance to be struck between two entirely incommensurable things'.[496] In essence the Court of Appeal felt that the HFEA 1990 had taken a reasonable approach between balancing these rights and so it could not be said to be incompatible with the Convention, although, had the Act permitted Ms Evans to implant the embryo, this too might have been a reasonable balance.

The case went to the European Court of Human Rights.[497] The European Court of Human Rights (Grand Chamber) held that English law in the HFEA 1990 did not improperly interfere with the parties' rights under the ECHR; although their judgment implies that a statute which would have decided that she could have used the embryos would also have been compliant with the ECHR. In other words, this was an area where states within their margin of appreciation could legislate as they felt appropriate. The European Court of Human Rights held that the case involved a complex clash of

---

[495] This was confirmed in *Vo v France* [2004] 2 FCR 577.

[496] [2004] 3 All ER 1025 at para 66.

[497] *Evans v UK* [2006] 1 FCR 585 and [2007] 2 FCR 5. See Wright (2008) and Morris (2007) for interesting discussions of the issues.

article 8 rights: in essence, the right to be a parent (of Ms Evans) and the right not to be a parent (of Mr Johnston). It also involved some broader social issues, such as the principle of primacy of consent and the need for certainty. The UK law which favoured the right not to be a parent could not be said to be improper. It could not be said that the state had a positive obligation to ensure that a woman should be permitted to implant her embryo notwithstanding the withdrawal of consent by the gamete provider. She had not been prevented from becoming a mother in a social, legal or physical sense because she could adopt a child or use donated gametes.

The case as an interpretation of the HFEA 1990 was relatively uncontroversial.[498] However, dealing with the human rights issues was less straightforward.[499] The Court of Appeal concluded that the article 8 rights of Ms Evans and Mr Johnston were equal and this was seen as acceptable by the ECtHR. However, the claimed right to implant the embryo and thereby become a mother and the claimed right to destroy the embryo and thereby avoid becoming a father both fall within the right to respect for private and family life under article 8; this does not mean that the rights are equal. Many people will agree with Thorpe LJ that these rights are incommensurate. Only the most hard-hearted can fail to find sympathy with Ms Evans being denied the only chance she had to have a child of her own. But many will also sympathise with Mr Johnston's principled objection to becoming a father against his wishes. One could go back to what is at the heart of the rights claimed here. In essence, this is the right of autonomy: the right to live your life as you wish. It is common to talk in terms of encouraging people to find and live out their version of the 'good life' free from interference from the state. This provides us some benchmark against which to measure these competing rights. Would it be a greater setback to their version of living their 'good life' for Ms Evans to be denied having the child she so desperately wanted or for Mr Johnston to have to live his life knowing there was a child of his whom he did not know and in whose life he was not able to play an effective role?[500]

### (ii) Should assisted reproduction be permitted?

Although assisted reproduction is now commonly available, whether it should be permitted is a topic which still engenders debate. Giesen[501] argues:

> Assisted reproduction with both gametes donated must be prohibited as departing too far from the traditional setting; donation of female gametes as well disturbs the natural unity of bearing and genetic motherhood. We feel that a separation of biological and social fatherhood should be avoided as well. Still, we must answer to reality: prohibiting AID would turn out to be unenforceable, since AID does not require medical assistance.

So, wherever possible, reproductive techniques should use gametes from the couple concerned. The validity of this argument partly turns on the idea of the 'natural'. Some would say that allowing a couple medical assistance to have a child is allowing them to have what nature intended (a child); others might argue that AID is equivalent to adultery. Whatever the views of individuals, it appears that Giesen's approach is in a minority.

---

[498] Department of Health (2005b) recommends improvements be made in explaining to couples the paperwork they sign when agreeing to treatment at a licensed clinic.

[499] An excellent discussion of the Court of Appeal case is Sheldon (2004).

[500] See Wright (2008).

[501] Giesen (1997: 260).

Another argument against assisted reproductive techniques is that the world is already overpopulated and there is no need to create more people. However, the number of children born through reproductive techniques is too small for this argument to carry much weight. Others argue that assisted reproduction overlooks the real problems connected with the issue: society's expectations which create the sadness often associated with infertility, and emphasises treating the symptoms of infertility, rather than considering its causes.[502] Further, it should be remembered that assisted reproduction carries with it far higher risks of adverse outcomes from babies than 'natural' conception.[503]

### (iii) Restricting access to assisted reproductive techniques

#### (a) *The legal restrictions*

Although the Human Fertilisation and Embryology Act 1990 provides regulations requiring the licensing of clinics it does not restrict who is permitted to have access to the treatment. The crucial provision is s 13(5), which requires clinics, in deciding whether to provide treatment to a particular patient, to take account of 'the welfare of any child who may be born as a result of the treatment (including the need of the child for supportive parenting), and of any other child who may be affected by the birth'.[504] Section 14 of the Human Fertilisation and Embryology Act 2008 had amended this provision, by removing the reference to a child's need for a father and replacing it by referring to the child's need for 'supportive parenting'.[505] There is also a non-binding code of practice.[506] This code of practice encourages clinics to start with a presumption that all those who seek infertility treatment should receive it. Clinics should consider whether there are things in a patient's medical or social background which might cause the child serious medical, physical or psychological harm. In law, then, the clinics have a wide discretion in deciding whether to provide treatment in individual cases.[507] Emily Jackson[508] has argued that it is not possible to assess the potential welfare of a child born as a result of assisted reproduction.[509] We do not assess whether fertile people should become parents, so we should not do that for infertile couples either. As Alghrani and Harris point out, paedophiles and abusers are allowed to become parents naturally, so why should they not be allowed to become parents using assisted reproduction? They state 'there is only one reliable criterion for inadequate parenting; it is the palpable demonstration of that inadequacy, in terms of cruelty, neglect or abuse of children'.[510] In other words, a person can only be labelled an inadequate parent once they have harmed a child; until then we should not try and predict who will be one. Their suggestion that we permit a known child abuser to receive assisted reproductive treatment and then wait until they have actually harmed the child before removing her is extraordinary. But is there a sensible way in which we can decide who will or will not make a good parent? Some ethicists suggest that the question to ask is whether a virtuous parent would choose to become a parent in these circumstances.[511] But under that test maybe very few people indeed should become parents!

---

[502] Morgan (1995).

[503] Blyth (2008).

[504] Discussed in Douglas (1993); Jackson (2002); Jackson (2007).

[505] HFEA 2008, s. 15. See Smith (2010) and McCandless and Sheldon (2010b) for a helpful discussion.

[506] Human Fertilisation and Embryology Authority (2010).

[507] Probert (2004: 274).

[508] Jackson (2002). See also House of Commons Science and Technology Committee (2005: paras 91–107) who are similarly critical.

[509] See Archard (2004a) who disagrees, arguing that it is wrong to bring into the world a child whose quality of life will be below a minimally decent level.

[510] Alghrani and Harris (2006: 202).

[511] McDougal (2007).

### (b) Restrictions in practice[512]

There is much evidence that clinics, in effect, ration access to reproductive treatments. Studies show that age, sexual orientation, and marital status are taken into account.[513] There have been complaints that clinics follow their own internal guidelines rather than considering each case on its own merits. Certainly there is a lack of consistency in approach, no doubt because the notion of the child's welfare is such an ambiguous concept.[514] This has led some lesbian couples to avoid using licensed clinics, for fear that they will be rejected.[515] Jackson has challenged the restrictions on access to assisted reproduction. She argues that doctors, legislators and regulators are ill equipped to make the decision about whether an individual deserves to be able to procreate.[516] Indeed no one should be making decisions about who can reproduce.

## (iv) Challenging a refusal to treat

If a parent wishes to challenge the decision of a health authority, the starting place is with the authority's own internal complaints procedure. The only legal remedy for an individual patient is to seek a judicial review.[517] But in *R v Ethical Committee of St Mary's Hospital (Manchester), ex p H*[518] it was indicated that it is very unlikely that the court will look into the merits of the decision made by a clinic. However, the court accepted that in extreme cases judicial review could succeed if, for example, the clinic denied treatment on grounds of race.

## (v) Should surrogacy be permitted?

### (a) Criminal offences

One writer has claimed that there are one hundred surrogate births per year.[519] Section 2(1) of the Surrogacy Arrangements Act 1985 states:

---

**LEGISLATIVE PROVISION**

**Surrogacy Arrangements Act 1985, section 2(1)**

No person shall on a commercial basis do any of the following acts in the United Kingdom, that is—

(a)  initiate or take part in any negotiations with a view to the making of a surrogacy arrangement,

(b)  offer or agree to negotiate the making of a surrogacy arrangement, or

(c)  compile any information with a view to its use in making, or negotiating the making of surrogacy arrangements;

and no person shall in the United Kingdom knowingly cause another to do any of those acts on a commercial basis.[520]

---

[512]  For further discussion, see Douglas (1993).
[513]  Six out of 66 clinics did not exclude from treatment anyone on principle; three of 65 clinics did not treat unmarried couples; 30 of 64 had a maximum age: Douglas (1993); Blyth (1995).
[514]  Blyth (1995).
[515]  Wallbank (2004a).
[516]  Jackson (2002: 259).
[517]  *R v Ethical Committee of St Mary's Hospital (Manchester), ex p H* [1988] 1 FLR 512.
[518]  [1988] 1 FLR 512.
[519]  Laurance (2000).
[520]  Section 3 outlaws advertising in relation to surrogacy.

To constitute an offence the arrangement needs to be made before the gestational mother becomes pregnant. It should be stressed that the gestational mother and the commissioning mother are not liable for the offence; only third parties who make the arrangements can be guilty of the offence. The UK will therefore never allow the situation which arises in the United States, where companies will advertise mothers at varying rates depending on their age, intelligence and health.[521]

It is also an offence to pay money that constitutes a reward or profit to the gestational mother under a surrogacy arrangement, but payment can cover expenses.[522] Any payments can be authorised under s 30(7) of the Human Fertilisation and Embryology Act 1990: *Re Q (Parental Order)*.[523] Some regard this as effectively permitting commercial surrogacy.[524]

Section 1A of the Surrogacy Arrangements Act 1985 states: 'No surrogacy arrangement is enforceable by or against any of the persons making it.' Without this provision a surrogacy contract might be thought to be enforced in the same way as any other contract. In *Briody* v *St Helens and Knowsley HA*,[525] the case mentioned earlier, where a woman sought damages from a health authority which she claimed had rendered her infertile through negligence to enable her to enter a surrogacy contract, Ebsworth J stated: 'It is one thing for a court retrospectively to sanction breaches of statute in the paramount interests of an existing child, it is quite another to award damages to enable such an unenforceable and unlawful contract to be entered into.'[526] However, it was left open whether in the future such damages may be available.

### (b) What happens when the baby is born?

If the arrangement goes to plan and the baby is handed over to the commissioning parents the following legal options are available:

1. The commissioning parents could take no legal steps. The gestational mother would be the mother and the genetic father the father. The commissioning parents (without a court order) would not have parental responsibility and so would be bringing up the child without formal legal authority. If the child's status ever did come to court, the judge may have little choice but to affirm the status quo and grant a residence order to the commissioning parents. This is demonstrated by *Re H (A Minor) (S.37 Direction)*,[527] where a mother gave birth, but did not want to care for the child. She handed the baby over to two friends, a lesbian couple. One had a history of mental illness and the other had a criminal conviction. Nine months after the birth the matter was brought to the court's attention. By now the child had bonded with the couple and the court accepted that unless there was danger of significant harm to the child it would have to affirm the present arrangements. Had the matter come to court shortly after the birth, with the couple applying for a residence order, it would have been highly unlikely that the court would have made the order. This case demonstrates the difficulties of legal intervention in this area. A surrogacy arrangement may not come to the court's attention until so much time has passed that the court has little option other than to affirm the transaction.

---

[521] Ince (1993).
[522] *Re Adoption Application AA 212/86 (Adoption Payment)* [1987] 2 FLR 291. In *Re C (Application by Mr and Mrs X)* [2002] Fam Law 351, £12,000 has been accepted as a payment covering expenses.
[523] [1996] 1 FLR 369, [1996] 2 FCR 345.
[524] Jackson (2002: 265).
[525] [2000] 2 FCR 13.
[526] At p. 36.
[527] [1993] 2 FLR 541, [1993] 2 FCR 277.

2. The commissioning parents could apply for a parental order. This has been discussed above.

3. The commissioning couple could apply for a residence order.[528] Leave to make the application will be required unless the commissioning husband is the genetic father of the child. In considering the application the court's paramount consideration will be the welfare of the child, and the court will not in any sense feel bound by the terms of the surrogacy agreement. However, if the gestational mother does not oppose the application it is likely to be granted.[529] Normally, if the child has bonded with the surrogate mother the court will be reluctant to order the child be handed over to the father. An exceptional case is *Re P (Surrogacy: Residence)*[530] where the surrogate mother lied to the father and told him that she had miscarried.[531] He later found out the truth and with his wife applied for a residence order. Although the child was now 18 months old and had spent all its life with the mother, it was held to be in the child's best long-term interests that the child be raised by the father and his wife. Evidence of the mother's psychological state indicated she would not be able to parent a child in the long term.

4. The commissioning parents may also apply for an adoption order if a parental order is not available.[532] One problem that may arise is that the Adoption Act 1976 clearly forbids any 'payment or reward' in private adoption placements. However, the courts have in practice been willing to overlook any payments made under the surrogacy arrangement and have authorised the adoption.[533]

5. The local authority may wish to investigate in order to decide whether to use any of its powers: for example, to apply for a care order. It may be that the court will make a direction under s 37 of the Children Act 1989,[534] asking the local authority to investigate the child's situation.

If there is a dispute between the commissioning parents and the gestational mother who refuses to hand over the child, then the commissioning parents could apply for a residence order. However, by the time the matter reaches the court it may well be that the child will have bonded with the gestational mother. This, in conjunction with the 'natural parent' presumption,[535] is likely to mean that the court will not grant the order and the child will stay with the gestational mother unless she is for some reason clearly unsuitable.[536] Although it is widely assumed that if the gestational mother is willing to hand the child over to the commissioning parents a parental order or adoption should be made in favour of the commissioning couple, this does not follow. It might be argued that if the birth mother does not want to care for the child, then the child should be placed with whoever is highest on the list of parents seeking to adopt a child.

The law's response to surrogacy is in a sense ambiguous. Surrogacy itself is not illegal, but on the other hand surrogacy contracts are not enforceable. Notably, two leading government reports on the subject found surrogacy widely 'accepted', but there were grave concerns that

---

[528] *Re C (A Minor) (Wardship: Surrogacy)* [1985] FLR 846; *Re P (Minor) (Wardship: Surrogacy)* [1987] 2 FLR 421, [1988] FCR 140.

[529] E.g. *Re C (A Minor) (Wardship: Surrogacy)* [1985] FLR 846.

[530] [2008] Fam Law 18.

[531] There was evidence she had done this to several men.

[532] *Re MW (Adoption Surrogacy)* [1995] 2 FLR 759, [1996] 3 FCR 128.

[533] *Re Adoption Application AA 212/86 (Adoption Payment)* [1987] 2 FLR 291; *Re MW (Adoption: Surrogacy)* [1995] 2 FLR 759.

[534] *Re H (A Minor) (S.37 Direction)* [1993] 2 FLR 541, [1993] 2 FCR 277.

[535] See Chapter 9.

[536] *A v C* [1985] FLR 445.

it was unethical.[537] Yet, as Deech has pointed out, where surrogacy runs smoothly there are no objections to surrogacy; it is when it does not that the media and general public become concerned.[538] The arguments for and against encouraging surrogacy arrangements will now be summarised.

---

### DEBATE

## Arguments over surrogacy

### Arguments against surrogacy

1. It has been argued that surrogacy arrangements are contrary to the best interests of children. Bainham has suggested that: 'It is difficult to see how it could be argued that surrogacy is designed *primarily* for the benefit of the child.'[539] However, he adds that talking of the benefits for the child is a little odd in this context. Would it be in a child's interests not to be born? Perhaps the strongest way the argument can be put is that it is not desirable for a child to be born in circumstances that are so likely to result in a dispute between adults, which may well harm the child. Some argue that children born as a result of surrogacy will be confused as to their identity.[540]

2. Surrogacy can be seen as demeaning to women – they are being used as little more than 'walking incubators'. There are some areas of life, it is argued, that are too intimate to be the subject of a contract.[541] Alternatively, it may be argued that the decision to give up a child is such a complex one that it cannot validly be made until after the birth.[542] There are particular concerns where women are forced through poverty to offer themselves as surrogate mothers.[543]

3. Surrogacy does not challenge the attitude of society towards infertility and means resources are not directed towards discovering the causes of infertility.

4. The Roman Catholic Church has argued that surrogacy is analogous to adultery, in that it brings a third party into the marriage.[544]

5. There are concerns expressed by some that the child after birth might be rejected by both the gestational mother and the commissioning parents, particularly if the child is born disabled.[545] Even if this does not happen, there are concerns that children will be confused over their biological origins[546] or that the child will be harmed by being denied contact with his or her birth mother.[547] Whether these concerns are such that it would be better for the child not to be born is hotly debated.

6. Commercial surrogacy arrangements commodify children and treat them as chattels to be bought and sold. Of course this argument is only really of weight when considering commercial surrogacy.

---

[537] Warnock Report (1984: para 8.17); Brazier, Campbell and Golombok (1998: para 2.23).
[538] Deech (1998).
[539] Bainham (1998a: 209).
[540] British Medical Association (1996).
[541] Field (1989), although Maclean (1990) provides arguments to the contrary.
[542] See the discussion in Lane (2003).
[543] Rao (2003).
[544] See also the opposition of the Roman Catholic Church (1987).
[545] For a disturbing example of where this occurred see Tong (1985: 56).
[546] See Morgan (2003) for argument that could be made in this regard under the Human Rights Act 1998.
[547] Lane (2003: 131).

## Arguments in favour of surrogacy

1. A woman should be allowed to do with her body as she wishes. If she wishes to enter into a surrogacy arrangement and use her body in that way, she should be allowed to. Surrogacy can also be argued as an aspect of procreative freedom. Indeed it is possible to regard surrogacy as a 'gift' to be encouraged.[548]

2. Some people believe that surrogacy is a more appropriate solution for infertile couples than AID or other forms of treatment.[549] However, as Bainham notes, 'surrogacy will be triggered by a man's desire to have his own *genetic* child where his wife or partner is unable to conceive or bear a child'.[550]

3. Surrogacy is inevitable, and therefore best regulated by the law. Its history goes back to biblical times, and, were it to be outlawed, this would simply lead to a black market in surrogacy.

4. It has been argued that surrogacy encourages and enables a variety of family forms. For example, a gay couple would be able to have a child through a surrogate. In early 2000 the media paid much attention to a gay couple who travelled over to the United States and produced a child, using a surrogacy arrangement, and then returned to Britain with the child.[551] In a different case a couple sought unsuccessfully to use a surrogate mother and the sperm of their dead son so that they could have a grandchild.[552] Some will see these examples as a welcome break from the traditional nuclear family form; but others will see them as a misuse of technology.

## Questions

1. *Should a surrogacy contract be enforced? If so, how?*

2. *Should surrogacy be regulated in the same way as adoption? Specifically should surrogate parents require approval from the local authority?*

## Further reading

Read **Horsey and Biggs** (2007) for a useful collection of essays on surrogacy.

The Government has reviewed the law on surrogacy following the disquiet concerning publicity surrounding Karen Roche.[553] The media claimed that she entered into a surrogacy arrangement with a Dutch couple but ended the arrangement, claiming (untruthfully) that she had terminated the pregnancy. It was alleged that she then entered into a second arrangement with a different couple. In 1998 there was a review of surrogacy[554] which led to proposals for a new code of practice aimed at controlling the payments to surrogate mothers and the regulation of surrogacy by the UK.[555]

---

[548] See the discussion of the use of gift in this context: Ragoné (2003).

[549] Even the BMA states that surrogacy is an acceptable option of last resort: British Medical Association (1996).

[550] Bainham (1998b: 202) (italics changed from the original).

[551] *Independent on Sunday* (2000).

[552] Laurance (2000). See Schiff (1997) for a general discussion surrounding the issues of 'posthumous parenthood'.

[553] See Hibbs (1997).

[554] Department of Health (1998a).

[555] As Morgan (2003) emphasises, the use of the Internet for 'procreative tourism' means that if surrogacy were banned in the UK it would be easy for someone to access surrogacy overseas.

## (vi) The right not to procreate

The law, to a limited extent, recognises a right not to procreate.[556] We will not consider the law relating to contraception and abortion in any detail here, only recognising that there is no legal impediment to access to contraception (at least for those over the age of 16), while access to abortion is restricted.[557] Douglas summarises the law's attitude to pregnancy:[558]

> The law therefore gives the woman the right to control her capacity to reproduce through contraception, through its recognition of a right to bodily autonomy in the sense of non-interference. But once the child has been conceived, her freedom to have an abortion depends on a balance which gradually shifts in the foetus's favour though never so far as to favour the life of the foetus over that of the woman.

## D 'Illegitimacy'

Historically, in England and Wales a lesser status has been accorded to children whose parents are not married. At common law an illegitimate child was referred to as a *filius nullius* and had no legal relationship with his or her father, nor even, at one time, with his or her mother. There has been a gradual shifting of the position by permitting a child to be legitimated by the parents' subsequent marriage,[559] and there has been a gradual removal of the legal disadvantages of children born outside of marriage. Now, as we shall see, very few consequences flow from illegitimacy. The key argument behind the reforms is that a child's legal position should not be affected by the parents' decision whether or not to marry. This is reflected in article 2(1) of the UN Convention on the Rights of the Child and in the European Convention on the Legal Status of Children Born out of Wedlock, which both state that a child's status should not depend on whether his or her parents were married. Some jurisdictions have removed the status of the illegitimate child altogether.[560] As confirmed by the European Court of Human Rights in *Sahin v Germany*,[561] the Human Rights Act 1998 means that any distinction between legitimate and illegitimate children may infringe article 8 in conjunction with article 14, unless that distinction can be justified as necessary under para 2 of article 8.[562]

The Family Law Reform Acts of 1969 and 1987 have done much to limit the distinction made between legitimate and illegitimate children. Now children whose parents are not married have nearly the same rights as children whose parents are married. Section 1(1) of the Family Law Reform Act 1987 states that for all future legislation any reference to a parent would (unless there was contrary indication) cover both married and unmarried parents. However, there are a few distinctions between children whose parents were married and those whose parents were unmarried, in the areas of citizenship,[563] titles of honour[564] and maintenance.[565] There is also a distinction drawn in the father's legal position because

---

[556] Jackson (2009); Priaulx (2009).
[557] See Herring (2010e: ch. 5) for a discussion of the issues surrounding abortion.
[558] Douglas (1991: 18).
[559] Legitimacy Act 1976.
[560] E.g. New Zealand.
[561] [2003] 2 FCR 619.
[562] *Camp and Bourimi v The Netherlands* [2000] 3 FCR 307.
[563] Discussed in detail in Cretney (1997: 606). In *Re Moynihan* [2000] 1 FLR 113 the House of Lords took the view that this was not in breach of article 8 of the European Convention, nor article 1 of the first Protocol.
[564] Family Law Reform Act 1987, s 19(14).
[565] See Chapter 5.

an unmarried father, unlike a married father, does not acquire parental responsibility. In *R (On the Application of Montana)* v *Secretary of State for the Home Department*[566] it was held that the denial of citizenship to the child of an unmarried father was not an infringement of the right to respect for family life, and therefore article 14 could not be invoked. It could be argued that the fact that children of unmarried parents do not benefit from their fathers having parental responsibility for them is discrimination on the grounds of their illegitimacy. It is also notable that the judiciary still in judgments refer to 'illegitimate' children, even in the House of Lords.[567] Indeed we still have a Legitimacy Act 1976 on the statue books and it is technically possible to apply for a declaration of legitimacy.[568] So despite the formal removal of legitimacy from family law, it still lingers around.[569]

## E  Licensing parenthood

As mentioned earlier, it would be possible to have a legal system where parents would only be able to keep children if they were approved by the state as suitable. This is sometimes known as licensing parenthood.[570] Few would support licensing; in fact there is a positive fear of 'social engineering'. In one case Butler-Sloss LJ stated: 'The mother must be shown to be entirely unsuitable before another family can be considered, otherwise we are in grave danger of slipping into social engineering.'[571] Despite this, there are some forms of parenting which are in effect licensed. Most obviously, adoption and parenting orders are made after the court is convinced that the parents are suitable.

## 13 Conclusion

It was not long ago when to ask, 'What is a parent?' would have appeared to be asking the obvious; but now the question is the subject of lengthy books. The complex sets of relationships within which children are raised require the law to recognise that a variety of people may act towards the child in a parental or quasi-parental way and those who are the child's genetic parents may play little part in the child's life. One major debate in this area concerns whether greater legal recognition should be given to those who are the genetic parents of the child or to those who act socially as the parents of the child.[572] The law is developing ways of recognising both these understandings of parenthood, but the 'balance of power' between the adults involved is controversial. This chapter has also considered other complex issues which have been created by the advent of assisted reproduction: Is there a right to be a parent? Does a child have a right to know his or her genetic origins? The future development of reproductive technologies will, no doubt, create many more legal problems.

---

[566] [2001] 1 FCR 358.
[567] *Dawson* v *Wearmouth* [1999] 1 FLR 1167; for criticism of them doing so, see Bainham (2000b: 482) and Bainham (2009c). Hale LJ in *Re R (A Child)* [2001] EWCA Civ 1344 was critical of case reporters who had used the word 'illegitimate' in the title of a case.
[568] Family Law Act 1986, s. 56.
[569] Bainham (2009c).
[570] Lafollete (1980).
[571] *Re K (A Minor) (Wardship: Adoption)* [1991] 1 FLR 57, [1991] FCR 142.
[572] Millbank (2008a).

## Further reading

**Bainham, A.** (2006b) 'The Rights and Obligations Associated with the Birth of a Child', in J. Spencer and A. du Bois-Pedain (eds) *Freedom and Responsibility in Reproductive Choice*, Oxford: Hart.

**Bainham, A.** (2008a) 'Arguments about parentage', *Cambridge Law Journal* 67: 322.

**Bainham, A.** (2008c) 'What is the point of birth registration?', *Child and Family Law Quarterly* 20: 449.

**Bainham, A., Day Sclater, S. and Richards, M. (eds)** (1999) *What is a Parent?*, Oxford: Hart.

**Baker, K.** (2004) 'Bargaining or Biology? The History and Future of Paternity Law and Parental Status', *Cornell Journal of Law and Public Policy* 14: 1.

**Blyth, E.** (2008) 'To Be or Not to Be? A Critical Appraisal of the Welfare of Children Conceived through New Reproductive Technologies', *International Journal of Children's Rights* 16: 505.

**Diduck, A.** (2007) 'If only we can find the appropriate terms to use the issue will be solved: law, identity and parenthood', *Child and Family Law Quarterly* 19: 458.

**Draper, H. and Ives, J.** (2009) 'Paternity testing: a poor test of fatherhood', *Journal of Social Welfare and Family Law* 31: 407.

**Eekelaar, J.** (1991c) 'Parental responsibility: State of nature or nature of the state?', *Journal of Social Welfare and Family Law* 13: 37.

**Fortin, J.** (2009a) 'Children's right to know their origins – too far, too fast?', *Child and Family Law Quarterly* 21: 336.

**Gilmore, S.** (2003) 'Parental responsibility and the unmarried father – a new dimension to the debate', *Child and Family Law Quarterly* 15: 21.

**Horsey, K. and Biggs, H.** (2007) *Human Fertilisation and Embryology: Reproducing Regulation*, London: Routledge.

**Jackson, E.** (2002) 'Conception and the irrelevance of the welfare principle', *Modern Law Review* 65: 176.

**Jones, C.** (2007) *Why donor insemination requires developments in family law: the need for new definitions of parenthood*, Lewiston: Edwin Mellen.

**Lind, C.** (2008) 'Responsible Fathers: paternity, the blood tie and family responsibility', in J. Bridgeman, H. Keating and C. Lind (eds), *Responsibility, Law and the Family*, London: Ashgate.

**Lind, C. and Hewitt, T.** (2009) 'Law and the complexities of parenting: parental status and parental function', *Journal of Social Welfare and Family Law* 31: 391.

**Masson, J.** (2006c) 'Parenting by being; parenting by doing – In search of Principles for Founding Families', in J. Spencer and A. du Bois-Pedain (eds) *Freedom and Responsibility in Reproductive Choice*, Oxford: Hart.

**McCandless, J. and Sheldon, S.** (2010a) 'The Human Fertilisation and Embryology Act 2008 and the Tenacity of the Sexual Family Form', *Modern Law Review* 73: 175.

**Millbank, J.** (2008a) 'Unlikely Fissures and Uneasy Resonances: Lesbian Co-mothers, Surrogate Parenthood and Fathers' Rights', *Feminist Legal Studies* 16: 141.

**Sheldon, S.** (2005) 'Fragmenting Fatherhood: The Regulation of Reproductive Technologies', *Modern Law Review* 68: 523.

**Smith, Leanne** (2006b) 'Is three a crowd? Lesbian mothers' perspectives on parental status', *Child and Family Law Quarterly* 18: 231.

**Smith, Leanne** (2010) 'Clashing symbols? Reconciling support for fathers and fatherless families after the Human Fertilisation and Embryology Act 2008', *Child and Family Law Quarterly* 22: 46.

**Turkmendag, I., Dingwall, R. and Murphy, T.** (2008) 'The removal of donor anonymity in the UK: The silencing of claims by would-be parents', *International Journal of Law, Policy and the Family* 22: 283.

Visit **www.mylawchamber.co.uk/herring** to access study support resources including interactive multiple choice questions, weblinks, discussion questions and legal updates.

*unrivalled support for legal education*

Use **Case Navigator** to read in full some of the key cases referenced in this chapter with commentary and questions:

POWERED BY LexisNexis

*Re G (Children) (Residence: Same-Sex Partner)* [2006] 4 All ER 241

*Leeds Teaching Hospital Trust* v *A* [2003] 1 FCR 599

*Lancashire CC* v *B* [2000] All ER 97

*Re S (A Minor) (Parental Responsibility)* [1995] 3 FCR 225

# 8 Parents' and children's rights

This chapter will consider the legal position of parents and children.[1] What rights do parents and children have? How can the law balance the interests of parents and children? Chapter 9 will look at how the courts resolve disputes between children and parents. This chapter is concerned with the legal position if no court order has been made. The chapter will start by considering when childhood begins or ends. It will then examine the position of parents: what obligations and rights does the law impose upon parents? The chapter will then turn to the legal position of children: how does the law protect the interests of children? Do children have any rights? The complex questions of how to deal with clashes between the interests of children and parents and also between different children will be examined. The chapter will conclude by looking at particular issues to see how, in practice, the interests of children and parents are balanced.

## 1 When does childhood begin?

English law takes the position that a person's life begins at birth. Before birth the foetus is not a person. But this does not mean that the unborn child is a 'nothing'. In the eyes of the law the foetus is a 'unique organism'[2] which is protected by the law in a variety of ways.[3] For example, it is an offence to procure a miscarriage unless the procedure is permitted under the Abortion Act 1967. However, the law is unwilling to protect the foetus at the expense of the rights of the mother to bodily integrity and self-determination. For example, in *Re F (In Utero)*[4] the social services were concerned about the well-being of the unborn child and wanted to make it a ward of court. The court stated that the unborn child could not be made a ward of court, as it was not a child; although once the child was born there was nothing to stop the court warding him or her.[5] It was held that to enable an unborn child to be warded would give the court inappropriate control over the mother's life.[6]

Fathers have no rights in relation to foetuses and are therefore not able to prevent an abortion.[7] The only possible route for a father seeking to prevent an abortion is to argue that

---

[1] See Fortin (2009b) for an excellent discussion of themes of this chapter.
[2] *Attorney-General's Reference (No. 3 of 1994)* [1998] AC 245 at p. 256.
[3] *St George's Healthcare NHS Trust v S* [1998] 2 FLR 728. *Vo v France* [2004] 2 FCR 577 made it clear that the foetus has no rights under the ECHR, although it is open to signatory states to pass legislation to protect foetuses if they wish. For discussion of this case see Mason (2005).
[4] [1988] Fam 122; Fortin (1988).
[5] See Chapter 11 for further discussion of when a care order can be obtained in such cases.
[6] For a general discussion of the law, see Seymour (2000); Herring (2000a).
[7] *C v S* [1987] 2 FLR 505; *Paton v BPAST* [1979] QB 276. Approved by the European Convention on Human Rights: *Paton v UK* (1981) 3 EHRR 408.

the proposed abortion is illegal. However, in *C v S*[8] it was suggested that the Director of Public Prosecutions is the person who should be bringing any such proceedings, rather than the father.[9]

## 2 When does childhood end?

Childhood is a concept in flux. Societies at different times and in different places have had a variety of ideas about when childhood ends.[10] In 1969 the legal age at which a child ceased to be a minor in England and Wales was reduced from 21 to 18.[11] The Children Act 1989 confirms this by defining a child as 'a person under the age of eighteen'.[12] However, there is not a straightforward transformation in the status of the child at age 18. For example, 16 is the age at which a child is entitled to perform some activities[13] and there are still some legal limitations that apply until the person is 21.[14] Further, in *Gillick v W Norfolk and Wisbech AHA*[15] the House of Lords accepted that the law must recognise that children develop and mature at different rates and a child under 16 should be recognised as competent to make some decisions for himself or herself. We shall discuss the notion of '*Gillick*-competence' and when under 16-year-olds can make decisions for themselves in further detail shortly.

Although childhood legally ends at age 18, the parental role does not necessarily end then. Many over-18-year-olds continue to live with parents, who will continue to provide them with practical, financial and emotional support. Indeed, under certain circumstances parents can be legally obliged to support children financially beyond the age of 18.[16]

## 3 The nature of childhood

As we have seen already there is no hard and fast line between childhood and adulthood. This has led some to claim that childhood is a social construction.[17] Certainly the notion of childhood is a powerful one in our society and the media are constantly concerned by the position of children. To some we are living in times when childhood is disappearing, with children becoming exposed to adult life at an earlier and earlier stage. In particular, there are concerns about the sexualisation and commercialisation of children.[18] These are rushing children through what should be an innocent and stress-free time of life.[19] However, others claim that the lines between childhood and adulthood are being reinforced more than ever. Children are being excluded from public places either because their parents fear for their

---

[8] [1987] 2 FLR 505.
[9] Infant Life (Preservation) Act 1929, s 1.
[10] Ariès (1986); Freeman (1997a).
[11] Family Law Reform Act 1969, s 1. Eighteen is the age used by the UN Convention on the Rights of the Child, Article 1.
[12] Children Act 1989, s 105(1); subject to exemptions relating to financial support.
[13] A child can marry at age 16.
[14] For example, applicants for adoption need to have reached the age of 21.
[15] [1986] 1 FLR 229, [1986] AC 112.
[16] E.g. *B v B (Adult Student: Liability to Support)* [1998] 1 FLR 373 and see Chapter 5.
[17] In other words, that there is not an objectively true definition of childhood, rather the concept is created by society. See further Fionda (2001); Stainton Rogers (2001); Smart, Neale and Wade (2001: 11).
[18] Although children's materialism simply reflects society's: Ashworth and Walker (1994).
[19] Stainton Rogers (2001); Mayall (2002: 3).

safety or because of concerns about their behaviour.[20] Children's play is nowadays made up of commercialised leisure activities, usually overseen by adults.[21] Much government legislation has been directed towards tackling truants and children with anti-social behaviour. Children have been regarded as a resource the state needs to invest in.[22] It may, in fact, be that both these perspectives have an element of truth:[23] that children are simultaneously being treated as dangerous young people in need of control in some areas of life, but also as vulnerable minors needing protection and/or restraint. Are they little angels or little devils?[24]

A similar division of opinion can be found in assessments of the position of children in society.[25] Much has been written of the innocence of children and the need to protect them from the vast array of dangers the modern world poses to them. However, others challenge this view. Jenks argues that children now have taken a central place in meeting the needs of adults. He argues:

> As we need children we watch them and we develop institutions and programmes to watch them and oversee the maintenance of that which they, and they only, now protect. We have always watched children, once as guardians of their own future and now because they have become the guardians.[26]

Jenks then suggests that adults' concern over the vulnerability of children says far more about the insecurity of adults than it does about the reality for children. He also challenges the orthodox view that children are nowadays economically unproductive and are (until they are older) a drain on the economy. James, Jenks and Prout suggest that such a view overlooks the way children contribute to the economy by the time they spend caring for themselves rather than relying on an adult to look after them; and by caring for sick or disabled adults and working for their parents in unpaid work.[27] There has also been much academic discussion of the notion of children as citizens. Bren Neale[28] writes of the need to see children 'not simply as welfare dependants but as young citizens with an active contribution to make to society'.

The last couple of decades have seen increasing interest in the role of children in family life from psychologists[29] and sociologists. The common perception that children are passive in family life, the victims of the decisions of the adults around them, has been challenged. Increasingly children are recognised as active participants in family life, sometimes offering as much support and help as they receive from their parents.[30] In relation to legal intervention on relationship breakdown Alison Diduck and Felicity Kaganas[31] suggest children are seen as both incompetent and dependent, but also as having agency and autonomy.

In all of this discussion there tends to be a separation into 'them' (the children) and 'us' the adults.[32] However, as already indicated, there is no clear divide.

---

[20] Valentine (2004).
[21] Mayhew, Finch, Beresford and Keung (2005).
[22] Piper (2009).
[23] Smart, Neale and Wade (2001) suggest that in the media children are often represented as either little angels or little devils.
[24] Valentine (2004: 1).
[25] See James and James (2004) and Prout (2005) for excellent sociological accounts of childhood.
[26] Jenks (1996: 69).
[27] James, Jenks and Prout (1998); Solberg (1997).
[28] Neale (2004: 1).
[29] E.g. Graham, Turk and Verhulst (1999).
[30] Smart, Neale and Wade (2001: 12).
[31] Diduck and Kaganas (2004).
[32] Mayall (2000).

## TOPICAL ISSUE

### Childhood in crisis?

In recent years the media paid much attention to the 'crisis' of childhood. In 2006 a letter was sent to the *Daily Telegraph* signed by leading academics and public figures. They expressed grave concern at the rates of depression and behavioural problems experienced by children. They saw 'modern life' as being part of the problem, explaining: 'Since children's brains are still developing, they cannot adjust – as full-grown adults can – to the effects of ever more rapid technological and cultural change. They still need what developing human beings have always needed, including real food (as opposed to processed "junk"), real play (as opposed to sedentary, screen-based entertainment), first-hand experience of the world they live in and regular interaction with the real-life significant adults in their lives.'[33] The Archbishop of Canterbury joined the expression of concern, complaining that children had become 'infant adults'.[34] A 2008 report blamed excessive individualism by adults as creating a mass of problems for children.[35] In one survey 89 per cent of adults felt that children had been damaged by materialsim.[36] But children are regarded not just as disadvantaged but dangerous. In one poll 43 per cent agreed with the statement that 'something has to be done to protect us from children'.[37] Whether children 'have never had it so bad' is hard to assess. In material ways there is much evidence that children are better off than their predecessors, but that seems to be bringing with it a range of other problems. The Children's Commissioner states that 'one in ten children and young people aged 5–16 have a mental disorder that is associated with "considerable distress and substantial interference with personal functions"'.[38]

## 4 Parents' rights, responsibilities and discretion

Parental responsibility is the key legal concept which describes the legal duties and rights that can flow from being a child's parent. It is significant that the Children Act 1989 talks of 'parental responsibility' rather than 'parental rights', because this stresses that children are not possessions to be controlled by parents, but instead children are persons to be cared for. Parents should have their responsibilities, rather than their rights, in the forefront of their minds. However, when the Children Act comes to define parental responsibility in s 3, it states:

## LEGISLATIVE PROVISION

### Children Act 1989, section 3

In this Act 'parental responsibility' means all the rights, duties, powers, responsibilities and authority which by law a parent of a child has in relation to the child and his property.

---

[33] Abbs et al. (2006).
[34] BBC Newsonline (2006e).
[35] Laylard and Dunn (2008).
[36] BBC Newsonline (2008i).
[37] Bernados (2008).
[38] 11 Million (2008a). See Morrow and Mayall (2009) for a discussion of the difficulties in assessing children's well-being.

It will be noted that the first word used to describe parental responsibility is 'rights'. This demonstrates that it would be quite wrong to say that parents do not have rights.[39]

## A Parental rights

Two important distinctions need to be made when we consider parental rights. The first is that when talking about parents' rights it is important to distinguish:

1. The rights a parent may have as a human being. These will be called a parent's human rights and would include, for example, the right to life, free speech, etc.

2. The rights that a parent may have because he or she is a parent. These will be called a parent's parental rights and would include the right to decide where the child will live.

Secondly, when talking about a parent's parental rights it is important to be clear what might be meant by such a phrase. Take, for example, the parent's right to feed the child. By this could be meant one (or more) of three things:

1. Third parties or the state cannot prevent the parent carrying out this particular activity. So, no one is entitled to prevent a parent feeding the child what food the parent believes appropriate.

2. The state must enable the parent to perform this activity. For example, in relation to the right to feed, the state is obliged to ensure that parents have sufficient money so that they can supply the food the child needs.

3. The acts of the parents are lawful. This means that although it may be unlawful for a stranger to feed a child,[40] the parental right means it is not unlawful for a parent to feed a child.

Having made these distinctions there are some difficult questions concerning parental rights that must be faced.[41]

## B Are parents' rights and responsibilities linked?

In the House of Lords decision in *Gillick*, Lord Scarman argued that parents' rights exist only for the purpose of discharging their duties to children: 'Parental rights are derived from parental duty and exist only so long as they are needed for the protection of the person and property of the child.'[42] Lord Scarman is talking here about a parent's parental rights and is making the important point that any parental rights a parent has exist for the purpose of promoting children's interests. Bainham, however, suggests that the position is not that straightforward. He has suggested that parents have rights *because* they have responsibilities and they have responsibilities *because* they have rights.[43] By contrast Michael Freeman claims that children have a right to responsible parents.[44]

---

[39] See Scherpe (2009) for a comparative analysis of the notion of parental rights.
[40] It is far from clear whether this would be a criminal offence (assuming the substance is not harmful), although it could be a battery.
[41] See Archard (2003: ch. 2) for a useful discussion of parents' rights.
[42] *Gillick v W Norfolk and Wisbech AHA* [1986] AC 112 at p. 184, per Lord Scarman.
[43] Bainham (1998a).
[44] Freeman (2008).

McCall Smith[45] has argued that not all parental rights exist for the benefit of children. He suggests that parents have two kinds of parental rights: parent-centred and child-centred rights. Child-centred rights are rights given to parents to enable them to carry out their duties. So, the parent has the right to clothe the child as an essential part of enabling the parent to fulfil his or her duty of ensuring the health of the child. By contrast, parent-centred rights exist for the benefit of the parent. One example McCall Smith gives is that of the parental right to determine the religious upbringing of children. He argues: that this right is given to enable parents to bring up children as they think is most appropriate. Parent-centred rights, he explains, are justified not because they positively promote the welfare of the child, but because they cannot be shown to harm the child, but can benefit the parent. Such an approach has been supported by Andrew Bainham. He argues: 'It is simply not reasonable to take the position that those who bear the legal and moral burdens which society expects of a parent should be denied all recognition of their independent claims or interests.'[46]

The distinction between child-centred and parent-centred rights is an important one, but there are difficulties with McCall Smith's approach. It can be difficult to decide whether a right is a parent-centred or child-centred right. Is the right to feed the child parent- or child-centred? Such a right is essential for the health of the child and so appears to be child-centred. But what kind of food is provided (for example, whether the parents choose to feed their children only vegetarian food) appears to be a parent-centred right. Further, it could be argued that parental rights do promote a child's welfare and do not exist solely for the benefit of parents. This is because many believe that living in a society where people like different kinds of food, have different religious beliefs, and different senses of humour is part of what makes life enjoyable. If so, it could be said to be in a child's interests to be brought up in a diverse society.

What is most useful about McCall Smith's distinction is that it stresses that there are certain areas of parenting over which parents do not have a discretion: they may not starve their child, the child must be adequately fed. There are, however, other areas of parenting where there is no state-approved standard of parenting (e.g. what kind of clothes the child should wear; whether children should be allowed to drink small amounts of alcohol[47]) and so the issue is left to the discretion of each individual parent. So, while it is clear that if an issue relating to a child's upbringing comes before the court it will give 'respect' to the wishes of a responsible parent, at the end of the day it is for the court to decide what is in the best interests of the child.[48] However, if the court finds that it is unclear what is in the best interests of the child, it will permit the resident parent to make the decision. The court may take the view that it cannot in practical terms force a parent to treat a child in a particular way and so to make an order would be pointless.[49] This can mean that it is difficult for a non-resident parent to obtain a court order seeking to change the way the resident parent raises the child. Nonetheless, the Court of Appeal in *Re B (Child Immunisation)*[50] was willing to permit the vaccination of a child with the MMR vaccine, against the wishes of the resident parent, following an application for such an order by the non-resident parent. This may be explained on the basis that the order did not involve an invasion of the resident parent's rights on how

---

[45] McCall Smith (1990), discussed in Bainham (1994b).
[46] Bainham (2009d).
[47] BBC Newsonline (2007d).
[48] *Re A (Conjoined Twins: Medical Treatment)* [2000] 3 FCR 577.
[49] *Re C (A Child) (HIV Test)* [1999] 2 FLR 1004, although see Strong (2000) for criticism of the argument on the facts of that case.
[50] [2003] 3 FCR 156, discussed in O'Donnell (2004).

to live her day-to-day life. It would, no doubt, have been quite different if the non-resident parent had sought an order that the resident parent feed the child at least five portions of fresh fruit or vegetables a day. It is unlikely that a court would make such a court order, despite the clear scientific evidence of the benefits of such a diet.[51]

Baroness Hale, in *R (On the Application of Williamson)* v *Secretary of State for Education and Employment*,[52] stated:

> Children have the right to be properly cared for and brought up so that they can fulfil their potential and play their part in society. Their parents have both the primary responsibility and the primary right to do this. The state steps in to regulate the exercise of that responsibility in the interests of children and society as a whole. But 'the child is not the child of the state' and it is important in a free society that parents should be allowed a large measure of autonomy in the way in which they discharge their parental responsibilities. A free society is premised on the fact that people are different from one another. A free society respects individual differences.

This is a remarkably different approach to parents' rights to that taken by Lord Scarman, mentioned above. In light of the points made by McCall Smith, it is respectfully suggested that it is also a more accurate one.

Jo Bridgeman has argued that any understanding of parental responsibilities should not be regarded as a set of abstract principles, but to flow from the parent–child relationship. She writes:

> In any relationship, responsibilities are partly determined by social expectation, in part individually interpreted, and depend upon current needs . . . In contrast to traditional philosophy, which insists that what the individual ought to do should be determined according to abstract principles, it is argued that a moral concept of responsibility should be informed by practices of caring responsibility. That is, that what parents ought to do with regard to the care of their children's health should be informed by guidelines developed through consideration of what parents do in caring for their children's health.[53]

This approach warns against trying to set out an abstract set of rights or responsibilities for parents, but rather suggests we look at the appropriate set of rights and responsibilities for the particular child–parent relationship at hand.

## C  Why do parents have rights and responsibilities?

It may seem self-evident that on the birth of a child the mother and father are under legal and moral obligations concerning the child and have the right to care for the child. But this need not be so. We could have a society where the state takes care of every child at birth in giant children's homes and the parents have no legal standing in relation to the child; or where on birth the child is handed over to the person who has scored highest in a parenting examination organised by the state. Most people would regard these alternatives with horror, but why is it that it seems so 'natural' that parents should be responsible for and should have rights over 'their' children? Philosophers and lawyers have struggled with this question and in truth there is no entirely satisfactory answer, but some of the suggestions are as follows:

---

[51] See Probert, Gilmore and Herring (2009) for a detailed discussion of parental discretion.
[52] [2005] 1 FCR 498 at para 72.
[53] Bridgeman (2007: 36).

## (i) Children as property

Children can be seen as the fruit of the parent's labour through procreation and therefore as the property of the parent.[54] This could be seen as the basis of parental rights. Indeed Arden LJ[55] has stated that the common law 'effectively treats the child as the property of the parent'.[56] At first sight, this is a rather unpleasant way of seeing children and such a theory has great difficulties.[57] We do not normally regard people as pieces of property which can be owned, and to describe parents' legal relationship with their children in the same terms used to describe their relationship with their cars seems clearly inappropriate.[58]

Despite these objections, Barton and Douglas[59] argue that the property notion has something to be said for it. If a child is removed from a hospital by a stranger shortly after birth, parents might naturally say 'their' baby had been stolen. Our society is based on a strong belief that parents should normally be allowed to bring up 'their' children, and children can only be removed from parents if there is sufficient justification. Such claims are similar to those made in respect of items of property. However, despite some similarities there are many other ways in which children are treated quite differently from property. One can legally destroy one's computer but not one's child, for example.

## (ii) Children on trust

This theory is that children have rights as people. As the child is unable to exercise these rights, the parents exercise these rights on the child's behalf. This version of explaining parents' rights is more popular than the property formulation.[60] It can take three forms:

1. The parents hold the rights of the child on trust for the child until he or she is old enough to claim these rights for him- or herself.

2. The parents hold the rights of the child on trust for the state. The parents care for the child until the child is able to become a citizen and a member of the state him- or herself.

3. The parents hold the rights of the child on a purpose trust – the purpose being the promotion of the welfare of the child.

The exact formulation matters little in practice, but the alternative approaches indicate important theoretical differences. The crucial difference is to whom the parent is responsible for the exercise of their rights: under 1 the parent is responsible to the child, whereas under 2 the parent is responsible to the state, while 3 leaves it unclear who has responsibility for enforcing the trust. The point to stress in all of these formulations is that the rights that parents exercise are not theirs, but those of the child and so should not be exercised for the benefit of the parent, but of the child.

There are three particular benefits of the trust analysis.[61] First, the law on trustees (fiduciaries) has been specifically developed to deal with fears that the trustee will misuse his or her powers as a trustee for his or her own benefit, rather than for the benefit of the subject of the trust. Such rules may be used by the law in ensuring that parents do not misuse their parental

---

[54] Montgomery (1988).
[55] *R (On the Application of Williamson)* v *Secretary of State for Education and Employment* [2003] 1 FLR 726, 793.
[56] See Reece (2005) for an argument that no one has ever taken seriously the claim that children are property.
[57] Archard (1993).
[58] Not least because once a child reaches majority parental rights cease.
[59] Barton and Douglas (1995).
[60] See Beck, Clavis, Barnes Jenkins and Nadi (1978); Scott and Scott (1995); Holgate (2005).
[61] O'Donovan (1993).

rights. Secondly, the law on trusts has developed realistic standards in policing the fiduciary's behaviour. The trustee cannot be expected always to make perfect choices, and is allowed a degree of discretion, but this does not permit the trustee to make manifestly bad decisions. These rules may also be useful in the parenting context. Thirdly, the trust approach means that the law would not need to see parents' interests and children's interests as in conflict.

There are, however, difficulties with the trusts approach. There are some uncertainties of a technical nature:[62] precisely what is the subject of the trust? (the rights of the child is the most common answer); who created the trust? Other problems are more practical. It may be justifiable to place on fiduciaries heavy obligations never to consider their own interests when dealing with the trust property, but for parents the obligation to care for children is a 24-hour-a-day obligation, involving decisions which profoundly affect their own private lives. To require the same standards as of a trustee (and never to consider their own interests) may seem therefore overly onerous.[63] Further, although the law can readily establish a widely accepted standard on, for example, the duty of investment upon a trustee, finding community standards as to what is reasonable parenting would be well-nigh impossible on many issues.[64] Also, the trust model does not readily capture the notion that children may have the right to make decisions for themselves. This could be dealt with by stating that the number of rights which are the subject of the trust lessen as the child becomes older and the child is able to exercise these for him- or herself.

## (iii) Imposition by society

The flip side of the question of why parents should have rights is to ask: Why should parents be under a duty to care for children? Eekelaar argues that there are two aspects of a parent's obligations to care for a child.[65] First, he suggests that every person owes a basic duty to other people to promote human flourishing. Secondly, on top of that basic duty there are special duties that society chooses to impose on particular people in particular circumstances. Our society chooses to impose special duties on parents to care for children. This is because children are vulnerable and need to be cared for by someone if society is to grow. Parents are best placed to provide the required care and that is widely accepted within our society. In other words, parents are only obliged especially to care for children because that is the choice of our society, not because of some underlying moral principle. Barton and Douglas[66] are unhappy with this approach because it suggests that there would be nothing morally objectionable for a state to require all children at birth to be removed from their parents and raised by state-approved agencies. They argue that most people would find such a system objectionable, even if it could be shown not to be particularly harmful to children, which is why they think that parents have something akin to an ownership right in respect of the child.

## (iv) Voluntary assumption by parents

Barton and Douglas[67] argue that the key element behind imposing the responsibilities of parenthood is that parents have voluntarily accepted the obligation. A parent who does not want to care for the child is not necessarily obliged to. For example, they argue that if a mother gives birth to a child following a rape she is not obliged to raise the child, although

---

[62] See, e.g., Bryan (1995).
[63] Schneider (1995).
[64] Schneider (1995).
[65] Eekelaar (1991b).
[66] Barton and Douglas (1995).
[67] Barton and Douglas (1995).

she is under a duty to ensure the child receives some care, as would someone who came across an abandoned baby. However, any parent who chooses to undertake the parental role is under a duty to carry out the role reasonably well. There is much to be said for this theory, but it cannot completely explain why parents are under parental obligations.[68] If Y notices that her neighbour has just had a baby and Y steals her and undertakes to care for her, this does not give Y the rights and duties of parenthood, despite her intent to be a parent. So, as Barton and Douglas[69] suggest, an element of the property argument or Eekelaar's argument needs to be relied upon in addition to the argument based on voluntary assumption of obligation if this theory is to explain the law's attitude towards parents.

### (v) The 'extensions claim'

It can be said that the rights of parents to raise their children as they think fit is connected with the right that the state should not interfere with parents' private lives. As Fried has put it, 'the right to form one's child's values, one's child's life plan and the right to lavish attention on the child are extensions of the right not to be interfered with in doing those things for one's self'.[70] The difficulty with such a claim is that it could be made in respect of close friends or fellow employees.[71]

To conclude, it is surprisingly difficult to find a single theory that adequately explains why parents should be responsible for their children. Perhaps the answer lies in the strength of a combination of these views. So far we have been looking at parents' rights and responsibility from a theoretical perspective. What is the law itself?

## 5 Parental responsibility

The law on the duties and rights of parenthood is covered by the notion of parental responsibility.

### A What is parental responsibility?

Given that parental responsibility is one of the key concepts in family law, one might have thought it would be easy to define it, but it is not.[72] The root cause of the uncertainty is that the notion of parental responsibility is required to fulfil a wide variety of functions.[73] Eekelaar has suggested that there are two aspects of parental responsibility:[74]

1. *What that responsibility means.* It encapsulates the legal duties and powers that enable a parent to care for a child or act on the child's behalf. Parents must exercise their rights 'dutifully' towards their children.

---

[68] See Chapter 5 for further discussion of such arguments in the context of child support.
[69] Barton and Douglas (1995).
[70] Fried (1978: 152).
[71] Archard (2003: 92).
[72] See Probert, Gilmore and Herring (2009) for a useful set of essays on the topic. For an attempt to produce a Europe-wide definition of parental responsiblity see Boele-Woelki et al. (2007).
[73] Piper (1999) discusses the difficulties solicitors face in practice when trying to explain what parental responsibility means.
[74] See Eekelaar (1991c).

2. *Who has the responsibility?* It explains that the law permits the person with parental responsibility rather than anyone else[75] to have parental responsibility. It determines who has the authority to make a decision relating to a child.

In an attempt to explain further what parental responsibility means we need to look at the legislative and judicial understanding of parental responsibility:

## (i) The Children Act

The starting point is s 3 of the Children Act 1989:

> **LEGISLATIVE PROVISION**
>
> **Children Act 1989, section 3**
>
> In this Act 'parental responsibility' means all the rights, duties, powers, responsibilities and authority which by law a parent of a child has in relation to the child and his property.

This leaves unanswered as many questions as it answers, because it fails to explain what those rights etc. are. The Law Commission decided against a statutory definition of the responsibilities of parents because they change from case to case and depend on the age and maturity of the child. For example, parental responsibility in relation to a disabled child might be thought to impose different obligations on a parent than if the child were not disabled.[76] In any event, it would not be possible to list all the responsibilities that attend parental responsibility. Lowe and Douglas have attempted a list and have suggested the following:

1. bringing up the child;
2. having contact with the child;
3. protecting and maintaining the child;
4. disciplining the child;
5. determining and providing for the child's education;
6. determining the child's religion;
7. consenting to the child's medical treatment;
8. consenting to the child's marriage;
9. agreeing to the child's adoption;
10. vetoing the issue of a child's passport;
11. taking the child outside the UK and consenting to the child's emigration;
12. administering the child's property;
13. protecting and maintaining the child;
14. naming the child;
15. representing the child in legal proceedings;
16. disposing of the child's corpse;
17. appointing a guardian for the child.[77]

---

[75] A point stressed in Lowe (1997b).

[76] See Corker and Davis (2000) for a discussion of the legal treatment of disabled children.

[77] Lowe and Douglas (2007: 377). See also Hendricson's proposals (2003) for a parenting code, setting out clearly the rights and responsibilities of parents.

No doubt this is not a complete list, but it gives an indication of the range of issues for which parents may be responsible. Occasionally Parliament adds to the responsibilities of parents. For example, under ss 8–10 of the Crime and Disorder Act 1998 the court may make a parenting order if a child has committed certain offences. This may require parents to control their child and require parents to attend guidance sessions; in effect, it imposes on parents a duty to ensure their children do not commit crimes. In *R (On the Application of M) v Inner London Crown Court*[78] the Divisional Court accepted that such an order interfered with a parent's right to respect for family life, under article 8 of the ECHR, but held that this was justified under article 8(2) by the need to protect the community from crime.

Rather than trying to list the issues over which parents can make decisions about a child, it may be more profitable to consider what limitations there are on the parental power to decide how to raise a child. The parent can make decisions about all areas of the child's life, subject to the following:

1. *The criminal law.* For example, it is a criminal offence to assault a child, which restricts the power[79] of parents to administer corporal punishment.

2. *Any requirement to consult or obtain the consent of anyone else with parental responsibility.* For example, s 13 of the Children Act 1989 requires a parent wishing to change a child's surname to obtain the consent of anyone else with parental responsibility, before doing so.

3. *The power of the local authority to take a child into care.* If a child is taken into care by a local authority then this effectively restricts the powers of parents to make decisions about their child's upbringing.[80]

4. *Any orders of the court.* There may be a court order in force which deals with a specific aspect of a child's upbringing, in which case a parent may not act in a way contrary to the court order.[81]

5. *The ability of a child who is sufficiently mature (**Gillick**-competent) to make decisions for him- or herself.* This will be discussed shortly.

The Children Act 1989 appears then to see parental responsibility in terms of being able to make decisions about a child's upbringing, even if it is not quite clear what those rights are.

## (ii) Judicial understanding of parental responsibility

Unfortunately the courts have not been consistent in their understanding of parental responsibility. Some cases have described parental responsibility as a 'stamp of approval' to mark the 'status' which nature has bestowed on the father.[82] In *Re S (A Minor) (Parental Responsibility)* the Court of Appeal spoke of the way in which parental responsibility may create a positive image of the father in the child's eyes.[83] So understood, parental responsibility appears to be little more than a pat on the back and an official confirmation that the father is a committed father. This is especially so in cases where the father is given parental responsibility, but then denied contact with the child.[84] Helen Reece looking at this case law

---

[78] [2004] 1 FCR 178.
[79] Offences Against the Person Act 1861, s 47.
[80] See Chapter 11.
[81] Children Act 1989, s 2(8).
[82] E.g. *Re S (A Minor) (Parental Responsibility)* [1995] 2 FLR 648, [1995] 3 FCR 225; *Re C and V (Minors) (Parental Responsibility and Contact)* [1998] 1 FCR 57.
[83] [1995] 2 FLR 648, [1995] 3 FCR 225.
[84] See also the odd use of a joint residence order in *W v A* [2004] EWCA Civ 1587 even though the mother was to take the child to South Africa. The joint residence order, Wall LJ explained, would emphasise that both parents shared parental responsibility.

has suggested that parental responsibility is being used as a form of therapy.[85] It is designed to make the father feel good about himself and his relationship with the child, even if, in reality, the relationship has little substance.

Other cases have, however, seen parental responsibility as about real rights and about the exercise of parental responsibility. For example, in *M v M (Parental Responsibility)*,[86] despite his obvious love and commitment to his child, the father was denied parental responsibility because he lacked the mental capacities to make decisions on behalf of the child. In *Re M (Sperm Donor Father)*[87] the court ordered contact to a father who did not know the child, and suggested that after a while the court might award him parental responsibility once he had got to know the child. The view that parental responsibility is about the making of decisions over children is further supported by those cases (which will be discussed shortly) which indicate that, with regard to important issues, the resident parent must consult with all parents with parental responsibility. In *Re G (Parental Responsibility Order)*,[88] where the father had no existing relationship with the child born as a result of a 'one-night stand', the judge granted him a 'suspended parental responsibility' which would come into effect if the mother failed to provide him with information about the child's health and education. On appeal the Court of Appeal held that such a 'suspended parental responsibility' was not possible under the Children Act 1989; the judge would have to decide either to give or not to give parental responsibility.

As this discussion shows, there is a real tension in the case law as to whether parental responsibility is about real decision-making power, or whether it is of more symbolic value, recognising the father's commitment to the child. It is, therefore, perhaps reassuring to read Black J's statement: 'parental responsibility can be an inaccessible concept at the best of times, not infrequently difficult for lawyers to grasp and often very challenging for those who are not lawyers'.[89]

## B Parental responsibility in practice

A person who does not have parental responsibility can, of course, act as a parent towards a child in a variety of ways. He or she can feed, clothe, educate, and play with the child. There are many men carrying out the tasks of parenthood, without parental responsibility. Indeed, no doubt, some people without parental responsibility act more like a parent towards a child than other people with parental responsibility. So when does it actually matter whether a person has parental responsibility? The following are rights and responsibilities that a father with parental responsibility has, which a father without parental responsibility does not have.[90]

1. He can withhold consent to adoption and freeing for adoption.[91]

2. He can object to the child being accommodated in local authority accommodation[92] and remove the child from local authority accommodation.[93]

---

[85] Reece (2009c).
[86] [1999] 2 FLR 737.
[87] [2003] Fam Law 94.
[88] [2006] Fam Law 744.
[89] *Re D (Contact and Parental Responsibility: Lesbian Mothers and Known Father)* [2006] 1 FCR 556.
[90] The issue relates only to fathers because all mothers have parental responsibility.
[91] Adoption Act 1976, s 72.
[92] Children Act 1989, s 20(7).
[93] Children Act 1989, s 20(8).

3. He can appoint a guardian.[94]

4. He can give legal authorisation for medical treatment.[95]

5. He has a right of access to his child's health records.

6. He can withdraw a child from sex education and religious education classes and make representations to schools concerning the child's education.[96]

7. His consent is required if the child's mother seeks to remove the child from the jurisdiction.[97]

8. He can sign a child's passport application and object to the granting of a passport.[98]

9. He has sufficient rights in relation to a child to invoke the international child abduction rules.[99]

10. He can consent to the marriage of a child aged 16 or 17.[100]

11. He will automatically be a party to care proceedings.[101]

Although this is a lengthy list, in fact these rights do not arise very often in practice. The most common situations are where a third party wishes to treat a child in a particular way which would be a crime or tort without the consent of someone who has parental responsibility:[102] for example, a doctor wishes to provide medical treatment for a child.[103] Ros Pickford[104] found that over 75 per cent of fathers were unaware that they lacked parental responsibility. Many of these fathers were fathers of teenagers. This indicates that it is quite possible to carry out a full parental role without having to rely on parental responsibility. Notably, even those fathers who were aware they lacked parental responsibility rarely went on to seek it.

If parental responsibility is of limited practical significance then why is it so important? Eekelaar sums up the position well: 'parental responsibility can best be understood as legal recognition of the exercise of social parenthood. It thus comprises a factual (recognition of a state of affairs) and a normative (giving the state of affairs the "stamp of approval") element.'[105]

As this implies, parental responsibility is more about confirming an existing situation or sending a message of approval to the parent, rather than actually creating rights. However, as most unmarried fathers are unaware of whether they have parental responsibility or not,[106] the effectiveness of such a stamp of approval may be questioned.

---

[94] Children Act 1989, s 5.

[95] Eekelaar (2001d: 429) argues that a father without parental responsibility can give effective consent to medical treatment because he has a duty to promote the health of his children and that duty can only realistically be imposed if he has the right to provide the consent necessary for that treatment. See Probert, Gilmore and Herring (2009) for a questioning of this view.

[96] Education Act 1996. Eekelaar (2001d) argues that a father without parental responsibility can make decisions in relation to the child's education.

[97] Children Act 1989, s 13.

[98] See Passport Agency (1994).

[99] See Chapter 9.

[100] Marriage Act 1949, s 3.

[101] A father without parental responsibility can also be a party in certain limited circumstances: Children Act 1989, Appendix 3.

[102] Or the consent of the court.

[103] *B v B (Grandparent: Residence Order)* [1992] 2 FLR 327, [1993] 1 FCR 211.

[104] Pickford (1999).

[105] Eekelaar (2001d: 428).

[106] Pickford (1999).

## C The rights of a parent without responsibility

Although parental responsibility is the primary source of parental rights, there are rights and responsibilities that flow simply from being a parent. These are the benefits and responsibilities that follow from parenthood in and of itself. Notice two things about this list. First, these right apply to a parent, whether or not they have parental responsibility. Second, that most of these do not apply to a person who has parental responsibility but is not a parent.

1. A parent has a right to apply without leave for a s 8 order.[107]

2. A parent has rights of succession to the estate of the child.[108]

3. There is a presumption that a child in local authority care should have reasonable contact with each parent.[109]

4. On application for an emergency protection order there is a duty to inform the child's parents.[110]

5. A parent can apply to discharge an emergency protection order.[111]

6. Rights of citizenship pass primarily through parentage.[112]

7. Parents are liable persons under social security legislation.[113]

8. A parent cannot marry his or her child.[114]

9. The criminal law on incest forbids sexual relations between parents and children.

10. A parent who is not living with his or her child will be liable to make payments under the child support legislation.

As can be seen from this list, the parent without parental responsibility has some rights, but they do not directly relate to the child's day-to-day upbringing. As Baroness Hale, in *Re G (Residence: Same-Sex Partner)*,[115] puts it:

> To be the legal parent of a child gives a person legal standing to bring and defend proceedings about the child and makes the child a member of that person's family, but it does not necessarily tell us much about the importance of that person to the child's welfare.

## D The extent of parental responsibility

Parental responsibility is for life. Once a parent has parental responsibility, this cannot be removed, except in a few special cases.[116] Even if the parent has behaved in such a way that the child has to be taken into care, he or she will not lose parental responsibility.[117] Although

---

[107] Children Act 1989, s 10(4).
[108] See Chapter 12.
[109] Children Act 1989, s 34.
[110] Children Act 1989, s 44(13).
[111] Children Act 1989, s 45(8).
[112] Cretney, Masson and Bailey-Harris (2002: 105–6).
[113] Cretney, Masson and Bailey-Harris (2002: ch. 11).
[114] Marriage Act 1949, s 1.
[115] [2006] 1 FCR 681 at para 32.
[116] If a non-parent has parental responsibility through a residence order then when the order comes to an end the parental responsibility ceases. In *Re F (Indirect Contact)* [2006] EWCA Civ 1426 a father's parental responsibility (given to him under a parental responsibility order) was revoked after a sustained campaign of violence and harassment against the mother and child.
[117] See Chapter 10.

a parent cannot surrender parental responsibility, it is possible to delegate it.[118] The fact that a new person acquires parental responsibility does not mean that anyone else loses it.[119] As shall be seen later, the nature of parental responsibility may change with the age and development of the child.

## 6  Sharing parental responsibility

It is clear from the scheme of the Children Act 1989 that there will be many situations where several people have parental responsibility. Although a child can have only two parents, any number of people can have parental responsibility. The question therefore arises whether each person with parental responsibility can exercise his or her parental responsibility alone or whether it is necessary to have the agreement of all those with parental responsibility in respect of each decision concerning the upbringing of the child.[120]

Although there are a few exceptions, s 2(7) appears to give a clear answer:

### LEGISLATIVE PROVISION

**Children Act 1989, section 2(7)**

Where more than one person has parental responsibility for a child, each of them may act alone and without the other (or others) in meeting that responsibility; but nothing in this Part shall be taken to affect the operation of any enactment which requires the consent of more than one person in a matter affecting the child.

There are two crucial points that appear clear from this subsection. The first is that, except where the statute provides otherwise, each person with parental responsibility can exercise parental responsibility alone without obtaining the consent of the others with parental responsibility or even consulting them. It has been suggested that in this way the Act promotes 'independent' rather than 'co-operative' parenting.[121]

The second is that there is no hierarchy among those with parental responsibility. So, in the Children Act 1989 there is no preference given to mothers over fathers, or between those with whom the child lives and those with whom the child does not live. If a child who normally lives with her mother is visiting her father (with parental responsibility), he can take her to a church service, arrange for her to have an unusual haircut, or feed her meat – even if the mother strongly opposes these activities. The mother could apply for a prohibited steps order[122] to prevent the father doing this, but in the absence of such an order he is free to do this.[123] Similarly, when the child lives with the mother, she can bring up the child as she believes best.[124]

---

[118]  Children Act 1989, s 2(9).

[119]  Children Act 1989, s 2(6), although an adoption order will end any existing parental responsibility.

[120]  See the discussion in Maidment (2001b).

[121]  Bainham (1990).

[122]  Under Children Act 1989, s 8.

[123]  A local authority has a duty to consult parents and people with parental responsibility about all decisions unless this is not reasonably practicable.

[124]  There is no question of the parties being bound by pre-birth agreements: *Re W (A Minor) (Residence Order)* [1992] 2 FLR 332.

There are a number of exceptions to the rule that there is no need to consult, although in all of these situations if the consent is not provided then the court may be able to dispense with the consent and authorise the act:

1. Adoption and freeing for adoption can take place only if *all* parents[125] with parental responsibility consent.[126]

2. If the child aged 16 or 17 wishes to marry then *all* parents with parental responsibility and any guardians must consent.[127]

3. If the child is to be accommodated by the local authority then *none* of those with parental responsibility must have objected.[128]

4. Section 13 of the Children Act 1989 states that if a residence order has been made and one party wishes to change the surname of the child then the consent of all those with parental responsibility is required.[129] In *Re PC (Change of Surname)*[130] it was suggested that even if there was not a residence order in force then it was necessary to have the consent of all those with parental responsibility.[131]

5. Section 13 of the Children Act 1989 states that if there is a residence order it is not possible to remove a child from the UK without the consent of all those with parental responsibility.[132] It is arguable, by analogy with the decisions relating to surnames, that in order to remove a child from the UK the consent of all those with parental responsibility is required.

6. There are cases which suggest that the consent of all those with parental responsibility is required for any decision which is of fundamental importance to the child and is irreversible.[133] Which decisions are of fundamental importance? This will, it seems, be decided on a case-by-case basis. We know the following are issues of fundamental importance:

   ● *Education.* In *Re G (A Minor) (Parental Responsibility: Education)*[134] it was suggested that there is a duty to consult over long-term decisions relating to education. Here the question was whether the child should be moved from one school to another.

   ● *Circumcision.* In *Re J (Specific Issue Orders)*[135] the Court of Appeal held that if a male child[136] is to undergo a circumcision all of those with parental responsibility should be consulted.

   ● *Changing the child's surname.* Consultation with all those with parental responsibility is required before a child's surname can be changed.[137]

   ● *The MMR vaccine.* If the resident parent decides not to give her child the MMR vaccine she should consult with the non-resident parent if he has parental responsibility.[138]

---

[125] And guardians.
[126] But not others with parental responsibility: Adoption Act 1976, s 16; Children Act 1989, ss 12(3), 33(6).
[127] Marriage Act 1949, s 3(1A).
[128] See Chapter 10.
[129] Children Act 1989, s 13.
[130] [1997] 2 FLR 730.
[131] Indeed, as we shall see in Chapter 9, it may be necessary to obtain the consent of every parent.
[132] Children Act 1989, s 13.
[133] Eekelaar (1998).
[134] [1994] 2 FLR 964, [1995] 2 FCR 53.
[135] [2000] 1 FLR 517, [2000] 1 FCR 307.
[136] Female circumcision is forbidden under the Female Genital Mutilation Act 2003.
[137] *Re PC (Change of Surname)* [1997] 2 FLR 730.
[138] *Re B (A Child) (Immunisation)* [2003] 3 FCR 156.

It is arguable that these decisions fly in the face of s 2(7) of the Children Act 1989,[139] which makes it clear that, in the absence of statutory provisions to the contrary, a parent can exercise parental responsibility without consultation.

It appears from the case law that the duty on the resident parent is to consult, rather than obtain the non-resident parent's consent. The significance of this consultation requirement is therefore that it gives the non-resident parent the opportunity to bring legal proceedings to prevent the resident parent from acting in the proposed way. However, it is far from clear what the court will do if the resident parent fails to consult. For example, if the mother arranges for the circumcision without consultation with the father, there is not much the law can do. The requirement to consult appears unenforceable in many cases.

## A Are all parental responsibilities equal?

It seems clear from s 2(7) of the Children Act 1989 that each parent with parental responsibility is equal. However, in *Re P (A Minor) (Parental Responsibility Order)*[140] the courts have suggested that the parent with whom the child lives is to have the power to decide 'day-to-day' issues relating to the child. So the non-residential parent cannot use his or her parental responsibility to upset the day-to-day parenting of the residential parent.[141] In *Re C (Welfare of Child: Immunisation)*, Sumner J stated: 'Where parents do not live together, the court recognizes the importance of the particular bond which exists in most cases between a child and the parent with the principal care of the child . . . It does not give that parent greater rights. It does mean that the court will take care to safeguard and preserve that bond in the best interests of the child.'[142] However, in *A v A (Children) (Shared Residence Order)*[143] it was suggested that a resident parent should not interfere in day-to-day issues in the way the non-resident parent treats the child during contact sessions.

## B Is the law in a sound state?

If a residential parent (the parent with whom the child lives) exercises parental responsibility in a way objected to by the non-residential parent, the latter could bring the matter before the court by way of a specific issue order or prohibited steps order. There is, therefore, a sense that it matters little whether there is a formal duty to consult because, whether or not there is a requirement to consult, if those with parental responsibility disagree, the matter will be brought before a court. There are, however, three points of practical significance in whether or not there is a duty to consult. The first is that it determines whose responsibility it is to bring the matter before the court. For example, if the law is that one parent cannot change the name of the child without the other's consent then the parent seeking to change the name will have the burden of bringing the matter before the court. However, if the law was that a parent could independently change a name, then it would be the responsibility of the person objecting to the change to bring the matter before the court. Secondly, the issue of who should be liable to pay the legal costs of both parties if the matter is brought before the court may depend on whether there was a duty to consult, with which a parent did not comply. Thirdly, there is the 'message' that the law wishes to send out. Does the law wish to encourage co-operative or independent parenting?

---

[139] Eekelaar (2001d).
[140] [1994] 1 FLR 578.
[141] E.g. *Re J (Specific Issue Orders)* [2000] 1 FLR 517, [2000] 1 FCR 307.
[142] [2003] 2 FLR 1054 at para 305.
[143] [2004] 1 FCR 201 at para 118.

The following are some of the approaches that the law could take regarding those who share parental responsibility:

1. All those with parental responsibility must agree on every issue relating to the child.

2. The residential parent can make all decisions relating to the child, and the non-residential parent has rights only to bring a matter to court.

3. The residential parent should make all important decisions, although the non-residential parent can make day-to-day decisions when the child is spending time with him or her.

4. The parents must consult on all important issues, otherwise each parent can take day-to-day decisions when the child is spending time with him or her.

5. Each parent with parental responsibility can exercise parental responsibility independently and does not need to consult with the other over any issue.

It should be clear that approach 1 is impractical. It would not be realistic to expect a parent to contact and discuss with the other parent the contents of every meal, for example. Approach 2 is likewise impractical, at least if the non-residential parent is to have contact with the child. The choice is therefore between the last three options. The issues seem to be as follows:

---

**DEBATE**

### Should parenting be co-operative?

1. *Fears of misuse.* There are fears that giving the non-residential parent a say in how the child is brought up by the residential parent could constitute a major infringement of the rights of private life of the residential parent.[144] For example, if the non-residential parent could compel the vegetarian parent to prepare meat for the child to eat, this may be seen as an infringement of the residential parent's rights. There are particular concerns in cases where there has been domestic violence, where there is evidence that abusers continue to exercise control over their victims through whatever route is available.[145] Giving powers to the non-residential parent to direct how the residential parent brings up the child is therefore open to abuse.

2. *Involvement of the non-residential parent.* There are concerns that the non-residential parent will be excluded from the child's life. If there is no duty to consult, the non-residential parent may not even be aware that there is a crucial issue to be decided in respect of the child and will not be able to carry out an effective parenting role.

3. *Lack of knowledge of non-residential parent.* Some claim that non-residential parents do not know the child well enough to make important decisions in relation to the child. Of course, this is a generalisation, but the law in this area must rest on generalisations and it may well be argued that, as a general rule, the residential parent will be better poised to make a decision in respect of a child than a non-residential parent.

4. *Onerous obligation on residential parent.* Some are concerned that an obligation to obtain consent could be unduly time-consuming, stressful and burdensome for the residential parent, especially where the other parent may be difficult to contact.[146]

---

[144] Roche (1991).
[145] Hester and Radford (1996).
[146] Law Commission Report 172 (1988: para 2.10).

5. *Disruption for child*. There is a concern that permitting each parent to exercise parental responsibility will lead to disruption for the child by constantly changing lifestyles. For example, in **Re PC (Change of Surname)**[147] it was argued that if each parent with parental responsibility could change the child's surname, this would lead to the child's name constantly being changed, first by one parent and then by the other. Similarly, a child receiving religious instruction from one parent and conflicting religious instruction from another could feel confused and pressurised.

6. *Law should stress 'doing'*. Smart and Neale[148] criticise the law for failing to place sufficient emphasis on the 'doing' aspects of caring. They argue it is wrong to stress 'caring about' children above 'caring for' children. They see a danger in giving non-residential parents rights, without having to perform the day-to-day care for children. Indeed the burden of ensuring there is co-operation seems to fall on the resident parent. It is she who must find and discuss the issue with the non-resident parent.

7. *Ignorance of the law*. Given the ignorance of the requirements of family law, it seems wrong to impose an obligation to consult, as it is likely to be unknown by most people. It would therefore be honoured more in the breach than the observance and would, as suggested above, effectively be unenforceable.

8. *Reality*. It could be argued that there is little the law can do here. Whether there will be co-operative or independent parenting will depend on the relationship and personality of the parties, rather than the requirements of the law. Compelling consultation or co-operation is unlikely to be productive.

## Questions

1. *Can the law do anything to encourage co-operative parenting?*
2. *If one parent spends more time with the child than the other should they have a greater say in disputes over the child's upbringing?*

## Further reading

Read **Bainham** (2009d) for a discussion of whether parents have rights.

As can be seen from the above, there are strong arguments on both sides. Whatever the law is, there will be some cases where a consultation requirement will be beneficial and others where it is open to abuse. This key issue is whether it is worth running the risks of misuse in the name of sending a message encouraging co-operation. Further, although we may generally want parents to consult over important issues concerning their children's upbringing, that does not mean that we should turn that into a legal obligation. Also, it is arguable that if there is to be a duty to consult we need to be a little more careful in deciding who should have parental responsibility.[149] Should the father in **Re S (A Minor) (Parental Responsibility)**,[150] who was known to be a possessor of paedophilic literature, be consulted about his daughter's

---

[147] [1997] 2 FLR 730, [1997] 3 FCR 544.
[148] Smart and Neale (1999).
[149] Eekelaar (2001d).
[150] [1995] 2 FLR 648, [1995] 3 FCR 225.

medical treatment? Even if he has not seen her for years? Should a mother be required to consult a father if he has been violent towards her in the past?

## C Co-parenting in practice

It seems that in practice there is only a limited degree of co-parenting after separation. This is particularly so where one of the parents remarries or starts cohabiting with a new partner. Eekelaar and Maclean write: 'Joint decision-making of any serious nature probably occurs in about one in ten cases where contact is regularly exercised, and then usually only on a limited number of issues.'[151] Indeed, the Law Commission accepted that, in reality, parental responsibility 'ran with child'. This might suggest that the independent parenting envisaged in s 2(9) of the Children Act 1989 is realistic, whatever the ideal may be.[152]

## 7 The welfare principle

At the heart of the law relating to children is the principle that whenever the court considers a question relating to the upbringing of children the paramount consideration should be the welfare of the children. Section 1(1) of the Children Act 1989 clearly states the central principle of child law:

> **LEGISLATIVE PROVISION**
>
> **Children Act 1989, section 1(1)**
>
> When a court determines any question with respect to—
>
> (a)  the upbringing of a child; or
>
> (b)  the administration of a child's property or the application of any income arising from it, the child's welfare shall be the court's paramount consideration.

This apparently simple principle is in fact complex. Several issues require explanation.

## A What does 'welfare' mean?

The Children Act has attempted to add some flesh to the concept of a child's welfare.[153] There is no definition of 'welfare' in the Children Act 1989, although there is a list of factors which a judge should consider when deciding what is in the child's welfare. These are listed in s 1(3):

---

[151] Eekelaar and Maclean (1997: 137). Trinder (2005: para 5.5) found that 78% of separated parents never discussed their children's problems together.
[152] See Smart and Neale (2000) for explanations for the lack of consultation.
[153] For an interesting discussion that it would be preferable to talk in terms of well-being rather than welfare see Eekelaar (2002a: 243).

---

**LEGISLATIVE PROVISION**

**Children Act 1989, section 1(3)**

(a) the ascertainable wishes and feelings of the child concerned (considered in the light of his age and understanding);

(b) his physical, emotional and educational needs;

(c) the likely effect on him of any change in his circumstances;

(d) his age, sex, background and any characteristics of his which the court considers relevant;

(e) any harm which he has suffered or is at risk of suffering;

(f) how capable each of his parents, and any other person in relation to whom the court considers the question to be relevant, is of meeting his needs;

(g) the range of powers available to the court under this Act in the proceedings in question.

---

The interpretation of these factors is discussed in detail in Chapter 9.

## B What does 'paramount' mean?

The courts' interpretation of the word 'paramount' is based on the decision of the House of Lords in *J v C*,[154] which considered the meaning of the words 'first and paramount' in the Guardianship of Infants Act 1925. Lord McDermott explained that the phrase means:

> more than the child's welfare is to be treated as the top item in a list of items relevant to the matter in question. [The words] connote a process whereby, when all the relevant facts, relationships, claims and wishes of parents, risks, choices and other circumstances are taken into account and weighed, the course to be followed will be that which is most in the interests of the child.[155]

This clearly expresses the view that the welfare of the child is the sole consideration. The interests of adults and other children are only relevant in so far as they might affect the welfare of the child in question.[156] *J v C*[157] itself was especially significant because the House of Lords made it quite clear that the interests of the children outweigh the interests of even 'unimpeachable' (perfect) parents.[158] So whether an order is 'fair' or infringes the rights of parents is not relevant; all that matters is whether the order promotes the interests of children. This is a surprising interpretation because, had Parliament intended welfare to be the only consideration, it could have said so. There was no need to interpret the word 'paramount' to mean sole. It is interesting to note that the UN Convention on the Rights of Children, in article 3, states that the child's welfare should be the primary consideration. This appears to place slightly less weight on children's interests than s 1 of the Children Act 1989. It has been argued that the Human Rights Act 1998 requires the courts to reinterpret the word paramount in s 1 to mean primary, so that the court can then take due account of the interests of parents and others.[159]

---

[154] [1970] AC 668.
[155] At pp. 710–11.
[156] See, e.g., Lord Hobhouse in *Dawson v Wearmouth* [1999] 1 FLR 1167.
[157] [1970] AC 668.
[158] Freeman (2000a) notes that unimpeachable parents were always fathers.
[159] See Choudhry and Fenwick (2005); Fortin (2006a). See Herring (1999b) for an argument that the courts can retain the paramountcy notion, while taking into account parents' interests.

In *M v H (A Child) (Educational Welfare)*[160] Charles J suggested that often all the courts were able to do was to find the 'least bad solution' for the child, The ideal solution may be for the parents to live together happily and raise the child together. That may not be possible and the court would have to select from the available options the one that caused least harm.

## C When does the welfare principle apply?

The welfare principle applies when the court is asked to determine any question that concerns a child's upbringing or the administration of their property. Bracewell J in *Re X (A Child) (Injunctions Restraining Publication)*[161] stated that upbringing means 'the bringing up, care for, treatment, education, and instruction of the child by its parents or by those who are substitute parents'. It is of wide application and not restricted to the Children Act 1989. For example, s 1(1) applies where the court considers making an order under s 8 of the Children Act 1989; where the High Court is exercising the inherent jurisdiction;[162] and when the court considers public law orders such as care orders.[163] Rather than listing all the orders when the welfare principle applies, it is in fact easier to consider the issue from the opposite perspective and ask when the welfare principle does not apply.

## D When does the welfare principle not apply?[164]

The welfare principle does not apply in the following cases:

1. *If the issue does not relate to the child's upbringing.* It is clear from the wording of s 1 of the Children Act 1989 that the welfare principle applies only if the issues involve the upbringing of the child. Even if the issue does not involve the upbringing of the child, the court may still pay special attention to the welfare of the child, although the welfare of the child will not be paramount.[165] It is not always easy, however, to know whether an issue relates to the upbringing of the child, as is clear from some of the following examples:

    (a) In *Re A (Minors) (Residence Orders: Leave to Apply)*[166] the Court of Appeal held that deciding whether or not to grant leave to an adult to apply for an order under s 8 of the Children Act 1989 was not an issue that involved the upbringing of a child and so the child's welfare was not paramount. However, the welfare principle does apply where a child is seeking leave to bring a s 8 application.[167]

    (b) In considering whether to order blood tests to determine who is the father of a child, the welfare principle does not apply, as the taking of blood does not relate to the child's upbringing.[168]

---

[160] [2008] 2 FCR 280.
[161] [2001] 1 FCR 541 at 546f.
[162] *Re T (A Minor) (Wardship: Medical Treatment)* [1997] 1 FLR 502, [1997] 2 FCR 363.
[163] *Humberside CC v B* [1993] 1 FLR 257, [1993] 1 FCR 613, per Booth J; applied in *F v Leeds City Council* [1994] 2 FLR 60, [1994] 2 FCR 428.
[164] See the discussion in Lowe (1997b).
[165] *S v S, W v Official Solicitor (or W)* [1972] AC 24; *Richards v Richards* [1984] AC 174.
[166] [1992] 2 FCR 174, [1992] 2 FLR 154.
[167] *Re SC (A Minor) (Leave to Seek Section 8 Orders)* [1994] 1 FCR 837, [1994] 1 FLR 96; *Re C (Residence: Child's Application for Leave)* [1995] 1 FLR 927, [1996] 1 FCR 461.
[168] *Re H (A Minor) (Blood Tests: Parental Rights)* [1996] 2 FLR 65, [1996] 3 FCR 201.

(c) It is held that the welfare principle does not apply when a court is deciding whether a parent should be committed to prison for breach of a court order concerning a child.[169]

(d) In *Re Z (A Minor) (Identity: Restrictions on Publication)*[170] the Court of Appeal held that the decision whether a television company be allowed to film a programme about a child's education related to her upbringing and so the welfare principle applied. However, if the television programme relates not to the child's upbringing, but rather to publicity about the child's parent, then the child's welfare is not paramount, although it may be a factor to be taken into account.[171]

2. *Part III of the Children Act.* The welfare principle does not apply to Part III of the Children Act 1989, which sets out the various duties that a local authority owes to children in its area. This was made clear in *Re M (A Minor) (Secure Accommodation Order)*.[172] The explanation is that, in considering what services to provide to children in its area and how to exercise its powers, the local authority must consider the needs of all children in its area and the financial limitations it faces. The welfare of a particular child cannot, therefore, be paramount.

3. *Express statutory provision.* The welfare principle does not apply if a statute expressly states it should not. A notable example is in relation to redistribution of property and financial issues on divorce: the child's interests are said to be 'first', but not paramount.[173] Perhaps most significantly, in deciding whether or not to grant a divoce to a child's parents, the child's welfare is not paramount; indeed the courts are not even required to consider the child's welfare.

4. *Outside the context of litigation.* It is arguable that the welfare principle does not apply to parents with respect to their day-to-day decisions relating to the child. For example, where to live or what jobs to do. However, there are some dicta which have suggested that the welfare principle does affect a parent's day-to-day life. Ward LJ suggested:

> a parent may choose to conduct himself in a way which has insufficient regard to his responsibilities to his children. If a person has no parental responsibilities, he is at liberty to conduct himself as he chooses . . . if he has parental responsibilities, those responsibilities may restrict his freedom of action. He is required, where his children's upbringing is involved, to have regard also to the welfare of his children.[174]

It is far from clear how to interpret these dicta. Perhaps the best way to understand the law is that there is a duty on parents to avoid causing the child harm, but not a duty positively to promote the child's welfare.

### E What if the case involves two children – whose interests are paramount?

There is a real difficulty in using the welfare principle in cases where two or more children are concerned and their interests are in conflict.

---

[169] *A v N (Committal: Refusal of Contact)* [1997] 2 FCR 475, [1997] 1 FLR 533.
[170] [1997] Fam 1.
[171] *Re LM (A Child) (Reporting Restrictions: Coroner's Inquest* [2007] 3 FCR 44.
[172] [1995] Fam 108.
[173] Matrimonial Causes Act 1973, s 25(1).
[174] *Re W (Wardship: Discharge: Publicity)* [1995] 2 FLR 466 at p. 477.

## (i) The basic rule: 'who is the subject of the application?'

*Birmingham City Council* v *H (A Minor)*[175] involved a mother who was herself a minor, being under 16, and her baby. The mother and baby had been taken into care, but had been separated. The mother applied for contact with the baby. It was felt that it was in the minor mother's interest that contact take place but that contact was not necessarily in the baby's interests. It was therefore crucial for the court to determine whose interest was paramount: the mother's or the baby's. The House of Lords took the view, relying on the wording of s 1(1) of the Children Act 1989, that it was the child who was the subject of the proceedings whose welfare was paramount. It was held that because the mother was applying for contact with the baby, the baby was the 'subject of the proceedings' and so it was the baby's interests which were paramount and therefore contact was not ordered.

This is not a very satisfactory approach because it may be a matter of chance what form the application takes and which child happens to be the subject of the application.[176] Although the approach of the House of Lords was correct as a matter of statutory interpretation, the House of Lords could have approached the issues on a more theoretical level: either by saying that in such cases the interests of the two children had to be balanced with each other; or that a minor mother's interests were always lower than her baby's. However, the House of Lords rejected these alternatives.

*Birmingham City Council* v *H (A Minor)*[177] has been applied in later cases. For example, in *Re S (Contact: Application by Sibling)*,[178] Y (an adopted child) sought leave to bring an application for contact with her birth sister, S (also adopted, but by other parents). In such a case it was S's and not Y's welfare which was paramount, because S was the 'subject' of the application.[179] In this case it was not in S's welfare to make a contact order, and so, however much contact may benefit Y, contact could not be ordered.

## (ii) Where there are two or more children who are the subject of an application under the Children Act 1989

What if an application[180] were made in respect of two children and it was in the interests of one child that the order be made, but not in the interests of the other? Wilson J in *Re T and E*[181] explained that in such a case both children's welfare had to be taken into account and balanced against each other. So, if the order would greatly benefit one child and slightly disadvantage the other, the order should be made. This approach was applied in *Re A (Conjoined Twins: Medical Treatment)*,[182] where there were two conjoined twins, J and M. If no medical treatment was provided then both would die. It was, however, possible to separate the twins with the result that J would live, but M would die. The operation would therefore be in J's interests, but not in M's (she would die sooner if the operation were performed than if it were not). The Court of Appeal was willing to balance the interests of the children. The interests of J were held to be more weighty than the interest of M and so the operation was authorised.

---

[175] [1994] 2 AC 212.
[176] See Douglas (1994a).
[177] [1994] 2 AC 212; see Douglas (1994a).
[178] [1998] 2 FLR 897.
[179] See also *Re F (Contact: Child in Care)* [1995] 1 FLR 510, [1994] 2 FCR 1354.
[180] Or two applications are heard together.
[181] [1995] 1 FLR 581, [1995] 3 FCR 260, noted in Cromack and Parry (1996).
[182] [2001] 1 FLR 1, [2000] 3 FCR 577.

### (iii) Where there are two or more children who are the subject of applications under different pieces of legislation

What if two children are the subject of connected applications under different pieces of legislation with different versions of the welfare principle? In *Re T and E*[183] T and E were half-sisters; both were in care. T's father wanted to revoke T's care order and sought a residence order under the Children Act 1989. The local authority sought an adoption order, hoping that T and E would be adopted together with the same family. The court decided that it was in T's interests for her to live with her father, but in E's interests for T and E to be adopted together. Wall J decided that under the adoption application the interests of both children were the 'first' consideration, but under the application for the revocation of the care order, T's welfare was paramount. The care order therefore had to be revoked, because it was in T's welfare to live with her father (even if that was contrary to E's interests).

## F Conflicts of interests between parents and children

One might expect that, given the welfare principle, if there is a clash between the interests of the children and parents, the interests of the child would be preferred.[184] As was stated by the Court of Appeal in *Re P (Contact: Supervision)*,[185] 'the court is concerned with the interests of the mother and the father only in so far as they bear on the welfare of the child'. So, however great the sacrifice demanded of parents, if there is overall a marginal increase in the child's welfare, the order should be made. In fact, despite the existence of the welfare principle, the English courts have been able to protect the interests of parents.[186] Four of the ways that have been used to do this will now be briefly examined, although there are more:

1. The law makes no attempt to ensure that everything that adults do in relation to children day to day promotes their welfare. There is no direct supervision of the way parents treat their children, unlike the close direct regulation of day-care centres or childminders.[187] Although there are regular inspections and assessments of day-care centres, there are no equivalent investigations into the way parents raise children. If the parents bring up the child in a way that harms the child then, unless one of the parents or the local authority or the child brings the matter before a court, there is unlikely to be any formal legal intervention.[188]

2. As already noted, there are various issues to which the welfare principle does not apply, even though the interests of the child may still be an important consideration. Such circumstances include the granting of a divorce; domestic violence; financial redistribution of property on divorce; and enforcement of court orders.[189] It may be noted that these are hardly topics where children's interests are insignificant, but rather cases where parents' interests are particularly weighty. A cynic may suggest that the law is only willing to promote a child's welfare where that does not greatly inconvenience adults.

---

[183] [1995] 1 FLR 581, [1995] 3 FCR 260.
[184] See Henricson and Bainham (2005) on, generally, tensions in the law and policy in balancing the interests of children and parents.
[185] [1996] 2 FLR 314 at p. 328.
[186] Herring (1999a).
[187] Children Act 1989, Part X, Sch 9; Department of Health (1991d).
[188] Though see Donzelot (1980) for discussion of indirect policing of families.
[189] *Re F (Contact: Enforcement: Representation of Child)* [1998] 1 FLR 691, [1998] 3 FCR 216.

3. A third way that the courts have protected the rights of parents is through closely identifying the interests of children and parents. Perhaps the best recent example to illustrate this is *Re T (A Minor) (Wardship: Medical Treatment)*.[190] This case concerned a dispute over whether life-saving medical treatment should be given to a child. The unanimous medical opinion was in favour, but the parents opposed it. The court decided that it would not be in the child's best interests for the treatment to go ahead, bearing in mind the pressure that this would put on the parents. Butler-Sloss LJ reasoned: 'the mother and this child are one for the purpose of this unusual case and the decision of the court to consent to the operation jointly affects the mother and son and so also affects the father. The welfare of the child depends upon his mother.'[191]

By suggesting that the interests of the parent and the child were 'one', the Court of Appeal was able to take account of the parents' interests under the umbrella of the child's welfare. It can be argued that this case failed to consider fully the possibility of the child being cared for by alternative carers if the parents felt unable to cope, and, further, that the court placed excessive weight on the parents' views and insufficient weight on the child's right to life. By seeing the mother and child as one, the child's independent interests were hidden.

4. The courts have sometimes protected parents' interests by explicitly limiting their jurisdiction. So, for example, in *Re E (Residence: Imposition of Conditions)*[192] the court refused to make it a condition of a mother's residence order that she remain in London because that would be to intervene in the mother's right to choose where to live.[193] There is nothing in the Children Act 1989 that limits the courts' jurisdiction in such a way, but decisions of this kind enable the court to protect the interests of parents.[194]

These indicate that, in fact, the courts are able to give effect to the interests of the parents despite purporting to uphold the welfare principle as a principle requiring the interests of parents to be subservient to the interests of children. In the light of the Human Rights Act 1998 the court will have to acknowledge explicitly that parents have human rights which cannot be automatically overridden simply by reference to the welfare principle.[195] So how should the law deal with clashes between the rights and interests of parents and children?

Here are some of the possibilities that could be adopted:[196]

---

**DEBATE**

## How should the interests of parents and children be balanced?

1. *The welfare principle.* It could be argued that, despite the acknowledgement of parents' rights in the Human Rights Act 1998, the court should continue to assert that the interests of children are the sole consideration.

---

[190] [1997] 1 FLR 502.
[191] [1997] 1 FLR 502 at p. 510.
[192] [1997] 2 FLR 638. Contrast *Re S (A Child: Residence Order: Condition) (No. 2)* [2003] 1 FCR 138.
[193] See Chapter 9 for further discussion.
[194] See also *D v N (Contact Order: Conditions)* [1997] 2 FLR 797, [1997] 3 FCR 721.
[195] Choudhry and Fenwick (2005); Bonner, Fenwick and Harris-Short (2003); Herring (1999b).
[196] When considering these theories it may be useful to look at the facts of an actual case. Consider, for example, *Re S (A Child: Residence Order: Condition) (No. 2)* [2003] 1 FCR 138.

2. *Primary and secondary interests (Bainham)*. One of the most developed considerations of how to balance the conflicting rights and interests of family members is the analysis made by Bainham. He suggests that the answer is to categorise parents' and children's interests as either primary or secondary interests.[197] A child's secondary interests would have to give way to a parent's primary interests and similarly a parent's secondary interests must give way to a child's primary interests. In addition, the court should consider the 'collective family interest'.[198] This, he argues, should also be taken into account in the balancing exercise, so that the interests of one family member may have to be weighed against the good of the family as a unit.

3. *Relationship-based welfare (Herring)*. This theory[199] argues that children should be brought up in relationships which overall promote their welfare.[200] It argues that families, and society in general, are based on mutual co-operation and support.[201] So it is important to encourage a child to adopt, to a limited extent, the virtue of altruism and an awareness of social obligation. Children should only be expected to be altruistic to the extent of not demanding from parents excessive sacrifices in return for minor benefits. It is beneficial for a child to be brought up in a family that is based on relationships which are fair and just. A relationship based on unacceptable demands on a parent is not furthering a child's welfare. Indeed, it is impossible to construct an approach to looking at a child's welfare which ignores the web of relationships within which the child is brought up. Supporting the child means supporting the caregiver and supporting the caregiver means supporting the child.[202] So a court can legitimately make an order which benefits a parent, but not a child, if that can be regarded as appropriate in the context of their past and ongoing relationship.[203]

4. *Modified least detrimental alternative (Eekelaar)*. Eekelaar summarises his theory in this way:

> The best solution is surely to adopt the course that avoids inflicting the most damage on the well-being of any interested individual . . . [I]f the choice was between a solution that advanced a child's well-being a great deal, but also damaged the interests of one parent a great deal, and a different solution under which the child's well-being was diminished, but damaged the parent to a far lesser degree, one should choose the second option, even though it was not the least detrimental alternative for the child.[204]

However, he adds an important qualification to this test and that is that 'no solution should be adopted where the detriments outweigh the benefits for the child, unless that would be the result of *any* available solution, so that is unavoidable.'[205] He also adds that there may be a degree of detriment to which a child should never be subjected, if that is avoidable.[206] He is concerned about cases where, for example, a disabled spouse would greatly suffer if on divorce the child were to live with the other parent.

➡

[197] Bainham (1998c).
[198] Bainham (1998c). See also Henricson and Bainham (2005: 11) where it is argued that the family 'as a group' have interests that deserve protection.
[199] Herring (1999b); see also Bridgeman (2010).
[200] Sevenhuijsen (2002) and Czapanskiy (1999).
[201] See Butler, Robinson and Scanlan (2005) for evidence that families are increasingly based on a democratic model with children being involved in decision making within families.
[202] Kavanagh (2004).
[203] See Bonthuys (2006) who complains that seeing parents' interests just through the prism of welfare fails to place sufficient weight on parents' interests.
[204] Eekelaar (2002a: 243–4).
[205] Eekelaar (2002a: 243).
[206] Eekelaar (2002a: 245).

5. *Balancing all interests*. This perspective[207] simply requires the courts to weigh up the interests of each party. There would be no particular preference for the interests of each of the parties. This approach would suggest that the court should make the order which would produce the most benefit and least detriment for the parties.

The difference between these approaches can be clarified by looking at the benefit or disadvantage of the proposed orders on a scale of +50 (the most beneficial) to −50 (the least beneficial). Consider these four possible orders (F being the father, M the mother and C the child):

Solution 1: C (−30); F (+30); M (+30)
Solution 2: C (−5); F (−5); M (+35)
Solution 3: C (+10); F (−30); M (−40)
Solution 4: C (+5); F (−5); M (−5)

The approach of balancing all the interests would support solution 1 because this is the one that produces the greatest total benefit adding together all the disadvantages and benefits for each party and treating them equally. Solution 1 would be unacceptable to the welfare principle because it harms the child. It would be unacceptable to Bainham because it involves the infringement of a primary interest of the child. It would also be unacceptable to Eekelaar because he refuses to accept making an order which causes a detriment to a child unless any order the court would make would cause a detriment to a child.

The welfare principle approach would promote solution 3. Despite the fact this may harm (quite seriously) the father and mother, under the welfare principle the harms caused to the parents are irrelevant and this is the solution that would best promote the child's welfare. Eekelaar would prefer solution 4. Although solution 3 promotes the child's welfare to the greatest extent, it does so by causing the parents significant harm. Solution 4 manages still to promote the child's welfare (albeit to a lesser extent than solution 3) and it does so causing less harm to the parents. Bainham might also approve of solutions 2 or 4 because they do not involve the infringement of anyone's primary or secondary interests.

Herring's approach is less straightforward because it requires an understanding of the nature of the relationship in the past, and the foreseeable future. If, for example, in the past the mother and father have had to make unusual and extreme sacrifices for the benefit of the child, solution 2 or even 1 may be acceptable.[208]

## Questions

1. *Are there any circumstances in which it is appropriate for a court to make a decision which will harm a child?*

2. *Should parents be taken to accept that by choosing to become parents their interests will count for less than their chidlren's?*

## Further reading

Compare **Eekelaar** (2002a) and **Herring** (1999b) for contrasting answers to this issue.

---

[207] This appears to be supported by Reece (1996).

[208] This perhaps indicates a concern with this approach. Most parents make enormous sacrifices for their children and so the approach might too easily lead to an argument that it is justifiable to promote parents' interests over those of children. See further Federele (1994: 356) for a concern that relational approaches can too easily overlook the power within the relationships.

## 8 The Human Rights Act 1998 and children's welfare and rights

It is generally accepted that the European Convention on Human Rights[209] does not provide adequately for the rights of children.[210] The Convention was clearly drawn up with adults (rather than children) as the focus of attention.[211] Indeed, there are no articles in the Convention explicitly dealing with children. However, that is not to say that children receive no protection under the Convention.[212] Children are entitled to the same rights under the Convention as adults.[213] Article 1 states: 'The High Contracting Parties shall secure to everyone within their jurisdiction the rights and freedoms in this Convention.'[214] The European Court has accepted that 'everyone' in article 1 includes children.[215] To give two examples: children have been able to bring applications before the European Court of Human Rights claiming that they are entitled to state protection under article 3 (to protect them from corporal punishment which constitutes torture or inhuman or degrading treatment)[216] and article 5 (to complain of being wrongfully detained in a hospital).[217] Children's interests can also sometimes be protected when an adult enforces his or her own rights. So the enforcement of a parent's rights of contact with his or her child inevitably leads to an enforcement of the right of the child to contact with his or her parent.[218]

Although children are in theory entitled to claim these rights, one leading commentator on child law has complained of the 'pitifully inadequate response thus far by the European Institutions to the equally independent rights of children under the Convention'.[219] This complaint is made because often the rights of the children concerned are not explicitly mentioned by the courts when cases are brought by adults even though the case concerns children. It is notable that many of the cases which have concerned children have involved parents bringing proceedings in respect of a breach of a parent's rights.[220] For example, some of the leading cases on the corporal punishment of children in schools concern claims by parents that hitting children infringes the rights of parents.[221] Indeed one leading academic has complained of 'judicial myopia' when considering children's rights.[222]

A notable case where the rights of children played an important role was *R (On the Application of Begum) v Headteacher and Governors of Denbigh High School*.[223] The House of Lords considered a school dress code that prevented Shabina Begum from wearing the *jilbab* (a long

---

[209] Choudhry and Herring (2010); Fortin (2006a); Harris-Short (2005); Fortin (1999a); Herring (1999b).
[210] Fortin (2002 and 2006a).
[211] Douglas (1988).
[212] For a thorough discussion of the rights of children under the European Convention see Kilkelly (2000).
[213] Smith (1993).
[214] Article 14 states that the rights must be granted without discrimination 'on any ground such as sex, race, colour . . .'. Although age is not specifically mentioned, the use of the words 'such as' indicates that the list is not intended to be exhaustive and so it could be argued that age should be included as a prohibited ground of discrimination.
[215] *Nielsen v Denmark* (1989) 11 EHRR 175.
[216] *A v UK (Human Rights: Punishment of Child)* [1998] 2 FLR 959.
[217] *Nielsen v Denmark* (1988) 11 EHRR 175.
[218] E.g. *Eriksson v Sweden* (1989) 12 EHRR 183.
[219] Bainham (1995a: 258).
[220] Hale (2006).
[221] Under article 2 of Protocol 1; *Campbell and Cosans v UK* (1982) 4 EHRR 293; *R (On the Application of Williamson) v Secretary of State for Education and Employment* [2005] 1 FCR 498.
[222] Fortin (2006b).
[223] [2006] 1 FCR 613, discussed in Edwards (2007).

coat-like garment) which she believed she was required to wear by her religion. Their Lordships accepted that children had a right to manifest their religion under article 9 of the ECHR, just as adults did. The majority held that there was no interference in her right to manifest her religious belief because she was free to go to another school where she could wear the *jilbab*. Unanimously their Lordships agreed that, in any event, even if there was a breach it could be justified in the name of protecting the freedoms of other pupils at the school (particularly girls) who might otherwise feel pressurised into wearing the *jilbab* against their wishes.[224]

The issue has returned to the courts. In *R (Playfoot) v Governing Body of Millais School*[225] Lydia Playfoot sought to wear a purity ring to school. The ring was said to symbolise her promise to God to abstain from sexual intercourse until marriage. She was told by the school that the ring infringed the school policy of 'no jewellery'. She claimed the school policy improperly infringed her right to manifest her religious beliefs, as protected under article 9 of the ECHR. This argument was rejected primarily on the basis that the wearing of the ring was not a manifestation of her religious belief. Her beliefs did not require her to wear the ring. While the case is primarily about the interpretation of manifestation of religious belief, it is remarkable that the court placed little right on the child's right to respect for her private life, which included wearing the clothing or jewellery she had wanted. The case should be contrasted with *R (Watkins-Singh) v Governing Body of Aberdare Girls' High School*[226] where a Sikh girl who was prohibited from wearing a *kara* (a religious steel band of about one-fifth of an inch wide). There it was found that the wearing of the *kara* was central to her religious beliefs, and barring it was indirect religious discrimination and hence unlawful.[227] Important in that case was the fact that there was no evidence that the wearing of the *kara* would impact on other pupils.

The relevance of particular rights of children under the Convention will be discussed where appropriate throughout the book; but now the way the Convention deals with clashes between the interests of adults and children will be considered.

## A Balancing the rights of parents and children under the Convention

The Convention, rather surprisingly, includes no explicit reference to ensure that the enforcement of adult rights does not harm a child's welfare. However, the European Court has been able to give weight to the interest of the child by considering the wording in the articles which restrict rights. For example, the most quoted article in cases concerning children is article 8:

---

### LEGISLATIVE PROVISION

**European Convention on Human Rights, article 8**

1. Everyone has the right to respect for his private and family life, his home and his correspondence.

2. There shall be no interference by a public authority with the exercise of this right except such as is in accordance with the law and is necessary in a democratic society in the interests of national security, public safety or the economic well-being of the country, for the prevention of disorder or crime, for the protection of health or morals, or for the protection of the rights and freedoms of others.

---

[224] The banning of headscarves in French schools was held not to infringe the ECHR in *Aktas v France* (Application 43563/08). See also *Lautsi v Italy* (App. No. 30814/06) on state sponsorship of religion in schools.

[225] [2007] 3 FCR 754.

[226] [2008] 2 FCR 203.

[227] Under s 1(1a) of the Race Relations Act 1976 and s 45(3) of the Equality Act 2006.

So, a permitted interference of the right must be in accordance with the law;[228] it must pursue a legitimate aim; it must be proportionate[229] and necessary.[230] It is clearly established that a 'legitimate aim' includes preserving the rights and welfare of children.[231] In other words, an infringement of an adult's right to respect for private and family life can be justified if necessary to protect the children's interests.

The correct approach, then, where there may be a clash between the rights of children and adults (or between any two parties) is to start by looking at the rights that each individual has and consider whether the issue engages a right under the ECHR. If it does then the court will need to consider whether an infringement of that right is justified. So, a parent may have a right under article 8(1) to have contact with a child, but under article 8(2) it may be permissible to interfere with that right if necessary in the interests of the child or the resident parent. It would be necessary then to consider the right of each party involved (each parent and the child) and consider in each case where the rights and interests of others are sufficiently strong to justify an interference with that right. The difficulty with this approach is that you may end up with a clash between two rights under the ECHR.[232]

There are a number of solutions to a case where there is a clash between the rights of the parties. According to the European Court of Human Rights when considering the competing rights of adults and children in this case, the rights of children should be regarded as being of crucial importance (see below). Shazia Choudhry and Helen Fenwick[233] have suggested that the rights of children should be 'privileged'. However, Jane Fortin[234] complains that this is too vague and, while she is generally supportive of this kind of approach, feels that how the interests of children are privileged needs to be explained. Is it claimed that if there is a clash of rights the rights of children always win out? If not, when will children's rights lose out to an adult's right?[235]

Rachel Taylor and the author have suggested that in a case of clashing rights the court should look at the values underpinning the right.[236] In the case of article 8, which is the most common right used in family cases, the underlying value is that of autonomy: the right to pursue one's vision of the 'good life'. We could then consider the extent to which the proposed order would constitute a blight on each of the party's opportunities to live the good life. The court should make the order which causes the least blight.

The European Court of Human Rights has not yet given much guidance on the issue. It is clear that in cases involving families, the interests of children must be considered. In *W v Federal Republic of Germany*[237] the Commission held that a national court should take into consideration the interests of children.[238] In *Hendriks v Netherlands*[239] it was stated: 'the

---

[228] The procedure must be accessible, foreseeable and reasonably quick: *W v UK* (1988) 10 EHRR 29.

[229] *Price v UK* (1988) 55 D&R 1988.

[230] States have a margin of appreciation in deciding whether the intrusion is necessary.

[231] E.g. *R v UK* [1988] 2 FLR 445.

[232] Choudhry and Herring (2010); Fenwick (2004); Choudhry and Fenwick (2005); R. Taylor (2006); Harris-Short (2005).

[233] Choudhry and Fenwick (2005).

[234] Fortin (2006a).

[235] Fortin (2006a) suggests that only if the rights are 'equal' should the child's win out; although it is not quite clear what 'equal' means here.

[236] Herring and Taylor (2006). This seeks to develop Choudhry and Fenwick (2005) and dicta of Lord Steyn in *Re S (A Child) (Identification: Restrictions on Publication)* [2005] 1 AC 593 at para 17 which refer to the need to consider the values underlying the right when considering cases of clashing rights.

[237] (1985) 50 D&R 219.

[238] *L v Sweden* (1982) 40 D&R 140.

[239] (1982) 5 D&R 225.

Commission has consistently held that, in assessing the question of whether or not the refusal of the right of access to the non-custodial parent was in conformity with article 8 of the Convention, the interests of the child would predominate'. This was accepted as an accurate statement of the approach of the Convention by the Court of Appeal in *Re L (A Child) (Contact: Domestic Violence)*.[240] The European Court of Human Rights in *Scott v UK*[241] has stated that the interests of the child are 'of crucial importance' in cases involving the interests of parents and child. In *Hoppe v Germany*[242] it was said that the interests of children were of 'particular importance'.[243] In *Yousef v The Netherlands*[244] it was held that, under the European Convention, where the rights of children and parents conflict, the rights of children will be the 'paramount consideration'. In *Neulinger and Shuruk v Switzerland* it was said: 'The Court notes that there is currently a broad consensus – including in international law – in support of the idea that in all decisions concerning children, their best interests must be paramount.'[245] This is very close to the interpretation by the English and Welsh courts of the welfare principle,[246] however a close reading of the judgments suggests that in these cases the ECtHR was not intending paramount to mean that the welfare of the child is the sole consideration. Most subsequent cases[247] have not used the term 'paramount' and preferred to say children's interests are particularly important[248] or crucial.[249] It is interesting to note that in *Paulik v Slovakia*[250] the ECtHR, considering a case involving a man who wished to disprove a presumption of paternity, thought it significant that the child was now aged 40 and therefore an adult. This meant that her rights had lost much of their importance.[251] It seems then that in cases involving clashes between the rights of adults and children, while under the Children Act 1989, only the interests of children should be considered, under the ECHR the interests of children and adults should be considered, but the interests of children will be regarded as having significant weight.[252]

Despite these findings there are concerns that the Human Rights Act 1998, by explicitly giving parents rights, will weaken the interests of children. As Fortin[253] argues:

> It is of fundamental importance that the judiciary shows a willingness to interpret the European Convention in a child-centred way, as far as its narrow scope allows. It would be unfortunate in the extreme, if such a change heralded in an increased willingness to allow parents to pursue their own rights under the Convention at the expense of those of their children.

[240] [2000] 2 FCR 404.
[241] [2000] 2 FCR 560 at p. 572.
[242] [2003] 1 FCR 176 at para 49.
[243] See also *Sahin v Germany* [2003] 2 FCR 619 and *Haase v Germany* [2004] 2 FCR 1.
[244] [2000] 2 FLR 118 at para 118.
[245] (Application 41615/07), para 135.
[246] In *Re S (A Child) (Contact)* [2004] 1 FCR 439 at para 15 Butler-Sloss cited *Yousef* as showing that the ECHR had recognised the principle of the paramountcy of the child's welfare.
[247] Harris Short (2005: 357) describes *Yousef* as an isolated decision. Although, see *Maire v Portugal* [2004] 2 FLR 653 at para 77, which followed *Yousef* in using the 'paramount' terminology. In *Kearns v France* [2008] 2 FCR 1, at para 79 the child's interests were said to be paramount, but that statement appears to relate to the particular context of the case.
[248] E.g. *Haase v Germany* [2004] 2 FCR 1 at para 93; *Suss v Germany* [2005] 3 FCR 66 at para 88; *Hunt v Ukraine* [2006] 3 FCR 756; *Chepelev v Russia* [2007] 2 FCR 649, para 27.
[249] *Nanning v Germany* [2007] 2 FCR 543, para 63. See also, *C v Finland* [2006] 2 FCR 195 at para 52; although in para 54 they use the 'particular importance' formulation.
[250] [2006] 3 FCR 323.
[251] Para 46.
[252] Choudhry and Herring (2010: chs 2 and 3).
[253] Fortin (1998: 56). See further Fortin (2006a and 2009b).

Kaganas and Piper[254] predict that the rights of adults under the Human Rights Act will only be upheld where these correspond to the current understanding of the welfare of the child. This will mean that there will be no conflict between the Human Rights Act and the welfare principle. If they are right then Fortin's concern will be overcome. However, if children's welfare and their rights are treated in the same way then it becomes difficult to see what point there is in considering children's rights.

## B  Is there any practical difference between the approaches of the European Convention and the Children Act 1989?

It has been seen that the European Convention, based upon rights, can take into account the welfare of children and that the Children Act 1989, based upon the welfare principle, has taken into account the rights of parents. It is therefore inevitable that the question be asked: is there any practical difference between the two approaches?[255]

It may certainly be argued that the difference between the approach in the Human Rights Act 1998 and that in the Children Act 1989 is semantic only. Indeed, when the House of Lords directly faced the question whether the welfare principle and the rights protected in the Convention were consistent, it suggested that the difference was negligible. Bainham has argued that the courts see it 'as business as usual' in applying the welfare principle after the Human Rights Act.[256] In *Re KD (A Minor) (Ward: Termination of Access)*[257] Lord Templeman specifically compared the welfare principle and the Convention: 'In my opinion there is no inconsistency of principle or application between the English rule and the Convention rule.' Lord Oliver suggested that:

> Such conflict as exists is, I think, semantic only and lies only in differing ways of giving expression to the single common concept that the natural bond and relationship between parent and child gives rise to universally recognised norms which ought not to be gratuitously interfered with and which, if interfered with at all, ought to be so only if the welfare of the child dictates it.[258]

Such an approach has been confirmed by the House of Lords in *Re B (Adoption by One Natural Parent to Exclusion of Other)*.[259] It is respectfully suggested that this statement is not entirely accurate and that there are important differences between the approach of the Children Act 1989 and the European Convention on Human Rights.[260] Imagine a case concerning contact between a child and a non-residential parent. Under the European Convention, the starting point is the parent's right to respect for family life which will be infringed if contact is denied. In order to justify the breach there must be clear and convincing evidence that the contact would infringe the rights and interests of the child or resident parent to such an extent that the infringement was necessary and proportionate. However, under the Children Act there is a factual assumption that contact will promote the child's

---

[254] Kaganas and Piper (2001).

[255] See Herring (1999b); Choudhry (2003).

[256] Bainham (2002b: 290). See also Harris-Short (2002: 338) for concerns that the courts have not taken the impact of the Human Rights Act seriously enough.

[257] [1988] 2 FLR 139, [1988] FCR 657.

[258] [1988] 1 All ER 577 at p. 588.

[259] [2002] 1 FLR 196.

[260] This view has been taken by many commentators: Fortin (2006a); Harris-Short (2005); Choudhry and Fenwick (2005); Herring and Taylor (2006). Indeed, the writer knows of no academic commentator who agrees that the welfare principle as interpreted by the courts and an approach based on the ECHR are the same.

welfare, although this could be rebutted by evidence that contact would not promote the child's welfare in this particular case.

The difference between the two approaches is twofold. First, less evidence would be required under the Children Act to show the assumption that contact promotes a child's welfare than would be required under the Convention to show that infringement of the parent's rights is necessary and proportionate. Secondly, the nature of the question is different. Under the Children Act the question is a factual one – will contact promote the child's welfare?; whereas under the European Convention approach it is a question of legal judgment – whether the harm to the child is sufficient to make the breach 'necessary' as understood by the law.

A further difference between the approach of the welfare principle and the Convention is that the Convention is in this area essentially restrictive – it tells governments and courts what they may not do;[261] while the welfare principle requires the court to act positively to promote the child's welfare.[262] A good example is article 2 of the first Protocol: 'no person shall be denied the right to education'. It should be noted that this does not give a positive right to education, just a right not to be denied any education offered by the state. Similarly, article 8 requires that the state should not interfere with respect for family life, but the wording does not appear to require the state to promote family life. That said, as seen in Chapter 7, article 8 has been interpreted to require the state in some circumstances to act positively to promote the child's welfare.

## 9 Criticisms of the welfare principle

The welfare principle seeks to ensure that children are not exploited for the interests of adults.[263] At least, judicial decisions concerning children's upbringing must be phrased in terms of benefit for children. This can be justified on the basis that children are likely to be the least responsible for the difficulties that have led to the court case. They are also the least likely to be able to escape from the family difficulties and are least equipped to respond positively to the effect of any order which is against their interests.

Despite its predominance in the law relating to children, the welfare principle has been criticised.[264] Some of the main objections will be now be outlined.

1. *The law has a narrow perception of welfare.* King and Piper have argued that 'the broad range of factors – genetic, financial, educational, environmental and relational – which science would recognise as capable of affecting the welfare of a child are narrowed by law to a small range of issues which fall directly under the influence of the judge, the social workers or the adult parties to the litigation process'.[265] As Jo Bridgeman writes:

    unless consideration is given to the individual child, to the person they are, their personality, character, feelings of pleasure and pain, and relational interests (relationships with those upon whom they depend), determinations about the best interests of the child are reached according to current ideas about the child and according to adult memories of childhood.[266]

---

[261] Hale (2006) sees this as a weakness of the ECHR from a child's point of view.
[262] Although note s 1(5) of the Children Act 1989.
[263] Eekelaar (2002a).
[264] See, e.g., Reece (1996). For support of the principle in the face of these criticisms see Herring (2005b).
[265] King and Piper (1995: 50). This is based on autopoietic theory: see Chapter 1.
[266] Bridgeman (2007: 9).

Further, the court's focus on child welfare tends not to consider issues such as pollution, the quality of public housing and wider political questions which can have a powerful effect on the interests of children.

2. *Uncertainty.* Mnookin[267] argues that the welfare principle gives rise to inconsistency and unpredictability.[268] Guggenheim[269] writes:

> However alluring and child-friendly the 'best interests' test appears, in truth it is a formula for unleashing state power, without any meaningful reassurance of advancing children's interests.

The uncertainty arises from the great many unknowns concerning welfare. The facts are not known because often there is only the conflicting evidence of the father and mother as to the history of the parents' relationship. Even if the facts are established, it is impossible to predict how well the parties will be able to care for children. Even if the court could predict how the parents will act, it may be hard to choose who is the better parent, given the lack of agreed values over what makes an ideal parent. These uncertainties in effect give a judge a wide discretion in deciding what is in a child's welfare.[270] Some have even suggested it enables a judge to give free reign to his or her prejudices.[271] The uncertainty also creates problems for parents in negotiating. As it is hard to anticipate how a judge might decide a case, the parties may well prefer chancing a judicial hearing, rather than reaching a negotiated settlement. By contrast, if it was predictable how a judge would resolve a dispute between the parties then there would be little point in incurring the expenses involved in taking the matter to court.

3. *Smokescreen.* There is a concern that, given the uncertainty surrounding the welfare principle, the real basis for the decision will be hidden.[272] In particular, the prejudices of the professionals involved (the judiciary, the expert witnesses and the lawyers) provide the true reason behind the decision. For example, an individual's ideology of what makes a good mother or father can be extremely significant.[273] This then can lead to the welfare presumption being used in a way which works against the interests of women.[274]

4. *Increased costs.* It can be argued that the welfare principle simply increases the costs for the parties. Its unpredictability means that it is harder to negotiate a settlement and the complexity of the test means that court hearings take longer and require more substantial preparation.

5. *Unfairness.* The welfare principle can be attacked for failing to give adequate (or indeed any) weight to the interests of adults.[275] Eekelaar explains: 'the very ease of the welfare test

---

[267] Mnookin (1975).
[268] For a good discussion of inconsistencies among Court of Appeal decisions in applying the welfare principle, see Gilmore (2004); although, as Schneider (1993) points out, rule-based systems tend to develop their own way of creating discretion.
[269] Guggenheim (2006: 41).
[270] Elster (1987). Although O'Halloran (1999: 305), for example, has argued that the existence of widely held legal presumptions and assumptions in relation to children's welfare has 'fixed a set agenda' for determining welfare.
[271] Millar and Goldenberg (1998) complain that judges are anti-fathers.
[272] Reece (1996: 296–7).
[273] Boyd (1996).
[274] Fineman (1988).
[275] Reece (1996: 303), although Ribbens McCarthy, Edwards and Gillies (2003: 140) argue that the position that the interests of children should be first is one of the few 'unquestionable moral assertions'.

encourages a laziness and unwillingness to pay proper attention to all the interests that are at stake in these decisions and, possibly, also a tendency to abdicate responsibility for decision making to welfare professionals'.[276] Those who see the force of such an approach would prefer the courts paid greater attention to the impact of the Human Rights Act 1998, which they say requires the court to pay attention to the rights of adults and children. The benefit of such an approach has been summarised by Sonia Harris-Short in this way:

> Rights-based reasoning has the potential to introduce much greater intellectual rigour and discipline to judicial reasoning in the family law context, ensuring the needs and interests of all family members are clearly articulated and considered in the decision-making process and preventing untested assumptions and prejudices, currently obscured behind the vagaries of the welfare principle, from determining the outcome of common family disputes.[277]

6. *Unrealistic.* If there is a dispute over the medical treatment for a child and the matter is brought before the court, a judge considering what is best for the child may decide that the child should be flown to the top medical hospital in America to be treated by the world's leading expert in the field, with no expense spared.[278] Of course a court could not make such an order. As this indicates, it is often for practical reasons impossible to make the order that would best promote the child's welfare.

7. *Children's rights.* As we will discuss later in this chapter, those who advocate children's rights and in particular those who support the idea that children should be allowed to make decisions for themselves, even if that slightly harms them, would not support the welfare principle.

In the face of such powerful criticisms is there anything that can be said in favour of the welfare principle?[279] Perhaps the most that can be said is that it is better than its alternatives (see below). As to indeterminacy, Gillian Douglas[280] has written that the 'uncertainty and inconsistency may be both the greatest strength and greatest weakness of the "welfare principle"'. The benefit of the uncertainty surrounding the welfare principle is that it enables courts to produce results which are flexible and responsive to the individual needs of each child. Further, the welfare principle sends an important symbolic message.[281] It recognises the value, the importance and the vulnerability of children. Quite simply, if a court order causes a loss or hurt, children have fewer resources open to them than adults do. Children lack the material, psychological, and relational resources that parents have. Another point is that without the welfare principle it would be easy in court proceedings for the interests of the children to be lost, especially because rarely in disputes over children is there an independent advocate for the child or is the child heard herself. Finally, the message sent to separating parents by the welfare principle is one they desperately need to hear: forget about your own rights; put the interests of your children first.

---

[276] Eekelaar (2002a: 248).
[277] Harris-Short (2005: 359).
[278] Archard (2003: 41).
[279] Herring (2005b).
[280] Douglas (2004: 173).
[281] More cynically, see Van Krieken (2005) who sees the welfare principle being used as a way of 'civilising parents'.

# 10 Alternatives to the welfare principle

If the law were to abandon the welfare principle, what alternatives could be used?[282]

1. *Presumptions.* The law could seek to rely on presumptions. These could be, for example, that children should live with their mothers and the view of the mother should be preferred over the view of the father in any issue of dispute or that on separation a child should spend an equal amount of time with each parent. We shall discuss such presumptions further in Chapter 9. A major difficulty is that they are based on generalisations. Opponents argue that courts should deal with the particular children and family before them, and not rely on assumptions about what is often good for families in general. Research from Australia which has developed a strong presumption in favour of shared residence is that it has worked against the interests of children in many families where the model is inappropriate.[283]

2. *Letting the child decide.* There is much evidence that although children wish to be listened to when their parents separate, most do not want to be forced to decide between their parents.[284] It is therefore unlikely that this would be appropriate except for mature teenagers who have strong views. There are further dangers that the approach might encourage parents to manipulate the child's views.

3. *Tossing a coin.* Elster suggests that disputes over children could be resolved by tossing a coin.[285] In part this approach is a counsel of despair: the courts are not able to predict what will promote the welfare of the child and so they may as well toss a coin. The approach is cheap and treats each side equally. However, the approach cannot really be acceptable, because it abdicates responsibility for children. It is true there are some cases where it is impossible to know what is in a child's interest, but there are many others where the court can ascertain what is in a child's interests or at least what is not in a child's interests. Not to protect the child in such a case would appear irresponsible.[286]

4. *Non-legal solutions.* It is perhaps too readily assumed that disputes between family members should be resolved by a court hearing.[287] It is certainly arguable that social work to assist the family may be more effective than legal intervention. Masson,[288] considering disputes over contact, suggests that rather than spending resources on lengthy bitter disputes in deciding whether or not there should be contact, resources may be better spent encouraging the parties to reach their own decision and facilitating contact. Thorpe LJ in *Re L (A Child) (Contact: Domestic Violence)*, also talking about disputes over contact, has suggested:

> The disputes are particularly prevalent and intractable. They consume a disproportionate quantity of private law judicial time. The disputes are often driven by personality disorders, unresolved adult conflicts or egocentricity. These originating or contributing factors would generally be better treated therapeutically, where at least there would be some prospect of beneficial change, rather than given vent in the family justice system.[289]

---

[282] Meli (1993).
[283] Rhoades (2010a).
[284] Cantwell and Scott (1995).
[285] Elster (1987).
[286] Schneider (1991).
[287] King (2000).
[288] Masson (2000b).
[289] [2000] 2 FCR 404 at p. 439.

Such thinking has been influential in the Children and Adoption Act 2006 which provides extra-legal methods of seeking to encourage parties to resolve their differences over contact. Whether such an approach could be justified in the light of the Human Rights Act 1998, and the requirement that the state protects the rights of parents and children, is open to debate. This gives rise to some of the debates over mediation which were considered in Chapter 3.

Of all of the alternatives to the welfare principle it is an approach based on children's rights which has been most influential and so we will consider that next.

## 11 Children's rights

So far we have looked at the law's attempts to promote the welfare of the child. However, in the last few decades there have been calls that, rather than adults attempting to promote the child's welfare, the law should recognise that children have rights of their own.[290] After all, it is hard to resist the argument 'children have human rights, because children are human'.[291] Michael Freeman has argued:

> Rights are important because they recognise the respect their bearers are entitled to. To accord rights is to respect dignity: to deny rights is to cast doubt on humanity and on integrity. Rights are an affirmation of the Kantian basic principle that we are ends in ourselves, and not means to the ends of others.[292]

Indeed, children's rights are protected by a variety of international instruments,[293] including most notably the United Nations Convention on the Rights of the Child.[294]

Katherine Federle[295] explains the significance of seeing that children have rights, rather than just being people who should be looked after:

> Rights have a transformative aspect because they have the potential to reduce victimization and dependence by changing the rights holder into a powerful individual who commands the respect of those in the legal system. . . . rights create mutual zones of respect, challenging those who want to act in the best interests of children to promote the empowerment of children instead.

There is relatively little dispute that children should have some of the basic rights, such as right to life, rights to education, or rights to protection from serious harm[296]; and so we will focus on whether children have rights in terms of two key questions:

1. Should children have all the rights that adults have or should we limit the rights available to children?

2. Should children be given extra rights over and above those given to adults?[297]

---

[290] For a consideration of children's rights from a broad perspective see John (2003), Freeman (2004b), Archard and Macleod (2002), Willems (2007) and Woodhouse (2000 and 2008).

[291] Herring (2003b: 146).

[292] Freeman (2007: 7).

[293] Fortin (2003b: ch. 2) provides an invaluable discussion on the rights of children in international law.

[294] MacDonald, A. (2009a). The Government had been criticised for failing fully to implement the Convention by the United Nations Committee on the Rights of the Child (2008). See HM Government (2010b) for the Government's report to the UN Committee on the Rights of the Child. For a discussion of gaps in the Convention see Freeman (2000e). In 2010 a private member's Children's Rights Bill was introduced to Parliament which, if passed, will enshrine the Convention into English law. It has little chance of becoming law.

[295] Federle (2009).

[296] Alderson (2008).

[297] See Herring (2003b) for more detailed discussion.

## A Should children have all the rights adults have?

A simple approach is that children are people and so should have all the rights that adults have.[298] These will include the right to vote,[299] work, travel, use drugs and to engage in sexual relations.[300] Such an approach is taken by a group of thinkers known as child liberationists or colloquially as 'kiddy libbers'.[301] For example, Holt[302] has written that the law supports the view of a child 'being wholly subservient and dependent . . . being seen by older people as a mixture of expensive nuisance, slave and super-pet'. Initially, the approach seems unacceptable: surely we cannot accept a society where children have the same rights to sexual freedom, to marry, or to drive cars as adults?[303] Farson replies to such arguments in this way:

> asking what is good for children is beside the point. We will grant children rights for the same reason we grant rights to adults, not because we are sure that children will then become better people, but more for ideological reasons, because we believe that expanding freedom as a way of life is worthwhile in itself. And freedom, we have found, is a difficult burden for adults as well as for children.[304]

In other words, he accepts that giving children rights might lead to them being harmed, but the same thing happens to adults when we give them rights.

The child liberationist position is often criticised for failing to appreciate the physical and mental differences between children and adults.[305] But this is not quite what most child liberationists nowadays claim; they argue that the same laws should apply to adults and children. It is quite permissible to ban from driving those incapable of driving competently, but the state should not ban people from driving on the grounds of age. So, children should not be barred from driving simply on the basis of their age, but can be on the basis of their inability at driving. Similarly, in sexual matters, if the child is not competent to consent then it would be unlawful for someone to have sexual relations with him or her.[306] But that would be true for all who have sexual relations with those who do not consent. Another way of putting this argument is that children should not be discriminated against on the grounds of their age.[307] It must be admitted that the present law on at what age young people are able to do something is illogical. To give one example: a 16-year-old is deemed old enough to consent to sexual relations with her or his MP, but not to vote for her or him!

This more moderate liberationist approach is harder to rebut. It is necessary to show some morally relevant distinction between children and adults in order to justify rejection of the liberationist position.[308] One argument may be based on bureaucratic difficulties in assessing competence. To expect a bar-tender to interview every person who orders a drink to ascertain

---

[298] Although still today some academic commentators take the view that it is appropriate to call a child 'it'.

[299] For a contemporary argument that children should have the right to vote see Olsson (2008).

[300] Holt (1975: 18). See Waites (2005) for a wide-ranging discussion on the age of consent to sexual relations.

[301] Children's liberationists include Foster and Freund (1972) and Holt (1975). For criticism see Archard (1993); Fox Harding (1996). On 'kiddy libbers' see Mnookin (1981).

[302] Holt (1975).

[303] Archard (2003: 9) suggests that some writers are 'rhetorical child liberationists' in that they do not really mean that children should have all the rights of adults, but that to make such a claim is eye-catching and therefore politically a useful way of increasing the number of rights children have.

[304] Farson (1978: 31).

[305] Fortin (2003b: 5).

[306] The Sexual Offences Act 2003 contains arrange of sexual offences that can be committed against children under the age of 16; s 5 makes it an offence for a man to have sex with a girl under the age of 13, whether or not she consents. See further *R v G* [2008] UKHL 37, confirming it was no defence if the man believed the victim to be over the age of 13 and consenting.

[307] Herring (2003b).

[308] Roche (1999).

whether they have sufficient understanding of the potential harms of alcohol to make a reasoned decision to purchase it would be unworkable.[309] A slightly different point is that using age provides a clear impersonal requirement, because the assessment of each individual's capacity can involve 'contested norms'.[310] Age also provides a predictable criterion which enables people to plan their lives, without fearing that they will be found incompetent.[311]

As can be seen already, much of the discussion about children's rights centres on the right to autonomy. The right to autonomy is essentially the right to decide how you wish to live your life. Eekelaar has called autonomy 'the most dangerous but precious of rights: the right to make their own mistakes'.[312] Most people accept that if an adult wishes to spend all his or her free time playing computer games or watching television or writing a law textbook he or she can, providing these activities do not harm anyone else. Sometimes writers talk about each person being permitted to pursue their own vision of the 'good life'. This is generally regarded as not only good for each individual but also good for society. Our society would be a less culturally rich society if everyone were to spend all their free time jogging, for example. It is good for society that there is diversity in the kinds of hobbies people enjoy. The difficulty is in applying this approach to children. Specifically, children do not have the capacity to develop their own version of their 'good life', at least in the sense of defining long-term goals. The essential problem is this: the way a child lives his or her childhood affects the range of choices and options available later on in life.[313] A simple example is that allowing a child to pursue their vision of a good life and allowing them not to go to school may mean that they will be prevented from pursuing what they regard as the good life once they reach majority because they will not have the education needed to pursue their goals. It may therefore be justifiable to infringe a child's autonomy during minority in order to maximise their autonomy later on in life. This, then, could explain why children cannot be treated as adults and why the state may be entitled to restrict autonomy rights in the name of promoting the child's welfare and ultimately their autonomy. John Eekelaar has developed a well-respected version of children's rights.[314] He started with Joseph Raz's definition of a right that: 'a law creates a right if it is based on and expresses the view that someone has an interest which is sufficient ground for holding another to be subject to a duty'.[315] Eekelaar suggests that three kinds of interest are relevant for children:

1. *Basic interests.* These are the essential requirements of living – physical, emotional and intellectual interests. They would include the interest in being provided with food and clothing and in developing emotionally and intellectually. Eekelaar argues that the duty to promote these basic needs lies on parents, but there is also a duty on the state to provide these where parents fail to do so.

2. *Developmental interests.* Eekelaar describes these as 'all children should have an equal opportunity to maximise the resources available to them during their childhood (including their own inherent abilities) so as to minimise the degree to which they enter adult life affected by avoidable prejudices incurred during childhood'.[316] Eekelaar accepts that, apart from education, these would be hard to enforce as legal rights.

---

[309] How many adults would pass the test?
[310] Haldane (1994).
[311] Teitelbaum (1999).
[312] Eekelaar (1986: 161).
[313] Eekelaar (1994b).
[314] Eekelaar (1994b and 2006b: ch. 6). Bevan (1989: 11) proposes a simple division of children's rights which are protective and those which are self-assertive. This has received the support of Fortin (2003b: 17).
[315] Raz (1994).
[316] Eekelaar (1994b).

3. *Autonomy interest*. This is the freedom for the child to make his or her own decisions about their life.

Of these three interests, Eekelaar would rank the autonomy interest as subordinate to the developmental and basic interests.[317] So children would not be able to claim autonomy interests in a way that would prejudice their basic or developmental interests. He would therefore allow children to make decisions for themselves, even if those were bad mistakes, unless the decision involved infringing one of the basic or developmental interests. This would mean that a child's decision not to go to school would be overridden, because this would be infringing their developmental interests. But their decision to wear jeans should not be overridden as it would not infringe their interests.[318] Of course, there may be borderline cases (would nose piercing be permitted?) but such borderline cases are present in every theory. Eekelaar's approach has the benefit of providing an explanation of why children do not have all the rights of adults – so that they can have greater autonomy as adults – and provides a sensible practical model enabling children to make some decisions for themselves, but not so as to cause themselves serious harm.[319]

Eekelaar has developed his thinking by suggesting that the law should promote a child's welfare by encouraging dynamic self-determinism.[320] He explains that:

> The process is dynamic because it appreciates that the optimal course for a child cannot always be mapped out at the time of decision, and may need to be revised as the child grows up. It involves self-determinism because the child itself is given scope to influence the outcome.[321]

The aim of this approach is:

> To bring a child to the threshold of adulthood with the maximum opportunities to form and pursue life-goals which reflect as closely as possible an autonomous choice.[322]

This means that:

> in making decisions about children's upbringing, care should be taken to avoid imposing inflexible outcomes at an early stage in a child's development which unduly limit the child's capacity to fashion his/her own identity, and the context in which it flourishes best.[323]

This approach would therefore give children an increasing role in making decisions for themselves as they grow up.

One way to test Eekelaar's theory would be to ask (as Eekelaar has) how as adults looking back on our childhood we would have wished to have been raised. The answer is probably that we would not have wanted every desire we had as children to be granted. It may well be that we would come up with a set of guidelines similar to Eekelaar's. Interestingly a survey of children's views found a general agreement that although children should be able to make some decisions, parents should make important ones.[324] Surely listening to children to find out what rights they think they ought to have is a productive way of considering the issue.[325]

---

[317] Eekelaar (1994b). Freeman (1997a) proposes a similar theory and agrees with the subordination of autonomy to other basic needs of the child.

[318] Unless he or she were not allowed to attend school while wearing jeans.

[319] Giddens (1998: 191–2) argues for the democratisation of family life, with children being treated as equal citizens in the family.

[320] Eekelaar (1994a).

[321] Eekelaar (1994a: 48).

[322] Eekelaar (1994a: 156).

[323] Eekelaar (2004: 186).

[324] Cherney (2010).

[325] Wall (2008).

A dramatic example of the exercise of children's rights concerned a 14-year-old Dutch sailor who wished (with her parents' consent) to sail around the world. The Dutch authorities were concerned about her welfare and she was put into care by the Dutch authorities.[326] She managed to escape and start her voyage. She was later given permission by the courts to undertake her expedition.[327]

However, Eekelaar's approach is problematic. David Archard[328] considers parents who face a choice of encouraging a child to play sport or music. If we ask what as an adult the child would want, this is problematic because what the child would think when he or she grows up will depend on the choice. If the parents choose music and the child grows up a talented musician he or she will approve of his or her parents' decisions. However, if the parents choose sport and the child becomes a successful sportsperson then the child will approve of that decision.[329] There are also problems because the hypothetical adult will decide using adult eyes. Would the adult let the child go to an expensive Santa's grotto at Christmas, or would the hypothetical adult regard that as a waste of money?

There are also difficulties with applying Eekelaar's theory practically in modern society. Imagine a child who is a highly gifted artist. What are the parents to do? Should the parents permit or encourage the child to devote most of her life to developing this talent? If the parents do, is it not arguable that that will limit the child's range of lifestyles in adulthood: she will be aged 18, a gifted artist, but with a limited range of alternatives in life. If, however, the parents seek to encourage her to develop a wide range of interests and hobbies and not dedicate a large portion of her life to art, it is unlikely that she will be sufficiently skilled to become a professional artist. With increased specialisation (especially in artistic, academic and sporting activities), dedication in childhood is essential in order to live out some life goals. A more common example is of children whose parents have undergone a bitter divorce. The court may have to decide whether the child will live with the mother or the father, knowing that contact with the other parent is unlikely to be effective. In such a case the court cannot keep the options open for the child to decide when they are an adult; the court must decide on some basis which is best for the child.[330] Indeed a parent who tried to ensure that a child had a maximum range of options available at adulthood would soon collapse with exhaustion!

A second problem with Eekelaar's approach is that it is not clear why it is restricted to child-hood. The university student who fails to work towards their degree and ends up failing their examinations could be said to have lessened their ability to choose their life choices. Is there a good reason for not permitting a child to limit their life choices but allowing young adults to do so?

A third objection is that Eekelaar's approach may lead to an open-ended solution. Leaving the question so that the child can make decisions when they are old enough may leave issues connected with the child's upbringing unresolved and open-ended.[331] For example, in relation to a dispute over religious upbringing, Eekelaar's approach may suggest that a child be brought up within both religions so that they can decide their religion for themselves later on in life. However, this may leave the child confused and unsettled.[332] Despite these

---

[326] BBC Newsonline (2009j).
[327] BBC Newsonline (2010d).
[328] Archard (2003: 51).
[329] A similar issue arises in raising a child with a particular religious belief, or ethnic identity. Eekelaar (2004) sees advantages in raising children with a variety of identities to choose from, although he sees nothing wrong with raising a child with a clear single sense of a single identity.
[330] C. Smith (1997b).
[331] C. Smith (1997b).
[332] Although see Eekelaar's (2004) reply to points of this kind. He rejects an argument that the child would find being raised with a variety of religions confusing.

difficulties it is submitted that Eekelaar's approach provides the best approach to examining children's rights.

It should not be thought that all supporters of children's rights are happy to give children the leeway to make decisions that even Eekelaar's model gives. Dwyer[333] is adamant that any rights that children have must protect their best interests; they have a right to have their welfare promoted.[334] Therefore, children should not be permitted to make decisions which will harm them. We will return to this issue later when we consider whether there is a difference between a rights-based approach and a welfare-based approach. There are, of course, a range of mid-way responses which suggest that children should be consulted over decisions concerning their upbringing, but their views will not be determinative.[335]

The Equality Act 2010 provide protection from discrimination on a broad range of characteristics, including age. However, it does not apply to children. The Government explained:[336]

> Age discrimination provisions do not extend to the under 18s because it is almost always appropriate to treat children of different ages in a way which is appropriate to their particular stage of development, abilities, capabilities and level of responsibility.

However, the fact that discrimination against children may often be justified does not mean that children should not be protected from it when it is not justified. Having recognised in the Equality Act that unjustified age discrimination is a degrading treatment which needs to be challenged, it is hard to justify why that should be only true in the case of adults.

## B The argument against rights for children

### DEBATE

#### Is there a case for children not having rights?

Here are some of the arguments that have been put forward against children having rights:

1. There are two main theories of rights: the will theory and the interest theory.[337] The will theory argues that rights can only exist where the right-holder can have choice in deciding whether or not to enforce the rights. This would mean that children (especially if very young) could not have rights.[338] MacCormick and other supporters of children's rights argue that this would be unacceptable and hence he rejects the will theory of rights in favour of the interest theory, which protects the interests of the right-holder and is not dependent on the ability to make a choice.[339] The arguments for and against these theories are discussed in detail in books on jurisprudence.[340]

➡

---

[333] Dwyer (2006: 11).
[334] Dwyer (2006: 132). See also Fortin (2006a) who rejects suggestions that rights can ever be used in a way which fundamentally harms a child.
[335] Archard and Skivenes (2009).
[336] HM Government (2010b: 11).
[337] MacCormick (1976).
[338] It could be argued by supporters of the will theory who wish to support children's rights that if children are not competent to choose whether or not to enforce their rights, parents are entitled to enforce those rights on children's behalf. See the discussion in Archard (2003: 7).
[339] The benefits and disadvantages of these approaches are beyond the scope of this book.
[340] See, e.g., MacCormick (1976); Archard (2003: ch. 1); Federle (2009).

2. A second objection would be that focusing on rights does not provide adequate protection for children.[341] Children are vulnerable and need protection from adults who can seek to take advantage of them and from children's own foolish decisions. As Archard puts it:

> [Children] need to be nurtured, supported and, more particularly, subjected to control and discipline. Without that context, giving children the rights that adults have is not only bad for the children but is also bad for the adults they will turn into, and for the society we share as adults and children.[342]

A moderate version of children's rights, such as Eekelaar's, would seem to diffuse such fears. However, there are still concerns that too much weight may be placed on children's wishes. Sir Thomas Bingham MR in **Re S (A Minor) (Independent Representation)**[343] has explained:

> First is the principle, to be honoured and respected, that children are human beings in their own right with individual minds and wills, views and emotions, which should command serious attention. A child's wishes are not to be discounted or dismissed simply because he is a child. He should be free to express them and decision-makers should listen. Second is the fact that a child is after all a child. The reason why the law is particularly solicitous in protecting the interests of children is that they are liable to be vulnerable and impressionable, lacking the maturity to weigh the longer term against the shorter, lacking the insight to know how they will react and the imagination to know how others will react in certain situations, lacking the experience to match the probable against the possible . . .

3. A further difficulty with rights for children is that an enforcement of a right of autonomy for a child will mean in many cases an infringement of a parent's or other carer's rights. Children live much of their childhood dependent on adults, and their relationship with adults is crucial.[344] That argument will be of less concern if we accept that there needs to be a fair balancing between the rights of children and parents.

4. It is arguable that the language of rights is quite inappropriate in intimate family relationships, where sacrifice and mutual support are the overriding values of the family unit, rather than the individual market-place philosophy where rights might make more sense.[345] It may be possible to produce a vision of rights that promotes individual autonomy *and* interpersonal connection, but these would not be identical to rights as they are commonly understood.[346]

   Much work among feminist writers sympathetic to such arguments has been in developing an 'ethic of care'.[347] Sevenhuijsen explains that the ethic of care: 'is encapsulated in the idea that individuals can exist only because they are members of various networks of care and responsibility, for good or bad. The self can exist only through and with others and vice versa . . .'.[348] Such a model would seem to emphasise the values of interdependence and relationships, rather than individualistic versions of rights. Smart has explained that the ethic of care:

---

[341] Purdy (1994).
[342] Archard (2003: 16).
[343] [1993] 2 FLR 437, [1993] 2 FCR 1.
[344] Guggenheim (2006).
[345] Regan (1993a); Wardle (1996); Diamantides (1999).
[346] Minow (1986); Herring (1999a).
[347] See, e.g., Sevenhuijsen (2000); Noddings (2003).
[348] Sevenhuijsen (2002: 131). See also Herring (2007a).

need not be carried forward on the basis of individual rights in which the child is construed as an autonomous individual consumer of oppositional rule-based entitlements, but more where the child is construed as part of a web of relationships in which outcomes need to be negotiated (not demanded) and where responsibilities are seen to be reciprocal.[349]

Fiona Kelly has argued that children must be seen as relational beings. An ethic of care approach can do this, but neither a welfare (protectionist) approach, nor a rights based approach does this:

> While protectionism and children's rights go some way towards understanding children as relational beings, both are fundamentally incompatible with such a construction. The protectionist model does acknowledge the parent/child relationship, but the relationship it protects is inherently unequal. It is premised on children's incapacity and the right of adults to speak on behalf of children. Similarly, while there is some acknowledgement under the children's rights model of the importance of connection in children's lives – for example, the Convention on the Rights of the Child gives the child a right to maintain relationships with caregivers if it is in his or her best interests – because the rights model is focused on producing a rational and autonomous adult, connection is treated as a stage in the maturity process which will ultimately be supplanted by detached individualism. In addition, the relationships a children's rights model envisages protecting arise out of the enforcement of rights, rather than the acknowledgement or valorisation of connection; caregiver relationships are protected because the child has a 'right' to maintain them.[350]

The author[351] has made a wider point, that the law in its emphasis on individualised rights can fail to attach sufficient significance to relationships of care:

> We are not self-sufficient but interdependent; not isolated individuals but people in relationship; not people with rights clashing with those who care for us and for whom we care, but people who live with entwined obligations and interests with those we love. We are not easily divided up into carers and cared for. We are in mutually supportive relationships. We need then a legal and ethical approach that promotes just caring: respects it; rewards it; and protects those rendered vulnerable by the caring role – an approach which has relationship at its heart.

It may, however be possible to deal with these concerns within a human rights framework, by developing an approach to rights which attaches appropriate weight to relational values.[352]

5. O'Neill[353] has suggested that it would be more profitable to focus on the notion of duties that adults owe towards children, than to stress the rights of children.[354] She is particularly concerned with impressive-sounding rights when it is unclear who has the duty to provide the child with the benefit. She warns:

> many of the rights promulgated in international documents are not perhaps spurious, but they are patently no more than 'manifesto' rights . . . that cannot be claimed unless or until practices and institutions are established that determine against whom claims on behalf of a particular child may be lodged. Mere insistence that certain ideals or goals are rights cannot make them into rights . . .[355]

➡

---

[349] Smart (2003: 239).

[350] Kelly (2005: 385).

[351] Herring (2007a). See also Rhoades (2010b).

[352] See Rhoades (2010b); Choudhry and Herring (2010: ch. 3); Wallbank, Choudhry and Herring (2010).

[353] O'Neill (1992). For a response, see Coady (1992).

[354] For a discussion over whether too much is expected of children's rights see Wardle (1996); King (1997); Freeman (2000c).

[355] Discussed further in Freeman (1997a).

She therefore argues that there are obligations owed to children, which cannot be recognised as rights, but that should still be recognised as obligations. This might be particularly desirable in cases where children lack maturity to be able to enforce rights themselves.[356] The main remedy she suggests to deal with children's powerlessness is to grow up. Her approach can be used to support the view that we should focus on dealing with the wrongs done to children, rather than giving them rights;[357] although rights supporters would argue that giving children rights is the best way of protecting them from wrongs. They might also agree with O'Neill that imposing obligations on adults is important, but this can be done in addition to giving children rights.

6. A further argument is that even if in theory children's rights are beneficial, in practice children's rights can be used to the disadvantage of women and children.[358] The fear is that rights are of use to those who have strength within society and, in particular, rights are of use to men to be used as tools of oppression. For example, children's rights could be used to investigate and control the intimate lives of women.

7. There are also concerns that children's rights reflect the norms within society, which may be discriminatory. Frances Olsen asks why getting children to help mother bake cookies at home is not a form of child labour.[359] This question, although a little tongue in cheek, does lead us to enquire how many of what we regard as human rights are in fact just a reflection of the cultural values of our society.

8. There is a concern over the enforcement of children's rights. If children's rights can only realistically be enforced by adults, it may be that such rights will be used only for the benefit of adults.[360] For example, the courts have held that a child has a right to know his or her genetic origins, but in practice this only occurs when a father seeks to have biological tests carried out to determine whether or not he is the father. This example may lead one to conclude that in reality this is a right for fathers to establish paternity, rather than for children to know their genetic identity. In *R (On the Application of Williamson)* v *Secretary of State for Education and Employment*[361] Baroness Hale memorably opened her speech: 'My lords, this is, and has always been, a case about children, their rights and the rights of their parents and teachers. Yet there has been no one here or in the courts below to speak on behalf of the children . . . The battle has been fought on ground selected by the adults.' She returned to the theme in *R (On the Application of Kehoe)* v *Secretary of State for Work and Pensions*:[362] 'My lords, this is another case which has been presented to us largely as a case about adults' rights when in reality it is a case about children's rights.'

   A slightly different point is about the problems the adult world may have in listening to children: children in our society are not used to being listened to. In schools and homes children become accustomed to not being expected to make decisions for themselves.[363] Lowe and Murch also raise the issue of difficulties over communication between children and adults:

---

[356] Federle (1994: 343).
[357] Simon (2000).
[358] Olsen (1992).
[359] Olsen (1992).
[360] Guggenheim (2006).
[361] [2005] 1 FCR 498 at para 71.
[362] [2005] 2 FCR 683 at para 49.
[363] Schofield and Thoburn (1996: 62).

children, in certain respects, inhabit different cultural worlds from adults. Moreover, they can be baffled by the language of adults, especially by professional jargon. Equally, adults are often unfamiliar with children's language codes which, in any event, can differ from age group to age group.[364]

The ease of misconception is demonstrated by the finding of one study which suggested that children associated courts with criminal wrongdoing, even if in fact the court is a family one.[365]

9. Some commentators have argued that the most important right children have is 'the right to be a child'.[366] This argument emphasises that children should not be expected to bear the responsibilities of adulthood. There is, for example, evidence from psychologists interviewing children whose parents are divorcing which suggests that, although children do wish to be listened to by their parents and the courts, they do not wish to be required to choose between their parents.[367] Neale found that children wanted to be involved in decision making, but to reach decisions with adults and not to be expected to reach decisions on their own.[368] Critics suggest that such arguments are based on an idealised childhood – a time of innocence, free from the concerns and responsibility of the adult world – that is a far cry from the poverty, bullying and abuse which is the lot of all too many children.[369]

10. Some commentators from a more traditionalist perspective have been concerned about the way children's rights could be used to interfere in the privacy rights accorded to the family. Lynette Burrows writes:

> State intervention into family life is feared and loathed by most children more than anything. They are more troubled by the state interfering than they are reassured by the protection offered. Children do not want rights, they want love and protection and the majority of them do not want social workers or anyone else coming into their families and telling their parents they are not behaving properly.[370]

However, you might wonder whether what she is saying is true for children who are being abused by their parents.

## Questions

1. *Should children who are as competent as adults be treated exactly the same as an adult?*

2. *Do rights work in the context of intimate relationships?*

3. *Do children want rights?*

## Further reading

Read **Archard and Skivenes** (2009) for a discussion of how to balance attaching weight to the wishes of children and to their protection.

---

[364] Lowe and Murch (2001: 145).
[365] Lowe and Murch (2001: 152).
[366] Campbell (1992).
[367] Tisdall et al. (2004); Cantwell and Scott (1995).
[368] Neale (2004). See also Smart (2002).
[369] See Phillips (2003) who discusses the pervasive violence faced by many children in their everyday lives.
[370] Burrows (1999: 54).

## C Extra rights for children

So far the chapter has focused on whether children are entitled to all the rights that adults have. But can children claim rights which adults do not have? It certainly seems so. Children may be thought to have rights to education, protection from abuse[371] and financial support to a greater extent than might be claimed by adults. These would reflect the developmental interests expounded in Eekelaar's approach. A clear example is that a parent is liable to support a child financially until (normally) the child reaches the age of 18.[372] These rights, then, are the rights of the child to enable him or her to become an adult and take on the full mantle of rights an adult has.

## D Children's rights for adults

Most of the discussion on children's rights has centred on the debate whether children are as competent as adults. Although difficult to gauge, probably most commentators appear to accept that the vulnerability of children and their dependency on their parents means that children cannot be granted the same rights as adults. However, it is interesting to ask the question the other way around: are adults as vulnerable and dependent as children? Although the law tends to assume that adults are self-sufficient, fully competent adults, this is an ideal which is unrealistic for many adults.[373] It can be argued that 'once co-operative, care-giving relationships among vulnerable people (rather than autonomous individuals) are seen as the basis around which rights work, the difficulties with children having the same rights to a large extent fall away'.[374]

## E Children's rights in practice

As we have seen, most of the academic discussion on children's rights has centred on children's rights of autonomy. However, this discussion of children's rights is skewed from a western perspective. Notably, looking at the main English and Welsh textbooks on family law it is easier to find a discussion on whether children should be allowed to pierce their noses than on children's right to clean water. We tend to take for granted that the basic needs of children are met.[375] However, Britain need not be complacent:[376]

> **KEY STATISTICS**
>
> - 3.9 million children live in poverty according to the figures for 2008–09.[377]
> - UNICEF in a report placed England bottom of a league of child well-being of 21 countries.[378]

---

[371] E.g. Children Act 1989, Part IV.
[372] See Chapter 5.
[373] Minow (1986); Lim and Roche (2000).
[374] Herring (2003b: 172).
[375] See UNICEF (2000) for an outline of the agonies facing the world's children.
[376] See United Kingdom Commissioners for Children (2008) and Mayhew (2005) for a discussion of the position of children in the UK.
[377] Department for Work and Pensions (2010). Poverty here defined as below 60% of contemporary median net disposable household income after housing costs.
[378] UNICEF (2007).

- 81% of 11–16-year-olds said that violence was a major problem for children;[379] 59% said that they had witnessed violence at school or on the street. In England and Wales 8,067 children aged 0 to 10 suffered injuries after violence was used against them in 2007.[380]

- 21% of children suffer physical abuse; 15% a serious or intermediate lack of care; 21% of girls and 11% of boys suffer sexual abuse.[381]

- There were 631,000 prescriptions for depression medications for those under 16 in 2006–07; an increase from 146,000 in the mid 1990s.[382]

- One-quarter of 16-year-olds failed to achieve any GCSEs above a grade D in 2001.[383]

- One-third of British teenagers are overweight.[384] Around one in four 11–15-year-olds are considered obese.[385]

- Over one-quarter of all rapes recorded by the police are committed against children under 16 years of age.[386]

- Of children aged 5–10, 8% suffer mental disorder and for those aged 11–15 the percentage rises to 11%.[387]

- In one survey 31% of those aged 11–16 had drunk alcohol in the past week and 20% smoked regularly; 30% of 11–15-year-olds watched four or more hours of television a week; only 32% of girls took the recommended amount of physical activity each day.[388]

- Just under one-quarter of all arrests are of under 17-year-olds.[389]

- The president of the Family Division pointed out that Britons give far more money by way of charitable giving to donkey sanctuaries than to children in need.[390]

- Despite all of the above statistics, a recent survey found 89% of children generally happy about life.[391]

Indeed the United Nations Committee on the Rights of the Child had no difficulty in providing extensive criticism of the position of children within the UK.[392]

It would, of course, be wrong to assume that all is doom and gloom for children.[393] A report in 2009, perhaps surprisingly, found that parents are spending more time with children than in previous decades.[394] Performance in exams continues to improve. A study of chidlren's views found that there were few areas where they believed they needed more rights.[395]

---

[379] BBC Newsonline (2007f).
[380] University of Cardiff (2008).
[381] Hooper (2005).
[382] Nuffield Foundation (2009a); BBC Newsonline (2007g).
[383] New Policy Institute (2002).
[384] BBC Newsonline (2002b).
[385] Information Centre (2006).
[386] NSPCC (2000).
[387] Quilgars, Searle and Keung (2005); National Statistics (2005d).
[388] Finch and Searle (2005) record all these statistics.
[389] Neale (2005).
[390] Butler-Sloss (2003).
[391] Willitts et al. (2005).
[392] United Nations Committee on the Rights of the Child (2008); UK Children's Commissioners (2009). See Bradshaw and Mayhew (2005: 15) for a discussion of the increased government spending on children.
[393] HM Government (2010b).
[394] Nuffield Foundation (2009b).
[395] Morgan (2009).

## F  Is there a difference between a welfare-based approach and a rights-based approach?

Does it really make any difference whether the law talks in terms of children's rights or their welfare?[396] Traditionally there has been seen to be a clash between those who are paternalists and those who are supporters of children rights. Paternalism takes as its starting point that children are vulnerable and in need of protection from the dangers posed by adults, other children and themselves. Children lack the knowledge, experience or strength to care for themselves, and therefore society must do all it can to promote the child's welfare.[397] Within paternalism there is some dispute over who should decide what is in the child's best interests: the child's parents or the state, taking the advice of expert psychologists.

After all, the rights of children to clothing, food, education, etc. could all equally be supported in terms of a child's right to their basic needs and as necessary in order to promote a child's welfare. Indeed, as Eekelaar has pointed out, 'if people have rights to anything, it must include the right that their well-being be respected'.[398] In fact, in the vast majority of situations there would be no difference in result whether a rights-based approach or a welfare-based approach was taken. But, in practical terms, when would it matter which approach is taken? Looking at Eekelaar's approach, the welfare approach would justify promoting a child's basic or developmental interests. The difference between the approaches is revealed when considering the autonomy approach. The rights-based approach would permit children to make decisions for themselves as long as there is no infringement of the developmental or basic interests. A welfare approach would also permit children to make some decisions for themselves. This is because it could be said to be in a child's interests to learn from their own mistakes. Alternatively, it could be argued that refusing to follow the child's wishes would cause the child emotional distress. The difference between a welfare approach and Eekelaar's rights-based approach would be over a small band of cases where allowing a child to decide for him- or herself would not infringe their basic or developmental interests, but would cause enough harm for a welfare approach to decide that more harm would be caused by allowing them to make the decision than not.

A child welfarist can, therefore, readily accept that children should be able to make decisions for themselves, and a children's rights proponent can readily accept that children's choices should be restricted in order to promote their welfare. Indeed, it would be quite possible for a children's rights advocate to be less willing than a child welfarist to allow children to make decisions for themselves. This would be so where a children's rights advocate emphasised children's rights to protection from harm, the right to a safe environment or the right to discipline and/or where a child welfarist placed much weight on the benefit to children of developing their own personalities through making decisions for themselves and learning from their mistakes.

Consider also this statement of Dame Elizabeth Butler-Sloss: 'The child has a right to a relationship with his father even if he [the child] does not want it.'[399] Indeed, it could be said that children have a right to have their welfare promoted.[400] However, Eekelaar[401] has rejected any suggestion of such a right:

---

[396] See the very useful discussion in Bainham (2002a) and Moylan (2010).
[397] Fox Harding (1996).
[398] Eekelaar (2002a: 243).
[399] *Re W (Contact Proceedings: Joinder of Child)* [2003] 2 FCR 175.
[400] See Fortin (2006) who is critical of those who see rights and welfare as incompatible.
[401] Eekelaar (1992: 221).

A claim simply that some should act to further my welfare as they define it is in reality to make no claim at all. Running behind these explicit propositions lies the suggestion that to treat someone fully as an individual of moral worth implies recognizing that that person makes claims and exercises choices: that is, is a potential right-holder.

Even if in practical terms there are few cases when the approaches would produce different results, there are important conceptual differences between the two approaches. The first is that although both rights and welfare models can be explained on the basis that they protect the child's interest, in the welfare model the courts or parents determine what children's interests are, whereas the rights-based model seeks to promote the interests as the child sees them to be, or would see them were they capable. A second important difference is that the existence of rights implies that there are duties: that is, that the child (or those acting on behalf of the child) can make claims against the court or parents. However, a welfare approach imposes no obligation on the parents or courts, unless we merge the two approaches and give the children a right to have their welfare promoted by the courts and their parents.[402] A third is that there may be rights which a child has, which cannot necessarily be demonstrated to promote his or her welfare. For example, it is increasingly recognised that a child has a right to know his or her genetic origins, even though it might not be possible to demonstrate that this knowledge promotes a child's welfare.

There is also an important difference between the two approaches in the form of reasoning used. Under the welfare approach the focus of the court is solely on what is best for the child, while under a rights-based approach all of the interests of the parties are considered. Supporters of a rights-based approach argue that that improves the quality of the reasoning and means that each party can leave court feeling that the case has been looked at from their perspective and that they had their rights considered.[403] Opponents might respond that as soon as the focus of the court's attention is diverted from considering the position of the child, the results are likely to harm children.

To see how the theoretical discussion operates in practice, this chapter will now briefly discuss cases where the interests of children, parents and the state have had to be balanced. The area that reveals the issues better than any other is medical law.

## 12 Children and medical law

Many of the cases involving disputes between children and adults have concerned medical treatment.[404] The cases are useful beyond the medical arena because they give some general guidance on how disputes between children and adults should generally be resolved.

The law on when a doctor can treat a child can be summarised as follows.[405] Unless there has been a court order forbidding the carrying out of the treatment, a doctor can provide treatment to a child which he or she believes to be in the child's best interests if, and only if:

1. the child is competent and consents to the treatment; or
2. those with parental responsibility consent; or
3. the court declares the treatment lawful; or
4. the defence of necessity applies.

[402] Eekelaar (1994d).
[403] Choudhry and Herring (2010: ch. 3).
[404] But see *Re Roddy (A Child) (Identification: Restriction on Publication)* [2004] 1 FCR 481 for an example of the use of children's rights in the area of freedom of expression.
[405] Freeman (2005) provides a useful summary and discussion of the current law.

The court cannot force a doctor to provide treatment which the doctor does not wish to provide. An understanding of the law must start with the fact that a doctor who touches a patient commits a battery, which is a criminal offence, unless he or she has a defence. A defence is provided in any one of the four circumstances listed above. These will now be considered in further detail.

## A 16- and 17-year-olds

Section 8(1) of the Family Law Reform Act 1969 states:

> **LEGISLATIVE PROVISION**
>
> **Family Law Reform Act 1969, section 8(1)**
>
> The consent of a minor who has attained the age of sixteen years to any surgical, medical or dental treatment . . . shall be as effective as it would be if he were of full age; and where a minor has by virtue of this section given an effective consent to any treatment it shall not be necessary to obtain any consent for it from his parent or guardian.

This indicates clearly that a child aged 16 or 17 can give legal effect to treatment, unless they are shown to be incompetent, using the same rules as for an adult. This might arise if they suffered from a mental disability.

What if a child aged 16 or 17 refused to consent but their parents did consent to the treatment? Following *Re W (A Minor) (Medical Treatment: Court's Jurisdiction)*,[406] a doctor can rely on the consent of the parents of a 16- or 17-year-old, despite the opposition of the child. However, this decision is subject to an important caveat. The doctor can only treat a patient if he or she believes the treatment is in the best interests of the patient. It would be most unusual for a doctor to decide that it would be in the interests of a 16- or 17-year-old to receive medical treatment against their wishes. Balcombe LJ stated in *Re W (A Minor) (Medical Treatment: Court's Jurisdiction)*:[407]

> As children approach the age of majority they are increasingly able to take their own decisions concerning their medical treatment . . . It will normally be in the best interests of a child of sufficient age and understanding to make an informed decision that the court should respect its integrity as a human being and not lightly override its decision on such a personal matter as medical treatment. All the more so if that treatment is invasive.

Even if a doctor did wish to treat such a patient, relying on the consent of the parents, he or she may well prefer to obtain the authorisation of the court before so doing.[408] In *Re C (Detention: Medical Treatment)*[409] C, aged 16, suffered from anorexia nervosa. The court under the inherent jurisdiction directed that C should remain as a patient at a clinic until discharged by her consultant or further order of the court. This power included the use of reasonable force to detain her for the purposes of treatment.[410] This is a highly controversial

---

[406] [1993] 1 FLR 1, [1992] 2 FCR 785.
[407] [1993] 1 FLR 1 at p. 19, [1992] 2 FCR 785 at p. 786.
[408] *Re W (A Minor) (Medical Treatment: Court's Jurisdiction)* [1992] 2 FCR 785.
[409] [1997] 2 FLR 180, [1997] 3 FCR 49.
[410] De Cruz (1999).

decision because it is unlikely that, had C been over 18, it would have been lawful to detain her. In *Re P (Medical Treatment: Best Interests)*[411] a blood transfusion was ordered on a young woman who was nearly 18. Johnson J emphasised his reluctance to make the order given that she was so nearly 18. However, in the life or death situation facing him he was willing to make the order authorising the transfusion if that was the only way to save her life.

## B Under 16-year-olds

The leading case here is *Gillick*.[412]

---

**CASE: *Gillick v W Norfolk and Wisbech AHA* [1985] 3 All ER 402; [1986] 1 FLR 229; [1986] AC 112 HL**

In 1980 the Department of Health and Social Security provided a notice that in 'exceptional circumstances' a doctor could give contraceptive advice to a girl under 16 without parental consent or consultation. Victoria Gillick, a committed Roman Catholic, sought to challenge the legality of the notice after she unsuccessfully requested assurances that none of her five daughters under 16 would receive advice without her permission. She lost at first instance, but won unanimously at the Court of Appeal, but lost 3–2 in the House of Lords.[413] The fact that the majority of judges who heard the case decided in her favour, even though she lost at the end of the day, reveals the difficulty of the issues involved.

The majority of the House of Lords accepted that if a doctor decided that it was in the best interests of an under-16-year-old that she be given the contraceptive advice she sought and that she was competent to understand the issues involved, then the doctor was permitted to provide the treatment without obtaining the consent of the parents first. This was a hugely important decision because it recognised that under-16-year-olds had the right to give effective legal consent to medical treatment.

---

The *Gillick* decision was reconsidered in the following case:[414]

---

**CASE: *R (On the Application of Axon) v Secretary of State for Health (Family Planning Association intervening)* [2006] 1 FCR 175**

Mrs Axon applied for judicial review of Department of Health guidance which said that medical professionals could provide advice on sexual matters, including abortion, to under-16-year-olds, without their parents being notified. Silber J, following *Gillick*, ruled that there was a duty of confidence owed to young people and so advice on abortion and other matters could be given without informing the parent. He placed particular weight on evidence that if confidentiality concerning sexual matters could not be guaranteed young people may be deterred from seeking medical advice and this ➡

---

[411] [2003] EWHC 2327 (Fam).
[412] Noted in Bainham (1986); Eekelaar (1986).
[413] The case also gave rise to some interesting issues of criminal law, which will not be discussed here.
[414] [2006] 1 FCR 175.

would have 'undesirable and troubled consequences'.[415] He rejected a claim that parents had a right to be informed of advice or treatment given to their children under article 8 of the ECHR, explaining that parents have no right to family life in respect of a competent child who does not want the parents to have that right.[416] Even if they did have a right to be told of treatment given to their children this could be justifiably interfered with in the name of promoting good sexual health among young people.[417] Having said all of that, Silber J stated that he hoped most young people would want to discuss sexual health issues with their parents.

It would be wrong to see *Axon* as a case which is a total victory for adolescent autonomy. Silber J listed five criteria that a doctor would have to be satisfied had been met before a doctor could give treatment to an under-16-year-old without informing his or her parents: they must understand all aspects of the advice; the medical professional had not been able to persuade the young person to inform his or her parents; (in the case of contraception) the young person is very likely to have sexual intercourse with or without the contraception; unless the young person receives the advice or treatment his or her physical or mental heath are likely to suffer; and it is in the best interests of the young person to receive the treatment on sexual matters without parental consent. Notably, then, a doctor may refuse to provide a competent minor with medical treatment where if the patient were an adult they would be entitled to receive it as of right.

The *Gillick* decision, recently followed in *Axon*, left a number of issues unanswered:

## (i) When is a child competent to give consent?[418]

The Mental Capacity Act 2005 sets out the test for mental capacity in relation to adults, but it does not apply to children. However, in developing the law in relation to children the courts may pay attention to the Act. In section 2 it is said that a person lacks capacity if he or she is unable to make a decision for him or her self. Section 3(1) explains that a person is unable to make a decision if he or she is unable:

### LEGISLATIVE PREVISION

**Mental Capacity Act 2005, section 3(1)**

(a) to understand the information relevant to the decision,

(b) to retain that information,

(c) to use or weigh that information as part of the process of making the decision, or

(d) to communicate his decision (whether by talking, using sign language or any other means).

---

[415] At para 66. See Gilbar (2004) for a wider discussion of confidentiality in children cases.

[416] See Douglas (2006a: 273) who questions this holding. It would seem preferable to say that the parent does have a right of family life in connection with the decision, although this right can be interfered with because that is necessary in the interests of the child. After all, if the decision is not to have an abortion this will have a huge impact on the parent's life.

[417] Although see Lee (2004) for a discussion of the practical difficulties young people face in accessing abortion services.

[418] See the discussion in Alderson (1993).

The term 'Gillick-competent' has been widely used to describe children who are sufficiently competent to give consent to treatment. In considering whether a child is *Gillick*-competent or not, the court will consider a number of issues:

1. *Does the child understand the nature of their medical condition and the proposed treatment?* Relevant here is not just the fact that the child understands what it is that is proposed to be done, but the possible side-effects of any treatment.[419] The child must also understand what will happen if the treatment is not performed. Rather controversially, in *Re L (Medical Treatment: Gillick Competency)*[420] L was found not to be competent because she did not appreciate the manner of her death if the treatment was not performed. The reason why she did not was because the doctors thought it would cause her undue distress if they were to tell her. It seems highly unsatisfactory that a child can be found not competent because the doctors have failed to give her the relevant information that she needs to be competent.[421]

2. *Does the child understand the moral and family issues involved?* This was stressed by Lord Scarman in *Gillick*. It was also thought relevant in *Re E (A Minor) (Wardship: Medical Treatment)*,[422] where the court was concerned that the child did not appreciate how much grief his parents would suffer if he were to die.

3. *How much experience of life does the child have?* The courts have relied on this ground in particular when considering children brought up by parents of strong religious views. In *Re L (Medical Treatment: Gillick Competency)*[423] a 14-year-old had been brought up by Jehovah's Witness parents. The court felt that she had lived a sheltered life and had not been exposed to a variety of different religious views. This pointed to the fact she was not competent.[424]

4. *Is the child in a fluctuating mental state?* If the child is fluctuating between competence and incompetence then the court will treat the child as not competent. This was the approach taken in *Re R (A Minor) (Wardship: Consent to Medical Treatment)*.[425] The decision could be justified on the basis that, otherwise, the hospital would be in a very difficult position in having to decide each time the child was touched whether she was competent or not. Opponents of the decision would argue that inconvenience for medical professionals should not justify not taking the rights of children seriously.

5. *Is the child capable of weighing the information appropriately to be able to reach a decision?*[426] Here the court will consider not only the child's ability to understand facts, but also the ability to weigh the facts in reaching a decision. Lord Scarman noted that it is necessary to ask whether the child 'has sufficient discretion to enable him or her to make a wise choice in his or her own interest'. Michael Freeman suggests this means the child needs to have 'wisdom', which is not necessarily the same thing as knowledge.[427] He argues there needs to be 'less emphasis on what these young persons know – less talk in other words of knowledge and understanding – and more on how the decision they have reached furthers their goals and coheres with their system of values'.[428]

---

[419] *Re R (A Minor) (Wardship: Consent to Medical Treatment)* [1992] 1 FLR 190, [1992] 2 FCR 229.
[420] [1998] 2 FLR 810.
[421] Indeed since this decision the British Medical Association has suggested that doctors should not fail to give minor patients information on the basis that to do so would cause them distress.
[422] [1993] 1 FLR 386.
[423] [1998] 2 FLR 810.
[424] See also *Re S (A Minor) (Medical Treatment)* [1993] 1 FLR 376. For criticism of such cases see Eekelaar (1994a: 57).
[425] [1992] 1 FLR 190, [1992] 2 FCR 229.
[426] *Re MB* [1997] Med LR 217.
[427] Freeman (2007).
[428] Freeman (2007).

## (ii) When the doctor can rely on the parent's consent

Lord Scarman had suggested in *Gillick* that 'the parental right yields to the child's right to make his own decisions when he reaches a sufficient understanding and intelligence to be capable of making up his own mind on the matter requiring decision'. This seemed to suggest that if the child was competent and refused to give consent then this refusal could not be overridden by someone with parental responsibility. However, the Court of Appeal has made it clear in cases following *Gillick* that, even if a competent child does not consent, the doctor can still treat a child if he or she believes that to do so would promote the welfare of the child, and someone with parental responsibility for the child gives consent. In *Re W (A Minor) (Medical Treatment: Court's Jurisdiction)*[429] it was explained that a doctor who wishes to treat a patient needs a 'flak jacket' of consent that would provide protection from liability in criminal or tort law. It was stated that this flak jacket could be provided by either the competent child *or* a person with parental responsibility *or* by the court.[430] So the fact that the child had refused to provide the flak jacket did not prevent someone with parental responsibility providing one. Indeed, in *Re K, W, and H (Minors) (Medical Treatment)*[431] it was held that, where someone with parental responsibility gives consent, it was unnecessary and inappropriate to bring the matter before the court; the doctors should simply provide the treatment. In *Re M (Medical Treatment: Consent)*[432] a 15-year-old girl refused a heart transplant, stating that she did not want to have someone else's heart. Her mother consented to the treatment. The Court of Appeal authorised the operation, stating that the preserving of the girl's life justified overriding her views. Notably here the Court of Appeal did not state whether she was or was not *Gillick*-competent. This was because it did not matter; someone with parental responsibility had provided the flak jacket and the operation was in the best interests of the girl so her views were irrelevant. In *Nielsen v Denmark*[433] the European Court of Human Rights appeared to accept that the European Convention would permit treatment to be carried out on children against their wishes, relying on the consent of the parent.[434]

A shadow of doubt may have been created by Silber J's judgment in *R (On the Application of Axon) v Secretary of State for Health*[435] where he stated: 'the parental right to determine whether a young person will have medical treatment terminates if and when the young person achieves a sufficient understanding and intelligence to understand fully what is proposed'.[436] This implies that if a child is competent then the parent has no right to determine what treatment a child shall receive. However, this is a single obiter statement of a first instance judge and it cannot, of course, overrule a well-established line of Court of Appeal cases.[437] It does, however, indicate some judicial unhappiness with the way the law has developed.[438]

---

[429] [1993] 1 FLR 1, [1992] 2 FCR 785.
[430] In an emergency, where the doctor cannot obtain the consent of the parent or the court the doctors may be able to rely on the defence of necessity if they are acting in the child's best interests. However, that is available only where there is no time to go to the courts: *Glass v UK* [2004] 1 FCR 553.
[431] [1993] 1 FLR 854, [1993] 1 FCR 240.
[432] [1999] 2 FLR 1097.
[433] (1988) 11 EHRR 175.
[434] In an *obiter* comment in *Re S (A Child) (Identification: Restriction on Publication)* [2003] 2 FCR 577 Hale LJ suggested that a child might be competent enough to consent to an interview with a newspaper and her parents would not have any power to stop her.
[435] [2006] 1 FCR 175.
[436] At para 56.
[437] See further Taylor (2007).
[438] See also *Mabon v Mabon* [2005] EWCA Civ 634, [2005] 2 FLR 1011, [2005] 2 FCR 354 where, at para 28, Thorpe LJ emphasised the importance of letting competent teenagers make decisions for themselves.

It may be that despite the official line taken by the courts in practice the views of children are given weight by doctors. In one much publicised case a 14-year-old, Hannah Jones, refused the heart transplant recommended by her doctors even though without it she was likely to die. The doctors decided to abide by her wishes, although she subsequently decided to accept the transplant.[439] In 2010 there were newpaper reports of a 15-year-old Jehovah's Witness, Joshua McAuley, who died after refusing a blood transfusion. In both these cases the issue was not brought to the courts.[440]

### (iii) If the matter is brought before the court, how should the court resolve the issue?

Where cases involving disputes over the medical treatment of children have been brought before them, the courts have been very willing to approve the treatment proposed by the doctors, even if the treatment is opposed by the parents and the children.[441] The cases that have come before either court have tended to be extreme: the children of Jehovah's Witnesses refusing to consent to a blood transfusion necessary to save their lives;[442] an anorexic girl refusing treatment necessary to treat her illness.[443] It would be quite wrong, however, to conclude that parents' wishes are largely ignored. The fact that only these rather extreme cases come before the court indicates that, normally, doctors abide by the parent's wishes and, if not, try very hard to persuade the child or parent to consent to the treatment.[444] In *NHS Trust v A*[445] although Holman J declared that receiving a bone marrow transplant would be in the best interests of the child, he refused to order the parents (who opposed the treatment) to present the child at the hospital. Notably this was a case where the judge found the arguments for and against the treatment fairly balanced. Had the treatment been better for the child beyond all doubt the judge could have used the inherent jurisdiction or wardship to ensure the child received the treatment.[446]

There is one notable case where the court sided with the parents, rather than the medical establishment: *Re T (A Minor) (Wardship: Medical Treatment)*.[447] Here a baby, C, had a life-threatening liver complaint. There was a unanimous prognosis from the medical experts that, without a liver transplant, C would not live beyond two-and-a-half years of age. However, if a transplant could be found the prognosis was very good. The parents refused to consent to the transplant. This time the courts sided with the parents and refused to authorise the transplant without the consent of the parents. Before examining the court's reasoning, it should be stressed that there were several facts that made the case rather unusual. First, both parents were health-care professionals who had experience of caring for sick children. Secondly, C had undergone earlier unsuccessful surgery and this had caused C much pain and distress. Thirdly, the parents at the time of the case had moved (for job reasons) to a distant Commonwealth country. The Court of Appeal, in deciding not to authorise the treatment, relied upon the welfare principle. It was stated that although there was a presumption

---

[439] BBC Newsonline (2010c).
[440] Roberts (2010).
[441] *Re E (A Minor) (Wardship: Medical Treatment* [1993] 1 FLR 386.
[442] *Re E (A Minor) (Wardship: Medical Treatment)* [1993] 1 FLR 386, [1992] 2 FCR 219; *Re S (A Minor) (Consent to Medical Treatment)* [1994] 2 FLR 1065, [1994] 1 FCR 604.
[443] E.g. *Re W (A Minor) (Medical Treatment: Court's Jurisdiction)* [1993] 1 FLR 1, [1992] 2 FCR 785.
[444] C. Bridge (1999).
[445] [2008] 1 FCR 34.
[446] For further discussion see Morris (2009).
[447] [1997] 1 FLR 502, [1997] 2 FCR 363; discussed Bainham (1997); Fox and McHale (1997); Michalowski (1997).

in favour of prolonging a child's life, this was not the court's sole objective. Ward LJ stated: 'in the last analysis the best interest of every child includes an expectation that difficult decisions affecting the length and quality of its life will be taken for it by the parent to whom its care had been entrusted by nature'.[448] The decision seemed to place much weight on the intrusion that ordering the treatment would make in the lives of the parents: they would need to return from their new country and would be required to provide extensive care for the child. Arguably, these concerns were misplaced because, even if the parents were unwilling to make these sacrifices, they could hand the child over to be cared for by a local authority. In fact, despite the Court of Appeal's ruling, the parents did return to the UK and the child received treatment.[449] The decision may be contrasted with *Re MM (Medical Treatment)*,[450] where the Russian parents opposed the treatment proposed by the doctors for what the court described as 'rational reasons' (they were not sure the treatment could be provided on their return to Russia; and did not want to depart from a treatment which had worked in the past). However, Black J authorised the proposed treatment, confirming the approach of most cases of this kind which have stressed that parents are not to be permitted to make martyrs of their children. A similar approach was taken in *Re A (Conjoined Twins: Medical Treatment)*[451] where the Court of Appeal authorised the separation of the conjoined twins despite the objections of the parents. Ward LJ added, however, that had the hospital decided to abide by the wishes of the parents and not operate this would have been a 'perfectly acceptable response'. However, that suggestion appears to overlook the rights of J (the stronger of the twins) to the life-saving treatment which the court decided she should receive.

There have been tragically difficult cases involving children who have been born severely disabled and there is dispute over the appropriate medical treatment for the child.[452] The criminal law prohibits any acts of doctors designed to end the child's life,[453] or acts aimed at shortening the child's life (as opposed to aimed at relieving pain).[454] What is strictly forbidden is the performing of any act designed to end the life of the child: that would be murder. However, the courts may authorise the doctors to refrain from offering treatment. The general approach has been that, if there is medical evidence that the child's life will be intolerable if the child lives, the court will approve the non-treatment, even if the parents are in favour of providing treatment.[455] If the child's life will not be intolerable, the doctors should provide the treatment, even if the parents object to it (*Re B (A Minor) (Disclosure of Evidence)*).[456] However, in *Re L (Medical Treatment: Benefit)* Butler-Sloss P emphasised that at the end of the day the key concept was not intolerability but rather what was in the best interests of the child.[457] There was a strong presumption in favour of life, but if the treatment was futile a court would not order doctors to provide it. It was necessary for the court to weigh up all the benefits and disadvantages of treatment to calculaion what would be in a child's interest, including his or her emotional well-being. In such a case the court must form its own

---

[448] The use of the term 'it' in reference to the child is revealing.

[449] C. Bridge (1999: 11).

[450] [2000] 1 FLR 224.

[451] [2000] 4 All ER 961.

[452] See Nuffield Council on Bioethics (2007) and Morris (2009). If there is a dispute between the parents and doctors, such cases should be brought before the court: *R v Portsmouth NHS Trust, ex p Glass* [1999] 2 FLR 905.

[453] Not reported but discussed in Gunn and Smith (1985).

[454] *Royal Wolverhampton Hospitals NHS Trust v B* [2000] 1 FLR 953 at p. 956, per Bodey J.

[455] *Re C (Medical Treatment)* [1998] 1 FLR 384; Fortin (1998).

[456] [1983] 3 FLR 117.

[457] [2005] 1 FCR 421. This point was emphasised by Heley J in *Portsmouth NHS Trust v Wyatt* [2005] 1 FLR 21 and Holman J in *An NHS Trust v MB* [2006] EWHC 507 (Fam).

view as to the child's best interests and is not bound to follow the views of the doctors nor the parents.[458]

During 2004 and 2005 a series of applications by the parents of Charlotte Wyatt were heard by courts, relating to their daughter's treatment in hospital.[459] Ever since her birth she has been ill and she has never left hospital. There have been ongoing disagreements between her parents and the medical team treating her concerning proposals for her treatment. A key dispute concerned the extent to which the medical team should attempt to provide ventilation to Charlotte if she were to suffer a major health crisis, requiring such life-saving intervention. In essence, the views of the doctors have been that in the event of a major crisis ventilation should not be offered, while her parents have wanted everything done to save her. The medical team have expressed concern that ventilation might kill Charlotte and, even if it was provided, it might not improve her condition. In summarising their approach to the welfare of the child in cases of this kind, the Court of Appeal stated:

> In our judgment, the intellectual milestones for the judge in a case such as the present are, therefore, simple, although the ultimate decision will frequently be extremely difficult. The judge must decide what is in the child's best interests. In making that decision, the welfare of the child is paramount, and the judge must look at the question from the assumed point of view of the patient (Re J). There is a strong presumption in favour of a course of action which will prolong life, but that presumption is not irrebuttable (Re J). The term 'best interests' encompasses medical, emotional, and all other welfare issues (Re A). The court must conduct a balancing exercise in which all the relevant factors are weighed . . .[460]

The Court of Appeal[461] rejected an argument that in cases of withdrawing or not offering treatment to seriously ill children the key question was whether or not the child's condition after the treatment would be intolerable. The court held that the test was simply to ask what was in the child's best interests. Although asking whether, if the treatment were provided, life would be intolerable might be a valuable guide, it did not replace the best interests test. This approach has been held by Cazalet J in *A NHS Trust v D*[462] not to be in breach of a child's right to life under article 2 of the European Convention on Human Rights. Indeed, not providing treatment which would extend an intolerable life was necessary under article 3, which required the state to ensure that the child was not subjected to inhuman or degrading treatment.

### (iv) Can a doctor be forced to treat a child?

The issue here relates to the situation where the doctor refuses to treat a child. This may be because the doctor believes that the treatment is not appropriate, or may be because of health-care rationing (e.g. that the treatment is too expensive). It is clear that if a doctor declines to offer treatment then the court cannot force him or her to perform the operation. One option in such a case is for a patient to apply for judicial review, although such an option is unlikely to succeed unless there is strong evidence that the decision is unreasonable.[463] In any event, even if judicial review is successful the NHS trust would be required only to reconsider the decision and would not necessarily be required to perform the operation. If

---

[458] *An NHS Trust v MB* [2006] EWHC 507 (Fam).
[459] *Wyatt v Portsmouth Hospital NHS Trust* [2004] EWHC 2247; [2005] EWHC 117; [2005] EWHC 693; [2005] 3 FCR 263; [2005] 4 All ER 1325.
[460] *Wyatt v Portsmouth Hospital NHS Trust* [2005] 3 FCR 263 at para 87.
[461] [2005] 3 FCR 263 at para 76.
[462] [2000] 2 FCR 577.
[463] *R v Cambridge District Health Authority, ex p B* [1995] 1 FLR 1055.

a doctor is unsure about the propriety of treatment (e.g. because it is a risky, untried procedure) the matter could be brought before a court for guidance.[464]

## (v) Can the parents be criminally liable for failing to arrange suitable medical care for a child?

It is an offence when anyone over 16 with responsibility for a child 'wilfully assaults, ill-treats, neglects, abandons, or exposes him . . . in a manner likely to cause him unnecessary suffering or injury to health'.[465] This means that a parent who wilfully fails to ensure that the child receives adequate medical treatment commits an offence. It should be stressed that it must be shown that the failure to arrange treatment is wilful. Therefore, as *R v Sheppard*[466] suggests, if parents do not provide treatment due to their low intelligence they will not be punished.[467] If the child dies after his or her parents fail to organise suitable medical treatment there is even the possibility of a manslaughter or murder conviction.[468]

## (vi) Are there some kinds of treatment which cannot be carried out on children?

Is there a limit to what the doctors, with the parents' consent, can do to a child? The dispute here surrounds non-therapeutic treatment, that is, treatment which has no direct medical benefit to the child. It seems that some non-therapeutic treatment can be carried out, but only if it can be shown that the treatment benefits the child in the wider sense. So, for example, the parent can consent to a blood test to determine a child's paternity. Although such a blood test does not provide medical benefits, it is thought to be in a child's interests as it enables his or her paternity to be ascertained. However, problems may arise where the child is asked to donate bone marrow or organs for the treatment of someone else. If the bone marrow or organ is to a close relative it may be possible to find a benefit to the child. For example, if a child is donating an organ to their sister and without the treatment the sister will die, the benefit to the child of maintaining the relationship with the sister may be sufficient to make the donation in the child's benefit.[469] In *Re B (Medical Treatment)*[470] Colderidge J was dealing with a very sick child and a question of whether the child should be resuscitated if the need arose. The local authority, who had parental responsibility, thought that parental responsibility did not give it authority to consent to the child not being resuscitated and that a court declaration was required. Colderidge J held that they were 'probably right'.[471] Even if they could have consented, bringing the matter to court was sensible. By contrast in *LA v SB*[472] parents refused to agree to the treatment recommended by the hospital in response to life-threatening seizures a child was having. The local authority and doctors decided to withdraw from legal proceedings they had initially instigated. Unsurprisingly Wall P concluded that he could not compel the local authority to continue litigation. More surprisingly he concluded that the court should not intervene on its own motion. As this indicates the court may be

---

[464] E.g. *Simms v Simms* [2003] 1 FCR 361.
[465] Children and Young Persons Act 1933, s 1(1).
[466] [1981] AC 394.
[467] It is no defence to show that even had one attempted to obtain medical assistance there would have been none available.
[468] *R v Senior* [1899] 1 QB 283, where for religious reasons a parent refused to obtain medical treatment. See also the offence of causing or allowing the death of a child or vulnerable adult under s 5 of the Domestic Violence, Crime and Victims Act 2004.
[469] By analogy with the reasoning in *Re Y (Mental Incapacity: Bone Marrow Transplant)* [1996] 2 FLR 787.
[470] [2009] 1 FLR 1264.
[471] Para 7.
[472] [2010] EWHC 1744 (Fam).

more willing to intervene where a parents wants to do something harmful to a child, than where a parent is failing to improve a child's situation.

A procedure that is clearly to the detriment of a child may not be lawful. For example, it may be that a parent could not effectively consent to multiple body piercing of a child.[473] One particularly controversial issue is circumcision.[474] Female circumcision is unlawful, unless necessary for medical reasons.[475] But the position as regards male circumcision seems to be that it is lawful. There are those who claim that this is an irreversible operation, which is an attack on the child's physical integrity, and unless there are medical benefits to the child it should be unlawful.[476] There are others who argue that a child has a right to a religious or cultural heritage and, at least where circumcision is an aspect of religious background, it should be permissible.[477]

## C Comments on the law

### (i) The case law and children's rights

Some have argued that the present law is illogical, by arguing as follows: the law permits a competent minor to consent to treatment, but not to refuse it. If the child is competent to decide the question, it seems a bit odd to say to him or her: 'You can decide this issue but only if you decide to answer "yes". If you decide "no" we may override your wishes.' It is especially odd because it is a far greater infringement of a child's rights to operate on him or her without their consent than to deny them treatment that they would like to have. If anything, the law would be more logical if it said that the doctor cannot operate on the child if he or she refuses but has a discretion if he or she consents. Such arguments have led Fortin to suggest that the present law may be open to challenge under the Human Rights Act in that forcing treatment on young people breaches their rights to protection from inhuman and degrading treatment and right to liberty and security of the person.[478]

However, the law is perfectly logical once it is recalled that the basis of the law relating to children is set out in s 1 of the Children Act 1989 – the welfare principle.[479] The law is based on the view that, if the doctor wants to perform treatment, this is in the best interests of the child because it is the view of the medical expert. The law is then engineered to make it as easy as possible to enable the doctor to go ahead. The doctor can operate if either the mature minor consents, or the parents consent, or the courts give approval. The law could hardly do more to enable the doctor to treat, once he or she has decided that the treatment is in the best interests of the child. Put this way, the law is a clear example of ensuring that the child's best interests are promoted. However, as the previous paragraph makes clear, the law is not logical if one looks at the question as one of children's autonomy rights.

---

[473] Similarly, sterilisation may be permitted if the child suffers from mental handicap, if that sterilisation can be said to be in the best interests of the child, and the court has given its approval: J v C [1990] 2 FLR 527, [1990] FCR 716; *Practice Note (Official Solicitor: Sterilisation)* [1993] 2 FLR 222; and *Practice Note (Official Solicitor: Sterilisation)* [1996] 2 FLR 111.

[474] I. Katz (1999).

[475] Female Genital Mutilation Act 2003.

[476] Fox and Thomson (2005).

[477] Circumcision of boys is regarded by many Jews and Muslims as an important aspect of their religious practice.

[478] Fortin (2003: 129). She also suggests that the law could be challenged using article 14 of the European Convention on Human Rights, arguing that the present law amounts to discrimination on the grounds of age. Although age is not included in article 14 as a prohibited ground of discrimination, the list of grounds under article 14 is not closed and a strong case can be made for adding age.

[479] See Gilmore (2009) for further discussion of this.

### (ii) The importance of doctors

There is some concern that the law places too much weight on the opinions of doctors. It has just been argued that the law relating to children is best understood on the basis that the doctor is presumed to make decisions that are in the child's interests. In effect, if the parent consents and the child does not, it is the doctor who has the final say unless the child decides to bring the matter before the court. Of course, generally, doctors will be best placed to decide whether a medical treatment is in a patient's best interests. However, where the issue involves moral as well as medical issues (abortion, for example), giving so much power to doctors may be controversial.[480] Also, in many areas of medicine there is more than one point of view as to the best kind of medical treatment. The present law favours the views of the particular doctor dealing with the patient, over what might be the reasonable objections of the patient.[481]

### (iii) Misuses of competence

It has been argued that the test for competence for children is too strict. Certainly the test of competence for children is stiffer than that for adults.[482] Further, there is a danger that the child will be found incompetent if the doctor or court believes the child's decision to be wrong, but the child will be found competent if the decision is one which is thought to promote his or her best interests.[483] However, arguments over the appropriate test for competence are complex. If the law was that a competent child's decision could not be vetoed by the courts or the parents, the law would wish to have a very strict test of competence. A further complaint about the law on competence for children is that it is wrong for the law to categorise children as either competent or not and, instead, decisions should be made with children, enabling them to participate in the decision-making process to as great an extent as possible.[484]

### (iv) Is the law not adequately protecting children?

As mentioned above, if the parents oppose a form of treatment, the doctors will seek to find alternative forms of treatment or persuade the parents to change their minds. It is only where this fails that the doctors are likely to turn to the courts for authorisation to treat the child contrary to the parents' wishes. For example, where a child's parents are Jehovah's Witnesses, who oppose blood transfusions, doctors may try to use non-blood substitutes before eventually seeking court intervention.[485] Bridge[486] has argued that this delay in providing the ideal treatment could be seen as protecting the parents' rather than the child's interests.

## 13 Children's rights in other cases

The reasoning in *Gillick* has been applied outside the context of medical cases. In *Re Roddy (A Child) (Identification: Restriction on Publication)*[487] a 16-year-old girl wanted to tell her story to the media. She had become pregnant at age 12. Munby J memorably stated:

---

[480] Herring (1997).
[481] Douglas (1992).
[482] See Dickenson and Jones (1995) for a general discussion of children's competence.
[483] Freeman (2005); Shaw (2002).
[484] Herring (1997).
[485] *Re S (A Minor) (Medical Treatment)* [1994] 2 FLR 1065, [1994] 1 FCR 604.
[486] C. Bridge (1999).
[487] [2004] 1 FCR 481.

We no longer treat our 17-year-old daughters as our Victorian ancestors did, and if we try to do so it is at our – and their – peril. Angela, in my judgment, is of an age, and has sufficient understanding and maturity, to decide for herself whether that which is private, personal and intimate should remain private or whether it should be shared with the whole world.[488]

He concluded that the court had to respect the right of free speech of a child who has sufficient understanding to make an informed decision. It was part of her dignity and integrity as a human being.[489] The implication from the case is that *Gillick* will be of general application and that a *Gillick*-competent child can give effective consent to what would otherwise be a legal wrong, unless there is a specific statutory provision saying otherwise.[490]

## 14 Children in court

Children's rights would mean little without an effective mode of enforcement. It is therefore crucial that children have access to courts.[491] It is also important that the decisions of courts are communicated and explained to children.[492] The fact that children should be heard in proceedings does not require that their views will necessarily determine the question. The right of a child to be heard is therefore less contentious than a right to autonomy. However, there is a delicate balance to be drawn between listening to children and not placing them in the position where they have to decide between their parents.[493] Many commentators have been persuaded by the view that if children have autonomy rights then they must have a means to bring applications to enforce those rights. However, there are also serious concerns about involving children in litigation.[494] There is considerable evidence that requiring a child to choose whether they live with their father or mother causes the child much harm. There is also a concern that children's rights to bring matters before a court are open to misuse, either from parents seeking to manipulate the children[495] or even from solicitors keen to promote their professional standing.[496]

There are three ways in which a child may be directly involved in family proceedings:

1. The child may bring proceedings through a solicitor in their own right.

2. The child's 'next friend' (normally one of their parents) can bring proceedings on the child's behalf.

3. The child's interests can be represented in the case between adults by a Guardian ad Litem.[497]

---

[488] At para 56.
[489] At para 57.
[490] As there is, for example, in relation to sexual activity: Sexual Offences Act 2003.
[491] UN Convention on the Rights of the Child, article 12. See also the European Convention on the Exercise of Children's Rights, not yet signed by the UK. See Lowe and Murch (2001) for an excellent discussion.
[492] Wilson J (2007).
[493] King (1987: 190).
[494] This was recognised by Thorpe LJ in *Re HB (Abduction: Children's Objections)* [1998] 1 FLR 422.
[495] In *Re K (Replacement of Guardian ad Litem)* [2001] 1 FLR 663 the court decided that the child had been pressurised by his father into applying to dispense with the services of his guardian.
[496] Thorpe LJ (1994).
[497] See Doughty (2008b) for a history of the role played by court welfare officers.

## A  Children bringing proceedings in their own right

Under rule 9.2A of the Family Proceedings Rules 1999, SI 1999/3491, a minor can bring (or defend) proceedings under the Children Act 1989 or involving the inherent jurisdiction either:

1. if the court gives leave; or

2. where a solicitor, acting for the child, considers[498] that the child is able to give instructions in relation to the proceedings.[499] However, the most likely proceedings that a child will want to bring is for an order under s 8 of the Children Act 1989 and, for such an application, the court must give leave, even if the child's solicitor is satisfied that the child is competent.[500]

There was a fear when the Children Act 1989 was first introduced that the courts would be swamped with applications from children seeking to 'divorce' their parents (although this has proved to be unfounded). Before granting leave, the court must be satisfied 'that [the child] has sufficient understanding to make the proposed application'.[501] There has been some dispute over whether the welfare of the child is relevant when considering whether or not to grant leave. Following *Re H (Residence Order: Child's Application for Leave)*,[502] it now seems to be accepted that the welfare of the child is not the paramount consideration. This was significant in that case because H was 15, and since the age of 6 he had come under the influence of a Mr R, who had been arrested for committing offences against children. As H was a mature and intelligent young man, it was held that he should have separate representation, even though there were grave concerns surrounding his desire to have unrestricted contact with Mr R. In considering whether to grant leave, the court will consider the following factors:

1. *Is the matter serious enough to justify a court hearing?* In *Re C (A Minor) (Leave to Seek Section 8 Order)*[503] a 14-year-old wanted to go on holiday with her friend's family to Bulgaria. Her parents opposed this and she applied for a specific issue order that she be permitted to go on the holiday. Johnson J refused to grant leave, claiming that the issue was too trivial to be suitable for resolution by the courts. If this issue is too trivial, it is likely that many other issues which children may want to raise before a court (e.g. what time they go to bed) will also be too trivial. Freeman has forcefully argued that, where the child has instituted proceedings, this is an indication that, to the child, it is an important issue and there is therefore a need for some kind of intervention for the child's benefit.[504] This is correct, but whether the intervention need be in the form of a court hearing or some kind of informal social work is a matter for debate. It should be recalled that issues that may appear trivial to adults, may appear hugely important from a child's perspective.

2. *Should the family resolve the issue themselves?* Johnson J in *Re C (A Minor) (Leave to Seek Section 8 Order)*[505] also considered the girl's application that she be allowed to move in

---

[498] Sawyer (1995).

[499] *Re H (A Minor) (Role of the Official Solicitor)* [1993] 2 FLR 552. Even if the solicitor decides that the child is competent, it is open to the court to stop the proceedings if the court is not satisfied that the child is competent: *Re CT (A Minor) (Child Representation)* [1993] 2 FLR 278, [1993] 2 FCR 445.

[500] *Practice Direction* [1993] 1 FLR 668; *Re N (Contact: Minor Seeking Leave to Defend and Removal of Guardian)* [2003] Fam Law 154.

[501] Section 10(8).

[502] [2000] 1 FLR 780.

[503] [1994] 1 FLR 26.

[504] Freeman (1997a: 168; 2000c).

[505] [1994] 1 FLR 26.

with her friend's family. He also refused to grant leave for that application on the basis that he thought the issue should be left to the family to sort out between themselves, rather than involving the courts. The court feared that giving the child leave might give her an advantage in her dispute with her parents, although it might be thought that denying her leave gave her parents an advantage point.

3. *How mature is the child?* In *Re S (A Minor) (Independent Representation)*[506] it was stressed that the real issue is not the child's age but her understanding.[507] The very fact that the child had applied to the court would indicate maturity.[508] In *Re H (A Minor) (Role of the Official Solicitor)*[509] it was stressed that what had to be considered was whether the child would be able to give instructions in the light of the evidence that would be produced to the court. Where the evidence might be complex there may be difficulty in demonstrating this. The court may also take the view that the emotional turmoil that would be caused to the child by becoming involved in the litigation would be contrary to his or her welfare.[510]

4. *What is the likelihood of the success of the application?*[511] In *SC (A Minor) (Leave to Seek Section 8 Orders)*[512] it was confirmed that the fact that the application was not a hopeless application would be a factor in favour of granting leave.

5. *Would the child suffer from being involved in a protracted dispute between the parents?* In *Re S (A Minor) (Independent Representation)*[513] an 11-year-old boy wanted to replace his Guardian ad Litem. In the Court of Appeal, Bingham MR said that it was necessary to respect the child's wishes but at the same time protect the child from danger. It was held here that the effect of being closely involved with a bitter dispute between parents could harm a child and it was better for the boy to have the 'buffer' of a Guardian ad Litem. In *Re C (Residence: Child's Application for Leave)*[514] it was thought not to be to the child's benefit to hear the evidence of his warring parents. Fortin has argued that, rather than using this as a reason for denying access to the courts, consideration should be given as to how court procedures can be altered to protect child litigants' psychological welfare.[515] Further, it should not be forgotten that children are likely to have heard far worse arguments between their parents at home than they might witness in a court setting.[516]

6. *Will all the arguments that a child wishes to raise be presented to the court?* In *Re H (Residence Order: Child's Application for Leave)*[517] a 12-year-old boy sought to apply to the court for a residence order in his father's favour on his parents' divorce. Although he was mature enough to make the application, Johnson J held that the child would not bring before the court any argument that the father would not be making in his application for a residence order. There was therefore nothing to gain from granting leave. This argument fails to appreciate the importance to the child of feeling that he or she is being listened to.

[506] [1993] 2 FLR 437, [1993] 2 FCR 1.
[507] In *Re S (Contact: Application by Sibling)* [1999] Fam 283, a 9-year-old was found to have sufficient understanding to apply for leave for a contact order with her half-brother.
[508] *Re C (A Minor) (Leave to Seek Section 8 Order)* [1995] 1 FLR 927, [1996] 1 FCR 461.
[509] [1993] 2 FLR 552.
[510] *Re N (Contact: Minor Seeking Leave to Defend and Removal of Guardian)* [2003] Fam Law 154.
[511] *Re C (A Minor) (Leave to Seek Section 8 Order)* [1995] 1 FLR 927, [1996] 1 FCR 461.
[512] [1994] 1 FLR 96, [1994] 1 FCR 837.
[513] [1993] 2 FLR 437, [1993] 2 FCR 1.
[514] [1995] 1 FLR 927, [1996] 1 FCR 461.
[515] Fortin (1998: 202–3).
[516] Wilson J (2007).
[517] [2000] 1 FLR 780, discussed in Sawyer (2001).

7. *The impact of the Human Rights Act 1998*. A child may have a right to be represented and heard in proceedings with which they are involved.[518] ***Re A (Contact: Separate Representation)***[519] accepted that a boy who wished to alert the judge to the dangers he believed his father posed to his young half-sister should have leave to do so.

In the light of this list of reasons for not permitting access, it is not surprising that it is rare for children successfully to bring applications before the court, or to find that research suggests that, generally, judges are opposed to children even attending court hearings.[520] It has been argued that the leave requirement improperly infringes a child's right to a fair hearing under article 6 of the European Convention, in a way which improperly discriminates on the basis of age, contrary to article 14.[521] In reply it could be said that children may need protection from the rigours of the court procedures such as cross-examination and this justifies the imposition of the leave requirement.[522] The ability of children to represent themselves would mean that the court could hear the child's views in his or her own words, rather than mediated through the reports of welfare officers.[523] Notably, Dame Margaret Booth has argued that children should not be required to seek leave from the High Court before applying for a s 8 order.[524]

If leave is granted, the full application will be heard. The welfare principle will govern the issue. The law governing the case is as discussed in Chapter 9.

## B Representation

In 2001 the Government created the Children and Family Court Advisory Support Service (CAFCASS).[525] This agency was created to provide courts with services in cases involving children.[526] It is in charge of ensuring that children's interests are properly represented in court cases.[527] It is necessary to distinguish public and private law cases.

### (i) Public law cases

In public law cases (e.g. where a child is being taken into care) the child's interests will be protected by a guardian. The guardian will appoint a solicitor whose job it will be to represent the child's interests in any court hearing. The guardian and solicitor will work together to ascertain the wishes of the child and present these to the court. Courts can allow children who are the subject of public law proceedings to attend their hearing, although research indicates that at present many children who wish to attend the court are not allowed to do so.[528] Fortin[529] suggests that the awareness of children's rights under articles 6 and 8 might lead to a change in practice. Although the representation of children in public cases is generally well thought of, it is under huge threat from cutbacks in legal aid in public law cases.[530]

---

[518] Lyon (2007).
[519] [2001] 1 FLR 715.
[520] Masson and Winn Oakley (1999).
[521] Lyon (2000).
[522] Lowe and Murch (2001).
[523] Butler and Williamson (1994).
[524] Her views are noted and discussed in Children Act Sub-Committee (2002a: para 12.6).
[525] Criminal Justice and Court Service Act 2000, s 11.
[526] Murch (2003) provides an excellent discussion of the issues.
[527] See Wall LJ (2006) and MacDonald (2008) for a discussion of the failures in child representation in court hearings.
[528] Fortin (2009b).
[529] Fortin (2009b: ch. 7).
[530] Blacklaws and Dowding (2006).

## (ii) Private law cases

The representation of children's interests in private law cases is less effective.[531] In a private case any of the following could occur:

1. The case proceeds without the court ever hearing of the child's views.
2. The court requests a child and family reporter[532] to prepare a report on the child, which will include a summary of the child's views.
3. The child could have party status (i.e. be treated as a party to the proceedings) and his or her interests be represented by his or her own lawyer.[533]
4. The child may be able to litigate and bring applications on his or her own behalf with the leave of the court.[534]

Many commentators have expressed concern that all too often point 1 is what happens and that children's wishes and interests are not specifically addressed in a court proceeding. The United Nations Committee on the Rights of Children has expressed concern about the lack of representation of children's wishes in private cases.[535] Fortin has gone so far as to complain that 'The most serious procedural weakness undermining the Children Act's direction to the courts to consider the child's wishes and feelings is that there is no guarantee that the court will receive any evidence indicating what those wishes are.'[536] In part the reluctance to call for reports can be explained by the delays that can result while a report is being prepared.[537] Further, courts are aware that CAFCASS is understaffed and underfunded. Judges are therefore, understandably, reluctant to ask for reports unless absolutely necessary. The situation has been worsened by the fact that the Government has asked CAFCASS officers to concentrate on assisting parents to reach agreements and thereby avoid a costly hearing. Ironically this means it is even less likely that the voices of children will be heard and CAFCASS officers, rather than listening to children and reporting their concerns, will be talking to parents and attempting to persuade them to reach an agreement, regardless of the views of the children.[538] It has been reported that guardians will only be appointed to assist in private children's cases in the most urgent of cases.[539]

In the last few years there has been an increasing acknowledgement of the need to ensure that children are heard in disputes over their upbringing.[540] Even if children's wishes are not to determine the case they should at least be heard and have their views taken seriously.[541] The case for child representation can be made on two bases.[542] First, it can be promoted as a way of advancing children's welfare. There is much evidence that children who are the subject

---

[531] James, James and McNamee (2003).
[532] A specialist social worker attached to CAFCASS.
[533] Although see Masson and Winn Oakley (1999) for an argument that, even though children's interests may be separately represented, the child may have only limited communication with their lawyer.
[534] It is very difficult for children to get leave in such cases: see *Re H (A Minor) (Care Proceedings: Child's Wishes)* [1993] 1 FLR 440 and *Re C (Secure Accommodation Order: Representation)* [1993] 1 FLR 440.
[535] Fortin (2009b: 254). See also Munby J (2004) for a powerful argument in favour of increasing child representation.
[536] Fortin (2009: 256).
[537] In *M v A (Contact: Domestic Violence)* [2002] 2 FLR 921 there was a seven-month delay in the preparation of a report.
[538] Fortin (2006b).
[539] Walsh (2010).
[540] Ruegger (2001); Murch (2003). Thomas (2001) emphasises that listening to children is also more likely to produce good decisions.
[541] Archard (2003: 54) emphasises that children have a right not just to be listened to, but also to be heard.
[542] Harold and Murch (2005).

of litigation can be confused and anxious.[543] They report feeling ignored; not surprisingly, when it is claimed that in only 2 per cent of cases are children listened to and given a response.[544] It is well established that the existence of conflict between parents can be more harmful for the child than the ending of the relationship.[545] Having children's representation can be seen as necessary to promote children's welfare. Secondly, it can be seen as part of the rights of a child, protected by the United Nations Convention on the Rights of the Child, article 12.[546]

The judiciary itself now recognises the importance of listening to the views of children.[547] This is even true (perhaps particularly true) where the parents appear to agree over what is best for the child. Indeed, arguably a child has a right under article 6 of the European Convention on Human Rights to have her or his views given due consideration.[548] This may require, as well as a report, separate representation of the child's interests.[549] The leading case is *Mabon* v *Mabon*.[550]

### CASE: *Mabon* v *Mabon* [2005] 2 FCR 354

The Court of Appeal overturned a judge's decision that three 'educated, articulate and reasonably mature' boys aged 17, 15 and 13 should not be separately represented in a bitterly contested application over residence and contact.[551] Thorpe LJ was blunt: 'It was simply unthinkable to exclude young men from knowledge of and participation in legal proceedings that affected them so fundamentally . . . I am in no doubt that the judge was plainly wrong.'[552] Indeed he thought that even if participation would be contrary to the welfare of the child that would not necessarily mean that it should not be permitted: 'the right of freedom of expression and participation outweighs the paternalistic judgement of welfare'.[553] However, he could imagine very limited circumstances in which it would not be appropriate to permit a competent child participation:

> If direct participation would pose an obvious risk of harm to the child arising out of the nature of the continuing proceedings and, if the child is incapable of comprehending that risk, then the judge is entitled to find that sufficient understanding has not been demonstrated. But judges have to be equally alive to the risk of emotional harm that might arise from denying the child knowledge of and participation in the continuing proceedings.[554]

This approach, Thorpe LJ held, was required in order to protect children's rights to autonomy under article 8 and also the right in article 12 of the UN Convention on the Rights of the Child for children to express their views.

---

[543] Douglas et al. (2006); Cashmore (2003).
[544] Harold and Murch (2005).
[545] Harold and Murch (2005).
[546] James, James and McNamee (2004); Davey (2010).
[547] *Re A (Contact: Separate Representation)* [2001] 1 FLR 715.
[548] Fortin (2009b: ch. 10).
[549] Adoption and Children Act 2002, s 122 means that applications under CA 1989, s 8 are now 'specified proceedings' for the purpose of CA 1989, s 41 and so separate representation can be ordered. *Re A (Contact: Separate Representation)* [2001] 1 FLR 715 CA. But *CAFCASS Practice Note (Officers of Legal Services and Special Casework: Appointment in Family Proceedings)* [2001] 2 FLR 151 suggests that separate representation is appropriate only in special cases.
[550] [2005] 2 FCR 354.
[551] Though see *Re N (Contact: Minor Seeking Leave to Defend and Removal of Guardian)* [2003] 1 FLR 652 where the 11-year-old boy lacked the maturity to be able to give instructions.
[552] [2005] 2 FCR 354. At paras 23–24.
[553] At para 29.
[554] Para 29.

In *Re C (Abduction: Separate Representation of Children)*[555] a case involving child abduction, Ryder J held that children aged 16, 13, 11 and 9 should be represented. He held that it would be harmful for some of the children but not others to have their views presented.

Despite the fine rhetoric in *Mabon*, the reality is that there is neither the funding nor the staff at CAFCASS to provide the representation for children Thorpe LJ would evidently like to see.[556] In fact research suggests that representation is used as a 'last resort' where there are complex disputes.[557] The latest guidance, issued in February 2005, states that only a circuit judge can appoint a guardian. This is a clear attempt to restrict the separate representation of children in private law cases. Indeed, the Department of Constitutional Affairs has complained that too many children are being given party status or separate representation.[558] The report warns of the dangers of rising legal costs and overburdening CAFCASS.

Despite the acknowledgement that listening to and appreciating children's wishes is important, there are still grave concerns over the way in which reports concerning children are prepared and the length of time taken to prepare them.[559] The problem that many commentators recount is that it is difficult for social workers to ascertain and report the wishes of children accurately. Children may feel intimidated and unable to say what they wish. Further, the questions asked of them by the Family Court Advisor may not reflect the way the problem is perceived by the child.[560] The reporter therefore (unintentionally) deprives children of the ability to express their views in their own terms.[561] James et al.[562] argue that their research indicates that the reporters have a particular image of childhood (e.g. that children become competent at particular ages) and this prevents an effective evaluation of every child. Indeed the very concept of 'listening' to children may too easily slip into taking a paternalistic approach to them. Bev Clucas[563] writes:

> the problem with focusing on children's views and interests at the expense of children's rights is that there is an increased emphasis on children as incompetent objects, recipients of our compassion and good will, rather than on children as subjects, developing citizens who may need guidance in the exercise of their will and the understanding of their responsibilities – but who are people, deserving of equal consideration and important entitlements.

Her concern is that listening to children is one thing, taking their views seriously is another.[564] A survey of cases by May and Smart[565] found that in only one-quarter of cases was there any kind of record on the paperwork of cases as to the wishes of the child; although this could be largely explained by the age of the child or the fact that the parents were in agreement. They found that where children's wishes did not coincide with the welfare officer's view it was rare for the children's views to prevail.

As well as preparing the reports, the child and family reporter can be responsible for communicating with the child after the order has been made. This is also important because

---

[555] [2008] 2 FLR 6.
[556] See *Re C (Children) (Appointment of Guardian)* [2008] 1 FCR 359 where the National Youth Advisory Service was asked to represent and assist the children.
[557] Douglas et al. (2006). Bellamy and Lord (2003) found that rule 9.5 was used in 7.3% of contested cases.
[558] Department of Constitutional Affairs (2006b). For a devastating critique of the report see Fortin (2007).
[559] Hunt and Lawson (1999); Lyon, Surrey and Timms (1999).
[560] Mayall (2002: 166).
[561] Buchanan et al. (2001);
[562] Murch (2003). James, James and McNamee (2003). See also HM Inspectorate of Court Administration (2005).
[563] Clucas (2005: 291).
[564] See Wilson (2004).
[565] May and Smart (2004).

part of taking a child's views seriously is reporting back to the child the court's decision and discussing it with him or her.[566]

### (iii) Appointment of Official Solicitor

The Official Solicitor has traditionally represented children in wardship. It is in the discretion of the Lord Chancellor whether the Official Solicitor should intervene. If the child is not represented by a Guardian ad Litem, then a judge may decide, in exceptional cases, to ask the Official Solicitor to become involved.[567] This will occur only in cases in the High Court and the office of the Official Solicitor should be used sparingly.[568]

## 15 The Children's Commissioner

The Children Act 2004 created the post Children's Commissioner for England. There are separate ones for Wales, Scotland and Northern Ireland. The first holder of the English post was Professor Al Aynsley-Green; Maggie Atkinson now holds the post; and the Children's Commissioner for Wales is currently Keith Towler.

### A The role of the Commissioner

The primary role of the English Commissioner is set out in s 2(1) of the Children Act 2004: 'to promote awareness of the views and interests of children in England'. In particular, under s 2(2) she or he must:

> **LEGISLATIVE PROVISION**
>
> **Children Act 2004, section 2(2)**
>
> (a) encourage persons exercising functions or engaged in activities affecting children to take account of their views and interests;
> (b) advise the Secretary of State on the views and interests of children;
> (c) consider or research the operation of complaints procedures so far as relating to children;
> (d) consider or research any other matter relating to the interests of children; publish a report on any matter researched by him under this section.

The Secretary of State can ask the Children's Commissioner to hold an inquiry into a case of an individual child if that would raise wider issues relevant for children.[569] The Children's Commissioner on his or her own initiative can consider the case of an individual child if it raises issues of public policy or relevance to other children.[570]

It is notable that rights are not mentioned in the remit of the Children's Commissioner for England. The Welsh, Northern Irish and Scottish Children's Commissioners are required to

---

[566] Buchanan, Hunt, Bretherton and Bream (2001: 93).
[567] *Practice Note (The Official Solicitor: Application in Family Proceedings)* [1995] 2 FLR 479.
[568] *Re CT (A Minor) (Child: Representation)* [1993] 2 FLR 278, [1993] 2 FCR 445.
[569] Children Act 2004, s 4.
[570] Children Act 2004, s 3.

promote and safeguard the rights of children.[571] It is remarkable that the rights of English children are seen as less requiring of protection than those of children elsewhere. The Children Act 2004 steadfastly talks in terms of the interests of children rather than their rights.[572] The Commissioner can consider the rights children have under the United Nations Convention on the Rights of the Child, but that convention is in no sense binding on the Commissioner.[573]

The Children's Commissioner for Wales[574] has as his or her principal aim to safeguard and promote the rights and welfare of children.[575] He or she should have regard to the United Nations Convention on the Rights of the Child when exercising his or her functions.[576] The Welsh Commissioner's remit appears notably more rights-focused than that of his or her English counterpart.[577]

## B What have the Commissioners done?

The English Commissioner, currently Maggie Atkinson, in the annual review of 2009–10[578] explains that her office's work has covered protection of children, encouraging children in participation and mental health issues.

The Welsh Commissioner for Children has been in post since 2001. He has produced a wide range of reports covering topics from school toilets to the teaching of drama. He has also sought to address wider issues such as child poverty and bullying.[579]

## 16 Children and education[580]

Article 2 of the first Protocol to the European Convention on Human Rights states:

> No person shall be denied the right to education. In the exercise of the functions which it assumes in relation to education, and to teaching, the state shall respect the right of parents to ensure such education and teaching is in conformity with their own religious and philosophical convictions.[581]

There are two notable points about this article of the Convention. First, rather than granting a positive right to education, the article says that children should not be *denied* education. This seems to imply that if the state decides to provide education, it must not prevent a child using the education, rather than requiring the state positively to provide education.[582] Secondly, the article protects the religious and philosophical beliefs of the parents, but not of the child.

---

[571] Care Standards Act 2000, s 72A; Commissioner for Children and Young People (Scotland) Act 2003; and Commissioner for Children and Young People (Northern Ireland) Order 2003. See Williams (2005) for a useful discussion of the work of the Commissioners.

[572] Clucas (2005).

[573] Children Act 2004, s 2(11).

[574] Children's Commissioner for Wales Act 2001 and Part V of Care Standards Act 2000.

[575] Care Standards Act 2000, s 72A.

[576] Children's Commissioner for Wales Regulations 2001, SI 2001/2787 (W237), reg 22.

[577] See Thomas et al. (2010) for a helpful assessment of the work of the commissioner to date.

[578] Children's Commissioner for England (2010).

[579] www.childcom.org.uk will provide up-to-date information on the Welsh Commissioner.

[580] For a discussion of the law on education, see Harris (2005); Fortin (2003b: ch. 6); Lundy (2005).

[581] Contrast the UN Convention on the Rights of the Child in article 28(1).

[582] See Monk (2009) for an excellent discussion on home education.

Children spend a large portion of their childhood in schools. Generally, our society believes that education is a crucial part of enabling a child to develop his or her own personality and become a productive member of society. Education gives rise to some interesting clashes between the rights of parents, children and the state over who should decide the form of education. This area is one where, surprisingly, the notion of children's rights has little sway and some children complain that being at school is like living under a dictatorship.[583] Monk has argued that it is meaningful to talk of children having rights in education: rights to be treated as subjects, not objects, and a recognition that children are social agents and active participants within the education system.[584] Others complain of suffering racial disadvantage within the education system and hope that recognising rights in education will combat that.[585]

It is not possible here to provide a detailed discussion of the law on education, which would require a book.[586] Section 7 of the Education Act 1996 imposes an obligation on parents to ensure a child receives effective full-time education. If necessary this duty can be enforced by a range of court orders. This is one of the few areas of parenting where the law requires something positive of parents.

## 17 Children and criminal law

Children are protected under the general criminal law.[587] There are also special offences that are designed to protect children from particular forms of abuse. The extreme child liberationists would be opposed to these laws on the ground that children should be treated in exactly the same way as adults and any special protection under the criminal law denies a child the autonomy that an adult has. It is important in considering the protection offered to children by the criminal law to note that a high proportion of crimes against children are committed by members of the child's family or household.

The offences involving children can be divided into three main groups.[588] First, there are those which are designed to protect children from abuse by adults. For example, there are special sexual offences against children[589] and the offence of neglecting children.[590] Secondly, there are offences designed to protect children's basic interests. For example, there are a host of protections for children from being employed in dangerous activities or for long periods.[591] Thirdly, there are offences which may be seen as protecting the general public from children. For example, a huge number of offences restrict what might be sold to a child under 16: these include alcohol,[592] tobacco,[593] firearms,[594] crossbows and fireworks.[595]

---

[583] See also Hill and Tisdall (1997: ch. 7).

[584] Monk (2002: 45). See also Harris (2009).

[585] Owusu-Bempah (2001).

[586] E.g. Harris (2007).

[587] See, e.g., Hayes (2005).

[588] See Hall (2009) for a discussion of the issues surrounding children giving evidence in criminal trials.

[589] E.g. Sexual Offences Act 2003.

[590] E.g. Children and Young Persons Act 1933.

[591] E.g. Employment of Young People Act 1993, s 1(1); Employment of Women, Young Persons and Children Act 1920; Mines and Quarries Act 1954, s 124; Employment Act 1989.

[592] Licensing Act 1964, s 169.

[593] Protection of Children (Tobacco) Act 1986; Children and Young Persons (Protection from Tobacco) Act 1991.

[594] Firearms Acts 1968 and 1982.

[595] Crossbows Act 1987 and Fireworks Act 2003, respectively.

One controversial area is the Sexual Offences Act 2003 which prohibits sexual contact with under-16-year-olds, even where there is consent. Bainham has described the act as 'capable of prohibiting the sort of innocuous, some may even think desirable, sexual experimentation between adolescents which is a normal part of growing up'.[596] It might be thought it shows a lack of appreciation of reality because about one-third of children first experience sexual intercourse before their sixteenth birthday.[597] On the other hand, supporters of the legislation argue that the Act will never be used to prosecute experimentation of the kind Bainham refers to, but it provides the prosecution with a powerful set of offences to use against those who sexually exploit children.[598] In *Re W (Children) (Abuse: Oral Evidence)*[599] the Supreme Court removed the presumption that children should not be required to give evidence against those accused of abusing them. This will help protect the rights of defendants accused of sexual abuse, but may deter the reporting and prosecution of sexual offences. The court can still decide not to require a child victim to give evidence and much will depend on how the court exercises its discretion in the future.

A different issue is how the law deals with children who have committed crimes.[600] Here the state needs to balance the protection of the public from criminal youngsters with the desire to help children who have committed crime. On the one hand, there are those who believe criminal activity in those aged under 18 reveals that the child is in need of social work assistance and support.[601] On the other, criminal activity among the under-18s constitutes a large percentage of criminal acts, and protection of the public might call for harsh treatment of young criminals. The Crime and Disorder Act 1998 now governs this area of the law: children under the age of 10 cannot be convicted of a criminal offence, however heinous their crime; children aged over 10 can be prosecuted for crimes, and special procedures and courts are used.[602] In *SC v UK*[603] the European Court of Human Rights emphasised that, when prosecuting a child aged 11, article 6 (protecting the right to a fair trial) requires that the child be able effectively to participate in the trial. If the defendant is not able to do so, criminal proceedings should not be used. Such a child may, of course, be subject to protective measures under Part III of the Children Act 1989. It is striking how readily the law finds children to be competent for the purposes of punishment under the criminal law, but, as we have seen, not competent to make decisions about their medical treatment.[604]

Sometimes special measures are enacted to deal with 'troublesome' children. In *R (On the Application of W) v Commissioner of Police*[605] the Court of Appeal considered s 30(6) of the Anti-Social Behaviour Act 2003 which gave police constables power to remove a person under the age of 16 who was not under the effective control of a responsible adult to his home using reasonable force. The Court of Appeal rejected the argument that the use of force against a young man under this provision was contrary to his rights protected under the Human Rights Act 1998.[606] There has been increasing concern at the use of anti-social behaviour orders to control the lawful conduct of young people.[607]

---

[596] Bainham (2006b: 622).
[597] BBC Newsonline (2006c).
[598] For a useful discussion of the age of consent see Waites (2005).
[599] [2010] UKSC 12.
[600] For general discussion on this see Keating (2007 and 2008); and Hollingsworth (2007a and b).
[601] See Stephen (2009). For concerns about the way the law treats children who get into trouble see Barnado's (2003).
[602] For criticisms of this see UN Committee on the Rights of the Child (2002).
[603] [2005] 1 FCR 347.
[604] Lyons (2010).
[605] [2006] EWCA Crim 458.
[606] For criticism of the legislation and discussion of case law see Hollingsworth (2006).
[607] Bateman (2007) and Macdonald (2007).

In recent years Parliament[608] has accepted that, in some cases, parents have parental responsibility for the criminal acts of their children.[609] There are two main arguments against the proposals. The first was that those families whose children are committing crimes are often the most deprived and it would be better for resources to be channelled into providing support for such families. The second was that it might encourage a greater use of corporal punishment which could become child abuse. Under s 8 of the Crime and Disorder Act 1998 a court may make a parenting order where a child safety order is made;[610] or where an anti-social behaviour order or a sex offender order is made in respect of a child or young person;[611] or if the child or young person is convicted of an offence (in which case the court shall make a parenting order unless it decides that to do so would be not desirable, in which case it must explain why in open court); or where a person is convicted of an offence under s 43 or s 44 of the Education Act 1996.[612] The order requires a parent to attend counselling or guidance sessions. These last no more than 12 weeks and occur no more than once a week.[613] There may be additional requirements. The most likely would be that a parent must ensure that a child attends school or that a child be home by a particular time. These requirements can last 12 months. The order is controversial, as Bainham suggests:

> The new order might be viewed by some as an attempt to provide support and encouragement to the parents of young offenders, while others will see it as fundamentally authoritarian, an attack on civil liberties and an extraordinary invasion by the State into family autonomy – so richly prized elsewhere in the law.[614]

Helen Reece has suggested that: 'In the case of parents, in recent years their responsibility *for* their children has been undermined by their responsibility *to* external agencies.'[615] Indeed she sees a move towards parental accountability:

> The shift in the meaning of parental responsibility enables the law to be uniquely intrusive and judgmental, because every parent, on being held up to scrutiny, is found lacking. Accordingly the blurry spectrum of facilitation and support that has recently replaced clear-cut punishment and enforcement can be explained by its much better fit with parental responsibility as accountability.[616]

Luckock is less negative about the Government's approach:

> The immediate aim of New Labour policy has been to remoralise and reskill parents as the primary influence on children as future citizens. This has led to policies of intrusion which appear to undermine parental autonomy and authority. However, the ultimate objective is precisely to restore that authority in the long run.[617]

---

[608] Home Office (1990a: paras 8.1 and 8.2).
[609] Hollingsworth (2007a and b); Koffman (2008).
[610] This order is available where a child under the age of 10 commits an act that would be a crime if the child were over 10, or where such an order is considered necessary to prevent the child committing such acts.
[611] Very basically, these orders are available where a person has caused distress, alarm or harassment to one or more people not in the person's own household and so their behaviour is deemed anti-social.
[612] In *R (On the Application of M) v Inner London Crown Court* [2003] 1 FLR 994 it was accepted that a parenting order did infringe a parent's rights under article 8 of the European Convention to a right to respect for family life, but that such an intervention was justifiable under para 2.
[613] For positive reports from parents who have attended the classes see Ghate and Ramella (2002).
[614] Bainham (1998a: 491). See further Moran and Ghate (2005). See also parenting contracts which schools can require parents of troublesome pupils to sign.
[615] Reece (2005: 468).
[616] Reece (2005: 483).
[617] Luckock (2008: 25).

# 18 Corporal punishment

Corporal punishment has been defined as 'the use of physical force with the intention of causing a child to experience pain but not injury for the purposes of correction or control of the child's behaviour'.[618] Corporal punishment is one of the most controversial topics surrounding parenting.[619] Although nearly everyone agrees that children require some form of discipline,[620] there is much dispute about what form that discipline should take. For some, the issue is straightforward: 'Hitting people is wrong – and children are people too.'[621] Indeed, it can be regarded as a basic human right not to be hit.[622] The impact on children can be underestimated. One child respondent to a Government survey stated 'the memory of how it made me feel inside was so much stronger than how it felt on my skin – that was over in a few seconds'.[623] Others argue that corporal punishment is an important part of bringing children up well and even cite some biblical support.[624] A third group (perhaps the majority of parents) do not think that corporal punishment is necessarily a positive good but admit that, when at the end of their tether, they use corporal punishment. A survey revealed that corporal punishment is widespread: 81 per cent of interviewees supported corporal punishment by parents of own children; 45 per cent by carers or nannies; 67 per cent by teachers; 71 per cent by head teachers; and (remarkably) 70 per cent by courts.[625] Another survey found that 88 per cent of parents stated that they felt it sometimes necessary to hit their children.[626] However, it may be that attitudes are changing, with the most recent survey finding only 59 per cent of those questioned believing that parents should be allowed to smack their children.[627] Corporal punishment starts surprisingly young: three-quarters of 1-year-olds have been smacked and among 4-year-olds 48 per cent were hit once a week.[628]

The present law is that corporal punishment is prima facie an assault. It could be a battery, an assault occasioning actual bodily harm,[629] or wounding or inflicting or causing grievous bodily harm,[630] depending on the severity of the punishment. However, under common law there is a defence to these offences if the conduct constitutes 'lawful chastisement'. Precisely what 'lawful chastisement' is, is not clear. Section 58 of the Children Act 2004 makes it clear that 'reasonable chastisement' cannot provide a defence to a charge of assault occasioning actual bodily harm or the offences involving grievous bodily harm. In other words, to rely on the defence of reasonable chastisement the level of harm used must cause less than actual bodily harm. As actual bodily harm includes a bruise, only 'mild corporal punishment' is permitted. The Crown Prosecution Service guidelines state:

---

[618] Strauss and Donnolly (1993: 420).
[619] For useful discussions of the use of force against children in a variety of contexts see Barton (2008c), Keating (2006), Fortin (2003) and Booth (2005).
[620] Rhona Smith (2004) suggests a child has a right to discipline.
[621] Newell (1989).
[622] United Nations Committee on the Rights of the Child (2002) called on the UK to remove the defence of 'reasonable chastisement'.
[623] Barton (2008c: 65).
[624] Proverbs 13: 24; see *R (On the Application of Williamson) v Secretary of State* [2005] 1 FCR 498.
[625] ICM poll (*The Guardian*, 7 November 1996).
[626] Sawyer (2000).
[627] Department for Education and Skills (2008: para 31).
[628] Phillips and Alderson (2003).
[629] Contrary to Offences Against the Person Act 1861, s 47.
[630] Contrary to Offences Against the Person Act 1861, s 18 or s 10.

. . . for minor assaults committed by an adult upon a child that result in injuries such as grazes, scratches, abrasions, minor bruising, swelling, superficial cuts or a black eye, the appropriate charge will normally be ABH[631] for which the defence of 'reasonable chastisement' is no longer available.

However, if the injury amounts to no more than reddening of the skin, and the injury is transient and trifling, a charge of common assault may be laid against the defendant for whom the reasonable chastisement defence remains available to parents or adults acting *in loco parentis*.[632]

The Government Review of the current law decided no change was necessary. Section 58 of the Children Act 2004 had improved the protection for children while not producing significant practical problems.[633] While the Government 'does not condone smacking and believes that other methods of managing children are more effective',[634] it 'does not believe the state should intervene in family life unnecessarily'. Therefore the current law remains, as the *Daily Telegraph* put it: 'Parents can smack – if they're gentle.'[635]

As well as involving potential criminal charges, corporal punishment might also lead to investigation by a local authority.[636] Corporal punishment is now forbidden in state and independent schools[637] and in residential care homes.[638] The European Court and Commission have had to address the issue of corporal punishment on a number of occasions.[639] The most recent case, *A v UK (Human Rights: Punishment of Child)*,[640] has had the biggest impact. A cane was used on more than one occasion by a mother's partner on her child. The European Court of Human Rights did not make a general statement on chastisement but did state that article 3 was breached. The defence of 'reasonable chastisement' was too vague and inadequately protected the child from inhuman and degrading treatment.[641] The European Court of Human Rights took the view that corporal punishment breached article 19 of the UN Convention, which requires the state to protect children from all forms of violence.[642]

In *R (On the Application of Williamson)* v *Secretary of State for Education and Employment* the House of Lords had to consider whether parents or teachers could claim a right to administer corporal punishment.

---

[631] Actual bodily harm.

[632] Crown Prosecution Service (2007: 1).

[633] See Choudhry (2009) for an excellent discussion of the current law.

[634] Department for Education and Skills (2008: para 55).

[635] Quoted Barton (2008c: 68).

[636] *Re F (Children)(Interim Care Order)* [2007] 2 FCR 639 where a single act of excessive force in punishment was found on the facts to be insufficient to justify an interim care order.

[637] Education Act 1996, s 548(1) as amended by the Schools Standards and Framework Act 1998, s 131 abolished corporal punishment in independent schools. A challenge that this provision infringed parents' rights under the European Convention on Human Rights failed in *R (On the Application of Williamson)* v *Secretary of State for Education and Employment* [2005] 1 FCR 498.

[638] Home Office (1993: para 5). Day Care and Child Minding (National Standards: England) Regulations 2003, SI 2003/1996, reg 5 prohibits childminders and day-care workers from 'smacking' children.

[639] Including *Tyrer v UK* (1978) 2 EHRR 1; *Campbell and Cosans v UK* (1982) 4 EHRR 293; *Warwick v UK* (1986) 60 DR 5; *Y v UK* (1992) 17 EHRR 238; *Costello-Roberts v UK* (1995) EHRR 112; *A v UK (Human Rights: Punishment of Child)* [1998] 2 FLR 959, [1998] 3 FCR 597; discussed Barton (1999).

[640] [1998] 2 FLR 959, [1998] 3 FCR 597.

[641] The court left open a possible claim under article 8.

[642] United Nations Human Rights Committee (1995: paras 16 and 31). See also United Nations Human Rights Committee (2008) where the concerns are repeated.

> **CASE: *R (On the Application of Williamson)* v *Secretary of State for Education and Employment* [2005] 1 FCR 498**
>
> The House of Lords rejected a claim by parents that the prohibition of corporal punishment in private schools (in Education Act 1996, s 548) infringed their right to respect for family life. They had sent their children to a private Christian school and the parents and teachers wanted the teachers to be able to use corporal punishment in the school. Their Lordships accepted that the Act did interfere with the right to religious freedom in article 9 of the ECHR, but held that the interference could be justified. Lord Nicholls explained: 'Corporal punishment involves deliberately inflicting physical violence. The legislation is intended to protect children against the distress, pain and other harmful effects infliction of physical violence may cause.' But it would be quite wrong to think that this case indicates that children have the right never to suffer corporal punishment. Lord Nicholls makes it clear he does not think that corporal punishment necessarily infringes a child's rights under article 3 or article 8. Baroness Hale is less clear. She states at one point: 'If a child has a right to be brought up without institutional violence, as he does, that right should be respected whether or not his parents and teachers believe otherwise.'[643] However, she earlier states that in a free society parents should have a 'large measure of autonomy' in deciding how to raise children.[644]

Despite the changes to the law in the Children Act 2004 there are many who argue that the law should never permit corporal punishment.[645]

> **TOPICAL ISSUE**
>
> **Should the law permit corporal punishment?**
>
> In this debate the following issues appear to be of particular significance:
>
> 1. The psychological evidence seems to suggest that corporal punishment harms children.[646] Opponents of corporal punishment argue that it teaches children that violence is an appropriate way to deal with situations of conflict and that it is appropriate for larger people to injure smaller people.[647] Further, it is argued that corporal punishment cultivates a culture within society which accepts violence towards children. Some fear that where there is regular corporal punishment this can too easily escalate to more serious abuse and violence for the child.[648] That said, there are many children who have been corporally punished, whom it cannot be shown have suffered particular harm as a result.
>
> 2. To some there are links between corporal punishment and sexual abuse. Freeman explains that it has been used as a form of grooming for further abuse. Others have linked corporal punishment to 'sexualised smacking'.

➡

---

[643] At para 84.
[644] At para 72.
[645] E.g. Keating (2006); United Nations Committee on the Rights of the Child (2008).
[646] Orentlicher (1998); Gershoff (2002); Newell (2002). Phillips and Alderson (2003) suggest it is striking how few experts in the area support smacking.
[647] Commission on Children and Violence (1995).
[648] Scottish Law Commission Report 135 (1992).

3. The most straightforward approach is that hitting children is an infringement of their rights. Freeman has stated that 'nothing is a clearer statement of the position that children occupy in society, a clearer badge of childhood, than the fact that children alone of all people in society can be hit with impunity'.[649]

4. It would be possible to reform the law so as to forbid the hitting of the child with certain kinds of implements or hitting children on certain parts of the body. However, any such list would draw arbitrary lines and would be unlikely to be effective.

5. It is difficult to distinguish physical restraint and corporal punishment. It is generally accepted that on occasion it is necessary to use force to restrain a child.[650] Some believe there is a very fine dividing line between restraining children who are about to harm themselves or another and punishment.[651] The same act (e.g. pushing a child) could be restraining a child who was about to harm him- or herself or a punishment, depending on the intention of the parent. This demonstrates that there is some difficulty in saying that the issue is simply that a child should not be hit.

6. Some fear that if corporal punishment is outlawed then trivial assaults (e.g. a light smack) might be seen as corporal punishment. However, in Sweden, in the 14 years since corporal punishment was made illegal[652] there has been only one punishment of a parent after a complaint by a child.[653] This suggests that fears that any prohibition would lead to a major intrusion into family life are exaggerated.

7. In a survey, 88 per cent of those questioned thought it sometimes necessary to smack naughty children.[654] It must be questioned whether a prohibition against all corporal punishment which would go against the views and practice of the vast majority of parents would be justifiable. Perhaps, however, a useful analogy could be made with speeding whilst driving. Clearly not all speeding is punished, and most people do break the speeding laws, yet the laws are still generally accepted.

## 19 Children's duties

Although much has been written on children's rights, there is very little said about children's duties.[655] Indeed, children appear to be under few duties under the law. By far the most significant is the duty to obey the criminal law, at least once they have reached the age of 10.[656] However, there is not even an obligation upon children to attend school.[657]

At a theoretical level, as children's rights are increasingly recognised, it is arguable that greater emphasis should be placed on children's responsibilities. If children are thought to

---

[649] Points 2 and 3: Freeman (1997a).
[650] Fortin (2001: 247).
[651] See, e.g., Education Act 1996, s 550A, which sets out when teachers can use force.
[652] Sweden, Finland, Denmark, Germany, Iceland, Norway, Austria, Latvia, Ukraine, Croatia and Cyprus have all prohibited corporal punishment: Booth (2005).
[653] Sawyer (2000). See further on the Swedish experience: Durrant (2003).
[654] Department of Health (2000a: Annexe A). See for further discussion on parents' atitudes: Bunting, Webb and Healy (2010).
[655] Bainham (1998c).
[656] Notably a young offender can be subject to a curfew order. Such orders cannot be made against adults.
[657] The obligation to ensure attendance at school is placed upon the parents, rather than the child.

have sufficient capacity to be able to make decisions for themselves, then it is arguable that they have sufficient capacity to have responsibilities. As Sir John Laws has written:

> A society whose values are defined by reference to individual rights is by that very fact already impoverished. Its existence says nothing about individual duty, nothing about virtue, self-discipline, self-restraint, to say nothing of self-sacrifice.[658]

However, the difficulty arises in enforcing any duties imposed upon children. Even though children are subject to the criminal law, the punishments imposed on children are not the same as those placed on adults. Certainly, where a child is exercising a right, like others she must ensure she respects the rights of others. In *Re Roddy (A Child) (Identification: Restriction on Publication)*[659] a 16-year-old was permitted to tell the media her story of how she became pregnant at age 12. However, she was not permitted, in doing so, to reveal the identity of her child nor of the father of the child, both of whom were under the age of 18. In *Re M (A Child) (Care Proceedings: Witness Summons)*[660] a child was forced to give evidence against her will in child abuse proceedings. The importance of discovering the truth about the alleged abuse in that case justified overruling her wishes.

## 20 Conclusion

This chapter has considered the ways in which the law looks at children. Two particular approaches have been contrasted: that in which the law seeks to promote the child's welfare; and that in which the law protects the rights of the child. In respect of many issues, despite their important theoretical differences, these approaches would adopt the same solution. The issue of most disagreement is over whether a child should be able to make decisions for him- or herself. The leading cases in this area have in fact focused on the medical arena. In the rather extreme circumstances of those cases, the courts have not been willing to permit children to make decisions which have the effect of ending their lives. These cases might give the impression that children's wishes will be readily overridden by the courts, whereas in fact forcing any form of action on an unwilling teenager is rare, although this may be as much because of the practical problems in compelling a person to do something against their will as any theoretical principle. In *Mabon v Mabon*, Thorpe LJ indicated that in the twenty-first century there was a keener awareness of children's autonomy rights.[661] We will wait and see if this leads to changes in the approaches of the courts. The chapter has also considered the ways in which the law must balance the interests of parents and children. The issue is often not made explicit in the case law. The simple approach that the interests of children are paramount and always trump those of the parent has been shown not to represent the law and not to be appropriate in theory. The Human Rights Act 1998 will no doubt lead to many more cases where the court will be required to balance the interests of parents, children and the state; and, hopefully, more well-thought-out principles will be developed.

---

[658] Laws (1998: 255).
[659] [2004] 1 FCR 481.
[660] [2007] 1 FCR 253.
[661] [2005] 2 FCR 354 at para 26.

## Further reading

**Archard, D.** (2004b) *Children: Rights and Childhood*, London: Routledge.

**Archard, D. and Skivenes, M.** (2009) 'Balancing a Child's Best Interests and a Child's Views', *International Journal of Children's Rights* 17 (2009) 1–21.

**Bainham, A.** (2009d) 'Is anything now left of parental rights?' in R. Probert, S. Gilmore and J. Herring, *Responsible Parents and Parental Responsibility*, Oxford: Hart.

**Bridgeman, J.** (2007) *Parental Responsibility, Young Children and Healthcare Law*, Cambridge: CUP.

**Cassidy, C.** (2009) *Thinking Children*, London: Continuum.

**Choudhry, S. and Fenwick, H.** (2005) 'Taking the rights of parents and children seriously: Confronting the welfare principle under the Human Rights Act', *Oxford Journal of Legal Studies* 25: 453.

**Eekelaar, J.** (1994a) 'The interests of the child and the child's wishes: the role of dynamic self-determinism', *International Journal of Law and the Family* 8: 42.

**Eekelaar, J.** (2004) 'Children between cultures', *International Journal of Law, Policy and the Family* 18: 178.

**Fortin, J.** (2006a) 'Accommodating Children's Rights in a Post Human Rights Act Era', *Modern Law Review* 69: 299.

**Fortin, J.** (2009b) *Children's Rights and the Developing Law*, London: LexisNexis Butterworths.

**Freeman, M.** (1983) *The Rights and Wrongs of Children*, London: Frances Pinter.

**Freeman, M.** (2000e) 'The future of children's rights', *Children and Society* 14: 277.

**Freeman, M.** (2007) 'Why it remains important to take children's rights seriously', *International Journal of Children's Rights* 15: 5.

**Gilmore, S.** (2009) 'The limits of parental responsibility', in R. Probert, S. Gilmore and J. Herring, *Responsible Parents and Parental Responsibility*, Oxford: Hart.

**Guggenheim, M.** (2005) *What's Wrong with Children's Rights?*, Cambridge, Mass.: Harvard University Press.

**Harris-Short, S.** (2005) 'Family law and the Human Rights Act 1998: judicial restraint or revolution?', *Child and Family Law Quarterly* 17: 329.

**Herring, J.** (1999b) 'The Human Rights Act and the welfare principle in family law – conflicting or complementary?', *Child and Family Law Quarterly* 11: 223.

**Herring, J.** (2005b) 'Farewell Welfare', *Journal of Social Welfare and Family Law* 27: 159.

**Hollingsworth, K.** (2007a) 'Responsibility and rights: Children and their parents in the youth justice system', *International Journal of Law, Family and Policy* 21: 190.

**Kelly, F.** (2005) 'Conceptualising the child through an ethic of care: lessons for family law', *International Journal of Law in Context* 1: 375.

**Lim, H. and Roche, J.** (2000) 'Feminism and Children's Rights', in J. Bridgeman and D. Monk (eds) *Feminist Perspectives on Child Law*, London: Cavendish.

**Lyons, B.** (2010) 'Dying to be responsible: adolescence, autonomy and responsibility', *Legal Studies* 30: 257.

**Parkinson, P. and Cashmore, J.** (2010) *The Voice of a Child in Family Law Disputes*, Oxford: OUP.

**Probert, R., Gilmore, S. and Herring, J.** (eds) (2009) *Responsible Parents and Parental Responsibility*, Oxford: Hart.

**Williams, Jane** (2007) 'Incorporating children's rights: The divergence in law and policy', *Legal Studies* 27: 261.

Visit **www.mylawchamber.co.uk/herring** to access study support resources including interactive multiple choice questions, weblinks, discussion questions and legal updates.

Use **Case Navigator** to read in full some of the key cases referenced in this chapter with commentary and questions:

*Gillick* v *West Norfolk and Wisbech AHA* [1985] 3 All ER 112
*Mabon* v *Mabon* [2005] 2 FCR 354
*Re S (A Minor) (Parental Responsibility)* [1995] 3 FCR 225
*Re G (Residence: Same-Sex Partner)* [2006] 4 All ER 241

# 9 Court resolution of private disputes over children

## 1 Introduction

This chapter will consider the law in situations when the court is required to resolve a private dispute concerning children. Chapter 10 will examine public law cases, that is, where the local authority is seeking to protect a child whom it fears is in danger of being abused. Here we will concentrate largely on the cases which involved disputes between parents over the upbringing of children, although, as will become apparent, adults other than parents, and indeed children themselves, may seek court orders over children.

The law is based on the assumption that parents promote the welfare of their children, and so there is normally no need for the intervention of the court.[1] The courts become involved only if there is a dispute between the parents over the upbringing of their child or, rarely, if the child him- or herself applies to the court. One exception is on divorce. Under s 41 of the Matrimonial Causes Act 1973:

---

**LEGISLATIVE PROVISION**

**Matrimonial Causes Act 1973, section 41**

In any proceedings for a decree of divorce or nullity of marriage, or a decree of judicial separation, the court shall consider—

(a) whether there are any children of the family to whom this section applies; and

(b) where there are any such children, whether (in the light of the arrangements which have been, or are proposed to be, made for their upbringing and welfare) it should exercise any of its powers under the Children Act 1989 with respect to any of them.

---

So, on the making of each divorce decree the court must consider the statement of arrangements concerning the children produced by the parents and decide whether it should exercise any of its powers in relation to the children of the divorcing couple. In practice, if neither party applies for an order, the court will normally assume that there is no need to make an order.[2] The thinking behind this approach has been explained by Douglas et al. in this way: 'parents may be trusted, in most cases, to plan what is best for their children's futures, and that, where they are in agreement on this, it is unnecessary and potentially damaging for the

[1] Probert, Gilmore and Herring (2009).
[2] Douglas et al. (2000).

state, in the guise of the court, to intervene'.[3] Research into the operation of s 41 has indicated that the procedure is flawed.[4] There are no means of checking whether the proposals in the statement are accurate. More significantly, researchers found that the parents' proposals were rarely discussed with the children.[5]

The Children Act 1989 brought together the orders appropriate for most private disputes involving children, but sometimes the courts must use their inherent jurisdiction if it is not possible to make the order needed to protect a child under the Children Act 1989.[6] This chapter will begin by setting out the orders available under the Children Act, then consider how the courts decide what order to make, followed by a discussion of the inherent jurisdiction, and concluding with the rules relating to child abduction.

## 2 Section 8 orders

In private cases involving children the courts may make one of the orders mentioned in s 8 of the Children Act 1989. A s 8 order cannot be made in respect of a person over the age of 18. If the child is 16 or 17 then (except for residence orders) s 8 orders should not be made unless the 'circumstances of the case are exceptional'.[7] There are a few cases where the court has thought it appropriate to make an order in respect of a 16- or 17-year-old. In *Re M (A Minor) (Immigration: Residence Order)*[8] the fact that the child did not have any relatives living in the UK was sufficiently exceptional to justify the making of an order that would last until the eighteenth birthday of the child.[9]

The different orders that can be made under s 8 will now be considered.

### A The residence order

#### (i) The effect of a residence order

A residence order is 'an order settling the arrangements to be made as to the person with whom a child is to live'.[10] A residence order determines where the child shall live, it cannot order who will care for the child.[11] It will normally be made in favour of one of the child's parents, but can be made in favour of a grandparent, an aunt, or, in fact, anyone.[12] It is even possible to impose a residence order on people against their wishes,[13] although it is very rare.

The residence order confers upon those to whom it is granted parental responsibility, if they do not have it already. It is therefore impossible to have a residence order without

---

[3] Douglas et al. (2000: 183–4).
[4] Douglas et al. (2000).
[5] Douglas et al. (2000).
[6] For an interesting discussion of the history of the making of the Children Act 1989 see Harris (2006).
[7] Children Act 1989 (hereafter CA 1989), s 9(6).
[8] [1993] 2 FLR 858.
[9] Children Act 1989 (CA 1989), s 12(5), allows a court to make a residence order in favour of a person who is not a parent or guardian to continue until a child is 18 years old.
[10] CA 1989, s 8(1).
[11] *Re S (A Child)* [2010] EWCA Civ 705.
[12] Booth J in *Re SC (A Minor) (Leave to Seek Section 8 Orders)* [1994] 1 FLR 96 at p. 100, suggested that a residence order could not be made in favour of a child. However, there is no statutory provision to this effect. It would not be impossible to imagine circumstances when it might be appropriate: for example, where a mature 15-year-old sister is to care for her younger sibling.
[13] *Re M (Adoption or Residence Order)* [1998] 1 FLR 570, [1998] 1 FCR 165; *Re K (Care Order or Residence Order)* [1995] 1 FLR 675, [1996] 1 FCR 365.

having parental responsibility. The reason for this is that if the child is to live with an adult then that adult will be exercising all the duties and responsibilities of parenthood on a day-to-day basis, and so giving him or her parental responsibility will make the legal position reflect the factual position. However, if the court is granting a residence order in favour of an unmarried father, then s 12(1) of the Children Act 1989 obliges the court to make a separate parental responsibility order. The significance of this is that, if the residence order is subsequently revoked, the unmarried father will retain parental responsibility, whereas a non-parent with a residence order would cease to have parental responsibility if the residence order was revoked. If there is a residence order requiring a child to live with one of two parents, the order will cease if the parents live together for longer than six months.[14]

## (ii) Shared residence orders

A residence order can be made in favour of two people under s 11(4), even if they do not live together.[15] The subsection explains that an order can require a child to spend a certain amount of time with one person and a certain amount of time with the other. For example, the order may state that the child should spend alternate weeks with the mother and father. This is commonly known as a 'shared residence order', although that is a rather adult-focused way of seeing it and 'dual residence' may be a preferable term.[16] The precise dividing line between a shared residence order and a liberal contact order is blurred. It has been suggested that a shared residence order is one which involves each parent seeing the child a substantial amount of time.[17] Some commentators suggest a shared residence order occurs when each parent sees the child between 30 per cent and 70 per cent of the time.[18] In *Re M (Children) (Residence Order)*[19] Thorpe LJ explained there were 'fine shades of distinction' between a shared residence order and an generous contact order. He held a judge had a broad discretion to decide how to phrase the order.[20] In *Re K (Shared Residence Order)*[21] it was suggested that the court should first determine the correct division of time between the parents and then decide whether or not a shared residence order was appropriate. As this approach indicates a shared residence order is, in fact, more than a mere statement about the division of time. Wilson LJ thought that the shared residence order would place 'a stamp that he has two parents of equal importance in the overall direction of his life, notwithstanding that the division of his time between the two homes will remain slightly unequal'.[22] That is a bit surprising because the principle continuing parental responsibility (see page 410) was intended to convey that message. It is perhaps unsurprising that there is quite some confusion over what is the role and significance of a shared residence.[23]

---

[14] CA 1989, s 11(5).

[15] Gilmore (2006b); Hoggett (1994); Baker and Townsend (1996); Bridge (1996).

[16] Neale, Flowerdew and Smart (2003). In *Re K (Shared Residence Order)* [2008] EWCA Civ 526 it was suggested that the term 'joint residence' should only be used where two people were living together.

[17] *Re D (Children) (Shared Residence Orders)* [2001] 1 FCR 147 at para 32.

[18] Macooby and Mnookin (1992). In *Re F (Children) (Shared Residence Order)* [2003] 2 FCR 164 a shared residence order where the father saw the children 38% of the time was approved, although Wilson J suggested that the court could just as well have made a residence order in favour of the mother and a generous contact order in favour of the father (para 32).

[19] [2010] 2 FCR 236.

[20] Para 55.

[21] [2008] EWCA Civ 526.

[22] Para 25.

[23] *Re R (A Child)* [2010] EWCA Civ 303; Gilmore (2010); George (2010).

## B The contact order

### (i) The effect of a contact order

As well as deciding with whom the child should live, the court must also consider whether the child should have regular meetings with their other parent (the contact parent), or indeed with other relatives or family friends. The hope is that regular meetings will enable the child to continue his or her relationship with both parents and both sides of the family. As is often (rather glibly) stated, the fact that the parents have separated should not affect their relationship with the child: parenthood is for life. Following a bitter separation, the resident parent[24] may be deeply opposed to the child seeing the other parent. This is particularly so if the resident parent repartners and tries to form a 'new family'. On the other hand, the contact parent will seek to do all he or she can to retain contact with the child and make the most of the contact permitted. This means that contact applications are often very bitterly disputed.

The contact order is defined as 'an order requiring the person with whom a child lives, or is to live, to allow the child to visit or stay with the person named in the order, or for that person and the child otherwise to have contact with each other'.[25] A contact order can only be made if a residence order has also been made.[26] This wording gives rise to some interesting questions about the effect of the order.

### (ii) Who has the obligation of enabling contact?

The definition of a contact order is interesting. It seems to suggest that there are two kinds of contact order available. First, and normally, the order can be directed at the residential parent requiring her or him to permit the child to have contact with the person named in the order. So if the residential parent prevents contact then she or he will be in breach of the order and could ultimately be imprisoned for contempt. Secondly, the order can simply state that the child and another person are to have contact. This seems to impose no obligation on the residential parent, and the residential parent would not be in breach of the order if the contact did not take place. In fact, no one would be in breach of the order if contact did not take place. However, the distinction between these different wordings of the orders has not been made explicit by the courts, and *Re H (Minors) (Prohibited Steps Order)*[27] appeared to assume that only the first kind of order could be made.

### (iii) Is a 'no contact' order a contact order?

The courts have interpreted the definition of a contact order to include an order that there is to be *no* contact between the child and a named person.[28] It is not clear whether such an order binds both the named party and the residential parent. *Re H (Minors) (Prohibited Steps Order)*[29] seemed to suggest that if a court wishes to bind the residential parent then a no contact order should be made, but if the aim is to bind a person who is not to have contact then a prohibited steps order should be made.[30] A no contact order may be appropriate where the residential parent has a friend who is a known paedophile and the courts wish to prevent the residential parent from introducing the friend to the child. A prohibited steps order may

---

[24] A 'resident parent' is the parent with whom the child is to live.
[25] CA 1989, s 8(1).
[26] *Re S (A Child)* [2010] EWCA Civ 705.
[27] [1995] 1 FLR 638, [1995] 2 FCR 547.
[28] *Nottingham CC v P* [1993] 2 FLR 134, [1994] 1 FCR 624.
[29] [1995] 1 FLR 638, [1995] 2 FCR 547.
[30] *Re H (Minors) (Prohibited Steps Order)* [1995] 1 FLR 638, [1995] 2 FCR 547.

be appropriate where a stepfather has abused his stepchildren and has then separated from the mother, but has been seeking to contact the children.[31] In such a case a no contact order may be inappropriate because there is little the mother could do to stop the step-parent seeing the children, if he was persistent enough.[32] It would therefore be more appropriate to make a prohibited steps order, directed against the step-parent. In some cases it might be best to make both a no contact and a prohibited steps order.

### (iv) Can the parent be forced to have contact with the child?

The law has not yet directly addressed the question of whether the non-residential parent can be *required* to have contact with the child. If the evidence is clear that the child would benefit from regular contact with the non-resident father, but the father does not wish to have contact, can he be compelled to see the child?[33] The definition of a contact order would not seem to include an order that binds the person named to have contact.[34] Indeed, Thorpe LJ in *Re L (A Child) (Contact: Domestic Violence)*[35] explicitly denied that a parent could be ordered to spend time with a child against the parent's wishes. In any event, it would probably be counter-productive to compel a reluctant parent to see a child.[36] In *Re S (A Child)*[37] it was confirmed that a parent could not be required to spend time caring for the child.

### (v) What can 'contact' involve?

A contact order will normally involve face-to-face meetings, but contact orders can also involve indirect contact, for example in the form of letters, e-mails, Skyping[38] or telephone calls. An indirect contact order may be appropriate if the contact parent cannot see the child: for example, if he or she is in prison.[39] An indirect contact order may also be appropriate if the child and the contact parent do not have a relationship at present, and they need to establish or re-establish links before direct contact would be appropriate.[40] It would be most unusual for a court to decide that even indirect contact would be inappropriate.[41]

If contact is to be face to face, it can be supervised by the social services.[42] This may be particularly appropriate where there is a fear that the contact parent may endanger the child.[43] If contact is to be supervised then it will often take place at a contact centre, a place set up by the local authority to assist in meetings between contact parents and children. The effectiveness of these centres will be considered later in this chapter. In *Re C (Abduction: Residence and Contact)*[44] it was held that the Human Rights Act 1998 indicated that there was a presumption in favour of normal contact and there had to be clear evidence to justify requiring

---

[31] *Re H (Minors) (Prohibited Steps Order)* [1995] 1 FLR 638, [1995] 2 FCR 547.

[32] *Re C (Contact: No Order for Contact)* [2000] Fam Law 699, [2000] 2 FLR 723.

[33] Of course, he could not physically be forced to do so, but he could be ordered to do so under threat of punishment.

[34] Although a specific issue order may have this effect.

[35] [2000] 2 FCR 404 at para 43.

[36] But see the discussions on the duties of contact later in this chapter. See Fortin, Ritchie and Buchanan (2006) for a discussion of children's experience of court ordered contact.

[37] [2010] EWCA Civ 705.

[38] E.g. *Re A (Contact: Witness Protection Scheme)* [2005] EWHC 2189 (Fam).

[39] *A v L (Contact)* [1998] 1 FLR 361, [1998] 2 FCR 204.

[40] *Re L (Contact: Transsexual Applicant)* [1995] 2 FLR 438, [1995] 3 FCR 125.

[41] *Re P (Contact: Indirect Contact)* [1999] 2 FLR 893.

[42] *Practice Direction (Access: Supervised Access)* [1980] 1 WLR 334.

[43] Although where there has been sexual abuse indirect contact is normally ordered: *Re M (Sexual Abuse Allegations: Interviewing Techniques)* [1999] 2 FLR 92.

[44] [2005] EWHC 2205 (Fam).

contact to be supervised. If supervised contact has successfully taken place for a considerable period of time, the court may well be minded to permit unsupervised contact.[45]

## C Specific issue orders and prohibited steps orders

A specific issue order (SIO) is 'an order giving directions for the purpose of determining a specific question which has arisen, or which may arise, in connection with any aspect of parental responsibility for a child'.[46] A prohibited steps order (PSO) is 'an order that no step which could be taken by a parent in meeting his parental responsibility for a child, and which is of a kind specified in the order, shall be taken by any person without the consent of the court'.[47]

The SIO may require someone to act positively in some way or may require someone to refrain from a particular activity.[48] It is designed to deal with a particular one-off issue relating to the child's upbringing: for example, in *Re C (A Child) (HIV Test)*[49] an SIO was made that a baby be tested for HIV and in *M v M (Specific Issue: Choice of School)*[50] an SIO was used to decide that the child should attend a voice test for a cathedral school. It is not designed to deal with ongoing disputes – for example, what kind of clothes the child may wear.[51] The PSO is entirely negative – it tells a parent what he or she may not do in respect of their child. The order can be used, for example, to prevent a child being known by a different name,[52] or to prevent a child being removed from the United Kingdom.

## D Restrictions on the use of section 8 orders

The s 8 orders are loosely defined and so could be open to abuse were they not restricted in their scope in the following ways.

### (i) The order must relate to an aspect of parental responsibility

This means that the order must relate to an issue concerning the upbringing of the child and not just concerning the relationship between the parents. So, for example, s 8 orders cannot prevent contact between adults,[53] nor require a husband to provide the wife with a *get* so that their divorce can be recognised within Jewish law.[54] By contrast requiring a mother to inform her children that a man is the children's father does fall under the scope of parental responsibility.[55] However, it is not always easy to tell whether a particular question does relate to an aspect of parental responsibility. For example, as we shall see there has been some dispute over whether restricting publicity about children is an aspect of parental responsibility.

Although the order can only concern an exercise of parental responsibility, the person at whom the order is directed need not actually have parental responsibility. It is sufficient if the order is stopping someone from doing something that would be an exercise of parental

---

[45] *R v P (Contact: Abduction: Supervision)* [2008] 2 FLR 936.
[46] CA 1989, s 8(1). It is possible to apply for an *ex parte* specific issue order: Family Proceedings Rules 1991, SI 1991/1247, r 4.4(c).
[47] CA 1989, s 8(1).
[48] Gilmore (2004c) provides an excellent discussion of the use of specific issue orders.
[49] [1999] 2 FLR 1004 CA.
[50] [2005] EWHC 2769 (Fam).
[51] Whether an SIO can state that in future a named person (e.g. the mother) can make decisions concerning a particular topic is unclear: see Gilmore (2004c: 369–71).
[52] *Dawson v Wearmouth* [1999] 1 FLR 1167, [1999] 1 FCR 625.
[53] *Croydon LB v A* [1992] 2 FLR 341, [1992] 1 FCR 522.
[54] *N v N (Jurisdiction: Pre-Nuptial Agreement)* [1999] 2 FLR 745.
[55] *Re F (Children) (Paternity: Jurisdiction)* [2008] 1 FCR 382.

responsibility if he or she had parental responsibility.[56] So it would be possible for a neighbour to be ordered not to speak to a child, even though the neighbour has no parental responsibility, because if the neighbour had parental responsibility speaking to the child would be an exercise of it.

### (ii) There is no power to make an occupation or non-molestation order through a s 8 order

A specific issue or prohibited steps order cannot be made if the effect is the same as an occupation or non-molestation order.[57] Any such order must be sought under the Family Law Act 1996, Part IV.[58] However, if it can be shown that the order sought is not identical to an order available under the Family Law Act 1996 then the order can be made. In *Re H (Minors) (Prohibited Steps Order)*[59] a PSO preventing a stepfather visiting a child could be made because a non-molestation order would only prevent molestation and not prohibit all contact with the child. The PSO was therefore not identical to a non-molestation order.

### (iii) There is no power to make a disguised residence or contact order using a PSO or SIO

Section 9(5)(a) of the Children Act 1989 states that neither a PSO nor an SIO can be made 'with a view to achieving a result which could be achieved by making a residence or contact order'.[60] The real significance of this restriction relates to local authorities: they can apply for specific issue orders or prohibited steps orders, but cannot apply for contact or residence orders. In *Nottingham CC v P*[61] the Court of Appeal held that a local authority could not apply for a s 8 order that a father vacate a matrimonial home. Such an order was essentially a residence order and local authorities were prohibited from applying for that. In *Re H (Minors) (Prohibited Steps Order)*[62] an order was made preventing a stepfather from contacting a child. This was not a no contact order in disguise because a contact order compels the residential parent to permit or forbid contact, but here the order was directed to be effective against the stepfather and so could not have been made as a contact order.

### (iv) A s 8 order cannot be made if the High Court would not be able to make the order acting under the inherent jurisdiction

The practical effect of this restriction is that a local authority is prevented from accommodating the child or obtaining the care or supervision of a child through a specific issue order. If the local authority wishes to accommodate, care for, or supervise a child, they must use their powers under the Children Act 1989, Part III, rather than use s 8 orders.

### (v) The courts will not normally make a PSO or SIO in relation to trivial matters

In *Re C (A Minor) (Leave to Seek Section 8 Order)*[63] Johnson J refused to give leave to apply for an SIO permitting a child to go on holiday to Bulgaria with her friend's family against her

---

[56] *Re H (Minors) (Prohibited Steps Order)* [1995] 1 FLR 638, [1995] 2 FCR 547.
[57] *Re D (Prohibited Steps Order)* [1996] 2 FLR 273, [1996] 2 FCR 496 CA; *Re D (Residence: Imposition of Conditions)* [1996] 2 FLR 281, [1996] 2 FCR 820.
[58] See Chapter 6.
[59] [1995] 1 FLR 638, [1995] 2 FCR 547.
[60] *Re B (Minors) (Residence Order)* [1992] 2 FLR 1, [1992] 1 FCR 555.
[61] [1993] 2 FLR 134, [1994] 1 FCR 624.
[62] [1995] 1 FLR 638, [1995] 2 FCR 547, discussed in M. Roberts (1995).
[63] [1994] 1 FLR 26.

parents' wishes. This was held to be too trivial an issue to be suitable for a s 8 order. If going on holiday is too trivial an issue for an SIO, many other questions that may concern a child or non-residential parent (such as whether the child has to eat green vegetables) can also be seen as too trivial.[64] Section 8 orders should deal with issues of great significance in the child's life, such as where the child is to go to school or whether he or she should have a medical operation. However, there is nothing in the wording of the statute to suggest that s 8 orders should not deal with what might appear to be trivial matters. A court might feel it is appropriate to deal with a 'trivial issue' (for example, what hairstyle the child should have)[65] if the issue has come to dominate the parents' and child's relationship to such an extent that it is harming the child. For example, in *M v M (Specific Issue: Choice of School)*[66] although attending the voice test for the cathedral school appeared minor, without attending the test he had no hope of a scholarship and hence the case was in reality about where the child would attend school.[67] So the better view is that SIOs or PSOs can be made in relation to trivial issues, but only rarely will it be appropriate to do so.

### (vi) The orders must be in precise terms

A prohibited steps or specific issue order must be in clear terms. An order prohibiting the publishing of 'any information' about two children was found to be in too general terms and restricted by the Court of Appeal to information that identified the children.[68]

### (vii) Only residence orders are available if the child is in care

Under s 9(1) of the Children Act 1989 the only s 8 order that can be applied for if a child is in care is a residence order. The reasoning is that the local authority, rather than the court, should make decisions relating to the upbringing of a child in care.[69]

### (viii) There may be restrictions on s 8 orders where the child is competent

There is some dispute over whether a PSO can overrule the decision of a competent child. For example, if a competent child and doctor agree on a form of contraception, could a court make a PSO to prevent the doctor providing the contraception? One view is that the PSO can only prevent an exercise of parental responsibility. As a parent cannot overrule the consent of a competent child to such treatment, neither can a PSO.[70] The opposite view is that the PSO can overrule the wishes of a competent minor because the definition of a PSO in s 8(1) refers to the decision that 'a' parent, rather than 'the' parent, could make. The best view of the present law is that the court is unlikely to make a s 8 order against the wishes of a competent child, but it is open to the court to do so if necessary for the child's welfare. Even if this view were not taken, it would still be open to the court to overrule the child's wishes through the use of the inherent jurisdiction.

---

[64] *Re C (A Minor) (Leave to Seek Section 8 Order)* [1994] 1 FLR 26.
[65] E.g. what time the child should go to bed: *B v B (Custody: Conditions)* [1979] 1 FLR 385.
[66] [2005] EWHC 2769 (Fam).
[67] Although in that case the child objected to attending the voice test and it is hard to imagine, therefore, much good would come from compelling the child to attend.
[68] *Re G (A Child) (Contempt: Committal Order)* [2003] 2 FCR 231.
[69] See Chapter 11 for further discussion.
[70] *Gillick v W Norfolk and Wisbech AHA* [1986] 1 FLR 229, [1986] AC 112.

## E Attaching conditions

When making any order under s 8, the court can attach conditions to the order. This power enables the court to 'fine-tune' the order. The conditions can give detailed arrangements as to how the order should be carried out. For example, there may be conditions stating where the contact is to take place. There is a fine balance here between encouraging the parties to be flexible and resolve minor issues between themselves, and making the order sufficiently detailed that it is clear what is required. Section 11(7) provides that an order under s 8 can:

---

### LEGISLATIVE PROVISION

**Children Act 1989, section 11(7)**

(a) contain directions about how it is to be carried into effect;

(b) impose conditions which must be complied with by any person—

    (i) in whose favour the order is made;
    (ii) who is a parent of the child concerned;
    (iii) who is not a parent of his but who has parental responsibility for him; or
    (iv) with whom the child is living,

    and to whom the conditions are expressed to apply;

(c) be made to have effect for a specified period, or contain provisions which are to have effect for a specified period;

(d) make such incidental, supplemental or consequential provision as the court thinks fit.

---

It will be noted that the conditions do not necessarily apply to the person who has the benefit of the s 8 order. They might bind the partner of the person who has the benefit of a contact order, for example. However, the power to attach conditions is not as wide as it might at first appear, and the courts have developed a number of restrictions on the use of the power:

1. Conditions are intended to be supplemental to the s 8 order and should not be used as the primary purpose of the order.[71] Hence a Jewish wife failed in an application for a condition to be attached to a contact order that a husband provided her with a *get* so that she could obtain a religious divorce. It was held that this condition would not be appropriate as it was not supplemental to a contact order and was raising a completely new issue.[72]

2. The condition must not be incompatible with the main order. In ***Birmingham CC v H***[73] Ward J said that a residence order could not contain a condition that the mother had to live at a specialised unit for mothers and children and comply with reasonable instructions from the staff at the unit. The court explained that the basis of a residence order is that the person with the benefit of the order can choose where the child should live and how to raise the child; the condition was inconsistent with both of these. In ***Re S (Children)***[74] the Court of Appeal considered a condition on a contact order which said: 'it is a condition of the contact . . . that the children have to decide for each contact whether to take it up or not'. In effect the condition meant that the children decided whether the

---

[71] *Re D (Prohibited Steps Order)* [1996] 2 FLR 273, [1996] 2 FCR 496.
[72] *N v N (Jurisdiction: Pre-Nuptial Agreement)* [1999] 2 FLR 745.
[73] [1992] 2 FLR 323.
[74] *Re S (Children)* [2010] EWCA Civ 447.

contact order had any effect. While the Court of Appeal did not say such a condition was impermissible Thorpe LJ described it as 'highly unusual' and held it was inappropriate on the facts of the case.

3. The condition cannot affect the fundamental rights of a parent. In *Re E (Residence: Imposition of Conditions)*[75] the judge sought to impose a condition on a residence order that the mother remain at a particular address. This was held by the Court of Appeal to be an inappropriate use of a condition, as it limited the mother's right to choose where to live.[76] However, in *Re S (A Child) (Residence Order: Condition) (No. 2)*[77] the Court of Appeal took the view that, in the truly exceptional circumstances of the case before it, it was permissible for the judge to make a residence order prohibiting the mother from moving to Cornwall to be with her new partner.[78] The exceptional circumstances were that the child in question suffered from Down Syndrome and other complications. She had a very good relationship with the mother and father. The judge was concerned that if the mother moved to Cornwall this would have the effect of dramatically reducing the contact between the father and child. The daughter would lack the capacity to understand why this had happened and would therefore suffer great distress. The condition was therefore necessary in the interests of the child, even though the condition would cause a significant infringement into the rights of the mother.[79] Another 'highly exceptional' case which justified restricting the mother's freedom of movement was *B v B (Residence: Condition Limiting Geographical Area)*[80] where it was held that the mother was wanting to move to Newcastle simply to frustrate the father's contact with the child. In *Re G (Children) (Residence: Same-Sex Partner)*[81] Baroness Hale confirmed that orders restricting where a parent should live are generally regarded as an unwarranted imposition on the right of the parent, although they can be justified in exceptional cases. However, if the child is subject to a shared residence order, but one of the parents wishes to move with the child to another part of the country then the court could make an order prohibiting the move if doing so would be in the child's best interests.[82]

In *Re D (Residence: Imposition of Conditions)*[83] children were returned to the mother under a residence order with a condition that the children should not be brought into contact with her partner and that her partner should not reside with her and the children. The Court of Appeal allowed an appeal against the imposition of the condition. Ward LJ explained that:

> the case concerned a mother seeking, as she was entitled to, to allow this man back into her life because that is the way she wished to live it. The court was not in a position so to override her right to live her life as she chose. What was before the court was whether, if she chose to have him back, the proper person with whom the children should reside was herself or whether it would be better for the children that they lived with their father or with the grandmother.

[75] [1997] 2 FLR 638, [1997] 3 FCR 245. Two other examples are *Re D (Residence: Imposition of Conditions)* [1996] 2 FLR 281, [1996] 2 FCR 820 CA; and *D v N (Contact Order: Conditions)* [1997] 2 FLR 797, [1997] 3 FCR 721.
[76] See *Re B (Prohibited Steps Order)* [2007] EWCA Civ 1055 where the Court of Appeal emphasised that only in the most exceptional cases could a condition restricting where the resident parent lived be imposed.
[77] [2003] 1 FCR 138.
[78] See for other examples *Re H (Children) (Residence Order: Condition)* [2001] 3 FCR 182; and *Mr E v Mrs E* [2006] EWCA Civ 843.
[79] This case is also discussed in Herring (2005b).
[80] [2004] 2 FLR 979.
[81] [2006] UKHL 43 at para 15.
[82] *E v E (Residence: Relocation: Ancillary Relief)* [2006] EWCA Civ 843.
[83] [1996] 2 FCR 820 at p. 825.

In other words, the court should not use conditions attached to residence orders to 'perfect' a parent. Instead, in deciding who should have a residence order, the court should choose between the parents as they are.

4. The condition cannot be used as a back-door route to obtaining an order that is available under other pieces of legislation. So in *D v N (Contact Order: Conditions)*[84] the Court of Appeal stated that it was inappropriate to use conditions to prevent the father molesting the mother, as such an order was available under the Family Law Act 1996.

5. The condition must be enforceable. In *B v B (Custody: Conditions)*[85] a condition that the child be in bed before 6.30 pm was struck out. There was no way that the court could realistically enforce such an order. Similarly, in *Re C (A Child) (HIV Test)*[86] the Court of Appeal agreed that it would be inappropriate to order a mother not to breastfeed her child, as this would be unenforceable.[87]

6. There is no power to use conditions to interfere with the local authority's exercise of its statutory or common law powers. So a condition cannot be used to require a local authority to supervise contact[88] or to exercise its powers in a particular way.[89]

### F Variation, discharge and appeals

It is possible to appeal against the granting of a s 8 order. However, it is clear from *G v G*[90] that there is no power in an appeal court to overturn a decision simply because it disagrees with the lower court's decision. It has to be shown that the lower court's decision was flawed in one of the following ways:

1. the lower court made an error of law;
2. the lower court relied upon evidence which should not have been taken into account;
3. the lower court failed to consider evidence that should have been taken into account; or
4. the decision of the lower court was 'plainly wrong'.

The aim is to provide a degree of certainty and to discourage appeals.

Section 8 orders can be discharged or varied. People who can apply as of right for a s 8 order can also apply for a variation or discharge of the order. In addition, a person can apply for variation of an order if the order was made on his or her application. A person who is named in a contact order can also apply for a variation or discharge of the order,[91] but that does not include the child who is the subject of the order.[92]

## 3 Who can apply for section 8 orders?

When considering who can apply for s 8 orders it is necessary to distinguish two separate groups of applicants: those who have the automatic right to apply for a s 8 order, and those who have the right to apply only if the court grants leave. The detailed law will be discussed

---

[84] [1997] 2 FLR 797, [1997] 3 FCR 721.
[85] [1979] 1 FLR 385.
[86] [1999] 2 FLR 1004.
[87] For criticism of this decision see Strong (2000).
[88] *Leeds CC v C* [1993] 1 FLR 269, [1993] 1 FCR 585.
[89] *D v D (County Court Jurisdiction: Injunctions)* [1993] 2 FLR 802, [1994] 3 FCR 28.
[90] [1985] FLR 894.
[91] CA 1989, s 10(7) states that additional categories can be added, although these powers have not been used.
[92] *Re H (Residence Order: Child's Application for Leave)* [2000] 1 FLR 780.

shortly but, generally, those who have a very close link with the child can automatically apply for a s 8 order. Anyone else must first seek the leave of the court to bring the application. Only if the court thinks there is an issue which requires a full hearing will it give leave for the application to be heard. If it thinks the application is frivolous or mischievous, the court will refuse to grant leave. The law in this area is seeking to strike a balance between making the court accessible to all those who have legitimate concerns about the upbringing of children, and protecting those who care for children from the stress of facing challenges to their parenting in the courts. The requirement for leave enables the court to filter out applications that the court thinks are inappropriate, without causing the residential parent the expense and stress of preparing a defence and attending the hearing.

## A Persons who can apply without leave

Those who can apply for any s 8 order without leave of the court are:

1. Parents. This includes an unmarried father without parental responsibility. It does not include former parents, for example those whose children have been freed for adoption.[93]

2. Guardians.

3. Those with the benefit of a residence order.

There is a special category of people who can apply without leave only for residence or contact orders. The explanation seems to be that the listed people have a sufficiently close relationship with the child to have a say in where the child should live (particularly where the parents have become incapable of caring for the child), but they do not have a right to have a say in the details of how the parent should bring up the child. Those who can apply for residence or contact orders (but not other orders) without leave are:

1. Any party to a marriage[94] or civil partnership if the child has been treated by the applicant as a 'child of the family'.[95] This includes step-parents.

2. Any person with whom the child has lived for at least three years, or a relative with whom the child has lived for at least one year.[96]

3. Any person who has the consent of

   (a) each of the persons in whose favour any residence order is in force; or

   (b) the local authority, if the child is subject to a care order; or

   (c) in any other case, each of the people who have parental responsibility for the child.[97]

## B People who need the leave of the court

Anyone else can apply for a s 8 order once they have obtained the leave of the court. This includes the child him- or herself. The one exception to this is local authority foster carers, who must have the consent of the local authority to apply for a s 8 order unless they are

---

[93] *M v C and Calderdale MBC* [1993] 1 FLR 505, [1993] 1 FCR 431.

[94] Even if the marriage has been dissolved.

[95] CA 1989, s 10(5)(a).

[96] CA 1989 s 10(5B). The period need not be continuous but needs to have started more than five years before the application and be subsisting three months before the making of the application.

[97] CA 1989, s 10(5)(b).

related to the child or the child has been living with them for at least three years preceding the application.[98]

## C How the court decides whether to grant leave

If it is necessary to obtain the leave of the court, the factors that the court will take into account in deciding whether to give leave depend on whether the applicant is an adult or a child.

### (i) Adults seeking leave

The factors to be considered are listed in s 10(9) of the Children Act 1989:[99]

---

**LEGISLATIVE PROVISION**

**Children Act 1989, section 10(9)**

(a) the nature of the proposed application for the section 8 order;

(b) the applicant's connection with the child;

(c) any risk there might be of that proposed application disrupting the child's life to such an extent that he would be harmed by it; and

(d) where the child is being looked after by a local authority—

    (i) the authority's plans for the child's future; and

    (ii) the wishes and feelings of the child's parents.

---

In *Re A (Minors) (Residence Orders: Leave to Apply)*[100] the Court of Appeal held that the paramountcy principle under s 1(1) of the Children Act 1989 does not apply when considering whether to grant leave. This is because the question of leave does not itself involve an issue relating to the child's upbringing.[101] The court can consider factors that are not listed in s 10(9), most notably the child's wishes.[102] In deciding whether or not to grant leave the courts must now take account of the applicant's rights under articles 6 and 8 of the European Convention.[103] This suggests that only where the application is thought frivolous, vexatious or otherwise harmful to the child will leave not be granted.[104] There is no need to show that the applicant has 'a good arguable case' before being granted leave.[105] Special considerations apply if the application concerns a child in care, and these will be discussed in Chapter 11.

It is clear that if leave is granted there is no presumption that the application will succeed at the full hearing.[106]

### (ii) Children seeking leave

This was discussed in Chapter 8.

---

[98] CA 1989, s 9(3).

[99] These do not apply to an application for leave following a s 91(14) application: *Re A (Application for Leave)* [1998] 1 FLR 1, [1999] 1 FCR 127.

[100] [1992] 2 FLR 154, [1992] 2 FCR 174.

[101] The Court of Appeal also argued that the criteria in s 10(9) would be otiose if s 1(3) applied.

[102] *Re A (A Minor) (Residence Order: Leave To Apply)* [1993] 1 FLR 425, [1993] 1 FCR 870.

[103] *Re J (Leave to Issue Application for Residence Order)* [2003] 1 FLR 114.

[104] *Re M (Care: Contact: Grandmother's Application for Leave)* [1995] 2 FLR 86, [1995] 3 FCR 550.

[105] *Re J (Leave to Issue Application for Residence Order)* [2003] 1 FLR 114.

[106] *Re W (Contact: Application by Grandmother)* [1997] 1 FLR 793, [1997] 2 FCR 643.

### (iii) Applying for s 8 orders in favour of someone else

It is not clear whether it is possible to apply for a s 8 order on behalf of someone else, although, as there is no statutory bar, it is presumably possible. Certainly an adult can apply for leave on behalf of a child.[107] It also seems that a child can apply for leave for a residence order in favour of someone else.[108] There is some debate over whether a local authority can apply for a residence order in favour of a third party. Such an application would fail if it were thought that a local authority was seeking to circumvent the prohibition on a local authority to apply for a residence or contact order themselves.

## D  Restricting section 8 applications: section 91(14)

One parent may be intent on pursuing applications against the other out of bitterness or desperation. For example, a non-residential parent may constantly apply to the court for SIOs relating to tiny aspects of the child's upbringing.[109] Repeated fruitless applications to the court could cause severe distress to the child and their carer, not least because each application must be defended in court.[110] In order to restrict such applications, the court under s 91(14) can require a party to obtain the leave of the court before applying for any further orders.[111] This way the child and their carer will not be bothered by having to defend an application unless the court has considered it worthy of a full hearing and granted leave. In *Re N (Section 91(14))*[112] a section 91(14) order against both parents was said to be required because the parties had been litigating for five years, causing the child serious anxiety and stress. A court can make a s 91(14) order whenever it disposes of an application for any order under the Children Act 1989. It is possible under the subsection to restrict only a certain kind of application: for example, applications for a residence order. A section 91(14) order cannot be made in relation to a child in care.[113] One interesting example of the use of the order was *K v M (Paternity: Contact)*,[114] where a lover was prevented from bringing further applications to establish that he was the father of a woman's child, after the woman had decided to remain with her husband and to raise the child with him. The court thought the use of the order necessary to prevent the spreading of rumours over the child's paternity.

A s 91(14) order is appropriate only where there is evidence that future applications are likely to be unreasonable, vexatious, or frivolous.[115] In deciding whether or not to make an order under s 91(14) the court should keep in mind, *inter alia*, the following factors:[116]

---

[107] There may be financial reasons for doing this, as the child may then be able to obtain legal aid: *Re HG (Specific Issue Order: Sterilisation)* [1993] 1 FLR 587, [1993] 1 FCR 553.

[108] So a child cannot apply for a residence order that he or she live by him- or herself.

[109] *Re N (Section 91(14) Order)* [1996] 1 FLR 356.

[110] *C v W (Contact: Leave to Apply)* [1999] 1 FLR 916. A resident parent improperly objecting to contact can also be ordered to pay costs: *Re T (A Child) (Orders for Costs)* [2005] 1 FCR 625.

[111] The order can be made even if the child is in care: *Re J (A Child) (Restrictions on Applications)* [2007] 3 FCR 123.

[112] [2010] 1 FLR 1110A.

[113] *Re M (Education: Section 91(14) Order)* [2008] 2 FLR 404.

[114] [1996] 1 FLR 312, [1996] 3 FCR 517.

[115] *F v Kent CC* [1993] 1 FLR 432, [1992] 2 FCR 433. So if there is no history of making inappropriate applications a s 91(14) order should not be made: *B v B (Residence Order: Restricting Applications)* [1997] 1 FLR 139, [1997] 2 FCR 518.

[116] A complete list of relevant factors is listed in *Re P (Section 91(14) Guidelines) (Residence and Religious Heritage)* [1999] 2 FLR 573.

1. The welfare of the child is the paramount consideration.[117]

2. It is a draconian order[118] which should be used sparingly and only as a last resort.[119] It should be regarded as an exceptional order.[120]

3. The court should weigh up the child's interests in being protected from inappropriate applications with the fundamental right of access to the courts: *Re R (Residence: Contact: Restricting Applications)*.[121]

4. The order is appropriate if there have been repeated and unreasonable applications.[122] However, the order can be made even if there is no history of making unreasonable applications,[123] but only if there is evidence that he or she will do so; otherwise, the order will be inappropriate.[124]

5. The order should be limited to only as long as it is necessary. A s 91(14) order made against a mother of an 8-year-old for five years was unnecessarily long.

If a s 91(14) order is made against a party, he or she can still apply for leave to make an application. The important point is that the hearing for leave will not require the attendance of the residential parent; indeed, they need not even know of the application.[125] This protects the residential parent from the worry that such applications may cause. If an application for leave is made then the test in deciding whether to grant leave is whether the application for leave demonstrates a need for renewed investigation by the court.[126] It is not possible to apply conditions to a s 91(14) order.[127] In *Re S (Children)*[128] the Court of Appeal allowed an appeal against an order which had said that a father could seek leave to apply for an order only once he had undergone therapy.

It might be argued that s 91(14) is inconsistent with the Human Rights Act 1998. However, the Court of Appeal explained in *Re P (Section 91(14) Guidelines) (Residence and Religious Heritage)*[129] that, as s 91(14) does not constitute a complete bar of access to the court but simply requires leave, it is probably consistent with the Act. Indeed, the European Convention itself includes similar provisions to prevent inappropriate applications to the European Court of Human Rights,[130] so it is unlikely that s 91(14) would infringe the Human Rights Act. However, in *Re B (A Child)*[131] the Court of Appeal suggested that to make a s 91(14) order that would last for the whole of the child's minority was a disproportionate infringement of the father's rights, given that the father had never sought to misuse court proceedings. It was held that the order should last only two years.

---

[117] *Re M (Section 91(14) Order)* [1999] 2 FLR 553.
[118] Butler-Sloss P in *Re G (A Child) (Contempt: Committal Order)* [2003] 2 FCR 231.
[119] *Re R (Residence: Contact: Restricting Applications)* [1998] 1 FLR 749; *Re C-J (Section (14) Order)* [2006] EWHC 1491 (Fam).
[120] *Re C (Litigant in Person: Section 91(14) Order)* [2009] 2 FLR 1461.
[121] [1998] 1 FLR 749.
[122] *Re R (Residence: Contact: Restricting Applications)* [1998] 1 FLR 749.
[123] *Re F (Children) (Restriction on Applications)* [2005] 2 FCR 176.
[124] *Re C (Contact: No Order for Contact)* [2000] Fam Law 699, [2000] 2 FLR 723.
[125] In *Re G and M (Child Orders: Restricting Applications)* [1995] 2 FLR 416 it was expressly ordered that the mother should not be informed of applications for leave.
[126] *Re A (Application for Leave)* [1998] 1 FLR 1, [1999] 1 FCR 127.
[127] *S v S* [2006] 3 FCR 614.
[128] [2006] EWCA Civ 1190.
[129] [1999] 2 FLR 573.
[130] Article 35, para 3.
[131] [2003] EWCA Civ 1966.

## 4 Children's welfare on divorce and relationship breakdown

The most common circumstance in which an application for a s 8 order is made is when the relationship of the parents breaks down. We will now consider the evidence of child psychologists that children suffer on the breakdown of their parents' relationship, and how the law responds to this.

It is widely accepted that, statistically, children whose parents separate are more likely to suffer in various ways than those whose parents stay together.[132] As one of the leading experts in the field, Martin Richards, has stated:[133]

> Compared with those of similar social backgrounds whose parents remain married, children whose parents divorce show consistent, but small differences in their behaviour throughout childhood and adolescence and a somewhat different life course as they move into adulthood. More specifically, the research indicates on average lower levels of academic achievement and self-esteem and a higher incidence of bad conduct and other problems of psychological adjustment during childhood. Also during childhood a somewhat earlier social maturity has been recorded. A number of transitions to adulthood are typically reached at earlier ages; these include leaving home, beginning heterosexual relationships and entering cohabitation, marriage and child bearing. In young adulthood there is a tendency toward more changes of job, lower socio-economic status, a greater propensity to divorce and there are some indications of a higher frequency of depression and lower measures of psychological well-being. The relationship (in adulthood) with parents and other kin relationships may be more distant.

It is important to appreciate what is *not* being claimed here. Clearly not all children whose parents separate suffer in these ways and some children whose parents do not separate do suffer in these ways. The point is merely that, on average, children whose parents separate are more likely to suffer these harms than those whose parents have not separated. In fact, only a minority of children whose parents separate suffer in these ways,[134] although they appear to be twice as likely to do so as children whose parents stay together.[135] It should also be stressed that although children whose parents have separated can suffer in these various ways, it does not necessarily follow that this is because their parents have separated. It may not be the separation that causes these problems, but the earlier tensions in the marital relationship;[136] or poverty connected to relationship breakdown; or society's reaction to separated families, although there is some evidence that the quality of parenting declines immediately following a divorce as the parents come to terms with lone parenthood.[137] Further, the research does not support the view that parents should 'stay together for the sake of the children'. Indeed, evidence suggests that children brought up in continually warring families do even less well than children whose parents separate.[138] There is also clear evidence that family beakdown affects the health of the parents.[139]

---

[132] Coleman and Glenn (2010b). Amato and Cheadle (2005) and Poussin and Martin-LeBrun (2002), although for a discussion on the limitations of such research, see Pryor and Seymour (1996). Coltrane and Adams (2003) express the concern that the statistics discussed here can be used for 'morality politics'.

[133] Richards (1997: 543); Pryor and Seymour (1996).

[134] Coleman and Glenn (2010b). Although nearly every child reports feelings of pain or distress at the time of divorce (Emery (1999)).

[135] Rogers and Pryor (1998).

[136] Kelly (2003). Notably, children who experience the death of a parent do not suffer in these ways to the same extent as children whose parents have divorced.

[137] Emery (1998).

[138] Richards (1994); Eekelaar and Maclean (1997: 53–7).

[139] Coleman and Glenn (2010b).

There do seem to be some factors that are particularly linked to the problems children suffer on their parents' divorce, namely: poverty before or after the separation; conflict before, during or after the separation;[140] a parent's psychological distress; multiple changes in family structures;[141] and a lack of high-quality contact with the non-residential parent.[142] Richards[143] suggests that there are steps that can be taken to lessen the harm caused to children on divorce. He argues that society should seek to encourage the maintenance of ties with both parents and kin; ensure adequacy of income for the child; reduce conflict over children involved; provide emotional support for parents; and limit the need for the child to move house or school.[144] As will be seen, these aims are pursued by the law only to a limited extent. There is also ample evidence that listening to children and keeping them informed during the separation process is important to their welfare.[145] Particularly significant is the way children are first told about the breakdown.[146] Research suggests that both children and parents avoid talking about the separation and this may exacerbate the harm suffered by children.[147] In an important study[148] children expressed the range of fears they felt when hearing of the parental separation. They were concerned at not only losing contact with the non-resident parent, but of losing friends or changing schools. Although children reported receiving support from their resident parents, best friends were found to be extremely important.[149]

One thing that is clear is that the behaviour of parents, especially on relationship breakdown, can cause children severe harm. Lord Justice Wall in *Re R (A Child)(Residence Order)*[150], a case where the disputes between parents had caused considerable emotional turmoil for the children, said the case reminded him of the poem 'This Be The Verse' by Philip Larkin which describes how your parents fill you with their own faults without meaning to, and even add some more just for good measure.[151]

He then explained:

> Separated parents, in my experience, frequently fail to understand that their children love both of them, and have loyalty to both. Such an attitude on the part of children is normally as it should be. The fact that one parent has come to hate the other, or that both hate each other is no reason for the child not to love both and have loyalty to both. It thus poses the most enormous difficulties for the children of separated parents when each parent vilifies the other, or makes it clear that he or she has no respect for the other.[152]

---

[140] As Wild and Richards (2003) emphasise, the child may experience conflict even though the parents attempt to keep the conflict under wraps in the presence of the child.

[141] E.g. living with a parent who has a number of partners during the child's minority.

[142] Rogers and Pryor (1998); Hawthorne et al. (2003).

[143] Richards (1994).

[144] See also Richards and Connell (2000).

[145] Rogers and Pryor (1998).

[146] Douglas et al. (2001).

[147] Douglas et al. (2001).

[148] Butler et al. (2003).

[149] Butler et al. (2003: 188).

[150] [2009] 2 FCR 203.

[151] Para 126. (Poem extract from 'This Be The Verse' by Philip Larkin, © the Estate of Philip Larkin, from *Collected Poems*, Faber and Faber Ltd.)

[152] Para 126.

# 5 How the court decides what is in the child's best interests: the checklist

In resolving any dispute relating to the upbringing of the child, the court must decide what is in the child's best interests. We discussed the general meaning of the welfare principle in Chapter 8. In this chapter we will explore how it is applied in particular cases. However, when doing so it is important to bear in mind the important observation of Baroness Hale:

> Family court orders are meant to provide practical solutions to the practical problems faced by separating families. They are not meant to be aspirational statements of what would be for the best in some ideal world which has little prospect of realisation.[153]

So, the courts are not concerned with what might be best for children in some mythical ideal world, but in the reality of the case before them. We need, therefore to be modest about what good court orders can do.[154]

Before looking at the kinds of issues that the courts have considered in deciding what will promote a child's welfare, the ways in which the court receives information about a child's well-being will be examined.

## A How the court obtains information on the child's welfare

Obviously not all children are alike and the arrangements which might promote one child's welfare will not benefit another.[155] Therefore the court needs to consider the position of each child before it as an individual. In deciding what is in the interests of the child's welfare the judge does not rely on his or her own instincts, but seeks expert advice.[156] Although the parties themselves are free to call witnesses to support their case, the court often needs independent evidence about a child and may seek a report, known as a welfare report.[157] The report is not requested in every case, but only when there is no realistic possibility that the parties can be persuaded to mediate the dispute.

These reports are normally prepared for the court by an appointed social worker or other expert.[158] The report considers issues over which there is dispute; the options that are available to the court; and, if appropriate, recommends a course of action. In preparing the report, the reporter should interview each party as well as the child. Normally quite a number of visits will be needed. The importance placed on the report means that great care should be taken in its preparation.[159] Often the report will be highly influential on the eventual outcome of the case, although it would be wrong to think that the court must follow the welfare report.[160] If the judge is minded to depart from the report, he or she should obtain oral evidence from the reporter.[161] The welfare report often records the child's wishes. However, there

---

[153] *Holmes-Moorhouse v Richmond-Upon-Thames London Borough Council* [2009] 1 FLR 904, para 38.
[154] Hedley (2009).
[155] Smart, Neale and Wade (2001: 166).
[156] In a private law case it is not possible to order a residential assessment of one parent and child against the wishes of the other parent (*R v R (Private Law Proceedings: Residential Assessment)* [2002] 2 FLR 953). This is possible in a public law case.
[157] CA 1989, s 7(1).
[158] CAFCASS (2005) discusses proposed reforms of CAFCASS.
[159] *Re P (A Minor) (Inadequate Welfare Report)* [1996] 2 FCR 285.
[160] *Re P (A Minor) (Inadequate Welfare Report)* [1996] 2 FCR 285.
[161] *Re CB (Access: Court Welfare Reports)* [1995] 1 FLR 622.

is increasing recognition of the desirability to the court of hearing the child's voice directly.[162] If necessary the judge can interview the child in private to protect them from the ordeal of appearing in court.[163]

There has been a growing interest in the right of children to express their views in any court case concerning their upbringing.[164] Indeed such a right is protected under article 12 of the United Nations Convention on the Rights of the Child 1989 and the European Convention on Children's Rights 1996.[165] There are, however, concerns that in problematic cases there may be difficulties in listening to children.[166] Children may not be used to being listened to by adults and find it disturbing talking to professionals.[167] One report on children's experiences of professionals depressingly concluded: 'Professionals may be perceived as inflexible, intrusive, condescending, deceitful and reinforcing in a myriad of ways their superiority to the child.'[168] Another research team found that children wanted a conversation with their parents about the separation, rather than being asked for a formal expression of their views.[169] A disturbing account of the way children's wishes were used by professionals and couples seeking to negotiate a settlement and thereby avoid a court hearing, showed that children's views were used as tools in the negotiation, rather than being the starting point of the discussion.[170]

## B The statutory checklist

When considering applications under s 8, the court must take into account the checklist of factors in s 1(3), in deciding what is in the welfare of the child.[171] The court is required to consider all the different factors and weigh them in the balance, although the court can also take into account other factors not mentioned in the list.[172]

There are contrasting attitudes towards the checklist among the judiciary. Waite LJ in *Southwood LBC v B*[173] referred to the checklist as an aide-mémoire.[174] To Staughton LJ in *H v H (Residence Order: Leave to Remove from the Jurisdiction)*[175] the checklist was not 'like the list of checks which an airline pilot has to make with his co-pilot, aloud one to the other before he takes off'. By contrast, *B v B (Residence Order: Reasons for Decisions)*[176] described going through the individual items on the checklist as a good discipline. Baroness Hale in *Re G (Children) (Residence: Same-Sex Partner)*[177] suggested that in difficult cases it would be

---

[162] Indeed this is required under article 12(1) of the UN Convention on the Rights of the Child. See further, e.g., in Smart and Neale (2000).

[163] *Re R (A Minor) (Residence: Religion)* [1993] 2 FLR 163, [1993] 2 FCR 525. For a fascinating discussion see Hunter (2008).

[164] Lowe and Murch (2003); Murch (2003).

[165] To which the UK is not a signatory.

[166] For encouraging evidence that courts are now more willing to listen to the views of mature children see Smart and May (2004a). See HM Inspectorate of Court Administration (2005) for suggestions as to how courts can improve even further their involvement of children.

[167] Lowe and Murch (2003: 18–19).

[168] Neale and Smart (1999: 33).

[169] Smart, Neale and Wade (2001: 169).

[170] Trinder, Jenks, and Firth (2010).

[171] CA 1989, s 1(4).

[172] Baroness Hale in *Re G (Children) (Residence: Same-Sex Partner)* [2006] UKHL 43 at para 40.

[173] [1993] 2 FLR 559 at p. 573.

[174] Magistrates use a pro forma listing the factors to guide their reasoning: *R v Oxfordshire CC (Secure Accommodation Order)* [1992] Fam 150 at p. 160.

[175] [1995] 1 FLR 529 at p. 532.

[176] [1997] 2 FLR 602.

[177] [2006] UKHL 43 at para 40.

helpful to consider each item of the checklist. This suggests that the exact use of the checklist differs from judge to judge. What is clear is that if it can be shown that a judge failed to take into account one of the factors on the checklist which was relevant to the case in hand, then the decision would be liable to be overturned on appeal.

The various factors listed in s 1(3) will now be considered.

### (i) The ascertainable wishes and feelings of the child concerned (considered in the light of his age and understanding)[178]

The child's wishes are only one of the factors to be taken into account, but where the child is mature it is likely to be the most important factor.[179] Sturge and Glaser, two leading psychologists, suggest that the wishes of children under the age of 6 should be regarded as indistinguishable from the wishes of the main carer, and the wishes of children over 10 should carry considerable weight, while those between 6 and 10 are at an intermediate state.[180] In *Re R (A Child) (Residence Order: Treatment of Child's Wishes)*[181] the Court of Appeal criticised a judge who failed to attach sufficient weight to a child aged 10. In deciding whether a child's views should be taken into account the court will consider whether the child is competent.[182] 'Full and generous' weight should be given to a mature child's wishes.[183]

Baroness Hale has explained why she regards hearing the views of children important:

> . . . there is now a growing understanding of the importance of listening to the children involved in children's cases. It is the child, more than anyone else, who will have to live with what the court decides. Those who do listen to children understand that they often have a point of view which is quite distinct from that of the person looking after them. They are quite capable of being moral actors in their own right. Just as the adults may have to do what the court decides whether they like it or not, so may the child. But that is no more a reason for failing to hear what the child has to say than it is for refusing to hear the parents' views.[184]

Even if a judge believes the child to be mistaken, it may still be appropriate to follow the child's views. There are two reasons why a judge may do this. First, there are practical considerations. If a teenager insists on not living with a particular parent then the child may simply ignore any court order awarding residence to that parent. There will be little point in making an order that the child will simply disobey. Secondly, the judge may also believe that it is beneficial for the child to learn from his or her mistakes. Indeed, it may damage a child psychologically to ignore his or her wishes. As Butler-Sloss LJ has argued:[185] 'nobody should dictate to children of this age, because one is dealing with their emotions, their lives, and they are not packages to be moved around. They are people entitled to be treated with respect.' That is not to say that the wishes of a mature minor can never be overridden, because the welfare principle is the paramount criterion.[186] There have, for example, been several cases

---

[178] CA 1989, s 1(3)(a).

[179] *B v B (M v M) (Transfer of Custody: Appeal)* [1987] 2 FLR 146; *Re T (Abduction: Child's Objections to Return)* [2000] 2 FLR 193. UN Convention on the Rights of the Child, article 12, requires the court to give due weight to children's views in accordance with their age and maturity; discussed in Parkes (2009).

[180] Sturge and Glaser (2000: 624). See also Parkinson and Cashmore (2010).

[181] [2009] 2 FCR 572.

[182] *Re S (Change of Surname)* [1999] 1 FLR 672.

[183] *Re H (Residence Order: Child's Application for Leave)* [2000] 1 FLR 780.

[184] *Re D (A Child) (Abduction: Rights of Custody)* [2006] UKHL 51, para 57.

[185] *Re S (Minors) (Access: Religious Upbringing)* [1992] 2 FLR 313 at p. 321.

[186] *Re P (A Minor) (Education)* [1992] 1 FLR 316, [1992] FCR 145. Contrast the position in Finland where children over the age of 12 can veto court decisions concerning residence and access (the Finnish law is conveniently summarised in *K and T v Finland* [2000] 2 FLR 79).

where the court has approved the provision of life-saving medical treatment, despite the opposition of the teenager who needed it.[187] In *C v Finland*[188] the European Court of Human Rights criticised the Finnish Supreme Court for placing 'exclusive weight' on the views of children aged 14 and 12 about whether they wished to live with their father or step-father following their mother's death. This suggests that a court which decided a case by following a child's views without any consideration of the wider issues could be open to a human rights challenge. By contrast in *Damnjanović v Serbia*[189] the ECtHR held that refusal of the children to leave the father justified not enforcing a residence order.

When the court considers the views of the child it will have regard to the following factors:

1. The weight to be attached to the child's views will depend on the maturity of the child.[190] In *Re B (Minors) (Change of Surname)*[191] it was held that it would be exceptional for a court to make orders contrary to the wishes of a teenager.[192] The Children Act states that the facts of the case must be exceptional before an order can be made in respect of children over 16.[193] In *Re S (Contact: Children's Views)*[194] Tyrer J followed the views of a 16- and a 14-year-old stating that their views were carefully thought out. He stated that if the law required young people to respect the law then the law must respect them. This might even mean permitting them to make mistakes.[195]

2. The importance of the issue is clearly relevant. The more important the issue, the more willing the court may be to overrule the wishes of a child. For example, if the child refuses to consent to medical treatment which would save his or her life, the court will readily override the child's decision.[196]

3. The courts are also concerned with the possibility that an adult may heavily influence the views of the child.[197] So before attaching weight to the child's views, the court will try to ensure that they truly are the views of the child and he or she is not simply repeating what they have been told by one of their parents.[198] In *Puxty v Moore*[199] Thorpe LJ, when considering the fact that a 9½-year-old girl wanted to live with her mother, noted she was influenced by the fact her mother had bought her a pony. In *Re M (Intractable Contact Dispute: Court's Positive Duty)*[200] the opposition of a 15-year-old girl and 13-year-old boy to contact with their mother was not given great weight because 'their understanding in this case is corrupted by the malignancy of the views, with which they have been force-fed [by the father] over many years of their life, until so blinded by them that they cannot see the truth either of their mother's good qualities or of the good it will do them to have some contact with her'.

---

[187] *Re M (Medical Treatment: Consent)* [1999] 2 FLR 1097.

[188] [2006] 2 FCR 195.

[189] [2009] 1 FLR 339.

[190] A 9-year-old's wishes were overridden in *Re R (A Minor) (Residence: Religion)* [1993] 2 FLR 163, [1993] 2 FCR 525.

[191] [1996] 1 FLR 791, [1996] 2 FCR 304.

[192] See also *Re M (Intractable Contact Dispute: Court's Positive Duty)* [2006] 1 FLR 627.

[193] CA 1989, s 9(6), (7).

[194] [2002] 1 FLR 1156.

[195] See also *Re W (Children) (Leave to Remove)* [2008] 2 FCR 420 where the Court of Appeal overturned a judgment in which it was held insufficient weight had been attached to the views of children aged 15, 13 and 11.

[196] *Re M (Medical Treatment: Consent)* [1999] 2 FLR 1097.

[197] *Re S (Transfer of Residence)* [2010] 1 FLR 1785.

[198] There are particular concerns where the child has been the victim of sexual abuse: see Jones and Parkinson (1995).

[199] [2005] EWCA Civ 1386.

[200] [2006] 1 FLR 627 at para 26.

4. There is some psychological evidence that requiring children to choose between parents is very harmful.[201] The court will readily be prepared to accept that the child has no wishes in such cases.[202] Interestingly, in one study only 55 per cent of children interviewed said they would like to have been asked whether they would prefer to live with their mother or father after the separation of their parents.[203] Another study reported that many children wanted to talk to the family court welfare officer, but did not want them to tell their parents or the court what they had said, largely for fear that to do so would hurt a parent they loved.[204]

5. The court will wish to examine the basis of the child's views. In *Re M (A Minor) (Family Proceedings: Affidavits)*[205] the wishes of a 12-year-old girl to live with her father were over-ridden because her decision was based on occasional visits to her father while she lived with her grandparents. It was felt that her occasional visits did not give her a clear view of what life with her father would be like.[206] The case indicates that where a child has a strong view based on factual error, the court will readily override that view. The courts have also expressed a concern that children may put undue weight on short-term gains and not take a long-term view of their welfare.[207]

The court may be able to find the child's views by means of a welfare report; although in one recent study it was found that some officers, admittedly a minority, rather than reporting the child's views, were reporting what they thought the child should want.[208] However, in difficult cases it may be appropriate for the child to be separately represented by his or her own counsel.[209] The National Youth Advocacy Service (a charitable organisation that helps children during family breakdown and can offer legal representation) and other organisations can assist with the legal representation of children in court cases.[210] It might even be appropriate in some cases for the judge to talk directly to the children.[211] This might remedy the widespread perception elicited by one study of children involved in private law cases concerning them, that, although they were listened to, they were not involved in the decision-making process.[212] Other studies have found that practitioners lack the skills necessary to listen effectively to children.[213] Ocassionally a judge will meet the child.[214]

Of course, what has been said so far deals with cases which reach the courts. Where the dispute is resolved without recourse to the court process children may have little voice in what happens to them. Remarkably, 45 per cent of children in one study said that on the breakdown of their parents' relationship they were not asked whether they preferred to live with their mother or father.[215] Recently CAFCASS officers have been told to focus on assisting

---

[201] King (1987: 190). Such an argument was influential in *Re A (Specific Issue Order: Parental Dispute)* [2001] 1 FLR 121.
[202] Schofield (1998).
[203] Douglas et al. (2001).
[204] Bretherton (2002).
[205] [1995] 2 FLR 100, [1995] 2 FCR 90.
[206] In particular, she did not appreciate that she might have to do a lot of housework!
[207] *Re C (A Minor) (Care: Children's Wishes)* [1993] 1 FLR 832, [1993] 1 FCR 810.
[208] Douglas (2006c).
[209] *Re A (A Child) (Separate Representation in Contact Proceedings)* [2001] 2 FCR 55.
[210] *Re H (A Child)* [2006] EWCA Civ 896; *Re A-H (Contact Order)* [2008] EWCA Civ 630.
[211] See *Re W (Children) (Leave to Remove)* [2008] 2 FCR 420 where there was a division of opinion over when and how the judge should talk to the children.
[212] Bretherton (2002); Douglas et al. (2006).
[213] Sawyer (1995); O'Quigley (1999).
[214] Family Justice Council (2010).
[215] Douglas et al. (2001).

parents to reach an agreement and so avoid a court hearing. Ironically this may well mean that children's voices will be heard even less.[216]

### (ii) The child's physical, emotional and educational needs[217]

In many cases the child's needs, together with the parents' capacity for meeting those needs, are the crucial issue. The emotional welfare of the child is particularly important.[218] The welfare report will consider the closeness of the relationship between the child and each of the parents. This might require the court to compare different styles of parenting. In *May* v *May*[219] the court preferred the father's parenting, partly because he stressed the importance of academic achievement, to the mother's more relaxed attitude towards school. As will be noted shortly, the courts have accepted that it is normally in the emotional interests of children to retain contact with both parents.

### (iii) The likely effect on the child of any change in his circumstances[220]

The courts have stressed the importance of maintaining the status quo for children if possible.[221] Changing children's schools and housing can cause even further disturbance for children at a time when their lives are already under stress. In practice, as empirical evidence shows, the court will normally confirm the presently existing arrangements for the child.[222] In effect, then, if a child has a settled life with one parent, good reasons will be needed to justify a move to the other parent.[223] This was stressed by the Supreme Court in *Re B (A Child)*[224] where it was emphasised that a child should not be moved from an arrangement which was thriving unless there was a good reason to do so.[225]

Indeed, in some cases the importance of maintaining the status quo has even been sufficient to prefer a third party over a natural parent[226] and to separate two siblings.[227] Of course, there are also cases where the status quo is disrupted, but they tend to involve fairly extreme factors, such as the drug-taking of parents.[228] Sometimes it is difficult to know what the status quo is. In *Re F (A Child) (Shared Residence Order)*[229] the children had been raised in Nottingham, but the after the separation the mother had taken the children for 12 months to Droitwich. The judge, upheld by the Court of Appeal, held that the children should live with their father in Nottingham as that was where they had been brought up for most of their lives and would reflect the status quo. The mother, of course, had argued that the staus quo was their living in Droitwich.

There are three particular concerns about placing much weight upon the status quo. The first is that it might encourage a parent to snatch their child from the other parent and then go into hiding, and later seek to rely on this principle. However, the courts have accepted that

---

[216] Fortin (2006b).
[217] CA 1989, s 1(3)(b).
[218] *Re J (Children) (Residence: Expert Evidence)* [2001] 2 FCR 44.
[219] [1986] 1 FLR 325.
[220] CA 1989, s 1(3)(c).
[221] *Re H (Children) (Residence Order)* [2007] 2 FCR 621.
[222] Smart and May (2004a).
[223] *Re L (Residence: Justices' Reasons)* [1995] 2 FLR 445.
[224] [2009] UKSC 5.
[225] [1998] 1 FCR 549.
[226] *Re B (A Child)* [2009] UKSC 5.
[227] *Re B (T) (A Minor) (Residence Order)* [1995] 2 FCR 240.
[228] *Re G (Minors) (Ex Parte Interim Residence Order)* [1993] 1 FLR 910.
[229] [2010] 2 FCR 163.

the status quo is not relevant if it is achieved by abduction.[230] The second concern is that there is a danger the principle will encourage the party with whom the child is living to delay the proceedings. There are now, however, various procedures that can be used by a court to speed up litigation if necessary. A third concern is that the status quo principle means that the parties in reality resolve the dispute between themselves when deciding where the child is to live while awaiting the court's decision, often not appreciating the significance of their decision.

### (iv) The child's age, sex, background and any characteristics of his which the court considers relevant[231]

These factors are likely to be of special relevance in choosing foster parents and potential adopters for children. The Children Act 1989 requires a local authority to take account of the child's 'religious persuasion, racial origin and cultural and linguistic background' in deciding what care arrangements are appropriate for the child. As we shall discuss shortly, there has been some debate in the case law as to whether girls are better looked after by their mothers and boys by their fathers.

### (v) Any harm which the child has suffered or is at risk of suffering[232]

Harm is defined in s 31(9): 'harm means ill-treatment or the impairment of health or development including, for example, impairment suffered from seeing or hearing ill-treatment of another'. The last 12 words of the subsection refer to the harm a child may suffer if aware of domestic violence in his or her household. The court, of course, would never make an order which it thought might place a child in a situation where there was a risk that the child would suffer harm. It has been made clear by the Court of Appeal in *Re M and R (Child Abuse: Evidence)*[233] that, before taking a risk into account, the court must find proved facts on the balance of probabilities which reveal that risk.[234] So the court must first consider what facts are proved. Once facts are proved, the next issue is whether those proven facts indicate a risk of harm.[235] The risk only needed to be of a real possibility of harm; it does not need to be shown that it is more likely than not that the child will be harmed.[236]

It is not always easy to tell whether an arrangement will cause harm to a child. In *Re W (Residence Order)*[237] the mother and her new partner had an uninhibited attitude towards nudity and were often nude in front of the children. The Court of Appeal thought the trial judge had been misled in assuming that this would harm the children. There was no clear evidence that the nudity would harm the children and so it should not have been taken into account. The risk need not be that the child will be directly harmed, but a risk of harm to someone close to the child (e.g. their primary carer) is often a risk that the child will thereby be harmed.[238]

---

[230] *Edwards v Edwards* [1986] 1 FLR 187.
[231] CA 1989, s 1(3)(d).
[232] CA 1989, s 1(3)(e).
[233] [1996] 2 FLR 195, [1996] 2 FCR 617.
[234] This is explained and discussed further in Chapter 10.
[235] *Re A (Contact: Witness Protection Scheme)* [2005] EWHC 2189 (Fam).
[236] *Re A (Contact: Witness Protection Scheme)* [2005] EWHC 2189 (Fam).
[237] [1999] 1 FLR 869.
[238] *Re A (Contact: Witness Protection Scheme)* [2005] EWHC 2189 (Fam).

### (vi) How capable each of the child's parents (and any other person in relation to whom the court considers the question to be relevant) is in meeting his needs[239]

This factor must be read in conjunction with the needs of the child. If, for example, the child has a medical condition requiring careful management which only one parent is capable of providing, this would be a crucial consideration.[240] In *Re M (Handicapped Child: Parental Responsibility)*[241] the father's inability to care effectively for his disabled daughter was fatal to his application for a residence order. The phrase 'other person' could include the new partner of the parent. The court may regard it as an advantage to the child to live in a two-adult household rather than a single-person one.[242]

### (vii) The range of powers available to the court under the Children Act 1989 in the proceedings in question[243]

The court has the power to make orders other than those sought by the parties.[244] The court, in considering an application for a particular order, must therefore decide whether the order sought would be better than any other order available under the Children Act 1989.

As well as the checklist of factors, the court must also take into account two further provisions of the Act which are relevant in deciding whether to make a s 8 order.

### (viii) The principle of no delay

Section 1(2) states:

---

**LEGISLATIVE PROVISION**

**Children Act 1989, section 1(2)**

In any proceedings in which any question with respect to the upbringing of a child arises, the court shall have regard to the general principle that any delay in determining the question is likely to prejudice the welfare of the child.

---

The legal process is notoriously slow, but the longer the court takes in cases involving children, the greater the uncertainty for the children and the higher the levels of stress felt by the parents.[245] It is therefore not surprising that the judiciary has been particularly critical of delay in family cases.[246] Indeed, article 6 of the European Convention on Human Rights may require a public hearing within a reasonable timescale, and so avoiding unnecessary delay is now required by the Human Rights Act 1998.[247]

The no delay principle in s 1(2) applies to all proceedings concerning a child's upbringing, except financial orders.[248] It should, however, be stressed that while delay is not necessarily

---

[239] CA 1989, s 1(3)(f).
[240] *Re C and V (Minors) (Parental Responsibility and Contact)* [1998] 1 FLR 392, [1998] 1 FCR 57.
[241] [2001] 3 FCR 454.
[242] *Re DW (A Minor) (Custody)* [1984] 14 Fam Law 17; *M v Birmingham CC* [1994] 2 FLR 141.
[243] CA 1989, s 1(3)(g).
[244] CA 1989, s 10(1).
[245] Lord Chancellor's Department (2002c).
[246] Ewbank J in *Stockport MBC v B; Stockport MBC v L* [1986] 2 FLR 80.
[247] *EO and VP v Slovakia* [2004] 2 FCR 242; *ZM and KP v Slovakia* [2005] 2 FCR 415; *Karcheva v Bulgaria* [2006] 3 FCR 434; *Adam v Germany* [2009] 1 FLR 560.
[248] See *Re TB (Care Proceedings: Criminal Trial)* [1995] 2 FLR 810, [1996] 1 FCR 101 for a discussion of how criminal and care proceedings should be co-ordinated.

detrimental to a child, unnecessary delay is.[249] There are occasions when delay may be beneficial. It might be important for there to be a delay in order that further crucial information can be obtained or for the parties' circumstances to settle so that the best long-term decision can be reached. But any delay should be planned and purposeful.[250]

This subsection on its own would probably do little to prevent delay. The Children Act 1989 gave more powers to the judges to speed up cases. In both private[251] and public[252] cases the court must draw up a timetable for the case and ensure that the timetable is followed. The timetable cannot be departed from unless the court grants leave.[253] The Law Commission set the goal for resolving cases within 12 weeks,[254] but this has not been met.[255] Practice directions have been produced which are designed to speed up the conduct of private proceedings.[256] There is a tension here between the desire to encourage speedy litigation and the desire to persuade the parties to settle without a court hearing. The faster the parties are propelled towards a court hearing, the less time there is for negotiation.[257]

## (ix) The no order principle

This fundamental principle is set out in s 1(5) of the Children Act 1989:

---

### LEGISLATIVE PROVISION

#### Children Act 1989, section 1(5)

Where a court is considering whether or not to make one or more orders under this Act with respect to a child, it shall not make the order or any of the orders unless it considers that doing so would be better for the child than making no order at all.

---

This provision emphasises that, before making an order under the Children Act concerning the upbringing of children,[258] there should be a demonstrable benefit to the child by making the order. If no positive benefit can be obtained by making the order then no order should be made. The Law Commission was particularly concerned that orders should not be made where parents were in complete agreement, and there was therefore no specific need for an order. This is sometimes referred to as the 'no order' principle. It can be argued that this principle is really just an aspect of the welfare principle: if an order does not promote a child's welfare, it should not be made. However, it was clearly thought necessary to stress this particular application of the welfare principle.

Some commentators have read more into s 1(5) and have suggested that it represents the principle of deregulation or non-intervention;[259] that is, that the subsection reflects the presumption that the parents are the best people to care for the child and they should decide

---

[249] *C v Solihull MBC* [1993] 1 FLR 290, [1992] 2 FCR 341.
[250] *C v Solihull MBC* [1993] 1 FLR 290, [1992] 2 FCR 341.
[251] CA 1989, s 11.
[252] CA 1989, s 32.
[253] Family Proceedings Rules 1991, SI 1991/1247, r 4.15(1), Part IV.
[254] Law Commission Report 172 (1988: para 4.54).
[255] Children Act Advisory Committee (1993: ch. 2).
[256] The Revised Private Law Programme [2010] 2 FCR 496.
[257] Bailey-Harris et al. (1998: 26).
[258] *K v H (Child Maintenance)* [1993] 2 FLR 61, [1993] 1 FCR 684 states that s 1(5) does not apply to applications under Sch 1 to CA 1989 for financial provision for children.
[259] See, e.g., Cretney and Masson (1997: 658).

what should happen to the child. Only if there are strong reasons should the law intervene. It can be said that this is in line with article 8 of the European Convention on Human Rights, which protects family privacy. However, other commentators stress that the statute itself does not suggest that there is a presumption that no order is best. Rather, it is neutral on the question of whether intervention is desirable.[260] All the subsection is saying is that it is necessary to show there is a positive benefit to be gained from making an order.[261] The disagreement over the meaning of the subsection is reflected in a study which found that practitioners and district judges took a variety of approaches to the sub-section.[262] In *Dawson v Wearmouth*[263] Lord Mackay interpreted s 1(5) to mean that a court should make an order only if there was some evidence that to do so would improve the child's welfare. In *Re P (Parental Dispute: Judicial Determination)*[264] the Court of Appeal stressed that if a dispute is brought before a court it must be adjudicated on and s 1(5) should not be used to abdicate responsibility. In *Re G (Children) (Residence Order: No Order Principle)*[265] Ward LJ explained: 'It does not, in my judgment, create a presumption one way or another. All it demands is that before the court makes any order it must ask the question: Will it be better for the child to make the order than making no order at all?'[266] Baroness Hale has commented: 'This means that there must be some tangible benefit to the children from making an order rather than leaving the parents to sort things out for themselves.'[267]

An example of the subsection in operation is *B v B (A Minor) (Residence Order)*,[268] where a child had been living with her grandmother for ten years. The grandmother applied for a residence order because she had encountered difficulties in providing consent to various school activities because she lacked parental responsibility. The court held that there were good reasons for making the order, even though there were only a few occasions when it would provide practical benefit. It was wrong to think that s 1(5) meant it was necessary to show that the making of the order would significantly benefit the child; it was enough if it was seen, on balance, as better to make the order than not to. The Court of Appeal has also warned of the dangers which might result from deciding to make no order simply because the parties appear to be in agreement. In *Re S (Contact: Grandparents)*[269] a grandparent sought a contact order. By the time the matter came to court, the judge was persuaded that the mother would permit contact, and therefore did not make a contact order, relying on s 1(5). The Court of Appeal felt that, having decided that it was in the child's welfare to have contact with the grandparent, the contact order should be made, even if the parties were in agreement at the time of the court hearing. The making of the order would ensure that contact did take place and avoid the need to return to court in the event of a disagreement. It should be stressed that this was a case where there was a history of antagonism between the parties and, therefore, there was a risk that the arrangement would break down. In *Re G (Children) (Residence Order: No Order Principle)*,[270] although the parties were in agreement after protracted negotiations, it was held appropriate to make the order so as to give the

---

[260] Bainham (1990: 221).
[261] As argued in Bainham (1998b: 2–4).
[262] Bailey-Harris, Barron and Pearce (1999); Doughty (2008a).
[263] [1999] 2 AC 308.
[264] [2003] 1 FLR 286.
[265] [2006] 1 FLR 771.
[266] At para 10.
[267] *Holmes-Moorhouse v Richmond-Upon-Thames London Borough Council* [2009] 1 FLR 904, para 30.
[268] [1992] 2 FLR 327, [1993] 1 FCR 211.
[269] [1996] 1 FLR 158, [1996] 3 FCR 30.
[270] [2006] 1 FLR 771.

mother peace of mind. If the parties have consistently been in agreement, s 1(5) may operate to make no order appropriate.[271] This reflects the practical reality that the role played by grandparents after divorce depends greatly on the relationship between the grandparents and children and parents before the divorce.[272]

If the court does not grant an order, it must be made clear whether the court is dismissing the application or is deciding to make 'no order'. This was stressed in *D v D (Application for Contact)*.[273] The actual number of 'no orders' has not been great. For example, in 2005, in relation to contact applications, 828 were disposed of by no order, while 76,759 orders were made.[274] That said, the number of applications for residence orders has fallen, especially when compared with the equivalent number before the Children Act 1989; so it may be that s 1(5) has the effect of discouraging applications.[275]

Now some of the issues which have caused the courts particular difficulty in applying the welfare principle will be considered.

## 6 Issues of controversy in applying the welfare principle

### A Is there a presumption in favour of mothers?

#### TOPICAL ISSUE

#### Are mothers preferred in residence cases?

One hotly disputed issue is whether there is or should be a presumption that children are better brought up by mothers rather than by fathers.[276] At one time it was thought that there was a presumption that babies and girls should be brought up by mothers, and boys by fathers.[277] It was made clear by the Court of Appeal in *Re A (Children: 1959 UN Declaration)*[278] that, although there is still a presumption that babies are better off with mothers,[279] with regard to other children there is no principle or presumption in favour of mothers or fathers.[280] The rule in relation to babies is partly based on the benefits of breastfeeding. The psychological evidence seems to support the view that there is no convincing evidence that girls are better off with mothers, or boys with fathers.[281] That said, there is some research that children prefer to be brought up by the parent of the same sex after divorce.[282]

Even though there is no presumption in favour of mothers, the sex of the parent can still be important in issues relating to children. Lord Jauncey, in the House of Lords in a Scottish case (*Brixley v Lynas*[283]), explained:[284]

---

[271] *Re A-H (Contact Order)* [2008] 2 FLR 1188.
[272] Douglas and Ferguson (2003).
[273] [1994] 1 FCR 694.
[274] Ministry of Justice (2009).
[275] Bailey-Harris, Barron and Pearce (1999).
[276] There is in fact little psychological evidence for this: see King (1974); Chambers (1984: 515–24).
[277] See *Re W (A Minor) (Residence Order)* [1992] 2 FLR 332, [1992] 2 FCR 461.
[278] [1998] 1 FLR 354, [1998] 2 FCR 633.
[279] *Re W (A Minor) (Residence Order)* [1992] 2 FLR 332, [1992] 2 FCR 461.
[280] See also *Re S (A Minor) (Custody)* [1991] 2 FLR 388.
[281] Downey and Powell (1993).
[282] Kaltenborn and Lemrap (1998).
[283] [1996] 2 FLR 499, [1997] 1 FCR 220, discussed in Sutherland (1997).
[284] [1996] 2 FLR 499 at p. 505.

the advantage to a very young child of being with its mother is a consideration which must be taken into account when deciding where lie its best interests in custody proceedings in which the mother is involved. It is neither a presumption nor a principle but rather recognition of a widely held belief based on practical experience and the workings of nature. Its importance will vary according to the age of the child and to the other circumstances of each individual case such as whether the child has been living with or apart from the mother and whether she is or is not capable of providing proper care. Circumstances may be such that it has no importance at all. Furthermore it will always yield to other competing advantages which more effectively promote the welfare of the child. However, where a very young child has been with its mother since birth and there is no criticism of her ability to care for the child only the strongest competing arguments are likely to prevail.

So the position seems to be that, although there is no legal presumption in favour of the mother,[285] the court will more easily be persuaded that the child is better cared for by the mother than by the father.[286] This is especially so in the case of younger children. Lord Scott has declared 'mothers are special',[287] but it is not quite clear what he meant by that. The Court of Appeal in **Re K (Residence Order: Securing Contact)**,[288] in awarding residence of a 2-year-old to a father, admitted that this was 'somewhat unusual'. Indeed, the research indicates that, on separation, it is far more common for children to live with mothers than with fathers.[289] In **Re N**[290] Munby J rejected an argument that there was a principle that 8-year-old boys should be raised by their fathers. The courts are wary of explicitly creating a presumption in favour of mothers, as this might constitute discrimination on the grounds of sex and so be in breach of the Human Rights Act 1998.[291] However, there is evidence that girls are particularly vulnerable to sexual abuse following divorce. Fretwell Wilson[292] points to a study which found that 50 per cent of girls living solely with their father reported sexual abuse by someone (not necessarily their father) and argues that these concerns must be addressed when the court is making decisions over residence.[293]

## B The 'natural parent presumption'

Where there is a dispute between a parent and a third party there used to be a strong presumption that: '[t]he best person to bring up a child is the natural parent. It matters not whether the parent is wise or foolish, rich or poor, educated or illiterate, provided the child's moral and physical health are not endangered.'[294]

The potential strength of the 'natural parent' presumption was revealed in the controversial case of *Re M (Child's Upbringing)*.[295]

[285] Stressed in *Re A (Children: 1959 UN Declaration)* [1998] 1 FLR 354, [1998] 2 FCR 633.
[286] *Re W (Residence)* [1999] 2 FLR 390.
[287] *Re G (Children)(Same-Sex Partner)* [2006] UKHL 43, para 3.
[288] [1999] 1 FLR 583.
[289] Trinder (2005).
[290] [2010] 1 FLR 272.
[291] Sutherland (1997).
[292] Fretwell Wilson (2002).
[293] Where allegations by a mother of sexual abuse are held to be unfounded by a court this does not, of course, mean that the mother will necessarily accept the court's findings: see *Re N (Sexual Abuse Allegations: Professionals Not Abiding By Findings of Fact)* [2005] Fam Law 529.
[294] *Re KD (A Minor) (Ward: Termination of Access)* [1988] 1 All ER 577 at p. 578. The Court of Appeal recently described this passage as being 'a bedrock of family jurisprudence' in *Re P (A Child) (Care and Placement Proceedings)* [2008] 3 FCR 243.
[295] [1996] 2 FLR 441, [1996] 3 FCR 99.

**CASE:** *Re M (Child's Upbringing)* [1996] 2 FLR 441, [1996] 3 FCR 99

The Court of Appeal had to consider what should happen to a 10-year-old Zulu boy who had been handed over by his parents to a white couple and raised in England for four years. The child had settled into life in England and expressed a strong wish to stay with the white couple. There was expert evidence that his immediate return to South Africa would cause psychological harm. However, his parents successfully applied for his return and Neill LJ in the Court of Appeal stated:

> Of course there will be cases where the welfare of the child requires that the child's right to be with his natural parents has to give way in his own interest to other considerations. But I am satisfied that in this case, as in other cases, one starts with the strong supposition that it is in the [child's] best interests . . . that he should be brought up with his natural parents.

The Court of Appeal therefore ordered his immediate return to the natural parents. The story did not end there because, following the court hearing and some unsuccessful attempts to force him onto the aeroplane, the boy was returned to South Africa. However, he failed to settle there and his family later consented to his being returned to the couple in England.[296]

However this presumption has been reconsidered by two important recent decisions of the House of Lords and the Supreme Court.

**CASE:** *Re G (Children) (Residence: Same-Sex Partner)* [2006] UKHL 43

A lesbian couple decided to have a child. One of them became pregnant through assisted reproductive techniques using donated sperm. In law the woman who gave birth to the child was the child's mother, but her partner did not have any parental status. The couple raised the child together. However, the couple broke up and a dispute arose over the residence of the child and contact arrangements. Initially residence was awarded to the mother, and the partner had regular contact. However, the mother removed the child to Cornwall in an attempt to prevent contact and in breach of court orders. The Court of Appeal held that residence should be transferred to the partner. In this case they had both raised the child together and were both the psychological parents of the child. The 'natural parent' presumption applied to them both equally, Thorpe LJ believed. However, in the House of Lords their Lordships re-emphasised the importance of the natural parenthood and Lord Nicholls stated that there needed to be cogent reasons for removing a child from a 'natural' parent, in this case the mother. He stated:

> In reaching its decision the court should always have in mind that in the ordinary way the rearing of a child by his or her biological parent can be expected to be in the child's best interests, both in the short term and also, and importantly, in the longer term. I decry any tendency to diminish the significance of this factor. A child should not be removed from the primary care of his or her biological parents without compelling reason.[297]

Baroness Hale explained that the fact that one of the parties was the natural mother was an important and significant factor to which the lower courts had failed to pay sufficient attention. However she rejected the view that there was a formal legal presumption in favour of the 'natural parent'.

---

[296] Freeman (1997b).
[297] See also *Re D (Care: Natural Parent Presumption)* [1999] 1 FLR 134 CA.

While the House of Lords in *Re G*[298] appeared to acknowledge that the biological link was an important figure, they did not use the language of a presumption. The Supreme Court returned to consider the issue again.

---

**CASE: *Re B (A Child)* [2009] UKSC 5**

The case concerned a 4-year-old boy, B, who had lived with his maternal grandparents since birth. His parents, who separated before B's birth, had not been able to care for him satisfactorily, although they were in regular contact with him. In 2009 the father married and had a child with his new wife. He sought a residence order in relation to B. A report from the social services stated that B was thriving with the grandmother, but also found that the father and his new wife could provide an adequate home for him. In March 2009 a residence order was made in favour of the grandmother, with staying contact with B's parents. This order was overturned in the Family Division, in an order upheld in the Court of Appeal. However, the Supreme Court affirmed the original order of residence in favour of the grandparents.

The central issue in the case was simple: what weight should be attached to the status quo and the good care that the boy was receiving from his grandmother and what weight should be attached to the possibility of the boy living with his father? Lord Kerr held that the error in the lower courts was to talk in terms of rights:

> We consider that this statement betrays a failure on the part of the judge to concentrate on the factor of overwhelming – indeed, paramount – importance which is, of course, the welfare of the child. To talk in terms of a child's rights – as opposed to his or her best interests – diverts from the focus that the child's welfare should occupy in the minds of those called on to make decisions as to their residence.[299]

Lord Kerr held that this led to the judge making the error of deciding that if the father's care was 'good enough' he should be preferred over the grandmother, even if she could offer a higher standard of care. Lord Kerr rejected that approach: 'The court's quest is to determine what is in the *best* interests of the child, not what might constitute a second best but supposedly adequate alternative.'[300]

This did not mean that Lord Kerr thought parenthood irrelevant in residence disputes. He was willing to accept that '[i]n the ordinary way one *can* expect that children will do best with their biological parents'.[301] But, as he then astutely pointed out, many disputes about residence and contact cases do not follow the ordinary way. He summarised his views thus:

> All consideration of the importance of parenthood in private law disputes about residence must be firmly rooted in an examination of what is in the child's best interests. This is the paramount consideration. It is only as a contributor to the child's welfare that parenthood assumes any significance. In common with all other factors bearing on what is in the best interests of the child, it must be examined for its potential to fulfil that aim.[302]

---

[298] [2006] UKHL 43.
[299] Para 19.
[300] Para 20.
[301] Para 35.
[302] Para 37.

Four points are particularly important about this decision. The first, is that their lordships decried the use of presumptions or rights. They preferred to look at the particular child and the particular relationships in issue, rather than rely on general assumptions or presumptions about what is good for children. Second, the case emphasised that the foucs of the court's attention is the child, and not the parents. However unfair the decision may appear to the father in *Re B*, the court's paramount concern was with the child. Third, it is remarkable that the Human Rights Act 1998 was not mentioned by their Lordships in *Re B* even once. This demonstrates how in section 8 cases this Act has had a fairly small impact. Finally the decision marks the demise of the natural parent presumption. Now the best we can say is that in deciding a residence dispute between a natural parent and a third party, the biological link is but one factor to take into account in assessing the child's welfare. In *Re G*, where the other factors were finely balanced, the biological link played an important role, but in most cases other factors will be decisive.

The decision has been fiercely criticised by Andrew Bainham[303] who decries the failure to recognise that parents do have rights in relation to their children, albeit rights that can be interfered with if necessary in order to protect the rights of children. He argues that our legal system does assume that a child is best cared for by a natural parent and this is shown by the fact that we do not routinely on birth check whether parents are suitable carers for a child or whether others may be better placed to care for the child.

Supporters of the decision will welcome the significance attached by the court to the strong relationship between the grandparents and the child. The quality of care provided by them and the strong emotional bond between them counted for more than the blood tie between the father and the child. The Supreme Court in *Re B* were not saying that the blood tie counted for nothing, simply that it was but one factor that needed to be taken into account alongside all of the others.

### C Is there a presumption that siblings should reside together?

The evidence of psychologists stresses the importance of the sibling relationship, especially on the breakdown of the parental relationship.[304] It is, therefore, not surprising that the courts have suggested that siblings should be kept in the same household unless there are strong reasons against this.[305] The same is true of half-siblings.[306] However, the further the siblings are apart in age, the weaker the presumption that they should stay together.[307] Of course, there still will be cases where the separation of the siblings is necessary. For example, in *B v B (Residence Order: Restricting Applications)*[308] the court decided that the mother should bring up two brothers, but the older brother simply refused to stay with the mother and lived with the father. The court felt that, as the older brother was intent on staying with the father and the younger brother had a close attachment to the mother, it was necessary for the brothers to live apart.[309] If the siblings are to live in different places, there is a strong

---

[303] Bainham (2010).

[304] Hill and Tisdall (1997: 85–9) and Edwards, Hadfield and Mauthner (2005), although in the study by Douglas (2001: 376) siblings were not found to be a significant source of emotional support on family breakdown and friends were far more important.

[305] E.g. *C v C (Minors: Custody)* [1988] 2 FLR 291.

[306] *Re H (A Child) (Leave to Apply for Residence Order)* [2008] 3 FCR 391.

[307] *B v B (Minors) (Custody: Care Control)* [1991] 1 FLR 402, [1991] FCR 1.

[308] [1997] 1 FLR 139, [1997] 2 FCR 518.

[309] See also *Re B (T) (A Minor) (Residence Order)* [1995] 2 FCR 240.

presumption that there should be contact between them.[310] It is clear that the relationship between two siblings will be regarded as family life and so protected under the Human Rights Act 1998.[311] This supports the presumption that there must be good reasons for separating siblings.

## D Racial and cultural background

Racial and cultural backgrounds are important issues which the court should not ignore.[312] Normally, a child should be brought up by carers who share his or her racial and cultural background. In *Re M (Section 94 Appeals)*[313] the Court of Appeal reversed the first instance judgment which did not consider the racial issues involved when denying a mixed-race girl contact with her father.[314] Although there may be concern that children who are raised by people of a different racial background to their own will suffer confusion,[315] these concerns can be lessened by arranging contact with relatives of the same background.[316] In *Re A (Children) (Specific Issue Order: Parental Dispute)*[317] the Court of Appeal approved of a judge's decision that children of a French father and an English mother should live with the mother, but attend a French school in London. This would enable the children to have close links with both aspects of their background. Despite these points, as was stressed in *Re A (A Minor) (Cultural Background)*,[318] racial and cultural issues are but one factor to be taken into account when considering a child's welfare. A child's racial or cultural interests will not be promoted at the cost of the child's overall welfare.

## E Religion

Disputes over the religious upbringing of children have a long history.[319] In one well-known eighteenth-century case, the poet Shelley was denied custody of his child on the basis that he was an atheist.[320] Nowadays the court would not deny a parent a residence order on the basis of their religious beliefs. Generally, if the child has no religious views, the present law is summed up in the dicta of Scarman LJ in *Re T (Minors) (Custody: Religious Upbringing)*[321] that the court should not 'pass any judgement on the beliefs of parents where they are socially acceptable and consistent with a decent and respectable life'. However, it may be that the court can be persuaded that a parent's religion is 'immoral and obnoxious' or inimical to good family life'.[322] In *Re B and G (Minors) (Custody)*[323] the court felt that this was true of Scientology, and ordered custody to the non-Scientologist parent. The court should consider

---

[310] *Re S (Minors: Access)* [1990] 2 FLR 166, [1990] 2 FCR 379.
[311] *Moustaquim v Belgium* (1991) 13 EHRR 802 at para 36. In *Senthuran v Secretary of State for the Home Dept* [2004] 3 FCR 273 it was held that adult siblings living together were capable of having family life together.
[312] *Re M (Section 94 Appeals)* [1995] 1 FLR 546 at p. 550.
[313] [1995] 1 FLR 546.
[314] *Re M (Child's Upbringing)* [1996] 2 FLR 441, [1996] 3 FCR 99 (discussed above) can be explained on these grounds.
[315] Gill and Jackson (1983).
[316] *Re O (Transracial Adoption: Contact)* [1995] 2 FLR 597, [1996] 1 FCR 540.
[317] [2001] 1 FCR 210.
[318] [1987] 2 FLR 429.
[319] For a discussion of the issues, see Taylor (2009); Hamilton (1995); M. Freeman (2003).
[320] *Shelley v Westbrook* (1817) Jac 266n.
[321] (1975) 2 FLR 239.
[322] *M v H (A Child: Educational Welfare)* [2008] 2 FCR 280, at para 30.
[323] [1985] FLR 493.

whether the religion involves practices that directly harm the child. So, for example, if the religion requires lengthy periods of fasting, causing medical harm to the child, then the court would be willing to take the parent's religious practices into account. The court might be willing to consider an argument that a religion caused the child to suffer social isolation[324] or indoctrination.[325] The court should always bear in mind that particular issues can be dealt with by means of a specific issue order. For example, the court should not be deterred from awarding a residence order to a Jehovah's Witness parent for fear that the parent might refuse to consent to a blood transfusion should the child require it, because if that issue arose the court could overrule the parent's decision by means of a specific issue order.[326]

Simply to deny residence to a parent on the basis of religious beliefs would be contrary to the Human Rights Act 1998 because the European Convention on Human Rights protects freedom of religion and outlaws discrimination on the grounds of religion.[327] In *Hoffman* v *Austria*[328] it was held that it would be contrary to the Convention for a state to deny custody to a parent simply because of her religion, although it would be permissible for courts to take into account the effect of any religious practices on a child. This approach seems in line with that of the English and Welsh courts,[329] although it is often impossible to distinguish a religion and its practices. To say 'the law does not discriminate against you on the grounds of your religion but on the grounds that you attend religious services' is to disguise the truth.[330] It may be more honest to accept that there are limits to religious freedom, and that discrimination against a religion that demonstrably harms children is permitted.[331]

If a child has religious beliefs[332] of his or her own the court is likely to make an order which enables the child to continue their religious practices.[333] Indeed, if the child has strong religious views shared by one parent but not the other, this might be a factor in that parent's favour.[334] If the child has religious views of his or her own, the residential parent could be required to permit the child to exercise their religious beliefs. For example, there could be a specific issue order requiring the residential parent to permit the child to attend religious services[335] or indeed preventing the parent from involving a child in his or her religion.[336] For example, in *Re T and M*[337] two boys were baptised as Roman Catholics and the mother converted to Islam. The mother wished to move the children from a Church of England school to an Islamic school. A prohibited steps order was made to stop the change of schools, although the mother was permitted to talk to the children about Islam. Such cases would now involve careful consideration of both the parents' and children's rights to freedom of

---

[324] *Hewison* v *Hewison* [1977] Fam Law 207.

[325] *Wright* v *Wright* [1980] 2 FLR 276.

[326] *Re S (A Minor) (Blood Transfusion: Adoption Order Conditions)* [1994] 2 FLR 416.

[327] Article 9 and article 14 respectively.

[328] (1993) 17 EHRR 293 ECtHR. See also *Palau-Martinez* v *France* [2004] Fam Law 412 and *Ismailova* v *Russia* [2008] 2 FCR 72.

[329] Adhar (1996).

[330] Bainham (1994c).

[331] See the general discussion in Mumford (1998).

[332] The court will focus on the religious practices of the child and will *not* automatically assume that a child acquires a religion simply through being born to parents of a particular religion: *Re J (Specific Issue Orders)* [2000] 1 FLR 517.

[333] *Re R (A Minor) (Residence: Religion)* [1993] 2 FLR 163, [1993] 2 FCR 525.

[334] E.g. *Robertson* v *Robertson* unreported 1980 CA, although that would be only one factor: *Re R (A Minor) (Residence: Religion)* [1993] 2 FLR 163, [1993] 2 FCR 525.

[335] *J* v *C* [1970] AC 668 HL (Protestants gave an undertaking to bring up the child as a Roman Catholic); *Re R (A Minor) (Residence: Religion)* [1993] 2 FLR 163 (where the Exclusive Brethren aunt was permitted contact on condition that she did not discuss religion).

[336] *Re S (Minors) (Access: Religious Upbringing)* [1992] 2 FLR 313.

[337] [1995] FLR 1.

religion in article 9 and private life in article 8 of the European Convention.[338] Even if the child does not have beliefs of his or her own as they are too young, the court may still take into account the religious heritage into which they were born. So, when a child who was born to an Orthodox Jewish couple was taken into care, then the court confirmed that the local authority should try to find Jewish foster parents and adopters if possible.[339]

Where the parents of a child have different religions there might be disputes over the religious upbringing of a child. If the child is not old enough to form his or her own religious beliefs the courts are likely to allow the resident parent to determine the religious upbringing of the child. In *Re S (Change of Names: Cultural Factors)*[340] Wilson J rejected the father's argument that the child should be raised as both a Muslim and a Sikh. Instead he should be raised in the religion of the mother (Islam), although he should be made aware of his Sikh identity and encouraged to respect Sikhism. Wilson J was persuaded that, having decided that the mother should have the residence order, the child would inevitably become integrated into the Muslim community of which she was part.

In *Re J (Specific Issue Orders: Muslim Upbringing and Circumcision)*[341] Wall J suggested that although the father might be able to claim to have his child circumcised in accordance with his freedom of thought, conscience and religion under article 9 of the European Convention, so too did the mother have the right not to have her son circumcised under the same article. In such a case, where two parents disagree, the Convention permits the courts to choose the approach which best furthers the welfare of the child. The Court of Appeal confirmed his approach and did not require the circumcision to be performed. In particular they rejected the argument that the child was a Muslim boy, arguing that the child was not yet old enough to belong to any faith.[342] In *Re S (Specific Issue Order: Religion: Circumcision)*[343] on separation there arose a dispute between a Muslim mother and a Jain Hindu father. The boy in issue was 8 years old, and had been raised by the parents as a Hindu. The children following separation lived with their mother, but had regular contact with the father. The mother sought permission to circumcise the boy in accordance with Muslim tradition and to raise both children as Muslims. The father opposed this as it was strongly against Jainist teaching. The Court of Appeal held that children raised with a mixed heritage should be allowed to decide for themselves what religion (if any) they wished to follow when they were older. Both parents should be allowed to teach the children about their religions.[344] The boy should not be circumcised, although when he was older he would be able to consent to a circumcision if that was what he wanted.

A powerful critique of the law's approach to minority religions has been presented by Suhraiya Jivraj and Didi Herman[345] who argue that unconsciously in these cases the judiciary are adopting a Christian perspective. In particular the assumption that religion is something that is chosen by an individual rather than being membership of a community reflects a Christian perspective on the nature of religious identity. Further, that the notion of attempting to raise a child in a religiously neutral way can be questioned, given must be understood in a society in which Christianty has a dominant position among religions.

---

[338] Barnett (2000).

[339] *Re P (Section 91(14) Guidelines) (Residence and Religious Heritage)* [1999] 2 FLR 573.

[340] [2001] 3 FCR 648.

[341] [1999] 2 FLR 678; approved in *Re J (Specific Issue Orders)* [2000] 1 FLR 517. Contrast in *Re S (Change of Names: Cultural Factors)* [2001] 3 FCR 648.

[342] For further discussion of how the religion of a child is ascertained see Van Praagh (1997).

[343] [2004] EWHC 1282 (Fam).

[344] See Eekelaar (2004) for an insightful analysis of children of mixed religious backgrounds.

[345] Jivraj and Herman (2009).

The issue of religious parenting has become controversial. It has even been suggested that where parents raise their children as members of a particular religion this is child abuse.[346] However a recent study of children raised by Christian and Muslim parents found children speaking positively about their religious upbringing.[347] The issue here takes us back to some of the arguments in Chapter 8 about the extent to which parents should, or can, provide a child with an 'open future'.

## F Employed parents

It used to be thought that a parent who stayed at home to spend as much time as possible with a child would be favoured regarding residency over a parent who spent substantial time in employed work. Such an approach tends to favour mothers over fathers; indeed a father who gave up work to look after a child was at one time criticised by a court for 'deliberately giv[ing] up work in order to go on social security'.[348] However, it seems now that a working parent will be slightly disadvantaged over a non-working parent.[349] In *Re Dhaliwal*, both parents originally offered full-time care of the child. However, during the hearing on residence the father explained that rather than offering the child full-time care he was about to take up a job which had hours from 9 o'clock in the morning to 6 or 7 o'clock in the evening. Thorpe LJ on appeal said: 'The whole balance inevitably tips significantly in favour of the mother's proposal once the father revealed that he would be heavily dependent on the unexplored availability of the extended family.'[350] In *Re R (A Minor) (Residence Order: Finance)*[351] the court preferred to make a shared residence order so that both parents were able to continue in employment, rather than giving sole residence to the mother, because that would mean she would have to give up her job which would cause financial disadvantage to the children and involve the Child Support Agency in the family's finances. However in *Re B (A Child)*[352] the Court of Appeal expressed very strongly the view that it was wrong in principle to let Child Support Act consequences affect residence or contact arrangements.

## G Sexual orientation of parents

> ### TOPICAL ISSUE
>
> ### Are gay or lesbian parents as good as straight ones?
>
> There have been several cases where the court has had to consider whether the fact that one of the parents is in a gay or lesbian relationship should have any bearing on a dispute over the residence of the child. The older cases suggested that this is a relevant factor: 'It is still the norm that children are brought up in a home with a father, mother and siblings (if  ➡

---

346 See the discussion in Taylor (2009).
347 Lees, and Horwarth (2009); Howarth et al (2008).
348 *Plant v Plant* [1983] 4 FLR 305 at p. 310. See also *B v B (Custody of Children)* [1985] FLR 166 CA; contrast *B v B (Custody of Children)* [1985] FLR 462.
349 Although see *Re B (Minors: Residence: Working Father)* [1996] CLY 615 and *Re O (Children) (Residence)* [2004] 1 FCR 169 where the court contrasted the care of a 'full-time mother' and the father who could only offer 'support' to the children's grandparents whom he proposed undertook the primary role of child caring.
350 [2005] 2 FCR 398, 402.
351 [1995] 2 FLR 612, [1995] 3 FCR 334.
352 [2006] EWCA Civ 1574. See the discussion of this case in Gilmore (2007).

any) and, other things being equal, such an upbringing is most likely to be conducive to their welfare.'[353] This was the approach taken in the case of *C v C (A Minor) (Custody: Appeal)*,[354] where the Court of Appeal had to decide between a mother who was in a lesbian relationship and a father who had remarried. It was noted: 'If [the child's] home was to be with the father that would be a normal home by the standards of our society; that would not be the case if the home were with the mother.'[355] More recently Black J in *Re M (Sperm Donor Father)*[356] has confirmed that a court could not ignore that there were special concerns where a child was being raised in a lesbian household, in particular about teasing at school and confusions a child may have about his or her background. However, in the Court of Appeal decision in *Re G (Children) (Residence: Same-Sex Partner)*[357] Thorpe LJ said that judicial attitudes towards homosexuality were very different today than they were 20 years ago.[358] He indicated that there should be no difference between a case involving a woman who had received assisted reproductive treatment with a partner who was male from where she was female. Indeed, notably, when *Re G (Children) (Residence: Same-Sex Partner)* went to the House of Lords the fact that the case involved a lesbian couple was not mentioned as a relevant factor in the legal debate. That, however, may have been unfortunate. Thorpe LJ, in the Court of Appeal, thought it unimaginable that, if there was a dispute over the upbringing of a child born using donated sperm between the mother and the father, the fact that the father was not the genetic father would be relevant. Why should it be any different if it is a same-sex couple? True, the partner of the mother will not have parental status under the Human Fertilisation and Embryology Act, but why should that matter?

The court must also consider the relevance of the Human Rights Act 1998. The European Court of Human Rights decision in *Da Silva Mouta v Portugal*[359] found that it was unlawful discrimination contrary to articles 14 and 8 to deny residence or contact to a parent on the ground of sexual orientation. The fact that a gay family was 'abnormal' did not constitute an objective or reasonable justification.[360] Whether concerns over possible teasing of a child will amount to a justification for discrimination remains to be seen; certainly, convincing evidence of it would be required before the court could take it into account.[361]

The court may wish to hear expert views on this issue. It is difficult to conduct research on how being raised by a gay parent affects a child, due to the relatively small number of children involved. However, the research to date does suggest that the courts are wrong to foresee any adverse side-effects. After a thorough review of the research, Golombok concludes: 'What the findings appear to suggest is that whether their mother is lesbian or heterosexual may matter less for children's psychological adjustment than a warm and supportive relationship with their parents and a harmonious family environment.'[362]

---

[353] Balcombe LJ in *C v C (A Minor) (Custody: Appeal)* [1991] 1 FLR 223 at p. 231.

[354] [1991] 1 FLR 223, [1991] FCR 254.

[355] [1991] 1 FLR 223 at p. 232. See also *B v B (Minors) (Custody: Care and Control)* [1991] 1 FLR 402, [1991] FCR 1. Tasker and Golombok (1991).

[356] [2003] Fam Law 94.

[357] [2006] EWCA Civ 372 at para 42. See also *Re G (Residence: Same-Sex Partner)* [2005] EWCA Civ 462 and *Re D (Contact and Parental Responsibility)* [2006] EWHC 2 (Fam).

[358] See further Leanne Smith (2006a and b).

[359] [2001] 1 FCR 653 ECtHR, discussed in Herring (2002a).

[360] See *G v F (Contact and Shared Residence)* [1998] 2 FLR 799 where it was held that there should be no discrimination against a lesbian applicant and that a mother and her lesbian partner should be given the benefit of a shared residence order.

[361] Concerns over teasing were seen as legitimate in *Re M (Sperm Donor Father)* [2003] Fam Law 94.

[362] Golombok (1999: 175). See also Golombok (2000), Patterson, Fulcher and Wainright (2002), Maccullum and Golombok (2004), Murray (2004) and Tasker and Patterson (2007) who likewise conclude that children do not suffer by being raised by a same-sex couple. But Morgan (2002) and Stacey and Biblarz (2001) argue that such studies fail to establish a convincing case and that it is wrong to carry out social experiments on children.

## H Disabled parents

The courts will take into account the abilities of parents to meet the needs of a child, and any disability of a parent will thus be relevant. In *M v M (Parental Responsibility)*[363] Wilson J decided that it would be inappropriate to give a father parental responsibility because he suffered from learning disabilities, aggravated by an accident, which meant that he would not be capable of exercising the rights and responsibilities of parenthood. Cases involving disabled parents must now be reconsidered in the light of the Human Rights Act 1998. Although the Human Rights Act does not explicitly prohibit discrimination on the basis of disability, it is arguable that it should be added to the list of prohibited grounds in article 14. The English and Welsh courts' approach is demonstrated in *Re V (Residence Review)*,[364] where a father suffered a collapse after witnessing the drowning of one of his children. He suffered post-traumatic stress syndrome and lost his job. The court decided it would be better for the child to live with the mother, although this was against the boy's wishes and the recommendation of the welfare report. The father had received severe head injuries which the court felt deprived him of the ability to react appropriately to the child. Direct contact would be dangerously destabilising to the child and therefore only indirect contact was deemed suitable.[365] It is suggested that, before taking such an approach, the court should ensure that a disabled parent cannot be enabled by the provision of suitable equipment or assistance to meet the child's needs. In *Re P (Non-Disclosure of HIV)*[366] Bodey J made it very clear that the HIV status of the mother was irrelevant to the residence/contact dispute between the parents. The mother did not need to disclose it to the father.

## I Poverty

The court should not place much weight on the fact that one parent can offer a higher standard of living than another.[367] This is explained on the basis that 'anyone with experience of life knows that affluence and happiness are not necessarily synonymous'.[368] Although this is true, if given a choice most children would rather their parents be rich than poor, all other factors being equal. In reality it is easier to explain the irrelevance of wealth on the basis that it would be unjust to distinguish rich and poor parents. The significance of this factor is lessened in relation to married couples because the court has the power to redistribute the couple's property.

## J The 'immoral' conduct of a parent

In general, the conduct of a parent will be relevant only if it affects his or her ability to be a parent. So, for example, the fact that a parent has committed adultery will nowadays, in and of itself, not be relevant to a dispute over residence or contact.[369] In *Re R (Minors) (Custody)*[370] the father had a drink problem and a criminal record and it was held that this affected his

---

[363] [1999] 2 FLR 737.
[364] [1995] 2 FLR 1010.
[365] See also *Re H (Children) (Contact Order) (No. 2)* [2001] 3 FCR 385.
[366] [2006] Fam Law 177.
[367] *Stephenson v Stephenson* [1985] FLR 1140 at p. 1148.
[368] *Re P (Adoption: Parental Agreement)* [1985] FLR 635 at p. 637.
[369] Although see Wardle (2002) for an argument that adultery should be a relevant factor.
[370] [1986] 1 FLR 6.

ability to be a parent. By contrast, in *Re P (Contact: Supervision)*[371] the fact that the father wore Nazi uniforms and had extreme political views did not mean that a contact order in his favour should not be made, as the court felt that this did not relate directly to his child-raising abilities.

It should be stressed that the court will not seek to achieve justice between the parents. So the fact that one party to the marriage may have behaved in a deeply reprehensible way and the other in an exemplary way will not necessarily affect how the court decides who is the best person to care for the child.[372] That said, the court will consider which parent is best able to bring up the child in the whole sense and this may include instilling moral values. It might therefore, for this reason, be open to a judge to consider a parent's lifestyle. However, as *Re W (Residence Order)*[373] (the case involving the nudist parent of a child) reveals, unless a particular way of life can be shown positively to harm a child, the court is unlikely to criticise it.

## K When is shared residence appropriate?

There are two situations where a court might consider a shared residence order.[374] The first is where it is intended that the child split his or her time between the two parents. For example, the child may spend alternate weeks with their mother and father. The second situation is where the primary purpose of the shared residence order is to grant parental responsibility to both parents. Lord Hoffmann has explained that joint residence orders are 'not unusual'.[375]

A shared residence order where the child is genuinely sharing his or her time between the two parents is not common, although it should not be regarded as appropriate only in exceptional circumstances.[376] In most cases the court will decide that it is better for a child to have the security of being based at one home. Also in many cases parents will after separation live in different parts of the country and so a joint residence order may not be practical.[377] Only where the shared residence order is in the interests of the child should it be made.[378] There is no presumption that a shared residence order should be made unless there is a good reason not to.[379]

A shared residence order is not appropriate if one of the parties lacks suitable accommodation.[380] Where the reality is that children are spending a roughly equal amount of time with each parent a shared residence order should be made to reflect that reality, unless to do so would harm the child.[381] Where the child has a good relationship with each parent and the child can move from one parent to the other without undue inconvenience (for example, if they live close to each other), the order may be suitable.[382] One interesting possibility is that

[371] [1996] 2 FLR 314, [1997] 1 FCR 458.
[372] *J v C* [1970] AC 668.
[373] [1999] 1 FLR 869.
[374] See Gilmore (2010) for a very clear summary of the current law.
[375] *Holmes-Moorhouse v Richmond Upon Thames London Borough Council* [2009] UKHL 7, para 7.
[376] *Re A (A Minor) (Shared Residence Order)* [1994] 1 FLR 669; *Re A (Children) (Shared Residence)* [2002] 1 FCR 177.
[377] *Holmes-Moorhouse v Richmond Upon Thames London Borough Council* [2009] UKHL 7,
[378] *D v D (Shared Residence Order)* [2001] 1 FLR 495 CA. See Weyland (1995), arguing that in practice the courts are reluctant to make the orders.
[379] *Re W (Shared Residence Order)* [2009] 2 FLR 436.
[380] In *Holmes-Moorhouse v Richmond-Upon-Thames London Borough Council* [2009] 1 FLR 904 it was held that a local authority cannot be required to provide accommodation to a parent simply because they have the benefit of a joint residence order.
[381] *Re A (Children) (Shared Residence)* [2003] 3 FCR 656; *Re P (Children) (Shared Residence Order)* [2006] 1 FCR 309.
[382] *Re M (Residence Order)* [2008] EWCA Civ 66; *Re A (Children) (Shared Residence)* [2003] 3 FCR 656. Dunn and Deater-Deckard (2001) found that children in such arrangements were very positive about them.

the child stays in one house and the parents move in and out.[383] A shared residence order is usually only suitable where there is a good relationship between the parents.[384] This is because, if a shared residence order is to work, it is essential that the parties can talk effectively to each other. However, in *Re R (Residence: Shared Care: Children's Views)*[385] the Court of Appeal emphasised that a shared residence order could be made even if there was hostility between the parties, if it would promote the children's welfare.[386]

One benefit of a shared residence order is that it may minimise the conflict between parents and rebut the all-too-common perception that disputes over custody involve a winner and a loser.[387] On the other hand, some express concern that a shared residence order is an ideal compromise for the two parents but not for the child, who can find it artificial and alienating.[388] There is particular concern if the child has to travel considerable distances between the two homes.[389] In *Puxty v Moore*[390] a 9½-year-old wanted to leave her father, who had residence for her, and move in with her mother. A shared residence order was made on the basis that denying contact with the mother altogether was likely to be counter-productive, as the child would not accept it, while granting shared residence might help prevent the mother from 'poisoning' the mind of the child against the father.[391]

An alternative reason for making a joint residence order is to confer parental responsibility upon one party. In *Re H (Shared Residence: Parental Responsibility)*[392] it was accepted that the child should live with the mother. However, it was felt that there was a strong case for the stepfather, who had brought up the child as his own and whom the child regarded as a father figure, to have parental responsibility. The court was willing to grant a joint residence order to the mother and stepfather primarily in order to give the stepfather parental responsibility, even though the child would spend most of her time with the mother. When a shared residence order is made for the purpose of conferring parental responsibility there is no need for the child to be spending an equal time with both parents, or indeed anything like an equal amount of time.[393] However, the court may balk at making a shared residence order if one of the parents is to have no contact at all.[394]

A shared residence order may also be used to reinforce the fact that both parents have an equal status. In *R v E and F (Female Parents: Known Father)*[395] a lesbian couple were raising a child born to one of them, using sperm from a friend. When the child was 5 there was a disagreement between the couple and the man who wanted greater involvement in the life of the child. Although the couple had already entered a parental responsibility agreement and

---

[383] Bridge (1996).
[384] *Re B (Leave to Remove)* [2006] EWHC 1783 (Fam); *Re R (A Minor) (Residence Order: Finance)* [1995] 2 FLR 612, [1995] 3 FCR 334, though see *Re D (Children) (Shared Residence Orders)* [2001] 1 FCR 147 for a case where the Court of Appeal held that there should be a shared residence order even though there was much animosity between the parents.
[385] [2005] EWCA Civ 542.
[386] See also *A v A (Shared Residence)* [2004] 1 FLR 1195 and *K v B and P* [2006] EWHC 1786 (Fam) where the bad relationship between the parents meant that shared residence was inappropriate.
[387] Bridge (1996).
[388] Macooby and Mnookin (1992); Baker and Townsend (1996).
[389] See *Re F (Shared Residence Order)* [2003] 2 FLR 397 for a case where a shared residence order was made despite the considerable distance between the two homes.
[390] [2006] 1 FCR 28.
[391] See Gilmore (2006) for a thorough review of the research evidence to date. He argues that it does not support a presumption of shared residence.
[392] [1995] 2 FLR 883, [1996] 3 FCR 321. See also *Re AB (Adoption: Joint Residence)* [1996] 1 FLR 27, [1996] 1 FCR 633.
[393] *Re W (Shared Residence Order)* [2009] 2 FLR 436.
[394] *Re A (Children) (Shared Residence)* [2002] 1 FCR 177 *Re H (Children)* [2009] EWCA Civ 902.
[395] [2010] EWHC 417 (Fam).

so both had parental responsibility, a shared residence order was made so that if the mother died, there would be no doubt that her partner (rather than the father) should care for the child. A shared residence order may also be suitable in a case where one parent is seeking to marginalise the other and the court wants to reinforce to separated parents that they both have an equal say in the upbringing of the child.[396] This argument can work the other way and form a reason for not making a shared residence order: if it is perceived that it would be used by one party inappropriately as a weapon against the other. As already mentioned, this justification is hard to support as the principle of shared parental responsibility underlines the fact that each parent has an equal say in the upbringing of the child. As Rob George and Peter Harris point out, there is a danger of having a multiplication of legal rules and court orders saying the same thing.[397] Indeed there are some signs that the courts are moving away from residence orders where the primary purpose is to reinforce the status of one of the parents. In *Re H (Children)* [2009] EWCA Civ 902 the Court of Appeal emphasised that shared residence orders are about where a child is to live and not about the rights and responsibilities of parents.

In *Re AR (A Child: Relocation)*[398] Mostyn J argued that shared residence was:

> the rule rather than the exception even where the quantum of care undertaken by each parent is decidedly unequal. There is very good reason why such orders should be normative for they avoid the psychological baggage of right, power and control that attends a sole residence order, which was one of the reasons that we were ridden of the notions of custody and care and control by the Act of 1989.[399]

This dicta seems to be contrary to the approach taken in most of the other case law. It also seems to ignore the importance of shared parental responsibility, and flies in the face of evidence that generally children in shared residence arrangements do less well than children with one primary residence.[400] It is hoped this approach is not followed, but it may herald a new era in judicial responses to shared residence.

It has been argued that the courts should adopt a presumption in favour of shared residence. However, that proposal seems to be motivated by adults' needs to be seen to be treated equally, rather than an assessment of what is in the child's best interests.[401] In the majority of cases both during a relationship and afterwards the mother undertakes the bulk of the care of a child. To use a presumption of shared care, where this does not reflect the reality masks the reality of the mother's care.[402] In Australia, where a presumption of shared residence has been enacted, mothers feel under great pressure to agree to shared care even in cases where there has been abuse.[403] Further, there is a particular concern that in many cases the presence of domestic violence or abuse will make any kind of shared residence order undesirable and dangerous.

A small-scale study by Neale, Flowerdew and Smart[404] of children living under a shared residence scheme showed a mixed picture. Some children valued the sense of fairness it created and the structure it provided for their lives. Others felt they were suffering inconvenience so that neither parent felt they had 'lost' and the structure of the order restricted their social lives.

---

[396] *Re W (Shared Residence Order)* [2009] 2 FLR 436; *Re A (Joint Residence: Parental Responsibility)* [2008] EWCA Civ 867. *Re P (Shared Residence Order)* [2005] EWCA Civ 1639.
[397] Harris and George (2010).
[398] [2010] EWHC 1346 (Fam).
[399] Para 52.
[400] Hunt et al. (2008).
[401] Daniel (2009).
[402] Barnett (2009).
[403] Rhoades (2010a).
[404] Neale, Flowerdew and Smart (2003).

Shared residence where the needs of parents were prioritised and which were inflexible in their structures worked least well.

## L Publicity

There has been a series of cases concerning publicity over children. The position seems to be as follows:

1. A child has a right to privacy. In *Murray v Big Pictures (UK) Ltd*[405] people who took photographs of JK Rowling's child in the street were held to have breached the child's privacy. The court took account of the child's attributes, the nature of what they were doing when photographed, where they were, the nature and purpose of the intrusion and the purpose for the intrusion and the lack of express or inferred consent, the effect on the child and his mother. The court indicated there may be a difference between cases where parents courted publicity through their child and cases where they had tried to keep their children out of the public gaze.

2. An order can be sought to prevent publicity. Where the child is not the subject of the publicity, the court has jurisdiction to prevent the publicity, but will rarely do so. So in *R v Central Independent Television plc*[406] a mother sought to prevent the broadcast of a television programme concerning the facts around the arrest of the child's father over charges of indecency. As the child was not the subject of the programme, the child's welfare was not paramount. In fact the child's welfare was not relevant at all, and the Court of Appeal stated that in such cases the freedom of the press prevailed.[407] Subsequently, in *Re S (A Child) (Identification: Restriction on Publication)*[408] the House of Lords said that in such cases the Human Rights Act 1998 had an important impact. In this case a child's parents were facing criminal proceedings and an injunction was sought to prevent revelation of their names. The court here had to weigh up the article 8 rights of the child and the article 10 rights protecting freedom of expression of the newspapers. Given that the publicity was only going to indirectly impact on the child and that the reporting of criminal trials was an important part of the rule of law, the newspapers' article 10 rights triumphed over the child's article 8 rights.[409] The injunction was therefore refused. In *Re LM (A Child) (Reporting Restrictions: Coroner's Inquest)*[410] Sir Mark Potter P held that only where there were exceptional circumstances would the interests of the child outweigh the importance of free press and open justice.[411]

3. Where the child is the subject of the publicity, a parent can apply to the court for a s 8 order and in such circumstances the welfare of the child will be the paramount consideration.[412] Similarly, if a parent permits publicity about the child, the other parent could seek a s 8 order to prohibit the publicity, or the court could prohibit it under the inherent jurisdiction.[413] If the court is very concerned about a parent seeking to use a child for

---

[405] [2008] EWCA Civ 446.
[406] [1994] 2 FLR 151.
[407] Although the right to respect for private life is now relevant because of the Human Rights Act 1998: *A v M (Family Proceedings: Publicity)* [2000] 1 FLR 562; *Kelly v BBC* [2001] 1 FCR 197.
[408] [2004] 3 FCR 407, discussed in Taylor (2006).
[409] See also *Clayton v Clayton* [2006] EWCA Civ 878.
[410] [2007] 3 FCR 44.
[411] See also *A Local Authority v W* [2007] 3 FCR 69.
[412] CA 1989, s 1(1).
[413] *Re Z (A Minor) (Identity: Restrictions on Publication)* [1996] 1 FLR 191, [1996] 2 FCR 164.

publicity purposes, the court may even make the child a ward of court.[414] Section 12 of the Human Rights Act 1998 requires the courts to pay particular regard to the importance of the right to freedom of expression under article 10 of the European Convention. This means that, in future, the court will not be able to state that the sole consideration is the child's welfare.[415] This led Butler-Sloss P in *Thompson and Venables v News Group Newspapers Ltd*[416] to make an injunction preventing the publication of information about the two boys who had killed Jamie Bulger. She relied on the law on protection of confidential information to do so, in this exceptional case. In *Re Steadman*[417] because so much information about the children was already made public, further publication, correcting earlier misleading reports, was justified.

It should be noted that the distinction between cases where the subject of the publicity is the child and those where it is someone else is artificial. Its basis is the wording of s 1 of the Children Act 1989, which states that the welfare of the child is paramount in cases involving the upbringing of the child. However, the child can be as harmed by publicity which indirectly relates to the child as by publicity which directly relates to the child. The issues of balancing the welfare of the child and the freedom of the press should be the same in both.

---

### CASE: *Clayton v Clayton* [2006] EWCA Civ 878

This case involved a lengthy and bitter residence and contact dispute. At one point the child had been abducted by the father to Portugal, which had resulted in a nine-month prison sentence for the father. On his release, the father resumed contact with the child. In 2004 the mother discovered that the father intended to publicise how his case had been dealt with by the family courts. The mother objected to the publicity, arguing that the contact and residence applications were currently adjourned and that s 97(2) Children Act 1989 stated that no person could publish material which was likely to identify any child as being involved in Children Act proceedings. The judge made an order that the father be restrained from communicating any matter relating to the education, maintenance, financial circumstances or family circumstances of the child to anyone except a list of permitted persons. Subsequently, the litigation was settled, with a shared care arrangement being agreed. The father sought to lift the order restraining publication, but the judge refused. The father appealed, arguing that the s 97(2) restriction applied only while the litigation was ongoing. Further, his right to freedom of expression under article 10 of the European Convention on Human Rights outweighed the rights of the child to a private life under article 8.

The Court of Appeal agreed with the father's argument that s 97 prevented the identification of children only while the proceedings continued. Once the litigation had finished, unless a specific order was made, there was nothing which prevented publication of information about the children, although information relating to the actual proceedings themselves could not be made public without a court's leave. Where a judge thought appropriate, she or he could make an order to protect the child's rights to privacy which could extend beyond

---

[414] *Re W (Wardship: Discharge: Publicity)* [1995] 2 FLR 466, [1996] 1 FCR 393.
[415] *Re Z (A Minor) (Identity: Restrictions on Publication)* [1996] 1 FLR 191, [1996] 2 FCR 164 was approved by the European Commission in *A and Byrne and Twenty-Twenty Television v UK* (1998) 25 EHRR 159 CD.
[416] [2001] 1 FLR 791.
[417] [2009] 2 FLR 852.

the proceedings and even to the age of 19. In deciding whether to make such an order, a balance had to be struck between the article 8 rights of the child and the article 10 rights of the parents or media, where appropriate. In this case the issues the father wished to raise were legitimate and his rights outweighed any rights of the child. Therefore, the injunction would be discharged, although a prohibited steps order prevented the taking of the child to Portugal and involving the child in any publicity concerning the child's abduction.

The Court of Appeal held (relying on *Re S (A Child) (Identification: Restriction on Publication)*[418]) that when weighing up the competing rights of the child and the adults, neither right was to have precedence. Where there is a conflict: 'an intense focus on the comparative importance of the specific rights being claimed in the individual cases is necessary. The justification for interfering with or restricting each right must be taken into account and, finally, the proportionality test must be applied to each' (at [57]). However, the court accepted that the balancing exercise here was not quite the same as in *Re S* because in that case the child's upbringing was not directly in question. The publicity concerned the parent, although it was accepted that that publicity would impact on the child. In *Clayton* the publicity directly related to the child. The significance of that was that s 1(1) of the Children Act 1989 became relevant with its insistence that the welfare of the child had to be the court's paramount consideration. Having established this, Sir Mark Potter stated that s 1(1):

> does not exclude the necessity for the court to consider (a) the right of the child under art 8 to privacy, both in relation to the proceedings and the confidentiality of his or her personal data, (b) the right of the parent under art 10 to tell his or her story to the world and, (c) in the case of an application by media interests, their wish to publish or broadcast the story and/or to comment on the issues involved.[419]

This is, with respect, not very helpful. The Court of Appeal tell us that where the child's upbringing is directly covered by the publicity, s 1(1) of the Children Act 1989 becomes relevant, but that the courts should still, nevertheless, carry out the balancing act of the relevant rights. What we are not told is what should happen if the application of the welfare principle indicates a different result from the weighing up of the rights. One view could be that the result never will be different. However, Sir Mark Potter stated:

> The court, after the conclusion of the proceedings, retains its welfare jurisdiction and will be able to intervene where a child's welfare is put at risk by inappropriate parental identification for publicity purposes. Quite where the line is to be drawn between CA 1989, s 1, and ECHR, Articles 8 and 10, in this context remains to be seen, although I venture to think that in practice most parents will recognise it. But let those parents who do not be in no doubt that the court's powers under the ss 1 and 8 of the 1989 Act remain, as do its powers to grant injunctions.[420]

This suggests that using the welfare principle and using a rights-based approach will not necessarily produce the same answer. This, it is submitted, is correct. Where the publicity may cause the child a tiny amount of harm this would be sufficient to justify making an order prohibiting it under the welfare principle. However, the tiny amount of harm may well not be enough to justify an interference in the parents' or media's article 10 rights. Which approach should be preferred was left by the Court of Appeal to another day.

---

[418] [2004] UKHL 47, [2004] 4 All ER 683.
[419] At para 59.
[420] Para 78.

We discussed in Chapter 1 the developments in the law over allowing the media to report on cases in the family courts.

## M Names

### (i) Registration of birth

A child must be registered within 42 days of the birth and the person registering the birth can declare 'the surname by which at the date of the registration of the birth it is intended that the child shall be known'.[421] The birth can be registered by the mother or the father, if he is married to the mother. An unmarried father has no right to register the birth. The father has no ground to insist that the child be given his surname. This position has been criticised.[422] It gives the unmarried father no say in the name of his child. It also enables the married father who has separated from the mother to register the child without consulting the mother.[423] As discussed in Chapter 7, the Welfare Reform Act 2010 paves the way for reform of the law in a way which will encourage joint birth registration.

If a father (or mother) objects to the initial registration he (or she) can apply for a specific issue order that the child have his (or her) surname. The Court of Appeal decision in *Dawson v Wearmouth*[424] suggests that as long as the mother's decision was not 'a maliciously or manifestly absurd choice', the courts will uphold her choice. So, presumably, if a mother chooses her own or the child's father's surname it could not successfully be challenged in court. If, however, she chooses the surname of a popular television personality, the father would be more likely to succeed in his appeal. Once the name is registered it cannot be changed unless there has been a clerical error.[425] Unlike other countries there is no restriction on a choice of name.[426] Parents are free to let their imagination run riot.

### (ii) What is a child's name?

In law a child's name is not necessarily the name which appears on the birth register. *Re T (Otherwise H) (An Infant)*[427] makes it clear that the child's surname in law is simply that by which he or she is customarily known, which does not, of course, have to be the registered name. It is possible through a deed poll to provide formal evidence of a change from the registered surname, although it is not essential.[428] If a deed poll is used to recognise the new surname of a child, it must be signed by all those with parental responsibility.[429]

### (iii) Can a parent allow a child to be known by a name with which he or she was not registered?

It is clear that only a person with parental responsibility can change the name of a child. What is not clear is whether a person with parental responsibility must consult with anyone else with parental responsibility before doing so. The following situations need to be distinguished.

---

[421] Registration of Births and Deaths Regulations 1987, SI 1987/2088, reg 9(3).
[422] Gosden (2003).
[423] This appeared to happen in *Re H and A (Children)* [2002] 2 FCR 469.
[424] [1997] 2 FLR 629 at p. 635.
[425] Births and Deaths Registration Act 1953, s 29.
[426] See, e.g., *Guillot v France* App 22500/93 (24 October 1996).
[427] [1962] 3 All ER 970.
[428] The procedure for this is set out in *Practice Direction (Minor: Change of Surname: Deed Poll)* [1995] 1 All ER 832.
[429] *Practice Direction (Minor: Change of Surname: Deed Poll)* [1995] 1 All ER 832.

### (a) Where a residence order is in force

Where a residence order is in force the position is governed by s 13(1) of the Children Act 1989:

---

**LEGISLATIVE PROVISION**

**Children Act 1989, section 13(1)**

Where a residence order is in force with respect to a child, no person may—

(a) cause the child to be known by a new surname; or

(b) remove him from the United Kingdom

without either the written consent of every person who has parental responsibility for the child or leave of the court.

---

So where a residence order is in force, the name of the child cannot be changed without the consent of all those with parental responsibility or the leave of the court.[430]

The section does not state that the consent of the child is needed. It was left open in *Re PC (Change of Surname)*[431] whether the consent of a *Gillick*-competent child was necessary or sufficient to change the name. Given that the mature child can in effect ensure that he or she is known by friends and others by a particular name, there may be little point in ordering an older child to be known by a particular name.[432] The fact that a child cannot choose his or her own name shows how little respect there is for children's autonomy in English law. The decision over one's name is deeply personal, but can hardly be harmful. If children cannot make such decisions one wonders what decisions the law thinks they can make.[433]

### (b) Where there is no residence order in force and both parents have parental responsibility

It was held in *Dawson v Wearmouth*[434] that if two people have parental responsibility, the child's name cannot be changed without the agreement of both. If there is no agreement the court's approval is required. They rejected an argument that s 2(7) allowed either parent to change the name arguing that if that was correct it could lead to a chaotic situation with the name being constantly changed and re-changed by each parent.

### (c) Where one person has parental responsibility

Holman J in *Re PC (Change of Surname)*[435] suggested that if only one parent has parental responsibility then he or she could unilaterally change a child's name. An unmarried father without parental responsibility could object to this by applying for a prohibited steps order, but the mother is entitled to change the name, and the burden is on the father to bring the matter to the court if he wishes to object. However, the law is unclear. Lord Mackay in *Dawson v Wearmouth*[436] in the House of Lords stated: 'Any dispute [over the registration of a

---

[430] Leave of the court should probably be obtained through a section 8 application. For a discussion see George (2008b).

[431] [1997] 2 FLR 730, [1997] 3 FCR 544.

[432] *Re B (Change of Surname)* [1996] 1 FLR 791, [1996] 2 FCR 304.

[433] Herring (2008d).

[434] [1997] 2 FLR 629 CA; affirmed [1999] 1 FLR 1167, [1999] 1 FCR 625.

[435] [1997] 2 FLR 730, [1997] 3 FCR 544.

[436] [1999] 1 FLR 1167, [1999] 1 FCR 625.

child's name] should be referred to the court for determination whether or not there is a residence order in force and whoever has or has not parental responsibility. No disputed registration or change should be made unilaterally.'[437] This implies that even if only the mother has parental responsibility she will need to apply to the court for permission to change a child's name. In *Re W, Re A, Re B (Change of Name)*[438] it was suggested that if only one person has parental responsibility, they ought to obtain the consent of the other parent or the leave of the court, although it is unclear where this requirement comes from and what the penalty is for breaching it. However, in *Re R (A Child)* Hale LJ appeared to suggest that a parent without parental responsibility did not have a right to be consulted over the surname of a child, but did have the right to challenge the choice in court.[439]

### (iv) Child in local authority care

Under s 33(7), if a child is in care then a child's name can only be changed in writing, if all those with parental responsibility consent or the court gives leave. It would be open for a child in care, if sufficiently competent, to apply him- or herself to have their name changed.[440] In *Re M, T, P, K and B (Care: Change of Name)*[441] a local authority was given leave to change the surname of children in care because they lived in fear that their parents would discover their whereabouts. This was seen as a valid reason for giving leave to change the surname.

### (v) How will the court resolve a disputed case?

If a dispute over a child's name is brought before the court then the child's welfare will be the paramount consideration.[442] Their Lordships in *Dawson v Wearmouth* made it clear there was no parental right to name a child.[443] The cases indicate that a court seeking to resolve a dispute over the surname of a child will consider the following issues:[444]

1. *The registered name.* The person seeking to change the name from the registered name must show 'good and cogent reasons' for changing the name.[445] On the other hand, it would be wrong to suggest that registration should be regarded as decisive;[446] rather that if the arguments for or against changing the name are equally balanced the registered name should prevail.[447]

2. *The child's views.* The child's views will be important, but not the sole consideration. Wilson J in *Re B (Change of Surname)*[448] ordered that three children (two teenagers) keep their father's surname, despite their opposition, in order to maintain the link with their father. However, it might be thought that little more could be done to damage the relationship

---

[437] [1999] 1 FLR 1167 at p. 1173.
[438] [1999] 2 FLR 930.
[439] [2002] 1 FCR 170 at para 9.
[440] *Re S (Change of Surname)* [1999] 1 FLR 672.
[441] [2000] 1 FLR 645.
[442] *Dawson v Wearmouth* [1999] 1 FLR 1167, [1999] 1 FCR 625.
[443] But see *Znamenskaya v Russia* [2005] 2 FCR 406 where a mother was held to have a right under article 8 to give her stillborn child the biological father's surname.
[444] *Stjerna v Finland* (1994) 24 EHRR 195 ECtHR. A man wanted to change his surname about which he was regularly taunted. The European Court accepted that article 8 included the right to change one's name, although the public interest in that case justified infringing his right. Contrast *Johansson v Finland* [2007] 3 FCR 420 where the public interest was insufficient.
[445] *Re C (Change of Surname)* [1999] 1 FCR 318.
[446] *Re W, Re A, Re B (Change of Name)* [1999] 2 FLR 930.
[447] *A v Y (Child's Surname)* [1999] 2 FLR 5.
[448] *Re B (Change of Surname)* [1996] 1 FLR 791, [1996] 2 FCR 304.

between a father and teenagers than forcing them to keep his name. Despite this decision, it was made clear in *Re S (Change of Surname)*[449] that the views of a *Gillick*-competent child over a surname should be given careful consideration.[450]

3. *Embarrassment. It* seems that simply arguing that the child is going to be embarrassed by having a different name from their residential parent is not a strong enough argument to justify changing the name.[451] In fact 'there [is] no opprobrium nowadays for a child to have a different surname from that of adults in the household'.[452]

4. *Informal use of names.* There is a difficulty where the child's surname has informally been changed and the child has used the new name for some time before the matter is brought before the court. In such circumstances the court may easily be persuaded that it would be harmful for the child to have the name changed back to the original name. For example, in *Re C (Change of Surname)*[453] the Court of Appeal felt that, although the mother's initial decision to change the surname had been undesirable, given the length of time the children had been known by the new surname it would be inappropriate to revert to the original name. It may be that a court will accept that the formal name will be different from the informal name. Wilson J in *Re B (Change of Surname)* accepted that, in practice, there is little the law can do to control the name by which a child is to be known on a day-to-day basis. The court can only control the name by which the child will be known in formal documents.[454]

5. *Strength of the child's relationship with their parents.* Where the residential parent is seeking to change the child's surname from the surname of the non-residential parent then the strength of the relationship between the child and non-residential parent will be taken into account.[455] However, it is not easy to tell how this relationship will be taken into account. If the child sees the non-residential parent only rarely then that is an argument *in favour* of retaining the non-residential parent's name, because the name may be the strongest link between the child and the non-residential parent. However, in the *B* case in *Re W, Re A, Re B (Change of Name)*,[456] approval was given to a change of name from the father's after the father had been imprisoned, because there was not likely to be a meaningful relationship between the child and her father in the future. In *Re S (Change of Surname)*[457] the fact that the children alleged the father had abused them was recognised as a strong reason for justifying a change from the father's name.

6. *Cultural factors.* A court might place weight on normal rules governing surnames from the parent's cultural background.[458] In *Re S (Change of Names: Cultural Factors)*[459] Wilson J held that the child's name should be changed for day-to-day purposes from a Sikh name to a Muslim name. This was because he had ordered residence to the Muslim mother and therefore the child would inevitably become part of the Muslim community; and the child

---

[449] [1999] 1 FLR 672.
[450] *Re R (Residence: Shared Care: Children's Views)* [2005] EWCA Civ 542.
[451] *Re F (Child: Surname)* [1993] 2 FLR 827n, [1994] 1 FCR 110; *Re T (Change of Name)* [1998] 2 FLR 620, [1999] 1 FCR 476.
[452] *Re B (Change of Surname)* [1996] 1 FLR 791, [1996] 2 FCR 304 CA; *Re T (Change of Name)* [1998] 2 FLR 620, [1999] 1 FCR 476.
[453] [1998] 2 FLR 656.
[454] [1996] 2 FCR 304. Accepted also in *Re F (Child: Surname)* [1993] 2 FLR 837n, [1994] 1 FCR 110.
[455] *Re P (Parental Responsibility: Change of Name)* [1997] 2 FLR 722, [1997] 3 FCR 739.
[456] [1999] 2 FLR 930.
[457] [1999] 1 FLR 672.
[458] *Re A (A Child) (Change of Name)* [2003] 1 FCR 493.
[459] [2001] 3 FCR 648.

should be helped to become accepted within that community. However, for formal purposes he held that the name should remain the Sikh name to remind him of his Sikh origins.

7. *Double-barrelled names.* It might be thought that suggesting the child have a double-barrelled name, linking the child to both the mother and father, would be a suitable compromise in many cases. In *Re R (A Child)*[460] it was suggested that using a combination of both surnames was to be encouraged because it would recognise the importance of both parents to the child.

### (vi) First names

In *Re H (Child's Name: First Name)*[461] it was held that the rules in relation to surnames do not apply to forenames. A court will not stop the resident parent from using whatever forename she wishes. The father had registered the child with one first name and that would remain the registered name, but for all practical purposes the mother could choose the name she wished. Foster carers and adoptive parents should not change their children's first names (even by using a shortened form of the name) without the local authority's approval. If there is no agreement the matter should be taken to the High Court.[462] To many this might sound bizarre, but the President of the Family Division so held, explaining that changes of forenames raised important issues. Notably, however, she held that the foster carers, who were 'marvellous people' in caring for a severely disabled child, should not be caused unhappiness or difficulty by requiring them not to use the name they wished.

### (vii) What should the law be?

There are three main issues here.[463] The first is whether the question of the surname is an important one. The House of Lords has accepted that changing the surname of the child is a 'profound issue',[464] so much so that the normal rule of independent parenting does not apply. Lord Jauncey in *Dawson v Wearmouth*[465] suggested that 'the surname is . . . a biological label which tells the world at large that the blood of the name flows in its veins'. But is it really a 'profound issue'?[466] More so than dispute over religious upbringing or medical issues to which s 2(7) does apply? It is arguable that although the surname may be important to the parents, it is rarely a profound issue for children, for whom first names are usually far more important.[467] The fact that the House of Lords felt it necessary to hear a case over surnames, when there are so many other issues of greater significance to children's welfare, may be thought to reveal how the court's involvement in the lives of children is driven by the concerns of adults, rather than the needs of children.

The second issue is how the law should treat stepfamilies. Many of these cases involve the mother remarrying or repartnering and wanting to take on her new partner's name. The issue then arises whether the child's name should be changed to reflect the mother's new name and so tie in the child to the new family, or whether the child should keep his or her biological

---

[460] [2002] 1 FCR 170. The option did not appeal to Tyrer J in *A v Y (Child's Surname)* [1999] 2 FLR 5 who thought that only the mother's half (the latter half) of the name would be used.

[461] [2002] 1 FLR 973.

[462] *Re D, L and LA (Care: Change of Forename)* [2003] 1 FLR 339.

[463] Bond (1998); Eekelaar (1998); Herring (1998a).

[464] *Dawson v Wearmouth* [1999] 1 FLR 1167 at p. 1173, per Lord Mackay.

[465] [1999] 1 FLR 1167 at p. 1175.

[466] Thorpe LJ in *Re R (A Child)* [2002] 1 FCR 170 called the surname issue a 'small issue' (para 1).

[467] Lord Hobhouse in *Dawson v Wearmouth* [1999] 1 FLR 1167 at p. 1178 was insistent that the issue was one of the welfare of the child rather than the rights of parents.

father's name to retain the link with him. Hale LJ in *Re R (A Child)*[468] expressed her view forcefully:

> It is also a matter of great sadness to me that it is so often assumed, and even sometimes argued, that fathers need that outward and visible link in order to retain their relationship with, and commitment to, their child. That should not be the case. It is a poor sort of parent whose interest in and commitment to his child depends upon that child bearing his name. After all, that is a privilege which is not enjoyed by many mothers, even if they are not living with the child. They have to depend upon other more substantial things.

Third, there are those who see the norm of wives and children taking the husband's surname as a way of reinforcing patriarchy. It symbolises the 'headship' of fathers over their family.[469] However, others see the use of a common name as reflecting family unity, rather than any statement of male authority.

## N  Removal from the UK

It is clear from s 13(1)(b) of the Children Act 1989[470] that if there is a residence order in force then a child cannot be removed from the UK for longer than one month unless there is the written consent of every person with parental responsibility, or the leave of the court.[471] Section 13(2) permits a child to be removed for less than one month by the person with the residence order without the consent of others with parental responsibility.[472] If there is a dispute between the parents over removal of the child from the UK an application for a specific issue order could be made.[473]

If leave to remove the child from the jurisdiction[474] is sought, the child's welfare is the paramount consideration.[475] The court must take a long-term view in deciding whether leave to remove will promote the child's welfare.[476] The most difficult cases involve the residential parent seeking to emigrate with a child. Refusing leave may be regarded as an infringement of the parent's right to respect for private and family life, which includes being able to choose where to live.[477] The non-residential parent may well object on the ground that permitting emigration will severely restrict the practicability of any contact with the child and infringe that parent's rights under article 8. The approach that the courts have taken is that leave will be granted if the request to emigrate is reasonable and bona fide,[478] unless it is shown that emigration would be contrary to the welfare of the child.[479] Where the children are older their

---

[468] [2002] 1 FCR 170 at para 13.
[469] Herring (2009d).
[470] See page 523.
[471] For a general discussion of this issue see Pressdee (2008).
[472] See also Child Abduction Act 1984.
[473] See *Re L (Removal from Jurisdiction: Holiday)* [2001] 1 FLR 241 where permission was given on condition (*inter alia*) that the mother and her family made solemn declarations on the Koran that they would return the child to the UK.
[474] That is, to remove the child from the country.
[475] CA 1989, s 1(1). See George (2008b) for a discussion of whether the welfare checklist in section 1(3) should apply.
[476] *Re B (Children) (Removal from Jurisdiction)* [2001] 1 FCR 108.
[477] European Convention on Human Rights, article 8; *Re G-A (A Child) (Removal from Jurisdiction: Human Rights)* [2001] 1 FCR 43.
[478] That is, it is not being made solely for the purpose of bringing the contact arrangement to an end. See, e.g., *Tyler v Tyler* [1989] 2 FLR 158, [1990] FCR 22; *Re K (Application to Remove from Jurisdiction)* [1988] 2 FLR 1006.
[479] *Re H (Application to Remove from Jurisdiction)* [1998] 1 FLR 848, [1999] 2 FCR 34.

views will be given weight.[480] Where leave is granted this may well be on the basis that the children will return to the UK for lengthy holidays.[481]

The leading case[482] on this issue is now ***Payne v Payne***.[483]

---

**CASE: *Payne v Payne* [2001] 1 FCR 425**

Thorpe LJ explained, 'refusing the primary carer's reasonable proposals for the relocation of her family life is likely to impact detrimentally on the welfare of her dependent children. Therefore her application to relocate will be granted unless the court concludes that it is incompatible with the welfare of the children'.[484] He went on to confirm that such an approach was consistent with the European Convention.[485] Thorpe LJ went on to warn of the dangers of stating that there was a legal presumption that if the primary carer's plans were reasonable she would be given leave. In each case the judge must assess what would be in the welfare of the child, using the following approach:

(a) Pose the question: is the mother's application genuine in the sense that it is not motivated by some selfish desire to exclude the father from the child's life? Then ask is the mother's application realistic, by which I mean founded on practical proposals both well researched and investigated? If the application fails either of these tests refusal will inevitably follow.

(b) If, however, the application passes these tests then there must be a careful appraisal of the father's opposition: is it motivated by genuine concern for the future of the child's welfare or is it driven by some ulterior motive? What would be the extent of the detriment to him and his future relationship with the child were the application granted? To what extent would that be offset by extension of the child's relationships with the maternal family and homeland?

(c) What would be the impact on the mother, either as the single parent or as a new wife, of a refusal of her realistic proposal?

(d) The outcome of the second and third appraisals must then be brought into an overriding review of the child's welfare as the paramount consideration, directed by the statutory checklist in so far as appropriate.[486]

Thorpe LJ emphasised that:

> In suggesting such a discipline I would not wish to be thought to have diminished the importance that this court has consistently attached to the emotional and psychological well-being of the primary carer. In any evaluation of the welfare of the child as the paramount consideration great weight must be given to this factor.[487]

---

[480] *M v M (Minors) (Jurisdiction)* [1993] 1 FCR 5.

[481] *Re B (Minors) (Removal from the Jurisdiction)* [1994] 2 FLR 309; *Re H (Application to Remove from Jurisdiction)* [1998] 1 FLR 848, [1999] 2 FCR 34.

[482] As confirmed in *Re H (Children) (Residence Order: Condition)* [2001] 2 FLR 1277 and *Re G (Leave to Remove)* [2007] EWCA Civ 1497, which rejected an argument that the decision was 'antiquated'.

[483] [2001] 1 FCR 425.

[484] [2001] 1 FCR 425 at para 26.

[485] [2001] 1 FCR 425 at para 34. See also *Re A (Permission to Remove Child from Jurisdiction: Human Rights)* [2000] 2 FLR 225.

[486] *Payne v Payne* [2001] 1 FCR 425 at para 40.

[487] At para 41.

The courts have insisted that welfare is the key test, but if the resident parent's proposals are reasonable leave is likely to be granted. Subsequent decisions show that normally leave will be granted.[488] Reasons for relocation which have been regarded as reasonable by the court include the pursuit of a career or educational opportunity;[489] the wish to return to the home country or to be close to family and friends;[490] the desire to join a new partner[491] or to enable that partner to pursue career or educational opportunities;[492] and the hope of establishing a new life in a new place.[493] Great weight will be placed on the impact on the emotional and psychological welfare of the resident parent of a refusal of leave to relocate.[494] Medical evidence will strengthen a mother's case.[495] In *Re C (Permission to Remove from Jurisdiction)*[496] the court held that the ideal solution would be for the mother to decide to stay in the UK rather than return to the country of birth. However, to order her to do so would in the long term harm the children because of its potential impact on the mother. The court asked the mother to reconsider her decision to leave, but refused to prevent her doing so.[497] The court will also scrutinise the proposals for contact. In *W v A*[498] the Court of Appeal accepted that technology had made international communication easier with telephone, e-mail, text messages, DVD and digital photography. All of these would help a non-resident parent keep up a relationship with the child even if they were now living overseas. In *B v S*[499] Sedley LJ suggested that a father might find occasional substantial periods of residence a more effective way of maintaining a relationship than regular short times of non-residential contact. Those cases where leave has been refused (e.g. *R v R*;[500] *H v F*[501]) tend to be those where the resident parent has failed to think out the plans adequately or where the court concludes that the move has been entirely motivated by a desire to stop contact taking place,[502] although in *Re F and H (Children)*[503] it was held that where a parent was returning to a country with which she was very familiar the court would be less strict about requiring detailed plans. In some cases the wishes of mature children will be weighty factors.[504]

The *Payne v Payne* approach is not to apply where the child is currently enjoying shared residence with both parents. In such a case if one is seeking leave to leave the jurisdiction they

---

[488] *Re W (A Child) (Removal from the Jurisdiction)* [2006] 1 FCR 346; *L v L (Leave to Remove Children from Jurisdiction: Effect on Children)* [2003] 1 FLR 900. But see *Re C (Leave to Remove from the Jurisdiction)* [2000] 2 FCR 40 CA for a controversial decision denying leave to remove the children.

[489] E.g. *W v A* [2004] EWCA Civ 1587.

[490] E.g. *Payne v Payne* [2001] 1 FLR 1052.

[491] E.g. *Re A (Leave To Remove: Cultural and Religious Considerations)* [2006] EWHC 421 (Fam).

[492] E.g. *L v L (Leave to Remove Children from Jurisdiction: Effect on Children)* [2002] EWHC 2577 (Fam); [2003] 1 FLR 900; *Re J (Children) (Residence Order: Removal Outside the Jurisdiction)* [2007] 2 FCR 149.

[493] Brasse (2005b).

[494] *Re B (Children) (Termination of Contact)* [2005] 1 FCR 481.

[495] In *Re TG* [2009] EWHC 3122 (Fam).

[496] [2003] FL 484.

[497] An important factor can be whether or not the resident parent has a network of friends in the UK to support him or her: *Re S (Children: Application for Removal from Jurisdiction)* [2005] 1 FCR 471. See also *Re B (Children) (Removal from the Jurisdiction), Re S (A Child) (Removal from the Jurisdiction)* [2003] 3 FCR 637 where the Court of Appeal gave leave to take children out of the jurisdiction so that the resident parents could marry men living abroad.

[498] [2004] EWCA Civ 1587 at para 19.

[499] [2003] EWCA Civ 1149 at para 34.

[500] [2005] 1 FLR 687.

[501] [2005] EWHC 2705 (Fam).

[502] Although see *Re H (Removal from the Jurisdiction)* [2007] EWCA Civ 222 where it was held that the harm to the children by loss of regular contact with the father and wider family members justified not granting leave.

[503] [2007] EWCA Civ 692.

[504] *Re J (Leave to Remove: Urgent Case)* [2006] EWCA Civ 1897.

will face an uphill task. In *Re Y (Leave to remove from Jurisdiction)*[505] an American mother and Welsh father were living in Wales. The mother wished to remove the child to America. It was held that, as the child's home was in Wales and he lived equally with both parents, the move to Texas would cause him disruption and a loss of his bicultural and bilingual life. Leave was therefore refused. Similarly, the *Payne* approach does not apply in cases of temporary removals, where permission will be granted for leave unless there is a good reason not to (*W v A*[506]).

There have also been cases where the resident parent has wished to move within the UK, but to such a distance that it will make contact difficult. The issue was considered in *Re L (A Child) (Internal Relocation: Shared Residence Order)*.[507] There was a joint residence order, but the mother found a new job and wished to move to Somerset from North London, where the father lived. The Court of Appeal held that the case should be determined simply by an application of the welfare principle. The judge held that the move should not be permitted because of the impact on the child's relationship with the father. Although the Court of Appeal questioned whether the judge had placed adequate weight on the impact of refusal on the mother, it upheld the judge's decision as within his judicial discretion. The fact that this was a joint residence case was said just to be a factor in deciding what was in the child's welfare.

There appears to be a head of steam building up to challenge the current approach. Mostyn J has urged the Supreme Court to consider the law's approach to relocation.[508] Similarly, in *Re D (Children)*,[509] while the Court of Appeal acknowledged that *Payne v Payne* still represented the law it accepted that there had been considerable criticism of the case and a respectable arguement could be made for saying that the law needed to be changed.[510]

The courts' approach has been controversial.[511] Hayes and Williams[512] argue that: 'The courts have been too ready to indulge the selfish feelings of mothers and second husbands . . . Restrictions on mobility should simply be regarded as one of the burdens of bringing up children.' It is sometimes said that resident parents are seeking to leave the country just as part of a lifestyle choice.[513] Mary Hayes,[514] in a powerful critique of the courts' reasoning, has suggested that, although the Court of Appeal says that the welfare of the child is the key criterion, it greatly restricts a judge's freedom to ascertain what is in a child's welfare by emphasising the importance of the reasonableness or otherwise of the mother's plans.[515] However, it should be noted that while the resident parent needs leave to go out of the jurisdiction with the child, the non-resident parent has freedom to move wherever he wishes. Stephen Gilmore

---

[505] [2004] 2 FLR 330.
[506] [2004] EWCA Civ 1587 at para 19.
[507] [2009] 1 FCR 584.
[508] *Re AR (A Child: Relocation)* [2010] EWHC 1346 (Fam).
[509] [2010] EWCA Civ 50.
[510] See also *Re H (A Child)* [2010] EWCA Civ 915.
[511] An international judicial conference produced the Washington Declaration on International Family Relocation. If it were to be adopted by England it would produce a notably different approach with a presumption against allowing relocation. Interestingly the Court of Appeal in *Re H (A Child)* [2010] EWCA Civ 915 questioned whether the Declaration provided sufficient protection for children's welfare.
[512] Hayes and Williams (1999: 316–17).
[513] But in *Re S (Children, Termination of Contact)* [2005] 1 FCR 489 Thorpe LJ (at para 16) stated that even if the application resulted from a lifestyle decision the *Payne* approach should still be used. See also *Re H (Removal from the Jurisdiction)* [2007] EWCA Civ 222 where the suggestion that the proposed move was a lifestyle choice was rejected in the Court of Appeal.
[514] Hayes (2006).
[515] Most of the cases have involved mothers seeking to leave the jurisdiction. For a case where a father was able to take the children with him out of the jurisdiction see *Re J (Children) (Residence Order: Removal Outside the Jurisdiction)* [2007] 2 FCR 149.

has noted that the importance attached to the emotional and psychological well-being of the primary carer is not matched in other areas of the law.[516]

While holding that the decision in *Payne* was justifiable, Bainham is concerned that the reasoning used:

> apparently attached more significance to the security and stability of the child with her mother, than it did to the preservation of the child's relationship with the father, as secondary carer, and the father's family. This, again, might be criticized as an inadequate response to the child's identity rights under the UN Convention.[517]

The approach can also be said to fail to attach sufficient weight to the rights of the child and non-resident parent as required by the Human Rights Act. However, it can be argued that adopting a human rights approach would not lead to a change in the results reached because the autonomy rights of the resident parent and child would normally be more weighty than the other rights of the non-resident parent and child.[518]

Psychologists have much debated whether it is more harmful for the child to relocate and suffer diminished contact with the non-resident parent, or not to be allowed to relocate, with the resulting emotional harm to the mother. In truth there is no clear evidence either way.[519]

## O When should there be contact between a child and parent?

Baroness Hale recently declared: 'Making contact happen and, even more importantly, making contact work is one of the most difficult and contentious challenges in the whole of family law.'[520] Contact disputes can become bitterly contested and become impossible to resolve satisfactorily.[521] Groups such as Fathers for Justice have claimed that the law on contact discriminates against fathers. The publicity they have generated has led the Court of Appeal to declare: 'No distinction is drawn between the rights and responsibilities of the mother and the father in residence or contact applications.'[522] Wall J has stated: 'The courts are not anti-father and pro-mother or vice versa.'[523] The fact that members of the judiciary feel it is necessary to make such comments indicates the pressure they feel under as regards this issue. Before considering the approach the courts have taken, the findings of psychologists on the benefits of contact will be considered.

### (i) Psychological evidence of the benefits of contact

There is much support among child psychologists for 'attachment theory': that at an early age a child forms a psychological attachment with a parent or parent figure. This normally takes place within the first three months of the child's life, but may occur even up to age 7.[524] Removing that child from the adult to whom they have become attached can cause the child serious harm. Of course, the quality of the attachment is of great significance, but the breaking

---

[516] Gilmore (2004c: 384).
[517] Bainham (2002a: 285). See also Barton (1997). See Judd and George (2010) for a comparative consideration of the law.
[518] Herring and Taylor (2006).
[519] See the analysis in Herring and Taylor (2006).
[520] *Re G (Children) (Residence: Same-Sex Partner)* [2006] UKHL 43 at para 41.
[521] Geldof (2003) is a vivid expression of the emotions that arise in disputed contact cases. See generally Bainham et al. (2003) for a useful discussion of the issues.
[522] *Re S (A Child) (Contact)* [2004] 1 FCR 439 at p. 445. For a discussion of these groups see Barton (2006) and Collier (2005).
[523] *Re O (A Child) (Contact: Withdrawal of Application)* [2003] EWHC 3031 (Fam) at para 3.
[524] Schaffer (1990).

of any attachment can cause harm.[525] The dominant view in England and Wales is that contact between a child and both parents is in general beneficial.[526] It has been argued that contact with the non-resident parent provides a number of benefits:

1. It avoids the child feeling rejected by the non-residential parent.

2. It enables the parent and child to maintain a beneficial relationship.

3. Contact may dispel erroneous fantasies that the child could have about the non-residential parent.[527]

4. Contact helps the child develop or retain a sense of identity. In particular, it may help in maintaining a sense of cultural identity.

5. Contact can help the child understand the parental separation.

6. It can ensure the child retains contact with the wider family of the non-residential parent.

7. It can help the child feel free to develop relationships with a step-parent without a sense of betrayal to his or her birth parent.[528]

However, proof of these benefits is not established beyond doubt.[529] As Eekelaar and Maclean explain:

> What has not been established is whether a child whose separated parents behave gently and reasonably to her and to one another, but who sees the outside parent rarely or never, somehow does 'less well' than a child of similar parents who sees the outside parent often.[530]

Others argue that benefits do not flow from the mere existence of the contact; what matters is the frequency and quality of the contact.[531] As Pryor and Daly Peoples put it:

> Fathers who are able to have a nurturing and monitoring role have a positive impact on their children in a variety of ways . . . Those fathers whose participation is confined to outings and having fun will, then, have little influence on their children's adjustment.[532]

After a major investigation of the research to date, by Rogers and Pryor,[533] they concluded:

> the relationship between the amount of access to the non-residential parent and child adjustment is not straightforward. Some studies find that frequent contact is associated with better adjustment for children; however, others find no relationship. A few find a negative relationship between frequent levels of contact and child well-being. These diverse findings suggest that the relationship between contact and well-being is moderated by other factors.[534]

Stephen Gilmore, summarising his extensive studies into the benefits of contact, states:[535]

---

[525] See, e.g. Schofield (1998).
[526] Willbourne and Stanley (2002).
[527] In *Re M (Sperm Donor Father)* [2003] Fam Law 94 a lesbian couple used a sperm donor to father a child. He applied for a contact order. It was held that on balance it would be beneficial for occasional contact to take place, so that the child could, at an early stage, be comfortable about his origins.
[528] Hill and Tisdall (1997: 227).
[529] As Eekelaar (2002b) points out, a number of studies cast doubt on the assumption that contact is beneficial: e.g. Emery (1994); Poussin and Martin-LeBrun (2002).
[530] Eekelaar and Maclean (1997: 55). See further Hunt (2006a); Dunn (2003) and Dunn et al. (2004).
[531] Lewis (2005); Rogers and Pryor (1998: 40); Hetherington and Kelly (2002: 133).
[532] Pryor and Daly Peoples (2001: 199). See further Hunt (2006a).
[533] Rogers and Pryor (1998). See also Gilmore (2006a and b) and Wilson (2006) for useful analyses of the research on the benefits and nature of contact.
[534] Rogers and Pryor (1998: 42). See also Pryor and Rogers (2001); Lewis and Lamb (2006).
[535] Gilmore (2008a). See also Gilmore (2006a and b and 2008b).

Research suggests that it is not contact *per se* but the nature and quality of contact that are important to children's adjustment, and there is a range of factors which impact upon the nature and quality of contact . . . The evidence does not suggest that we can, or should, generalise about the benefits of contact.

Even if there are benefits of contact, it must be recognised that there are also potential disadvantages:[536]

1. Contact often leads to bitter disputes between the resident and non-resident parent, and this atmosphere of conflict may harm the child.[537]

2. The child may feel torn between the residential and non-residential parent, a feeling which may be exacerbated by emotionally intense contact sessions. This may cause psychological disturbance.[538]

3. The relationship between the child and the non-residential parent may be an abusive or bullying one whose continuance will harm the child.[539]

A recent study on children in stepfamilies[540] found that contact with the non-resident parent had no discernable impact on children's welfare. Crucial to a child's welfare were the relationships in the home where the child was living. This suggests that the law should not seek to promote contact where this will cause severe disturbance in the child's home.[541]

To conclude on the current state of the evidence on the benefits of contact between a child and non-resident parent: what the evidence certainly does show is that it should not be assumed that contact is always beneficial.[542] On the other hand, there are numerous benefits that *can* flow from contact in many cases where the contact is part of a constructive relationship.[543] Certainly there is evidence that children value the contact they have with their non-resident parent and would like to have more.[544] It should not be forgotten in all the debate over whether children benefit or not from contact that contact arrangements can have significant impact on the welfare of fathers[545] and mothers.[546] Most importantly it must not be assumed that because contact is beneficial, forcing contact through court orders will be beneficial. Despite the ambiguity of the research, the law has been willing to accept that contact promotes the welfare of the child.

## (ii) The courts' approach to contact: is there a right to contact?

Some cases have talked of children having a right to contact.[547] Sir Stephen Brown suggested in *Re W (A Minor) (Contact)*:[548] 'It is quite clear that contact with a parent is a fundamental right of a child, save in wholly exceptional circumstances.' Those cases which have referred to a right to contact have stressed that contact is the right of the child and not the parent.[549]

---

[536] Discussed in *Re L (A Child) (Contact: Domestic Violence)* [2000] 2 FCR 404.
[537] This was accepted by Wall J in *A v A (Children) (Shared Residence Order)* [2004] 1 FCR 201.
[538] Wallerstein and Kelly (1980: 311).
[539] Jones and Parkinson (1995).
[540] Smith et al. (2001).
[541] Maclean and Mueller-Johnson (2003).
[542] Rogers and Pryor (1998); Kaganas and Piper (1999).
[543] Hetherington and Kelly (2002); Poussin and Martin-LeBrun (2002); Trinder (2003a).
[544] Dunn (2003).
[545] Simpson, Jessop and McCarthy (2003).
[546] Day Sclater and Kaganas (2003).
[547] E.g. *Re S (Minors) (Access)* [1990] 2 FLR 166 at p. 170, per Balcombe LJ; *Re F (Contact: Restraint Order)* [1995] 1 FLR 956 at p. 963.
[548] [1994] 2 FLR 441 CA at p. 447.
[549] *M v M (Child: Access)* [1973] 2 All ER 81. See further the discussion in Wallbank (1998).

However, to talk of a right to contact is a misnomer because s 1(1) of the Children Act 1989 applies to contact applications and so the key question is whether or not the contact will promote the child's welfare.[550] In *Re M (Contact: Welfare Test)* it was held that contact was not a fundamental right of the child. Instead, the Court of Appeal accepted that there was a strong presumption in favour of contact, and the test was:

> whether the fundamental emotional need of every child to have an enduring relationship with both his parents [s 1(3)(b)] is outweighed by the depth of harm which in the light, inter alia, of his wishes and feelings [s 1(3)(a)] this child would be at risk of suffering [s 1(3)(e)] by virtue of a contact order.[551]

This quotation has been approved in the Court of Appeal in *Re L (A Child) (Contact: Domestic Violence)*,[552] where Thorpe LJ and Butler-Sloss P explained that it was not appropriate to talk of a right to contact. Thorpe LJ was not keen even on referring to a presumption in favour of contact and preferred to talk of an assumption of the benefit of contact which was 'the base of knowledge and experience from which the court embarks upon its application of the welfare principle'.[553] He suggested that the strength of the case in favour of contact depended on the quality of the relationship between the non-resident parent and the child. Where there is a high-quality existing relationship, the case for contact is at its strongest, but if the child does not know the parent, or the relationship is an abusive one, the argument for contact is much weaker.[554] Whether or not the father is married to the mother should not be a relevant characteristic.[555] However, Kaganas and Day Sclater[556] suggested that Butler-Sloss P, who gave the other main judgment in *Re L*, was more willing than Thorpe LJ to assume that contact was to the benefit of the child. She agreed with statements in *Re O (Imposition of Conditions)*[557] that contact was 'almost always' in the child's interests. However, it is submitted that, rather than suggesting a different approach, Butler-Sloss P was agreeing with Thorpe LJ that each case should be considered on its own merits, and only pointed out that in most cases contact will be found beneficial.[558] In *Re K (A Child)*[559] Wilson LJ referred to 'the need in principle for a child to have some sort of a relationship with both her parents and at least an informed sense of her own identity'. This, however, is short of an assumption that there be contact.

It seems that now the courts will consider more carefully what benefits and disadvantages contact would provide, both in the short and long term.[560] Empirical studies indicate that courts do tend to operate with the assumption that contact is beneficial.[561] Stephen Gilmore[562] suggests that Thorpe LJ's talk of an assumption of contact can be viewed either as a reference to an 'assumed general fact' that contact is good for children, which is just part of the

---

[550] See the discussion in Bailey-Harris (2001d).
[551] [1995] 1 FLR 274 at p. 275. A useful summary of the law is set out in *Re P (Contact: Supervision)* [1996] 2 FLR 314 at p. 318.
[552] [2000] 2 FLR 334, [2000] 2 FCR 404 CA.
[553] *Re L (A Child) (Contact: Domestic Violence)* [2000] 2 FCR 404 at p. 437. Although in HM Inspectorate of Court Administration (2005: para 3.8) it was said that in practice there is a presumption in favour of contact. See also Standley (2006: 336) who also claims there is a presumption in favour of contact.
[554] *Re L (A Child) (Contact: Domestic Violence)* [2000] 2 FCR 404 at p. 437.
[555] *Sahin v Germany* [2003] 2 FCR 619.
[556] Kaganas and Day Sclater (2000).
[557] [2000] Fam Law 631.
[558] This appears to be her view in an extra-judicial article: Butler-Sloss (2001).
[559] [2010] EWCA Civ 478, para 15.
[560] *Re J-S (A Child) (Contact: Parental Responsibility)* [2002] 3 FCR 433 and *Carp v Byron* [2006] 1 FCR 1.
[561] Smart and May (2004b).
[562] Gilmore (2008b).

background knowledge upon which a decision is made in a particular case, or an assumption that contact will be best for the child in the particular case. He argues that only the former can be supported on the research evidence.

Bainham is adamant that there is a right to contact. He explains that by a right he is talking about 'fundamental presumptions' which may be rebutted – but only for good reasons.[563] He claims that 'those who assert that there is no right or presumption of contact are not merely misguided, but are plainly wrong'.[564] He argues that children have a right of contact with mothers and fathers and mothers and fathers have rights of contact with their children.[565] This is a bold statement in the light of the clear statement of Lord Justice Thorpe that there is no right or presumption in favour of contact in English and Welsh law. Bainham's argument is focused on the right to contact which parents and children have under the European Convention on Human Rights.[566] The European Court of Human Rights has made it quite clear that the right to respect for family and private life under article 8 of the European Convention on Human Rights includes the right of contact between parents and children.[567] In *Elsholz v Germany*[568] it was confirmed that to deny contact between a father and a child where they had an established relationship infringed article 8, although denial of contact could be justified under paragraph 2 if necessary in the interests of the child or resident parent.[569] When weighing up the interests of parents and child in relation to contact, the welfare of the child will be of 'crucial importance'.[570] However, it must be shown that the concerns over the welfare of the child render the infringement of the father's right necessary.[571] In other words, contact should not be denied simply because it will very slightly harm the child; a significant harm to the child is required to justify denying contact. However, Bainham also accepts that violence of the father against the mother or child may lead to a forfeiture of his right to contact.[572]

It is perhaps possible to reconcile the approach of Thorpe LJ with the approach of the European Convention. Thorpe LJ appeared to take the view that the human rights to contact were protected by the application of the welfare principle used by the English courts. So Thorpe LJ was not denying that the rights existed, but believed that their existence did not require the court to depart from the statutory formulation under the Children Act, based on the welfare principle. Thorpe LJ's argument could be that, given the court's willingness to assume that contact was beneficial, the English court, just like the European Court, will order contact unless there is clear evidence that the child will be harmed by it.[573] In *Re S (Contact: Promoting Relationship with Absent Parent)*[574] Butler-Sloss P referred to the statement in *Yousef v Netherlands*[575] that 'where the rights under art 8 of parents and those of a child are

---

[563] Bainham (2003a: 75). See also the excellent discussion in Gilmore (2008b).

[564] Bainham (2003a: 74).

[565] Bainham (2003a: 74).

[566] He also relies on the UN Convention on the Rights of the Child, although this is not binding on English or Welsh courts.

[567] *Hokkanen v Finland* (1995) 19 EHRR 139 and *Ignaccolo-Zenide v Romania* (2001) 31 EHRR 7.

[568] [2000] 2 FLR 486 ECtHR.

[569] *Sahin v Germany* [2003] 2 FCR 619 ECtHR. Although see *Hansen v Turkey* [2004] 1 FLR 142 where the fact that the child did not want to have contact was in that case not sufficient to justify an interference in the right of the father to see the child.

[570] *Sahin v Germany* [2002] 3 FCR 321 ECtHR at para 40.

[571] *Elsholz v Germany* [2000] 2 FLR 486 ECtHR; *Suss v Germany* [2005] 3 FCR 666.

[572] Bainham (2003a: 72).

[573] *Suss v Germany* [2005] 3 FCR 666.

[574] [2004] 1 FLR 1279; [2004] 1 FCR 439.

[575] [2002] ECHR 33711/96 at para 73.

at stake, the child's rights must be the "paramount" consideration' to argue that there is no conflict between the Human Rights Act 1998 and the welfare principle in contact cases; although, as we saw at page 427, later decisions of the European Court have not used the 'paramount' terminology.

In truth it may be better to accept that there is a difference between the welfare principle and an approach based on human rights.[576] In cases where it is clear that contact will benefit the child, the two approaches will be the same. Similarly, in cases where it is clear that the child will be significantly harmed by contact, there will be no difference. Any right the non-resident parent may claim to contact can be justifiably interfered with in order to protect the interests of the child. The difference between the approaches will arise in a case where contact is very slightly harmful to the child; then, although contact would not be ordered under the welfare principle, a human rights approach might say that the small amount of harm to the child is insufficient to justify an interference with the non-resident parent's right of contact, and so contact should be ordered.

The Court of Appeal has accepted that the Human Rights Act 1998 has had an impact on contact cases. In *Elsholz v Germany*[577] the failure of the state to obtain a psychological report meant that it could not be demonstrated that termination of the contact was necessary.[578] Similarly, in *Sahin v Germany*[579] the German courts, in failing to hear the child directly or receive an expert report recording her view on contact, infringed the human rights of the father who was seeking contact. Not surprising you might think, except that the child was aged 4. In the light of these cases, in *Re A (A Child) (Separate Representation in Contact Proceedings)*[580] the Court of Appeal suggested that following the Human Rights Act 1998 it may be necessary for children to be separately represented to ensure that their views are heard by the court. Further, if a parent is to be denied contact, expert reports may be required before contact is denied to ensure that the infringement of rights is justified.

In summary, the present law on contact is that the courts will consider the benefits and disadvantages of contact in each particular case. There is no presumption in favour of contact, although its benefits will readily be found in an appropriate case. In each case the courts will weigh up the benefits and disadvantages of contact.[581] The courts have therefore not accepted the arguments of some commentators that there should be a presumption in favour of equal parenting after divorce[582] nor that the Human Rights Act 1998 requires a different approach.[583]

We will now consider certain types of contact cases which have raised particular difficulties.

### (iii) The opposition of the residential parent

There has in recent years been a change in approach in cases where the resident parent is strongly opposed to contact.[584] At one time opposition was thoroughly castigated. In *Re O (Contact: Imposition of Conditions)*[585] it was stated:

---

[576] Herring and Taylor (2006).
[577] [2000] 2 FLR 486 ECtHR.
[578] *Hoppe v Germany* [2003] 1 FCR 176 is an example of where the procedural requirements were met.
[579] [2002] 3 FCR 321 ECtHR.
[580] [2001] 2 FCR 55.
[581] For an example of where the disadvantages outweighed the advantages see *Re F (Children) (Contact: Change of Surname)* [2007] 3 FCR 832.
[582] Bartlett (1999).
[583] For arguments that the Human Rights Act 1998 does require a new approach to contact cases see Choudhry and Fenwick (2005).
[584] Wallbank (1998) discusses these cases.
[585] [1995] 2 FLR 124 at pp. 129–30.

The courts should not at all readily accept that the child's welfare will be injured by direct contact . . . Neither parent should be encouraged or permitted to think that the more intransigent, the more unreasonable, the more obdurate and the more uncooperative they are, the more likely they are to get their own way.

As explained in *Re W (A Minor) (Contact)*,[586] the mother has no right to deny the child the benefit of contact. More recently, in *Re P (Contact Discretion)*,[587] the courts have accepted that there may be very good reasons for the residential parent to oppose contact, and it is now necessary to distinguish two types of cases.[588] First, where the opposition of the parent is justified: in such a case if the residential parent's fears are 'genuine and rationally held'[589] then the court may refuse contact.[590] Where the resident parent claims that there is a risk of violence to the children, that would be a reasonable ground to oppose contact, unless that risk can be eliminated.[591] The resident parent may also reasonably fear that the non-resident parent will, during a contact session, seek to abduct the child and take him or her out of the jurisdiction.[592] Secondly, those cases where the opposition is 'emotional' and there is no rational basis for it: in such a case contact will be ordered unless it can be shown that the residential parent will suffer such distress if forced to permit contact that the child will be harmed.[593] In *Re H (Children) (Contact Order) (No. 2)*[594] Wall J held that the child's need to have a competent and confident primary carer outweighed their need to have direct contact with their father in a case where there was evidence that the mother might have a nervous breakdown if contact was ordered. In *Re H (Children) (Contact Order)* Hale LJ supported such an approach, explaining that research showed that having a competent and confident primary carer was a better predictor of a child's success following separation than contact.[595]

A few recent cases have focused on the father's conduct and have accepted the argument that the father, if he wishes to have contact, must behave in a more suitable way.[596] This is important because the earlier case law had concentrated on the mother and regarded her opposition as the problem, rather than considering whether it was the father's behaviour which created the difficulties.[597] Some commentators have suggested that the law is predicated on an image of a 'good' or 'bad' mother or father. A mother is automatically 'bad' if she denies contact to a father, even when she fears that the father may harm the child; whereas a father is 'good' if he seeks contact with the child, even though he may have shown disregard of the child's welfare during the parents' relationship.[598] There are concerns that the increased emphasis on encouraging contact will reinforce this message.[599]

---

[586] [1994] 2 FLR 441, [1994] 2 FCR 1216.

[587] [1998] 2 FLR 696, [1999] 1 FCR 566.

[588] See also *Re D (Contact: Reasons for Refusal)* [1997] 2 FLR 48, [1998] 1 FCR 321.

[589] *Re D (Contact: Reasons for Refusal)* [1997] 2 FLR 48 at p. 53.

[590] For a thorough discussion see Children Act Sub-Committee (2002a) and *Re H (A Child) (Contact: Mother's Opposition)* [2001] 1 FCR 59.

[591] *Re H (Children) (Contact Order) (No. 2)* [2001] 3 FCR 385. The court may leave open the possibility of contact in the future: *Re D (A Minor) (Contact: Mother's Hostility)* [1993] 2 FLR 1, [1993] 1 FCR 964.

[592] D. Smith (2003).

[593] *Re C (Contact: Supervision)* [1996] 2 FLR 314 suggested that it may be difficult to persuade a court of this.

[594] [2001] 3 FCR 385. See also *Re M (Handicapped Child: Parental Responsibility)* [2001] 3 FCR 454.

[595] [2001] 1 FCR 49 at para 58.

[596] *Re M (Minors) (Contact: Violent Parent)* [1999] 2 FCR 56; *Re O (A Child) (Contact: Withdrawal of Application)* [2004] 1 FCR 687.

[597] Smart and Neale (1999a).

[598] Kaganas and Day Sclater (2004); Boyd (1996).

[599] Rhoades (2002a).

There are also practical issues here. In *Re D (A Child) (IVF Treatment)*[600] Butler-Sloss P held that in relation to a young baby who did not know the father it would be impossible to remove the child from the mother to enable contact to take place, at least until she was aged 3.[601] In other words, the co-operation of the resident parent may be essential to the working of the contact order. This may mean that if the resident parent strongly opposes contact, then to order it may be ineffective. Some commentators take the wider point that for contact to be productive there must be trust and co-operation between the parents.[602] Contact where the parents still fear and distrust each other (whether justifiably or not) is likely to lead to the child being used as a pawn in their dispute. Research suggests that the most common reason for resident mothers refusing contact is fear that violence or sexual abuse will be carried out against them or the child.[603] Where these fears are justified, of course, contact will not be ordered.[604] But even if they are unjustified fears some commentators argue that contact in the context of such fear is likely to be traumatic for the child, rather than beneficial.[605] Consider, for example, the case of *Re U (Children) (Contact)*[606] where the father had, when 22, been convicted of 'a particularly unpleasant and brutal' indecent assault on a child aged 11. He was convicted to a sentence of four years' imprisonment. After his release he married, but never told his wife of his conviction. The marriage broke down with the wife alleging violence. When she discovered his previous conviction she refused to permit contact with their two daughters. However, the Court of Appeal held that the father should have been permitted to produce evidence that he had received therapy and did not pose a threat to them. One can imagine that, whatever evidence he might introduce, the mother is unlikely to be convinced he is safe. One wonders whether in such an atmosphere contact could be beneficial. As Julie Wallbank has argued, there is a danger that the weight placed on the importance of maintaining contact means that where contact does not take place the problem is seen as lying at the mother's feet, rather than there being a consideration of whether it is the father whose behaviour has caused the suspicions and difficulties.[607]

### (iv) Domestic violence and contact

In recent years there has been much debate in the courts and among commentators concerning cases in which there is a dispute over contact where the parental relationship had been marked by domestic violence. One study of separated parents found that 56 per cent of parents interviewed reported domestic violence and 78 per cent feared it.[608] Eighty per cent of resident parents disputing contact cited violence concerns in one study.[609] Some commentators have argued in favour of a legal presumption against contact where there has been domestic violence.[610] Those who take such an approach point to the following:[611]

---

[600] [2001] 1 FCR 481.

[601] In *Re H (A Child)* [2010] EWCA Civ 448 the Court of Appeal dealt with a case involving a $4\frac{1}{2}$-month-old baby, while recognising there was an 'issue' over breastfeeding, they still awarded overnight contact to the father.

[602] Herring (2003a).

[603] Rhoades (2002b); Day Sclater and Kaganas (2003).

[604] See *Re C (A Child) (Contact Order)* [2005] 3 FCR 571.

[605] Imagine what a mother with such fears will say to her child as she sends him or her off for the contact session.

[606] [2004] 1 FCR 768.

[607] Wallbank (2007).

[608] Buchanan, Hunt, Bretherton and Bream (2001: 15); Trinder (2005). See Humphreys (2006) for statistics on the rates of violence after separation. See CAFCASS and HMCS (2005) for an acknowledgement that some CAFCASS officers insufficiently appreciate the significance or effect of domestic violence.

[609] Hunt and Macleod (2008).

[610] Kaye (1996); Hester and Pearson (1997); Fineman (2002); Perry (2006). See Wallerstein and Lewis (1998: 375–7) for a general discussion of these cases.

[611] For a helpful summary see Bell (2008).

1. Children who live in an atmosphere of domestic violence suffer psychological harm,[612] even if they do not actually witness the abuse.[613]

2. There is evidence that there are statistical links between child abuse and spousal abuse.[614] Judge Wall[615] quoted research that if a man is abusing his wife there is a 40–60 per cent chance he is also abusing his child.[616]

3. There is also a fear that a father may be able to continue to dominate and exercise power over the mother through the arrangements over contact.[617] For example, contact arrangements can be used to discover the mother's address, or to threaten or abuse her.[618] Hale LJ has expressed her concern 'that some women are being pursued and oppressed by controlling or vengeful men with the full support of the system'.[619] A study by Woman's Aid highlighted 29 cases where children had been killed during or in connection with contact meetings.[620]

4. One survey, which looked at cases where contact had been ordered even though there had been domestic violence, suggested that 25 per cent of children were abused[621] as a result of the contact.[622]

The leading case on the law is *Re L (A Child) (Contact: Domestic Violence)*.[623] The Court of Appeal decided to hear four cases together so as to analyse the law in this area.[624] It was emphasised that the fact that there had been domestic violence is not a bar to contact. However, it is one important factor in the balancing exercise. The Court of Appeal stressed that a judge should approach such cases in two stages:[625]

1. If domestic violence is alleged, the court has to decide whether the allegations are made out or not.[626]

2. The court should weigh up the risks involved, and the impact of contact on the child, against the positive benefits (if any) of contact. Any risk of harm to the residential parent should also be considered.

Butler-Sloss P explained:[627]

---

[612] Kaye (1996); Barnett (2000); Hester, Pearson and Harwin (2000).

[613] *Re L (A Child) (Contact: Domestic Violence)* [2000] 2 FCR 404. Note also the definition of harm in CA 1989, s 31(3A) including the witnessing of ill-treatment of another.

[614] Bowker, Arbitell and McFerron (1989).

[615] Wall HHJ (1997).

[616] See also Bowker, Arbitell and McFerron (1989).

[617] E.g. Kaye, Stubbs and Tolmie (2003); Masson and Humphreys (2005); Hardesty and Chung (2006); Humphreys and Thiara (2003).

[618] Hester and Radford (1996); Wall HHJ (1997: 817); Women's Aid (2003).

[619] Hale LJ (1999).

[620] Saunders (2004). See Wall LJ (2006) who argues that in only three cases could the court possibly have foreseen any kind of risk. Tragically it seems such killings are becoming increasingly common; BBC Newsonline (2008b).

[621] A term the researchers used to include emotional harm. Ten per cent were sexually abused and 15 per cent physically abused.

[622] Radford (1999); Hester (2002).

[623] [2000] 2 FCR 404.

[624] The Court of Appeal paid particular attention to Children Act Sub-Committee (2002a). See further Sturge and Glaser (2000).

[625] In *Re H (A Child) (Contact: Domestic Violence)* [2006] 1 FCR 102 the Court of Appeal was strongly critical of a judge who failed to follow the approach set out in *Re L, V, M and H (Children) (Contact: Domestic Violence)* [2000] 2 FCR 404.

[626] *Re K and S* [2006] 1 FCR 316. In cases of interim contact when it is not possible to assess the facts, special care should be taken to protect the child.

[627] See Gilmore (2008b) for criticism of the Court of Appeal's handling of the expert evidence in that case.

a court hearing a contact application in which allegations of domestic violence are raised, should consider the conduct of both parties towards each other and towards the children, the effect on the children and on the residential parent and the motivation of the parent seeking contact. Is it a desire to promote the best interests of the child or a means to continue violence and/or intimidation or harassment of the other parent? In cases of serious domestic violence, the ability of the offending parent to recognise his or her past conduct, to be aware of the need for change and to make genuine efforts to do so, will be likely to be an important consideration.[628]

In particular, the court should consider the following factors when considering contact where there has been domestic violence:

1. The child might be abused during contact.

2. Contact might exacerbate the bitterness between the parents, and this would be detrimental to the child.

3. A bullying or dominating relationship between the child and contact parent might be perpetuated.

4. If the child had witnessed domestic violence between their parents then contact might reawaken old fears.[629]

5. If the child opposes contact, weight should be placed on their views.[630]

When considering the benefits the court should recall in particular:

1. That seeing a father may be beneficial to the child's identity.

2. The 'male contribution to parenting'[631] that a father can offer.

3. The loss of opportunity to know the paternal grandparents if contact does not take place with the father.

4. The opportunity 'to mend the harm done' may be lost if contact is not ordered.

The President of the Family Division has issued a Practice Direction which lists factors a court must consider when considering making a contact order in a case where there has been domestic violence:

(a) the effect of the domestic violence which has been established on the child and on the parent with whom the child is living;

(b) the extent to which the parent seeking residence or contact is motivated by a desire to promote the best interests of the child or may be doing so as a means of continuing a process of violence, intimidation or harassment against the other parent;

(c) the likely behaviour during contact of the parent seeking contact and its effect on the child;

(d) the capacity of the parent seeking residence or contact to appreciate the effect of past violence and the potential for future violence on the other parent and the child;

(e) the attitude of the parent seeking residence or contact to past violent conduct by that parent; and in particular whether that parent has the capacity to change and to behave appropriately.[632]

---

[628] *Re L (A Child) (Contact: Domestic Violence)* [2000] 2 FCR 404 at p. 416. In *G (A Child) (Domestic Violence: Direct Contact)* [2001] 2 FCR 134 the father's failure to recognise the distress caused by the past violence was a powerful consideration in denying contact.

[629] This factor was relied upon when denying contact in *Re G (Domestic Violence: Direct Contact)* [2000] Fam Law 789.

[630] Morrisson (2009).

[631] It is not clear exactly what this means.

[632] *Practice Direction: Residence and Contact Orders: Domestic Violence and Harm* [2009] 2 FLR 1400, para 27.

The Direction also states:

> When deciding the issue of residence or contact the court should, in the light of any findings of fact, apply the individual matters in the welfare checklist with reference to those findings; in particular, where relevant findings of domestic violence have been made, the court should in every case consider any harm which the child has suffered as a consequence of that violence and any harm which the child is at risk of suffering if an order for residence or contact is made and should only make an order for contact if it can be satisfied that the physical and emotional safety of the child and the parent with whom the child is living can, as far as possible, be secured before during and after contact.[633]

However, overriding all such factors it is the welfare of the child which is the paramount consideration and domestic violence is but one factor to be taken into account. Hence, in *Re J-S (A Child) (Contact: Parental Responsibility)*,[634] despite the fact that the father had thrown a shoe at the mother, forced his way into her home, had pushed a hot tea bag in her face, and hit her across the face chipping her tooth, he was permitted contact. It was explained that the child had established a strong attachment with the father and that to end contact with the father would therefore harm the child.[635] In *Re A (Suspended Residence Order)*[636] a court ordered a mother to allow her daughter to visit the father even though the father had been found to have sexually abused one of the mother's other daughters and despite the strong opposition of the daughters to contact. Such cases will be opposed by those commentators who are concerned that too great a willingness to permit contact following serious domestic violence may endanger mothers and children.[637] Indeed, one may well ask in that case how a father can claim to be committed to the child when he treats the child's primary carer or half-sisters in that way.

The real difficulty is that in many cases there is an allegation of domestic violence, but the court is unable to determine the facts of the case.[638] The fear is that the current pro-contact climate will mean that unless there is the clearest of evidence of domestic violence contact will be ordered. This may well endanger the child and mother.

The emphasis that is placed on benefits of contact raises the concern that couples will agree contact orders even where there has been domestic violence and contact will not benefit the children. As Jane Craig[639] has argued, it should not be assumed that in cases where the couple agree to contact taking place that contact is necessarily beneficial or even safe for the child. As she notes, of the 29 children killed by their fathers during contact in one study, in three of the cases contact had been ordered by the court. Research by Judith Masson[640] also supported the view that consent orders for contact pay insufficient attention to safeguarding children, particularly in cases where there has been domestic violence. It seems the desire to persuade the parties to reach agreement, and the overemphasis on the benefits of contact, is leading some lawyers to encourage their clients to agree to contact in circumstances where doing so harms or endangers children. There is also disturbing evidence that in cases of mediated agreement mediators sideline and downplay allegations of domestic violence to encourage the parties to agree to contact taking place.[641]

---

[633] Para 26.
[634] [2002] 3 FCR 433.
[635] See *Carp v Byron* [2006] 1 FCR 1 for a case where the violence justified an order for no contact.
[636] [2010] 1 FLR 1679.
[637] Hester (2002).
[638] *S v S (Interim Contact)* [2009] 2 FLR 1586.
[639] Craig (2007).
[640] Masson (2006d).
[641] Trinder, Jenks and Firth (2010).

## (v) Step-parents and hostility

Sometimes the courts are willing to accept the opposition of a step-parent to the contact order as reason enough for denying contact. In *Re SM (A Minor) (Natural Father: Access)*[642] the fear that contact with the natural father would destabilise the relationship between the mother and the stepfather was seen as a reason for denying contact. A similar finding was made in *Re B (Contact: Stepfather's Opposition)*,[643] where the stepfather gave evidence that he would leave the mother if the father were allowed contact with the child. The Court of Appeal accepted that the stepfather was sincere[644] and noted that, had contact with the father been ordered, the contact would have been very limited. These cases are very controversial, with some arguing that a step-parent's views should not be taken into account.

## (vi) The relevance of the child's opposition

As has already been discussed, in deciding what is in the welfare of a child the court will place much weight on the child's views,[645] taking into account the age of the child, the reasons behind the child's views and the seriousness of the issues.[646] In *M v M (Defined Contact Application)*[647] a father was granted residence of his children. The eldest daughter insisted on regularly visiting her mother. Her father sought a defined contact order to limit the contact between the mother and the daughter. The court made 'no order'; the argument being that if a defined order was made, the child would be in a position deliberately to flout it. In effect, the court accepted that in relation to mature children the law can do little to encourage or discourage contact with parents and so there is usually little benefit in making contact orders.[648] For younger children courts may not be unduly perturbed by the apparent distress of children,[649] believing that the long-term benefits of contact normally outweigh short-term distress.[650] However, in *Re C (Contact: No Order for Contact)*[651] the child (aged nearly 4) was terrified of the father and this justified an order that even indirect contact be prohibited. In *Re M and B (Children) (Contact: Domestic Violence)*[652] Thorpe LJ held that it was a misdirection for the trial judge to hold that an 8-year-old was too immature to express a view on contact. Less controversially, in *Re S (Contact: Children's Views)*[653] the strong views of 16-, 14- and 12-year-olds that they did not want to have contact with their father were followed by the court. The Court of Appeal wisely stated:

> They [the children] might obey, perhaps they will obey an order of the court, but with what result? What would be the quality of what is being asked of them by me to do if I order them

---

[642] [1996] 2 FLR 333, [1997] 2 FCR 475.
[643] [1997] 2 FLR 579, [1998] 3 FCR 289.
[644] Evidence was given that his attitude was common among the Asian community.
[645] Buchanan, Hunt, Bretherton and Bream (2001: 18) suggest that children often feel that their views are not properly taken into account in contact cases.
[646] In *Re F (Minors) (Denial of Contact)* [1993] 2 FLR 677, [1993] 1 FCR 945 CA contact was not ordered because the children (aged 12 and 9) strongly opposed contact following the father's 'sex change' operation.
[647] [1998] 2 FLR 244.
[648] See Smart and Neale (1999a: 189) for an argument that children could be said to have a right not to have contact with parents against their wishes.
[649] *Re H (Minors) (Access)* [1992] 1 FLR 148, [1992] 1 FCR 70.
[650] *Re F (Minors) (Denial of Contact)* [1993] 2 FLR 677, [1993] 1 FCR 945, where the boys did not want contact to see their transsexual father.
[651] [2000] Fam Law 699.
[652] [2001] 1 FCR 116 at para 19.
[653] [2002] 1 FLR 1156.

to do it? . . . If young people are to be brought up to respect the law, then it seems to me that the law must respect them and their wishes, even to the extent of allowing them, as occasionally they do, to make mistakes.[654]

In recent years some commentators have sought to attach significance to what has been called 'parental alienation syndrome'.[655] This controversial 'syndrome' is said to lead to the resident parent turning the child against the non-resident parent. Supporters claim that appreciation of this syndrome means that if the child opposes contact the court should readily ignore his or her view and order contact. Indeed, the opposition of the child may indicate that the residential parent suffers from this syndrome and that residence should be changed. An example of the 'syndrome' may be found in *Re M (Intractable Contact Dispute: Interim Care Order)*[656] where it was found that a mother had falsely persuaded her children that their father had physically and sexually assaulted them. In *Re S (Transfer of Residence)*[657] the court also acknowledged the existence of alienation. There the child said he would prefer to be taken into care than live with his father. Despite the courts granting a residence order in the father's favour, the boy refused to talk to or look at the father. Many contact visits were arranged to ease the transfer of residence but they simply caused the boy great distress. Finally the father agreed that the boy should live with the mother.[658] However, in other cases the courts have rejected suggestions that the resident parent suffered from the syndrome. In *Re O (A Child) (Contact: Withdrawal of Application)*[659] Wall J suggested the father's allegation of the syndrome was denial of his own responsibility for the problems relating to contact.[660] In fact most commentators argue such a syndrome does not exist.[661] In *Re C (Children: Contact)*[662] Butler-Sloss P thought that the more likely explanation for the children's objection to seeing their father was that he had left his wife and children for another woman, rather than parental alienation syndrome. Indeed, she suggested the father's obsession with his view that the mother suffered from the syndrome was blocking his appreciation of the reality. Evidence from Australia suggests that it is far more common for non-resident parents to seek to turn children against resident parents than vice versa.[663] The courts, to date, have not found evidence to support the existence of the syndrome,[664] although they do recognise the importance of ensuring that the expressed views of the children are genuinely their own views.[665] Indeed the UK courts have accepted that in complex cases the child should be separately represented to ensure their views are clearly heard by the court.[666] This is in line with the approach taken by the European Court of Human Rights.[667]

[654] At p. 1169.
[655] Hobbs (2002a) provides a basic introduction to this alleged syndrome. Gardner et al. (2005) provide a book-length treatment of the subject. See also Clarkson and Clarkson (2007).
[656] [2004] 1 FCR 687. See *Re M (Children)* [2005] EWCA Civ 1090 where the resident father was found to have turned the children against the non-resident mother.
[657] See also *Re S (Transfer of Residence)* [2010] 1 FLR 1785.
[658] *Warwick CC v TE* [2010] EWHC B19 (Fam).
[659] [2004] 1 FCR 687.
[660] See also *Re Bradford, Re O'Connell* [2006] EWCA Civ 1199.
[661] Sturge and Glaser (2000); Burch (2002).
[662] [2002] 3 FCR 183, [2002] 1 FLR 1136. Hobbs (2002b) claims that the decision supports the existence of the syndrome, but this appears to be a misinterpretation (see Masson (2002b)).
[663] Rhoades (2002a).
[664] *Re P (A Child) (Expert Evidence)* [2001] 1 FCR 751; *Re S (Contact: Children's Views)* [2002] 1 FLR 1156.
[665] *Re T (A Child: Contact)* [2003] 1 FCR 303, [2003] 1 FLR 531.
[666] *Re A (A Child) (Separate Representation in Contact Proceedings)* [2001] 2 FCR 55.
[667] *Ignaccolo-Zenide v Romania* (2001) 31 EHRR 7.

## (vii) Indirect contact

Even if direct contact is not appropriate, the court will make an order for indirect contact in all but exceptional cases.[668] That can take the form of letters or e-mails. If necessary a third party can be asked to pass on the communications to ensure there is no contact between the parents.[669] In *Re L (Contact: Genuine Fear)*,[670] indirect contact was ordered even though the mother suffered a 'phobia' of the father (he had been a Hell's Angel who had stabbed his ex-wife, and her solicitor and boyfriend). Although it was felt that the 'phobia'[671] meant that direct contact could not take place, this was no reason for denying indirect contact. The judge asked for professional help in ensuring the indirect contact took place because it was feared that the mother might destroy any correspondence. Only very rarely will the court not even order indirect contact. In *Re C (Contact: No Order for Contact)*[672] the child was terrified of his father and destroyed all letters sent by the father. This persuaded Connell J to make an order which prohibited indirect contact between the father and the child.[673]

## (viii) Enforcement of contact orders

There is much debate over how the court should enforce contact.[674] For example, if a mother refused to permit a father to have contact with a child, despite the existence of a contact order, should she be sent to prison? In such a case, *A v N (Committal: Refusal of Contact)*,[675] it was confirmed that, when considering imprisonment, the welfare of the child was a material consideration but was not the paramount consideration.[676] Holman J accepted that the daughter would suffer if the mother were imprisoned but held that this was not due to the law's approach but that 'this little child suffers because the mother chooses to make her suffer'.[677] However, in more recent cases the courts have sought to avoid such a drastic conclusion. In *Re F (Contact: Enforcement: Representation of Child)*,[678] where the baby suffered cerebral palsy, it was held that the harm to the child if the mother was imprisoned was such that it would be inappropriate to attach a penal notice to a contact order. In *Re K (Children: Committal Proceedings)*[679] the Court of Appeal emphasised that imprisonment of the resident parent would infringe the article 8 rights of both the mother and child and therefore before committal the court should ensure that the committal is justifiable under article 8(2).[680] The Court of Appeal in *Re M (Contact Order: Committal)*[681] stated that, before committal to prison, other remedies such as further contact orders, a fine,[682] family therapy[683] and even changing residence should be explored.[684] Despite this decision the courts are still

---

[668] *Re K (Contact: Mother's Anxiety)* [1999] 2 FLR 703; *Re F (A Child) (Indirect Contact through Third Party)* [2006] 3 FCR 553.

[669] *Re F (A Child) (Indirect Contact through Third Party)* [2006] 3 FCR 553.

[670] [2002] 1 FLR 621.

[671] Bruce Blair QC described her fears as 'irrational', perhaps surprisingly.

[672] [2000] Fam Law 699.

[673] See Perry and Rainey (2007) for a discussion of the use of indirect contact orders.

[674] Smart and Neale (1997).

[675] [1997] 1 FLR 533, [1997] 2 FCR 475.

[676] This was approved by the Court of Appeal in *M v M (Breaches of Orders: Committal)* [2005] EWCA Civ 1722.

[677] See also *F v F (Contact: Committal)* [1998] 2 FLR 237, [1999] 2 FCR 42.

[678] [1998] 1 FLR 691, [1998] 3 FCR 216.

[679] [2003] 2 FCR 336.

[680] The non-resident parent's and child's rights under article 8 must also be considered.

[681] [1999] 1 FLR 810.

[682] *Re M (Contact Order)* [2005] 2 FLR 1006. Of course many mothers cannot afford to pay a fine: Butler-Sloss P in *Re S (A Child) (Contact)* [2004] 1 FCR 439 at para 29.

[683] *Re S (Uncooperative Mother)* [2004] EWCA Civ 597.

[684] Baroness Hale suggested that this was more often threatened than actually done.

occasionally willing to imprison a resident parent who is refusing to allow contact. In *Re S (Contact Dispute: Committal)*[685] Hedley J was willing to uphold a committal to prison for seven days after a mother failed to allow a father to see his 6-year-old daughter. It was a last resort, he accepted, but respect for the rule of law required obedience to orders of the court, and punishment if they were not obeyed. In *B v S (Contempt: Imprisonment of Mother)*[686] the Court of Appeal stated that the 'days were long gone' when a mother could assume her care of the child protected her from imprisonment following breach of an order. Nevertheless, the Court emphasised that the interference in the baby's right to family life had to be justified. Where the prison authorities allowed mothers to take babies into prison that may make imprisonment easier to justify.

Another option is to change the residence order. So if a mother is refusing to comply with a contact order the court may make a residence order in favour of the father. Of course, that will only be an option if the making of the order is in the child's welfare. A court which believes that it is important that the child retain a relationship with both parents, may determine that the child will be better off with the father who will allow contact, than with the mother who will not. However, changing residence was described by the Court of Appeal in *Re A (Residence Order)*[687] as 'a judicial weapon of last resort'.[688] In that case a transfer of residence was said to be premature because although the mother had prevented the father from having contact, no formal contact orders had in fact been made so she was not in breach of a court order. When deciding whether to transfer residence the court must be persuaded that the benefits of contact with both parents outweighed any disadvantages that would flow from the child being with the other parent.

Baroness Hale stated that transferring residence is more often used as a threat, than is carried out.[689] Colderidge J described it as 'putting a gun to a parent's head to force her or him to rethink'.[690] Many resident parents who are told that if they do not allow contact the children will be removed to the other parent will be thereby persuaded to allow contact. In *Re S (Transfer of Residence)*[691] Bellamy J transferred the residence of an 11-year-old boy from the mother to the father, after contact with the father had failed. Notably this was done despite the strong opposition of the boy to the change. Bellamy J dismissed his views as being the result of 'alienation' and claimed that the mother was guilty of causing severe harm to the boy by her attitude to contact. This case could be contrasted with *Re C (A Child)*[692] where the mother's 'viciously corrupting influence' had persuaded the child that she had been abused by the father. The court concluded that contact with the father would harm the child and so could not be ordered. In so doing the court accepted that the father justifiably felt let down by the court system.

It seems that the courts are making increasing efforts to enforce contact orders; giving up on enforcement should be a 'last resort'.[693] Ward LJ in *Re M (Contact Dispute: Court's Positive Duty)* held:

> Where, as in this case, the court has the picture that a parent is seeking, without good reason, to eliminate the other parent from the child's, or children's, lives, the court should not stand by

[685] [2004] EWCA Civ 1790.
[686] [2009] 2 FLR 1005.
[687] [2010] 1 FLR 1083.
[688] Para 18.
[689] In *Re G (Children) (Residence: Same-Sex Partner)* [2006] UKHL 43 at para 42.
[690] *Re A (Suspended Residence Order)* [2010] 1 FLR 1679.
[691] [2010] 1 FLR 1785.
[692] [2008] EWCA Civ 551.
[693] *Re P (Children) (Contact Order)* [2009] 2 FCR 402.

and take no positive action. Justice to the children and the deprived parent, in this case the mother, requires the court to leave no stone unturned that might resolve the situation and prevent long-term harm to the children.[694]

It should not be thought that problems with contact are always caused by resident mothers. In *Re Bradford; Re O'Connell*[695] the Court of Appeal concluded that problems with contact leading to contact breaking down were more often on account of the father's conduct than the mother's. Those cases involved fathers who falsely blamed the mothers for turning the children against them and attacked the courts and professionals without foundation for not enforcing higher levels of contact.

The greater efforts taken by the court to enforce contact are a response both to judicial acceptance that previously not enough had been done to ensure the child saw both parents[696] and also to the Human Rights Act 1998.

The European Court of Human Rights in *Hokkanen v Finland*[697] interpreted article 8 to mean that not only may the state prevent contact between a parent and child only where permitted to do so under paragraph 2 of article 8, but, further, that there is a positive obligation on the state to ensure that other people do not prevent contact.[698] In that case a father had been granted rights of contact, but the grandparents, who were caring for the child, refused to permit him to have access to the child. The state was found to be in breach of article 8 because it failed to provide an effective means by which the father could enforce his right of contact. However, the state is required only to take reasonable steps to enforce contact and must do so without undue delay.[699] The European Court in *Glaser v UK*[700] accepted that, at the end of the day, if the only means of enforcement were imprisonment of the residential parent or changing residence, the state may justifiably decide not to take these steps.[701] As it was put in *Kosmopoulou v Greece*,[702] 'any obligation to apply coercion in this area must be limited since the interests as well as the rights and freedoms of all concerned must be taken into account, and more particularly the best interests of the child and his or her rights under art 8 of the Convention'.[703] In deciding whether the national courts have acted sufficiently to protect a person's right of contact, one factor to take into account is the importance of respect for the rule of law.[704] The speed of the response of the state was an important issue to take into account too.[705] In *Hansen v Turkey*[706] the European Court of Human Rights held that coercive measures against children (e.g. requiring them to meet non-resident parents they did not want to see) were not desirable but could not be ruled out.[707] Applying this approach in *Kaleta v Poland*[708] the European Court accepted that where a 15-year-old did not want to see her father there was little the state could do.

---

[694] [2006] 1 FLR 621 at para 41.
[695] [2006] EWCA Civ 1199.
[696] *Re D (A Child) (Intractable Contact Dispute: Publicity)* [2004] 3 FCR 234.
[697] [1996] 1 FLR 289, [1995] 2 FCR 320.
[698] See also *Hansen v Turkey* [2003] 3 FCR 97.
[699] *Karadzic v Croatia* [2006] 1 FCR 36.
[700] [2000] 3 FCR 193.
[701] *Nuutinen v Finland*, App no. 32842/96, unreported, 27.6.2000, ECtHR.
[702] [2004] 1 FCR 427.
[703] At para 45.
[704] *Sobota-Gajjc v Bosnia* [2007] 3 FRC 591.
[705] *M v Serbia* [2007] 1 FCR 760.
[706] [2004] 1 FLR 142.
[707] See *Damnjanović v Serbia* [2009] 1 FLR 339 for a case where the children's refusal to leave the father justified the state in not enforcing the mother's residence order.
[708] [2009] 1 FLR 927.

As a result of this judicial pressure and increasing complaints from fathers' groups and the media, the Government passed the Children and Adoption Act 2006. This has increased the range of orders available to a court in a disputed contact case, by inserting a new sections into the Children Act 1989. The thinking behind the Act is revealed in the following statement by Ruth Kelly, introducing a draft of the legislation:

> We recognise also that, after a separation, parents are the people who know best what will work for their family and how to bring up their children.
>
> There is a role for Government, though, in helping to ease people's passage through what is undoubtedly one of the most difficult times of their lives, and support them in finding what is best for their family.[709]

Note that the issue is seen as one for parents to resolve, albeit with government help. The picture is not the usual one of the courts telling parents what should happen and promoting the welfare of the child, but rather the dispute is seen as a private one, for the couple to sort out. The assumption is that they will reach a solution which promotes the welfare of the child. The Government also appears to accept that the solution to the issue lies in social changes whereby it will become socially unacceptable for a non-resident parent not to be involved in his or her child's life or for a resident parent to impede a non-resident in having contact.[710] Diduck and Kaganas reject any suggestion that in the Act the state is in a straight-forward way relegating contact disputes to a private matter:

> The state is seeking to 'radiate' messages about how to separate or divorce well and these messages are rights-orientated and rule-like. The state is seeking to promote 'responsible' decision-making by families, so allowing for the preservation of the liberal idea of family privacy. At the same time, the state is seeking to promote a particular construction of welfare, one that 'responsible' families will embrace.[711]

The Government in introducing the 2006 Act accepted that there were problems with the way the current law worked. Many found the courts slow, impenetrable and unsatisfactory.[712] However, there is no 'magic bullet' to solve the solution of bitterly contested contact cases.[713]

The new orders include the following:

### (a) A contact activity direction

A contact activity direction is a direction to engage in the following activities:

---

**LEGISLATIVE PROVISION**

**Children's Act 1989, section 11A(5)**

(a) programmes, classes and counselling or guidance sessions of a kind that—

    (i) may assist a person as regards establishing, maintaining or improving contact with a child;

    (ii) may, by addressing a person's violent behaviour, enable or facilitate contact with a child;

(b) sessions in which information or advice is given as regards making or operating arrangements for contact with a child, including making arrangements by means of mediation.[714]

---

[709] HM Government (2005b: 1).
[710] HM Government (2005b: 6).
[711] Diduck and Kaganas (2006: 323).
[712] HM Government (2005b: 5).
[713] Hunt and Roberts (2004) make this point having surveyed a wide range of jurisdictions.
[714] See Perry and Rainey (2007) for a welcome response to such orders.

These must not include medical or psychiatric examination, assessment or treatment, or the taking of medication.[715] Rather they will require a person to attend group sessions, lectures or individual meetings in an attempt to encourage the parties to reach an appropriate agreement over contact.[716] The parties may both be required to attend or may attend separately. Children cannot be required to attend.[717] In deciding whether to make a contact activity direction the welfare of the child is the paramount consideration.[718]

Section 11B(1) of the Children Act 1989 states: 'A court may not make a contact activity direction in any proceedings unless there is a dispute as regards the provision about contact that the court is considering whether to make in the proceedings.' Presumably this is designed to prevent a court making a contact activity direction where the parties have come to an agreement with which the court is unhappy: for example, where the couple agree there should be only negligible contact, but the court would like to see more. However, in such a case it could be argued under s 11B(1) that there is a dispute between the judge and the parties and so a direction can be made; that interpretation would probably be contrary to the intention of the drafters of the legislation.

Before making a contact activity direction the court must be satisfied of three matters as set out in s 11E:

## LEGISLATIVE PROVISION

**Children's Act 1989, section 11E**

(2) The first matter is that the activity proposed to be specified is appropriate in the circumstances of the case.

(3) The second matter is that the person proposed to be specified as the provider of the activity is suitable to provide the activity.

(4) The third matter is that the activity proposed to be specified is provided in a place to which the individual who would be subject to the direction (or the condition) can reasonably be expected to travel.

The court is also required to consider the likely effect of imposing the condition on the individual;[719] in particular, whether there will be a conflict with religious beliefs, employment or education.[720] A fee may be charged for the contact activities, although help may be provided to those who cannot afford it.[721]

This section is an acknowledgement by the law that formal court-based intervention may not be the most effective way of dealing with a hotly contested contact dispute. It is better to assist and inform the couple so that they can reach an agreement between themselves. It may be questioned whether or not telling parents about the importance of putting children first will be of much assistance. Generally couples accept this; where they are in dispute is whether contact will promote the welfare of the child.[722] The studies from the pilot projects on family

---

[715] CA 1989, s 11A(6).
[716] See Rhoades (2003) for the negative Australian experience of these, although P. Parkinson (2006) appears more positive about it.
[717] CA 1989, s 11B(2), unless they are the parents of the child whose case is before the court.
[718] CA 1989, s 11A(9).
[719] CA 1989, s 11E(5).
[720] CA 1989, s 11E(6).
[721] CA 1989, s 11F.
[722] Smart (2006); Kaganas and Day Sclater (2004).

resolution of contact disputes is mixed. Only half of the parents completed the programme, but those who did found the group sessions useful, with a change in form of contact taking place in two-thirds of cases.[723] The researchers concluded that the programmes offered little for the really hard cases.[724] However, it seems that around 40 per cent return to court within two years because the agreement has broken down.[725]

Vanessa May and Carol Smart argue that there are political pressures on courts to resolve disputed contact cases. They argue:

> This is producing a kind of modern folly in which family courts are being increasingly set up as if they can and should solve complex human relationship problems. When they fail, as our research suggests they are likely to, they will be required to produce a greater intensification of effort and so the cycle will repeat itself. The question that therefore perhaps requires greater attention is whether, if the aims of family policy are to protect and promote the well-being of children, this is ultimately the best use of scarce resources.[726]

### (b) Contact activity condition

This matches the contact activity direction, but is used where the court has made a contact order.[727] The same restrictions and requirements apply to a contact activity condition that apply to a contact activity direction. The condition must specify the activity and who is to provide the activity.[728] The order can require the resident parent, the parent who will be having contact or both to attend a contact activity.

### (c) Monitoring contact activity conditions or directions

When making a contact activity condition or direction the court can require a family proceedings officer to monitor whether the condition or direction is being complied with and to report to the court any failure to attend an activity.

### (d) Monitoring contact

When the court makes or varies a contact order it can require a family proceedings officer to monitor whether the order is complied with by the resident parent or the parent who is to have contact with the child.[729] The court can require the officer to report on such non-compliance as the court requests.

### (e) Contact warning notices

Section 11I of the Children Act 1989 states: 'Where the court makes (or varies) a contact order, it is to attach to the contact order (or the order varying the contact order) a notice warning of the consequences of failing to comply with the contact order.' No doubt this will often be backed up with an oral warning given by the judge to the parties, where appropriate.

### (f) Enforcement orders

If the court has made a contact order and is satisfied beyond reasonable doubt that a person has failed to comply with that order the court may make an enforcement order, unless the court is satisfied that the person has a reasonable excuse for not complying with the

---

[723] Trinder et al. (2006). See Trinder (2006) for a discussion of in-court mediation.
[724] Trinder et al. (2006).
[725] Trinder and Kellett (2007).
[726] May and Smart (2007: 79).
[727] CA 1989, s 11C.
[728] CA 1989, s 11C(4).
[729] CA 1989, s 11H.

order.[730] The resident parent, the parent who is to have contact or the child[731] can apply for the enforcement order. The enforcement order will require the person breaching the contact order to undertake unpaid work. Presumably this will be of the kind undertaken by a person convicted of a criminal offence who is required to serve a community sentence.

It should be emphasised that it must be shown beyond reasonable doubt that the contact order has been breached. This is the criminal burden of proof which is, perhaps, a recognition that the unpaid work order is a punishment. The defence of reasonable excuse will no doubt be often relied upon. Whether fear of violence, particularly if the court believes it to be genuine but unjustified, is a reasonable excuse is an interesting question.[732]

Section 11L of the Children Act 1989 opens:

## LEGISLATIVE PROVISION

**Children Act 1989, section 11L**

(1) Before making an enforcement order as regards a person in breach of a contact order, the court must be satisfied that—

(a)  making the enforcement order proposed is necessary to secure the person's compliance with the contact order or any contact order that has effect in its place;

(b)  the likely effect on the person of the enforcement order proposed to be made is proportionate to the seriousness of the breach of the contact order.

The court is required specifically to consider the effect of the order on the individual; in particular, whether it will interfere with his or her religious beliefs, employment or education.[733] Most significantly, s 11L(7) of the CA 1989 states: 'In making an enforcement order in relation to a contact order, a court must take into account the welfare of the child who is the subject of the contact order.' Notably this does not require the court to treat the welfare of the child as the paramount consideration. The child's welfare must only be taken into account.

### (g) Compensation for financial loss

Section 11O(2) of the Children Act 1989 states:

## LEGISLATIVE PROVISION

**Children Act 1989, section 11O(2)**

(2) If the court is satisfied that—

(a)  an individual has failed to comply with the contact order, and

(b)  a person falling within subsection (6) has suffered financial loss by reason of the breach,

it may make an order requiring the individual in breach to pay the person compensation in respect of his financial loss.

---

[730] The person claiming to have a reasonable excuse has the burden of proving this on the balance of probabilities: CA 1989, s 11J(4).

[731] The child will require leave: s 11J(6).

[732] CA 1989, s 11K states that an enforcement order cannot be made if the individual has not been served with the order.

[733] CA 1989, s 11L(4).

The people falling within subsection (6) are the resident parent, the parent who is to have contact with the child, a person subject to a condition attached to a contact order or the child.[734] The individual is not required to pay if they can show that they have reasonable excuse for failing to comply with the contact order.[735] The amount payable can be any sum up to the total lost.[736] In deciding whether to make an order the court must take into account the welfare of the child.[737] Again note that the welfare of the child is not the paramount consideration.

This provision deals with the situation where the non-resident parent buys tickets in order to take the children on an outing during a contact session, but the resident parent then refuses to hand the children over, for no good reason. In such a case the court could now order the resident parent to compensate the non-resident parent for any financial loss. It should be emphasised that, as it is not possible to make an order requiring the non-resident parent to have contact with the child if the non-resident parent does not turn up for a contact session, technically speaking that is not a breach of the order. It appears, therefore, that the resident parent cannot seek compensation for expenses they have incurred on the assumption that the non-resident parent will have the children for the day. Possibly the court will take a broad interpretation of the statute and award damages in such a case.

### (h) Family assistance orders

The Children and Adoption Act 2006 has extended the provisions dealing with a family assistance order so that they can be useful in the context of a disputed contact case. It inserts a new s 16(4A) of the Children Act 1989 which means that on making a family assistance order the court officer can 'give advice and assistance as regards establishing, improving and maintaining contact to such of the persons named in the order as may be specified in the order'. It also creates s 16(6) of the Children Act 1989 under which a court officer can be required to report to the court on matters relating to contact.

The Act is almost as notable for what it does not say as for what it does. Notably there is no presumption that a child should spend an equal amount of time with both parents, as many fathers' groups had sought.[738] The Government explained:

> The Government does not, however, believe that an automatic 50:50 division of the child's time between the two parents would be in the best interests of most children. In many separated families, such arrangements would not work in practical terms, owing to living arrangements or work commitments. Enforcing this type of arrangement through legislation would not be what many children want and could have a damaging impact on some of them. Children are not a commodity to be apportioned equally after separation. The best arrangements for them will depend on a variety of issues particular to their circumstances: a one-size-fits-all formula will not work.[739]

Indeed, there is no recognition of a right to contact or even a presumption in favour of contact. The Government stated: 'The Government firmly believes that both parents should continue to have a meaningful relationship with their children after separation as long as it

---

[734] CA 1989, s 11O(6). The child can apply only with leave and must have sufficient understanding to bring the proceedings (s 11O(7)).

[735] CA 1989, s 11O(3). The individual must have been served with a copy of the order: s 11P.

[736] CA 1989, s 11O(9).

[737] CA 1989, s 11O(14).

[738] Of course not all resident parents are mothers. See Kielty (2006) for a discussion of non-resident mothers.

[739] HM Government (2004: 42). See Cohen and Gershbain (2001) who warn of the dangers they see shared parenting presenting.

is safe and in the child's best interests.' On the other hand, there is no presumption that in cases of domestic violence there should not be contact, as some women's groups had sought.[740]

It should not be forgotten that many cases concerning contact disputes in fact raise a host of issues for the couple. They tend to be troubled families in many ways.[741] As Wall J suggests, often contact disputes are no more than a continuation of a power struggle between the couple which has been going on for some time.[742] There is, therefore, no easy solution in cases of contested contact. Academics have hotly contested the correct way of responding to a breach of a contact order:

---

### DEBATE

## How should contact orders be enforced, if at all?

Here are some of the views that have been expressed on how (if at all) contact should be enforced:

1. Smart and Neale[743] have suggested: 'Questions must be asked about where family law is going, because in its current form the law is beginning to look like a lever for the powerful to use against the vulnerable, rather than a measure to safeguard the welfare of children.' They see these cases as too often involving strong fathers using the law on contact as a tool against mothers they have abused or terrified. Contact can then become a way of continuing to exercise power over the mothers. Bainham has maintained that such an argument is in danger of equating the interests of children with those of their mothers.[744] Helen Reece puts the argument in terms of enforcement of contact maintaining gender roles:

   > These critiques point to the division of labour that still exists within the intact traditional nuclear family, characterised primarily by women taking the main responsibility for childcare, and secondarily by gendered roles in relation to shared childcare, with fathers tending to perform discrete, fun activities (such as taking children to the park) and mothers tending to remain in charge of the more repetitive, continuous and mundane day-to-day care. They argue that the strong assumption of substantial post-separation contact between fathers and children is one mechanism by which the law ensures that parental separation does not fundamentally disrupt this division of labour: instead, the nuclear family is replicated post-separation.[745]

2. Some groups promoting the interests of fathers have claimed that the non-enforcement of contact orders means that they are not worth the paper they are written on. If court orders are not enforced the law is seen as powerless and unwilling to enforce people's rights.[746] Opponents of this view may argue that if contact has taken place only following threats of imprisonment or pressure from judges or professionals there will not be effective contact.[747]

---

[740] HM Government (2005b: para 22).
[741] Kelly and Emery (2003). See also Smyth (2005) for a discussion of what causes contact problems.
[742] Wall J (2005).
[743] Smart and Neale (1997: 336).
[744] Bainham (1998b: 7).
[745] Reece (2006b: 547).
[746] Jolly (1995: 234).
[747] Herring (2003a).

3. Bainham suggests that there must be an attempt to enforce contact in order to send the message that contact is an important right of the child which the law will protect.[748] He writes:

> Unless the courts are seen to be taking the contact issue seriously, the message of the law that contact is an important right of the child may be lost. And caution needs to be exercised in equating too readily the interests of women (usually the so-called 'primary carers') and children in this matter. Moreover . . . the ECHR requires the State to take action to enforce orders for contact.[749]

4. Even if at the end of the day contact orders are not enforced, they should be made and steps should be taken to try to enforce them, he argues. Carol Smart[750] has argued against the use of rights in this context. She argues that children see contact issues not in terms of rights, but in terms of care and love. We need a law reflecting those values, rather than emphasising rights.

5. Eekelaar has warned: 'it is important not to jump from the fact that an outcome is optimally desirable to the conclusion that it should, therefore, be legally enforceable'.[751] It certainly seems odd to enforce an order designed to further a child's welfare in a way that harms a child. However, the law might be justified by the argument that the imprisonment of the mother in the case harms the child, but this promotes the welfare of children generally by encouraging parents to obey court orders.

6. Some commentators[752] have argued that where contact orders are ignored the solution lies not in imprisonment but in the use of extra-legal facilities. In *Re H (A Child) (Contact: Mother's Opposition)*[753] the mother opposed contact. The Court of Appeal took the view that the mother's opposition was without foundation and amounted to an attempt to blackmail the court. The Court of Appeal sought the assistance of a psychiatrist who was to assist the family and advise on how contact could be progressed. This indicates a recognition that some cases of this kind involve emotional and psychological difficulties more suitable for the help of a counsellor or psychiatrist than a judge or a lawyer.

7. Many commentators take the view that there is little the law can do in these cases.[754] We have to acknowledge that family law cannot always provide an answer. A recent study[755] found that couples who rely on the law to resolve their contact disputes risk making matters worse for everyone concerned. By contrast, those parents who resolve matters without recourse to the law avoid stress and distress. The researchers argued that in dealing with contentious contact cases it would be more profitable to spend time and money on services to improve the relations between the parents and children, rather than on lawyers and the legal process.

8. Several commentators[756] have noted the contrast in treatment of resident and non-resident parents. If the resident parent deprives the child of the benefit of contact he or she risks

---

[748] Bainham (2003). See also Jolly (1995); Willbourne and Stanley (2002: 688).
[749] Bainham (2005a: 160).
[750] Smart (2004).
[751] Eekelaar (2002b: 272).
[752] E.g. Masson (2000b); Buchanan and Hunt (2003).
[753] [2001] 1 FCR 59.
[754] Trinder, Beek and Connolly (2002) emphasise the harm children can suffer due to stress and dispute over contact.
[755] Trinder, Beek and Connolly (2002).
[756] E.g. Smart and Neale (1997).

imprisonment. However, if the non-resident parent does not want contact with the child (equally depriving the child of the benefit of contact) he or she will not face any legal sanction.

### Questions

1. *Is the real answer to contact disputes to rely on non-legal remedies, such as counselling and mediation? Is that appropriate in cases of domestic violence?*

2. *Normally when a court order is deliberately breached imprisonment will follow, why not in relation to contact orders?*

3. *Would it be better for the courts to be more reluctant to make contact orders, but then stricter in enforcing them?*

### Further reading

See **Bainham, Lindley, Richards, and Trinder** (2003) for a useful set of essays on contact. See **Gilmore** (2008b) for an insightful analysis of the the data on the benefits of contact.

### (ix) Contact centres

There has been increased interest in and use of contact centres.[757] These provide a neutral venue in which contact can take place. Although not designed to deal with potentially violent cases,[758] they are often used by courts and solicitors in cases where the resident parent has concerns over his or her own or his or her child's safety.[759] The contact can be supervised by a social worker or untrained volunteer, who can make sure that there is no abuse of the child. Also it would be possible for the arrangements to be such that the resident parent and contact parent do not meet.

Not everyone is convinced that the use of contact centres is the solution to the intractable problem of contact. Key to the success of such studies is that they create a safe and pleasant atmosphere for contact. One study suggested that (predictably) resident parents feel that the supervision at such centres is inadequate, while non-resident parents feel that the supervision is unnecessarily invasive and humiliating.[760] The study went on to note that in a significant minority of centres the well-being of women and children was being compromised due to a lack of staff and expertise, leading to inadequate supervision.[761] Indeed, it should be appreciated that in the UK many contact centres are run in community buildings such as church halls.[762] It should also be recalled that very young children might require the resident parent to remain in sight during the contact session.[763]

### (x) Linking contact and residence

The court might take the parents' attitudes to contact into account when deciding to whom to grant a residence order, and this can be an important consideration.[764] If, for example, the

---

[757] Lord Chancellor's Department (2002a); Humphreys and Harrison (2003a). See Wall (2010) for guidance on when contact centres should be used.

[758] A point emphasised by Humphreys and Harrison (2003b).

[759] Humphreys and Harrison (2003a).

[760] Aris, Harrison and Humphreys (2002).

[761] There is grave concern over decisions like *Re P (Parental Responsibility)* [1998] 2 FLR 96 where a paedophilic father who had been 'grooming a child' was allowed contact at a contact centre.

[762] Maclean and Mueller-Johnson (2003).

[763] Aris, Harrison and Humphreys (2002) found this to be so in a significant minority of cases.

[764] *Re A (Minors) (Custody)* [1991] 2 FLR 394 at p. 400.

mother is bitterly opposed to contact and the father is happy to allow contact, that will be a factor in favour of awarding residence to the father. Richards has even suggested it should be the most important factor.[765] Some supporters of 'parental alienation syndrome'[766] have argued that if a child is manipulated in this way by the residential parent, the residence should be changed.

## (xi) Other relatives

Step-parents[767] and grandparents[768] can apply for contact, but there is not the same assumption of the benefits of contact that exists in relation to parents.[769] Step-parents and grandparents must persuade the court that they have a close relationship with the child and that the child will benefit from continued contact. In *Re W (Contact: Application by Grandparent)*[770] Hollis J accepted that it can be extremely beneficial for a child to have contact with her grandparents, even if that contact is opposed by the parents. However, some campaigners claim that other judges too readily deny contact to grandparents, especially if that is opposed by the child's parents.[771] Grandparents with an established relationship with a child may be able to claim that they have rights to contact under article 8 of the EHCR.[772]

## (xii) Duties of contact

Although there has been much discussion of the rights of contact, there has been less about the duties of contact. Yet as Bainham has pointed out: 'to talk of contact as a *right* of anyone is devoid of meaning unless considered alongside the *obligations* which go with that right'.[773]

Bainham argues that if we acknowledge that children have a right of contact then parents have a duty to exercise it. This is controversial because it suggests that a parent who does not want to have contact with his or her child could be required by a court order (on pain of imprisonment) to have contact.[774] Bainham accepts that such a duty may be unenforceable, but this does not mean that the duty should not be recognised as a way of underlining the fact that society values relationships between parents and children. Thorpe LJ in *Re L (A Child) (Contact: Domestic Violence)* suggested that such an order cannot be made: 'The errant or selfish parent cannot be ordered to spend time with his child against his will however much the child may yearn for his company and the mother desire respite.'[775]

Bainham[776] also controversially suggests that if a parent has a right of contact with a child then the child can be said to be under a duty to permit that contact. Without such a duty the parent's right is not meaningful. Again he accepts there may be difficulties in forcing children to see parents they do not want to see, but he suggests attempts should be made to do so. John Eekelaar forcefully rejects the notion that children may be under a duty of contact: 'to put a child under a legal duty to submit to the care and attentions of someone who is not the daily caregiver simply because that person is the child's parent . . . is to put the child under

---

[765] Richards (1989).
[766] Maidment (1998).
[767] *Re H (A Minor) (Contact)* [1994] 2 FLR 776, [1994] FCR 419.
[768] *Re A (Section 8 Order: Grandparent Application)* [1995] 2 FLR 153, [1996] 1 FCR 467.
[769] For a useful discussion of grandparents and contact see Kaganas and Piper (2001).
[770] [2001] 1 FLR 263.
[771] Drew and Smith (1999).
[772] *Adam v Germany* [2009] 1 FLR 560.
[773] Bainham (2003a: 61).
[774] See also Wallbank (2010).
[775] [2000] 4 All ER 609 at p. 637e–f.
[776] Bainham (2003a).

legal constraints based not on the child's interests, but on the demands of adults, or one adult, which have arisen as a result of events in which the child had no part.'[777]

## (xiii) Encouraging contact

The problem of the lack of contact between children and non-resident parents is only partly due to non-resident parents wanting, but not being able to have, contact. A far more common cause of the lack of contact is that non-resident parents do not seek contact with children. It is notable that those who seek to emphasise the right of the child to contact use this right as a means of forcing resident parents (normally mothers) to have contact with the non-resident parents (normally fathers) but arguably more could be done by those wishing to promote the child's rights to contact if those fathers who do not have contact with their children were encouraged to do so.[778] The reality is that after separation many non-resident fathers find their relationship with their children strained.[779] Further, it is often difficult to fit in contact sessions with the work life of the non-resident parent and the social life of the child.[780]

## (xiv) The role of solicitors in contact disputes

There is evidence that family law solicitors,[781] mediators[782] and district judges[783] are keen to promote contact and will strongly discourage opposition to contact. This creates a culture where contact is seen as the norm. It may be that the attitudes of these professionals is in practical terms more important than the views of the Court of Appeal.[784]

## (xv) Contact in practice

The statistics suggest that contact arrangements often break down. Eekelaar and Clive[785] found that although two-thirds of non-residential parents had contact in the first six months, by five years after the divorce only one-third did. However, other studies have shown higher rates of contact. Eekelaar and Maclean in their study found contact rates of 69 per cent where the parents had been married, but 45 per cent where unmarried.[786] In the survey by Bradshaw et al.[787] only 21 per cent of the sample had not seen their children in the last year. Trinder et al.[788] found that for only 27 of the 61 families were contact arrangements 'working'. A study by the Office for National Statistics found that 10 per cent of children saw both parents daily.[789] Around 30 per cent of resident parents reported that the child never saw the non-resident parent. However, all the studies show a decline in the rate of contact as the years since parental separation pass. This drop-off has been explained on three grounds: the first is that some fathers may (falsely) believe they do not have to pay (or can escape payment of)

---

[777] Eekelaar (2006b: 68).
[778] See Herring (2003a) for a discussion of how the law might do this, including a suggestion of collecting child support more effectively. Where child support is paid there is evidence that this increases the rate of contact (see Smart et al. (2005)).
[779] Bradshaw et al. (1999).
[780] Buchanan et al. (2001: 18); Buchanan and Hunt (2003).
[781] Neale and Smart (1997).
[782] Piper (1993: 118).
[783] Bailey-Harris et al. (1998).
[784] Eekelaar, Maclean and Beinart (2000).
[785] Eekelaar and Clive (1977).
[786] Eekelaar and Maclean (1997).
[787] Bradshaw et al. (1999).
[788] Trinder, Beek and Connolly (2002).
[789] National Statistics (2008a).

child support if they do not see the child; secondly, some find occasional contact painful;[790] thirdly, some fathers believe that the child will settle down better if contact is stopped. Another important factor is that the father may remarry or repartner[791] and his new partner may discourage contact, especially once the new couple have children of their own. Long-term contact works best where both the resident and non-resident parent are committed to making contact succeed and are willing to work through the practical difficulties.[792]

As already mentioned, contact disputes are often the most bitter cases. Many believe that too often fathers are denied contact: the courts refuse to order contact, or, where they do, the orders are not enforced. Others claim that the courts too readily order contact, placing mothers and children in danger. In fact the evidence is that where contact is applied for it is nearly always granted. In 2006 there were 26,605 orders for contact. In only 126 did the judge refuse to make contact.[793] Where couples negotiate and avoid the need for a court hearing they nearly always agree some degree of contact.[794] This shows that the argument that judges are denying fathers contact because they are anti-father is false. In fact, given that around 90 per cent of contact disputes are resolved through negotiations[795] and only the most contested reach court, the number of applications refused looks worryingly low, especially given the rates of domestic violence and child abuse. A major study of the way contact cases are dealt with found no evidence of bias against fathers. In the very few cases where contact was denied there were very good reasons for this.[796] In fact a much stronger case can be made for saying that the legal process is too ready to grant contact than it is for refusing it.

## 7 Wardship and the inherent jurisdiction

The inherent jurisdiction provides the court with powers which do not originate from statute but from the common law. The jurisdiction flows from the ancient *parens patriae* jurisdiction which the Crown owes to those subjects who are unable to protect themselves. The classic example of such subjects are children. The basis of the jurisdiction is that if a child needs protection the courts should not be inhibited from acting merely because of 'technical' difficulties. It is readily understandable that children should not be left without the protection of the law.[797] However, there is concern that use of the inherent jurisdiction bypasses the protection of the rights of children and adults in statutes. It is notable that, following the Children Act 1989, there is a limited role for the inherent jurisdiction.

The following are examples of cases where wardship has proved useful:

1. Wardship might be appropriate where the parents refuse to consent to medical treatment and it is necessary to take long-term decisions about the child.[798] In *Re C (A Baby)*[799] a

---

[790] Trinder, Beek and Connolly (2002) found that children experienced difficulty in establishing a meaningful relationship with the non-resident parent.

[791] Eekelaar and Maclean (1997) found that sometimes repartnering encouraged contact and sometimes discouraged it.

[792] Trinder, Beek and Connolly (2002).

[793] Ministry of Justice (2008).

[794] Hunt and Macleod (2008).

[795] Dyer et al. (2008).

[796] Hunt and Macleod (2008).

[797] In *W v J (Child: Variation of Financial Provision)* [2004] 2 FLR 300 it was said to be inappropriate to use wardship as a way of getting one parent to pay the other's legal fees because that would not be for the benefit of the child.

[798] Eekelaar and Dingwall (1990).

[799] [1996] 2 FLR 43, [1996] 2 FCR 569.

child was abandoned and there was no one with parental responsibility for the child who could be found. Sir Stephen Brown suggested that wardship was useful, especially as the child was severely ill, having developed brain damage after meningitis.[800]

2. Wardship might also be useful if third parties such as the press are intruding on the child's life. A prohibited steps order or specific issue order cannot be obtained against someone who is not exercising an aspect of parental responsibility. Wardship would be able to protect the child as the court has the power under wardship to prevent publicity relating to children.

3. In *Re W (Wardship: Discharge: Publicity)*[801] a father had care and control of four sons. He permitted the children to talk to the press, which led to the publication of various articles. The father also changed the children's schooling without consulting the mother. The Court of Appeal saw the need for wardship because a specific issue order could not be made which was wide enough – it was not possible to predict how the father might act in the future. It was also thought beneficial that the Official Solicitor could remain involved in the case and act as a buffer between the parents.

4. In *Re KR (Abduction: Forcible Removal by Parents)*[802] wardship was used to protect a child who, it was feared, was about to be removed from the jurisdiction to be forced to enter an arranged marriage.

5. Wardship has been found useful in cases involving children of asylum seekers where there are concerns about their welfare.[803]

The exercise of the inherent jurisdiction is quite different from wardship. The order will simply resolve a single issue relating to the child and have no wider effect. It does not provide ongoing supervision by the court of the child's welfare. The Court of Appeal has stated that its powers under the inherent jurisdiction are unlimited.[804] Specifically, it is accepted that the court, acting under the inherent jurisdiction, has wider powers than a parent.[805]

## 8 Child abduction

There is a special set of rules that deals with child abduction: that is, where a child is removed from the care of the residential parent, often to another jurisdiction. This area of law is complex, and what follows is an outline of the legal position.

### A General

The popular image of child abduction is the harrowing one of a father, having lost his battles in the court, who steals his child from his or her school and removes the child to another country: the distraught mother despairs of seeing her child again. While there are cases such as this, in fact the majority of child abductions are carried out by women. It has been

---

[800] Although see *LA v SB, AB & MB* [2010] EWCA Civ 1744 for a case where the court refused to intervene after parents refused to consent to recommended treatment.
[801] [1995] 2 FLR 466, [1996] 1 FCR 393.
[802] [1999] 2 FLR 542.
[803] Welstead and Edwards (2006: 278). However in *S v S* [2009] 1 FLR 241 it was held to be a misuse of wardship to attempt to interfere in an immigration decision.
[804] *Re W (A Minor) (Medical Treatment: Court's Jurisdiction)* [1993] Fam 64, [1992] 2 FCR 785, [1993] 1 FLR 1.
[805] *Re R (A Minor) (Wardship: Consent to Medical Treatment)* [1992] Fam 11 at p. 25.

suggested that many women are removing themselves and their children to other countries to escape from their partner's abuse and violence.[806]

As one would expect, there is clear evidence that abducted children suffer distress.[807] However, this is one of those areas of the law where there is a difference between the interests of the child in the case and the interests of children generally. If a child is abducted and lives with his or her abducting parent for several years before they are finally traced, it may be in the child's interests to stay with the abducting parent with whom they may have settled into a new way of life. On the other hand, to make such an order may send the wrong message, suggesting that parents who abduct children and keep them hidden for long enough will be permitted to keep the children.[808] Such a message may harm the interests of children generally.

It is partly a sign of the growth of international travel and cross-national relationships that international child abduction has become a growing problem. In 2007 the Official Solicitor took on 369 new cases of children abducted from the UK.[809] It must not, of course, be assumed that once the child is returned the difficulties for the resident parent are over. Fear of repeat abduction and harassment of the family may continue for some time.[810]

In a united effort to combat the problem of child abduction two international conventions have been produced which aim to facilitate the location and return of abducted children.[811] The UK has signed both the Hague Convention[812] and the European Convention,[813] which are effected by the Child Abduction and Custody Act 1985.[814] There seems to be widespread agreement that the Hague Convention works well. This is not to say that there are not enormous problems in recovering abducted children, but the Hague Convention provides as effective a legal response as might reasonably be expected. In England and Wales the returns are completed within $6^1/_2$ weeks on average (in outgoing cases the average is $11^1/_2$ weeks). The European Convention on Human Rights also requires states to take reasonable steps to return abducted children to their residential parent.[815]

Before considering the Conventions, this section will look at attempts to prevent children being taken from the country. First, there are the criminal offences created by the Child Abduction Act 1984.

## B Child Abduction Act 1984

The Child Abduction Act 1984 states that it is an offence for a person unconnected with a child to remove from or keep a child under 16 from a person who has lawful control of the

---

[806] Lowe and Perry (1998) show that 70% of abductions are by mothers and a high proportion of those may be mothers escaping violence.

[807] Marilyn Freeman (2006) discusses the effect on children of international child abduction.

[808] For explicit recognition of this argument see Wilson J in *Re L (Abduction: Pending Criminal Proceedings)* [1999] 1 FLR 433 at p. 442.

[809] Official Solicitor and Public Trustee (2009).

[810] Marilyn Freeman (2003).

[811] Required by the United Nations Convention on the Rights of the Child 1989, articles 11, 13.

[812] The full title is the Hague Convention on Civil Aspects of International Child Abduction 1980 (1981 Cmnd 8281).

[813] The European Convention on the Recognition and Enforcement of Decisions Concerning Custody of Children and Restoration of Custody of Children 1980 (Luxembourg Convention) (1981 Cmnd 8155).

[814] Although see Armstrong (2002) for an argument that the 1985 Act has failed to implement effectively the 1980 Hague Convention.

[815] *Gil and AUI v Spain* [2005] 1 FCR 210. Notice that in *Maire v Portugal* [2004] Fam Law 644 the ECtHR said that the ECHR should be interpreted in accordance with international law including the UN Convention on the Rights of the Child and the Hague Convention.

child.[816] There are two separate offences: one of removal and the other of keeping.[817] Of perhaps greater significance for the purposes of this topic is that it is an offence for a person connected with a child to remove a child under 16 from the UK,[818] without the consent[819] of everyone with parental responsibility, unless the leave of the court has been granted.[820] So, even if the parents are happily married, it could be an offence for a husband to take the children out of the country without the consent of the mother.[821] However, it is not an offence for a mother of a child to take the child out of the UK without the consent of a father without parental responsibility. There is one exception and that is where a parent has a residence order, in which case he or she can remove the child for a period of up to one month without the consent of others with parental responsibility, unless there is a prohibited steps order in effect to prevent it.

There is no offence if one of the defences under s 1(5) is proved. These are that the removal was done:

---

### LEGISLATIVE PROVISION

**Child Abduction Act 1984, section 1(5)**

(a)  . . . in the belief that the other person—

    (i)  has consented; or

    (ii)  would consent if he was aware of all the relevant circumstances; or

(b)  he has taken all reasonable steps to communicate with the other person but has been unable to communicate with him; or

(c)  the other person has unreasonably refused to consent.

---

There are other offences which could be relied upon in a child abduction case, most notably kidnapping and false imprisonment.[822]

## C Prevention of abduction, and court orders preventing removal

Once a child has been removed to a foreign country, locating the child and obtaining effective court orders for the return of the child will be extremely difficult. It is therefore far better, if possible, to prevent removal from the UK. Although the Child Abduction Act 1984 makes it clear that removal of a child can be a criminal offence, there is much to be said for applying for a court order specifically prohibiting the removal if there is a fear that the child is about to be removed. Having the court order will help in obtaining the assistance of the police and public authorities in preventing a removal.[823] For example, it will assist in utilising the 'port

---

[816] Child Abduction Act 1984, s 2.

[817] *Foster v DPP* [2005] 1 FCR 153.

[818] England, Wales, Scotland and Northern Ireland. The Channel Islands and Isle of Man are not included.

[819] Written or oral.

[820] There are a number of limited defences in s 1(5).

[821] Although there is a defence if the father believes that the mother consents even though in fact she does not (Child Abduction Act 1984, s 1(5)).

[822] E.g. *R v D* [1984] AC 778; *R v Rahman* (1985) 81 Cr App R 349; *R v C (Kidnapping: Abduction)* [1991] 2 FLR 252.

[823] The obtaining of the court order can assist in acquiring the help of government agencies (such as the Office for National Statistics or National Health Service) to locate the child or the abductor: *Practice Direction (Disclosure of Addresses)* [1989] 1 All ER 765 and *Practice Direction* [1995] 2 FLR 813. The court can order the Child Support Agency to disclose information: *Re C (A Minor) (Child Support Agency: Disclosure)* [1995] 1 FLR 201.

alert' facility, which will be discussed shortly. There are two main kinds of order that may be appropriate:

1. *Prohibited steps orders*. A prohibited steps order under s 8 of the Children Act 1989 can prohibit a parent from removing a child from the jurisdiction.[824] If there is any doubt in the mind of the would-be abductor that he or she might be permitted to take the child abroad, a court order will make it clear that the answer is no.

2. *Wardship*. If the child is made a ward of court then there is an automatic ban on taking the child out of the country. The bar operates as soon as the application for wardship is received by the court, and so it is the swiftest way of obtaining the desired protection. To remove a warded child would be a contempt of court, even if the abductor were unaware of the wardship.[825]

If there are concerns that a child may be abducted, a court may be persuaded to make additional orders that can assist in preventing the child's removal. For example, the High Court can require a person who has information concerning an abducted child to reveal it to the court.[826] The court can also order the return of a child's passport[827] or that a passport not be issued for a child. Very occasionally the courts have approved the electronic tagging of a would-be abductor.[828]

## (i) All ports warning system

The police national computer can warn all airports and ports throughout the country of a suspected abduction. The warning includes descriptions of the individuals concerned; how it is feared they may try to leave the country; and a statement of the likely ports of exit. The police organise this facility[829] and must be persuaded that the complaint is bona fide and that the danger of removal is real and imminent (i.e. within the next 24 to 48 hours). The existence of a court order is clear evidence to the police of the gravity of the issue. Of course, although the system is effective, it is by no means foolproof. The police will have the right to arrest anyone they believe to be taking a child out of the country contrary to the Child Abduction Act 1984.[830]

## D  Recovery in the UK

If the child is removed from one part of the UK to another then the situation is dealt with by the Family Law Act 1986.[831] Under Part 1 of the Family Law Act 1986 an order made by a court in one part of the UK is recognised and enforceable in any other part of the UK.[832] For example, if a father was granted the benefit of a contact order by a Scottish court and the child

---

[824] *Re D (A Minor) (Child: Removal From Jurisdiction)* [1992] 1 FLR 637.
[825] *Re J (An Infant)* (1913) 108 LT 554.
[826] Family Law Act 1986, s 33. This includes a solicitor: *Re B (Abduction: Disclosure)* [1995] 1 FLR 774. See also *Practice Direction* [1980] 2 All ER 806.
[827] Family Law Act 1986, s 37. This can include surrender of a foreign national's passport: *Re A-K (Foreign Passport)* [1997] 2 FLR 569.
[828] *Re A (Family Proceedings: Electronic Tagging)* [2009] 2 FLR 891.
[829] *Practice Direction (Child: Removal from Jurisdiction)* [1986] 1 All ER 983.
[830] *R v Griffin* [1993] Crim LR 515.
[831] The Act is not to be used where the dispute is between England and another country which is not part of the UK (*Re S (A Child: Abduction)* [2003] Fam Law 298).
[832] Section 25. For an excellent critique of the Act see Lowe (2002).

was removed to England, the father could register the Scottish court order in the local English court and then apply to have the order enforced. Once the order is registered it can be enforced as if the order had been made in that court. The only objection to registration that can be raised is that the court which made the original order had no jurisdiction to do so; or, in the light of subsequent events, the local court may be persuaded that it should reconsider the original order.[833]

## E The Hague Convention

The Hague Convention on the Civil Aspects of International Child Abduction is a remarkably successful example of international legal co-operation. The concern over the harm that child abduction can cause has led to more than 50 countries signing the Convention. The principle at the heart of the Hague Convention is that disputes over children should be resolved in the child's country of habitual residence. For example, if a child is removed from Australia and brought to Britain, there is a presumption that the dispute should be resolved in Australia. The Hague Convention is also useful in non-abduction cases: for example, where a parent living in Britain has a right of contact with a child living abroad but is being prevented from seeing that child.[834]

Baroness Hale recently summarised the purpose of the Convention in this way:

> The whole object of the Convention is to secure the swift return of children wrongfully removed from their home country, not only so that they can return to the place which is properly their 'home', but also so that any dispute about where they should live in the future can be decided in the courts of their home country and in accordance with the evidence which will mostly be there rather than in the country to which they have been removed.[835]

### (i) Who can invoke the Convention?

Article 8 of the Hague Convention provides that 'any person, institution or other body claiming that a child has been removed or retained in breach of custody rights' can invoke the Convention. So anyone can claim that the child has been wrongfully removed or retained, even the child him- or herself. However, the applicant must have some interest in the matter. Rather surprisingly *Ansari v Ansari*[836] held that even where the Convention applied a parent could still rely on wardship or the inherent jurisdiction to obtain an order for the return of the child.

### (ii) To whom does the Convention apply?

Article 4 explains that the Convention applies to any child under the age of 16[837] who is habitually resident in one contracting state but has been wrongfully removed to or retained in another contracting state.[838] These terms need some clarification.

---

[833] *Re M (Minors) (Custody: Jurisdiction)* [1992] 2 FLR 382 at pp. 386–7.
[834] Lowe (1994).
[835] *D (A Child) (Abduction: Foreign Custody Rights)* [2007] 1 FCR 1, para 48.
[836] [2009] 1 FLR 1121.
[837] The Convention does not apply to over 16-year-olds: *Re H (Abduction: Child of 16)* [2000] 2 FLR 51, although the inherent jurisdiction could be invoked for over 16-year-olds who have been abducted.
[838] See *Al Habtoor v Fotheringham* [2001] Fam Law 352 for an unsuccessful attempt to use wardship in relation to a child who was no longer habitually resident in the UK.

## (a) Habitual residence

The key question is where the habitual residence of the child is immediately before the wrongful removal.[839] Normally children will take on the residence of their parents,[840] but if the parents agree that a child should live elsewhere, this may change a child's residence. However, if the child is living overseas simply for education, while the parents remain in the UK, the child's habitual residence will remain in the UK.[841] If parents separate then the child's residence normally follows that of the primary carer.[842] A wrongful removal cannot change a child's habitual residence.[843] To change habitual residence it is necessary to show a settled purpose to stay in the new country;[844] although it is not necessary to show that the person has no plans to return to their original country.[845] In *Cannon v Cannon*[846] a mother managed to remove her child from the USA to England, and by subterfuge prevented the father from discovering their whereabouts for four years. The Court of Appeal held that on these facts it was unlikely that the child could be said to have settled into life in England. But on the rehearing in *Re C (Abduction: Settlement)*[847] Kirkwood J found that the girl was flourishing. She was well integrated into her local community and thriving at her school. She could therefore be said to have been settled. Further, the emotional harm to the child that would be caused by returning her to the United States meant that she would not be returned. Although the case might be seen as setting a dangerous precedent as an 'abductor's charter', the judge was clearly influenced by the fact that the father was in prison in the USA for cruelty to children. If the child was returned the mother was likely to be imprisoned too (for the abduction) and this could lead to the child entering care. The facts of this case were, therefore, rather unusual. The final part (hopefully) of the long-running litigation came in *Re C (Abduction: Residence and Contact)*[848] where a residence order was made in the mother's favour with unsupervised contact for the father.[849]

## (b) 'Wrongful' removal or retention

In order to use the Convention it is necessary to find the taking or retention to be wrongful, within the meaning of article 3. The removal or retention is wrongful if the act is contrary to the rights of custody under the law of the contracting state in which the child is habitually resident.[850] The judge must first decide what rights the claimant has under the relevant state and then decide whether those rights amount to rights of custody for the purposes of the Hague Convention.[851] Article 5(a) explains that: '"rights of custody" includes rights relating to the care of the person of the child, and, in particular, the right to determine the child's

---

[839] *Re S (A Minor) (Abduction)* [1991] 2 FLR 1 CA. For a case where a newborn child was found to have no country of habitual residence see *W and B v H (Child Abduction: Surrogacy)* [2002] Fam Law 345.

[840] It seems that older children may be able to form the necessary intention to establish a residence apart from their parents. This was suggested *obiter* in *B v H (Children) (Habitual Residence)* [2002] 2 FCR 329.

[841] *Ansari v Ansari* [2009] 1 FLR 1121.

[842] But not always. See, e.g., *Re M (Minors) (Residence Order: Jurisdiction)* [1993] 1 FLR 495, [1993] 1 FCR 718.

[843] *N v N (Child Abduction: Habitual Residence)* [2000] 3 FCR 84.

[844] *Re A (Abduction: Consent: Habitual Residence)* [2005] EWHC 2998 (Fam).

[845] *Re P-J (Children) (Abduction: Habitual Residence: Consent)* [2010] 1 FCR 32.

[846] [2004] 3 FCR 438.

[847] [2005] 1 FLR 938.

[848] [2005] EWHC 2205 (Fam).

[849] Even where a child is found to be settled in the UK the court may still decide to return the child if the courts of the original jurisdiction are best suited to determining the case: *F v M and Another (Abduction: Acquiescence: Settlement)* [2008] 3 FCR 718.

[850] It is necessary to show that the rights of custody were actually exercised or would have been exercised but for the removal or retention.

[851] *Kennedy v Kennedy* [2010] 1 FLR 782.

place of residence'.[852] Clearly the removal will be wrongful if it is contrary to an express court order[853] or contrary to the general law of the relevant state,[854] although the Court of Appeal in *Re V-B (Abduction: Custody Rights)*[855] stated that a right to be consulted before removing a child, but not to veto the removal, did not amount to custody rights. The removal is wrongful even if the taker was ignorant of the wrongfulness.[856] If a child has been taken to England from another country the courts will accept that other country's courts' assessment of whether the removal was wrongful under their law,[857] unless their characterisation of parental rights was clearly out of line with the international understanding.[858]

The majority of the Court of Appeal in *Re B (Minors) (Abduction)*[859] and Cazalet J in *Re O (Abduction: Custody Rights)*[860] gave a wider meaning to rights of custody and accepted that exceptionally rights of custody could include factual day-to-day care of the child, even though this is not technically supported by a legal right. So if a relative had for some time been caring for a child without the formal legal right to do so and the father of the child suddenly removed the child, that could still be regarded as a wrongful taking.[861] Similarly, if a mother had abandoned care of her daughter to someone else they could obtain rights of custody.[862] However, if the unmarried father did not have parental responsibility and was not the primary carer of the child then he will not have custody rights.[863] In *A v H (Registrar General for England and Wales and Another Intervening)*[864] a father who cohabited for under a year with the mother and children following a religious service of marriage, but who was not officially married, did not thereby have custody rights. The mother had not abandoned care to him, nor did he have any rights to decide where the child should live. Rights to contact are not enough to be rights of custody.[865] These are controversial decisions, not readily justified by the meaning of the Convention, but they do recognise that often children are cared for by those who do not formalise their position as carers in the eyes of the law.

If an application is made to a court to decide the child's future, the court thereby acquires rights of custody over the child. This was confirmed by the House of Lords in *Re H (Abduction: Rights of Custody)*.[866] Therefore, if a father or relative who does not have legal rights of custody applies to have rights over the child, then any removal of the child will be wrongful as in breach of the *court's* rights of custody. Although this may appear to be a rather strained interpretation of the phrase 'rights of custody', it overcomes the problem of a parent

---

[852] A parent can have rights of custody even if he has been imprisoned and so restricted in the way he can exercise those rights: *Re L (A Child)* [2005] EWHC 1237 (Fam).

[853] *Re C (A Minor) (Abduction)* [1989] 1 FLR 403.

[854] *C v C (Minors) (Child Abduction)* [1992] 1 FLR 163.

[855] [1999] 2 FLR 192. See also the discussion in *Re S (Minors) (Abduction: Wrongful Retention)* [1994] Fam 530.

[856] *C v C (Minors) (Child Abduction)* [1992] 1 FLR 163.

[857] *Re D (A Child) (Abduction: Foreign Custody Rights)* [2007] 1 FCR 1. The case went to the ECtHR: *D v Romania and the UK* [2008] 2 FCR 303.

[858] This might be so if, for example, the country only allowed fathers to have parental rights.

[859] [1993] 1 FLR 988. Stressed in *Re W, Re B (Child Abduction: Unmarried Father)* [1998] 2 FLR 146, per Hale J, although the dicta are hard to reconcile with the House of Lords' decision in *Re J (A Minor) (Abduction: Custody Rights)* [1990] 2 AC 562.

[860] [1997] 2 FLR 702.

[861] See *Re F (Abduction: Unmarried Father: Sole Carer)* [2003] Fam Law 222; *Re G (Abduction: Rights of Custody)* [2002] Fam Law 732.

[862] *Re B (A Minor) (Abduction)* [1994] 2 FLR 249.

[863] *Re C (Child Abduction) (Unmarried Father: Rights of Custody)* [2003] 1 FLR 252; *Re J (Abduction: Acquiring Custody Rights by Caring for Child)* [2005] Fam Law 605.

[864] [2009] 3 FCR 95.

[865] *Hunter v Murrow* [2005] 3 FCR 1.

[866] [2000] 1 FLR 374.

removing a child when an application for custody rights has been lodged but the court has not yet heard the case.[867]

There has been some doubt over whether a removal or retention is wrongful if it has been done with the consent of the parent with custody rights.[868] In *Re C (Abduction: Consent)*[869] it was suggested that consent could not render a wrongful removal justifiable, because consent is specifically mentioned as a defence under article 13(a) and the issue should be relevant under article 13(a), rather than as negating the wrongfulness of the custody. However, Bennett J in *Re O (Abduction: Consent and Acquiescence)*[870] disagreed and said that consent is relevant for both article 3 and article 13(a).[871]

### (c) Removal or retention

The Convention refers to both removal and retention. In *Re H, Re S*[872] the House of Lords stressed that removal and retention were different concepts. Removal was defined as: 'when a child, which has previously been in the state of its habitual residence, is taken away across the frontier of that state'; whereas retention 'occurs where a child, which has previously been for a limited period of time outside the state of its habitual residence, is not returned on the expiry of such limited period'.[873] *Re G* also explained that retention arises where a child who has been taken outside of their country of habitual residence for an approved period of time is not returned there when the time is up.[874]

### (iii) The presumption in favour of returning the child

Under article 12 of the Convention, if an application is brought within 12 months of the removal, the court must order the return of the child unless one of the defences in article 13 applies.[875] If more than a year has passed then the child should be returned 'unless it is demonstrated that the child is now settled in its new environment'. The courts have clarified some of the terminology. 'Now' refers to the date of the commencement of the proceedings and not the date of the hearing, explained Bracewell J in *Re N (Minors) (Abduction)*.[876] As to 'settled', Bracewell J stated that this involves both a physical element of being established in a community and an emotional one, indicating security.[877] Wilson J in *Re L (Abduction: Pending Criminal Proceedings)*[878] suggested that a year living in hiding could not lead to 'a settled life'.[879]

The House of Lords in *Re M (Children) (Abduction)*[880] confirmed that even though a child had settled into her new environment the court had a discretion to return the child. In exercising that discretion the court should take into account the welfare and rights of the

---

[867] For a controversial application see *Re H (Child Abduction) (Unmarried Father: Rights of Custody)* [2003] Fam Law 469, discussed Beevers (2006).
[868] See *Re P-J (Children) (Abduction: Habitual Residence: Consent)* [2010] 1 FCR 32 for a helpful discussion of the issues, but which did not resolve the issue.
[869] [1996] 1 FLR 414.
[870] [1997] 1 FLR 924.
[871] The agreement may be vitiated by deceit.
[872] *Re S (Minors) (Abduction: Custody Rights)* [1991] 2 AC 476.
[873] [1991] 2 AC 476 at p. 500, per Lord Brandon.
[874] *Re G (Abduction: Withdrawal of Proceedings, Acquiescence and Habitual Residence)* [2007] EWHC 2807 (Fam).
[875] Delays in dealing with abduction cases could infringe the article 6 rights of the parties: *Deak v Romania and United Kingdom* [2008] 2 FLR 994.
[876] [1991] 1 FLR 413.
[877] See also *Re M (A Minor) (Abduction: Acquiescence)* [1996] 1 FLR 315.
[878] [1999] 1 FLR 433.
[879] See also *Re H (Abduction: Child of 16)* [2000] 2 FLR 51.
[880] [2008] 1 FCR 536.

child, the broad circumstances of the case, and the general policy considerations underlying the Convention. Baroness Hale stated that these included 'not only the swift return of abducted children, but also comity between the contracting states and respect for one another's judicial processes'.[881] She also referred to the need to deter would-be abductors: 'The message should go out to potential abductors that there are no safe havens among the contracting states.'[882] She did not elaborate on how the balancing between the welfare of the child and the policies of the Convention should be carried out. Baroness Hale went on to note that in a settlement case the ideal of the swift return was no longer possible and it can no longer be assumed that the original country is the best place to hear the dispute.[883]

### (iv) The exceptions in article 13

There are exceptions to the general principle that the child should be returned, and these are set out in article 13. The burden of proving the existence of the exception lies on the party seeking to establish it. Even if the exception is established, the court still has discretion to order a return of the child under article 18.[884] It has been suggested that in the most exceptional of cases the court might be willing to refuse to return the child on grounds other than those set out in articles 12 and 13,[885] but that would be most unusual. It should be emphasised that the child's welfare is not the paramount consideration when deciding child abduction cases.[886]

### (a) Article 13(a): consent or acquiescence

Under article 13(a) of the Hague Convention, the child might not be returned if 'the person, institution or other body having care of the child was not actually exercising the custody rights at the time of the removal or retention, or has consented to or acquiesced in the removal or retention'.[887]

The evidence of consent needs to be clear and unequivocal,[888] although it need not be in writing, as was made clear in *Re K (Abduction: Custody)*.[889] So consent to removal 'if our relationship breaks down' may be too imprecise to amount to consent.[890] Consent can also be withdrawn at any time up until the removal, in which case the earlier consent will provide no defence.[891] Consent could be conditional or for a limited time.[892] Consent is to be judged by the realities of family life and not the strict rules of contract law.[893] Statements made in anger or distress may not amount to consent.[894] Holman J in *Re C (Abduction: Consent)*[895] suggested that consent could even be inferred from conduct.[896] In *C v W*[897] the fact that the

---

[881] Para 42.

[882] Para 42.

[883] Para 44.

[884] *Re L (Abduction: Pending Criminal Proceedings)* [1999] 1 FLR 433.

[885] *Re B (Minors) (Abduction)* [1993] 1 FLR 988.

[886] *Re R (Abduction: Consent)* [1999] 1 FLR 828.

[887] A claim that a parent consented should be seen as raising an issue under article 13(a), rather than a claim under article 3 that the removal was not wrongful: *Re P (A Child) (Abduction: Acquiescence)* [2004] 2 FCR 698.

[888] *Re P-J (Children) (Abduction: Habitual Residence: Consent)* [2010] 1 FCR 32.

[889] [1997] 2 FLR 22.

[890] *Re P-J (Children) (Abduction: Habitual Residence: Consent)* [2010] 1 FCR 32.

[891] *Re P-J (Children) (Abduction: Habitual Residence: Consent)* [2010] 1 FCR 32.

[892] *BT v JRT (Abduction: Conditional Acquiescence and Consent)* [2008] 2 FLR 972.

[893] *Re P-J (Children) (Abduction: Habitual Residence: Consent)* [2010] 1 FCR 32.

[894] *C v W* [2007] 3 FCR 243.

[895] [1996] 1 FLR 414.

[896] Approved in *Re M (Abduction) (Consent: Acquiescence)* [1999] 1 FLR 171.

[897] [2007] 3 FCR 243.

child and father concealed the removal from the mother was evidence that she did not consent. The fact that the consent is reluctant does not negate the fact that it is consent,[898] although the fact that it was obtained as a result of a fraud would.[899] Once acted upon, consent cannot be withdrawn.[900]

What is acquiescence? *Re H (Minors) (Abduction: Acquiescence)*[901] is a leading case on the topic. It involved an Orthodox Jewish couple. The mother and children moved to the UK without the father's consent. The father pursued the matter in the religious rabbinical courts in Israel; only later did he turn to the secular court. The House of Lords rejected the distinction which had been drawn in some earlier cases[902] between active and passive acquiescence. The new approach was set out by Lord Browne-Wilkinson, who stated that the question of whether or not there is acquiescence is a subjective question. It depends on the actual state of mind of the person said to have acquiesced and not whether the other parent believed them to have acquiesced. However, he qualified this by adding:

> Where the words or actions of the wronged parent clearly and unequivocally show and have led the other parent to believe that the wronged parent is not asserting or going to assert his right to the summary return of the child and are inconsistent with such return, justice requires that the wronged parent be held to have acquiesced.[903]

Delay can be evidence of acquiescence,[904] but there may be an explanation for the delay that negates any suggestion that the delay implies acquiescence.[905] For example, if the applicant failed to make any attempt to have the child returned as a result of wrong legal advice then the delay would not necessarily indicate acquiescence.[906] The fact that a parent has not applied for custody does not, in and of itself, indicate that there is acquiescence. In *B-G v B-G*[907] the father had sought legal advice in his home country when the children were removed to England. He was improperly advised and not informed of his rights under the Hague Convention. It was held he had acquiesced in their removal because he had led the mother to believe that he would not challenge the removal.

### (b) Article 13(b): grave risk

Under article 13(b) of the Convention the court may refuse to return the child if 'there is a grave risk that his or her return would expose the child to physical or psychological harm or otherwise place the child in an intolerable situation'. In what might be regarded as a rather strained piece of statutory interpretation, Ward LJ in *Re S (A Child) (Abduction: Grave Risk of Harm)*[908] suggested that it is necessary to show both that there was a risk of physical or psychological harm, *and* that that risk of harm put the child in an intolerable situation. This was not followed in *Re W (A Child) (Abduction: Conditions for Return)*[909] where the Court of Appeal held the article 13(b) defence could be established without findings of violence or abuse to the child, although Thorpe LJ added that that would be 'rare'.[910] But a case where the

---

[898] *Re M (Abduction) (Consent: Acquiescence)* [1999] 1 FLR 171.
[899] *Re B (A Minor) (Abduction)* [1994] 2 FLR 249.
[900] *Re K (Abduction: Consent)* [1997] 2 FLR 212.
[901] [1998] AC 72; noted McClean (1997).
[902] E.g. *Re A (Minors) (Abduction: Custody Rights)* [1992] Fam 106.
[903] *Re H (Minors) (Abduction: Acquiescence)* [1998] AC 72 at p. 90002E.
[904] *W v W (Child Abduction: Acquiescence)* [1993] 2 FLR 211.
[905] *Re AZ (A Minor)* [1997] 1 FLR 682.
[906] *Re S (Minors) (Abduction: Acquiescence)* [1994] 1 FLR 819; *De L v H* [2010] 1 FLR 1229.
[907] [2008] EWHC 688 (Fam).
[908] [2002] 3 FCR 43 at para 41.
[909] [2004] 3 FCR 559, [2004] EWCA Civ 1366.
[910] At para 22.

return would put the mother at grave risk of violence might fall within article 13(b). In *Re D (Article 13(b): Non-return)*[911] the mother had fled from Venezuela after an assassination attempt on her life. This clearly fell within article 13(b).[912] The fact a child will be stressed by being returned is insufficient in itself to amount to a grave harm.[913]

It should be noted that if the child is returned this does not mean that the other parent will automatically take over care of the child. So in *Re H (Children: Abduction)*,[914] although there were grave concerns about the father's past violence and threats, the Court of Appeal ordered the return of the child to Belgium. It was held that there was no evidence that the father was such an uncontrollable risk that the Belgian authorities were not able to control him.[915]

The courts have been reluctant to find that a case falls into the 'grave risk' category and the evidential burden is high.[916] A mere allegation, even of serious abuse, will not necessarily be sufficient.[917] There must be clear and compelling evidence[918] of a grave and serious harm.[919] The harm must be much more than the inevitable disruption that would inevitably follow from an unwelcome return to a country of habitual residence.[920] In *C v B*[921] Sir Mark Potter found that, although there was a risk that the mother would suffer depression if she was required to return to Australia, the court did not think there was a grave risk that she would do so to the extent of losing her parenting ability.[922] Ward LJ justified setting the hurdle high in order that it not prevent the dominant purpose of the Convention, namely to return the child to the country of habitual residence. In *Re M (Abduction: Intolerable Situation)*[923] the mother argued that, if she were forced to return to Norway with the child, she would be at risk of physical harm from her husband, who had been imprisoned for murdering a man whom he thought was having an affair with the mother. He was soon to be released, but Charles J was willing to assume that the Norwegian authorities would be able to protect the mother and would keep her address secret. This suggests that the courts will rarely find the defence proved. In *Re S (A Child) (Abduction: Grave Risk of Harm)*[924] concerns of returning the child to Israel, given the security situation in the Middle East, were insufficient to justify not returning the child.[925] The Court of Appeal in *Re C (Abduction: Grave Risk of Physical or Psychological Harm)*[926] indicated that it was necessary to distinguish cases where the intolerable situation existed before the abduction itself (e.g. where the abductor removed the child from an abusive situation), and where the risk of harm arose from the abduction (e.g. where the child has become attached to the abductor and it would harm the child to be returned). In the latter kind of case it would be very rare for the defence to succeed, although in the former there was a higher chance of success.

---

[911] [2006] EWCA Crim 146.
[912] See *S v B (Abduction: Human Rights)* [2005] Fam Law 610 for a firm rejection of the view that the Human Rights Act 1998 required the court to reconsider its approach to article 13(b).
[913] *De L v H* [2010] 1 FLR 1229.
[914] [2003] 2 FCR 151.
[915] See also *Re W (A Child) (Abduction: Conditions for Return)* [2004] 3 FCR 559.
[916] *Re M (Abduction: Undertakings)* [1995] 1 FLR 1021; *M v T (Abduction)* [2009] 1 FLR 1309.
[917] *N v N (Abduction: Article 13 Defence)* [1995] 1 FLR 107.
[918] *Re C (Abduction: Grave Risk of Psychological Harm)* [1999] 1 FLR 1145.
[919] *Re H (Children: Abduction)* [2003] 2 FCR 151 at para 30.
[920] *C v B* [2005] EWHC 2988 (Fam).
[921] [2005] EWHC 2988 (Fam).
[922] It might be questioned whether an inevitable consequence of the debilitating effects of depression is a loss of parenting ability.
[923] [2000] 1 FLR 930.
[924] [2002] EWCA Civ 908, [2002] 3 FCR 43.
[925] See Freedman (2002) who is wary of ever using security concerns as a reason for not returning a child.
[926] [1999] 2 FLR 478.

Despite the courts' reluctance to find this defence made out, there have been cases where it has succeeded. For example, in *Re F (A Minor) (Abduction: Custody Rights Abroad)*[927] the abducting mother removed the children from the father who had abused and harassed the children and the mother. A rather controversial case is *Re G (Abduction: Psychological Harm)*,[928] where it was found that if the children were returned to the father this would have a severe effect on the mother's psychological health and this would harm the children. In *TB v JB (Abduction: Grave Risk of Harm)* it was accepted that psychological harm to the mother if she were forced to return to New Zealand could lead to grave harm to the children, but it was held that on the facts of the case the English court could assume that the New Zealand courts would protect the mother and children from being contacted or harassed by the father and that therefore the mother could be protected from psychological harm. Further, the mother could receive medical assistance for any depression or other illness and thereby alleviate the harm to the children. Hale LJ vigorously dissented:

> primary carers who have fled from abuse and maltreatment should not be expected to go back to it, if this will have a seriously detrimental effect upon the children. We are now more conscious of the effects of such treatment, not only on the immediate victims but also on the children who witness it.[929]

However, in *Re S (A Child) (Abduction: Grave Risk of Harm)*[930] Ward LJ emphasised that just because returning the child would produce an intolerable position for the mother, it did not mean that the position would be intolerable for the child, which was the question the court had to consider.[931] However, in *Re E (Abduction: Intolerable Situation)*[932] if the boy were returned to Oregon the mother would have to choose between following him to Oregon or remaining in Enland with her other child. The court felt the boy, aged 11, would suffer severe psychological harm if he saw his mother in such a dilemma. The boy too would feel great pain in being separated from his half-brother. Freeman[933] argues on cases like these: 'So keen are we to uphold our international obligations to secure the return of abducted children that we forget that we also have an international obligation towards the children themselves . . . to protect them from abuse.'

Generally speaking, if the abducting parent has created the situation causing a grave risk of harm they cannot then seek to rely on a defence. Under the Hague Convention,[934] however, article 13(b) specifies that if a child is facing a grave risk of harm the defence should be available even if the abducting parent is responsible for creating the situation.[935]

### (c) The objection of children

A further defence under article 13 is when 'the child objects to being returned and has attained an age and degree of maturity at which it is appropriate to take account of its views'.[936] The court can consider not only whether the child objects to being returned to a particular country, but also whether the child objects to being returned to a particular

[927] [1995] Fam 224.
[928] [1995] 1 FLR 64.
[929] [2001] 2 FCR 497, [2001] 2 FLR 515, at para 46.
[930] [2002] 3 FCR 43.
[931] For an argument that the courts have failed adequately to protect mothers who have abducted children to avoid violent situations, see Kaye (1999).
[932] [2009] 2 FLR 485.
[933] Freeman (2000d: 7).
[934] *Re C (A Minor) (Abduction)* [1989] 1 FLR 403.
[935] *S v B (Abduction: Human Rights)* [2005] Fam Law 610.
[936] See McEleavy (2008) for an excellent discussion of the recent case law.

person.[937] However, it should be stressed that the child's wishes will never determine the issue.[938] A court may decide that an objecting child is mature, but still decide to go against his or her wishes. A court can decide to go against the child's wishes based on the policies behind the Convention,[939] concerns about the child's welfare, or because the child does not adequately understand the issues.[940] It is not necessary to show that the case is exceptional before a child's views can be followed.[941] The court will consider whether there are in fact objections from the child;[942] then whether the age and maturity of the child are such that they should be taken into account; and then whether to exercise their discretion to determine whether or not to return the child.[943] Normally, a trained officer will interview a child to ascertain his or her maturity and whether he or she has been subject to coercion.[944] Sometimes a child may be given separate representation in Hague Convention cases.[945] The test to consider when deciding whether children should have separate representation was 'whether the separate representation of the child will add enough to the court's understanding of the issues that arise under the Hague Convention to justify the intrusion and the expense and delay that may result'.[946] In *W v W (Abduction: Joinder as Party)* [2010] 1 FLR 1342 a 17-year-old sister was joined as a party to Hague Convention proceedings after arguing that she had a protective role towards her younger sister and that their mother could not protect the sister from the violent father.

There is no particular age which must have been reached before the child's wishes can be taken into account.[947] Obviously, the older the child, the more likely it is that the court will decide the child is mature.[948] In *W v W (Abduction: Acquiescence: Children's Objections)*[949] the views of children aged 8 and 6 were taken into account.[950] The court will want to listen carefully to the views of the child. In *Re G (Abduction)*[951] it was held that the child's real objections were to living with the father, rather than returning to her country of origin. Her views were not, therefore, a strong reason against returning her.

In the most authoritative statement on the significance of children's wishes in these cases, Baroness Hale in *Re M (Children) (Abduction)*[952] held:

---

[937] *Re M (A Minor) (Child Abduction)* [1994] 1 FLR 390.

[938] *Re S (Minors) (Abduction: Acquiescence)* [1994] 1 FLR 819; *Re L (Abduction: Child's Objections to Return)* [2002] 2 FLR 1042; *Re J and K (Abduction: Objections of Child)* [2004] EWHC 1985 (Fam).

[939] *C v W* [2007] 3 FCR 243, where the child was 14.

[940] *Z v Z (Abduction: Children's Views)* [2005] EWCA Civ 1012.

[941] *Re M (Abduction: Zimbabwe)* [2007] UKHL 55.

[942] In *M v M (Abduction: Settlement)* [2008] 2 FLR 1884 the views of a 5-year-old were said to be simply a reflection of her father's views and so carried no weight.

[943] *AF v MB-F (Abduction: Rights of Custody)* [2008] FL 966; *De L v H* [2010] 1 FLR 1229.

[944] *Re D (A Child) (Abduction: Foreign Custody Rights)* [2007] 1 FCR 1. For a case where this did not happen because that would place too much of an emotional burden on the child, see *Re M (Abduction: Habitual Residence: Relocation)* [2005] Fam Law 441.

[945] *Re H (A Child) (Child Abduction)* [2007] 1 FCR 345.

[946] *Re C (Abduction: Separate Representation of Children)* [2008] 2 FLR 6, para 31.

[947] *Re P (Abduction: Minor's Views)* [1998] 2 FLR 825.

[948] Although children as young as 7 years of age have had their views taken into account: *B v K (Child Abduction)* [1993] 1 FCR 382; *Re R (Child Abduction: Acquiescence)* [1995] 1 FLR 716; *Re S (A Minor) (Abduction: Custody Rights)* [1993] Fam 242; *M (Abduction: Child's Objections)* [2007] 3 FCR 631. Contrast *Re C (Abduction: Grave Risk of Psychological Harm)* [1999] 1 FLR 1145 where boys aged 9 and 7 who had suffered severe physical abuse at their father's hands were found to be insufficiently mature to object to their return to him. It is rare for teenagers to be returned against their wishes (see *Re L (Abduction: Child's Objections to Return)* [1999] 1 FCR 739).

[949] [2010] EWHC 332 (Fam).

[950] See also *Re T (Abduction: Child's Objections to Return)* [2000] 2 FLR 193.

[951] [2009] 1 FLR 760.

[952] [2008] 1 FCR 536, at para 46.

the court may have to consider the nature and strength of the child's objections, the extent to which they are 'authentically her own' or the product of the influence of the abducting parent, the extent to which they coincide or are at odds with other considerations which are relevant to her welfare, as well as the general convention considerations . . . The older the child, the greater the weight that her objections are likely to carry. But that is far from saying the child's objections should only prevail in the most exceptional circumstances.

Cases relying on the child's objection must now consider the impact of the Human Rights Act 1998. In **Sylvester v Austria**[953] the Austrian Supreme Court overturned an enforcement order requiring the return of a child to her father on the basis that so much time had passed since the original order that the child had become alienated from her father. The European Court of Human Rights held that the delay had been caused by the Austrian state's failure to enforce the original order and hence it had infringed the father's and child's rights under article 8.

### (d) Infringement of fundamental rights and freedoms

An English or Welsh court could refuse to return a child if that would be contrary to respect for human rights and fundamental freedoms. This ground is very rarely relied upon. In **Re S (Abduction: Intolerable Situation: Beth Din)**[954] a mother argued that if the child returned to Israel the case would be decided by a Jewish religious court, which would discriminate against her on the ground that she was a woman. However, Connell J rejected her argument, holding that as the mother was herself an Orthodox Jew and because it was her choice that the religious rather than civil courts in Israel would hear the case, her objection had little merit.[955]

### (e) The residual discretion

Even if one of the defences above is not proved, the court still has a residual discretion to refuse to return a child. In **H v H (Abduction: Acquiescence)** Waite LJ suggested that in considering exercising the residual discretion the following factors should be considered:

(a) the comparative suitability of the forum in the competing jurisdictions to determine the child's future in the substantive proceedings;

(b) the likely outcome (in whatever forum they be heard) of the substantive proceedings;

(c) the consequences of the acquiescence, with particular reference to the extent to which a child may have become settled in the requested state;

(d) the situation which would await the absconding parent and the child if compelled to return to the requesting jurisdiction;

(e) the anticipated emotional effect upon the child of an immediate return order (a factor which is to be treated as significant but not as paramount);

(f) the extent to which the purpose and underlying philosophy of the Hague Convention would be at risk of frustration if a return order were to be refused.[956]

In **B v El-B**[957] it was held that children should be returned to Lebanon, from where the mother had removed them. Although the trial there would be under Sharia law, which would

---

[953] [2003] 2 FCR 128.
[954] [2000] 1 FLR 454.
[955] For an interesting discussion of child abduction cases and the issue of cultural diversity, see Khaliq and Young (2001).
[956] [1996] 2 FLR 570 at p. 576.
[957] [2003] 1 FLR 811.

be very different from the approach in the English courts, the family were Muslim by birth and upbringing and it could not be concluded that Sharia law would not be concerned with the welfare of children. However, on an appeal from an immigration tribunal, in the House of Lords in *EM (Lebanon) v Secretary of State for the Home Department*[958] their Lordships held it would breach a child and mother's rights under article 8 of the ECHR to return them to Lebanon where a custody dispute concerning the child would be resolved under Sharia law. Because that would give far stronger rights to the father and inevitably lead to separation of the mother and child, it was held that removal to Lebanon would infringe their ECHR rights. However, their Lordships found this to be an exceptional case because: 'His mother has cared for him since his birth. He has a settled and happy relationship with her in this country. Life with his mother is the only family life he knows. Life with his father or any other member of his family in Lebanon, with whom he has never had any contact, would be totally alien to him.'[959]

## F  Brussels II (European Council Regulation (EC) 2201/2003)

This European Council Regulation governs the jurisdiction, recognition and enforcement of judgments in matrimonial matters and matters of parental responsibility.[960] Article 10 means that if a child is removed from one member state to another then issues relating to parental responsibility should be resolved in the child's country of origin.[961] Under article 20 in urgent cases orders can be made to protect the child, but these should be with a view to returning the child to her home country. Article 11(3) imposes a six-week timetable for courts dealing with an application for return of a child, made under the Convention.

Even if there are concerns about the well-being of the child article 11(4) requires the return of the child 'if it is established that adequate arrangements have been made to secure the protection of the child after his or her return'. This, in effect, limits the article 13(b) defence that would otherwise apply in a Hague Convention case.[962]

Brussells II attaches notable weight to the views of children. By article 11(2) a child must be heard in a Hague abduction application to which the regulation applies, irrespective of whether or not a 'child's objections' defence is raised.

## G  Neither convention applies

### (i) Children abducted to a non-Convention country

If the child has been removed from the UK to a country that is neither in the EU nor a signatory to the Hague Convention, there are grave difficulties in recovering the child. There are two alternatives, although both are expensive and have only a limited chance of success. The first is to bring proceedings in the country to which the child has been taken; the second, to seek extradition of the abducting parent to England in connection with a criminal offence under the Child Abduction Act 1984. The latter is only an option if there is an extradition treaty between the UK and the country to which the child has been taken.

---

[958] [2008] UKHL 64.

[959] Para 18.

[960] European Communities (Jurisdiction and Judgments in Matrimonial and Parental Responsibility Matters) Regulations 2005, SI 2005/265.

[961] In *Re I (A Child) (Contact Application: Jurisdiction)* [2010] 1 FLR 361 Brussels II was used for a Pakistani child who had substantial connections with England.

[962] *F v M (Abduction: Grave Risk of Harm)* [2008] 2 FLR 1263.

## (ii) Children abducted to UK from a non-Convention country

Where a child is brought to England and Wales from a non-Convention country, the common law governs the position. Wardship is often used. The High Court, as always in wardship, will make its own assessment of what is in the child's best interests.[963] However, there is a presumption that it is in the best interests of the child for the child's future to be decided by the courts of the country from which the child has been abducted.[964] There are two crucial questions for the courts to look at:

1. Will the foreign court use principles similar to the ones used by the English or Welsh court? The court must be satisfied that the country will give sufficient protection to the children's interests.[965] This will be assumed where the state is a member of the European Union,[966] or where the state has historical roots with the UK.[967] It is not necessary to show that the other country has exactly the same attitude to children and their interests. In *Re JA (Child Abduction: Non-Convention Country)*[968] Ward LJ stressed that the courts have a responsibility to ensure that the child's welfare will be adequately protected by the courts in the other country.[969] However, more recently, in *Re E (Abduction: Non-Convention Country)*[970] the Court of Appeal took a rather different approach and argued that it was proper for a dispute within a Muslim family to be resolved according to the Muslim law in Sudan. They held that it would not be appropriate for the English courts to scrutinise the family justice regime of a particular country.

2. Is there any evidence that the child will suffer significant harm if he or she is returned to their country of origin?

---

**CASE: *Re J (A Child) (Return to Foreign Jurisdiction: Convention Rights)*
[2005] UKHL 40, [2005] 3 All ER 291**

The child's father was Saudi Arabian. The mother had both British and Saudi nationality. The couple were married according to Sharia law in Saudi Arabia. The mother took the child to the United Kingdom with the consent of the father. The mother petitioned for divorce in the English courts. The father sought a specific issue order under s 8 of the Children Act 1989 demanding the return of the child to Saudi Arabia. Saudi Arabia is not a party to the Hague Convention and so the case did not fall under the regulations provided there. The trial judge held that he would have ordered the child to return but for the fact that the husband had alleged that the wife had been unfaithful to him. The judge's concern was that under Sharia law allegations of adultery can have a significant impact on residence cases. The Court of Appeal allowed the father's appeal on the basis that the concerns over the way that Sharia law might impact on the welfare of the child had been given too much weight.

➡

---

[963] *Re L (Minors) (Wardship: Jurisdiction)* [1974] 1 All ER 913.

[964] *U v U* [2010] 2 FCR 447; *Re F (A Minor) (Abduction: Jurisdiction)* [1991] Fam 25; McClean and Beevers (1995).

[965] *Re S (Minors) (Abduction)* [1994] 1 FLR 297.

[966] *Re M (Abduction: Non-Convention Country)* [1995] 1 FLR 89.

[967] *Re M (Jurisdiction: Forum Conveniens)* [1995] 2 FLR 224, concerning Malta.

[968] [1998] 1 FLR 231, concerning the Arab Emirates.

[969] *Re M (Minors) (Abduction: Peremptory Return Order)* [1996] 1 FLR 478, by contrast, suggested that the courts could presume that any state was in line with Britain's attitude.

[970] [1999] 2 FLR 642.

The House of Lords emphasised that in any case concerning the upbringing of a child the welfare of the child was the court's paramount consideration, whether the application be under the Children Act or the inherent jurisdiction. This welfare principle applied to cases of child abduction which involved countries that were not signatories to the Hague Convention. Baroness Hale explicitly rejected an argument that in such cases there would be a strong presumption that children should be returned to their country of habitual residence. She did, however, think that:

> the judge may find it convenient to start from the proposition that it is likely to be better for a child to return to his home country for any disputes about his future to be decided there. A case against his doing so has to be made. But the weight to be given to that proposition will vary enormously from case to case.[971]

A factor that could be relevant in assessing whether a child should be returned is the degree of connection of the child with each country. In particular, attention will be paid to the length of time a child has spent in each country. Attention would also be paid as to who could be regarded as the primary carer of the child and the effect upon them of having the case heard here or overseas. Baroness Hale also accepted that it was relevant to consider whether the law in the country to which the child was to be sent worked in a way which would be described as discriminatory by our courts.

In this case the trial judge had indeed focused on the welfare of the individual child. The differences between the legal systems in England and Saudi Arabia were clearly important in an assessment of the child's welfare. In particular, the judge was entitled to take into account that under the Saudi legal system the mother would not be permitted to take the child to the UK without the father's permission. Therefore, the judge's decision should not be interfered with and the child would not be returned to Saudi Arabia.

This approach was applied in *Re H (Abduction: Dominica: Corporal Punishment)*[972] where Bracewell J refused to return the child to Dominica, a country which has not signed the Hague Convention, having heard evidence of cruel physical ill-treatment by the father. She referred to the UN Committee on the Rights of the Child which noted that in Dominica corporal punishment is widely used and sanctioned. As Gillian Douglas noted, there is an irony here in that the same committee has criticised the use of and law on corporal punishment in the UK![973]

## 9 Conclusion

This chapter has considered those cases where the courts have had to resolve private disputes concerning the upbringing of children. Much of this area of the law depends on the judiciary exercising their discretion and deciding each case on its own particular facts. Indeed, increasingly the courts are willing to accept that there is no one view which represents the child's best

---

[971] [2005] UKHL 40 at para 33.
[972] [2006] EWHC 199 (Fam).
[973] Douglas (2006b: 523).

interests and it is rather a case of deciding which of the parents' wishes are to predominate. That said, there are some presumptions or assumptions (e.g. in favour of the 'natural' parent; in favour of contact with parents) which the courts have developed to provide a degree of predictability for some kinds of cases. Interestingly, some of the judiciary have begun to question whether the courtroom is the appropriate forum in which to resolve family disputes. Whether this marks the beginning of the end for court resolution of family disagreements is unlikely, but it may well be that in the future the legal aid rules will be tightened so that courts will only be troubled by arguments between members of richer families.

## Further reading

Bailey-Harris, R. (2001d) 'Contact – Challenging conventional wisdom', *Child and Family Law Quarterly* 13: 361.

Bainham, A., Lindley, B., Richards, M. and Trinder, L. (eds) (2003) *Children and Their Families*, Oxford: Hart.

Collier, R. (2005) 'Fathers 4 Justice, law and the new politics of fatherhood', *Child and Family Law Quarterly* 17: 511.

Gilmore, S. (2006a) 'Contact/Shared Residence and child well-being: Research evidence and its decisions for legal decision-making', *International Journal of Law, Policy and the Family* 20: 344.

Gilmore, S. (2006b) 'Court decision-making in shared residence order cases: A critical examination', *Child and Family Law Quarterly* 18: 478.

Gilmore, S. (2008a) 'The Assumption That Contact is Beneficial: Challenging the "Secure Foundation"', *Family Law* 38: 1226.

Gilmore, S. (2008b) 'Disputing contact: challenging some assumptions', *Child and Family Law Quarterly* 20: 285.

Hayes, M. (2006) 'Relocation Cases: Is the Court of Appeal Applying the Correct Principles?', *Child and Family Law Quarterly* 19: 351.

Herring, J. and Taylor, R. (2006) 'Relocating Relocation', *Child and Family Law Quarterly* 18: 517.

Jivraj, S. and Herman, D. (2009) '"It is difficult for a white judge to understand": orientalism, racialisation, and Christianity in English child welfare cases', *Child and Family Law Quarterly* 21: 283.

Maclean, M. (ed.) (2007) *Parenting after Partnering*, Oxford: Hart.

Reece, H. (2006b) 'UK women's groups' child contact campaign: "so long as it is safe"', *Child and Family Law Quarterly* 18: 538.

Smart, C., May, V., Wade, A. and Furniss, C. (2003 and 2005) *Residence and Contact Disputes in Court Vols 1 and 2*, London: DCA.

Smart, C. and Neale, B. (1999a) *Family Fragments?* Cambridge: Polity Press.

Trinder, L., Beek, M. and Connolly, J. (2002) *Making Contact: How Parents and Children Negotiate and Experience Contact After Divorce*, York: Joseph Rowntree.

Trinder, L. and Kellett, J. (2007) 'Fairness, efficiency and effectiveness in court-based dispute resolution schemes in England', *International Journal of Law, Policy and the Family* 21: 322.

Wall LJ (2009) 'Making contact work in 2009', *Family Law* 39: 590.

Visit **www.mylawchamber.co.uk/herring** to access study support resources including interactive multiple choice questions, weblinks, discussion questions and legal updates.

Use **Case Navigator** to read in full some of the key cases referenced in this chapter with commentary and questions:

*Gillick* v *West Norfolk and Wisbech AHA* [1985] 3 All ER 402 112
*Re G (Children) (Residence: Same-Sex Partner)* [2006] 4 All ER 241
*Payne* v *Payne* [2001] 1 FCR 425
*Re L, V, M and H (Children) (Contact: Domestic Violence)* [2000] 2 FCR 404

# 10 Child protection

Although the law generally assumes that parents will promote the interests of their children, some parents do not. In such cases the state has the power to remove children from their parents in order to protect them from harm.[1] This power is one of the greatest that the state has. For many parents, having their children compulsorily removed by the state would be one of the worst things that could happen to them. On the other hand, the appalling harm that children can suffer at the hands of their parents means that the state must intervene if children's rights are to be protected.[2]

One of the great problems in the law concerning the protection of children is that if the wrong decision is made, enormous harm can be caused. Imagine that a social worker visits a home where a child has a broken arm and bruises. The social worker suspects this may have been caused by the parents, while the parents claim that the injuries were caused by a fall down the stairs. If the parents' explanation is untrue, but the social worker decides to believe it, she would be leaving the child with abusive parents and there would be a danger that the child could suffer serious injury or even death.[3] On the other hand, if the explanation is true and the social worker decides to remove the child, then the child and parents may suffer great harm through the separation. The history of the law on child protection reveals tragedies resulting from excessive intervention in family life as well as gross failure to intervene.[4] The difficulty is that it is only with hindsight that it would be apparent that in a particular case the approach was inappropriate.

This puts social workers in an impossible position. Many are happy to rush to criticise them when they are seen to be too interventionist. Wall LJ in *EH v Greenwich London Borough Council*[5] has noted

> What social workers do not appear to understand is that the public perception of their role in care proceedings is not a happy one. They are perceived by many as the arrogant and enthusiastic removers of children from their parents into an unsatisfactory care system, and as trampling on the rights of parents and children in the process.

Yet social workers face equal levels of blame when they fail to protect children from harm, as seen in the media outcry following the Baby Peter case.[6] The report into the case found it was not so much a case of inadequate guidelines, as a failure to follow them. The frustration

---

[1] For a magnificent lengthy discussion of the issues see Hoyano and Keenan (2007).
[2] For a disturbing account of the long-term effects of child abuse see e.g. Colquhoun (2009).
[3] For recent horrific examples see Laming (2003 and 2009); Brandon et al. (2008).
[4] Butler-Sloss (1989: 12); Department of Health (1995a); Masson (2000b).
[5] [2010] 2 FCR 106, para 109.
[6] Laming (2009).

in Lord Laming's report into the many failings that meant there was in adequate intervention to protect the child are palpable:

> [T]his document, and its recommendations, are aimed at making sure that good practice becomes standard practice in every service. This includes recommendations on improving the inspection of safeguarding services and the quality of serious case reviews as well as recommendations on improving the help and support children receive when they are at risk of harm. The utility of the policy and legislation has been pressed on me by contributors throughout this report. In such circumstances it is hard to resist the urge to respond by saying to each of the key services, if that is so 'NOW JUST DO IT!'[7]

It is easy when looking at individual dramatic failures to obtain a false picture. Many social workers engage in hugely important work for families. The difficulties have largely arisen as a result of inadequate funding, low morale and poor management. A Channel Four under-cover documentary[8] revealed overworked, underpaid and terrified social workers struggling to deal with cases of enormous complexity. Given the huge importance of the issues at stake, social work requires significantly greater levels of funding and support from the state. As Alistair MacDonald put it:

> If we are to escape the corrosive effects of the caustic dichotomy created by a soaring vision for the care system that is chained by inadequate resources, then the Government must not only recognise and react to the urgent need for proper human, structural and financial provision within the care system, it must also see clearly the *value* of that system. It must recognise that, by reason of the terrible truths that require its existence, the care system is both integral to the safety and welfare of individual children *and* fundamental to the integrity and fairness of our democratic society. It must recognise that both children *and* society are threatened by the system's weaknesses. Above all, the Government must recognise that to achieve its political vision for the care system, true commitment lies in resources not in rhetoric.[9]

As this discussion suggests many of the difficulties in this area lie not so much in the substantive law, as practical issues.[10] Nevertheless there are important legal issues to address. Here are three major difficulties that the law faces.

1. There are evidential problems. Lord Nicholls in the House of Lords recognised the difficulties facing a judge in care cases of having to 'penetrate the fog of denials, evasions, lies and half-truths which all too often descends'.[11] In other words, social workers and the courts often simply do not know the facts and have to deal with possibilities. Even experts examining the same injuries can differ widely in their interpretation of them.[12] Indeed, as the decision in *R v Cannings*[13] revealed, there are dangers in placing excessive weight on the opinion of experts in the field.[14] In that case a mother's conviction of murder of her babies was quashed after it was found that the prosecution expert's evidence was flawed. Similarly, there are the difficulties of predicting the future. Predicting the likelihood that a

---

[7] Laming (2009: 1).
[8] *Dispatches*, Undercover social worker, 7 June 2010.
[9] MacDonald (2009b: 45). See also Masson (2008).
[10] See also the increase in fees for public law applications, which were unsuccessfully challenged in *R (Hillingdon London Borough Council) and Others v Lord Chancellor and Secretary of State for Communities and Local Government* [2009] 1 FLR 39.
[11] *Lancashire CC v B* [2000] 1 FLR 583 at p. 589.
[12] *Re U (A Child) (Serious Injury: Standard of Proof)* [2004] 2 FCR 257; *Re W (A Child) (Non-accidental Injury: Expert Evidence)* [2005] 3 FCR 513.
[13] [2004] 1 FCR 193.
[14] For a useful discussion of how the courts should use expert evidence in care cases see *A County Council v K, D and L* [2005] 1 FLR 851.

parent will abuse a child on the basis of past conduct is far from easy. Yet such predictions are essential to child care in practice. Hence 'experts' on child abuse play an important role in the way the law works, yet it may be that reference to expertise is used to disguise the fact we know very little about the prediction of child abuse.[15] The problems of proof in part explain the lengthy delays which can occur in child protection proceedings.[16]

2. Even if the facts are known, there is much controversy over how much suffering the child should face before it is suitable for the state to intervene to protect him or her. If a local authority finds a child living in a home which is dirty and untidy, where the family's diet is unhealthy, and the children spend nearly all their time watching television, what should be done? Many would argue that this kind of situation is not sufficiently serious to justify intervention. Others would argue that the state must offer support and help to the parents to improve the family's lifestyle, for the sake of the child. The issue here is whether protection of family privacy means the state should intervene only in the most serious cases, or whether the local authority is justified in acting in order to prevent abuse.

Fox Harding has outlined four basic approaches that the law could take in relation to suspected child abuse:[17]

(a) *Laissez-faire and patriarchy.*[18] Here, the core approach is that the role of the state should be kept to a minimum. The privacy of the original family should be respected. This is an 'all or nothing' approach. Family privacy should be protected unless it is absolutely necessary to remove a child. Critics argue that the approach promotes non-intervention except in the most extreme cases of violence, enabling men to exercise control over women and children within their families.

(b) *State paternalism and child protection.* This approach favours the intervention of the state in order to protect the child. It encourages state intervention, to whatever extent is necessary, to promote the welfare of children. Opponents of this policy claim that the approach places insufficient weight on the rights of birth families. The approach, they claim, can too easily slip into 'social engineering', and presumes that the state knows what is best for the child.

(c) *The defence of the birth family and parents' rights.* The emphasis in this approach is on the benefits of psychological and biological bonds between children and parents.[19] The birth family is seen as the 'optimal context' for bringing up children. Even where parents fail, the state should see its role as doing as much as possible to preserve the family ties. The approach is not opposed to state intervention, but argues that such intervention should be aimed at supporting the family as much as possible. Even where children do have to be removed, contact with the family should be retained and the aim should be to reunite the family if at all possible. Opponents of such an approach argue that it does not provide adequate protection for children.[20] Given the levels of abuse within families, we cannot assume that children are always best cared for by their families.

---

[15] Ashenden (2004: 164).

[16] BBC Newsonline (2010b). See *Practice Direction: Public Law Proceedings – Guide to Case Management* [2010] 2 FCR 468 for guidance designed to speed up cases.

[17] Fox Harding (1996).

[18] The leading proponents of this are Goldstein, Solnit, Goldstein and Freud (1996).

[19] For a radical challenge to the presumption that, wherever possible, children should be brought up by their parents, see Bartholet (1999).

[20] See *Re R (Care: Rehabilitation in Context of Domestic Violence)* [2006] EWCA Civ 1638 for a case where the Court of Appeal thought that the judge's attempts to rehabilitate the parents and child were unrealistic.

(d) *Children's rights and child liberation.* Here the emphasis is on the child's viewpoints, feelings and wishes.[21] There is a range of approaches focusing on children's rights. At one extreme it could be argued that the state should intervene only if the child requests it.[22] In areas of suspected abuse placing weight on children's views must be treated with great caution, given the complex psychological interplay that can exist between a child and his or her abuser.[23]

Fox Harding argues that aspects of all of these approaches can be found in the Children Act 1989. This, she suggests, is not necessarily a bad thing. In some areas the law may wish to place greater weight on the powers of parents, in other areas children's rights, and in others the protection of children.

3. Even where abuse is proved, there is much debate over the correct response to it.[24] Of particular concern is the level of abuse of children in care, and in particular of those in children's homes.[25] Removing a child from an abusive family only to place him or her into an abusive situation in a children's home is to heap harm upon harm.

## 1 The Children Act 1989 and child protection

The duties and responsibilities of local authorities towards families are located in Part III of the Children Act 1989. The powers granted to a local authority can be divided between those powers which give the local authority a discretion and those which impose a duty. Those which impose duties require local authorities to act in a particular way. Those which give a discretion leave the decision whether to use a power up to the local authority. It is also necessary to distinguish between those powers that permit the local authority to intervene in family life without the family's consent, and those which permit the local authority to offer voluntary services that a family may use as it wishes. However, this distinction is not watertight. This is because if there is the threat of compulsory intervention then the family may 'consent' to 'voluntary' intervention, aware that if they did not the local authority may intervene against the family's consent. So, to distinguish those services which are voluntary and those which are compulsory is not straightforward.[26]

It would be quite wrong to see the state's protection of children as limited to court intervention. Indeed, there has been much work by sociologists on the subtle ways in which the state polices families. Health visitors, social workers, teachers and doctors can encourage the voluntary co-operation of parents and thereby encourage them to adhere to prevailing expectations about the appropriate care of children. This has been called the 'soft' policing of families.[27]

The Children Act 1989 was produced after a major rethink over child protection policy, and two major themes emerged:

---

[21] Schofield (1998: 366) argues that many abused children want to remain with their parents, but the abuse to stop.

[22] For a more moderate approach based on children's rights, see Freeman (1983: 57).

[23] Jones and Parkinson (1995).

[24] Department of Health (1999c).

[25] E.g. Levy and Kahan (1991); Stationery Office (2000b).

[26] Masson (2005; 1992).

[27] Parton (1991).

1. There should be a clear line drawn between the child being in care or not in care. A child in care is one looked after by the local authority, where the local authority effectively takes over the parental role. Under the previous legislation a child could be in an ambiguous position – formally not in care, but effectively in care. Under the Children Act a child can only enter care as a result of a court order and there are clear criteria which govern when a care order can be made.

2. The Act promotes 'partnership' between parents and local authorities. Parents and local authorities should work together for the good of the child. This has two aspects. The first is that the local authority should be regarded as a resource for parents to use, especially if the family is having difficulties.[28] The aim, therefore, is that parents experiencing difficulties in parenting will regard the local authority as there to provide support and assistance, rather than as a body to be feared. For example, if a mother is struggling in caring for her child, she should have the option of asking the local authority to accommodate her child temporarily, without there being a fear that the child will 'slip into care'. Local authorities are encouraged to use Family Group Conferences where the child's family and the professionals involved in the case meet to discuss a child over whom there are concerns.[29] However, in a recent survey of parents whose children had been taken into care, 59 per cent said they had received no support from the local authority before their child was removed.[30] Further, parents had little understanding of the local authority's reasons for concern about their children.[31]

The second aspect is that, even if the child is taken into care, parents should be involved with the care for the child to the greatest extent possible.[32] Government guidance explains:

> The objective of any partnership between families and professionals must be the protection and welfare of the child; partnership should not be an end in itself. From the outset workers should consider the possibility of a partnership with each family based on openness, mutual trust, joint decision making and a willingness to listen to families and to capitalise on their strengths. However, words such as equality, choice and power have a limited meaning at certain points in the child protection process. There are times when professional agencies have statutory responsibilities that they have to fulfil and powers that they have to use for the benefit of the child.[33]

There is a fear that there cannot be a partnership, or at least anything like an equal partnership, between a parent and a local authority.[34] The local authority has the 'sword of Damocles' of a care order hanging over the parents, and so there can be little equality in the 'partnership'.[35] The fear is that, under the guise of 'partnership', social workers will be able to exercise even more power over parents than they would if they acknowledged the intervention was compulsory. In particular there is concern with the increased use of informal understandings between parents and the local authority concerning the child.[36] These agreements may be entered into without the parents receiving legal advice or without the protection of legal procedural safeguards. While a child cannot be taken into care

[28] Masson (1995).
[29] See the discussion in Welbourne (2008: 342).
[30] Ofsted (2008).
[31] Brophy (2006).
[32] Department for Children, Schools and Families (2008a).
[33] Department of Health (1995b: 2.13).
[34] Kaganas (1995).
[35] For concerns, see Masson (1995).
[36] The increase in court fees may well increase the use of these.

on the basis of an agreement between the local authority and parents, there are concerns that agreements which fail to adequately protect the child, or which are overly interventionist in the life of the family may be entered into.[37] Alison Diduck and Felicity Kaganas have suggested that the term 'partnership' can be used to promote the ideology that it is the family, rather than the state, which should be responsible for children.[38]

Not only should parents and local authorities work in partnership, so also should local authorities and all the other bodies involved in child work (for example, the NSPCC, hospitals).[39] The Children Act in various ways encourages co-operation between these different agencies. Reports into failings of the child protection system regularly cite a lack of communication between different bodies as being a cause of the absence of proper care.[40]

A study by Judith Masson, Julia Pearce and Kay Barder into the bringing of care proceedings made some interesting findings.[41] It found no evidence of care proceedings being brought without a good reason. Neglect was the most common basis for the application, but 40 per cent had resulted from a crisis situation. In only a third of the cases was the father involved in care of the child. Sixty per cent of applications resulted in a care order and 23 per cent in a residence order. Julia Brophy, in her study, highlighted the difficulties facing the parents of children facing care proceedings:

> Over 40% are likely to have mental health problems, many (20–30%) are likely to have drug/alcohol problems, many lead chaotic lifestyles (about 36%). Many mothers also endure domestic violence (45–50%); many parents (some 61% in the latest study) are unable to control their children.[42]

## 2 The Human Rights Act 1998 and child protection

English and Welsh law after the Human Rights Act 1998 must now start with a strong presumption that the state must respect the right to family and private life (article 8).[43] In *EH v Greenwich London Borough Council*[44] the Court of Appeal said that in all cases involving care orders the court must consider whether any infringement of human rights by the court orders are justified.[45] However, it would be wrong to assume that the Human Rights Act supports a non-interventionist approach in child protection cases. There are three ways in which the Human Rights Act can permit or even require intervention:

1. Any removal by the state of a child from his or her parents will automatically constitute an infringement of article 8, but this may be justified by taking into account the welfare of the child.[46] Paragraph 2 of article 8 permits an infringement of the right if it is necessary

---

[37] Welbourne (2008).
[38] Diduck and Kaganas (2006: 358).
[39] See Children Act 2004, Part II which is designed for better integration of the delivery of children's services. See *A County Council v A Mother* [2005] Fam Law 350 for an example suggesting work still needs to be done in this area.
[40] Laming (2003).
[41] Masson, Pearce and Bader (2008).
[42] Brophy (2006).
[43] Choudhry and Herring (2010: ch. 8); Kaganas (2010).
[44] [2010] 2 FCR 106, para 63.
[45] See also *G v Neath Port Talbot CBC* [2010] EWCA Civ 821.
[46] Although see the argument in Herring (2008c) that abusive forms of family life may not be entitled to respect under article 8.

in the interests of others, and this would clearly include the interests of the child.[47] In deciding whether the infringement is necessary, the consideration of the welfare of the child is 'crucial'.[48] There is little difficulty justifying an intervention in family life in order to protect a child from abuse.[49] Just because it turns out that the removal of the child was based on a false belief does not mean there was a breach of human rights[50] – as long as the belief was a genuine and reasonably held concern.[51]

2. Although article 8 may readily be invoked to protect parents from state intervention, it could be argued that abused children have rights to respect for private life that can be protected only by intervention. Article 8 imposes positive obligations on the state and these will include obligations to protect a child from abuse.

3. Article 3 requires the state to protect children and adults from torture and inhuman and degrading treatment[52] and article 2 requires the state to protect children from the risk of death.[53] This is an absolute right in the sense that a breach of it cannot be justified by reference to the interests of others.[54] Therefore, if a local authority knows or should know that a child is suffering serious abuse then it is obliged to protect the child from that harm.[55] Similarly if the local authority knows or ought to know that there is a 'real immediate risk' of death, torture, inhuman or degrading treatment it must intervene.[56] A local authority will have infringed a child's rights under article 3 if it has failed to take measures that could have prevented the abuse. It is not necessary to show that had the local authority acted as it should the abuse would not have occurred.[57] A child who was not protected by a local authority from abuse could sue it under s 7 of the Human Rights Act 1998.

So, when a local authority removes a child from her family, although that may be an interference with the parents' rights under article 8 (albeit justified under article 8(2)) the local authority may itself have been required to remove the child under its obligations under article 8.[58]

A significant concept which was introduced by the Human Rights Act 1998 is the notion of proportionality.[59] If the state is to intervene in a child's life, it must be shown that the level of state intervention is proportionate to the risk that the child is suffering.[60] In *K and T v Finland*[61] a newborn baby was removed from the mother at birth. There were concerns that the mother suffered from various psychoses. As the mother had never behaved violently towards her other children and appeared calm at the birth, it was held to be a disproportionate

---

[47] See Chapter 8 for a general discussion.

[48] *K and T v Finland* [2000] 2 FLR 79; *L v Finland* [2000] 2 FLR 118.

[49] *Re B* [2008] 2 FCR 339 at para 77.

[50] *R v United Kingdom* (38000(1)/05).

[51] *R v United Kingdom* (38000(1)/05).

[52] *A v UK (Human Rights: Punishment of Child)* [1998] 3 FCR 597 ECtHR; *X v UK* [2000] 2 FCR 245 EComHR.

[53] *R (Plymouth CC) v Devon* [2005] 2 FCR 428.

[54] Therefore, in *Re B (Care Proceedings: Diplomatic Immunity)* [2003] Fam Law 8 a child had to be taken into care, even though the father might have been able to plead diplomatic immunity in relation to criminal and civil proceedings.

[55] *Z v UK* [2001] 2 FCR 246 and *E v UK* [2003] 1 FLR 348. See *DP v UK* [2002] 3 FCR 385 for an example of a case where it was held that because the local authority could not have known of the abuse it had not harmed the child's article 3 rights.

[56] *R (Plymouth CC) v Devon* [2005] 2 FCR 428 at para 73.

[57] *E v UK* [2002] 3 FCR 700.

[58] Munby J (2004b: 342).

[59] *Re C and B (Children) (Care Order: Future Harm)* [2000] 2 FCR 614; *Re S (Children)* [2010] EWCA Civ 421.

[60] *Re V (A Child) (Care Proceedings: Human Rights Claims)* [2004] 1 FCR 338; *Westminster CC v RA* [2005] EWHC 970 (Fam).

[61] [2000] 2 FLR 79.

response to remove the child.[62] In *MAK v United Kingdom*[63] while on the facts of the case an investigation of sexual abuse was justified, the taking of blood tests and intimate photographs without parental consent was not.

In all of the recent cases in the public law area, the European Court has stressed that in deciding whether to remove a child the individual countries have a wide margin of appreciation.[64] This concept of margin of appreciation has been used by the European Court to recognise that different states covered by the European Convention have different religious and cultural backgrounds and so states should be given some room for manoeuvre. Only where the state's response is clearly disproportionate, as in *K and T v Finland*,[65] will the Convention be infringed. A crucial question under the Human Rights Act 1998 will be how this margin of appreciation will be treated. It could be that the English courts will state that the local authority has a margin of appreciation and, unless the intervention in the right to respect for family life is clearly inappropriate, the courts will not hold a decision of the local authority to infringe the Act. However, it is possible that the doctrine has no place under the Human Rights Act because the Act applies just to the UK and so there is no need to take account of the different social and cultural backgrounds of different states. In such a case the court may be willing to take a stronger line than the European Court in requiring that a local authority acts proportionately when infringing a parent's rights. Bracewell J in *Re N (Leave to Withdraw Care Proceedings)*[66] has taken the latter view. She held that the margin of appreciation is not relevant and the question when considering whether a child should be taken into care is whether it has been shown that 'there is a pressing social need for intervention by the State at this stage in family life and is the response proportionate to the need?'[67] This is a question for the courts, not the local authority. However, the Court of Appeal in *Langley v Liverpool*[68] took the view that when deciding whether the local authority has acted disproportionately some deference is due to decision makers.[69] This appears to indicate that if the case is 'borderline' and could reasonably be regarded as either proportionate or disproportionate the courts should accept the local authority's decision that the intervention is appropriate.

The Human Rights Act 1998 also has important implications in the procedures used by a local authority before taking a child into care and in the decision-making process once a child has been taken into care.[70] Both articles 6 (the right to a fair trial) and 8 have an impact when deciding the extent to which parents of children should be involved in local authority decision-making processes concerning their children.[71] This includes not only court hearings, but also meetings within the local authority about the child.[72] The key test is to be found in *W v UK*:[73]

> The decision-making process must . . . be such as to secure that [the parents'] views and interests are made known to and duly taken into account by the local authority and that they are able to exercise in due time any remedies available to them . . . what therefore has to be determined is

---

[62] See also *P, C, S v UK* [2002] 3 FCR 1, [2002] 2 FLR 631 ECtHR; *Haase v Germany* [2004] Fam Law 500.
[63] (2010) 13 CCLR 241.
[64] *Moser v Austria* [2006] 3 FCR 107.
[65] [2000] 2 FLR 79.
[66] [2000] 1 FLR 134 at p. 141.
[67] [2000] 1 FLR 134 at p. 141.
[68] [2005] 3 FCR 303.
[69] At para 63.
[70] Actions taken by a local authority before the birth of a child cannot amount to an interference with a parent's procedural rights under article 6: *Re V (A Child) (Care: Pre-birth Actions)* [2006] 2 FCR 121.
[71] *Re L (Care: Assessment: Fair Trial)* [2002] 2 FLR 730.
[72] *TP and KM v UK* [2001] 2 FCR 289; *Berecova v Slovakia* [2007] 2 FCR 207.
[73] (1988) 10 EHRR 29, at paras 63–4.

whether, having regard to the particular circumstances of the case and notably the serious nature of the decisions to be taken, the parents have been involved in the decision-making process, seen as a whole, to a degree sufficient to provide them with the requisite protection of their interests.

Here are some examples of the potential impact of the Human Rights Act 1998 on the procedural protections for parents' rights:[74]

1. Reports which a local authority intends to rely upon in a court hearing should be disclosed to the parents,[75] unless there is a compelling justification rendering it necessary not to disclose the documents.[76] If there is any doubt over whether relevant information should be disclosed to parents the local authority should submit the issue to the court for approval.[77]

2. If the local authority has instructed the report of an expert (e.g. a psychologist's report) which is likely to have a preponderant effect on a court case, then, before the report is produced, parents should have the opportunity to examine and comment on the documents being considered by the expert and to cross-examine witnesses interviewed by the expert.[78]

3. The parent must be provided with a lawyer during a hearing of an application for a care order or an application to free or place a child for adoption. This has been held to be an indispensable requirement of article 6.[79]

4. The parents should be kept informed of the local authority's plans in relation to the children.[80]

The courts and local authorities have struggled in some cases to comply with these obligations. In *Re S (Children)*[81] the Court of Appeal identified seven breaches of the mother and children's human rights. Felicity Kaganas suggests that the procedural human rights obligations may have caused some local authorities to by-pass them by using more informal measures of protecting children.[82]

The courts have emphasised that in assessing whether or not there was unfairness in the local authority's procedure the court will consider the process as a whole. This means that although initially the local authority may have treated the parent unfairly, by subsequently fully involving the parents they can overcome the earlier unfairness.[83] Indeed, in an extreme case a parent can be excluded from involvement in care proceedings, where, for example, they pose a serious risk to the child and have no interest in being involved in the child's life.[84]

The courts have shown a reluctance readily to find an interference with a parent's procedural rights under article 8. In *Re J (A Child) (Care Proceedings: Fair Trial)*[85] the Court of Appeal held that judges should be extremely cautious in finding that a failure to follow good practice

---

[74] And indeed for anyone who has family life with the child.
[75] *McMichael v UK* (1995) 20 EHRR 205.
[76] *Re B (Disclosure to Other Parties)* [2002] 2 FCR 32; *Venema v Netherlands* [2003] 1 FCR 153.
[77] *TP and KM v UK* [2001] 2 FCR 289.
[78] *Re C (Care Proceedings: Disclosure of Local Authority's Decision-Making Process)* [2002] 2 FCR 673.
[79] *P, C, S v UK* [2002] 3 FCR 1, [2002] 2 FLR 631 ECtHR, although see Lindley, Richards and Freeman (2001) for concerns over the legal advice and advocacy for parents in child protection cases.
[80] *Re S (Children)* [2010] EWCA Civ 421; *C v Bury MBC* [2002] 3 FCR 608, [2002] 2 FLR 868.
[81] [2010] EWCA Civ 421, discussed Herring (2010f).
[82] Kaganas (2010).
[83] E.g. *Re C (Care Proceedings: Disclosure of Local Authority's Decision-Making Process)* [2002] 2 FCR 673. The courts may be willing to assume that the parent has only him- or herself to blame for the lack of involvement: *Re P (Care Proceedings: Father's Application)* [2001] 2 FCR 279.
[84] *A Local Authority v M and F* [2010] 1 FLR 1355.
[85] [2006] 2 FCR 107.

amounted to an infringement of parents' human rights. There had to be a substantial departure from good practice, which infected the fairness of the proceedings. Munby J in *Re L (Care Proceedings: Human Rights Claims)*[86] has warned of the dangers of the 'terrible irony'[87] that protecting the procedural rights of parents may cause delay which would harm the rights of children.[88] Where there is an infringement of a procedural right, a parent may be entitled to the payment of damages, but only where it is just and necessary to do so.[89] In considering damages it should be emphasised that just because the intervention was based on fears which turned out to be groundless does not mean it is necessarily unlawful.[90]

So, then, under the Human Rights Act 1998 there are heavy demands on local authorities to ensure both that children are protected and that the rights of the family are protected if they do intervene. Henricson and Bainham[91] point out that these obligations can pull in separate directions. Cash-strapped local authorities face difficult choices when considering their obligations both to protect children at risk and to offer appropriate support to families where children have been removed.

## 3 Defining and explaining abuse

There are great difficulties in defining child abuse.[92] The problem is the great stigma attached to conduct which is labelled abuse. If the definition is too wide, there is a danger that the stigma will be lessened. If the definition is too narrow then this may weaken the protection offered to children. One definition is:

> Child abuse consists of anything which individuals, institutions, or processes do or fail to do which directly or indirectly harms children or damages their prospects of safe and healthy development into adulthood.[93]

Some would regard this as too wide a definition. Arguably, letting a child watch too much television or eat too much chocolate could fall into this definition, but most would not regard that as abuse.[94]

It is notable that the phrase 'child abuse' conjures up the notion of physical or sexual abuse of a child by an adult. However, this is far too narrow an understanding. In fact, a significant proportion of abuse is committed by children on other children. Further, other harms that children suffer, such as pollution, inadequate education or poverty are often not labelled abuse, but perhaps should be.[95]

What is widely accepted is that children who have been abused suffer in emotional, educational and social terms.[96] Given the difficulty in defining abuse and detecting it[97] there is little consensus over the level of abuse which exists.

---

[86] [2004] 1 FCR 289.
[87] At para 29.
[88] See Ministry of Justice (2010a) for the latest attempt to speed up care proceedings.
[89] *Re C (Breach of Human Rights: Damages)* [2007] 3 FCR 288.
[90] *A v East Sussex CC* [2010] EWCA Civ 743.
[91] Henricson and Bainham (2005: 368–9). See Freeman (2004a) for a brief history of child abuse.
[92] Archard (1999).
[93] Department of Health (1995a: para 1.4).
[94] For a description of the potential impact of emotional neglect and abuse on children, see Hobbs, Hanks and Wynne (1999).
[95] King (1997).
[96] Department of Health (1995a: 62).
[97] Particularly where the victim suffers from mental disability (see *Re D (A Child) (Wardship: Evidence of Abuse)* [2001] 1 FCR 707).

> **KEY STATISTICS**
>
> - The NSPCC, the highly respected children's charity, has claimed that one in eight people was abused as a child. An NSPCC study found that 38% of children suffered serious or intermediate level maltreatment.[98] A quarter (25%) of children experienced one or more forms of physical violence during childhood.[99] 31% of children claim to have experienced bullying.[100]
>
> - Fretwell Wilson[101] claims that in Great Britain between 12% and 24% of girls[102] and 8 and 9% of boys experience sexual abuse before their sixteenth birthday.[103] 11% of children suffer sexual abuse from someone known to them but unrelated to them; 4% are sexually abused by a parent or relative; and 5% by a stranger.[104]
>
> - There is a common misperception that children are at greater risk of abuse from strangers than families. On average five or six children die a year at the hands of strangers, while between 70 and 100 will die at the hands of their families.[105]
>
> - On 31 March 2007 there were 29,200 children on child protection registers in England.[106] Of these, 13,400 were at risk of neglect; 3,400 of physical abuse; 2,000 of sexual abuse; and 5,100 of emotional abuse. In 2008 7,077 care orders were made.[107]
>
> - On average, every week in England and Wales one to two children are killed at the hands of another person.[108]

It is perhaps easy to label child abuse as caused by social deviants. But we live in a country where one-third of children live in poverty; over 1 million schoolchildren work illegally; each year over 9,000 children are permanently excluded from schools; over 100,000 children live in temporary accommodation; 5,000 children under the age of 16 are used for prostitution; about 2,800 children aged between 15 and 17 are imprisoned in young offender's institutes; and with the highest teenage pregnancy rate in Europe.[109] Abuse is the lot of far too many children in the UK and it is not just the 'sick' few who are to blame. If we are looking at the causes of child abuse we must look at society as a whole as well as the 'abusers'.[110]

## A Explanations for abuse

Not surprisingly, there is no consensus on what causes abuse. The following are some of the explanations:

---

[98] Cawson (2002: 52).
[99] NSPCC (2007).
[100] NSPCC (2007).
[101] Fretwell Wilson (2002).
[102] Whether it is 12% or 24% depends on the definition of sexual abuse used.
[103] See Freeman (2004a) and Smallbone, Marshall and Wortley (2008) for a discussion of the nature and extent of child sexual abuse.
[104] NSPCC (2007).
[105] Lyon (2001).
[106] NSPCC (2008).
[107] Ministry of Justice (2009).
[108] NSPCC (2007).
[109] These statistics are taken from Butler-Sloss (2003).
[110] See, e.g., Masson (2006b).

1. *Psychological factors.* This explanation of the abuse lies in the psychology of the abuser. For example, there is some evidence that those who were themselves abused as children are more likely to abuse children when they become adults, although the fact that by no means all abused children then later abuse indicates that this cannot be the sole explanation.

2. *Sociological factors.* This explanation focuses on the position of children within society. For example, the sexualisation of children in advertising is pointed to as indicating the ambivalent attitude of society towards children and sexual relations.

3. *Feminist perspectives.* These focus on child sexual abuse as an example of patriarchy – the exercise of male power.[111] It reflects the fact that male sexual desire is often linked with themes of superiority and performance.[112] It is notable that the vast majority of sexual abuse is carried out by men.[113]

4. *Family systems.* Others point to family relationships as the key to explaining sexual abuse in the home. Furniss[114] argues that it is only if the other members of the family permit the abuse to occur (whether consciously or not) that it can. Some even claim that child abuse is caused by the wife's failure to meet the husband's sexual needs. Feminists have objected to this explanation on the basis that it can be read as blaming the mother for the abuse.[115]

## 4 Protection of children by the criminal law

If a child is abused, as well as the question of whether the child should be taken into care there is the issue of whether criminal proceedings should be brought against the abuser. There is no one offence of child abuse; the general criminal law protects children, and so children could be the victims of the whole range of assaults in the Offences Against the Person Act 1861. There are also special offences designed to protect children.[116] For example, s 1 of the Children and Young Persons Act 1933 states that any wilful violent or non-violent neglect or ill-treatment which is 'likely to cause him unnecessary suffering or injury to health (including injury to or loss of sight, or hearing, or limb, or organ of the body, and any mental derangement)' is an offence. The Sexual Offences Act 2003 has radically reformed the criminal law on sexual offences against children.[117]

The arguments in favour of criminal prosecution centre on the fact that prosecution demonstrates society's condemnation of child abuse. To the child, the prosecution sends the message that the state acknowledges the abuse suffered and that harm has been done. If the perpetrator is imprisoned then, even if this does not guarantee that the abuser will not abuse again, at least it ensures that during the imprisonment he or she will commit no further

---

[111] Edwards (1996: ch. 7).
[112] Liddle (1993: 112–16).
[113] Cawson (2002: 5); Smart (1989).
[114] Furniss (1991).
[115] Day Sclater (2000).
[116] See, e.g., Punishment of Incest Act 1908; Sexual Offences Act 1956, ss 10–11, 14, 25 and 28. There has been an increasing number of criminal cases where the abuse is alleged to have taken place many years previously: Lewis and Mullis (1999).
[117] See also Gillespie (2010) for a discussion of legal regulation of child pornography.

abuse. On the other hand, if the prosecution fails, the abuser may feel vindicated and the child less protected. Fortin argues:

> There is a widespread perception among child-care practitioners that, as presently organized, the criminal justice system does not promote the welfare of children caught up in its processes and that its use may even victimize them over again. At every stage of the child protection process, efforts to help the child recover from the effects of abuse may be undermined by the prospect of criminal proceedings against the abuser.[118]

While she accepts that an argument could be made that the benefits to children as a class could justify criminal proccedings, she doubts this is made out given the low conviction rates.

## 5 Voluntary services provided by local authorities

The powers and duties of local authorities in respect of children whom it is feared may be suffering harm can be divided into three categories: provision of services; investigation; compulsory intervention. First, the provision of services will be considered.

### A Voluntary accommodation

One of the most basic needs of a vulnerable child is accommodation. Not surprisingly, the Children Act 1989 sets out duties on a local authority to accommodate certain children in need.[119] The Act draws a sharp distinction between children whose parents ask the local authority to accommodate their children ('voluntary accommodation') and children who have been compulsorily removed from parents under a care order and accommodated by the local authority ('compulsory accommodation'). In this section voluntary accommodation will be discussed.

### (i) Duty to accommodate

Section 20 of the Children Act 1989 sets out the circumstances in which a local authority *must* accommodate a child in need:

---

**LEGISLATIVE PROVISION**

**Children Act 1989, section 20**

Every local authority shall provide accommodation for any child in need within their area who appears to them to require accommodation as a result of:

(a) there being no person who has parental responsibility for him;

(b) his being lost or having been abandoned; or

(c) the person who has been caring for him being prevented (whether or not permanently, and for whatever reason) from providing him with suitable accommodation or care.

---

[118] Fortin (2009b: 644).
[119] CA 1989, s 22A imposes a duty on local authorities to ensure there is sufficient accommodation for looked-after children in their area. The provision of housing for homeless families is referred to in Chapter 6.

There are basically two categories of people whom a local authority must accommodate. First, a local authority must accommodate orphaned or abandoned children (although a local authority will often prefer to apply for a care order in respect of an orphaned child so that it acquires parental responsibility for the child). Secondly, there is a duty to accommodate those children whose carers are prevented from looking after them.[120]

One issue which has proved greatly troublesome in practice is where an asylum seeker claims to be a child and therefore must be accommodated by the local authority, but the local authority is unconvinced that they are in fact under 18. The key issue is whether it is for the local authority or the courts to determine someone's age in this kind of case. The issue reached the House of Lords in *R (A) v Croydon London Borough Council*,[121] where it was held that the issue is for the local authority, although their determination could be challenged in the courts by way of judicial review.[122]

It should be stressed that there is no need for a court to approve the voluntary accommodation. But if a parent with parental responsibility for the child objects to the accommodation, the local authority may not accommodate the child. If the local authority wishes to accommodate a child despite the parent's objection, then the local authority must resort to compulsory measures, such as a care order. The accommodation is usually provided for by the local authority through foster parents or children's homes. However, s 22C of the Children and Young Persons Act 2008 imposes a duty on the local authority to explore placement for children with friends or relatives. That said, the local authority cannot avoid having to pay foster carers financial support by saying that there is a private fostering arrangement, when the local authority have in fact made the arrangements.[123]

## (ii) Discretion to accommodate

In addition to the duty outlined above, local authorities have a discretion to provide accommodation to a child even if the child is not in need, 'if they consider that to do so would safeguard or promote the child's welfare' under s 20(4).[124] This discretion exists even if there is a person who has parental responsibility who can provide accommodation. However, all those with parental responsibility must consent to the local authority accommodating the child.

## (iii) The consent or objection of those with parental responsibility

As already mentioned, under s 20(7) no child under the age of 16 can be accommodated without a court order where a person with parental responsibility objects; but there is no need for anyone positively to consent to the accommodation. If a person with parental responsibility objects, then he or she must show that he or she is willing and able to provide accommodation for the child. There seems to be no requirement that the accommodation be

---

[120] Article 27(3) of the UN Convention on the Rights of the Child requires the signatory states to provide needy children with assistance with housing.
[121] [2010] 1 FLR 959.
[122] Detailed guidance on how age is to be assessed is found in *R (F) v Lewisham London Borough Council* [2010] 1 FLR 1463.
[123] *R (A) v Coventry City Council* [2009] 1 FLR 1202; *R (C) v Knowsley Metropolitan Borough Council* [2009] 1 FLR 493.
[124] Any person aged 16–21 can be accommodated if a local authority believes that this would safeguard or promote the young person's welfare under the Children Act 1989 (hereafter CA 1989), s 20(5).

suitable, although a court may decide that such a requirement be read into the statute. If the local authority believes that the child will be endangered if accommodated by that person, it must apply for a care order or other protective order. If a person is caring for a child under a residence order,[125] then only that person can object. If in such a case the non-resident parent objects, he or she could apply for a residence order or a prohibited steps order to prevent the child being accommodated by the local authority.[126]

The unmarried father without parental responsibility has no right to object to voluntary accommodation. If an unmarried father objects to the accommodation, he would need to apply for a residence order. If the parent with parental responsibility objects to the child being accommodated with a particular foster parent, the local authority must accede to that wish. It may return the child to the parents, or apply for a care order, but may not accommodate the child under s 20 against the objection of the parents.[127]

### (iv) Children requesting accommodation

If the child requests accommodation him- or herself, the position depends on whether the child is above or below the age of 16.

#### (a) Children aged 16 and over

The local authority must accommodate any child aged 16 or 17 'in need', whose welfare it considers 'is likely to be seriously prejudiced if they do not provide him with accommodation'.[128] If the child is aged over 16 then there is no need for parental approval.[129] If the child is not in such dire need, the local authority is required only to provide advice on accommodation or housing and is not required to accommodate the child. In a case where the child no longer wishes to live with her parents, but her parents are able to offer accommodation, the duty to accommodate does not arise.[130] In *R (On the Application of FL)* v *Lambeth London Borough Council*[131] a girl had been raped by a member of a gang and wished to move away from her mother as she did not feel safe in her mother's neighbourhood. The court held that the local authority was entitled to determine that the immediate surroundings of the mother's house were safe and the rapist did not know her address. There was, therefore, no duty to provide accommodation as accommodation was available. The concern was that if the duty was not limited, local authorities might be inundated with requests for accommodation from 16- and 17-year-olds.[132] However, the high rates of homelessness among this age group have led some to call for this area of the law to be reconsidered. Another concern is that teenagers may seek local authority care as an act of rebellion, rather than really being in need. To prevent the teenager seeking accommodation, a parent could apply for a residence order, although that would succeed only in exceptional circumstances.[133]

---

[125] Or an order under the inherent jurisdiction allowing the child to stay with him or her.

[126] By analogy: *D* v *D (County Court Jurisdiction: Injunctions)* [1993] 2 FLR 802.

[127] *R* v *Tameside MBC, ex p J* [2000] 1 FLR 942, [2000] 1 FCR 173.

[128] CA 1989, s 20(3). If these requirements are met the local authority cannot seek to accommodate the child under section 17, rather than section 20: *R (W)* v *North Lincolnshire Council* [2008] 2 FLR 2150.

[129] CA 1989, s 20(3).

[130] *R (M)* v *London Borough of Barnet* [2009] 2 FLR 725, discussed in Driscoll and Hollingsworth (2008).

[131] [2010] 1 FCR 269.

[132] Fortin (2009b: ch. 4).

[133] CA 1989, s 9(7).

> ### CASE: *R (On the Application of G)* v *Southwark London Borough Council* [2009] 3 All ER 189
>
> G was 16 when his mother excluded him from her home and he approached his local authority requesting an assessment of his needs under s 17. He also sought accommodation under s 20. The local authority assessment concluded that he had a need for housing, but this could be provided by the authority's homeless person's unit. He was also referred to the family resource team which could help him apply for benefits. He brought legal proceedings claiming that he had a right to be housed by the local authority under s 20.
>
> Their Lordships were clear that where a child has been excluded from the family home and asks their local authority for accommodation it was not open to a local authority to arrange for accommodation under the homelessness provisions of the 1996 Housing Act. Having determined that he was a child who was in need and that he had no permenant accommodation the authority was liable to accommodate him. It could be said that he had need for accommodation because his mother was prevented from offering him accommodation. Baroness Hale approved the comments of Rix LJ in the Court of Appeal:
>
> > a child, even one on the verge of adulthood, is considered and treated by Parliament as a vulnerable person to whom the state, in the form of a relevant local authority, owes a duty which goes wider than the mere provision of accommodation.[134]

### (b) Children under 16

There is much doubt concerning the position of under-16-year-olds requesting local authority accommodation. It might be argued that, following *Gillick*,[135] a competent minor should have a decisive say as to whether they are accommodated by a local authority. Eekelaar and Dingwall have suggested that when a child is *Gillick*-competent then the parents lose the power to decide where the child is to live.[136] Those who oppose this view note that *Gillick*-competent children do not have a power of consent where there are express statutory provisions to the contrary.[137] Here s 20(6) states that the court should:

> ### LEGISLATIVE PROVISION
>
> **Children Act 1989, section 20(6)**
>
> so far as is reasonably practicable and consistent with the child's welfare—
>
> (a) ascertain the child's wishes regarding the provision of accommodation; and
>
> (b) give due consideration (having regard to his age and understanding) to such wishes of the child as they have been able to ascertain.

This seems explicitly to fall short of giving the competent child the exclusive right to have themselves accommodated. Section 20(7) appears to be quite clear that a child cannot be accommodated under the Children Act 1989 against the wishes of a parent with parental

---

[134] [2009] 1 FCR 357 at [35].
[135] *Gillick v West Norfolk and Wisbech AHA* [1986] 1 FLR 229, [1986] AC 112.
[136] Eekelaar and Dingwall (1990: 78).
[137] *Re W (A Minor) (Medical Treatment: Court's Jurisdiction)* [1993] 1 FLR 1, [1992] 2 FCR 785.

responsibility. Bainham therefore argues that if a parent objects, then the competent child's wishes cannot prevail.[138] The matter could, however, be brought before the court by way of a s 8 application.[139]

## (v) Removal from accommodation

Under s 20(8) of the Children Act 1989, anyone with parental responsibility 'may at any time remove the child from accommodation provided by or on behalf of the local authority'.[140] There is not even a requirement that parents give notice to the local authority of their intention to remove their child from voluntary accommodation. It is not possible for the local authority to stop a removal by obtaining a s 8 order preventing the removal by the parent,[141] nor even to require a formal undertaking from parents not to remove their child.[142] But a parent with parental responsibility is not able to remove a child if the child was placed by another person with a residence order. Some argue that this is an inappropriate limitation on the rights of a parent with parental responsibility,[143] while others argue that the core element of a residence order is that the holder of the residence order can determine where the child should live.[144]

There are two main arguments in favour of the right of a parent to remove their children from accommodation. First, it is important to keep a clear distinction between voluntary and compulsory care, and the power of immediate removal maintains the clarity of this distinction. Secondly, it has been suggested that voluntary accommodation should be made as attractive an option as possible, so that parents feeling under great pressure will be willing to use the 'service'.

There have been concerns that parents may misuse their power of automatic removal and remove their children in unsuitable circumstances. For example, a parent could turn up at the foster parents' house drunk, demanding the return of his or her child. The Children Act 1989 appears to suggest that the foster parents must hand the child over to the parent, but there are four options available for a local authority in such a case:

1. Some commentators[145] argue that a local authority is permitted to prevent the unsuitable removal of children by relying on s 3(5) of the Children Act 1989. However, a strong opposing argument is that s 3(5) cannot be used to prevent the exercise of the parental right to remove the child, especially where the parental right is explicitly granted in a statute.

2. A local authority could apply for an emergency protection order if the child is likely to suffer significant harm.

3. A foster parent from whom a child was removed could apply for a residence order or even rely on wardship[146] or the inherent jurisdiction.

4. Police protection may also be available in an extreme case.[147]

---

[138] Bainham (2005: 341).

[139] Although a child cannot apply for a residence order in favour of him- or herself nor in favour of the local authority. CA 1989, s 9( 2): *Re SC (A Minor) (Leave to Seek Section 8 Orders)* [1994] 1 FLR 96, [1994] 1 FCR 837.

[140] This might include an unmarried father with parental responsibility.

[141] *Nottinghamshire County Council v J* unreported 26 November 1993, cited in Lowe and Douglas (1998: 526).

[142] CA 1989, s 9(5), although *Re G (Minors) (Interim Care Order)* [1993] 2 FLR 839 at p. 843 suggested it was.

[143] Bainham (1998a: 339).

[144] Hayes and Williams (1999: 144).

[145] See the discussion in Cretney, Masson and Bailey-Harris (2002: 709).

[146] Although if foster parents started caring for the child as a ward of court they may lose the financial assistance of the local authority.

[147] CA 1989, s 46. See the discussion in Masson (2005).

It may be that the threat of the local authority applying for a care order provides a suitable deterrent to children being inappropriately removed.

It seems that a child who is aged 16 or 17 can leave voluntary accommodation provided by the local authority at will. There is no statutory basis on which a local authority can detain a child against his or her wishes.[148]

### (vi) Accommodation agreements[149]

If a child is accommodated, the local authority should enter an agreement with the person with parental responsibility. The agreement is likely to cover issues such as schooling, religious practices and contact arrangements. The agreement is not legally binding, but is intended to clarify the expectations of all involved and hence avoid any potential disputes.

### (vii) Refusals to accommodate

If a local authority refuses to accommodate a child, parents have only a limited right to challenge that decision. It seems that, by analogy with *Re J (Specific Issue Order: Leave to Apply)*,[150] a specific issue order could not be relied upon to compel a local authority to accommodate a child. Judicial review of a decision not to accommodate may be possible but it would be difficult to demonstrate that the local authority's decision was unlawful. For example, it would be difficult to show that the decision not to accommodate was so unreasonable that no reasonable local authority could have reached that decision.[151] The best route to challenge the decision would be to rely on the local authority's internal complaints procedure.[152]

### (viii) Effect of child being accommodated

A child accommodated by the local authority under s 20 is not put into care, and the local authority does not acquire parental responsibility. But the child will be 'looked after' by the local authority, and therefore the local authority will owe such a child the various duties discussed in Chapter 11. In *D v London Borough of Southwark*[153] a local authority social worker took a child away from her abusive father and placed the child with the father's former girlfriend. The local authority refused to pay for the child's support. It was held that the local authority had a duty to accommodate the child and could not side-step that by making an informal arrangement with someone. The child was being looked after by the local authority and they were accommodating her with the girlfriend. The council was therefore liable to pay for the child's care and maintenance.

## B  Services for children in need

Clearly, prevention of abuse is better than dealing with its consequences. Section 7 of the Children and Young Persons Act 2008 imposes a general duty on the Secretary of State to promote the well-being of children. The Children Act 1989 attempts to focus local authorities'

---

[148] There is a severe lack of resources for housing: see Fortin (2009b: ch. 4). Also see the problems in *R v Northavon DC, ex p Smith* [1994] 2 FCR 859, [1994] 2 FLR 671, with families being shunted around from department to department. The House of Lords case made it clear that there is an obligation for local authorities to change their housing policies in the light of CA 1989, s 27.

[149] Detailed in Department of Health (1991a: para 2.13 et seq.).

[150] [1995] 1 FLR 669, [1995] 3 FCR 799, where the child sought a declaration under CA 1989, s 8 that he was in need.

[151] *R v Kingston-upon-Thames RB, ex p T* [1994] 1 FLR 798, [1994] 1 FCR 232; *R v Birmingham City Council, ex p A* [1997] 2 FLR 841.

[152] *A and S v Enfield London Borough Council* [2008] 2 FLR 1945.

[153] [2007] 1 FCR 788.

attention on children in their area who are 'in need' and at danger of suffering significant harm.[154] The fact that a child is in need does not necessarily mean that his or her parents are mistreating them. A child may be 'in need' but be cared for so well by his or her parents that there is no fear of abuse or neglect[155] (e.g. such as a child brought up in an impoverished family). Part III of the Children Act 1989 requires the local authority to provide certain services to those children who are 'in need'. Once a local authority has decided that a child is in need, then it must provide services. Although a local authority cannot decide to provide no assistance to children in need, it is left to the local authority to decide what form the assistance will take.[156] In considering what services to supply, a child's welfare is a relevant factor, but it is not paramount. Financial considerations will often play a significant role.[157]

The law governing children in need is a rather strange area because it appears there is no effective court enforcement of a local authority's duties, so the 'duties' are largely of a non-enforceable nature. However, a child whose needs are inadequately assessed could use judicial review, although that would be hard to prove.[158] The importance of the Children Act 1989 here is that it helps focus a local authority's attention towards vulnerable children. That said, after the Human Rights Act 1998 it is arguable that local authorities must ensure that children do not suffer torture and inhuman or degrading treatment.[159] If the child is suffering so much that it could be said to be suffering inhuman and degrading treatment, then the local authority may be under an enforceable duty under the Human Rights Act to supply such protection necessary to prevent the child so suffering.[160] However, as we shall see, the House of Lords in *R (On the Application of G) v Barnet London Borough Council*[161] has held that s 17 of the Children Act 1989 does not give rights to individual children.

Crucial to understanding the extent of the local authority's responsibilities under the Children Act 1989 is the concept of being 'in need'.

### (i) What does 'in need' mean?

A child is 'in need' if:

---

**LEGISLATIVE PROVISION**

**Children Act 1989, section 17(10)**

(a) he is unlikely to achieve or maintain, or to have the opportunity of achieving or maintaining, a reasonable standard of health or development without the provision for him of services by a local authority under this part;

(b) his health or development is likely to be significantly impaired, or further impaired, without the provision for him of such services; or

(c) he is disabled.

---

[154] Detailed guidance is found in Department of Health (1999c), and Children and Young Persons Act 2008.

[155] For a useful discussion of the significance of child neglect see Tanner and Turney (2002).

[156] See Piper (2004) for a discussion of assessment.

[157] *Re M (Secure Accommodation Order)* [1995] 1 FLR 418. The issues are discussed in Masson (1992). Parry (2000) expresses concerns about the local authorities' care for ethnic minority children.

[158] See *Re T (Judicial Review: Local Authority Decisions Concerning Children in Need)* [2003] EWHC 2515 (Admin); *R (On the Application of AB and SB) v Nottingham CC* [2001] 3 FCR 350; *R (EW and BW) v Nottinghamshire County Council* [2009] 2 FLR 974 for successful applications for judicial review.

[159] Applying *A v UK (Human Rights: Punishment of Child)* [1998] 2 FLR 959, [1998] 3 FCR 597.

[160] For a thorough discussion of the difficulties in enforcing a local authority's obligations under CA 1989, Part III, see Murphy (2003).

[161] [2003] UKHL 57, [2003] 3 FCR 419, discussed in Cowan (2004).

'Development' includes 'physical, intellectual, emotional, social or behavioural development'; health includes 'physical or mental health'.[162] A disabled child is one who is 'blind, deaf, or dumb or suffers from mental disorder of any kind or is substantially and permanently handicapped by illness, injury or congenital deformity or such other disability as may be prescribed'.[163] The law here is not concerned with the causes of the need, but rather the fact of need. The need may arise from the lack of skills of the parent, or may be due to the disabilities of the child.

### (ii) What services should be supplied?

Part III of the Children Act 1989 was intended to establish a single code to govern the voluntary services to children and all decisions of a local authority.[164] The general duty to provide services is set out in s 17(1):

---

**LEGISLATIVE PROVISION**

**Children Act 1989, section 17(1)**

It shall be the general duty of every local authority (in addition to the other duties imposed on them by this Part)—

(a) to safeguard and promote the welfare of children within their area who are in need; and

(b) so far as is consistent with that duty, to promote the upbringing of such children by their families

by providing a range and level of services appropriate to those children's needs.

---

The duty is described as a general duty to indicate that an individual child cannot seek to compel a local authority to provide services by relying on this section.[165] The House of Lords in *R (On the Application of G) v Barnet LBC*[166] has held that the section does not create a right for a particular child to services, but rather describes a duty that the local authority owes to a section of the public (i.e. children in need). This is because it is for the local authority to decide how to spend its resources. The majority of their Lordships held that s 17 did not impose a duty on a local authority even to assess the needs of a particular child. Lord Steyn, for the minority argued:

> On the local authorities' approach, since s 17(1) does not impose a duty in relation to an individual child, it follows that a local authority is not under a duty to assess the needs of a child in need under s 17(1). That cannot be right. That would go far to stultify the whole purpose of Pt III of the 1989 Act.[167]

What concerned the majority appears to be an attempt by the parents in this case, who were temporarily homeless and not entitled to housing, to make a claim to be housed through their children. Further, the courts recognised that delicate issues such as the distribution of

---

[162] CA 1989, s 17(11).

[163] CA 1989, s 17(11). Some have argued that this terminology is inappropriate: Freeman (1992a: 57).

[164] See Department of Health (1998b).

[165] *R (On the Application of G) v Barnet London Borough Council* [2003] UKHL 57; *Re M (Secure Accommodation Order)* [1995] 1 FLR 418.

[166] [2003] UKHL 57.

[167] At para 32.

public housing and the support of immigrants were best left to elected local authorities, rather than the decisions of courts looking at the merits of a particular case.

Services are to be made available not only to children, but also to their parents and family members,[168] as long as the services are aimed at safeguarding the welfare of the child. 'Family' is defined to include 'any person who has parental responsibility for the child and any other person with whom he has been living'.[169] 'Services' can include the provision of assistance in kind and even cash in exceptional circumstances.[170] There is also a list of special duties in Sch 2 to the Children Act 1989. For example, there are duties to take reasonable steps to avoid the need to bring proceedings for care or supervision orders; duties to encourage children not to commit criminal offences; and duties to publicise the services that the local authority offers.[171]

### (iii) Every Child Matters

The Children Act 2004 was passed as a response to the Victoria Climbié scandal. Following that tragedy two important documents were produced: the Laming Report into what went wrong in that case[172] and the Government's *Every Child Matters*[173] which recommended policies to ensure that it never happened again. The documents accepted that the current legislative framework was basically sound. The difficulty was in using it effectively on the ground. A key theme, and one which has been repeated in many inquiries into public failings in child abuse cases, was failures of communications between the different bodies dealing with children.[174] Housing, education, medical and social work departments had failed to keep each other informed; had they done so, the picture of abuse would have been apparent. The Children Act 2004 seeks to improve this position. In Part I the Children's Commissioner for England was created;[175] Part II seeks to improve co-operation between the different agencies who deal with children, such as the police, health authorities, education authorities and the probation service;[176] and s 13 creates Local Safeguarding Boards, to co-ordinate efforts to safeguard children in their area.[177]

Another theme of *Every Child Matters* was the need to ensure that where there were concerns with children, these were not left until they reached the point of crisis.[178] In other words, there should be a less sharp line between services offered to children generally and special services offered to children 'in need'. The *Every Child Matters* document believed that there was broad agreement in respect of five key outcomes for children:

- **Being healthy**: enjoying good physical and mental health and living a healthy lifestyle.
- **Staying safe**: being protected from harm and neglect and growing up able to look after themselves.

---

[168] This includes any person with parental responsibility or any other person with whom the child is living (CA 1989, s 17(10)).

[169] CA 1989, s 17(10).

[170] CA 1989, s 17(6).

[171] A local authority is under a duty to provide day-care facilities to children in need as appropriate under CA 1989, s 18.

[172] Laming (2003).

[173] Department for Education and Skills (2003).

[174] Children Act 2004 (hereafter CA 2004), Part X is designed to improve the communications between the different organisations that work with children, including the police and medical professionals.

[175] CA 2004, Part I. See pages 466–7 for a discussion of the Commissioner.

[176] CA 2004, Part II.

[177] CA 2004, s 13. Now there are Children's Trust Arrangements which involve those working with children and are designed to improve communication between the bodies. See National Children's Bureau (2005) for early signs of success.

[178] Department for Education and Skills (2003: para 1.2).

- **Enjoying and achieving**: getting the most out of life and developing broad skills for adulthood.

- **Making a positive contribution**: to the community and to society and not engaging in anti-social or offending behaviour.

- **Economic well-being**: overcoming socio-economic disadvantage to achieve their full potential in life.

These were goals that local authorities could seek in relation to all children, not just those 'in need'. Indeed, by doing that the state could seek to prevent children falling into need rather than just responding once an emergency had occurred.

From one perspective this is sensible. Surely it is better to offer support and help to children and their families before there is a crisis than to rush in 'all guns blazing' when suddenly there is an emergency. Further, there is a danger that a child who is genuinely suffering will be known to the local authority, but never, quite, be regarded as suffering sufficiently to justify intervention. In such a case the child could suffer perhaps years of harm and serious hardship.[179] The difficulty, however, is that marginalised families may end up being the focus of local authority interest and have 'middle-class moral values' imposed upon them.[180] What to a social worker is 'helping a family who is struggling', to the family may appear as 'coercive state interference'. Another concern is that there are insufficient funds to deal with those children who are at serious risk, let alone deal with those children who might become at risk.[181] Nigel Parton argues:

> England is witnessing the emergence of 'the preventive-surveillance state' which aims to intervene earlier in order to ensure that all children develop to their full potential rather than simply aim to detect, investigate, and respond to problems once they have arisen. The approach to prevention on which the strategy is premised is derived from a particular scientific explanation of cause and effect which assumes both the possibility of predicting future outcomes and the belief in the capacity for positive intervention by government in social life. Policies and practices that emphasize such an approach to prevention and early intervention are intimately connected to the need to expand systems of surveillance and information sharing.[182]

## C The family assistance order

The family assistance order (FAO) is governed by s 16 of the Children Act 1989 and is a form of voluntary assistance provided to a family by the local authority.[183] The order requires either a probation officer or an officer of the local authority ('the officer') to be made available 'to advise, assist and (where appropriate) befriend any person named in the order'. The order can benefit anyone with whom the child is living and is not restricted to parents. The order is designed to provide short-term help to a family and may be as much directed at the parents as the child.[184] It might be particularly appropriate in a case where the parent is affectionate towards the child but lacks the skills to care for the child practically.[185]

---

[179] Brandon (2005).
[180] See Gillies (2005) for a discussion of concerns of this kind.
[181] Cooper, Hetherington and Katz (2003: 21).
[182] Parton (2008: 185).
[183] Thorough reviews of the use of family assistance orders are to be found in HM Inspectorate of Court Administration (2007); James and Sturgeon-Adams (1999) and Seden (2001).
[184] Department of Health (1991b: 2.50).
[185] See Iwaniec, Donaldson and Allweis (2004) for a discussion of such cases.

The order can be made only in exceptional circumstances[186] and only by the court acting on its own motion. In other words, a parent cannot apply for an FAO. However, it is necessary that the person in whose favour the order is made has consented to the making of the order.[187] It seems the local authority must consent to the making of the order as well.[188]

The maximum length of the order is six months.[189] The only power of enforcement that the officer has is to refer the case to the court if he or she believes there is a need for variation. He or she could also report their concerns to the local authority, which may wish to intervene by applying for a care order. The FAO should not be used for purposes unrelated to its primary purpose of assisting the family. So in *S v P (Contact Application: Family Assistance Order)*[190] it was said to be a misuse of the order to make it for the purpose of providing someone to accompany a child visiting his father in prison. An appropriate use of the order was found in *Re U (Application to Free for Adoption)*[191] when the court decided that a child should reside with her grandparents and thought that an FAO could assist the child and grandparents in establishing a new life together.

In practice, FAOs appear to be little used.[192] It has been suggested that this is because of concerns about the extent to which the order intervenes in family life. It also appears that there is much confusion among social workers as to their purpose.[193]

## 6 Investigations by local authorities

There are two provisions in the Children Act 1989 under which the local authority may be required to investigate a child's welfare. Section 47 sets out specific circumstances in which a local authority must investigate a child's well-being. Section 37 permits a court to require a local authority to investigate a child's welfare.

### A Section 47 investigations

Under s 47 of the Children Act 1989 the local authority is under a duty to investigate the welfare of a child in their area when:

1. a child is subject to an emergency protection order;
2. a child is in police protection;
3. a child has contravened a curfew notice;[194] or
4. the local authority has reasonable cause to suspect that a child is suffering, or is likely to suffer, significant harm.[195]

Local authorities may obtain information about potential abuse of children from a wide variety of sources. Neighbours, teachers, doctors, even children themselves may provide

---

[186] CA 1989, s 16(3)(a).
[187] CA 1989, s 16(3).
[188] CA 1989, s 16(7); *Re C (Family Assistance Order)* [1996] 1 FLR 424, [1996] 3 FCR 514.
[189] CA 1989, s 16(5).
[190] [1997] 2 FLR 277, [1997] 2 FCR 185.
[191] [1993] 2 FLR 992.
[192] Seden (2001).
[193] James and Sturgeon-Adams (1999).
[194] Under Ch. 1, Part 1 of the Crime and Disorder Act 1998.
[195] CA 1989, s 47.

information.[196] The local authority does not need proved facts before it carries out an investigation; suspicions are sufficient.[197] This means that even if a criminal prosecution against an alleged perpetrator of sexual abuse had failed, the local authority might still be authorised to carry out a s 47 investigation.[198]

Under these circumstances the local authority must make 'such enquiries as they consider necessary to enable them to decide whether they should take any action to safeguard or promote the child's welfare'.[199] There is no power to enter a child's home against the parents' will. However, if parents fail to permit social workers to see a child then the local authority must apply for either an emergency protection order, a child assessment order, a supervision order, or a care order unless they are satisfied that the child can be satisfactorily safeguarded in other ways.[200] However, if the parents have permitted the local authority to see the child, the legislation leaves the choice of what to do next to the local authority. The main options are: to do nothing; to offer the family services; or to apply to the court for a child assessment order, emergency protection order, or supervision or care order. As Eekelaar has pointed out, a local authority is not under a duty to apply for an order, even if it decides that the child would be best protected by applying for such an order. There is a duty to investigate and to decide what it *should* do, but there is no duty to do anything as a result of the investigation.[201] It may be that financial limitations would cause a local authority not to apply for an order which it thought desirable but not essential. In practice few s 47 enquiries are undertaken, due to staff shortages and lack of staff training.[202]

A court has no jurisdiction to prevent a local authority carrying out its investigative duties.[203] If a court was convinced that the investigations by a local authority were unjustified and causing harm to a child, it could make a prohibited steps order under s 8 of the Children Act 1989 to restrain a parent from co-operating with the investigation.[204] However, it would require a most unusual case for this to be an appropriate course of action.

## B Section 37 directions

The court cannot require a local authority to apply for a care order, nor can it force a care order upon a local authority which does not apply for one.[205] What the court may do is direct a local authority to investigate a child's circumstances under s 37 of the Children Act 1989. The court can make such a direction wherever 'a question arises with respect to the welfare of any child', and it appears to the court that 'it may be appropriate for a care or supervision order to be made with respect to him'.[206] The court must not make a s 37 direction if the case is not one where it may be appropriate to make a care or supervision order.[207] The local authority must report back to the court within eight weeks. The court

---

[196] Department of Health (2000c).
[197] *R (On the Application of S)* v *Swindon BC* [2001] EWHC 334, [2001] 3 FCR 702.
[198] *R (On the Application of S)* v *Swindon BC* [2001] EWHC 334, [2001] 3 FCR 702.
[199] CA 1989, s 47(1)(b).
[200] CA 1989, s 47(6).
[201] Eekelaar (1990).
[202] Department of Health (2002a: 6.8).
[203] *D* v *D (County Court Jurisdiction: Injunctions)* [1993] 2 FLR 802.
[204] *D* v *D (County Court Jurisdiction: Injunctions)* [1993] 2 FLR 802.
[205] *Nottingham CC* v *P* [1993] 2 FLR 134, [1994] 1 FCR 624.
[206] CA 1989, s 37(1).
[207] *Re L (Section 37 Direction)* [1999] 1 FLR 984.

cannot seek to control the local authority's investigation.[208] If, following an investigation under s 37, the local authority does not apply for an order, it must explain this to the court and describe what services or assistance it intends to provide.[209] If the local authority after its investigations decides not to apply for a court order, the court cannot force it to do so.[210] It is submitted that, following the Human Rights Act 1998, where the local authority is aware that a child is suffering serious abuse following a s 37 or s 47 investigation, it is under a duty to protect the child.[211]

A different concern in the light of the Human Rights Act 1998 is the number of investigations in which it was found that there was no evidence of abuse of children. In the year ending March 2003 there were 65,000 investigations, of which only 37,400 led to a child protection conference.[212] Arguably, an investigation launched without justification could constitute a lack of respect for family life and so breach article 8 of the European Convention on Human Rights.

## C Child assessment orders

A child assessment order is a preliminary order that allows assessments to take place to determine whether further orders may be necessary.

### (i) When is a child assessment order appropriate?

A child assessment order (CAO) is appropriate where the local authority has concerns about a child but needs more information before it is able to decide what action to take.[213] The guidance makes it clear the CAO is 'emphatically not for emergencies'.[214] If the grounds for an emergency protection order (EPO) are made out, s 43(4) of the Children Act 1989 states that the court may not make a CAO but must make an EPO. In fact, it is difficult to envisage when a CAO may be appropriate.[215] If there is a serious concern that the child is being abused, and the parents refuse to have the child examined, then an EPO will normally be more appropriate; whereas if the parents are happy to agree to the examination, then there may be no need for a CAO at all.[216] It is therefore not surprising that few CAOs are granted.[217]

### (ii) When can the CAO be made?

A CAO can only be requested by a local authority or an 'authorised person' (at present, only the NSPCC).[218] The court can make a CAO under s 43(1) where:

---

[208] *Re M (Official Solicitor's Role)* [1998] 3 FLR 815 suggested that it was inappropriate to use the Official Solicitor to ensure that a local authority carried out an investigation in the manner requested by the judge.
[209] CA 1989, s 37(3).
[210] *Nottingham CC v P* [1993] 2 FLR 134, [1994] 1 FCR 624.
[211] Choudhry and Herring (2006b).
[212] Department for Education and Skills (2004b).
[213] Discussed in Lavery (1996).
[214] Department of Health (1991b: 4.4).
[215] Parton (1991: 188–90).
[216] Dickens (1993: 94).
[217] The numbers are so small that the Government stopped collecting statistics on CAOs after 1993.
[218] Contrast with the emergency protection order, which can be applied for by anyone.

> **LEGISLATIVE PROVISION**
>
> **Children Act 1989, section 43(1)**
>
> (a) the applicant has reasonable cause to suspect that the child is suffering, or is likely to suffer, significant harm;
>
> (b) an assessment of the state of the child's health or development, or of the way in which he has been treated, is required to enable the applicant to determine whether or not the child is suffering, or is likely to suffer, significant harm; and
>
> (c) it is unlikely that such an assessment will be made, or be satisfactory, in the absence of an order under this section.

The phrase 'significant harm' has the same meaning as in s 31, which will be discussed later in this chapter. The focus of the test is the applicant's belief of the risk of significant harm: it must be reasonable. The hurdle is lower than that for a care order, for example, because the CAO is less intrusive into family life.[219] Once the court is satisfied that s 43(1) is satisfied, it must still be persuaded that the making of the CAO is in the child's welfare under s 1(1) and satisfies s 1(5) of the Children Act 1989.[220]

### (iii) The effects of a CAO

There are two automatic results of a CAO. First, the order requires any person who is able to do so to produce the child to a person named in the order (normally a social worker). The second effect is that the order authorises the named person to carry out an assessment of the child.[221] There are likely to be specific directions in the order relating to medical or psychiatric examinations: for example, who should conduct the examinations and where they should take place.[222] The local authority does not acquire parental responsibility, which remains with the parents. It seems that a child may refuse to submit to an examination if he or she is of sufficient understanding.[223]

The maximum duration of a CAO is seven days from the starting date specified in the order.[224] There is no power to extend this time period. Seven days is unlikely to be long enough for some psychological examinations.[225] The justification for the limitation is that seven days should be enough to tell the authority whether further orders are required.

## 7 Compulsory orders: care orders and supervision orders

There are three main orders under which a local authority can intervene in a family's life even without the family's consent. For emergencies, the emergency protection order (EPO) is

---

[219] One important difference between the CAO and the EPO is that an application for the CAO can be applied for *ex parte*.

[220] The checklist of factors in s 1(3) does not apply: *Re R (Recovery Orders)* [1998] 2 FLR 401.

[221] CA 1989, s 43(7).

[222] If the child is to be removed from home, this should be set out in the order: CA 1989, s 43(10).

[223] CA 1989, s 43(8); but note the interpretation of *South Glamorgan County Council v W and B* [1993] 1 FLR 574, [1993] 1 FCR 626 on the similarly worded s 44(7), that the court may override the refusal of a child.

[224] CA 1989, s 43(5).

[225] Dickens (1993: 96).

available. To provide long-term solutions the choice is between care or supervision orders.[226] Care and supervision orders should only be applied for as a last resort, if voluntary arrangements and the provision of services cannot adequately protect a child. As Bainham has put it: 'Court orders for care and supervision are . . . very much the ambulance at the bottom of the cliff while the support services are the (however inadequate) fence at the top.'[227] The Children Act 1989 makes it clear that a child can only be taken into care through one route, that is s 31.[228] The local authority cannot take a child into care except by applying for a care order. This was dramatically revealed in *R (G) v Nottingham CC*[229] where a local authority removed a newborn baby from a mother. They did so without any court authorisation. The authority relied on the fact that she had not opposed the taking of the baby, but Munby J held that fell well short of the consent required. As he put it 'helpless acquiescence' could not be equated with consent. The local authority, even if acting in the best interests of the child, had failed to obtain proper legal authorisation for what they did.[230]

## A Who can apply?

Section 31(1) states that only a local authority or the NSPCC can apply for a care or supervision order. There is provision for the Secretary of State to add to that list, but to date there have been no additions. Before the NSPCC brings care proceedings, it should consult the local authority in whose area the child is ordinarily resident.[231]

## B Who can be taken into care?

Care and supervision orders can only be made in respect of a child who is under 18.[232] Orders should only be made if the child is habitually resident in the UK, or currently present there.[233] A married child cannot be taken into care. Can a care order be made in respect of a foetus?[234] There have been several cases where a local authority has become aware that a pregnant women is harming her unborn child, perhaps by taking drugs or excessive alcohol; or there may be a history of the woman abusing other children. The local authority may feel that the mother needs antenatal help and may even seek to restrict her behaviour. The court has consistently held that the unborn child is not a person and so cannot be the subject of a care order, as was established in *Re F (In Utero)*.[235] However, harm done to the foetus might be relied upon as evidence to place a child in care shortly after birth.[236] Exceptionally a court can make an *ex parte* declaration that on birth a local authority may remove the baby for its own safety.[237] The local authority can only intervene to protect an unborn child if the mother consents to the intervention. The policy here seems to be that any intervention designed to assist the foetus will inevitably interfere with the mother's autonomy. The mother's freedom

---

[226] The effects of the orders will be discussed in detail in Chapter 11.
[227] Bainham (2005: 325).
[228] *Re T (A Minor) (Care Order: Conditions)* [1994] 2 FLR 423, [1994] 2 FCR 721.
[229] [2008] EWHC 152 (Admin) and [2008] EWHC 400 (Admin).
[230] See Bainham (2008b).
[231] CA 1989, s 31(6) and (7).
[232] CA 1989, s 105.
[233] *Lewisham London Borough Council v D (Criteria for Territorial Jurisdiction in Public Law Proceedings)* [2008] 2 FLR 1449.
[234] Discussion in Wagstaff (1998).
[235] [1988] Fam 122.
[236] *Re D (A Minor)* [1987] 1 FLR 422; *Re N (Leave to Withdraw Care Proceedings)* [2000] 1 FLR 134.
[237] *Re D (Unborn Baby)* [2009] 2 FLR 313.

to take such alcohol as she thinks fit, or refuse medication, for example, overrides any interest that the foetus has.[238]

It is, of course, quite possible for a local authority to obtain an emergency court order once the child has been born.[239] However, the issue is not straightforward. If the child is born with foetal alcohol syndrome, for example, it is arguable that he or she might not be suffering harm (at least as compared with a similar child with foetal alcohol syndrome). Further, even if the child is suffering harm, it is arguable that the suffering is not caused by the parenting. The argument would be that if the foetus is not a child, then the care during the pregnancy cannot be parenting. Perhaps the best argument for the local authority would be that the lack of care shown towards the foetus during pregnancy is evidence that the parent is likely to cause the child significant harm in the future.[240] However, in *K and T v Finland*[241] the European Court of Human Rights took the view that removing a child at birth infringed the mother's rights under article 8 of the European Convention on Human Rights. The case concerned a mother who suffered on occasion from schizophrenia, although at the time of the child's birth she was in good health. The removal of the baby, without consultation, from the parents and without exploring the possibilities of reuniting the family, infringed the Convention. This was particularly so in the light of the fact that the mother had no history of being violent towards children and the child had been taken from the hospital, which was a safe environment for the child and therefore there was no need for immediate intervention. The court was particularly concerned that the removal of the child prevented the mother from bonding with or breastfeeding the child.[242] That said, where there is strong evidence that the mother will pose a serious risk to the baby at birth, for example where she has said she will kill the baby, the local authority will be permitted to remove the child. If necessary an *ex parte* declaration authorising that can be obtained in advance.[243]

## C The effect of a care order

The main effect of a care order is to give parental responsibility for the child to the local authority. The local authority may then remove the child from the parents (but does not have to). The local authority will be authorised to make decisions about the child and will be responsible for the child's welfare and deciding where the child will live. The effects of the care order will be discussed in more detail in Chapter 11.

## D The nature and purpose of the supervision order

The supervision order aims to give the local authority some control over the child, without the degree of intervention involved in a care order.[244] Under a supervision order the child will remain at home, but will be under the watch of a designated officer of a local authority, or a probation officer.[245] The making of the order does not alter the legal position of the parents: they retain full parental responsibility; the supervision order does not give parental

---

[238] *St George's Healthcare NHS Trust v S* [1998] 2 FLR 728. Herring (2008b: ch. 5) for a fuller discussion of the legal and ethical issues.
[239] *Re R (A Child) (Care Proceedings: Teenage Pregnancy)* [2000] 2 FCR 556.
[240] *Re A (A Minor) (Care Proceedings)* [1993] 1 FLR 824.
[241] [2000] 2 FLR 79.
[242] See also *Re M (Care Proceedings: Judicial Review)* [2004] 1 FCR 302.
[243] *Re D (Unborn Baby)* [2009] 2 FLR 313.
[244] If the problems relate specifically to education then a special education supervision order is available.
[245] CA 1989, s 31(1)(b).

responsibility to the local authority. The court cannot make a care order at the same time as a supervision order, although it can make a s 8 order and a supervision order.[246]

Although the supervision order is usually regarded as a less serious intervention in family life than a care order, the grounds for the orders are the same. Although the intervention into family life is less serious than with the care order, it is nevertheless a significant intrusion into the family's life.

## E Care or supervision order?

Where the threshold criteria have been made out, the local authority must decide whether a care order or a supervision order is more appropriate.[247]

The following factors are relevant:

1. If the local authority wishes to remove a child from the home then it must apply for a care order.[248] It is not possible to remove a child under a supervision order.[249] If the local authority decides that the child should stay with the family, either a care order or a supervision order can be made. If a care order is made then the child can be removed by the local authority at any time.[250] If a supervision order is made then the child can only be removed if a further application is made to the court, for an emergency protection order for example. The supervision order, combined with the power to apply for an emergency protection order, should be regarded as a 'strong package', especially as the supervision order gives instant access into the child's home.[251] However, where there is very serious harm or sexual abuse, the courts have suggested that a care order should be made.[252]

2. Hale J in *Re O (Care or Supervision Order)*[253] stated that a supervision order normally requires co-operation from the parents and is therefore appropriate only where there is at least a reasonable relationship between the parent and the local authority. In *Oxfordshire CC v L (Care or Supervision Order)*[254] the parents had co-operated with the local authority and responded well to assistance in the past. This indicated that a supervision order would be appropriate.

3. Where the local authority wishes to acquire parental responsibility, a care order is appropriate.[255] *Re V (Care or Supervision Order)*[256] demonstrates this point well. There was a dispute between the parents and the local authority over what kind of education was appropriate for a disabled child. The local authority wanted to be able to make decisions relating to the child's education and so a care order was made, even though the child was to remain with the parents.

4. If a child was injured through an act of a parent that was thought to be out of character, then a supervision order may be more appropriate than a care order.[257]

---

[246] E.g. *Re DH (A Minor) (Child Abuse)* [1994] 1 FLR 679, [1994] 2 FCR 3.
[247] For a useful summary of the relevant factors, see *Re D (Care or Supervision Order)* [2000] Fam Law 600.
[248] *Oxfordshire CC v L (Care or Supervision Order)* [1998] 1 FLR 70.
[249] Unless the child is voluntarily accommodated under CA 1989, s 20.
[250] *Re T (A Child) (Care Order)* [2009] 2 FCR 367; *Re B (Care Order or Supervision Order)* [1996] 2 FLR 693, [1997] 1 FCR 309.
[251] *Re S (J) (A Minor) (Care or Supervision)* [1993] 2 FLR 919 at p. 947.
[252] *Re S (Care or Supervision Order)* [1996] 1 FLR 753.
[253] [1996] 2 FLR 755, [1997] 2 FCR 17.
[254] [1998] 1 FLR 70.
[255] *Re T (A Child) (Care Order)* [2009] 2 FCR 367.
[256] [1996] 1 FLR 776.
[257] *Manchester CC v B* [1996] 1 FLR 324.

5. If the parents would react very negatively to the making of a care order, but not to a supervision order, this could be a significant factor, especially if the children are going to remain with the parents.[258]

## F Grounds for supervision and care orders

The grounds for a supervision or care order are set out in s 31 of the Children Act 1989. Before a care order or a supervision order can be made, it is necessary to show four things:

1. The court must be satisfied that 'the child concerned is suffering, or is likely to suffer, significant harm'.[259]

2. '[T]hat the harm, or likelihood of harm, is attributable to: (i) the care given to the child, or likely to be given to him if the order were not made, not being what it would be reasonable to expect a parent to give him; or (ii) the child's being beyond parental control.'[260]

3. The making of the order would promote the welfare of the child.[261]

4. That making the order is better for the child than making no order at all.[262]

The first two requirements are commonly known as the 'threshold criteria'.[263] It should be stressed that a care order or supervision order cannot be made simply on the basis that the child's parents agree that the child should be taken into care.[264] By contrast, simply because there is significant harm does not mean that an order must be made; it must also be shown that the making of the order will advance the child's welfare.[265] If there are several children involved each child should be considered separately. For example, in *Re B (Care Proceedings: Interim Care Order)*[266] the evidence was that the parents cared for the daughter perfectly well, but treated their son very badly. The threshold criteria were only made out in respect of the son.

These four requirements will now be considered separately.

### (i) 'Is suffering or is likely to suffer significant harm'

The following terms need to be examined.

### (a) Harm

Harm is defined in s 31(9) of the Children Act 1989 as 'ill-treatment or the impairment of health or development, including, for example, impairment suffered from seeing or hearing the ill-treatment of another'. This last clause covers, for example, the harm a child may suffer while witnessing the domestic violence of her mother.[267] 'Ill-treatment' includes 'sexual abuse and forms of ill-treatment which are not physical, including, for example, impairment suffered from seeing or hearing the ill-treatment of another'; 'development' is defined as 'physical, intellectual, emotional, social or behavioural development'; and 'health' means

---

[258] *Re B (Care Order or Supervision Order)* [1996] 2 FLR 693, [1997] 1 FCR 309.
[259] CA 1989, s 31(2)(a).
[260] CA 1989, s 31(2)(b).
[261] CA 1989, s 1(1).
[262] CA 1989, s 1(5).
[263] See Wilkinson (2009) for a critical assessment of these.
[264] *Re G (A Minor) (Care Proceedings)* [1994] 2 FLR 69.
[265] *Humberside CC v B* [1993] 1 FLR 257, [1993] 1 FCR 613. See *Re B (Children) (Care: Interference with Family Life)* [2004] 1 FCR 463 for an example of a case where, although the threshold criteria were made out, the Court of Appeal thought a care order should not be made.
[266] [2010] 1 FLR 1211.
[267] *Re R (Care: Rehabilitation in Context of Domestic Violence)* [2006] EWCA Civ 1638.

'physical or mental health'.[268] Therefore, harm is not limited to physical abuse. For example, children can be harmed if their parents do not talk to them, or deprive them of opportunities of developing social skills. Similarly, not attending school[269] or not receiving adequate medical treatment[270] could amount to harm.

The harm can be due to positive or negative acts.[271] Of course, harm can be caused unintentionally. In *Re V (Care or Supervision Order)*[272] a mother, who was very protective of her son, sought to keep her son at home rather than sending him to a special school (he suffered from cystic fibrosis). This was held as amounting to harm, even though she was acting from the best of motives.

There can be difficulties in defining harm. Imagine a child who is brought up by devoutly religious parents who require the child to spend two hours a day in prayer and memorising holy texts. Some may say this is providing the child with an invaluable spiritual basis for his or her life. Others may regard this as abuse, hindering the child's social development. In *Re W (Minors) (Residence Order)*[273] the Court of Appeal considered a case involving a mother and stepfather who were naturists. The court accepted that nudity of adults before children per se did not fall within the definition of sexual abuse; it required clear evidence that such conduct harmed the children. It did not follow that, because it might be disapproved of by many parents, it was therefore abuse. Another, perhaps controversial, example of harm is the following case:

---

## TOPICAL ISSUE

### The 'miracle' baby case

In *London Borough of Haringey v Mrs E, Mr E*[274] a couple were caring for a child they claimed was theirs, produced as a result of a miracle following a prayer session with a religious leader. It was clear that the child was not biologically theirs and there were very strong suspicions that the child had been illegally brought into the country from overseas. It was held that the child was likely to suffer significant harm because the child was not Mr and Mrs E's and the child would be misled by them when he was older as to the origins of his birth. While it is understandable that authorities do not wish to encourage a practice which on one view of what happened amounted to 'baby selling', it is not obvious that this was a case where the child was suffering or was likely to suffer significant harm in the immediate future.[275]

---

### (b) Significant harm

In the Department of Health's *Guidance and Regulations*[276] it is explained that 'minor shortcomings in health or minor deficits in physical, psychological or social development should not require compulsory intervention unless cumulatively they are having, or are likely to have, serious and lasting effects upon the child'. *Significant* harm can therefore be the result

---

[268] CA 1989, s 31(9).
[269] *Re O (A Minor) (Care Order: Education: Procedure)* [1992] 2 FLR 7, [1992] 1 FCR 489.
[270] *F v Solfolk* [1981] 2 FLR 208.
[271] Bracewell J in *Re M (A Minor) (Care Order: Threshold Conditions)* [1994] Fam 95; approved [1994] 2 AC 424 HL.
[272] [1996] 1 FLR 776.
[273] [1998] 1 FCR 75.
[274] [2004] EWHC 2580 (Fam).
[275] The child was subsequently freed for adoption: *Haringey v Mr and Mrs E* [2006] EWHC 1620 (Fam).
[276] Department of Health (1991b: 3.2).

of several minor harms. Booth J in *Humberside CC v B*[277] suggested that 'significant' here meant 'considerable, noteworthy or important'. The court will readily assume that an abandoned child will be likely to suffer significant harm.[278]

It should be stressed that the word 'significant' focuses on the harm suffered by the child, rather than the blameworthiness of the parent's act. However, an act committed by a parent against their child which shows enormous indifference to the child's welfare, but in fact only causes a small amount of harm, might indicate that the child is likely to suffer significant harm in the future, which would be enough to establish the threshold criteria.

In the following case the Court of Appeal controversially found there was not a risk of significant harm.

---

### CASE: *Re MA (Care Threshold)* [2009] EWCA Civ 853

The case involved a Pakistani family, who were illegally residing in the UK. They had three children of their own and a 'mystery' girl, aged 5. She was not their biological child and there was no information about her identity. She was kept secretly by the family and it was found that she was very badly treated. The children were accommodated by the local authority after the oldest child alleged physical abuse, although there was no evidence to support those allegations. The key issue in the case was whether the serious abuse of the mystery girl could found the basis of a finding that the couple's own children would be likely to suffer significant harm. The judge decided not. The fact that they mistreated the mystery child was not evidence that they would treat their own children in the same way. The children's guardian appealed.

The Court of Appeal by a majority upheld the judge's ruling, which could not be said to be plainly wrong. To amount to significant harm, the harm had to be significant enough to justify the intervention of the state and justify an intervention in the family life of the parents, under article 8 of the ECHR. The judge had been entitled to find that in this case there was not a sufficient risk to justify making an order. The court report noted that the childen were 'well nourished, well cared for and with close attachments to their parents'. The Court aeccepted that the position of the 'mystery child' was unclear and the judge was permitted to conclude that the way the parents had treated her was not sufficient evidence of a risk of serious harm to their natural children. Wilson LJ dissented, concluding that the way the mystery child had been treated was so 'grossly abnormal' she had suffered physical and emotional harm. This showed a capacity for cruelty and so gave rise to a real possibility that they would harm their own children.

---

The case shows how difficult it can be to determine whether harm is significant. There was evidence from one of the children that they had been hit and slapped by the parents. On this Hallett LJ commented:

> Reasonable physical chastisement of children by parents is not yet unlawful in this country. Slaps and even kicks vary enormously in their seriousness. A kick sounds particularly unpleasant, yet many a parent may have nudged their child's nappied bottom with their foot in gentle play, without committing an assault. Many a parent will have slapped their child on the hand to make the point that running out into a busy road is a dangerous thing to do. What M alleged, therefore, was not necessarily indicative of abuse. It will all depend on the circumstances.[279]

---

[277] [1993] 1 FLR 257, [1993] 1 FCR 613.
[278] *Re M (Care Order: Parental Responsibility)* [1996] 2 FLR 84, [1996] 2 FLR 521.
[279] Para 39.

Not everyone would take such a sanguine view of the child's evidence, particularly in the light of the way the parents had treated the 'mystery girl'.[280] Particularly concerning is the majority's argument that because the parents had not provided an explanation for the slaps and kicks it was better to assume they were innocuous. That appears to encourage parents not to provide an explanation for injuires.[281]

In deciding whether the child is suffering significant harm, 'the child's health or development shall be compared with that which could reasonably be expected of a similar child'.[282] Precisely what this means is open to debate. However, it seems clear that, for example, in determining whether a child with learning difficulties is suffering it is necessary to compare the child in question with a hypothetical child who also has learning difficulties. In other words, it cannot be said that the child with learning difficulties is suffering significant harm because he or she is less educationally developed than a child without such difficulties. The question is whether an average child with learning difficulties would have reached the same level of educational achievement. There are a number of debatable issues in considering the 'similar child' test:

1. There is particular controversy over the extent to which the cultural background of the child should be taken into account.[283] For example, if a particular religion or culture teaches that a teenage girl should not talk to anyone who is not related to her, and a local authority thought this was harming a girl's social development, should the girl be compared only with a girl brought up in the same culture?

   There are two main views on this. One is that 'Muslim children, Rastafarian children, the children of Hasidic Jews may be different and have different needs from children brought up in the indigenous white nominally Christian culture.'[284] This perspective would require the court to compare the child with a child from a similar culture or background. The other view is that there should be a minimum standard for all children;[285] what is considered harmful to children should not depend on their cultural background. However, the fact that the harm was an aspect of cultural or religious practice may be very relevant in deciding whether making a care order would promote the welfare of the child.[286] In *Re D (Care: Threshold Criteria)*[287] the Court of Appeal adopted the second view, declaring that what amounts to significant harm should not depend on the child's cultural or ethnic background. On the other hand, there are concerns also that a lack of appreciation of cultural differences may lead social workers to perceive harm where there is none.[288] In *A Local Authority v N*[289] Munby J in considering an application for a supervision order in relation to a girl it was claimed was being forced into a marriage, emphasised the need to consider the 'underlying cultural, social or religious realities'. Controversially he added that if the parents had recently arrived in England, the court should be slow to find that their parenting fell below an acceptable standard if they had done nothing wrong by the standards of their own community. Julie Brophy has, however, warned of the dangers of assuming that an alleged practice is an acceptable cultural practice, simply on the say-so of an individual.[290]

---

[280] See the powerful analysis of Hayes, Hayes and Williams (2010) which is highly critical of the decision.
[281] Hayes, Hayes and Williams (2010).
[282] CA 1989, s 31(10).
[283] Freeman (1992a: 107). See also Brophy, Jhotti-Johal and Owen (2003).
[284] Freeman (1992a: 153). See also Freeman (1997a: ch. 7).
[285] Bainham (2005: 383–4).
[286] CA 1989, s 1(3)(d).
[287] [1998] Fam Law 656.
[288] Prevatt Goldstein (2009); Brophy, Jhotti-Johal and Owen (2003); Brophy (2008).
[289] [2005] EWHC 2956 (Fam).
[290] Brophy (2008).

2. To what extent are the characteristics or capabilities of the parents to be taken into account? If a child is brought up by a parent with a disability, should the child be considered only in comparison with a similar child living with disabled parents?[291] The statutory test seems to focus on the child rather than the parents. The better view, therefore, is that the capabilities of the parents are not taken into account in the definition of harm.[292] In *Re L (Children) (Threshold Criteria)*[293] the Court of Appeal warned that it would be inappropriate to remove a child from parents with learning difficulties on the assumption that the children would be at risk.[294] There was a risk of 'social engineering' if such assumptions were made.

3. What if the child has brought about the harm him- or herself? In *Re O (A Minor) (Care Order: Education: Procedure)*[295] it was suggested that in relation to a 15-year-old truant, the 'similar child' was 'a child of equivalent intellectual and social development who has gone to school and not merely an average child who may or may not be at school'.[296] Crucially, the child was not to be compared with another truant child. The reason why truancy was not a relevant characteristic is not clear, but one interpretation of the decision is that factors that the child has brought upon himself or herself are not to be taken into account.

### (c) Is suffering

Section 31 requires proof on the balance of probability[297] that the child either is suffering or is likely to suffer significant harm. Notably, proof that the child has suffered harm in the past is insufficient, although harm in the past may be evidence that the child is likely to suffer harm in the future.

There has been much debate over what 'is' means in this context.[298] The leading case is now *Re M (A Minor) (Care Order: Threshold Conditions)*,[299] decided in the House of Lords.

---

**CASE: *Re M (A Minor) (Care Order: Threshold Conditions)* [1994] 2 FLR 577, [1994] 2 FCR 871**

The father murdered the mother in front of the children. The father was convicted of murder and given a life sentence, and there was a recommendation that he be deported on his release. Three of the four children were placed with W (the children's aunt). The remaining child, M, was initially placed with foster parents, but later joined her siblings with W. By the time the case came before the House of Lords it was agreed by everyone that M should live with W, but the local authority still wanted a care order just in case it became necessary in due course to remove M from W's house.

The crucial issue in the case was whether the phrase 'is suffering' meant that it had to be shown that the child was suffering at the time of the hearing before the court. This was important because, by the time the matter came to court, the child was safely with the foster parents and it could not have been found by the court that 'she is suffering

---

[291] See Freeman (1992a: 107).
[292] More debatable may be whether the poverty of the family should be taken into account.
[293] [2007] FL 17.
[294] *G v Neath Port Talbot CBC* [2010] EWCA Civ 821.
[295] [1992] 2 FLR 7, [1992] 1 FCR 489.
[296] Noted Fortin (1993).
[297] *Re H (Minors) (Sexual Abuse: Standard of Proof)* [1996] AC 563.
[298] Only lawyers . . . !
[299] [1994] 2 FLR 577, [1994] 2 FCR 871; discussed in Bainham (1994a); Masson (1994).

significant harm'. Lord Mackay LC rejected such a reading. He stated that the date at which the child must be suffering significant harm was 'the date at which the local authority initiated the procedure for protection under the Act'. If the child was suffering significant harm at the time the local authority first intervened, and the social work continued to the date of the court hearing, then the child 'is suffering significant harm' for the purpose of the Act.

Applying this to the facts of the case in *Re M* it was clear that, at the time when the social work intervention started (i.e. just after the murder of the mother), it could have been said the child was suffering significant harm, and therefore a care order could be made. Lord Nolan explained:

> Parliament cannot have intended that temporary measures taken to protect the child from immediate harm should prevent the court from regarding the child as one who is suffering, or is likely to suffer, significant harm within the meaning of s 31(2)(a), and should thus disqualify the court from making a more permanent order under the section. The focal point of the inquiry must be the situation which resulted in the temporary measures taken, and which has led to the application for a care or supervision order.[300]

The decision is clearly correct because, if it is necessary to show that at the time of a court hearing a child is suffering significant harm, then the local authority may have to delay taking measures to protect the child until there has been a court hearing.[301] Subsequently, the Court of Appeal in *Re G (Care Proceedings: Threshold Conditions)*[302] held that the local authority could rely on facts which subsequently came to light to demonstrate that at the time when the local authority first intervened the child was suffering significant harm, even if it did not know of those facts at that time.[303] Although the House of Lords' interpretation of 'is' has been widely praised,[304] another aspect of the decision has given cause for concern.

By the time the case was before the House of Lords, M was settled with W, but their Lordships approved the making of a care order. It may be questioned whether there really was a need for a care order at all. Lord Templeman justified their Lordships' decision by suggesting there was a need for 'a watching brief' on the child's behalf.[305] Although it is understandable that the local authority wanted to keep an eye on M, and also might want in emergency circumstances to be able to remove M, a supervision order and the potential to apply for an emergency protection order would seem to provide adequate protection.

### (d) Is likely to suffer significant harm[306]

It is generally agreed that the state should be able to intervene and remove a child who is in real danger of suffering significant harm in the future, rather than wait until the harm occurs. However, removing a child on the basis of speculative harm, especially harm that may be a long way off, is controversial, because it is impossible to know whether or not the harm would materialise.

---

[300] [1994] 2 FCR 871 at para 32.
[301] Lord Templeman and Lord Nolan specifically took this point.
[302] [2001] FL 727.
[303] Although the Court of Appeal warned of 'Micawberish' actions being taken in the hope that the intervention will be justified by what will later be found out.
[304] The decision has been applied in *Re SH (Care Order: Orphan)* [1996] 1 FCR 1 and *Re M (Care Order: Parental Responsibility)* [1996] 2 FLR 84.
[305] *Re M (A Minor) (Care Order: Threshold Conditions)* [1994] 2 AC 424 at p. 440.
[306] CA 1989, s 31(2)(a).

The simple words 'is likely to suffer significant harm' were discussed in detail by the House of Lords in *Re H (Minors) (Sexual Abuse: Standard of Proof)*.[307] The case divided the House of Lords three to two and revealed the real problems at issue.

---

**CASE:** *Re H (Minors) (Sexual Abuse: Standard of Proof)* [1996] AC 563

A 15-year-old girl alleged that she had been sexually abused by her mother's cohabitant. The cohabitant was tried for rape but he was acquitted by a jury. The local authority was still concerned about the situation, especially because the cohabitant continued to live with the mother and her three younger children.[308] The local authority sought a care order in respect of the three younger girls. It argued that, although it had not been proved beyond all reasonable doubt[309] that the older child had been abused, there was a substantial risk that the younger children could be abused. The judge at first instance accepted that there was 'a real possibility' that the older girl had been abused, but he felt that the 'high standard of proof' required for a care order had not been satisfied. He therefore dismissed the application for a care order. The House of Lords looked at five questions:

1. *What does 'likely' mean?* It was held unanimously that 'likely' meant that significant harm was a real possibility; that is, a possibility that could not sensibly be ignored.[310] This is a comparatively 'low' risk of harm.[311] The phrase 'likely' did *not* require the court to find that the harm was more likely than not to occur. This is a remarkably 'pro-child protection' stance of the law to take. A child can be taken away from parents, even though the child has not been harmed and it is not even more likely than not that the child will be, if it can be shown that there is a real possibility the child will suffer significant harm.

2. *When must the harm be likely?* It needs to be shown that the child was likely to be harmed at the time the local authority first intervened; in other words, the *Re M (A Minor) (Care Order: Threshold Conditions)*[312] approach to 'is' was also followed for 'is likely'. In *Re N (Leave to Withdraw Care Proceedings)*[313] Bracewell J stressed that the court was not restricted to looking at harm in the immediate future, but could also consider longer-term harms.

3. *What is the burden of proof?* It must be shown on the balance of probabilities that harm is likely. In other words, it must be more likely than not that there is a real possibility of harm.[314] This was not controversial. However, the question has been made far more complex by dicta of Lord Nicholls in *Re H (Minors) (Sexual Abuse: Standard of Proof)*,[315] who argued: 'the more serious the allegation the less likely it is that the event occurred and, hence, the stronger should be the evidence before the court concludes

---

[307] [1996] AC 563; noted in Keating (1996); Hayes (1997); Keenan (1997). A powerful criticism of the reasoning can be found in Freeman (2004a: 331–3).

[308] The 15-year-old child had moved to live elsewhere.

[309] The standard of proof in criminal proceedings. See Cobley (2006) for an excellent discussion of the differences in this context for the different burdens of proof and justifications for them.

[310] Applied in *Re R (Care Order: Threshold Criteria)* [2010] 1 FLR 673.

[311] *Re O and N (Children) (Non-Accidental Injury)* [2003] 1 FCR 673 at para 16.

[312] [1994] 2 FCR 871.

[313] [2000] 1 FLR 134.

[314] See, for an application of this, *A Local Authority v S, W and T* [2004] 2 FLR 129.

[315] [1996] AC 563; noted in Keating (1996); Hayes (1997); Keenan (1997).

that the allegation is established on the balance of probability'.[316] This decision was interpreted by some to mean that in cases of more serious allegation more evidence was required to prove them than where less serious allegations were made. His statement was subsequently revised by the House of Lords in *Re B (Children)(Sexual Abuse: Standard of Proof (see below)* which made it clear that in all cases the normal balance of probabilities test applies.

4. *Who has to prove that the child is likely to suffer significant harm?* The House of Lords agreed that the local authority had to prove that the significant harm was likely to occur. The burden did not lie on the parents to show that it was not likely to occur.

5. *From what evidence can the risk of harm be established?* The majority argued that, in order to find that harm was likely, it was necessary first to find certain 'primary facts'. Each of these primary facts would have to be proved on the balance of probabilities.[317] Then, looking at these primary facts, the court could consider whether they demonstrated that significant harm was likely (that is, that there was a real possibility of significant harm).[318] In *Re H*, because it had not been found on the balance of probabilities that the older child had been abused (there was only a strong suspicion that she had), there were no primary facts proved. Therefore, it could not be shown that the younger girls were likely to suffer significant harm. Suspicion itself was an insufficient basis on which to decide that there was a significant likelihood of abuse. One reason is that it would be unjustifiable for a parent to have his or her child removed (with the attendant shame and social exclusion which would probably follow) on the basis of a suspicion. Another reason is that, as Lord Nicholls explained subsequently in *Re O and N (Children) (Non-Accidental Injury)*,[319] otherwise a suspicion that a parent had harmed a child would not be sufficient to show that the child had suffered significant harm, but could be relied upon to show that the child was likely to suffer significant harm. That would be 'extraordinary', he suggested.[320]

The majority's approach in *Re H* has been subject to several criticisms:

(a) 'Parliament has asked a simple question: is the court satisfied that there is a serious risk of significant harm in the future? The question should be capable of being answered without too much over-analysis.'[321] The minority argued that, looking at the case as a whole, there were sufficient worries (especially the fact that there was a strong suspicion that the cohabitant had abused the older girl) to justify the finding of likely harm. This, they thought, was sufficient to justify making the care order.[322] This argument was particularly strong on the facts of that case because, if the older girl had been abused as she had alleged, there was a very serious danger facing the younger children.

---

[316] [1996] AC 563 at p. 586; applied in *Re ET (Serious Injuries: Standard of Proof)* [2003] 2 FLR 1205.

[317] The court can look at medical evidence as well as matters such as explanations given by parents for injuries and the credibility of those caring for the child (*Re B (Threshold Criteria: Fabricated Illness)* [2004] Fam Law 565).

[318] In *Lancashire County Council v R* [2010] 1 FLR 387 Ryder J held it to be wrong to assume that a person who engaged in domestic violence had a propensity to child abuse.

[319] [2003] 1 FCR 673. See the excellent discussion in Hayes (2004).

[320] [2003] 1 FCR 673 at para 16.

[321] *Re H (Minors) (Sexual Abuse: Standard of Proof)* [1996] AC 563 at p. 581.

[322] The majority did admit that the totality of the evidence established a worrying number of circumstances, but, as no facts were proved, this belief was mere suspicion.

(b) Mathematically, the majority's approach looks dubious. Imagine two cases: in case A there are ten alleged facts pointing to abuse and there is a 45 per cent chance that each alleged fact was true; in case B there is one alleged fact pointing to abuse for which there is a 60 per cent chance that it is true.[323] The approach of the majority would allow for a finding of likely harm only in case B. In case A, as none of the facts were proved on the balance of probabilities, an order could not be made. Yet, in statistical terms, case A would be a stronger case than case B. The approach of the minority, looking at the totality of the circumstances, would permit the making of a care order in case A.

(c) The key underlying issue in the case has been explained by Hayes: 'The dilemma to be resolved is how the legal framework, and the legal process, can best reconcile safeguards for children suffering from significant harm with the obligation to respect parental autonomy and family privacy.'[324] There is an option of either threatening the parents' rights by removing the child from them without clear evidence, or threatening the child's rights by not providing protection even where there is a serious risk of danger. The House of Lords clearly preferred upholding parents' rights. Whether this is consistent with the welfare principle in s 1 of the Children Act 1989 is open to debate.

(d) The question must now be viewed in the light of the European Convention on Human Rights. A child must be protected from 'torture' and 'inhuman and degrading treatment'.[325] Yet at the same time the state is required to respect the private and family life of all the family members.[326] It is certainly arguable that the approach taken in *Re H* places more weight on the parents' right to respect for family life than on the child's right to respect for private life and to be protected from inhuman and degrading treatment.

Despite these criticisms Lord Steyn's speech was confirmed as setting out the current law by the House of Lords in their reconsideration of the issue.

---

**CASE: *Re B (Children) (Sexual Abuse: Standard of Proof)* [2008] 2 FCR 339**

The local authority were concerned about the sexualised behaviour of a 9-year-old girl. After investigations it was decided that she and her younger sister, and their stepsister aged 16, should be removed from their mother and placed with their father who lived elsewhere. When they were about to be removed from the mother, the 16-year-old alleged that the stepfather had abused her. The key issue was the standard of proof required on such an allegation. The House of Lords unanimously concluded that it was a simple balance of probabilities. Neither the seriousness of the allegations nor the seriousness of the consequences if they were true affected the standard of proof. The approach in *Re H (Minors) (Sexual Abuse: Standard of Proof)*[327] was confirmed. Care orders could only be made on the basis of proven facts and not suspicions. Baroness Hale explained: 'To allow the courts to make decisions about the allocation of parental responsibility for children on the basis of unproven allegations and unsubstantiated suspicions would be to deny them their essential role in protecting both children and their families from the

---

[323] Assuming that the ten facts, if true, would provide as good evidence that future harm was likely as the single fact, if true.
[324] Hayes (1997: 1–2).
[325] Article 3.
[326] Article 8.
[327] [1996] AC 563.

> intervention of the state, however well intentioned that intervention may be.'[328] Baroness Hale wanted there to be no doubt about the law:
>
> > I . . . announce loud and clear that the standard of proof in finding the facts necessary to establish the threshold under s 31(2) or the welfare considerations in s 1 of the 1989 Act is the simple balance of probabilities, neither more nor less. Neither the seriousness of the allegation nor the seriousness of the consequences should make any difference to the standard of proof to be applied in determining the facts. The inherent probabilities are simply something to be taken into account, where relevant, in deciding where the truth lies.[329]

This makes it clear that for all issues the test is the balance of probabilities, but that some allegations were inherently unlikely and might be harder to prove on the balance of probabilities.[330] The error in *Re H* was to suggest that it was the severity of the allegation that indicated its unlikelihood. That was incorrect. It was rather whether what was being alleged was particularly bizarre, or inherently unlikely. Their lordships' approach was later relied upon in *R (D) v Life Sentences Review Commission*[331] which was not a care case, but one about whether a prisoner's licence should be revoked. The question was whether it had been proved on the balance of probabilities that he had committed buggery on his 13-year-old niece. The House of Lords, following *Re B*[332] stated that although it was a serious allegation, it was not inherently unlikely that a girl had been sexually assaulted by her uncle. On the balance of probabilities there was evidence that the prisoner had committed the buggery.

Baroness Hale approved of the approach taken in *Re H*, stating: 'The Threshold is there to protect both the children and their parents from unjustified intervention in their lives. It would provide no protection at all if it could be established on the basis of unsubstantiated suspicions: that is, where a judge cannot say that there is no real possibility that abuse took place, so concludes that there is a real possibility that it did not.'[333] She explained that the decisions of the House of Lords produced a coherent picture:

> The court must first be satisfied that the harm or likelihood of harm exists. Once that is established, as it was in both the *Lancashire*[334] and *Re O*[335] cases, the court has to decide what outcome will be best for the child. It is very much easier to decide upon a solution if the relative responsibility of the child's carers for the harm which she or another child has suffered can also be established. But the court cannot shut its eyes to the undoubted harm which has been suffered simply because it does not know who was responsible.[336]

The House of Lords emphasised the importance of building cases on the assumption that either a fact is true or it is not. Lord Hoffman stated that either a fact happened (1) or it did not (0); and there was nothing in between. This makes it clear that a judge should only find the care order made on the basis of facts. It is harder to apply in a case where it is unclear who was the perpetrator.[337]

---

[328] *Re B (Children) (Sexual Abuse: Standard of Proof)* [2008] 2 FCR 339, at para 59. See also Hayes (2010).
[329] Para 70.
[330] *Re S-B (Children)* [2009] UKSC 17, discussed Bainham (2009b).
[331] [2009] 1 FLR 700.
[332] Unfortunately there was some uncertainty with some of their comments, although it was clear they were trying to following *Re B*, see Douglas (2009).
[333] Para 54.
[334] *Lancashire CC v B* [2000] 1 FCR 509.
[335] *Re O and N (Children) (Non-Accidental Injury)* [2003] 1 FCR 673.
[336] Para 61.
[337] Hayes (2008).

### (ii) Harm attributable to the care given or likely to be given or the child's being beyond parental control

The court must be satisfied that the harm is attributable to the care of the child not being what it would be reasonable to expect a parent to give. It is important to remember that, as Wall LJ stated in *Re L (A Child) (Care Proceedings: Responsibility for Child's Injury)*,[338] 'a child may receive serious accidental injuries whilst in the care of his or her parents, even where those parents are both conscientious and competent'. The obvious point is that the fact a child has suffered a serious injury does not mean the child has not been given the care by her parents that she should have been. However, Wall LJ then went on to say that in everyday language the effect of s 31(2) is that 'the local authority must prove that an injury is non-accidental'. This could be misleading. Surely a local authority should be able to obtain a care order in a case where a child has repeatedly suffered injuries due to the negligence of a parent, even if there was no deliberate infliction of harm? In *X v Liverpool City Council*[339] an emergency protection order was obtained after a parent repeatedly, and despite warnings, drove in a car with the children, despite the fact he was legally classified as blind. No doubt he did not intend to injure the children, but that should not mean no care order can be obtained. The best reading of Wall LJ's comments, it is suggested, is that if the injury is just the result of the kind of accident that can happen at the hands of any parent a care order cannot be obtained. But if the injury is deliberately inflicted or the result of serious negligence it can be.

Care in this context is not defined in the Act. The government Guidance[340] on the Act states: '"Care" is not defined but in the context is interpreted as including responsibility for making proper provision for the child's health and welfare (including promoting his physical, intellectual, emotional, social and behavioural development) and not just meeting basic survival needs.' This makes it clear that failure to ensure the child's general developmental needs are met is a failure to provide care.

In the following case the court considered further the extent to which it had to be shown that the parent's care was inadequate.

---

**CASE:** *Re L (Children)* [2006] EWCA Civ 1282, [2006] 3 FCR 301

The local authority were concerned about parents with learning difficulties who were raising a girl aged 10 and a boy aged 7. In particular, in the past the father had allowed a paedophile to visit the home, where he had abused the girl. There were also unproven allegations that the father had whipped the children with belts and proven allegations of domestic violence. The children were taken into foster care, but stated they wished to be with their parents. The judge found that the threshold criteria had been met.

The most interesting part of the Court of Appeal's judgment, which ordered that the case be reheard, were the comments that (at [49]):

> family courts do not remove children from their parents into care because the parents in question are not intelligent enough to care for them or have low intelligence quotients. Children are only removed into care (1) if they are suffering or likely to suffer significant harm in the care of their parents; and (2) if it is in their interests that a care order is made. Anything else is social engineering and wholly impermissible.

---

[338] [2006] 1 FCR 285.
[339] [2005] EWCA Civ 1173.
[340] Department of Health (1991a).

The case was reheard *Re L (Care: Threshold Criteria)*,[341] where some similar sentiments were issued by Hedley J who held:

> society must be willing to tolerate very diverse standards of parenting, including the eccentric, the barely adequate and the inconsistent. It follows too that children will inevitably have both very different experiences of parenting and very unequal consequences flowing from it. It means that some children will experience disadvantage and harm, while others flourish in atmospheres of loving security and emotional stability. These are the consequences of our fallible humanity and it is not the provenance of the state to spare children all the consequences of defective parenting. In any event, it simply could not be done.[342]

He went on to make it clear that 'at least something more than the commonplace human failure or inadequacy'[343] was required. In this case: 'Certainly they have suffered harm; certainly it is likely they will do so in the future and certainly that has been and will be attributable to the parenting they receive'; but that was insufficient to justify a finding that the threshold criteria had been met.[344]

The case raises some difficult and interesting issues, which the courts to some extent side-stepped. Should we accept that treatment of a child of parents with learning difficulties will not meet the threshold criteria, while the same treatment of a child by parents without learning difficulties will? Should there be minimum standards of parenting which children are entitled to expect regardless of the personal characteristics of their parents? Or is the lesson to be learned from cases such as these that parents with difficulties need special support and help from society? Taking the children of parents with learning difficulties into care, rather than offering them support, is merely perpetuating prejudice.

Harm will be attributable to the parent's care either where there are acts by the parent harming the child, or where there is a failure to protect the child from harm.[345] The requirement also means that if the harm is caused by someone who is not a carer of the child (e.g. if the child was abused by a stranger), that harm cannot form the basis of a care order, unless it could be argued that the harm is attributable to the parents because they failed to stop the third party from causing it.[346] In *A Local Authority v J*[347] a care order was justified in a case where a mother failed to protect her children from her partner who posed a serious risk to the children. There is an exception to this where a parent shares the regular care of the child with a third party, which we shall discuss shortly. So, if the child is subject to bullying at school and suffers significant harm as a result, a care order could only be made if it could be shown that the parents had not taken reasonable steps to prevent the bullying. This requirement is in part explained on the basis that a parent who cannot be blamed for the harm should not have his or her child taken into care.

An argument which has been particularly difficult for the court is where it is clear that the child had been harmed, but it is not clear who caused the harm.

---

[341] [2007] 1 FLR 2050.
[342] Para 50.
[343] Para 51.
[344] Para 52.
[345] *Re A (Children) (Interim Care Order)* [2001] 3 FCR 402.
[346] Although see *Re W (A Child)(Care Proceedings)* [2007] 2 FCR 160 where the Court of Apeeal held that a judge who decided that a father had not abused his daughter could not then make a care order on the basis that the mother had failed to protect the daughter from abuse.
[347] [2008] 2 FLR 1389.

It is necessary to distinguish three situations:

1. *It is not clear which parent injured the child.* If it is shown that a child had suffered non-accidental injury at the hands of his or her parents but it could not be proved which of them caused the injury the threshold criteria will be met.[348]

2. *It is not clear whether the parent or a third party (other than a carer) harmed the child.* In such a case, unless it is proved on the balance of probabilities that a parent or carer had harmed the child, a care order cannot be made.

3. It is not clear whether a parent or another carer harmed the child. The House of Lords in *Lancashire CC v B* examined this issue.[349]

---

**CASE:** *Lancashire CC v B* [2000] 1 FCR 509

The case involved child A, who was being cared for by a childminder while her parents were out at work. It became clear that A had suffered serious non-accidental head injuries, but it was impossible to establish whether these injuries were caused by the mother, the father or the childminder. The parents argued that s 31(2)(b) required proof that it was the care of the parents (or primary carers) which was not of the standard expected of a reasonable parent and, as it was not clear that they had harmed the child, the care order should not be made. The local authority argued that all that needed to be shown was that the care given by *someone* who was caring for the child was below the standard expected of a reasonable parent. In other words, the reference to parents in s 31(2)(b) was a reference to the standard of care expected and not a requirement that it was a parent whose care was less than the required standard.

---

The House of Lords acknowledged that there were difficulties with either interpretation. If the parents' argument was accepted, then a child might undoubtedly be suffering significant harm but, because it was not clear who had caused the harm, no protection could be offered. As Lord Nicholls maintained: '[s]uch an interpretation would mean that the child's future health, or even her life, would have to be hazarded on the chance that, after all, the non-parental carer rather than one of the parents inflicted the injuries'.[350] On the other hand, if the view of the local authority was accepted, then a child could be taken into care even though the parents were blameless. The approach taken by the House of Lords was that if it is clear that either of the parents or one of the primary carers caused the harm, the attributable condition has been made out.[351]

The difficulty with the House of Lords' decision is that it is far from clear who is 'a carer' in this context. If a child should not be denied protection because it is unclear whether the harm is caused by a parent or childminder, why should he or she be denied protection if it is unclear whether the harm is caused by a parent or a non-carer (e.g. a bully at school)? If, in the name of child protection, we are to permit children to be taken into care even if their parents may well be blameless, surely this should be so whoever else may have caused the harm?[352] The

---

[348] *Re O and N (Children) (Non-Accidental Injury)* [2003] 1 FCR 673.
[349] [2000] 1 FCR 509, discussed in Bainham (2000a).
[350] *Lancashire CC v B* [2000] 1 All ER 97 at p. 103.
[351] See *Merton LBC v K* [2005] Fam Law 446 for an application of this approach.
[352] Herring (2000b).

real problem at the heart of the House of Lords' decision is that it does not consider the purpose of the 'attributable' condition. Its purpose could have been seen as a form of protection of parental rights: 'your child will only be removed if you do not treat your child as a reasonable parent would'; or as a way of protecting children's interests: it will only be best for a local authority to remove a child from his or her parents if he or she is suffering significant harm. But the House of Lords' decision is not consistent with either approach and leaves the attributable condition without a clear role.

Although the House of Lords in *Lancashire CC v B*[353] provided clear guidance on when the threshold criteria would be satisfied in a case of an unknown perpetrator, they gave little guidance on how the court should deal with an unknown perpetrator when deciding whether or not to make a care order. They returned to that issue in *Re O and N (Children) (Non-Accidental Injury)*[354] and *Re S-B.*[355]

In *Re O and N (Children) (Non-Accidental Injury)*[356] the House of Lords heard two appeals which they called cases of the 'uncertain perpetrator'. The cases concerned children who it was clear had been harmed. In one case it was thought likely to be the father who had caused the harm, but the mother could not be ruled out. In the other case it was clear one of the parents caused harm, but it was unclear which. In both cases the mother and father had since separated. It was clear that in both cases the threshold criteria had been satisfied. The difficulty was at the stage when the court considered the welfare principle. Should the court not make a care order and return the child to the mother on the basis that it had not been established that she was a threat to the child, or were the suspicions over the mother sufficient to justify making a care order? Lord Nicholls thought it would be 'grotesque' if, because it could not be shown which parent had harmed the child, the child had to be treated as not at risk from either of them. Instead he suggested that:

> The preferable interpretation of the legislation is that in such cases the court is able to proceed at the welfare stage on the footing that each of the possible perpetrators is, indeed, just that: a possible perpetrator.[357]

He went on to emphasise that social workers should be careful in such cases to treat the parents as potential perpetrators, not proved perpetrators.

---

### CASE: *Re S-B (Children)* [2009] UKSC 17

A child aged 4 weeks old was found with non-accidental bruising. The local authority decided that either parent might have caused the injuries, but that the parent who did not cause the bruising was guilty of a failure to protect the child. On this basis the local authority successfully applied for a care order and the child was placed with a foster family. The mother and father then separated. The mother gave birth to a second child who was placed with the same foster parent. The mother sought to challenge the care orders. The judge at first instance ruled that neither parent could be ruled out as a perpetrator, but suggested that there was only a 40 per cent likelihood it was the mother. However, as there was a real possibility it was the mother it was in the welfare of the ➡

---

[353] [2000] 1 All ER 97.
[354] [2003] 1 FCR 673, [2003] UKHL 18.
[355] Discussed in Keating (2009); Cobley and Lowe (2009).
[356] [2003] 1 FCR 673, [2003] UKHL 18.
[357] [2003] 1 FCR 673 at para 28.

children that they be placed with adoption. The mother's case before the House of Lords was that as it had been held only 40 per cent likely that she was the perpetrator the case should have proceeded on the basis that the father was the perpetrator.

The House of Lords confirmed, again, that when deciding what the facts of the case were, the simple balance of probabilities test applied. This was true when deciding who the perpetrator was, as with any other question. However, the judge could determine that it was not possible to determine who was the perpetrator on the balance of probabilities. In that case the judge should not 'strain' to identify the perpetrator and instead the finding should be that a list of people were possible perpetrators. In rare cases the judge could indicate who among that list was more likely than others to be the perpetrator. When deciding what order would promote the welfare of the children the judge could consider these findings, always remembering that this was a case with no certainty as to who was the perpetrator. If, however, the judge feels that on the balance of probability one person is the perpetrator, other suspects should be treated as innocent.

While these decisions do not really make the job of the judge any easier, they make the law relatively clear.[358] If it is not possible to decide who is the perpetrator then all should be treated as possible perpetrators. That is of little help to a judge deciding whether to leave a child with a parent, who may be an abuser, or may be entirely innocent. Perhaps a key issue at that point is the extent to which the local authority and others can supervise the child and look out for any warning signs of abuse.

One issue which may well require further attention is how likely does it have to be that a person is a perpetrator to add them to the 'pool of possible perpetrators'?[359] One could imagine a case where the judge concludes that any person in regular contact with the child could have caused the injuries, and it is impossible to say who. In such a case should all those in regular contact be labelled as potential abusers? It seems so, but perhaps that is the kind of case where the judge should give an indication of who is most likely to be the abuser(s).

The effect of *Re O and N and Re S-B* is that suspicions (i.e. allegations which cannot be proved on the balance of probabilities) cannot be relied upon in establishing the threshold criteria, but they can be when the court decides what order, if any, to make under the welfare test. The mothers in *Re O and N* could with some justification feel that the decision enables the court to remove their children *from them* on the basis of suspicions. This was the very thing that Lord Nicholls in *Re H* said should not happen. A strong argument can be made that the law should be amended to permit suspicions to be relevant in deciding whether or not a supervision order should be made, but suspicions should not be relied upon to make a care order.[360]

It should be stressed that when the court is considering whether the harm was attributable to the parenting the test is essentially an objective one. The test refers to *a* parent, and not *this* parent. This makes clear that the test is satisfied even if the parent was doing his or her best, if the parent's best caused the child significant harm.

The subsection also includes cases where the child is suffering harm or is likely to suffer harm because he or she is beyond parental control. The kind of situation here is where the child behaves in an uncontrolled manner. Commonly it is used where the child is dependent

---

[358] *Re N (A Child) (Non-Accidental Injury)* [2010] 2 FCR 58.
[359] Colbey and Lowe (2010).
[360] Bainham (2000b).

upon illegal drugs. It does not matter if it is unclear whether the harm is caused by the parent or the child being beyond parental control. Ewbank J in *Re O (A Minor) (Care Order: Education: Procedure)*[361] suggested: '. . . where a child is suffering harm in not going to school and is living at home it will follow that either the child is beyond her parents' control or that they are not giving the child the care that it would be reasonable to expect a parent to give'.

### (iii) The order must promote the child's welfare

The court must not reason that, because the threshold criteria are satisfied, the care order must be made. It is crucial for the court to consider whether the making of the order is in the child's welfare.[362] When considering the welfare principle, the checklist of factors in s 1(3) must be taken into account.[363] Particularly relevant is whether there are any relatives[364] (or perhaps even a family friend) who can look after the child. A residence order in their favour, rather than a care order, may be more in the child's welfare. In *Re U (Care Proceedings: Criminal Conviction: Refusal to Give Evidence)*[365] a father was found to have caused 'brutal' injuries to the child and the mother had failed to protect the child from his violence. However, Holman J emphasised that in this case the mother was a victim of the father's aggression too and so ordered a further hearing to ascertain whether the mother, now that the father had left, could protect the child in the future. In considering the welfare of the child the views of the child may be relevant. In *Re H (Care Order: Contact)*[366] the Court of Appeal criticised the judge for failing to put sufficient weight on the view of a mature 10-year-old who very much wished to remain with her mother.

A crucial issue under the welfare criteria is whether the proposals of the local authority are proportionate to the harm and therefore permissible from a Human Rights Act perspective.[367] So, even if there is significant harm, it may well be that taking the child into care would not be a proportionate response.[368] For example, in *Kutzner v Germany*[369] the European Court of Human Rights considered a case involving a married couple with learning difficulties. They had two children about whom the local authority became concerned. A psychologist's report suggested that there were concerns about the applicants' intellectual capacity to bring up children and the local authority placed the children with foster parents (and denied contact for the first six months). The European Court of Human Rights found that the parents' article 8 rights had been infringed. Although the local authority was justified in having concerns about the children, it had failed to consider whether additional measures of support to the couple would have sufficiently protected the children and thereby avoided the need for the 'most extreme measure' of removing the children. In *Re K (Care Order)*[370] it was held that a care order should not be made because a mother had not been given the chance of being assessed at a specialist centre and so demonstrate her parenting abilities.

The notion of proportionality is particularly important in cases based on a risk of harm. It should be remembered that there needed to be a 'pressing social need' for intervention and

---

[361] [1992] 2 FLR 7.
[362] *Re O and N (Children) (Non-Accidental Injury)* [2003] 1 FCR 673 at para 23, per Lord Nicholls.
[363] CA 1989, s 1(4)(b). Section 1(3)(g) is perhaps especially important in that it means that the court must consider whether making an s 8 order in favour of a relative is a better option than taking the child into care.
[364] *Re N-B and Others (Children) (Residence: Expert Evidence)* [2002] 3 FCR 259. See Hunt (2001) for a discussion of the important role that relatives can play in child-care cases.
[365] [2006] Fam Law 521.
[366] [2009] 2 FLR 55.
[367] *Re V (A Child) (Care Proceedings: Human Rights Claims)* [2004] 1 FCR 338.
[368] *Re O (A Child) (Supervision Order: Future Harm)* [2001] 1 FCR 289.
[369] [2003] 1 FCR 249.
[370] [2007] EWCA Civ 697.

it was not sufficient for the court to determine that a child would be better off living with another family.[371] When considering risks of harm the court will consider the likelihood of harm and the severity of the feared harm. So while a possibility of death may justify the making of a care order, the possibility that the child might not be sent to school would not.[372]

The welfare stage is the point at which the court will consider whether it is more appropriate to make a care order or a supervision order. In theory, a court could grant a care order even though the local authority only applied for a supervision order,[373] although this would require 'urgent and strong reasons'.[374] In *Re K (Supervision Orders)*[375] Wall J considered a case which was borderline between making a supervision order or no order. He stressed that the benefits of a supervision order were that the social workers would make the case a higher priority if a supervision order were granted and the mother would be more likely to co-operate if such an order were made.

In *Re K (Care Order or Residence Order)*[376] the question was whether it would be more appropriate to make a residence order or a care order. It was agreed that the children should be brought up by their grandparents. The local authority argued that the grandparents should be granted a residence order, whereas the grandparents argued that a care order was appropriate. This may sound odd, but the explanation lies in the financial consequences. If a care order were made and the children placed with the grandparents, the local authority would be responsible for providing financial support for the care of the children. However, if a residence order were made the local authority would not be obliged to make any financial contribution. Given that the children were disabled and needed specialist equipment, and that the grandparents were not well off, the Court of Appeal made a care order. It was fortunate for the grandparents that the local authority had originally applied for a care order and that its application was technically before the court, because the court could not have made a care order if the local authority had never applied for one.[377]

### (iv) Section 1(5)

Section 1(5) requires the court to be persuaded that it is better for the child to make the care or supervision order than not to make an order at all. This provision was discussed in detail in Chapter 9.

### (v) The role of the threshold criteria

One issue behind many of the cases interpreting s 31 is the role of the threshold criteria. Here are three popular views:

1. According to Lord Nicholls in *Re O and N*[378] the purpose of the threshold criteria is 'to protect families, both adults and children, from inappropriate interference in their lives by public authorities through the making of care and supervision orders'.

---

[371] *Re S-B (Children)* [2009] UKSC 17, para 7.

[372] *Re S-B (Children)* [2009] UKSC 17, para 9.

[373] In *Re M (A Minor) (Care Order: Threshold Conditions)* [1994] 2 AC 424 the House of Lords made a care order even though the local authority wished to withdraw its application; see also *Re K (Care Order or Residence Order)* [1995] 1 FLR 675, [1996] 1 FCR 365, where a care order was made contrary to the local authority's wishes.

[374] *Oxfordshire CC v L (Care or Supervision Order)* [1998] 1 FLR 70.

[375] [1999] 2 FLR 303.

[376] [1995] 1 FLR 675, [1996] 1 FCR 365.

[377] Grandparents with a residence order may apply for residence order allowance: *R (H) v Essex County Council* [2009] 2 FLR 91.

[378] [2003] 1 FCR 673 at para 14.

2. The threshold criteria are there to reinforce the welfare principle and to remind courts that children are normally best brought up by their parents and only where there is a real danger will it be in the child's welfare for a care order to be made.

3. The threshold criteria exist to protect parents' rights. The state in effect guarantees to parents that, unless they cause significant harm to their children, their children will not be removed.

## G Care plans

When a local authority is applying for a care order it must prepare a care plan.[379] This sets out what the local authority proposes should happen to the child while he or she is in care. It will suggest, for example, where he or she should live and what contact there should be with his or her family. The court, when considering whether to make the care order, should take into account the care plan.[380] We shall discuss the exact status of the plan in Chapter 11.

## H Interim care orders

It may be that, having heard all the evidence, the court still feels it is not in a position to make a final decision of whether to make a care order or supervision order, or no order at all.[381] In such cases an interim order is appropriate.[382] An interim care order can only be made if the threshold and s 1 criteria are met and making an interim care order is proportionate to the risk faced by the child.[383] If, when hearing an application for a care order or supervision order, the court is not convinced that the child is in need of immediate local authority care, it may consider just making an interim residence order[384] in favour of a relative. However, it may do so only if the court is persuaded that the child will be adequately protected without an interim care order or supervision order.[385] Children should only be removed from their parents under an interim care order if their safety demands it.[386] Removal might be necessary so that a proper assessment of the parents can be made, which cannot safely be done while the children remain at home.[387]

These interim orders provide a legal framework until a final order can be made. In *Re G (A Child) (Interim Care Order: Residential Assessment)*[388] Lord Scott explained: 'an "interim" care order is a temporary order, applied for and granted in care proceedings as an interim measure until sufficient information can be obtained about the child, the child's family, the child's circumstances and the child's need to enable a final decision in the care proceedings to be made'. It is important to stress that, as was made clear in *Re G (Minors) (Interim Care Order)*,[389] the fact that an interim order is made does not weigh on the court one way or the other in deciding the final order.[390] To make an interim supervision order or interim care order the court must be satisfied that there are reasonable grounds for believing that the

---

[379] CA 1989, s 31A; *Manchester City Council v F* [1993] 1 FLR 419, [1993] 1 FCR 1000; Department of Health (1991a: 2.62).

[380] CA 1989, s 31(3A).

[381] *Re S, Re W (Children: Care Plan)* [2002] 1 FCR 577 at para 90.

[382] *Re CH (Care or Interim Care Order)* [1998] 1 FLR 402, [1998] 2 FCR 347.

[383] *Re H (A Child) (Interim Care Order)* [2003] 1 FCR 350.

[384] CA 1989, s 1(1) and (5) would have to be satisfied.

[385] CA 1989, s 38(3).

[386] *Re LA (Care: Chronic Neglect)* [2010] 1 FLR 80.

[387] *Re B (Interim Care Order)* [2010] EWCA Civ 324.

[388] [2005] 3 FCR 621 at para 2.

[389] [1993] 2 FLR 839, [1993] 2 FCR 557.

[390] *Re B (Care Proceedings: Interim Care Order)* [2009] EWCA Civ 1254.

criteria under s 31(2) of the Children Act 1989 (the threshold criteria) have been satisfied, but they do not have to prove the conditions exist.[391]

On the making of an interim care order the local authority gains all the benefits and obligations of a care order: parental responsibility is placed on the local authority and the child is in the care of the local authority. There is a danger, therefore, that a court would be tempted to make an interim care order so that it could retain some control over the local authority and its care plan. However, Lord Nicholls in *Re S, Re W (Children: Care Plan)*[392] held that it would be wrong for a court to make an interim care order so that a court could exercise a supervisory role over the local authority. Lord Nicholls approved of the making of an interim care order in *C v Solihull MBC*[393] where the court was awaiting a report from an assessment of the parent's parenting skills and without that report it was not possible to decide whether or not to make a care order. However, when deciding whether there is sufficient certainty to make a care order the court should remember that to an extent uncertainty is inevitable and the local authority might have to be trusted to amend its care plan to deal appropriately with events as they unfold.[394]

What about cases where the care plan itself is rather unclear? Lord Nicholls explained that care plans had to be 'sufficiently firm and particularized for all concerned to have a reasonably clear picture of the likely way ahead for the foreseeable future'. He added that the plan had to be sufficiently clear to enable the parents and child to claim that the order would inappropriately interfere with their rights to respect for family life.[395] If the care plan is uncertain an interim care order may be appropriate.

While it is not possible for a court to attach a condition to a full care order, it can to an interim care order. There are two leading cases. The first is *Re C (Interim Care Order: Residential Assessment)*.[396] The House of Lords had to consider s 38(6), which states:

> Where the court makes an interim care order, or interim supervision order, it may give such directions (if any) as it considers appropriate with regard to the medical or psychiatric examination or other assessment of the child . . .

The local authority had obtained an emergency protection order and an interim care order in relation to a child who had been taken to hospital with serious non-accidental injuries. The parents were young: 17 and 16 years old. The social workers involved favoured an assessment of the parents and child at a residential unit. The local authority disagreed on the basis of the cost of the programme (between £18,000 and £24,000) and because they feared that it would expose the child to risks. The House of Lords thought it was permissible for the court to make an emergency protection order with conditions under s 38(6) that the parents and the child attend the centre. The House of Lords rejected two arguments of the local authority. The first was that under s 38(6) the assessment could be ordered only if it was of a medical or psychiatric nature, whereas here the assessment concerned the parents' abilities.[397] The House of Lords held that the assessment in question could fall within the definition of 'other assessment' in s 38(6), and so it was permitted.[398] The second argument of the local authority

---

[391] *Re B (A Minor) (Care Order: Criteria)* [1993] 1 FLR 815, [1993] 1 FCR 565.
[392] [2002] 1 FCR 577 at para 90.
[393] [1992] 2 FCR 341.
[394] *Re S, Re W (Children: Care Plan)* [2002] 1 FCR 577 HL at para 98.
[395] *TP and KM v UK* [2001] 2 FCR 289 at para 72.
[396] [1997] 1 FLR 1, [1997] 1 FCR 149; see C. Smith (1997a).
[397] See the useful discussion in Kennedy (2001) on the distinction between treatment and assessment.
[398] See also *Re B (A Child: Interim Care Order)* [2002] 2 FCR 367 where the court was willing to state precisely where the assessment should be carried out. Note also *Lambeth LBC v S, C, V and J* [2005] Fam Law 685 in which Ryder J ordered that the costs of the assessment be shared between the local authority and the Legal Services Commission (who were funding the parents' case).

was that the condition was a wrongful attempt by the court to interfere with its care plan. The House of Lords rejected this argument, stating that, although it was the preserve of the local authority to decide what should happen to a child in its care, it was the preserve of the court to decide whether a care order should be made. Here the assessment was necessary to enable the court to decide what order should be made. The decision in *Re C* does not sit easily with the general approach taken in the Children Act 1989 that the courts should not compel local authorities to spend their social services budget in a particular way.[399] In *Re C (Children) (Residential Assessment)*[400] the local authority argued that to be required to provide a residential assessment for the particular family would be to involve a disproportionate level of expenditure on one family, among all of those they had to care for. The Court of Appeal rejected this argument, but significantly on the basis that the local authority had not produced evidence to substantiate its claim. It was accepted that if such evidence had been forthcoming then the decision would have been different.

The second leading case on attaching conditions to a care order is *Re G (A Child) (Interim Care Order: Residential Assessment)*.[401] There a judge had attached a condition to an interim residence order requiring the local authority to fund an assessment of a mother, her new partner and their child at a hospital which specialised in multi-problem families. Their Lordships held that conditions attached through s 38(6) had to have as their purpose the gathering of information. In this case the hospital would be engaged in providing treatment, advice and help for the family, as much as, if not more than, gathering information. Any assessment or examination must be for the purpose of gathering information and to provide treatment to the child or her parents. To use s 38(6) as the judge had done was to contravene the 'cardinal principle' in the Children Act that the courts could not order local authorities to provide particular services to children in care. Lord Scott indicated that it was not the job of the state to make better parents. Baroness Hale did, however, admit that a hard and fast line cannot always be drawn between information gathering and information providing. It may be necessary to observe child and parents interacting in different settings in order to obtain information.[402] Dr Kennedy, a consultant at a leading hospital involved in such cases, has written: 'No assessment of a child ordered by a court could be complete without knowing how the parent responds to the child, how the parent's emotional state may or may not be in tune with the child's own emotional state or whether or not a parent has the capacity to change in their handling of the child's physical and emotional well-being.'[403] Despite these benefits of parental assessments, one factor influencing their Lordships was that if s 38(6) could be used to authorise treatment then this would slow down a system already burdened with delay. It is noticeable that in *Re L (Children) (Care Order: Residential Assessment)*[404] the Court of Appeal referred to article 6 of the ECHR and held that failing to provide the parents with an opportunity to take part in a residential assessment of the child would be unfair, as it would deny them the opportunity of having evidence to demonstrate they had the capacity to parent M. This suggests that the courts might interpret *Re G* quite strictly.[405]

Section 38(6) states that children can refuse to participate in the assessment if they have sufficient understanding. Very controversially, in *South Glamorgan County Council v*

---

[399] In *Re A (Residential Assessment)* [2009] EWHC 865 (Fam) it was confirmed that an assessment could be required, while the child lived with an aunt and great grandmother.

[400] [2001] 3 FCR 164.

[401] [2005] 3 FCR 621.

[402] See *Re L (Children) (Care Order: Residential Assessment)* [2007] 3 FCR 259.

[403] Kennedy (2006: 382).

[404] [2007] 3 FCR 259.

[405] See also *Re S (Residential Assessment)* [2009] 2 FLR 397.

*W and B*,[406] the court held that a court order under the inherent jurisdiction could override the refusal of a child. This seems to go against the normal position that an order under the inherent jurisdiction cannot run counter to a statutory provision. Here s 38(6) explicitly gives the child the right to refuse.

## **I** Exclusion orders

Under ss 38A and 44A of the Children Act 1989[407] exclusion orders are available to the local authority in addition to an emergency protection order and interim care orders. The exclusion requirement may include one or more of the following (s 38A(3)):

---

**LEGISLATIVE PROVISION**

**Children Act 1989, section 38A(3)**

(a) a provision requiring the relevant person to leave a dwelling-house in which he is living with the child;

(b) a provision prohibiting the relevant person from entering a dwelling-house in which the child lives; and

(c) a provision excluding the relevant person from a defined area in which a dwelling-house in which the child lives is situated.

---

The circumstances in which an exclusion order can be made are (s 38A(2)):

---

**LEGISLATIVE PROVISION**

**Children Act 1989, section 38A(2)**

(a) that there is reasonable cause to believe that, if a person ('the relevant person') is excluded from a dwelling-house in which the child lives, the child will cease to suffer, or cease to be likely to suffer, significant harm, and

(b) that another person living in the dwelling-house (whether a parent of the child or some other person)—

    (i) is able and willing to give to the child the care which it would be reasonable to expect a parent to give him, and

    (ii) consents to the inclusion of the exclusion requirement.

---

There are two important limitations on the exclusion order. First, the exclusion order can only be made if the grounds for an emergency protection order or interim care order are made out. Both of these orders are short-lived, and so the exclusion requirement offers only short-term protection. The second requirement is that there must be another person in the home who is able and willing to care for the child, and who consents to the inclusion of

---

[406] [1993] 1 FLR 574, [1993] 1 FCR 626.
[407] Inserted by Family Law Act 1996.

the exclusion requirement.[408] If, for example, the mother wishes to continue her relationship with the suspected abuser, she may well refuse to consent. She may then have to choose between consenting to the removal of her partner and having her child removed under a care order.

## 8 Emergencies: police protection and emergency protection orders

There are two main remedies available if children need immediate assistance.[409]

### A Police protection

In cases requiring urgent action, the police have some powers to protect children. The powers enable the police to act immediately, without the delay of having to apply to a court. For example, in *Re M (A Minor) (Care Order: Threshold Conditions)*[410] the police were called to a house where a husband had murdered his wife in front of the children; the police were able to take the children immediately into their care.

These powers exist under s 46(1) of the Children Act 1989: if a police constable has reasonable cause to believe that a child would be likely to suffer significant harm then the child can be removed by the constable to 'suitable accommodation'.[411] However, this section does not give the police the power to enter and search a building. This is an important limitation and means that, if the parents refuse to co-operate with the police, and the child is in the parents' house, the police have no powers under the Children Act 1989 to protect the child.[412]

The children can be kept in police protection for up to 72 hours. Once a child is taken into police protection, a designated officer will be appointed to be in charge of the case. He or she must inform the local authority of the decision to protect the child, and must let the parents or persons with parental responsibility know of the steps taken.[413] The police do not acquire parental responsibility when a child is in police protection, but the designated officer is required to do what is reasonable in all the circumstances to promote the child's welfare.[414] He or she must permit reasonable contact between the child and anyone with parental responsibility, or anyone else with whom the child was living.[415] The child must be released to the parent or person with parental responsibility unless there are reasonable grounds to believe that he or she is likely to suffer significant harm if released.[416]

---

[408] *W v A Local Authority* [2000] 2 FCR 662.
[409] See Masson (2005) and Masson, McGovern, Pick and Winn Oakley (2007) for excellent discussions of this topic.
[410] [1994] 2 AC 424.
[411] The constable may also take reasonable steps to remove the child to a hospital or other place. The power exists even if the child has been made the subject of an emergency protection order: *Langley v Liverpool CC* [2005] 3 FCR 303. But the Court of Appeal added that the police should only use their powers where an EPO could not be used.
[412] Unless the police are able to use their general powers to arrest people or search houses under the Police and Criminal Evidence Act 1984.
[413] CA 1989, s 46(3).
[414] CA 1989, s 46(9)(b).
[415] CA 1989, s 46(10).
[416] CA 1989, s 46(5).

## B The emergency protection order

### (i) When Is an emergency protection order appropriate?

Where it is clear that the child is suffering significant harm, but the local authority is not in a position to decide the long-term future of the child, then an emergency protection order (EPO) is appropriate.[417] The guidance explains that the purpose of an EPO is 'to enable the child in a genuine emergency to be removed from where he is, or be kept where he is, if and only if this is what is necessary to provide immediate short-term protection'.[418] The EPO should only be used in emergencies, as it involves the immediate removal of a child, often without notice to the parents or time to prepare the child appropriately.[419] Munby J has said that an EPO requires exceptional circumstances and there must be no less drastic alternatives available.[420]

### (ii) Who may apply?

Anyone can apply for an EPO. This is by contrast with a child assessment order, care order or supervision order. Restrictions on who can apply for the order seem inappropriate, given the kind of urgent situations in which the EPO is appropriate. The police, local authorities, teachers, doctors or close relatives are most likely to be the ones who will apply. If someone apart from the local authority is applying for the EPO, the local authority can take over the application if appropriate. As it is an emergency application, the EPO will normally be applied for *ex parte*.[421] It is arguable that an *ex parte* hearing would be in breach of article 6 of the European Convention on Human Rights. However, in *KA v Finland*[422] the European Court of Human Rights recognised that in urgent cases it was not possible always to involve the parents fully in the decision-making processes.

### (iii) What are the grounds for the order?

There are three grounds for obtaining an EPO.

1. Where 'there is reasonable cause to believe that the child is likely to suffer significant harm if . . . (i) he is not removed to accommodation provided by or on behalf of the applicant'.[423] This ground could be satisfied, for example, if there is reasonable cause to believe that the child is being abused.

2. Where 'there is reasonable cause to believe that the child is likely to suffer significant harm if . . . (ii) he does not remain in the place in which he is then being accommodated'.[424] This might apply where the child is currently safe, but there is a fear that he or she will be removed to a place where they may be harmed. For example, if the child has run away to his or her grandparents, but the local authority fears that the father may be on the point of finding the child and taking him or her back to an abusive home life.

---

[417] For detailed judicial guidance on the procedures and purposes of the EPO see *Re X (Emergency Protection Orders)* [2006] EWHC 510 (Fam).

[418] Department of Health (1991b: 4.28).

[419] *Re X (Emergency Protection Orders)* [2006] EWHC 510 (Fam). If used when there is no real emergency then there may well be an infringement of parents' human rights: *Haase v Germany* [2004] Fam Law 500.

[420] *X Council v B (Emergency Protection Orders)* [2004] EWHC 2015 (Fam). See *Haringey LBC v C* [2005] Fam Law 351 for a case where Ryder J believed an emergency protection order was unnecessary.

[421] Family Proceedings Court (Children Act) Rules 1991, SI 1991/1395, r 4(5).

[422] [2003] 1 FCR 201 at para 95.

[423] CA 1989, s 44(1)(a)(i).

[424] CA 1989, s 44(1)(a)(ii).

3. Under s 44(1)(b) a local authority or the NSPCC[425] can apply for an EPO where: the applicant is making enquiries into the child's welfare; and 'those enquiries are being frustrated by access to the child being unreasonably refused to a person authorised to seek access and that the applicant has reasonable cause to believe that access to the child is required as a matter of urgency'.[426]

The NSPCC (but not local authorities) need to show also that there is reasonable cause to suspect that the child is suffering or is likely to suffer significant harm.

These grounds are all prospective; they relate to the fear of harm in the future. So an EPO cannot be made on the basis of past harm unless the fact of past harm is evidence of a fear of future significant harm. The test attempts to strike a balance between ensuring that proceedings in these emergency situations do not get bogged down in complex questions of evidence, while at the same time ensuring that children are removed only when there is evidence to justify rapid intervention.

Even if the grounds for an EPO are satisfied, the court must still decide whether or not to make an EPO using the welfare principle. Under article 8 of the European Convention on Human Rights the local authority will be required to consider whether there were any alternatives to removing the children under the emergency order.[427]

---

**CASE: *X Council v B and Others (Emergency Protection Orders)* [2004] EWHC 2015 (Fam)**

Munby J provided authoritative guidance on the use of the emergency protection order (EPO). The case concerned three children who had a variety of difficulties. The parents, not surprisingly, struggled with the care of these children and there was evidence that the children suffered and were likely to suffer harm at the hands of their parents. An EPO was applied for and obtained. The case concerned an appeal against that order.

Munby J emphasised that an EPO was a drastic order to make. His description shows why:

> An EPO, summarily removing a child from his parents, is a terrible and drastic remedy . . . After all, the child of five or ten who, as in the present case, is suddenly removed from the parents with whom he has lived all his life is exposed to something the new-born baby is mercifully spared: being suddenly wrenched away in frightening – perhaps terrifying – circumstances from everything he has known and loved and taken away by people and placed with other people who, however caring and compassionate they may be, are in all probability total strangers.[428]

Partly with these concerns in mind, Munby J listed the features of the statutory regime that he believes are not entirely satisfactory. In particular, he noted that an EPO can be made without notice and the application need only be served on the parent 48 hours after the order is made; and that there is no appeal against the making or extension of an EPO. These concerns led him to consider the impact of the Human Rights Act 1998 on the law. He emphasised that the Human Rights Act 1998 requires that an EPO is  ➡

---

[425] CA 1989, s 31(9).
[426] CA 1989, s 44(1)(b).
[427] *KA v Finland* [2003] 1 FCR 201.
[428] Para 34.

appropriate only where there is an imminent danger and the order is necessary. If a less interventionist order (e.g. a child assessment order) can adequately protect the child then it should be used.[429] Similarly, if an EPO is to be made it should last for as short a period as is necessary, and a child should be returned by a local authority to the parents as soon as it is safe to do so. Munby J stated:

> An EPO, summarily removing a child from his parents, is a 'draconian' and 'extremely harsh' measure, requiring 'exceptional justification' and 'extraordinarily compelling reasons'. Such an order should not be made unless the FPC [Family Proceedings Court] is satisfied that it is both necessary and proportionate and that no other less radical form of order will achieve the essential end of promoting the welfare of the child. Separation is only to be contemplated if immediate separation is essential to secure the child's safety; 'imminent danger' must be 'actually established'.[430]

Not just that, but the evidence supporting the claim must be effective:

> The evidence in support of the application for an EPO must be full, detailed, precise and compelling. Unparticularised generalities will not suffice. The sources of hearsay evidence must be identified. Expressions of opinion must be supported by detailed evidence and properly articulated reasoning.[431]

The judgment is likely to mean that courts will be far more wary about making EPOs. Where they are made, they will be of shorter duration and local authorities will exercise their powers under EPOs with even greater care. The significance of Munby J's judgment was shown by McFarlane J's recommendation in *Re X (Emergency Protection Orders)*[432] that it should be made available to every court which hears an application for an EPO.

### (iv) The effects of an EPO

Section 44(4) sets out the three legal effects of an EPO. The order:

## LEGISLATIVE PROVISION

**Children Act 1989, section 44(4)**

(a) operates as a direction to any person who is in a position to do so to comply with any request to produce the child to the applicant;

(b) authorises—

    (i) the removal of the child at any time to accommodation provided by or on behalf of the applicant and his being kept there; or

    (ii) the prevention of the child's removal from any hospital, or other place, in which he was being accommodated immediately before the making of the order; and

(c) gives the applicant parental responsibility for the child.

---

[429] Para 49.
[430] Para 57.
[431] Para 58.
[432] [2006] EWHC 510 (Fam), [2007] 1 FCR 551.

These will now be considered in more detail:

### (a) Production of the child

The EPO requires any person who can comply with the request to produce the child to do so. The order also forbids the removal of the child from the place where the applicant has accommodated the child. If necessary, the applicant can enter any premises named in the EPO to search for the child,[433] although if force is required then the police should be involved and a warrant is required.[434]

### (b) Acquisition of parental responsibility by applicant

The applicant will acquire parental responsibility on the making of the EPO. This is appropriate, as the applicant will remove the child and will be responsible for the child's welfare. However, the applicant obtains only limited parental responsibility – parental responsibility should only be exercised 'as is reasonably required to safeguard or promote the welfare of the child (having regard in particular to the duration of the order)'.[435] The applicant should therefore not make any decisions which are major or irreversible. For example, important medical treatment should not be performed under an EPO. Any major decisions should be brought before the court by way of an application for a specific issue order. The child should be returned home as soon as it appears to the applicant safe to do so.[436] If the child is returned to their parents, this will not automatically bring the EPO to an end. The applicant could again remove the child, if necessary, providing the EPO has not yet expired.

### (c) Reasonable contact

During the length of the EPO there is a presumption of reasonable contact between the child and certain prescribed individuals, including parents; persons with parental responsibility; those with contact orders; those with whom the child was living before the EPO; and any person acting on their behalf.[437] If the court wishes, it can restrict any right of contact or impose conditions upon it when making the EPO.[438]

### (d) Other directions

The court has the power when making an EPO to insert additional directions. The most likely additional directions are that medical or psychiatric examinations be carried out.[439] The competent child has a right to refuse such examinations under s 44(7).[440] An exclusion requirement can be added under s 44A of the Children Act 1989, as discussed above.

## (v) How long does the EPO last?

Section 45(1) states that 8 days is the maximum length of an EPO. The local authority or NSPCC can apply for an extension to a maximum total length of 15 days.[441] There is no appeal from the making of an EPO,[442] but it is possible to apply to discharge the order.

---

[433] CA 1989, s 48(3) and (4).
[434] CA 1989, s 48(9).
[435] CA 1989, s 44(5)(b).
[436] CA 1989, s 44(10).
[437] CA 1989, s 44(13).
[438] CA 1989, s 44(6).
[439] CA 1989, s 44(6)(b) and (8).
[440] CA 1989, s 44(7); but see *South Glamorgan County Council v W and B* [1993] 1 FLR 574, [1993] 1 FCR 626, which suggests that a court can override refusal, although this is a controversial decision.
[441] On application by the NSPCC or local authority under CA 1989, s 45(4).
[442] CA 1989, s 45(10).

The application to discharge can be brought by the child; the parents; persons with parental responsibility; and any person with whom the child was living immediately before the order. But the application for the discharge cannot be made until 72 hours have elapsed since the making of the EPO.[443] There is also no appeal against a refusal to grant an EPO.[444] It may be that if an application for an EPO fails, the local authority could seek to invoke the court's inherent jurisdiction.

A local authority has no right of appeal against the refusal to extend an EPO. This can give rise to problems, as revealed in *Re P (Emergency Protection Order)*.[445] In this case a young baby nearly died after what was thought to be an attempt to suffocate him. There was clear medical evidence by a paediatrician of the abuse. The magistrates, however, refused to extend the EPO. Johnson J subsequently heard an application for a care order and criticised the justices for failing to extend the EPO in the face of the life-threatening abuse. The only option available to a local authority whose application for an extension is denied is to apply for a care order or interim care order.

## 9 Local authorities and section 8 orders

A local authority may obtain a specific issue order or a prohibited steps order subject to the following restrictions:

1. A local authority may not apply for a specific issue order or prohibited steps order which has the same effect as a residence order or a contact order.[446] The policy behind this restriction is that if the child is not suffering sufficiently for a care order to be made then a local authority should not be seeking to arrange accommodation for the child against the parents' wishes.

2. If the child is in care then no s 8 order may be made apart from a residence order. As a local authority cannot apply for a residence order, the effect is that a local authority cannot apply for a s 8 order in respect of a child it has in its care.

So there is limited scope for a local authority to use s 8 orders. They are appropriate, however, when a local authority might be concerned about a specific aspect of a parent's care of the child and, while not wanting to take the child into care, may wish to protect the child. For example, if parents are refusing to consent to necessary medical treatment the local authority might apply to the court for a specific issue order authorising the operation.[447] Thorpe LJ in *Langley v Liverpool CC*[448] stated that he had never encountered a case where a local authority had decided to use a prohibited steps order to deal with a child protection case. According to Charles J in *Re P (Care Orders: Injunctive Relief)*[449] a court can make injunctions under s 37 of the Supreme Court Act 1981 (now renamed as the Senior Courts Act 1981) which are ancillary to a care order. In that case, in addition to a care order, injunctions were made stopping the parents from preventing the child from attending college.

---

[443] CA 1989, s 45(9).
[444] *Essex CC v F* [1993] 1 FLR 847, [1993] 2 FCR 289.
[445] [1996] 1 FLR 482, [1996] 1 FCR 637.
[446] See Chapter 9.
[447] E.g. *Re R (A Minor) (Wardship: Consent to Medical Treatment)* [1992] 1 FLR 190, [1992] 2 FCR 229.
[448] [2005] 3 FCR 303 at para 77.
[449] [2000] 3 FCR 426.

## 10 The problem of ousting the abuser

One situation which has troubled the courts and local authorities is where a child is living with the mother and a man who is suspected of abusing the child. The ideal solution may be to remove the suspected abuser, while leaving the child with the mother. This is certainly an acceptable solution where the mother agrees that the man should be removed.[450] However, where the mother wants the man to stay, there is a complex clash between the rights of the child and the rights of adults. For the state to force the mother to separate from her partner against her will would be a grave invasion of her rights, but that may be the only solution which protects the child. In such cases the options for the local authority are as follows:

1. The local authority will no doubt prefer to deal with the issue by informal co-operation and persuade the suspected abuser to leave the house voluntarily. The local authority may be able to offer assistance or alternative housing.[451]

2. The local authority could encourage the mother to apply for an occupation order, under the Family Law Act 1996, Part IV, to remove the man from the house.

3. The local authority could apply for a care order or a supervision order. It could then remove the child from the home under the care order. Alternatively, the child could remain with the mother under a care or supervision order and the local authority would request that the abuser leave the home, with the threat that the child would be removed from the mother immediately if the abuser returns. However, the local authority cannot be forced to apply for a care or supervision order, and the court cannot make a care or supervision order unless the local authority applies for one. This is clear from *Nottingham CC v P*,[452] in which the Court of Appeal was deeply concerned that there was no power to compel the local authority to take steps to protect the children. A local authority may be wary of applying for a care order and permitting a child to remain in the house because of the potential liability in tort if the child were abused. Further, if either a supervision or a care order was relied upon, a local authority may have grave difficulty in ensuring that the suspected abuser did not live in the house. A local authority, for these reasons, may prefer to remove a child from the house if a care order is made, and enable substantial contact between the child and his or her mother.

4. The availability of s 8 orders for the local authority in this kind of case is very limited. In *Nottingham CC v P* it was stressed that it was not possible for the local authority to obtain a s 8 order to remove the suspected abuser. Removing the man from the home is in the nature of a residence or contact order. Local authorities cannot apply for residence or contact orders. Nor may they apply for prohibited steps or specific issue orders which have the same effect as residence or contact orders. The Court of Appeal stressed that where the local authority was seeking to protect children who were suffering significant harm, it should look to Part IV of the Children Act 1989 for care and supervision orders, and not use private orders to protect children. The core reasoning behind this restriction is that a prohibited steps or specific issue order does not vest any power in the local authority. In *Nottingham CC v P* if a residence order with conditions had been made in the mother's favour then the local authority would not have been able to enforce it. The mother could have applied to discharge the order and the local authority would have had no standing to intervene. Therefore such an order provides inadequate protection for children in such cases.

---

[450] Cobley and Lowe (1994).
[451] CA 1989, Sch 2, para 5.
[452] [1993] 2 FLR 134, [1994] 1 FCR 624.

The *Nottingham CC v P* decision does not prevent a prohibited steps order being granted on the application of a local authority where a suspected abuser is living apart from the mother and children. In *Re H (Minors) (Prohibited Steps Order)*[453] Butler-Sloss LJ argued that it was permissible to use a prohibited steps order to prevent a stepfather having contact with the children with whom he was no longer living.[454]

5. Exclusion orders are available under ss 38A and 44A of the Children Act 1989. These can only offer a short-term solution, as explained above.

6. The courts have also been willing to grant orders under the inherent jurisdiction removing a suspected abuser from the home, although the limits of this are unclear.[455] In *Devon CC v S* it was argued that where the court could not make an order which adequately protected the child then the court should rely on the inherent jurisdiction.[456] The court distinguished *Nottingham CC v P* on the basis that the court had found that it could have made an order that would have protected the child (a care order), but it had not been applied for by a local authority. If the court is persuaded that the child needs protection, and no order could be made which would protect the child, then an order under the inherent jurisdiction can protect the child. Although this decision is controversial in the light of the Human Rights Act 1998 and article 3 of the European Convention on Human Rights, as interpreted in *Z v UK*,[457] the state is under an obligation to protect children suffering serious abuse and so the use of the inherent jurisdiction may be required.

7. The local authority could apply for a family assistance order, although this might provide only very limited protection to the child.

The ideal solution is to enable or encourage the mother to separate from the abuser. Indeed in *EH v Greenwich London Borough Council*[458] the local authority were criticised for not seeing the mother on her own and explaining the dangers to the children of continuing the relationship. Wall LJ was shocked: 'Here was a mother who needed and was asking for help to break free from an abusive relationship. She was denied that help abruptly and without explanation. That, in my judgment is very poor social work practice.'[459]

## 11 Conclusion

This chapter has considered the circumstances in which it is appropriate to take a child into care. This is a notoriously problematic and controversial issue. It is all too easy, with hindsight, to claim that the local authority was too interventionist or not interventionist enough, but making the decisions in some of these cases must be agonising. The practical problems increase with the shortage of appropriately trained social workers. The Children Act 1989 has given the local authority the powers to provide services which are designed to prevent the authority having to use its more interventionist powers. Although the Children Act 1989 set up the threshold criteria before significant intervention in family life could be permitted, the

---

[453] [1995] 1 FLR 638, [1995] 2 FCR 547; discussed in M. Roberts (1995).
[454] See Chapter 9 for discussion of this case.
[455] *Re S (Minors) (Inherent Jurisdiction: Ouster)* [1994] 1 FLR 623; *Devon CC v S* [1994] 1 FLR 355, [1994] 2 FCR 409.
[456] [1994] 1 FLR 355, [1994] 2 FCR 409.
[457] [2000] 2 FCR 245.
[458] [2010] 2 FCR 106.
[459] Para 105.

interpretation of the criteria, particularly by the House of Lords, has had the effect of lessening the hurdle that they represent. The Human Rights Act 1998 will now play an important role, at least in formulating the language which will be used: it must be shown that the intervention in family life by the state is a necessary and proportionate response to the threat faced by the child. The change in language will not fundamentally change the key question, which is when the state is entitled to remove a child from his or her parents against their wishes. The issue involves the exercise by the state of one of its most coercive powers in order to fulfil its fundamental duties to protect the most vulnerable of its citizens.

## Further reading

Brophy, J. (2006) *Research Review: Child care proceedings under the Children Act 1989*, London: DCA.

Brophy, J. (2008) 'Child maltreatment and diverse households', *Journal of Law and Society* 35: 75.

Fox Harding, L. (1996) *Family, State and Social Policy*, Basingstoke: Macmillan.

Hayes, M. (1998) 'Child protection – from principles and policies to practice', *Child and Family Law Quarterly* 10: 119.

Hayes, M. (2004) 'Uncertain evidence and risk taking in child protection cases', *Child and Family Law Quarterly* 16: 63.

Hoyano, L. and Keenan, C. (2007) *Child Abuse: Law and Policy Across Boundaries*, Oxford: OUP.

Masson, J. (2000a) 'From Curtis to Waterhouse', in S. Katz, J. Eekelaar and M. Maclean (eds) *Cross Currents*, Oxford: OUP.

Masson, J. (2005) 'Emergency intervention to protect children: using and avoiding legal controls', *Child and Family Law Quarterly* 17: 75.

Masson, J. (2007) 'Reforming care proceedings – time for a review', *Child and Family Law Quarterly* 19: 411.

Masson, J. (2008a) 'The state as parent: Reluctant parent? The problem of parents of last resort', *Journal of Law and Society* 35: 52.

Masson, J. (2008b) 'Controlling costs and maintaining services – the reform of legal aid fees for care proceedings', *Child and Family Law Quarterly* 20: 425.

# 11 Children in care

## 1 Introduction

This chapter will consider the law governing those children who are in the care of the local authority.

### KEY STATISTICS

- For the year ending March 2009 there were 547,000 referrals of children to social service departments and 60,900 were being looked after by local authorities.[1]
- For the year ending March 2009 there were 34,100 children who were the subject of a plan. That figure represents 31 children per 10,000 of the population.[2] 45% of the care plans were created to deal with neglect.

As article 20 of the UN Convention on the Rights of the Child explains, states owe duties of 'special protection and assistance' to children harmed by their families. Unfortunately, the history of state-organised child care in England and Wales is bleak, with widespread evidence of abuse and mistreatment of children in children's homes.[3] Indeed, it is not difficult to find cases where the intervention of the state has made matters worse, not better, for children.[4] Claire Taylor states that her study of residential care for children in care paints an 'incredibly bleak and depressing picture' which is a 'national disgrace'.[5] The Government has accepted that children in care have a less advantageous start in life and cite the following statistics:[6]

---

[1] Department for Children, Schools and Families (2009).
[2] Department for Children, Schools and Families (2009).
[3] For a survey, see Department of Health (1995a; 1999c). Tragically, the stories of abuse seem not to be abating: Waterhouse (2000). There is evidence of a small number of children being abused during foster care (Social Services Inspectorate (2002: para 5.4)), especially private fostering (Philpot (2001)). Private fostering is now subject to regulation under the Children Act 2004, Part V.
[4] E.g. *Re F* [2002] 1 FLR 217. For difficulties in assessing how effective interventions are see McAuley et al. (2006).
[5] C. Taylor (2006: 175).
[6] Department for Children, Schools and Families (2008b).

Despite this gloomy picture, 74 per cent of parents of children in care believed that their children were being well looked after,[7] although only 42 per cent believed that the child's emotional needs were being met. A recent study found that where there was early intervention, stability in care and a swift transition to independence the care system worked well for childen.[8] The authors of the report criticise media presentations suggesting that children in care are doomed to a life of disadvantage.[9] Rather, care can be a positive intervention for many children.[10] The Labour Government produced a programme known as *Care Matters*, designed to improve the outcomes for children in care.[11]

The basic position under the Children Act 1989 is that local authorities (rather than courts) are responsible for deciding how children taken into care should be cared for. This is partly because the law recognises that decisions on how to look after a child in care involve careful interaction between the local authority, the parents, alternative carers and maybe other charitable bodies. These relationships might require ongoing and flexible negotiations of a kind unsuitable for court supervision. However, local authorities do not have unlimited discretion on how to bring up the child. There are four particular restrictions on local authorities' powers. First, there are financial restrictions which may limit the resources available to a local authority.[12] Evidence suggests that this has meant that local authorities have failed to provide services needed by children in care.[13] The Government also launched an initiative entitled *Quality Protects*, intended to improve the funding for support services for children in care.[14] The Children and Young Persons Act 2008 allows local authorities to use private bodies to provide services. Whether this will lead to cheaper or higher quality care remains to be seen.[15] Secondly, there are a few issues over which the courts retain some control. In particular, only a court can discharge a care order[16] and a court order is required to approve the termination

---

[7] Ofsted (2008).

[8] Hannon et al. (2010). See also Stein (2009) and Owusu-Bempah (2010) for an analysis of when care works well.

[9] See Morgan (2010) and CAFCASS (2010) for a discussion of the views of children in care.

[10] Hannon et al. (2010).

[11] Department for Children, Schools and Families (2010c).

[12] E.g. *Re C (Children) (Residential Assessment)* [2001] 3 FCR 164.

[13] Lansdown (2001).

[14] This is discussed in Roberts (2001). See May (2004) for the problems concerning the education of children in care.

[15] Cardy (2010).

[16] Children Act 1989 (hereafter CA 1989), s 39.

of contact between the child in care and his or her parents.[17] Thirdly, parents retain parental responsibility (even when a child is taken into care) and will be encouraged to be involved in decisions relating to the way their child is brought up while in care. Fourthly, the children in care themselves play an important role in determining the way they are brought up under the care system.

The chapter will start with an outline of the approach to children in care taken by the European Convention on Human Rights because this will be highly influential on the development of the law in the future. We will then discuss the effect of supervision orders and care orders. In the light of these, we will consider the role of parents and courts following the making of a supervision or care order. The chapter will end by considering the role of adoption, which has traditionally been seen as an ideal way to treat many children removed by the state from their parents.

## 2 Human Rights Act 1998 and children in care

As noted in Chapter 10, because removing a child from his or her family automatically constitutes an infringement of the parents' and child's right to respect for family and private life, the removal must be justified under article 8(2) of the European Convention.[18] However, the significance of the right to respect for family life continues even after a child is taken into care.[19] The approach of the European Court of Human Rights is summarised in *L v Finland*:[20]

> The Court recalls that taking a child into care should normally be regarded as a temporary measure to be discontinued as soon as circumstances permit, and that any measure of implementation of temporary care should be consistent with the ultimate aim of reuniting the natural parent and the child . . . In this regard a fair balance has to be struck between the interests of the child in remaining in public care and those of the parent in being reunited with the child . . . In carrying out this balancing exercise the Court will attach particular importance to the best interests of the child, which, depending on their nature and seriousness, may override those of the parent. In particular the parent cannot be entitled under Art 8 of the Convention to have such measure taken as would harm the child's health and development.[21]

There are three points of particular note. First, care measures should be regarded as temporary and, if at all possible, should be designed to enable the child to be reunited with his or her parent.[22] In *R v Finland*[23] the European Court of Human Rights held that the local authority who failed to make a 'serious and sustained' effort to facilitate reunion between the child and his birth family had infringed their human rights under article 8. The local authority should keep under review the possibility of rehabilitation with the birth family.[24] This means that adoption should be used as a last resort because it normally terminates the link between the birth parent and child.[25] However, the European Court in *KA v Finland*[26] and *R v Finland*[27]

---

[17] CA 1989, s 34.
[18] *W v UK* (1988) 10 EHRR 29.
[19] See further, Lindley, Herring and Wyld (2001); Choudhry and Herring (2010).
[20] [2000] 2 FLR 118.
[21] At p. 140.
[22] This was emphasised recently in *Haase v Germany* [2004] 2 FCR 1.
[23] [2006] 2 FCR 264 at para 92.
[24] *K and T v Finland* [2001] 2 FCR 673 at paras 154–5.
[25] Harris-Short (2008: 31).
[26] [2003] 1 FCR 230 at para 138.
[27] [2006] 2 FCR 264.

accepted that there may come a time when the child's interests in not being moved from the stable arrangements that the state has made override the interests of the parents in being reunited with their child. In *Re P (Adoption: Breach of Care Plan)*[28] the two older siblings of P had been successfully reintegrated with their father, but the local authority wanted to pursue adoption for P. The Court of Appeal thought that this was unsuitable given that the two older children had returned to their father, which indicated that reunification of all the children with the father could not be dismissed as a possibility.

Secondly, the rights of the parents to contact with children in care should be protected and any restriction on the rights of parents to see or have contact with their children must be justified as necessary and proportionate under article 8(2).[29] In *Eriksson v Sweden*[30] the court emphasised that the length and severity of the restriction on contact would be taken into account when considering whether the infringement was permitted. The burden will be on the local authority to justify any restriction on contact between children and parents.[31] The European Court in *Olsson v Sweden (No. 1)*[32] explained that the court 'cannot confine itself to considering the impugned decisions in isolation, but must look at them in the light of the case as a whole; it must determine whether the reasons adduced to justify the interference at issue are "relevant and sufficient"'. Thirdly, the response of the local authority to a child who is suffering harm must be proportionate to the harm which the child faced, as stressed by Bracewell J in *Re N (Leave to Withdraw Care Proceedings)*.[33] Hale LJ in *Re C and B (Children) (Care Order: Future Harm)*[34] explained:

> one comes back to the principle of proportionality. The principle has to be that the local authority works to support, and eventually to reunite, the family, unless the risks are so high that the child's welfare requires alternative family care.[35]

The local authority must demonstrate that there is no lesser level of intervention that would adequately protect the child.

In addition to article 8, article 6 of the Convention is important. It requires the state to provide a right of access to a court or tribunal to determine the parents' rights and obligations and this includes enabling parents to protect their rights under article 8.[36] In particular, this may mean that parents should have a right to challenge in court decisions of the local authority concerning children in care. In *Re G (Care: Challenge to Local Authority's Decision)*[37] the local authority had obtained a care order, but the child remained with the parents for two years. Then the local authority (without consulting the parents) decided to remove the children from their home. This was held to be in clear breach of the family's article 8 rights. If the local authority wished to carry out a significant change in the way a child in care was being looked after, then it would have to involve the parents effectively in the decision-making process (unless the case was an emergency).

---

[28] [2004] EWCA Civ 355.
[29] *HK v Finland* [2006] 3 FCR 199.
[30] (1989) 12 EHRR 183.
[31] *R v Finland* [2006] 2 FCR 264.
[32] (1988) 11 EHRR 259 at para 68.
[33] [2000] 1 FLR 134.
[34] [2000] 2 FCR 614.
[35] At p. 624.
[36] *McMichael v UK* (1995) 20 EHRR 205.
[37] [2003] Fam Law 389.

## 3 The effect of a supervision order

On the making of a supervision order a supervisor will be appointed. Under s 35(1) of the Children Act 1989 the supervisor has three duties:[38]

---

**LEGISLATIVE PROVISION**

**Children Act 1989, section 35(1)**

(a) to advise, assist and befriend the supervised child;

(b) to take such steps as are reasonably necessary to give effect to the order; and

(c) where—

(i) the order is not wholly complied with; or
(ii) the supervisor considers that the order may no longer be necessary,

to consider whether or not to apply to the court for its variation or discharge.

---

So the key element of a supervision order is that a supervisor advises, assists and befriends the child. As well as befriending the child, the supervisor can advise the parents and make recommendations about the upbringing of children. For example, the supervisor might offer suggestions on methods of disciplining children. It is also possible to add specific conditions to a supervision order. Schedule 3 to the Children Act 1989[39] lists the conditions that a court can impose. These include requiring a child to live at a particular place, requiring the child to present him- or herself at a relevant place, or to participate in special activities. It is possible to impose conditions on a supervision order not listed in Sch 3, but only with the parents' consent.[40]

The whole ethos of the supervision order is based on the parents' consent and co-operation. The supervision order does not give the supervisor the right to enter any property and remove a child. Nor does the supervisor have the power to direct the child to undergo medical or psychiatric examination or treatment. It is not even possible to force the parents to comply with the conditions in the order or the requests of the supervisor. However, the failure to comply with requests from the supervisor may lead to the supervisor applying for a care order or emergency protection order. As the threshold criteria for the making of a care and supervision order are the same, the court may well be convinced that it would be appropriate to make a care order if the parents are refusing to co-operate with the supervisor. This means that, although the supervision order is apparently based on partnership and voluntary co-operation between the local authority and the parents, the threat of having the children removed under a care order gives the supervision order a coercive edge. However, supervision orders appear to be unpopular with some social workers who told researchers that the orders were 'a complete waste of time' and toothless.[41] A different kind of concern is indicated by research that children left with abusive parents are at risk of further abuse. In one study 40 per cent of children left with parents following local authority intervention suffered maltreatment in the 12 months following protective intervention. Fifteen per cent

---

[38] CA 1989, Sch 3 sets out their duties in further detail.
[39] *Re V (Care or Supervision Order)* [1996] 1 FLR 776.
[40] CA 1989, Sch 3, para 3(1).
[41] Hunt and McLeod (1998: 237).

suffered serious maltreatment.[42] On the other hand, another study into cases where a care order or interim care order had been made found that in 46 per cent of cases the end result of the case could have been obtained without making an order[43] and that care orders were used to encourage parents to co-operate in the performance of assessment, rather than as a response to proved harms or risks.

## 4 The effects of a care order

### A Distinguishing a child in care and a child voluntarily accommodated

In Chapter 10 it was noted that the Children Act 1989 draws a clear distinction between children in care and those voluntarily accommodated by the local authority under s 20 of the Act. The key difference is that local authorities have parental responsibility for a child in care,[44] whereas local authorities do not acquire parental responsibility over children who are voluntarily accommodated. The most significant practical consequence of this is that a person with parental responsibility can at any time remove a child who has been voluntarily accommodated, but cannot remove a child in care, without the consent of the local authority or approval of the court.[45]

### B The legal effects of the care order

Section 33 of the Children Act 1989 sets out the effects of a care order, which are as follows.

#### (i) Care orders and parental responsibility

Section 33(3) of the Children Act 1989 states that the local authority acquires parental responsibility by virtue of the care order and has 'the power (subject to the following provisions of this section) to determine the extent to which a parent or guardian of the child may meet his parental responsibility for him'.[46] So, on the making of a care order, the local authority acquires parental responsibility, but parents or guardians retain theirs. However, those who have parental responsibility by virtue of a residence order lose parental responsibility on the making of a care order. This is because a care order automatically brings to an end any residence order. Even though parents and guardians retain parental responsibility, they cannot exercise it in a way which is incompatible with the local authority's plans.[47] This means that, although parental responsibility is shared between parents and local authorities, in fact it is the local authority that very much controls what happens to the children in its care. However, that is not to say that local authorities are completely unrestrained in their use of parental responsibility and parents are powerless. The Children Act 1989 sets out a number of limitations on the exercise of a local authority's powers over children in its care, which protect the interests of parents. The list is interesting because it reflects those issues which the law regards as so fundamental to the concept of being a parent that the local authority should not be able to override the parents' wishes:

---

[42] Brandon (1999: 200–1).
[43] Brandon (1999: 151).
[44] CA 1989, s 33(3)(a).
[45] The court would have to discharge the care order.
[46] Although under CA 1989, s 33(4) the local authority can only restrict a parent's parental authority if satisfied that to do so is necessary to safeguard or promote the child's welfare.
[47] CA 1989, s 33(3).

- Local authorities cannot permit the child to be brought up in a different religion from that which the parents intended for the child.[48]

- Local authorities do not have the right to consent (or refuse to consent) to the making of an application for adoption.[49] The consent of the parents is required before an adoption order is made.[50]

- Local authorities cannot appoint a guardian.[51]

- Local authorities cannot cause the child to be known by a different surname, unless they have the consent of all those with parental responsibility, or the leave of the court.[52] An example of the kind of circumstances in which the court may be willing to give leave to change a surname is *Re M, T, P, K and B (Care: Change of Name)*,[53] where the children were in terror of their parents and had a pathological fear that their parents would remove them from their foster parents. Changing the children's name was seen as a means of preventing the parents from discovering the whereabouts of the children.

- The child cannot be removed from the UK unless all those with parental responsibility consent or the court grants leave.[54]

- The mother of a child in care is at liberty to enter a parental responsibility agreement, thereby giving the father parental responsibility, despite the local authority's opposition.[55]

The sharing of the parental responsibility between the parents and the local authority is highly controversial.[56] Some argue that it is inappropriate that parents who have appallingly abused their children, so that their children have been taken into care, retain parental responsibility. Others argue that the retention of parental responsibility by parents weakens the powers of local authorities. A different objection is that the sharing of parental responsibility is artificial. It is claimed that parents have parental responsibility in name alone. The strength of this objection depends on the nature of parental responsibility.[57] If parental responsibility is essentially a status then maybe it is correct that a care order does not affect the status of parenthood. But if parental responsibility reflects the performance of day-to-day parenting of children then the retention of parental responsibility on the making of a care order may well be artificial.[58] The law can be seen as a compromise between those who wish to protect the rights of parents of children who have been taken into care and the concerns of social work professionals that giving parents too many rights will hamper their protection of children within their care. The present law on parental responsibility is consistent with the Human Rights Act 1998, as it can be seen as the minimum intervention in the rights of parents compatible with effective protection of children. Indeed, despite the academic criticism of the concept of shared parental responsibility, the reported cases do not indicate that local authorities are finding their powers unduly restricted by parents' retention of

---

[48] CA 1989, s 33(6)(a); Foster Placement (Children) Regulations 1991, SI 1991/910, reg 5(2); Children's Homes Regulations 1991, SI 1991/1506, reg 11.

[49] CA 1989, s 33(6)(b)(i).

[50] See pages 681–4.

[51] CA 1989, s 33(6)(b)(iii). See Chapter 7.

[52] CA 1989, s 33(7).

[53] [2000] 1 FLR 645.

[54] CA 1989, Sch 2, para 19(3).

[55] *Re X (Parental Responsibility Agreement)* [2000] 1 FLR 517.

[56] Eekelaar (1991c: 43).

[57] See Chapter 7.

[58] See Chapters 7 and 8 for discussion of the different understandings of parental responsibility.

parental responsibility.[59] In fact, local authorities may be relieved that the parents must resolve controversial issues, such as religious upbringing and surnames.

The local authority should enter an agreement with the parents or those with parental responsibility concerning the arrangements for children in care. The agreement should deal with questions such as where the child should live and what services should be provided to the child.[60] The agreements are not binding contracts and they are not enforceable in the courts. They should be in writing and copies of the agreement should be provided to those with parental responsibility. If appropriate, a copy should be given to the child in a comprehensible form.[61] The agreement may include a delegation to foster carers of the right to consent to medical treatment or give consent for the child to be involved in various activities arranged by the local authority.[62]

## (ii) Duties imposed upon a local authority

The Children Act 1989 imposes upon local authorities a number of duties owed towards children who are looked after by them.[63] These duties are owed to children who are voluntarily accommodated by the local authority for more than 24 hours[64] and to those who are the subject of a care order.[65]

### (a) The general duty

The general duty of the local authority is contained in s 22(3):

---

**LEGISLATIVE PROVISION**

**Children Act 1989, section 22(3)**

It shall be the duty of a local authority looking after any child—

(a) to safeguard and promote his welfare; and

(b) to make such use of services available for children cared for by their own parents as appears to the authority reasonable in his case.

---

This duty is self-explanatory, but it should be noted that the local authority can owe duties to children even if the children are cared for by their parents.

### (b) The duty to decide where the child should live

The local authority must 'receive the child into their care and . . . keep him in their care while the order remains in force'.[66] So on the making of the care order the local authority becomes responsible for deciding where the child should live.

---

[59] For an example of where the father did continue to pose a risk to the children in care and where the local authority were able to rely on CA 1989, s 33(3)(b) to limit the father's powers, see *Re P (Children Act 1989, ss 22 and 26: Local Authority Compliance)* [2000] 2 FLR 910.

[60] Arrangements for Placement of Children (General) Regulations 1991, SI 1991/890, reg 4 and Sch 4.

[61] Regulation 5(3).

[62] Department for Children, Schools and Families (2008a).

[63] CA 1989, s 22, inserted by Children and Young Persons Act 2008. See HM Government (2010c) for detailed guidance.

[64] CA 1989, s 22(2).

[65] CA 1989, s 22(1).

[66] CA 1989, s 33(1).

### (c) The duty to consult

The Children Act 1989, s 22(4) requires a local authority to consult with the child and his or her family:

---

**LEGISLATIVE PROVISION**

**Children Act 1989, section 22(4)**

Before making any decision with respect to a child whom they are looking after, or proposing to look after, a local authority shall, so far as is reasonably practicable, ascertain the wishes and feelings of—

(a)  the child;

(b)  his parents;

(c)  any person who is not a parent of his but who has parental responsibility for him; and

(d)  any other person whose wishes and feelings the authority consider to be relevant regarding the matter to be decided.

---

The local authority must then give 'due consideration' to these views. The views of the child are taken into account as would be appropriate given the age and understanding of the child.[67] The local authority must also give due consideration to the child's 'religious persuasion, racial origin and cultural and linguistic background'.[68] These factors are likely to be most relevant when considering the placement of children with foster carers. Where possible, foster carers should be of the same religious and cultural background as the child, although that will be only one consideration when selecting suitable foster carers.[69]

### (d) The duty to provide accommodation

The local authority has a duty to accommodate a child in care.[70] The Children Act 1989 sets out the alternative ways of providing accommodation:

- to place the child with the parents, family or relatives;[71]
- to place the child with foster carers;
- to place the child in a community home;
- to place the child in a voluntary home;
- to place the child in a registered children's home;
- to place the child in a home for special families;
- such other arrangements as seem appropriate to the local authority.[72]

Before considering any other alternative accommodation, the local authority should first consider whether the child should be allowed to remain at home. There is a specific duty to make

---

[67] CA 1989, s 22(5)(a) and (b). If the local authority fails to consult with a parent or child, their decision is not necessarily void: *Re P (Children Act 1989, ss 22 and 26: Local Authority Compliance)* [2000] 2 FLR 910.
[68] CA 1989, s 22(5)(c).
[69] There are reports of severe shortages of foster carers: BBC Newsonline (2010a).
[70] CA 1989 s 22A.
[71] CA 1989, s 23(5); Placement with Parents etc. Regulations 1991, SI 1991/893.
[72] CA 1989, s 22C.

arrangements for the child to live with his or her family or friends unless it is not reasonably practicable or consistent with his or her welfare.[73] There is also a duty to accommodate the child as close as possible to the parents' home and to any siblings accommodated by the local authority.[74]

It is a common misconception that children taken into care spend the rest of their childhood in children's homes. One study found that in less than half the cases where care proceedings were instigated were children removed from their parents.[75] In fact nine out of ten children taken into care are eventually returned to their families.[76] Indeed, it is becoming less common for children in care to be accommodated in children's homes, at least as a long-term solution. In part this is in response to a depressing procession of scandals about the physical and sexual abuse of children in children's homes. Foster carers are often seen as a preferable solution.

### (e) The duty to maintain

There is a duty on the local authority to maintain a child, but in some circumstances it can recoup the cost by requiring a financial contribution to the child's maintenance from their parents or others, if reasonable to do so.[77]

### (f) The duty to promote contact

A local authority is under a positive obligation[78] to promote contact between children and parents, family or friends unless such contact is not reasonably practicable or is inconsistent with the child's welfare. This is required under s 34 of the Children Act 1989 and would be required under article 8 of the European Convention.[79] Local authorities are also required to keep in touch with persons who have parental responsibility for the child and specifically to keep them informed of the child's whereabouts. However, there is no duty on the local authority to provide finance to promote the contact.[80] Parents and those with parental responsibility are required to keep the local authority informed of their addresses. In a survey of parents whose children were in care 61 per cent said they had contact with their child at least once a week. Only 8 per cent said they had no contact at all.[81] In another study[82] while at the end of court proceedings it was intended that nearly all the children in care in the study would retain contact with at least one parent, three years later just under a half were seeing their parents at least once a month. It was contact with fathers which was particularly likely to tail off and cease. Where the placement was with members of their family the researchers found a high level of strained or conflicted relationships between carers and parents which could cause harm to the child.

### (g) Other miscellaneous powers and duties

There are other duties which are set out in Part II of Sch 2 to the Children Act 1989, and the Children and Young Persons Act 2008. These include, for example, assistance with travelling

---

[73] CA 1989, s 22C.
[74] CA 1989, s 22C(8).
[75] Hunt (1998: 287).
[76] Bullock, Malos and Millham (1993).
[77] CA 1989, s 22B.
[78] CA 1989, Sch 2, para 15.
[79] *L v Finland* [2000] 2 FLR 118.
[80] CA 1989, Sch 2, para 16.
[81] Ofsted (2008).
[82] Hunt, Waterhouse and Lutman (2010).

expenses for children in care; the appointment of an independent visitor; the arrangement for funeral expenses if a child dies while in care.

### (h) Duty to review

The local authority is required to keep under review the long-term plans for each child in care. The local authority must review a child's case within four weeks of the child being first accommodated by the authority. A second review should be carried out within three months of the first and, thereafter, reviews every six months. The purpose of the review is to ensure that the child does not 'drift through care' and instead that the time in care is part of a co-ordinated programme designed to promote the child's welfare.[83] So it should be decided as early as possible whether the child is to be adopted and, if so, what steps should be put in place to enable that to take place. Parents and children should be included in the review, or at least consulted.[84] Following the Human Rights Act 1998, the review should constantly ensure that the children's and parents' rights to respect for family life be maintained to the greatest extent possible and that, where appropriate, the care plan progresses towards reuniting the child and the parent.[85]

### (iii) Empowering children in care

A variety of provisions seek to protect the rights of children in care:

- Children's views must be given due consideration when making decisions about their time in care.[86]
- Children can apply to the court for an order authorising contact with another person.[87]
- Children can apply for a s 8 order.[88]
- The child can institute the complaints procedures.[89]
- The child can apply to discharge a care order.[90]

Despite these provisions, research suggests that children in care feel that their wishes are not being taken into account and are not listened to.[91] Some argue that the high levels of anti-social behaviour and running away among children in care is explained by the fact that they feel they are not being heard. There are particular concerns with the complaints procedure, which should be readily accessible to children in care. Some local authorities appoint a children's rights officer to promote good practice and to assist children to use the complaints procedure.[92] The hope was that the complaints procedures set out in s 26(3) of the Children Act 1989 would do much to resolve the problems of abuse. Lyon reports[93] that this has not happened because children are not confident about using the complaints procedure through fear of reprisals.[94] She also argues that even when complaints are made by children in care,

---

[83] For an appalling example of such drift see *Re F, F v Lambeth LBC* [2002] Fam Law 8.
[84] Review of Children's Cases Regulations 1991, SI 1991/895.
[85] *L v Finland* [2000] 2 FLR 118.
[86] CA 1989, s 22(4)(a) and (5)(a).
[87] CA 1989, s 34(2) and (4).
[88] See Chapter 8.
[89] CA 1989, s 26(3)(a). Complaints procedures will be further discussed shortly.
[90] CA 1989, s 39(1).
[91] Department of Health (1996).
[92] CA 1989, Sch 2A; Ellis and Franklin (1995).
[93] Lyon (1997a).
[94] Dalrymple and Payne (1994).

they are not investigated effectively.[95] At least two separate reports[96] have found that both staff and children were not sufficiently informed about the existence of the complaints procedures.[97] The Waterhouse Report[98] found that children in care still feel that there is no one to whom they can complain and that they have little contact with people outside the care homes in which they live.

## (iv) Contact arrangements for children in care

Even though a child has been taken into care, it may still be appropriate for the child to retain contact with his or her parents or other relatives.[99] There may be a number of reasons for encouraging contact between a child in care and their birth family. It may be that contact is part of a care plan designed ultimately to return the child to the parent. Even if that is not a possibility, contact may be regarded as important for providing the emotional support of a continuous relationship with his or her parents or providing the child with a sense of identity. Indeed, even in a permanent placement, the success of that placement may depend on the benefit of contact with family members.[100] As already stressed, parents' rights to respect for family life under the Human Rights Act 1998 require the local authority to encourage contact unless it is necessary to prevent it in the child's interests. However, despite the legal position there can be practical and psychological problems which make contact between a child in care and his or her parents problematic.[101] One study found that 51 per cent of children in care would like to see more of their family.[102]

The issue of contact between the child in care and his or her family is one of the few issues concerning children in care where the court has a major say. There are two ways that the court may exercise control over contact between a child in care and his or her natural parents:

1. The making of the care order. When applying for a care order a local authority must present a 'care plan', which will include its proposals for contact.[103] If the court is dissatisfied with the arrangements for contact, it can refuse to make the care order, although it cannot make a care order on condition that a certain kind of contact take place.[104] This can leave the court with the choice between two evils: leave the child without the protection of a court order, or make a care order with a care plan of which the court disapproves.[105]

2. Section 34 creates a presumption in favour of contact between a child in care and his or her parents, guardians and anyone with whom the child had lived[106] under a residence order (or an order under the inherent jurisdiction).[107] Except in an emergency, the local authority can only refuse contact between the child and those people after applying to the court. If necessary a penal notice can be attached to an order requiring the local authority

---

[95] Lyon (1997a).
[96] Williams and Jordan (1996a).
[97] Williams and Jordan (1996b).
[98] Waterhouse (2000).
[99] Department for Children, Schools and Families (2008a: ch 6).
[100] Macaskill (2002), although contrast Browne and Moloney (2002).
[101] Miles and Lindley (2003).
[102] Who Cares? Trust (2000).
[103] CA 1989, s 31(3A).
[104] *Re T (A Minor) (Care Order: Conditions)* [1994] 2 FLR 423, [1994] 2 FCR 721; see also Contact with Children Regulations 1991, SI 1991/891. However, the care order can contain a s 34 order authorising prohibition of contact.
[105] *Re S and D (Children: Powers of Court)* [1995] 2 FLR 456.
[106] Immediately before the making of the care order.
[107] Brasse (1993: 57).

to allow contact.[108] In an emergency, s 34(6) of the Children Act 1989 permits a local authority to refuse contact for up to seven days if: If the local authority wishes to prohibit contact for a period longer than seven days, it must apply for an order under s 34 of the Children Act 1989 permitting it to do so. If such an application is made, the court must determine whether there is to be contact and, if there is, the frequency and place of contact.[109] However, the court has no jurisdiction to prohibit the local authority from permitting contact between the child and his or her parents.[110] All the court has the power to do is permit the local authority to prohibit contact.

---

## LEGISLATIVE PROVISION

### Children Act 1989, section 34(6)

(a) they are satisfied that it is necessary to do so in order to safeguard or promote the child's welfare; and

(b) the refusal—

    (i) is decided upon as a matter of urgency; and
    (ii) does not last for more than seven days.

---

When the courts consider cases where the local authority has sought to end contact between the child and his or her family the welfare principle and the s 1(3) checklist govern the discretion of the court.[111] A number of particular issues should be taken into account by the court in such cases.

### (a) A presumption in favour of contact

*Re E (A Minor) (Care Order: Contact)*[112] confirms that there is a presumption in favour of contact. The burden of establishing that contact should be terminated rests on the local authority. Simon Brown LJ explained:

> Even when the s 31 criteria are satisfied, contact may well be of singular importance to the long-term welfare of the child: first in giving the child the security of knowing that his parents love him and are interested in his welfare; secondly, by avoiding any damaging sense of loss to the child in seeing himself abandoned by his parents; thirdly, by enabling the child to commit himself to the substitute family with the seal of approval of the natural parents; and fourthly, by giving the child the necessary sense of family and personal identity. Contact, if maintained, is capable of reinforcing and increasing the chances of a permanent placement, whether on a long-term fostering basis or by adoption.

Even in *Re DH (A Minor) (Child Abuse)*,[113] where there were fears that the mother suffered from Munchausen's syndrome, it was accepted that there was value in maintaining contact so that the mother did not become a fantasy figure to the child. Contact should be prohibited in the kind of cases where there is no likelihood of rehabilitation with the birth family and

---

[108] *Re P-B (Contact: Committal)* [2009] 2 FLR 66.
[109] CA 1989, s 34(3).
[110] *Re W (Section 34(2)) (Orders)* [2000] 1 FLR 512.
[111] *Re B (Minors) (Termination of Contact: Paramount Consideration)* [1993] 1 FLR 543, [1993] 1 FCR 363; *Re H (Children) (Termination of Contact)* [2005] 1 FCR 658.
[112] [1994] 1 FLR 146, [1994] 1 FCR 584.
[113] [1994] 1 FLR 679, [1994] 2 FCR 3.

the child has been placed for adoption.[114] It is not appropriate to make a s 34 order simply because there might in the future be circumstances that would make contact undesirable.[115]

### (b) The Human Rights Act 1998

Under the Human Rights Act 1998 parents have a right of contact with their children and children a right of contact with their parents.[116] To justify a termination of contact under the Act, it would have to be shown that it was necessary in the child's interests and that it was proportionate to the harm faced by the child.[117] This approach will normally coincide with the application of the welfare principle.[118] However, the requirement that the parents' rights can be infringed only if *necessary* in the child's interests might suggest that only if there is clear evidence that the child's interests require it can contact be terminated. Although the Human Rights Act 1998 may alter the language used to express the arguments, Wall J in *Re F (Care Proceedings: Contact)*[119] was of the view that it is unlikely that the Act will alter the ways decisions are reached in relation to s 34 applications.

### (c) The plans of the local authority

When a local authority seeks to terminate contact this is often because contact is inconsistent with its plans for the child: for example, it wishes to place the child for adoption. So the issue is raised whether the court can refuse to permit termination of contact if the refusal will scupper the local authority's plans for the child. The approach taken by the courts to date is that, where an application is made under s 34, the court should give respect to the plans of the local authority, but at the end of the day the welfare principle governs the issue.[120] As was explained by Butler-Sloss LJ in *Re B (Minors) (Termination of Contact: Paramount Consideration)*:

> The proposals of the local authority, based on their appreciation of the best interests of the child, must command the greatest respect and consideration from the court, but Parliament has given to the court, and not to the local authority, the duty to decide on contact between the child and those named in section 34(1).[121]

So, if the court, even having given the plans of the local authority the greatest respect,[122] decides that the child's welfare requires the continuation of the contact, it will refuse the local authority's application to terminate contact.[123]

### (d) Weight to be placed on the child's view

In *L v L (Child Abuse: Access)*[124] it was confirmed that the wishes of the children were to be taken into account when deciding whether to terminate contact. However, the weight placed

---

[114] *Re L (Sexual Abuse: Standard of Proof)* [1996] 1 FLR 116 at p. 127, per Butler-Sloss LJ.
[115] *Re S (Care: Parental Contact)* [2004] EWCA Civ 1397.
[116] *R v UK* [1988] 2 FLR 445. Although it will be easier to justify ending contact with a father who has had little contact with the child, than with a mother who has formed a close bond to the child: *Söderbäck v Sweden* [1999] 1 FLR 250.
[117] *S and G v Italy* [2000] 2 FLR 771.
[118] *Re F (Care: Termination of Care)* [2000] FCR 481.
[119] [2000] 2 FCR 481.
[120] *Berkshire CC v B* [1997] 1 FLR 171, [1997] 3 FCR 88.
[121] [1993] Fam 301 at p. 311. Supported in *Re E (A Minor) (Care Order: Contact)* [1994] 1 FLR 146, [1994] 1 FCR 584.
[122] In *Re D and H (Care: Termination of Contact)* [1997] 1 FLR 841 it was said to be inadvisable to disrupt the local authority plans by refusing to permit the termination of contact.
[123] *Berkshire CC v B* [1997] 1 FLR 171, [1997] 3 FCR 88; *Re S (Children) (Termination of Contact)* [2005] 1 FCR 489.
[124] [1989] 2 FLR 16, [1989] FCR 697.

on the child's wishes depends on the age of the child and circumstances of the case. Jones and Parkinson[125] have warned of the dangers of placing weight on abused children's wishes. This is because abuse can cause a complex psychological relationship between the child and an abuser. This factor was relevant in *Re G (A Child) (Domestic Violence: Direct Contact)*[126] in which an order was made under s 34 to deny contact between a child aged nearly 4 and her father. The child suffered from post-traumatic stress disorder and long-term trauma, having witnessed her father being violent to her mother, and the evidence was that contact would cause the child great harm.

### (e) Contact with relatives other than parents

Section 34 provides a presumption of contact only between children and parents, guardians and those with whom the child has lived. The Court of Appeal has held that the duty of the local authority to promote contact extended to 'any relative, friend or other person connected with him'.[127] However, it needs to be stressed that unlike parents, the local authority does not require the consent of the court to terminate contact with those not listed in s 34. This means that if a local authority does not permit contact, these other relatives and friends need to apply for a contact order under s 8 of the Children Act 1989.[128] In deciding whether to grant leave to a person seeking contact with a child, the court will be governed by the welfare principle, but will take into account the criteria set out in s 10(9):[129]

- the nature of the contact being sought;
- the connection of the applicant to the child;
- any disruption to the child's stability or security; and
- the wishes of the parents and local authority which are important but not determinative.

In *Re M (Care: Contact: Grandmother's Application for Leave)*[130] the Court of Appeal considered that grandparents do not have a right of contact with children in care and must show that contact would be in the interests of the child. The court may well be prepared to assume that it is good for a child in care to maintain links with as many family members as possible if they are willing to go to the effort of visiting him or her. In *Re W (Care Proceedings: Leave to Apply)*[131] it was held that where an aunt applied for contact with a child in care the court would consider the criteria set out in s 10(9).[132]

### (f) Application by children under s 34

The child can apply without leave of the court for contact with a named person and for an order permitting the authority to refuse to allow contact with a person.

### (g) Forcing an adult to have contact with children in care

The court has no power to force an adult to have contact with the child, according to Wilson J in *Re F (Contact: Child in Care)*.[133] The only person who can be forced to behave in

---

[125] Jones and Parkinson (1995).
[126] [2001] 2 FCR 134.
[127] CA 1989, Sch 2, para 15(1)(c).
[128] CA 1989, s 34(3)(b).
[129] *Re M (Care: Contact: Grandmother's Application for Leave)* [1995] 2 FLR 86, [1995] 3 FCR 550.
[130] [1995] 2 FLR 86, [1995] 3 FCR 550.
[131] [2004] EWHC 3342 (Fam).
[132] See page 490.
[133] [1995] 1 FLR 510, [1994] 2 FCR 1354.

a particular way by an order under s 34 is the local authority, which can be required to allow the parents to have contact with the child.

## (v) Abducting children from care

It is a criminal offence to abduct children from care.

---

**LEGISLATIVE PROVISION**

**Children Act 1989, section 49(1)**

A person shall be guilty of an offence if, knowingly and without lawful authority or reasonable excuse, he—

(a) takes a child to whom this section applies away from the responsible person;

(b) keeps such a child away from the responsible person; or

(c) induces, assists or incites such a child to run away or stay away from the responsible person.

---

A 'responsible person' here means a person who has care of the child by virtue of a care order, an emergency protection order, or powers of police protection. The section is therefore designed to deal with people taking children away from public care, rather than people removing children from their parents or relatives.

## 5 Questioning local authority decisions

### A Avoiding disputes

The Children Act 1989 is designed to prevent disputes between parents and local authorities arising in the first place. There are two main ways in which this is done. The first is through the concept of partnership: this is the idea that local authorities should work in partnership with the child's family and others interested in the child's welfare. The second is through regular reviews: local authorities are required periodically to review each child looked after by them and have a duty to establish procedures to hear complaints or representations. The Review of Children's Cases Regulations 1991 require the local authority to take into account the views of parents, those with parental responsibility, and any other persons whose views are considered relevant, when reviewing the care for children.

### B Procedures to challenge local authority decisions

Despite these attempts to avoid disputes, inevitably they do arise and there are a number of routes of appeal for those seeking to challenge local authority decisions.[134]

---

[134] See Bailey-Harris and Harris (2002) for an excellent discussion.

### (i) Internal complaints procedures[135]

The internal complaints procedure is primarily designed to work in cases where there is no dispute over what the facts are or the law is. The complaints procedure is most appropriate where the dispute is whether the local authority has misused its powers. *R v Kingston-upon-Thames RB, ex p T*[136] suggested that the complaints procedure should be preferred to judicial review in most cases.

Local authorities are required to establish procedures to deal with complaints.[137] The following can initiate the complaints procedure: children cared for by the local authority; parents of children in care; those with parental responsibility for children in care; and local authority foster carers.[138] The local authority may add to that list if it decides that an individual has sufficient interest in the child. The representations can relate to the way a particular child is cared for or refer to the carrying out of any of the local authority's functions under Part III of the Children Act 1989. The kinds of issues that might be involved include: complaints relating to day care; after care; accommodation; or support services if the child lives at home. The procedures should involve a two-stage process. The local authority must appoint an officer who will be responsible for co-ordinating the complaint. The authority and an independent person must consider the complaint and formulate a response. If the complainant is not happy with the initial response then he or she has the right to have the complaint considered by a panel. The decision reached by the panel is not binding at law on the authority, but a local authority will normally abide by it.[139] If the local authority does not follow the recommendation of the panel then a judicial review application may well succeed.[140]

Local authorities are required to appoint independent reviewing officers (IROs) to review the care of children in care and other looked-after children.[141] If IROs have concerns (e.g. the local authority inappropriately departs from a care plan) which the local authority does not deal with, they can refer cases to CAFCASS, which will then have the power to bring legal proceedings (e.g. for judicial review or for an application under the Human Rights Act).[142]

### (ii) Human Rights Act 1998

Under s 7 of the Human Rights Act 1998 an individual can bring a claim against a local authority which has infringed or is about to infringe that individual's rights under that Act.[143] Section 8 provides that if the application is successful then the court can provide such relief or remedy as is appropriate. This could include requiring the local authority to pay damages[144] or reverse its decision and reconsider what should happen to the child.[145] Proceedings should

---

[135] General guidance is found in Representation Procedure (Children) Regulations 1991, SI 1991/894 and Department for Children, Schools and Families (2008a). C. Williams (2002) provides a study of how the complaints procedures work in practice.

[136] [1994] 1 FLR 798, [1994] 1 FCR 232.

[137] Department for Children, Schools and Families (2008a: ch. 10); Williams and Jordan (1996a; b).

[138] CA 1989, s 26(3).

[139] See *R v Brent LBC, ex p S* [1994] 1 FLR 203.

[140] As suggested in *R v Kingston-upon-Thames RB, ex p T* [1994] 1 FLR 798 at p. 814, although not necessarily: *Re T (Accommodation by Local Authority)* [1995] 1 FLR 159, [1995] 1 FCR 517; *R v Avon County Council, ex p M* [1994] 2 FCR 259, [1994] 1 FCR 1006.

[141] Children Act 1989, s 26, as amended by Adoption and Children Act 2002, s 118.

[142] Review of Children's Cases (Amendment) (England) Regulations 2004 (SI 2004/1419).

[143] Actions can only be brought in respect of acts after 2 October 2000 (Human Rights Act 1998, s 22(4)).

[144] Although even if an interference with articles 6 or 8 is found the court may decide not to award damages. Damages are to be ordered only if just and appropriate: Human Rights Act 1998, ss 7 and 8. See *Re V (A Child) (Care: Pre-birth Actions)* [2006] 2 FCR 121.

[145] *Re M (Challenging Decisions by Local Authority)* [2001] 2 FLR 1300.

only be brought under s 8 if there are no ongoing care proceedings. If care proceedings are ongoing, human rights arguments should be made in the context of those proceedings.[146] In *C v Bury Metropolitan Borough Council*[147] a mother brought an action against a local authority under the Human Rights Act 1998 claiming that it had infringed her article 8 rights and those of her son who was in care. The case centred on the decision by the local authority to move the son to a residential school 350 miles away from the mother. Although it was accepted that their article 8 rights had been infringed it was held that the infringement was lawful, being in the son's interests and a proportionate interference. Perhaps of significance was the fact that the mother did not have a settled lifestyle and moved around the United Kingdom, and the finding that the local authority had acted reasonably given its financial responsibilities to all the children in its care. The decision has led one commentator to speculate that the Human Rights Act remedies may rarely differ in outcome from judicial review.[148] That would be surprising, but time will tell.

## (iii) Judicial review

Judicial review is another court-based remedy when an individual is claiming that a local authority is acting illegally. Leave is required before an application for judicial review can be launched.[149] The court must be persuaded that the applicant has sufficient interest in the matter.[150] Clearly, a parent will have sufficient standing, as will other relatives if their relationship to the child was close enough. Before the court grants leave it will need to be satisfied that the applicant has a reasonable prospect of winning the case.[151] In *Re M; R (X and Y) v Gloucestershire CC*[152] Munby J held that judicial review was not an appropriate means of seeking to prevent a local authority from commencing emergency protection or care proceedings, unless there were exceptional circumstances.[153] In *A and S v Enfield London Borough Council*[154] Blair J suggested that it would be rare that judicial review should be used in the field of child protection. The purpose of judicial review is not to decide whether or not the decision was the right one but to decide whether the decision was reached in accordance with the law. So, even if the court thinks that the decision was the wrong one, it cannot overturn it unless the decision was outside the bounds of the law.

### (a) Grounds for judicial review

There are three main grounds on which judicial review of a decision of a local authority could be sought:[155]

1. *Unreasonableness.* This phrase is given a special meaning in the law relating to judicial review. It must be shown that the local authority has acted in a way in which no reasonable local authority would act.[156]

---

[146] *Re L (Care Proceedings: Human Rights Claims)* [2004] 1 FCR 289; *Re V (Care Proceedings: Human Rights Claims)* [2004] Fam Law 238. The same is true if a claim is made in habeas corpus.

[147] [2002] 2 FLR 868.

[148] Bailey-Harris (2002).

[149] Rules of the Supreme Court, Order 53, r 3.

[150] Clearly, parents and the child him- or herself will have sufficient interest but more remote relatives might have difficulty.

[151] *R v Lancashire CC, ex p M* [1992] 1 FLR 109, [1992] FCR 283.

[152] [2003] Fam Law 444.

[153] See also *Re M (Care Proceedings: Judicial Review)* [2004] 1 FCR 302.

[154] [2008] 2 FLR 1945.

[155] *Council of Civil Service Unions v Minister for the Civil Service* [1985] AC 374.

[156] E.g. *R v Kingston-upon-Thames RB, ex p T* [1994] 1 FLR 798, [1994] 1 FCR 232.

2. *Illegality.* Several notions are included under this head. The core notion is that the local authority has acted outside the powers given to it by the law: for example, that the local authority has changed the surname of the child without the approval of the parents or the court. Another form of illegality is where the local authority has fettered its discretion. This means that it would be unlawful for a local authority to adopt a rigid policy or rule which determines every case that comes up for consideration (for example, that a child can never be adopted by a person of a different race). The reasoning is that where a local authority has been given a discretion by Parliament over a particular issue the local authority is obliged to consider each case separately and not apply a blanket rule. Of course, a local authority can adopt general policies which usually apply as long as each case is considered on its own merits. A local authority may also be acting illegally if it fails to take into account a factor it is required to take into account,[157] or takes a factor into account which it should not have taken into account.

3. *Procedural impropriety.* This would be relevant where the local authority has breached the rules of natural justice.[158] An example might be where a child is removed from foster carers without the child, foster carers or biological parents being consulted.[159]

The following list indicates the kinds of complaints that have led to judicial review proceedings:

1. Removing a child from foster carers without consultation.[160]
2. Improperly removing a person from a list of approved adopters.[161]
3. Unjustifiably placing a child on a child protection register.[162]
4. Disclosing to third parties allegation of child abuse.[163]
5. Failing to take into account the views of a 15-year-old child in care about where she was to live.[164]

Even if a local authority is found to have acted illegally, the remedies after a successful claim for judicial review are limited. The court will declare the decision unlawful and require the local authority to reconsider the issue. The court does not normally have the power to compel the local authority to act in a particular way. The limited remedies available under judicial review indicate that it is best used when an applicant is attempting to challenge a general policy of a local authority. Where the complaint is about the way a particular individual was treated, an application under the Human Rights Act 1998 may be more appropriate. Munby J has described judicial review in this context as a 'singularly blunt and unsatisfactory tool' and 'a remedy of last resort'.[165]

---

[157] E.g. *R v Avon CC, ex p K* [1986] 1 FLR 443, where a children's home was closed without considering the welfare of the children in the home.

[158] E.g. *R v Bedfordshire CC, ex p C* [1987] 1 FLR 239.

[159] *R v Wandsworth LBC, ex p P* [1989] 1 FLR 387. In *Re M (A Child)* [2002] 1 FCR 88 and *Haringey v Mr and Mrs E* [2006] EWHC 1620 (Fam) the child was found to have established the right to family life with the foster carer.

[160] *R v Hereford and Worcester County Council, ex p R* [1992] 1 FLR 448, [1992] FCR 497; *R v Lancashire CC, ex p M* [1992] 1 FLR 109, [1992] FCR 283.

[161] *R v Wandsworth LBC, ex p P* [1989] 1 FLR 387.

[162] E.g. *R v Hampshire CC, ex p H* [1999] 2 FLR 359.

[163] *R v Devon CC, ex p L* [1991] 2 FLR 541.

[164] *R (CD) v Isle of Anglesey CC* [2004] 3 FCR 171.

[165] *Re M (Care Proceedings: Judicial Review)* [2004] 1 FCR 302.

## (iv) Secretary of State's default powers

The Secretary of State has the power to intervene in an extreme case. The Secretary of State will be reluctant to use this power in an individual complaint but may be persuaded to do so where a local authority has adopted what he or she regards as an undesirable policy. An example may be a local authority which has failed to set up a satisfactory complaints system.[166]

## (v) The local government ombudsman

A complaint can be made to the relevant local government ombudsman if there is maladministration. Recourse to the local government ombudsman is only possible where there is no remedy by way of the internal complaints procedure or it would be unreasonable to use that procedure. The ombudsman will issue a report and can award an ex gratia payment.[167] However, the ombudsman has no power to order the local authority to act towards a child in a particular way.

## (vi) Civil actions

There have in recent years been several attempts by parents and children to sue local authorities under the law of tort for compensation for harms caused by local authorities when performing their child-care obligations.[168] These claims are usually based on either the tort of negligence or the breach of statutory duty.[169] The cases involve some highly complex issues of tort law and so only a broad outline can be provided here. The position that the law has now reached is that each case depends on its facts. There is no blanket immunity that a local authority can rely upon when facing a claim of negligence. Instead a duty of care is owed where it is fair, just and reasonable. For example, in *W v Essex CC*[170] foster parents specifically told a local authority that they would not be willing to care for a child who was himself a known child abuser. Nevertheless, the local authority housed such a child with them and he abused the foster parents' own children. The House of Lords were willing to accept that, potentially, the local authority could be liable in tort for the harm caused to the foster parents and their children. In *Barrett v Enfield LBC*[171] a local authority was held liable for damages to a child whom it had taken into care but then unsatisfactorily placed with foster carers. It was held that the courts should be more ready to find a duty of care where the claim was that a child taken into care had been mistreated, than in cases where the argument was that the taking into care was improper.[172]

*JD v East Berkshire Community Health NHS Trust*[173] marked a noticeable shift in the approach of the law. The House of Lords held, in line with the cases outlined above, that parents could not sue doctors or social workers who had acted negligently in child protection work. However, they indicated that the children concerned did have a right of action. Lord Nicholls explained why parents could not sue:

---

[166] *R v Brent LBC, ex p S* [1994] 1 FLR 203.

[167] This is not enforceable.

[168] See Palser (2009) for a helpful summary of the law.

[169] For an important recent decision on the doctrine of vicarious liability in the child-care context see *Lister v Hesley Hall Ltd* [2001] 2 FLR 307.

[170] [2000] 1 FLR 657.

[171] [1999] 3 WLR 79.

[172] See further *Pierce v Doncaster Metropolitan Borough Council* [2009] 1 FLR 1189.

[173] [2005] 2 AC 373. The Court of Appeal in *Lawrence v Pembrokeshire CC* [2007] 2 FCR 329 confirmed that the case still stands even in the light of the Human Rights Act 1998. In *L v Reading BC* [2008] 1 FCR 295 it was confirmed that the same principles would bar a claim against the social workers individually.

A doctor is obliged to act in the best interests of his patient. In these cases the child is his patient. The doctor is charged with the protection of the child, not with the protection of the parent. The best interests of a child and his parent normally march hand-in-hand. But when considering whether something does not feel 'quite right', a doctor must be able to act single-mindedly in the interests of the child. He ought not to have at the back of his mind an awareness that if his doubts about intentional injury or sexual abuse prove unfounded he may be exposed to claims by a distressed parent.[174]

In *B v A CC*[175] the Court of Appeal held that a county council owed a duty of care in negligence towards adoptive parents with whom it was placing a child. Doing so would be 'fair, just and reasonable'. The parents lost their case because they were unable to prove that the county council had revealed the adoptive parents' identity to the birth family, despite a guarantee not to, and that as a result the adoptive parents had suffered a campaign of harassment. Had they succeeded in proving those allegations damages may well have been awarded. In *Merthyr Tydfil County Borough Council v C*[176] a mother reported sexual abuse of her children by a neighbour. The local authority failed to deal with the complaint properly and later denied a complaint had been made. The mother suffered psychological harm and it was held that there was a reasonable prospect of a later court finding that the local authority did owe her a duty of care, created by virtue of the fact she had reported the abuse.

The law involves a delicate balance. On the one hand, in favour of liability of the local authority under the law of tort are arguments that tort liability will encourage the local authority to see that it has in place procedures to ensure that negligent acts do not take place. Also in favour of liability are arguments that children or adults who suffer as a result of local authority intervention or non-intervention deserve compensation for their loss. Indeed, they may be entitled to a remedy under article 6 of the European Convention on Human Rights. On the other hand, there are also arguments against tortious liability. Local authorities may become too 'litigation conscious' in carrying out the delicate task of child protection, leading to social workers always adopting the safest course of action, which may not be the course which is the best policy for the child. A further complexity is that sometimes the decision over the form of intervention to protect a child is essentially a political one, involving allocation of resources. Such decisions, partly economic or political, are normally thought inappropriate for judicial review. Due to the difficulties in pursuing a tort action an applicant may prefer, where possible, to use the Human Rights Act 1998.[177]

## (vii) Private orders

An aggrieved parent or relative could use a s 8 order.[178] In *Re A (Minors) (Residence Orders: Leave to Apply)*[179] a foster mother sought to challenge a local authority's decision that she was no longer permitted to foster four children by applying for a residence order in respect of the children. The Court of Appeal took the view that, in considering whether to give leave, the authority's plans were very important.[180] The court was willing to assume that departure from the local authority's plan would not promote the child's welfare and therefore it declined to grant leave. This case indicates that it will be rare for a court to grant leave for a s 8 application

---

[174] [2005] 2 AC 373, para 85.
[175] *B v A County Council* [2006] 3 FCR 568.
[176] [2010] 1 FLR 1640.
[177] *Lawrence v Pembrokeshire CC* [2007] 2 FCR 329.
[178] Non-parents may require the leave of the court: see Chapter 9.
[179] [1992] 2 FLR 154, [1992] 2 FCR 174.
[180] As required under CA 1989, s 10(9)(d)(i).

which the local authority opposes. Whether a court will have to be more willing to grant leave, relying on article 6 of the European Convention on Human Rights, is open to debate.

### (viii) Inherent jurisdiction

If a child is in need and no other route is open to protect the child's welfare, the court may be willing to use the inherent jurisdiction in exceptional cases. In *Re M (Care: Leave to Interview Child)*[181] a father successfully applied under the inherent jurisdiction for an order that he could have his child interviewed to assist in his defence to a rape charge. The court will only make an order under the inherent jurisdiction if persuaded that the order sought will promote the welfare of the child. The inherent jurisdiction cannot be used to compel a public authority to act in a particular way.[182]

### (ix) The Care Quality Commission

The Care Quality Commission has the job of supervising, registering and inspecting children's homes and care homes. Whether the work of the Commission will improve the position of those who leave care remains to be seen.

## 6 The position of local authority foster carers

Foster carers have proved highly successful in looking after children who have been taken into care. Children will live in the foster carers' homes and be brought up with their families. Foster carers are normally paid an allowance by local authorities to cover the costs of bringing up the child.[183] Evidence suggests that children cared for by foster carers suffer less than children living in children's homes; and even children who have been adopted.[184] However, foster care is rarely intended to be a long-term solution for children in care. It is crucial that at the outset it is made clear to the foster carers and the child whether the arrangement is intended to be a long- or short-term one. Failure to do this could cause great hardship to all the parties. In *Kirklees MDC v S*[185] Bodley J dismissed an appeal against an order that there be daily supervised contact between the birth parents and children now living with foster carers. He felt this was appropriate so that the links between the child and birth family were maintained. The foster carers had to appreciate that they were not to become substitute parents.

The law is structured with the policy of making fostering an attractive option for both foster carers and local authorities. It seeks to strike a balance between enabling foster carers to make decisions in respect of children in their care and ensuring that the local authority's long-term plans for the child are not hindered. Normally, the relationships between the local authority and foster carers are good and negotiations can deal with any problems that arise. However, the courts may become involved when the local authority and foster carers disagree over what should happen to the child and in particular if the local authority wishes to remove the child from the foster carers against their wishes.

---

[181] [1995] 1 FLR 825, [1995] 2 FCR 643.
[182] *Re L (Care Proceedings: Human Rights Claims)* [2004] 1 FCR 289 at para 12.
[183] See Bostock (2004) for a discussion of 'private foster arrangements'. Private fostering is now regulated by Children Act 2004, Part V.
[184] Gibbons, Gallagher, Bell and Gordon (1995).
[185] [2005] Fam Law 769.

The legal position of foster carers is precarious. Their status gives them the right to retain the child until there is a request from the local authority to return the child. The foster carers have limited recourse to the courts if required by the local authority to return the child:

1. The foster carers could apply for a residence or contact order. Foster carers can only seek leave to bring an application for a contact or residence order if:[186]

   (a) the child has lived with the foster carers for at least one year;[187] or
   (b) the local authority consents; or
   (c) they are relatives of the child.

   If none of these conditions exists then foster carers cannot bring an application. This puts foster carers in a weaker position than anyone else. Anyone else can apply for leave to bring an application for a s 8 order in respect of a child.

2. The foster carers could apply to adopt the child.[188] If the foster carers issue a notice of their intention to apply to adopt the child, the court will refuse leave to remove the child until there has been a proper investigation of the adoption application.[189]

3. The foster carers could apply for judicial review of the local authority's decision to remove the child.

4. Foster carers are prevented by s 9(3) from applying for a residence order unless they fall into one of the categories mentioned in point 1, above. However, in a controversial decision,[190] *Gloucestershire CC v P*,[191] the Court of Appeal stated that a court can make a residence order in favour of the foster carers on its own motion under s 10(1)(b), although only in exceptional cases.[192] Thorpe LJ dissented on the ground that this was to use s 10(1)(b) to get around the bar in s 9(3) preventing foster carers applying for residence orders.

It is possible that the relationship between a foster carer and a child could constitute family life and so be protected under article 8 of the European Convention on Human Rights. Whether the relationship does constitute family life seems to depend on the strength of the relationship between the child and foster carers.[193] In the light of this, local authorities will have to have strong justification before removing children from foster carers with whom they have lived for many years.

## 7 Duration of care and supervision orders

A supervision order lasts for up to one year initially, although it can be made for a shorter period.[194] It is possible for the supervisor to apply for an extension for up to three years. The

---

[186] These are the rules if the child is in care. If the child is not in care but accommodated by the local authority the position is slightly different: see Hayes and Williams (1999: 112–15).
[187] Not ending more than three months before the date of the application: CA 1989, s 10(5)(b).
[188] See e.g. *Re A (A Child)(Adoption)* [2008] 1 FCR 55.
[189] *Re C (A Minor) (Adoption)* [1994] 2 FLR 513, [1994] 2 FCR 839.
[190] For criticism, see Lowe and Douglas (1998: 432).
[191] [1999] 2 FLR 61.
[192] See also Wall J in *Re MD and TD (Minors) (No. 2)* [1994] Fam Law 489.
[193] *Gaskin v UK* (1989)12 EHRR 36 at para 49.
[194] See, e.g., *M v Warwickshire* [1994] 2 FLR 593.

welfare principle will cover any application for an extension.[195] Any existing supervision order will be terminated if the court subsequently makes a care order.[196]

A care order lasts until any of the following events occur:

- The child reaches the age of 18.

- The court discharges the care order.[197] The child, the local authority and anyone with parental responsibility may apply for the discharge of a care order.[198] It should be noted that unmarried fathers without parental responsibility cannot therefore apply for a discharge, although the father could apply for a residence order which, if granted, would automatically discharge the care order.[199] According to *Re A (Care: Discharge Application by Child)*,[200] a child applying for discharge of a care order to which he or she is subject does not need leave. The welfare principle[201] governs applications to discharge care orders.[202] In some cases it may be appropriate to discharge a care order and replace it with a supervision order.[203] A care order in relation to a 15-year-old was discharged after the child ran away from authority care and the local authority was unable to return him to their care. The order was doing nothing and so there was no point in maintaining it.[204]

- If the court grants a residence order in respect of a child, this will bring to an end any care order relating to that child.

- An adoption order will bring to an end a care order.

## 8 Duties to children leaving care

Children leaving care are often vulnerable. For example, one in seven girls leaving care is pregnant or has children of her own. It is therefore essential to ensure that there is proper provision for children who are moving out of care.[205] The basic duty of the local authority to a child leaving care is to 'advise, assist and befriend him with a view to promoting his welfare when he ceases to be looked after by them'.[206] The local authority can provide assistance, even exceptionally in cash.[207] Assistance in finding employment may be provided. The provision of services to children leaving care has been widely seen as inadequate.[208] Seven per cent of authorities did not monitor what happened to their children at all and 9 per cent did not monitor what had happened to children who had left their care. This area is now governed

---

[195] *Re A (A Minor) (Supervision Extension)* [1995] 1 FLR 335.

[196] CA 1989, Sch 3, para 10.

[197] A supervision order can be varied or discharged on the application of the child, any person with parental responsibility, or the supervisor. Applications to discharge supervision orders are also governed by the welfare principle, although if the court wished to substitute a supervision order with a care order this does necessitate proof of the significant harm test.

[198] CA 1989, s 39(1). Variation of a care order is not permitted because there is nothing to vary apart from discharging it.

[199] CA 1989, s 91(1).

[200] [1995] 1 FLR 599, [1995] 2 FCR 686, Thorpe J.

[201] CA 1989, s 1.

[202] *Re T (Termination of Contact: Discharge of Order)* [1997] 1 FLR 517.

[203] E.g. *Re O (Care: Discharge of Care Order)* [1999] 2 FLR 119.

[204] *Re C (Care: Discharge of Care Order)* [2010] 1 FLR 774. The court made it clear that even if a care order was being ineffective there may be circumstances which made its retention useful.

[205] Recognised in Department of Health (1999b) and Social Exclusion Unit (1999b).

[206] CA 1989, s 24(1).

[207] CA 1989, s 24(8) and (9); restrictively construed in *R v Kent CC, ex p S* [2000] 1 FLR 155.

[208] Department of Health (2000c: para 2.4).

by the Children (Leaving Care) Act 2000. The aim of the Act is to ensure that children can move successfully from care to 'real life'. The local authority must have 'a pathway plan' which applies until the children are aged 21. The plan should cover their education, training and general plans for the future. There is a general duty to assess the needs of those leaving care. The Act is certainly an improvement on the law as it was previously. The Children and Young Persons Act 2008 will provide a new framework for local authority duties owed to children leaving care.

## 9 The balance of power between courts and local authorities

A recurring theme through the past two chapters has been the delicate balance of power between the courts and local authorities.[209] Courts and local authorities have each complained that the other has exceeded its powers. In *Nottingham CC v P*[210] the court criticised the local authority for failing to apply for a care order, leaving the court powerless to help the child; while in *Re C (Interim Care Order: Residential Assessment)*[211] the local authority felt that the courts were exceeding their powers in ordering the local authority to assess the child at a specialist centre.

How does the Children Act 1989 balance the power between the courts and the local authority? At a simple level the answer is that the courts decide whether to make an order, but the local authority decides how to implement the order. The position has been summarised by the Court of Appeal in *Re R (Care Proceedings: Adjournment)*:[212]

> [T]he judge is not a rubber stamp. But if the threshold criteria have been met and there is no realistic alternative to a care order and to the specific plans proposed by the local authority, the court is likely to find itself in the position of being obliged to hand the responsibility for the future decisions about the child to the local authority . . . To make other than a full care order on the facts of this case was to trespass into the assumption by the court of a control over the local authority which was specifically disallowed by the passing of the Children Act.

However, it is more complex than that. Dewar[213] has suggested two models that could describe the way that the court operates:

1. The first is the adjudicative or umpire model. Here the court simply decides whether a local authority has made out the threshold criteria for an order and will make the order without involving itself in planning issues. In other words, once the court is persuaded that the grounds for an order are made out, the local authority takes over control of what should happen during the order.

2. The second is the active or participatory model. The court should decide not only whether or not there should be an order but also what should happen once the order is made.

There is support for both models in the Children Act 1989 and the case law. In favour of the adjudicative model being an accurate description of the role of the court in this area is

---

[209] Hayes (1996).
[210] [1993] 2 FLR 134, [1994] 1 FCR 624.
[211] [1997] 1 FLR 1, [1997] 1 FCR 149.
[212] [1998] 2 FLR 390, [1998] 3 FCR 654.
[213] Dewar (1995). See also Hayes (1996).

the ethos of partnership, indicating that disputes over what should happen to the child in care should be resolved between the local authority, the parents and the child, without court intervention.[214] In particular, the local authority is required to set up a complaints procedure which is designed to resolve any disputes and avoid the need to refer issues to the court.[215] In favour of the participative model is the fact that the courts retain control over the contact arrangements, although it should be noted that the courts have the power only to require the local authority to ensure contact continues. The courts have no power to order a local authority to prevent contact.[216] The courts also have the power to revoke a care order, for example, by making a residence order.

There have been several cases revealing clashes between the courts and local authorities.[217] The leading case is the following:

## CASE: *Re S, Re W (Children: Care Plan)* [2002] 1 FCR 577[218]

Here the House of Lords was required to consider the extent to which a court could require a local authority to carry out its care order. The Court of Appeal in that case clearly felt frustrated that a judge makes a care order on the basis of a particular care plan, but the local authority may then decide to do something completely different with a child, without having to return to the court.[219] An extreme example might be that the local authority in the care plan proposes keeping the child with the birth family, but providing them with services. The judge, approving of this, makes a care order but the local authority could then decide to place the child with fosterers, with a view ultimately to adoption: quite a different prospect from that foreseen by the judge who made the original care order.[220] It should be added that local authorities tend to depart from care plans not because of malice, but a shortage of funds. One study found that only 60 of the 100 children studied had their care plans fulfilled.[221] The same study suggests that where care plans are implemented this normally promotes the child's welfare better than where the plan is departed from.[222]

The Court of Appeal in *Re S, Re W* therefore came up with a scheme under which, on making the care order, the court could star various items on the care plan (e.g. where the child was to live, crucial services which the local authority was to provide). If subsequently the local authority wished to depart from one of the starred items the local authority should take the matter back to court and seek approval of the course of action. If they failed to do so the matter could be brought before the judge by the guardian.

It must be admitted that there were no sections in the Children Act 1989 which mentioned this starring system. However, the Court of Appeal justified its creation of it ➡

---

[214] Department for Children, Schools and Families (2008a).

[215] CA 1989, s 26(3).

[216] *Re W (Section 34(2) Orders)* [2000] 1 FLR 512.

[217] For an extraordinary judicial expression of outrage at the 'disgraceful' conduct of an adoption agency see *Re F (A Child)(Placement Order)* [2008] 2 FCR 93.

[218] Discussed in Herring (2002b); Miles (2002); Mole (2002); Smith (2002).

[219] In *Re O (Care: Discharge of Care Order)* [1999] 2 FLR 119 the care order was discharged because the care plan had been departed from so radically.

[220] A more realistic example may be that the child is placed with the birth parents under the care order but the promised services are not provided. For an example of a child 'lost in care' while a local authority failed to carry out a care plan see *F v Lambeth LBC* [2001] 3 FCR 738.

[221] Harwin and Owen (2003: 72).

[222] Harwin and Owen (2003: 78). See also Hunt and McLeod (1998: chs 7–9).

by reference to the Human Rights Act 1998. The argument was that on making a care order the state would, inevitably, be interfering in article 8 rights of the child and family. The court would have to make sure that the interference was justified and that the extent of the intervention was proportionate. The only way the court could do this would be to approve the extent of the intervention as set out in the care plan, and require court approval for any further intervention. The House of Lords, however, felt that the Court of Appeal's approach was illegitimate. The Court of Appeal had crossed the line from using the Human Rights Act to interpret legislation, which was permissible, to amending legislation, which was not.[223] The House of Lords pointed out that there were no words in the Children Act which the Court of Appeal were 'interpreting' to produce their starred system; rather, in effect, a new section was being added to the legislation.

The House of Lords went further and claimed that the Court of Appeal's interpretation infringed a cardinal principle in the Children Act 1989. Lord Nicholls explained:

> The court operates as the gateway into care, and makes the necessary care order when the threshold conditions are satisfied and the court considers a care order would be in the best interests of the child. That is the responsibility of the court. Thereafter the court has no continuing role in relation to the care order. Then it is the responsibility of the local authority to decide how the child should be cared for.[224]

In other words, the court has the task of deciding whether or not to make a care order, but the local authority has the task of deciding what should happen to a child who has been taken into care.[225] As Lord Nicholls acknowledges, this principle is not without exception. A local authority cannot, for example, terminate contact between a child in care and his or her family, nor change the child's name or religion without the permission of the court. Indeed, supporters of the Court of Appeal's approach might even claim that the Children Act does leave the courts with control over crucial issues concerning the upbringing of a child in care and therefore the issue is not as straightforward as the House of Lords might have suggested. It is worth noting that Lord Nicholls was clearly not unsympathetic to what the Court of Appeal was doing. He described the Court of Appeal's approach as 'understandable'[226] and made it clear that his objection was that such an approach should be created by Parliament, not the courts.[227]

Having decided that the Court of Appeal's use of the starring system was illegitimate Lord Nicholls then held that the present law (whereby the local authority could decide how to bring up a child in its care free from court supervision) was not incompatible with the rights of the child and his or her family under article 8. He explained that although the law gave the local authority the power to infringe the child's rights (e.g. by disproportionately interfering in his or her article 8 rights) that did not mean that the law itself thereby infringed the child's rights. The fact that the Children Act provided only limited remedies where it was claimed that the local authority had interfered with the child's or his or her family's right to family life did not thereby render the Act itself

---

[223] *Re S, Re W (Children: Care Plan)* [2002] 1 FCR 577 at para 39. This approach to the balance of power between the courts and local authorities was approved in *Kent CC v G* [2005] UKHL 68.

[224] *Re S, Re W (Children: Care Plan)* [2002] 1 FCR 577 at para 28.

[225] For criticism of this see Herring (2002b).

[226] *Re S, Re W (Children: Care Plan)* [2002] 1 FCR 577 at para 35.

[227] For calls for Parliament to reform the law and a useful summary of possible reform proposals see Geekie (2002).

incompatible with the European Convention. This was because the absence of a provision in a statute could not render that statute incompatible with the European Convention.[228] In any event, as Lord Nicholls pointed out, whenever a local authority infringed a child's or his or her family's article 8 rights they could bring proceedings against the local authority under s 7 of the Human Rights Act 1998. This also provided protection for an individual's article 6 rights.[229] He accepted that relying on parents bringing proceedings to protect the rights of a child in care was not fail-proof. A parent may not want or be unable to litigate. In such a case (unless the child was particularly mature) there would be no one who could enforce the child's rights.

In some ways the lesson to be learned from this litigation is that all too often local authorities lack the resources to implement care plans and this might lead to the infringement of the human rights of children in care. Although the temptation may be to enable the court to compel a local authority to abide by care plans, to do so might mean that local authorities will have to withdraw funding from other children in their care. The fact that all too often insufficient funds are available to ensure that the human rights of children in care are protected should shame our society.[230]

In *Re S and W (Children) (Care Proceedings: Care Plan)*[231] the Court of Appeal felt it necessary to return to the issue of how the courts should deal with an unsatisfactory care plan. In that case there was no question but that a care order should be made in respect of three siblings and that they should be removed from their parents. There was, however, substantial dispute among the professionals involved over whether the children should be adopted by strangers or whether they should be fostered by a great-aunt and uncle or grandparents. In relation to one of the three children the local authority care plan was that the child be fostered by the great-uncle and aunt, but the judge clearly thought that plan inappropriate. He adjourned the application to enable the director of social services of the local authority to reconsider the care plan. On appeal it was argued that the judge was acting inappropriately in adjourning the case and asking the local authority to reconsider its plans. It was argued before the Court of Appeal that when a judge was faced with an application for a care order, supported by a care plan, the judge's role was to decide whether or not to make a care order, but not to interfere with the content of the care plan. That argument was fiercely rejected by the Court of Appeal. In fact, they held, the judge had to scrutinise the care plan rigorously and if the judge did not think it met the needs of the child, the court could refuse to make the care order.

In *Nottingham CC v P*[232] the Court of Appeal held that courts have no power to order a local authority to apply for a care order, even though it was convinced that a care order was necessary to protect the child. Sir Stephen Brown stated:

> The court is deeply concerned at the absence of any power to direct this authority to take steps to protect the children. In the former wardship jurisdiction it might well have been able to do so. The operation of the Children Act 1989 is entirely dependent upon the full co-operation of

---

[228] *Re S, Re W (Children: Care Plan)* [2002] 1 FCR 577 at para 59.
[229] Theoretically, if a parent's parental rights were infringed in a way which did not constitute an infringement of their article 8 rights, then it may be that the parent's article 6 rights could be infringed, but, as Lord Nicholls said, it is hard to think of an instance where this would happen.
[230] Herring (2002b).
[231] [2007] EWCA Civ 232.
[232] [1994] Fam 18, [1993] 2 FLR 134, [1994] 1 FCR 624, discussed in Chapter 10.

all those involved. This includes the courts, local authorities, social workers, and all who have to deal with children. Unfortunately, as appears from this case, if a local authority doggedly resists taking the steps which are appropriate to the care of children at risk of suffering significant harm it appears that the court is powerless.

No doubt concerns of this kind led Bracewell J in *Re N (Leave to Withdraw Care Proceedings)*[233] to hold that the court had the power to refuse to permit the local authority to withdraw an application for care proceedings when it felt that the children needed the protection of a care order. This does not sit easily with the argument that a care order cannot be made against the wishes of a local authority.

There is much to be said for the general approach of leaving day-to-day issues relating to the treatment of a child in care to the local authority. The first is a practical one and that is that the court cannot provide continuous guidance relating to children in care, responding to particular issues as they arise. Secondly, some issues relating to the care of abused children lie in the expertise of the local authority's social workers. Thirdly, the local authority will have to balance the needs of all children (and other vulnerable people) in their area with the resources they have available to spend. Although courts are adept in deciding specific issues relating to a particular child, court procedures are not suitable for formulating general policies in allocation of resources. Indeed this may have been the key policy behind the House of Lords' decision in *Re S, Re W (Children: Care Plan)*.[234]

In *G v N County Council*[235] a care order had been made in respect of two children living with their mother. The plan was that the children were to remain with the mother under close supervision. The local authority was worried that the children were being neglected and moved quickly to remove them. The mother successfully challenged the local authority's actions under the Human Rights Act 1998. Macfarlane J emphasised that even though the local authority had a care order they still, in a case such as this, were required to act in a proportionate way in accordance with the law, and ensure that the mother was involved fairly in the decision-making process.

## 10 Secure accommodation orders

The secure accommodation order is available only to local authorities and is used to control the aggressive behaviour of children.[236] The aim is not necessarily to provide treatment, but to ensure that problematic children are in an environment where they pose no danger to themselves or others. If the child is to be placed in secure accommodation[237] for more than 72 hours, court approval through a secure accommodation order is required. The order should be used only as a 'last resort'.[238] The grounds on which a child can be subject to a secure accommodation order are set out in s 25(1) of the Children Act 1989:[239]

---

[233] [2000] 1 FLR 134.

[234] [2002] 1 FCR 577.

[235] [2009] 1 FLR 774.

[236] As well as the secure accommodation order, children can be detained under the Mental Health Act 1983; s 23 of the Children and Young Persons Act 1969; and s 38(6) of the Police and Criminal Evidence Act 1984.

[237] For a discussion of what is secure accommodation, see *Re C (Detention: Medical Treatment)* [1997] 2 FLR 180, [1997] 3 FCR 49.

[238] Department for Children, Schools and Families (2008a: para 5.1).

[239] Detailed regulation is found in the Child (Secure Accommodation) Regulations 1991, SI 1991/1505.

---

**LEGISLATIVE PROVISION**

**Children Act 1989, section 25(1)**

(a) that—
- (i) he has a history of absconding and is likely to abscond from any other description of accommodation; and
- (ii) if he absconds, he is likely to suffer significant harm; or

(b) that if he is kept in any other description of accommodation he is likely to injure himself or other persons.

---

The word 'likely' in this section means a real possibility that cannot sensibly be ignored.[240] The court has no power to make a secure accommodation order in respect of a child over the age of 16.[241] The child's welfare is not the paramount consideration in deciding whether to make a secure accommodation order, as was made clear in *Re M (Secure Accommodation Order)*.[242] It will be recalled that one of the purposes of the order is for the protection of the public, in which case the order may be justifiable, even if it is not for the child's benefit. The court's role is simply to test the evidence and fix the duration of the order, but not to determine what happens to the child during the accommodation.[243] A local authority must review the detention one month after the making of the order and thereafter every three months. The local authority must be satisfied that the criteria are still met and that detention is necessary.[244]

In *Re K (A Child) (Secure Accommodation Order: Right to Liberty)*[245] the Court of Appeal held that a secure accommodation order deprived a child of liberty and therefore fell within article 5 of the European Convention on Human Rights, which makes it clear that 'nobody shall be deprived of his liberty save in the following cases and in accordance with a procedure prescribed by law'.[246] The article lists the circumstances in which a detention may be permitted. A secure accommodation order could be compliant with the article on the basis of article 5(1)(d), which permits: 'the detention of a minor by lawful order for the purpose of educational supervision or his lawful detention for the purpose of bringing him before the competent legal authority'. Dame Elizabeth Butler-Sloss explained that education in article 5(1)(d) included education broadly defined. However, it would not be possible to use a secure accommodation order simply to punish or detain a child if there was no educational element in what was being done.[247]

---

[240] *S v Knowsley BC* [2004] EWHC 491 (Fam).
[241] A child under the age of 16 in whose favour a secure accommodation order is made, but who subsequently becomes 16, could be accommodated under CA 1989, s 20(5): *Re G (Secure Accommodation)* [2000] 2 FLR 259, [2000] 2 FCR 385.
[242] [1995] 1 FLR 418.
[243] *Re W (A Minor) (Secure Accommodation Order)* [1993] 1 FLR 692.
[244] *LM v Essex CC* [1999] 1 FLR 988. A failure to do this could lead to a successful judicial review: *S v Knowsley BC* [2004] Fam Law 653.
[245] [2001] 1 FCR 249 CA, discussed in Masson (2002b).
[246] In *Bouamar v Belgium* (1987) 11 EHRR 1, where a person with a history of aggressive behaviour was detained, the court suggested that the detention was lawful only if the matter was brought speedily before the court.
[247] *Re M (A Child) (Secure Accommodation)* [2001] 1 FCR 692 emphasises that children have rights under article 6 to a fair trial in applications for secure accommodation orders.

## 11 Adoption

### A The use of adoption today

The history of adoption reveals changes within our society.[248] Legal adoption started with the passing of the Adoption of Children Act 1926.[249] Before then informal adoption had taken place under the guise of wet-nursing, apprenticeship and informal arrangements for the care of a child.[250] Traditionally, adoption was regarded as a convenient way of handing children born to an unmarried mother to a married infertile couple.[251] It was seen as a blessing to all concerned: the unmarried mother could quietly and without embarrassment get rid of the child, who would otherwise be a public witness to her sin, and the married couple would be provided with the child they so longed for. Nowadays adoption is viewed rather differently, with the interests of the child, rather than the adults, being at the forefront of the law's concern.

Adoption is now seen as a service for children, rather than provision for infertile couples.[252] It is one of the ways in which the state may arrange care for children whose parents are unable or unwilling to care for them. Infertile couples are now more likely to turn to assisted reproduction than an adoption agency. Unmarried mothers are unlikely to feel that such is the stigma of extramarital birth that they should put up their children for adoption. Indeed, only about 50 mothers a year place their babies for adoption and this is usually because of the child's disability or their mother's personal circumstances.[253] Further, in recent years half of all adoptions have involved the mother and stepfather adopting the mother's child,[254] so that the stepfather can become the child's father in the eyes of the law.

Traditionally, adoption was based on the 'transplant' model, namely that children would be transplanted from one family and inserted into a new family. The child would cease to be a member of his or her 'old family' and would become a full member of the new family. Baroness Hale has explained:

> an adoption order does far more than deprive the birth parents of their parental responsibility for bringing up the child and confer it upon her adoptive parents (provided for in article 12 [of the ECHR]). It severs, irrevocably and for all time, the legal relationship between a child and her family of birth. It creates, irrevocably and for all time (unless the child is later adopted again into another family), a new legal relationship, not only between the child and her adoptive parents, but between the child and each of her adoptive parent's families.[255]

However, increasingly the transplant model is under challenge.[256] One of England's leading family lawyers has written: 'Much of the case for adoption seems to rest on meeting the insecurities of long-term carers, but it is questionable whether the only or best means of addressing these understandable insecurities is through what has been called a "constructed affiliation".'[257] While not arguing for the abolition of adoption, he sees it as suitable only in

---

[248] Goody (1983), Douglas and Philpot (2003), O'Halloran (2003) discuss the changing nature of adoption.
[249] Bridge and Swindells (2003: ch. 1). Cretney (2003a: ch. 17) provides an excellent history of adoption.
[250] Goody (1983).
[251] Department of Health (1999a).
[252] Lewis (2004). See Thoburn (2003) for a useful discussion of the effectiveness of adoption.
[253] Parker (1999: 4).
[254] Lord Chancellor's Department (2000).
[255] *Re P* [2008] UKHL 38, para 85.
[256] As Lewis (2004) points out, many children are used to having several parent figures in their lives.
[257] Bainham (2008a: 349).

rare cases. One of the significant changes in the nature of adoption is that the average age of children being adopted has risen.[258] The older the child is, the more likely it is that he or she will be aware of who his or her biological parents are and that it will be appropriate for the adopted child to retain contact with his or her natural parents.[259] In such cases the transplant model is unsuitable. Further, the skills required of a parent adopting a newborn baby are different from those for taking care of an older child with a troubled history. So the kind of people who are adopting is changing too.[260]

---

### KEY STATISTICS

The following statistcs relate to England and only to children looked after by local authorities.[261] They do not include children adopted by relatives.

- 3,300 children were adopted in 2009. That was the same number as in 2007, but slightly down on the number in 2005 (3,800).

- Only 2% of children adopted were under the age of 1. Seventy-two per cent were aged 1–4.[262]

- The reason give for the adoption was neglect or abuse in 73% of cases, and the child's disability in only 1% of cases.

- 82% of children adopted were white and in only 3% were the child listed as black or black British.

- Two people adopted in 92% of cases, while a single person adopted in 8% of cases.

- Three per cent of adoptions were to a same-sex couple, with the couple being in a civil partnership in two-thirds of those cases, 82% of adoptions were to a married couple and 6% to an unmarried opposite-sex couple.

---

The Government has sought to increase the number of adoption orders, but to date has had relatively little success: 5,680 adoption orders were made in England and Wales during 2002, this had fallen to 4,637 in 2007.[263] Despite the falling numbers there have been claims, rejected by the Government, that local authorities have been inappropriately placing children for adoption in order to meet targets.[264] It should be noted that adoption is still used for only a small number of children looked after by local authorities (around 6 per cent).[265] Of children in England and Wales who were entered on the adoption register in 2008, 793 were born to a married couple and 3,960 to an unmarried couple.[266]

The law on adoption was significantly reformed by the Adoption and Children Act 2002. The Act was premised on the belief that adoption was underused by local authorities, was uncoordinated[267] and riddled with delays.[268] One of the primary motivations behind the legislation was to increase the number of children being adopted. The Government is

---

[258] Lowe (1997a).
[259] Ryburn (1998).
[260] *Re P* [2008] UKHL 38, para 91.
[261] Department for Children, Schools and Families (2010a). For discussion see Hayden (2010).
[262] Department for Children, Schools and Families (2010a).
[263] There has been a delay in production of the statistics on court orders.
[264] BBC Newsonline (2008g). See also the discussion in Sagar and Hitchings (2007).
[265] Selwyn, Fraser and Quinton (2006).
[266] 312 were listed as unknown: National Statistics (2010a).
[267] Department of Health (2000e).
[268] See, e.g., Morgan (1999a).

convinced that adoption benefits children. This could be supported on the basis of psychological evidence that children in care permanently placed with a family suffer less than children living in institutional children's homes.[269] Research on adopted children even indicates
that there is no difference between the well-being of adopted children and children living
with their biological parents.[270] Indeed, the majority of adopted children fare better on various
indicia than children with comparable starts in life who live with their birth parents.[271] Despite
the widespread assumption that adoption benefits children, in fact there has been remarkably
little research into the benefits of adoption. Those studies that have been carried out tend
to suggest that adoption is beneficial, but the picture is not straightforward and much more
research needs to be done before we can confidently assert that adoption is superior to
long-term fostering.[272] That said, when considering the benefits of adoption it should not be
forgotten that the statistics on children who remain in care are grim.[273]

The Government has stated that the following principles will govern the law and practice
under the Adoption and Children Act 2002:

- Children are entitled to grow up as part of a loving family which can meet their needs
during childhood and beyond.
- It is best for children where possible to be brought up by their own birth family.
- The child's wishes and feelings will be actively sought and fully taken into account at all
stages.
- Children's ethnic origin, cultural background, religion and language will be fully recognised and positively valued and promoted when decisions are made.
- The role of adoptive parents in offering a permanent family to a child who cannot live
with their birth family will be valued and respected.[274]

In *Re F (A Child) (Placement Order)*[275] Wall LJ set out the four objectives of the Act:

> The first was to simplify the process. The second was to enable a crucial element of the decision
> making process to be undertaken at an earlier stage. The third was to shift the emphasis to a
> concentration on the welfare of the child; and the fourth was to avoid delay.

We will now consider these issues in more detail.

## B Encouraging adoption

For many years the numbers of adoptions have been in gradual decline and it had been
forecast that adoption would become of little practical relevance for family lawyers. However,
the Government indicated its desire to greatly increase the number of adoption orders being
made. This aim has surprised some, given that the adoption rate from care of children in
the UK is already one of the highest in the world.[276] Lowe and Murch express the concern

---

[269] Quinton and Selwyn (2006a and b); Barton and Douglas (1995: 350); Department of Health (2000e).
Judicially acknowledged in *Re F (A Minor) (Adoption: Parental Agreement)* [1982] 3 FLR 101.
[270] Bohman and Sigvardsson (1990).
[271] Ryburn (1998: 55–6); Rushton (2002).
[272] Eekelaar (2003a); Warman and Roberts (2003). Grotevant and McRoy (1998), for example, in a US study
find no evidence that adoption benefits children.
[273] Performance and Innovation Unit (2000a: report box 2.3).
[274] Department of Health (2003d).
[275] [2008] 2 FCR 93, para 72.
[276] Tolson (2002).

that 'authorities, keen to meet their percentage target for adoption, may too hastily rule out rehabilitation with the birth parents or wider family, particularly for young children who are likely to be thought more adoptable'.[277] The Adoption and Children Act 2002 seeks to improve the adoption rates by the following means:

1. There will be a national register of people who wish to adopt a child and children who need to be adopted. Before the 2002 Act each local adoption agency made its own efforts in trying to match would-be adopters and children. In cases where children had particular needs (e.g. children from minority religious or cultural backgrounds) it could be difficult for small adoption agencies to find suitable adopters. The setting up of the national register should assist in such cases.

2. Local authorities are required to maintain an adoption service under s 3 of the Adoption and Children Act 2002. The adoption service must make arrangements for adoption and provide adoption support services.[278] Under s 5 of the 2002 Act local authorities must prepare a plan for adoption services in their area. Prior to the 2002 Act, how adoption services were carried out was very much a matter for an individual local authority. A study by Lowe and Murch[279] found wide variations in the use made of adoption by different local authorities. These variations could not be explained simply on the basis of the kind of children in their care. The 2002 Act is intended to create a more co-ordinated approach which will be subject to greater central government control. The Secretary of State has issued National Adoption Standards and other regulations which govern the way local authorities must perform their obligations concerning adoption.[280]

3. Section 1 of the Adoption and Children Act 2002 states: 'Whenever a court or adoption agency is coming to a decision relating to the adoption of a child the paramount consideration must be the child's welfare, throughout his life.' This is intended to discourage the court from refusing to make an adoption order because of the rights of the birth family.

## C Adoption and secret birth

There have been several cases where a mother has not wanted the wider family (including her parents) to be informed about the birth of a child.[281] Generally in such a case the rights of the mother to anonymity have been seen to trump any rights of the wider family to be considered as carers of the child. This was explained by Holman J in *Z CC v R*:[282]

> There is, in my judgment, a strong social need, if it is lawful, to continue to enable some mothers, such as this mother, to make discreet, dignified and humane arrangements for the birth and subsequent adoption of their babies, without their families knowing anything about it, if the mother, for good reason, so wishes.

However, it would be wrong to think that the privacy rights of the parents will always win out in such cases. In *Birmingham CC v S, R and A*[283] a father did not want his parents to be told about the birth or considered as adopters. However, the Court of Appeal held that the

---

[277] Lowe and Murch (2002: 149).
[278] In this regard they must work in conjunction with other services.
[279] Lowe and Murch (2002).
[280] E.g. Department for Education and Skills (2005c); Suitability of Adopters Regulations 2005, SI 2005/1712; The Adoption Agency Regulations 2005, SI 2005/389.
[281] *Re R (A Child) (Adoption: Disclosure)* [2001] 1 FCR 238.
[282] [2001] Fam Law 8.
[283] [2006] EWHC 3065 (Fam).

father's objections could not carry weight because it could not be assumed that his parents would not be interested in caring for the child. They explained:

> Adoption is a last resort for any child. It is only to be considered when neither of the parents nor the wider family and friends can reasonably be considered as potential carers for the child. To deprive a significant member of the wider family of the information that the child exists who might otherwise be adopted, is a fundamental step that can only be justified on cogent and compelling grounds.[284]

Such grounds were not found in that case. It is interesting to note that this case involved the father, rather than the mother, wishing to keep the birth secret. The court made little of this point, but it is interesting to speculate whether the courts think that a mother has a greater right to secrecy than a father.

A rather different attitude can be detected in *C v XYZ CC*[285] where the Court of Appeal confirmed that there was nothing in the Adoption and Children Act 2002 which compelled a local authority to disclose the identity of a child to the extended family against the mother's wishes. The mother wanted neither the father nor their wider families to know of the birth. The Court of Appeal held that section 1 of the 2002 Act did not privilege the birth family over adoptive parents, 'simply because they are the birth family', although placing a child with a birth family will 'often be in the best interests of the child'.[286] The Court of Appeal believed that the requirement in section 1(4)(f) of the 2002 Act to consider the relationships which a child has could include relationships which have the potential to develop in the future, even if there is currently no relationship. That included, in this case, the grandparents. However, the overall conclusion of the court was that in this particular case informing the family would further delay finding an alternative home for the child. As to any Human Rights Act claims, it was held that the father had no family right with the child and so he could not claim any right to be informed of the birth. Interestingly, it was held that the grandparents did have a right to be informed of the birth under article 8(1), but that interference in their rights was justified. Brief mention was made of the argument that the child may have a right to family life, but any interference in that could be justified if the adoption was approved under article 8(2). It is surprising that the grandparents, but not the father, were found to have a right to be informed of the birth. This is not fully explained in the judgment, but it may have been because the father had indicated that he had no interest in the child and wanted to play no role in the child's life, while the grandparents had not had an opportunity to develop family life with the child.

The contrast between the two cases is striking and it is clear that there are a number of issues at play. First, there is the argument in *Birmingham CC v S, R and A*[287] that care within the family is less interventionist in family life than arranging care outside the family, and so that possibility should be investigated properly to ensure that extra-familial care is a proportionate response to the risks of harm facing the child. Second, there is the argument in *Re C v XYZ CC*[288] over whether the father or wider family had rights protected by the ECHR, with the rather surprising conclusion that the father did not, but the grandparents did.[289] Both of these arguments reflect an interesting issue about the definition of family life and

---

[284] Para 75.
[285] [2007] EWCA Civ 1206, discussed in Sloan (2009).
[286] Para 18.
[287] [2006] EWHC 3065 (Fam).
[288] [2007] EWCA Civ 1206.
[289] For strong opposition to this decision see Bainham (2008b: 350).

whose family life we are talking about. If the focus is on the right of the child to family life and this is taken to include a right to be raised by her family then it could be argued that a court should be satisfied that wider family members are appropriate as carers of a child. However, if a child's primary right to family life is to be cared for by her parents, or at least have contact with them, it is not hard to imagine cases where contact is more likely to flourish where the child is cared for outside the family – where the relationship between the child's grandparents and parents is bad, for example.

## D Who can adopt?

As part of the attempt to encourage an increase in the rate of adoption, the 2002 Act extends the category of those who can adopt. Now anyone can adopt, subject to the following restrictions:

1. An adoptive parent must be at least 21 years old. However, if a parent is adopting his or her own child then he or she need only be 18.[290]

2. If a couple wish to adopt together they must be married, civil partners or 'living as partners in an enduring family relationship'.[291] If a couple are in a casual relationship this would mean they could not adopt together, but one of them could adopt a child alone.

3. A single person can adopt. But a married person can only adopt alone if he or she satisfies the court that his or her spouse cannot be found; or is incapable by reason of ill-health of applying for the adoption; or that the spouses have separated and it is likely to be a permanent separation.[292]

4. There are complex rules which set out domicile or habitual residence requirements for would-be adopters.[293]

5. An adoption agency cannot place any child for adoption where a person over the age of 18 has been convicted or cautioned for a specified offence (e.g. child abuse).

At the time, one of the most controversial aspects of the 2002 Act was that it permitted adoption by a same-sex couple. In fact the change was not as dramatic as might at first appear, for two reasons. First, even before the Act a gay or lesbian person could adopt alone and then, together with his or her partner, apply for a joint residence order, granting them both parental responsibility for the child.[294] Secondly, although the Act states that a same-sex couple may adopt a child, the Act says nothing about whether or not the sexual orientation or marital status of an applicant should count for or against a couple being considered for adoption. It is submitted that it should be uncontroversial that if it is in the best interests of a child to be adopted by a same-sex or unmarried couple the court should be able to permit the adoption to go ahead.[295] Otherwise one would have to take the view that it would *always* be preferable for a child to remain in state care, rather than be adopted by the most suitable unmarried or same-sex couple – a view it would be hard to accept.[296] Indeed for that very reason the House

---

[290] Adoption and Children Act 2002 (hereafter ACA 2002), s 50.
[291] ACA 2002, s 144(4). See A. Marshall (2003).
[292] ACA 2002, s 51.
[293] ACA 2002, s 49(2), (3). See *Re A (Adoption: Removal)* [2009] 2 FLR 597.
[294] *Re AB (Adoption: Joint Residence)* [1996] 1 FLR 27, [1996] 1 FCR 633.
[295] *Re P* [2008] UKHL 38, discussed Herring (2009a).
[296] *Re P (Adoption: Unmarried Couple)* [2008] 2 FCR 366 finding it would be contrary to the Human Rights Act 1998 not to allow an unmarried couple to adopt. But see Wardle (2004) for an argument that unmarried couples should not be permitted to adopt.

of Lords, when considering Northern Irish legislation, held that it would be contrary to the Human Rights Act 1998 to forbid unmarried couples to adopt. In fact, the evidence available generally on parenting by same-sex parents suggests there is no reason to believe children adopted by same-sex couples will be in any way disadvantaged.[297] Despite this, one small-scale study found same-sex couples were disadvantaged in the adoption process.[298]

## E Who can be adopted?

Only a person under the age of 19 can be adopted, although the application must be made before that person's eighteenth birthday.[299] In other countries it is possible for one adult to adopt another. This is normally done to enable them legally to become family members, which may have significance in relation to, for example, inheritance rights. It has been used by some gay couples in the United States as a way of enabling their relation to be recognised as a family one.[300] Although the child does not need to consent to the adoption, in the case of a child with sufficient understanding they should be consulted through the process and offered counselling. It is hard to imagine that an adoption agency would want to place a child for adoption who opposed it.

## F Selecting adopters and matching adopters and children

Before setting out the procedures for matching adopters and children, we need to appreciate a tension in the law's goals here. A court will be willing to make an adoption order only if it is decided that there is no realistic hope of the child living with the birth family in the foreseeable future and that the adoption will promote the child's welfare. There are, therefore, difficulties in cases where the birth family objects to the adoption. When are their objections to be considered? If they are left to the end of the process, there could be a situation where the child has been placed with adopters for a trial period which has gone very well, with raised hope of the adopters and perhaps the child, which are dashed when at the final hearing the judge decides that the birth parents are justifiably objecting to the proposed adoption. However, if the consent of the birth parents is dealt with as the first issue the judge is in the difficult position of having to decide whether to dispense with the parents' consent, without knowing whether or not the proposed adopters will be suitable. The solution adopted by the 2002 Act is that the consent issue should be dealt with early on in the process, at the stage of the placement. However, if there is a change in circumstances then at the final hearing the parents have a further chance to object.

The road to adoption under the Adoption and Children Act 2002 involves the following stages:

1. *Planning for adoption.* The local authority should consider whether adoption is suitable for every child in its care. If it decides that the birth family are unable to meet a child's needs in the foreseeable future and that adoption is likely to provide the best means of doing so, then a plan for adoption should be drawn up.[301] As with all decisions that a local

---

[297] Tasker and Bellamy (2008).

[298] Hitchings and Sagar (2007).

[299] ACA 2002, ss 47(9) and 49(4). In *Re B (Adoption Order: Nationality)* [1999] 1 FLR 907 the House of Lords approved of the making of an adoption order of a 16-year-old to enable her grandparents to take care of her in this country.

[300] See also *Bedinger v Graybill's Trustee* (1957) (302) SW (2nd) 594 where a husband adopted his wife!

[301] ACA 2002, s 1.

authority makes in relation to a child in care, his or her parents must be sufficiently involved in the planning process. This does not mean that they must be involved in every meeting, but they must be sufficiently involved to protect their interests.[302] In deciding whether to pursue adoption the local authority must also consider the likelihood of finding appropriate adopters. A severely disabled child may be harder to place; a child under the age of 4 with no direct links to family members will be much easier.[303]

In making the decision to consider adoption, a delicate balance has to be drawn. On the one hand, if the local authority believes that there is a hope of rehabilitation with the birth parents it will be reluctant to pursue an adoption. On the other hand, delaying adoption because of a faint hope of rehabilitation may mean the child has to spend years in limbo, making the chance of success of any later adoption more remote. Some local authorities use a process known as twin-tracking to deal with this difficulty: at the same time, work is done on the one hand with the family in an effort to pursue rehabilitation with the birth parent, while on the other hand preparations are made to find an alternative secure home for the child.[304] Such procedures can be difficult for all involved and require trust and commitment all round. There may also be concerns that such procedures may cause confusion for the child. Another scheme is known as concurrent planning, where a child is placed with foster carers on the understanding that they will assist in attempts to rehabilitate the child with the birth parents, but, if that fails, the foster carers will be considered as adopters.[305]

2. *Assessing would-be adopters.* When a couple or an individual approaches an adoption agency, wishing to be considered as an adopter, they will be assessed by the agency.[306] Many agencies take the view that the process should be as much about the agency deciding whether the couple are suitable to be adopters, as about assisting the couple to decide whether they wish to adopt. Applicants must be treated fairly, openly and with respect.[307] In the past there were concerns over the assessment of would-be adopters. Television programmes and newspaper articles claimed that some adoption agencies attached improper significance to irrelevant factors such as people's weight, smoking habits and religious beliefs.[308] There were also complaints that the assessments used were improperly invasive. In response the Adoption Agency Regulations 2005 set out the grounds that should be taken into account.[309] This should at least ensure there is consistency in practice between the different agencies.

3. *The preparation of the report.* The adoption agency must interview and assess anyone who puts themselves forward as potential adopters and then prepare a detailed report for the agency's adoption panel.[310] The report might comment on the applicant's relationships, health and lifestyle, and will take up references. Attitudes to child care, and the use of corporal punishment will be considered too.[311]

---

[302] *Scott v UK* [2000] 1 FLR 958.
[303] Lowe and Murch (2002: 141).
[304] The courts have approved such schemes: e.g. *Re R (Child of Teenage Mother)* [2000] 2 FLR 660.
[305] Monck, Reynolds and Wigfall (2003).
[306] See Suitability of Adopters Regulations 2005, SI 2005/1712 for the procedures which should be followed.
[307] Department for Education and Skills (2005c: standards B 1–7).
[308] See Kamil (2009) for a discussion of fattism in the adoption process. See Selwyn and Sempik (2010) for a discussion of the decline of voluntary adoption agencies.
[309] See, further, Department for Education and Skills (2006b).
[310] This is required by the Department for Education and Skills (2006b).
[311] *R (A) v Newham London Borough Council* [2009] 1 FCR 545.

4. *The adoption agency's decision on the applicant's suitability.* In the light of the report, the adoption agency will decide whether or not to approve the adopters. Although the report prepared by the panel will be taken into account, the decision is ultimately one for the agency. At present it appears that 95 per cent of applicants put before the agency are approved. This figure may seem very high, but it should be appreciated that most candidates thought unsuitable for adoption will have withdrawn from the process before the final report is placed before the panel.

An applicant who was rejected as an adopter by a local authority could apply for judicial review of the local authority's decision.[312] Alternatively, a claim could be made under the Human Rights Act. There is no right to adopt under the ECHR.[313] However, if an applicant could demonstrate that he or she was denied an adoption in a way which discriminated against him or her in a way prohibited by article 14 (e.g. on the grounds of race) then arguably that would infringe his or her rights. In *Fretté v France*[314] the European Court found that it was permissible for a state to prohibit a single homosexual man from adopting. It was held that the right to respect for family life presupposed the existence of a family and did not provide the right to found a family. Therefore it was not possible to claim a right to adopt a child under article 8. Given that no Convention right had been infringed it was not possible for the applicant to rely on article 14 and claim that his Convention rights had been infringed in a way which had unlawfully discriminated against him. However, in *EB v France*[315] the ECtHR in Grand Chamber held that it was unlawful discrimination not to allow a same-sex couple to adopt a child.[316] Although *Fretté v France*[317] was not overruled, it appears unlikely to be followed in the future.

5. *Matching the child and adopter.* If the adopter(s) is (or are) approved, the agency must then consider whether there are any children needing to be adopted who are an appropriate match. If there are, the applicants will be given brief details of the children. If the applicants are keen to proceed then the adoption panel will prepare a report for the adoption agency on the proposed match.[318]

6. *The agency approves the match.* The adoption agency will need to approve of the proposal that adoption between the child and would-be adopter should be pursued. It should be remembered that s 1 of the Act applies to the agency. Thus the agency should approve the match if to do so would promote the child's welfare. The agency will have to pay due regard to the child's religious persuasion, racial origin and cultural and linguistic background.[319] However, political policies (e.g. political objections to transracial adoption) should not be allowed to prevent the pursuing of an adoption which would promote the child's best interests.[320]

---

[312] *R (AT, TT and S) v Newham London Borough Council* [2009] 1 FLR 311.

[313] *Fretté v France* [2003] 2 FCR 39.

[314] [2003] 2 FCR 39.

[315] [2008] 1 FCR 236.

[316] See Curry-Sumner (2009) for a helpful discussion of the case.

[317] [2003] 2 FCR 39.

[318] A child may be placed with it being undecided whether adoption or long-term fostering will be more appropriate: *Re P (Placement Orders: Parental Consent)* [2008] EWCA Civ 535.

[319] See the discussion in *Re C (Adoption: Religious Observance)* [2002] 1 FLR 1119 and *Haringey v Mr and Mrs E* [2006] EWHC 1620 (Fam).

[320] Lowe and Murch (1999): 31% of agencies said that they would not place a child transracially.

---

**TOPICAL ISSUE**

### Transracial adoption

The issue of transracial adoption is a controversial one.[321] At one extreme there are concerns that adoption can become a means of taking children away from deprived black families and giving them to infertile middle-class white couples. There is also conflicting evidence concerning whether children whose race differs from that of their primary carers suffer from confusions over their cultural identity. To others transracial adoption is to be encouraged as part of the creation of a racially and culturally diverse and mixed society.[322] Section 1(5) of the Adoption and Children Act 2002 requires the court when considering the placement of children to give 'due consideration' to the child's racial origin. The guidance states that although there are 'clearly benefits' from the child being placed with adopters who share the child's ethnic background, that may not always be possible.[323] Certainly there should not be undue delay in trying to ensure that the child is placed with an adopter of the same background.[324]

---

7. *The adopters are provided with a full report on the child.* The would-be adopters at this stage will be provided with a full report on the child's health, needs and history.[325]

8. *Placement of the child with the would-be adopters.* The next stage will be the placement of the child with the adopters for what is, in effect, a trial period.[326] To place a child, the agency must either have the consent of each parent with parental responsibility[327] or must have obtained a placement order from the court.[328] The issue of placement is complex and will be discussed in more detail shortly.

9. *The agency applies for an adoption order.* If the placement has worked well, the final stage will be for the adoption agency to apply for an adoption order. It is not possible to apply for an adoption order unless there has been a placement order or the parents are consenting to the adoption, with one exception: that is, foster carers who have looked after the child for at least 12 months, who can apply without satisfying any further requirements.[329] This will be discussed further shortly.

## G Placement for adoption

As we have just seen, the placement of a child with potential adopters plays a crucial role in the process for adoption. To place a child, the agency must either have the consent of each

---

[321] See the discussions in Hayes (1995); Morgan (1999a); Gupta (2002).

[322] Murphy (2000).

[323] Department for Education and Skills (2006c; 62). See, further, Hayes (2003).

[324] In *Re B-M (Care Orders)* [2009] 2 FLR 20 where there had been extensive threats to the children as a result of 'honour violence' it was thought best to foster the children outside the Muslim community,

[325] A local authority may be liable in tort if it fails to provide relevant information which, if disclosed, would have persuaded the adopters not to go ahead with the adoption: *A and B v Essex CC* [2002] EWHC 2709 (Fam).

[326] See the speech of Baroness Hale in *Down Lisburn v H* [2006] UKHL 36 for a powerful critique of the law prior to the 2002 Act on 'freeing' (the procedure which was replaced by placement).

[327] ACA 2002, s 19(1), unless care proceedings are pending (s 19(3)).

[328] ACA 2002, ss 21(3), 52.

[329] ACA 2002, s 47.

parent with parental responsibility[330] or must have obtained a placement order from the court.[331] These two alternatives will now be considered:

1. *Placement by consent.* Parental consent can be specific (i.e. the parents consent to the child being placed with a particular person or people) or general (i.e. the parents consent to the child being placed with whomever the local authority believes to be appropriate). However, if at any time a parent withdraws his or her consent then the agency must apply for a placement order or return the child to the parents.[332] Once consent to placement is granted, the agency acquires parental responsibility, but the birth parents do not lose it. However, the agency is entitled to restrict the way parents can exercise their parental responsibility.

2. *Placement by placement order.*[333] The court can make a placement order only if all of the following are satisfied:

   (a) Either a care order has already been made in respect of the child or the court is satisfied that the significant harm test in s 31 of the Children Act 1989 (see Chapter 10) is satisfied.

   (b) Parental consent has been given or been dispensed with.[334] Dispensing with parental consent will be dealt with in more detail in a later section, but in brief this can happen if to do so will promote the child's welfare.

   (c) The court is persuaded that it is better to make the placement order than not to do so.[335]

The welfare principle applies when the court is making a placement order. The placement order can be made, even if it is foreseen that there may be difficulties in placing the child or even concerns that adoption may not be able to take place.[336] However, where the children are not even suitable for placement (e.g. due to their emotional state), a placement order would not be appropriate.[337] In *NS-H v Kingston Upon Hull City Council and MC*[338] the Court of Appeal explained that placement was only suitable where 'the child is presently in a *condition* to be adopted and is *ready* to be adopted'. If that was not true, then a placement order was not appropriate, and if necessary could be revoked.

The placement order grants the local authority parental responsibility.[339] It brings to an end any contact order in operation.[340] On the making of a placement order the prospective adopters will acquire parental responsibility while the child is with them. If the child is not with prospective adopters then the agency will have parental responsibility. The birth parents will retain parental responsibility if they have it, but the agency can decide the extent to which it can be exercised.[341] A placement order also prohibits the removal of the child from the adopters by anyone (including, most importantly, the birth parents) except the local authority.[342]

---

[330] ACA 2002, s 19(1), unless care proceedings are pending (s 19(3)).
[331] ACA 2002, ss 21(3), 52.
[332] ACA 2002, ss 22, 31 and 32. If the birth parent(s) do not wish to be involved any further in the process they are entitled to ask that they not be informed of any application for adoption (s 20(4)).
[333] Article 6 of the European Convention on Human Rights requires that legal aid be made available: *P, C, S v UK* [2002] 2 FLR 631.
[334] If consent has been given the local authority is likely to go down the route of placement by consent.
[335] ACA 2002, s 1(6).
[336] *Re T (Children: Placement Order)* [2008] 1 FCR 633.
[337] *Re T (Children: Placement Order)* [2008] 1 FCR 633.
[338] [2008] 2 FLR 918.
[339] ACA 2002, s 25(1).
[340] ACA 2002, s 26(1).
[341] ACA 2002, s 25.
[342] ACA 2002, ss 34(1), 47(4).

Once a placement order has been made, only in exceptional circumstances will the birth family be able to raise objections to an adoption order.[343] This means that once the placement order has been made the would-be adopters can go ahead with the placement secure in the knowledge that if the placement works well the birth family are very unlikely to undermine it.

Before making a placement order, the court is required to consider the arrangements for contact between the child and birth family.[344] The placement order will terminate any existing contact order, but on making the placement order the court can make a contact order. It can also authorise the agency to refuse contact between the child and any named person.[345] The placement order can be subject to conditions. In particular the court can make the placement order subject to condition that the child keeps contact with the birth family.

The placement order can be revoked if it is decided that there is no plan for adoption.[346] The adoption agency can apply for a revocation. Once the child has been placed,[347] birth parents cannot apply for revocation unless they have the leave of the court,[348] which will be granted only if there has been a change of circumstances and granting leave would promote the welfare of the child.[349] If the child was in care then the revocation of the placement order will lead to the care order taking full effect.[350]

It is illegal for anyone except an adoption agency to place a child for adoption with a person who is not a relative.[351] If parents wish to have their child adopted they should contact an adoption agency. Only local authorities and adoption societies can run adoption services.[352] There are even criminal offences if an unauthorised person seeks to run an adoption service.[353] Where a couple have unlawfully brought a child to the UK the court will not normally then allow the couple to adopt the child.[354]

## H The making of an adoption order

It is not possible for an adoption to occur without a court order. So, if a couple take into their home a child and raise him or her as their own child this will not be an adoption. Before considering an adoption order the court will have to be satisfied that the placement criteria have been met. The exact requirement depends on the nature of the applicants:

- If the adoption is arranged by an adoption agency then the child must have lived with the applicants for at least ten weeks before the application is made.

- If the adoption is a non-agency case and the applicant is a step-parent or partner of the parent then the minimum period is six months.

---

[343] ACA 2002. s 47.

[344] ACA 2002, ss 26, 27(4).

[345] ACA 2002, s 27.

[346] The child is treated as placed for adoption when the local authority has approved the panel's matching recommendation: *R (W) v Brent London Borough Council* [2010] 1 FLR 1914.

[347] *Re S (Placement Order: Revocation)* [2009] 1 FLR 503.

[348] See *S-H v Kingston-Upon-Hull* [2008] EWCA Civ 493 for a case where the parent was granted leave to apply to revoke the placement order, because the child was not thriving during placement. See also *Re B (Placement Order)* [2008] 2 FLR 1404 where a placement order was revoked following incorrect procedures being used by the adoption panel.

[349] *Re M (Children) (Placement Order)* [2007] 3 FCR 681. If an application for revocation has been made a child may not be placed for adoption: s 24 ACA 2002, although that does not apply to an application for leave to apply for revocation: *Re F (A Child) (Placement Order)* [2008] 2 FCR 93.

[350] ACA 2002, s 29(1).

[351] ACA 2002, ss 92, 93. See *Re MW (Adoption: Surrogacy)* [1995] 2 FLR 759, for a pre-2002 Act example.

[352] ACA 2002, s 92.

[353] ACA 2002, s 93.

[354] *Northumberland County Council v Z* [2010] 1 FCR 494.

- If the adoption is a non-agency case and the applicant is a local authority foster carer then a continuous period of one year is required.

- If the adoption is a non-agency case and the applicant is a relative then the child must have lived with the applicant for a cumulative period of three years during the preceding five years.[355]

These requirements ensure that the child and would-be adopters have spent a sufficient amount of time together for the court to be able properly to assess whether the adoption is likely to benefit the child. If the placement criteria are satisfied[356] the court will go on to consider the two key crucial requirements for an adoption order:

1. that the making of the adoption order is in the child's welfare, and

2. that the birth parent consents to the adoption or that consent has been dispensed with.[357]

These requirements will be considered separately.

### (i) That the making of the adoption order is in the child's welfare

In deciding whether or not an adoption order is in the welfare of the child the court must consider the checklist in s 1(4) of the Adoption and Children Act 2002. This is the following:

---

**LEGISLATIVE PROVISION**

**Adoption and Children Act 2002, section 1(4)**

(a) the child's ascertainable wishes and feelings regarding the decisions (considered in the light of the child's age and understanding);

(b) the child's particular needs;

(c) the likely effect on the child (throughout his life) of having ceased to be a member of the original family and become an adopted person;

(d) the child's age, sex, background and any of the child's characteristics which the court or agency considers relevant;

(e) any harm (within the meaning of the Children Act 1989) which the child has suffered or is at risk of suffering;

(f) the relationship which the child has with relatives, and with any other person in relation to whom the court or agency considers the relationship to be relevant, including—

　(i)　the likelihood of any such relationship continuing and the value to the child of its doing so;

　(ii)　the ability and willingness of any of the child's relatives, or of any such person, to provide the child with a secure environment in which the child can develop, and otherwise to meet the child's needs;

　(iii)　the wishes and feelings of the child's relatives, or of any such person, regarding the child.

---

[355] ACA 2002, s 42.

[356] If they are not satisfied, the court must grant leave to apply for the order. In such a case the court will consider the child's welfare and the likelihood of the application succeeding: *Re A (A Child) (Adoption)* [2008] 1 FCR 55.

[357] See *Down Lisburn v H* [2006] UKHL 36 which highlights the problem with the 'reasonable person test' for dispensing with consent under the old law.

Four points in particular will be emphasised about this list.[358] First, it should be noted that the court must consider the child's welfare not only during the child's minority, but for the rest of his or her life.[359] Thus, a court may be persuaded that making an adoption order in favour of a child just short of his or her eighteenth birthday will promote his or her welfare, if doing so will give him or her British citizenship. Secondly, as usual, the child's own views about the proposed adoption are likely to be very important, if not crucial, to a determination of the child's welfare. At one time it was proposed that an adoption order could not be made in respect of a child over the age of 12 without his or her consent. This did not appear in the final Act. However, it is hard to imagine a case where a court will decide that an adoption, against the wishes of a teenager, will promote his or her welfare.[360] Thirdly, the Act requires the court specifically to consider the child's relationships with his or her birth family: not just his or her birth parents, but his or her wider family.[361] In particular the court must consider whether the child's blood relatives are in a position to care for the child. In *Re C (Family Placement)*[362] the Court of Appeal preferred to make a residence order to a 5-year-old's grandmother, rather than place the child for adoption with strangers, as the local authority wished to do. They referred to the law's preference that children be raised within their family. The grandmother's age was noted (she was 70), but the court believed other family members would rally round if the grandmother became unable to care for the child.

The fourth point is that when considering an application for an adoption order the court must recall the alternative orders that it can make.[363] These include: (i) a residence order in favour of the applicants;[364] (ii) a special guardianship; (iii) no order. The key issue in many contested adoptions is whether adoption is a preferable alternative to a residence order in favour of the would-be adopters, or a special guardianship in their favour. All of these options would lead to the child living with the applicants, but, unlike adoption, the birth parents would not lose their parental status. Also, significantly, the formal links between the child and his or her wider family (e.g. siblings, grandparents, etc.) would remain. The court will have to weigh up the benefits of retaining the broad links with the birth family with the benefits of security offered by an adoption. Holman J in *Re H (Adoption Non-patrial)*[365] summarised the benefits of an adoption order over and above a residence order in favour of the would-be adopters:

> It is well recognised that adoption confers an extra and psychologically and emotionally important sense of 'belonging'. There is real benefit to the parent/child relationship in knowing that each is legally bound to the other and in knowing that the relationship thus created is as secure and free from interference by outsiders as the relationship between natural parents and their child.

In *Re B (A Child) (Sole Adoption by Unmarried Father)*[366] the Court of Appeal declined to make an adoption on the basis that the present fostering arrangements were working well and there was no particular benefit to be gained by an adoption. Masson has argued that it

---

[358] The list is similar, but not identical to, CA 1989, s 1(3).
[359] *Re P (Children) (Adoption: Parental Consent)* [2008] 2 FCR 185.
[360] Adoption Agencies Regulations 2005 require the agency to counsel the child and ascertain his or her wishes and feelings and report on these to the adoption panel, if appropriate.
[361] Parkinson (2003).
[362] [2009] 1 FLR 1425.
[363] *Re P (Children) (Adoption: Parental Consent)* [2008] 2 FCR 185.
[364] The ACA 2002 has amended s 12 of the Children Act 1989 so that a residence order can last until the child's eighteenth birthday.
[365] [1996] 1 FLR 717 at p. 726.
[366] [2002] 1 FCR 150.

will be particularly difficult to justify making an adoption order, rather than a residence order, if a relative is seeking to adopt the child.[367]

In *Re M (Adoption or Residence Order)*[368] the views of a 12-year-old that she did not want to be regarded as no longer the sibling of her siblings were decisive in ordering a residence order in favour of the applicants, rather than an adoption. The Court of Appeal was brave in doing this because the applicants had stated that they would not be able to care for the child if only granted a residence order and threatened that if they were denied an adoption order they would return the child to the local authority. In the face of strong evidence that it was in the interests of the child to live with the applicants, the Court of Appeal trusted that the applicants would not carry through with their threats. In addition to a residence order, it also made an order under s 91(14) of the Children Act 1989, preventing the birth mother making an application for an order under that Act without the leave of the court. This would provide some limited protection to the applicants from concerns that the birth mother would be constantly seeking to interfere with the way they were raising the child.

When considering whether the adoption will promote the child's welfare the court will be aware of potential rights under the Human Rights Act 1998.[369] The approach of the European Court of Human Rights towards adoption is rather ambiguous. In *Johansen v Norway*[370] the European Court considered the placement of the applicant's daughter in a foster home with a view to adoption. The court stated:

> These measures were particularly far-reaching in that they totally deprived the applicant of the family life with the child and were inconsistent with the aim of reuniting them. Such measures should only be applied in exceptional circumstances and could only be justified if they were motivated by an overriding requirement pertaining to the child's best interests.[371]

This statement, subsequently repeated in many cases, appears to suggest that adoption is only permissible in exceptional cases and only if there is a very strong case for it based on the child's interests. However, later cases suggested a more positive attitude towards adoption. In *Söderbäck v Sweden*[372] the European Court of Human Rights approved the making of an adoption order in favour of a mother and her new husband, despite the opposition of the child's father, who only ever had limited contact with the child. The court accepted that the stability that the adoption order would provide justified the making of the order.[373] However, it is hard to see how the circumstances of that case were in any way exceptional. The case can be read as signifying a change in the European Court's attitudes towards adoption. Or it may be that as the only right to family life being infringed by the adoption order was that of the father and child who had only limited contact with each other, an adoption order was easier to justify than a case like *Johansen* where a child is being removed from a parent who has an established relationship with the child.[374] In *Görgülü v Germany*[375] a child was placed by his mother with foster parents for adoption, shortly after birth. When the father sought custody

---

[367] Masson (2003: 32).
[368] [1998] 1 FLR 570.
[369] *Re P (Children) (Adoption: Parental Consent)* [2008] 2 FCR 185.
[370] (1996) 23 EHRR 33.
[371] At para 78.
[372] [1999] 1 FLR 250.
[373] See similarly *Eski v Austria* [2007] 1 FCR 453 and *Chepelev v Russia* [2007] 2 FCR 649 where in both cases the ECtHR held that an adoption order in favour of the mother and her new husband did not improperly infringe the child's father's rights. In both, the limited relationship the birth father had with the child was emphasised.
[374] *Söderbäck v Sweden* [1999] 1 FLR 250; paras 13–33 in the judgment appear to draw this distinction.
[375] [2004] 1 FCR 410.

and contact these were refused by the German courts. The European Court found that the father's article 8 rights had been interfered with. Too much weight had been put on the child's bond with the foster parents and the hope that adoption offered, and insufficient weight had been given to the possibility of reuniting the father and son. This emphasises the requirement that adoption should be used only when there is no realistic chance of the birth parents providing appropriate care.

## (ii) The consent of the parents

Before an adoption order can be made, the court must have the consent of the parents or dispense with that consent.

### (a) Who must consent?

The consent of all parents with parental responsibility and any guardians is required. The consent of an unmarried father without parental responsibility is not required. The 1996 draft Adoption Bill required the consent of children over the age of 12 to being adopted, but this is not required under the 2002 Act.[376] The British Agencies for Adoption and Fostering (BAAF) objected to the consent requirement on the basis that children may feel they are being asked actively to reject their birth parents by consenting to adoption.[377]

If the birth parents consent to the adoption it might be thought that adoption is uncontroversial. Lord Nicholls expressed the view that if a mother consented to the adoption it could not be said to infringe her article 8 rights.[378] However, the right to respect for family life of the child should not be forgotten. Even where the parent is consenting to the adoption the child's rights are still being interfered with by the order.[379]

### (b) The unmarried father without parental responsibility

As just noted, it is not necessary to have the consent of a father without parental responsibility before the court makes an adoption order;[380] but that does not mean that he can be ignored by the adoption agency. The adoption agency should normally notify the father of the adoption proceedings.[381] Where the father has family life for the purposes of article 8, the courts have held that he must be notified of the proceedings and involved sufficiently to protect his interests. Not to do so might infringe his rights under articles 8 and 6.[382] This human rights dimension now means that he should be informed of the proposed adoption unless there are very good reasons for not involving the father (e.g. where there is a concern that he will be violent towards the mother if he should learn of the child's birth and proposed adoption).[383]

---

[376] See Piper and Miakishev (2003) for support for this proposal.
[377] Masson (2003: 26) complains that children are not able to be parties to the adoption proceedings.
[378] *Re B (Adoption by One Natural Parent to the Exclusion of Other)* [2001] 1 FLR 589 at para 29.
[379] Harris-Short (2002).
[380] See Davis (2005) for criticism of the lack of clear protection for unmarried fathers in this context.
[381] This includes anyone believed to be a father by the agency: see *Re B (A Child) (Parentage: Knowledge of Proceedings)* [2004] 1 FCR 473 where the Court of Appeal ordered that the mother's husband be notified of the plan to adopt the mother's newborn baby (about which, remarkably, the husband was unaware), even though the wife insisted that the child was not her husband's.
[382] *Re R (Adoption: Father's Involvement)* [2001] 1 FLR 302.
[383] *Re C (Adoption: Disclosure to Father)* [2006] Fam Law 624; *Re M (Adoption: Rights of Natural Father)* [2001] 1 FLR 745; *Re J (Adoption: Contacting Father)* [2003] Fam Law 368; *Re S (A Child) (Adoption Proceedings: Joinder of Father)* [2001] 1 FCR 158; *Re H (A Child) (Adoption: Disclosure)*; *Re G (A Child) (Adoption: Disclosure)* [2001] 1 FCR 726.

### (c) What is consent?

Consent must be given 'unconditionally and with full understanding of what it involved'.[384] It is therefore not possible for a birth parent to consent to an adoption only under certain circumstances (e.g. that the adopter is a Chelsea supporter!).[385] The consent must be in writing on a form which sets out the effect of adoption and is witnessed by a CAFCASS officer. The intention of these requirements is that the consent be given freely and with full understanding.[386] This also explains why a birth mother's consent to adoption is valid only if the child is at least six weeks old.[387] Until this time she may not have full understanding of the significance of the decision she is making. A birth mother could consent to placement immediately following birth, but then would need to provide later consent to adoption.[388]

### (d) Consent to what?

The consent to the adoption can be consent to adoption by a specific person or general consent for the child to be adopted by anyone. The consent can be given at the time of placement or subsequently. This reflects the variety of roles that the birth family may wish to play in an adoption case. It may be that the birth parents do not want any involvement in adoption and hand over the child to the adoption agency, happy for them to select an appropriate adopter. On the other hand, it may be that the birth family want a say in the selection of the adopter (particularly if the adoption is to be an open one), in which case they may prefer to consent to a particular adopter of whom they approve.

### (e) Changes of mind

If the consent is given in advance of the adoption order it can subsequently be withdrawn, as long as an application for an adoption order has not been made. But, if a placement order has been made a parent cannot object to the making of the adoption order without the leave of the court.[389] Similarly, if consent has been given and not withdrawn by the time of the application, the parent cannot object to the making of the adoption order without the leave of the court. The court will give leave only if there has been a change in circumstances; although the effect of the Human Rights Act 1998 might mean that a court will be very unlikely to deny a parent the right to withdraw their consent.[390]

### (iii) Dispensing with consent

The court can dispense with the consent of a parent whose consent is required, in two circumstances:

---

[384] ACA 2002, s 52(5).
[385] If the birth parent is willing to consent to adoption only if the adopter has certain characteristics (e.g. is of a certain religion), he or she may be willing to give specific consent to adoption to named individuals, but not a general consent.
[386] Although see *Re A (Adoption: Agreement: Procedure)* [2001] 2 FLR 455 where the consent of a 15-year-old Kosovan rape victim to a freeing order was revoked on the basis that she had not understood what she was signing.
[387] ACA 2002, s 52(3). See *Sandwell Metropolitan Borough Council* v *GC* [2008] EWHC 2555 (Fam) and *A Local Authority* v *GC and Others* [2009] 1 FLR 299 for the procedure to be used if the child to be adopted is under ten weeks old.
[388] *A Local Authority* v *GC and Others* [2009] 1 FLR 299.
[389] ACA 2002, s 47(3).
[390] Davis (2005: 295). Although see *Kearns* v *France* [2008] 2 FCR 1 where the ECtHR upheld the restrictions under French law on withdrawal of a parent's consent to adoption.

1. 'The parent or guardian cannot be found or is incapable of giving consent.'[391] This provision will be used in cases where the parent or guardian has disappeared or is unknown (e.g. if the baby was found abandoned outside a hospital and the mother has never been identified). It is also used if the parent is suffering a mental disability which means she lacks capacity to consent.

2. 'The welfare of the child requires the consent to be dispensed with.'[392] Under the Adoption Act 1976, parents' objections to adoption could only be overridden if they were unreasonably withholding their consent to the adoption. Section 1 of the Adoption and Children Act 2002 makes clear that now the sole consideration for the court in dispensing with consent is the child's welfare. So the rights of the parents and questions about whether or not the parents were reasonable in their objections are irrelevant. This has led to heavy criticism by some who fear that to permit the adoption of children against the wishes of parents simply on the basis that it would be better for the child rides roughshod over the importance attached to parental rights. Can any parent be particularly confident that it is impossible to find someone else who would be better at raising his or her child?[393] Such concerns, however, may be overblown. There are a number of ways in which, despite the wording of s 52(1)(b), the interests of parents could be taken into account:

   (i) The subsection uses the word 'requires'. This might suggest that, if it is shown that adoption is only slightly in the interests of the child, this will be insufficient to *require* the consent to be dispensed with.[394] In *Re P (Placement Orders: Parental Consent)*[395] the Court of Appeal held that the word requires carries a connotation of being imperative: that dispensing with the consent is not just reasonable or desirable but required in the interests of the child.

   (ii) Under the Human Rights Act 1998 this subsection must be read in a way which is compatible with the European Convention if at all possible.[396] Clearly an adoption order is a grave interference with the right to respect for family life between the parent and child.[397] Indeed, it is hard to think of a graver one. It must therefore be a proportionate intervention. Only a substantial benefit to the child of adoption might be thought sufficient to make adoption a proportionate response and therefore permissible under article 8(2).[398]

   (iii) It should be added that if the child has lived with the would-be adopters and has developed a close relationship with them it is arguable that the would-be adopters and child have developed family life which is also protected under article 8. Such an argument is likely to be strongest where the child has lived with the applicants for a considerable period of time.[399]

   (iv) In interpreting the welfare test in the Children Act 1989 the courts have developed the 'natural parent presumption': that is, it is presumed that the child is best brought up by the natural (i.e. birth) family. It is true that this presumption has been questioned

---

[391] ACA 2002, s 52(1)(a). See *Haringey v Mr and Mrs E* [2006] EWHC 1620 (Fam) for such a case.
[392] ACA 2002, s 52(1)(b).
[393] Barton (2001).
[394] Davis (2005).
[395] [2008] EWCA Civ 535.
[396] Welbourne (2002), Ball (2003) and Choudhry (2003) provide useful discussions on the potential impact of the Human Rights Act 1998 in this context.
[397] *P, C, S v UK* [2002] 2 FLR 631.
[398] *P, C, S v UK* [2002] 2 FLR 631 at para 118. See also *Re C and B (Children) (Care Order: Future Harm)* [2001] 1 FLR 611.
[399] *Re B (A Child) (Adoption Order)* [2001] EWCA 347, [2001] 2 FCR 89.

in recent years (see Chapter 9) but that has been in cases where there has been no effective relationship between the birth parent and child.

(v)   Professional practice. Most social workers working in this area regard adoption as a last resort, to be tried only where any hope of rehabilitation with the birth parents has been lost.[400] This means that, even if theoretically the law does not protect parents' rights, the practice of the professionals involved might mean that adoption will only be sought when there are very strong child welfare reasons for seeking it.

(vi)  Although at the adoption order stage the welfare test applies, at the placement stage the s 31 threshold criteria (see Chapter 10) will have to be satisfied. Therefore it will have to have been shown that the parenting of the child caused or risked the child significant harm before a child can be adopted against the parent's wishes.

Despite such arguments, Bridge and Swindells argue that there is a change in the law in that: 'Whereas parents (under the former law) could take a different view of their child's welfare and not be unreasonable, the court will now be able to impose its view on them.'[401] The point is that under the 1976 Act if it would be reasonable to take the view both that the child should be adopted and that the child should not (i.e. it was a borderline case) it would not be possible to dispense with the parent's consent. However, in such a case under the 2002 Act it would be open to the court to decide that an adoption was (just) in a child's welfare and therefore to dispense with parental consent. This is revealed in *Re R (Placement Order)*[402] where Sumner J dispensed with the consent of Muslim parents to adoption. They opposed adoption as being contrary to Muslim practice. The judge held that the children's welfare required adoption despite the objections of the parents.

## I   The effect of an adoption order

An adopted child is to be treated as the 'legitimate child of the adopter or adopters'.[403] This means that the adoption order will have the following effects:

1.  Parental responsibility for the child is given to the adopters.[404]

2.  Adoptive parents can make all decisions about the child which other parents can make, including appointing a guardian.[405]

3.  An adoption order extinguishes the parental status and parental responsibility of any other person. There is one exception to this and that is where a step-parent adopts their partner's child, where their partner will retain parental responsibility and status.[406]

4.  After the making of an adoption order an adopted child no longer has any right to inherit their birth parent's property.

5.  On the making of an adoption order an adopted child who is not a British citizen will acquire British citizenship if the adopter is a British citizen.[407]

There are, however, some circumstances in which the adoption order does not treat the adopted child in exactly the same way as a natural child.

---

[400]  Harris-Short (2008) argues that such an approach is required in the Human Rights Act 1998.
[401]  Bridge and Swindells (2003: 152).
[402]  [2007] EWHC 3031 (Fam).
[403]  ACA 2002, s 67(1)–(3).
[404]  ACA 2002, s 46(1).
[405]  ACA 2002, s 67.
[406]  ACA 2002, ss 51(2), 67(3)(d).
[407]  British Nationality Act 1981, s 1(5).

- An adopted person is deemed within the prohibited degrees of relations for the purpose of marrying his or her birth relations.[408] Therefore, for example, if an adopted man marries his birth sister, entirely innocently, the marriage will be void. However, he can marry his adoptive relatives, including an adoptive sister, but not his adoptive mother.

- A minor may retain the nationality he or she had acquired from his or her birth. However, a minor adopted in the UK court will be a British citizen if one of the adopters is a British citizen.[409]

- Adoptions do not affect the right to succeed to peerages.

- Section 69 of the Adoption and Children Act 2002 states that an adoption will not affect certain dispositions of property.[410]

The European Convention on Human Rights, under article 14, prohibits improper discrimination between adopted children and birth children.[411] Of course, the legal effects are only a small part of the significance of adoption. As Thorpe LJ said in *Re J (A Minor) (Adoption: Non-Patrial)*[412] the result of adoption is 'the creation of the psychological relationship of parent and child with all its far-reaching manifestations and consequences'.

## J  Open adoption

As originally conceived, adoption was seen as a closed and secretive process.[413] Birth parents were not told who had adopted the child, adoptive parents were not told who the birth parents were, and the child was not told that he or she had been adopted. Even if the child did find out, this was a secret to be kept from the rest of the world.[414] This secrecy model changed with evidence that some adopted children needed detailed information of their birth background to establish a secure sense of who they were,[415] and birth parents needed to know that their child had been successfully and happily adopted.[416]

These concerns have led to an increase in willingness for local authorities to encourage open adoption. These are adoptions where the child maintains links with the birth parents or wider family. This may be indirectly through e-mails, or directly through face-to-face meetings. Research suggests that open adoptions more often involve contact between the birth mother and her side of the family, rather than the birth father.[417] Research also suggests that in fact the possibility of contact is effectively determined at the time when the care order is made. If after the care order there is no contact, it is unlikely that contact will arise after adoption, while, if contact has taken place after the care order, this is likely to continue once the adoption order has been made.[418] At present at least 70 per cent of children who have been adopted retain some kind of contact with their birth families.[419]

---

[408] ACA 2002, s 74(1).
[409] British Nationality Act 1981, s 1(5).
[410] Bridge and Swindells (2003: 215–17) explain the detail of the law, and Swindells and Heaton (2006) the procedure.
[411] *Pla and Puncernau v Andorra* [2004] 2 FCR 630.
[412] [1998] 1 FCR 125 at 130.
[413] See Smith (2004) for an autopoietic approach to open adoption.
[414] Cretney (2003a: ch. 17).
[415] Triseliotis (1973).
[416] Howe and Feast (2000).
[417] Neil (2000).
[418] Richards (1994).
[419] Department of Health (2002d: 15). Thoburn (2003: 394) says the figure is around 80%.

---

### DEBATE

## Is open adoption a good idea?

The issue of open adoption is controversial.[420] In favour it is said that openly adopted children will feel less of a sense of being rejected by their birth families;[421] it will provide them with a greater sense of security; and it might encourage birth families to be supportive of the adoption.[422] Indeed, one study interviewing adopted children found that many wanted greater contact with their birth families.[423] Against open adoption it must be recalled that some cases of adoption are those where the child has suffered or been at risk of significant harm because of the parenting they have received. Particularly where the birth family have abused the child, the benefits of contact may be questioned. Further, there are concerns that contact with the birth family might undermine the position of the adopters.[424] It may also deter some would-be adopters from going through with the adoption.[425]

### Questions

1. *What would happen if adoption were abolished? What could replace it?*
2. *Is there a case for amending the law on adoption so that the birth parents retain some status in respect of the child?*

### Further reading

See **Harris-Short** (2008) for a useful discussion of the law on adoption.

---

Interestingly, the courts have been reluctant to make a court order requiring contact between the child and the birth family.[426] The argument the courts have accepted is that if the adopters are happy for there to be contact then there is no need for the court to make an order requiring it;[427] and if the adopters do not want there to be contact it would be wrong to force them to do so.[428] This means that trust between the birth families and adopters is key.[429] Section 46(6) of the 2002 Act now requires the court to consider, when making an adoption order, whether to make a contact order in respect of the child. It remains to be seen whether this will be interpreted as encouraging the courts to make contact orders. Under the old law what tended to happen was that agencies produced written agreements which clearly set out the kind of contact between the child and the birth family that was expected.[430] These agreements

[420] Smith and Logan (2002) and Neil (2003) provide useful discussions. For an article sceptical about the benefits of open adoption see Quinton, Selwyn, Rushton and Dance (1998).

[421] Casey and Gibberd (2001). In *Re G (Adoption: Contact)* [2003] Fam Law 9 the fear was expressed that without contact the children might view their birth families as 'ogres'.

[422] Lowe et al. (1999: 324); Smith and Logan (2002). *Re G (Child: Contact)* [2002] 3 FCR 377 acknowledges that research is generally in favour of open adoption.

[423] Thomas (2001).

[424] Lowe et al. (1999: 313). For an example see *Re C (Contempt: Committal)* [1995] 2 FLR 767.

[425] Lowe and Murch (2002: 62).

[426] *Re R (Adoption: Contact)* [2005] EWCA Civ 1128.

[427] *Re T (Adoption: Contact)* [1995] 2 FLR 251.

[428] *Re T (Adoption: Contact)* [1995] 2 FLR 251.

[429] Smith (2005).

[430] Masson (2003: 57).

are not, however, enforceable. If the adopted parents refuse to permit contact as expected, it would be possible for the birth parents to apply for a s 8 contact order.[431] However, they will need the leave of the court before the court will hear their application. The courts are likely to grant leave only where the maintenance of contact with the birth family is of such benefit to the child as to justify overriding the privacy of the adoptive family. Forcing contact against the wishes of the adopters is unlikely to benefit the child in the long run[432] and would be 'extremely unusual'.[433]

One of the few cases where the Court of Appeal held that leave should be granted was *Re T Minors (Adopted Children: Contact)*[434] where the adopters had failed to provide an annual report to the adopted children's adult half-sister. Notably this case did not greatly interfere in the private and family life of the adoptive parents.[435] In *Re P (Children) (Adoption: Parental Consent)*[436] it was held to be of fundamental importance that two siblings keep in contact.[437] The Court of Appeal held that in such a case the court should order contact, rather than leaving it to be dealt with informally by the local authorities and adopters. But such a case is still rare. Contact orders made in favour of birth family members against adoptive parents will be 'extremely unusual'.[438] In *A Local Authority v J*[439] the local authority's plans to have a 15-month-old child adopted were approved, even though this was likely to mean that contact between the child and the siblings would probably cease. Perhaps it was significant in that case that the child in issue was too young to have an established relationship with the older children.

In *Oxfordshire County Council v X*[440] the adoptive parents objected to providing the birth parents with a photograph of the child, for fear they would use it on the Internet to find out where the child was. The Court of Appeal in deciding that the adoptive parents should not be required to supply the photographs held that the question was not whether or not their fears were correct, but whether the views of the adoptive parents were unreasonable. The court held they were not. It was emphasised that the welfare of the child depended on the parents feeling secure and this feeling would be challenged if it was ordered that they supply photographs. Perhaps at the heart of this case is the blunt message: 'The adoptive parents are J's parents; the natural parents are not.'[441]

Sometimes it is very important that the birth families do not know where the child is now living. This would be so where the birth family pose a risk to the child or adopters. In *B v A County Council*[442] the adopters were the victims of a campaign of harassment by the birth family after the Council revealed the adopters' names. The adopters' claim for damages failed primarily because the council had specifically refused to guarantee that their details would be kept confidential.

---

[431] Bridge and Swindells (2003: 233) discuss whether the welfare checklist in the CA 1989 or the ACA 2002 would be used.

[432] *Down Lisburn v H* [2006] UKHL 36; Eekelaar (2003a).

[433] *Oxfordshire County Council v X* [2010] 2 FCR 355, para 6.

[434] [1995] 2 FLR 792.

[435] *Contrast Re S (Contact: Application by Sibling)* [1998] 2 FLR 897.

[436] [2008] 2 FCR 185.

[437] See also *Re H (Leave to Apply for Residence Order)* [2008] EWCA Civ 503.

[438] *Re R (A Child)(Adoption: Contact)* [2007] 1 FCR 149. Although see *X and Y v A Local Authority (Adoption: Procedure)* [2009] 2 FLR 984.

[439] [2008] 2 FLR 1389.

[440] [2010] 2 FCR 355.

[441] Para 36.

[442] [2006] 3 FCR 568.

## K Adoption by a parent

A parent may decide to adopt his or her own child. The reason for doing this is usually to eliminate the other parent from the picture. Nowadays this is very rare, but it sometimes arises. In *Re B (Adoption by the Natural Parent to Exclusion of Other)*[443] very shortly after the birth of her child a mother decided to place her child for adoption. The father, by chance, discovered this and offered to raise his child. The mother agreed to the arrangement. She did not want to play any role in the child's upbringing and was therefore happy for her maternal role to be ended. The Official Solicitor was appointed and objected on the basis that it was not in the child's welfare to terminate the link with her mother. At first instance the adoption order was made but the Court of Appeal allowed an appeal. Hale LJ held that only exceptional circumstances (e.g. disappearance of a parent or anonymous sperm donation) could justify single-parent adoptions. The House of Lords, however, allowed a further appeal and restored the adoption. It held, controversially, that an order which was in the child's best interests could not breach the child's rights. The decision was reached under the Adoption Act 1976 under which the child's welfare was the first, but not paramount, consideration in any decision. It was held that, as the mother did not want to have anything to do with the child, an adoption could not be said to interfere improperly with the human rights of the mother or child.[444]

## L Adoption by parent and step-parent

Twenty-two per cent of all adoptions in 2005 involved step-parents.[445] Typically, such adoptions arise where a mother remarries and her new husband wishes to have formal recognition of his status. He could enter into an agreement with his wife in relation to the child which would grant him parental responsibility.[446] However, he might still want the formal label of father and/or he may be concerned that the birth father may seek to interfere with the way that the stepfamily will care for the child; he may therefore consider adoption.[447] The stepfather might have two options:

1. The mother and her new husband adopt the mother's child. So, rather strangely, the mother adopts her own child. The purpose of doing this is that the birth father will lose entirely his parental status. The stepfather and birth mother will become the legal parents of the child. However, to some the attraction of adoption is that it means the stepfamily need no longer fear that the birth family will interfere with the way they raise the child.

2. The Adoption and Children Act 2002 enables the partner of a parent to adopt a child, without that affecting the parental status of the birth parents.[448] Thus a stepfather can adopt the child. He will become the father, but the mother will remain as the mother. Notably the procedure can be used not only by the spouse of a parent, but any partner (including a same-sex partner).

---

[443] [2002] 1 FLR 196.
[444] See Bainham (2002b) and Harris-Short (2002) for criticism of this decision.
[445] Department of Constitutional Affairs (2006a).
[446] CA 1989, s 4A.
[447] Note the comments of Thorpe LJ, in *Re PJ (Adoption: Practice on Appeal)* [1998] 2 FLR 252 at p. 260, about the complex motives and emotions that surround a step-parent adoption.
[448] ACA 2002, s 52(2).

If there is an application for adoption involving a step-parent the application will be governed by the principles already outlined. It must be shown that the adoption will promote the welfare of the child, and the necessary parental consents must be obtained or dispensed with. It should be emphasised that the court must be persuaded that it is better to make an adoption order than to make no order at all.[449]

Many take the view that step-parent adoptions should not be permitted. In particular, while it is understandable why the stepfather might want some kind of recognition of his position in the child's life, that should not mean that the birth father and his side of the family lose their status in respect of the child.

## M Adoption by relatives

Relatives of the child may wish to adopt the child.[450] This may be under an arrangement with the mother or through discussions with the local authority. A teenager may ask her mother to raise her child for her. It may also be that the local authority asks a relative to consider being an adopter, although this is rare.[451] There has been a fair amount of criticism of adoption by relatives because it can distort the child's family relationships (e.g. the child's birth grandmother becomes her mother and her birth mother becomes her adopted sister). It is also thought to be unnecessary. A residence order or special guardianship provides sufficient protection for the relative's position.[452] The Adoption and Children Act 2002 permits relatives to apply to adopt, but only if they have cared for the child for at least three of the five previous years or obtain the leave of the court to make the application.[453] The relative must then satisfy the court that adoption is a better option than a residence order or special guardianship. These hurdles may mean that very few adoptions by relatives occur.

## N Post-adoption support

Lowe has suggested that adoption has changed from the gift/donation model to a contract/ services model.[454] He points out that at one time a child being adopted was regarded as a gift to be handed over by an adoption agency to an infertile couple. Once the child was received by the couple, the local authority's role was at an end and the adopter would be treated in the same way as a birth parent. Nowadays adoption is seen as one of the ways of arranging the care of a child taken into care. As the age of adopted children has increased, and as a result children being adopted may present a range of emotional and physical problems, it has become necessary to rethink the assumption that the local authority carries no responsibility for adopted children. This has led to increased awareness of the importance of providing support to children who have been adopted.[455] The task of adopting a child who has been severely abused or suffers from complex physical disability may be beyond all but the most gifted of parents without the assistance, advice and support of a local authority. The offering of services may help to decrease the rate of adoption breakdown and may encourage prospective

---

[449] ACA 2002, s 1(6). For an argument which is more positive towards kinship adoption see Talbot and Williams (2003).
[450] Waterhouse, Hunt and Lutman (2008); and Hall (2008a and b).
[451] Murch, Lowe, Borkowski et al. (1993: 11).
[452] This was the view taken by the Performance and Innovation Unit (2000a: para 5.8).
[453] ACA 2002, s 42(5), (6).
[454] Lowe (1997a).
[455] Lowe, Murch, Borkowski et al. (1999).

adopters to adopt 'difficult' children.[456] A more cynical view is that these 'services' may in effect amount to regulation of and intervention in the family life of the adoptive family.[457]

The Adoption and Children Act 2002 now requires adoption agencies to provide for a wide range of adoption support services.[458] However, this does not create a strong right to such services. Although adopted parents and children have the right to request that they be assessed for the provision of adoption support, the Act does not require the local authority to meet the need.[459] This would mean that the local authority may assess an adopted child to be in need of services, but then decide that it is unable to afford to provide them.[460] Special guardians (who will be discussed shortly) do not even have the right to be assessed, although a local authority may, if it wishes, provide services to them.[461]

## O Revocation of an adoption order

The adoption order continues to have effect unless another adoption order is made. In particular, the adoption order does not come to an end when the child reaches the age of 18. As mentioned above, one of the main advantages of adoption is the security it creates. If adoption could be brought to an end it would undermine that benefit.[462] There are just three circumstances in which an adoption order can be overturned:[463]

1. If the child is adopted by his or her father, but his or her mother then marries the father. In such a case the father could apply under s 55 of the Adoption and Children Act 2002 for the adoption to be revoked and the child would then in law be the child of his or her parents. This provision is very rarely invoked.

2. It is possible to appeal against the making of the adoption order,[464] although it is necessary to show a flaw in the making of the order itself and demonstrate exceptional circumstances. The case law provides two examples of exceptional circumstances:

   (i) Where the consent of the parent to the adoption was given on the basis of a fundamental mistake. In *Re M (A Minor) (Adoption)*[465] a father agreed to the adoption of his children by his former wife and her new husband. Unknown to him, his ex-wife was terminally ill and she died shortly afterwards. The court allowed the appeal in what they regarded as a 'very exceptional case' on the basis that ignorance of the wife's condition negated his consent, which was based on a fundamental mistake.

   (ii) Where the adoption procedures involved a fundamental defect in natural justice. In *Re K (Adoption and Wardship)*[466] an English foster carer had adopted a Muslim baby, who had been found under a pile of bodies in the former Yugoslavia. Unfortunately, the adoption process had been deeply flawed. The adoption order was set aside due to the lack of protection for the birth family and the breach of natural justice caused

---

[456] Douglas and Philpot (2003: 109) emphasise that birth parents may also require services from the local authority.

[457] Harris-Short (2008).

[458] ACA 2002, s 4(7); Adoption Support Services (Local Authorities) (England) Regulations 2003, SI 2003/1348; Department of Health (2003b); Department for Education and Skills (2005c).

[459] ACA 2002, s 4.

[460] See, by analogy, *R (On the Application of A) v Lambeth* [2003] 3 FCR 419.

[461] CA 1989, s 14F(1), (2).

[462] *Re B (Adoption: Setting Aside)* [1995] 1 FLR 1 at p. 7.

[463] *Re B (Adoption: Jurisdiction to Set Aside)* [1995] 2 FLR 1, [1994] 2 FLR 1297.

[464] If necessary, leave can be given to appeal out of time.

[465] [1991] 1 FLR 458; [1990] FCR 993.

[466] [1997] 2 FLR 221; [1997] 2 FLR 230.

by the faulty procedure. At the rehearing[467] for the adoption order it was decided that the child should be made a ward of court but that he remain with the foster carers who were required to bring him up with instruction in the Bosnian language and Muslim religion. Every three months they were required to report back to the Bosnian family.

3. If the child is adopted by a new set of parents this will end (but not revoke) the original adoption.

In the absence of one of these three grounds an adoption order cannot be set aside, however sympathetic the court may be to the application.[468] If the birth family are seeking to challenge an adoption order and are not able to overturn the adoption order, they could still apply for a residence order in respect of the child. It would be unlikely that such an application would succeed unless the adoption had completely broken down.[469]

A dramatic example of the application of these principles was the following case:

---

**CASE: *Webster v Norfolk CC* [2009] EWCA Civ 59**

Mr and Mrs Webster had three children in three years, born between 2000 and 2003. In late 2003 their middle child, B, was taken to hospital suffering multiple fractures. The hospital and local authority assessed the injuries to be non-accidental and caused by his parents. The children were adopted by late 2005.

In 2006 Mrs Webster became pregnant again. In the course of care proceedings relating to the new baby the Websters obtained fresh expert evidence in relation to B. The new report was powerfully of the opinion that the injuries to B were caused by scurvy and iron deficiency rather than abuse. At the time scurvy was considered as unknown in the West and had not been considered as an explanation for the injuries. As a result the care proceedings in relation to the baby were discontinued. The parents then sought to set aside all the orders relating to their three younger children.

Wall LJ confirmed that 'only in highly exceptional and very particular circumstances' can adoption be set aside. Why? Wall LJ thought the answer lay in the dicta of Swinton Thomas LJ in *Re B (Adoption: Jurisdiction to Set Aside)*:[470]

> An adoption order has a quite different standing to almost every other order made by a court. It provides the status of the adopted child and of the adoptive parents. The effect of an adoption order is to extinguish any parental responsibility of the natural parents. Once an adoption order has been made, the adoptive parents stand to one another and the child in precisely the same relationship as if they were his legitimate parents, and the child stands in the same relationship to them as to legitimate parents. Once an adoption order has been made the adopted child ceases to be the child of his previous parents and becomes the child for all purposes of the adopters as though he were their legitimate child.

In the Websters' case there was nothing in the procedure that led to the making of the order which rendered the procedure flawed, and hence the adoption order could not be set aside. Wilson LJ emphasised that the children had been with the adopters for four years in an arrangement they had been told was permanent.

---

[467] [1997] 2 FLR 230.
[468] *Re B (Adoption: Jurisdiction to Set Aside)* [1995] 2 FLR 1, [1994] 2 FLR 1297.
[469] *Re O (A Minor) (Wardship: Adopted Child)* [1978] Fam 196.
[470] [1995] Fam 239, at 245C.

The decision has proved controversial. The author has argued that the reasoning of the case failed to place appropriate weight on the human rights of the parties and the welfare of the children.[471] While the decision placed weight on the importance for adopters in having the security of knowing adoptions will not be set aside unless there are exceptional circumstance, it did not mention the importance for birth parents feeling secure that their children will not be permanently removed without good cause.[472] Andrew Bainham goes further and suggests that the decision requires a reconsideration of whether adoption should be a preferred model for children in care.[473] Not everyone has objected to the decision. Caroline Bridge has described it as a 'model of clarity and common sense'.[474]

## P The breakdown of adoption

Surprisingly there are no official statistics on the rate of breakdown of adoptions.[475] One study found that 9 per cent of the placements studied broke down before an adoption order was made and 8 per cent broke down after the order was made.[476] Another found the average breakdown rate of adoption to be around 20 per cent, although a lot depends on age.[477] If the child is under 6 months at the time of adoption the breakdown rate falls below 5 per cent, but where the child is over the age of 10 around 50 per cent of adoptions break down.[478] Of adults who have been adopted around 20 per cent express significant dissatisfaction with the adoption.[479] The impact of a failed adoption on the child and adoptive parents can only be imagined. Indeed, it is possible that failed adoptions will cause the child more harm than would have been suffered by the child if the adoption had not been attempted. It is therefore important that the Government's attempts to increase the number of adoptions do not lead to an increase in the rate of adoption breakdown.

## Q Access to birth and adoption register

One study estimated that one-third of adopted people seek to obtain access to their birth records.[480] Of course, others may make less formal attempts to find the background to their births. One study found that 75 per cent in their sample sought their birth mother and 38 per cent their father.[481] An adopted person seeking to discover information about his or her birth family could seek access to the following:[482]

1. *Birth certificates.* The Registrar-General is required under s 79 of the Adoption and Children Act 2002 to keep records to enable adopted people to trace their original birth registration. This would enable a person to discover the details of their birth, including the name of their mother. There is no absolute right to obtain a copy of the birth certificate. This is demonstrated by *R v Registrar-General, ex p Smith*,[483] where the Court of Appeal

---

[471] Herring (2009h).
[472] Herring (2010g).
[473] Bainham, A. (2009a).
[474] Bridge (2009: 381).
[475] Department of Health (2002b).
[476] Parker (1999: 10).
[477] Quinton and Selwyn (2006).
[478] Thoburn (2003: 394).
[479] Thoburn (2003: 394).
[480] Rushbrooke (2001).
[481] Howe and Feast (2000).
[482] Disclosure of Adoption Information (Post Commencement Adoptions) Regulations 2005, SI 2005/888.
[483] [1991] FLR 255, [1991] FCR 403.

held that the Registrar-General was entitled to restrict the access of Smith to his birth records. Smith was in prison in Broadmoor, having killed his cell-mate in the belief that he was killing his mother. It was held that he might use the knowledge of his birth mother to harm her and the court held that it was therefore proper for the Registrar to deny him access.

2. *Information from adoption agencies.* When the Adoption and Children Bill was first introduced it sought to restrict access of adopted children to information about their birth. This was justified on the basis of data protection concerns and a need to protect the human rights of the birth parents. However, these proposals were highly controversial and it was felt by many groups involved that they paid insufficient attention to the rights of adopted people to know their genetic identity. As a result, the Government amended the Bill and the Act requires adoption agencies to provide details which would enable an adopted person to obtain their birth certificate. They will also be able to obtain information from the court which made the adoption order.[484] If the agency does not wish to disclose the information, it can obtain a court order permitting non-disclosure.[485] If it is 'protected information', in that it concerns private information about other people, then the agency can fail to disclose it although they should also take reasonable steps to ascertain the views of the people involved.

3. *The Adoption Contact Register.* If birth families wish to contact adopted children then they can use the Adoption Contact Register. This is provided by the National Organisation for Counselling Adoptees and Parents (NORCAP); it facilitates contact between adopters and birth families. As at 2010 it had some 63,000 names on the register. In 2008–09 the organisation helped 229 relatives to be reunited with their birth families.[486]

Now a parent who has given up his or her child for adoption can seek an intermediary to find out further information about the adopted person. The individual must use an agency; this will normally be an adoption agency. The intermediary will contact the Registrar-General and seek to obtain the name of the agency who arranged the adoption. The intermediary will then seek to contact that agency, the court or local authority in an attempt to find out more information. The intermediary will only be able to disclose information to the birth family if they have the informed consent of the adopted adult.[487]

These measures go some way towards recognising a person's rights to know about their genetic origins,[488] which has been held to be an important aspect of a person's right to private life, protected by article 8 of the European Convention on Human Rights.[489] It should be noted that in fact adopted children who do seek information about their birth parents are particularly interested in finding out about their mothers.[490] It is also important to appreciate that even where contact is made this does not usually lead to an ongoing relationship.[491]

---

[484] ACA 2002, s 60(4).
[485] ACA 2002, s 60(3).
[486] NORCAP (2010).
[487] ACA 2002, ss 64(4), 65(1), 98(2) and (3).
[488] Howe and Feast (2000).
[489] *MG v UK* [2002] 3 FCR 289. See further O'Donovan (1988); Van Bueren (1995).
[490] Sachdev (1992) found that only 20% of adopted children said they ever thought about their birth father.
[491] Howe and Feast (2000) report a study that only 51% of adopted children who had found their birth mother had continued the contact. However, 97% of adopted people who had located their birth parents had no regrets about doing so.

## R Inter-country adoption

The limits on the number of children available for adoption has caused some people to turn to adoption of babies from overseas. This practice is governed by the Adoption (Inter-country Aspects) Act 1999 and the Adoption and Children Act 2002, which give effect to the Hague Conference on Private International Law's Convention on Intercountry Adoption.[492] This topic is not covered in detail in this book.[493]

## S Special guardianship

As already indicated, one of the major concerns over the nature of adoption in England and Wales is the way that it terminates the parental status of the birth parents. Those troubled by this have sought to replace adoption with an institution which will provide security and an appropriate status for the new carer of the child, without ending completely the status of the birth parents.[494] In the Adoption and Children Act 2002 the status of special guardian was introduced.[495] This is not a replacement for adoption, but is an alternative to it. The White Paper mentions the kind of cases where special guardianship may be appropriate:

> Some older children do not wish to be legally separated from their birth families. Adoption may not be best for some children being cared for on a permanent basis by members of their wider birth family. Some minority ethnic communities have religious and cultural difficulties with adoption as it is set out in law. Unaccompanied asylum seeking children may also need secure, permanent homes, but have strong attachments to their families abroad.[496]

The Special Guardianship Guidance[497] lists some of the things special guardianship will do:

- Give the carer clear responsibility for all aspects of caring for the child and for taking the decisions to do with their upbringing. The child will no longer be looked after by a local authority.

- Provide a firm foundation on which to build a lifelong permanent relationship between the child and their carer.

- Be legally secure.

- Preserve the basic link between the child and their birth family.

- Be accompanied by access to a full range of support services including, where appropriate, financial support.[498]

There were 2,071 special guardianship orders made in 2008.[499] Most people using special guardianship are relatives, especially grandparents.[500] Typically orders were made in favour of

---

[492] See Bainham (2003b) for a useful discussion on why restrictions on inter-country adoption may be needed.
[493] An excellent summary of the law on inter-country adoption can be found in Bridge and Swindells (2003: ch. 14).
[494] Department of Health (2000e: 248).
[495] See also Special Guardianship Regulations 2005 (SI 2005/1109) and Department for Education and Skills (2005c). Jordan and Lindley (2007) provide useful discussion of special guardianship.
[496] Department of Health (2000e: para 5.9).
[497] Department for Education and Skills (2005a); Special Guardianship Regulations 2005, SI 2005/1109.
[498] A local authority scheme which paid special guardians at a reduced rate was found to be unlawful in *B v Lewisham BC* [2008] EWHC 738 (Admin).
[499] Ministry of Justice (2009).
[500] Wade, Dixon and Richards (2009).

relatives with whom the child had been living for some time.[501] The children involved tend to be young, with 52 per cent under the age of 5. Most children had come from troubled backgrounds marked by maltreatment or parental difficulties.[502]

In *A Local Authority v Y, Z and Others*[503] a special guardianship order was made in favour of an uncle and aunt who had looked after two children for nearly two years. The children supported the applications, wanting the security the status provided. The order was therefore made. By contrast, in *Haringey v Mr and Mrs E*[504] the court felt that special guardianship would not offer the child the security needed. It was unclear how the child had entered the UK or who his parents were. The court held that the child needed the permanence and security offered by adoption. A study of special guardianship found that the order gave the guardians a sense of security and a secure legal foundation. However, many also reported that taking on care of the child had caused economic and psychological hardship, especially where they were the grandparents of the child.[505]

Special guardianship does not terminate the parental status of the birth parents, and special guardians are not treated as the parents of the child.[506] However, they are given many of the rights of a parent. They are able to make almost every decision about a child's upbringing. They can even change the child's name, with the consent of those with parental responsibility.[507] As Andrew Bainham puts it, in terms of taking decisions over the child the special guardians are 'in the driving seat'.[508] They cannot change the child's surname or remove the child from the jurisdiction for longer than three months without the written consent of all those with parental responsibility. The status of special guardianship remains until revoked by an order of the court. It is, in a sense, a halfway house between a residence order and an adoption order.[509] A special guardianship can be varied or discharged on the application of the following:[510]

a. The special guardian.

b. The child's birth parents or guardian, with the leave of the court.

c. The child with the leave of the court.

d. Any individual who presently has the benefit of a residence order.

e. Any individual who had parental responsibility immediately before the making of the special guardianship order, with the leave of the court.

f. The local authority, but only where a care order is made in respect of the child.

g. The court on its own motion in any case where the welfare of the child arises.

---

[501] Wade, Dixon and Richards (2009).
[502] Wade, Dixon and Richards (2009).
[503] [2006] Fam Law 449.
[504] [2006] EWHC 1620 (Fam).
[505] Wade, Dixon and Richards (2009).
[506] Even where a special guardian has been appointed the birth parents will retain their rights in respect of adoption.
[507] CA 1989, s 14C(3).
[508] Bainham (2005: 253).
[509] Johnstone (2006: 116).
[510] CA 1989, s 14D.

Any application to revoke special guardianship must obtain the leave of the court.[511] Unless the application is by the local authority, the child or the special guardian him- or herself it needs to be shown that there has been a significant change in the circumstances from when the special guardianship order was made. This makes the special guardianship a little more secure than a residence order.[512]

Special guardianship is likely to be appropriate where there are good reasons why the child should retain formal links with the birth family. For example, in *Re M (Adoption or Residence Order)*[513] the child was strongly of the opinion that she did not want her links with her mother and siblings to be destroyed, even though she wished to live with the applicants in a permanent relationship. This is the kind of case where special guardianship will now be considered. It may also be appropriate for some children from ethnic minorities. For example, the concept of adoption sits unhappily with Islamic law, which does not recognise the notion of the extinguishment of parental rights.[514] Special guardianship may therefore be more acceptable than adoption to some Muslim parents.

The success of special guardianship will depend on the extent to which both children and would-be adopters are satisfied that it will provide them with the sense of security and belonging together as a family which adoption has been said traditionally to provide.[515] One difficulty, an odd but important one, is terminology. Most people are very familiar with the concept of adoption, and a child can introduce her adoptive parents (and vice versa) without explanation. A special guardianship order might require more explanation until it becomes a familiar term. An earlier attempt to introduce a similar concept was labelled 'custodianship'. This proved deeply unpopular, perhaps in part because, for example, of the difficulties a child might face in introducing her carer to her friends: 'Meet my custodian.'[516]

Anyone (including the child himself or herself![517]) can apply to be a special guardian of a child with the leave of the court.[518] Section 14A of the Children Act 1989 also provides a list of those who can apply without leave.[519] This includes those who have a residence order in respect of a child; relatives with whom the child has lived for a year; anyone else with whom a child has lived for three of the last five years, and those who have the consent of all those with parental responsibility. It is possible for a cohabiting couple to apply to be special guardians. They do not need to be married or of opposite sex, but they must be over 18.[520] When considering an application for a special guardianship the court will, *inter alia*, take into account the applicant's connection with the child and (if the child is being looked after by a local authority) the local authority's plans for the child's future.[521]

---

[511] One exception is where the child is applying (CA 1989, s 14D(5)).
[512] Department of Health (2002e: 50).
[513] [1998] 1 FLR 570.
[514] Pearl and Menski (1998: 410).
[515] It has been suggested that the practice of local authorities of paying a lower level of allowance to special guardians was making them unpopular. That practice may become less widespread following the court's criticism of it in *B v Lewisham BC* [2008] EWHC 738 (Admin).
[516] Custodianship was introduced by the Children Act 1975.
[517] The court must be satisfied that the child has sufficient understanding to make the application (CA 1989, s 10(8)).
[518] CA 1989, s 14A(3)(b).
[519] Those not included need to apply for leave to apply for an order or give notice of an intention to do so: *Re R (A Child) (Special Guardianship Order)* [2007] 1 FCR 121.
[520] CA 1989, s 14A(1). Birth parents cannot apply to be special guardians (CA 1989, s 14A(2)).
[521] CA 1989, s 14A(12).

> **CASE:** *Re S (A Child) (Adoption Order or Special Guardianship Order)*
> [2007] 1 FCR 271;[522] *Re J (A Child) (Adoption Order or Special Guardianship
> Order)* [2007] 1 FCR 308; *Re M-J (A Child) (Adoption Order or Special
> Guardianship Order)* [2007] 1 FCR 329

The cases all involved applicants who originally sought adoption, but for whom the local authority had proposed special guardianship. The courts made the following important points:

First, the court explained that there were fundamental differences between adoption and special guardianship. Of course, the most significant is that while adoption ends the parental status of the birth parents, special guardianship does not. The Court of Appeal was clear that these differences should be considered carefully when deciding between an adoption and special guardianship order.

Secondly, the court refused to accept that there were particular categories of cases where a special guardianship order was preferable to an adoption order or vice versa. In every case the question was simply one of asking what order would best promote the welfare of the child in question. In particular, there was no presumption that, where the child was to be raised within the wider family, a special guardianship was preferable to an adoption order. In *Re J* the argument that it would be confusing for a child to be raised under an adoption order by his uncle and aunt was rejected because the child knew the true family relationship. There was, therefore, no danger that the family relationships would be 'distorted' by an adoption order.

Thirdly, the court emphasised that, under the Human Rights Act 1998, the court must ensure that the intervention in family life was necessary and proportionate. As a special guardianship order was a less fundamental intervention than an adoption order, it should be preferred if it protects the welfare of the child to the same extent as an adoption order. In *Re S* it was held:

> In choosing between adoption and special guardianship, in most cases Art 8 is unlikely to add anything to the considerations contained in the respective welfare checklists. Under both statutes the welfare of the child is the court's paramount consideration, and the balancing exercise required by the statutes will be no different to that required by Art 8. However, in some cases, the fact that the welfare objective can be achieved with less disruption of existing family relationships can properly be regarded as helping to tip the balance.[523]

Fourthly, when considering whether to make a special guardianship order, it should be remembered that the child's parents will still be able to apply for s 8 orders. This is not true in the case of adoption. The special guardianship does not, therefore, provide the same permanency of protection as adoption. In a case (like *Re J*) where the carers and child needed an assurance that the placement could not be disturbed, then adoption may well be more appropriate. While it was true that, where a special guardianship order was made, a parent would need leave before making an application for a residence order, that did not provide the same level of security as an adoption order. A court could also make

---

[522] [2007] 1 FCR 271. For helpful discussions of these cases see Bond (2007) and Bainham (2007).
[523] [2007] 1 FCR 271, para 49.

an order under s 91(14) of the Children Act 1989 to require a parent seeking any s 8 order to obtain leave of the court first. Even then the level of security for special guardians would not match that available for adoption.

Fifthly, special guardianship orders can be made by the court on its own motion. In deciding whether to do so, the court must consider whether making the order against the wishes of the parties will promote the welfare interests of the child. A court can only make a guardianship order on its own motion when a report has been prepared by the local authority.[524]

The following are the main differences between adoption and special guardianships:[525]

1. *The status of the carer.* The adopter becomes a parent for all purposes; the special guardian does not become a parent.

2. *The status of the birth family.* In adoption the child ceases to be a child of the birth family. That is not so in a case of special guardianship. In adoption the birth parents lose parental responsibility, while it is retained for birth parents in a case of special guardianship.[526] In a case of special guardianship birth parents can seek contact orders or prohibited steps orders or specific issue orders without leave of the court.

3. *Duration.* An adoption order is life long[527] while a special guardianship order ceases on reaching age 18 or when it is revoked.

4. *Parental responsibility.* Adopters have full parental responsibility in the same way any other parent has. A special guardian's parental responsibility has limitations.[528] In particular:

   i. Removal from the jurisdiction. A special guardian can remove a child from the country without leave for three months, but if they wish to remove the child for longer they need the written consent of all those with parental responsibility or the leave of the court.

   ii. Changing the name. Special guardians cannot change the child's surname without the written consent of all those with parental responsibility or an order of the court.

   iii. Consent to adoption. The consent of both special guardians and birth parents is required before an adoption order can be made.

   iv. Medical procedures. It may be that in the case of certain serious medical procedures (e.g. sterilisation) the consent of all those with parental responsibility will be required.

   v. Voluntary accommodation. If a parents objects, it seems that a local authority cannot accommodate a child, even if the special guardians consent, without a court order.

5. *Death of the child.* Adopters have all the rights of a parent. Special guardians may not arrange for burials if the parents wish to undertake the arrangements.

---

[524] CA 1989, s 14A(8).
[525] See Schedule at the end of *Re AJ (A Child)(Adoption Order or Special Guardianship Order)* [2007] 1 FCR 308.
[526] CA 1989, s 14C.
[527] ACA 2002, s 67.
[528] CA 1989, s 14C.

6. *Revocation.* An adoption order is irrevocable, unless there are exceptional circumstances. Birth parents can apply for a special guardianship order to be revoked, with leave of the court.[529] Leave to apply for a revocation will only be granted if the application has a real prospect of showing there has been a significant change in circumstances.[530]

7. *Financial support.* Following an adoption birth parents cease to have any financial responsibilities for children. This is not so in a case of special guardianship. The guardians are entitled to special guardianship allowance which is designed to cover the cost of caring for the child.[531]

8. *Intestacy.* If adopters die their adopted children have rights of intestate successions. This is not so for children whose special guardians die.

The following case provides a vivid example of how special guardianship can produce tensions between the parents and special guardians.

---

**CASE: *Re L (A Child) (Special Guardianship Order and Ancillary Orders)*
[2007] 1 FCR 804**

The parents of child L were drug addicts in a volatile relationship. When L was just 3 months old she was placed with her grandparents, who were granted a residence order. Two years later, the grandparents sought an adoption order, but the judge made a special guardianship order. On appeal to the Court of Appeal there were two key issues. First, was whether there should be contact with the parents. The trial judge had ordered that contact take place six times a year, away from the grandparents' house, supervised by the local authority. Further contact could be agreed between the mother and grandparents if approved by a social worker. Second, was whether the grandparents were entitled to change the surname of the child to their own. This, they explained, would mean that they would not need to explain the family history to everyone who came into contact with the child and queried the difference in surname. The trial judge had refused to grant this request, a conclusion the Court of Appeal agreed with.

At the heart of both of these issues was the extent to which special guardians are permitted to make decisions concerning the child. At the general level, the Court of Appeal explained that special guardianship did give guardians the right to exercise parental responsibility in the best interests of the child. However, that did not mean that there was no judicial control over the decisions of the guardians. Indeed in the two issues under consideration s 14B of the Children Act 1989 required the court, when making a special guardianship order, to consider whether to make a contact order and enabled the court to give leave to change the surname. The response by the parents was:

> What real value ... does the name tag have if it does not give the guardians the autonomy to bring up the child in a normal way without 'big brother', the social workers, exercising the real control which, absent a care order, the local authority does not have.[532]

---

[529] CA 1989, s 14D.

[530] *Re G (Special Guardianship Order)* [2010] EWCA Civ 300.

[531] *R (Barrett) v Kirklees Metropolitan Council* [2010] 2 FCR 153. Although the local authority can determine the level of the award there need to be good reasons for it to be lower than the amounts paid to foster carers.

[532] Para 30.

The court's response was that:

> It is intended to promote and secure stability for the child cemented into this new family relationship. Links with the natural family are not severed as in adoption but the purpose undoubtedly is to give freedom to the special guardians to exercise parental responsibility in the best interests of the child. That, however, does not mean that the special guardians are free from the exercise of judicial oversight.[533]

On the surname issue, the court held that it was important that the child know of her background and live with the fact she is being brought up by her grandparents. However, given that the child was to have regular contact with her birth parents, it is not realistic to assume the child could be misled as to the relationship. As the court admitted:[534] 'In the scale of things in this child's life, her surname is a fact of little real significance.' With that in mind one might have thought that allowing the special guardians, who had undertaken, somewhat reluctantly, the enormous task of raising this troubled child, the liberty to change the name would be a minor concession. The court accepted 'that the care offered by the grandparents was exemplary' but the litigation and surrounding dispute had left them 'not far short from breaking point'.[535]

On the contact issue the relationship between the grandparents and mother was volatile and so having them together at the time of the contact session was potentially harmful to the child. However, it was held that the requirement that a social worker approve of contact in excess of that ordered was unnecessary.

## 12 Conclusion

The history of state care for children in England and Wales is littered with findings of abuse and mistreatment of these vulnerable children. It is therefore not surprising that there is now a move away from caring for children in children's homes and towards the use of adoption or fostering. The law on children in care involves a delicate balance between giving the local authority a discretion to care for a child as it thinks best and enabling parents to play an effective role in their children's lives, even though they have been taken into care. The Human Rights Act 1998 emphasises the rights of parents over children in care. Any intervention in family life must now be proportionate with the needs of the children. This might mean that the courts may be required to play a greater role in supervising the position of children in care than they have done to date. This chapter has also considered adoption, the most serious intervention by the state in family life. The Adoption and Children Act 2002 aims to increase adoption rates and produce a more co-ordinated approach to adoption. Time will tell whether adoption will be used at an increasing rate, or whether it will become an outdated institution.

---

[533] Para 33.
[534] Para 40.
[535] Para 22.

# Further reading

**Bridge, C. and Swindells, H.** (2003) *Adoption. The Modern Law*, Bristol: Jordans.

**Choudhry, S.** (2003) 'The Adoption and Children Act 2002, the welfare principle and the Human Rights Act 1998 – a missed opportunity', *Child and Family Law Quarterly* 15: 119.

**Cullen, D.** (2005b) 'Adoption – a (fairly) new approach', *Child and Family Law Quarterly* 17: 475.

**Dey, I.** (2005) 'Adapting Adoption: A case of closet politics', *International Journal of Law, Policy and the Family* 19: 289.

**Harris-Short, S.** (2002) 'Putting the child at the heart of adoption?', *Child and Family Law Quarterly* 14: 325.

**Harris-Short, S.** (2008) 'Making and breaking family life: Adoption, the state and human rights', *Journal of Law and Society* 35: 28.

**Lewis, J.** (2004) 'Adoption: The Nature of Policy Shifts in England and Wales', *International Journal of Law, Policy and the Family* 18: 235.

**Parton, N.** (2008) 'The Change for Children Programme in England: Towards the prevention-surveillance state', *Journal of Law and Society* 35: 208.

**Quinton, D. and Selwyn, J.** (2006b) 'Adoption: research, policy and practice', *Child and Family Law Quarterly* 19: 459.

**Sloan, B.** (2009) '*Re C (A Child) (Adoption: Duty of Local Authority)* – Welfare and the rights of the birth family in "fast track" adoption cases', *Child and Family Law Quarterly* 21: 87.

Visit **www.mylawchamber.co.uk/herring** to access study support resources including interactive multiple choice questions, weblinks, discussion questions and legal updates.

Use **Case Navigator** to read in full some of the key cases referenced in this chapter with commentary and questions:

*Re S, Re W (Children: Care Plan)* [2002] 2 All ER 192

# 12 Families and older people

## 1 Introduction

There is no legislative definition of 'older people'. It is most common to draw a definition in terms of the retirement age, or the age at which state pension becomes payable.[1] However defined, older people hardly constitute a homogeneous group.[2] As the catchphrase states: 'you are only as old as you feel'.[3] Certainly there are stereotypes attached to old age – frailty and failing mental capacities – but many older people are highly active in their communities. This has led to a flurry of government publications seeking to improve the autonomy and quality of life of older people: *Developing Effective Services for Older People*;[4] *Independence, Well-Being and Choice*;[5] *Living Well in Later life*.[6] Some may argue that it makes more sense to distinguish people with or without mental capacity or employment, rather than by using the category of age.[7] Indeed, as we shall see later in relation to elder abuse, in more recent years government policy has focused on the abuse of vulnerable people, rather than specifically elder abuse. Nevertheless, there are a number of particular issues that affect older people and this is recognised by the fact that the Government has set up a Ministerial Group for Older People[8] and produced a National Service Framework for Older People.[9]

In the family law context there are increasingly important questions about the extent to which families are and should be responsible for their older relatives.[10] This chapter will consider whether adult children should be liable to support their impoverished parents in their old age, and how to balance the interests of the old and young within society. It will also examine the complexities that surround the abuse of older people. The chapter will then outline what happens when older people are no longer able to look after themselves. Finally, the chapter will discuss what happens to the property of older people on their death. Before considering these issues it is necessary to quote some statistics which reveal something of the position of older people within our society.

[1] See the discussion in Herring (2009d: ch. 1).
[2] Hence this chapter will use the phrase 'older people' rather than 'elderly people'.
[3] For a discussion of the biological process of ageing see Grimley Evans (2003).
[4] National Audit Office (2003).
[5] Department of Health (2005c).
[6] Healthcare Commission (2006).
[7] For discussion of this issue see Herring (2008e).
[8] Department of Health (2000d).
[9] Philp (2006).
[10] Herring (2009g).

## 2 Statistics on older people

### A Number of older people

There has been much talk of a 'generational time bomb'. It has been claimed that there is an increasing number of older people and that a growing proportion of the population is older.[11] Certainly the statistics support this, although whether it is a 'bomb' and therefore something which should be a cause for concern is another issue.

### KEY STATISTICS

- In 2008 for the first time there were more people over 60 than children under the age of 18.[12]
- In 2009, 19% of the population were over the pensionable age (65 for men, 60 for women).[13]
- 2% of the population (1.3 million people) are over the age of 85. This percentage is expected to rise to 4% by 2031.

### B Older people and their families

It has been estimated that almost one-third of all adults in the UK are grandparents.[14] Grandparents are now the single most important source of pre-school child care after parents.[15] One survey found that 44 per cent of children were receiving regular care from grandparents.[16] Even if they are not taking part in child care, it appears that most older people are able to keep in contact with family or friends. In the OASIS survey, 75 per cent of older people in the UK had face-to-face contact at least weekly with their children; 61 per cent received instrumental help; and 76 per cent felt very close to their children.[17] However, there is also evidence that older people, especially men, who divorce early on in life have weaker links with their families in old age.[18] Society has yet to see the full consequences of the increased rate of divorce.

The sharing of accommodation by adult children and their parents is not common, with only 2 per cent of men and 7 per cent of women over 65 living with their son or daughter.[19] Increasing percentages of older people are living alone.[20] This increase (again partly caused by higher divorce rates) has important social consequences because older people who live alone are much more likely to enter institutional care than those who live with a spouse.[21] In fact there is evidence that older people much prefer to live in their own homes than in

---

[11] Ethnic minorities are under-represented, with only 2% of the over 60s being from black and ethnic communities. Ethnic minorities make up 7% of the total population: Fredman (2003: 25).
[12] National Statistics (2010a).
[13] National Statistics (2010a).
[14] Walsh (1998).
[15] Eden (2000).
[16] Fergusson, Maughan and Golding (2008).
[17] Lowenstein and Daatland (2006).
[18] Solomou, Richards, Huppert et al. (1998).
[19] Office of Population and Census Surveys (1996). See for further discussion Stewart (2007).
[20] Phillipson, Bernard, Phillips and Ogg (1999).
[21] Grundy (1992).

institutional care.[22] Ninety-five per cent of those aged 65 or over live in private households and only 4.5 per cent live in communal establishments.[23] However, that 4.5 per cent constitutes about 500,000 older people living in some form of institutional setting. Although it is rare for adult children to live with their infirm parents, it is common for them to provide day-to-day care for their parents. Most care is carried out by women aged 45–64.[24] It has been estimated that 2.8 million carers in the UK are over 60.[25]

## C Income

Poverty is endemic in old age. There were 2.3 million pensioners in poverty in 2008–09.[26] Poverty does not lie equally on gender or race[27] lines. It has been estimated that one in ten older women are very poor, living on less than half the median household income.[28] There is a particular problem with poverty among divorced women,[29] caused by the failure to ensure divorce settlements provide adequately for women on retirement.[30] Not only are there are an increasing number of pensioners below the poverty line, but the gap between the income of pensioners and employees has widened. One cause of this is the linking of pensions with the increase in the prices of goods rather than wages. There are further difficulties because many pensioners do not claim all of the credits and benefits to which they are entitled.

A Joseph Rowntree study found that:

> The risk of poverty among older people in the UK is about three to four times higher than the typical risk of poverty in Europe. People aged 75 and over rely more on benefits as a source of income and get a smaller proportion of their income from occupational pensions and investments than younger pensioners.[31]

## D Age discrimination

Much of the recent legal discussion concerning older people has centred on the concept of age discrimination.[32] The Employment Equality (Age) Regulations 2006[33] require legislation to outlaw discrimination on the grounds of age in employment matters. However, discrimination in employment is only part of the picture.[34] As Fredman has argued, unless discrimination against older people in health, housing and social security is combated, there will not be equality in the employment market.[35] It is easy to find evidence that older workers find it difficult to obtain or remain in employment. About 30 per cent of those aged between 50 and the state pension retirement age did not participate in paid employment.[36] Notably,

[22] Gibson (1998).
[23] Office of Population and Census Surveys (1993).
[24] Moynagh and Worsley (2000).
[25] Age UK (2010a).
[26] Department for Work and Pensions (2010); Age UK (2010b).
[27] On gender see Burholt and Windle (2006). On race see Platt (2007).
[28] Price (2006).
[29] Bardasi and Jenkins (2002).
[30] The increased number of divorces is linked to poverty and old age: Burholt and Windle (2006).
[31] Burholt and Windle (2006: 1).
[32] For an excellent discussion of age discrimination see Fredman (2003). See also Herring (2009d).
[33] SI 2006/1031. These implement Council Directive 2000/78/EC, discussed Herring (2010h).
[34] See also Hepple (2003).
[35] Fredman (2003: 23).
[36] National Statistics (2005e).

although younger women are 50 per cent more likely to be employed than 20 years ago, the proportion of women in employment when approaching retirement has not increased. There is also evidence that older women of Indian, Pakistani or Bangladeshi origin are particular victims of discrimination.[37]

The Equality Act 2010 outlaws discrimination on the ground of age. It covers both direct discrimination[38] (where the discrimination is blatantly on the grounds of age) and indirect discrimination[39] (where the discrimination does not refer explicitly to age, but to other grounds which in effect discriminate on the basis of age). The Act only applies to those over the age of 18. A child, therefore, cannot complain that they were discriminated against on the basis of their age. It applies to the provision of services.[40] However, unlike other forms of discrimination age discrimination can be justified if it is a 'proportionate means of achieving a legitimate aim'.[41]

## 3 Do children have an obligation to support their parents?

Some legal systems require adult children to support their aged parents.[42] In Britain such a legal obligation has not generally been accepted.[43] There is no equivalent of the Child Support Act which requires an adult child to support a parent in old age. Further, the social security system does not treat an adult child as a 'liable relative' of a parent, meaning that an adult child's resources are not taken into account when considering a parent's claim for income support. However, with the debate raging over how care for older people is to be financed, this question must be reconsidered. There is widespread feeling that there is at least a moral obligation on adult children to provide some support for their infirm parents; however, it is hard to find a convincing basis for this sense of obligation. There are a number of ways that one could establish an obligation on adult children to support parents:

1. *Reciprocated duty.* It could be argued that an obligation to support parents is a reflection of the obligation on parents to support young children. In other words, because parents provided for children in their vulnerability, children should support parents when parents become infirm. Despite the initial attraction of such an argument, there are difficulties with it. First, although parents can be said to have caused the child to be born in his or her vulnerable state, the adult child cannot be said to have caused the vulnerable state of his or her parents. A similar point is that, although parents can be said to have chosen to have the child and so impliedly undertaken the obligation to care for the child, the same could not be said of children.[44] In the light of these objections it is clear that there is not necessarily a straightforward link between the duty of parents to care for children and an adult child's obligation to care for parents.

2. *Relational support.* It could be argued that an obligation to support parents flows from the relationship of love that exists between parents and children. The difficulty is that clearly

---

[37] Fredman (2003: 25).
[38] Section 13.
[39] Section 19.
[40] Section 29.
[41] Section 13(2).
[42] See e.g. the discussion in Blair (1996); Deech (2010a).
[43] Herring (2008d). See also Oldham (2001) for an excellent discussion of the English and French approaches to this issue.
[44] Daniels (1988).

not all parents and children are in loving relationships. However, even where children and parents do not love each other, adult children may feel a sense of obligation to support their parents. This suggests that the obligation to support comes not so much from a relationship of mutual love, but from some other source. A further difficulty with the relational argument is that people do not feel an obligation to support all those with whom they are in a loving relationship. Most people would not feel obliged to support a good friend in his or her old age, even though they may choose to do so. It has been suggested that what distinguishes family relationships from friendships is the notion of intimacy. The argument here is that family life involves bonds of sharing and intimacy, unlike that in any other relationship.[45] Parents and children reveal to each other aspects of their lives that they show to no other person. However, whether this intimacy is unique to families may be questioned. Some people may feel that they are more open to their friends than to their families. All these points suggest that, although a loving relationship might form the basis of an obligation to support parents, there are other aspects that together complete a more complex picture of obligation.

3. *Implied contract*. It could be argued that there is an implied contract between parents and children that they will support each other. An obvious objection is that children are unable to consent to such a contract at birth. However, the law could assume that the child would have agreed to the contract at birth had he or she been competent to do so. This approach might carry some weight, especially if children were free to rescind the contract once they had reached sufficient maturity to decide whether to uphold it. Another objection to the contract approach is that to see the relationship between family members in terms of contract would not seem in accordance with the realities of family life. A family which regarded its relationships as governed by the terms of a formal contract would be rather unusual.

4. *Dependency*. Here the argument is that the obligation to support flows from the vulnerability of the parent. There is no doubt that some older people need care and financial help from someone. Our society would not accept that older people could be abandoned without any support. It is, then, a matter for society to decide who should provide that support. It could be argued that children are in the best position to give that care, and therefore society is entitled to require adult children to supply it.[46] This is a similar argument to the one used by Eekelaar to explain why parents are under a duty to care for their children.[47] Although children may be uniquely placed to provide emotional comfort for their older parents, whether the same is true for financial support is a different issue. This argument at its strongest could lead us to conclude that society would be entitled, if it wished, to require some kind of support of older parents by adult children. However, although there is widespread acceptance that the law is right to require parents to fulfil their parental duties, the idea that children must support their parents is much more controversial.[48]

## A Moral obligations or legal obligations?

English[49] has argued that although there may be moral obligations to support older relatives, these should not give rise to legal obligations. She argues that the law does not generally

---

[45] English (1979).
[46] Kellet (2006).
[47] Eekelaar (1991b).
[48] See Oldham (2006) for an excellent discussion.
[49] English (1979).

enforce obligations that arise out of love or friendship. Family members do not add up all they have given and all they have received from a relative in order to work out whether they should help them. Parents do not change nappies out of a sense of legal obligation, but as part of sacrificial love. These are strong arguments, but they could be used equally well in relation to adults and young children. We do place legal obligations on parents to care for young children, even though their relationship is one based on love. The law sets out the minimum required of parents, while accepting that it is just part of what is morally required of them. However, as we shall see, there is a fine line between legal obligations which compel people to provide care they may not wish to give, and the law encouraging and enabling people to give care and support voluntarily. So, before deciding what the law's response should be, it is necessary to consider what obligations family members actually feel towards older people.

## B  What obligations do people actually feel?

Despite the fact that it is difficult to pin down precisely *why* adult children owe a moral obligation to their parents, there is a widespread feeling that they do. However, such feelings of obligation are complex. Finch,[50] in her wide-ranging study of family obligations, distinguishes two kinds of moral obligation: a normative guideline; and a negotiated commitment. In basic terms, the normative guideline is an accepted standard that applies across the board to certain relationships: for example, that parents should care for their young children. The negotiated commitment is an agreement reached between two people which governs their behaviour: for example, the relationship between an elderly aunt and her nephew may develop over time to the stage where the nephew feels obliged to support his aunt even though, generally, nephews are not expected to support aunts. Finch found that, in deciding whether a person felt under an obligation to provide assistance to another, there were guidelines rather than strict rules in operation. She[51] suggests that people tend to ask two key questions: Who is this person? (e.g. are they a relative?); and How well do I get on with this person? She found that parent–child links were the strongest family ties. In parent–child relationships the second question (How well do I get on with this person?) is less significant than the needs of the older person. So an adult child may feel little responsibility for a spry elderly parent, even if their relationship is close; whereas an adult child might feel a burden of responsibility for an infirm parent, even if their relationship is not close. That said, Finch notes that most people do not clearly reason out why they act in the way they do.

A further important aspect in the obligations that family members feel they owe to each other is gender. Ungerson[52] found that women have a clearer sense of obligation to family members than men. As noted earlier, it is women who perform the majority of practical care for older relatives.

## C  Integrating family and state care

If, then, there is a sense of moral obligation towards older parents, how should the law respond? There has been some debate over whether the provision of state aid for older people has weakened the feeling of responsibility of adult children to support their parents. Finch

[50] Finch (1994).
[51] Finch (1989).
[52] Ungerson (1987).

thinks not, arguing: 'If anything it has been the state's assuming some responsibility for individuals – such as the granting of old age pensions – which has freed people to develop closer and more supportive relationships with their kin.'[53] Indeed, the existence of state services for older people has not meant that relatives do not care for each other. A high level of acceptance that children should care for their older parents has also been found. Although Finch argues that the sense of family obligation has not lessened, she accepts that the circumstances of modern life (e.g. the fact that more women are working) mean that the way people carry out their obligations has changed.[54] Such changes may lead to the result that social services will be required to perform more day-to-day services for older people.

There is increasing acceptance that it is necessary to integrate state support for older people with the support of relatives. Tinker suggests the aim should be:

> the interleaving of informal, usually family, care with statutory services that is so necessary but so difficult to achieve. What does seem evident is that without good basic statutory services, such as community nursing and help in the home, informal carers will not be able to support older people without cost to their mental and physical health. It is no use paying lip service to support for informal carers if help from professionals is not forthcoming.[55]

Not only can the role of the state be regarded as a necessary support for carers, there is also some evidence that older people perceive direct financial support from their children embarrassing and, in a sense, a lessening of their autonomy.[56] There is evidence that older people find it difficult to be in relationships with their children where they are receiving rather than giving. Therefore, receiving money directly from the Government in the form of pensions, rather than from their children, may be regarded by many as a more acceptable form of financial assistance.

## D Conclusion

A case can be made for imposing obligations on adult children. Starting with the vulnerability and needs of older people, and accepting that they should be met somehow, society *could* choose to require adult children to provide that care, as they are often best placed to provide it. Such an obligation appears to be reflected in the attitudes and practices of most adult children. However, there are good reasons why our society may prefer to support older people through taxation rather than require financial support from relatives. First, there is the evidence mentioned above that older people dislike feeling that they are a drain on their younger relatives. Enforcing financial support and practical care may therefore damage the family relationships which can be so important in old age. Secondly, such a system could work against the interests of those older people who have no children. Thirdly, as we shall see shortly, there is clear evidence of the strain often incurred by those caring for vulnerable older relatives, and such strain may be exacerbated with an explicit legal obligation. So, it is submitted, a better option is for the state to seek to enable and encourage caring among family members, rather than compel it.[57] As we shall now see, there is some attempt to do this in the present benefits system.

---

[53] Finch (1994: 243).
[54] Finch (1989: 242); Qureshi and Walker (1989).
[55] Tinker (1997: 250).
[56] Wenger (1984).
[57] For further discussion see Herring (2008d).

## 4 Financial support for older people and their carers

The state provides a wide selection of benefits to the retired. Most obviously there is the basic state pension, supplemented by the state earnings-related pension if paid into by the claimant during his or her employment. There is also a raft of other benefits including housing benefit, disability living allowance, incapacity benefit, and income benefit, as well as payments from the Social Fund, which are available to meet particular needs of the retired person. However, as mentioned earlier, these benefits are often not claimed by retired people. In addition to the state provision, the Government in recent years has encouraged people to take out private pensions if their employers have not provided occupational pensions. Oldham, considering the public provision for older people, states: 'Public provision is in a mess. Levels of under-funding are such that the welfare system is no longer straining – it is actually failing – to achieve its goals.'[58]

Of particular interest is the state's support of those who care for older people and disabled adults.[59] There is ample evidence that carers suffer great strain, both emotional[60] and financial.[61] The Government has in recent years recognised the pressures that can be caused through caring for dependent relatives and has, following its report, *Caring About Carers*,[62] set up a national strategy for carers. Indeed the Government announced a *National Strategy for Carers*, with the then Prime Minister declaring:

> What carers do should be properly recognised, and properly supported – and the Government should play its part. Carers should be able to take pride in what they do. And in turn, we should take pride in carers. I am determined to see that they do – and that we all do.[63]

Despite this, there is ample evidence that carers fail to receive much support or recognition.[64] There is, however, more help than there was in the past. For example, the local authority has the power to make special grants to enable carers to have breaks. Further, there are special benefits available for those who spend significant time caring for dependent relatives: for example, invalid care allowance.[65] By offering these funds the state is recognising the benefits that carers provide not only to their dependants, but also to the state through saving the state the cost of providing the care. The details of these benefits are beyond the scope of this book, but three important points on a theoretical level can be made:

1. Parents who do not seek employment, and instead care for children, receive no special benefits in respect of their care.[66] Further, the Government has developed the New Deal (now Flexible New Deal), through which the benefits system and other forms of assistance are designed to encourage lone parents with children to find employment.[67] So here the voluntary care by mothers (and especially lone mothers) of young children is not positively valued and encouraged by the state.[68] By contrast, the care of older people is supported

---

[58] Oldham (2001: 168).
[59] For a detailed discussion, see Herring (2007a).
[60] Healy and Yarrow (1997).
[61] Wright (1998).
[62] Department of Health (2002g). See also Carers (Recognition and Services) Act 1995.
[63] Department of Health (2005b: 1).
[64] Herring (2007a and 2008b).
[65] For the details see West (2000).
[66] Apart from child benefit, which is available to all parents.
[67] See Douglas (2000a).
[68] Morgan (2000) argues that lone parenthood is encouraged by the benefits system.

and encouraged through the benefits system, although many argue that the support given to such carers is inadequate.[69] It may be that the Government feels that carers of older people need financial incentives to provide care, which the parents of children do not need.

2. There are grave concerns that carers are inadequately valued within society. Gibson[70] suggests that social provision for frail and older people is predicated on the expectation that women provide the vast majority of the care at no fiscal cost to the state, and that the care the state does provide is subsidised by underpaid female care assistants. It has been claimed that the value of the care provided for older people and other dependent relatives is a staggering £57.4 billion per year, the equivalent to the spending on the NHS.[71] However, there is a dark side to care of older people at home. The majority of carers described themselves as 'extremely tired' and some were depressed.[72] Both the older people and carers were terrified about the possibility of having to move the older person into a nursing home. It should not be assumed that, once the older person is in residential care, their carers are then free from strain.[73]

3. What is the state's obligation towards an older person who is wealthy enough to pay for support him- or herself? To what extent can the National Health Service and social services be expected to provide free care for an older person? There are large sums of money involved, with £10.5 billion being spent on long-term care in the year 2000.[74] The Government undertook a review of the funding of long-term care for older people following a Royal Commission report.[75] The Royal Commission had argued that the state should be responsible for ensuring that older people receive the basic care necessary for their health, and therefore the state should provide the health and essential personal care without charge. They proposed distinguishing between care which involves touching the patient and care which does not: if it does, it should be provided free of charge. Other expenses, including housing[76] and non-essential personal care, would not be provided without charge under the NHS. The Government rejected this proposal, essentially on the ground that it would be too expensive. Instead, the Government decided to distinguish between health care, which would be provided free of charge, and personal care (e.g. washing patients), which would only be provided free of charge if the patient had low income and few assets.[77] This distinction is problematic.[78] As had been pointed out by the Royal Commission, a person would soon fall ill without washing. Further, if the inability to wash is caused by an illness, is it not a health issue? The Government has supported its approach by arguing that there needs to be a 'fairer and lasting balance between taxpayers and individuals' over the financing of long-term care. It is clear that the approach proposed by the Government will create artificial distinctions (between personal care and medical care), although this would happen wherever the line is drawn between what care is paid for and what is not. However, the idea that our society could accept that an older person who refuses to pay should be left unwashed seems unjustifiable in the light of the duty that society owes to all citizens to ensure that people do not suffer inhuman or degrading treatment under the Human Rights Act 1998.

---

[69] See the campaigns of Carers UK. See also Oldham (2001).
[70] Gibson (2000).
[71] Carers UK (2005).
[72] Healy and Yarrow (1997).
[73] Wright (1998).
[74] Department of Health (2000b: 1.2).
[75] Royal Commission (1999).
[76] Unless they had to be housed in a hospital.
[77] Department of Health (2000b).
[78] See Law Commission Consultation Paper 192 (2010).

# 5 Inter-generational justice

In the introduction to its plans for older people and the NHS, the Government states: 'older people are not and must never be seen as a burden on society'.[79] It is revealing that the Government felt it necessary to reject such a perception. There are few who would overtly claim that older people are a drain on society's resources. However, in the United States in particular, there has been much discussion of inter-generational justice.[80] This is an ethos that there should be fairness between the older members of society and the younger. There are some who argue that older people receive a disproportionate level of society's resources. Although those over 65 constitute 20 per cent of the population in the UK, half of all hospital and community health service expenditure is spent on them.[81] Some talk almost in terms of a battle between the older and younger generations, with the older generation calling for even greater health and pension provision for which the younger generation would have to pay through taxes.[82] There is no easy way of avoiding the fact that a society which distributes resources on the basis of need may well prefer one age group over another.

Daniels[83] wishes to move away from the image of competition between generations. He proposes the 'lifespan approach', in which he suggests that society needs to consider whether the state should provide people with special resources in their young, middle or old age. The fact that the state might provide an especially high level of services in old age is not preferring the old to the young, because the young will receive the same benefits when older. Across each person's lifetime the state expenditure will be the same, Daniels argues. In other words, 'transfers between age groups are really transfers within lives'.[84] Although his approach has much to recommend it to society, medicine and technology are changing too quickly for his approach to provide a satisfactory solution. For example, when a person is born, social attitudes and medical advances may mean that society wishes to focus provision on children, but by the time the person is older, social advances may mean that there is no need to spend so much on the young, and those funds might be better spent on older people.

## A Health care and older people: health care rationing

It is generally accepted that it is not possible for the National Health Service to provide all of the treatments and medical services that are requested. It is therefore necessary to restrict medical provision; in other words, to ration it. The issue for this chapter is whether age should be a factor in deciding who should receive a particular treatment.[85] The official view is that age rationing is not permitted. Indeed following the Equality Act 2010 any difference in treatment based on age would need to be justified. The *National Service Framework for Older People* states:

> Denying access to services on the basis of age alone is not acceptable. Decisions about treatment and health care should be made on the basis of health needs and ability to benefit rather than

---

[79] Department of Health (2000b: 1.2).
[80] E.g. G. Smith II (1997).
[81] Fox Harding (1996: 39).
[82] An American organisation, Americans for Generational Equity (AGE), argues that older people receive an undue proportion of available public resources and that it would be unreasonable to divert more funds to them.
[83] Daniels (1988: 5).
[84] Daniels (1988: 63).
[85] For a very useful discussion see Robinson (2003).

a patient's age . . . That is not to say that everyone has the same health needs; the overall health status of the individual, their assessed social care need and their own wishes and aspirations and those of their carers, should shape the package of health and social care.[86]

The National Institute for Health and Clinical Excellence has made it clear that in allocating health resources age should not be a relevant factor.[87] However, the reality may be different. Jeffreys found in her survey that, in practice, surgeons and GPs accept that age is a factor in rationing health care.[88]

It is not controversial that if, because of someone's age, a certain form of treatment is not effective then the treatment should not be offered. What is controversial is whether effective treatment should be denied simply because of age. Two examples which highlight the issues are as follows: a heart becomes available for transplantation and a hospital must choose between a 25-year-old and a 50-year-old. Apart from their age, there are no other significant differences between the patients. Should the 25-year-old be given the heart on the basis of youth? Or, take a health service trust which, because of budgetary constraints, can fund treatment either, but not both, of a disease which is most common among the elderly or a disease which more commonly afflicts the young. Should it fund the latter because of the age factor?

One approach to such questions which has gained much support has become known as Quality-Adjusted Life Years (QALYs).[89] Alan Williams explains:

> The essence of a QALY is that it takes a year of healthy life expectancy to be worth 1, but regards a year of unhealthy life expectancy as worth less than 1. Its precise value is lower the worse the quality of life of the unhealthy person (which is what the quality adjusted bit is all about) . . . The general idea is that a beneficial health care activity is one that generates a positive amount of QALYs, and that an efficient health care activity is one where the cost-per-QALYs is as low as it can be. A high priority health care activity is one where the cost-per-QALY is low, and a low priority activity is one where the cost-per-QALY is high.[90]

So the approach attempts to calculate the improvement in life quality and life expectancy caused by the treatment. A key difficulty with the approach is that it can be hard to assess 'quality': how can one compare the increase in quality of life resulting from infertility treatment with that resulting from a hip replacement? In Oregon, in the United States, a vote was taken among the population to assess which operations were regarded as most improving the quality of life. Cosmetic breast surgery scored very highly on QALYs, in fact higher than hip replacements. This might suggest that relying on public opinion to decide what constitutes 'quality of life' would produce unacceptable results.

There are three particular difficulties in the way the QALY approach would operate in relation to elderly patients. First, the approach does not have built-in protection for the dignity of the patient. It is arguable that some treatments could be necessary even though they would not score highly on a QALYs assessment (e.g. pain relief in the last few days of a person's life). The second difficulty with the approach is that it assumes that time is equally precious to all people. A treatment denied to a person on their deathbed that would give them six months more to live is not directly comparable to treatment given to a 30-year-old, not in any mortal

---

[86] Quoted in Fredman (2003: 41). See also Health Advisory Service (2000).
[87] National Institute for Health and Clinical Excellence (2005).
[88] Jeffreys (1995). See E. Roberts (2000) finding rationing on the basis of age throughout the NHS. For a useful general discussion see Robinson (2003: 101).
[89] For a detailed discussion see Herring (2008b: ch 2).
[90] Williams (1985: 3).

danger, which would increase their life expectancy by six months. Thirdly, some claim that the QALY calculation constitutes age discrimination as it would always work against older people. The elderly would always be at a disadvantage in their ability to demonstrate as many improved years as a younger person.

Some who reject QALY argue that like patients should be treated alike and, if a patient would benefit from a hip replacement, the age of the patient should not be a relevant consideration. Treatment should instead focus on need,[91] although it is arguable that it is not age discrimination to distinguish between individuals on the basis of life expectancy.

In a highly controversial book, Callahan argues that we need to work towards a society which appreciates the concept of 'a tolerable death'. He explains:

> My definition of a 'tolerable death' is this: the individual event of death at that stage in a life span when (a) one's life possibilities have on the whole been accomplished; (b) one's moral obligations to those for whom one has had responsibility have been discharged; and (c) one's death will not seem to others an offence to sense or sensibility, or tempt others to despair and rage at the finitude of human existence.[92]

He contrasts intolerable death (such as the death of a child) with tolerable death (that of a person in old age). He suggests that once someone has reached their natural life span (which he asserts may be late 70s or early 80s) then medical resources should not be used to resist death, although treatment can be provided to mitigate pain and suffering. At the heart of his argument is a belief that medicine must have limited aims and cannot be involved in a relentless effort to save life. Therefore, resources should not be spent on those who have reached their natural life span and should instead be focused on preventing intolerable (early) death. The problem with Callahan's argument is that while his concept of a timely and tolerable death may be acceptable to many, it will not be to all. Some may spend their youth and middle age working hard and looking forward to retirement, seeing their 70s and 80s as the prime of their life. Is it justifiable for our society to rule out this version of 'the good life'? Callahan's argument, however, makes a powerful case. If our society wishes not to adopt his approach, it must be willing to pay the extra taxes or health insurance payments to ensure that it does not occur.

## 6 Incapable older people

### A Do older people have rights?

Clearly, old people who have mental capacity have rights. However, more difficult is the position of older people who through illness or old age lack capacity.[93] Of all people aged 80 or more, over one in five will suffer some kind of dementia.[94] When children's rights were discussed in Chapter 8, it was noted that there are some difficulties in claiming that children have rights because they cannot choose whether to exercise their rights. The approach propounded by Eekelaar was that children's basic, developmental and autonomy interests should be promoted so that once children were sufficiently mature they would be in a position

---

[91] Banner (1995).
[92] Callahan (1997: 66).
[93] Goodin and Gibson (1997).
[94] Gibson (2000: 42).

to make life choices for themselves.[95] Such an approach is not possible for incapable older people. Older people will already have developed their own style of life and values. Therefore the law cannot take a neutral position and make decisions for older people that would enable them to make their own once competent; this is because, having lost competence, most older people will not regain it.

Goodin and Gibson suggest that, for these reasons, it is inappropriate to hold that an incompetent older person has rights and instead the law should move towards a different approach: 'A much more apt description of our duties and their due is couched in terms of a broader but in many ways more demanding notion of "right conduct" towards dependent others.'[96] So, rather than talking about the protection of interests, 'it is rather, that there are certain sorts of things that we must, and certain sorts of things that we must not, do to and for particular sorts of people'.[97] This view therefore says that we cannot talk about rights for the older incapable person, because they cannot choose what they want, and the law cannot ascertain the interests that should be protected. However, this does not mean that older people should be unprotected because others are obliged to treat them with 'right conduct'. There is much to be said for such an approach, although talk of 'right conduct' lacks the punch of 'rights' in political rhetoric.

## B When does an older person lose capacity in the eyes of the law?

The answer to this question is the same as that for any adult.[98] A patient must be competent in order to be able to provide legally effective consent. Section 1(2) of the Mental Capacity Act 2005 (MCA 2005) makes it clear it should be presumed that a patient is competent, unless there is evidence that he or she is not.[99] If the case comes to court the burden is on the doctor or whoever treated the patient in a particular way to demonstrate that the patient lacks capacity on the balance of probabilities.[100] But what exactly does it mean to say that the patient is incompetent? Section 2(1) of the MCA 2005 states:

---

**LEGISLATIVE PROVISION**

**Mental Capacity Act 2005, section 2(1)**

. . . a person lacks capacity in relation to a matter if at the material time he is unable to make a decision for himself in relation to the matter because of an impairment of, or a disturbance in the functioning of, the mind or brain.

---

So, for a person to be incompetent it must be shown that he or she is unable to make a decision for him- or herself. Section 3(1) explains:

---

[95] Eekelaar (1986).
[96] Goodin and Gibson (1997: 186).
[97] Goodin and Gibson (1997: 186).
[98] See Herring (2010e) for a detailed discussion of the law.
[99] *R v Sullivan* [1984] AC 156 at 170–1.
[100] *R (On the Application of N) v Dr M, A NHS Trust and Dr O* [2002] EWHC 1911 (Fam).

LEGISLATIVE PROVISION

**Mental Capacity Act 2005, section 3(1)**

. . . a person is unable to make a decision for himself if he is unable—

(a)  to understand the information relevant to the decision,

(b)  to retain that information,

(c)  to use or weigh that information as part of the process of making the decision, or

(d)  to communicate his decision (whether by talking, using sign language or any other means).

As this indicates, there are a number of ways in which a person may be said to be unable to make a decision. It may be a case of lack of comprehension: the person is not capable of understanding their condition or the proposed treatment or the consequences of not receiving treatment.[101] A patient may be found to have sufficient understanding to be able to consent to a minor straightforward piece of medical treatment, but not have sufficient understanding to be able to consent to a far more complex procedure.[102] The MCA 2005, however, emphasises that a patient should not be treated as lacking capacity 'unless all practical steps to help him' reach capacity 'have been taken without success'. Further, under s 2(2):

LEGISLATIVE PROVISION

**Mental Capacity Act 2005, section 2(2)**

A person is not to be regarded as unable to understand the information to a decision if he is able to understand an explanation of it given to him in a way that is appropriate to his circumstances (using simple language, visual aids or any other means).

To be competent the patient must also be able to use the information: weigh it and be able to make a decision. This means that, even though a patient may fully understand the issues involved, if she is in such a panic that she is unable to process this knowledge to reach a decision then she will be incompetent. Section 1(3) of the MCA 2005 states that: 'A person is not to be treated as unable to make a decision merely because he makes an unwise decision.'[103] There is a careful line to be trodden between not allowing the line of reasoning: this decision is irrational therefore the patient is incompetent; but permitting the reasoning: this decision is irrational because the individual is not able to properly weigh up the different issues and therefore is incompetent.[104]

[101] MCA 2005, s 2(4).

[102] A point emphasised in *Re W* [2002] EWHC 901 and *Gillick v West Norfolk and Wisbech Area Health Authority and Another* [1986] AC 112, 169 and 186.

[103] Despite the clear statement of this principle, commentators have claimed that the judges have done exactly this to ensure patients receive the treatment they need: Montgomery (2000).

[104] See Savulescu and Momeyer (1997) who insist that a patient's decision must be based on rational belief if it is to be respected.

In order to show that a person lacks capacity under the MCA 2005 it is not enough just to show that they are unable to make a decision for themselves; it must be shown that this is as a result of an impairment of, or disturbance in the functioning of, the mind or the brain. The significance of this is that a patient has capacity if there is no mental impairment or disturbance, however impaired their reasoning process may have been. So, for example, a patient with no mental impairment who refuses all treatment because of her religious belief that God will cure her will not lack capacity, even if the doctors try to argue that she does not properly understand the reality of her situation.

A final point on competence is that the MCA 2005 makes special provision to ensure that patients are not assessed as lacking capacity in a prejudicial way. Section 2(3) states:

## LEGISLATIVE PROVISION

**Mental Capacity Act 2005, section 2(3)**

A lack of capacity cannot be established merely by reference to—

a person's age or appearance, or

a condition of his, or an aspect of his behaviour, which might lead others to make unjustified assumptions about him.

This is designed to ensure that a patient who appears unkempt or disordered is not assessed as lacking capacity purely on that basis. The use of the word 'merely' is perhaps surprising because it suggests prejudicial attitudes can be a factor taken into account in assessing capacity.[105] Of course, even if a patient has mental capacity, if their consent is as a result of deceit or undue influence[106] it will be legally ineffective.

The Mental Capacity Act 2005 enables a competent adult (P) to create a lasting power of attorney which enables its donee (i.e. the person appointed to act under the lasting power of attorney) to make decisions on P's behalf when P becomes incompetent.[107] The MCA 2005 also enables the court to appoint a deputy to make certain decisions on behalf of a person who has become incompetent.[108] Perhaps most significantly, the Act allows competent people to create advance decisions rejecting treatment in the event that they become incompetent.[109] If the patient then becomes incompetent the advance decision must be respected.

The treatment of a patient lacking capacity is now governed by the Mental Capacity Act 2005. The Act applies only to those over the age of 16.[110] It will be remembered that the Act makes it clear that a patient should be presumed to be competent.[111] If it is found that the patient is incompetent and a medical professional wishes to treat the patient, then the following questions must be considered.

---

[105] Bartlett (2005: 28).
[106] See Burns (2002).
[107] MCA 2005, s 9.
[108] MCA 2005, s 19.
[109] MCA 2005, s 24.
[110] Although the offence of ill-treatment or wilful neglect of a person lacking capacity in s 44 has no limit. Also, in s 18(3) there is power for the court to deal with the property of an incapable minor.
[111] MCA 2005, s 1(2).

1. Has the patient created an effective advance decision (sometimes called a 'living will') which refuses the treatment in question? If so, the advance decision must be respected.

2. Has the patient effectively created a lasting power of attorney (LPA)? If so, the donee of the LPA may be able to make the decision.

3. Has the court appointed a deputy? If so, the deputy in some cases can make the decision.

4. If there is no effective advance decision and no LPA or deputy who can make the decision, then the question is whether the treatment is in the best interests of the patient.

We need, therefore, to consider the four scenarios separately:

## C  Advance decisions

An advance decision is defined in MCA 2005, s 24 thus:

---

### LEGISLATIVE PROVISION

**Mental Capacity Act 2005, section 24**

'Advance Decision' means a decision made by a person ('P'), after he has reached 18 and when he has capacity to do so, that if—

at a later time and in such circumstances as he may specify, a specified treatment is proposed to be carried out or continued by a person providing health care for him, and

at that time he lacks capacity to consent to the carrying out or continuation of the treatment, the specified treatment is not to be carried out or continued.

---

A number of points should be noted about this definition. First, the advance decision is only effective if, when it was made, P (the patient) was over 18 and competent. Secondly, the advance decision is only to be relevant if the patient lacks capacity to consent to the treatment. So, if a patient has signed an advance decision refusing to consent to a blood transfusion, but at the time is competent and consents, then the advance decision should be ignored.[112] Thirdly, the definition of advance decisions only allows 'negative' decisions; decisions to refuse treatment. An advance decision cannot be used to compel a medical professional to provide treatment. The definition of advance decision covers both treatment and the continuation of treatment. An advance decision could, therefore, indicate that P is willing to receive treatment, but only for a certain period of time. If the advance decision does reject life-saving treatment it must be in writing and signed by P and witnessed by a third party.[113] Otherwise the decision does not need to be in writing.

Section 25 explains how an advance decision may be invalid. This is where P, with capacity, has withdrawn the advance decision; where P has created an LPA after making the advance decision and given the LPA the power to make the decision in question; or where P has done anything else which is clearly inconsistent and to which the decision related.

Section 26(1) of the MCA 2005 explains:

---

[112] MCA 2005, s 25(3).
[113] MCA 2005, s 25(6).

> **LEGISLATIVE PROVISION**
>
> **Mental Capacity Act 2005, section 26(1)**
>
> If P has made an advance decision which is—
>
> (a) valid, and
>
> (b) applicable to the treatment,
>
> the decision has the effect as if he had made it, and had had capacity to make it, at the time when the question arises whether the treatment should be carried out or continued.

This means that if P has a valid and applicable advance decision which rejects treatment the medical professional should not provide it. If she or he does then there is the potential for a criminal or tortious action. However, under s 26(2): 'A person does not incur liability for carrying out or continuing the treatment unless, at the time, he is satisfied that an advance decision exists which is valid and applicable to the treatment.'

## D Lasting powers of attorney

If a person wants someone else to make decisions on their behalf when they become incompetent they can make a lasting power of attorney (LPA) under s 9 of the MCA 2005. The donee or donees of the LPA can make decisions for general matters relating to someone's welfare, including some medical decisions. In order to execute an LPA the person (P) must be over 18 years old and have capacity to do so.[114] There are strict regulations as to the formalities surrounding the LPA and its registration. These are set out in Schedule 1 to the MCA 2005. If they are not complied with the LPA will be ineffective.

The donee of the LPA must be over the age of 18. It is possible to appoint more than one LPA. Unless the LPA says so, where more than one donee is appointed they are to act jointly.[115] In other words, all of them must agree on the decision in question before using the LPA. An LPA can be revoked at any time if P has the capacity to do so.[116]

Where an LPA has been validly appointed and the donee has the power to make decisions about P's personal welfare then this can extend to giving or refusing to the carrying out of health care. However, this is subject to an important restriction in that the donee must make the decision based on what would be in P's best interests, as described in s 4 (which will be discussed below).

## E Deputies

Under the MCA 2005, s 16, if P lacks capacity in relation to a matter concerning her or his personal welfare (e.g. a health issue) then the court can make the decision on P's behalf or decide to appoint a deputy to make decisions on P's behalf. In deciding whether to appoint a deputy the court should consider whether to do so would be in P's best interests (considering the factors in s 4 which we shall be looking at shortly) and also the following principles:

[114] MCA 2005, s 9.
[115] MCA 2005, s 9(5).
[116] MCA 2005, s 13(2).

(a) a decision by the court is to be preferred to the appointment of a deputy to make a decision, and

(b) the powers conferred on a deputy should be as limited in scope and duration as is reasonably practicable in the circumstances.

This suggests that where there is a 'one off' decision to be made about P, appointing a deputy is unlikely to be appropriate. Where decisions need to be made about P on a regular basis then a deputy may be more suitable. A deputy must be over the age of 18 and have consented to take on the role.[117] The court can appoint more than one deputy; and it can revoke the appointment of a deputy.[118]

## F Court decision based on best interests

An application can be made to court in respect of any person who lacks capacity. The court can make a declaration as to the lawfulness of any act concerning the individual. The decision will be made based on what is in the best interests of the patient, as that is understood under MCA 2005, s 4.

## G The best interests of the person

If an advance decision is valid and applicable that must be respected and the issue of what is in P's best interests does not arise. However, where a court or donee of an LPA or deputy or a person caring for or providing treatment to P is making a decision concerning P, the decision must be made based on what is in P's best interests.[119] Section 1(6) emphasises that:

> Before the act, is done, or decision is made, regard must be had to whether the purpose for which it is needed can be effectively achieved in a way that is less restrictive of the person's rights and freedom of action.

So, whenever a decision is being made about an incompetent patient it is not enough just to show that the action is in P's best interests; it must be shown there is not an equally good way of promoting P's interests which is less invasive of his rights or freedom.

Section 4 of the MCA 2005 states that, in deciding what is in a patient's best interests, the court or deputy must consider all the relevant circumstances, including the following factors:

(i) '(a) whether it is likely that the person will at some time have capacity in relation to the matter in question, and (b) if it appears likely that he will, when that is likely to be'.[120] Clearly if the person is soon to regain capacity it may be better, if possible, to postpone making a decision so she or he can make it for her- or himself.

(ii) The decision-maker must 'so far as reasonably practicable, permit and encourage the person to participate, or to improve his ability to participate, as fully as possible in any act done for him and any decision affecting him'.[121] This is a recognition that even if it is not possible for the person to make a decision for himself, he should still be involved to a reasonable extent in the decision-making process and his views listened to.

---

[117] MCA 2005, s 19.
[118] MCA 2005, s 16(8).
[119] MCA 2005, s 1(5).
[120] MCA 2005, s 4(3).
[121] MCA 2005, s 4(4). See Herring (2009f) for further discussion.

(iii) The decision-maker must consider, so far as is reasonably ascertainable, '(a) the person's past and present wishes and feelings (and, in particular, any relevant written statement made by him when he had capacity), (b) the beliefs and values that would be likely to influence his decision if he had capacity, and (c) the other factors that he would be likely to consider if he were able to do so'.[122] It should be emphasised that the MCA 2005 does not adopt a substituted judgment test (see below). In other words, it does not require decision-makers to make their decision based on what they guess the person would have decided if she or he had been competent. However, as this factor makes clear, the views of the person while competent, and assessment of what decision she or he would have made if competent, can be taken into account in deciding what are in her or his best interests.

(iv) The decision-maker should, if practical and appropriate, consider the views of '(a) anyone named by the person as someone to be consulted on the matter in question or on matters of that kind, (b) anyone engaged in caring for the person or interested in his welfare, (c) any donee of a lasting power of attorney granted by the person, and (d) any deputy appointed for the person, by the court, as to what would be in the patient's best interests'. The decision-maker may choose to consult a wider group of people than this, but is not required to do so.[123] It is unclear how much weight should be placed on the views of a family. If P's family are all Jehovah's Witnesses and oppose the required blood transfusion, should their views carry the day? Probably not; the views of family members are only one factor and in such a case it would be hard to see P's death as in P's best interests, as that term is generally understood in society. If the court decides that it is important that the relative has an on-going relationship with P, then their views may be relevant to ensure that continues.[124]

There are two factors which the decision-maker should not take into account:

(i) A decision as to what is in a person's best interests should not be made merely on the basis of '(a) the person's age or appearance, or (b) a condition of his, or an aspect of his behaviour, which might lead others to make unjustified assumptions about what might be in his best interests'. This might be most relevant in combating assumptions about older people and what is best for them.

(ii) Section 4(5) states: 'Where the determination relates to life-sustaining treatment [the decision-maker], in considering whether the treatment is in the best interests of the person concerned, may not be motivated by a desire to bring about his death.'

These factors have been described as 'open ended' and 'quite broad'.[125] This is probably inevitable. People, their circumstances, their families and beliefs are so different that it would be difficult to produce a more concrete list that would not lead to undesirable results in some cases. However, the looseness of the definition of best interests means it will be very difficult to challenge a decision-maker's determination as to what is in P's best interests.

Where an incompetent patient is opposing treatment, articles 3 and 8 of the European Convention on Human Rights may become relevant. These require the state to protect the patient from torture or inhuman or degrading treatment. In *Herczegfalvy v Austria*[126] the

---

[122] MCA 2005, s 4(6).
[123] Department of Constitutional Affairs (2004: para 4.23).
[124] *A Primary Care Trust and P v AH and A Local Authority* [2008] 2 FLR 1196.
[125] Bartlett (2005: 35–6).
[126] (1993) 50 EHRR 437, at para 82.

European Court held that 'as a general rule, treatment which is a therapeutic necessity cannot be regarded as inhuman or degrading. The court must nevertheless satisfy itself that the medical necessity has been convincingly shown to exist.'

In recent years the courts have shown an increasing willingness to use the Mental Capacity Act 2005 to make orders in relation to those who have lost capacity or are classified as vulnerable adults.[127] In *Surrey Council v MB*,[128] a woman was removed from her home and put into a nursing home against her wishes, after it was found that she was unable to care for herself and posed a risk of causing herself serious harm. As this case indicates, under the Act a patient can be deprived of their liberty, although there are strict requirements which need to be satisfied.[129] Before someone is removed to a care home the local authority should convince themselves that there are no relatives who can care for the patient.[130]

## 7 Succession and intestacy

This section will consider what happens to people's property on their death. What is particularly revealing is the law's acknowledgement that family members may have legally enforceable claims on the estate, even if there is no will. Before considering the law, the theoretical issues will be discussed.

### A Theory

It is important to distinguish between two situations: first, where the deceased has left a will; and, secondly, where the deceased has not left a will or has left a will that does not deal with all of the deceased's property. These two scenarios give rise to quite different problems.

### (i) Where there is a will

Where someone leaves a will it might be thought that the issue is straightforward. Our society accepts that people should be free to dispose of their property in whatever ways they wish, however foolish others may think them to be. If during their lives people wish to spend all of their hard-earned money on gambling or purchasing law textbooks, they may, and unless they are mentally incompetent there is no way of stopping them. If this is true in life, should it not also be true in death? Not necessarily, because on divorce the law feels entitled to redistribute a spouse's property to achieve a fair result. If the law is willing to do this when a relationship is ended by divorce, should it not also be able to do so if the relationship is ended by death?

As we shall see, the law's response to these arguments is to seek a middle course. A person is permitted to make a will directing what should happen to his or her property on death, but if anyone feels that the will has not provided for them adequately then they are allowed to apply to the court for an order that they receive a payment out of the estate under the Inheritance (Provision for Family and Dependants) Act 1975. What is interesting is that the class of potential claimants is not restricted to spouses. Other relatives may claim that the

---

[127] See Herring (2009g).
[128] [2007] EWHC 3085 (Fam).
[129] Ministry of Justice (2008); *GJ v Foundation Trust, PCT and the Secretary of State for Health* [2010] 1 FLR 1251. These cases can involve some complex issues concerning the interaction of the Mental Capacity Act 2005 and the Mental Health Act 1983, see Richardson (2010).
[130] *LLBC v TG, JG and KR* [2009] 1 FLR 414.

deceased has not adequately provided for them in the will. The intervention of the law could be based on two grounds. First, it could be argued that even though the deceased had made a will, he or she could not really have intended not to provide for the claimant and the law is intervening to ensure that the will truly reflects the wishes of the deceased. Alternatively, the law could be explained as being a recognition that legal claims can be made on the deceased's income. Neither of these arguments is satisfactory. With the first there is the difficulty that an award can be made under the Act even if the evidence is clear that the deceased did not want the claimant to receive any of his or her money. The problem with the second is that, while a person is alive, the law does not recognise a liability to provide for other relatives apart from spouses.[131] There does not seem to be a strong reason to explain why these obligations suddenly spring into existence on the death of a person. It may be argued that, while alive, a person has the right to govern what happens to their property and this trumps the claims of other family members; however, once deceased, a person has no rights and so the law can give effect to the claims of other family members.

### (ii) Where there is no will: intestacy

There are different issues where the deceased has left no will. Here there are two main possible approaches: the law could attempt to ascertain what the wishes of the deceased were, considering all the evidence available; or the law could decide objectively what would be a fair and just distribution of the property. The two approaches could be intermingled: we might presume that a deceased's intention would be a fair and just settlement, but there may be occasions when there is evidence that the deceased did not wish a fair distribution to be made.

In a way, the law on intestacy is easier to defend than the law where there is a will. The law makes it clear that if an individual does not make a will then the law will decide how the property will be distributed. If the deceased decides not to make a will, he or she can make no objection (were they able to!) about the distribution of the property. Given the difficulties and litigation that would inevitably surround a law based on attempting to ascertain the deceased's wishes, the law has developed a set formula which operates in cases of intestacy. It has been estimated that about 40 per cent of people aged over 60 have not made a will[132] and so it is important that the formula is predictable and discourages litigation. However, because a formula is not appropriate in every case, English and Welsh law has established a procedure by which an application can be made to the court if the result of the statutory rules would produce injustice.

### B The law in cases where there is a will

The starting point is that the will is enacted and property is distributed according to it. There are, of course, ways to challenge a will. It can be argued that a will does not comply with the formalities in the Wills Act 1837, or that the will was made by the deceased while of unsound mind or as a result of undue influence[133] or that the will has been revoked.[134] The detail of the law cannot be covered here,[135] but if the will is invalid for any of these reasons then the

---

[131] Unless a legally binding contract has been entered into.
[132] Law Commission Report 187 (1989).
[133] See Kerridge (2000) for concerns that the law may fail adequately to protect vulnerable testators.
[134] E.g. divorce will revoke a will.
[135] An excellent summary can be found in *Cattermole v Prisk* [2006] Fam Law 98.

estate will be dealt with using the rules of intestacy. There may also be arguments that a particular piece of property does not belong (or does not wholly belong) to the deceased. For example, it may be argued that the house, although being in the name of the deceased, was in fact held on trust for the deceased and his wife under a constructive trust or proprietary estoppel.[136] In such a case, if the deceased purported in his will to give the house to his daughter, he would only be able to give her his share of the house.

If someone feels that they have not been adequately provided for under the will they may be able to make a claim under the Inheritance (Provision for Family and Dependants) Act 1975, which will be discussed shortly.

## C Intestacy

The rules that operate on intestacy apply where the deceased has not made a will or has made a will that does not dispose of his or her entire estate.[137] The rules are rather complex and depend on whether the deceased has a surviving spouse or any surviving issue (that is, children of the deceased, including adopted children and children born outside marriage).

### (i) If there is a surviving spouse and children or grandchildren

If there is a surviving spouse[138] and issue then the surviving spouse is entitled to all of the personal chattels,[139] and £125,000 (known as the statutory legacy), if there is that much in the deceased's estate. If there is still money or property left in the estate after these transfers are made then the spouse has a life interest in half the remainder. The balance of the estate (subject to the spouse's life interest) is held on statutory trust for the children. This will mean that the children will be entitled to maintenance until they are 18 and then they will be entitled to the capital.[140]

### (ii) If there is a surviving spouse, no issue, but close relatives

If there is a surviving spouse and no children, but there are surviving parents, brothers or sisters,[141] then the spouse is entitled to the personal chattels absolutely, £200,000 statutory legacy and half of the balance absolutely (rather than just a life interest). The parents, or if no parents then brothers or sisters (or their issue[142]), are entitled to the other half of the remainder.

### (iii) If there is a surviving spouse, but no issue or close relatives

If there is a surviving spouse but no parents or brothers or sisters or issue of brothers and sisters then the spouse will take the intestate's estate absolutely.

---

[136] See Chapter 4.

[137] See Law Commission Consultation Paper 191 (2009) for proposals for reform of the law which would increase rights of cohabitants.

[138] It is necessary for the spouse to have survived the deceased by 28 days if he or she is to be seen as a surviving spouse: Administration of Estates Act 1925, s 46.

[139] In basic terms the furniture and personal objects of the parties. The term is defined in the Administration of Estates Act 1925, s 55(1)(x).

[140] Cretney (1995). The Law Commission Report 187 (1989) found that the majority of people thought the surviving spouse should receive everything on the death of a spouse.

[141] They must be of the whole blood.

[142] 'Issue' here means the children of the brother and sister. They will take their parent's share if the parent has died.

## (iv) If there is no surviving spouse

If there is no spouse then there is a list of relatives who may be entitled to the estate in the following order. Whichever relatives are highest up the list will take the estate absolutely and those lower down the list will take nothing:

1. children of the deceased or grandchildren;
2. parents of the deceased;
3. brothers or sisters of the whole blood, or their issue;
4. brothers or sisters of the half blood, or their issue;
5. grandparents of the deceased;
6. aunts or uncles of the deceased, or their issue.

If there is more than one relative in a category they will share the estate equally. If there is no one related to the deceased in this list then the estate will go to the Crown, *bona vacantia*. It is open to the Crown to give as a matter of grace some of the property to friends or others who fall outside the terms of the intestacy rules.[143] This power is most likely to be used in the case of cohabitants. Any person who is unhappy about the operation of the intestacy rules can apply to the court under the Inheritance (Provision for Family and Dependants) Act 1975.

As has been noted, a spouse is entitled to the personal chattels of the deceased: for example, the television, the bed, any pets, etc. This seems only sensible and is largely uncontroversial. In addition, the spouse is given absolutely a lump sum which he or she may use to purchase somewhere to live,[144] and a life interest in the rest of the estate which will provide him or her with an income. The rules do not mean that the spouse will automatically be able to live in the house. This may seem harsh but it is mitigated by two rules. The first is that if the family home is in the joint names of the deceased and the spouse then, on the deceased's death, under the rules of land law, the house will belong to the spouse absolutely and will not normally be regarded as part of the deceased's estate. So the spouse would have the house as well as the statutory legacy, and so should be well provided for. Secondly, even if the house is not in joint names then there are rules permitting the spouse to use his or her statutory legacy to purchase the house from the estate. Nevertheless, if the house is in the sole name of the deceased and is worth more than the statutory legacy, then the house may have to be sold. This has led some to argue that the spouse should be entitled to the entire estate of the deceased.[145] However, others argue that the present law is too generous to spouses. The circumstances in which it might appear too generous are where the deceased had remarried and the second spouse acquires the estate under the intestacy rules. The children of the deceased, especially if they do not get on well with their step-parent, may fear that the estate will ultimately be diverted to the step-parent's 'family' rather than the deceased's family. Another very important point about the intestacy rules is that they do not provide for unmarried cohabiting partners, nor good friends. The focus is very much on blood relations and spouses, not social relations. This is in contrast to other parts of the law[146] where social relationships are emphasised.

---

[143] See Williams, Potter, and Douglas (2008) for evidence of support among the public for increased provision in the intestacy rules for cohabitants.
[144] The spouse is entitled to take the matrimonial home in lieu of his or her lump sum.
[145] Law Commission Report 187 (1989).
[146] See Chapter 7, for example.

## D  The Inheritance (Provision for Family and Dependants) Act 1975

Where relatives or dependants feel that an inadequate sum has been left to them as a result of the deceased's will or the rules on intestacy, an application can be made to the court for an order. The burden of persuading the court to make the order rests on the applicant. There are no rights to property under the Act; the legislation simply gives the court a discretion to decide the appropriate amount, if any, to be paid to a claimant. The court is entitled to provide for someone who is not mentioned in the will or would not be entitled to money on intestacy. An individual can claim under the Act even if the deceased had made it quite plain that he or she did not wish the individual to receive any money on their death. The policy of the Act has been to ensure that a person who has become dependent upon the deceased does not suffer an injustice on the deceased's death.[147]

### (i)  Who can apply?

The following can apply under the Act:

1. The spouse or civil partner of the deceased.[148]

2. The former spouse or civil partner of the deceased, providing the applicant has not remarried or entered another civil partnership.[149]

3. A person who '... during the whole of the period of two years ending immediately before the date when the deceased died ... was living—(a) in the same household as the deceased, and (b) as the husband or wife [or civil partner] of the deceased'.[150]

    This category would include many cohabiting couples.[151] The test to be applied is whether a reasonable person with normal powers of perception would say the couple was living together as husband and wife.[152] In using this test the reasonable person should be aware of the multifarious nature of marriages.[153] Therefore, in *Re Watson*[154] a couple in their fifties who started living together companionably without engaging in sexual relations could be said to be living as husband and wife. Indeed, Neuberger J noted that many married couples in their mid-fifties do not have sexual relations. In *Baynes v Hedger*[155] it was held that living as the deceased's civil partner or spouse required that the relationship was publicly acknowledged. A clandestine same-sex relationship could not be categorised as living as civil partners.[156] In *Lindop v Agus, Bass and Hedley*[157] the couple lived together, had a sexual relationship, shared finances and on occasions cared for children together. It was held that the woman could claim under the Act, even though she had retained a separate address for many formal purposes. The requirement that the cohabitation last until

---

[147] *Jelley v Iliffe* [1981] Fam 128 CA.

[148] Inheritance (Provision for Family and Dependants) Act 1975 (hereafter I(PFD)A 1975), s 1(1)(a). This includes people who in good faith entered a void marriage with the deceased: I(PFD)A 1975, s 25(4), but does not include former spouses.

[149] I(PFD)A 1975, s 1(1)(b).

[150] I(PFD)A 1975, s 1A. This category of claimants is available only if the deceased died on or after 1 January 1996.

[151] See the reasoning in *Fitzpatrick v Sterling Housing Association Ltd* [2000] 1 FCR 21 HL.

[152] *Re Watson* [1999] 1 FLR 878.

[153] See Chapter 1 for a discussion of the factors a court is likely to take into account in deciding whether there was cohabitation.

[154] [1999] 1 FLR 878.

[155] [2008] 3 FCR 151.

[156] It may be argued that this fails to take into account the prejudice that can be shown towards open same-sex couples.

[157] [2010] 1 FLR 631.

'immediately' before the death has to be interpreted sensibly. In *Re Watson*[158] the deceased spent the last few weeks of his life in hospital and that did not prevent the section applying. In *Gully v Dix*[159] the claimant and deceased had cohabited for over 25 years, but she left the house three months before his death, saying she would return when he stopped drinking. The Court of Appeal took the view that in light of the length of the relationship she was still living in the same household as the deceased, even if she had temporarily moved out. There had not been an irretrievable breakdown in relations. In *Churchill v Roach*[160] Judge Norris QC said that to live in the same household it was necessary to have 'elements of permanence, to involve a consideration of the frequency and intimacy of contact, to contain an element of mutual support, to require some consideration of the degree of voluntary restraint upon personal freedom which each party undertakes, and to involve an element of community of resources'.

4. Any child of the deceased, including posthumous, adopted and grown-up children.[161] An adopted child cannot claim under this ground against their biological parents, but can claim against their adopted parents.[162]

5. Any person 'treated by the deceased as a child of the family in relation to' a marriage or civil partnership.[163] This is similar to the concept 'child of the family' discussed in Chapter 7. It most commonly applies in relation to stepchildren.[164] It should be stressed that this category exists only in the context of a marriage or civil partnership. If the deceased cohabits with a woman and her child from a previous relationship, the child could not rely on this category.[165]

6. Any other person 'who immediately before the death of the deceased was being maintained, either wholly or partly, by the deceased'.[166] The phrase 'maintained' in this definition is clarified in s 1(3):

> a person shall be treated as being maintained by the deceased, either wholly or partly, as the case may be, if the deceased, otherwise than for full valuable consideration, was making a substantial contribution in money or money's worth towards the reasonable needs of that person.

This could include unmarried cohabitees as well as two friends living together without a sexual relationship but with a degree of maintenance. A few points need to be stressed about fulfilling the definition of this category:

(a) The maintenance must be substantial. In *Rees v Newbery and the Institute of Cancer Research*[167] the deceased had provided the applicant (an actor) with a flat in London at a low rent. There was no cohabitation nor sexual or emotional relationship between them, but it was found that the applicant had been maintained by the deceased, by providing the flat. It does not need to be shown that but for the financial assistance the claimant would have been in dire poverty.[168]

---

[158] [1999] 1 FLR 878.
[159] [2004] 1 FCR 453.
[160] [2004] 3 FCR 744 at p. 761.
[161] I(PFD)A 1975, s 1(1)(c).
[162] *Re Collins* [1990] Fam 56.
[163] I(PFD)A 1975, s 1(1)(d).
[164] See *Re Leach* [1986] Ch 226 CA for an example of the potential breadth of the section.
[165] Although they may be able to rely on I(PFD)A 1975, s 1(1)(e).
[166] I(PFD)A 1975, s 1(1)(e).
[167] [1998] 1 FLR 1041.
[168] *Churchill v Roach* [2004] 3 FCR 744.

(b) The contribution must be in 'money or money's worth'. There is some debate whether companionship and care could count as maintenance for 'money's worth'. As housework and nursing services and even 'companionship' can be bought, it is submitted that these can be regarded as being for money's worth.[169]

(c) It has to be shown that the maintenance was not paid for by valuable consideration.[170] This requirement has caused difficulties. Could it be said that, although a deceased cohabitant provided the claimant with free accommodation, this was in return for care and companionship and so the applicant was 'paid for' by valuable consideration? Although at one time it was suggested that it was necessary to weigh up the financial value of the maintenance provided by the deceased against the benefits to the deceased provided by the claimant, the courts no longer take such an approach. The courts will readily accept that one cohabitant was being maintained by the other. In *Bouette v Rose*[171] the Court of Appeal accepted that a mother was maintained by her disabled child. The child had been awarded a substantial sum of money as a result of her disability. The court took a practical approach and explained that the fund was used to support the lifestyle of both the mother and the child, and so the child was effectively maintaining the mother.

(d) The deceased must have been maintaining the claimant immediately before the death of the deceased. As *Re Watson*[172] makes clear, the fact that the deceased's last few weeks were spent in a hospital or a nursing home will not prevent the applicant's claim being accepted. However, if a couple clearly separate shortly before the death then a claim cannot be made. This is controversial: although the separation may indicate that the deceased would not have wanted to leave a former cohabitant any property, it does not necessarily mean that it would not be fair to make such an award.

## (ii) What is reasonable financial provision?

The key question in deciding an order is whether reasonable financial provision was made for the claimant in the will. Rather strangely, the concept of reasonable provision depends on the exact relationship between the deceased and the claimant. If the claimant is the spouse, the question is simply whether the *provision* is 'reasonable'. For other cases, the question is whether the *maintenance* is reasonable. The emphasis on maintenance is important. A non-spouse applicant who is 'comfortably off' may have difficulty in persuading the court that they need to be maintained.[173] A spouse who is well off will more easily be able to argue that the provision was not reasonable. This is because a spouse may be entitled to a share in his or her spouse's property because of the length of the marriage, even though he or she may not need to be maintained.[174] Reasonable provision is not necessarily restricted to the minimum necessary to survive,[175] but will not stretch to luxuries.[176]

---

[169] This seems to have been accepted in *Jelley v Illiffe* [1981] Fam 128.
[170] This, in simple terms, requires that the contribution had not been paid for.
[171] [2000] 1 FLR 363.
[172] [1999] 1 FLR 878.
[173] *Re Jennings (Deceased)* [1994] Ch 256.
[174] I(PFD)A 1975, s 1(2).
[175] *Re Coventry* [1990] Fam 561.
[176] *Re Dennis* [1981] 2 All ER 140.

Under s 3, in considering a claim, the court should consider:

---

**LEGISLATIVE PROVISION**

**Inheritance (Provision for Family and Dependants) Act 1975, section 3**

(a) the financial resources and financial needs which the applicant has or is likely to have in the foreseeable future;

(b) the financial resources and financial needs which any other applicant for an order . . . has or is likely to have in the foreseeable future;

(c) the financial resources and financial needs which any beneficiary of the estate of the deceased has or is likely to have in the foreseeable future;

(d) any obligations and responsibilities which the deceased had towards any applicant for an order . . . or towards any beneficiary of the estate of the deceased;

(e) the size and nature of the net estate of the deceased;

(f) any physical or mental disability of any applicant for an order . . . or any beneficiary of the estate of the deceased;

(g) any other matter, including the conduct of the applicant or any other person, which in the circumstances of the case the court may consider relevant.

---

These factors are largely self-explanatory. It should be noted that factors (b), (c), (d), (f) and (g) require the court to consider the position of all those who may be seeking money from the estate. So, although a claimant may show a close relationship to the deceased and be in great need, his or her claim may fail if there are others interested in the estate who are of greater need. Although it is not stated explicitly, the wishes of the deceased can be taken into account.[177] For example, in *Re Hancock (Deceased)*[178] there was a dramatic increase in the value of the estate (from £100,000 to £650,000) and the Court of Appeal accepted evidence that, had the deceased been aware that his estate would increase to this level, he would have provided for the applicant. There are some additional considerations that apply for specific kinds of applicants:

### (a) Spouses

For a surviving spouse reasonable financial provision means 'such financial provision as it would be reasonable in all the circumstances of the case for a husband or wife to receive, whether or not that provision is required for his or her maintenance'.[179] When considering the appropriate level for a spouse, the court will have regard to the age of the applicant; the duration of the marriage; the applicant's contribution to the welfare of the family of the deceased; and the provision the applicant may reasonably have expected to receive if the marriage had been terminated by divorce rather than by death.[180] Miller[181] has suggested that the court should separate two elements of provision for spouses: first, the spouse's share of the 'family property', and, secondly, the proportion of the estate which would be necessary to provide the spouse with sufficient support.

---

[177] According to I(PFD)A 1975, s 21, a statement of the deceased is admissible evidence.
[178] [1998] 2 FLR 346.
[179] I(PFD)A 1975, s 1(2)(a).
[180] I(PFD)A 1975, s 3(2).
[181] Miller (1997).

This emphasis on the amount that might have been awarded on divorce reflects the argument that a spouse whose marriage is ended by death should not be worse off than if the marriage had been ended by divorce. However, death and divorce are distinguishable. On divorce, the crucial question is how to divide up the property fairly between the two parties. On death, there is no division required except between the spouse and the other relatives. It could be argued, therefore, that on death a spouse might expect a greater share than on divorce.[182] There has been some dispute in the case law whether the divorce analogy should be seen as just one factor, or the guiding criterion. *Re Krubert*,[183] preferred the view that the divorce analogy was only one factor to be taken into account. Applying this in *Fielden* v *Cunliffe*[184] the Court of Appeal suggested that the reasoning in *White v White*[185] could be used, with its yardstick of equality guideline, but only with caution.[186] This seems correct. First, as a matter of statutory interpretation – the divorce analogy relates to only one of several factors which should be taken into account. Secondly, as has already been mentioned, the two scenarios – death and divorce – are quite different.[187] The Court of Appeal in *Fielden* indicated that the obligation to make reasonable provision is not the same as the goal of fairness emphasised in ancillary relief cases. In *P* v *G*[188] it was held that where a wealthy husband died after a lengthy marriage the wife might be entitled to more than the half share that a *White v White* approach might indicate in a divorce. This was because, unlike a divorce case, there was only the one spouse's needs and contributions to take into account; although Black J added that the court still needed to give due weight to the importance of testamentary freedom.

### (b) Former spouses

A former spouse can only claim under the Act if he or she has not remarried.[189] It is rare for former spouses to claim under the Act because it is common on divorce for a court to order that an applicant cannot make a claim under the Act if the ex-spouse subsequently dies. If such an order is in place then an application cannot be made, whether or not the ex-spouse has remarried. Even if an ex-spouse is not prevented from bringing an application, the court may well take the view that it is reasonable provision for the deceased to leave a former spouse nothing in the will.[190]

### (c) Child of the deceased

The court should have regard to the manner in which the child was being, or in which he or she might expect to be, educated or trained.[191] So if the intention was that the child be privately educated, money from the estate could be claimed to provide such education.

### (d) Adult children

The courts are generally reluctant to allow adult children who have sufficient earning capacity to succeed in making a claim against their parents' estate. The difficulty facing an employed adult child claimant is in showing that an award would be reasonable for his or her maintenance.

---

[182] See, e.g., *Fielden v Cunliffe* [2005] 3 FCR 593 at p. 603, where it was said that the shortness of the marriage was a less critical factor in applications under the Act than in cases of divorce.

[183] [1997] Ch 97.

[184] [2005] 3 FCR 593. See Maguire and Frankland (2006) for a useful discussion.

[185] [2001] 1 AC 596.

[186] See also *Baker v Baker* [2008] EWHC 977 (Ch).

[187] Miller (1997).

[188] [2006] Fam Law 179.

[189] I(PFD)A 1975, s 1(1)(b).

[190] E.g. *Cameron v Treasury Solicitor* [1996] 2 FLR 716 CA; *Barrass v Harding* [2001] 1 FCR 297.

[191] I(PFD)A 1975, s 3(3).

The courts have usually required that an adult child establish a 'moral obligation' or some other special circumstances if the claim is to succeed. Examples of a moral obligation or special circumstances include a son who had worked on the family farm in the expectation that he would inherit it;[192] and an applicant whose father was left money by the applicant's mother on the understanding that he would leave the money in his will to the applicant but did not.[193] In *Re Hancock (Deceased)*[194] the Court of Appeal stressed that it would be wrong to say that an adult child can never succeed in an application unless there is a moral obligation or other special circumstances, but without those the application would be unlikely to succeed, especially if the applicant is in paid employment. In *Espinosa v Bourke*[195] the daughter had for a while cared for her father, but somewhat abandoned him when she ran off to Spain to live with a Spanish fisherman. Despite this being what some would regard as reprehensible conduct, she was entitled to an award based on her need, her doubtful earning capacity, and having no formal employment. Similarly in *H v J's Personal Representatives, Blue Cross, RSPB and RSPCA*[196] a daughter failed in her claim against the estate of her mother who left her nothing after she had married a man the mother disapproved of. The court held that while many would not agree with the mother's actions she was entitled to leave her money to animal charities if she wished. Similarly in *Garland v Morris*[197] it was found to be reasonable for the deceased to make no provision given his daughter had not spoken to him for several years. These decisions stress that moral obligation is but one factor to be taken into account.[198] As these decisions indicate, something more than the ordinary obligation a parent owes a child is required.[199]

### (e) Child of the deceased's family

When the court is considering a child who was not biologically the deceased's, but whom he or she treated as a child of the family, the court should consider whether the deceased had assumed responsibility for the child and whether, in assuming responsibility, the deceased knew that the applicant was not his or her own child. The liability of any other person to maintain the applicant should also be taken into account.

### (f) Dependants

In addition to the general factors, the court will consider 'the extent to which and the basis upon which the deceased assumed responsibility for the maintenance of the applicant, and . . . the length of time for which the deceased discharged that responsibility'.[200] Megarry V-C stressed that the deceased must have assumed responsibility for the applicant: that maintenance on its own would not be enough, if the deceased had not undertaken responsibility.[201] The Court of Appeal, however, has suggested that it is willing to infer assumption of responsibility from maintenance.[202] In determining the amount awarded to such claimants the court can take into account the lifestyle they enjoyed while being maintained by the deceased.[203]

---

[192] *Re Pearce (Deceased)* [1998] 2 FLR 705.
[193] *Re Goodchild* [1996] 1 WLR 694.
[194] [1998] 2 FLR 346.
[195] [1999] 1 FLR 747.
[196] [2010] 1 FLR 1613.
[197] [2007] EWHC 2 (Ch).
[198] Borkowski (1999).
[199] [2010] 1 FLR 1613.
[200] I(PFD)A 1975, s 3(4).
[201] *Re Beaumont* [1980] Ch 444.
[202] *Jelley v Iliffe* [1981] Fam 128; *Bouette v Rose* [2000] 1 FLR 363, [2000] 1 FCR 385.
[203] *Negus v Bahouse* [2008] 1 FCR 768.

### (g) Cohabitants

If the claimant relies on s 1A the following special factors apply:

(a) the age of the applicant and the length of the period [of cohabitation] . . . ;

(b) the contribution made by the applicant to the welfare of the family of the deceased, including any contribution made by looking after the home or caring for the family.

However, a cohabitant cannot normally expect an award at a level which would enable him or her to retain the same standard of living as the couple had enjoyed together, even if it had been a lengthy relationship.[204] Nevertheless, the previous lifestyle was a factor to consider, as was the length of the relationships, whether there were any children and the needs of other claimants. In *Webster v Webster*[205] a woman who had cohabited with the deceased for 28 years and had two children with him was awarded the bulk of the estate. In *Re Watson*[206] the needs of the frail applicant were particularly significant.

## 8 Elder abuse

### A Defining elder abuse

The National Council on Ageing has defined elder abuse as 'the mistreatment of an older person . . . it can be a single incident or part of a repeated pattern'.[207] The kinds of abuse include physical, sexual, psychological and financial abuse. The Social Services Inspectorate[208] found that physical abuse was the most frequent form of abuse among older people, and the most common class of victim was women aged 81 or over.[209] The abuser is often the principal carer and a close relative.[210]

The Law Commission has defined abuse in this context as the:

ill-treatment of that person (including sexual abuse and forms of ill-treatment that are not physical), the impairment of, or an avoidable deterioration in, the physical or mental health of that person or the impairment of his physical, intellectual, emotional, social or behavioural development.[211]

Notably, this definition includes abuse by omission (not providing the appropriate level of care) as well as abuse by act. It also makes it clear that abuse includes acts that were not intended to harm the dependent person. The most recent government publications have emphasised that elder abuse should be regarded as part of a wider problem of abuse of vulnerable people.[212]

Statistics on the level of abuse are hard to obtain, not least because much abuse goes unreported. The leading study in England and Wales found that 2 per cent of older people

---

[204] *Graham v Murphy* [1997] 1 FLR 860.
[205] [2009] 1 FLR 1240.
[206] [1999] 1 FLR 878.
[207] Quoted Pollard (1995: 257). For a fuller discussion, see Williams (2008); House of Commons Health Committee (2004); Pollard (1995); Brogden and Nijhar (2000); Pritchard (2002). Alternative definitions of elder abuse are discussed in Brammer and Biggs (1998).
[208] Social Services Inspectorate (1992; 1993).
[209] Although see Pritchard (2002) for a discussion of the abuse of older men.
[210] Ogg and Bennett (1992).
[211] Law Commission Report 231 (1995: 9.8).
[212] Department of Health (2002f).

had suffered financial abuse and 5 per cent verbal abuse.[213] A smaller-scale study found that 27.5 per cent of pensioners had been the victim of abuse or neglect.[214]

## B The law

The criminal law applies as it does with any other group of people. The Government rejected a proposal that there should be a new offence of ill-treatment or wilful neglect of a person without capacity.[215] The law provides a number of routes whereby an older person can obtain protection from abuse. Some of these remedies are the same as those available to cohabitants or spouses.

1. Non-molestation orders and occupation orders are available under the Family Law Act 1996.[216] To obtain a non-molestation order it is necessary to show that the older person is associated with the abuser. This can readily be established if the abuser is a relative. However, an older person who is living in a residential home will normally not be associated with a care assistant at the home.

2. The Protection from Harassment Act 1997 may afford protection. There is no need to prove that the parties are associated persons to use this legislation.

3. Under the Mental Capacity Act 2005 the court can make orders based on what is in the best interests of a person lacking capacity. There have been cases where the court has restricted contact between such a person and others due to concerns that they pose a risk to them.[217] It is even possible to use the Act to remove the individual from an abusive house.[218] The Act can only be relied upon if the person has lost capacity. If they retain capacity, but are classified as vulnerable adults because they are unable to protect themselves then orders under the inherent jurisdiction may be used, although the preference is to assist individuals to help themselves.[219]

4. Older people are protected from abuse by the criminal law. However, this depends on the police being made aware of the abuse, which, given the private nature of abuse and the reluctance or inability of the older person to report the abuse, may mean that it is rare for the criminal law to be invoked. The Mental Capacity Act 2005 created an offence of ill treating or neglecting a person without capacity,[220] but otherwise it will be rare that a failure to obtain care will amount to an offence.[221]

5. Under the Registered Homes Act 1984, local authorities have the right to cancel registration of an old persons' home; this Act could be invoked if there were allegations of serious abuse. The local authority has the right to enter the home;[222] inspect records; and cancel or refuse registration.[223] There is an emergency procedure available to cancel registration if there is a serious risk to the life, health, or well-being of the residents.[224] There are,

---

[213] Ogg and Bennett (1992).
[214] Ogg and Munn-Giddings (1993).
[215] Department of Constitutional Affairs (2004).
[216] Discussed in detail in Chapter 6.
[217] *Re MM (An Adult)* [2009] 1 FLR 487.
[218] *G v E* [2010] EWCA Civ 822; *Re SK* [2008] EWHC 636 (Fam).
[219] *A Local Authority v A* [2010] EWHC 1549 (Fam).
[220] Mental Capacity Act 2005, s 44.
[221] Herring (2010a).
[222] Registered Homes Act 1984, s 17.
[223] The Care Standards Act 2000 creates the National Care Standards Commission, which monitors care services.
[224] Registered Homes Act 1984, s 11.

however, concerns that moving older people from their homes can lead to great distress and even premature death.[225]

6. There is a limited power in s 47 of the National Assistance Act 1948 to remove a person from care in a domestic setting. The application is on seven days' notice by a local authority to a magistrates' court. The main ground for such an application is that the person is living in unsanitary conditions and not receiving proper care and attention from other persons. The order initially lasts for three days. An emergency order can be applied for *ex parte* under the National Assistance (Amendment) Act 1951 for a maximum of three weeks. These powers are rarely used. This is in part because of the stigma that attaches to the phrase 'unsanitary conditions'.

The contrast with the protection available for children who are being abused is notable. In particular, there is no duty on a local authority to investigate a suspected case of abuse, as there is for children under s 47 of the Children Act 1989. Also, there is no equivalent to a child's being taken into care.

## C  Issues concerning elder abuse

The question of the abuse of older people gives rise to some complex issues, which might explain why the law has struggled to find an effective response. The following are some of the difficulties:

1. *Autonomy.* Normally in a liberal democracy the state is not willing to remove adults from their homes, or to prevent them from seeing someone simply on the basis that it would not be good for them. We have seen when considering family violence that the law seeks to respect the autonomy of the victim, although there is a tension with other values that the law may seek to uphold. An example of the problem is that an older person may prefer to be cared for by a relative who is abusive, rather than being placed in a residential home. Should the state deprive the older person of that choice? One answer may be that it depends on whether the older person is competent to make that decision or not. However, there are real difficulties in deciding the level of competence of an older person, especially as the level of understanding may vary considerably from day to day. In any event, can we be sure that residential care is better for an older person than personal care by a loved one who is occasionally abusive? But does this last question reveal an attitude that would be regarded as unacceptable if we were talking about the care of a child?

2. *Definitions of self-neglect.* What might appear to be self-neglect to one person may be eccentricity to another. An older person who insists on sleeping all day and being awake at night might be exhibiting signs of self-neglect or neglect by carers, or might be eccentric. If older people are exhibiting eccentric behaviour, does this justify state intervention to protect them from themselves, or is this an unwarranted intrusion into the autonomy of older people?

3. *Problems in defining violence and neglect.* A carer who is rough in handling an older person or is irritable might be said to be abusive to the older person. But others might regard ill-temper as an inevitable part of the stresses involved in giving personal care.

---

[225] *McKellar v Hounslow LBC*, unreported, 28 October 2003, QBD.

4. *Proof.* As always with issues of abuse, there are great problems in proving the abuse. One solution would be regular visits of social workers to older people who are perceived to be vulnerable. However, there is a widespread feeling among older people that visits of social workers are an infringement of privacy.

5. *Remedies.* If the abuse is taking place in the older person's home, there is the difficult question of remedy. Placing the older person in a residential home against his or her wishes could itself be seen as a form of abuse. Another issue is that, even if the carer has physically abused the older person, this may be due in part to the lack of provision of adequate resources by the social services.

6. *Relationship of care-giver and care-receiver.* The relationship between the care-giver and care-receiver can be a complex one. The exhaustion and desperation that care-givers might feel could even be regarded as a form of abuse itself. Indeed, many cases of elder abuse are simply deeply sad stories that do not necessarily lead to blame of the kind that we place on the child abuser. Landau and Osmo[226] have pointed out that sometimes it is not clear who should be regarded as the social worker's client: the abused older person or the desperate carer. There is, in fact, an almost equal number of care-givers who report abuse as there are elderly charges who report being abused.[227]

## 9 Conclusion

The position of elderly people and their relatives is of increasing importance in family law. One key issue is the extent to which adult children should be required to provide financial support for elderly parents. Although there is widespread acceptance that there is a moral obligation owed by adult children to their parents, there are complex issues in the debate whether the obligation should become a legal one. The law on succession indicates that, at least once a person is dead, the law will give legal effect to moral obligations between a variety of relationships, including those between adult children and their parents. The chapter has also considered an issue which will become of increasing importance – inter-generational justice: how should society distribute its resources between the younger and older sections of society? The concluding discussion looked at the topic of abuse of older people and the complex issues that arise in protecting the rights, interests and dignity of the older person.

---

[226] Landau and Osmo (2003).
[227] Wilson (1994).

# Further reading

**Fredman, S.** (2003) 'The Age of Equality', in S. Fredman and S. Spencer (eds), *Age as an Equality Issue*, Oxford: Hart.

**Herring, J.** (2008d) 'Together forever? The rights and responsibilities of adult children and their parents', in J. Bridgeman, H. Keating and C. Lind (eds), *Responsibility, Law and the Family*, London: Ashgate.

**Herring, J.** (2008e) 'Older People and the Law', in C. O'Cinneide and J. Holder (eds), *Current Legal Problems*, Oxford: OUP.

**Herring, J.** (2009d) *Older People in Law and Society*, Oxford: OUP.

**House of Commons Health Committee** (2004) *Elder Abuse*, London: The Stationery Office.

**Kellet, S.** (2006) 'Four Theories of Filial Duty', *The Philosophical Quarterly* 56: 254.

**Oldham, M.** (2001) 'Financial obligations within the family – aspects of intergenerational maintenance and succession in England and France', *Cambridge Law Journal* 60: 128.

**Oldham, M.** (2006) 'Maintenance and the Elderly: Legal Signalling Kinship and the State', in F. Ebtehaj, B. Lindley and M. Richards (eds), *Kinship Matters*, Hart: Oxford.

**Stewart, A.** (2007) 'Home or Home: Caring about and for elderly family members in a welfare state', in R. Probert (ed.), *Family Life and the Law*, Aldershot: Ashgate.

**Williams, J.** (2008) 'State responsibility and the abuse of vulnerable older people: Is there a case for a public law to protect vulnerable older people from abuse?', in J. Bridgeman, H. Keating and C. Lind (eds), *Responsibility, Law and the Family*, London: Ashgate.

# Bibliography and further reading

Abbs et al. (2006) 'Modern life leads to more depression among children', *Daily Telegraph*, 12 September.

Abrahams, H. (2010) *Rebuilding Lives after Domestic Violence: Understanding Long-Term Outcomes*, London: Jessica Kingsley.

Adam, B. (2004) 'Care, Intimacy and Same-Sex Partnership in the 21st Century', *Current Sociology* 52: 265.

Adams, D. (2000) 'The Emerge Program', in J. Hanmer and C. Itzin (eds) *Home Truths About Domestic Violence*, London: Routledge.

Adams, L., McAndrew, F. and Winterbotham, M. (2005) *Pregnancy Discrimination at Work*, London: ECO.

Adhar, R. (1996) 'Religion as a factor in custody and access disputes', *International Journal of Law, Policy and the Family* 10: 177.

Advicenow (2006) *Living Together*, London: DCA.

Age UK (2010a) *Older Carers*, London: Age UK.

Age UK (2010b) *Response to latest poverty figures*, London: Age UK.

Ahmed, F. (2010) 'Personal Autonomy and the Option of Religious Law', *International Journal of Law, Policy and the Family* 24: 222.

Ahuja, K., Simons, E., Mostyn, B. and Bowen Simkins, P. (1998) 'An assessment of the motives and morals of egg share donors', *Human Reproduction* 2671.

Alderson, P. (1993) *Children's Consent to Surgery*, Buckingham: Open University Press.

Alderson, P. (2008) *Young Children's Rights*, London: Jessica Kingsley.

Aldgate, J. and Jones, D. (2006) 'The Place of Attachment in Children's Development', in J. Aldgate et al. (eds) *The Developing World of the Child*, London: Jessica Kingsley.

Alexander, G. (1998) 'The new marriage contract and the limits of private ordering', *Indiana Law Review* 1998: 503.

Alghrani, A. and Harris, J. (2006) 'Reproductive liberty: should the foundation of families be regulated?', *Child and Family Law Quarterly* 18: 191.

Allen, N. and Williams, H. (2009) 'The Law and Financial Provision on the Dissolution of Civil Partnerships', *Family Law* 39: 836.

Almack, K. (2006) 'Seeking Sperm: Accounts of Lesbian couples reproductive decision-making and understanding of the needs of the child', *International Journal of Law, Policy and the Family* 20: 1.

Almond, B. (2006) *The Fragmenting Family*, Oxford: Oxford University Press.

Altman, S. (1996) 'Divorcing threats and offers', *Law and Philosophy* 15: 209.

Altman, S. (2003) 'A theory of child support', *International Journal of Law, Policy and the Family* 17: 173.

Amato, P. (2001) 'Children of divorce in the 1990s', *Journal of Family Psychology* 15: 355.

Amato, P. and Cheadle, J. (2005) 'The long reach of divorce', *Journal of Marriage and the Family* 67: 191.

Anderson, L. (1997) 'Registered personal relationships', *Family Law* 27: 174.

Andrews, E. (2009) 'Facebook "sex chats" blamed for one in five divorces', *Daily Mail*, 22 December 2009.

Anitha, S. and Gill, A. (2009) 'Coercion, consent and the forced marriage debate', *Feminist Legal Studies* 17: 165.

Arber, S. and Ginn, J. (2004) *Social Trends*, London: National Statistics.

Archard, D. (1993) 'Do parents own their children?', *International Journal of Children's Rights* 1: 293.

Archard, D. (1995) 'What's blood got to do with it? The significance of natural parenthood', *Res Publica* 1: 91.

Archard, D. (1999) 'Can Child Abuse Be Defined?', in M. King (ed.) *Moral Agendas for Children's Welfare*, London: Routledge.

Archard, D. (2001) 'Philosophical Perspectives on Childhood', in J. Fionda (ed.) *Legal Concepts of Childhood*, Oxford: Hart.

Archard, D. (2003) *Children, Family and The State*, Aldershot: Ashgate.

Archard, D. (2004a) 'Wrongful life', *Philosophy* 79: 403.

Archard, D. (2004b) *Children: Rights and Childhood*, London: Routledge.

Archard, D. and Macleod, M. (eds) (2002) *The Moral and Political Status of Children*, Oxford: OUP.

Archard, D. and Skivenes, M. (2009) 'Balancing a Child's Best Interests and a Child's Views', *International Journal of Children's Rights* 17: 1–21.

Ariès, P. (1986) *Centuries of Childhood*, London: Penguin.

Aris, R., Harrison, C. and Humphreys, C. (2002) *Safety and Child Contact*, London: LCD.

Armstrong, S. (2002) 'Is the jurisdiction of England and Wales correctly applying the 1980 Hague Convention on the Civil Aspects of International Child Abduction?', *International and Comparative Law Quarterly* 51: 427.

Arnold, W. (2000) 'Implementation of Part II: Lessons Learned', in Thorpe LJ and E. Clarke (eds) *No Fault or Flaw: The Future of the Family Law Act 1996*, Bristol: Jordans.

Ashenden, S. (2004) *Governing Child Sexual Abuse*, London: Routledge.

Ashworth, K. and Walker, K. (1994) 'Reeboks, a Game Boy and a cat', in S. Middleton, K. Ashworth and R. Walker (eds) *Family Fortunes*, London: Child Poverty Action Group.

Atiyah, P. (1982) 'Economic duress and the overborne will', *Law Quarterly Review* 98: 147.

Atkin, B. (2003) 'The rights of married and unmarried couples in New Zealand – Radical new laws on property and succession', *Child and Family Law Quarterly* 15: 173.

Atkinson, A., McKay, S. and Dominy, N. (2006) *Future policy options for child support: The views of parents*, London: DWP.

Attwood, C., Singh, G., Prime, D. and Creasey, R. (2003) *Home Office Citizenship Survey*, London: Home Office.

Atwood, B. (1993) 'Ten years later: Lingering concerns about the Uniform Pre-marital Agreement Act', *Journal of Legislation* 19: 127.

Auchmuty, R. (2003) 'When equality is not equity: homosexual inclusion in undue influence law', *Feminist Legal Studies* 11: 163.

Auchmuty, R. (2004) 'Same-sex marriage revived: feminist critique and legal strategy', *Feminism and Psychology* 14: 101.

Auchmuty, R. (2008) 'What's so special about marriage? The impact of *Wilkinson* v *Kitzinger*', *Child and Family Law Quarterly* 20: 475.

Auchmuty, R. (2009) 'Beyond Couples', *Feminist Legal Studies* 17: 205.

Babb, P., Butcher, H., Church, J. and Zealey, L. (2006) *Social Trends*, London: ONS.

Bailey-Harris, R. (1995) 'Financial rights in relationships outside marriage: A decade of reform in Australia', *International Journal of Law, Policy and the Family* 9: 223.

Bailey-Harris, R. (1996) 'Law and unmarried couples: Oppression or liberation?' *Child and Family Law Quarterly* 8: 137.

Bailey-Harris, R. (1998a) 'Dividing the Assets on Breakdown of Relationships Outside Marriage: Challenges for Reformers', in R. Bailey-Harris (ed.) *Dividing the Assets on Family Breakdown*, Bristol: Jordans.

Bailey-Harris, R. (1998b) 'Equality or Inequality Within the Family? Ideology, Reality and the Law's Response', in J. Eekelaar and T. Nhlapo (eds) *The Changing Family: International Perspectives on the Family and Family Law*, Oxford: Hart.

Bailey-Harris, R. (2000) 'New Families for a New Society', in S. Cretney (ed.) *Family Law – Essays for the New Millennium*, Bristol: Jordans.

Bailey-Harris, R. (2001a) 'Comment on *White* v *White*', *Family Law* 31: 14.

Bailey-Harris, R. (2001b) 'Dividing the assets on family breakdown: the content of fairness', *Current Legal Problems* 53: 533.

Bailey-Harris, R. (2001c) 'Same-Sex Partnerships in English Family Law', in R. Wintemute and M. Andenæs (eds) *Legal Recognition of Same-Sex Partnerships*, Oxford: Hart.

Bailey-Harris, R. (2001d) 'Contact – challenging conventional wisdom', *Child and Family Law Quarterly* 13: 361.

Bailey-Harris, R. (2002) 'Comment on *C* v *Bury MBC*', *Family Law* 32: 810.

Bailey-Harris, R. (2003a) 'Comment on *GW* v *RW*', *Family Law* 33: 386.

Bailey-Harris, R. (2003b) 'Lambert v Lambert – towards the recognition of marriage as a partnership of equals', *Child and Family Quarterly* 15: 417.

Bailey-Harris, R. (2005) 'The paradoxes of principle and pragmatism: ancillary relief in England and Wales', *International Journal of Law, Policy and the Family* 19: 229.

Bailey-Harris, R., Barron, J. and Pearce, J. (1999) 'Settlement culture and the use of the "No Order" Principle under the Children Act 1989', *Child and Family Law Quarterly* 11: 53.

Bailey-Harris, R., Davis, G., Barron, J. and Pearce, J. (1998) *Monitoring Private Law Applications Under the Children Act: A Research Report to the Nuffield Foundation*, Bristol: University of Bristol.

Bailey-Harris, R. and Harris, M. (2002) 'Local authorities and child protection – the mosaic of accountability', *Child and Family Law Quarterly* 14: 117.

Bainham, A. (1986) 'The balance of power in family decisions', *Cambridge Law Journal* 45: 262.

Bainham, A. (1989) 'When is a parent not a parent? Reflections on the unmarried father and his children in English law', *International Journal of Family Law* 3: 208.

Bainham, A. (1990) 'The privatisation of the public interest in children', *Modern Law Review* 53: 206.

Bainham, A. (1994a) 'The temporal dimension of care', *Cambridge Law Journal* 53: 458.

Bainham, A. (1994b) 'Non-Intervention and Judicial Paternalism', in P. Birks (ed.) *Frontiers of Liability*, Oxford: OUP.

Bainham, A. (1994c) 'Religion, human rights and the fitness of parents', *Cambridge Law Journal* 53: 39.

Bainham, A. (1995a) 'Contact as a fundamental right', *Cambridge Law Journal* 54: 255.

Bainham, A. (1995b) 'Family Law in a pluralistic society', *Journal of Law and Society* 23: 234.

Bainham, A. (1996) 'Sex Education: A Family Lawyer's Perspective', in N. Harris (ed.) *Children, Sex Education and the Law*, London: National Children's Bureau.

Bainham, A. (1997) 'Do babies have rights?', *Cambridge Law Journal* 56: 48.

Bainham, A. (1998a) *Children: The Modern Law*, Bristol: Jordans.

Bainham, A. (1998b) 'Changing families and changing concepts: Reforming the language of family law', *Child and Family Law Quarterly* 10: 1.

Bainham, A. (1998c) 'Honour Thy Father and Thy Mother: Children's Rights and Children's Duties', in G. Douglas and L. Sebba (eds) *Children's Rights and Traditional Values*, Aldershot: Dartmouth.

Bainham, A. (1999) 'Parentage, Parenthood and Parental Responsibility: Subtle, Elusive Yet Important Distinctions', in A. Bainham, S. Day Sclater and M. Richards (eds) *What is a Parent?*, Oxford: Hart.

Bainham, A. (2000a) 'Attributing harm: child abuse and the unknown perpetrator', *Cambridge Law Journal* 59: 458.

Bainham, A. (2000b) 'Children Law at the Millennium', in S. Cretney (ed.) *Family Law – Essays for the New Millennium*, Bristol: Jordans.

Bainham, A. (2000c) 'Family rights in the next millennium', *Current Legal Problems* 53: 471.

Bainham, A. (2001a) 'Men and women behaving badly: Is fault dead in English family law?', *Oxford Journal of Legal Studies* 21: 219.

Bainham, A. (2001b) 'Resolving the unresolvable: The case of the conjoined twins', *Cambridge Law Journal* 60: 49.

Bainham, A. (2002a) 'Can we protect children and protect their rights?', *Family Law* 32: 279.

Bainham, A. (2002b) 'Unintentional parenthood: The case of the reluctant mother', *Cambridge Law Journal* 61: 288.

Bainham, A. (2002c) 'Sexualities, Sexual Relations and the Law', in A. Bainham, S. Day Sclater and M. Richards (eds) *Body Lore and Laws*, Oxford: Hart.

Bainham, A. (2003a) 'Contact as a Right and Obligation', in A. Bainham, B. Lindley, M. Richards and L. Trinder (eds) *Children and Their Families*, Oxford: Hart.

Bainham, A. (2003b) 'International Adoption from Romania – why the moratorium should not be ended', *Child and Family Law Quarterly* 15: 223.

Bainham, A. (2005) *Children: The Modern Law*, Bristol: Jordans.

Bainham, A. (2006a) 'Status Anxiety? The Rush for Family Recognition', in F. Ebtehaj, B. Lindley and M. Richards (eds) *Kinship Matters*, Hart: Oxford.

Bainham, A. (2006b) 'The Rights and Obligations Associated with the Birth of a Child', in J. Spencer and A. du Bois-Pedain *Freedom and Responsibility in Reproductive Choice*, Oxford: Hart.

Bainham, A. (2007) 'Permanence for children: Special guardianship or adoption?', *Cambridge Law Journal* 66: 520.

Bainham, A. (2008a) 'Arguments about parentage', *Cambridge Law Journal* 67: 322.

Bainham, A. (2008b) 'Removing babies at birth: a more than questionable practice', *Cambridge Law Journal* 67: 260.

Bainham, A. (2008c) 'What is the point of birth registration?', *Child and Family Law Quarterly* 20: 449.

Bainham, A. (2009a) 'The peculiar finality of adoption', *Cambridge Law Journal* 68: 238.

Bainham, A. (2009b) 'Striking the balance in child protection', *Cambridge Law Journal* 68: 42.

Bainham, A. (2009c) 'Is legitimacy legitimate?', *Family Law* 39: 673.

Bainham, A. (2009d) 'Is anything now left of parental rights?', in R. Probert, S. Gilmore and J. Herring, *Responsible Parents and Parental Responsibility* Oxford: Hart.

Bainham, A. (2010) 'Rowing Back from *Re G*? Natural Parents in the Supreme Court', *Family Law* 40: 394.

Bainham, A., Day Sclater, S. and Richards, M. (eds) (1999) *What is a Parent?*, Oxford: Hart.

Bainham, A., Lindley, B., Richards, M. and Trinder, L. (eds) (2003) *Children and Their Families*, Oxford: Hart.

Baker, A. and Townsend, P. (1996) 'Post divorce parenting – rethinking shared residence', *Child and Family Law Quarterly* 8: 217.

Baker, H. (2009a) ' "Potentially violent men?": teenage boys, access to refuges and constructions of men, masculinity and violence', *Journal of Social Welfare and Family Law* 31: 435.

Baker, H. (2009b) 'New Cohabitation Law in Australia', *Family Law* 39: 1201.

Baker, K. (2004) 'Bargaining or Biology? The History and Future of Paternity Law and Parental Status', *Cornell Journal of Law and Public Policy* 14: 1.

Bala, N. and Jaremko Bromwich, R. (2002) 'Context and inclusivity in Canada's evolving definition of the family', *International Journal of Law, Policy and the Family* 16: 145.

Ball, C. (2003) 'The Changed Nature of Adoption', in G. Miller (ed.) *Frontiers of Family Law*, Aldershot: Ashgate.

Bamforth, N. (2001) 'Same-Sex Partnerships and Arguments of Justice', in R. Wintemute and M. Andenæs (eds) *Legal Recognition of Same-Sex Partnerships*, Oxford: Hart.

Bamforth, N. (2005) 'The role of philosophical and constitutional arguments in the same-sex marriage debate: a response to John Murphy', *Child and Family Law Quarterly* 17: 165.

Bamforth, N. (2007) ' "The benefits of marriage in all but name"? Same-sex couples and the Civil Partnership Act 2004', *Child and Family Law Quarterly* 19: 133.

Banda, F. (2003) 'Global standards: local values', *International Journal of Law, Policy and the Family* 17: 1.

Banda, F. (2005) *Women, Law and Human Rights*, Oxford: Hart.

Banner, R. (1995) 'Economic Devices and Ethical Pitfalls', in A. Grubb (ed.) *Choices and Decisions in Health Care*, Chichester: John Wiley & Sons.

Bar-Hava, G. and Pryor, J. (1998) 'Cinderella's challenge – adjustment to stepfamilies in the 1990s', *Child and Family Law Quarterly* 10: 257.

Barker, K. (2006) 'Sex and the Civil Partnership Act: the future of (non) conjugality?', *Feminist Legal Studies* 14: 214.

Barker, N. (2004) 'For better or worse?', *Journal of Social Welfare and Family Law* 26: 313.

Barlow, A. (2007) 'Family law and housing law: A symbiotic relationship?', in R. Probert (ed.) *Family Life and the Law*, Aldershot: Ashgate.

Barlow, A. (2009a) 'Legal rationality and family property', in J. Miles and R. Probert (eds) *Sharing Lives, Dividing Assets*, Oxford: Hart.

Barlow, A. (2009b) 'What does community of property have to offer English law?', in A. Bottomley and S. Wong (eds) *Changing Contours of Domestic Life, Family and Law*, Oxford: Hart.

Barlow, A., Burgoyne, C., Clery, E. and Smithson, J. (2008) 'Cohabitation and the law: Myths, money and the media', in *British Social Attitudes Survey*, London: Sage.

Barlow, A., Burgoyne, C. and Smithson, J. (2008) 'The Living Together Campaign – The Impact on Cohabitants', *Family Law* 37: 165.

Barlow, A., Callus, T. and Cooke, E. (2004) 'Community of property – A study for England and Wales', *Family Law* 34: 47.

Barlow, A., Duncan, S., James, G. and Park, A. (2001) 'Just a Piece of Paper. Marriage and Cohabitation in Britain', in *British Social Attitudes: the 18th Report*, London: Sage.

Barlow, A., Duncan, S., James, G. and Park, A. (2003) *Family Affairs: Cohabitation, Marriage and the Law*, London: Nuffield Foundation.

Barlow, A., Duncan, S., James, G. and Park, A. (2005) *Cohabitation, Marriage and the Law*, Oxford: Hart.

Barlow, A. and James, G. (2004) 'Regulating Marriage and Cohabitation in 21st Century Britain', *Modern Law Review* 67: 143.

Barlow, A. and Lind, C. (1999) 'A matter of trust: the allocation of rights in the family home', *Legal Studies* 19: 468.

Barnado's (2003) *Children in Trouble: Time for Change*, London: Barnado's.

Barnado's (2004) *Bitter Legacy*, London: Barnado's.

Barnardo's (2008) *Don't Give Up On Us*, London: Barnardo's.

Barnes, M., Lyon, N. and Sweiry, D. (2006) *Families with Children in Britain*, London: DWP.

Barnett, A. (2000) 'Contact and Domestic Violence: The Ideological Divide', in J. Bridgeman and D. Monk (eds) *Feminist Perspectives on Child Law*, London: Cavendish.

Barnett, A. (2009) 'The Welfare of the Child Re-Visited: In Whose Best Interests? Part I', *Family Law* 39: 50 and 135.

Barnett, S. (2000) 'Compatibility and religious rights', *Family Law* 30: 494.

Barnish, M. (2004) *Domestic Violence: A Literature Review*, London: HMIP.

Barrett, D. and Melrose, M. (2003) 'Courting controversy – children sexually abused through prostitution – are they everybody's distant relatives but nobody's children?', *Child and Family Law Quarterly* 15: 371.

Barrett, M. and MacIntosh, M. (1991) *The Anti-Social Family*, London: Verso.

Barron, J. (2002) *5 Years On: A Review of Legal Protection from Domestic Violence*, Bristol: Women's Aid.

Barrow, S. and Bartley, J. (2006) *What Future for Marriage?*, London: Ekklesia.

Barter, C., McCarry, M., Berridge, D. and Evans, K. (2009) *Partner Exploitation and Violence in Teenage Intimate Relationships*, London: NSPCC.

Bartholet, E. (1999) *Nobody's Children*, Boston: Beacon Press.

Bartlett, K. (1984) 'Rethinking parenthood', *Virginia Law Review* 70: 879.

Bartlett, K. (1999) 'Improving the Law Relating to Postdivorce Arrangements for Children', in R. Thompson and P. Amato (eds) *The Postdivorce Family*, Thousand Oaks, Calif.: Sage.

Barton, C. (1996b) 'The homosexual in the family', *Family Law* 26: 626.

Barton, C. (1997) 'When did you next see your father?' *Child and Family Law Quarterly* 9: 73.

Barton, C. (1999) 'A v *United Kingdom* – The Thirty-Thousand Pound Caning – An "English Vice" in Europe', *Child and Family Law Quarterly* 11: 63.

Barton, C. (2002a) 'Parental hitting – the "Responses" to "Protecting Children, Supporting Parents"', *Family Law* 32: 124.

Barton, C. (2002b) 'White Paper weddings – the beginnings, muddles and the ends of wedlock', *Family Law* 32: 421.

Barton, C. (2003) 'The mediator as midwife – a marketing opportunity', *Family Law* 33: 195.

Barton, C. (2004) 'Bigamy & Marriage – Horse & Carriage', *Family Law* 34: 517.

Barton, C. (2005) 'The FMA Annual Conference', *Family Law* 35: 992.

Barton, C. (2006) 'Pressure Groups and Family Law – what will the men want next?', *Family Law* 36: 202.

Barton, C. (2007) 'Contract – A Justifiable Taboo?', in R. Probert (ed.), *Family Life and the Law*, Aldershot: Ashgate.

Barton, C. (2008a) 'Domestic Partnership Contracts: Sliced Bread or A Slice of the Bread?', *Family Law* 38: 900.

Barton, C. (2008b) 'Joint Birth Registration: "Recording Responsibility" Responsibly?', *Family Law* 38: 789.

Barton, C. (2008c) 'Hitting your Children: Common Assault or Common Sense?', *Family Law* 38: 64.

Barton, C. (2008d) 'British Minority Ethnics, Religion and Family Law(yers)', *Family Law* 38: 1217.

Barton, C. (2009) 'Stepfathers, Mothers' Cohabitants and "Uncles"', *Family Law* 39: 326.

Barton, C. and Bissett-Johnson, A. (2000) 'The declining number of Ancillary Relief Orders', *Family Law* 30: 94.

Barton, C. and Douglas, G. (1995) *Law and Parenthood*, London: Butterworths.

Barton, C. and Hibbs, M. (2002) 'Ancillary financial relief and fat cat(tle) divorce', *Modern Law Review* 65: 79.

Bateman, R. (2007) 'Ignoring necessity: the court's decision to impose an ASBO on a child', *Child and Family Law Quarterly* 19: 304.

Battersby, G. (1996) 'How not to judge the quantum (and priority) or a share in the family home', *Child and Family Law Quarterly* 8: 261.

Battersby, G. (2005) '*Oxley* v *Hiscock* in the Court of Appeal: the search for principle continues', *Child and Family Law Quarterly* 17: 259.

Bayne, T. (2003) 'Gamete donation and parental responsibility', *Journal of Applied Philosophy* 20: 77.

BBC (2003) 'Internet Sperm Bank', www.bbc.co.uk/radio4

BBC Newsonline (2002a) 'Children want a voice in government', 7 October.

BBC Newsonline (2002b) 'One third of British teenagers are overweight', 17 September.

BBC Newsonline (2004) 'Dads shun nappy changing for work', 26 July.

BBC Newsonline (2005a) 'Male abusers targeted in campaign', 5 March.

BBC Newsonline (2005b) 'Girls reveal abuse by boyfriends', 21 March.

BBC Newsonline (2005c) 'Divorced women miss pension share', 20 May.

BBC Newsonline (2006a) 'Britons put fun before babies', 2 May.

BBC Newsonline (2006b) 'Worry over sperm donor shortage', 31 July.

BBC Newsonline (2006c) 'Third have sex below legal age', 13 August.

BBC Newsonline (2006d) 'IVF Sperm donor shortage revealed', 13 September.

BBC Newsonline (2006e) 'Archbishop warns of child crisis', 18 September.

BBC Newsonline (2006g) 'Raising a child costs £180,137', 10 November.

BBC Newsonline (2006h) 'Twenty-one-year old father's seventh child', 2 July.

BBC Newsonline (2006i) 'Tories warn on couple break-up', 8 December.

BBC Newsonline (2007a) 'Tories consider marriage tax help', 10 July.

BBC Newsonline (2007c) 'Sir Paul likens divorce to hell', 16 October.

BBC Newsonline (2007d) 'Call to stop children's drinking', 27 Febuary.

BBC Newsonline (2007e) 'How much is family life changing?', 5 November.

BBC Newsonline (2007f) 'Violence a problem for children', 21 May.

BBC Newsonline (2007g) 'Child depression drug use soars', 23 July.

BBC Newsonline (2007h) 'Sperm donor to pay child support', 3 December.

BBC Newsonline (2007i) 'Parents struggle to find balance', 17 July.

BBC Newsonline (2007j) 'The UK family', 6 November.

BBC Newsonline (2008a) 'Budget bride's basement bargains', 16 August.

BBC Newsonline (2008b) 'Father jailed for murdering son', 5 March.

BBC Newsonline (2008c) 'US "pregnant man" has baby girl', 3 July.

BBC Newsonline (2008d) 'Horses for divorces', 23 September.

BBC Newsonline (2008f) 'Three parent embryo formed in lab', 5 February.

BBC Newsonline (2008g) 'Forced adoption claims dismissed', 2 February.

BBC Newsonline (2008h) 'More children living in poverty', 10 June.

BBC Newsonline (2008i) 'Unpaid child support at 1.8bn', 25 October.

BBC Newsonline (2008j) 'Children "damaged" by materialism', 25 Febuary.

BBC Newsonline (2008k) 'Brown targets "problem families"', 14 July.

BBC Newsonline (2008l) 'Support for working mums falls', 6 August.

BBC Newsonline (2009a) 'Vicar in "sham marriages" arrest', 1 July.

BBC Newsonline (2009b) 'Scientists claim sperm "first"', 7 July.

BBC Newsonline (2009c) 'Couples to test "intimacy" device', April 21.

BBC Newsonline (2009d) 'Fathers "cool on parental leave"', 18 May.

BBC Newsonline (2009e) '"Most unfortunate names" revealed', 25 February.

BBC newsonline (2009f) 'Police probed over woman's murder', 9 March.

BBC Newsonline (2009g) 'Secret world of sperm donation', 18 September.

BBC newsonline (2009h) 'Divorce man "wants kidney back"', 8 January.

BBC Newsoline (2009i) 'Gay marriage row at Miss USA show', 20 April.

BBC Newsonline (2009j) 'Dutch sailor girl put under care', 28 August.

BBC Newsonline (2010a) 'Foster carers "urgently" needed says charity', 5 August.

BBC Newsonline (2010b) 'Barnardo's says court delays damage children', 9 August.

BBC newsonline (2010c) 'Heart refusal girl back at school', 5 January 2010.

BBC Newsonline (2010d) 'Court says Dutch teenager Laura Dekker can set sail', 27 July.

Beck, C., Clavis, G., Barnes Jenkins, M. and Nadi, R. (1978) 'The rights of children: A trust model', *Fordham Law Review* 46: 669.

Beck, U. (2002) *Individualization*, London: Sage.

Beck, U. and Beck-Gernsheim, G. (1995) *The Normal Chaos of Love*, Cambridge: Polity Press.

Beck-Gernsheim, E. (2002) *Reinventing the Family*, Cambridge: Polity Press.

Beesson, S. (2007) 'Enforcing the child's right to know her origins: contrasting approaches under the Convention on the Rights of the Child and the European Convention on Human Rights', *International Journal of Law, Policy and the Family* 21: 137.

Beevers, K. (2006) 'Child abduction: inchoate rights of custody and the unmarried father', *Child and Family Law Quarterly* 18: 499.

Belhorn, S. (2005) 'Settling beyond the shadow of the law: how mediation can make the most of social norms', *Ohio State Journal on Dispute Resolution* 20: 981.

Bell, C. (2008) 'Domestic violence and contact', *Family Law* 38: 1139.

Bellamy, C. and Lord, G. (2003) 'Reflections on Family Proceedings Rule 9.5', *Family Law* 33: 265.

Benatar, D. (1999) 'The unbearable lightness of bringing into being', *Journal of Applied Philosophy* 16: 173.

Bennett, F. (1997) *Child Support: Issues for the Future*, London: Child Poverty Action Group.

Bennett, R. (2009) 'Church "out of touch" as public supports equal rights for homosexuals', *The Times*, 27 June.

Benson, H. (2009) *Married and Unmarried Family Breakdown*, Bristol: Community Family Trust.

Beresford, S. and Falkus, C. (2009) 'Abolishing marriage: can civil partnership cover it?', *Liverpool Law Review* 30: 1.

Berger, P. and Kellner, H. (1980) 'Marriage and the Construction of Reality', in B. Cosin (ed.) *School and Society: A Sociological Reader*, London: Routledge.

Bergman, B. (1986) *The Economic Emergence of Women*, New York: Basic Books.

Bernardes, J. (1997) *Family Studies*, London: Routledge.

Bernstein, A. (2003) 'For and Against Marriage: A Revision', *Michigan Law Review* 102: 129.

Bernstein, A. (ed.) (2006) *Marriage Proposals: Questioning A Legal Status*, New York: New York University Press.

Bessant, C. (2005) 'Enforcing non-molestation orders in the civil and criminal courts', *Family Law* 35: 640.

Bevan, G. and Davis, G. (1999) 'A preliminary exploration of the impact of family mediation on legal aid costs', *Child and Family Law Quarterly* 11: 411.

Bevan, H. (1989) *The Law Relating to Children*, London: Butterworths.

Bird, R. (1996) *Domestic Violence: The New Law*, Bristol: Jordans.

Bird, R. (2000) 'Pension sharing', *Family Law* 30: 455.

Bird, R. (2002) 'The reform of section 25', *Family Law* 32: 428.

Bird, R. and Cretney, S. (1996) *Divorce: The New Law – The Family Law Act 1996*, Bristol: Jordans.

Biz/ed (2005) *What Price a Wedding?* London: Biz/ed.

Björnberg, U. and Kollind, A.-K. (2005) *Individualism and Families*, Abingdon: Routledge.

Blacklaws, C. and Dowding, S. (2006) 'The representation of children: from aspiration to extinction', *Family Law* 36: 777.

Blackstone, W. (1770) *Commentaries on the Laws of England*.

Blackwell, F. and Dawe, F. (2003) *Non-Resident Parental Contact*, London: DCA.

Blair, J. (1996) ' "Honour thy father and thy mother" – but for how long? Adult children's duty to care for and protect elderly parents', *Journal of Family Law* 35: 765.

Blustein, J. (1982) *Parents and Children: The Ethics of the Family*, Oxford: OUP.

Blyth, E. (1995) 'The United Kingdom's Human Fertilisation and Embryology Act 1990 and the welfare of the child: A critique', *International Journal of Children's Rights* 3: 417.

Blyth, E. (2008) 'To be or not to be? A critical appraisal of the welfare of children conceived through new reproductive technologies', *International Journal of Children's Rights* 16: 505.

Blyth, E. and Farrand, A. (2004) 'Anonymity in donor-assisted conception and the UN Convention on the Rights of the Child', *International Journal of Children's Rights* 12: 89.

Blyth, E. and Frith, L. (2009) 'Donor-conceived people's access to genetic and biographical history', *International Journal of Law, Policy and the Family* 23: 174.

Blyth, E. and Landau, R. (2004) *Third Party Assisted Conception Across Cultures*, London: Jessica Kingsley.

Blyth, E., Jones, C., Frith, L. and Speirs, J. (2009) 'The role of birth certificates in relation to access to biographical and genetic history in donor conception', *International Journal of Children's Rights* 17: 207.

Boele-Woelki, K., Ferrand, F., Beilfuss, C., Jantera-Jareborg, M., Lowe, N., Martiny, D. and Pintens, W. (2007) *Principles of European Family Law Regarding Parental Responsibilities*, Antwerp: Intersentia.

Bohman, M. and Sigvardsson, S. (1990) 'Outcomes in Adoption: Lessons from Longitudinal Studies', in D. Brodzinsky and M. Schechter (eds) *The Psychology of Adoption*, Oxford: OUP.

Bond, A. (1998) 'Reconstructing families – changing children's surnames', *Child and Family Law Quarterly* 10: 17.

Bond, A. (2007) 'Special Guardianship after *Re S, Re AJ* and *Re M-J*', *Family Law* 37: 321.

Bonner, D., Fenwick, H. and Harris-Short, S. (2003) 'Judicial approaches to the Human Rights Act', *International and Comparative Law Quarterly* 52: 549.

Bonthuys, E. (2006) 'The best interests of children in the South African Constitution', *International Journal of Law, Policy and the Family*, 20: 23.

Booth, J. (1985) *Report of the Matrimonial Causes Procedure Committee*, London: HMSO.

Booth, J. (2002) *A Scoping Study on Delay*, London: LCD.

Booth, P. (2004) 'Parental responsibility – what changes', *Family Law* 34: 353.

Booth, P. (2005) 'The punishment of children', *Family Law* 45: 33.

Booth, P. (2008) 'Judging Sharia', *Family Law* 38: 935.

Borkowski, A. (1994) 'Wilful refusal to consummate: "Just excuse"', *Family Law* 24: 684.

Borkowski, A. (1999) 'Moral obligation and family provision', *Child and Family Law Quarterly* 11: 305.

Borkowski, A. (2002) 'The presumption of marriage', *Child and Family Law Quarterly* 14: 250.

Borkowski, A., Murch, M. and Walker, V. (1983) *Marital Violence. The Community Response*, London: Tavistock Publications.

Bornat, J., Dimmock, B., Jones, D. and Peace, S. (1999) 'The Impact of Family Change on Older People: The Case of Stepfamilies', in S. McRae (ed.) *Changing Britain*, Oxford: OUP.

Bostock, L. (2004) 'By private arrangement? Safeguarding the welfare of private foster children', *Child and Family Law Quarterly* 18: 66.

Bottomley, A. and Wong, S. (2007) 'Shared households: A new paradigm for thinking about the reform of domestic property relations', in A. Diduck and K. O'Donovan (eds) *Feminist Perspectives on Family Law*, London: Routledge.

Bottomley, A. and Wong, S. (2009) *Changing Contours of Domestic Life, Family and Law*, Oxford: Hart.

Bourreau-Dubois, C., Jeandidier, B. and Berger, F. (2003) *Poverty Dynamics, Family Events and Labour Market Events: Are there any differences between men and women?*, London: ISER.

Bowen, E., Brown, L. and Gilchrist, E. (2002) 'Evaluating probation-based offender programmes for domestic violence offenders', *Howard Journal of Criminal Justice* 41: 221.

Bowker, L., Arbitell, M. and McFerron, J. (1989) 'On the Relationship Between Wife Beating and Child Abuse', in K. Yllo and M. Bograd (eds) *Feminist Perspectives on Wife Abuse*, London: Sage.

Bowlby, J. (1973) *Attachment and Loss*, London: Hogarth.

Boyd, S. (1996) 'Is there an ideology of motherhood in (post) modern child custody law?', *Social and Legal Studies* 5: 495.

Boyd, S. (2008) 'Equality enough? Fathers' rights and women's rights', in R. Hunter (ed.) *Rethinking Equality Projects in Law*, Oxford: Hart.

Boyd, S. and Young, C. (2003) 'From same-sex to no-sex?', *Seattle Journal for Social Justice* 1: 575.

Bracher, M., Morgan, S. and Trussell, J. (1993) 'Marriage dissolution in Australia: Models and explanations', *Population Studies* 47: 403.

Bradley, D. (1987) 'Homosexuality and child custody in English law', *International Journal of Law and the Family* 1: 155.

Bradley, D. (1998) 'Politics, culture and family law in Finland: Comparative approaches to the institution of marriage', *International Journal of Law, Policy and the Family* 12: 288.

Bradley, D. (2001) 'Regulation of unmarried cohabitation in West-European Jurisdictions – determinants of legal policy', *International Journal of Law, Policy and the Family* 15: 22.

Bradney, A. (1983) 'Duress and arranged marriages', *Modern Law Review* 46: 499.

Bradney, A. (1993) *Religious Rights and Laws*, London: Sweet & Maxwell.

Bradney, A. (1994) 'Duress, family law and the coherent legal system', *Modern Law Review* 57: 963.

Bradshaw, J. (2005) 'Child poverty and deprivation', in J. Bradshaw and E. Mayhew, *The Well-Being of Children in the UK*, London: Save the Children.

Bradshaw, J. and Mayhew, E. (2005) 'Introduction', in J. Bradshaw and E. Mayhew, *The Well-Being of Children in the UK*, London: Save the Children.

Bradshaw, J. and Millar, J. (1991) *Lone Parent Families in the UK*, DSS Research Report No. 6, London: HMSO.

Bradshaw, J., Stimson, C., Skinner, C. and Williams, J. (1999) *Absent Fathers?* London: Routledge.

Brake, E. (2005) 'Fatherhood and child support: Do men have a right to choose?', *Journal of Applied Philosophy* 22: 56.

Brammer, A. and Biggs, S. (1998) 'Defining elder abuse', *Journal of Social Welfare and Family Law* 20: 285.

Brandon, M. (1999) *Safeguarding Children with the Children Act 1989*, London: The Stationery Office.

Brandon, M., Thoburn, J., Rose, S. and Belderson, P. (2005) *Living with Significant Harm*, Norwich: Centre for Research on the Child and Family.

Brandon, J., Belderson, P., Warren, C., Howe, D., Gardner, R., Dodsworth, J. and Black, J. (2008) *Analysing Child Deaths and Serious Injury Through Abuse and Neglect*, London: DCFS.

Brannen, J., Meszaros, G., Moss, P. and Poland, G. (1994) *Employment and Family Life*, London: University of London.

Brasse, G. (1993) 'Section 34: A Trojan horse?', *Family Law* 23: 55.

Brasse, G. (2004) 'Conciliation is working', *Family Law* 34: 722.

Brasse, G. (2005) 'The *Payne* threshold: Leaving the jurisdiction', *Family Law* 35: 780.

Brasse, G. (2006) 'It's payback time! *Miller, McFarlane* and the compensation culture', *Family Law* 36: 647.

Brazier, M. (1999) 'Can you buy children?', *Child and Family Law Quarterly* 11: 345.

Brazier, M., Campbell, A. and Golombok, S. (1998) *Surrogacy: Review for Health Ministers*, London: HMSO.

Brecher, B. (1994) 'What Is Wrong with the Family', in D. Morgan and G. Douglas (eds) *Constituting Families*, Stuttgart: Franz Steiner Verlag.

Bretherton, H. (2002) ' "Because it's me the decisions are about" – Children's experiences of private law proceedings', *Family Law* 32: 450.

Bridge, C. (1996) 'Shared residence in England and New Zealand – A comparative analysis', *Child and Family Law Quarterly* 8: 12.

Bridge, C. (1999) 'Religion, culture and conviction – the medical treatment of young children', *Child and Family Law Quarterly* 11: 1.

Bridge, C. (2000) 'Diversity, divorce and information meetings – ensuring access to justice', *Family Law* 30: 645.

Bridge, C. (2009) 'Comment', *Family Law* 39: 381.

Bridge, C. and Swindells, H. (2003) *Adoption. The Modern Law*, Bristol: Jordans.

Bridge, S. (2001) 'Marriage and Divorce: The Regulation of Intimacy', in J. Herring (ed.) *Family Law – Issues, Debates, Policy*, Cullompton: Willan.

Bridge, S. (2002) 'The property rights of cohabitants – where do we go from here?', *Family Law* 31: 743.

Bridge, S. (2006) 'Money, Marriage and Cohabitation', *Family Law* 36: 641.

Bridge, S. (2007a) 'Financial Relief for cohabitants: eligibility, opt out and provision on death', *Family Law* 37: 1076.

Bridge, S. (2007b) 'Financial Relief for cohabitants: How the Law Commission's Scheme would work', *Family Law* 37: 998.

Bridge, S. (2007c) 'Cohabitation: Why Legislative Reform is Necessary', *Family Law* 37: 911.

Bridgeman, J. (2007) *Parental Responsibility, Young Children and Healthcare Law*, Cambridge: CUP.

Bridgeman, J. (2010) 'Children with exceptional needs: Welfare, rights and caring responsibilities', in J. Wallbank, S. Choudhry and J. Herring (eds) *Rights, Gender and Family Law*, Abingdon: Routledge.

Bridgeman, J., Keating, H. and Lind, C. (2008) *Responsibility, Law and the Family*, London: Ashgate.

Bright, S. and McFarlane, B. (2005) 'Proprietary estoppel and property rights', *Cambridge Law Journal* 64: 449.

Brinig, M. (2000) *From Contract to Covenant. Beyond the Law and Economics of the Family*, New York: Harvard University Press.

Brinig, M. (2010) *Family, Law and Community*, Chicago: Chicago University Press.

British Medical Association (2001) *Consent, Rights and Choices in Health Care for Children and Young People*, London: BMJ Books.

Broberg, P. (1996) 'The registered partnership for same-sex couples in Denmark', *Child and Family Law Quarterly* 8: 149.

Brogden, M. and Nijhar, P. (2000) *Crime, Abuse and the Elderly*, Cullompton: Willan.

Brophy, J. (1985) 'Child Care and the Growth of Power', in J. Brophy and C. Smart (eds) *Women in Law*, London: Routledge.

Brophy, J. (2000) ' "Race" and ethnicity in public law proceedings', *Family Law* 30: 740.

Brophy, J. (2006) *Research Review: Child care proceedings under the Children Act 1989*, London: DCA.

Brophy, J. (2008) 'Child maltreatment and diverse households', *Journal of Law and Society* 35: 75.

Brophy, J. (2010) *The Views of Children and Young People Regarding Media Access to Family Courts*, London: 11 Million.

Brophy, J., Jhotti-Johal, J. and Owen, C. (2003) *Significant Harm*, London: Department for Constitutional Affairs.

Brophy, J. and Roberts, C. (2009) 'Openness and Transparency' in Family Courts: What the Experience of Other Countries Tells Us About Reform in England and Wales Oxford: OXFLAP.

Brown, J. and Day Sclater, S. (1999) 'Divorce: A Psychodynamic Perspective', in S. Day Sclater and C. Piper (eds) *Undercurrents of Divorce*, Aldershot: Ashgate.

Browne, D. and Moloney, A. (2002) ' "Contact irregular": A qualitative analysis of the impact of visiting patterns of natural parents on foster placements', *Child and Family Social Work* 7: 35.

Brunner, K. (2001) 'Nullity in unconsummated marriages', *Family Law* 31: 837.

Bryan, M. (1995) 'Parents as fiduciaries: A special place in equity', *International Journal of Children's Rights* 3: 227.

Bryan, P. (1992) 'Killing us softly: Divorce mediation and the politics of power', *Buffalo Law Review* 40: 441.

Bryson, C., Budd, T., Lewis, J. and Elam, G. (2000) *Women's Attitudes to Combining Paid Work and Family Life*, London: Social and Community Planning Research.

Bryson, C., Kazimirski, A. and Soutwood, H. (2006) *Childcare and Early Years Provision*, London: DES.

Buchanan, A. and Hunt, J. (2003) 'Disputed Contact Cases in the Courts', in A. Bainham, B. Lindley, M. Richards and L. Trinder (eds) *Children and Their Families*, Oxford: Hart.

Buchanan, A., Hunt, J., Bretherton, H. and Bream, V. (2001) *Families in Conflict*, Cambridge: Polity Press.

Bullock, K., Sarre, S., Tarling, R. and Wilkinson, M. (2010) *The Delivery of Domestic Abuse Programmes*, London: Ministry of Justice.

Bullock, R., Malos, E. and Millham, S. (1993) *Going Home: The Return of Children Separated from Their Families*, Aldershot: Dartmouth.

Bunting, A. (2005) 'Stages of Development; Marriage of girls and teens as an international human rights issue', *Social and Legal Studies* 14: 17.

Bunting, L., Webb, M. and Healy, J. (2010) 'In Two Minds? – Parental attitudes toward physical punishment in the UK', *Children and Society* 24: 359.

Burch, C. (1983) 'Of work, family wealth and equality', *Family Law Quarterly* 17: 99.

Burch, C. (2002) 'Parental Alienation Syndrome and alienated children – getting it wrong in child custody cases', *Child and Family Law Quarterly* 14: 381.

Burch, R. and Gallup, G. (2004) 'Pregnancy as a stimulus for domestic violence', *Journal of Family Violence* 19: 243–7.

Burggraf, S. (1997) *The Feminine Economy*, New York: Addison-Wesley.

Burgoyne, C., Clarke, V., Reibstein, J. and Edmunds, A. (2006) '"All my worldly goods I share with you"? Managing money at the transition to heterosexual marriage', *Sociological Review* 54: 619.

Burgoyne, C. and Sonnenberg, S. (2009) 'Financial practices in cohabiting heterosexual couples', in J. Miles and R. Probert (eds) *Sharing Lives, Dividing Assets*, Oxford: Hart.

Burholt, V. and Windle, G. (2006) *The Material Resources and Well-Being of Older People*, York: Joseph Rowntree Foundation.

Burman, E., Smailes, S. and Chantler, K. (2004) '"Culture" as a barrier to service provision and delivery: domestic violence services for minoritized women', *Critical Social Policy* 24: 332.

Burns, F. (2002) 'The elderly and undue influence inter vivos', *Legal Studies* 23: 251.

Burrows, D. (2000) 'Mediation – the king's new clothes?', *Family Law* 30: 363.

Burrows, D. (2006) 'The CSA: Judicial review and compensation for maladministration', *Family Law* 36: 44.

Burrows, D. (2010) 'In Practice: "Objectives" for CMEC: a new beginning or a false dawn?', *Family Law* 40: 658.

Burrows, L. (1999) *The Fight for the Family*, Oxford: Family Education Trust.

Burton, M. (2004) '*Lomas v Parle* – Coherent and effective remedies for victims of domestic violence: time for an integrated domestic violence court', *Child and Family Law Quarterly* 16: 317.

Burton, M. (2006) 'Judicial Monitoring of Compliance', *International Journal of Law, Policy and the Family* 20: 366.

Burton, M. (2008a) *Legal Responses to Domestic Violence*, London: Routledge.

Burton, M. (2008b) '"Scream quietly or the neighbours will hear": domestic violence, "nuisance neighbours" and the public/private dichotomy revisited', *Child and Family Law Quarterly* 20: 95.

Burton, M. (2009a) 'The civil law remedies for domestic violence: Why are applications for non-molestation orders declining?', *Journal of Social Welfare and Family Law* 31: 109.

Burton, M. (2009b) *Domestic Violence: Literature Review*, London: LSC.

Burton, M. (2010) 'The human rights of victims of domestic violence: *Opuz* v *Turkey*', *Child and Family Law Quarterly* 22: 131.

Butler, A., Noaks, L., Douglas, G. et al. (1993) 'The Children Act and the issue of delay', *Family Law* 23: 412.

Butler, I., Robinson, M. and Scanlan, L. (2005) *Children and Decision Making*, York: Joseph Rowntree.

Butler, I., Scanlan, L. and Robinson, M. et al. (2002) 'Children's involvement in their parents' divorce: implications for practice', *Children and Society* 16: 89.

Butler, I., Scanlan, L., Robinson, M. et al. (2003) *Divorcing Children*, London: Jessica Kingsley.

Butler-Sloss, E. (1989) *Report of the Inquiry into Child Abuse in Cleveland 1987*, London: HMSO.

Butler-Sloss, E. (2001) 'Contact and domestic violence', *Family Law* 31: 355.

Butler-Sloss, E. (2003) *Are we failing the family? Human rights, children and the meaning of family in the 21st century*, London: LCD.

Butler-Sloss, E. (2004) *The Private Law Programme*, London: DCA.

Butler-Sloss, E. (2006) 'Ethical considerations in family law', *Web Journal of Current Legal Issues* 2.

Buzawa, E. and Buzawa, C. (2003) *Domestic Violence: The Criminal Justice Response*, 3rd edn, London: Sage.

Cabinet Office (2008) *Families in Britain*, London: The Stationery Office.

CAFCASS (2008) *Health and Wellbeing Review*, London: CAFCASS.

CAFCASS (2010) *How It Looks To Me*, London: CAFCASS.

CAFCASS and HMCS (2005) *Domestic Violence, Safety and Family Proceedings*, London: HMCS.

Cahn, N. and Carbone, J. (2010) *Red Families v Blue Families*, Oxford: OUP.

Cahn, N. and Collins, J. (2009) 'Eight is enough', *Wake Forest University Legal Studies Paper No. 1365975*.

Callahan, D. (1992) 'Bioethics and Fatherhood', *Utah Law Review* 735.

Callahan, D. (1997) *Setting Limits*, Georgetown, DC: Georgetown University Press.

Callus, T. (2004) 'Tempered Hope? A qualified right to know one's genetic origin', *Modern Law Review* 67: 658.

Callus, T. (2008) 'First "designer babies", now à la carte parents', *Family Law* 38: 143.

Campbell, T. (1992) 'The Rights of the Minor', in P. Alston, S. Parker and J. Seymour (eds) *Children, Rights and the Law*, Oxford: Clarendon Press.

Cantwell, B. and Scott, S. (1995) 'Children's wishes, children's burdens', *Journal of Social Welfare and Family Law* 17: 337.

Capper, D. (2008) 'Marrying financial provision and insolvency avoidance', *Law Quarterly Review* 124: 361.

Carbone, J. (1996) 'Feminism, Gender and the Consequences of Divorce', in M. Freeman (ed.) *Divorce: Where Next?* Aldershot: Dartmouth.

Carbone, J. (2000) *From Partners to Parents*, New York: Columbia University Press.

Carbone, J. and Brinig, M. (1988) 'The reliance interest of marriage', *Tulane Law Review* 62: 855.

Carbone, J. and Brinig, M. (1991) 'Rethinking marriage', *Tulane Law Review* 65: 953.

Cardy, S. (2010) '"Care Matters" and the privatization of looked after children's services in England and Wales: Developing a critique of independent "social work practices"', *Critical Social Policy* 30: 430.

Carers UK (2005) *Facts About Carers*, London: Carers UK.

Carling, A. (2002) 'Family Policy, Social Theory and the State', in A. Carling, S. Duncan and R. Edwards (eds) *Analysing Families*, London: Routledge.

Carter, H. (2003) 'Marriage falls out of fashion . . . or does it?' *The Guardian*, 21 March 2003.

Case, M A (2010) 'What feminists have to lose in same-sex marriage litigation', *UCLA Law Review* 57: 1119.

Casey, D. and Gibberd, A. (2001) 'Adoption and Contact', *Family Law* 31: 39.

Cashmore, J. (2003) 'Children's participation in family law matters', in H. Hallet and A. Prout (eds) *Hearing the Voices of Children*, London: Routledge/Falmer.

Cassidy, C. (2009) *Thinking Children*, London: Continuum.

Cavadino, M. (2002) 'New Mental Health Law for old – safety-plus equals human rights minus', *Child and Family Law Quarterly* 14: 175.

Cawson, P. (2002) *Child Maltreatment in the Family*, London: NSPCC.

Cawson, P., Wattam, C., Brooker, S. and Kelly, G. (2000) *Child Maltreatment in the United Kingdom*, London: NSPCC.

Centre for Social Justice (2009) *Every Family Matters*, London: Centre for Social Justice.

Centre for Social Justice (2010) *Green Paper on the Family*, London: Centre for Social Justice.

Chambers, C. (2007) *Sex, Culture and Justice: The Limits of Choice*, University Park: Pennsylvania State University Press.

Chambers, D. (1984) 'Rethinking the substantive rules for custody in divorce', *Michigan Law Review* 83: 477.

Chantler, K., Gangoli, G. and Hester, M. (2009) 'Forced marriage in the UK: Religious, cultural, economic or state violence?', *Critical Social Policy* 29: 587.

Chau, P.-L. and Herring, J. (2002) 'Defining, assigning and designing sex', *International Journal of Law, Policy and the Family* 16: 327.

Chau, P.-L. and Herring, J. (2004) 'Men, Women and People: The Definition of Sex', in B. Brooks-Gordon, L. Goldsthorpe, M. Johnson and A. Bainham (eds) *Sexuality Repositioned*, Oxford: Hart.

Cherney, I. (2010) 'Mothers', fathers', and their children's perceptions and reasoning about nurturance and self-determination rights', *International Journal of Children's Rights* 18: 79.

Child Maintenance and Enforcement Commission (2008a) *Choice for all Parents Starts Today*, London: CMEC.

Child Maintenance and Enforcement Commission (2008b) *Child Maintenance Options*, London: CMEC.

Child Maintenance and Enforcement Commission (2008c) *Child Maintenance: Getting Started*, London: CMEC.

Child Maintenance and Enforcement Commission (2010) *Child Support Statistics*, London: CMEC.

Child Poverty Action Group (1994) *Putting the Treasury First*, London: CPAG.

Child Poverty Action Group (2010) *Poverty in the UK*, London: CPAG.

Child Support Agency (2006) *Operational Improvement Plan*, London: CSA.

Children Act Advisory Committee (1993) *Annual Report*, London: HMSO.

Children Act Sub-Committee (2002a) *Making Contact Work*, London: LCD.

Children Act Sub-Committee (2002b) *Parental Contact with Children where there is Violence*, London: LCD.

Children's Commissioner for England (2010) *Annual Report*, London: Children's Commissioner.

Children's Law Centre (1999) *At What Age Can I . . . ?*, London: Children's Law Centre.

Choudhry, S. (2001) 'The Child Protection Conference and the Human Rights Act 1998', *Family Law* 31: 531.

Choudhry, S. (2003) 'The Adoption and Children Act 2002, the welfare principle and the Human Rights Act 1998 – a missed opportunity', *Child and Family Law Quarterly* 15: 119.

Choudhry, S. (2009) 'Parental responsibility and corporal punishment', in R. Probert, S. Gilmore and J. Herring, *Responsible Parents and Parental Responsibility*, Oxford: Hart.

Choudhry, S. (2010) 'Mandatory prosecution and arrest as a form of compliance with due diligence duties in domestic violence – the gender implications', in J. Wallbank, S. Choudhry and J. Herring (eds) *Rights, Gender and Family Law*, Abingdon: Routledge.

Choudhry, S. and Fenwick, H. (2005) 'Taking the rights of parents and children seriously: Confronting the welfare principle under the Human Rights Act', *Oxford Journal of Legal Studies* 25: 453.

Choudhry, S. and Herring, J. (2006a) 'Righting Domestic Violence', *International Journal of Law, Policy and the Family* 20: 95.

Choudhry, S. and Herring, J. (2006b) 'Domestic Violence and the Human Rights Act 1998: A new means of legal intervention', *Public Law* 752.

Choudhry, S. and Herring, J. (2010) *European Human Rights and Family Law*, Oxford: Hart.

Christian Concern for the Nation (2009) *New European Union Directive could Silence Christians across Europe*, London: CCFN.

Christian Institute (2002) *Counterfeit Marriage*, Newcastle-upon-Tyne: Christian Institute.

Churchill, H. (2008) 'Being a responsible mother', in J. Bridgeman, H. Keating and C. Lind (eds) *Responsibility, Law and the Family*, London: Ashgate.

Circuit Judges Family Sub-Committee (2008) *Response* at www.judiciary.gov.uk

Clark, B. (2004) 'Should greater prominence be given to pre-nuptial contracts in the law of ancillary relief?', *Child and Family Law Quarterly* 16: 399.

Clark, M., Graham, S. and Grote, N. (2002) 'Bases for giving benefits in marriage: What is ideal? What is realistic? What really happens?', in P. Noller and J. Feeney (eds) *Understanding Marriage*, Cambridge: CUP.

Clark, V., Burgoyne, C. and Burns, M. (2006) 'Just a piece of paper? A qualitative exploration of same-sex couples' multiple conceptions of civil partnership and marriage', *Lesbian and Gay Psychology Review* 7: 141.

Clarke, A. (1993) 'Insolvent Families', in H. Rajak (ed.) *Insolvency Law, Theory and Practice*, London: Sweet & Maxwell.

Clarkson, H. and Clarkson, D. (2007) 'Confusion and Controversy in Parental Alienation', *Journal of Social Welfare and Family Law* 29: 265.

Cleary, A. (2004) 'Cohabitation – A word of caution', *Family Law* 34: 62.

Cleland, A. and Tisdall, K. (2005) 'The challenge of anti-social behaviour', *International Journal of Law, Policy and the Family* 19: 395.

Clive, E. (1994) 'Marriage: An Unnecessary Legal Concept?', in J. Eekelaar and M. Maclean (eds) *A Reader on Family Law*, Oxford: OUP.

Clucas, B. (2005) 'The Children's Commissioner for England: The Way Forward?', *Family Law* 35: 290.

Coady, C. (1992) 'Theory, Rights and Children', in P. Alston, S. Parker and J. Seymour (eds) *Children, Rights and the Law*, Oxford: Clarendon Press.

Cobley, C. (1998) 'Financial compensation for victims of child abuse', *Journal of Social Welfare and Family Law* 20: 721.

Cobley, C. (2006) 'The quest for truth: substantiating allegations of physical abuse in criminal proceedings and care proceedings', *International Journal of Law, Policy and the Family* 20: 317.

Cobley, C. and Lowe, N. (1994) 'Ousting Abusers – public or private solution?' *Law Quarterly Review* 110: 38.

Cobley, C. and Lowe, N. (2009) 'Interpreting the threshold criteria under section 31(2) of the Children Act 1989: the House of Lords decision in *Re B*', *Modern Law Review* 72: 463.

Cohen, J. and Gershbain, N. (2001) 'For the Sake of the Fathers? Child Custody Reform and the Perils of Maximum Contact', *Canadian Family Law Quarterly* 19: 121.

Cohen, J. and Hale, C. (2006) 'Treatment or Therapy: The House of Lords Decision in Re G (Interim Care Order: Residential Assessment)', *Family Law* 36: 294.

Cohen, L. (2002) 'Marriage: the Long-Term Contract', in A. Dnes and R. Rowthorn (eds) *The Law and Economics of Marriage and Divorce*, Cambridge: CUP.

Coleman, L. and Glenn, F. (2010a) 'The varied impact of couple relationship breakdown on children: implications for practice and policy', *Children and Society* 24: 238.

Coleman, L. and Glenn, F. (2010b) *When Couples Part: Understanding the Consequences for Adults And Children*, London: One plus One.

Coleridge J (2008) 'Family Life – Family Justice – Fairness', *Family Law* 38: 388.

Collier, R. (1995) *Masculinity, Law and the Family*, London: Routledge.

Collier, R. (1999) 'The dashing of a "liberal dream"? – The information meeting, the "new family" and the limits of law', *Child and Family Law Quarterly* 11: 257.

Collier, R. (2000) 'Anxious Parenthood, the Vulnerable Child and the "Good Father"', in J. Bridgeman and D. Monk (eds) *Feminist Perspectives on Child Law*, London: Cavendish.

Collier, R. (2003) 'In Search of the "Good Father"', in J. Dewar and S. Parker (eds) *Family Law Processes, Practices, Pressures*, Oxford: Hart.

Collier, R. (2005) 'Fathers 4 Justice, law and the new politics of fatherhood', *Child and Family Law Quarterly* 17: 511.

Collier, R. (2007) 'Feminist legal studies and the subject(s) of men', in A. Diduck and K. O'Donovan (eds) *Feminist Perspective on Family Law*, London: Routledge.

Collier, R. (2008) 'Engaging fathers? Responsibility, law and the "problem of fatherhood"', in J. Bridgeman, H. Keating and C. Lind (eds) *Responsibility, Law and the Family*, London: Ashgate.

Collier, R. (2009a) 'Fathers' rights, gender and welfare: some questions for family law', *Journal of Social Welfare and Family Law* 31: 237.

Collier. R. (2009b) 'Rethinking fathers' rights', *Family Law* 39: 45.

Collier. R. (2010) *Men, Law and Gender*, London: Routledge.

Collier, R. and Sheldon, S. (2008) *Fragmenting Fatherhood*, Oxford: Hart.

Colquhoun, F. (2009) *The Relationship between Child Maltreatment, Sexual Abuse and Subsequent Suicide Attempts*, London: NSPCC.

Coltrane, S. and Adams, M. (2003) 'The social construction of the "divorce problem"', *Family Relations* 52: 363.

Connelly, C. and Cavanagh, K. (2008) 'Domestic abuse, civil protection orders and the "new criminologies": is there any value in engaging with the law?', *Feminist Legal Studies* 16: 139.

Constitutional Affairs Committee (2005) *Family Justice: the Operation of the Family Courts*, London: House of Commons.

Conway, H. (2004) 'The Domestic Violence, Crime and Victims Bill', *Family Law* 34: 132.

Cook, R. (2002) 'Villain, Hero or Masked Stranger: Ambivalence in Transaction with Human Gametes', in A. Bainham, S. Day Sclater and M. Richards (eds) *Body Lore and Laws*, Oxford: Hart.

Cook, R., Day Sclater, S. and Kaganas, F. (2003) *Surrogate Motherhood*, Oxford: Hart.

Cooke, E. (1994) 'Making the break squeaky clean', *Family Law* 24: 268.

Cooke, E. (1998) 'Children and real property – trusts, interests and considerations', *Family Law* 28: 349.

Cooke, E. (2005) 'Cohabitants, common intention and contributions', *Conveyancer* 69: 55.

Cooke, E. (2007) 'Miller/McFarlane: law in search of a definition', *Child and Family Law Quarterly* 19: 98.

Cooke, E. (2009) 'The future for ancillary relief', in G. Douglas and N. Lowe (eds) *The Continuing Evolution of Family Law*, Bristol: Family Law.

Cooper, A., Hetherington, R. and Katz, I. (2003) *The Risk Factor: Making the Child Protection System Work for Children*, London: Demos.

Cooper, D. (2001) '"Like Counting Stars"? Restructuring Equality and the Socio-Legal Space of Same-Sex Marriage', in R. Wintemute and M. Andenæs (eds) *Legal Recognition of Same-Sex Partnerships*, Oxford: Hart.

Corbett, M. (1999) *Independent on Sunday*, 14 March 1999: 16.

Corker, M. and Davis, J. (2000) 'Disabled Children: Invisible under the Law', in J. Cooper and S. Vernon (eds) *Disability and the Law*, London: Jessica Kingsley.

Council of Europe (2002) *The Protection of Women Against Violence*, Brussels: Council of Europe.

Council of Europe (2005) *Eliminating Corporal Punishment: A Human Rights Imperative for Children*, Brussels: Council of Europe.

Cowan, D. (2004) 'On need and gatekeeping', *Child and Family Law Quarterly* 16: 331.

Cowan, S. and Hodgson, J. (2007) 'Violence in the family context', in R. Probert (ed.) *Family Life and the Law*, Aldershot: Ashgate.

Craig, P. (1999) 'What Next for the Children?', in P. Morgan (ed.) *Adoption: The Continuing Debate*, London: IEA.

Craig, P. (2007) 'Everybody's business: Applications for contact orders by consent', *Family Law* 37: 26.

Crawford, S. and Pierce, J. (2010) 'Reporting proceedings', *Family Law* 40: 825.

Creighton, P. (1990) 'Spouse competence and compellability', *Criminal Law Review* 34.

Cretney, A. and Davis, G. (1996) 'Prosecuting "domestic" assault', *Criminal Law Review* 162.

Cretney, S. (1972) 'The Nullity of Marriage Act 1971', *Modern Law Review* 35: 57.

Cretney, S. (1995) 'Reform of intestacy: the best we can do?', *Law Quarterly Review* 111: 77.

Cretney, S. (1996a) 'Right and wrong in the Court of Appeal', *Law Quarterly Review* 112: 33.

Cretney, S. (1996b) 'Divorce Reform in England: Humbug and Hypocrisy or a Smooth Transition?', in M. Freeman (ed.) *Divorce: Where Next?* Aldershot: Dartmouth.

Cretney, S. (1996c) 'From Status to Contract?' in F. Rose (ed.) *Consensus Ad Idem*, London: Sweet & Maxwell.

Cretney, S. (1997) 'The Children Act 1948 – Lessons for today?', *Child and Family Law Quarterly* 9: 359.

Cretney, S. (1998) *Law, Law Reform and the Family*, Oxford: OUP.

Cretney, S. (1999) 'Contract not apt in divorce deal', *Law Quarterly Review* 115: 356.

Cretney, S. (2000) 'Trusting the judges: Money after divorce', *Current Legal Problems* 53: 286.

Cretney, S. (2001) 'Black and white', *Family Law* 31: 3.

Cretney, S. (2002) 'Marriage, divorce and the courts', *Family Law* 32: 900.

Cretney, S. (2003a) *Family Law in the Twentieth Century – a History*, Oxford: OUP.

Cretney, S. (2003b) 'Private ordering and divorce – how far can we go?', *Family Law* 33: 399.

Cretney, S. (2003c) 'A Community of Property System Imposed by Judicial Decision', *Law Quarterly Review* 119: 349.

Cretney, S. (2003d) 'The family and the law – status or contract?', *Child and Family Law Quarterly* 15: 403.

Cretney, S. (2006a) *Same-sex relationships*, Oxford: OUP.

Cretney, S. (2006b) 'Marriage, mothers-in-law and human rights', *Law Quarterly Review* 122: 8.

Cretney, S. and Masson, J. (1997) *Principles of Family Law*, London: Sweet and Maxwell.

Cretney, S., Masson, J. and Bailey-Harris, R. (2002) *Principles of Family Law*, London: Sweet & Maxwell.

Cromack, V. and Parry, M. (1996) 'Welfare of the child – conflicting interest and conflicting principles: Re T and E (Proceedings: Conflicting Interests)', *Child and Family Law Quarterly* 8: 72.

Crompton, L. (2004) 'Civil Partnerships Bill 2004: The illusion of equality', *Family Law* 34: 888.

Crompton, R. and Lyonette, C. (2008) 'Who does the housework? The division of labour within the home', in A. Park, J. Curtice, K. Thomson, M. Phillips and M. Johnson (eds) *British Social Attitudes: the 24th Report*, London: Sage.

Cronin, H. and Curry, O. (2000) 'The Evolved Family', in H. Wilkinson (ed.) *Family Business*, London: Demos.

Crook, H. (2001) '*Troxel et vir* v *Granville* – grandparent visitation rights in the United States Supreme Court', *Child and Family Law Quarterly* 13: 101.

Crown Prosecution Service (2007) *Reasonable Chastisement Research Report*, London: CPS.

Crown Prosecution Service (2009) *Policy for Prosecuting Cases of Domestic Violence*, London: CPS.

Crown Prosecution Service and Department of Constitutional Affairs (2004) *Specialist Domestic Violence Courts*, London: DCA.

Crown Prosecution Service Inspectorate (1998) *The Inspectorate's Report on Cases Involving Domestic Violence*, London: Crown Prosecution Service Inspectorate.

Cullen, D. (2005a) 'Challenges of the new adoption law', *Family Law* 35: 594.

Cullen, D. (2005b) 'Adoption – a (fairly) new approach', *Child and Family Law Quarterly* 17: 475.

Curry-Sumner, I. (2009) '*EB v France*: A Missed Opportunity', *Child and Family Law Quarterly* 21: 356.

Czapanskiy, K. (1999) 'Interdependencies, Families, and Children', *Santa Clara Law Review* 39: 957.

Da Costa, E. (1998) 'Back door occupation orders', *Family Law* 28: 167.

*Daily Telegraph* (2005) 'Sir Elton John leads England's gay marriage rush', 21 December.

Daly, M. and Scheiwe, K. (2010) 'Individualisation and personal obligations – Social Policy, family policy and law reform in Germany and the UK', *International Journal of Law, Policy and the Family* 24: 177.

Daniel, L. (2009) 'Australia's Family Law Amendment (Shared Responsibility) Act 2006: A policy critique', *Journal of Social Welfare and Family Law* 31: 147.

Daniels, C. (2006) *Exposing Men: The Science and Politics of Male Reproduction*, Oxford: OUP.

Daniels, N. (1988) *Am I My Brother's Keeper?* Oxford: OUP.

Dauvergne, C. and Millbank, J. (2010) 'Forced Marriage as a Harm in Domestic and International Law', *Modern Law Review* 73: 57.

Davey, C. (2010) *Children' Participation in Decision-making*, London: Children's Commissioner.

Davey, M. (1997) 'Creditors and the Family Home', in C. Bridge (ed.) *Family Law Towards the Millennium: Essays for PM Bromley*, London: Butterworths.

Davies, L. and Krane, J. (2006) 'Collaborate with caution: protecting children, helping mothers', *Critical Social Policy* 26: 412.

Davis, G. (1988) *Partisans and Mediators*, Oxford: Clarendon Press.

Davis, G. (2000) *Monitoring Publicly Funded Family Mediation*, London: Legal Services Commission.

Davis, G. (2001) 'Informing policy in the light of research findings', *Family Law* 31: 822.

Davis, G., Bevan, G., Clisby, S., Cumming, Z. et al. (2000) *Monitoring Publicly Funded Family Mediation*, London: Legal Services Commission.

Davis, G., Bevan, G. and Pearce, J. (2001) 'Family mediation – where do we go from here?', *Family Law* 31: 265.

Davis, G., Clisby, S., Cumming, Z. et al. (2003) *Monitoring Publicly Funded Family Mediation*, London: Legal Services Commission.

Davis, G., Cretney, S., Barder, K. and Collins, J. (1991) 'The Relationship Between Public and Private Financial Support Following Divorce in England and Wales', in M. Maclean and L. Weitzman (eds) *The Economic Consequences of Divorce: The International Perspective*, Oxford: Clarendon Press.

Davis, G., Cretney, S. and Collins, J. (1994) *Simple Quarrels*, Oxford: Clarendon Press.

Davis, G., Finch, S. and Barnham, L. (2003) 'Family solicitors and the LSC', *Family Law* 33: 327.

Davis, G., Finch, S. and Fitzgerald, R. (2001) 'Mediation and Legal Services – The Client Speaks', *Family Law* 31: 110.

Davis, G. and Murch, M. (1988) *Grounds for Divorce*, Oxford: Clarendon Press.

Davis, G., Pearce, J., Bird, R. et al. (2000) 'Ancillary Relief Outcomes', *Child and Family Law Quarterly* 12: 1243.

Davis, G. and Roberts, S. (1989) 'Mediation and the battle of the sexes', *Family Law* 19: 305.

Davis, G. and Wikeley, N. (2002) 'National survey of Child Support Agency clients – the relationship dimension', *Family Law* 32: 523.

Davis, G., Wikeley, N. and Young, R. (1998) *Child Support in Action*, Oxford: Hart.

Davis, L. (2005) 'Adoption and Children Act 2002 – some concerns', *Family Law* 35: 294.

Davis, S. (2008) 'Equal Sharing: a Judicial Gloss too Far?', *Family Law* 38: 429.

Daycare Trust, The (2003) *Towards Universal Child Care*, London: The Daycare Trust.

Day Sclater, S. (1999) *Divorce: A Psychological Study*, Aldershot: Dartmouth.

Day Sclater, S. (2000) *Families*, London: Hodder & Stoughton.

Day Sclater, S. and Kaganas, F. (2003) 'Contact: Mothers, Welfare Rights', in A. Bainham, B. Lindley, M. Richards and L. Trinder (eds) *Children and Their Families*, Oxford: Hart.

Day Sclater, S. and Piper, C. (1999) *Undercurrents of Divorce*, Aldershot: Ashgate.

Day Sclater, S. and Yates, C. (1999) 'The Psycho-Politics of Post-Divorce Parenting', in A. Bainham, S. Day Sclater and M. Richards (eds) *What is a Parent?* Oxford: Hart.

Dayton, J. (2003) 'The silencing of a woman's choice: mandatory arrest and no drop prosecution policies in domestic violence cases', *Cardozo Women's Law Journal* 9: 281.

De Cruz, P. (1999) 'Adolescent autonomy, detention for medical treatment and *Re C*', *Modern Law Review* 62: 595.

De Cruz, P. (2010) *Family Law, Sex and Society*, Abingdon: Routledge.

Deech, R. (1980) 'The Case Against Legal Recognition of Cohabitation', in J. Eekelaar and S. Katz (eds) *Marriage and Cohabitation in Contemporary Societies*, Toronto: Butterworths.

Deech, R. (1990) 'Divorce law and empirical studies', *Law Quarterly Review* 106: 229.

Deech, R. (1993) 'The Rights of Fathers: Social and Biological Concepts of Parenthood', in J. Eekelaar and P. Sarcevic (eds) *Parenthood in Modern Society*, London: Martinus Nijhoff.

Deech, R. (1994) 'Comment: Not just marriage breakdown', *Family Law* 24: 121.

Deech, R. (1996) 'Property and Money Matters', in M. Freeman (ed.) *Divorce: Where Next?* Aldershot: Dartmouth.

Deech, R. (1998) 'Family law and genetics', *Modern Law Review* 61: 697.

Deech, R. (2000) 'The Legal Regulation of Infertility Treatment in Britain', in S. Katz, J. Eekelaar and M. Maclean (eds) *Cross Currents*, Oxford: OUP.

Deech, R. (2009a) 'What's a woman worth?', *Family Law* 39: 1140.

Deech, R. (2009b) 'Divorce – A disaster?', *Family Law* 39: 1048.

Deech, R. (2010a) 'Sisters sisters – and other family members', *Family Law* 40: 375.

Deech, R. (2010b) 'Civil Partnership', *Family Law* 40: 468.

Deech, R. (2010c) 'Cousin Marriage', *Family Law* 40: 619.

Deech, R. (2010d) 'Cohabitation', *Family Law* 40: 39.

Deech, R. and Smajdor, A. (2007) *From IVF to Immortality*, Oxford: OUP.

Delphy, C. and Leonard, D. (1992) *Familiar Policy: A New Analysis of Marriage in Contemporary Western Societies*, Cambridge: Polity Press.

Dempsey, D. (2004) 'Donor, Father or Parent? Conceiving paternity in the Australian Family Court', *International Journal of Law, Policy and the Family* 18: 76.

Dench, G. and Ogg, J. (2002) *Grandparenting in Britain*, London: Institute of Community Studies.

Department for Children, Schools and Families (2007) *Care Matters: Time for Change*, London: DCSF.

Department for Children, Schools and Families (2008a) *Children Act 1989: Guidance and Regulations*, London: DCSF.

Department for Children, Schools and Families (2008b) *Children Looked After in England*, London: DCSF.

Department for Children, Schools and Families (2009) *Forced Marriage: Prevalence and Service, Response*, London: The Stationery Office.

Department for Children, Schools and Families (2010a) *Support for All*, London: DCSF.

Department for Children, Schools and Families (2010b) *Referrals, Assessment and Children and Young People who are the Subject of a Child Protection Plan*, London: DCSF.

Department for Children, Schools and Families (2010c) *Care Matters: Ministerial Stocktake Report*, London: DCSF.

Department for Education and Skills (2003) *Every Child Matters*, London: The Stationery Office.

Department for Education and Skills (2004a) *Every Child Matters, Next Steps*, London: The Stationery Office.

Department for Education and Skills (2004b) *The Children Act Report 2003*, London: DfES.

Department for Education and Skills (2005a) *Special Guardianship Guidance*, London: DfES.

Department for Education and Skills (2005b) *Children Looked After by Local Authorities,* London: DfES.

Department for Education and Skills (2005c) *Adoption Support Agencies: National Minimum Standards,* London: DfES.

Department for Education and Skills (2006a) *Adoption Guidance,* London: DfES.

Department for Education and Skills (2006b) *Preparing and Assessing Prospective Adopters,* London: DfES.

Department for Education and Skills (2007) *Children Looked After by Local Authorities,* London: DfES.

Department for Education and Skills (2008) *Review Report: Reasonable Chastisement,* London: DfES.

Department for Work and Pensions (2005) *Opportunity for All,* London: DWP.

Department for Work and Pensions (2006a) *A New Deal for Welfare,* London: DWP.

Department for Work and Pensions (2006b) *Making a Difference,* London: DWP.

Department for Work and Pensions (2006c) *A Fresh Start: Child Support Redesign – the Government's response to Sir David Henshaw,* London: DWP.

Department for Work and Pensions (2008a) *Joint Birth Registration: Recording Responsibility,* London: DWP.

Department for Work and Pensions (2008b), *Opportunity Age,* London: DWP.

Department for Work and Pensions (2010) *Households Below Average Income,* London: DWP.

Department of Constitutional Affairs (2004) *Mental Incapacity: Who Decides?* London: DCA.

Department of Constitutional Affairs (2005) *The Government Response to the Constitutional Affairs Select Committee Report: Family Justice,* London: HMSO.

Department of Communities and Local Government (2006) *Homelessness Code of Guidance for Local Authorities,* London: The Stationery Office.

Department of Health (1995a) *Child Protection: Messages from Research,* London: HMSO.

Department of Health (1995b) The Challenge of Partnership in Child Protection: Practice Guide, London: HMSO.

Department of Health (1996) *Focus on Teenagers: Research into Practice,* London: HMSO.

Department of Health (1998a) *Surrogacy Review,* London: The Stationery Office.

Department of Health (1998b) *Working Together to Safeguard Children,* London: The Stationery Office.

Department of Health (1999a) *Adoption Now,* Chichester: John Wiley & Sons.

Department of Health (1999b) *Me Survive Out There?* London: DoH.

Department of Health (1999c) *The Government's Objectives of Children's Social Services,* London: DoH.

Department of Health (2000a) *Protecting Children, Supporting Parents,* London: The Stationery Office.

Department of Health (2000b) *The NHS Plan. The Government's Response to the Royal Commission on Long Term Care,* London: The Stationery Office.

Department of Health (2002a) *Homelessness: Code of Guidance for Local Authorities,* London: DoH.

Department of Health (2002b) *Monitoring Adoption Disruption Rates Post Adoption Order,* London: DoH.

Department of Health (2002c) *Safeguarding Children,* London: DoH.

Department of Health (2002d) *Adoption and Permanence Taskforce Second Report,* London: DoH.

Department of Health (2002e) *Friends and Family Care (Kinship Care),* London: DoH.

Department of Health (2002f) *No Secrets,* London: DoH.

Department of Health (2002g) *Adopter Preparation and Assessment and the Operation of Adoption Panels,* London: DoH.

Department of Health (2002h) *Caring About Carers,* London: DoH.

Department of Health (2003a) *Children Looked After in England 2001/2002,* London: DoH.

Department of Health (2003b) *Adoption Support Services Guidance,* London: DoH.

Department of Health (2003c) *Adoption and Permanence Project,* London: DoH.

Department of Health (2003d) *Adoption National Minimum Standards,* London: DoH.

Department of Health (2005a) *Review of the Human Fertilisation and Embryology Act: a Public Consultation,* London: DoH.

Department of Health (2005b) *Caring About Carers,* London: DoH.

Department of Health (2005c) *Independence, Well-Being and Choice,* London: DoH.

Department of Health (2010) *Review of Arm's Length Bodies to Cut Bureaucracy*, London: DoH.

Department of Social Security (1990) *Children Come First*, London: HMSO.

Department of Social Security (1998) *Children First: A New Approach to Child Support*, London: DSS.

Department of Social Security (2000) *Children's Rights and Parents' Responsibilities*, London: DSS.

Devlin, P. (1965) *The Enforcement of Morals*, Oxford: OUP.

Dewar, J. (1992) *Law and the Family*, London: Butterworths.

Dewar, J. (1995) 'The courts and local authority autonomy', *Child and Family Law Quarterly* 7: 15.

Dewar, J. (1997) 'Reducing discretion in family law', *Australian Journal of Family Law* 11: 309.

Dewar, J. (1998) 'The normal chaos of family law', *Modern Law Review* 61: 467.

Dewar, J. (2000a) 'Family law and its discontents', *International Journal of Law, Policy and the Family* 14: 59.

Dewar, J. (2000b) 'Making Family Law New?', in M. McLean (ed.) *Making Law for Families*, Oxford: Hart.

Dewar, J. and Parker, S. (2000) 'English Family Law since World War II: From Status to Chaos', in S. Katz, J. Eekelaar and M. Maclean (eds) *Cross Currents*, Oxford: OUP.

Dex, S., Ward, K. and Joshi, H. (2006) *Changes in Women's Occupations and Occupational Mobility over 25 Years*, London: Centre for Longitudinal Studies.

Dey, I. (2005) 'Adapting Adoption: A case of closet politics', *International Journal of Law, Policy and the Family* 19: 289.

Diamantides, M. (1999) 'Meditations on Parental Love', in M. King (ed.) *Moral Agendas for Children's Welfare*, London: Routledge.

Dickens, J. (1993) 'Assessment and the control of social work: Analysis of reasons for the non-use of the Child Assessment Order', *Journal of Social Welfare and Family Law* 15: 88.

Dickens, J. (2005) 'Being "the epitome of reason": The challenges for lawyers and social workers in child care proceedings', *International Journal of Law, Policy and the Family* 19: 73.

Dickenson, D. and Jones, D. (1995) 'True wishes: The philosophy and developmental psychology of children's informed consent', *Philosophy, Psychiatry and Psychology* 2: 287.

Diduck, A. (1995) 'The unmodified family: the Child Support Act and the construction of legal subjects', *Journal of Law and Society* 22: 527.

Diduck, A. (2000) 'Solicitors and Legal Subjects', in J. Bridgeman and D. Monk (eds) *Feminist Perspectives on Child Law*, London: Cavendish.

Diduck, A. (2001a) 'A family by any other name . . . or Starbucks comes to England', *Journal of Law and Society* 28: 290.

Diduck, A. (2001b) 'Fairness and justice for all?', *Feminist Legal Studies* 9: 173.

Diduck, A. (2003) *Law's Families*, London: LexisNexis Butterworths.

Diduck, A. (2005) 'Shifting Familiarity', in J. Holder and C. O'Cinneide (eds) *Current Legal Problems*, Oxford: OUP.

Diduck, A. (2007) 'If only we can find the appropriate terms to use the issue will be solved: law, identity and parenthood', *Child and Family Law Quarterly* 19: 458.

Diduck, A. (2008) 'Family law and family responsibility' in J. Bridgeman, H. Keating and C. Lind (eds) *Responsibility, Law and the Family*, London: Ashgate.

Diduck, A. (2009) 'Relationship fairness', in Bottomley, A. and Wong, S. (eds) *Changing Contours of Domestic Life, Family and Law*, Oxford: Hart.

Diduck, A. (2010) 'Public norms and private lives: Rights, fairness and family law' in J. Wallbank, S. Choudhry and J. Herring (eds) *Rights, Gender and Family Law*, Abingdon: Routledge.

Diduck, A. and Kaganas, F. (2004) 'Incomplete citizens: changing images of post-separation children', *Modern Law Review* 67: 959.

Diduck, A. and Kaganas, F. (2006) *Family Law, Gender and the State*, Oxford: Hart.

Diduck, A. and O'Donovan, K. (2007) 'Feminism and families: Plus ça change?' in A. Diduck and K. O'Donovan (eds) *Feminist Perspectives on Family Law*, London: Routledge.

Diduck, A. and Orton, H. (1994) 'Equality and support for spouses', *Modern Law Review* 57: 681.

Dingwall, R. (1988) 'Empowerment or Enforcement? Some Questions about Power and Control in Divorce Mediation', in J. Eekelaar and R. Dingwall (eds) *Divorce, Mediation and the Legal Process*, Oxford: Clarendon Press.

Dingwall, R. and Greatbatch, D. (1994) 'The Virtues of Formality', in J. Eekelaar and M. Maclean (eds) *A Reader on Family Law*, Oxford: OUP.

Dingwall, R. and Greatbatch, D. (2001) 'Family mediators – What are they doing?', *Family Law* 31: 379.

Dispatches (2010) *Undercover Social Worker*, broadcast 7 June.

Dixon, M. (1998) 'Combating the mortgagee's right to possession: New hope for the mortgagor in chains?', *Legal Studies* 18: 279.

Dixon, M. (2007) 'The never-ending story – co-ownership after *Stack* v *Dowden*', *Conveyancer and Property Lawyer* 71: 456.

Dixon, M. (2010) 'Confining and defining proprietary estoppel: the role of unconscionability', *Legal Studies* 30: 408.

Dnes, A. (1998) 'The division of marital assets following divorce', *Journal of Law and Society* 25: 336.

Dnes, A. (2002) 'Cohabitation and Marriage', in A. Dnes and R. Rowthorn (eds) *The Law and Economics of Marriage and Divorce*, Cambridge: CUP.

Dobash, R. and Dobash, R. (1992) *Women, Violence and Social Change*, London: Routledge.

Dobash, R. and Dobash, R. (2000) 'Violence Against Women in the Family', in S. Katz, J. Eekelaar and M. Maclean (eds) *Cross Currents*, Oxford: OUP.

Dobash, R. and Dobash, R. (2004) 'Women's violence to men in intimate relationships', *British Journal of Criminology* 44: 324.

Doggett, M. (1992) Marriage, Wife-Beating and the Law in Victorian England, London: Weidenfeld & Nicholson.

Dolgin, J. (1998) *Defining the Family*, New York: New York University Press.

Donovan, C. (2006) 'Genetics, fathers and families: Exploring the implications of changing the law in favour of identifying sperm donors', *Social Legal Studies* 15: 494.

Donzelot, J. (1980) *The Policing of Families*, London: Hutchinson.

Doughty, J. (2008a) 'The "no order principle": A myth revived', *Family Law* 38: 561.

Doughty, J. (2008b) 'From court missionaries to conflict resolution: a century of family

court welfare', *Child and Family Law Quarterly* 20: 131.

Doughty, J. (2009) 'Identity crisis in the family courts? Different approaches in England and Wales and Australia', *Journal of Social Welfare and Family Law* 31: 231.

Douglas, A. and Philpot, T. (2003) *Adoption – Changing Families, Changing Times*, London: Routledge.

Douglas, G. (1988) 'The family and the state under the European Convention on Human Rights', *International Journal of Law and the Family* 2: 76.

Douglas, G. (1992) 'The retreat from *Gillick*', *Modern Law Review* 55: 569.

Douglas, G. (1993) 'Assisted reproduction and the welfare of children', *Current Legal Problems* 46: 53.

Douglas, G. (1994a) 'In whose best interests?', *Law Quarterly Review* 110: 379.

Douglas, G. (1994b) 'The intention to be a parent and the making of mothers', *Modern Law Review* 57: 636.

Douglas, G. (2000a) 'Supporting Families', in A. Bainham (ed.) *The International Survey of Family Law*, 2000 Edition, Bristol: Jordans.

Douglas, G. (2000b) 'Marriage, Cohabitation and Parenthood – from Contract to Status', in S. Katz, J. Eekelaar and M. Maclean (eds) *Cross Currents*, Oxford: OUP.

Douglas, G. (2004) 'Comment: *Co* v *Co*', *Family Law* 34: 406.

Douglas, G. (2005) *An Introduction to Family Law*, Oxford: OUP.

Douglas, G. (2006a) 'Comment: *R (Axon)* v *Secretary of State for Health*', *Family Law* 36: 272.

Douglas, G. (2006b) 'Comment: *Re H (Abduction: Dominica: Corporal Punishment)*', Family Law 36: 523.

Douglas, G. (2006c) 'The separate representation of children – in whose best interests?', in M. Thorpe and R. Budden (eds) *Durable Solutions*, Bristol: Jordans.

Douglas, G. (2006d) *Children and Family Breakdown*, Cardiff: Cardiff Centre for Ethics, Law and Society.

Douglas, G. (2009) 'Comment', *Family Law* 39: 381.

Douglas, G. and Ferguson, N. (2003) 'The role of grandparents in divorced families', *International Journal of Law, Policy and the Family* 17: 41.

Douglas, G. and Lowe, N. (1992) 'Becoming a parent in English Law', *Law Quarterly Review* 108: 414.

Douglas, G. and Murch, M. (2002a) *The Role of Grandparents in Divorced Families*, Cardiff: Family Studies Research Centre, University of Wales.

Douglas, G. and Murch, M. (2002b) 'Taking account of children's needs at divorce', *Child and Family Law Quarterly* 14: 57.

Douglas, G., Murch, M., Miles, C. and Scanlan, L. (2006) *Research into the Operation of Rule 9.5 of the Family Proceedings Rules 1991*, London: DCA.

Douglas, G., Murch, M., Robinson, M. et al. (2001) 'Children's perspectives and experience of the divorce process', *Family Law* 31: 373.

Douglas, G., Murch, M., Scanlan, L. and Perry, A. (2000) 'Safeguarding children's welfare in non-contentious divorce: towards a new conception of the legal process', *Modern Law Review* 63: 177.

Douglas, G., Pearce, J. and Woodward, H. (2007) *A Failure of Trust: Resolving Property Issues on Cohabitation Breakdown*, Cardiff: Cardiff University.

Douglas, G., Pearce, J. and Woodward, H. (2008) 'The law commission's cohabitation proposals: applying them in practice', *Family Law* 38: 351.

Douglas, G., Pearce, J. and Woodward, H. (2009a) 'Money, property, cohabitation and separation', in J. Miles and R. Probert (eds) *Sharing Lives, Dividing Assets*, Oxford: Hart.

Douglas, G., Pearce, J. and Woodward, H. (2009b) 'Cohabitants, Property and the Law: A Study of Injustice', *Modern Law Review* 72: 24.

Douglas, G. and Philpot, T. (eds) (2003) *Adoption: Changing Families: Changing Times*, London: Routledge.

Downey, D. and Powell, B. (1993) 'Do children in single-parent households fare better living with same-sex parents?' *Journal of Marriage and the Family* 55: 55.

Draper, H. and Ives, J. (2009) 'Paternity testing: a poor test of fatherhood', *Journal of Social Welfare and Family Law* 31: 407.

Drew, L. and Smith, P. (1999) 'The impact of parental separation on grand-parent–grandchild relationships', *International Journal of Ageing and Human Development* 48: 191.

Driscoll, J. and Hollingsworth, K. (2008) 'Accommodating Children in Need: *R (M)* v *Hammersmith and Fulham London Borough Council*', *Child and Family Law Quarterly* 20: 522.

Duckworth, P. (2002a) 'We are family. Really?', *Family Law* 32: 91.

Duckworth, P. (2002b) 'What is family? A personal view', *Family Law* 32: 367.

Duckworth, P. and Hodson, D. (2001) '*White* v *White* – bringing section 25 back to the people', *Family Law* 31: 24.

Dunn, G. (1999) 'A Passion for Sameness? Sexuality and Gender Accountability', in E. Silva and C. Smart (eds) *The New Family*, London: Sage.

Dunn, J. (2003) 'Contact and Children's Perspectives on Parental Relationships', in A. Bainham, B. Lindley, M. Richards and L. Trinder (eds) *Children and Their Families*, Oxford: Hart.

Dunn, J. (2006) 'Contact with non-resident fathers', in M. Thorpe and R. Budden (eds) *Durable Solutions*, Bristol: Jordans.

Dunn, J., Chung, H., O'Connor, T. and Bridges, L. (2004) 'Children's perspectives on their relationships with their nonresident fathers: influences, outcomes and implications', *Journal of Child Psychology and Psychiatry* 45: 553.

Dunn, J. and Deater-Deckard, K. (2001) *Children's Views of Their Changing Family*, London: YPS.

Dunne, G. (2000) 'Opting into motherhood', *Gender and Society* 14: 11.

Durrant, J. (2003) 'Legal reform and attitudes towards physical punishment in Sweden', *International Journal of Children's Rights* 11: 147.

Dwyer, J. (2006) The Relationship Rights of Children, Cambridge: CUP.

Dyer, C. (2000) 'Government drops plan for no-fault divorce', *The Guardian*, 2 September.

Dyer, C., McCrum, S., Thomas, R., Ward, R. and Wookey, S. (2008) 'Making Contact Work: Is the Children and Adoption Act 2006 Enough for Resident Parents and Children?', *Family Law* 38: 1237.

Eaton, M. (1994) 'Abuse By Any Other Name: Feminism, Difference and Intralesbian Violence', in N. Fine and R. Myktiuk (eds) *The Public Nature of Private Violence. The Discovery of Domestic Abuse*, New York: Routledge.

Economic and Social Research Council (2005) *Welfare and Single Parenthood in the UK*, London: ESRC.

Eden, R. (2000) *Traditional Family Life 'is in Decline'*, London: Family Policy Studies Centre.

Edwards, L. (2004) *The Lever Faberge Family Report 2004*, London: Lever Faberge.

Edwards, R., Gillies, V. and McCarthy, J. (1999) 'Biological parents and social families: legal discourses and everyday understandings of the position of step-parents', *International Journal of Law, Policy and the Family* 13: 78.

Edwards, R., Hadfield, L. and Mauthner, M. (2005) *Children's Understanding of Their Sibling Relationships*, York: Joseph Rowntree Foundation.

Edwards, S. (1996) *Sex and Gender in the Legal Process*, London: Blackstone.

Edwards, S. (2000) *Briefing Note: Reducing Domestic Violence*, London: Home Office.

Edwards, S. (2004) 'Division of assets and fairness – "Brick Lane" – Gender culture and ancillary relief on divorce', *Family Law* 34: 809.

Edwards, S. (2007) 'Imagining Islam . . . of meaning and metaphor symbolizing and jilbab', *Child and Family Law Quarterly* 19: 247.

Edwards, S., Gould, C. and Halpern, A. (1990) 'The continuing saga of maintaining the family after divorce', *Family Law* 20: 31.

Edwards, S. and Halpern, A. (1991) 'Protection for the victims of domestic violence: Time for radical revision', *Journal of Social Welfare and Family Law* 13: 94.

Edwards, S. and Halpern, A. (1992) 'Parental responsibility: An instrument of social policy', *Family Law* 22: 113.

Eekelaar, J. (1984) *Family Law and Social Policy*, London: Weidenfeld & Nicholson.

Eekelaar, J. (1986) 'The eclipse of parental rights', *Law Quarterly Review* 102: 4.

Eekelaar, J. (1987a) 'Second thoughts on illegitimacy reform', *Family Law* 17: 261.

Eekelaar, J. (1987b) 'Family Law and Social Control', in J. Eekelaar and J. Bell (eds) *Oxford Essays in Jurisprudence*, Oxford: OUP.

Eekelaar, J. (1988) 'Equality and the purpose of maintenance', *Journal of Law and Society* 15: 188.

Eekelaar, J. (1989) 'What is "critical" family law?', *Law Quarterly Review* 105: 244.

Eekelaar, J. (1990) 'Investigation under the Children Act 1989', *Family Law* 20: 486.

Eekelaar, J. (1991a) *Regulating Divorce*, Oxford: Clarendon Press.

Eekelaar, J. (1991b) 'Are parents morally obliged to care for their children?', *Oxford Journal of Legal Studies* 11: 51.

Eekelaar, J. (1991c) 'Parental responsibility: State of nature or nature of the state?', *Journal of Social Welfare and Family Law* 13: 37.

Eekelaar, J. (1991d) 'The wardship jurisdiction, children's welfare and parents' rights', *Law Quarterly Review* 107: 386.

Eekelaar, J. (1992) 'The importance of thinking that children have rights', *International Journal of Law, Policy and the Family* 6: 221.

Eekelaar, J. (1994a) 'The interests of the child and the child's wishes: the role of dynamic self-determinism', *International Journal of Law and the Family* 8: 42.

Eekelaar, J. (1994b) 'Non-Marital Property', in P. Birks (ed.) *Frontiers of Liability*, Oxford: OUP.

Eekelaar, J. (1994c) 'A jurisdiction in search of a mission: Family proceedings in England and Wales', *Modern Law Review* 57: 839.

Eekelaar, J. (1994d) 'Families and Children', in C. McCrudden and D. Chambers (eds) *Individual Rights and the Law in Britain*, Oxford: OUP.

Eekelaar, J. (1995) 'Family justice: Ideal or illusion? Family law and communitarian values', *Current Legal Problems* 48: 191.

Eekelaar, J. (1996) 'Parental responsibility – a new legal status?', *Law Quarterly Review* 112: 233.

Eekelaar, J. (1998) 'Do parents have a duty to consult?', *Law Quarterly Review* 114: 337.

Eekelaar, J. (1999) 'Family law: Keeping us "on message"', *Child and Family Law Quarterly* 11: 387.

Eekelaar J. (2000a) 'Family Law and the Responsible Citizen', in M. Maclean (ed.) *Making Law for Families*, Oxford: Hart.

Eekelaar, J. (2000b) 'Post-Divorce Financial Obligations', in S. Katz, J. Eekelaar and M. Maclean (eds) *Cross Currents*, Oxford: OUP.

Eekelaar, J. (2000c) 'The End of an Era?', in S. Katz, J. Eekelaar and M. Maclean (eds) *Cross Currents*, Oxford: OUP.

Eekelaar, J. (2001a) 'Asset distribution on divorce – the durational element', *Law Quarterly Review* 117: 24.

Eekelaar, J. (2001b) 'Back to basics and forward into the unknown', *Family Law* 31: 30.

Eekelaar, J. (2001c) 'Family law: The communitarian message', *Oxford Journal of Legal Studies* 21: 181.

Eekelaar, J. (2001d) 'Rethinking parental responsibility', *Family Law* 31: 426.

Eekelaar, J. (2002a) 'Beyond the welfare principle', *Child and Family Law Quarterly* 14: 237.

Eekelaar, J. (2002b) 'Contact – over the limit', *Family Law* 32: 271.

Eekelaar J. (2003a) 'Contact and the Adoption Reform', in A. Bainham, B. Lindley, M. Richards and L. Trinder (eds) *Children and Their Families*, Oxford: Hart.

Eekelaar, J. (2003b) 'Corporal punishment, parents' religion, and children's rights', *Law Quarterly Review* 119: 370.

Eekelaar, J. (2003c) 'Asset distribution on divorce – time and property', *Family Law* 33: 838.

Eekelaar, J. (2004) 'Children between cultures', *International Journal of Law, Policy and the Family* 18: 178.

Eekelaar, J. (2005a) '*Miller* v *Miller*: The descent into chaos', *Family Law* 35: 870.

Eekelaar J. (2005b) 'Shared income after divorce: a step too far', *Law Quarterly Review* 121: 1.

Eekelaar, J. (2006a) 'Property and Financial Settlement on Divorce – Sharing and Compensating', *Family Law* 36: 754.

Eekelaar, J. (2006b) *Family Life and Personal Life*, Oxford: OUP.

Eekelaar, J. (2007) 'Why people marry: The many faces of an institution', *Family Law Quarterly* 41: 413.

Eekelaar, J. (2009) 'Law, family and community' in G. Douglas and N. Lowe (eds), *The Continuing Evolution of Family Law* Bristol: Family Law.

Eekelaar, J. and Clive, E. (1977) *Custody After Divorce*, Oxford: OUP.

Eekelaar, J. and Dingwall, R. (1990) *The Reform of Child Care Law*, London: Routledge.

Eekelaar, J. and Maclean, M. (1986) *Maintenance After Divorce*, Oxford: Clarendon Press.

Eekelaar, J. and Maclean, M. (1990) 'Divorce law and empirical studies – a reply', *Law Quarterly Review* 106: 621.

Eekelaar, J. and Maclean, M. (1997) *The Parental Obligation*, Oxford: Hart.

Eekelaar, J. and Maclean, M. (2004) 'Marriage and the moral bases of personal relationships', *Journal of Law and Society* 4: 510.

Eekelaar, J. and Maclean, M. (2009) *Family Law Advocacy*, Oxford; Hart.

Eekelaar, J., Maclean, M. and Beinart, S. (2000) *Family Lawyers*, Oxford: Hart.

Eekelaar, J. and Nhlapo, T. (1998) 'Introduction', in J. Eekelaar and T. Nhlapo (eds) *The Changing Family: International Perspectives on the Family and Family Law*, Oxford: Hart.

Eijkholt, M. (2010) 'The right to found a family as a stillborn right to procreate?', *Medical Law Review* 18: 127.

Ellis, S. and Franklin, A. (1995) 'Children's Rights Officers: Righting Wrongs and Promoting Rights', in B. Franklin (ed.) *The Handbook of Children's Rights*, London: Routledge.

Ellison, L. (2002a) 'Responding to victim withdrawal in domestic violence prosecutions', *Criminal Law Review* 760.

Ellison, L. (2002b) 'Prosecuting domestic violence without victim participation', *Modern Law Review* 65: 834.

Ellison, R. (1998) 'Strengths and Weaknesses of the Law on Pension Splitting in the United Kingdom', in R. Bailey-Harris (ed.) *Dividing the Assets on Family Breakdown*, Bristol: Jordans.

Ellman, I. (1989) 'The theory of alimony', *California Law Review* 77: 3.

Ellman, I. (2000a) 'Divorce in the United States', in S. Katz, J. Eekelaar and M. Maclean (eds) *Cross Currents*, Oxford: OUP.

Ellman, I. (2000b) 'The Misguided Movement to Revive Fault Divorce', in M. King White (ed.) *Marriage in America*, Lanham, Md.: Rowman & Littlefield.

Ellman, I. (2005) 'Do Americans Play Football?', *International Journal of Law, Policy and the Family* 19: 257.

Ellman, I. (2007) 'Financial settlement on divorce: two steps forward, two to go', *Law Quarterly Review* 123: 2.

Elmalik, K. and Wheeler, R. (2007) 'Consent: Luck or law?', *Annals of the Royal College of Surgeons England* 89: 627.

Elster, J. (1987) 'Solomonic judgments: Against the best interests of the child', *University of Chicago Law Review* 54: 1.

Emens, E. (2004) 'Just Monogamy?', in M. Lyndon Shanley (ed.) *Just Marriage*, Oxford: OUP.

Emery, R. (1994) *Renegotiating Family Relationships: Divorce, Child Custody and Mediation*, Guildford: Guildford Press.

Emery, R. (1998) *Marriage, Divorce and Children's Adjustment*, Thousand Oaks, Calif.: Sage.

Emery, R. (1999) 'Post Divorce Family Life for Children', in R. Thompson and P. Amato (eds) *The Postdivorce Family*, Thousand Oaks, Calif.: Sage.

Engels, F. (1978) *The Origin of the Family, Private Property and the State*, Peking: Foreign Languages Press.

English, J. (1979) 'What Do Grown Children Owe Their Parents?', in O. O'Neill and W. Ruddick (eds) *Having Children*, New York: OUP.

Equal Opportunities Commission (2001) *Men and Women in Britain: The Life Cycle of Inequality*, London: EOC.

Equal Opportunities Commission (2006a) *Facts about Men and Women in Great Britain*, London: EOC.

Equal Opportunities Commission (2006b) *Sex Equality and the Modern Family*, London: EOC.

Ermisch, J. (2006) *Births Outside Marriage*, London: ESRC.

Ermisch, J. (2008) *Births Outside Marriage*, London: ESRC.

Ermisch, J. and Francesconi, M. (1998) *Cohabitation in Great Britain*, Colchester: University of Essex.

Ermisch, J. and Francesconi, M. (2001) *The Effects of Parents' Employment on Children's Lives*, London and York: Family Policy Studies Centre and Joseph Rowntree Foundation.

Ermisch, J. and Francesconi, M. (2003) *Working Parents: The Impact on Kids*, London: Institute for Social and Economic Research.

Ermisch, J. and Murphy, M. (2006) *Changing Household and Family Structures and Complex Living Arrangements*, London: ESRC.

Eskridge, W. (2001) 'The Ideological Structure of the Same-Sex Marriage Debate', in R. Wintemute and M. Andenæs (eds) *Legal Recognition of Same-Sex Partnershps*, Oxford: Hart.

Eskridge, W. and Spedale, D. (2006) *Gay marriage? For better or for worse?* Cambridge: Cambridge University Press.

Ettlebrick, P. (1992) 'Since when is marriage a path to liberation?', in S. Sherman (ed.) *Gay and Lesbian Marriage*, Philadelphia: Temple University Press.

Evans State, J. (1992) 'Mandatory planning for divorce', *Vanderbilt Law Review* 45: 397.

Families Need Fathers (2003) *Safety and Justice: Reply to Consultation*, London: FNF.

Family and Parenting Institute (2009) *Family Trends*, London: FPI.

Family Justice Council (2010) 'Guidelines for judges meeting children who are subject to family proceedings', *Family Law* 40: 647.

Family Matters Institute (2009) *Do Grandparents Matter?*, London: Family Matters Institute.

Family Policy Studies Centre (1995) *Families in Britain*, London: Family Policy Studies Centre.

Farson, R. (1978) *Birthrights*, London: Penguin.

Fatherhood Institute (2008) *The Difference a Dad Makes*, London: Fatherhood Institute.

Fawcett Society (2010) *Keeping Mum*, London: Fawcett Society.

Featherstone, B. (2009) *Contemporary Fathering*, Bristol: Policy Press.

Featherstone, B. (2010a) 'Gender, rights, responsibilities and social policy', in J. Wallbank, S. Choudhry and J. Herring (eds) *Rights, Gender and Family Law*, Abingdon: Routledge.

Featherstone, B. (2010b) 'Writing fathers in but mothers out!!!', *Critical Social Policy* 30: 208.

Federle, K. (1994) 'Rights flow downhill', *International Journal of Children's Rights* 2: 343.

Federle, K. (2009) 'Rights, Not Wrongs', *International Journal of Children's Rights* 17: 321.

Fehlberg, B. (1997) *Sexually Transmitted Debt*, Oxford: OUP.

Fehlberg, B. (2004) 'Spousal maintenance in Australia', *International Journal of Law, Policy and the Family* 18: 1.

Fehlberg, B. (2005) '"With all my worldly goods I thee endow"?: The partnership theme in Australian matrimonial property law', *International Journal of Law, Policy and the Family* 19: 176.

Fehlberg, B. and Smyth, B. (2002) 'Binding pre-nuptial agreements in Australia: The first year', *International Journal of Law, Policy and the Family* 16: 127.

Feldman, D. (1997) 'The developing scope of article 8 of the European Convention on Human Rights', *European Human Rights Law Review* 1: 265.

Fenwick, H. (2004) 'Clashing Rights, the welfare of the child and the Human Rights Act', *Modern Law Review* 67: 889.

Ferguson, E., Maughan, B. and Golding, J. (2008) 'Which children receive grandparental care and what effect does it have?', *Journal of Child Psychology and Psychiatry* 49: 161.

Ferguson, L. (2008) 'Family, social inequalities and the persuasive force of interpersonal obligation', *International Journal of Law, Policy and the Family* 22: 61.

Ferguson, N. (2004) *Grandparenting in Divorced Families*, Bristol: Policy Press.

Ferguson, P. (1993) 'Constructive trusts – a note of caution', *Law Quarterly Review* 109: 114.

Ferri, E. and Smith, K. (1998) *Step-Parenting in the 1990s*, London: Family Policy Studies Centre.

Field, M. (1989) 'Is Surrogacy Exploitative?', in S. Maclean (ed.) *Legal Issues in Human Reproduction*, Aldershot: Gower.

Finch, J. (1989) *Family Obligations and Social Change*, Cambridge: Polity Press.

Finch, J. (1994) 'The Proper Thing to Do', in J. Eekelaar and M. Maclean (eds) *A Reader on Family Law*, Oxford: OUP.

Finch, J. (2007) 'Displaying families', *Sociology* 41: 65.

Finch, N. and Searle, B. (2005) 'Children's Lifestyles', in J. Bradshaw and E. Mayhew (eds) *The Well-Being of Children in the UK*, London: Save the Children.

Fineman, M. (1988) 'Dominant discourse, professional language and legal change in child custody decision-making', *Harvard Law Review* 101: 727.

Fineman, M. (1995) *The Neutered Mother, the Sexual Family and Other Twentieth-Century Traditions*, London, New York: Routledge.

Fineman, M. (2002) 'Domestic violence, custody and visitation', *Family Law Quarterly* 36: 211.

Fineman, M. (2004) *The Autonomy Myth*, New York: The New Press.

Fineman, M. (2006) 'The Meaning of Marriage', in A. Bernstein (ed.) *Marriage Proposals*, New York: New York University Press.

Fink, H. and Carbone, J. (2003) 'Between private ordering and public fiat: A new paradigm for family law decision-making', *Journal of Law and Family Studies* 5: 1.

Finlay, A. (2002) 'Delay and the Challenges of the Children Act', in Thorpe LJ and C. Cowton (eds) *Delight and Dole*, Bristol: Jordans.

Finlay, H. (1976) 'Farewell to affinity and the celebration of kinship', *University of Tasmania Law Review* 5: 10.

Finnis, J. (1994) 'Law, morality and "sexual orientation"', *Notre Dame University Law Review* 69: 1.

Fionda, J. (2001) 'Legal Concepts of Childhood: An Introduction', in J. Fionda (ed.) *Legal Concepts of Childhood*, Hart: Oxford.

Fisher, L. (2002) 'The unexpected impact of *White* – taking "Equality" too far', *Family Law* 32: 108.

Fisher, H. and Low, H. (2009) 'Who wins, who loses and who recovers from divorce?', in J. Miles and R. Probert (eds) *Sharing Lives, Dividing Assets*, Oxford: Hart.

Flatley, J., Kershaw, C., Smith, K., Chaplin, R. and Moon, D. (2010) *Crime in England and Wales 2009/10*, London: Home Office.

Forced Marriage Unit (2006) *Forced Marriage: A Wrong not a Right. Summary of Responses*, London: Home Office.

Ford, M. and Morgan, D. (2003) 'Addressing a misconception', *Child and Family Law Quarterly* 15: 199.

Forder, C. (1987) 'Might and right in matrimonial property law: A comparative study of England and the German Democratic Republic', *International Journal of Law and the Family* 1: 47.

Fortin, J. (1988) 'Can you ward a foetus?', *Modern Law Review* 51: 768.

Fortin, J. (1993) 'Significant harm revisited', *Journal of Child Law* 5: 151.

Fortin, J. (1996) 'Re F: The gooseberry bush approach', *Modern Law Review* 57: 296.

Fortin, J. (1998) 'Re C (Medical Treatment) – A baby's right to die', *Child and Family Law Quarterly* 10: 411.

Fortin, J. (1999a) 'The HRA's impact on litigation involving children and their families', *Children and Family Law Quarterly* 11: 237.

Fortin, J. (1999b) 'Re D (Care: Natural Parent Presumption): Is Blood Really Thicker than Water?', *Child and Family Law Quarterly* 11: 435.

Fortin, J. (2001) 'Children's rights and the use of physical force', *Child and Family Law Quarterly* 13: 243.

Fortin, J. (2002) 'Children's Rights and the Impact of Two International Conventions: The UNCRC and the ECHR', in Thorpe LJ and C. Cowton (eds) *Delight and Dole*, Bristol: Jordans.

Fortin, J. (2003) 'Children's Rights and the Use of Force "In Their Own Best Interests"', in J. Dewar and S. Parker (eds) *Family Law Processes, Practices, Pressures*, Oxford: Hart.

Fortin, J. (2004) 'Children's Rights: Are the Courts Now Taking Them More Seriously?', *King's College Law Journal* 15: 253.

Fortin, J. (2006a) 'Accommodating Children's Rights in a Post Human Rights Act Era', *Modern Law Review* 69: 299.

Fortin, J. (2006b) 'Children's Rights – Substance or Spin?', *Family Law* 36: 759.

Fortin, J. (2007) 'Children's Representation Through the Looking Glass', *Family Law* 37: 500.

Fortin, J. (2009a) 'Children's right to know their origins – too far, too fast?', *Child and Family Law Quarterly* 21: 336.

Fortin, J. (2009b) *Children's Rights and the Developing Law*, London: Butterworths.

Fortin, J., Ritchie, C. and Buchanan, A. (2006) 'Young adults' perceptions of court-ordered contact', *Child and Family Law Quarterly* 18: 211.

Foster, H. and Freund, D. (1972) 'A Bill of Rights for children', *Family Law Quarterly* 6: 343.

Fox, L. (2003) 'Reforming family property – comparisons, compromises and common dimensions', *Child and Family Law Quarterly* 15: 1.

Fox, L. (2005) 'Creditors and the concept of "family home": a functional analysis', *Legal Studies* 25: 201.

Fox, L. (2006) *Conceptualising Home: Theories, Law and Policies*, Oxford: Hart.

Fox, M. and McHale, J. (1997) 'In whose best interests?', *Modern Law Review* 58: 700.

Fox, M. and Thomson, M. (2005) 'Short changed? The law and ethics of male circumcision', *International Journal of Children's Rights* 13: 161.

Fox Harding, L. (1996) *Family, State and Social Policy*, Basingstoke: Macmillan.

Francis, N. (2006) 'If it's broken – fix it', *Family Law* 36: 104.

Francis, N. and Philipps, S. (2003) 'New light on prenuptial agreements', *Family Law* 33: 164.

Franck, J-U (2009) '"So hedge therefore, who join forever": Understanding the interrelation of no-fault divorce and premarital contracts', *International Journal of Law, Policy and the Family* 23: 235.

Francoz-Terminal, L. (2009) 'From same-sex couples to same-sex families? Current French legal issues', *Child and Family Law Quarterly* 21: 485.

Frantz, C. and Dagan, H. (2002) *On Marital Property: Research Paper 45*, New York University Law School.

Frantz, C. and Dagan, H. (2004) 'Properties of Marriage', *Columbia Law Review* 104: 75.

Fredman, S. (2002) *Discrimination Law*, Oxford: OUP.

Fredman, S. (2003) 'The Age of Equality', in S. Fredman and S. Spencer (eds) *Age as an Equality Issue*, Oxford: Hart.

Freedman, E. (2002) 'International terrorism and the grave physical risk defence of the Hague Convention on International Child Abduction', *International Family Law* 6: 60.

Freeman, M. (1983) *The Rights and Wrongs of Children*, London: Frances Pinter.

Freeman, M. (1984) 'Legal Ideologies: Patriarchal Precedents and Domestic Violence', in M. Freeman (ed.) *The State, The Law and the Family*, London: Sweet & Maxwell.

Freeman, M. (1985) 'Towards a critical theory of family law', *Current Legal Problems* 40: 179.

Freeman, M. (1992a) *Children, Their Families and the Law*, Basingstoke: Macmillan.

Freeman, M. (1992b) 'Taking children's rights more seriously', *International Journal of Law, Policy and the Family* 6: 52.

Freeman, M. (1996) 'The new birth right?', *International Journal of Children's Rights* 4: 273.

Freeman, M. (1997a) *The Moral Status of Children*, London: Martinus Nijhoff.

Freeman, M. (1997b) 'The best interests of the child? Is the best interests of the child in the best interests of children?', *International Journal of Law, Policy and the Family* 11: 360.

Freeman, M. (1999) 'Not such a queer idea. Is there a case for same-sex marriages?', *Journal of Applied Philosophy* 16: 1.

Freeman, M. (2000a) 'Disputing Children', in S. Katz, J. Eekelaar and M. Maclean (eds) *Cross Currents*, Oxford: OUP.

Freeman, M. (2000b) 'Feminism and Child Law', in J. Bridgeman and D. Monk (eds) *Feminist Perspectives on Child Law*, London: Cavendish.

Freeman, M. (2000c) 'The end of the century of the child?', *Current Legal Problems* 55: 505.

Freeman, M. (2000d) 'Images of Child Welfare in Child Abduction Appeals', in J. Murphy (ed.) *Ethnic Minorities, Their Families and the Law*, Oxford: Hart.

Freeman, M. (2000e) 'The future of children's rights', *Children and Society* 14: 277.

Freeman, M. (2002a) *Human Rights*, Cambridge: Polity Press.

Freeman, M. (2002b) 'Human rights, children's rights and judgment', *International Journal of Children's Rights* 10: 345.

Freeman, M. (2003) 'The State, Race and the Family in England Today', in J. Dewar and S. Parker (eds) *Family Law Processes, Practices, Pressures*, Oxford: Hart.

Freeman, M. (2004a) 'The Sexual Abuse of Children', in B. Brooks-Gordon, L. Goldsthorpe, M. Johnson and A. Bainham (eds) *Sexuality Repositioned*, Oxford: Hart.

Freeman, M. (2004b) 'Introduction', in M. Freeman (ed.) *Children's Rights*, Dartmouth: Ashgate.

Freeman, M. (2005) 'Rethinking *Gillick*', *International Journal of Children's Rights* 13: 201.

Freeman, M. (2007) 'Why it remains important to take children's rights seriously', *International Journal of Children's Rights* 15: 5.

Freeman, M. (2008) 'The right to responsible parents', in J. Bridgeman, H. Keating and C. Lind (eds) *Responsibility, Law and the Family*, London: Ashgate.

Freeman, M. (2009) 'Fifty years of family law: an opinionated review', in G. Douglas and N. Lowe (eds), *The Continuing Evolution of Family Law*, Bristol: Family Law.

Freeman, Marilyn (2003) *Outcomes for Children Returned after Hague Orders*, London: Reunite.

Freeman, Marilyn (2006) *International Child Abduction: The Effects*, London: Reunite.

Freeman, T. and Richards, M. (2006) 'DNA Testing and Kinship', in F. Ebtehaj, B. Lindley and M. Richards (eds) *Kinship Matters*, Hart: Oxford.

Fretwell Wilson, R. (2002) 'Fractured families, fragile children – the sexual vulnerability of girls in the aftermath of divorce', *Child and Family Law Quarterly* 14: 1.

Fried, C. (1978) *Right and Wrong*, Cambridge, Mass.: Harvard University Press.

Funder, K. (1988) 'Women, Work and Post-Divorce Economic Self-Sufficiency: An Australian Perspective', in M. Meulders-Klein and J. Eekelaar (eds) *Family, State and Individual Economic Security*, Brussels: Kluwer.

Funder, K. (1994) 'Australia: A Proposal for Reform', in J. Eekelaar and M. Maclean (eds) *A Reader on Family Law*, Oxford: OUP.

Furniss, T. (1991) *The Multi-Professional Handbook of Child Sexual Abuse, Integrated Management Therapy and Legal Intervention*, London: Routledge.

Gaffney-Rhys, R. (2005) 'The relating to affinity after *B and L v UK*', *Family Law* 35: 955.

Gaffney-Rhys, R. (2006) '*Sheffield City Council v E and another* – capacity to marry and the rights and responsibilities of married couples', *Child and Family Law Quarterly* 18: 139.

Gallagher, M. (2001) 'What is marriage for? The public purposes of marriage law', *Louisiana Law Review* 62: 1.

Gallagher, M. and Waite, L. (2001) *The Case for Marriage*, New York: Doubleday.

Galston, W. (1991) *Liberal Purposes*, Cambridge: CUP.

Gangoli, G., McCarry, M. and Razak, A. (2009) 'Child marriage or forced marriage? South Asian communities in North East England', *Children and Society* 23: 418.

Gangoli, G. and Chantler, K. (2009) 'Protecting victims of forced marriage: Is age a protective factor?', *Feminist Legal Studies* 17: 267.

Gardner, J. (1998) 'On the ground of her sex(uality)', *Oxford Journal of Legal Studies* 18: 167.

Gardner, R., Sauber, R. and Lorandos, D. (2005) *The International Handbook of Parental Alienation Syndrome*, New York: Haworth Press.

Gardner, S. (1993) 'Rethinking family property', *Law Quarterly Review* 109: 263.

Gardner, S. (1998) 'Stalking', *Law Quarterly Review* 114: 33.

Gardner, S. (1999) 'Wives' guarantees of their husbands' debts', *Law Quarterly Review* 115: 1.

Gardner, S. (2004) 'Quantum in *Gissing* v *Gissing* Constructive Trusts', *Law Quarterly Review* 120: 541.

Gardner, S. (2006) 'The remedial element in proprietary estoppel – again', *Law Quarterly Review* 122: 492.

Gardner, S. (2008) 'Family property today', *Law Quarterly Review* 122: 422.

Garrison, M. (2004) 'Is consent necessary? An evaluation of the emerging laws of cohabitant obligation', *UCLA Law Review* 52: 815.

Garrison, M. (2007) 'The Decline of Formal Marriage: Inevitable or Reversible?', *Family Court Review* 41: 439.

Gatrell, C. (2005) *Hard Labour*, Maidenhead: Open University Press.

Gavison, R. (1994) 'Feminism and the Public–Private Distinction', in J. Eekelaar and M. Maclean (eds) *A Reader on Family Law*, Oxford: OUP.

Geekie, C. (2002) 'Protecting children's rights After *Re S* – the pressing need for reform', *Family Law* 32: 534.

Geist, C. (2010) 'Men and women's reports about housework', in J. Trew and S. Drobnic (eds) *Dividing the Domestic*, Stanford: University of Stanford Press.

Geldof, B. (2003) 'The Real Love that Dare Not Speak its Name', in A. Bainham, B. Lindley, M. Richards and L. Trinder (eds) *Children and Their Families*, Oxford: Hart.

Gender Recognition Users Panel (2010) *Minutes of Meeting* London: Gender Recognition Panel.

George, R. (1999) *In Defense of Natural Law*, New York: OUP.

George, R.H. (2008a) '*Stack* v *Dowden* – Do as we say, not as we do?', *Journal of Social Welfare and Family Law* 30: 49.

George, R.H. (2008b) 'Changing Names, Changing Places: Reconsidering S 13 of the Children Act 1989', *Family Law* 38: 1121.

George, R.H. (2010) '*Re L (Internal Relocation: Shared Residence Order)*', *Journal of Social Welfare and Family Law* 32: 71.

George, R.H., Harris, P. and Herring, J. (2009) 'Pre-Nuptial Agreements: For Better or for Worse?', *Family Law* 39: 934.

George, R.H. and Roberts, C. (2009) *The Media and the Family Courts*, Oxford: OXFLAP.

Gerlis, S. (1996) 'Undertakings reconsidered', *Family Law* 26: 233.

Gershoff, E. (2002) 'Corporal punishment by parents and associated child behaviours and experiences: a meta-analytic and theoretical review', *Psychological Bulletin* 128: 539.

Ghandhi, P. and MacNamee, E. (1991) 'The family in UK law and the International Covenant on Civil and Political Rights', *International Journal of Law and the Family* 5: 104.

Ghate, D. and Hazel, N. (2002) *Parenting in Poor Environments*, London: Jessica Kingsley.

Ghate, D. and Ramella, M. (2002) *Positive Parenting: The National Evaluation of the Youth Justice Board's Parenting Programme*, London: Youth Justice Board for England and Wales.

Ghysels, J. (2004) *Work, Family and Childcare*, Cheltenham: Edward Elgar Publishing.

Gibson, C. (1994) *Dissolving Wedlock*, London: Routledge.

Gibson, D. (1998) *Aged Care*, Cambridge: CUP.

Giddens, A. (1989) *Sociology*, Cambridge: Polity Press.

Giddens, A. (1992) *The Transformation of Intimacy*, Cambridge: Polity Press.

Giddens, A. (1998) *The Third Way: The Renewal of Social Democracy*, Cambridge: Polity Press.

Giesen, D. (1997) 'Artificial Reproduction Revisited: Status Problems and Welfare of the Child – A Comparative View', in C. Bridge (ed.) *Family Law Towards the Millennium: Essays for PM Bromley*, London: Butterworths.

Gilbar, R. (2004) 'Medical confidentiality within the family', *International Journal of Law, Policy and the Family* 18: 195.

Gill, D. and Jackson, B. (1983) *Adoption and Race*, London: Batsford.

Gill, A. and Anitha, S. (2009) 'The illusion of protection? An analysis of forced marriage legislation and policy in the UK', *Journal of Social Welfare and Family Law* 31: 257.

Gillespie, A. (2010) 'Defining child pornography: challenges for the law', *Child and Family Law Quarterly* 22: 200.

Gillies, R. (2005) 'Meeting parents' needs? Discourses of "support" and "inclusion" in family policy', *Critical Social Policy* 25: 70.

Gillies, V. (2008) 'Perspectives on parenting responsibility: Contextualizing values and practices', *Journal of Law and Society* 35: 95.

Gilligan, C. (1982) *In a Different Voice*, London: Harvard University Press.

Gilmore, S. (2003a) 'Parental responsibility and the unmarried father – a new dimension to the debate', *Child and Family Law Quarterly* 15: 21.

Gilmore, S. (2003b) '*Bellinger* v *Bellinger* – Not quite between the ears and between the legs – Transsexualism and marriage in the Lords', *Child and Family Law Quarterly* 15: 295.

Gilmore, S. (2004a) 'Duration of marriage and seamless preceding cohabitation', *Family Law* 34: 205.

Gilmore, S. (2004b) 'The Gender Recognition Act 2004', *Family Law* 34: 741.

Gilmore, S. (2004c) 'The nature, scope and use of the specific issue order', *Child and Family Law Quarterly* 16: 367.

Gilmore, S. (2004d) 'Shoeboxes and Comical Shopping Trips – Child Support from the Affluent to Fabulously Rich', *Child and Family Law Quarterly* 16: 103.

Gilmore, S. (2006a) 'Contact/Shared Residence and child well-being: Research evidence and its decisions for legal decision-making', *International Journal of Law, Policy and the Family* 20: 344.

Gilmore, S. (2006b) 'Court decision-making in shared residence order cases: A critical examination', *Child and Family Law Quarterly* 18: 478.

Gilmore, S. (2007) 'Horses and carts: contact and child support', *Child and Family Law Quarterly* 19: 357.

Gilmore, S. (2008a) 'The Assumption that Contact is Beneficial: Challenging the "Secure Foundation"', *Family Law* 38: 1226.

Gilmore, S. (2008b) 'Disputing contact: challenging some assumptions', *Child and Family Law Quarterly* 20: 285.

Gilmore, S. (2009) 'The limits of parental responsibility', in R. Probert, S. Gilmore and J. Herring (eds), *Responsible Parents and Parental Responsibility* Oxford: Hart.

Gilmore, S. (2010) 'Shared Residence: A Summary of the Courts' Guidance', *Family Law* 40: 285.

Ginn, J. and Price, D. (2002) 'Do divorced women catch up in pension building?', *Child and Family Law Quarterly* 14: 157.

Gittens, D. (1993) *The Family in Question: Changing Households and Familiar Ideologies*, Basingstoke: Macmillan.

Glendon, M. (1989) *The Transformation of Family Law*, Chicago: University of Chicago Press.

Glennon, L. (2000) '*Fitzpatrick* v *Sterling Housing Association Ltd* – An Endorsement of the Functional Family', *International Journal of Law, Policy and the Family* 14: 226.

Glennon, L. (2005) 'Displacing the "conjugal family" in legal policy – a progressive move?', *Child and Family Law Quarterly* 17: 141.

Glennon, L. (2006) 'Strategizing for the future through the Civil Partnership Act', *Journal of Law and Society* 33: 244.

Glennon, L. (2008) 'Obligations between adult partners: Moving from form to function?', *International Journal of Law, Policy and the Family* 22: 22.

Glennon, L. (2010) 'The limitations of equality discourses on the contours of intimate obligations', in J. Wallbank, S. Choudhry and J. Herring (eds) *Rights, Gender and Family Law*, Abingdon: Routledge.

Goldstein, J., Solnit, A., Goldstein, S. and Freud, A. (1996) *The Best Interests of the Child*, New York: Free Press.

Golombok, S. (1999) 'Lesbian Mother Families', in A. Bainham, S. Day Sclater and M. Richards (eds) *What is a Parent?* Oxford: Hart.

Golombok, S. (2000) *Parenting: What Really Counts?* London: Routledge.

Golombok, S. and Cook, R. (1993) *A Survey of Semen Donations*, London: HFEA.

Golombok, S., Cook, R., Bish, A. and Murray, C. (1995) 'Families created by the new reproductive technologies: Quality of parenting and social and emotional development of the children', *Child Development* 64: 285.

Golombok, S., MacCallum, F., Goodman, E. and Rutter, M. (2002) 'Families with children conceived by donor insemination', *Child Development* 73: 952.

Goodin, R. and Gibson, D. (1997) 'Rights, young and old', *Oxford Journal of Legal Studies* 17: 185.

Goodman, A. and Greaves, E. (2010a) *Cohabitation, Marriage and Child Outcomes*, London: Institute for Fiscal Studies.

Goodman, A. and Greaves, E. (2010b) *Cohabitation, Marriage and Relationship Stability*, London: Institute for Fiscal Studies.

Goody, E. (1982) *Parenthood and Social Responsibility*, Cambridge: CUP.

Goody, J. (1983) *The Development of the Family and Marriage in Europe*, Cambridge: CUP.

Gordon, D., Adelman, L., Ashworth, K. et al. (2000) *Poverty and Social Exclusion in Britain*, York: Joseph Rowntree Foundation.

Gosden, N. (2003) 'Children's surnames – how satisfactory is the current law?', *Family Law* 33: 186.

Gottlieb, C., Lalos, O. and Lindblad, E. (2000) 'Disclosure of donor insemination to the child: The impact of Swedish legislation', *Human Reproduction* 15: 2052.

Grace, S. (1995) *Home Office Research Study 139: Policing Domestic Violence in the 1990s*, London: HMSO.

Grace, V. and Daniels, K. (2007) 'The (ir)relevance of genetics: engendering parallel worlds of procreation and reproduction', *Sociology of Health and Illness* 29: 692.

Gray, K. (1977) *Reallocation of Property on Divorce*, Abingdon: Professional Books.

Greenwich London Borough Council (1987) *A Child in Mind: The Report of the Commission of Inquiry into the Circumstances Surrounding the Death of Kimberly Carlile*, London: Greenwich LBC.

Grenfell, L. (2003) 'Making sex: Law's narratives of sex, gender and identity', *Legal Studies* 23: 66.

Grillo, T. (1991) 'The mediation alternative: Process dangers for women', *Yale Law Journal* 100: 1545.

Grimley Evans, J. (2003) 'Age Discrimination: Implications of the Ageing Process', in S. Fredman and S. Spencer (eds) *Age as an Equality Issue*, Oxford: Hart.

Grotevant, H. and McRoy, R. (1998) *Openness in Adoption: Exploring Family Connections*, New York: Sage.

Gruber, A. (2007) 'The feminist war on crime', *Iowa Law Review* 92: 741.

Guggenheim, M. (2005) *What's Wrong with Children's Rights?*, Cambridge, Mass.: Harvard University Press.

Guggenheim, M. (2006) 'Ratify the UN Convention on the Rights of the Child, but don't expect any miracles', *Emory International Law Review* 20: 43.

Gunn, M. and Smith, J. (1985) 'Arthur's case and the right of life of a Down Syndrome child', *Criminal Law Review* 705.

Gupta, A. (2002) 'Adoption, Race and Identity', in A. Douglas and T. Philpot (eds) *Adoption – Changing Families, Changing Times*, London: Routledge.

Gupta, S., Evertsson, M., Grunow, D., Nermo, M., Sayer, L. (2010) 'Economic inequality and housework' in J. Trew and S. Drobnic (eds) *Dividing the Domestic*, Stanford: University of Stanford Press.

Hague, G., Thiara, R. and Mullender, A. (2010) 'Disabled women, domestic violence and social care: the risk of isolation, vulnerability and neglect', *British Journal of Social Work* 40: 1.

Hakim, C. (2003) *Models of the Family of Modern Societies*, Aldershot: Ashgate.

Haldane, J. (1994) 'Children, Families, Autonomy and the State', in D. Morgan and G. Douglas (eds) *Constituting Families*, Stuttgart: Franz Steiner Verlag.

Hale, Baroness (2004a) 'Unmarried couples in family law', *Family Law* 34: 419.

Hale, Baroness (2004b) 'Homosexual Rights', *Child and Family Law Quarterly* 16: 125.

Hale, Baroness (2006) 'Understanding children's rights: theory and practice', *Family Court Review* 44: 350.

Hale, Baroness (2009a) 'Families and the law: the forgotten international dimension', *Child and Family Law Quarterly* 21: 413.

Hale, Baroness (2009b) 'The future of marriage' in G. Douglas and N. Lowe (eds), *The Continuing Evolution of Family Law*, Bristol: Family Law.

Hale LJ (1999) 'The view from Court 45', *Child and Family Law Quarterly* 11: 377.

Hale LJ (2000) 'The Family Law Act 1996 – Dead Duck or Golden Goose?' in S. Cretney (ed.) *Family Law – Essays for the New Millennium*, Bristol: Jordans.

Hall HHJ (2000) 'Care Planning', *Family Law* 30: 343.

Hall, A. (2008a) 'Special Guardianship: A Missed Opportunity', *Family Law*, 38: 760.

Hall, A. (2008b) 'Special guardianship and permanency planning', *Child and Family Law Quarterly* 20: 359.

Hall, M. (2009) 'Children giving evidence through special measures in the criminal courts: progress and problems', *Child and Family Law Quarterly* 21: 65.

Hamilton, C. (1995) *Family, Law and Religion*, London: Sweet & Maxwell.

Hamilton, C. and Watt, D. (2004) 'The employment of children', *Child and Family Law Quarterly* 16: 135.

Hanlon, J. (2001) 'Till divorce do our pension plan part', *Child and Family Law Quarterly* 31: 51.

Hanmer, J. (2000) 'Domestic Violence and Gender Relations', in J. Hanmer and C. Itzin (eds) *Home Truths About Domestic Violence*, London: Routledge.

Hanna, C. (1996) 'No right to choose: Mandated victim participation in domestic violence prosecutions', *Harvard Law Review* 109: 1850.

Hannon, C., Wood, C. and Bazalgett, L. (2010) *In Loco Parentis*, London: Demos.

Hantrais, L. (2004) *Family Policy Matters*, Bristol: Policy Press.

Hantrais, L. and Letablier, M.-T. (1996) *Families and Family Policy in Europe*, London: Longman.

Hardesty, J. and Chung, G. (2006) 'Intimate Partner Violence, Parental Divorce, and Child Custody: Directions for Intervention and Future Research', *Family Relations* 55: 200.

Harding, M. (2009) 'Defending *Stack v Dowden*', *Conveyancer and Property Lawyer* 73: 309.

Harding, R. (2007) 'Sir Mark Potter and the protection of the traditional family: why same sex marriage is (still) a feminist issue', *Feminist Legal Studies* 15: 223.

Harkness, S. (2005) *Employment, Work Patterns and Unpaid Work*, London: ESRC.

Harne, L. and Radford, J. (2008) *Tackling Domestic Violence: Theories, Policies and Practice*, Maidenhead: Open University Press.

Harold, G. and Murch, M. (2005) 'Inter-parental conflict and children's adaptation to separation and divorce', *Child and Family Law Quarterly* 17: 185.

Harris, J. (1998) 'Rights and Reproductive Choice', in J. Harris and S. Holm (eds) *The Future of Human Reproduction*, Oxford: Clarendon Press.

Harris, J. (1999) 'Clones, Genes and Human Rights', in J. Burley (ed.) *The Genetic Revolution and Human Rights*, Oxford: OUP.

Harris, J. (2003) 'Assisted Reproductive Technological Blunders (ARTBs)', *Journal of Medical Ethics* 29: 205.

Harris, M. (2006) *President's Guidance No. 1*, London: Gender Recognition Panel.

Harris, N. (2005) 'Empowerment and state education', *Modern Law Review* 68: 925.

Harris, N. (2009) 'Playing catch-up in the schoolyard? Children and young people's "voice" and education rights in the UK', *International Journal of Law, Policy and the Family* 23: 331.

Harris, P. (2006) 'The Making of the Children Act: A Private History', *Family Law* 36: 1054.

Harris, P. (2008) 'The Miller Paradoxes', *Family Law* 38: 1096.

Harris, P. and George, R.H. (2010) 'Parental responsibility and shared residence orders: parliamentary intentions and judicial interpretations', *Child and Family Law Quarterly* 22: 151.

Harris-Short, S. (2002) 'Putting the child at the heart of adoption?', *Child and Family Law Quarterly* 14: 325.

Harris-Short, S. (2005) 'Family law and the Human Rights Act 1998: judicial restraint or revolution?', *Child and Family Law Quarterly* 17: 329.

Harris-Short, S. (2008) 'Making and breaking family life: Adoption, the state and human rights', *Journal of Law and Society* 35: 28.

Harrison, M. (2002) 'Australia's Family Law Act', *International Journal of Law, Policy and the Family* 16: 1.

Harvard Law Review (1991) 'Looking for a family resemblance: The limits of the functional approach to the legal definition of family', *Harvard Law Review* 104: 1640.

Harwin, J. and Owen, M. (2003) 'The Implementation of Care Plans and its Relationship to Children's Welfare', *Child and Family Law Quarterly* 15: 71.

Haskey, J. (1983) 'Marital status before marriage and age at marriage: Their influence on the chance of divorce', *Population Trends* 32: 4.

Haskey, J. (1984) 'Social class and socio-economic differentials in divorce in England and Wales', *Population Trends* 38: 419.

Haskey, J. (1992) 'Pre-marital cohabitation and problems of subsequent divorce', *Population Trends* 69: 70.

Haskey, J. (1994) 'Stepfamilies and stepchildren in Great Britain', *Population Trends* 76: 17.

Haskey, J. (1996a) 'Divorce statistics', *Family Law* 26: 301.

Haskey, J. (1996b) 'Population review: (6) Families and households in Great Britain', *Population Trends* 85: 7.

Haskey, J. (1997) 'Children who experience divorce in their family', *Population Trends* 87: 5.

Haskey, J. (2001) 'Demographic aspects of cohabitation in Great Britain', *International Journal of Law, Policy and the Family* 15: 51.

Haskey, J. (2005) 'Living arrangements in contemporary Britain: Having a partner who usually lives elsewhere and Living Apart Together (LAT)', *Population Trends* 122: 35.

Haskey, J. (2008) 'Divorce trends in England and Wales', *Family Law* 38: 1133.

Haskey, J. and Lewis, J. (2006) 'Living-apart-together in Britain: context and meaning', *International Journal of Law in Context* 2: 37.

Hasson, E. (2003) 'Divorce law and the Family Law Act 1996', *International Journal of Law, Policy and the Family* 17: 338.

Hasson, E. (2004) 'The street-level response to relationship breakdown: A lesson for national policy', *Journal of Social Welfare and Family Law* 26: 35.

Hauari, H. and Hollingworth, K. (2010) *Understanding Fatherhood: Masculinity, Diversity and Change*, York: JRF.

Hawthorne, J., Jessop, J., Pryor, J. and Richards, M. (2003) *Supporting Children Through Family Change*, York: Joseph Rowntree Foundation.

Hayden, A. (2010) 'Teenage Children in the UK: The Lost Generation?', *Family Law* 40: 69.

Hayes, J. (2008) 'Farewell to the cogent evidence test', *Family Law* 38: 859.

Hayes, J. (2010) 'Ensuring equal protection for siblings', *Family Law* 40: 505.

Hayes, J., Hayes, M., and Williams, J. (2010) '"Shocking" Abuse Followed By A "Staggering" Ruling: *Re MA (Care Threshold)*', *Family Law* 40: 166.

Hayes, M. (1994) '"Cohabitation clauses" in financial provision and property adjustment orders – law, policy and justice', *Law Quarterly Review* 110: 124.

Hayes, M. (1996) 'The proper role of courts in child care cases', *Child and Family Law Quarterly* 8: 201.

Hayes, M. (1997) 'Reconciling protection of children with justice for parents in cases of alleged child abuse', *Legal Studies* 17: 1.

Hayes, M. (1998) 'Child protection – from principles and policies to practice', *Child and Family Law Quarterly* 10: 119.

Hayes, M. (2004) 'Uncertain evidence and risk taking in child protection cases', *Child and Family Law Quarterly* 16: 63.

Hayes, M. (2005) 'Criminal trials where a child is the victim: extra protection for children or a missed opportunity?', *Child and Family Law Quarterly* 17: 307.

Hayes, M. (2006) 'Relocation Cases: Is the Court Of Appeal Applying the Correct Principles?' *Child and Family Law Quarterly* 19: 351.

Hayes, M. and Williams, C. (1999) *Family Law Principles, Policy and Practice*, London: Butterworths.

Hayes, P. (1995) 'The ideological attack on transracial adoption in the USA and Britain', *International Journal of Law and the Family* 9: 1.

Hayes, P. (2003) 'Giving due consideration to ethnicity in adoption placements', *Child and Family Law Quarterly* 15: 255.

Hayton, D. (1993) 'Constructive trusts of homes – a bold approach', *Law Quarterly Review* 109: 485.

Hayward, A. (2009) 'Family values in the home: *Fowler v Barron*', *Child and Family Law Quarterly* 21: 242.

Healthcare Commission (2006) *Living Well in Later Life*, London: Healthcare Commission.

Healy, J. and Yarrow, S. (1997) *Family Matters*, Bristol: Policy Press.

Heath, S. (2004) 'Peer shared households, quasi-communes and neo-tribes', *Current Sociology* 52: 161.

Hedley, J. (2009) 'Illusion and Disillusion? Perceptions of Children in the Family Justice System', *Family Law* 39: 118.

Held, V. (2006) *The Ethics of Care*, Cambridge: CUP.

Henricson, C. (2003) *Government and Parenting*, York: Joseph Rowntree Foundation.

Henricson, C. and Bainham, A. (2005) *The Child and Family Policy Divide*, York: Joseph Rowntree Foundation.

Henshaw, D. (2006) *Recovering child support: routes to responsibility*, London: DWP.

Hepple, B. (2003) 'Age Discrimination in Employment: Implementing the Framework Directive 2000/78/EC', in S. Fredman and S. Spencer (eds) *Age as an Equality Issue*, Oxford: Hart.

Herring, J. (1997) 'Children's abortion rights', *Medical Law Review* 5: 257.

Herring, J. (1998a) ' "Name this child" ', *Cambridge Law Journal* 57: 266.

Herring, J. (1998b) 'Book review', *Cambridge Law Journal* 57: 213.

Herring, J. (1998c) 'The criminalisation of harassment', *Cambridge Law Journal* 57: 10.

Herring, J. (1999a) 'The Welfare Principle and the Rights of Parents', in A. Bainham, S. Day Sclater and M. Richards (eds) *What is a Parent?* Oxford: Hart.

Herring, J. (1999b) 'The Human Rights Act and the welfare principle in family law – conflicting or complementary?', *Child and Family Law Quarterly* 11: 223.

Herring, J. (2000a) 'The Caesarean Section Cases and the Supremacy of Autonomy', in M. Freeman and A. Lewis (eds) *Law and Medicine*, Oxford: OUP.

Herring, J. (2000b) 'The suffering children of blameless parents', *Law Quarterly Review* 116: 550.

Herring, J. (2001) 'Parents and Children', in J. Herring (ed.) *Family Law: Issues, Debates, Policy*, Cullompton: Willan.

Herring, J. (2002a) 'Gay rights come quietly', *Law Quarterly Review* 118: 31.

Herring, J. (2002b) 'The human rights of children in care', *Law Quarterly Review* 118: 534.

Herring, J. (2003a) 'Connecting Contact', in A. Bainham, B. Lindley, M. Richards and L. Trinder (eds) *Children and Their Families*, Oxford: Hart.

Herring, J. (2003b) 'Children's Rights for Grown-Ups', in S. Fredman and S. Spencer (eds) *Age as an Equality Issue*, Oxford: Hart.

Herring, J. (2005a) 'Why Financial Orders on Divorce should be Unfair', *International Journal of Law, Policy and the Family* 19: 218.

Herring, J. (2005b) 'Farewell Welfare', *Journal of Social Welfare and Family Law* 27: 159.

Herring, J. (2007a) 'Where are the carers in healthcare law and ethics?', *Legal Studies* 27: 51.

Herring, J. (2007b) 'Familial Homicide, Failure to Protect and Domestic Violence: Who's the victim?', *Criminal Law Review* 923.

Herring, J. (2008a) 'Mum's not the word: An analysis of Section 5, Domestic Violence, Crime and Victims Act 2004', in C. Clarkson and S. Cunningham, *Criminal Liability for Non-Aggressive Death*, Aldershot: Ashgate.

Herring, J. (2008b) 'The Place of Carers', in M. Freeman (ed.) *Law and Bioethics*, Oxford: OUP.

Herring, J. (2008c) 'Respecting family life', *Amicus Curiae* 75: 21.

Herring, J. (2008d) 'Together forever? The rights and responsibilities of adult children and their parents', in J. Bridgeman, H. Keating, and C. Lind, (eds) *Responsibility, Law and the Family*, London: Ashgate.

Herring, J. (2008e) 'Older People and the Law', in C. O'Cinneide and J. Holder (eds) *Current Legal Problems*, Oxford: OUP.

Herring, J. (2009a) 'Who decides on human rights?', *Law Quarterly Review* 125: 1.

Herring (2009b) *The Woman Who Tickled Too Much*, Harlow: Pearson.

Herring, J. (2009c) *Criminal Law*, Basingstoke: Palgrave.

Herring, J. (2009d) *Older People in Law and Society*, Oxford: OUP.

Herring, J. (2009e) 'The shaming of naming', in R. Probert, S. Gilmore and J. Herring (eds) *Responsible Parents and Parental Responsibility*, Oxford: Hart.

Herring, J. (2009f) 'Losing it? Losing what? The Law and Dementia', *Child and Family Law Quarterly* 21: 3.

Herring, J. (2009g) 'Protecting vulnerable adults: A critical review of recent case law', *Child and Family Law Quarterly* 21: 498.

Herring, J. (2009h) 'Revoking adoptions', *New Law Journal* 159: 379.

Herring, J. (2010a) 'The legal duties of carers', *Medical Law Review* 18: 248.

Herring, J. (2010b) 'Relational autonomy and family law', in J. Wallbank, S. Choudhry and J. Herring, (eds) *Rights, Gender and Family Law*, London: Routledge.

Herring, J. (2010c) 'Sexless Family Law', *Lex Familiae* 11: 3.

Herring, J. (2010d) 'Money, Money, Money . . .', *New Law Journal* 160: 300.

Herring, J. (2010e) *Medical Law and Ethics*, Oxford: OUP.

Herring, J. (2010f) 'Seven ways of getting it wrong', *New Law Journal* 160: 715.

Herring, (2010g) 'Family Law' in *All England Law Review 2009*, London: LexisNexis.

Herring, J. (2010h) 'Age discrimination and the law: Forging the way ahead', in S. Tyson and E. Perry (eds) *Managing an Age-diverse Workforce*, Basingstoke: Macmillan.

Herring, J. (2010i) *Criminal Law*, Oxford: OUP.

Herring, J. (2011) 'No more holding and having', in S. Gilmore, J. Herring and R. Probert (eds) *Landmark Cases in Family Law*, Oxford: Hart.

Herring, J. and Chau, P.-L. (2001) 'Assigning sex and intersexuals', *Family Law* 31: 762.

Herring, J. and Taylor, R. (2006) 'Relocating Relocation', *Child and Family Law Quarterly* 18: 517.

Hester, M. (2002) 'One step forward and three steps back? Children, Abuse and Parental Contact in Denmark', *Child and Family Law Quarterly* 14: 267.

Hester, M. (2009) *Who Does What to Whom? Gender and Domestic Violence Perpetrators*, London: Northern Rock.

Hester, M. (2010) 'Commentary on "Mothers, Domestic Violence, and Child Protection"', *Violence against Women* 16: 516.

Hester, M. and Pearson, C. (1997) 'Domestic violence and children – the practice of Family Court Welfare Officers', *Child and Family Law Quarterly* 9: 281.

Hester, M., Pearson, C. and Harwin, N. (2007) *Making an Impact – Children and Domestic Violence: A Reader*, 2nd edn, London: Jessica Kingsley.

Hester, M., Pearson, C. and Radford, L. (1997) *Domestic Violence*, Bristol: Policy Press.

Hester, M. and Radford, L. (1996) *Domestic Violence and Child Contact Arrangements in England and Wales*, Bristol: Policy Press.

Hester, M. and Westmarland, N. (2005) *Tackling Domestic Violence*, London: Home Office.

Hester, M., Westmarland, N., Pearce, J. and Williamson, E. (2008) *Early Evaluation of the Domestic Violence, Crime and Victims Act 2004*, London: Ministry of Justice.

Hetherington, M. and Kelly, J. (2002) *For Better or For Worse*, New York: WW Norton & Co.

Hewlett, P. (2003) *Baby Hunger*, New York: Atlantic Books.

Hibbs, M. (1997) 'Surrogacy legislation – time for change', *Family Law* 27: 564.

Hibbs, M., Barton, C. and Beswick, J. (2001) 'Why marry? Perceptions of the affianced', *Family Law* 31: 197.

Hill, J. (1991) 'What does it mean to be a "parent"? The claims of biology as the basis for parental rights', *New York University Law Review* 66: 353.

Hill, M. (1995) 'Family Policies in Western Europe', in M. Hill, R. Hawthorne-Kirk and D. Part (eds) *Supporting Families*, Edinburgh: HMSO.

Hill, M. and Tisdall, K. (1997) *Children and Society*, London: Longman.

Hill, R. (2005) 'The Domestic Violence, Crime and Victim Act 2004', *Family Law* 35: 281.

Hitchings, E. (2005) 'A consequence of blurring the boundaries – Less choice for victims of domestic violence', *Social Policy and Society* 5: 91.

Hitchings, E. (2008) 'Everyday Cases in the Post-White Era', *Family Law* 38: 873.

Hitchings, E. (2009a) 'From Pre-Nups to Post-Nups: Dealing with Marital Property Agreements', *Family Law* 39: 1056.

Hitchings, E. (2009b) 'Chaos or consistency?' in J. Miles and R. Probert (eds) *Sharing Lives, Dividing Assets*, Oxford: Hart.

Hitchings, E. (2010) 'The impact of recent ancillary relief jurisprudence in the "everyday" ancillary relief case', *Child and Family Law Quarterly* 22: 93.

Hitchings, E. and Sagar, T. (2007) 'The Adoption and Children Act 2002: A Level Playing Field for Same-Sex Adopters', *Child and Family Law Quarterly* 19: 60.

HM Government (2004) *Parental Separation: Children's Needs and Parents' Responsibilities*, London: The Stationery Office.

HM Government (2005a) *Draft Children (Contact) and Adoption Bill*, London: The Stationery Office.

HM Government (2005b) *Parental Separation: Children's Needs and Parents' Responsibilities: Next Steps: Report of the Responses to Consultation*, London: The Stationery Office.

HM Government (2007) *UN Convention on the Rights of the Child: UK Report*, London: The Stationery Office.

HM Government (2008) *Thinking Family: Improving the Life Chances of Families at Risk*, London: The Stationery Office.

HM Government (2009) *Handling Cases of Forced Marriage*, London: The Stationery Office.

HM Government (2010a) *State of the Nation Report*, London: The Stationery Office.

HM Government (2010b) *Government's Response to the Joint Committee on Human Rights' (JCHR) Report, Children's Rights*, London: Children's Rights.

HM Government (2010c) *Care Planning, Placement and Case Review*, London: Stationery Office.

HM Inspectorate of Court Administration (2005) *Safeguarding Children in Family Proceedings*, London: The Stationery Office.

HM Inspectorate of Court Administration (2007) *Assisting Families by Court Order*, London: The Stationery Office.

HMIC/CPSI (2004) *A Joint Inspection of the Investigation and Prosecution of Cases Involving Domestic Violence*, London: HMIC.

Hobbs, C., Hanks, H. and Wynne, J. (1999) *Child Abuse and Neglect*, London: Churchill Livingston.

Hobbs, T. (2002a) 'Parental Alienation Syndrome and the UK Family Courts, Part 1', *Family Law* 32: 182.

Hobbs, T. (2002b) 'Parental Alienation Syndrome and the UK Family Courts – The dilemma', *Family Law* 32: 568.

Hochschild, A. (1996) 'The Emotional Geography of Work and Family Life', in L. Morris and S. Lyons (eds) *Gender Relations in Public and Private: Changing Research Perspectives*, London: Macmillan.

Hodson, D. (2006) 'Spare the child and hit the pocket', *Family Court Report* 44: 387.

Hodson, D. (2009) 'Report from the Family Law Review of the Centre for Social Justice: "Every Family Matters"', *Family Law* 39: 864.

Hodson, D., Green, M. and De Souza, N. (2003) '*Lambert* – shutting Pandora's box', *Family Law* 33: 37.

Hofferth, S. and Anderson, K. (2003) 'Are all Dads equal? Biology versus marriage for a basis for parental investment', *Journal of Marriage and the Family* 65: 213.

Hoggett, B. (1994) 'Joint parenting systems: The English experiment', *Journal of Child Law* 6: 8.

Hoggett, B., Pearl, D., Cooke, E. and Bates, P. (2003) *Family Law and Society*, London: Butterworths.

Holgate, L. (2005) *Children's Rights, State Intervention, Custody and Divorce*, New York: Edwin Mellen Press.

Hollingsworth, K. (2006) 'Interpreting child curfews: a question of rights?', *Child and Family Law Quarterly* 18: 253.

Hollingsworth, K. (2007a) 'Responsibility and rights: Children and their parents in the youth justice system', *International Journal of Law, Policy and the Family* 21: 190.

Hollingsworth, K. (2007b) 'Judicial approaches to children's rights in youth crime', *Child and Family Law Quarterly* 19: 42.

Hollingsworth, K. and Douglas, K. (2002) 'Creating a children's champion for Wales? The Care Standards Act 2000 (Part V) and the Children's Commissioner for Wales Act 2001', *Modern Law Review* 65: 58.

Holt, J. (1975) *Escape from Childhood*, London: Dutton.

Home Affairs Select Committee (2008) *Domestic Violence, Forced Marriage and 'Honour' Based Violence*, London: Hansard.

Home Office (1990a) *Crime, Justice and Protecting the Public*, London: HMSO.

Home Office (1990b) *Children Come First*, London: HMSO.

Home Office (1993) *Local Authority Circular* (93) (13), London: HMSO.

Home Office (1997) *Bringing Rights Home: The Human Rights Bill*, London: HMSO.

Home Office (1998) *Supporting Families. A Consultation Document*, London: The Stationery Office.

Home Office (1999) *Living Without Fear*, London: Home Office.

Home Office (2000a) *Report of the Interdepartmental Working Group on Transsexual People*, London: Home Office.

Home Office (2000b) *Setting the Boundaries*, London: Home Office.

Home Office (2000c) *A Choice By Right*, London: Home Office.

Home Office (2000d) *Domestic Violence: Break the Chain*, London: Home Office.

Home Office (2000e) *Government Policy Around Domestic Violence*, London: Home Office.

Home Office (2000f) *Reforming the Mental Health Act*, London: Home Office.

Home Office (2002) *Civil Registration: Vital Change; Birth, Marriage and Death Registration in the 21st Century*, London: The Stationery Office.

Home Office (2003a) *Safety and Justice*, London: Home Office.

Home Office (2003b) *Government Policy Around Domestic Violence*, London: Home Office.

Home Office (2004) *Alcohol and Intimate Partner Violence*, London: Home Office.

Home Office (2005a) *Domestic Violence: A National Report*, London: Home Office.

Home Office (2005b) *Parents Tasked to Take More Responsibility for the Problem Behaviour of their Children: Press Release*, London: Home Office.

Home Office (2006a) *National Domestic Violence Delivery Plan*, London: Home Office.

Home Office (2006b) *Wrong not a Right: Further Measures to Combat Forced Marriage*, London: Home Office.

Home Office (2009a) *Together We Can End Violence Against Women and Girls: A Strategy*, London: Home Office.

Homer, S. (1994) 'Against marriage', *Harvard Civil-Rights Civil-Liberties Law Review* 29: 505.

Hood, H. (2009) 'The Role of Conduct in Divorce Suits and Claims for Ancillary Relief', *Family Law* 39: 948.

Hooper, C.-A. (2005) 'Child maltreatment', in J. Bradshaw and E. Mayhew, (eds) *The Well-being of Children in the UK*, London: Save the Children.

Horsey, K. (2006) 'Who are the UK Sperm Donors?' *Bionews*, 14 February.

Horsey, K. (2007) 'Unconsidered inconsistencies: parenthood and assisted reproduction', in K. Horsey and H. Biggs (eds) *Human Fertilisation and Embryology: Reproducing Regulation*, London: Routledge.

Horsey, K. and Biggs, H. (eds) (2007) *Human Fertilisation and Embryology: Reproducing Regulation*, London: Routledge.

House of Commons Health Committee (2004) *Elder Abuse*, London: The Stationery Office.

House of Commons Home Affairs Select Committee (2008) *Domestic Violence, Forced Marriage and 'Honour-Based' Violence*, London: The Stationery Office.

House of Commons Joint Committee on Human Rights (2003) *Eighth Report*, London: The Stationery Office.

House of Commons Public Accounts Committee (2007) *Legal Services Commission: Legal Aid and Mediation for People Involved in Family Breakdown*, London: The Stationery Office.

House of Commons Science and Technology Committee (2005) *Human Reproductive Technologies and the Law*, London: The Stationery Office.

House of Commons Work and Pensions Committee (2005) *The Performance of the Child Support Agency*, London: The Stationery Office.

House of Commons Work and Pensions Committee (2010) *The Child Maintenance and Enforcement Commission and the Child Support Agency's Operational Improvement Plan*, London: The Stationery Office.

Howard, M. and Wilmott, M. (2000) 'The Networked Family', in H. Wilkinson (ed.) *Family Business*, London: Demos.

Howarth, E., Stimpson, L., Baran, D. and Robinson, A. (2009) *Safety in Numbers*, London: Hestia Fund.

Howarth, J., Lees, J., Sidebotham, P., Higgins, J. and Imtiaz, A. (2008) *Religion, Beliefs and Parenting Practices*, York: JRF.

Howe, D., Brandon, M., Hinings, J. and Schofield, G. (1999) *Attachment Theory, Child Maltreatment and Family Support*, Basingstoke: Palgrave.

Howe, D. and Feast, J. (2000) *Adoption, Search and Reunion*, London: The Children's Society.

Hoyano, L. and Keenan, C. (2007) *Child Abuse: Law and Policy Across Boundaries*, Oxford: OUP.

Hoyle, C. (1998) *Negotiating Domestic Violence: Police, Criminal Justice and Victims*, Oxford: Clarendon Press.

Hoyle, C. and Sanders, A. (2000) 'Police responses to domestic violence: from victim choice to victim empowerment', *British Journal of Criminology* 40: 14.

Hubin, D. (2003) 'Daddy dilemmas: Untangling the puzzles of paternity', *Cornell Journal of Law and Public Policy* 13: 29.

Hull, K. (2005) *Same-Sex Marriage*, Cambridge: Cambridge University Press.

Human Fertilisation and Embryology Authority (2005) *Tomorrow's Children*, London: HFEA.

Human Fertilisation and Embryology Authority (2006) *Sperm Egg and Embryo Donation Review*, London: HFEA.

Human Fertilisation and Embryology Authority (2010) *Code of Practice*, London: HFEA.

Humphreys, C. (2001) 'The Impact of Domestic Violence on Children', in P. Foley, J. Roche and S. Tucker (eds) *Children in Society*, Buckingham: Open University Press.

Humphreys, C. (2006) 'Thinking the unthinkable: the implication of research on women and children in relation to domestic violence', in M. Thorpe and R. Budden, *Durable Solutions*, Bristol: Jordans.

Humphreys, C. and Harrison, C. (2003a) 'Squaring the circle – contact and domestic violence', *Family Law* 33: 419.

Humphreys, C. and Harrison, C. (2003b) 'Focusing on safety – domestic violence and the role of child contact centres', *Child and Family Law Quarterly* 15: 237.

Humphreys, C., Hester, M., Hague, G. et al. (2002) *From Good Intentions to Good Practice: Mapping Services Working with Families where there is Domestic Violence*, York: Policy Press.

Humphreys, C. and Thiara, R. (2002) *Routes to Safety*, Bristol: Women's Aid.

Humphreys, C. and Thiara, R. (2003) 'Neither justice nor protection; women's experiences of post separation violence', *Journal of Social Welfare and Family Law* 25: 195.

Hunt, J. (2001) 'Kinship Care, Child Protection and the Courts', in B. Broad (ed.) *Kinship Care*, Lyme Regis: Russell House.

Hunt, J. (2006a) 'Contact with non-resident parents after separation and divorce', in M. Thorpe and R. Budden, *Durable Solutions*, Bristol: Jordans.

Hunt, J. (2006b) 'Substitute Care of Children by Members of their Extended Families and Social Networks', in F. Ebtehaj, B. Lindley and M. Richards (eds) *Kinship Matters*, Oxford: Hart.

Hunt, J. and Lawson, J. (1999) *Cross the Boundaries*, London: National Council for Family Proceedings.

Hunt, J. and Macleod, A. (1998) *The Best-Laid Plans*, London: The Stationery Office.

Hunt, J. and Macleod, A. (2008) *Outcomes of Applications to Court for Contact Orders after Parental Separation or Divorce*, London: Ministry of Justice.

Hunt, J., Masson, J. and Trinder, L. (2009) 'Shared Parenting: The Law, the Evidence and Guidance from Families need Fathers', *Family Law* 39: 831.

Hunt, J. and Roberts, C. (2004) *Intervening in Litigated Contact: Ideas from other jurisdictions*, Oxford: Oxford University Press.

Hunt, J., Waterhouse, S. and Lutman, E. (2008) *Keeping them in the Family: Outcomes for Abused and Neglected Children Placed with Family or Friends Carers through Care Proceedings*, London: BAAF.

Hunt, J., Waterhouse, S. and Lutman, E. (2010) 'Parental contact for children placed in kinship care through care proceedings', *Child and Family Law Quarterly* 22: 71.

Hunter, C., Nixon, J. and Parr, S. (2010) 'Mother abuse: A matter of youth justice, child welfare or domestic violence', *Journal of Law and Society* 37: 264.

Hunter, R. (2007) 'Close encounters of a judicial kind: "hearing" children's "voices" in family law proceedings', *Child and Family Law Quarterly* 19: 283.

Huntington, C. (2008) 'Repairing family law', *Duke Law Journal* 57: 101.

Huston, T. and Melz, H. (2004) 'The case for (promoting) marriage: the devil is in the detail', *Journal of Marriage and the Family* 66: 943.

Huxtable, R. (2004) '*Glass v United Kingdom*: maternal instinct v medical opinion', *Child and Family Law Quarterly* 16: 339.

Iacovou, M. (2004) 'The third age: And then the lover: can we all now choose individual fulfilment?', in R. Stewart and R. Vaitilingham (eds) *Seven Ages of Man and Woman*, London: ESRC.

ICM Poll (2002a) *Sex Uncovered*, London: ICM.

ICM Poll (2002b) *Marriage Survey*, London: ICM.

ICM Poll (2004) *Generation Survey*, London: ICM.

Illman, J. (1996) *The Guardian*, 9 July.

Ince, S. (1993) 'Inside the Surrogacy Industry', in M. Minow (ed.) *Family Matters*, New York: New York Press.

*Independent on Sunday* (2000) 'Gay couple's twins to get right to stay', 9 January.

Information Centre (2006) *Rise in Childhood Obesity Rates*, London: NHS.

Ingleby, R. (1992) *Solicitors and Divorce*, Oxford: OUP.

Ingleby, R. (1997) 'The De-Bromleyfication of Australian Family Law', in C. Bridge (ed.) *Family Law Towards the Millennium: Essays for PM Bromley*, London: Butterworths.

Ingleby, R. (2005) 'Lambert and Lamposts: The End of Equality in Anglo-Australian Matrimonial Property Law?', *International Journal of Law, Policy and the Family* 19: 137.

Inglis, A. (2001a) 'We are family (after all) – inclusive family law', *Family Law* 31: 895.

Inglis, A. (2001b) 'We are family? The uneasy engagement between gay men, lesbians and family law', *Family Law* 31: 830.

Inglis, A. (2003) '"The ordinary run of fighting"? Domestic violence and financial provision', *Family Law* 33: 181.

Instone-Brewer, D. (2002) *Divorce and Remarriage in the Bible*, Amsterdam: William B. Eerdmans.

Irvine, C. (2009) 'Mediation and Social Norms', *Family Law* 39: 351.

Iwaniec, D., Donaldson, T. and Allweis, M. (2004) 'The plight of neglected children – social work and judicial decision-making, and management of neglect cases', *Child and Family Law Quarterly* 16: 432.

Jackson, E. (2002) 'Conception and the irrelevance of the welfare principle', *Modern Law Review* 65: 176.

Jackson, E. (2007a) 'Rethinking the pre-conception welfare principle', in K. Horsey and H. Biggs, *Human Fertilisation and Embryology: Reproducing Regulation*, London: Routledge.

Jackson, E. (2007b) 'Prisoners, their partners and the right to family life', *Child and Family Law Quarterly Review* 19: 239.

Jackson, E. (2008) 'Degendering reproduction?', *Medical Law Review* 16: 346.

Jackson, E., Wasoff, F., Maclean, M. and Dobash, R. (1993) 'Financial support on divorce: The right mixture of rules and discretion?', *International Journal of Law, Policy and the Family* 7: 230.

Jagger, G. and Wright, C. (1999) *Changing Family Values*, London: Routledge.

James, A. (1992) 'An open or shut case? Law as an autopoietic system', *Journal of Law and Society* 19: 271.

James, A. (2002) 'The Family Law Act 1996', in A. Carling, S. Duncan and R. Edwards, *Analysing Families*, London: Routledge.

James, A. (2003) 'The Social, Legal and Welfare Organisation of Contact', in A. Bainham, B. Lindley, M. Richards and L. Trinder (eds) *Children and Their Families*, Oxford: Hart.

James, A. and James, A. (2004) *Constructing Childhood*, Basingstoke: Palgrave.

James, A., James, A. and McNamee, S. (2003) 'Constructing Children's Welfare in Family Proceedings', *Family Law* 33: 889.

James, A., James, A. and McNamee, S. (2004) 'Turn down the volume? – not hearing children in family proceedings', *Child and Family Law Quarterly* 16: 189.

James, A., Jenks, C. and Prout, A. (1998) *Theorizing Childhood*, Cambridge: Polity Press.

James, A. and Sturgeon-Adams, L. (1999) *Helping Families after Divorce: Assistance by Order*, London: Policy Press.

James, G. (2009) 'Mothers and fathers as parents and workers: family-friendly employment policies in an era of shifting identities', *Journal of Social Welfare and Family Law* 31: 271.

Jenks, C. (1996) *Childhood*, London: Routledge.

John, M. (2003) *Children's Rights and Power*, London: Jessica Kingsley.

Jivraj, S. and Herman, D. (2009) '"It is difficult for a white judge to understand": orientalism, racialisation, and Christianity in English child welfare cases', *Child and Family Law Quarterly* 21: 283.

Johnson, A., Mercer, C., Erens, B. et al. (2001) 'Sexual Behaviour in Britain', *The Lancet* 358: 1835.

Johnson, M. (1999) 'A Biomedical Perspective on Parenthood', in A. Bainham, S. Day Sclater and M. Richards (eds) *What is a Parent?* Oxford: Hart.

Johnson, M., Derrington, R., Menard, A., Ooms, T. and Stanley, S. (2010) *Making Distinctions Between Different Kinds of Intimate Partner Violence*, Washington: National Healthy Marriage Resource Centre.

Jolly, S. (1995) 'Implacable hostility, contact and the limits of law', *Child and Family Law Quarterly* 7: 228.

Jones, C. (2007) 'Parents in law: Subjective impacts and status implications around the use of licensed donor insemination', in A. Diduck and K. O'Donovan (eds) *Feminist Perspectives on Family Law*, London: Routledge.

Jones, C. (2007) *Why Donor Insemination Requires Developments in Family Law: The Need For New Definitions of Parenthood*, Lewiston: Edwin Mellen.

Jones, C. (2010) 'The identification of "parents" and "siblings"', in J. Wallbank, S. Choudhry and J. Herring (eds) *Rights, Gender and Family Law*, Abingdon: Routledge.

Jones, J. and Perrin, C. (2009) 'Third time lucky? The third child support reforms replace the Child Support Agency with the new C-MEC', *Journal of Social Welfare and Family Law* 31: 333.

Jones, E. and Parkinson, P. (1995) 'Child sexual abuse, access and the wishes of children', *International Journal of Law, Policy and the Family* 9: 54.

Jones, G., Lockton, D., Wood, R. and Kashefi, E. (1995) 'Divorce applications: An empirical study of one court', *Journal of Social Welfare and Family Law* 17: 67.

Jones-Purdy, C. (1998) 'The Law and Morality of Support in the Wider Family', in J. Eekelaar and T. Nhlapo (eds) *The Changing Family: International Perspectives on the Family and Family Law*, Oxford: Hart.

Jordan, A. (2009) '"Dads aren't Demons. Mums aren't Madonnas". Constructions of fatherhood and masculinities in the (real) Fathers 4 Justice campaign', *Journal of Social Welfare and Family Law* 31: 419.

Jordan, L. and Lindley, B. (2007) *Special Guardianship: What Does it Offer to Children who Cannot Live with their Parents?*, London: Family Rights Group.

Joshi, H. and Davies, H. (1992) 'Pensions, divorce and wives' double burden', *International Journal of Law and the Family* 6: 289.

Judd, F. and George, R. (2010) 'International relocation: Do we stand alone?', *Family Law* 40: 63.

Kaganas, F. (1995) 'Partnership Under the Children Act 1989 – An Overview', in F. Kaganas, M. King and C. Piper (eds) *Legislating for Harmony*, London: Jessica Kingsley.

Kaganas, F. (1996) 'Responsible or feckless fathers?', *Child and Family Law Quarterly* 8: 165.

Kaganas, F. (2002) 'Domestic Homicide, Gender and the Expert', in A. Bainham, S. Day Sclater and M. Richards (eds) *Body Lore and Laws*, Oxford: Hart.

Kaganas, F. (2007a) 'Domestic violence, Men's Groups and the equivalence argument', in A. Diduck and K. O'Donovan (eds) *Feminist Perspectives on Family Law*, London: Routledge.

Kaganas, F. (2007b) 'Grandparents' rights and grandparents' campaigns', *Child and Family Law Quarterly* 19: 17.

Kaganas, F. (2010) 'Child protection, gender and rights', in J. Wallbank, S. Choudhry and J. Herring (eds) *Rights, Gender and Family Law*, Abingdon: Routledge.

Kaganas, F. and Day Sclater, S. (2000) 'Contact and domestic violence – the winds of change?' *Family Law* 30: 630.

Kaganas, F. and Day Sclater, S. (2004) 'Contact Disputes: Narrative Constructions of "Good Parents"', *Feminist Legal Studies* 12: 1.

Kaganas, F. and Murray, C. (2001) 'Law, Women and the Family: The Question of Polygamy in a New South Africa', *Acta Juridica* 116.

Kaganas, F. and Piper, C. (1994) 'Domestic violence and divorce mediation', *Journal of Social Welfare and Family Law* 16: 265.

Kaganas, F. and Piper, C. (1999) 'Divorce and Domestic Violence', in S. Day Sclater and C. Piper (eds) *Undercurrents of Divorce*, Aldershot: Ashgate.

Kaganas, F. and Piper, C. (2001) 'Grandparents and contact: "rights v welfare" revisited', *International Journal of Law, Policy and the Family* 15: 250.

Kaganas, F. and Piper, C. (2002) 'Shared parenting – a 70% solution?', *Child and Family Law Quarterly* 14: 365.

Kaltenborn, K. and Lemrap, R. (1998) 'The welfare of the child in custody disputes after parental separation or divorce', *International Journal of Law, Policy and the Family* 12: 74.

Kamil, G. (2009) 'Fattism and adoption', *Family Law* 39: 1068.

Kamp Dush, C., Cohan, C. and Amato, P. (2003) 'The relationship between cohabitation and marital quality and stability', *Journal of Marriage and the Family* 65: 539.

Kandel, R. (1994) 'Which came first: The mother or the egg? A kinship solution to gestational survey', *Rutgers Law Review* 47: 165.

Karsten, I. (2001) 'The Draft EC Regulation on Parental Responsibility', *Family Law* 31: 885.

Katz, I. (1999) 'Is Male Circumcision Morally Defensible?', in M. King (ed.) *Moral Agenda for Children's Welfare*, London: Routledge.

Katz, S. (1999) 'Emerging models for alternatives to marriage', *Family Law Quarterly* 33: 663.

Kavanagh, L. (2000) 'Independent yet committed', *The Times*, 29 February.

Kavanagh, M. (2004) 'Rewriting the legal family: beyond exclusivity to a care-based standard', *Yale Journal of Law and Feminism* 16: 83.

Kaye, M. (1996) 'Domestic violence, residence and contact', *Child and Family Law Quarterly* 8: 285.

Kaye, M. (1999) 'The Hague Convention and the flight from domestic violence: how women and children are being returned by coach and four', *International Journal of Law, Policy and the Family* 13: 191.

Kaye, M., Stubbs, J. and Tolmie, J. (2003) 'Domestic Violence and Child Contact Arrangements', *Australian Journal of Family Law* 17: 1.

Keating, H. (1996) 'Shifting standards in the House of Lords – *Re H and Others (Minors) (Sexual Abuse: Standard of Proof)*', *Child and Family Law Quarterly* 8: 157.

Keating, H. (2006) 'Protecting or punishing children: physical punishment, human rights and English law reform', *Legal Studies* 26: 394.

Keating, H. (2007) 'The "responsibility" of children in the criminal law', *Child and Family Law Quarterly* 19: 183.

Keating, H. (2008) 'Being responsible, becoming responsible, and having responsibility thrust upon them: Constructing the "responsibility" of children and parents', in J. Bridgeman, H. Keating and C. Lind (eds) *Responsibility, Law and the Family*, London: Ashgate.

Keating, H. (2009) 'Suspicions, sitting on the fence and standards of proof', *Child and Family Law Quarterly* 21: 230.

Keenan, C. (1997) 'Finding that a child is at risk from sexual abuse', *Modern Law Review* 60: 857.

Keenan, C., Davis, G., Hoyano, L. and Maitland, L. (1999) 'Interviewing allegedly abused children with a view to criminal prosecution', *Criminal Law Review* 863.

Kellet, S. (2006) 'Four Theories of Filial Duty', *The Philosophical Quarterly* 56: 254.

Kelly, F. (2004) 'Nuclear Norms or Fluid Families? Incorporating Lesbian and Gay Parents and Their Children into Canadian Family Law', *Canadian Journal of Family Law* 21: 133.

Kelly, F. (2005) 'Conceptualising the child through an ethic of care: lessons for family law', *International Journal of Law in Context* 1: 375.

Kelly, J. (2003) 'Legal and Education Interventions for Families in Residence and Contact Disputes', in J. Dewar and S. Parker (eds) *Family Law Processes, Practices, Pressures*, Oxford: Hart.

Kelly, J. and Emery, R. (2003) 'Children's adjustment following divorce', *Family Relations* 52: 352.

Kelly, J. and Johnson, M. (2008) 'Differentiation among types of intimate partner violence: research update and implications for interventions', *Family Court Review* 46: 476.

Kelly, L. and Lovett, J. (2005) *What a Waste*, London: Women's National Commission.

Kennedy, R. (2001) 'Assessment and treatment in family law – a valid distinction?', *Family Law* 31: 676.

Kennedy, R. (2006) 'Assessing life after *Re G*', *Family Law* 36: 379.

Kerridge, R. (2000) 'Wills made in suspicious circumstances: the problem of the vulnerable testator', *Cambridge Law Journal* 59: 310.

Khaliq, U. (1996) 'Transsexuality and English law: latest developments', *Journal of Social Welfare and Family Law* 18: 365.

Khaliq, U. and Young, J. (2001) 'Cultural diversity, human rights and inconsistency in the English courts', *Legal Studies* 21: 192.

Kielty, S. (2006) 'Similarities and differences in the experiences of non-resident fathers and non-resident mothers', *International Journal of Law, Policy and the Family* 20: 74.

Kiernan, K. (2001) 'The rise of cohabitation and childbearing outside marriage in Western Europe', *International Journal of Law, Policy and the Family* 15: 1.

Kiernan, K. (2005) *Non-resident Fatherhood and Child Involvement*, London: LSE.

Kiernan, K., Barlow, A. and Merlo, R. (2006) 'Cohabitation Law Reform and its impact on marriage', *Family Law* 36: 1074.

Kiernan, K., Barlow, A. and Merlo, R. (2007) 'Cohabitation Law Reform and its Impact on Marriage: Evidence from Australia and Europe', *International Family Law* 71.

Kiernan, K. and Mensah, F. (2010) 'Partnership trajectories: parent and child wellbeing', in K. Hansen, H. Joshi and S. Dex (eds) *Children of the Twenty First Century*, Bristol: Policy Press.

Kiernan, K. and Mueller, G. (1999) 'Who Divorces?', in S. McRae (ed.) *Changing Britain*, Oxford: OUP.

Kiernan, K. and Wicks, M. (1990) *Family Change and Future Policy*, York: Rowntree and Family Policy Studies Centre.

Kilkelly, U. (2000) *The Child and the European Convention on Human Rights*, Aldershot: Ashgate.

Kilkelly, U. (2003) 'Economic Exploitation of Children', *Saint Louis University Public Law Review* 321.

Kilkey, M. (2006) 'New Labour and Reconciling Work and Family Life: Making It Fathers' Business?', *Social Policy and Society* 5: 167.

King, A. (1988) 'No legal aid without mediation – section 29', *Family Law* 18: 331.

King, M. (1974) 'Maternal love, fact or myth', *Family Law* 4: 61.

King, M. (1987) 'Playing the symbols – custody and the Law Commission', *Family Law* 17: 186.

King, M. (1997) *A Better World for Children*, London: Routledge.

King, M. (1999) 'Introduction', in M. King (ed.) *Moral Agendas for Children's Welfare*, London: Routledge.

King, M. (2000) 'Future uncertainty as a challenge to law's programmes: the dilemma of parental disputes', *Modern Law Review* 63: 523.

King, M. (2007) 'The right decision for the child', *Modern Law Review* 70: 857.

King, M. and Piper, C. (1995) *How the Law Thinks About Children*, Aldershot: Arena.

King, T. and Jobling, M. (2009) 'What's in a name?', *Trends in Genetics* 25: 351.

Kirby, J. (2005) *The Price of Parenthood*, London: Centre for Policy Studies.

Kiss, E. (1997) 'Alchemy or Fool's Gold? Assessing Feminist Doubts About Rights', in M. Lyndon Shanley and U. Narayan (eds) *Reconstructing Political Theory: Feminist Perspectives*, University Park: Pennsylvania State University Press.

Kitzmann, K., Gaylord, N., Holt, A. and Kenny, E. (2003) 'Child witnesses to domestic violence: a meta-analytic review', *Journal of Consultative Clinical Psychology* 71: 339.

Koffman, L. (2008) 'Holding parents to account', *Journal of Law and Society* 35: 113.

Krause, H. (1994) 'Child Support Reassessed: Limits of Private Responsibility and the Public Interest', in J. Eekelaar and M. Maclean (eds) *A Reader on Family Law*, Oxford: OUP.

Krause, H. and Meyers, M. (2002) 'What family for the 21st century?', *American Journal of Comparative Law* 50: 101.

Krinsky, C. (ed.) (2008) *Moral Panics over Contemporary Children and Youth*, Farnham: Ashgate.

Kruk, E. (1998) 'Power imbalance and spouse abuse in domestic disputes', *International Journal of Law, Policy and the Family* 12: 1.

Kurdek, L. (2004) 'Are gay and lesbian cohabiting couples really different from heterosexual married ones?', *Journal of Marriage and the Family* 66: 880.

Lacey, L. (1992) 'Mandatory marriage "for the sake of the children": A feminist reply to Elizabeth Scott', *Tulane Law Review* 66: 1434.

Lacey, N. (1993) 'Theory into Practice? Pornography and the Public/Private Dichotomy', in A. Bottomley and J. Conaghan (eds) *Feminist Theory and Legal Strategy*, Oxford: Blackwell.

Lafollete, H. (1980) 'Licensing parents', *Philosophy and Public Affairs* 9: 182.

Laming, Lord (2003) *The Victoria Climbié Report*, London: The Stationery Office.

Laming, Lord (2009) *The Protection of Children in England*, London: The Stationery Office.

Land, V. and Kitzinger, C. (2007) 'Contesting same-sex marriage in talk-in-interaction', *Feminist Psychology* 17: 173.

Landau, R. and Osmo, R. (2003) 'Professional and Personal Hierarchies of Ethical Principles', *International Journal of Social Work* 12: 42.

Lane, M. (2003) 'Ethical Issues in Surrogacy Arrangements', in R. Cook, S. Day Sclater and F. Kaganas (eds) *Surrogate Motherhood*, Oxford: Hart.

Lansdown, G. (2001) 'Children's Welfare and Children's Rights', in P. Foley, J. Roche and S. Tucker (eds) *Children in Society*, Buckingham: Open University Press.

Lasch, C. (1977) *Haven in a Heartless World*, New York: Basic Books.

Laslett, P. (1979) *The World We Have Lost*, Methuen: London.

Laufer-Ukeles, P. (2008) 'Selective recognition of gender difference in the law: revaluing the caretaker role', *Harvard Journal of Law and Gender* 31: 1.

Laurance, J. (2000) 'The booming baby market', *Independent on Sunday*, 7 April.

Lavery, R. (1996) 'The Child Assessment Order – a re-assessment', *Child and Family Law Quarterly* 8: 41.

Law Commission Consultation Paper 179 (2006) *Cohabitation: The Financial Consequences of Relationship Breakdown*, London: The Stationery Office.

Law Commission Consultation Paper 191 (2009) *Intestacy and Family Provision Claims on Death*, London: The Stationery Office.

Law Commission Consultation Paper 192 (2010) *Adult Social Care*, London: The Stationery Office.

Law Commission of Canada (2002) *Beyond Conjugality*, Ottawa: Law Commission of Canada.

Law Commission Report 6 (1966) *Reform of the Grounds of Divorce – The Field of Choice*, London: HMSO.

Law Commission Report 26 (1969) *Breach of Promise of Marriage*, London: HMSO.

Law Commission Report 33 (1970) *Report on Nullity of Marriage*, London: HMSO.

Law Commission Report 170 (1988) *Facing the Future*, London: HMSO.

Law Commission Report 175 (1988) *Family Law: Matrimonial Property*, London: HMSO.

Law Commission Report 192 (1990) *Family Law: The Ground of Divorce*, London: HMSO.

Law Commission Report 207 (1992) *Report on Domestic Violence and Occupation of the Family Home*, London: HMSO.

Law Commission Report 231 (1995) *Mental Incapacity*, London: HMSO.

Law Commission Report 234 (1995) *Sixth Programme of Reform*, London: HMSO.

Law Commission Report 278 (2002) *Sharing Homes*, London: The Stationery Office.

Law Commission Report 307 (2007) *Cohabitation: The Financial Consequences of Relationship Breakdown*, London: The Stationery Office.

Law Society (2002) *Cohabitation: The Case for Clear Law*, London: Law Society.

Law Society (2003) *Financial Provision on Divorce: Clarity and Fairness*, London: Law Society.

Law Society (2006) *Family Law Protocol*, London: Law Society.

Laws, J. (1998) 'The limitation of human rights', *Public Law* 254.

Layard, R. and Dunn, J. (2009) *A Good Childhood*, London: Penguin.

Lazarus-Black, M. (2007) *Everyday Harm: Domestic Violence, Court Rites and Cultures of Reconciliation*, Chicago: University of Illinois Press.

Leach, V. (2005) *Family Mediation: the Context*, London: Family Justice Council.

Leapman, B. (2007) 'Third of graduate women will be childless', *The Sunday Telegraph* 22 April, p. 1.

Leckey, R. (2008) *Contextual Subjects*, Toronto: University of Toronto.

Leckey, R. (2009) 'Cohabitation and comparative method', *Modern Law Review* 72: 48.

Lee, E. (2004) 'Young Women, Pregnancy and Abortion in Britain', *International Journal of Law, Policy and the Family* 18: 283.

Lees, J. and Horwarth, J. (2009) 'Religious parents . . . just want the best for their kids': Young people's perspectives on the influence of religious beliefs on parenting', *Children and Society* 23: 162:

Lefaucheur, N. (2004) 'The French "Tradition" of Anonymous Birth', *International Journal of Law, Policy and the Family* 18: 319.

Legal Services Commission (2007) *Annual Report*, London: LSC.

Legal Services Commission (2010) 'Mediation Results', *Family Law* 40: 122.

Lenard, D. (1980) *Sex and Generation: A Study of Courtship and Weddings*, London: Tavistock.

Levin, I. (2004) 'Living apart together: a new family form', *Current Sociology* 52: 223.

Levy, A. and Kahan, B. (1991) *The Pindown Experience and the Protection of Children*, London: HMSO.

Lewis, C. and Lamb, M. (2006) 'Father–Child Relationships and Children's Development', in M. Thorpe and R. Budden, *Durable Solutions*, Bristol: Jordans.

Lewis, J. (1999) 'Marriage and cohabitation and the nature of commitment', *Child and Family Law Quarterly* 11: 355.

Lewis, J. (2001a) 'Debates and issues regarding marriage and cohabitation in the English and American Literature', *International Journal of Law, Policy and the Family* 15: 159.

Lewis, J. (2001b) *The End of Marriage?* Cheltenham: Edward Elgar.

Lewis, J. (2004) 'Adoption: The Nature of Policy Shifts in England and Wales', *International Journal of Law, Policy and the Family* 18: 235.

Lewis, J. (2006) 'Repartnering and the management of risk', *International Journal of Law, Policy and the Family* 20: 151.

Lewis, J. (2009) *Work–Family Balance, Gender and Policy*, Cheltenham: Edward Elgar.

Lewis, J., Arthur, A., Fitzgerald, R. and Maclean, M. (2000) *Settling Up*, London: NCSR.

Lewis, J. and Campbell, M. (2007) 'Work/Family Balance Policies in the UK since 1997: A New Departure?', *Journal of Social Policy* 36: 365.

Lewis, J. and Welsh, E. (2006) 'Fathering practices in twenty-six intact families and the implications for child contact', *International Journal of Law in Context* 1: 81.

Lewis, M. (2005) *Unilever Family Report 2005: Home Alone*, London: Unilever.

Liddle, A. (1993) 'Gender, desire and child sexual abuse', *Theory, Culture and Society* 10: 103.

Liddy, J. (1998) 'The concept of family law under the ECHR', *European Human Rights Law Review* 1: 15.

Lim, H. and Roche, J. (2000) 'Feminism and Children's Rights', in J. Bridgeman and D. Monk (eds) *Feminist Perspectives on Child Law*, London: Cavendish.

Lind, C. (1995) 'The time for lesbian and gay marriages', *New Law Journal* 145: 1553.

Lind, C. (1997) 'Perceptions of sex in the legal determination of fatherhood – *X, Y, Z v UK*', *Child and Family Law Quarterly* 9: 401.

Lind, C. (2003) '*Re R (Paternity of IVF Baby)* – Unmarried Paternity under the Human Fertilisation and Embryology Act 1990', *Child and Family Law Quarterly* 15: 327.

Lind, C. (2004) 'Sexuality and Same-Sex Relationships in Law', in B. Brooks-Gordon, L. Gelsthorp, M. Johnson and A. Bainham, *Sexuality Repositioned*, Oxford: Hart.

Lind, C. (2008) 'Responsible Fathers: paternity, the blood tie and family responsibility' in J. Bridgeman, H. Keating and C. Lind (eds), *Responsibility, Law and the Family*, London: Ashgate.

Lind, C. and Hewitt, T. (2009) 'Law and the complexities of parenting: parental status and parental function', *Journal of Social Welfare and Family Law* 31: 391.

Lindley, B. (1997) 'Open adoption – is the door ajar?', *Child and Family Law Quarterly* 9: 115.

Lindley, B., Herring, J. and Wyld, N. (2001) 'Public Law Children's Cases', in J. Herring (ed.) *Family Law – Issues, Debates, Policy*, Cullompton: Willan.

Lindley, B., Richards, M. and Freeman, P. (2001) 'Advice and advocacy for parents in child protection cases – what is happening in current practice', *Child and Family Law Quarterly* 13: 167.

Lister, R. (2006) 'Children (but not women) first: New Labour, child welfare and gender', *Critical Social Policy* 26: 351.

Lord Chancellor's Advisory Committee on Legal Education and Conduct (1999)

Mediating Family Disputes: Education and Conduct for Mediators, London: LCD.

Lord Chancellor's Department (1995) *Looking to the Future: Mediation and the Ground for Divorce*, London: HMSO.

Lord Chancellor's Department (1996) *Striking the Balance. The Future of Legal Aid in England and Wales*, London: HMSO.

Lord Chancellor's Department (1997) *The Children Act Advisory Committee Final Report*, London: LCD.

Lord Chancellor's Department (1998) *Court Procedures for the Determination of Paternity*, London: HMSO.

Lord Chancellor's Department (2001) *Guidelines for Good Practice on Parental Contact in Cases where there is Domestic Violence*, London: LCD.

Lord Chancellor's Department (2002a) *Making Contact Work*, London: LCD.

Lord Chancellor's Department (2002b) *Moving Forward Together*, London: LCD.

Lord Chancellor's Department (2002c) *Scoping Study on Delay in Children Act Cases*, London: LCD.

Lord Chancellor's Department (2003a) *Reducing Delays in Family Proceedings Courts*, London: LCD.

Lord Chancellor's Department (2003b) *Domestic Violence. A Guide to Civil Remedies and Criminal Sanctions*, London: LCD.

Lord Chancellor's Department (2003c) *Results of the 2003–04 Grant Programme to Marriage and Relationship Support Services*, London: LCD.

Lord Chancellor's Department (2003d) *Judicial Statistics*, London: LCD.

Lord Chancellor's Department (2006) *Judicial Statistics*, London: LCD.

Lowe, N. (1988) 'The limits of the wardship jurisdiction: who can be made a ward?', *Journal of Child Law* 1: 6.

Lowe, N. (1994) 'Problems relating to access disputes under the Hague Convention on International Child Abduction', *International Journal of Family Law* 8: 374.

Lowe, N. (1997a) 'The changing face of adoption – the gift/donation model versus the contract services model', *Child and Family Law Quarterly* 9: 371.

Lowe, N. (1997b) 'The House of Lords and the Welfare Principle', in C. Bridge (ed.) *Family Law Towards the Millennium: Essays for PM Bromley*, London: Butterworths.

Lowe, N. (1997c) 'The meaning and allocation of parental responsibility – a common lawyer's perspective', *International Journal of Law, Policy and the Family* 11: 192.

Lowe, N. (2000) 'English Adoption Law', in S. Katz, J. Eekelaar and M. Maclean (eds) *Cross Currents*, Oxford: OUP.

Lowe, N. (2002) 'The Family Law Act 1986 – a critique', *Family Law* 32: 39.

Lowe, N. and Douglas, G. (1998) *Bromley's Family Law*, London: Butterworths.

Lowe, N. and Douglas, N. (2007) *Bromley's Family Law*, London: Butterworths.

Lowe, N. and Murch, M. (1999) *Supporting Adoption*, London: BAAF.

Lowe, N. and Murch, M. (2001) 'Children's participation in the family justice system – translating principles into practice', *Child and Family Law Quarterly* 13: 137.

Lowe, N. and Murch, M. (2002) *The Plan for the Child*, London: BAAF.

Lowe, N. and Murch, M. (2003) 'Translating Principles into Practice', in J. Dewar and S. Parker (eds) *Family Law: Processes, Practices, Pressures*, Oxford: OUP.

Lowe, N., Murch, M., Borkowski, M. et al. (1999) *Supporting Adoption*, London: BAAF.

Lowe, N. and Perry, M. (1998) 'The operation of the Hague and European Conventions on International Child Abduction between England and Germany', *International Family Law* 1: 8.

Lowenstein, A. and Daatland, S. (2006) 'Filial norms and family support in a comparative cross-national context: evidence from the OASIS study', *Ageing and Society* 26: 203.

Luckock, B. (2008) 'Adoption support and the negotiation of ambivalence in family policy and children's services', *Journal of Law and Society* 35: 3.

Lui, S. and Weaver, S. (1994) 'A survey of demand donors' attitudes', *Human Reproduction* 1994: 9.

Lundy, L. (2005) 'Family values in the classroom?', *International Journal of Law, Policy and the Family* 19: 346.

Lye, D. and Waldron, I. (1997) 'Attitudes towards cohabitation, family and gender roles', *Sociological Perspectives* 410: 199.

Lyndon Shanley, M. (2004) 'Just Marriage', in M. Lyndon Shanley (ed.) *Just Marriage*, Oxford: OUP.

Lyon, C. (1997a) 'Children Abused within the Care System', in N. Parton (ed.) *Child Protection and Family Support*, London: Routledge.

Lyon, C. (1997b) 'Children and the Law – Towards 2000 and Beyond', in C. Bridge (ed.) *Family Law Towards the Millennium: Essays for PM Bromley*, London: Butterworths.

Lyon, C. (2000) 'Children's Participation in Private Law Proceedings', in Thorpe LJ and E. Clarke (eds) *No Fault or Flaw: The Future of the Family Law Act 1996*, Bristol: Family Law.

Lyon, C. (2001) 'Children's rights and human rights', *Family Law* 31: 329.

Lyon, C. (2007) 'Children's Participation and the Promotion of their Rights', *Journal of Social Welfare and Family Law* 29: 99.

Lyon, C., Surrey, E. and Timms, N. (1999) *Effective Support Services for Children and Young People when Parental Relationships Break Down*, Liverpool: Liverpool University.

Lyon, N., Barnes, M. and Sweiry, M. (2006) *Families with Children in Britain*, London: DWP.

Lyons, B. (2010) 'Dying to be responsible: adolescence, autonomy and responsibility', *Legal Studies* 30: 257.

Macaskill, C. (2002) *Safe Contact? Children in Permanent Placement and Contact with their Birth Relatives*, Lyme Regis: Russell House.

McAuley, C., Pecora, P. and Rose, W. (2006) *Enhancing the Well-Being of Children and Families through Effective Intervention*, London: Jessica Kingsley.

McCall Smith, A. (1990) 'Is Anything Left of Parental Rights', in E. Sutherland and A. McCall Smith (eds) *Family Rights: Family Law and Medical Ethics*, Edinburgh: Edinburgh University Press.

McCandless, J. and Sheldon, S. (2010a) 'The Human Fertilisation and Embryology Act (2008) and the Tenacity of the Sexual Family Form', *Modern Law Review* 73: 175.

McCandless, J. and Sheldon, S. (2010b) '"No Father Required"? Rewriting the Family through the Welfare Clause of the HFE Act (2008)', in G. Haddow, M. Richards and C. Smart (eds) *Reproducing Parents and Kin: Assisted Reproduction and DNA Testing*, Basingstoke: Palgrave.

McCarthy, P. (2001) *The Provision of Information and the Prevention of Marriage Breakdown*, London: The Stationery Office.

McCarthy, P., Walker, J. and Hooper, D. (2000) 'Saving marriage – a role for divorce law?', *Family Law* 30: 412.

McClain, L. (2006) *The Place of Families,* Cambridge, Mass.: Harvard University Press.

McClean, D. (1997) 'International child abduction – some recent trends', *Child and Family Law Quarterly* 9: 387.

McClean, D. and Beevers, K. (1995) 'International child abduction – back to common law principles', *Child and Family Law Quarterly* 7: 128.

McColgan, A. (1993) 'In defence of battered women who kill', *Oxford Journal of Legal Studies* 13: 219.

MacCormick, N. (1976) 'Children's rights: a test-case for theories of rights', *Archiv für Rechts und Sozialphilosophie* 62: 305.

Maccullum, F. and Golombok, S. (2004) 'Children raised in fatherless families from infancy', *Journal of Child Psychology and Psychiatry* 48: 5.

MacDonald, A. (2008) 'The voice of the child: still a faint cry', *Family Law* 38: 648.

MacDonald, A. (2009a) 'Bringing Rights Home for Children: Arguing the UNCRC', *Family Law* 39: 1073.

MacDonald, A. (2009b) 'The caustic dichotomy – political vision and resourcing in the care system', *Child and Family Law Quarterly* 21: 30.

MacDonald, S. (2007) 'ASBO prohibitions and young people', *Child and Family Law Quarterly* 374.

McDougal, R. (2007) 'Parental virtue: A new way of thinking about the morality of reproductive actions', *Bioethics* 21: 181.

McEleavy, P. (2008) 'Evaluating the views of abducted children: trends in appellate case-law', *Child and Family Law Quarterly* 20: 230.

McFarlane, B. and Robertson, A. (2009) 'Apocalypse averted: proprietary estoppel in the House of Lords', *Law Quarterly Law Review* 125: 535.

MacFarlane, J. (2002) 'Mediating Ethically: the Limits of Codes of Conduct and the Potential of a Reflective Practice Model', *Osgoode Hall Law Journal* 40: 49.

McGee, C. (2000) 'Children's and Mother's Experiences of Support and Protection Following Domestic Violence', in J. Hanmer and C. Itzin (eds) *Home Truths About Domestic Violence,* London: Routledge.

McGillivray, A. (1994) 'Why children do have equal rights: In reply to Laura Purdy', *International Journal of Children's Rights* 2: 243.

McGillivray, A. (1997) '"He'll learn it on his body": Disciplining childhood in Canadian law', *International Journal of Children's Rights* 5: 193.

Mackay, Lord (2000) 'Family Law Reform', in S. Cretney (ed.) *Family Law – Essays for the New Millennium,* Bristol: Jordans.

Mackinnon, C. (1987) *Feminism Unmodified,* Cambridge, Mass.: Harvard University Press.

McLanahan, S. and Bumpass, L. (1988) 'Intergenerational consequences of marital disruption', *American Journal of Sociology* 94: 130.

Maclean, M. (1991) *Surviving Divorce,* New York: New York University Press.

Maclean, M. (2000) 'Access to Justice in Family Matters', in S. Katz, J. Eekelaar and M. Maclean (eds) *Cross Currents,* Oxford: OUP.

Maclean, M. (2002) 'The Green Paper: Supporting Families 1998', in A. Carling, S. Duncan and R. Edwards (eds) *Analysing Families,* London: Routledge.

Maclean, M. (ed.) (2007) *Parenting after Partnering,* Oxford: Hart.

Maclean, M. and Eekelaar, J. (2005a) 'Taking the plunge: perceptions of risk-taking associated with formal and informal partner relationships', *Child and Family Law Quarterly* 17: 247.

Maclean, M. and Eekelaar, J. (2005b) 'The significance of marriage: Contrasts between white British and ethnic minority groups in England', *Law and Policy* 27: 379.

Maclean, M., Eekelaar, J., Lewis, J., Arthur, S. et al. (2002) 'When cohabiting parents separate – law and expectations', *Family Law* 32: 373.

Maclean, M. and Mueller-Johnson, K. (2003) 'Supporting Cross-Household Parenting', in A. Bainham, B. Lindley, M. Richards and L. Trinder (eds) *Children and Their Families,* Oxford: Hart.

Maclean, M. and Fehlberg, B. (2009) 'Child support policy in Australia and the United Kingdom', *International Journal of Law, Policy and the Family* 23: 1.

Maclean, M. and Eekelaar, J. (2009) 'The perils of reforming family law and the increasing need for empirical research', in J. Miles and

R. Probert (eds) *Sharing Lives, Dividing Assets*, Oxford: Hart.

Maclean, S. (1990) 'Mothers and Others: The Case for Surrogacy', in E. Sutherland and A. McCall Smith (eds) *Family Rights: Family Law and Medical Ethics*, Edinburgh: Edinburgh University Press.

Maclean, S. and Maclean, M. (1996) 'Keeping secrets in assisted reproduction – the tension between donor anonymity and the need of the child for information', *Child and Family Law Quarterly* 8: 243.

McLellan, D. (1996) 'Contract marriage – the way forward or dead end?', *Journal of Law and Society* 23: 234.

Macooby, E. (1999) 'The Custody of Children of Divorcing Families', in R. Thompson and P. Amato (eds) *The Postdivorce Family*, Thousand Oaks, Calif.: Sage.

McRae, S. (1997) 'Cohabitation: A trial run for marriage?' *Sexual and Marital Therapy* 12: 259.

Madden Dempsey, M. (2006) 'What counts as domestic violence? A conceptual analysis', *William and Mary Journal of Women and the Law* 12: 301.

Madden Dempsey, M. (2007) 'Toward a Feminist State: What Does "Effective" Prosecution of Domestic Violence Mean?', *Modern Law Review* 70: 908.

Madden Dempsey, M. (2009) *Prosecuting Domestic Violence*, Oxford: OUP.

Maguire, J. and Frankland, E. (2006) ''Til death do us part: Inheritance claims and the short marriage', *Family Law* 36: 374.

Mahoney, M. (1991) 'Legal images of battered women: Redefining the issue of separation', *Michigan Law Review* 90: 1.

Maidment, S. (1998) 'Parental Alienation Syndrome – A judicial response?', *Family Law* 28: 264.

Maidment, S. (2001a) 'Children and psychiatric damage – parents' duty of care to their children', *Family Law* 31: 440.

Maidment, S. (2001b) 'Parental responsibility – is there a duty to consult?', *Family Law* 31: 518.

Malik, M. (2007) '"The branch on which we sit": Multiculturalism, minority women and family law', in A. Diduck and K. O'Donovan (eds) *Feminist Perspectives on Family Law*, London: Routledge.

Mallender, P. and Rayson, J. (2006) *The Civil Partnership Act 2004*, Cambridge: CUP.

Mama, A. (2000) 'Violence Against Black Women in the Home', in J. Hanmer and C. Itzin (eds) *Home Truths About Domestic Violence*, London: Routledge.

Manthorpe, J. and Price, E. (2005) 'Lesbian Carers: Personal Issues and Policy Responses', *Social Policy and Society* 5: 15.

Mantle, G. (2001) *Helping Families in Dispute*, Aldershot: Ashgate.

Marshall, A. (2003) 'Comedy of adoption – when is a parent not a parent?', *Family Law* 33: 840.

Marshall, J. (2008) 'Giving birth, but refusing motherhood', *International Journal of Law in Context* 4: 169.

Marshall, P. (2003) 'Divorce and the family business', *Family Law* 33: 407.

Martin, C. and Thery, I. (2001) 'The PACS and marriage and cohabitation in France', *International Journal of Law, Policy and the Family* 15: 135.

Mason, J. (2005) 'What's in a name? The vagaries of *Vo v France*', *Child and Family Law Quarterly* 17: 97.

Masson, J. (1984) 'Old Families into New: A Status for Step-Parents', in M. Freeman (ed.) *State, Law and the Family*, London: Tavistock.

Masson, J. (1992) 'Managing risk under the Children Act 1989: Diversion in child care?', *Child Abuse Review* 1: 103.

Masson, J. (1994) 'Social engineering in the House of Lords: *Re M*', *Journal of Child Law* 6: 17.

Masson, J. (1995) 'Partnership with Parents: Doing Something Together under the Children Act 1989', in F. Kaganas, M. King and C. Piper (eds) *Legislating for Harmony*, London: Jessica Kingsley.

Masson, J. (1996) 'Right to Divorce and Pension Rights', in M. Freeman (ed.) *Divorce: Where Next?* Aldershot: Dartmouth.

Masson, J. (2000a) 'From Curtis to Waterhouse', in S. Katz, J. Eekelaar and M. Maclean (eds) *Cross Currents*, Oxford: OUP.

Masson, J. (2000b) 'Thinking about contact – a social or a legal problem?', *Child and Family Law Quarterly* 12: 15.

Masson, J. (2002a) 'Letter', *Family Law* 32: 568.

Masson, J. (2002b) 'Securing human rights for children and young people in secure accommodation', *Child and Family Law Quarterly* 14: 77.

Masson, J. (2003) 'Paternalism, participation and placation: young people's experiences of representation in child protection proceedings in England and Wales', in J. Dewar and S. Parker (eds) *Family Law: Processes, Practices, Pressures*, Oxford: Hart.

Masson, J. (2005) 'Emergency intervention to protect children: using and avoiding legal controls', *Child and Family Law Quarterly* 17: 75.

Masson, J. (2006a) 'Making contact safe', *Family Law* 36: 253.

Masson, J. (2006b) 'The Climbié Inquiry – Context and Critique', *Journal of Law and Society* 33: 221.

Masson, J. (2006c) 'Parenting by Being; Parenting by Doing – In search of Principles for Founding Families', in J. Spencer and A. du Bois-Pedain, *Freedom and Responsibility in Reproductive Choice*, Oxford: Hart.

Masson, J. (2006d) 'Consent orders in contact cases', *Family Law* 36: 1041.

Masson, J. (2007) 'Reforming care proceedings – time for a review', *Child and Family Law Quarterly* 19: 411.

Masson, J. (2008a) 'The state as parent: Reluctant parent? The problem of parents of last resort', *Journal of Law and Society* 35: 52.

Masson, J. (2008b) 'Controlling costs and maintaining services – the reform of legal aid fees for care proceedings', *Child and Family Law Quarterly* 20: 425.

Mason, J. (2009) 'Caring for future generations', in G. Douglas and N. Lowe (eds), *The Continuing Evolution of Family Law*, Bristol: Family Law.

Masson, J. and Humphreys, C. (2005) 'Facilitating and enforcing contact: the Bill and the ten per cent', *Family Law* 35: 548.

Masson, J. and Lindley, B. (2006) 'Recognising Carers for What They Do – Legal Problems and Solutions for the Kinship Care of Children', in F. Ebtehaj, B. Lindley and M. Richards (eds) *Kinship Matters*, Hart: Oxford.

Masson, J., McGovern, D., Pick, K. and Winn Oakley, M. (2007) *Protecting Powers: Emergency Intervention for Children's Protection*, Chichester: John Wiley.

Masson, J., Pearce, J. and Bader, K. (2008) *Case Profiling Study*, London: Ministry of Justice.

Matheson, J. and Babb, T. (2003) *Social Trends 2002*, London: The Stationery Office.

Maushart, S. (2001) *Wifework*, London: Bloomsbury.

May, K. (2004) 'The education of children in care', *Family Law* 34: 259.

May, V. and Smart, C. (2004) 'Silence in court? – hearing children in residence and contact disputes', *Child and Family Law Quarterly* 16: 305.

May, V. and Smart, C. (2007) 'The parenting contest: problems of ongoing conflict over children', in M. Maclean (ed.) *Parenting after Partnering*, Oxford: Hart.

Mayall, B. (2000) 'The sociology of children in relation to children's rights', *International Journal of Children's Rights* 8: 243.

Mayall, B. (2002) *Towards a Sociology for Childhood*, Buckingham: Open University Press.

Mayes, G., Gillies, J., MacDonald, R. and Wilson, G. (2000) 'Evaluation of an information programme for divorced or separated parents', *Child and Family Law Quarterly* 15: 85.

Mayhew, E. (2005) 'Demography of childhood', in J. Bradshaw and E. Mayhew (eds) *The Well-being of Children in the UK*, London: Save the Children.

Mayhew, E., Finch, N., Beresford, B. and Keung, A. (2005) 'Children's time and space', in J. Bradshaw and E. Mayhew (eds) *The Well-being of Children in the UK*, London: Save the Children.

Mears, M. (1991) 'Getting it wrong again', *Family Law* 21: 231.

Mee, J. (1999) *The Property Rights of Cohabitees*, Oxford: Hart.

Mee, J. (2004) 'Property rights and personal relationships: reflections on reform', *Legal Studies* 24: 414.

Mee, J. (2009) 'The limits of proprietary estoppel: *Thorner v Major*', *Child and Family Law Quarterly* 21: 367.

Meehan, A. (2006) '*Miller* and *McFarlane*: An Opportunity missed?', *Family Law* 36: 566.

Meli, M. (1993) 'Towards a Restructuring of Custody Decision-Making at Divorce: An Alternative Approach to the Best Interests of the Child', in J. Eekelaar and P. Sarcevic (eds) *Parenthood in Modern Society*, London: Martinus Nijhoff.

Melville, A. and Laing, K. (2010) 'Closing the gate: family lawyers as gatekeepers to a holistic service', *International Journal of Law in Context* 6: 167.

Merrick, R. (2000) *Grandparents Suffering as Divorces Rise*, London: Family Policy Studies Centre.

Meyer, D. (2006) 'Parenthood in a time of transition: tensions between legal, biological, and social conceptions of parenthood', *American Journal of Comparative Law* 125.

Miccio, G. (2005) 'A house divided: mandatory arrest, domestic violence, and the conservatization of the battered women's movement', *Houston Law Review* 42: 237.

Michalowski, S. (1997) 'Is it in the best interests of a child to have a life-saving liver transplantation?', *Child and Family Law Quarterly* 9: 179.

Middleton, S. and Adelman, L. (2003) 'The Poverty and Social Exclusion Survey of Britain', in J. Bradshaw (ed.) *Children and Social Security*, Aldershot: Ashgate.

Middleton, S., Ashworth, K. and Braithwaite, I. (1997) *Small Fortunes*, York: Joseph Rowntree Foundation.

Miles, J. (2001) 'Domestic Violence', in J. Herring (ed.) *Family Law: Issues, Debates, Policy*, Cullompton: Willan.

Miles, J. (2002) 'Mind the gap . . . : Child protection, statutory interpretation and the Human Rights Act', *Cambridge Law Journal* 61: 533.

Miles, J. (2003) 'Property law v family law: resolving the problems of family property', *Legal Studies* 23: 624.

Miles, J. (2005) 'Principle or pragmatism in ancillary relief: the virtues of flirting with academic theories and other jurisdictions', *International Journal of Law, Policy and the Family* 19: 242.

Miles, J. (2008) '*Charman* v *Charman* (no. 4) [2007] EWCA Civ 503 – making sense of need, compensation and equal sharing after *Miller; McFarlane*', *Child and Family Law Quarterly* 20: 378.

Miles, J. and Lindley, B. (2003) 'Contact for Children Subject to State Intervention', in A. Bainham, B. Lindley, M. Richards and L. Trinder (eds) *Children and Their Families*, Oxford: Hart.

Miles, J. and Probert, R. (eds) (2009a) *Sharing Lives, Dividing Assets*, Oxford: Hart.

Miles, J. and Probert, R. (2009b) 'Legal principles and real life', in J. Miles and R. Probert (eds) *Sharing Lives, Dividing Assets*, Oxford: Hart.

Miles, J., Pleasence, P. and Balmer, N. (2009) 'The experience of relationship breakdown and civil law problems by people in different forms of relationship', *Child and Family Law Quarterly* 21: 47.

Millar, P. and Goldenberg, S. (1998) 'Explaining child custody determinations in Canada', *Canadian Journal of Law and Society* 13: 209.

Millbank, J. (2008a) 'Unlikely Fissures and Uneasy Resonances: Lesbian Co-mothers, Surrogate Parenthood and Fathers' Rights', *Feminist Legal Studies* 16: 141.

Millbank, J. (2008b) 'The role of "functional family" in same-sex family recognition trends', *Child and Family Law Quarterly* 20: 155.

Miller, G. (1997) 'Provision for a surviving spouse', *Conveyancer* 61: 442.

Miller, G. (2002) 'Bankruptcy as a means of enforcement in family proceedings', *Family Law* 32: 21.

Miller, G. (2003) 'Pre-nuptial agreements and financial provision', in G. Miller (ed.) *Frontiers of Family Law*, Aldershot: Ashgate.

Miller, G. (2004) *The Family, Creditors and Insolvency*, Oxford: OUP.

Million, 11 (2008a) *Making Children's Mental Health Matter*, London: 11 Million.

Million, 11 (2008b) *Annual Review*, London: 11 Million.

Mills, L. (2003) *Insult to Injury: Rethinking Our Responses to Intimate Abuse*, Princeton: Princeton University Press.

Mills, C. (2003) 'The child's right to an open future?', *Journal of Social Philosophy* 34: 499.

Ministerial Taskforce on Child Support (2005) *In the Best Interests of Children*, Canberra: Commonwealth of Australia.

Ministry of Justice (2007) *Openness in family courts – a new approach*. London: The Stationery Office.

Ministry of Justice (2008) *Deprivation of Liberty Safeguards*, London: The Stationery Office.

Ministry of Justice (2008) *Judicial and Court Statistics*, London: The Stationery Office.

Ministry of Justice (2009) *Judicial and Court Statistics* London: The Stationery Office.

Ministry of Justice (2010a) *Establishment of a System-Wide Target for Reducing Unnecessary Delay in Care and Supervision Proceedings*, London: The Stationery Office.

Ministry of Justice (2010b) *Family Justice Review*, London: The Stationery Office.

Minow, M. (1986) 'Rights for the next generation: A feminist approach to children's rights', *Harvard Women's Law Journal* 9: 1.

Mintel (2004) *Mintel Housework Survey*, London: Mintel.

Mirless-Black, C. (1999) *Home Office Research Study 191: Domestic Violence*, London: Home Office.

Mirless-Black, C. and Bayron, C. (2000) *Domestic Violence: Findings from the BCS Self-Completion Questionnaire*, London: Home Office.

Mnookin, R. (1975) 'Child custody adjudication', *Law and Contemporary Problems* 39: 226.

Mnookin, R. (1981) 'Thinking about children's rights – beyond kiddie libbers and child savers', *Stanford Lawyer* 1981: 24.

Moen, P. (2003) *It's About Time*, Ithaca, NY: Cornell University Press.

Mole, N. (2002) 'A note on the judgment from the perspective of the European Convention for the Protection of Human Rights and Fundamental Freedoms 1950', *Child and Family Law Quarterly* 14: 447.

Monck, E., Reynolds, J. and Wigfall, V. (2003) *The Role of Concurrent Planning*, London: BAAF.

Monk, D. (2002) 'Children's rights in education – making sense of contradictions', *Child and Family Law Quarterly* 14: 45.

Monk, D. (2009) 'Regulating home education: negotiating standards, anomalies and rights', *Child and Family Law Quarterly* 21: 155.

Montgomery, J. (1988) 'Children as property', *Modern Law Review* 51: 323.

Montgomery, J. (2000) 'Time for a paradigm shift', *Current Legal Problems* 53: 363.

Mookherjee, M. (2008) 'Autonomy, force and cultural plurality', *Res Publica* 14: 147.

Mooney, J. (2000) 'Women's Experiences of Violence', in J. Hanmer and C. Itzin (eds) *Home Truths About Domestic Violence*, London: Routledge.

Moor, P. and Le Grice, V. (2006) 'Periodical Payment Orders following *Miller* and *McFarlane*', *Family Law* 36: 655.

Moran, P. and Ghate, D. (2005) 'The effectiveness of parent support', *Children and Society* 19: 239.

Morgan, D. (1994) 'A surrogacy issue: Who is the other mother?', *International Journal of Law and the Family* 8: 386.

Morgan, D. (1995) 'Undoing What Comes Naturally – Regulating Medically Assisted Families', in A. Bainham, D. Pearl and R. Pickford (eds) *Frontiers of Family Law*, London: John Wiley & Co.

Morgan, D. (2003) 'Enigma Variations: Surrogacy, Rights and Procreative Tourism', in R. Cook, S. Day Sclater and F. Kaganas (eds) *Surrogate Motherhood*, Oxford: Hart.

Morgan, P. (1999a) 'Adoption and the Care of Children', in P. Morgan (ed.) *Adoption: The Continuing Debate*, London: IEA.

Morgan, P. (1999b) *Farewell to the Family?* London: IEA.

Morgan, P. (2000) *Marriage-Lite*, London: Institute for the Study of Civil Society.

Morgan, P. (2002) *Children as Trophies*, Newcastle: Christian Institute.

Morgan, P. (2007) *The War between the State and the Family*, London: IEA.

Morgan, R. (2009) *Children on Rights and Responsibilities*, London: Ofsted.

Morgan, R. (2010) *Children's Care Monitor 2009*, London: CAFCASS.

MORI (1999) *Families and Marriage*, London: MORI.

MORI (2004) *Youth Survey*, London: MORI.

Morley, P. (2000) 'Domestic Violence and Housing', in J. Hanmer and C. Itzin (eds) *Home Truths About Domestic Violence*, London: Routledge.

Morley, R. and Mullender, A. (1992) 'Hype or hope? The importance of pro-arrest policies and batterers' programmes from North America to Britain as key measures for preventing violence to women in the home', *International Journal of Law and the Family* 6: 265.

Morley, R. and Pascall, C. (1996) 'Women and homelessness: Proposals from the Department of the Environment, Part II, Domestic Violence', *Journal of Social Welfare and Family Law* 18: 327.

Morris, A. (2009) 'Selective treatment of irreversibly impaired infants: decision-making at the threshold', *Medical Law Review* 17: 347.

Morris, A. and Nott, S. (1995) *All My Worldly Goods*, Aldershot: Dartmouth.

Morris, C. (2005) 'Divorce in a multi-faith society', *Family Law* 35: 727.

Morris, C. (2007) '*Evans v United Kingdom*: Paradigms Of Parenting', *Modern Law Review* 70: 797.

Morrisson, F. (2009) *After Domestic Abuse: Children's Perspectives On Contact With Fathers*, Edinburgh: CRFR.

Morrow, V. (1998) *Understanding Families*, London: National Children's Bureau.

Morrow, V. and Mayall, B. (2009) 'What is wrong with children's well-being in the UK? Questions of meaning and measurement', *Journal of Social Welfare and Family Law* 31: 217.

Mouffe, O. (1995) 'Democracy and pluralism: A critique of the rationalist approach', *Cardozo Law Review* 16: 1533.

Mount, F. (1982) *The Subversive Family*, London: Jonathan Cape.

Mowbray, A. (2004) *The Development of Positive Obligations under the European Convention on Human Rights by the European Court of Human Rights*, Oxford: Hart.

Moylan HHJ (2010) *What Have Human Rights Done for Family Justice?* London: Resolution.

Moynagh, M. and Worsley, R. (2000) *Tomorrow*, King's Lynn: Tomorrow Project.

Muir, H. (2003) 'Women's baby hope cut back', *The Guardian*, 27 June.

Mullender, A. (2005) *Tackling Domestic Violence: Providing Support For Children Who Have Witnessed Domestic Violence*, London: Home Office.

Mullender, A. and Burton, S. (2000) *Domestic Violence. What Works? Perpetrator Programmes*, London: Home Office.

Mullender, A., Hague, G., Iman, U., Kieely, L., Malos, E. and Regan, L. (2002) *Children's Perspectives on Domestic Violence*, London: Sage.

Mumford, A. (2007) 'Working towards credit for parenting: A consideration of tax credits as a feminist enterprise', in A. Diduck and K. O'Donovan (eds) *Feminist Perspectives on Family Law*, London: Routledge.

Munby J (2004a) 'Making sure the child is heard. Part 1', *Family Law* 34: 338.

Munby J (2004b) 'Making sure the child is heard. Part 2', *Family Law* 34: 427.

Munby J (2004c) 'The family justice system', *Family Law* 34: 574.

Munby J (2005) 'Access to and reporting of family proceedings', *Family Law* 35: 945.

Munby J (2006) 'Families old and new – the family and Article 8', *Child and Family Law Quarterly* 17: 487.

Munro, V. (2007) *Law and Politics at the Perimeter: Re-evaluating Key Debates in Feminist Theory*, Oxford: Hart.

Murch, M. (2003) *The Voice of the Child in Private Family Law Proceedings*, Bristol: Family Law.

Murch, M., Douglas, G., Scanlan, L. et al. (1999) *Safeguarding Children's Welfare in Uncontentious Divorce*, Cardiff: Cardiff University.

Murch, M., Lowe, N., Borkowski, M. et al. (1993) *Pathways to Adoption*, London: HMSO.

Murch, M., Lowe, N., Borkowski, M. et al. (1999) *Adoption: Reframing the Approach*, London: Department of Health.

Murphy, J. (2000) 'Child Welfare in Transracial Adoption', in J. Murphy (ed.) *Ethnic Minorities, Their Families and the Law*, Oxford: Hart.

Murphy, J. (2002) 'The recognition of same-sex families in Britain: The role of private international law', *International Journal of Law, Policy and the Family* 16: 181.

Murphy, J. (2003) 'Children in need: the limits of local authority accountability', *Legal Studies* 23: 103.

Murphy, J. (2004) 'Same-sex marriage in England: a role for human rights', *Child and Family Law Quarterly Review* 16: 245.

Murphy, J. (2005) *International Dimensions in Family Law*, Manchester: Manchester University Press.

Murphy, M. and Wang, D. (1999) 'Forecasting British Families into the Twenty-First Century', in S. McRae (ed.) *Changing Britain*, Oxford: OUP.

Murray, A. (2008) 'Guidelines on Compensation', *Family Law* 38: 756.

Murray, C. (2004) 'Same-sex families: Outcomes for children and parents', *Family Law* 34: 136.

Musgrove, A. and Groves, N. (2007) 'The Domestic Violence, Crime and Victims Act 2004: Relevant or "Removed" Legislation?', *Journal of Social Welfare and Family Law* 29: 233.

National Audit Office (2003) *Developing Effective Services for Older People*, London: National Audit Office.

National Centre for Social Research (2008) *British Social Attitudes Survey*, London: Sage.

National Centre for Social Research (2010) *British Social Attitudes Survey*, London: Sage.

National Children's Bureau (2005) *National Evaluation of Children's Trusts*, Norwich: UEA.

National Institute for Health and Clinical Excellence (2005) *Social Value Judgements*, London: NICE.

National Statistics (2007) *Population Trends*, London: ONS.

National Statistics (2008a) *Populations Trends*, London: ONS.

National Statistics (2008b) *Living Arrangements*, London: ONS.

National Statistics (2008c) *Live Births*, London: ONS.

National Statistics (2008d) *Social Trends*, London: ONS.

National Statistics (2008e) *Divorces*, London: ONS.

National Statistics (2008f) *Lone Parents in Employment*, London: ONS.

National Statistics (2008g) *Ageing*, London: ONS.

National Statistics (2009a) *Gender Pay Gap*, London: ONS.

National Statistics (2010a) *Social Trends*, London: ONS.

National Statistics (2010b) *Marriages in England and Wales*, London: ONS.

National Statistics (2010c) *Civil Partnerships Down 18 per cent*, London: ONS.

National Statistics (2010d) *Divorces*, London: ONS.

Neale, B. (2004) *Young Children's Citizenship*, York: Joseph Rowntree Foundation.

Neale, B., Flowerdew, J. and Smart, C. (2003) 'Drifting towards shared residence?', *Family Law* 33: 904.

Neale, B. and Smart, C. (1997) 'Good and bad lawyers? Struggling in the shadow of the new law?' *Journal of Social Welfare and Family Law* 19: 377.

Neale, B. and Smart, C. (1999) *Agents or Dependants?* Leeds: Centre for Research on Family, Kinship and Childhood, Leeds University.

Neale, J. (2005) 'Children, crime and illegal drug use', in J. Bradshaw and E. Mayhew (eds) *The Well-Being of Children in the UK*, London: Save the Children.

Neil, E. (2000) 'The reasons why young children are placed for adoption', *Child and Family Social Work* 11: 303.

Neil, E. (2003) 'Adoption and Contact: A Research Review', in A. Bainham, B. Lindley, M. Richards and L. Trinder (eds) *Children and Their Families*, Oxford: Hart.

Nelson, H. and Nelson, J. (1989) 'Cutting motherhood in two: Some suspicions concerning surrogacy', *Hypatia* 4: 85.

Newcastle Centre for Family Studies (2004) *Picking up the Pieces*, London: DCA.

Newcastle Conciliation Project (1989) *Report to the Lord Chancellor on the Costs and Effectiveness of Conciliation in England and Wales*, London: Lord Chancellor's Department.

Newell, P. (1989) *Children Are People Too*, London: Bedford Square Press.

Newell, P. (1995) 'Respecting Children's Right to Physical Integrity', in B. Franklin (ed.) *The Handbook of Children's Rights*, London: Routledge.

Newell, P. (2002) 'Global Progress on Giving Up the Habit of Hitting Children', in B. Franklin (ed.) *The New Handbook of Children's Rights*, London: Routledge.

Nicholas, S., Kershaw, C. and Walker, A. (2007) *Crime in England and Wales 2006/7*, London: Home Office.

Nield, S. (2003) 'Constructive trusts and estoppel', *Legal Studies* 23: 311.

Nielsen, L. (1990) 'Family rights and the "Registered Partnership" in Denmark', *International Journal of Law and the Family* 4: 297.

Noddings, N. (2003) *Caring*, Berkeley: University of California Press.

NORCAP (2010) *Annual Report 2008–9*, London: NORCAP.

Northern Ireland Office of Law Reform (2001) *Physical Punishment in the Home*, Belfast: Office of Law Reform.

Nourin Shah-Kazemi, S. (2000) 'Cross-cultural mediation', *International Journal of Law, Policy and the Family* 14: 302.

NSPCC (2000) *Child Maltreatment Survey*, London: NSPCC.

NSPCC (2005) *Teen Abuse Survey of Great Britain*, London: NSPCC.

NSPCC (2007) *Key Child Protection Statistics*, London: NSPCC.

Nuffield Council on Bioethics (2007) *Critical Care and Decisions In Fetal and Neonatal Medicine: Ethical Issues*, London: Nuffield Council.

Nuffield Foundation (2009a) *Time Trends in Adolescent Well-Being*, London: Nuffield Foundation.

Nuffield Foundation (2009b) *Time Trends in Parenting and Outcomes for Young People*, London: Nuffield Foundation.

O'Brien, M. (2005) *Shared Care: Bringing Fathers into the Frame*, London: EOC.

O'Donnell, K. (2004) *'Re C (Welfare of Child: Immunisation) – Room to refuse? Immunisation, welfare and the role of parental decision making'*, *Child and Family Law Quarterly* 16: 213.

O'Donovan, K. (1982) 'Should all maintenance of spouses be abolished?', *Modern Law Review* 45: 424.

O'Donovan, K. (1984) 'Legal marriage – who needs it?', *Modern Law Review* 47: 111.

O'Donovan, K. (1988) 'A right to know one's parentage', *International Journal of Law, Policy and the Family* 2: 27.

O'Donovan, K. (1993) *Family Law Matters*, London: Pluto.

O'Donovan, K. (1998) 'Who is the Father? Access to Information on Genetic Identity', in G. Douglas and L. Sebba (eds) *Children's Rights and Traditional Values*, Aldershot: Ashgate.

O'Donovan, K. (2000) 'Constructions of Maternity and Motherhood in Stories of Lost Children', in J. Bridgeman and D. Monk (eds) *Feminist Perspectives on Child Law*, London: Cavendish.

O'Donovan, K. (2005) 'Flirting with academic categorisations', *Child and Family Law Quarterly* 17: 415.

Office of the Children's Commissioner (2006) *Annual Report*, London: OCC.

Office of Population and Census Surveys (1993) *Great Britain 1991 Census*, London: HMSO.

Office of Population and Census Surveys (1996) *Living in Britain: Results from the 1994 General Household Survey*, London: OPCS.

Office for National Statistics (2001) *The 2001 Census*, London: ONS.

Official Solicitor and Public Trustee (2009) *Annual Report*, London: HMSO.

Ofsted (2008) *Parents on Council Care*, London: The Stationery Office.

Ogg, J. and Bennett, G. (1992) 'Elder abuse in Britain', *British Medical Journal* 305: 990.

Ogg, J. and Munn-Giddings, M. (1993) 'Researching elder abuse', *Ageing and Society* 13: 389.

Ogus, A., Jones-Lee, M., Cloes, M. and McCarthy, P. (1990) 'Evaluating alternative dispute resolution: Measuring the impact of family conciliation on costs', *Modern Law Review* 53: 57.

O'Halloran, K. (2003) 'Adoption – A Public or Private Legal Process?', in J. Dewar and S. Parker (eds) *Family Law: Processes, Practices, Pressures*, Oxford: Hart.

Okin, S. (1992) *Justice, Gender and The Family*, New York: Basic Books.

Oldham, M. (1995) ' "Neither a borrower nor a lender be" – The life of *O'Brien*', *Child and Family Law Quarterly* 7: 104.

Oldham, M. (2001) 'Financial obligations within the family – aspects of intergenerational maintenance and succession in England and France', *Cambridge Law Journal* 60: 128.

Oldham, M. (2006) 'Maintenance and the Elderly: Legal Signalling Kinship and the State', in F. Ebtehaj, B. Lindley and M. Richards (eds) *Kinship Matters*, Hart: Oxford.

Oliver, D. (1982) 'Why do people live together?', *Journal of Social Welfare and Family Law* 4: 209.

Oliver, D. (1999) *Common Values and the Public–Private Divide*, London: Butterworths.

Olsen, F. (1992) 'Children's Rights: Some Feminist Approaches to the United Nations Convention on the Rights of the Child', in P. Alston, S. Parker and J. Seymour (eds) *Children, Rights and the Law*, Oxford: Clarendon Press.

Olsen, F. (1998) 'Asset Distribution after Unmarried Cohabitation: A United States Perspective', in R. Bailey-Harris (ed.) *Dividing the Assets on Family Breakdown*, Bristol: Jordans.

Olsson, S. (2008) 'Children's Suffrage: A Critique of the Importance of Voters' Knowledge for the Well-Being of Democracy', *International Journal of Children's Rights* 16: 55.

Ombudsman (2004) *Annual Report*, London: The Stationery Office.

One Parent Families (2006) *One Parent Families Today: The Facts*, London: One Parent Families.

O'Neill, O. (1992) 'Children's rights and children's lives', *International Journal of Law and the Family* 6: 24.

O'Neill, O. (2002) *Autonomy and Trust in Bioethics*, Cambridge: CUP.

O'Neill, O. and Ruddick, W. (1979) *Having Children*, Oxford: OUP.

O'Quigley, A. (1999) *Listening to Children's Views and Representing Their Best Interests*, York: Joseph Rowntree Foundation.

Orentlicher, D. (1998) 'Spanking and other corporal punishment of children by parents: Overvaluing pain, undervaluing children', *Houston Law Review* 35: 1478.

Ouazzani, S. (2009) 'Ancillary relief and the public/private divide', *Family Law* 40: 842.

Owusu-Bempah, K. (2001) 'Racism: An Important Factor in Practice with Ethnic Minority Children and Families', in P. Foley, J. Roche and S. Tucker (eds) *Children in Society*, Buckingham: Open University Press.

Owusu-Bempah, K. (2010) *The Wellbeing of Children in Care*, Abingdon: Routledge.

Pahl, J. (1989) *Money and Marriage*, Basingstoke: Macmillan.

Pahl, J. (2004) *Ethics review in social care research*, London: Department of Health.

Pahl, J. (2005) 'Individualisation in couple's finances', *Social Policy and Society* 4: 4.

Palmer, E. (2010) 'The Child Poverty Act 2010: holding government to account for promises in a recessionary climate?', *European Human Rights Law Review* 17: 305.

Palmer, G., Rahman, M. and Kenway, R. (2002) *Monitoring Poverty and Social Exclusion*, York: Joseph Rowntree Foundation.

Palser, E. (2009) 'Shutting the door on negligence liability: *Lawrence* v *Pembrokeshire County Council* and *L* v *Reading Borough Council*', *Child and Family Law Quarterly* 21: 384.

Parentline Plus (2006) *Parental Responsibility*, London: Parentline Plus.

Park, A., Phillips, M. and Johnson, M. (2004) *Young People in Britain: The Attitudes and Experiences of 12 to 19 Year Olds*, London: National Centre for Social Research.

Parker, A. (2002) 'Mutual Consent Divorce', in A. Dnes and R. Rowthorn (eds) *The Law and Economics of Marriage and Divorce*, Cambridge: CUP.

Parker, R. (1999) *Adoption Now*, London: DoH.

Parker, S. (1991) 'Child support in Australia: Children's rights or public interest?', *International Journal of Law and Family* 5: 24.

Parker, S. (1992) 'Rights and utility in Anglo-Australian family law', *Modern Law Review* 55: 311.

Parker, S. (1998) *New Balances in Family Law*, Melbourne: Griffith University.

Parkes, A. (2009) 'The Right of the Child to be Heard in Family Law Proceedings: Article 12 UNCRC', *International Family Law Journal* 4: 238.

Parkinson, L. (2006) 'Child-inclusive family mediation', *Family Law* 36: 483.

Parkinson, P. (1996) 'Multiculturalism and the Recognition of Marital Status in Australia', in G. Douglas and N. Lowe (eds) *Families Across Frontiers*, London: Kluwer.

Parkinson, P. (2003) 'Child protection, permanency planning and children's right to family life', *International Journal of Law, Policy and the Family* 17: 147.

Parkinson, P. (2005) 'The Yardstick of Equality: Assessing contributions in Australia and England', *International Journal of Law, Policy and the Family* 19: 163.

Parkinson, P. (2006) 'Keeping in contact: the role of family relationship centres in Australia', *Child and Family Law Quarterly* 18: 157.

Parkinson, P. (2007) 'Re-engineering the Child Support Scheme: An Australian Perspective on the British Government's Proposals', *Modern Law Review* 70: 812.

Parkinson, P. and Cashmore, J. (2010) *The Voice of a Child in Family Law Disputes*, Oxford: OUP.

Parkinson, P. and Humphreys, C. (1998) 'Children who witness domestic violence – the implications for child protection', *Child and Family Law Quarterly* 10: 147.

Parry, M. (2000) 'Local Authority Support for Ethnic Minority', in J. Murphy (ed.) *Ethnic Minorities, Their Families and the Law*, Oxford: Hart.

Parsons, T. and Bales, B. (1955) *Family, Socialization and Interaction Process*, Glencoe: Free Press.

Parton, N. (1991) *Governing the Family*, London: Macmillan.

Parton, N. (2008) 'The Change for Children Programme in England: Towards the prevention-surveillance state', *Journal of Law and Society* 35: 208.

Pascoe, S. (1998) 'Can English law uphold the sanctity of marriage?', *Family Law* 28: 620.

Patel, H. (2009) 'Dowry abuse', *Family Law* 39: 1092.

Patterson, C., Fulcher, M. and Wainright, J. (2002) 'Children of Lesbian and Gay Parents', in B. Bottoms, M. Kovera and B. McAuliff (eds) *Children, Social Science and the Law*, Cambridge: CUP.

Pawlowski, M. (2002) 'Beneficial entitlement – do indirect contributions suffice?' *Family Law* 32: 190.

Pawlowski, M. (2006) 'Family home: Doing justice to the parties', *Family Law* 36: 462.

Pawlowski, M. and Brown, J. (2002) *Undue Influence and the Family Home*, London: Cavendish.

Peacey, V. and Rainford, L. (2004) *Attitudes Towards Child Support*, London: ONS.

Pearce, J., Davis, G. and Barron, J. (1999) 'Love in a cold climate – section 8 applications under the Children Act 1989', *Family Law* 29: 22.

Pearl, D. and Menski, W. (1998) *Muslim Family Law*, Bristol: Jordans.

Pedain, A. (2005) 'Doctors, parents, and the courts: legitimizing restrictions on the continued provision of lifespan maximising treatments of severely handicapped non-dying babies', *Child and Family Law Quarterly* 17: 535.

Perry, A. (2006) 'Safety first? Contact and family violence in New Zealand', *Child and Family Law Quarterly* 18: 1.

Perry, A. and Rainey, B. (2007) 'Supervised, supported and indirect contact orders: research findings', *International Journal of Law, Policy and the Family* 21: 21.

Perry, P., Douglas, G., Murch, M. et al. (2000) *How Parents Cope Financially on Marriage Breakdown*, London: Joseph Rowntree Foundation.

Petre, J. (2006) 'Lesbians seeking first "gay divorce"', *Daily Telegraph*, 19 May.

Phillips, B. and Alderson, P. (2003) 'Beyond "anti-smacking": challenging violence and coercion in parent–child relationships', *International Journal of Children's Rights* 115: 175.

Phillips, C. (2003) 'Who's who in the pecking order?', *British Journal of Criminology* 43: 710.

Phillipson, C. (1998) *Reconstructing Old Age*, London: Sage.

Phillipson, C., Bernard, M., Phillips, J. and Ogg, J. (1999) 'Older People in Three Urban Areas: Household Composition, Kinship and Social Networks', in S. McRae (ed.) *Changing Britain*, Oxford: OUP.

Philp, I. (2006) *A New Ambition for Old Age*, London: DoH.

Philpot, T. (2001) *A Very Private Practice*, London: BAAF.

Pickford, R. (1999) 'Unmarried Fathers and the Law', in A. Bainham, S. Day Sclater and M. Richards (eds) *What is a Parent?* Oxford: Hart.

Piper, C. (1993) *The Responsible Parent: A Study in Divorce Mediation*, Hemel Hempstead: Harvester Wheatsheaf.

Piper, C. (1996) 'Norms and Negotiation in Mediation and Divorce', in M. Freeman (ed.) *Divorce: Where Next?* Aldershot: Dartmouth.

Piper, C. (1999) 'How do you define a family lawyer?', *Legal Studies* 19: 93.

Piper, C. (2004) 'Assessing Assessment', *Family Law* 34: 736.

Piper, C. (2009) *Investing in Children: Policy, Law and Practice in Context*, Cullompton: Willan.

Piper, C. (2010) 'Investing in a child's future: too risky?', *Child and Family Law Quarterly* 21: 1.

Piper, C. and Miakishev, A. (2003) 'A child's right to veto in England and Russia – another welfare ploy', *Child and Family Law Quarterly* 15: 57.

Piska, N. (2009) 'A common intention or a rare bird? Proprietary interests, personal claims and services rendered by lovers post-acquisition: *James v Thomas; Morris v Morris*', *Child and Family Law Quarterly* 21: 104.

Pizzey, E. (1978) *Scream Quietly or the Neighbours will Hear*, Harmondsworth: Pelican.

Platt, J. (2008) 'The Domestic Violence, Crime and Victims Act 2004 Part 1: Is it Working?', *Family Law* 38: 642.

Platt, L. (2007) *Poverty and Ethnicity in the UK*, York: Joseph Rowntree Foundation.

Pleasence, P., Balmer, N., Buck, A. et al. (2003) 'Family problems – what happens to whom', *Family Law* 33: 497.

Plomer, A. and Martin-Clement, N. (1996) 'The limits of beneficence: Egg donation under the Human Embryology and Fertilisation Act 1990', *Legal Studies* 16: 434.

Pollack, D. and Mason, S. (2004) 'Mandatory Visitation', *Family Court Review* 42: 74.

Pollard, J. (1995) 'Elder Abuse – The public law failure to protect', *Family Law* 25: 257.

Pontifical Council for the Family (2000) *Family, Marriage, and 'De Facto' Unions*, Rome: Pontifical Council for the Family.

Potter, G. and Williams, C. (2005) 'Parental responsibility and the duty to consult – the public's view', *Child and Family Law Quarterly* 17: 207.

Poulter, S. (1979) 'The definition of marriage in English law', *Modern Law Review* 42: 409.

Poulter, S. (1987) 'Ethnic minority cultural customs, English law and human rights', *International and Comparative Law Quarterly* 36: 589.

Poulter, S. (1998) *Ethnicity, Law and Human Rights*, Oxford: OUP.

Poussin, E. and Martin-LeBrun, G. (2002) 'A French study of children's self-esteem after parental separation', *International Journal of Law, Policy and the Family* 16: 313.

Povey, D. (2008) *Homicides, Firearm Offences and Intimate Violence 2006/07*, London: Home Office.

Powell, R. and Iowe, M. (2009) 'Annulment of Bankruptcy in Ancillary Relief Proceedings', *Family Law* 39: 401.

Pressdee, P. (2008) 'Relocation, Relocation, Relocation: Rigorous Security Revisited', *Family Law* 38: 220.

Prevatt Goldstein, B. (2009) 'Organisational Change: Good Practice and Black Minority Ethnic Families', *Family Law* 39: 859.

Priaulx, N. (2009) 'Rethinking Reproductive Injury', *Family Law* 39: 1161.

Price, D. (2006) 'The Poverty of Older People in the UK', *Journal of Social Work Practice* 20: 251.

Price, D. (2009) 'Pension accumulation and gendered household structures', in J. Miles and R. Probert (eds) *Sharing Lives, Dividing Assets*, Oxford: Hart.

Price, F. and Cook, R. (1995) 'The donor, the recipient and the child – human egg donation in UK licensed clinics', *Child and Family Law Quarterly* 7: 145.

Priolo, L. (2007) *The Complete Husband: A Practical Guide to Biblical Husbanding*, Washington: Baptist Press.

Pritchard, J. (2002) *Male Victims of Elder Abuse*, London: Jessica Kingsley.

Probert, R. (2002a) 'Sharing homes – a long-awaited paper', *Family Law* 32: 834.

Probert, R. (2002b) 'When are we married? Void, non-existent and presumed marriages', *Legal Studies* 22: 398.

Probert, R. (2003) 'Family law and property law: competing spheres in the regulation of the family home?', in A. Hudson (ed.) *New Perspectives on Family Law, Human Rights and the Home*, London: Cavendish Publishing.

Probert, R. (2004a) 'Families, assisted reproduction and the law', *Child and Family Law Quarterly* 16: 273.

Probert, R. (2004b) '*Sutton* v *Mischon de Reya and Gawor & Co* – Cohabitation contracts and Swedish sex slaves', *Child and Family Law Quarterly* 16: 453.

Probert, R. (2005) 'How would *Corbett* v *Corbett* be decided today?', *Family Law* 35: 382.

Probert, R. (2007a) 'Cohabitants and Joint Ownership: The implications of *Stack* v *Dowden*', *Family Law* 37: 924.

Probert, R. (2007b) 'Why couples still believe in common-law marriage', *Family Law* 37: 403.

Probert, R. (ed.) (2007c) *Family Life and the Law*, Aldershot: Ashgate.

Probert, R. (2007d) 'The security of the home and the home as security', in R. Probert (ed.) *Family Life and the Law*, Aldershot: Ashgate.

Probert, R. (2007e) '*Hyde* v *Hyde*: defining or defending marriage?' *Child and Family Law Quarterly* 19: 322.

Probert, R. (2008a) 'Hanging on the telephone', *Child and Family Law Quarterly* 20: 395.

Probert, R. (2008b) 'Common-law marriage: myths and misunderstandings', *Child and Family Law Quarterly* 20: 1.

Probert, R. (2009a) *Marriage Law and Practice in the Long Eighteenth Century: A Reassessment*, Cambridge: CUP.

Probert, R. (2009b) 'Parental responsibility and children's partnership choices', in R. Probert, S. Gilmore and J. Herring (eds) *Responsible Parents and Parental Responsibility*, Oxford: Hart.

Probert, R., Gilmore, S. and Herring, J. (2009) *Responsible Parents and Parental Responsibility*, Oxford: Hart.

Prout, A. (2005) *The Future of Childhood*, London: Routledge.

Pryor, J. (2003) 'Children's Contact with Relatives', in A. Bainham, B. Lindley, M. Richards and L. Trinder (eds) *Children and Their Families*, Oxford: Hart.

Pryor, J. and Daly Peoples, R. (2001) 'Adolescent attitudes toward living arrangements after divorce', *Child and Family Law Quarterly* 13: 197.

Pryor, J and Rogers B. (2001) *Children in Changing Families*, Oxford: Blackwells.

Pryor, J. and Seymour, F. (1996) 'Making decisions about children after parental separation', *Child and Family Law Quarterly* 8: 229.

Purdy, L. (1994) 'Why children shouldn't have equal rights', *International Journal of Children's Rights* 2: 223.

Quilgars, D., Searle, B. and Keung, A. (2005) 'Mental health and well-being', in J. Bradshaw and E. Mayhew (eds) *The Well-Being of Children in the UK*, London: Save the Children.

Quinton, D. (2004) *Supporting Parents*, London: Jessica Kingsley.

Quinton, D. and Selwyn, J. (2006a) 'Adoption in the UK', in C. McAuley, P. Pecora and W. Rose (eds) *Enhancing the Well-Being of Children and Families through Effective Intervention*, London: Jessica Kingsley.

Quinton, D. and Selwyn, J. (2006b) 'Adoption: research, policy and practice', *Child and Family Law Quarterly* 19: 459.

Quinton, D., Selwyn, J., Rushton, A. and Dance, C. (1998) 'Contact with birth parents in adoption – a response to Ryburn', *Child and Family Law Quarterly* 10: 349.

Qureshi, H. and Walker, A. (1989) *The Caring Relationship*, London: Macmillan.

Rabinovitch, D. (2002) 'Mothers matter more', *The Guardian*, 20 April.

Radford, L. (1999) *Unreasonable Fears? Child Contact in the Context of Domestic Violence*, London: Women's Aid.

Radford, L. and Hester, M. (2006) *Mothering through Domestic Violence*, London: Jessica Kingsley.

Ragoné, H. (2003) 'The Gift of Life', in R. Cook, S. Day Sclater and F. Kaganas (eds) *Surrogate Motherhood*, Oxford: Hart.

Rao, R. (2003) 'Surrogacy Law in the United States', in R. Cook, S. Day Sclater and F. Kaganas (eds) *Surrogate Motherhood*, Oxford: Hart.

Rasmusen, E. (2002) 'An Economic Approach to Adultery Law', in A. Dnes and R. Rowthorn (eds) *The Law and Economics of Marriage and Divorce*, Cambridge: CUP.

Rasmusen, E. and Evans State, J. (1998) 'Lifting the veil of ignorance: Personalising the marriage contract', *Indiana Law Journal* 73: 453.

Raz, J. (1984) 'Legal rights', *Oxford Journal of Legal Studies* 4: 1.

Raz, J. (1986) *The Morality of Freedom*, Oxford: OUP.

Raz, J. (1994) 'Multiculturalism: A liberal perspective', *Dissent* 1994: 67.

Readhead, P. (2006) *Same-Sex Couples Tie the Knot*, London: ESRC.

Reece, H. (1996) 'The paramountcy principle: consensus or construct?', *Current Legal Problems* 49: 267.

Reece, H. (2000) 'Divorcing the Children', in J. Bridgeman and D. Monk (eds) *Feminist Perspectives on Child Law*, London: Cavendish.

Reece, H. (2003) *Divorcing Responsibly*, Oxford: Hart.

Reece, H. (2005) 'From Parental Responsibility to Parenting Responsibly', in M. Freeman (ed.) *Law and Sociology*, Oxford: OUP.

Reece, H. (2006a) 'The End of Domestic Violence', *Modern Law Review* 69: 770.

Reece, H. (2006b) 'UK women's groups' child contact campaign: "so long as it is safe"', *Child and Family Law Quarterly* 18: 538.

Reece, H. (2008) 'The autonomy myth: A theory of dependency', *Child and Family Law Quarterly* 20: 109.

Reece, H. (2009a) 'Feminist Anti-Violence Discourse as Regulation', in E. Jackson, F. Ebtehaj, M. Richards and S. Day Sclater, *Regulating Autonomy: Sex, Reproduction and Families*, Oxford: Hart.

Reece, H. (2009b) 'The degradation of parental responsibility', in R. Probert, S. Gilmore and J. Herring, *Responsible Parents and Parental Responsibility*, Oxford: Hart.

Reece, H. (2009c) 'Parental Responsibility as Therapy', *Family Law* 39: 1167.

Rees, O. (2002) 'Beyond the hype – A year in the life of the Children's Commissioner for Wales', *Family Law* 32: 748.

Regan, M. (1993a) *Family Law and the Pursuit of Intimacy*, New York: New York University Press.

Regan, M. (1993b) 'Reason, tradition and family law: A comment on social constructionism', *Virginia Law Review* 79: 1515.

Regan, M. (1996) 'Post-modern Family Law: Toward a New Model of Status', in D. Popenoe, J. Elshtane and D. Blackenhorn (eds) *Promises to Keep: Decline and Renewal of Marriage in America*, New York: Rowman & Littlefield.

Regan, M. (1999) *Alone Together: Law and the Meaning of Marriage*, New York: OUP.

Regan, M. (2000) 'Morality, Fault and Divorce Law', in M. King White, *Marriage in America*, Lanham, Md.: Rowman & Littlefield.

Regan, M. (2004) 'Between Justice and Commitment', in M. Lyndon Shanley (ed.) *Just Marriage*, Oxford: OUP.

Reid, V. (2009) 'ADR: An Alternative to Justice', *Family Law* 39: 981.

Resolution (2010) *Survey into attitudes on divorce and relationship breakdown*, London: Resolution.

Rhoades, H. (2002a) 'The "No contact mother": Reconstructions of motherhood in the era of the "new father"', *International Journal of Law, Policy and the Family* 16: 71.

Rhoades, H. (2002b) 'The rise and rise of shared parenting laws: a critical reflection', *Canadian Journal of Family Law* 19: 75.

Rhoades, H. (2003) 'Enforcing contact or supporting parents?' Unpublished paper presented to the Oxford Centre for Family Law and Policy.

Rhoades, H. (2004) 'Contact Enforcement and Parenting Programmes – Policy Aims in Confusion?', *Child and Family Law Quarterly* 16: 1.

Rhoades, H. (2010a) 'Revising Australia's parenting laws: a plea for a relational approach to children's best interests', *Child and Family Law Quarterly* 22: 172.

Rhoades, H. (2010b) 'Concluding thoughts: The enduring chaos of family law', in J. Wallbank, S. Choudhry and J. Herring (eds) *Rights, Gender and Family Law*, Abingdon: Routledge.

Rhoades, H. and Boyd, S. (2004) 'Reforming Custody Law: A Comparative Study', *International Journal of Law, Policy and the Family* 18: 119.

Ribbens McCarthy, J., Edwards, R. and Gillies, V. (2003) *Making Families*, Durham: Sociology Press.

Richards, C. (2001) 'Allowing blame and revenge into mediation', *Family Law* 31: 775.

Richards, C. (2005) 'Equal opportunities: Who decides', *Family Law* 35: 389.

Richards, M. (1989) 'Joint custody revisited', *Family Law* 19: 83.

Richards, M. (1994) 'Divorcing Children: Roles for Parents and the State', in M. Maclean and J. Kurczewski (eds) *Families, Politics and the Law: Perspectives for East and West Europe*, Oxford: Clarendon Press.

Richards, M. (1995a) 'Private Worlds and Public Intentions: The Role of the State at Divorce', in A. Bainham, D. Pearl and R. Pickford (eds) *Frontiers of Family Law*, London: John Wiley & Co.

Richards, M. (1995b) 'But What About the Children? Some Reflections on the Divorce White Paper', *Child and Family Law Quarterly* 4: 223.

Richards, M. (1996a) *Community Care for Older People*, Bristol: Jordans.

Richards, M. (1996b) 'Divorce and divorce legislation', *Family Law* 26: 151.

Richards, M. (1997) 'The Interests of Children at Divorce', in M. Meulders-Klein (ed.) *Familles et Justice*, Brussels: Bruylant.

Richards, M. (2003) 'Assisted Reproduction and Parental Relationships', in A. Bainham, B. Lindley, M. Richards and L. Trinder (eds) *Children and Their Families*, Oxford: Hart.

Richards, M. (2006) 'Genes, Genealogies and Paternity', in J. Spencer and A. du Bois-Pedain (eds) *Freedom and Responsibility in Reproductive Choice*, Oxford: Hart.

Richards, M. and Connell, J. (2000) 'Children and the Family Law Act', in Thorpe LJ and E. Clarke (eds) *No Fault or Flaw: The Future of the Family Law Act 1996*, Bristol: Jordans.

Richards, M. and Dyson, M. (1982) *Separation, Divorce and the Development of Children*, London: DHSS.

Richards, M. and Stark, C. (2000) 'Children, parenting and information meetings', *Family Law* 30: 484.

Richardson, G. (2010) 'Mental capacity at the margin: the interface between two Acts', *Medical Law Review* 18: 56.

Rights of Women (2004) *Response to the Home Office Consultation Paper Society and Justice*, London: Rights of Women.

Rippon, P. (1998) 'Mistresses I have known – unmarried cohabitants and land ownership', *Family Law* 28: 682.

Roberts, E. (2000) *Age Discrimination in Health and Social Care*, London: King's Fund.

Roberts, L. (2010) 'Teenage Jehovah's Witness refuses blood transfusion and dies', *Daily Telegraph* 18 May 2010.

Roberts, M. (1995) 'Ousting abusers – Children Act 1989 or inherent jurisdiction *Re H (Prohibited Steps Order)*', *Child and Family Law Quarterly* 7: 243.

Roberts, M. (2000) 'Children by Donation: Do they have a Claim to their Genetic Parentage?', in J. Bridgeman and D. Monk (eds) *Feminist Perspectives on Child Law*, London: Cavendish.

Roberts, M. (2001) 'Childcare Policy', in P. Foley, J. Roche and S. Tucker (eds) *Children in Society*, Buckingham: Open University Press.

Roberts, S. (1988) 'Three Models of Family Mediation', in J. Eekelaar and R. Dingwall (eds) *Divorce, Mediation and the Legal Process*, Oxford: Clarendon.

Roberts, S. (1995) 'Decision-making for life apart', *Modern Law Review* 58: 714.

Roberts, S. (1996) 'Family mediation and the interests of women – facts and fears', *Family Law* 26: 239.

Roberts, S. (2000) 'Family Mediation in the New Millennium', in S. Cretney (ed.) *Family Law – Essays for the New Millennium*, Bristol: Jordans.

Robertson, J. (1994) *Children of Choice*, Princeton: Princeton University Press.

Robinson, J. (2003) 'Age Equality in Health and Social Care', in S. Fredman and S. Spencer (eds) *Age as an Equality Issue*, Oxford: Hart.

Roche, J. (1991) 'The Children Act 1989: Once a Parent Always a Parent', *Journal of Social Welfare and Family Law* 345.

Roche, J. (1999) 'Children and Divorce: A Private Affair?', in S. Day Sclater and C. Piper (eds) *Undercurrents of Divorce*, Aldershot: Ashgate.

Rodger, J. (1996) *Family Life and Social Control*, Basingstoke: Macmillan.

Rogers, B. and Pryor, J. (1998) *Divorce and Separation*, York: Joseph Rowntree Foundation.

Rogers, B. and Pryor, J. (2001) *Children in Changing Families*, Oxford: Blackwell.

Rogers, C. (2003) *Children at Risk 2003–4*, London: NFPI.

Roman Catholic Church (1987) *Instruction on Respect for Human Life in its Origin and on the Dignity of Procreation*, London: Catholic Truth Society.

Rose, N. (1987) 'Beyond the Public/Private Division: Law, Power and the Family', in P. Fitzpatrick and A. Hunt (eds) *Critical Legal Studies*, Oxford: Basil Blackwell.

Roseneil, S. and Budgeon, S. (2004) 'Cultures of Intimacy and Care: Beyond the "family"', *Sociology* 52: 135.

Rosettenstein, D. (2005) '"Big money" divorces and unequal distributions; value, risk, liquidity and other issues on the road to unfairness', *International Journal of Law, Policy and the Family* 19: 206.

Rothstein, M., Murray, T., Kaebnick, G. and Majumder, M. (2006) *Genetic Ties and the Family*, New York: Johns Hopkins University Press.

Rowthorn, R. (1999) 'Marriage and trust', *Cambridge Journal of Economics* 23: 661.

Rowthorn, R. (2002) 'Marriage as a Signal', in A. Dnes and R. Rowthorn (eds) *The Law and Economics of Marriage and Divorce*, Cambridge: CUP.

Royal Commission (1999) *Royal Commission Report on Long Term Care*, London: HMSO.

Rubens, T. (2008) 'Domestic violence and priority need', *Journal of Housing Law* 11: 28.

Rushbrooke, R. (2001) *The Proportion of Adoptees who have Received their Birth Records*, London: ONS.

Rushton, P. (2002) *Adoption as a Placement Choice*, London: King's College London.

Rusk, P. (1998) 'Same sex spousal benefits', *Toronto Faculty of Law Review* 52: 170.

Ryburn, M. (1998) 'In whose best interests? Post adoption contact with the birth family', *Child and Family Law Quarterly* 10: 53.

Ryder, J (2009) 'The autonomy of the citizen in the context of family law disputes', *International Family Law* 2: 88.

Sachdev, P. (1992) *Adoption, Reunion and After*, Washington: Child Welfare.

Sagar, T. and Hitchings, E. (2007) '"More Adoptions, More Quickly": A Study of Social Workers' Responses to the Adoption and Children Act 2002', *Journal of Social Welfare and Family Law* 29: 119.

Salter, D. (2000) 'A practitioner's guide to pension sharing', *Family Law* 30: 489.

Salter, D. (2003) 'Maskell unmasked', *Family Law* 33: 344.

Salter, D. (2008) 'Pension transfer values: The new regime', *Family Law* 38: 1205.

Samad, Y. (2010) 'Forced marriage among men: An unrecognized problem', *Critical Social Policy* 30: 189.

Sandland, R. (2005) 'Feminism and the Gender Recognition Act 2004', *Feminist Legal Studies* 14: 43.

Sarat, A. and Felstiner, W. (1995) *Divorce Lawyers and their Clients*, New York: OUP.

Saunders, H. (2004) *Twenty Nine Child Homicides*, Bristol: Women's Aid.

Savas, D. (1996) 'Parental participation in case conferences', *Child and Family Law Quarterly* 8: 57.

Save the Children and National Children's Bureau (1998) *It Hurts You Inside – Children Talking About Smacking,* London: Save the Children and National Children's Bureau.

Savulescu, J. and Momeyer, R. (1997) 'Should informed consent be based on rational beliefs?', *Journal of Medical Ethics* 23: 282.

Sawyer, C. (1995) 'The competence of children to participate in family proceedings', *Child and Family Law Quarterly* 7: 180.

Sawyer, C. (2000) 'Hitting people is wrong', *Family Law* 30: 654.

Sawyer, C. (2001) 'Applications by children: Still seen but not heard?', *Law Quarterly Review* 117: 203.

Sawyer, C. (2004) 'Equity's children – constructive trusts for the new generation', *Child and Family Law Quarterly* 16: 31.

Sayer, L. (2010) 'Gender differences in the relationship between long employment hours and multitasking', in B. Ruben (ed.) *Research in the Sociology of Work,* Amsterdam: Elsevier.

Schaffer, R. (1990) *Making Decisions About Children: Psychological Questions and Answers,* Oxford: Blackwell.

Schaffer, L. (2007) 'Taking the gloves off', *Family Law* 37: 439.

Scherpe, J. (2009) 'Establishing and ending parental responsibility: A comparative view', in R. Probert, S. Gilmore and J. Herring (eds), *Responsible Parents and Parental Responsibility,* Oxford: Hart.

Scherpe, J. (2010) 'Pre-Nups, Private Autonomy and Paternalism', *Cambridge Law Journal* 69: 35.

Schiff, A. (1997) 'Arising from the dead. Problems of posthumous reproduction', *North Carolina Law Review* 75: 901.

Schneider, C. (1991) 'Discretion, rules and law: Child custody and the UMDA's Best Interest Standard', *Michigan Law Review* 89: 2215.

Schneider, C. (1993) 'The tension between rules and discretion in family law: A Report and Reflection', *Family Law Quarterly* 27: 29.

Schneider, E. (1994) 'The Violence of Privacy', in M. Fineman and R. Myktiuk (eds) *The Public Nature of Private Violence,* London: Routledge.

Schneider, C. (1995) 'On the duties and rights of parents', *Virginia Law Review* 81: 2477.

Schneider, E. (2000a) *Battered Women and Feminist Law Making,* New Haven: Yale University Press.

Schneider, E. (2000b) 'Law and Violence Against Women in the Family at Century's End', in S. Katz, J. Eekelaar and M. MacLean (eds) *Cross Currents,* Oxford: OUP.

Schofield, G. (1998) 'Making sense of the ascertainable wishes and feelings of insecurely attached children', *Child and Family Law Quarterly* 10: 363.

Schofield, G. and Thoburn, J. (1996) *Child Protection: The Voice of the Child in Decision Making,* London: Institute for Public Policy Research.

Schuz, R. (1996) 'Divorce and Ethnic Minorities', in M. Freeman (ed.) *Divorce: Where Next?* Aldershot: Dartmouth.

Schwartz, P. (2000) 'Peer marriages', in M. Whyte (ed.) *Marriage in America,* Lanham, Md.: Rowman & Littlefield.

Scott, E. (1990) 'Rational decision making about marriage and divorce', *Virginia Law Review* 76: 9.

Scott, E. (2003) 'Marriage Commitment and the Legal Regulation of Divorce', in A. Dnes and R. Rowthorn (eds) *The Law and Economics of Marriage and Divorce,* Cambridge: CUP.

Scott, J. and Dex, S. (2009) 'Paid and unpaid work', in J. Miles and R. Probert (eds) *Sharing Lives, Dividing Assets,* Oxford: Hart.

Scott, E. and Scott, R. (1995) 'Parents as fiduciaries', *Virginia Law Review* 81: 2401.

Scott, K. and Warren, M. (2001) *Perspectives on Marriage,* New York: OUP.

Scott Hunt, S. (2009) 'Intentional communities and care-giving: Co-housing possibilities', in A. Bottomley and S. Wong (eds) *Changing Contours of Domestic Life, Family and Law,* Oxford: Hart.

Scottish Law Commission Report 135 (1992) *Report on Family Law,* Edinburgh: HMSO.

Scully, A. (2003) 'Big money cases, judicial discretion and equality of division', *Child and Family Law Quarterly* 15: 205.

Secretary of State for Constitutional Affairs and Lord Chancellor (2006) *Confidence and Confidentiality,* London: DCA.

Seden, J. (2001) 'Family Assistance Orders and the Children Act 1989: Ambivalence about intervention or a means of safeguarding and promoting children's welfare?', *International Journal of Law, Policy and the Family* 15: 226.

Select Committee (1975) *Report on Violence in Marriage*, HC 553, London: HMSO.

Select Committee (1977) *Violence in the Family*, HC 329, London: HMSO.

Selwyn, J., Fraser, L. and Quinton, D. (2006) 'Paved with good intentions', *British Journal of Social Work* 36: 561.

Selwyn, J. and Sempik, J. (2010) 'Recruiting Adoptive Families: The Costs of Family Finding and the Failure of the Inter-Agency Fee', *British Journal of Social Work* 40: 1.

Sevenhuijsen, S. (1997) *Citizenship and the Ethics of Care*, London: Routledge.

Sevenhuijsen, S. (2000) 'Caring in the third way', *Critical Social Policy* 20: 5.

Sevenhuijsen, S. (2002) 'An approach through the ethic of care', in A. Carling, S. Duncan and R. Edwards (eds) *Analysing Families*, London: Routledge.

Seymour, J. (2000) *Childbirth and the Law*, Oxford: OUP.

Shah, P. (2003) 'Attitudes to Polygamy in English Law', *International and Comparative Law Quarterly* 52: 369.

Sharpe, A. (2002) *Transgender Jurisprudence*, London: Cavendish.

Sharpe, A. (2007) 'Endless sex: the Gender Recognition Act 2004 and the persistence of a legal category', *Feminist Legal Studies* 15: 57.

Shaw, M. (2002) 'When Young People Refuse Treatment: Balancing Autonomy and Protection', in Thorpe LJ and C. Cowton (eds) *Delight and Dole*, Bristol: Jordans.

Shaw Spaht, K. (2002) 'Louisiana's Covenant Marriage Law', in A. Dnes and R. Rowthorn (eds) *The Law and Economics of Marriage and Divorce*, Cambridge: CUP.

Sheldon, S. (2001a) '"Sperm bandits", birth control fraud and the battle of the sexes', *Legal Studies* 21: 460.

Sheldon, S. (2001b) 'Unmarried fathers and parental responsibility: A convincing case for reform?' *Feminist Legal Studies* 9: 93.

Sheldon, S. (2003) 'Unwilling fathers and abortion: Terminating men's child support obligations', *Modern Law Review* 66: 175.

Sheldon, S. (2004) 'Evans v Amicus – Revealing cracks in the "twin pillars"?', *Child and Family Law Quarterly* 16: 437.

Sheldon, S. (2005) 'Fragmenting Fatherhood: The Regulation of Reproductive Technologies', *Modern Law Review* 68: 523.

Sheldon, S. (2009) 'From "absent objects of blame" to "fathers who want to take responsibility": reforming birth registration law', *Journal of Social Welfare and Family Law* 31: 373.

Shepherd, N. (2009) 'Ending the blame game: Getting no fault divorce back on the agenda', *Family Law* 39: 122.

Shultz, M. (1982) 'Contractual ordering of marriage', *California Law Review* 70: 204.

Shultz, M. (1990) 'Reproductive technology and intent-based parenthood: An opportunity for gender neutrality', *Wisconsin Law Review* 1990: 297.

Sifris, A. (2009) 'The legal recognition of lesbian-led families: justifications for change', *Child and Family Law Quarterly* 21: 197.

Sigle-Rushton, W. (2009) 'Great Britain: "Things can only get better . . ."', in André, H-J and Hummelsheim, D. (eds) *When Marriage Ends*, Cheltenham: Edward Elgar.

Silva, E. and Smart, C. (1999) *The New Family*, London: Sage.

Simon, T. (2000) 'United National Conventions on Wrongs to the Child', *International Journal of Children's Rights* 8: 1.

Simons, J. (1999) *Can Marriage Preparation Courses Influence the Quality and Stability of Marriage?*, London: One Plus One.

Simpson, B., Jessop, J. and McCarthy, P. (2003) 'Fathers after Divorce', in A. Bainham, B. Lindley, M. Richards and L. Trinder (eds) *Children and Their Families*, Oxford: Hart.

Singer HHJ (2001) 'Sexual discrimination in ancillary relief', *Family Law* 31: 115.

Singer, J. (1997) 'Husbands, wives and human capital: Why the shoe won't fit', *Family Law Quarterly* 31: 119.

Singh, A. (2010) 'Kirsty Young: Britain has become a child-centric society with too many pushy parents', *Daily Telegraph*, 5 January.

Slaughter, M. (2002) 'Marital Bargaining', in M. Maclean (ed.) *Making Law for Families*, Oxford: Hart.

Sloan, B. (2009) 'Re C (A Child) (Adoption: Duty of Local Authority) – Welfare and the rights of the birth family in "fast track" adoption cases', *Child and Family Law Quarterly* 21: 87.

Smallbone, S., Marshall, W. and Wortley, R. (2008) *Preventing Child Sexual Abuse*, Cullompton: Willan.

Smart, C. (1984) *The Ties that Bind*, London: Routledge.

Smart, C. (1989) *Feminism and the Power of Law*, London: Routledge.

Smart, C. (1991) 'The legal and moral ordering of child custody', *Journal of Law and Society* 19: 485.

Smart, C. (2000a) 'Divorce in England 1950–2000: A Moral Tale', in S. Katz, J. Eekelaar and M. Maclean (eds) *Cross Currents*, Oxford: OUP.

Smart, C. (2000b) 'Stories of a family life', *Canadian Journal of Family Law* 17: 20.

Smart, C. (2002) 'From children's shoes to children's voices', *Family Court Review* 40: 307.

Smart, C. (2003) 'Children and the Transformation of Family Law', in J. Dewar and S. Parker (eds) *Family Law: Processes, Practices, Pressures*, Oxford: Hart.

Smart, C. (2004) 'Equal shares? Rights for fathers or recognition for children?' *Critical Social Policy* 24: 484.

Smart, C. (2006) 'Parenting Disputes, Gender Conflict and the Courts', in M. Thorpe and R. Budden (eds) *Durable Solutions*, Bristol: Jordans.

Smart, C. (2007a) *Personal Life*. Bristol: Polity.

Smart, C. (2007b) 'The ethic of justice strikes back: Changing narratives of fatherhood' in A. Diduck and K. O'Donovan (eds) *Feminist Perspective on Family Law*, London: Routledge.

Smart, C. (2009) 'Making Kin: Relationality and Law', in A. Bottomley and S. Wong (eds) *Changing Contours of Domestic Life, Family and Law*, Oxford: Hart.

Smart, C., Masson, J. and Shipman, B. (2006) *Gay and Lesbian 'Marriage'*, Manchester: Morgan Centre.

Smart, C. and May, V. (2004a) 'Residence and contact disputes in court', *Family Law* 34: 36.

Smart, C. and May, V. (2004b) 'Why can't they agree? The underlying complexity of contact and residence disputes', *Journal of Social Welfare and Family Law* 26: 347.

Smart, C., May, V., Wade, A. and Furniss, C. (2003) *Residence and Contact Disputes in Court Vol. 1*, London: DCA.

Smart, C., May, V., Wade, A. and Furniss, C. (2005) *Residence and Contact Disputes in Court Vol. 2*, London: DCA.

Smart, C. and Neale, B. (1997) 'Argument against virtue – must contact be enforced?', *Family Law* 27: 332.

Smart, C. and Neale, B. (1999a) *Family Fragments?* Cambridge: Polity Press.

Smart, C. and Neale, B. (1999b) '"I hadn't really thought about it": new identities/new fatherhoods', in J. Seymour and P. Bagguley (eds) *Relating Intimacies: Power and Resistance*, Basingstoke: Macmillan.

Smart, C. and Neale, B. (2000) '"It's my life too": Children's perspectives on post-divorce parenting', *Family Law* 30: 163.

Smart, C., Neale, B. and Wade, A. (2001) *The Changing Experience of Childhood*, Cambridge: Polity Press.

Smart, C. and Stevens, P. (2000) *Cohabitation Breakdown*, London: Joseph Rowntree Foundation.

Smeaton, D. (2006) *Dads and their Babies*, London: Policy Studies Institute.

Smith, C. (1997a) 'Judicial power and local authority discretion – the contested frontier', *Child and Family Law Quarterly* 9: 243.

Smith, C. (1997b) 'Children's rights: Judicial ambivalence and social resistance', *International Journal of Law, Policy and the Family* 11: 103.

Smith, C. (2002) 'Human rights and the Children Act 1989', *Child and Family Law Quarterly* 14: 427.

Smith, C. (2004) 'Autopoietic law and the "epistemic trap": a case study of adoption and contact', *Journal of Law and Society* 31: 318.

Smith, C. (2005) 'Trust v Law: Promoting and safeguarding post-adoption contact', *Journal of Social Welfare and Family Law* 27: 315.

Smith, C. and Logan, J. (2002) 'Adoptive parenthood as a "legal fiction" – its consequences for direct post-adoption contact', *Child and Family Law Quarterly* 14: 281.

Smith, D. (2003) 'Making Contact Work in International Cases: Promoting Contact Whilst Preventing International Parental Child Abduction', in A. Bainham, B. Lindley, M. Richards and L. Trinder (eds) *Children and Their Families*, Oxford: Hart.

Smith II, G. (1997) *Legal and Healthcare Ethics for the Elderly*, Washington: Taylor and Francis.

Smith, L. (1989) *Home Office Research Study 107: Domestic Violence: An Overview of the Literature*, London: Home Office.

Smith, L. (1993) 'Children, Parents and the European Human Rights Convention', in

J. Eekelaar and P. Sarcevic (eds) *Parenthood in Modern Society*, London: Martinus Nijhoff.

Smith, Leanne (2006a) 'Principle or pragmatism? Lesbian parenting, shared residence and parental responsibility after *Re G (Residence: Same-Sex Partner)*', *Child and Family Law Quarterly* 18: 125.

Smith, Leanne (2006b) 'Is three a crowd? Lesbian mothers' perspectives on parental status?' *Child and Family Law Quarterly* 18: 231.

Smith, Leanne (2007) '*Re G (Children) (Residence: Same-sex Partner)* [2006] UKHL 43, [2006] 1 WLR 2305', *Journal of Social Welfare and Family Law* 29: 307.

Smith, Leanne (2010) 'Clashing symbols? Reconciling support for fathers and fatherless families after the Human Fertilisation and Embryology Act 2008', *Child and Family Law Quarterly* 22: 46.

Smith, M. (2003) 'New stepfamilies – a descriptive study of a largely unseen group', *Child and Family Law Quarterly* 15: 185.

Smith, M., Robertson, J., Dixon, J. and Quigley, M. (2001) *A Study of Step Children and Step Parenting*, London: Thomas Coram Research Unit.

Smith, Rhona (2004) '"Hands-off parenting?" – towards a reform of the defence of reasonable chastisement in the UK', *Child and Family Law Quarterly* 16: 261.

Smith, S. and Cook, R. (1991) 'Ovarian hyperstimulation: actual and theoretical risks', *British Medical Journal* 1991: 127.

Smyth, B. (2005) 'Parent–child contact in Australia: Exploring five different post-separation patterns of parenting', *International Journal of Law, Policy and the Family* 19: 1.

Snodgrass, G. (1998) 'Creating family without marriage: The advantages and disadvantages of adult adoption among gay and lesbian partners', *Journal of Family Law* 36: 75.

Social and Community Planning Research (2000) *Women's Attitudes to Combining Paid Work and Family Life*, London: SCPR.

Social Exclusion Unit (1999a) *Teenage Pregnancy*, London: SEU.

Social Exclusion Unit (1999b) *Bridging the Gap*, London: SEU.

Social Services Inspectorate (1992) *Confronting Elder Abuse*, London: HMSO.

Social Services Inspectorate (1993) *No Longer Afraid: The Safeguard of Older People in Domestic Settings*, London: HMSO.

Social Services Inspectorate (2002) *Fostering for the Future*, London: DoH.

Solberg, A. (1997) 'Negotiating Childhood', in A. James and A. Prout (eds) *Constructing and Reconstructing Childhood*, 2nd edn, London: Falmer.

Solicitors Family Law Association (2003) *Protection Before Punishment*, London: SFLA.

Solicitors Family Law Association (2004) *A More Certain Future*, London: SFLA.

Solomou, W., Richards, M., Huppert, F. et al. (1998) 'Divorce, current marital status and well-being in an elderly population', *International Journal of Law, Policy and the Family* 12: 323.

Spencer, J. and Pedain, A. (2006) *Freedom and Responsibility in Reproductive Choice*, Oxford: Hart.

Spon-Smith, R. (2005) 'Civil Partnership Act 2004', *Family Law* 35: 369.

Stacey, J. and Biblarz, T. (2001) '(How) does sexual orientation of parents matter?', *American Sociological Review* 66: 159.

Stainton Rogers, W. (2001) 'Constructing Childhood, Constructing Child Concerns', in P. Foley, J. Roche and S. Tucker (eds) *Children in Society*, Buckingham: Open University Press.

Stalford, H. (2002) 'Concepts of family under EU law – lessons from the ECHR', *International Journal of Law, Policy and the Family* 16: 410.

Stanko, E. (2000) *Press Release*, London: Reuters.

Stanko, E., Crisp, D., Hale, C. and Lucraft, H. (1998) *Counting the Costs: Estimating the Impact of Domestic Violence in the London Borough of Hackney*, Swindon: Crime Concern.

Stanley, N., Miller, P., Richardson Foster, H. and Thomson, G. (2010a) 'A Stop–Start Response: Social Services' Interventions with Children and Families Notified following Domestic Violence Incidents', *British Journal of Social Work* 40: 1.

Stanley, N., Miller, P., Richardson Foster, H. and Thomson, G. (2010b) *Children and Families Experiencing Domestic Violence: Police and Children's Social Services' Responses*, London: NSPCC.

Stark, B. (2005) *International Family Law*, Aldershot: Ashgate.

Stark, E. (2005) 'Reconsidering state intervention in domestic violence cases', *Social Policy and Society* 5: 149.

Stark, E. (2007) *Coercive Control: How Men Entrap Women in Personal Life*, Oxford: OUP.

Stein, M. (2009) *Quality Matters in Children's Services: Messages from research*, London: Jessica Kingsley.

Steinbock, B. (2005) 'Defining parenthood', *International Journal of Children's Rights* 13: 287.

Steiner, E. (2003) '*Odièvre* v *France*: Desperately seeking mother – anonymous births in the European Court of Human Rights', *Child and Family Law Quarterly* 15: 425.

Stepan, M. (2010) 'Mediation is moving on', *Family Law* 40: 545.

Stephen, D. (2009) 'Time to stop twisting the knife: a critical commentary on the rights and wrongs of criminal justice responses to problem youth in the UK', *Journal of Social Welfare and Family Law* 31: 193.

Sterling, V. (2009) 'DNA, Paternity Deceit and Reliability of the Birth Certificate as a Historical Document', *Family Law* 39: 701.

Stewart, A. (2007) 'Home or Home: Caring about and for elderly family members in a welfare state', in R. Probert (ed.) *Family Life and the Law*, Aldershot: Ashgate.

Stewart, M. (2004) 'Judicial Redefinition of Marriage', *Canadian Journal of Family Law* 21: 11.

Stewart, M., Wilkes, L., Jackson, D. and Mannix, J. (2006) 'Child-to-mother violence: A pilot study', *Advances in Nursing and Interpersonal Violence* 29: 217.

Strauss, M. and Donnolly, P. (1993) 'Corporal punishment of adolescents by American parents', *Society* 24: 419.

Strong, S. (2000) 'Between the baby and the breast', *Cambridge Law Journal* 59: 259.

Stumpf, A. (1986) 'Redefining mother: A legal matrix for the new reproductive technologies', *Yale Law Journal* 96: 187.

Sturge, C. and Glaser, D. (2000) 'Contact and domestic violence – the experts' court report', *Family Law* 30: 615.

Stychin, C. (2006) 'Not (quite) a horse and carriage', *Feminist Legal Studies* 14: 79.

Stychin, C. (2007) 'Family friendly? Rights, responsibilities and relationship recognition', in A. Diduck and K. O'Donovan (eds) *Feminist Perspectives on Family Law*, London: Routledge.

Sutherland, E. (1997) 'The unequal struggle – fathers and children in Scots law', *Child and Family Law Quarterly* 9: 191.

Sutherland, E. (2001) 'Parentage and Parenting', in J. Scoular (ed.) *Family Dynamics: Contemporary Issues in Family Law*, London: Butterworths.

Sutherland, E. (2003) '"Man not included" – single women, female couples and procreative freedom in the UK', *Child and Family Law Quarterly* 15: 155.

Swindells, H. and Heaton, C. (2006) *Adoption: The Modern Procedure*, Bristol: Jordans.

Swisher, P. (1997) 'Reassessing fault factors in no-fault divorce', *Family Law Quarterly* 31: 269.

Symes, P. (1985) 'Indissolubility and the clean break', *Modern Law Review* 48: 44.

Taitz, J. (1988) 'A transsexual's nightmare: The determination of sexual identity in English Law', *International Journal of Family Law* 2: 139.

Talbot, C. and Williams, M. (2003) 'Kinship care', *Family Law* 33: 502.

Tan, Y. (2002) 'New Forms of Cohabitation in Europe: Challenges for English Private International Law', in K. Boelle-Woelki (ed.) *Perspectives for the Unification and Harmonisation of Family Law in Europe*, Antwerp: Intersentia.

Tanner, K. and Turney, D. (2002) 'What do we know about child neglect?', *Child and Family Social Work* 8: 25.

Tasker, F. and Bellamy HHJ (2007) 'Reviewing lesbian and gay adoption and foster care', *Family Law* 37: 524.

Tasker, F. and Golombok, S. (1991) 'Children raised by lesbian mothers', *Family Law* 21: 184.

Tasker, F. and Patterson, C. (2007) 'Research on lesbian and gay parenting: Retrospect and prospect', *Journal of GLBT Family Studies* 7.

Tax Law Review Committee (2003) *Response to Civil Partnerships*, London: Tax Law Review Committee.

Taylor, A. (2008) 'Cousin marriage: a cause for concern?', *Bionews* 461: 1.

Taylor, C. (2006) *Young People in Care and Criminal Behaviour*, London: Jessica Kingsley.

Taylor, R. (2006) 'Children's Privacy and Press Freedom in Criminal Cases', *Child and Family Law Quarterly* 18: 269.

Taylor, R. (2007) 'Reversing the Retreat from *Gillick*?', *Child and Family Law Quarterly* 19: 81.

Taylor, R. (2009) 'Parental responsibility and religion', in R. Probert, S. Gilmore and J. Herring, (2009) *Responsible Parents and Parental Responsibility*, Oxford: Hart.

Tee, L. (2001) 'Division of Property upon Relationship Breakdown', in J. Herring (ed.) *Family Law: Issues, Debates, Policy*, Cullompton: Willan.

Teitelbaum, L. (1999) 'Children's rights and the problems of equal respect', *Hofstra Law Review* 27: 799.

Teitelbaum, L. and Dupaix, L. (1994) 'Alternative Dispute Resolution and Divorce: Natural Experimentation in Family Law', in J. Eekelaar and M. Maclean (eds) *A Reader on Family Law*, Oxford: OUP.

Thatcher, M. (1990) *The Independent*, 19 July.

Thatcher, M. (1995) *The Downing Street Years*, London: HarperCollins.

Thatcher, M. (1999) *Marriage After Modernity*, Sheffield: Sheffield Academic Press.

Thoburn, J. (1988) *Child Placement: Principles and Practice*, London: Wildwood.

Thoburn, J. (2003) 'The risks and rewards of adoption for children in the public care', *Child and Family Law Quarterly* 15: 391.

Thomas, N. (2001) 'Listening to Children', in P. Foley, J. Roche and S. Tucker (eds) *Children in Society*, Buckingham: Open University Press.

Thomas, N., Cook, M., Cook, J., France, H., Hillman, J., Jenkins, C., Pearson, T., Pugh-Dungey, R., Sawyers, B., Taylor, M. and Crowley, A. (2010) 'Evaluating the Children's Commissioner for Wales', *International Journal of Children's Rights* 18: 19.

Thompson, G. (2010) *Domestic Violence Statistics*, London: Hansard.

Thompson, M., Vinter, L. and Young, V. (2005) *Dads and their Babies*, London: EOC.

Thomson, M. (2009) *Endowed: Regulating the Male Sexed Body*, Abingdon, Routledge.

Thornton, A., Azinn, W. and Xie, Y. (2007) *Cohabitation and Marriage*, Chicago: University of Chicago.

Thornton, M. (1997) 'The judicial gendering of citizenship: A look at property interests during marriage', *Journal of Law and Society* 24: 486.

Thornton, R. (1989) 'Homelessness through relationship breakdown', *Journal of Social Welfare Law*, 11: 67.

Thorpe LJ (1994) 'Independent representation for minors', *Family Law* 24: 20.

Thorpe LJ (1998a) 'Should Section 25 be reformed?' *Family Law* 28: 469.

Thorpe LJ (1998b) 'The English System of Ancillary Relief', in R. Bailey-Harris (ed.) *Dividing the Assets on Family Breakdown*, Bristol: Jordans.

Thorpe LJ (1998c) *Report to the Lord Chancellor of the Ancillary Relief Advisory Group*, London: Ancillary Relief Advisory Group.

Thorpe LJ (2000) 'Introduction', in Thorpe LJ and E. Clarke (eds) *No Fault or Flaw: The Future of the Family Law Act 1996*, Bristol: Jordans.

Thorpe LJ (2002) 'Property rights on family breakdown', *Family Law* 32: 891.

Thorpe, LJ (2009) 'London – The Divorce Capital of the World', *Family Law* 39: 21.

Tilley, J. (2000) 'Cultural relativism', *Human Rights Quarterly* 19: 461.

Tilley, S. (2007) 'Recognising gender differences in all issues mediation', *Family Law* 37: 352.

Tisdall, K., Bray, R., Marshall, K. and Celeand, A. (2004) 'Children's participation in family law proceedings', *Journal of Social Welfare and Family Law* 26: 17.

Todd, R. (2006) 'The inevitable triumph of the ante-nuptial contract', *Family Law* 36: 539.

Tolson, R. (2002) 'Goals and the team's performance', *Family Law* 32: 491.

Toner, H. (2004) *Partnership Rights, Free Movement and EU Law*, Oxford: Hart.

Tong, R. (1985) 'Feminist Perspectives and Gestational Motherhood', in J. Callaghan (ed.) *Reproduction, Ethics and the Law*, Bloomington, Ind.: Indiana University Press.

Toren, A. (2004) *Survey of Domestic Violence Services*, London: Women's Aid.

Trew, J. and Drobnic, S. (2010) *Dividing the Domestic*, Stanford: University of Stanford Press.

Trinder, L. (2003a) 'Working and not Working Contact after Divorce', in A. Bainham, B. Lindley, M. Richards and L. Trinder (eds) *Children and Their Families*, Oxford: Hart.

Trinder, L. (2003b) 'Contact after Divorce: What has the Law to Offer', in G. Miller (ed.) *Frontiers of Family Law*, Aldershot: Ashgate.

Trinder, L. (2005) *A profile of applicants and respondents in contact cases in Essex*, London: DCA.

Trinder, L. (2006) 'In Court Conciliation', in M. Thorpe and R. Budden, *Durable Solutions*, Bristol: Jordans.

Trinder, L. (2008) 'Conciliation, The Private Law Programme and Children's Well-Being', *Family Law* 38: 338.

Trinder, L., Beek, M. and Connolly, J. (2002) *Making Contact: How Parents and Children Negotiate and Experience Contact After Divorce*, York: Joseph Rowntree Foundation.

Trinder, L., Connolly, J., Kellett, J. and Notley, C. (2006) *Evaluation of Family Resolutions Pilot Project*, London: DfES.

Trinder, L., Connolly, J., Kellett, J. and Thoday, C. (2004) 'Families in contact disputes: a profile', *Family Law* 24: 877.

Trinder, L., Firth, A., and Jenks, C. (2010) ' "So presumably things have moved on since then?" The management of risk allegations in child contact dispute resolution', *International Journal of Law, Policy and the Family* 24: 29.

Trinder, L., Jenks, C. and Firth, A. (2010) 'Talking children into being *in absentia*? Children as a strategic and contingent resource in family court dispute resolution', *Child and Family Law Quarterly* 22: 234.

Trinder, L. and Kellett, J. (2007) 'Fairness, efficiency and effectiveness in court-based dispute resolution schemes in England', *International Journal of Law, Policy and the Family* 21: 322.

Triseliotis, J. (1973) *In Search of Origins*, London: Routledge.

Turkmendag, I., Dingwall, R. and Murphy, T. (2008) 'The removal of donor anonymity in the UK: The silencing of claims by would-be parents', *International Journal of Law, Policy and the Family* 22: 283.

Twenge, J., Campbell, W. and Foster, C. (2003) 'Parenthood and marital satisfaction', *Journal of Marriage and the Family* 65: 574.

Ungerson, C. (1987) *Policy is Personal: Sex, Gender and Informal Care*, London: Tavistock.

UK Children's Commissioners (2008) *Report to UN Committee on the Rights of the Child*. London: 11 Million.

UK Children's Commissioners (2009) *Joint Position Statement on Progress on the 2008 United Nations Committee on the Rights of the Child's Concluding Observations*, London: 11 Million.

UNICEF (2000) *The State of the World's Children*, Geneva: UNICEF.

UNICEF (2006) *Behind Closed Doors: The Impact of Domestic Violence on Children*, Geneva: UNICEF.

UNICEF (2007) *Child Poverty in Perspective: An Overview of Child Well-being*, Geneva: UNICEF.

United Kingdom College of Mediators (1998) *Standards and Code of Practice*, London: UK College of Mediators.

United Kingdom College of Mediators (2000) *Code of Practice for Family Mediators*, London: UK College of Mediators.

United Nations Committee on the Rights of the Child (2008) *Concluding observations: United Kingdom*, Geneva: United Nations.

University of Cardiff (2008) *Violence Injuries Fall 12 per cent*, Cardiff: University of Cardiff.

Valentine, G. (2004) *Public Space and the Culture of Childhood*, Aldershot: Ashgate.

Van Bueren, G. (1995) 'Children's access to adoption records – State discretion or an enforceable right?', *Modern Law Review* 58: 37.

Van Krieken, R. (2005) 'The "best interests of the child" on parental separation: on the "civilising of parents"', *Modern Law Review* 68: 25.

Van Praagh, S. (1997) 'Children, custody and a child's identity', *Osgoode Law Journal* 35: 309.

Veitch, E. (1976) 'The essence of marriage – A comment on the homosexuality challenge', *Anglo-American Law Review* 5: 41.

Vogler, C. (2009) 'Managing money in intimate relationships', in J. Miles and R. Probert (eds) *Sharing Lives, Dividing Assets*, Oxford: Hart.

Vonk, M. (2007) *Children and Their Parents*, Antwerp: Intersentia.

Waal, de, A. (2008) *Second Thoughts on the Family*, London: Civitas.

Waddington, W. (2000) 'Marriage: An Institution in Transition and Redefinition', in S. Katz, J. Eekelaar and M. Maclean (eds) *Cross Currents*, Oxford: OUP.

Wade, J. (2003) 'Children on the edge – patterns of running away in the UK', *Child and Family Law Quarterly* 15: 343.

Wade, J., Dixon, J. and Richards, A. (2009) *Implementing Special Guardianship*, London: Department for Children, Schools and Families.

Wagstaff, C. (1998) 'Harming the unborn child – the foetus and the threshold criteria', *Family Law* 28: 160.

Waite, L. (2000) 'Cohabitation: A Communitarian Perspective', in M. Whyte (ed.) *Marriage in America*, Lanham, Md.: Rowman & Littlefield.

Waite, L. and Gallagher, M. (2001) *The Case for Marriage*, New York: Broadway Books.

Waites, M. (2005) *The Age of Consent: Young People, Sexuality and Citizenship*, Basingstoke: Palgrave.

Walby, S. (2004) *The Cost of Domestic Violence*, London: Home Office.

Walby, S. and Allen, J. (2004) *Domestic Violence, Sexual Assault and Stalking*, London: Home Office.

Waldman, E. (1997) 'Identifying the Role of Social Norms in Mediation: A Multiple Model Approach', *Hastings Law Journal* 48: 703.

Walker, J. (ed.) (1998) *Information Meetings and Associated Provision within FLA 1996. Second Interim Evaluation Report*, Newcastle: Newcastle Centre for Family Studies.

Walker, J. (ed.) (1999) *Information Meetings and Associated Provision within FLA 1996. Third Interim Evaluation*, Newcastle: Newcastle Centre for Family Studies.

Walker, J. (2000a) 'Whither the FLA, Part II?', in Thorpe LJ and E. Clarke (eds) *No Fault or Flaw: The Future of the Family Law Act 1996*, Bristol: Jordans.

Walker, J. (2000b) 'Information meetings revisited', *Family Law* 30: 330.

Walker, J. (2001a) *Information Meetings and Associated Provisions within the Family Law Act 1996*, London: Lord Chancellor's Department.

Walker, J. (2001b) 'The information pilots – using and abusing evidence', *Family Law* 31: 817.

Walker, J. (2004a) 'FAInS – A new approach for family lawyers', *Family Law* 34: 436.

Walker, J. (2004b) *Picking Up The Pieces: Marriage and Divorce Two Years After Information Provision*, London: DCA.

Walker, J. and McCarthy, P. (2004) 'Picking up the pieces', *Family Law* 34: 580.

Walker, J., McCarthy, P. and Timms, N. (1994) *Mediation: The Making and Remaking of Co-operative Relationships*, Newcastle: Relate Centre for Family Studies.

Wall HHJ (1997) 'Domestic violence and contact', *Family Law* 27: 813.

Wall, J. (2008) 'Human Rights in the Light of Childhood', *International Journal of Children's Rights* 16: 523.

Wall LJ (2005) 'Enforcement of contact orders', *Family Law* 35: 26.

Wall LJ (2006) *A Report to the President of the Family Division*, London: DCA.

Wall LJ (2007) 'Separate representation of children', *Family Law* 37: 124.

Wall LJ (2008a) 'Unreliable Evidence', Radio 4, 10 May 2008.

Wall LJ (2008b) 'Judge Speaks Out', *Family Law* 38: 584.

Wall LJ (2008c) 'Medical Evidence in Child Abuse Cases', *Family Law* 38: 320.

Wall LJ (2009) 'Making contact work in 2009', *Family Law* 39: 590.

Wall LJ (2010) 'Justice for Children: Welfare or Farewell?', *Family Law* 40: 29.

Wall, P. (2010) 'Revised Protocol for Referrals of Families to Supported Child Contact Centres by Judges and Magistrates', *Family Law* 40: 858.

Wallbank, J. (1998) 'Castigating mothers: The judicial response to wilful women in cases concerning contact', *Journal of Social Welfare and Family Law* 20: 257.

Wallbank, J. (2002a) 'Clause 106 of the Adoption and Children Bill: Legislation for the "good" father?', *Legal Studies* 22: 276.

Wallbank, J. (2002b) *Challenging Motherhoods*, London: Prentice Hall.

Wallbank, J. (2004a) 'Reconstructing the HFEA 1990: is blood really thicker than water?', *Child and Family Law Quarterly* 16: 387.

Wallbank, J. (2004b) 'The role of rights and utility in instituting a child's right to know her genetic history', *Social and Legal Studies* 13: 245.

Wallbank, J. (2007) 'Getting tough on mothers: regulating contact and residence', *Feminist Legal Studies* 15: 189.

Wallbank, J. (2009) '"Bodies in the Shadows": joint birth registration, parental responsibility and social class', *Child and Family Law Quarterly* 21: 267.

Wallbank, J. (2009) '(En)Gendering the fusion of rights and responsibilities in the law of contact', in J. Wallbank, S. Choudhry and J. Herring (eds), *Rights, Gender and Family Law*, Abingdon: Routledge.

Wallbank, J., Choudhry, S. and Herring, J. (eds) (2009) *Rights, Gender and Family Law*, London: Routledge.

Wallerstein, J. and Kelly, J. (1980) *Surviving the Breakup*, New York: Basic Books.

Wallerstein, J. and Lewis, J. (1998) 'The long-term impact of divorce on children', *Family and Conciliation Courts Review* 12: 368.

Walsh, E. (2009a) 'Increased reporting of forced marriage', *Family Law* 39: 988.

Walsh, E. (2009b) 'Parental Responsibility: A National Statement', *Family Law* 39: 632.

Walsh, E. (2009c) 'Domestic violence literature review', *Family Law* 39: 360.

Walsh, E. (2010) 'Children's guardians', *Family Law* 40: 783.

Walsh, J. (1998) *Across the Generations*, London: Age Concern.

Wardle, L. (1996) 'The use and abuse of rights rhetoric', *Loyola University Chicago Law Journal* 27: 321.

Wardle, L. (1998) 'Same-Sex Marriage and the Limits of Legal Pluralism', in J. Eekelaar and T. Nhlapo (eds) *The Changing Family: International Perspectives on the Family and Family Law*, Oxford: Hart.

Wardle, L. (2002) 'Parental infidelity and the "no harm" rule in custody litigation', *Catholic University Law Review* 52: 81.

Wardle, L. (2004) 'Adult sexuality, the best interests of children, and placement liability of foster care and adoption agencies', *Journal of Law and Family Studies* 6: 59.

Wardle, L. (2006) 'The "end" of marriage', *Family Court Review* 44: 45.

Warman, C. and Roberts, C. (2003) *Adoption and Looked After Children – an International Comparison*, Oxford: Oxford Centre for Family Law and Policy.

Warner, K. (2000) 'Sentencing in cases of marital rape: Towards changing the male imagination', *Legal Studies* 20: 592.

Warnock Report (1984) *Report of the Committee of Inquiry into Human Fertilisation and Embryology*, London: HMSO.

Warnock, M. (2002) *Making Babies*, Oxford: OUP.

Warnock, M. (2006) 'The Limits of Rights-based Discourse', in J. Spencer and A. du Bois-Pedain, *Freedom and Responsibility in Reproductive Choice*, Oxford: Hart.

Warren, E. (2002) 'Bankrupt Children', *Minnesota Law Review* 86: 1003.

Waterhouse, R. (2000) *Lost in Care*, London: The Stationery Office.

Waterhouse, S., Hunt, J. and Lutman, E. (2008) 'Children Placed with Kinship Carers Through Care Proceedings', *Family Law* 38: 435.

Watson-Lee, P. (2004) 'Financial Provision on Divorce: Clarity and Fairness', *Family Law* 34: 348.

Weeks, J. (2004) 'The Rights and Wrongs of Sexuality', in B. Brooks-Gordon, L. Goldsthorpe, M. Johnson and A. Bainham (eds) *Sexuality Repositioned*, Oxford: Hart.

Weeks, J., Donovan, C. and Heaphy, B. (2001) *Same-Sex Intimacies: Families of Choice and Other Life Experiments*, London: Routledge.

Weitzman, L. (1985) *The Divorce Revolution*, New York: The Free Press.

Welbourne, P. (2002) 'Adoption and the rights of children in the UK', *International Journal of Children's Rights* 10: 269.

Welbourne, P. (2008) 'Safeguarding children on the edge of care', *Child and Family Law Quarterly* 20: 335.

Wells, C. (1997) 'Stalking: The criminal law's response', *Criminal Law Review* 463.

Welsh, E., Buchanan, A., Flouri, E. and Lewis, J. (2004) *Involved Fathering and Child Well-being*, London: National Children's Bureau.

Welstead, M. and Edwards, S. (2006) *Family Law*, Oxford: OUP.

Wenger, G. (1984) *The Supportive Network*, London: Allen & Unwin.

West, S. (2000) *Your Rights*, London: Age Concern.

Westcott, H. (2006) 'Child witness testimony: what do we know and where are we going?', *Child and Family Law Quarterly* 18: 175.

Westendorp, I. and Wolleswinkel, R. (2005) *Violence in the Domestic Sphere*, Antwerp: Intersentia.

Weyland, I. (1995) 'Judicial attitudes to contact and shared residence since the Children Act 1989', *Journal of Social Welfare and Family Law* 17: 445.

Weyland, I. (1997) 'The blood tie: Raised to the status of a presumption', *Journal of Social Welfare and Family Law* 19: 173.

Weyrauch, W. (1980) 'Metamorphosis of marriage', *Family Law Quarterly* 13: 415.

White House Working Group on the Family (1985) *The Family: Possessing America's Future*, Washington: White House.

White, M. (2010) 'Same-sex marriage: the irrelevance of the economic approach to law', *International Journal of Law in Context* 6: 139.

Whittle, S. (2002) *Respect and Equality*, London: Cavendish.

Who Cares? Trust (2000) *Remember my Messages*, London: Who Cares? Trust.

Wicks, R. and Asato, J. (2002) *The Family Report 2002*, London: Lever Fabergé.

Wikeley, N. (2005) '*R (Kehoe)* v *Secretary of State*: No Redress when the Child Support Agency Fails to Deliver', *Child and Family Law Quarterly* 16: 97.

Wikeley, N. (2006a) 'A duty but not a right: child support after *R (Kehoe)* v *Secretary of State for Work and Pensions*', *Child and Family Law Quarterly* 18: 287.

Wikeley, N. (2006b) 'Child support – back to the drawing board', *Family Law* 36: 312.

Wikeley, N. (2006c) *Child Support: Law and Policy*, Oxford: Hart.

Wikeley, N. (2007a) 'Family law and social security', in R. Probert (ed.) *Family Life and the Law*, Aldershot: Ashgate.

Wikeley, N. (2007b) 'Child support reform – throwing the baby out with the bathwater', *Child and Family Law Quarterly* 19: 435.

Wikeley, N. (2008a) 'Child support: The brave new world', *Family Law* 38: 1024.

Wikeley, N. (2008b) 'Child support: carrots and sticks', *Family Law* 38: 1102.

Wikeley, N. (2009) 'Financial support for children after parental separation: Parental responsibility and responsible parenting', in R. Probert, S. Gilmore and J. Herring (eds), *Responsible Parents and Parental Responsibility*, Oxford: Hart.

Wikeley, N., Ireland, E., Bryson, C. and Smith, R. (2008). *Relationship separation and child support study*, DWP Research Report 503, London: DWP.

Wikeley, N. and Young, L. (2005) '*Smith* v *Secretary of State for Work and Pensions*: child support, the self-employed and the meaning of "total taxable profits" – total confusion reigns', *Child and Family Law Quarterly* 17: 267.

Wikeley, N. and Young, L. (2008) 'Secrets and lies: No deceit down under for patenity fraud', *Child and Family Law Quarterly* 20: 81.

Wild, L. and Richards, M. (2003) 'Exploring parent and child perceptions of interparental conflict', *International Journal of Law, Policy and Family* 17: 366.

Wilkinson, B. (2009) 'Child Protection: The Statutory Failure', *Family Law* 39: 420.

Willbourne, C. and Stanley, G. (2002) 'Contact under the microscope', *Family Law* 32: 687.

Willems, J. (2007) *Developmental and Autonomy Rights of Children*, Antwerp: Intersentia.

Williams, A. (1985) 'The value of QALYs', *Health and Social Service Journal*, July 1985: 3.

Williams, C. (2002) 'The practical operation of the Children Act complaints procedure', *Child and Family Law Quarterly* 14: 25.

Williams, C. and Jordan, H. (1996a) *The Children Act 1989 Complaints Procedure*, Sheffield: University of Sheffield.

Williams, C. and Jordan, H. (1996b) 'Factors relating to publicity surrounding the complaints procedure under the Children Act 1989', *Child and Family Law Quarterly* 6: 337.

Williams, C., Potter, G. and Douglas, G. (2008) 'Cohabitation and intestacy: public opinion and law reform', *Child and Family Law Quarterly* 20: 499.

Williams, D. and Blain, S. (2008) 'Voices in the Wilderness', *Family Law* 38: 135.

Williams, J. (2002) 'Prisoners and artificial insemination – Have the courts got it right?', *Child and Family Law Quarterly* 14: 216.

Williams, Jane (2005) 'Effective government structures for children? The UK's four Children's Commissioners', *Child and Family Law Quarterly* 17: 37.

Williams, Jane (2007) 'Incorporating children's rights: The divergence in law and policy', *Legal Studies* 27: 261.

Williams, Joan (1994) 'Is coverture dead? Beyond a new theory of alimony', *Georgetown Law Journal* 82: 2227.

Williams, John (2008) 'State responsibility and the abuse of vulnerable older people: Is there a case for a public law to protect vulnerable older people from abuse?', in J. Bridgeman, H. Keating and C. Lind (eds) *Responsibility, Law and the Family*, London: Ashgate.

Willitts, M., Anderson, T., Tait, C. and Williams, G. (2005) *Children in Britain*, London: DWP.

Willmott, M. and Nelson, W. (2003) *Complicated Lives*, Chichester: Wiley.

Wilson, B. (2004) 'Emotion, rationality and decision-making in mediation', *Family Law* 34: 682.

Wilson, B. and Smallwood, S. (2008) 'The proportion of marriages ending in divorce', *Population Trends* 131: 28.

Wilson, B. (2009) 'ADR Professional: Do Mediators Care?', *Family Law* 39: 201.

Wilson, G. (1994) 'Abuse of elderly men and women among clients of a community psycho-geriatric service', *British Journal of Social Work* 24: 81.

Wilson, G. (2006) 'The Non-Resident Parental Role for Separated Fathers: A Review', *International Journal of Law, Policy and the Family* 20: 286.

Wilson, G. (2007) 'Financial provision in civil partnerships', *Family Law* 37: 31.

Wilson J (1999) 'Ancillary relief reform', *Family Law* 29: 159.

Wilson J (2003) 'The misnomer of family law', *Family Law* 33: 29.

Wilson J (2007) 'The ears of the child in family proceeding', *Family Law* 37: 808.

Wilson, S. (1997) 'Identity, genealogy and the social family: The case of donor insemination', *International Journal of Law, Policy and the Family*, 11: 270.

Wintemute, R. (2005) 'From "sex rights" to "love rights": partnership rights as human rights', in N. Bamforth (ed.) *Sex Rights: The Oxford Amnesty Lectures*, Oxford: OUP.

Wintemute, R. and Andenæs, M. (eds) (2001) *Legal Recognition of Same-Sex Partnerships*, Oxford: Hart.

Woelke, A. (2002) 'Family credo', *Family Law* 32: 475.

Women and Equality Unit (2003) *Civil Partnership*, London: DTI.

Women and Equality Unit (2006a) *Domestic Violence*, London: DTI.

Women and Equality Unit (2006b) *Domestic Violence: Key Facts*, London: DTI.

Women's Aid (1998) *Women's Aid Annual Report 1997/8*, Bristol: Women's Aid Federation.

Women's Aid (2003) *Failure to Protect*, London: Women's Aid.

Women's Aid (2005) *Survey of Domestic Violence Service Finding*, London: Women's Aid.

Wong, S. (2004) 'Property regimes for home-sharers: the Civil Partnership Bill and other antipodean models', *Journal of Social Welfare and Family Law* 26: 361.

Wong, S. (2005) 'The Human Rights Act 1998 and the shared home: issues for cohabitants', *Journal of Social Welfare and Family Law* 27: 265.

Wong, S. (2006) 'Cohabitation and the Law Commission's Project', *Feminist Legal Studies* 14: 145.

Wong, S. (2009) 'Caring and sharing: Interdepency as a basis for property redistribution', in A. Bottomley and S. Wong (eds) *Changing Contours of Domestic Life, Family and Law*, Oxford: Hart.

Woodhouse, B. (2000) 'The Status of Children', in S. Katz, J. Eekelaar and M. Maclean (eds) *Cross Currents*, Oxford: OUP.

Woodhouse, B. (2008) *Hidden in Plain Sight*, Princeton: Princeton University Press.

Woolf, M. (2000) 'Children to get details of sperm donor men', *The Independent*, 18 September.

Wright, C. (2006) 'The divorce process: a view from the other side of the desk', *Child and Family Law Quarterly* 18: 93.

Wright, K. (2007) 'The role of solicitors in divorce: A note of caution', *Child and Family Law Quarterly* 19: 481.

Wright, K. (2008) 'Competing Interests in Reproduction: The Case of Natallie Evans', *King's College Law Journal* 19: 135.

Wright, W. (2006) 'The tide of equality: Same-sex marriage in Canada and England and Wales', *International Journal of Law, Policy and the Family* 30: 249.

Yaxley, D., Vinter, L. and Young, V. (2005) *Dads and their Babies: the Mother's Perspective*, London: Equal Opportunities Commission.

Yell, G. (1992) 'Point of order', *Law Society's Guardian Gazette* 89: 20.

Yllo, K. and Bograd, M. (1988) *Feminist Perspectives on Wife Abuse*, London: Sage.

Young, I. (1999) 'Mothers, Citizenship and Independence', in U. Narayan and J. Bartkowiak (eds) *Having and Raising Children*, Pennsylvania: Pennsylvania State University Press.

# Index

# LawExpress

## Understand quickly. Revise effectively. Take exams with confidence.

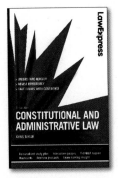
CONSTITUTIONAL AND ADMINISTRATIVE LAW
CHRIS TAYLOR

CONTRACT LAW
STEFAN FAFINSKI AND EMILY FINCH

LAND LAW
JOHN DUDDINGTON

EMPLOYMENT LAW
DAVID CABRELLI

BUSINESS LAW
EWAN MACINTYRE

COMPANY LAW
CHRIS TAYLOR

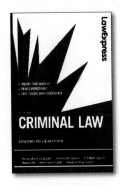
CRIMINAL LAW
EMILY FINCH AND STEFAN FAFINSKI

EQUITY AND TRUSTS
JOHN DUDDINGTON

FAMILY LAW
JONATHAN HERRING

EU LAW
EWAN KIRK

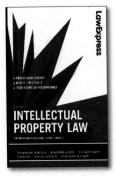
INTELLECTUAL PROPERTY LAW
DAVID BAINBRIDGE AND CLAIRE HOWELL

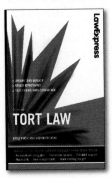
TORT LAW
EMILY FINCH AND STEFAN FAFINSKI

Other titles in the series are available from all good bookshops
or at www.pearsoned.co.uk/law

> UNDERSTAND QUICKLY  > REVISE EFFECTIVELY  > TAKE EXAMS WITH CONFIDENCE